BASIC WRITINGS OF
SAINT AUGUSTINE

EDITED, WITH AN INTRODUCTION AND NOTES BY

WHITNEY J. OATES

Ewing Professor of Greek Languages and Literature, Chairman
of the Department of Classics, Chairman of the Special Program
in the Humanities, Princeton University

VOLUME TWO

RANDOM HOUSE *Publishers* NEW YORK

CONTENTS

VOLUME ONE

THE CITY OF GOD

THE CITY OF GOD

Introductory Note

For a discussion of this, Saint Augustine's masterpiece, the reader is referred to the general Introduction, pp. xxxiii-xxxvi. One suggestion may be inserted here in connection with his use of the word history. It should be remembered that Saint Augustine sometimes uses the term in the way in which it is employed by the classical historians, but more often it has a wider connotation and one to which a modern so-called "scientific" historian would take sharp exception. However, if the comprehensiveness of Saint Augustine's vision is held firmly in mind, it is not difficult to see that he could never think of anything in time apart from eternity—he could not think of "history" apart from ultimate destiny.

THE CITY OF GOD

BOOK ONE

ARGUMENT

Augustine censures the pagans, who attributed the calamities of the world, and especially the recent sack of Rome by the Goths, to the Christian religion, and its prohibition of the worship of the gods. He speaks of the blessings and ills of life, which then, as always, happened to good and bad men alike. Finally, he rebukes the shamelessness of those who cast up to the Christians that their women had been violated by the soldiers.

PREFACE

EXPLAINING HIS DESIGN IN UNDERTAKING THIS WORK

THE glorious city of God is my theme in this work, which you, my dearest son Marcellinus,[1] suggested, and which is due to you by my promise. I have undertaken its defence against those who prefer their own gods to the Founder of this city—a city surpassingly glorious, whether we view it as it still lives by faith in this fleeting course of time, and sojourns as a stranger in the midst of the ungodly, or as it shall dwell in the fixed stability of its eternal seat, which it now with patience waits for, expecting until righteousness shall return unto judgment,[2] and it obtain, by virtue of its excellence, final victory and perfect peace. A great work this, and an arduous one; but God is my helper. For I am aware what ability is requisite to persuade the proud how great is the virtue of humility, which raises us, not by a quite human arrogance, but by a divine grace, above all earthly dignities that totter on this shifting scene. For the King and Founder of this city of which we speak, has in Scripture uttered to His people a dictum of the divine law in these words: "God resisteth the proud, but giveth grace unto the humble."[3] But this, which is God's prerogative, the inflated ambition of a proud spirit also affects, and dearly loves that this be numbered among its attributes, to

[1] Marcellinus was a friend of Augustine, and urged him to write this work. He was commissioned by the Emperor Honorius to convene a conference of Catholic and schismatic Donatist bishops in the summer of 411, and conceded the victory to the Catholics; but on account of his rigor in executing the laws against the Donatists, he fell a victim to their revenge, and was honored by a place among the martyrs.

[2] Ps. xciv. 15   [3] Jas. iv. 6 and 1 Pet. v. 5

Show pity to the humbled soul,
And crush the sons of pride.[4]

And therefore, as the plan of this work we have undertaken requires, and as occasion offers, we must speak also of the earthly city, which, though it be mistress of the nations, is itself ruled by its lust of rule.

CHAPTER I

OF THE ADVERSARIES OF THE NAME OF CHRIST, WHOM THE BARBARIANS FOR CHRIST'S SAKE SPARED WHEN THEY STORMED THE CITY

For to this earthly city belong the enemies against whom I have to defend the city of God. Many of them, indeed, being reclaimed from their ungodly error, have become sufficiently creditable citizens of this city; but many are so inflamed with hatred against it, and are so ungrateful to its Redeemer for His signal benefits, as to forget that they would now be unable to utter a single word to its prejudice, had they not found in its sacred places, as they fled from the enemy's steel, that life in which they now boast themselves. Are not those very Romans, who were spared by the barbarians through their respect for Christ, become enemies to the name of Christ? The reliquaries of the martyrs and the churches of the apostles bear witness to this; for in the sack of the city they were open sanctuary for all who fled to them, whether Christian or Pagan. To their very threshold the blood-thirsty enemy raged; there his murderous fury owned a limit. Thither did such of the enemy as had any pity convey those to whom they had given quarter, lest any less mercifully disposed might fall upon them. And, indeed, when even those murderers who everywhere else showed themselves pitiless came to those spots where that was forbidden which the license of war permitted in every other place, their furious rage for slaughter was bridled, and their eagerness to take prisoners was quenched. Thus escaped multitudes who now reproach the Christian religion, and impute to Christ the ills that have befallen their city; but the preservation of their own life—a boon which they owe to the respect entertained for Christ by the barbarians—they attribute not to our Christ, but to their own good luck. They ought rather, had they any right perceptions, to attribute the severities and hardships inflicted by their enemies, to that divine providence which is wont to reform the depraved manners of men by chastisement, and which exercises with similar afflictions the righteous and praiseworthy—either translating them, when they have passed through the trial, to a better world, or detaining them still on earth for ulterior purposes. And they ought to attribute it to the spirit of these Christian times, that, contrary to the custom of war, these blood-thirsty barbarians

[4] *Aeneid*, vi. 854 (The translations from Virgil are taken from the version of Conington.—Ed.)

spared them, and spared them for Christ's sake, whether this mercy was actually shown in promiscuous places, or in those places specially dedicated to Christ's name, and of which the very largest were selected as sanctuaries, that full scope might thus be given to the expansive compassion which desired that a large multitude might find shelter there. Therefore ought they to give God thanks, and with sincere confession flee for refuge to His name, that so they may escape the punishment of eternal fire—they who with lying lips took upon them this name, that they might escape the punishment of present destruction. For of those whom you see insolently and shamelessly insulting the servants of Christ, there are numbers who would not have escaped that destruction and slaughter had they not pretended that they themselves were Christ's servants. Yet now, in ungrateful pride and most impious madness, and at the risk of being punished in everlasting darkness, they perversely oppose that name under which they fraudulently protected themselves for the sake of enjoying the light of this brief life.

CHAPTER II

THAT IT IS QUITE CONTRARY TO THE USAGE OF WAR, THAT THE VICTORS SHOULD SPARE THE VANQUISHED FOR THE SAKE OF THEIR GODS

There are histories of numberless wars, both before the building of Rome and since its rise and the extension of its dominion; let these be read, and let one instance be cited in which, when a city had been taken by foreigners, the victors spared those who were found to have fled for sanctuary to the temples of their gods; or one instance in which a barbarian general gave orders that none should be put to the sword who had been found in this or that temple. Did not Aeneas see

> Dying Priam at the shrine,
> Staining the hearth he made divine? [5]

Did not Diomede and Ulysses

> Drag with red hands, the sentry slain,
> Her fateful image from your fane,
> Her chaste locks touch, and stain with gore
> The virgin coronal she wore? [6]

Neither is that true which follows, that

> Thenceforth the tide of fortune changed,
> And Greece grew weak. [7]

[5] *Aeneid*, ii. 501-2   [6] *Ibid*. ii. 166   [7] *Ibid*.

For after this they conquered and destroyed Troy with fire and sword; after this they beheaded Priam as he fled to the altars. Neither did Troy perish because it lost Minerva. For what had Minerva herself first lost, that she should perish? Her guards perhaps? No doubt; just her guards. For as soon as they were slain, she could be stolen. It was not, in fact, the men who were preserved by the image, but the image by the men. How, then, was she invoked to defend the city and the citizens, she who could not defend her own defenders?

CHAPTER III

THAT THE ROMANS DID NOT SHOW THEIR USUAL SAGACITY WHEN THEY TRUSTED THAT THEY WOULD BE BENEFITED BY THE GODS WHO HAD BEEN UNABLE TO DEFEND TROY

And these be the gods to whose protecting care the Romans were delighted to entrust their city! O too piteous mistake! And they are enraged at us when we speak thus about their gods, though, so far from being enraged at their own writers, they part with money to learn what they say; and, indeed, the very teachers of these authors are reckoned worthy of a salary from the public purse, and of other honors. There is Virgil, who is read by boys, in order that this great poet, this most famous and approved of all poets, may impregnate their virgin minds, and may not readily be forgotten by them, according to that saying of Horace,

The fresh cask long keeps its first tang.[8]

Well, in this Virgil, I say, Juno is introduced as hostile to the Trojans, and stirring up Aeolus, the king of the winds, against them in the words,

A race I hate now ploughs the sea,
Transporting Troy to Italy,
And home-gods conquered [9] . . . .

And ought prudent men to have entrusted the defence of Rome to these conquered gods? But it will be said, this was only the saying of Juno, who, like an angry woman, did not know what she was saying. What, then, says Aeneas himself—Aeneas who is so often designated "pious?" Does he not say,

Lo! Panthus, 'scaped from death by flight,
Priest of Apollo on the height,
His conquered gods with trembling hands
He bears, and shelter swift demands? [10]

[8] *Ep.* I. ii. 69   [9] *Aeneid,* i. 71   [10] *Ibid.,* ii. 319

Is it not clear that the gods (whom he does not scruple to call "conquered")
were rather entrusted to Aeneas than he to them, when it is said to him,

> The gods of her domestic shrines
> Your country to your care consigns? [11]

If, then, Virgil says that the gods were such as these, and were conquered, and that when conquered they could not escape except under the protection of a man, what madness is it to suppose that Rome had been wisely entrusted to these guardians, and could not have been taken unless it had lost them! Indeed, to worship conquered gods as protectors and champions, what is this but to worship, not good divinities, but evil omens? Would it not be wiser to believe, not that Rome would never have fallen into so great a calamity had not they first perished, but rather that they would have perished long since had not Rome preserved them as long as she could? For who does not see, when he thinks of it, what a foolish assumption it is that they could not be vanquished under vanquished defenders, and that they only perished because they had lost their guardian gods, when, indeed, the only cause of their perishing was that they chose for their protectors gods condemned to perish? The poets, therefore, when they composed and sang these things about the conquered gods, had no intention to invent falsehoods, but uttered, as honest men, what the truth extorted from them. This, however, will be carefully and copiously discussed in another and more fitting place. Meanwhile I will briefly, and to the best of my ability, explain what I meant to say about these ungrateful men who blasphemously impute to Christ the calamities which they deservedly suffer in consequence of their own wicked ways, while that which is for Christ's sake spared them in spite of their wickedness they do not even take the trouble to notice; and in their mad and blasphemous insolence, they use against His name those very lips wherewith they falsely claimed that same name that their lives might be spared. In the places consecrated to Christ, where for His sake no enemy would injure them, they restrained their tongues that they might be safe and protected; but no sooner do they emerge from these sanctuaries, than they unbridle these tongues to hurl against Him curses full of hate.

CHAPTER IV

OF THE ASYLUM OF JUNO IN TROY, WHICH SAVED NO ONE FROM THE GREEKS; AND OF THE CHURCHES OF THE APOSTLES, WHICH PROTECTED FROM THE BARBARIANS ALL WHO FLED TO THEM

Troy itself, the mother of the Roman people, was not able, as I have said, to protect its own citizens in the sacred places of their gods from the

[11] *Ibid.*, 293

fire and sword of the Greeks, though the Greeks worshipped the same gods.
Not only so, but

> Phoenix and Ulysses fell
> In the void courts by Juno's cell
> Were set the spoils to keep;
> Snatched from the burning shrines away,
> There Ilium's mighty treasure lay,
> Rich altars, bowls of massy gold,
> And captive raiment, rudely rolled
> In one promiscuous heap;
> While boys and matrons, wild with fear,
> In long array were standing near.[12]

In other words, the place consecrated to so great a goddess was chosen, not
that from it none might be led out a captive, but that in it all the captives
might be immured. Compare now this "asylum"—the asylum not of an
ordinary god, not of one of the rank and file of gods, but of Jove's own
sister and wife, the queen of all the gods—with the churches built in memory of the apostles. Into it were collected the spoils rescued from the blazing temples and snatched from the gods, not that they might be restored
to the vanquished, but divided among the victors; while into these was
carried back, with the most religious observance and respect, everything
which belonged to them, even though found elsewhere. There liberty was
lost; here preserved. There bondage was strict; here strictly excluded. Into
that temple men were driven to become the chattels of their enemies, now
lording it over them; into these churches men were led by their relenting
foes, that they might be at liberty. In fine, the "gentle" Greeks appropriated that temple of Juno to the purposes of their own avarice and pride;
while these churches of Christ were chosen even by the savage barbarians
as the fit scenes for humility and mercy. But perhaps, after all, the Greeks
did in that victory of theirs spare the temples of those gods whom they
worshipped in common with the Trojans, and did not dare to put to the
sword or make captive the wretched and vanquished Trojans who fled
thither; and perhaps Virgil, in the manner of poets, has depicted what
never really happened? But there is no question that he depicted the usual
custom of an enemy when sacking a city.

[12] *Aeneid*, ii. 761

CHAPTER V

CAESAR'S STATEMENT REGARDING THE UNIVERSAL CUSTOM OF AN ENEMY WHEN SACKING A CITY

Even Caesar himself gives us positive testimony regarding this custom; for, in his deliverance in the senate about the conspirators, he says (as Sallust, a historian of distinguished veracity, writes[13]) "that virgins and boys are violated, children torn from the embrace of their parents, matrons subjected to whatever should be the pleasure of the conquerors, temples and houses plundered, slaughter and burning rife; in fine, all things filled with arms, corpses, blood, and wailing." If he had not mentioned temples here, we might suppose that enemies were in the habit of sparing the dwellings of the gods. And the Roman temples were in danger of these disasters, not from foreign foes, but from Catiline and his associates, the most noble senators and citizens of Rome. But these, it may be said, were abandoned men, and the parricides of their fatherland.

CHAPTER VI

THAT NOT EVEN THE ROMANS, WHEN THEY TOOK CITIES, SPARED THE CONQUERED IN THEIR TEMPLES

Why, then, need our argument take note of the many nations who have waged wars with one another, and have nowhere spared the conquered in the temples of their gods? Let us look at the practice of the Romans themselves: let us, I say, recall and review the Romans, whose chief praise it has been "to spare the vanquished and subdue the proud," and that they preferred "rather to forgive than to revenge an injury;" [14] and among so many and great cities which they have stormed, taken, and overthrown for the extension of their dominion, let us be told what temples they were accustomed to exempt, so that whoever took refuge in them was free. Or have they really done this, and has the fact been suppressed by the historians of these events? Is it to be believed, that men who sought out with the greatest eagerness points they could praise, would omit those which, in their own estimation, are the most signal proofs of piety? Marcus Marcellus, a distinguished Roman, who took Syracuse, a most splendidly adorned city, is reported to have bewailed its coming ruin, and to have shed his own tears over it before he spilt its blood. He took steps also to preserve the chastity even of his enemy. For before he gave orders for the storming of the city, he issued an edict forbidding the violation of any free person. Yet the city was sacked according to the custom of war; nor do we anywhere read, that even by so chaste and gentle a commander orders were

---

[13] *Cat.* 51   [14] Sallust, *Cat.* 9

given that no one should be injured who had fled to this or that temple. And this certainly would by no means have been omitted, when neither his weeping nor his edict preservative of chastity could be passed in silence. Fabius, the conqueror of the city of Tarentum, is praised for abstaining from making booty of the images. For when his secretary proposed the question to him, what he wished done with the statues of the gods, which had been taken in large numbers, he veiled his moderation under a joke. For he asked of what sort they were; and when they reported to him that there were not only many large images, but some of them armed, "Oh," says he, "let us leave with the Tarentines their angry gods." Seeing, then, that the writers of Roman history could not pass in silence, neither the weeping of the one general nor the laughing of the other, neither the chaste pity of the one nor the facetious moderation of the other, on what occasion would it be omitted, if, for the honor of any of their enemy's gods, they had shown this particular form of leniency, that in any temple slaughter or captivity was prohibited?

CHAPTER VII

THAT THE CRUELTIES WHICH OCCURRED IN THE SACK OF ROME WERE IN ACCORDANCE WITH THE CUSTOM OF WAR, WHEREAS THE ACTS OF CLEMENCY RESULTED FROM THE INFLUENCE OF CHRIST'S NAME

All the spoiling, then, which Rome was exposed to in the recent calamity —all the slaughter, plundering, burning, and misery—was the result of the custom of war. But what was novel, was that savage barbarians showed themselves in so gentle a guise, that the largest churches were chosen and set apart for the purpose of being filled with the people to whom quarter was given, and that in them none were slain, from them none forcibly dragged; that into them many were led by their relenting enemies to be set at liberty, and that from them none were led into slavery by merciless foes. Whoever does not see that this is to be attributed to the name of Christ, and to the Christian temper, is blind; whoever sees this, and gives no praise, is ungrateful; whoever hinders any one from praising it, is mad. Far be it from any prudent man to impute this clemency to the barbarians. Their fierce and bloody minds were awed, and bridled, and marvellously tempered by Him who so long before said by His prophet, "I will visit their transgression with the rod, and their iniquities with stripes; nevertheless my loving-kindness will I not utterly take from them." [15]

[15] Ps. lxxxix. 32

CHAPTER VIII

OF THE ADVANTAGES AND DISADVANTAGES WHICH OFTEN
INDISCRIMINATELY ACCRUE TO GOOD AND WICKED MEN

Will some one say, Why, then, was this divine compassion extended even to the ungodly and ungrateful? Why, but because it was the mercy of Him who daily maketh His sun to rise on the evil and on the good, and sendeth rain on the just and on the unjust.[16] For though some of these men, taking thought of this, repent of their wickedness and reform, some, as the apostle says, "despising the riches of His goodness and long-suffering, after their hardness and impenitent heart, treasure up unto themselves wrath against the day of wrath and revelation of the righteous judgment of God, who will render to every man according to his deeds:"[17] nevertheless does the patience of God still invite the wicked to repentance, even as the scourge of God educates the good to patience. And so, too, does the mercy of God embrace the good that it may cherish them, as the severity of God arrests the wicked to punish them. To the divine providence it has seemed good to prepare in the world to come for the righteous good things, which the unrighteous shall not enjoy; and for the wicked evil things, by which the good shall not be tormented. But as for the good things of this life, and its ills, God has willed that these should be common to both; that we might not too eagerly covet the things which wicked men are seen equally to enjoy, nor shrink with an unseemly fear from the ills which even good men often suffer.

There is, too, a very great difference in the purpose served both by those events which we call adverse and those called prosperous. For the good man is neither uplifted with the good things of time, nor broken by its ills; but the wicked man, because he is corrupted by this world's happiness, feels himself punished by its unhappiness. Yet often, even in the present distribution of temporal things, does God plainly evince His own interference. For if every sin were now visited with manifest punishment, nothing would seem to be reserved for the final judgment; on the other hand, if no sin received now a plainly divine punishment, it would be concluded that there is no divine providence at all. And so of the good things of this life: if God did not by a very visible liberality confer these on some of those persons who ask for them, we should say that these good things were not at His disposal; and if He gave them to all who sought them, we should suppose that such were the only rewards of His service; and such a service would make us not godly, but greedy rather, and covetous. Therefore, though good and bad men suffer alike, we must not suppose that there is no difference between the men themselves, because there is no difference in what they both suffer. For even in the likeness of the sufferings, there remains an unlikeness in the sufferers; and though exposed to the same anguish, virtue and vice are not the same thing. For as the same fire causes gold to glow brightly, and chaff to smoke; and under the same flail the straw is beaten small, while the grain is cleansed; and as the lees are not mixed with the oil, though squeezed out of the vat by the same pressure, so the same violence of affliction proves, purges, clarifies the good, but damns, ruins, exterminates the wicked. And thus it is that in the same affliction the wicked detest God and blaspheme, while the good pray and praise. So material a difference does it make, not what ills are suffered, but what kind of man suffers them. For, stirred up with the same movement, mud exhales a horrible stench, and ointment emits a fragrant odor.

CHAPTER IX

OF THE REASONS FOR ADMINISTERING CORRECTION
TO BAD AND GOOD TOGETHER

What, then, have the Christians suffered in that calamitous period, which would not profit every one who duly and faithfully considered the following circumstances? First of all, they must humbly consider those very sins which have provoked God to fill the world with such terrible disasters; for although they be far from the excesses of wicked, immoral, and ungodly men, yet they do not judge themselves so completely removed from all faults as to be too good to suffer for these temporal ills. For every man, however laudably he lives, yet yields in some points to the lust of the flesh. Though he do not fall into gross enormity of wickedness, and abandoned viciousness, and abominable profanity, yet he slips into some sins, either rarely or so much the more frequently as the sins seem of less account. But not to mention this, where can we readily find a man who holds in fit and just estimation those persons on account of whose revolting pride, luxury, and avarice, and cursed iniquities and impiety, God now smites the earth as His predictions threatened? Where is the man who lives with them in the style in which it becomes us to live with them? For often we wickedly blind ourselves to the occasions of teaching and admonishing them, sometimes even of reprimanding and chiding them, either because we shrink from the labor or are ashamed to offend them, or because we fear to lose good friendships, lest this should stand in the way of our advancement, or injure us in some worldly matter, which either our covetous disposition desires to obtain, or our weakness shrinks from losing. So that, although the conduct of wicked men is distasteful to the good, and therefore they do not fall with them into that damnation which in the next life awaits such persons, yet, because they spare their damnable sins through fear, therefore, even though their own sins be slight and venial, they are justly scourged with the wicked in this world, though in eternity they quite escape punishment. Justly, when God afflicts them in common with the wicked, do they find this life bitter, through love of whose sweetness they declined to be bitter to these sinners.

If any one forbears to reprove and find fault with those who are doing wrong, because he seeks a more seasonable opportunity, or because he fears they may be made worse by his rebuke, or that other weak persons may be disheartened from endeavoring to lead a good and pious life, and may be driven from the faith; this man's omission seems to be occasioned not by covetousness, but by a charitable consideration. But what is blameworthy is, that they who themselves revolt from the conduct of the wicked, and live in quite another fashion, yet spare those faults in other men which they ought to reprehend and wean them from; and spare them because they fear to give offence, lest they should injure their interests in those things which good men may innocently and legitimately use—though they use them more greedily than becomes persons who are strangers in this world, and profess the hope of a heavenly country. For not only the weaker brethren who enjoy married life, and have children (or desire to have them), and own houses and establishments, whom the apostle addresses in the churches, warning and instructing them how they should live, both the wives with their husbands, and the husbands with their wives, the children with their parents, and parents with their children, and servants with their masters, and masters with their servants—not only do these weaker brethren gladly obtain and grudgingly lose many earthly and temporal things on account of which they dare not offend men whose polluted and wicked life greatly displeases them; but those also who live at a higher level, who are not entangled in the meshes of married life, but use meagre food and raiment, do often take thought of their own safety and good name, and abstain from finding fault with the wicked, because they fear their wiles and violence. And although they do not fear them to such an extent as to be drawn to the commission of like iniquities, nay, not by any threats or violence soever; yet those very deeds which they refuse to share in the commission of, they often decline to find fault with, when possibly they might by finding fault prevent their commission. They abstain from interference, because they fear that, if it fail of good effect, their own safety or reputation may be damaged or destroyed; not because they see that their preservation and good name are needful, that they may be able to influence those who need their instruction, but rather because they weakly relish the flattery and respect of men, and fear the judgments of the people, and the pain or death of the body; that is to say, their non-intervention is the result of selfishness, and not of love.

Accordingly this seems to me to be one principal reason why the good are chastised along with the wicked, when God is pleased to visit with temporal punishments the profligate manners of a community. They are punished together, not because they have spent an equally corrupt life, but because the good as well as the wicked, though not equally with them, love this present life; while they ought to hold it cheap, that the wicked, being admonished and reformed by their example, might lay hold of life eternal. And if they will not be the companions of the good in seeking life everlasting, they should be loved as enemies, and be dealt with patiently. For so long as they live, it remains uncertain whether they may not come to a better mind. These selfish persons have more cause to fear than those to whom it was said through the prophet, "He is taken away in his iniquity, but his blood will I require at the watchman's hand." [18] For watchmen or overseers of the people are appointed in churches, that they may unsparingly rebuke sin. Nor is that man guiltless of the sin we speak of, who, though he be not a watchman, yet sees in the conduct of those with whom the relationships of this life bring him into contact, many things that should be blamed, and yet overlooks them, fearing to give offence, and lose such worldly blessings as may legitimately be desired, but which he too eagerly grasps. Then, lastly, there is another reason why the good are afflicted with temporal calamities—the reason which Job's case exemplifies: that the human spirit may be proved, and that it may be manifested with what fortitude of pious trust, and with how unmercenary a love, it cleaves to God.

CHAPTER X

THAT THE SAINTS LOSE NOTHING IN LOSING TEMPORAL GOODS

These are the considerations which one must keep in view, that he may answer the question whether any evil happens to the faithful and godly which cannot be turned to profit. Or shall we say that the question is needless, and that the apostle is vaporing when he says, "We know that all things work together for good to them that love God?" [19]

They lost all they had. Their faith? Their godliness? The possessions of the hidden man of the heart, which in the sight of God are of great price? [20] Did they lose these? For these are the wealth of Christians, to whom the wealthy apostle said, "Godliness with contentment is great gain. For we brought nothing into this world, and it is certain we can carry nothing out. And having food and raiment, let us be therewith content. But they that will be rich fall into temptation and a snare, and into many foolish and hurtful lusts, which drown men in destruction and perdition. For the love of money is the root of all evil; which, while some coveted after, they have erred from the faith, and pierced themselves through with many sorrows." [21]

They, then, who lost their worldly all in the sack of Rome, if they owned their possessions as they had been taught by the apostle, who him-

[18] Ezek. xxxiii. 6   [19] Rom. viii. 28   [20] 1 Pet. iii. 4   [21] 1 Tim. vi. 6-10

self was poor without, but rich within—that is to say, if they used the world as not using it—could say in the words of Job, heavily tried, but not overcome: "Naked came I out of my mother's womb, and naked shall I return thither: the Lord gave, and the Lord hath taken away; as it pleased the Lord, so has it come to pass: blessed be the name of the Lord." [22] Like a good servant, Job counted the will of his Lord his great possession, by obedience to which his soul was enriched; nor did it grieve him to lose, while yet living, those goods which he must shortly leave at his death. But as to those feebler spirits who, though they cannot be said to prefer earthly possessions to Christ, do yet cleave to them with a somewhat immoderate attachment, they have discovered by the pain of losing these things how much they were sinning in loving them. For their grief is of their own making; in the words of the apostle quoted above, "they have pierced themselves through with many sorrows." For it was well that they who had so long despised these verbal admonitions should receive the teaching of experience. For when the apostle says, "They that will be rich fall into temptation," and so on, what he blames in riches is not the possession of them, but the desire of them. For elsewhere he says, "Charge them that are rich in this world, that they be not high-minded, nor trust in uncertain riches, but in the living God who giveth us richly all things to enjoy; that they do good, that they be rich in good works, ready to distribute, willing to communicate; laying up in store for themselves a good foundation against the time to come, that they may lay hold on eternal life." [23] They who were making such a use of their property have been consoled for light losses by great gains, and have had more pleasure in those possessions which they have securely laid past, by freely giving them away, than grief in those which they entirely lost by an anxious and selfish hoarding of them. For nothing could perish on earth save what they would be ashamed to carry away from earth. Our Lord's injunction runs, "Lay not up for yourselves treasures upon earth, where moth and rust doth corrupt, and where thieves break through and steal; but lay up for yourselves treasures in heaven, where neither moth nor rust doth corrupt, and where thieves do not break through nor steal: for where your treasure is, there will your heart be also." [24] And they who have listened to this injunction have proved in the time of tribulation how well they were advised in not despising this most trustworthy teacher, and most faithful and mighty guardian of their treasure. For if many were glad that their treasure was stored in places which the enemy chanced not to light upon, how much better founded was the joy of those who, by the counsel of their God, had fled with their treasure to a citadel which no enemy can possibly reach! Thus our Paulinus, bishop of Nola,[25] who

[22] Job i. 21   [23] 1 Tim. vi. 17-19   [24] Matt. vi. 19-21
[25] Paulinus was a native of Bordeaux, and both by inheritance and marriage acquired great wealth, which, after his conversion in his thirty-sixth year, he distributed to the

voluntarily abandoned vast wealth and became quite poor, though abundantly rich in holiness, when the barbarians sacked Nola, and took him prisoner, used silently to pray, as he afterwards told me, "O Lord, let me not be troubled for gold and silver, for where all my treasure is Thou knowest." For all his treasure was where he had been taught to hide and store it by Him who had also foretold that these calamities would happen in the world. Consequently those persons who obeyed their Lord when he warned them where and how to lay up treasure, did not lose even their earthly possessions in the invasion of the barbarians; while those who are now repenting that they did not obey Him have learnt the right use of earthly goods, if not by the wisdom which would have prevented their loss, at least by the experience which follows it.

But some good and Christian men have been put to the torture, that they might be forced to deliver up their goods to the enemy. They could indeed neither deliver nor lose that good which made themselves good. If, however, they preferred torture to the surrender of the mammon of iniquity, then I say they were not good men. Rather they should have been reminded that, if they suffered so severely for the sake of money, they should endure all torment, if need be, for Christ's sake; that they might be taught to love Him rather who enriches with eternal felicity all who suffer for Him, and not silver and gold, for which it was pitiable to suffer, whether they preserved it by telling a lie or lost it by telling the truth. For under these tortures no one lost Christ by confessing Him, no one preserved wealth save by denying its existence. So that possibly the torture which taught them that they should set their affections on a possession they could not lose, was more useful than those possessions which, without any useful fruit at all, disquieted and tormented their anxious owners. But then we are reminded that some were tortured who had no wealth to surrender, but who were not believed when they said so. These too, however, had perhaps some craving for wealth, and were not willingly poor with a holy resignation; and to such it had to be made plain, that not the actual possession alone, but also the desire of wealth, deserved such excruciating pains. And even if they were destitute of any hidden stores of gold and silver, because they were living in hopes of a better life—I know not indeed if any such person was tortured on the supposition that he had wealth; but if so, then certainly in confessing, when put to the question, a holy poverty, he confessed Christ. And though it was scarcely to be expected that the barbarians should believe him, yet no confessor of a holy poverty could be tortured without receiving a heavenly reward.

Again, they say that the long famine laid many a Christian low. But this, too, the faithful turned to good uses by a pious endurance of it. For those whom famine killed outright it rescued from the ills of this life, as a

poor. He became bishop of Nola in A. D. 409, being then in his fifty-sixth year. Nola was taken by Alaric shortly after the sack of Rome.

kindly disease would have done; and those who were only hunger-bitten were taught to live more sparingly, and inured to longer fasts.

CHAPTER XI

OF THE END OF THIS LIFE, WHETHER IT IS MATERIAL THAT IT BE LONG DELAYED

But, it is added, many Christians were slaughtered, and were put to death in a hideous variety of cruel ways. Well, if this be hard to bear, it is assuredly the common lot of all who are born into this life. Of this at least I am certain, that no one has ever died who was not destined to die some time. Now the end of life puts the longest life on a par with the shortest. For of two things which have alike ceased to be, the one is not better, the other worse—the one greater, the other less.[a] And of what consequence is it what kind of death puts an end to life, since he who has died once is not forced to go through the same ordeal a second time? And as in the daily casualties of life every man is, as it were, threatened with numberless deaths, so long as it remains uncertain which of them is his fate, I would ask whether it is not better to suffer one and die, than to live in fear of all? I am not unaware of the poor-spirited fear which prompts us to choose rather to live long in fear of so many deaths, than to die once and so escape them all; but the weak and cowardly shrinking of the flesh is one thing, and the well-considered and reasonable persuasion of the soul quite another. That death is not to be judged an evil which is the end of a good life; for death becomes evil only by the retribution which follows it. They, then, who are destined to die, need not be careful to inquire what death they are to die, but into what place death will usher them. And since Christians are well aware that the death of the godly pauper whose sores the dogs licked was far better than of the wicked rich man who lay in purple and fine linen, what harm could these terrific deaths do to the dead who had lived well?

CHAPTER XII

OF THE BURIAL OF THE DEAD: THAT THE DENIAL OF IT TO CHRISTIANS DOES THEM NO INJURY

Further still, we are reminded that in such a carnage as then occurred, the bodies could not even be buried. But godly confidence is not appalled by so ill-omened a circumstance; for the faithful bear in mind that assurance has been given that not a hair of their head shall perish, and that, therefore, though they even be devoured by beasts, their blessed resurrection will not hereby be hindered. The Truth would nowise have said, "Fear not them which kill the body, but are not able to kill the soul," [26] if

[a] A thought often expressed by M. Aurelius (ii. 14).—Ed.   [26] Matt. x. 28

anything whatever that an enemy could do to the body of the slain could be detrimental to the future life. Or will some one perhaps take so absurd a position as to contend that those who kill the body are not to be feared before death, and lest they kill the body, but after death, lest they deprive it of burial? If this be so, then that is false which Christ says, "Be not afraid of them that kill the body, and after that have no more that they can do;" [27] for it seems they can do great injury to the dead body. Far be it from us to suppose that the Truth can be thus false. They who kill the body are said "to do something," because the deathblow is felt, the body still having sensation; but after that, they have no more that they can do, for in the slain body there is no sensation. And so there are indeed many bodies of Christians lying unburied; but no one has separated them from heaven, nor from that earth which is all filled with the presence of Him who knows whence He will raise again what He created. It is said, indeed, in the Psalm: "The dead bodies of Thy servants have they given to be meat unto the fowls of the heaven, the flesh of Thy saints unto the beasts of the earth. Their blood have they shed like water about Jerusalem; and there was none to bury them." [28] But this was said rather to exhibit the cruelty of those who did these things, than the misery of those who suffered them. To the eyes of men this appears a harsh and doleful lot, yet precious in the sight of the Lord is the death of His saints.[29] Wherefore all these last offices and ceremonies that concern the dead, the careful funeral arrangements, and the equipment of the tomb, and the pomp of obsequies, are rather the solace of the living than the comfort of the dead. If a costly burial does any good to a wicked man, a squalid burial, or none at all, may harm the godly. His crowd of domestics furnished the purple-clad Dives with a funeral gorgeous in the eye of man; but in the sight of God that was a more sumptuous funeral which the ulcerous pauper received at the hands of the angels, who did not carry him out to a marble tomb, but bore him aloft to Abraham's bosom.

The men against whom I have undertaken to defend the city of God laugh at all this. But even their own philosophers[30] have despised a careful burial; and often whole armies have fought and fallen for their earthly country without caring to inquire whether they would be left exposed on the field of battle, or become the food of wild beasts. Of this noble disregard of sepulture poetry has well said: "He who has no tomb has the sky for his vault." [31] How much less ought they to insult over the unburied bodies of Christians, to whom it has been promised that the flesh itself shall be restored, and the body formed anew, all the members of it being gathered not only from the earth, but from the most secret recesses of any other of the elements in which the dead bodies of men have lain hid!

[27] Luke xii. 4   [28] Ps. lxxix. 2, 3   [29] Ps. cxvi. 15
[30] Cf. Seneca, *De Tranq.* c. 14, and *Epist.* 92 ; Cicero, *Tusc. Disp.* i. 43
[31] Lucan, *Pharsalia*, vii. 819, of those whom Caesar forbade to be buried after the battle of Pharsalia

of these last offices, this is neither the fault of the living, for they could
not render them; nor an indication to the dead, for they cannot feel the loss

CHAPTER XIII

REASONS FOR BURYING THE BODIES OF THE SAINTS

Nevertheless the bodies of the dead are not on this account to be despised and left unburied; least of all the bodies of the righteous and faithful, which have been used by the Holy Spirit as His organs and instruments
for all good works. For if the dress of a father, or his ring, or anything
he wore, be precious to his children, in proportion to the love they bore
him, with how much more reason ought we to care for the bodies of those
we love which they wore far more closely and intimately than any clothing!
For the body is not an extraneous ornament or aid, but a part of man's
very nature. And therefore to the righteous of ancient times the last offices
were piously rendered, and sepulchres provided for them, and obsequies
celebrated;[32] and they themselves, while yet alive, gave commandment to
their sons about the burial, and, on occasion, even about the removal of
their bodies to some favorite place.[33] And Tobit, according to the angel's
testimony, is commended, and is said to have pleased God by burying
the dead.[34] Our Lord Himself, too, though He was to rise again the third
day, applauds, and commends to our applause, the good work of the religious woman who poured precious ointment over His limbs, and did it
against His burial.[35] And the Gospel speaks with commendation of those
who were careful to take down His body from the cross, and wrap it
lovingly in costly cerements, and see to its burial.[36] These instances certainly do not prove that corpses have any feeling; but they show that God's
providence extends even to the bodies of the dead, and that such pious
offices are pleasing to Him, as cherishing faith in the resurrection. And we
may also draw from them this wholesome lesson, that if God does not
forget even any kind office which loving care pays to the unconscious dead,
much more does He reward the charity we exercise towards the living.
Other things, indeed, which the holy patriarchs said of the burial and
removal of their bodies, they meant to be taken in a prophetic sense; but
of these we need not here speak at large, what we have already said
being sufficient. But if the want of those things which are necessary for
the support of the living, as food and clothing, though painful and trying,
does not break down the fortitude and virtuous endurance of good men,
nor eradicate piety from their souls, but rather renders it more fruitful,
how much less can the absence of the funeral, and of the other customary
attentions paid to the dead, render those wretched who are already reposing
in the hidden abodes of the blessed! Consequently, though in the sack of
Rome and of other towns the dead bodies of the Christians were deprived

[32] Gen. xxv. 9, xxxv. 29, etc.   [33] Gen. xlvii. 29, l. 24   [34] Tob. xii. 12   [35] Matt.
xxvi. 10-13   [36] John xix. 38

of these last offices, this is neither the fault of the living, for they could not render them; nor an infliction to the dead, for they cannot feel the loss.

CHAPTER XIV

OF THE CAPTIVITY OF THE SAINTS, AND THAT DIVINE CONSOLATION NEVER FAILED THEM THEREIN

But, say they, many Christians were even led away captive. This indeed was a most pitiable fate, if they could be led away to any place where they could not find their God. But for this calamity also sacred Scripture affords great consolation. The three youths[37] were captives; Daniel was a captive; so were other prophets: and God, the comforter, did not fail them. And in like manner He has not failed His own people in the power of a nation which, though barbarous, is yet human—He who did not abandon the prophet[38] in the belly of a monster. These things, indeed, are turned to ridicule rather than credited by those with whom we are debating; though they believe what they read in their own books, that Arion of Methymna, the famous lyrist, when he was thrown overboard, was received on a dolphin's back and carried to land. But that story of ours about the prophet Jonah is far more incredible—more incredible because more marvellous, and more marvellous because a greater exhibition of power.

CHAPTER XV

OF REGULUS, IN WHOM WE HAVE AN EXAMPLE OF THE VOLUNTARY ENDURANCE OF CAPTIVITY FOR THE SAKE OF RELIGION; WHICH YET DID NOT PROFIT HIM, THOUGH HE WAS A WORSHIPPER OF THE GODS

But among their own famous men they have a very noble example of the voluntary endurance of captivity in obedience to a religious scruple. Marcus Attilius Regulus, a Roman general, was a prisoner in the hands of the Carthaginians. But they, being more anxious to exchange their prisoners with the Romans than to keep them, sent Regulus as a special envoy with their own ambassadors to negotiate this exchange, but bound him first with an oath, that if he failed to accomplish their wish, he would return to Carthage. He went, and persuaded the senate to the opposite course, because he believed it was not for the advantage of the Roman republic to make an exchange of prisoners. After he had thus exerted his influence, the Romans did not compel him to return to the enemy; but what he had sworn he voluntarily performed. But the Carthaginians put him to death with refined, elaborate, and horrible tortures. They shut him up in a narrow box, in which he was compelled to stand, and in which finely sharpened nails were fixed all round about him, so that he could not

[37] Dan. iii. [38] Jonah

lean upon any part of it without intense pain; and so they killed him by depriving him of sleep. With justice, indeed, do they applaud the virtue which rose superior to so frightful a fate. However, the gods he swore by were those who are now supposed to avenge the prohibition of their worship, by inflicting these present calamities on the human race. But if these gods, who were worshipped specially in this behalf, that they might confer happiness in this life, either willed or permitted these punishments to be inflicted on one who kept his oath to them, what more cruel punishment could they in their anger have inflicted on a perjured person? But why may I not draw from my reasoning a double inference? Regulus certainly had such reverence for the gods, that for his oath's sake he would neither remain in his own land nor go elsewhere, but without hesitation returned to his bitterest enemies. If he thought that this course would be advantageous with respect to this present life, he was certainly much deceived, for it brought his life to a frightful termination. By his own example, in fact, he taught that the gods do not secure the temporal happiness of their worshippers; since he himself, who was devoted to their worship, as both conquered in battle and taken prisoner, and then, because he refused to act in violation of the oath he had sworn by them, was tortured and put to death by a new, and hitherto unheard of, and all too horrible kind of punishment. And on the supposition that the worshippers of the gods are rewarded by felicity in the life to come, why, then, do they calumniate the influence of Christianity? why do they assert that this disaster has overtaken the city because it has ceased to worship its gods, since, worship them as assiduously as it may, it may yet be as unfortunate as Regulus was? Or will some one carry so wonderful a blindness to the extent of wildly attempting, in the face of the evident truth, to contend that though one man might be unfortunate, though a worshipper of the gods, yet a whole city could not be so? That is to say, the power of their gods is better adapted to preserve multitudes than individuals—as if a multitude were not composed of individuals.

But if they say that M. Regulus, even while a prisoner and enduring these bodily torments, might yet enjoy the blessedness of a virtuous soul, then let them recognize that true virtue by which a city also may be blessed. For the blessedness of a community and of an individual flow from the same source; for a community is nothing else than a harmonious collection of individuals. So that I am not concerned meantime to discuss what kind of virtue Regulus possessed; enough, that by his very noble example they are forced to own that the gods are to be worshipped not for the sake of bodily comforts or external advantages; for he preferred to lose all such things rather than offend the gods by whom he had sworn. But what can we make of men who glory in having such a citizen, but dread having a city like him? If they do not dread this, then let them acknowledge that some such calamity as befell Regulus may also befall a community, though they be worshipping their gods as diligently as he; and let them no longer throw the blame of their misfortunes on Christianity. But as our present concern is with those Christians who were taken prisoners, let those who take occasion from this calamity to revile our most wholesome religion in a fashion not less imprudent than impudent, consider this and hold their peace; for if it was no reproach to their gods that a most punctilious worshipper of theirs should, for the sake of keeping his oath to them, be deprived of his native land without hope of finding another, and fall into the hands of his enemies, and be put to death by a long-drawn and exquisite torture, much less ought the Christian name to be charged with the captivity of those who believe in its power, since they, in confident expectation of a heavenly country, know that they are pilgrims even in their own homes.

CHAPTER XVI

OF THE VIOLATION OF THE CONSECRATED AND OTHER CHRISTIAN VIRGINS, TO WHICH THEY WERE SUBJECTED IN CAPTIVITY, AND TO WHICH THEIR OWN WILL GAVE NO CONSENT; AND WHETHER THIS CONTAMINATED THEIR SOULS

But they fancy they bring a conclusive charge against Christianity, when they aggravate the horror of captivity by adding that not only wives and unmarried maidens, but even consecrated virgins, were violated. But truly, with respect to this, it is not Christian faith, nor piety, nor even the virtue of chastity, which is hemmed into any difficulty; the only difficulty is so to treat the subject as to satisfy at once modesty and reason. And in discussing it we shall not be so careful to reply to our accusers as to comfort our friends. Let this, therefore, in the first place, be laid down as an unassailable position, that the virtue which makes the life good has its throne in the soul, and thence rules the members of the body, which becomes holy in virtue of the holiness of the will; and that while the will remains firm and unshaken, nothing that another person does with the body, or upon the body, is any fault of the person who suffers it, so long as he cannot escape it without sin. But as not only pain may be inflicted, but lust gratified on the body of another, whenever anything of this latter kind takes place, shame invades even a thoroughly pure spirit from which modesty has not departed—shame, lest that act which could not be suffered without some sensual pleasure, should be believed to have been committed also with some assent of the will.

CHAPTER XVII

OF SUICIDE COMMITTED THROUGH FEAR OF PUNISHMENT OR DISHONOR

And consequently, even if some of these virgins killed themselves to avoid such disgrace, who that has any human feeling would refuse to forgive them? And as for those who would not put an end to their lives, lest they might seem to escape the crime of another by a sin of their own, he who lays this to their charge as a great wickedness is himself not guiltless of the fault of folly. For if it is not lawful to take the law into our own hands, and slay even a guilty person, whose death no public sentence has warranted, then certainly he who kills himself is a homicide, and so much the guiltier of his own death, as he was more innocent of that offence for which he doomed himself to die. Do we justly execrate the deed of Judas, and does truth itself pronounce that by hanging himself he rather aggravated than expiated the guilt of that most iniquitous betrayal, since, by despairing of God's mercy in his sorrow that wrought death, he left to himself no place for a healing penitence? How much more ought he to abstain from laying violent hands on himself who has done nothing worthy of such a punishment! For Judas, when he killed himself, killed a wicked man; but he passed from this life chargeable not only with the death of Christ, but with his own: for though he killed himself on account of his crime, his killing himself was another crime. Why, then, should a man who has done no ill do ill to himself, and by killing himself kill the innocent to escape another's guilty act, and perpetrate upon himself a sin of his own, that the sin of another may not be perpetrated on him?

CHAPTER XVIII

OF THE VIOLENCE WHICH MAY BE DONE TO THE BODY BY
ANOTHER'S LUST, WHILE THE MIND REMAINS INVIOLATE

But is there a fear that even another's lust may pollute the violated? It will not pollute, if it be another's: if it pollute, it is not another's, but is shared also by the polluted. But since purity is a virtue of the soul, and has for its companion virtue, the fortitude which will rather endure all ills than consent to evil; and since no one, however magnanimous and pure, has always the disposal of his own body, but can control only the consent and refusal of his will, what sane man can suppose that, if his body be seized and forcibly made use of to satisfy the lust of another, he thereby loses his purity? For if purity can be thus destroyed, then assuredly purity is no virtue of the soul; nor can it be numbered among those good things by which the life is made good, but among the good things of the body, in the same category as strength, beauty, sound and unbroken health, and, in short, all such good things as may be diminished without at all diminishing the goodness and rectitude of our life. But if purity be nothing better than these, why should the body be perilled that it may be preserved? If, on the other hand, it belongs to the soul, then not even when the body is violated is it lost. Nay more, the virtue of holy continence, when it resists the uncleanness of carnal lust, sanctifies even the body, and therefore when this continence remains unsubdued, even the sanctity of the body is preserved, because the will to use it holily remains, and, so far as lies in the body itself, the power also.

For the sanctity of the body does not consist in the integrity of its members, nor in their exemption from all touch; for they are exposed to various accidents which do violence to and wound them, and the surgeons who administer relief often perform operations that sicken the spectator. A midwife, suppose, has (whether maliciously or accidentally, or through unskillfulness) destroyed the virginity of some girl, while endeavoring to ascertain it: I suppose no one is so foolish as to believe that, by this destruction of the integrity of one organ, the virgin has lost anything even of her bodily sanctity. And thus, so long as the soul keeps this firmness of purpose which sanctifies even the body, the violence done by another's lust makes no impression on this bodily sanctity, which is preserved intact by one's own persistent continence. Suppose a virgin violates the oath she has sworn to God, and goes to meet her seducer with the intention of yielding to him, shall we say that as she goes she is possessed even of bodily sanctity, when already she has lost and destroyed that sanctity of soul which sanctifies the body? Far be it from us so to misapply words. Let us rather draw this conclusion, that while the sanctity of the soul remains even when the body is violated, the sanctity of the body is not lost; and that, in like manner, the sanctity of the body is lost when the sanctity of the soul is violated, though the body itself remains intact. And therefore a woman who has been violated by the sin of another, and without any consent of her own, has no cause to put herself to death; much less has she cause to commit suicide in order to avoid such violation, for in that case she commits certain homicide to prevent a crime which is uncertain as yet, and not her own.

CHAPTER XIX

OF LUCRETIA, WHO PUT AN END TO HER LIFE BECAUSE OF THE OUTRAGE DONE HER

This, then, is our position, and it seems sufficiently lucid. We maintain that when a woman is violated while her soul admits no consent to the iniquity, but remains inviolably chaste, the sin is not hers, but his who violates her. But do they against whom we have to defend not only the souls,

Lucretia dilemma

but the sacred bodies too of these outraged Christian captives—do they, perhaps, dare to dispute our position? But all know how loudly they extol the purity of Lucretia, that noble matron of ancient Rome. When King Tarquin's son had violated her body, she made known the wickedness of this young profligate to her husband Collatinus, and to Brutus her kinsman, men of high rank and full of courage, and bound them by an oath to avenge it. Then, heart-sick, and unable to bear the shame, she put an end to her life. What shall we call her? An adulteress, or chaste? There is no question which she was. Not more happily than truly did a declaimer say of this sad occurrence: "Here was a marvel: there were two, and only one committed adultery." Most forcibly and truly spoken. For this declaimer, seeing in the union of the two bodies the foul lust of the one, and the chaste will of the other, and giving heed not to the contact of the bodily members, but to the wide diversity of their souls, says: "There were two, but the adultery was committed only by one."

But how is it, that she who was no partner to the crime bears the heavier punishment of the two? For the adulterer was only banished along with his father; she suffered the extreme penalty. If that was not impurity by which she was unwillingly ravished, then this is not justice by which she, being chaste, is punished. To you I appeal, ye laws and judges of Rome. Even after the perpetration of great enormities, you do not suffer the criminal to be slain untried. If, then, one were to bring to your bar this case, and were to prove to you that a woman not only untried, but chaste and innocent, had been killed, would you not visit the murderer with punishment proportionably severe? This crime was committed by Lucretia; that Lucretia so celebrated and lauded slew the innocent, chaste, outraged Lucretia. Pronounce sentence. But if you cannot, because there does not appear any one whom you can punish, why do you extol with such unmeasured laudation her who slew an innocent and chaste woman? Assuredly you will find it impossible to defend her before the judges of the realms below, if they be such as your poets are fond of representing them; for she is among those:

> Who guiltless sent themselves to doom,
> And all for loathing of the day,
> In madness threw their lives away.

And if she with the others wishes to return,

> Fate bars the way: around their keep
> The slow unlovely waters creep,
> And bind with ninefold chain.[39]

[39] *Aeneid*, vi. 434

Or perhaps she is not there, because she slew herself conscious of guilt, not of innocence? She herself alone knows her reason; but what if she was betrayed by the pleasure of the act, and gave some consent to Sextus, though so violently abusing her, and then was so affected with remorse, that she thought death alone could expiate her sin? Even though this were the case, she ought still to have held her hand from suicide, if she could with her false gods have accomplished a fruitful repentance. However, if such were the state of the case, and if it were false that there were two, but one only committed adultery; if the truth were that both were involved in it, one by open assault, the other by secret consent, then she did not kill an innocent woman; and therefore her erudite defenders may maintain that she is not among that class of the dwellers below "who guiltless sent themselves to doom." But this case of Lucretia is in such a dilemma, that if you extenuate the homicide, you confirm the adultery: if you acquit her of adultery, you make the charge of homicide heavier; and there is no way out of the dilemma, when one asks, If she was adulterous, why praise her? if chaste, why slay her?

Nevertheless, for our purpose of refuting those who are unable to comprehend what true sanctity is, and who therefore revile our outraged Christian women, it is enough that in the instance of this noble Roman matron it was said in her praise, "There were two, but the adultery was the crime of only one." For Lucretia was confidently believed to be superior to the contamination of any consenting thought to the adultery. And accordingly, since she killed herself for being subjected to an outrage in which she had no guilty part, it is obvious that this act of hers was prompted not by the love of purity, but by the overwhelming burden of her shame. She was ashamed that so foul a crime had been perpetrated upon her, though without her abetting; and this matron, with the Roman love of glory in her veins, was seized with a proud dread that, if she continued to live, it would be supposed she willingly did not resent the wrong that had been done her. She could not exhibit to men her conscience, but she judged that her self-inflicted punishment would testify her state of mind; and she burned with shame at the thought that her patient endurance of the foul affront that another had done her, should be construed into complicity with him. Not such was the decision of the Christian women who suffered as she did, and yet survive. They declined to avenge upon themselves the guilt of others, and so add crimes of their own to those crimes in which they had no share. For this they would have done had their shame driven them to homicide, as the lust of their enemies had driven them to adultery. Within their own souls, in the witness of their own conscience, they enjoy the glory of chastity. In the sight of God, too, they are esteemed pure, and this contents them; they ask no more: it suffices them to have opportunity of doing good, and they decline to evade the distress of human suspicion, lest they thereby deviate from the divine law.

CHAPTER XX

THAT CHRISTIANS HAVE NO AUTHORITY FOR COMMITTING SUICIDE IN ANY CIRCUMSTANCES WHATEVER

It is not without significance, that in no passage of the holy canonical books there can be found either divine precept or permission to take away our own life, whether for the sake of entering on the enjoyment of immortality, or of shunning, or ridding ourselves of anything whatever. Nay, the law, rightly interpreted, even prohibits suicide, where it says, "Thou shalt not kill." [40] This is proved especially by the omission of the words "thy neighbor," which are inserted when false witness is forbidden: "Thou shalt not bear false witness against thy neighbor." Nor yet should any one on this account suppose he has not broken this commandment if he has borne false witness only against himself. For the love of our neighbor is regulated by the love of ourselves, as it is written, "Thou shalt love thy neighbor as thyself." [41] If, then, he who makes false statements about himself is not less guilty of bearing false witness than if he had made them to the injury of his neighbor; although in the commandment prohibiting false witness only his neighbor is mentioned, and persons taking no pains to understand it might suppose that a man was allowed to be a false witness to his own hurt; how much greater reason have we to understand that a man may not kill himself, since in the commandment, "Thou shalt not kill," there is no limitation added nor any exception made in favor of any one, and least of all in favor of him on whom the command is laid! And so some attempt to extend this command even to beasts and cattle, as if it forbade us to take life from any creature. But if so, why not extend it also to the plants, and all that is rooted in and nourished by the earth? For though this class of creatures have no sensation, yet they also are said to live, and consequently they can die; and therefore, if violence be done them, can be killed. So, too, the apostle, when speaking of the seeds of such things as these, says, "That which thou sowest is not quickened except it die;" [42] and in the Psalm it is said, "He killed their vines with hail." [43] Must we therefore reckon it a breaking of this commandment, "Thou shalt not kill," to pull a flower? Are we thus insanely to countenance the foolish error of the Manichaeans? Putting aside, then, these ravings, if, when we say, Thou shalt not kill, we do not understand this of the plants, since they have no sensation, nor of the irrational animals that fly, swim, walk, or creep, since they are dissociated from us by their want of reason, and are therefore by the just appointment of the Creator subjected to us to kill or keep alive for our own uses; if so, then it remains that we understand that commandment simply of man. The commandment is, "Thou shalt not kill man;"

[40] Exod. xx. 13, 16   [41] Matt. xxii. 39   [42] 1 Cor. xv. 36   [43] Ps. lxxviii. 47

therefore neither another nor yourself, for he who kills himself still kills nothing else than man.

CHAPTER XXI

OF THE CASES IN WHICH WE MAY PUT MEN TO DEATH WITHOUT INCURRING THE GUILT OF MURDER

However, there are some exceptions made by the divine authority to its own law, that men may not be put to death. These exceptions are of two kinds, being justified either by a general law, or by a special commission granted for a time to some individual. And in this latter case, he to whom authority is delegated, and who is but the sword in the hand of him who uses it, is not himself responsible for the death he deals. And, accordingly, they who have waged war in obedience to the divine command, or in conformity with His laws, have represented in their persons the public justice or the wisdom of government, and in this capacity have put to death wicked men; such persons have by no means violated the commandment, "Thou shalt not kill." Abraham indeed was not merely deemed guiltless of cruelty, but was even applauded for his piety, because he was ready to slay his son in obedience to God, not to his own passion. And it is reasonably enough made a question, whether we are to esteem it to have been in compliance with a command of God that Jephthah killed his daughter, because she met him when he had vowed that he would sacrifice to God whatever first met him as he returned victorious from battle. Samson, too, who drew down the house on himself and his foes together, is justified only on this ground, that the Spirit who wrought wonders by him had given him secret instructions to do this. With the exception, then, of these two classes of cases, which are justified either by a just law that applies generally, or by a special intimation from God Himself, the fountain of all justice, whoever kills a man, either himself or another, is implicated in the guilt of murder.

CHAPTER XXII

THAT SUICIDE CAN NEVER BE PROMPTED BY MAGNANIMITY

But they who have laid violent hands on themselves are perhaps to be admired for their greatness of soul, though they cannot be applauded for the soundness of their judgment. However, if you look at the matter more closely, you will scarcely call it greatness of soul, which prompts a man to kill himself rather than bear up against some hardships of fortune, or sins in which he is not implicated. Is it not rather proof of a feeble mind, to be unable to bear either the pains of bodily servitude or the foolish opinion of the vulgar? And is not that to be pronounced the greater mind, which rather faces than flees the ills of life, and which, in comparison of the light and purity of conscience, holds in small esteem the judgment of men, and specially of the vulgar, which is frequently involved in a mist of error? And, therefore, if suicide is to be esteemed a magnanimous act, none can take higher rank for magnanimity than that Cleombrotus, who (as the story goes), when he had read Plato's book in which he treats of the immortality of the soul, threw himself from a wall, and so passed from this life to that which he believed to be better. For he was not hard pressed by calamity, nor by any accusation, false or true, which he could not very well have lived down; there was, in short, no motive but only magnanimity urging him to seek death, and break away from the sweet detention of this life. And yet that this was a magnanimous rather than a justifiable action, Plato himself, whom he had read, would have told him; for he would certainly have been forward to commit, or at least to recommend suicide, had not the same bright intellect which saw that the soul was immortal, discerned also that to seek immortality by suicide was to be prohibited rather than encouraged.

Again, it is said many have killed themselves to prevent an enemy doing so. But we are not inquiring whether it has been done, but whether it ought to have been done. Sound judgment is to be preferred even to examples, and indeed examples harmonize with the voice of reason; but not all examples, but those only which are distinguished by their piety, and are proportionately worthy of imitation. For suicide we cannot cite the example of patriarchs, prophets, or apostles; though our Lord Jesus Christ, when He admonished them to flee from city to city if they were persecuted, might very well have taken that occasion to advise them to lay violent hands on themselves, and so escape their persecutors. But seeing He did not do this, nor proposed this mode of departing this life, though He were addressing His own friends for whom He had promised to prepare everlasting mansions, it is obvious that such examples as are produced from the nations that forget God, give no warrant of imitation to the worshippers of the one true God.

CHAPTER XXIII

WHAT WE ARE TO THINK OF THE EXAMPLE OF CATO, WHO SLEW HIMSELF BECAUSE UNABLE TO ENDURE CAESAR'S VICTORY

Besides Lucretia, of whom enough has already been said, our advocates of suicide have some difficulty in finding any other prescriptive example, unless it be that of Cato, who killed himself at Utica. His example is appealed to, not because he was the only man who did so, but because he was so esteemed as a learned and excellent man, that it could plausibly be maintained that what he did was and is a good thing to do. But of this action of his, what can I say but that his own friends, enlightened men as he, prudently dissuaded him, and therefore judged his act to be that of a feeble rather than a strong spirit, and dictated not by honorable feeling forestalling shame, but by weakness shrinking from hardships? Indeed, Cato condemns himself by the advice he gave to his dearly loved son. For if it was a disgrace to live under Caesar's rule, why did the father urge the son to this disgrace, by encouraging him to trust absolutely to Caesar's generosity? Why did he not persuade him to die along with himself? If Torquatus was applauded for putting his son to death, when contrary to orders he had engaged, and engaged successfully, with the enemy, why did conquered Cato spare his conquered son, though he did not spare himself? Was it more disgraceful to be a victor contrary to orders, than to submit to a victor contrary to the received ideas of honor? Cato, then, cannot have deemed it to be shameful to live under Caesar's rule; for had he done so, the father's sword would have delivered his son from this disgrace. The truth is, that his son, whom he both hoped and desired would be spared by Caesar, was not more loved by him than Caesar was envied the glory of pardoning him (as indeed Caesar himself is reported to have said[44]); or if envy is too strong a word, let us say he was *ashamed* that this glory should be his.

CHAPTER XXIV

THAT IN THAT VIRTUE IN WHICH REGULUS EXCELS CATO, CHRISTIANS ARE PRE-EMINENTLY DISTINGUISHED

Our opponents are offended at our preferring to Cato the saintly Job, who endured dreadful evils in his body rather than deliver himself from all torment by self-inflicted death; or other saints, of whom it is recorded in our authoritative and trustworthy books that they bore captivity and the oppression of their enemies rather than commit suicide. But their own books authorize us to prefer to Marcus Cato, Marcus Regulus. For Cato had never conquered Caesar; and when conquered by him, disdained to submit himself to him, and that he might escape this submission put himself to death. Regulus, on the contrary, had formerly conquered the Carthaginians, and in command of the army of Rome had won for the Roman republic a victory which no citizen could bewail, and which the enemy himself was constrained to admire; yet afterwards, when he in his turn was defeated by them, he preferred to be their captive rather than to put himself beyond their reach by suicide. Patient under the domination of the Carthaginians, and constant in his love of the Romans, he neither deprived the one of his conquered body, nor the other of his unconquered spirit. Neither was it love of life that prevented him from killing himself. This was plainly enough indicated by his unhesitatingly returning, on account of his promise and oath, to the same enemies whom he had more grievously provoked by

[44] Plutarch, *Cato,* 72

his words in the senate than even by his arms in battle. Having such a
contempt of life, and preferring to end it by whatever torments excited
enemies might contrive, rather than terminate it by his own hand, he
could not more distinctly have declared how great a crime he judged suicide
to be. Among all their famous and remarkable citizens, the Romans have
no better man to boast of than this, who was neither corrupted by prosperity, for he remained a very poor man after winning such victories; nor
broken by adversity, for he returned intrepidly to the most miserable end.
But if the bravest and most renowned heroes, who had but an earthly
country to defend, and who, though they had but false gods, yet rendered
them a true worship, and carefully kept their oath to them; if these men,
who by the custom and right of war put conquered enemies to the sword,
yet shrank from putting an end to their own lives even when conquered
by their enemies; if, though they had no fear at all of death, they would yet
rather suffer slavery than commit suicide, how much rather must Christians, the worshippers of the true God, the aspirants to a heavenly citizenship, shrink from this act, if in God's providence they have been for a season delivered into the hands of their enemies to prove or to correct them!
And certainly, Christians subjected to this humiliating condition will not
be deserted by the Most High, who for their sakes humbled Himself.
Neither should they forget that they are bound by no laws of war, nor
military orders, to put even a conquered enemy to the sword; and if a man
may not put to death the enemy who has sinned, or may yet sin against
him, who is so infatuated as to maintain that he may kill himself because
an enemy has sinned, or is going to sin, against him?

CHAPTER XXV

THAT WE SHOULD NOT ENDEAVOR BY SIN TO OBVIATE SIN

But, we are told, there is ground to fear that, when the body is subjected
to the enemy's lust, the insidious pleasure of sense may entice the soul to
consent to the sin, and steps must be taken to prevent so disastrous a result. And is not suicide the proper mode of preventing not only the enemy's
sin, but the sin of the Christian so allured? Now, in the first place, the
soul which is led by God and His wisdom, rather than by bodily concupiscence, will certainly never consent to the desire aroused in its own flesh
by another's lust. And, at all events, if it be true, as the truth plainly declares, that suicide is a detestable and damnable wickedness, who is such
a fool as to say, Let us sin now, that we may obviate a possible future sin;
let us now commit murder, lest we perhaps afterwards should commit
adultery? If we are so controlled by iniquity that innocence is out of the
question, and we can at best but make a choice of sins, is not a future and
uncertain adultery preferable to a present and certain murder? Is it not
better to commit a wickedness which penitence may heal, than a crime

which leaves no place for healing contrition? I say this for the sake of those
men or women who fear they may be enticed into consenting to their vio-
lator's lust, and think they should lay violent hands on themselves, and so
prevent, not another's sin, but their own. But far be it from the mind of a
Christian confiding in God, and resting in the hope of His aid; far be it,
I say, from such a mind to yield a shameful consent to pleasures of the
flesh, howsoever presented. And if that lustful disobedience, which still
dwells in our mortal members, follows its own law irrespective of our will,
surely its motions in the body of one who rebels against them are as blameless as its motions in the body of one who sleeps.

CHAPTER XXVI

THAT IN CERTAIN PECULIAR CASES THE EXAMPLES OF THE SAINTS ARE NOT TO BE FOLLOWED

But, they say, in the time of persecution some holy women escaped those
who menaced them with outrage, by casting themselves into rivers which
they knew would drown them; and having died in this manner, they are
venerated in the Catholic Church as martyrs. Of such persons I do not presume to speak rashly. I cannot tell whether there may not have been vouchsafed to the Church some divine authority, proved by trustworthy evidences,
for so honoring their memory: it may be that it is so. It may be they were
not deceived by human judgment, but prompted by divine wisdom, to their
act of self-destruction. We know that this was the case with Samson. And
when God enjoins any act, and intimates by plain evidence that He has
enjoined it, who will call obedience criminal? Who will accuse so religious
a submission? But then every man is not justified in sacrificing his son to
God, because Abraham was commendable in so doing. The soldier who
has slain a man in obedience to the authority under which he is lawfully
commissioned, is not accused of murder by any law of his state; nay, if
he has not slain him, it is then he is accused of treason to the state, and of
despising the law. But if he has been acting on his own authority, and at
his own impulse, he has in this case incurred the crime of shedding human
blood. And thus he is punished for doing without orders the very thing
he is punished for neglecting to do when he has been ordered. If the commands of a general make so great a difference, shall the commands of God
make none? He, then, who knows it is unlawful to kill himself, may nevertheless do so if he is ordered by Him whose commands we may not neglect.
Only let him be very sure that the divine command has been signified. As
for us, we can become privy to the secrets of conscience only in so far as
these are disclosed to us, and so far only do we judge: "No one knoweth
the things of a man, save the spirit of man which is in him." [45] But this we

---

[45] 1 Cor. ii. 11

affirm, this we maintain, this we every way pronounce to be right, that no man ought to inflict on himself voluntary death, for this is to escape the ills of time by plunging into those of eternity; that no man ought to do so on account of another man's sins, for this were to escape a guilt which could not pollute him, by incurring great guilt of his own; that no man ought to do so on account of his own past sins, for he has all the more need of this life that these sins may be healed by repentance; that no man should put an end to this life to obtain that better life we look for after death, for those who die by their own hand have no better life after death.

CHAPTER XXVII

WHETHER VOLUNTARY DEATH SHOULD BE SOUGHT IN ORDER TO AVOID SIN

There remains one reason for suicide which I mentioned before, and which is thought a sound one—namely, to prevent one's falling into sin either through the blandishments of pleasure or the violence of pain. If this reason were a good one, then we should be impelled to exhort men at once to destroy themselves, as soon as they have been washed in the font of regeneration, and have received the forgiveness of all sin. Then is the time to escape all future sin, when all past sin is blotted out. And if this escape be lawfully secured by suicide, why not then specially? Why does any baptized person hold his hand from taking his own life? Why does any person who is freed from the hazards of this life again expose himself to them, when he has power so easily to rid himself of them all, and when it is written, "He who loveth danger shall fall into it?" [46] Why does he love, or at least face, so many serious dangers, by remaining in this life from which he may legitimately depart? But is any one so blinded and twisted in his moral nature, and so far astray from the truth, as to think that, though a man ought to make away with himself for fear of being led into sin by the oppression of one man, his master, he ought yet to live, and so expose himself to the hourly temptations of this world, both to all those evils which the oppression of one master involves, and to numberless other miseries in which this life inevitably implicates us? What reason, then, is there for our consuming time in those exhortations by which we seek to animate the baptized, either to virginal chastity, or vidual continence, or matrimonial fidelity, when we have so much more simple and compendious a method of deliverance from sin, by persuading those who are fresh from baptism to put an end to their lives, and so pass to their Lord pure and well-conditioned? If any one thinks that such persuasion should be attempted, I say not he is foolish, but mad. With what face, then, can he say to any man, "Kill yourself, lest to your small sins you add a heinous sin,

[46] Ecclus. iii. 27

while you live under an unchaste master, whose conduct is that of a barbarian?" How can he say this, if he cannot without wickedness say, "Kill yourself, now that you are washed from all your sins, lest you fall again into similar or even aggravated sins, while you live in a world which has such power to allure by its unclean pleasures, to torment by its horrible cruelties, to overcome by its errors and terrors?" It is wicked to say this; it is therefore wicked to kill oneself. For if there could be any just cause of suicide, this were so. And since not even this is so, there is none.

CHAPTER XXVIII

BY WHAT JUDGMENT OF GOD THE ENEMY WAS PERMITTED TO INDULGE HIS LUST ON THE BODIES OF CONTINENT CHRISTIANS

Let not your life, then, be a burden to you, ye faithful servants of Christ, though your chastity was made the sport of your enemies. You have a grand and true consolation, if you maintain a good conscience, and know that you did not consent to the sins of those who were permitted to commit sinful outrage upon you. And if you should ask why this permission was granted, indeed it is a deep providence of the Creator and Governor of the world; and unsearchable are His judgments, and His ways past finding out.[47] Nevertheless, faithfully interrogate your own souls, whether ye have not been unduly puffed up by your integrity, and continence, and chastity; and whether ye have not been so desirous of the human praise that is accorded to these virtues, that ye have envied some who possessed them. I, for my part, do not know your hearts, and therefore I make no accusation; I do not even hear what your hearts answer when you question them. And yet, if they answer that it is as I have supposed it might be, do not marvel that you have lost that by which you can win men's praise, and retain that which cannot be exhibited to men. If you did not consent to sin, it was because God added His aid to His grace that it might not be lost, and because shame before men succeeded to human glory that it might not be loved. But in both respects even the faint-hearted among you have a consolation, approved by the one experience, chastened by the other; justified by the one, corrected by the other. As to those whose hearts, when interrogated, reply that they have never been proud of the virtue of virginity, widowhood, or matrimonial chastity, but, condescending to those of low estate, rejoiced with trembling in these gifts of God, and that they have never envied any one the like excellences of sanctity and purity, but rose superior to human applause, which is wont to be abundant in proportion to the rarity of the virtue applauded, and rather desired that their own number be increased, than that by the smallness of their numbers each of them should be conspicuous—even such faithful women, I

[47] Rom. xi. 33

say, must not complain that permission was given to the barbarians so grossly to outrage them; nor must they allow themselves to believe that God overlooked their character when He permitted acts which no one with impunity commits. For some most flagrant and wicked desires are allowed free play at present by the secret judgment of God, and are reserved to the public and final judgment. Moreover, it is possible that those Christian women, who are unconscious of any undue pride on account of their virtuous chastity, whereby they sinlessly suffered the violence of their captors, had yet some lurking infirmity which might have betrayed them into a proud and contemptuous bearing, had they not been subjected to the humiliation that befell them in the taking of the city. As, therefore, some men were removed by death, that no wickedness might change their disposition, so these women were outraged lest prosperity should corrupt their modesty. Neither those women, then, who were already puffed up by the circumstance that they were still virgins, nor those who might have been so puffed up had they not been exposed to the violence of the enemy, lost their chastity, but rather gained humility; the former were saved from pride already cherished, the latter from pride that would shortly have grown upon them.

We must further notice that some of those sufferers may have conceived that continence is a bodily good, and abides so long as the body is inviolate, and did not understand that the purity both of the body and the soul rests on the steadfastness of the will strengthened by God's grace, and cannot be forcibly taken from an unwilling person. From this error they are probably now delivered. For when they reflect how conscientiously they served God, and when they settle again to the firm persuasion that He can in nowise desert those who so serve Him, and so invoke His aid; and when they consider, what they cannot doubt, how pleasing to Him is chastity, they are forced to the conclusion that He could never have permitted these disasters to befall His saints, if by them that saintliness could be destroyed which He Himself had bestowed upon them, and delights to see in them.

CHAPTER XXIX

WHAT THE SERVANTS OF CHRIST SHOULD SAY IN REPLY TO THE UNBELIEVERS WHO CAST IN THEIR TEETH THAT CHRIST DID NOT RESCUE THEM FROM THE FURY OF THEIR ENEMIES

The whole family of God, most high and most true, has therefore a consolation of its own—a consolation which cannot deceive, and which has in it a surer hope than the tottering and falling affairs of earth can afford. They will not refuse the discipline of this temporal life, in which they are schooled for life eternal; nor will they lament their experience of it, for the good things of earth they use as pilgrims who are not detained by them, and its ills either prove or improve them. As for those who insult over them in their trials, and when ills befall them say, "Where is thy

God?" [48] we may ask them where their gods are when they suffer the very calamities for the sake of avoiding which they worship their gods, or maintain they ought to be worshipped; for the family of Christ is furnished with its reply: our God is everywhere present, wholly everywhere; not confined to any place. He can be present unperceived, and be absent without moving; when He exposes us to adversities, it is either to prove our perfections or correct our imperfections; and in return for our patient endurance of the sufferings of time, He reserves for us an everlasting reward. But who are you, that we should deign to speak with you even about your own gods, much less about our God, who is to be feared above all gods? For all the gods of the nations are idols; but the Lord made the heavens. [49]

CHAPTER XXX

THAT THOSE WHO COMPLAIN OF CHRISTIANITY REALLY DESIRE TO LIVE WITHOUT RESTRAINT IN SHAMEFUL LUXURY

If the famous Scipio Nasica were now alive, who was once your pontiff, and was unanimously chosen by the senate, when, in the panic created by the Punic war, they sought for the best citizen to entertain the Phrygian goddess, he would curb this shamelessness of yours, though you would perhaps scarcely dare to look upon the countenance of such a man. For why in your calamities do you complain of Christianity, unless because you desire to enjoy your luxurious license unrestrained, and to lead an abandoned and profligate life without the interruption of any uneasiness or disaster? For certainly your desire for peace, and prosperity, and plenty is not prompted by any purpose of using these blessings honestly, that is to say, with moderation, sobriety, temperance, and piety; for your purpose rather is to run riot in an endless variety of sottish pleasures, and thus to generate from your prosperity a moral pestilence which will prove a thousandfold more disastrous than the fiercest enemies. It was such a calamity as this that Scipio, your chief pontiff, your best man in the judgment of the whole senate, feared when he refused to agree to the destruction of Carthage, Rome's rival; and opposed Cato, who advised its destruction. He feared security, that enemy of weak minds, and he perceived that a wholesome fear would be a fit guardian for the citizens. And he was not mistaken; the event proved how wisely he had spoken. For when Carthage was destroyed, and the Roman republic delivered from its great cause of anxiety, a crowd of disastrous evils forthwith resulted from the prosperous condition of things. First concord was weakened, and destroyed by fierce and bloody seditions; then followed, by a concatenation of baleful causes, civil wars, which brought in their train such massacres, such bloodshed, such lawless and cruel proscription and plunder, that those Romans who,

[48] Ps. xlii. 10   [49] Ps. xcvi. 4, 5

in the days of their virtue, had expected injury only at the hands of their enemies, now that their virtue was lost, suffered greater cruelties at the hands of their fellow-citizens. The lust of rule, which with other vices existed among the Romans in more unmitigated intensity than among any other people, after it had taken possession of the more powerful few, subdued under its yoke the rest, worn and wearied.

CHAPTER XXXI

BY WHAT STEPS THE PASSION FOR GOVERNING INCREASED AMONG THE ROMANS

For at what stage would that passion rest when once it has lodged in a proud spirit, until by a succession of advances it has reached even the throne. And to obtain such advances nothing avails but unscrupulous ambition. But unscrupulous ambition has nothing to work upon, save in a nation corrupted by avarice and luxury. Moreover, a people becomes avaricious and luxurious by prosperity; and it was this which that very prudent man Nasica was endeavoring to avoid when he opposed the destruction of the greatest, strongest, wealthiest city of Rome's enemy. He thought that thus fear would act as a curb on lust, and that lust being curbed would not run riot in luxury, and that luxury being prevented avarice would be at an end; and that these vices being banished, virtue would flourish and increase the great profit of the state; and liberty, the fit companion of virtue, would abide unfettered. For similar reasons, and animated by the same considerate patriotism, that same chief pontiff of yours—I still refer to him who was adjudged Rome's best man without one dissentient voice—threw cold water on the proposal of the senate to build a circle of seats round the theatre, and in a very weighty speech warned them against allowing the luxurious manners of Greece to sap the Roman manliness, and persuaded them not to yield to the enervating and emasculating influence of foreign licentiousness. So authoritative and forcible were his words, that the senate was moved to prohibit the use even of those benches which hitherto had been customarily brought to the theatre for the temporary use of the citizens. How eagerly would such a man as this have banished from Rome the scenic exhibitions themselves, had he dared to oppose the authority of those whom he supposed to be gods! For he did not know that they were malicious devils; or if he did, he supposed they should rather be propitiated than despised. For there had not yet been revealed to the Gentiles the heavenly doctrine which should purify their hearts by faith, and transform their natural disposition by humble godliness, and turn them from the service of proud devils to seek the things that are in heaven, or even above the heavens.

CHAPTER XXXII

OF THE ESTABLISHMENT OF SCENIC ENTERTAINMENTS

Know then, ye who are ignorant of this, and ye who feign ignorance be reminded, while you murmur against Him who has freed you from such rulers, that the scenic games, exhibitions of shameless folly and license, were established at Rome, not by men's vicious cravings, but by the appointment of your gods. Much more pardonably might you have rendered divine honors to Scipio than to such gods as these. The gods were not so moral as their pontiff. But give me now your attention, if your mind, inebriated by its deep potations of error, can take in any sober truth. The gods enjoined that games be exhibited in their honor to stay a physical pestilence; their pontiff prohibited the theatre from being constructed, to prevent a moral pestilence. If, then, there remains in you sufficient mental enlightenment to prefer the soul to the body, choose whom you will worship. Besides, though the pestilence was stayed, this was not because the voluptuous madness of stage-plays had taken possession of a warlike people hitherto accustomed only to the games of the circus; but these astute and wicked spirits, foreseeing that in due course the pestilence would shortly cease, took occasion to infect, not the bodies, but the morals of their worshippers, with a far more serious disease. And in this pestilence these gods find great enjoyment, because it benighted the minds of men with so gross a darkness, and dishonored them with so foul a deformity, that even quite recently (will posterity be able to credit it?) some of those who fled from the sack of Rome and found refuge in Carthage, were so infected with this disease, that day after day they seemed to contend with one another who should most madly run after the actors in the theatres.

CHAPTER XXXIII

THAT THE OVERTHROW OF ROME HAS NOT CORRECTED THE VICES OF THE ROMANS

Oh infatuated men, what is this blindness, or rather madness, which possesses you? How is it that while, as we hear, even the eastern nations are bewailing your ruin, and while powerful states in the most remote parts of the earth are mourning your fall as a public calamity, ye yourselves should be crowding to the theatres, should be pouring into them and filling them; and, in short, be playing a madder part now than ever before? This was the foul plague-spot, this the wreck of virtue and honor that Scipio sought to preserve you from when he prohibited the construction of theatres; this was his reason for desiring that you might still have an enemy to fear, seeing as he did how easily prosperity would corrupt and destroy you. He did not consider that republic flourishing whose walls stand, but whose morals are in ruins. But the seductions of evil-minded devils had more influence with you than the precautions of prudent men. Hence the injuries you do, you will not permit to be imputed to you: but the injuries you suffer, you impute to Christianity. Depraved by good fortune, and not chastened by adversity, what you desire in the restoration of a peaceful and secure state, is not the tranquillity of the commonwealth, but the impunity of your own vicious luxury. Scipio wished you to be hard pressed by an enemy, that you might not abandon yourselves to luxurious manners; but so abandoned are you, that not even when crushed by the enemy is your luxury repressed. You have missed the profit of your calamity; you have been made most wretched, and have remained most profligate.

CHAPTER XXXIV

OF GOD'S CLEMENCY IN MODERATING THE RUIN OF THE CITY

And that you are yet alive is due to God, who spares you that you may be admonished to repent and reform your lives. It is He who has permitted you, ungrateful as you are, to escape the sword of the enemy, by calling yourselves His servants, or by finding asylum in the sacred places of the martyrs.

It is said that Romulus and Remus, in order to increase the population of the city they founded, opened a sanctuary in which every man might find asylum and absolution of all crime—a remarkable foreshadowing of what has recently occurred in honor of Christ. The destroyers of Rome followed the example of its founders. But it was not greatly to their credit that the latter, for the sake of increasing the number of their citizens, did that which the former have done, lest the number of their enemies should be diminished.

CHAPTER XXXV

OF THE SONS OF THE CHURCH WHO ARE HIDDEN AMONG THE WICKED, AND OF FALSE CHRISTIANS WITHIN THE CHURCH

Let these and similar answers (if any fuller and fitter answers can be found) be given to their enemies by the redeemed family of the Lord Christ, and by the pilgrim city of King Christ. But let this city bear in mind, that among her enemies lie hid those who are destined to be fellow-citizens, that she may not think it a fruitless labor to bear what they inflict as enemies until they become confessors of the faith. So, too, as long as she is a stranger in the world, the city of God has in her communion, and bound to her by the sacraments, some who shall not eternally dwell in the lot of the saints. Of these, some are not now recognized; others declare themselves, and do not hesitate to make common cause with our enemies in murmuring against God, whose sacramental badge they wear. These men you may to-day see thronging the churches with us, to-morrow crowding the theatres with the godless. But we have the less reason to despair of the reclamation even of such persons, if among our most declared enemies there are now some, unknown to themselves, who are destined to become our friends. In truth, these two cities are entangled together in this world, and intermixed until the last judgment effects their separation. I now proceed to speak, as God shall help me, of the rise, progress, and end of these two cities; and what I write, I write for the glory of the city of God, that, being placed in comparison with the other, it may shine with a brighter lustre.

CHAPTER XXXVI

WHAT SUBJECTS ARE TO BE HANDLED IN THE FOLLOWING DISCOURSE

But I have still some things to say in confutation of those who refer the disasters of the Roman republic to our religion, because it prohibits the offering of sacrifices to the gods. For this end I must recount all, or as many as may seem sufficient, of the disasters which befell that city and its subject provinces, before these sacrifices were prohibited; for all these disasters they would doubtless have attributed to us, if at that time our religion had shed its light upon them, and had prohibited their sacrifices. I must then go on to show what social well-being the true God, in whose hand are all kingdoms, vouchsafed to grant to them that their empire might increase. I must show why He did so, and how their false gods, instead of at all aiding them, greatly injured them by guile and deceit. And, lastly, I must meet those who, when on this point convinced and confuted by irrefragable proofs, endeavor to maintain that they worship the gods, not hoping for the present advantages of this life, but for those which are to be enjoyed after death. And this, if I am not mistaken, will be the most difficult part of my task, and will be worthy of the loftiest argument; for we must then enter the lists with the philosophers, not the mere common herd of philosophers, but the most renowned, who in many points agree with ourselves, as regarding the immortality of the soul, and that the true God created the world, and by His providence rules all He has created. But as they differ from us on other points, we must not shrink from the task of exposing their errors, that, having refuted the gainsaying of the wicked with such ability as God may vouchsafe, we may assert the city of God, and true piety, and the worship of God, to which alone the promise of true and everlasting felicity is attached. Here, then, let us conclude, that we may enter on these subjects in a fresh book.

BOOK TWO

Book II, Chapters 1-13

Summary

Chapter 1: It is very difficult, even after the fullest possible demonstration, to convince an obstinate opponent. Saint Augustine recognizes the necessity of speaking more fully on points which should be clear, even though this makes it hard to bring an end to his discussion.

Chapter 2: In the first book Saint Augustine has replied to those who attribute the sack of Rome to the religion of Christ.

Chapter 3: One needs only to read history to see the calamities which Rome suffered even before Christianity began to compete with the worship of the pagan gods.

Chapter 4: No pagan god ever gave a worshipper anything whereby he could improve his morals. On the contrary, the ceremonies of pagan worship often contained many obscenities.

Chapter 5: Such even was the case in connection with the shameful rites in honor of the mother of the gods.

Chapter 6: It is therefore not difficult to understand why these gods did not inculcate holiness of life.

Chapter 7: But, Saint Augustine asks, what of the effect of the philosophers? In the first place, they are not Roman but Greek. In the second place, though some of them made important discoveries, they did not have divine authority. Man tends towards evil, and thus will follow the evil examples of the gods rather than obey the precepts of men.

Chapter 8: But these stories of the gods may be but the fables of poets. On the contrary, the theatrical productions of poets have become part of the celebrations in honor of the gods. Yet these gods have shown no sign of being offended by these exhibitions.

Chapter 9: The Greeks allowed a poetical license which the ancient Romans found expedient to restrain.

Chapter 10: The devils, who permit many crimes to be attributed to them through human infatuation, do so to work men ill.

Chapter 11: The Greeks permitted actors to become officers of the state, because they were men who pleased the gods.

Chapter 12: The Romans were really more sensible in regard to themselves than they were with the gods, for they did not permit the same license towards man as they believed acceptable in connection with the gods.

CHAPTER XIV

THAT PLATO, WHO EXCLUDED POETS FROM A WELL-ORDERED CITY, WAS BETTER THAN THESE GODS WHO DESIRE TO BE HONORED BY THEATRICAL PLAYS

WE HAVE still to inquire why the poets who write the plays, and who by the law of the twelve tables are prohibited from injuring the good name of the citizens, are reckoned more estimable than the actors, though they so shamefully asperse the character of the gods? It is right that the actors of these poetical and God-dishonoring effusions be branded, while their authors are honored? Must we not here award the palm to a Greek, Plato, who, in framing his ideal republic,[1] conceived that poets should be banished from the city as enemies of the state? He could not brook that the gods be brought into disrepute, nor that the minds of the citizens be depraved and besotted, by the fictions of the poets. Compare now human nature as you see it in Plato, expelling poets from the city that the citizens be uninjured, with the divine nature as you see it in these gods exacting plays in their own honor. Plato strove, though unsuccessfully, to persuade the light-minded and lascivious Greeks to abstain from so much as writing such plays; the gods used their authority to extort the acting of the same from the dignified and sober-minded Romans. And not content with having them acted, they had them dedicated to themselves, consecrated to themselves, solemnly celebrated in their own honor. To which, then, would it be more becoming in a state to decree divine honors—to Plato, who prohibited these wicked and licentious plays, or to the demons who delighted in blinding men to the truth of what Plato unsuccessfully sought to inculcate?

This philosopher, Plato, has been elevated by Labeo to the rank of a demigod, and set thus upon a level with such as Hercules and Romulus. Labeo ranks demigods higher than heroes, but both he counts among the deities. But I have no doubt that he thinks this man whom he reckons a demigod worthy of greater respect not only than the heroes, but also than the gods themselves. The laws of the Romans and the speculations of Plato have this resemblance, that the latter pronounce a wholesale condemnation of poetical fictions, while the former restrain the license of satire, at least so far as men are the objects of it. Plato will not suffer poets even to dwell in his city: the laws of Rome prohibit actors from being enrolled as citizens; and if they had not feared to offend the gods who had asked the services of the players, they would in all likelihood have banished them

[1] *Republic*, Bk. III

altogether. It is obvious, therefore, that the Romans could not receive, nor reasonably expect to receive, laws for the regulation of their conduct from their gods, since the laws they themselves enacted far surpassed and put to shame the morality of the gods. The gods demand stage-plays in their own honor; the Romans exclude the players from all civic honors;[2] the former commanded that they should be celebrated by the scenic representation of their own disgrace; the latter commanded that no poet should dare to blemish the reputation of any citizen. But that demigod Plato resisted the lust of such gods as these, and showed the Romans what their genius had left incomplete; for he absolutely excluded poets from his ideal state whether they composed fictions with no regard to truth, or set the worst possible examples before wretched men under the guise of divine actions. We for our part, indeed, reckon Plato neither a god nor a demigod; we would not even compare him to any of God's holy angels; nor to the truth-speaking prophets, nor to any of the apostles or martyrs of Christ, nay, not to any faithful Christian man. The reason of this opinion of ours we will, God prospering us, render in its own place. Nevertheless, since they wish him to be considered a demigod, we think he certainly is more entitled to that rank, and is every way superior, if not to Hercules and Romulus (though no historian could ever narrate nor any poet sing of him that he had killed his brother, or committed any crime) yet certainly to Priapus, or a Cynocephalus,[3] or the Fever[4]—divinities whom the Romans have partly received from foreigners, and partly consecrated by home-grown rites. How, then, could gods such as these be expected to promulgate good and wholesome laws, either for the prevention of moral and social evils, or for their eradication where they had already sprung up?—gods who used their influence even to sow and cherish profligacy, by appointing that deeds truly or falsely ascribed to them should be published to the people by means of theatrical exhibitions, and by thus gratuitously fanning the flame of human lust with the breath of a seemingly divine approbation. In vain does Cicero, speaking of poets, exclaim against this state of things in these words: "When the plaudits and acclamation of the people, who sit as infallible judges, are won by the poets, what darkness benights the mind, what fears invade, what passions inflame it!"[5]

Book II, Chapters 15-20

Summary

Chapter 15: Vanity rather than reason regulated the choice by the Romans of some of their false gods.

Chapter 16: If the gods had really given the Romans a set of good laws they would not have borrowed from others, as they borrowed Solon's laws from the Athenians.

[2] Tertullian, *De Spectac.*, Chapter 22
[3] Lucan, VIII, 832
[4] Cicero, *De Nat. Deor.*, III, 25 and Aelian, *Var. Hist.*, XII, 11
[5] Cicero, *De Republica*, V. Compare the third *Tusculan Quaest.*, Chapter II

Chapter 17: The Romans may have been neglected by their gods, because, as Sallust has suggested, "equity and virtue prevailed among the Romans not more by force of laws than of nature." (Cat. Con. ix). Saint Augustine ironically suggests that the rape of the Sabine women was to be attributed to inborn equity.

Chapter 18: Sallust has recorded in his history how the Romans after the expulsion of the kings enjoyed a brief period of harmony and justice. But soon a group of more powerful men began to act unjustly, and in turn, between the second and third Punic wars, enjoyed a greater harmony and a purer state of society than at any other time. After the destruction of Carthage, Rome fell victim to all the vices which prosperity generates. Saint Augustine emphasizes the fact that Rome had become a sink of iniquity before the advent of Christ.

Chapter 19: A Roman writer pointed to the degradation of Rome. The Romans can see in the Christian teaching the Christian attitude towards such corruption. But yet they do not impute to their gods the fact that their society had become corrupt.

Chapter 20: Saint Augustine describes the kind of happiness which results from love of power, money, and pleasure.

CHAPTER XXI

CICERO'S OPINION OF THE ROMAN REPUBLIC

But if our adversaries do not care how foully and disgracefully the Roman republic be stained by corrupt practices, so long only as it holds together and continues in being, and if they therefore pooh-pooh the testimony of Sallust to its "utterly wicked and profligate" condition, what will they make of Cicero's statement, that even in his time it had become entirely extinct, and that there remained extant no Roman republic at all? He introduces Scipio (the Scipio who had destroyed Carthage) discussing the republic, at a time when already there were presentiments of its speedy ruin by that corruption which Sallust describes. In fact, at the time when the discussion took place, one of the Gracchi, who, according to Sallust, was the first great instigator of seditions, had already been put to death. His death, indeed, is mentioned in the same book. Now Scipio, at the end of the second book, says: "As among the different sounds which proceed from lyres, flutes, and the human voice, there must be maintained a certain harmony which a cultivated ear cannot endure to hear disturbed or jarring, but which may be elicited in full and absolute concord by the modulation even of voices very unlike one another; so, where reason is allowed to modulate the diverse elements of the state, there is obtained a perfect concord from the upper, lower, and middle classes as from various sounds; and what musicians call harmony in singing, is concord in matters of state, which is the strictest bond and best security of any republic, and which by no ingenuity can be retained where justice has become extinct." Then, when he had expatiated somewhat more fully, and had more copiously illustrated the benefits of its presence and the ruinous effects of its absence upon a state, Philus, one of the company present at the discussion, struck in and demanded that the question should be more thoroughly sifted, and that the subject of justice should be freely discussed for the sake of ascertaining what truth there was in the maxim which was then becoming daily more current, that "the republic cannot be governed without injustice." Scipio expressed his willingness to have this maxim discussed and sifted, and gave it as his opinion that it was baseless, and that no progress could be made in discussing the republic unless it was established, not only that this maxim, that "the republic cannot be governed without injustice," was false, but also that the truth is, that it cannot be governed without the most absolute justice. And the discussion of this question, being deferred till the next day, is carried on in the third book with great animation. For Philus himself undertook to defend the position that the republic cannot be governed without injustice, at the same time being at special pains to clear himself of any real participation in that opinion. He advocated with great keenness the cause of injustice against justice, and endeavored by plausible reasons and examples to demonstrate that the former is beneficial, the latter useless, to the republic. Then, at the request of the company, Laelius attempted to defend justice, and strained every nerve to prove that nothing is so hurtful to a state as injustice; and that without justice a republic can neither be governed, nor even continue to exist.

When this question has been handled to the satisfaction of the company, Scipio reverts to the original thread of discourse, and repeats with commendation his own brief definition of a republic, that it is the weal of the people. "The people" he defines as being not every assemblage or mob, but an assemblage associated by a common acknowledgment of law, and by a community of interests. Then he shows the use of definition in debate; and from these definitions of his own he gathers that a republic, or "weal of the people," then exists only when it is well and justly governed, whether by a monarch, or an aristocracy, or by the whole people. But when the monarch is unjust, or, as the Greeks say, a tyrant; or the aristocrats are unjust, and form a faction; or the people themselves are unjust, and become, as Scipio for want of a better name calls them, themselves the tyrant, then the republic is not only blemished (as had been proved the day before), but by legitimate deduction from these definitions, it altogether ceases to be. For it could not be the people's weal when a tyrant factiously lorded it over the state; neither would the people be any longer a people if it were unjust, since it would no longer answer the definition of a people—"an assemblage associated by a common acknowledgment of law, and by a community of interests."

When, therefore, the Roman republic was such as Sallust described it, it was not "utterly wicked and profligate," as he says, but had altogether ceased to exist, if we are to admit the reasoning of that debate maintained on the subject of the republic by its best representatives. Tully himself, too, speaking not in the person of Scipio or any one else, but uttering his own sentiments, uses the following language in the beginning of the fifth book, after quoting a line from the poet Ennius, in which he said, "Rome's severe morality and her citizens are her safeguard." "This verse," says Cicero, "seems to me to have all the sententious truthfulness of an oracle. For neither would the citizens have availed without the morality of the community, nor would the morality of the commons without outstanding men have availed either to establish or so long to maintain in vigor so grand a republic with so wide and just an empire. Accordingly, before our day, the hereditary usages formed our foremost men, and they on their part retained the usages and institutions of their fathers. But our age, receiving the republic as a *chef-d'oeuvre* of another age which has already begun to grow old, has not merely neglected to restore the colors of the original, but has not even been at the pains to preserve so much as the general outline and most outstanding features. For what survives of that primitive morality which the poet called Rome's safeguard? It is so obsolete and forgotten, that, far from practising it, one does not even know it. And of the citizens what shall I say? Morality has perished through poverty of great men; a poverty for which we must not only assign a reason, but for the guilt of which we must answer as criminals charged with a capital crime. For it is through our vices, and not by any mishap, that we retain only the name of a republic, and have long since lost the reality."

This is the confession of Cicero, long indeed after the death of Africanus, whom he introduced as an interlocutor in his work *De Republica*, but still before the coming of Christ. Yet, if the disasters he bewails had been lamented after the Christian religion had been diffused, and had begun to prevail, is there a man of our adversaries who would not have thought that they were to be imputed to the Christians? Why, then, did their gods not take steps then to prevent the decay and extinction of that republic, over the loss of which Cicero, long before Christ had come in the flesh, sings so lugubrious a dirge? Its admirers have need to inquire whether, even in the days of primitive men and morals, true justice flourished in it; or was it not perhaps even then, to use the casual expression of Cicero, rather a colored painting than the living reality? But, if God will, we shall consider this elsewhere. For I mean in its own place to show that—according to the definitions in which Cicero himself, using Scipio as his mouthpiece, briefly propounded what a republic is, and what a people is, and according to many testimonies, both of his own lips and of those who took part in that same debate—Rome never was a republic, because true justice had never a place in it. But accepting the more feasible definitions of a republic, I grant there was a republic of a certain kind, and certainly much better administered by the more ancient Romans than by their modern representatives. But the fact is, true justice has no existence save in that republic whose founder and ruler is Christ, if at least any choose to call this a republic; and indeed we cannot deny that it is the people's weal. But if perchance this name, which has become familiar in other connections, be considered alien to our common parlance, we may at all events say that in this city is true justice; the city of which Holy Scripture says, "Glorious things are said of thee, O city of God."

Book II, Chapters 22-29

Summary

Chapter 22: It is certain that the Roman gods never did anything to prevent the Republic from being ruined by immorality.

Chapter 23: The careers of Marius and Regulus, with their various vicissitudes, show that good or ill fortune is not a matter of the favor or ill-favor of the gods, but rather depend upon the will of the one true God.

Chapter 24: The gods boasted that they had given their help to Sylla in his various deeds.

Chapter 25: These evil spirits strive by their example to lend divine authority to crime. Rome had really been ruined by moral depravity before the advent of Christ.

Chapter 26: Certain of these demons are supposed to have given good moral instructions to some of their initiates in secret, but in the light of the corruption which they inculcate by their public solemnities, this merely reveals their malicious craft.

Chapter 27: The propitiation of divinities by wicked means contributed in great measure to the overthrow of the public order.

Chapter 28: The religion of Christ works powerfully against this uncleanness, and in its ceremonies are found righteousness and purity.

Chapter 29: Saint Augustine exhorts the Romans to renounce paganism; they have had their share of popular glory. Let them embrace the true religion of Christ.

BOOK THREE

Book III, Chapters 1-31

Summary

Chapter 1: Saint Augustine has already spoken of moral and spiritual ills. Now he proposes to discuss physical evils, such as war, disease, and captivity which evil men count alone as evil. Many of these befell Rome prior to the advent of Christ.

Chapter 2: Why did the gods permit the destruction of Troy? Was it because of Trojan perjury? Can it be that the gods hated Trojan perjury but loved Roman?

Chapter 3: The gods could hardly be offended by the adultery of Paris, when they themselves are so frequently guilty of this crime.

Chapter 4: Varro, a very learned man, all but admits that these stories are false, but also points how useful it is for men to feign that they are descended from the gods.

Chapter 5: It is not believable that the gods would punish such acts as the adultery of Paris, when, for example, they were not indignant over the adultery of the mother of Romulus.

Chapter 6: The gods certainly did not exact any penalty for Romulus' murder of his brother.

Chapter 7: In the early part of the civil war of Rome, why did the gods permit Fimbria, one of Marius' evil partisans, to destroy Troy, which had done no wrong?

Chapter 8: There would seem to be little wisdom in entrusting Rome to the Trojan gods who had demonstrated their weakness in the loss of Troy.

Chapter 9: It is difficult to attribute the peace of Numa to the power of the gods.

Chapter 10: It was hardly desirable for Rome to have expanded by a series of wars, when it might have remained quiet and peaceful by following the ways of Numa.

Chapter 11: Remember the story of the weeping statue of Apollo at Cumae. These tears presaged the defeat of the Greeks whom he was too weak to assist.

Chapter 12: Rome added numberless gods in addition to those introduced by Numa, and even this great number failed to help her.

Chapter 13: The gods could not assist the children of Aeneas to find wives by equitable means. Rather these early Romans took them by force.

Chapter 14: The Roman war against the Albans was wicked, and their victories were won through a lust for power.

48

Chapter 15: It is said that Romulus died a violent death. Tullus Hostilius was destroyed by lightning. With the exception of Numa and Ancus Maricus, all the other Roman kings met horrible deaths.

Chapter 16: Of the first Roman consuls, one banished his colleagues, and then was slain by an enemy after he had committed several unnatural murders.

Chapter 17: After the consulship was established in the Republic, Rome faced many disasters, with which the gods did not interfere.

Chapter 18: The Romans also suffered terribly in the Punic wars, during which the gods gave no protection.

Chapter 19: There is no need to recount all the disasters to Rome and Carthage in the second Punic war.

Chapter 20: The Saguntines were destroyed because they were faithful to Rome, and they received no assistance from the gods.

Chapter 21: Rome showed great ingratitude to her deliverer, Scipio. In this period after the second Punic war, when Roman manners and morals were supposed to have been at their best, Asiatic luxury was introduced.

Chapter 22: Saint Augustine recalls how all the Roman citizens in Asia were slain by an edict of Mithridates. Yet all those slain were worshippers of the gods.

Chapter 23: Remember the sea of Roman blood shed in the civil wars.

Chapter 24: Also there were the disasters which attended the seditions of the Gracchi.

Chapter 25: The senate ordered the temple of Concord to be built on the spot where the Gracchan rising took place.

Chapter 26: Think of the various wars which followed the building of the temple of Concord.

Chapter 27: Vast numbers were slaughtered in the civil war between Marius and Sylla.

Chapter 28: Sylla was victorious, but took murderous revenge, in a "rage of peace," for the cruelties of Marius.

Chapter 29: Saint Augustine points out that the ferocity of the war between Sylla and Marius, with its attendant disasters, was worse than either the ancient Gallic invasion and the more recent Gothic invasion.

Chapter 30: It is effrontery for the Romans to refuse to impute these former disasters to their gods, and then impute the present calamity to Christ. There were many and great wars before His coming.

Chapter 31: It is effrontery to assign the present troubles to Christ and the prohibition of pagan worship, since in the past such worship did not prevent calamities from befalling the Romans.

BOOK FOUR

Book IV, Chapter 1

Summary

Chapter 1: In discussing the city of God, it is first necessary to reply to the enemies of the one salutary and true religion. Their gods are false, unclean and most deceitful demons.

CHAPTER II

OF THOSE THINGS WHICH ARE CONTAINED IN BOOKS
SECOND AND THIRD

We had promised, then, that we would say something against those who attribute the calamities of the Roman republic to our religion, and that we would recount the evils, as many and great as we could remember or might deem sufficient, which that city, or the provinces belonging to its empire, had suffered before their sacrifices were prohibited, all of which would beyond doubt have been attributed to us, if our religion had either already shone on them, or had thus prohibited their sacrilegious rites. These things we have, as we think, fully disposed of in the second and third books, treating in the second of evils in morals, which alone or chiefly are to be accounted evils; and in the third, of those which only fools dread to undergo —namely, those of the body or of outward things—which for the most part the good also suffer. But those evils by which they themselves become evil, they take, I do not say patiently, but with pleasure. And how few evils have I related concerning that one city and its empire! Not even all down to the time of Caesar Augustus. What if I had chosen to recount and enlarge on those evils, not which men have inflicted on each other, such as the devastations and destructions of war, but which happen in earthly things, from the elements of the world itself. Of such evils Apuleius speaks briefly in one passage of that book which he wrote, *De Mundo*, saying that all earthly things are subject to change, overthrow, and destruction. For, to use his own words, by excessive earthquakes the ground has burst asunder, and cities with their inhabitants have been clean destroyed: by sudden rains whole regions have been washed away; those also which formerly had been continents, have been insulated by strange and new-come waves, and others, by the subsiding of the sea, have been made passable by the foot of man: by winds and storms cities have been overthrown; fires have flashed forth from the clouds, by which regions in the East being burnt up have perished; and

on the western coasts the like destructions have been caused by the bursting
forth of waters and floods. So, formerly, from the lofty craters of Etna,
rivers of fire kindled by God have flowed like a torrent down the steeps. If
I had wished to collect from history wherever I could, these and similar instances, where should I have finished what happened even in those times
before the name of Christ had put down those of their idols, so vain and
hurtful to true salvation? I promised that I should also point out which of
their customs, and for what cause, the true God, in whose power all kingdoms are, had deigned to favor to the enlargement of their empire; and how
those whom they think gods can have profited them nothing, but much
rather hurt them by deceiving and beguiling them; so that it seems to me
I must now speak of these things, and chiefly of the increase of the Roman
empire. For I have already said not a little, especially in the second book,
about the many evils introduced into their manners by the hurtful deceits
of the demons whom they worshipped as gods. But throughout all the three
books already completed, where it appeared suitable, we have set forth how
much succor God, through the name of Christ, to whom the barbarians beyond the custom of war paid so much honor, has bestowed on the good and
bad, according as it is written, "Who maketh His sun to rise on the good
and the evil, and giveth rain to the just and the unjust." [1]

Book IV, Chapter 3

Summary

*Chapter 3: It cannot be assumed that the great extent of empire, acquired by wars,
can be accounted among the goods of the wise or the happy. For example, a good
man, even though a slave, is free, while a bad man, even though he reigns, is a slave.*

CHAPTER IV

HOW LIKE KINGDOMS WITHOUT JUSTICE ARE TO ROBBERIES

Justice being taken away, then, what are kingdoms but great robberies?
For what are robberies themselves, but little kingdoms? The band itself is
made up of men; it is ruled by the authority of a prince, it is knit together
by the pact of the confederacy; the booty is divided by the law agreed on.
If, by the admittance of abandoned men, this evil increases to such a degree
that it holds places, fixes abodes, takes possession of cities, and subdues
peoples, it assumes the more plainly the name of a kingdom, because the
reality is now manifestly conferred on it, not by the removal of covetousness, but by the addition of impunity. Indeed, that was an apt and true
reply which was given to Alexander the Great by a pirate who had been
seized. For when that king had asked the man what he meant by keeping
hostile possession of the sea, he answered with bold pride, "What thou

[1] Matt., V, 45

meanest by seizing the whole earth; but because I do it with a petty ship, I am called a robber, whilst thou who dost it with a great fleet art styled emperor." [1]

Book IV, Chapters 5-34

Summary

Chapter 5: Saint Augustine asks what god it was who supported the rebel band of gladiators who for a time withstood the force of Rome.

Chapter 6: King Ninus, because he was covetous, extended by war the kingdom of the Assyrians. Was this not a great robbery?

Chapter 7: The kingdom of Ninus was great and lasting without the help of the gods. Why then should the size and long duration of the Roman empire be ascribed to the Roman gods? Do the rise and fall of earthly kingdoms come through the aid of the gods?

Chapter 8: The Romans have so many gods, that each individual thing has its separate parts committed to the care of different divinities. It is difficult to see how they could find any one god who would be able to preside over the increase and the preservation of the empire.

Chapter 9: Jove, the king of the gods, is thought to rule over Rome. Yet he has been badly used, because the Romans have set up an image of him.

Chapter 10: There is a great variety of opinion as to the assignment of the several parts of the world to the different gods.

Chapter 11: Learned men have insisted that many gods are really only one and the same Jupiter.

Chapter 12: The theory that God is the soul of the world and the world is the body of God must be rejected for obvious reasons.

Chapter 13: It is equally untenable to believe that only rational animals are parts of the one God.

Chapter 14: It is not correct to assign the enlargement of kingdoms to Jove. If Victoria is really a goddess, she alone would be sufficient for this business.

Chapter 15: It is proper to consider the question whether it is right for good men to wish to rule more widely.

Chapter 16: The fact that the temple to Quiet was erected outside the city gates may indicate that no peace of mind could be found in worshipping the multitude of gods within the city.

Chapter 17: It seems unnecessary to worship Victoria, if the supreme power resides in Jove.

[1] Cicero, *De Republica*, III

BOOK FIVE[1]

ARGUMENT

Augustine first discusses the doctrine of fate, for the sake of confuting those who are disposed to refer to fate the power and increase of the Roman Empire, which could not be attributed to false gods, as has been shown in the preceding book. After that, he proves that there is no contradiction between God's prescience and our free will. He then speaks of the manners of the ancient Romans, and shows in what sense it was due to the virtue of the Romans themselves, and in how far to the counsel of God, that he increased their dominion, though they did not worship him. Finally, he explains what is to be accounted the true happiness of the Christian emperors.

PREFACE

SINCE, then, it is established that the complete attainment of all we desire is that which constitutes felicity, which is no goddess, but a gift of God, and that therefore men can worship no god save Him who is able to make them happy—and were Felicity herself a goddess, she would with reason be the only object of worship—since, I say, this is established, let us now go on to consider why God, who is able to give with all other things those good gifts which can be possessed by men who are not good, and consequently not happy, has seen fit to grant such extended and long-continued dominion to the Roman empire; for that this was not effected by that multitude of false gods which they worshipped, we have both already adduced, and shall, as occasion offers, yet adduce considerable proof.

CHAPTER I

THAT THE CAUSE OF THE ROMAN EMPIRE, AND OF ALL KINGDOMS, IS NEITHER FORTUITOUS NOR CONSISTS IN THE POSITION OF THE STARS

The cause, then, of the greatness of the Roman empire is neither fortuitous nor fatal, according to the judgment or opinion of those who call those things *fortuitous* which either have no causes, or such causes as do not proceed from some intelligible order, and those things *fatal* which happen independently of the will of God and man, by the necessity of a certain *order*. In a word, human kingdoms are established by divine providence. And if any one attributes their existence to fate, because he calls the will or the power of God itself by the name of fate, let him keep his opinion, but correct his

[1] Written in the year 415

54

language. For why does he not say at first what he will say afterwards, when some one shall put the question to him, What he means by *fate?* For when men hear that word, according to the ordinary use of the language, they simply understand by it the virtue of that particular position of the stars which may exist at the time when any one is born or conceived, which some separate altogether from the will of God, whilst others affirm that this also is dependent on that will. But those who are of opinion that, apart from the will of God, the stars determine what we shall do, or what good things we shall possess, or what evils we shall suffer, must be refused a hearing by all, not only by those who hold the true religion, but by those who wish to be the worshippers of any gods whatsoever, even false gods. For what does this opinion really amount to but this, that no god whatever is to be worshipped or prayed to? Against these, however, our present disputation is not intended to be directed, but against those who, in defence of those whom they think to be gods, oppose the Christian religion. They, however, who make the position of the stars depend on the divine will, and in a manner decree what character each man shall have, and what good or evil shall happen to him, if they think that these same stars have that power conferred upon them by the supreme power of God, in order that they may determine these things according to their will, do a great injury to the celestial sphere, in whose most brilliant senate, and most splendid senate-house, as it were, they suppose that wicked deeds are decreed to be done— such deeds as that, if any terrestrial state should decree them, it would be condemned to overthrow by the decree of the whole human race. What judgment, then, is left to God concerning the deeds of men, who is Lord both of the stars and of men, when to these deeds a celestial necessity is attributed? Or, if they do not say that the stars, though they have indeed received a certain power from God, who is supreme, determine those things according to their own discretion, but simply that His commands are fulfilled by them instrumentally in the application and enforcing of such necessities, are we thus to think concerning God even what it seemed unworthy that we should think concerning the will of the stars? But, if the stars are said rather to signify these things than to effect them, so that that *position of the stars* is, as it were, a kind of speech predicting, not causing future things—for this has been the opinion of men of no ordinary learning—certainly the mathematicians are not wont so to speak, saying, for example, Mars in such or such a position *signifies* a homicide, but *makes* a homicide. But, nevertheless, though we grant that they do not speak as they ought, and that we ought to accept as the proper form of speech that employed by the philosophers in predicting those things which they think they discover in the position of the stars, how comes it that they have never been able to assign any cause why, in the life of twins, in their actions, in the events which befall them, in their professions, arts, honors, and other things pertaining to human life, also in their very death, there is often so great a difference, that, as far as these things are concerned, many entire strangers are more like them than they are like each other, though separated at birth by the smallest interval of time, but at conception generated by the same act of copulation, and at the same moment?

CHAPTER II

ON THE DIFFERENCE IN THE HEALTH OF TWINS

Cicero says that the famous physician Hippocrates has left in writing that he had suspected that a certain pair of brothers were twins, from the fact that they both took ill at once, and their disease advanced to its crisis and subsided in the same time in each of them. Posidonius the Stoic, who was much given to astrology, used to explain the fact by supposing that they had been born and conceived under the same constellation. In this question the conjecture of the physician is by far more worthy to be accepted, and approaches much nearer to credibility, since, according as the parents were affected in body at the time of copulation, so might the first elements of the foetuses have been affected, so that all that was necessary for their growth and development up till birth having been supplied from the body of the same mother, they might be born with like constitutions. Thereafter, nourished in the same house, on the same kinds of food, where they would have also the same kinds of air, the same locality, the same quality of water—which, according to the testimony of medical science, have a very great influence, good or bad, on the condition of bodily health—and where they would also be accustomed to the same kinds of exercise, they would have bodily constitutions so similar that they would be similarly affected with sickness at the same time and by the same causes. But, to wish to adduce that particular position of the stars which existed at the time when they were born or conceived as the cause of their being simultaneously affected with sickness, manifests the greatest arrogance, when so many beings of most diverse kinds, in the most diverse conditions, and subject to the most diverse events, may have been conceived and born at the same time, and in the same district, lying under the same sky. But we know that twins do not only act differently, and travel to very different places, but that they also suffer from different kinds of sickness; for which Hippocrates would give what is in my opinion the simplest reason, namely, that, through diversity of food and exercise, which arises not from the constitution of the body, but from the inclination of the mind, they may have come to be different from each other in respect of health. Moreover, Posidonius, or any other asserter of the fatal influence of the stars, will have enough to do to find anything to say to this, if he be unwilling to impose upon the minds of the uninstructed in things of which they are ignorant. But, as to what they attempt to make out from that very small interval of time elapsing between the births of twins, on account of that point in the heavens where the mark of the natal hour is placed, and which they call the "horoscope," it is either disproportionately small to the diversity which is found in the dispositions, actions, habits, and fortunes of twins, or it is disproportionately great when compared with the estate of twins, whether low or high, which is the same for both of them, the cause for whose greatest difference they place, in every case, in the hour on which one is born; and, for this reason, if the one is born so immediately after the other that there is no change in the horoscope, I demand an entire similarity in all that respects them both, which can never be found in the case of any twins. But if the slowness of the birth of the second give time for a change in the horoscope, I demand different parents, which twins can never have.

CHAPTER III

CONCERNING THE ARGUMENTS WHICH NIGIDIUS THE MATHEMATICIAN DREW FROM THE POTTER'S WHEEL, IN THE QUESTION ABOUT THE BIRTH OF TWINS

It is to no purpose, therefore, that that famous fiction about the potter's wheel is brought forward, which tells of the answer which Nigidius is said to have given when he was perplexed with this question, and on account of which he was called *Figulus*.[2] For, having whirled round the potter's wheel with all his strength he marked it with ink, striking it twice with the utmost rapidity, so that the strokes seemed to fall on the very same part of it. Then, when the rotation had ceased, the marks which he had made were found upon the rim of the wheel at no small distance apart. Thus, said he, considering the great rapidity with which the celestial sphere revolves, even though twins were born with as short an interval between their births as there was between the strokes which I gave this wheel, that brief interval of time is equivalent to a very great distance in the celestial sphere. Hence, said he, come whatever dissimilitudes may be remarked in the habits and fortunes of twins. This argument is more fragile than the vessels which are fashioned by the rotation of that wheel. For if there is so much significance in the heavens which cannot be comprehended by observation of the constellations, that, in the case of twins, an inheritance may fall to the one and not to the other, why, in the case of others who are not twins, do they dare, having examined their constellations, to declare such things as pertain to that secret which no one can comprehend, and to attribute them to the precise moment of the birth of each individual? Now, if such predictions in connection with the natal hours of others who are not twins are to be vindicated on the ground that they are founded on the observation of more extended spaces in the heavens, whilst those very small moments of time which separated the births of twins, and correspond to minute portions of

[2] *I.e.* the potter

celestial space, are to be connected with trifling things about which the mathematicians are not wont to be consulted—for who would consult them as to when he is to sit, when to walk abroad, when and on what he is to dine? —how can we be justified in so speaking, when we can point out such manifold diversity both in the habits, doings, and destinies of twins?

CHAPTER IV

CONCERNING THE TWINS ESAU AND JACOB, WHO WERE VERY UNLIKE EACH OTHER BOTH IN THEIR CHARACTER AND ACTIONS

In the time of the ancient fathers, to speak concerning illustrious persons, there were born two twin brothers, the one so immediately after the other, that the first took hold of the heel of the second. So great a difference existed in their lives and manners, so great a dissimilarity in their actions, so great a difference in their parents' love for them respectively, that the very contrast between them produced even a mutual hostile antipathy. Do we mean, when we say that they were so unlike each other, that when the one was walking the other was sitting, when the one was sleeping the other was waking—which differences are such as are attributed to those minute portions of space which cannot be appreciated by those who note down the position of the stars which exists at the moment of one's birth, in order that the mathematicians may be consulted concerning it? One of these twins was for a long time a hired servant; the other never served. One of them was beloved by his mother; the other was not so. One of them lost that honor which was so much valued among their people; the other obtained it. And what shall we say of their wives, their children, and their possessions? How different they were in respect to all these! If, therefore, such things as these are connected with those minute intervals of time which elapse between the births of twins, and are not to be attributed to the constellations, wherefore are they predicted in the case of others from the examination of their constellations? And if, on the other hand, these things are said to be predicted, because they are connected, not with minute and inappreciable moments, but with intervals of time which can be observed and noted down, what purpose is that potter's wheel to serve in this matter, except it be to whirl round men who have hearts of clay, in order that they may be prevented from detecting the emptiness of the talk of the mathematicians?

CHAPTER V

IN WHAT MANNER THE MATHEMATICIANS ARE CONVICTED OF PROFESSING A VAIN SCIENCE

Do not those very persons whom the medical sagacity of Hippocrates led him to suspect to be twins, because their disease was observed by him to develop to its crisis and to subside again in the same time in each of them—

do not these, I say, serve as a sufficient refutation of those who wish to attribute to the influence of the stars that which was owing to a similarity of bodily constitution? For wherefore were they both sick of the same disease, and at the same time, and not the one after the other in the order of their birth? (For certainly they could not both be born at the same time.) Or, if the fact of their having been born at different times by no means necessarily implies that they must be sick at different times, why do they contend that the difference in the time of their births was the cause of their difference in other things? Why could they travel in foreign parts at different times, marry at different times, beget children at different times, and do many other things at different times, by reason of their having been born at different times, and yet could not, for the same reason, also be sick at different times? For if a difference in the moment of birth changed the horoscope, and occasioned dissimilarity in all other things, why has that simultaneousness which belonged to their conception remained in their attacks of sickness? Or, if the destinies of health are involved in the time of conception, but those of other things be said to be attached to the time of birth, they ought not to predict anything concerning health from examination of the constellations of birth, when the hour of conception is not also given, that its constellations may be inspected. But if they say that they predict attacks of sickness without examining the horoscope of conception, because these are indicated by the moments of birth, how could they inform either of these twins when he would be sick, from the horoscope of his birth, when the other also, who had not the same horoscope of birth, must of necessity fall sick at the same time? Again, I ask, if the distance of time between the births of twins is so great as to occasion a difference of their constellations on account of the difference of their horoscopes, and therefore of all the cardinal points to which so much influence is attributed, that even from such change there comes a difference of destiny, how is it possible that this should be so, since they cannot have been conceived at different times? Or, if two conceived at the same moment of time could have different destinies with respect to their births, why may not also two born at the same moment of time have different destinies for life and for death? For if the one moment in which both were conceived did not hinder that the one should be born before the other, why, if two are born at the same moment, should anything hinder them from dying at the same moment? If a simultaneous conception allows of twins being differently affected in the *womb*, why should not simultaneousness of birth allow of any two individuals having different fortunes in the *world?* and thus would all the fictions of this art, or rather delusion, be swept away. What strange circumstance is this, that two children conceived at the same time, nay, at the same moment, under the same position of the stars, have different fates which bring them to different hours of birth, whilst two children, born of two different mothers, at the same moment of time, under one and the same position of the stars, cannot have different fates which shall conduct them by necessity to diverse manners of life and of death? Are they at conception as yet without destinies, because they can only have them if they be born? What, therefore, do they mean when they say that, if the hour of the conception be found, many things can be predicted by these astrologers? from which also arose that story which is reiterated by some, that a certain sage chose an hour in which to lie with his wife, in order to secure his begetting an illustrious son. From this opinion also came that answer of Posidonius, the great astrologer and also philosopher, concerning those twins who were attacked with sickness at the same time, namely, that this had happened to them because they were conceived at the same time, and born at the same time. For certainly he added "conception," lest it should be said to him that they could not both be *born* at the same time, knowing that at any rate they must both have been conceived at the same time; wishing thus to show that he did not attribute the fact of their being similarly and simultaneously affected with sickness to the similarity of their bodily constitutions as its proximate cause, but that he held that even in respect of the similarity of their health, they were bound together by a sidereal connection. If, therefore, the time of conception has so much to do with the similarity of destinies, these same destinies ought not to be changed by the circumstances of birth; or, if the destinies of twins be said to be changed because they are born at different times, why should we not rather understand that they had been already changed in order that they might be born at different times? Does not, then, the will of men living in the world change the destinies of birth, when the order of birth can change the destinies they had at conception?

CHAPTER VI

CONCERNING TWINS OF DIFFERENT SEXES

But even in the very conception of twins, which certainly occurs at the same moment in the case of both, it often happens that the one is conceived a male, and the other a female. I know two of different sexes who are twins. Both of them are alive, and in the flower of their age; and though they resemble each other in body, as far as difference of sex will permit, still they are very different in the whole scope and purpose of their lives (consideration being had of those differences which necessarily exist between the lives of males and females)—the one holding the office of a count, and being almost constantly away from home with the army in foreign service, the other never leaving her country's soil, or her native district. Still more—and this is more incredible, if the destinies of the stars are to be believed in, though it is not wonderful if we consider the wills of men, and the free gifts of God—he is married; she is a sacred virgin: he has begotten a numerous offspring; she has never even married. But is not the virtue of the horoscope very great? I think I have said enough to show the absurdity of that. But, say those astrologers, whatever be the virtue of the horoscope in other respects, it is certainly of significance with respect to birth. But why not also with respect to conception, which takes place undoubtedly with one act of copulation? And, indeed, so great is the force of nature, that after a woman has once conceived, she ceases to be liable to conception. Or were they, perhaps, changed at birth, either he into a male, or she into a female, because of the difference in their horoscopes? But, whilst it is not altogether absurd to say that certain sidereal influences have some power to cause differences in bodies alone—as, for instance, we see that the seasons of the year come round by the approaching and receding of the sun, and that certain kinds of things are increased in size or diminished by the waxings and wanings of the moon, such as sea-urchins, oysters, and the wonderful tides of the ocean— it does not follow that the *wills of men* are to be made subject to the position of the stars. The astrologers, however, when they wish to bind our actions also to the constellations, only set us on investigating whether, even in these bodies, the changes may not be attributable to some other than a sidereal cause. For what is there which more intimately concerns a body than its sex? And yet, under the same position of the stars, twins of different sexes may be conceived. Wherefore, what greater absurdity can be affirmed or believed than that the position of the stars, which was the same for both of them at the time of conception, could not cause that the one child should not have been of a different sex from her brother, with whom she had a common constellation, whilst the position of the stars which existed at the hour of their birth could cause that she should be separated from him by the great distance between marriage and holy virginity?

CHAPTER VII

CONCERNING THE CHOOSING OF A DAY FOR MARRIAGE, OR FOR PLANTING, OR SOWING

Now, will any one bring forward this, that in choosing certain particular days for particular actions, men bring about certain new destinies for their actions? That man, for instance, according to this doctrine, was not born to have an illustrious son, but rather a contemptible one, and therefore, being a man of learning, he chose an hour in which to lie with his wife. He made, therefore, a destiny which he did not have before, and from that destiny of his own making something began to be fatal which was not contained in the destiny of his natal hour. Oh, singular stupidity! A day is chosen on which to marry; and for this reason, I believe, that unless a day be chosen, the marriage may fall on an unlucky day, and turn out an unhappy one. What then becomes of what the stars have already decreed at the hour of birth? Can a man be said to change by an act of choice that which has already been determined for him, whilst that which he himself has determined in the choosing of a day cannot be changed by another power? Thus, if men alone, and not all things under heaven, are subject to the influence of the stars, why do they choose some days as suitable for planting vines or trees, or for sowing grain, other days as suitable for taming beasts on, or for putting the males to the females, that the cows and mares may be impregnated, and for things of this sort? If it be said that certain chosen days have an influence on these things, because the constellations rule over all terrestrial bodies, animate and inanimate, according to differences in moments of time, let it be considered what innumerable multitudes of beings are born or arise, or take their origin at the very same instant of time, which come to ends so different, that they may persuade any little boy that these observations about days are ridiculous. For who is so mad as to dare affirm that all trees, all herbs, all beasts, serpents, birds, fishes, worms, have each separately their own moments of birth or commencement? Nevertheless, men are wont, in order to try the skill of the mathematicians, to bring before them the constellations of dumb animals, the constellations of whose birth they diligently observe at home with a view to this discovery; and they prefer those mathematicians to all others, who say from the inspection of the constellations that they indicate the birth of a beast and not of a man. They also dare tell what kind of beast it is, whether it is a wool-bearing beast, or a beast suited for carrying burdens, or one fit for the plough, or for watching a house; for the astrologers are also tried with respect to the fates of dogs, and their answers concerning these are followed by shouts of admiration on the part of those who consult them. They so deceive men as to make them think that during the birth of a man the births of all other beings are suspended, so that not even a fly comes to life at the same time that he is being born, under the same region of the heavens. And if this be admitted with respect to the fly, the reasoning cannot stop there, but must ascend from flies till it lead them up to camels and elephants. Nor are they willing to attend to this, that when a day has been chosen whereon to sow a field, so many grains fall into the ground simultaneously, germinate simultaneously, spring up, come to perfection, and ripen simultaneously; and yet, of all the ears which are coeval, and, so to speak, *congerminal*, some are destroyed by mildew, some are devoured by the birds, and some are pulled by men. How can they say that all these had their different constellations, which they see coming to so different ends? Will they confess that it is folly to choose days for such things, and to affirm that they do not come within the sphere of the celestial decree, whilst they subject men alone to the stars, on whom alone in the world God has bestowed free wills? All these things being considered, we have good reason to believe that, when the astrologers give very many wonderful answers, it is to be attributed to the occult inspiration of spirits not of the best kind, whose care it is to insinuate into the minds of men, and to confirm in them, those false and noxious opinions concerning the fatal influence of the stars, and not to their marking and inspecting of horoscopes, according to some kind of art which in reality has no existence.

CHAPTER VIII

CONCERNING THOSE WHO CALL BY THE NAME OF FATE, NOT THE POSITION OF THE STARS, BUT THE CONNECTION OF CAUSES WHICH DEPENDS ON THE WILL OF GOD

But, as to those who call by the name of fate, not the disposition of the stars as it may exist when any creature is conceived, or born, or commences its existence, but the whole connection and train of causes which makes everything become what it does become, there is no need that I should labor and strive with them in a merely verbal controversy, since they attribute the so-called order and connection of causes to the will and power of God most high, who is most rightly and most truly believed to know all things before they come to pass, and to leave nothing unordained; from whom are all powers, although the wills of all are not from Him. Now, that it is chiefly the will of God most high, whose power extends itself irresistibly through all things which they call fate, is proved by the following verses, of which, if I mistake not, Annaeus Seneca is the author:—

> Father supreme, Thou ruler of the lofty heavens,
> Lead me where'er it is Thy pleasure; I will give
> A prompt obedience, making no delay,
> Lo! here I am. Promptly I come to do Thy sovereign will;
> If Thy command shall thwart my inclination, I will still
> Follow Thee groaning, and the work assigned,
> With all the suffering of a mind repugnant,
> Will perform, being evil; which, had I been good,
> I should have undertaken and performed, though hard,
> With virtuous cheerfulness.
> The Fates do lead the man that follows willing;
> But the man that is unwilling, him they drag.[3]

Most evidently, in this last verse, he calls that "fate" which he had before called "the will of the Father supreme," whom, he says, he is ready to obey that he may be led, being willing, not dragged, being unwilling, since "the Fates do lead the man that follows willing, but the man that is unwilling, him they drag."

The following Homeric lines, which Cicero translates into Latin, also favor this opinion:—

> Such are the minds of men, as is the light
> Which Father Jove himself doth pour
> Illustrious o'er the fruitful earth.[4]

Not that Cicero wishes that a poetical sentiment should have any weight in a question like this; for when he says that the Stoics, when asserting the

---

[3] *Epist.* 107   [4] *Odyssey*, xviii. 136, 137

power of fate, were in the habit of using these verses from Homer, he is not treating concerning the opinion of that poet, but concerning that of those philosophers, since by these verses, which they quote in connection with the controversy which they hold about fate, is most distinctly manifested what it is which they reckon fate, since they call by the name of Jupiter him whom they reckon the supreme god, from whom, they say, hangs the whole chain of fates.

CHAPTER IX

CONCERNING THE FOREKNOWLEDGE OF GOD AND THE FREE WILL OF MAN, IN OPPOSITION TO THE DEFINITION OF CICERO

The manner in which Cicero addresses himself to the task of refuting the Stoics, shows that he did not think he could effect anything against them in argument unless he had first demolished divination.[5] And this he attempts to accomplish by denying that there is any knowledge of future things, and maintains with all his might that there is no such knowledge either in God or man, and that there is no prediction of events. Thus he both denies the foreknowledge of God, and attempts by vain arguments, and by opposing to himself certain oracles very easy to be refuted, to overthrow all prophecy, even such as is clearer than the light (though even these oracles are not refuted by him).

But, in refuting these conjectures of the mathematicians, his argument is triumphant, because truly these are such as destroy and refute themselves. Nevertheless, they are far more tolerable who assert the fatal influence of the stars than they who deny the foreknowledge of future events. For, to confess that God exists, and at the same time to deny that He has foreknowledge of future things, is the most manifest folly. This Cicero himself saw, and therefore attempted to assert the doctrine embodied in the words of Scripture, "The fool hath said in his heart, There is no God." [6] That, however, he did not do in his own person, for he saw how odious and offensive such an opinion would be; and therefore, in his book on the nature of the gods,[7] he makes Cotta dispute concerning this against the Stoics, and preferred to give his own opinion in favor of Lucilius Balbus, to whom he assigned the defence of the Stoical position, rather than in favor of Cotta, who maintained that no divinity exists. However, in his book on divination, he in his own person most openly opposes the doctrine of the prescience of future things. But all this he seems to do in order that he may not grant the doctrine of fate, and by so doing destroy free will. For he thinks that, the knowledge of future things being once conceded, fate follows as so necessary a consequence that it cannot be denied.

But, let these perplexing debatings and disputations of the philosophers go on as they may, we, in order that we may confess the most high and true God Himself, do confess His will, supreme power, and prescience. Neither let us be afraid lest, after all, we do not do by will that which we do by will, because He, whose foreknowledge is infallible, foreknew that we would do it. It was this which Cicero was afraid of, and therefore opposed foreknowledge. The Stoics also maintained that all things do not come to pass by necessity, although they contended that all things happen according to destiny. What is it, then, that Cicero feared in the prescience of future things? Doubtless it was this—that if all future things have been foreknown, they will happen in the order in which they have been foreknown; and if they come to pass in this order, there is a certain order of things foreknown by God; and if a certain order of things, then a certain order of causes, for nothing can happen which is not preceded by some efficient cause. But if there is a certain order of causes according to which everything happens which does happen, then by fate, says he, all things happen which do happen. But if this be so, then is there nothing in our own power, and there is no such thing as freedom of will; and if we grant that, says he, the whole economy of human life is subverted. In vain are laws enacted. In vain are reproaches, praises, chidings, exhortations had recourse to; and there is no justice whatever in the appointment of rewards for the good, and punishments for the wicked. And that consequences so disgraceful, and absurd, and pernicious to humanity may not follow, Cicero chooses to reject the foreknowledge of future things, and shuts up the religious mind to this alternative, to make choice between two things, either that something is in our own power, or that there is foreknowledge—both of which cannot be true; but if the one is affirmed, the other is thereby denied. He therefore, like a truly great and wise man, and one who consulted very much and very skillfully for the good of humanity, of those two chose the freedom of the will, to confirm which he denied the foreknowledge of future things; and thus, wishing to make men free, he makes them sacrilegious. But the religious mind chooses both, confesses both, and maintains both by the faith of piety. But how so? says Cicero; for the knowledge of future things being granted, there follows a chain of consequences which ends in this, that there can be nothing depending on our own free wills. And further, if there is anything depending on our wills, we must go backwards by the same steps of reasoning till we arrive at the conclusion that there is no foreknowledge of future things. For we go backwards through all the steps in the following order: —If there is free will, all things do not happen according to fate; if all things do not happen according to fate, there is not a certain order of causes; and if there is not a certain order of causes, neither is there a certain order of things foreknown by God—for things cannot come to pass except they are preceded by efficient causes—but, if there is no fixed and certain order of causes foreknown by God, all things cannot be said to happen according as He foreknew that they would happen. And further, if it is not true that all things happen just as they have been foreknown by Him, there is not, says he, in God any foreknowledge of future events.

Now, against the sacrilegious and impious darings of reason, we assert both that God knows all things before they come to pass, and that we do by our free will whatsoever we know and feel to be done by us only because we will it. But that all things come to pass by fate, we do not say; nay we affirm that nothing comes to pass by fate; for we demonstrate that the name of fate, as it is wont to be used by those who speak of fate, meaning thereby the position of the stars at the time of each one's conception or birth, is an unmeaning word, for astrology itself is a delusion. But an order of causes in which the highest efficiency is attributed to the will of God, we neither deny nor do we designate it by the name of fate, unless, perhaps, we may understand fate to mean that which is spoken, deriving it from *fari*, to speak; for we cannot deny that it is written in the sacred Scriptures, "God hath spoken once; these two things have I heard, that power belongeth unto God. Also unto Thee, O God, belongeth mercy: for Thou wilt render unto every man according to his works." [8] Now the expression, "Once hath He spoken," is to be understood as meaning *"immovably,"* that is, unchangeably hath He spoken, inasmuch as He knows unchangeably all things which shall be, and all things which He will do. We might, then, use the word fate in the sense it bears when derived from *fari*, to speak, had it not already come to be understood in another sense, into which I am unwilling that the hearts of men should unconsciously slide. But it does not follow that, though there is for God a certain order of all causes, there must therefore be nothing depending on the free exercise of our own wills, for our wills themselves are included in that order of causes which is certain to God, and is embraced by His foreknowledge, for human wills are also causes of human actions; and He who foreknew all the causes of things would certainly among those causes not have been ignorant of our wills. For even that very concession which Cicero himself makes is enough to refute him in this argument. For what does it help him to say that nothing takes place without a cause, but that every cause is not fatal, there being a fortuitous cause, a natural cause, and a voluntary cause? It is sufficient that he confesses that whatever happens must be preceded by a cause. For we say that those causes which are called fortuitous are not a mere name for the absence of causes, but are only latent, and we attribute them either to the will of the true God, or to that of spirits of some kind or other. And as to natural causes, we by no means separate them from the will of Him who is the author and framer of all nature. But now as to voluntary causes. They are referable either to God, or to angels, or to men, or to animals of whatever description, if indeed those instinctive movements of animals devoid of reason, by which, in accordance with their own nature, they seek or shun various things, are to be called wills. And when I speak of the wills of angels, I mean either the wills of good angels, whom we call the angels of God, or of the wicked angels, whom we call the angels of the devil, or demons. Also by the wills of men I mean the wills

[8] Ps. lxii. 11, 12

either of the good or of the wicked. And from this we conclude that there are no efficient causes of all things which come to pass unless voluntary causes, that is, such as belong to that nature which is the spirit of life. For the air or wind is called spirit, but, inasmuch as it is a body, it is not the spirit of life. The spirit of life, therefore, which quickens all things, and is the creator of every body, and of every created spirit, is God Himself, the uncreated spirit. In His supreme will resides the power which acts on the wills of all created spirits, helping the good, judging the evil, controlling all, granting power to some, not granting it to others. For, as He is the creator of all natures, so also is He the bestower of all powers, not of all wills; for wicked wills are not from Him, being contrary to nature, which is from Him. As to bodies, they are more subject to wills: some to our wills, by which I mean the wills of all living mortal creatures, but more to the wills of men than of beasts. But all of them are most of all subject to the will of God, to whom all wills also are subject, since they have no power except what He has bestowed upon them. The cause of things, therefore, which makes but is not made, is God; but all other causes both make and are made. Such are all created spirits, and especially the rational. Material causes, therefore, which may rather be said to be made than to make, are not to be reckoned among efficient causes, because they can only do what the wills of spirits do by them. How, then, does an order of causes which is certain to the foreknowledge of God necessitate that there should be nothing which is dependent on our wills, when our wills themselves have a very important place in the order of causes? Cicero, then, contends with those who call this order of causes fatal, or rather designate this order itself by the name of fate; to which we have an abhorrence, especially on account of the word, which men have become accustomed to understand as meaning what is not true. But, whereas he denies that the order of all causes is most certain, and perfectly clear to the prescience of God, we detest his opinion more than the Stoics do. For he either denies that God exists—which, indeed, in an assumed personage, he has labored to do, in his book *De Natura Deorum*—or if he confesses that He exists, but denies that He is prescient of future things, what is that but just the fool saying in his heart there is no God? For one who is not prescient of all future things is not God. Wherefore our wills also have just so much power as God willed and foreknew that they should have; and therefore whatever power they have, they have it within most certain limits; and whatever they are to do, they are most assuredly to do, for He whose foreknowledge is infallible foreknew that they would have the power to do it, and would do it. Wherefore, if I should choose to apply the name of fate to anything at all, I should rather say that fate belongs to the weaker of two parties, will to the stronger, who has the other in his power, than that the freedom of our will is excluded by that order of causes, which, by an unusual application of the word peculiar to themselves, the Stoics call *Fate*.

CHAPTER X

WHETHER OUR WILLS ARE RULED BY NECESSITY

Wherefore, neither is that necessity to be feared, for dread of which the Stoics labored to make such distinctions among the causes of things as should enable them to rescue certain things from the dominion of necessity, and to subject others to it. Among those things which they wished not to be subject to necessity they placed our wills, knowing that they would not be free if subjected to necessity. For if that is to be called *our necessity* which is not in our power, but even though we be unwilling effects what it can effect—as, for instance, the necessity of death—it is manifest that our wills by which we live uprightly or wickedly are not under such a necessity; for we do many things which, if we were not willing, we should certainly not do. This is primarily true of the act of willing itself—for if we will, it *is;* if we will not, it *is* not—for we should not will if we were unwilling. But if we define necessity to be that according to which we say that it is necessary that anything be of such or such a nature, or be done in such and such a manner, I know not why we should have any dread of that necessity taking away the freedom of our will. For we do not put the life of God or the fore-knowledge of God under necessity if we should say that it is necessary that God should live forever, and foreknow all things; as neither is His power diminished when we say that He cannot die or fall into error—for this is in such a way impossible to Him, that if it were possible for Him, He would be of less power. But assuredly He is rightly called omnipotent, though He can neither die nor fall into error. For He is called omnipotent on account of His doing what He wills, not on account of His suffering what He wills not; for if that should befall Him, He would by no means be omnipotent. Wherefore, He cannot do some things for the very reason that He is omnipotent. So also, when we say that it is necessary that, when we will, we will by free choice, in so saying we both affirm what is true beyond doubt, and do not still subject our wills thereby to a necessity which destroys liberty. Our wills, therefore, *exist* as *wills*, and do themselves whatever we do by willing, and which would not be done if we were unwilling. But when any one suffers anything, being unwilling, by the will of another, even in that case will retains its essential validity—we do not mean the will of the party who inflicts the suffering, for we resolve it into the power of God. For if a will should simply exist, but not be able to do what it wills, it would be overborne by a more powerful will. Nor would this be the case unless there had existed will, and that not the will of the other party, but the will of him who willed, but was not able to accomplish what he willed. Therefore, whatsoever a man suffers contrary to his own will, he ought not to attribute to the will of men, or of angels, or of any created spirit, but rather to His will who gives power to wills. It is not the case, therefore, that because God foreknew what would be in the power of our wills, there is for that reason nothing in the power of our wills. For He who foreknew this did not foreknow nothing. Moreover, if He who foreknew what would be in the power of our wills did not foreknow nothing, but something, assuredly, even though He did foreknow, there is something in the power of our wills. Therefore we are by no means compelled, either, retaining the prescience of God, to take away the freedom of the will, or, retaining the freedom of the will, to deny that He is prescient of future things, which is impious. But we embrace both. We faithfully and sincerely confess both. The former, that we may believe well; the latter, that we may live well. For he lives ill who does not believe well concerning God. Wherefore, be it far from us, in order to maintain our freedom, to deny the prescience of Him by whose help we are or shall be free. Consequently, it is not in vain that laws are enacted, and that reproaches, exhortations, praises, and vituperations are had recourse to; for these also He foreknew, and they are of great avail, even as great as He foreknew that they would be of. Prayers, also, are of avail to procure those things which He foreknew that He would grant to those who offered them; and with justice have rewards been appointed for good deeds, and punishments for sins. For a man does not therefore sin because God foreknew that he would sin. Nay, it cannot be doubted but that it is the man himself who sins when he does sin, because He, whose foreknowledge is infallible, foreknew not that fate, or fortune, or something else would sin, but that the man himself would sin, who, if he wills not, sins not. But if he shall not will to sin, even this did God foreknow.

CHAPTER XI

CONCERNING THE UNIVERSAL PROVIDENCE OF GOD IN THE LAWS OF WHICH ALL THINGS ARE COMPREHENDED

Therefore God supreme and true, with His Word and Holy Spirit (which three are one), one God omnipotent, creator and maker of every soul and of every body; by whose gift all are happy who are happy through verity and not through vanity; who made man a rational animal consisting of soul and body, who, when he sinned, neither permitted him to go unpunished, nor left him without mercy; who has given to the good and to the evil, being in common with stones, vegetable life in common with trees, sensuous life in common with brutes, intellectual life in common with angels alone; from whom is every mode, every species, every order; from whom are measure, number, weight; from whom is everything which has an existence in nature, of whatever kind it be, and of whatever value; from whom are the seeds of forms and the forms of seeds, and the motion of seeds and of forms; who gave also to flesh its origin, beauty, health, reproductive fecundity, disposition of members, and the salutary concord of its parts; who also to the irrational soul has given memory, sense, appetite, but to the rational soul, in addition to these, has given intelligence and will; who has not left, not to speak of heaven and earth, angels and men, but not even the entrails of the smallest and most contemptible animal, or the feather of a bird, or the little flower of a plant, or the leaf of a tree, without a harmony, and, as it were, a mutual peace among all its parts—that God can never be believed to have left the kingdoms of men, their dominations and servitudes, outside of the laws of His providence.

CHAPTER XII

BY WHAT VIRTUES THE ANCIENT ROMANS MERITED THAT THE TRUE GOD, ALTHOUGH THEY DID NOT WORSHIP HIM, SHOULD ENLARGE THEIR EMPIRE

Wherefore let us go on to consider what virtues of the Romans they were which the true God, in whose power are also the kingdoms of the earth, condescended to help in order to raise the empire, and also for what reason He did so. And, in order to discuss this question on clearer ground, we have written the former books, to show that the power of those gods, who, they thought, were to be worshipped with such trifling and silly rites, had nothing to do in this matter; and also what we have already accomplished of the present volume, to refute the doctrine of fate, lest any one who might have been already persuaded that the Roman empire was not extended and preserved by the worship of these gods, might still be attributing its extension and preservation to some kind of fate, rather than to the most powerful will of God most high. The ancient and primitive Romans, therefore, though their history shows us that, like all the other nations, with the sole exception of the Hebrews, they worshipped false gods, and sacrificed victims, not to God, but to demons, have nevertheless this commendation bestowed on them by their historian, that they were "greedy of praise, prodigal of wealth, desirous of great glory, and content with a moderate fortune." [9] Glory they most ardently loved: for it they wished to live, for it they did not hesitate to die. Every other desire was repressed by the strength of their passion for that one thing. At length their country itself, because it seemed inglorious to serve, but glorious to rule and to command, they first earnestly desired to be free, and then to be mistress. Hence it was that, not enduring the domination of kings, they put the government into the hands of two chiefs, holding office for a year, who were called consuls, not kings or lords. But royal pomp seemed inconsistent with the administration of a ruler (*regentis*), or the benevolence of one who consults (that is, for the public good) (*consulentis*), but rather with the haughtiness of a lord (*dominantis*). King Tarquin, therefore, having been banished, and the consular government having been instituted, it followed, as the same author already alluded to says in his praises of the Romans, that "the state grew with amazing rapidity after it had obtained liberty, so great a desire of glory had taken

[9] Sallust, *Cat.* vii

possession of it." That eagerness for praise and desire of glory, then, was that which accomplished those many wonderful things, laudable, doubtless, and glorious according to human judgment. The same Sallust praises the great men of his own time, Marcus Cato, and Caius Caesar, saying that for a long time the republic had no one great in virtue, but that within his memory there had been these two men of eminent virtue, and very different pursuits. Now, among the praises which he pronounces on Caesar he put this, that he wished for a great empire, an army, and a new war, that he might have a sphere where his genius and virtue might shine forth. Thus it was ever the prayer of men of heroic character that Bellona would excite miserable nations to war, and lash them into agitation with her bloody scourge, so that there might be occasion for the display of their valor. This, really, is what that desire of praise and thirst for glory did. Wherefore, by the love of liberty in the first place, afterwards also by that of domination and through the desire of praise and glory, they achieved many great things; and their most eminent poet testifies to their having been prompted by all these motives:

> Porsenna there, with pride elate,
> Bids Rome to Tarquin ope her gate;
> With arms he hems the city in,
> Aeneas' sons stand firm to win.[10]

At that time it was their greatest ambition either to die bravely or to live free; but when liberty was obtained, so great a desire of glory took possession of them, that liberty alone was not enough unless domination also should be sought, their great ambition being that which the same poet puts into the mouth of Jupiter:

> Nay, Juno's self, whose wild alarms
> Set ocean, earth, and heaven in arms,
> Shall change for smiles her moody frown,
> And vie with me in zeal to crown
> Rome's sons, the nation of the gown.
> So stands my will. There comes a day,
> While Rome's great ages hold their way,
> When old Assaracus's sons
> Shall quit them on the myrmidons,
> O'er Phthia and Mycenae reign,
> And humble Argos to their chain.[11]

Which things, indeed, Virgil makes Jupiter predict as future, whilst, in reality, he was only himself passing in review in his own mind, things which were already done, and which were beheld by him as present realities. But I have mentioned them with the intention of showing that, next to liberty, the Romans so highly esteemed domination, that it received a place among

[10] *Aeneid,* viii. 646   [11] *Ibid.* i. 279

those things on which they bestowed the greatest praise. Hence also it is that that poet, preferring to the arts of other nations those arts which peculiarly belong to the Romans, namely, the arts of ruling and commanding, and of subjugating and vanquishing nations, says,

> Others, belike, with happier grace,
> From bronze or stone shall call the face,
> Plead doubtful causes, map the skies,
> And tell when planets set or rise;
> But Roman thou, do thou control
>   The nations far and wide;
> Be this thy genius, to impose
> The rule of peace on vanquished foes,
> Show pity to the humble soul,
> And crush the sons of pride.[12]

These arts they exercised with the more skill the less they gave themselves up to pleasures, and to enervation of body and mind in coveting and amassing riches, and through these corrupting morals, by extorting them from the miserable citizens and lavishing them on base stage-players. Hence these men of base character, who abounded when Sallust wrote and Virgil sang these things, did not seek after honors and glory by these arts, but by treachery and deceit. Wherefore the same says, "But at first it was rather ambition than avarice that stirred the minds of men, which vice, however, is nearer to virtue. For glory, honor, and power are desired alike by the good man and by the ignoble; but the former," he says, "strives onward to them by the true way, whilst the other, knowing nothing of the good arts, seeks them by fraud and deceit."[13] And what is meant by seeking the attainment of glory, honor, and power by good arts, is to seek them by virtue, and not by deceitful intrigue; for the good and the ignoble man alike desire these things, but the good man strives to overtake them by the true way. The way is virtue, along which he presses as to the goal of possession—namely, to glory, honor, and power. Now that this was a sentiment engrained in the Roman mind, is indicated even by the temples of their gods; for they built in very close proximity the temples of Virtue and Honor, worshipping as gods the gifts of God. Hence we can understand what they who were good thought to be the end of virtue, and to what they ultimately referred it, namely, to honor; for, as to the bad, they had no virtue though they desired honor, and strove to possess it by fraud and deceit. Praise of a higher kind is bestowed upon Cato, for he says of him, "The less he sought glory, the more it followed him."[14] We say praise of a higher kind; for the glory with the desire of which the Romans burned is the judgment of men thinking well of men. And therefore virtue is better, which is content with no human judgment save that of one's own conscience. Whence the apostle says, "For

---

[12] *Ibid*. vi. 847   [13] Sallust, *Cat*. xi.   [14] Sallust, *Cat*. liv.

this is our glory, the testimony of our conscience."[15] And in another place he says, "But let every one prove his own work, and then he shall have glory in himself, and not in another."[16] That glory, honor, and power, therefore, which they desired for themselves, and to which the good sought to attain by good arts, should not be sought after by virtue, but virtue by them. For there is no true virtue except that which is directed towards that end in which is the highest and ultimate good of man. Wherefore even the honors which Cato sought he ought not to have sought, but the state ought to have conferred them on him unsolicited, on account of his virtues.

But, of the two great Romans of that time, Cato was he whose virtue was by far the nearest to the true idea of virtue. Wherefore, let us refer to the opinion of Cato himself, to discover what was the judgment he had formed concerning the condition of the state both then and in former times. "I do not think," he says, "that it was by arms that our ancestors made the republic great from being small. Had that been the case, the republic of our day would have been by far more flourishing than that of their times, for the number of our allies and citizens is far greater; and, besides, we possess a far greater abundance of armor and of horses than they did. But it was other things than these that made them great, and we have none of them: industry at home, just government without, a mind free in deliberation, addicted neither to crime nor to lust. Instead of these, we have luxury and avarice, poverty in the state, opulence among citizens; we laud riches, we follow laziness; there is no difference made between the good and the bad; all the rewards of virtue are got possession of by intrigue. And no wonder, when every individual consults only for his own good, when ye are the slaves of pleasure at home, and, in public affairs, of money and favor, no wonder that an onslaught is made upon the unprotected republic."[17]

He who hears these words of Cato or of Sallust probably thinks that such praise bestowed on the ancient Romans was applicable to all of them, or, at least, to very many of them. It is not so; otherwise the things which Cato himself writes, and which I have quoted in the second book of this work, would not be true. In that passage he says, that even from the very beginning of the state wrongs were committed by the more powerful, which led to the separation of the people from the fathers, besides which there were other internal dissensions; and the only time at which there existed a just and moderate administration was after the banishment of the kings, and that no longer than whilst they had cause to be afraid of Tarquin, and were carrying on the grievous war which had been undertaken on his account against Etruria; but afterwards the fathers oppressed the people as slaves, flogged them as the kings had done, drove them from their land, and, to the exclusion of all others, held the government in their own hands alone. And to these discords, whilst the fathers were wishing to rule, and the people were unwilling to serve, the second Punic war put an end; for again great

[15] 2 Cor. i. 12   [16] Gal. vi. 4   [17] Sallust, *Cat*. lii.

fear began to press upon their disquieted minds, holding them back from those distractions by another and greater anxiety, and bringing them back to civil concord. But the great things which were then achieved were accomplished through the administration of a few men, who were good in their own way. And by the wisdom and forethought of these few good men, which first enabled the republic to endure these evils and mitigated them, it waxed greater and greater. And this the same historian affirms, when he says that, reading and hearing of the many illustrious achievements of the Roman people in peace and in war, by land and by sea, he wished to understand what it was by which these great things were specially sustained. For he knew that very often the Romans had with a small company contended with great legions of the enemy; and he knew also that with small resources they had carried on wars with opulent kings. And he says that, after having given the matter much consideration, it seemed evident to him that the pre-eminent virtue of a few citizens had achieved the whole, and that that explained how poverty overcame wealth, and small numbers great multitudes. But, he adds, after the state had been corrupted by luxury and indolence, again the republic, by its own greatness, was able to bear the vices of its magistrates and generals. Wherefore even the praises of Cato are only applicable to a few; for only a few were possessed of that virtue which leads men to pursue glory, honor, and power by the true way—that is, by virtue itself. This industry at home, of which Cato speaks, was the consequence of a desire to enrich the public treasury, even though the result should be poverty at home; and therefore, when he speaks of the evil arising out of the corruption of morals, he reverses the expression, and says, "Poverty in the state, riches at home."

CHAPTER XIII

CONCERNING THE LOVE OF PRAISE, WHICH, THOUGH IT IS A VICE, IS RECKONED A VIRTUE, BECAUSE BY IT GREATER VICE IS RESTRAINED

Wherefore, when the kingdoms of the East had been illustrious for a long time, it pleased God that there should also arise a Western empire, which, though later in time, should be more illustrious in extent and greatness. And, in order that it might overcome the grievous evils which existed among other nations, He purposely granted it to such men as, for the sake of honor, and praise, and glory, consulted well for their country, in whose glory they sought their own, and whose safety they did not hesitate to prefer to their own, suppressing the desire of wealth and many other vices for this one vice, namely, the love of praise. For he has the soundest perception who recognizes that even the love of praise is a vice; nor has this escaped the perception of the poet Horace, who says,

> You're bloated by ambition? take advice:
> Yon book will ease you if you read it thrice.[18]

And the same poet, in a lyric song, has thus spoken with the desire of repressing the passion for domination:

> Rule an ambitious spirit, and thou hast
> A wider kingdom than if thou shouldst join
> To distant Gades Lybia, and thus
> Shouldst hold in service either Carthaginian.[19]

Nevertheless, they who restrain baser lusts, not by the power of the Holy Spirit obtained by the faith of piety, or by the love of intelligible beauty, but by desire of human praise, or, at all events, restrain them better by the love of such praise, are not indeed yet holy, but only less base. Even Tully was not able to conceal this fact; for, in the same books which he wrote, *De Republica*, when speaking concerning the education of a chief of the state, who ought, he says, to be nourished on glory, goes on to say that their ancestors did many wonderful and illustrious things through desire of glory. So far, therefore, from resisting this vice, they even thought that it ought to be excited and kindled up, supposing that that would be beneficial to the republic. But not even in his books on philosophy does Tully dissimulate this poisonous opinion, for he there avows it more clearly than day. For when he is speaking of those studies which are to be pursued with a view to the *true good*, and not with the vainglorious desire of human praise, he introduces the following universal and general statement:

Honor nourishes the arts, and all are stimulated to the prosecution of studies by glory; and those pursuits are always neglected which are generally discredited.[20]

CHAPTER XIV

CONCERNING THE ERADICATION OF THE LOVE OF HUMAN PRAISE, BECAUSE ALL THE GLORY OF THE RIGHTEOUS IS IN GOD

It is, therefore, doubtless far better to resist this desire than to yield to it, for the purer one is from this defilement, the liker is he to God; and, though this vice be not thoroughly eradicated from his heart—for it does not cease to tempt even the minds of those who are making good progress in virtue—at any rate, let the desire of glory be surpassed by the love of righteousness, so that, if there be seen anywhere "lying neglected things which are generally discredited," if they are good, if they are right, even the love of human praise may blush and yield to the love of truth. For so hostile is this vice to pious faith, if the love of glory be greater in the heart than the fear or love of God, that the Lord said, "How can ye believe, who look for glory

[18] Horace, *Epist.* i. 1. 36, 37   [19] Hor. *Carm.* ii. 2   [20] *Tusc. Quaest.* i. 2

from one another, and do not seek the glory which is from God alone?" [21]
Also, concerning some who had believed on Him, but were afraid to confess
Him openly, the evangelist says, "They loved the praise of men more than
the praise of God;" [22] which did not the holy apostles, who, when they proclaimed the name of Christ in those places where it was not only discredited,
and therefore neglected—according as Cicero says, "Those things are always
neglected which are generally discredited"—but was even held in the utmost
detestation, holding to what they had heard from the Good Master, who
was also the physician of minds, "If any one shall deny me before men, him
will I also deny before my Father who is in heaven, and before the angels
of God," [23] amidst maledictions and reproaches, and most grievous persecutions and cruel punishments, were not deterred from the preaching of human
salvation by the noise of human indignation. And when, as they did and
spoke divine things, and lived divine lives, conquering, as it were, hard
hearts, and introducing into them the peace of righteousness, great glory
followed them in the church of Christ, they did not rest in that as in the end
of their virtue, but, referring that glory itself to the glory of God, by whose
grace they were what they were, they sought to kindle, also by that same
flame, the minds of those for whose good they consulted, to the love of Him,
by whom they could be made to be what they themselves were. For their
Master had taught them not to seek to be good for the sake of human glory,
saying, "Take heed that ye do not your righteousness before men to be seen
of them, or otherwise ye shall not have a reward from your Father who is in
heaven." [24] But again, lest, understanding this wrongly, they should, through
fear of pleasing men, be less useful through concealing their goodness, showing for what end they ought to make it known, He says, "Let your works
shine before men, that they may see your good deeds, and glorify your
Father who is in heaven." [25] Not, observe, "that ye may be seen by them,
that is, in order that their eyes may be directed upon you"—for of yourselves
ye are nothing—but "that they may glorify your Father who is in heaven,"
by fixing their regards on whom they may become such as ye are. These the
martyrs followed, who surpassed the Scaevolas, and the Curtiuses, and the
Deciuses, both in true virtue, because in true piety, and also in the greatness
of their number. But since those Romans were in an earthly city, and had
before them, as the end of all the offices undertaken in its behalf, its safety,
and a kingdom, not in heaven, but in earth—not in the sphere of eternal life,
but in the sphere of demise and succession, where the dead are succeeded by
the dying—what else but glory should they love, by which they wished even
after death to live in the mouths of their admirers?

[21] John v. 44   [22] John xii. 43   [23] Matt. x. 33   [24] Matt. vi. 1   [25] Matt. v. 16

CHAPTER XV

CONCERNING THE TEMPORAL REWARD WHICH GOD GRANTED TO THE VIRTUES OF THE ROMANS

Now, therefore, with regard to those to whom God did not purpose to give eternal life with His holy angels in His own celestial city, to the society of which that true piety which does not render the service of religion, which the Greeks call λατρεία, to any save the true God conducts, if He had also withheld from them the terrestrial glory of that most excellent empire, a reward would not have been rendered to their good arts—that is, their virtues—by which they sought to attain so great glory. For as to those who seem to do some good that they may receive glory from men, the Lord also says, "Verily I say unto you, they have received their reward."[26] So also these despised their own private affairs for the sake of the republic, and for its treasury resisted avarice, consulted for the good of their country with a spirit of freedom, addicted neither to what their laws pronounced to be crime nor to lust. By all these acts, as by the true way, they pressed forward to honors, power, and glory; they were honored among almost all nations; they imposed the laws of their empire upon many nations; and at this day, both in literature and history, they are glorious among almost all nations. There is no reason why they should complain against the justice of the supreme and true God—"they have received their reward."

CHAPTER XVI

CONCERNING THE REWARD OF THE HOLY CITIZENS OF THE CELESTIAL CITY, TO WHOM THE EXAMPLE OF THE VIRTUES OF THE ROMANS ARE USEFUL

But the reward of the saints is far different, who even here endured reproaches for that city of God which is hateful to the lovers of this world. That city is eternal. There none are born, for none die. There is true and full felicity—not a goddess, but a gift of God. Thence we receive the pledge of faith, whilst on our pilgrimage we sigh for its beauty. There rises not the sun on the good and the evil, but the Sun of Righteousness protects the good alone. There no great industry shall be expended to enrich the public treasury by suffering privations at home, for there is the common treasury of truth. And, therefore, it was not only for the sake of recompensing the citizens of Rome that her empire and glory had been so signally extended, but also that the citizens of that eternal city, during their pilgrimage here, might diligently and soberly contemplate these examples, and see what a love they owe to the supernal country on account of life eternal, if the ter-

[26] Matt. vi. 2

restrial country was so much beloved by its citizens on account of human glory.

CHAPTER XVII

TO WHAT PROFIT THE ROMANS CARRIED ON WARS, AND HOW MUCH THEY CONTRIBUTED TO THE WELL-BEING OF THOSE WHOM THEY CONQUERED

For, as far as this life of mortals is concerned, which is spent and ended in a few days, what does it matter under whose government a dying man lives, if they who govern do not force him to impiety and iniquity? Did the Romans at all harm those nations, on whom, when subjugated, they imposed their laws, except in as far as that was accomplished with great slaughter in war? Now, had it been done with consent of the nations, it would have been done with greater success, but there would have been no glory of conquest, for neither did the Romans themselves live exempt from those laws which they imposed on others. Had this been done without Mars and Bellona, so that there should have been no place for victory, no one conquering where no one had fought, would not the condition of the Romans and of the other nations have been one and the same, especially if that had been done at once which afterwards was done most humanely and most acceptably, namely, the admission of all to the rights of Roman citizens who belonged to the Roman empire, and if that had been made the privilege of all which was formerly the privilege of a few, with this one condition, that the humbler class who had no lands of their own should live at the public expense—an alimentary impost, which would have been paid with a much better grace by them into the hands of good administrators of the republic, of which they were members, by their own hearty consent, than it would have been paid with had it to be extorted from them as conquered men? For I do not see what it makes for the safety, good morals, and certainly not for the dignity, of men, that some have conquered and others have been conquered, except that it yields them that most insane pomp of human glory, in which "they have received their reward," who burned with excessive desire of it, and carried on most eager wars. For do not their lands pay tribute? Have they any privilege of learning what the others are not privileged to learn? Are there not many senators in the other countries who do not even know Rome by sight? Take away outward show, and what are all men after all but men? But even though the perversity of the age should permit that all the better men should be more highly honored than others, neither thus should human honor be held at a great price, for it is smoke which has no weight. But let us avail ourselves even in these things of the kindness of God. Let us consider how great things they despised, how great things they endured, what lusts they subdued for the sake of human glory, who merited that glory, as it were, in reward for such virtues; and let this be useful to

us even in suppressing pride, so that, as that city in which it has been promised us to reign as far surpasses this one as heaven is distant from the earth,
as eternal life surpasses temporal joy, solid glory empty praise, or the society of angels the society of mortals, or the glory of Him who made the
sun and moon the light of the sun and moon, the citizens of so great a country may not seem to themselves to have done anything very great, if, in
order to obtain it, they have done some good works or endured some evils,
when those men for this terrestrial country already obtained, did such great
things, suffered such great things. And especially are all these things to
be considered, because the remission of sins which collects citizens to the
celestial country has something in it to which a shadowy resemblance is
found in that asylum of Romulus, whither escape from the punishment of
all manner of crimes congregated that multitude with which the state was
to be founded.

CHAPTER XVIII

HOW FAR CHRISTIANS OUGHT TO BE FROM BOASTING, IF THEY HAVE DONE ANYTHING FOR THE LOVE OF THE ETERNAL COUNTRY, WHEN THE ROMANS DID SUCH GREAT THINGS FOR HUMAN GLORY AND A TERRESTRIAL CITY

What great things, therefore, is it for that eternal and celestial city to
despise all the charms of this world, however pleasant, if for the sake of this
terrestrial city Brutus could even put to death his son—a sacrifice which
the heavenly city compels no one to make? But certainly it is more difficult
to put to death one's sons, than to do what is required to be done for the
heavenly country, even to distribute to the poor those things which were
looked upon as things to be amassed and laid up for one's children, or to let
them go, if there arise any temptation which compels us to do so, for the
sake of faith and righteousness. For it is not earthly riches which make us
or our sons happy; for they must either be lost by us in our lifetime, or be
possessed when we are dead, by whom we know not, or perhaps by whom
we would not. But it is God who makes us happy, who is the true riches of
minds. But of Brutus, even the poet who celebrates his praises testifies that
it was the occasion of unhappiness to him that he slew his son, for he says,

> And call his own rebellious seed
> For menaced liberty to bleed.
> Unhappy father! howsoe'er
> The deed be judged by after days.[27]

But in the following verse he consoles him in his unhappiness, saying,

> His country's love shall all o'erbear.

[27] *Aeneid*, vi. 820

There are those two things, namely, liberty and the desire of human praise, which compelled the Romans to admirable deeds. If, therefore, for the liberty of dying men, and for the desire of human praise which is sought after by mortals, sons could be put to death by a father, what great thing is it, if, for the true liberty which has made us free from the dominion of sin, and death, and the devil—not through the desire of human praise, but through the earnest desire of freeing men, not from King Tarquin, but from demons and the prince of the demons—we should, I do not say put to death our sons, but reckon among our sons Christ's poor ones? If, also, another Roman chief, surnamed Torquatus, slew his son, not because he fought against his country, but because, being challenged by an enemy, he through youthful impetuosity fought, though for his country, yet contrary to orders which he his father had given as general; and this he did, notwithstanding that his son was victorious, lest there should be more evil in the example of authority despised, than good in the glory of slaying an enemy—if, I say, Torquatus acted thus, wherefore should they boast themselves, who, for the laws of a celestial country, despise all earthly good things, which are loved far less than sons? If Furius Camillus, who was condemned by those who envied him, notwithstanding that he had thrown off from the necks of his countrymen the yoke of their most bitter enemies, the Veientes, again delivered his ungrateful country from the Gauls, because he had no other in which he could have better opportunities for living a life of glory—if Camillus did thus, why should he be extolled as having done some great thing, who, having, it may be, suffered in the church at the hands of carnal enemies most grievous and dishonoring injury, has not betaken himself to heretical enemies, or himself raised some heresy against her, but has rather defended her, as far as he was able, from the most pernicious perversity of heretics, since there is not another church, I say not in which one can live a life of glory, but in which eternal life can be obtained? If Mucius, in order that peace might be made with King Porsenna, who was pressing the Romans with a most grievous war, when he did not succeed in slaying Porsenna, but slew another by mistake for him, reached forth his right hand and laid it on a red-hot altar, saying that many such as he saw him to be had conspired for his destruction, so that Porsenna, terrified at his daring, and at the thought of a conspiracy of such as he, without any delay recalled all his warlike purposes, and made peace—if, I say, Mucius did this, who shall speak of his meritorious claims to the kingdom of heaven, if for it he may have given to the flames not one hand, but even his whole body, and that not by his own spontaneous act, but because he was persecuted by another? If Curtius, spurring on his steed, threw himself all armed into a precipitous gulf, obeying the oracles of their gods, which had commanded that the Romans should throw into that gulf the best thing which they possessed, and they could only understand thereby that, since they excelled in men and arms, the gods had commanded that an armed man should be cast headlong into that destruction—if he did this, shall we say that that man has done a great thing for the eternal city who may have died by a like death, not, however, precipitating himself spontaneously into a gulf, but having suffered this death at the hands of some enemy of his faith, more especially when he has received from his Lord, who is also King of his country, a more certain oracle, "Fear not them who kill the body, but cannot kill the soul?" [28] If the Decii dedicated themselves to death, consecrating themselves in a form of words, as it were, that falling, and pacifying by their blood the wrath of the gods, they might be the means of delivering the Roman army—if they did this, let not the holy martyrs carry themselves proudly, as though they had done some meritorious thing for a share in that country where are eternal life and felicity, if even to the shedding of their blood, loving not only the brethren for whom it was shed, but, according as had been commanded them, even their enemies by whom it was being shed, they have vied with one another in faith of love and love of faith. If Marcus Pulvillus, when engaged in dedicating a temple to Jupiter, Juno, and Minerva, received with such indifference the false intelligence which was brought to him of the death of his son, with the intention of so agitating him that he should go away, and thus the glory of dedicating the temple should fall to his colleague—if he received that intelligence with such indifference that he even ordered that his son should be cast out unburied, the love of glory having overcome in his heart the grief of bereavement, how shall any one affirm that he had done a great thing for the preaching of the gospel, by which the citizens of the heavenly city are delivered from divers errors, and gathered together from divers wanderings, to whom his Lord has said, when anxious about the burial of his father, "Follow me, and let the dead bury their dead?" [29] Regulus, in order not to break his oath, even with his most cruel enemies, returned to them from Rome itself, because (as he is said to have replied to the Romans when they wished to retain him) he could not have the dignity of an honorable citizen at Rome after having been a slave to the Africans, and the Carthaginians put him to death with the utmost tortures, because he had spoken against them in the senate. If Regulus acted thus, what tortures are not to be despised for the sake of good faith toward that country to whose beatitude faith itself leads? Or what will a man have rendered to the Lord for all He has bestowed upon him, if, for the faithfulness he owes to Him, he shall have suffered such things as Regulus suffered at the hands of his most ruthless enemies for the good faith which he owed to them? And how shall a Christian dare vaunt himself of his voluntary poverty, which he has chosen in order that during the pilgrimage of this life he may walk the more disencumbered on the way which leads to the country where the true riches are, even God Himself— how, I say, shall he vaunt himself for this, when he hears or reads that Lucius Valerius, who died when he was holding the office of consul, was so

[28] Matt. x. 28   [29] Matt. viii. 22

poor that his funeral expenses were paid with money collected by the people? —or when he hears that Quintius Cincinnatus, who, possessing only four acres of land, and cultivating them with his own hands, was taken from the plough to be made dictator—an office more honorable even than that of consul—and that, after having won great glory by conquering the enemy, he preferred notwithstanding to continue in his poverty? Or how shall he boast of having done a great thing, who has not been prevailed upon by the offer of any reward of this world to renounce his connection with that heavenly and eternal country, when he hears that Fabricius could not be prevailed on to forsake the Roman city by the great gifts offered to him by Pyrrhus king of the Epirots, who promised him the fourth part of his kingdom, but preferred to abide there in his poverty as a private individual? For if, when their republic—that is, the interest of the people, the interest of the country, the common interest—was most prosperous and wealthy, they themselves were so poor in their own houses, that one of them, who had already been twice a consul, was expelled from that senate of poor men by the censor, because he was discovered to possess ten pounds weight of silver-plate—since, I say, those very men by whose triumphs the public treasury was enriched were so poor, ought not all Christians, who make common property of their riches with a far nobler purpose, even that (according to what is written in the *Acts of the Apostles*) they may distribute to each one according to his need, and that no one may say that anything is his own, but that all things may be their common possession[30]—ought they not to understand that they should not vaunt themselves, because they do that to obtain the society of angels, when those men did well-nigh the same thing to preserve the glory of the Romans?

How could these, and whatever like things are found in the Roman history, have become so widely known, and have been proclaimed by so great a fame, had not the Roman empire, extending far and wide, been raised to its greatness by magnificent successes? Wherefore, through that empire, so extensive and of so long continuance, so illustrious and glorious also through the virtues of such great men, the reward which they sought was rendered to their earnest aspirations, and also examples are set before us, containing necessary admonition, in order that we may be stung with shame if we shall see that we have not held fast those virtues for the sake of the most glorious city of God, which are, in whatever way, resembled by those virtues which they held fast for the sake of the glory of a terrestrial city, and that, too, if we shall feel conscious that we have held them fast, we may not be lifted up with pride, because, as the apostle says, "The sufferings of the present time are not worthy to be compared to the glory which shall be revealed in us." [31] But so far as regards human and temporal glory, the lives of these ancient Romans were reckoned sufficiently worthy. Therefore, also, we see, in the light of that truth which, veiled in the Old Testament, is revealed in the

[30] Acts ii. 45   [31] Rom. viii. 18

New, namely, that it is not in view of terrestrial and temporal benefits, which divine providence grants promiscuously to good and evil, that God is to be worshipped, but in view of eternal life, everlasting gifts, and of the society of the heavenly city itself—in the light of this truth we see that the Jews were most righteously given as a trophy to the glory of the Romans; for we see that these Romans, who rested on earthly glory, and sought to obtain it by virtues, such as they were, conquered those who, in their great depravity, slew and rejected the giver of true glory, and of the eternal city.

CHAPTER XIX

CONCERNING THE DIFFERENCE BETWEEN TRUE GLORY AND THE DESIRE OF DOMINATION

There is assuredly a difference between the desire of human glory and the desire of domination; for, though he who has an overweening delight in human glory will be also very prone to aspire earnestly after domination, nevertheless they who desire the true glory even of human praise strive not to displease those who judge well of them. For there are many good moral qualities, of which many are competent judges, although they are not possessed by many; and by those good moral qualities those men press on to glory, honor and domination, of whom Sallust says, "But they press on by the true way."

But whosoever, without possessing that desire of glory which makes one fear to displease those who judge his conduct, desires domination and power, very often seeks to obtain what he loves by most open crimes. Therefore he who desires glory presses on to obtain it either by the true way, or certainly by deceit and artifice, wishing to appear good when he is not. Therefore to him who possesses virtues it is a great virtue to despise glory; for contempt of it is seen by God, but is not manifest to human judgment. For whatever any one does before the eyes of men in order to show himself to be a despiser of glory, if they suspect that he is doing it in order to get greater praise—that is, greater glory—he has no means of demonstrating to the perceptions of those who suspect him that the case is really otherwise than they suspect it to be. But he who despises the judgment of praisers, despises also the rashness of suspectors. Their salvation, indeed, he does not despise, if he is truly good; for so great is the righteousness of that man who receives his virtues from the Spirit of God, that he loves his very enemies, and so loves them that he desires that his haters and detractors may be turned to righteousness, and become his associates, and that not in an earthly but in a heavenly country. But with respect to his praisers, though he sets little value on their praise, he does not set little value on their love; neither does he elude their praise, lest he should forfeit their love. And, therefore, he strives earnestly to have their praises directed to Him from whom every one receives whatever in him is truly praiseworthy.

But he who is a despiser of glory, but is greedy of domination, exceeds the beasts in the vices of cruelty and luxuriousness. Such, indeed, were certain of the Romans, who, wanting the love of esteem, wanted not the thirst for domination; and that there were many such, history testifies. But it was Nero Caesar who was the first to reach the summit, and, as it were, the citadel, of this vice; for so great was his luxuriousness, that one would have thought there was nothing manly to be dreaded in him, and such his cruelty, that, had not the contrary been known, no one would have thought there was anything effeminate in his character. Nevertheless power and domination are not given even to such men save by the providence of the most high God, when He judges that the state of human affairs is worthy of such lords. The divine utterance is clear on this matter; for the Wisdom of God thus speaks: "By me kings reign, and tyrants possess the land."[32] But, that it may not be thought that by "tyrants" is meant, not wicked and impious kings, but brave men, in accordance with the ancient use of the word, as when Virgil says,

> For know that treaty may not stand
> Where king greets king and joins not hand,[33]

in another place it is most unambiguously said of God, that He "maketh the man who is an hypocrite to reign on account of the perversity of the people."[34] Wherefore, though I have, according to my ability, shown for what reason God, who alone is true and just, helped forward the Romans, who were good according to a certain standard of an earthly state, to the acquirement of the glory of so great an empire, there may be, nevertheless, a more hidden cause, known better to God than to us, depending on the diversity of the merits of the human race. Among all who are truly pious, it is at all events agreed that no one without true piety—that is, true worship of the true God —can have true virtue; and that it is not true virtue which is the slave of human praise. Though, nevertheless, they who are not citizens of the eternal city, which is called the city of God in the sacred Scriptures, are more useful to the earthly city when they possess even that virtue than if they had not even that. But there could be nothing more fortunate for human affairs than that, by the mercy of God, they who are endowed with true piety of life, if they have the skill for ruling people, should also have the power. But such men, however great virtues they may possess in this life, attribute it solely to the grace of God that He has bestowed it on them—willing, believing, seeking. And, at the same time, they understand how far they are short of that perfection of righteousness which exists in the society of those holy angels for which they are striving to fit themselves. But however much that virtue may be praised and cried up, which without true piety is the slave of human glory, it is not at all to be compared even to the feeble beginnings of

[32] Prov. viii. 15   [33] *Aeneid*, vii. 266   [34] Job xxxiv. 30

the virtue of the saints, whose hope is placed in the grace and mercy of the true God.

CHAPTER XX

THAT IT IS AS SHAMEFUL FOR THE VIRTUES TO SERVE HUMAN GLORY AS BODILY PLEASURE

Philosophers—who place the end of human good in virtue itself, in order to put to shame certain other philosophers, who indeed approve of the virtues, but measure them all with reference to the end of bodily pleasure, and think that this pleasure is to be sought for its own sake, but the virtues on account of pleasure—are wont to paint a kind of word-picture, in which Pleasure sits like a luxurious queen on a royal seat, and all the virtues are subjected to her as slaves, watching her nod, that they may do whatever she shall command. She commands Prudence to be ever on the watch to discover how Pleasure may rule, and be safe. Justice she orders to grant what benefits she can, in order to secure those friendships which are necessary for bodily pleasure; to do wrong to no one, lest, on account of the breaking of the laws, Pleasure be not able to live in security. Fortitude she orders to keep her mistress, that is, Pleasure, bravely in her mind, if any affliction befall her body which does not occasion death, in order that by remembrance of former delights she may mitigate the poignancy of present pain. Temperance she commands to take only a certain quantity even of the most favorite food, lest, through immoderate use, anything prove hurtful by disturbing the health of the body, and thus Pleasure, which the Epicureans make to consist chiefly in the health of the body, be grievously offended. Thus the virtues, with the whole dignity of their glory, will be the slaves of Pleasure, as of some imperious and disreputable woman.

There is nothing, say our philosophers, more disgraceful and monstrous than this picture, and which the eyes of good men can less endure. And they say the truth. But I do not think that the picture would be sufficiently becoming, even if it were made so that the virtues should be represented as the slaves of human glory; for, though that glory be not a luxurious woman, it is nevertheless puffed up, and has much vanity in it. Wherefore it is unworthy of the solidity and firmness of the virtues to represent them as serving this glory, so that Prudence shall provide nothing, Justice distribute nothing, Temperance moderate nothing, except to the end that men may be pleased and vain glory served. Nor will they be able to defend themselves from the charge of such baseness, whilst they, by way of being despisers of glory, disregard the judgment of other men, seem to themselves wise, and please themselves. For their virtue—if, indeed, it is virtue at all—is only in another way subjected to human praise; for he who seeks to please himself seeks still to please man. But he who, with true piety towards God, whom he loves, believes, and hopes in, fixes his attention more on those things in which he displeases himself, than on those things, if there are any such, which please himself, or rather, not himself, but the truth, does not attribute that by which he can now please the truth to anything but to the mercy of Him whom he has feared to displease, giving thanks for what in him is healed, and pouring out prayers for the healing of that which is yet unhealed.

CHAPTER XXI

THAT THE ROMAN DOMINION WAS GRANTED BY HIM FROM WHOM IS ALL POWER, AND BY WHOSE PROVIDENCE ALL THINGS ARE RULED

These things being so, we do not attribute the power of giving kingdoms and empires to any save to the true God, who gives happiness in the kingdom of heaven to the pious alone, but gives kingly power on earth both to the pious and the impious, as it may please Him, whose good pleasure is always just. For though we have said something about the principles which guide His administration, in so far as it has seemed good to Him to explain it, nevertheless it is too much for us, and far surpasses our strength, to discuss the hidden things of men's hearts, and by a clear examination to determine the merits of various kingdoms. He, therefore, who is the one true God, who never leaves the human race without just judgment and help, gave a kingdom to the Romans when He would, and as great as He would, as He did also to the Assyrians, and even the Persians, by whom, as their own books testify, only two gods are worshipped, the one good and the other evil —to say nothing concerning the Hebrew people, of whom I have already spoken as much as seemed necessary, who, as long as they were a kingdom, worshipped none save the true God. The same, therefore, who gave to the Persians harvests, though they did not worship the goddess Segetia, who gave the other blessings of the earth, though they did not worship the many gods which the Romans supposed to preside, each one over some particular thing, or even many of them over each several thing—He, I say, gave the Persians dominion, though they worshipped none of those gods to whom the Romans believed themselves indebted for the empire. And the same is true in respect of men as well as nations. He who gave power to Marius gave it also to Caius Caesar; He who gave it to Augustus gave it also to Nero; He also who gave it to the most benignant emperors, the Vespasians, father and son, gave it also to the cruel Domitian; and, finally, to avoid the necessity of going over them all, He who gave it to the Christian Constantine gave it also to the apostate Julian, whose gifted mind was deceived by a sacrilegious and detestable curiosity, stimulated by the love of power. And it was because he was addicted through curiosity to vain oracles, that, confident of victory, he burned the ships which were laden with the provisions necessary for his army, and therefore, engaging with hot zeal in rashly audacious enterprises, he was soon slain, as the just consequence of his recklessness, and left his army unprovisioned in an enemy's country, and in such a predicament that it never could have escaped, save by altering the boundaries of the Roman empire, in violation of that omen of the god Terminus of which I spoke in the preceding book; for the god Terminus yielded to necessity, though he had not yielded to Jupiter. Manifestly these things are ruled and governed by the one God according as He pleases; and if His motives are hid, are they therefore unjust?

CHAPTER XXII

THE DURATIONS AND ISSUES OF WAR DEPEND ON THE WILL OF GOD

Thus also the durations of wars are determined by Him as He may see meet, according to His righteous will, and pleasure, and mercy, to afflict or to console the human race, so that they are sometimes of longer, sometimes of shorter duration. The war of the Pirates and the third Punic war were terminated with incredible celerity. Also the war of the fugitive gladiators, though in it many Roman generals and the consuls were defeated, and Italy was terribly wasted and ravaged, was nevertheless ended in the third year, having itself been, during its continuance, the end of much. The Picentes, the Marsi, and the Peligni, not distant but Italian nations, after a long and most loyal servitude under the Roman yoke, attempted to raise their heads into liberty, though many nations had now been subjected to the Roman power, and Carthage had been overthrown. In this Italian war the Romans were very often defeated, and two consuls perished, besides other noble senators; nevertheless this calamity was not protracted over a long space of time, for the fifth year put an end to it. But the second Punic war, lasting for the space of eighteen years, and occasioning the greatest disasters and calamities to the republic, wore out and well-nigh consumed the strength of the Romans; for in two battles about seventy thousand Romans fell. The first Punic war was terminated after having been waged for three-and-twenty years. The Mithridatic war was waged for forty years. And that no one may think that in the early and much belauded times of the Romans they were far braver and more able to bring wars to a speedy termination, the Samnite war was protracted for nearly fifty years; and in this war the Romans were so beaten that they were even put under the yoke. But because they did not love glory for the sake of justice, but seemed rather to have loved justice for the sake of glory, they broke the peace and the treaty which had been concluded. These things I mention, because many, ignorant of past things, and some also dissimulating what they know, if in Christian times they see any war protracted a little longer than they expected, straightway make a fierce and insolent attack on our religion, exclaiming that, but for it, the deities would have been supplicated still, according to ancient rites; and then, by that bravery of the Romans, which, with the help of Mars and Bellona, speedily brought to an end such great wars, this war also would be speedily terminated. Let them, therefore, who have read history recollect what long-continued wars, having various issues and entailing woeful slaughter, were waged by the ancient Romans, in accordance with the general truth that the earth, like the tempestuous deep, is subject to agitations from tempests—tempests of such evils, in various degrees—and let them sometimes confess what they do not like to own, and not, by madly speaking against God, destroy themselves and deceive the ignorant.

CHAPTER XXIII

CONCERNING THE WAR IN WHICH RADAGAISUS, KING OF THE GOTHS, A WORSHIPPER OF DEMONS, WAS CONQUERED IN ONE DAY, WITH ALL HIS MIGHTY FORCES

Nevertheless they do not mention with thanksgiving what God has very recently, and within our own memory, wonderfully and mercifully done, but as far as in them lies they attempt, if possible, to bury it in universal oblivion. But should we be silent about these things, we should be in like manner ungrateful. When Radagaisus, king of the Goths, having taken up his position very near to the city, with a vast and savage army, was already close upon the Romans, he was in one day so speedily and so thoroughly beaten, that, whilst not even one Roman was wounded, much less slain, far more than a hundred thousand of his army were prostrated, and he himself and his sons, having been captured, were forthwith put to death, suffering the punishment they deserved. For had so impious a man, with so great and so impious a host, entered the city, whom would he have spared? what tombs of the martyrs would he have respected? in his treatment of what person would he have manifested the fear of God? whose blood would he have refrained from shedding? whose chastity would he have wished to preserve inviolate? But how loud would they not have been in the praises of their gods! How insultingly they would have boasted, saying that Radagaisus had conquered, that he had been able to achieve such great things, because he propitiated and won over the gods by daily sacrifices—a thing which the Christian religion did not allow the Romans to do! For when he was approaching those places where he was overwhelmed at the nod of the Supreme Majesty, as his fame was everywhere increasing, it was being told us at Carthage that the pagans were believing, publishing, and boasting, that he, on account of the help and protection of the gods friendly to him, because of the sacrifices which he was said to be daily offering to them, would certainly not be conquered by those who were not performing such sacrifices to the Roman gods, and did not even permit that they should be offered by any one. And now these wretched men do not give thanks to God for His great mercy, who, having determined to chastise the corruption of men, which was worthy of far heavier chastisement than the corruption of the barbarians, tempered His indignation with such mildness as, in the first instance, to cause that the king of the Goths should be conquered in a wonderful manner, lest glory should accrue to demons, whom he was known to be supplicating, and thus the minds of the weak should be overthrown; and then, afterwards, to cause that, when Rome was to be taken, it should be taken by those barbarians who, contrary to any custom of all former wars, protected, through reverence for the Christian religion, those who fled for refuge to the sacred places, and who so opposed the demons themselves, and the rites of impious sacrifices, that they seemed to be carrying on a far more terrible war with them than with men. Thus did the true Lord and Governor of things both scourge the Romans mercifully, and, by the marvellous defeat of the worshippers of demons, show that those sacrifices were not necessary even for the safety of present things; so that, by those who do not obstinately hold out, but prudently consider the matter, true religion may not be deserted on account of the urgencies of the present time, but may be more clung to in most confident expectation of eternal life.

CHAPTER XXIV

WHAT WAS THE HAPPINESS OF THE CHRISTIAN EMPERORS, AND HOW FAR IT WAS TRUE HAPPINESS

For neither do we say that certain Christian emperors were therefore happy because they ruled a long time, or, dying a peaceful death, left their sons to succeed them in the empire, or subdued the enemies of the republic, or were able both to guard against and to suppress the attempt of hostile citizens rising against them. These and other gifts or comforts of this sorrowful life even certain worshippers of demons have merited to receive, who do not belong to the kingdom of God to which these belong; and this is to be traced to the mercy of God, who would not have those who believe in Him desire such things as the highest good. But we say that they are happy if they rule justly; if they are not lifted up amid the praises of those who pay them sublime honors, and the obsequiousness of those who salute them with an excessive humility, but remember that they are men; if they make their power the handmaid of His majesty by using it for the greatest possible extension of His worship; if they fear, love, worship God; if more than their own they love that kingdom in which they are not afraid to have partners; if they are slow to punish, ready to pardon; if they apply that punishment as necessary to government and defence of the republic, and not in order to gratify their own enmity; if they grant pardon, not that iniquity may go unpunished, but with the hope that the transgressor may amend his ways; if they compensate with the lenity of mercy and the liberality of benevolence for whatever severity they may be compelled to decree; if their luxury is as much restrained as it might have been unrestrained; if they prefer to govern depraved desires rather than any nation whatever; and if they do all these things, not through ardent desire of empty glory, but through love of eternal felicity, not neglecting to offer to the true God, who is their God, for their sins, the sacrifices of humility, contrition, and prayer. Such Christian emperors, we say, are happy in the present time by hope, and are destined to be so in the enjoyment of the reality itself, when that which we wait for shall have arrived.

CHAPTER XXV

CONCERNING THE PROSPERITY WHICH GOD GRANTED TO THE CHRISTIAN EMPEROR CONSTANTINE

For the good God, lest men, who believe that He is to be worshipped with a view to eternal life, should think that no one could attain to all this high estate, and to this terrestrial dominion, unless he should be a worshipper of the demons—supposing that these spirits have great power with respect to such things—for this reason He gave to the Emperor Constantine, who was not a worshipper of demons, but of the true God Himself, such fullness of earthly gifts as no one would even dare wish for. To him also He granted the honor of founding a city,[35] a companion to the Roman empire, the daughter, as it were, of Rome itself, but without any temple or image of the demons. He reigned for a long period as sole emperor, and unaided held and defended the whole Roman world. In conducting and carrying on wars he was most victorious; in overthrowing tyrants he was most successful. He died at a great age, of sickness and old age, and left his sons to succeed him in the empire.[36] But again, lest any emperor should become a Christian in order to merit the happiness of Constantine, when every one should be a Christian for the sake of eternal life, God took away Jovian far sooner than Julian, and permitted that Gratian should be slain by the sword of a tyrant. But in his case there was far more mitigation of the calamity than in the case of the great Pompey, for he could not be avenged by Cato, whom he had left, as it were, heir to the civil war. But Gratian, though pious minds require not such consolations, was avenged by Theodosius, whom he had associated with himself in the empire, though he had a little brother of his own, being more desirous of a faithful alliance than of extensive power.

CHAPTER XXVI

ON THE FAITH AND PIETY OF THEODOSIUS AUGUSTUS

And on this account, Theodosius not only preserved during the lifetime of Gratian that fidelity which was due to him, but also, after his death, he, like a true Christian, took his little brother Valentinian under his protection, as joint emperor, after he had been expelled by Maximus, the murderer of his father. He guarded him with paternal affection, though he might without any difficulty have got rid of him, being entirely destitute of all resources,

[35] Constantinople   [36] Constantius, Constantine, and Constans

had he been animated with the desire of extensive empire, and not with the ambition of being a benefactor. It was therefore a far greater pleasure to him, when he had adopted the boy, and preserved to him his imperial dignity, to console him by his very humanity and kindness. Afterwards, when that success was rendering Maximus terrible, Theodosius, in the midst of his perplexing anxieties, was not drawn away to follow the suggestions of a sacrilegious and unlawful curiosity, but sent to John, whose abode was in the desert of Egypt—for he had learned that this servant of God (whose fame was spreading abroad) was endowed with the gift of prophecy—and from him he received assurance of victory. Immediately the slayer of the tyrant Maximus, with the deepest feelings of compassion and respect, restored the boy Valentinianus to his share in the empire from which he had been driven. Valentinianus being soon after slain by secret assassination, or by some other plot or accident, Theodosius, having again received a response from the prophet, and placing entire confidence in it, marched against the tyrant Eugenius, who had been unlawfully elected to succeed that emperor, and defeated his very powerful army, more by prayer than by the sword. Some soldiers who were at the battle reported to me that all the missiles they were throwing were snatched from their hands by a vehement wind, which blew from the direction of Theodosius' army upon the enemy; nor did it only drive with greater velocity the darts which were hurled against them, but also turned back upon their own bodies the darts which they themselves were throwing. And therefore the poet Claudian, although an alien from the name of Christ, nevertheless says in his praises of him, "O prince, too much beloved by God, for thee Aeolus pours armed tempests from their caves; for thee the air fights, and the winds with one accord obey thy bugles." [37] But the victor, as he had believed and predicted, overthrew the statues of Jupiter, which had been, as it were, consecrated by I know not what kind of rites against him, and set up in the Alps. And the thunderbolts of these statues, which were made of gold, he mirthfully and graciously presented to his couriers, who (as the joy of the occasion permitted) were jocularly saying that they would be most happy to be struck by such thunderbolts. The sons of his own enemies, whose fathers had been slain not so much by his orders as by the vehemence of war, having fled for refuge to a church, though they were not yet Christians, he was anxious, taking advantage of the occasion, to bring over to Christianity, and treated them with Christian love. Nor did he deprive them of their property, but, besides allowing them to retain it, bestowed on them additional honors. He did not permit private animosities to affect the treatment of any man after the war. He was not like Cinna, and Marius, and Sulla, and other such men, who wished not to finish civil wars even when they were finished, but rather grieved that they had arisen at all, than wished that when they were finished they should harm any one. Amid all these events,

[37] *Panegyr. de tertio Honorii consulatu,* 96-98

from the very commencement of his reign, he did not cease to help the troubled church against the impious by most just and merciful laws, which the heretical Valens, favoring the Arians, had vehemently afflicted. Indeed, he rejoiced more to be a member of this church than he did to be a king upon the earth. The idols of the Gentiles he everywhere ordered to be overthrown, understanding well that not even terrestrial gifts are placed in the power of demons, but in that of the true God. And what could be more admirable than his religious humility, when, compelled by the urgency of certain of his intimates, he avenged the grievous crime of the Thessalonians, which at the prayer of the bishops he had promised to pardon, and, being laid hold of by the discipline of the church, did penance in such a way that the sight of his imperial loftiness prostrated made the people who were interceding for him weep more than the consciousness of offence had made them fear it when enraged? These and other similar good works, which it would be long to tell, he carried with him from this world of time, where the greatest human nobility and loftiness are but vapor. Of these works the reward is eternal happiness, of which God is the giver, though only to those who are sincerely pious. But all other blessings and privileges of this life, as the world itself, light, air, earth, water, fruits, and the soul of man himself, his body, senses, mind, life, He lavishes on good and bad alike. And among these blessings is also to be reckoned the possession of an empire, whose extent He regulates according to the requirements of His providential government at various times. Whence, I see, we must now answer those who, being confuted and convicted by the most manifest proofs, by which it is shown that for obtaining these terrestrial things, which are all the foolish desire to have, that multitude of false gods is of no use, attempt to assert that the gods are to be worshipped with a view to the interest, not of the present life, but of that which is to come after death. For as to those who, for the sake of the friendship of this world, are willing to worship vanities, and do not grieve that they are left to their puerile understandings, I think they have been sufficiently answered in these five books; of which books, when I had published the first three, and they had begun to come into the hands of many, I heard that certain persons were preparing against them an answer of some kind or other in writing. Then it was told me that they had already written their answer, but were waiting a time when they could publish it without danger. Such persons I would advise not to desire what cannot be of any advantage to them; for it is very easy for a man to seem to himself to have answered arguments, when he has only been unwilling to be silent. For what is more loquacious than vanity? And though it be able, if it like, to shout more loudly than the truth, it is not, for all that, more powerful than the truth. But let men consider diligently all the things that we have said, and if, perchance, judging without party spirit, they shall clearly perceive that they are such things as may rather be shaken than torn up by their most impudent garrulity, and, as it were, satirical and mimic levity, let them restrain their absurdities, and let them choose rather to be corrected by the wise than to be lauded by the foolish. For if they are waiting an opportunity, not for liberty to speak the truth, but for license to revile, may not that befall them which Tully says concerning some one, "Oh, wretched man! who was at liberty to sin?" [38] Wherefore, whoever he be who deems himself happy because of license to revile, he would be far happier if that were not allowed him at all; for he might all the while, laying aside empty boast, be contradicting those to whose views he is opposed by way of free consultation with them, and be listening, as it becomes him, honorably, gravely, candidly, to all that can be adduced by those whom he consults by friendly disputation.

[38] *Tusc. Quaest.* v. 19

BOOK SIX

Book VI, Chapters 1-4

Summary

Preface: The first five books of the work have been directed against those who maintain that the pagan gods are to be worshipped for the advantage of this mortal life.

Chapter 1: In the next place Saint Augustine insists that we must refute those who believe that the gods should be worshipped not for the sake of this life, but for the sake of the life after death. They are so numerous and so attached to minute aspects of this life that it seems hardly credible that they be worthy objects of worship so far as the next life is concerned.

Chapter 2: The most learned Varro has discussed the various kinds of these gods and their sacred rites in such a way as to suggest that he would have been more reverential towards them, had he kept silent about them.

Chapter 3: Saint Augustine describes the long work of Varro, in forty-one books, which he wrote concerning human and divine antiquities.

Chapter 4: The learned work of Varro seems to give priority to things human over things divine.

CHAPTER V

CONCERNING THE THREE KINDS OF THEOLOGY ACCORDING TO VARRO,
NAMELY, ONE FABULOUS, THE OTHER NATURAL, THE THIRD CIVIL

Now what are we to say of this proposition of his, namely, that there are three kinds of theology, that is, of the account which is given of the gods; and of these, the one is called mythical, the other physical, and the third civil? Did the Latin usage permit, we should call the kind which he has placed first in order *fabular*, but let us call it *fabulous* for mythical is derived from the Greek μῦθος, a fable; but that the second should be called *natural*, the usage of speech now admits; the third he himself has designated in Latin, calling it *civil*. Then he says, "they call that kind *mythical* which the poets chiefly use; *physical*, that which the philosophers use; *civil*, that which the people use. As to the first I have mentioned," says he, "in it are many fictions, which are contrary to the dignity and nature of the immortals. For we find in it that one god has been born from the head, another from the thigh, another from drops of blood; also, in this we find that gods have stolen, committed adultery, served men; in a word, in this all manner of things are attributed to the gods, such as may befall, not merely any man, but even the most contemptible man." He certainly, where he could, where he dared, where he thought he could do it with impunity, has manifested, without any of the haziness of ambiguity, how great injury was done to the nature of the gods by lying fables; for he was speaking, not concerning natural theology, not concerning civil, but concerning fabulous theology, which he thought he could freely find fault with.

Let us see, now, what he says concerning the second kind. "The second kind which I have explained," he says, "is that concerning which philosophers have left many books, in which they treat such questions as these: what gods there are, where they are, of what kind and character they are, since what time they have existed, or if they have existed from eternity; whether they are of fire, as Heraclitus believes; or of number, as Pythagoras; or of atoms, as Epicurus says; and other such things, which men's ears can more easily hear inside the walls of a school than outside in the Forum." He finds fault with nothing in this kind of theology which they call *physical*, and which belongs to philosophers, except that he has related their controversies among themselves, through which there has arisen a multitude of dissentient sects. Nevertheless he has removed this kind from the Forum, that is, from the populace, but he has shut it up in schools. But that first kind, most false and most base, he has not removed from the citizens. Oh, the religious ears of the people, and among them even those of the Romans, that are not able to bear what the philosophers dispute concerning the gods! But when the poets sing and stage-players act such things as are derogatory to the dignity and the nature of the immortals, such as may befall not a man merely, but the most contemptible man, they not only bear, but willingly listen to. Nor is this all, but they even consider that these things please the gods, and that they are propitiated by them.

But some one may say, Let us distinguish these two kinds of theology, the mythical and the physical—that is, the fabulous and the natural—from this civil kind about which we are now speaking. Anticipating this, he himself has distinguished them. Let us see now how he explains the civil theology itself. I see, indeed, why it should be distinguished as fabulous, even because it is false, because it is base, because it is unworthy. But to wish to distinguish the natural from the civil, what else is that but to confess that the civil itself is false? For if that be natural, what fault has it that it should be excluded? And if this which is called civil be not natural, what merit has it that it should be admitted? This, in truth, is the cause why he wrote first concerning human things, and afterwards concerning divine things; since in divine things he did not follow nature, but the institution of men. Let us look at this civil theology of his. "The third kind," says he, "is that which citizens in cities, and especially the priests, ought to know and to administer. From it is to be known what god each one may suitably worship, what sacred rites and sacrifices each one may suitably perform." Let us still attend to what follows. "The first theology," he says, "is especially adapted to the theatre, the second to the world, the third to the city." Who does not see to which he gives the palm? Certainly to the second, which he said above is that of the philosophers. For he testifies that this pertains to the world, than which they think there is nothing better. But those two theologies, the first and the third—to wit, those of the theatre and of the city—has he distinguished them or united them? For although we see that the city is in the world, we do not see that it follows that any things belonging to the city pertain to the world. For it is possible that such things may be worshipped and believed in the city, according to false opinions, as have no existence either in the world or out of it. But where is the theatre but in the city? Who instituted the theatre but the state? For what purpose did it constitute it but for scenic plays? And to what class of things do scenic plays belong but to those divine things concerning which these books of Varro's are written with so much ability?

Book VI, Chapters 6-12

Summary

Chapter 6: Varro's mythic or fabulous gods are adapted to the theatre, the natural to the world, and the civil to the city. How can one seek eternal life from the fabulous gods? Nor can it be obtained by civil theology.

Chapter 7: There are many obvious similarities between the fabulous gods and the civil gods.

Chapter 8: Some say that all these things have a natural or physical interpretation. For example, they say that the gods were once men. This sort of interpretation, which is strictly "natural," really does not bear upon theology.

Chapter 9: The duties and functions of the gods, which are so meanly and minutely portioned out, are more consistent with mimic buffoonery than with divine majesty.

Chapter 10: Seneca with full liberty criticized more vehemently the civil theology, than Varro did the theatrical or "fabulous" theology.

Chapter 11: Seneca found fault with the sacred things of the Jews, particularly their sabbath observance, but he did not dare to mention the Christians.

Chapter 12: It is clear that, in terms of Varro's three types of theology—the mythical, physical, and political (in Latin, the fabulous, the natural, and the civil)—the gods cannot bestow eternal life nor can they help in the things of temporal life.

BOOK SEVEN

Book VII, Chapters 1-5

Summary

Preface: Saint Augustine asks for patience from his readers while he continues his attack upon the false opinions of the ancients.

Chapter 1: It should be clear by now that the true Deity is not to be found in civil theology. Nor can it be found among select gods.

Chapter 2: Varro has given us a list of twenty select gods.

Chapter 3: There is actually no reason upon the basis of which certain gods should be selected, when many more important functions are performed by many inferior gods.

Chapter 4: Many of these non-select inferior gods are never associated with infamy, whereas the infamies of the select gods are celebrated.

Chapter 5: There are secret doctrines which are erroneous, as well as certain physical interpretations of the gods.

CHAPTER VI

CONCERNING THE OPINION OF VARRO, THAT GOD IS THE SOUL OF
THE WORLD, WHICH NEVERTHELESS, IN ITS VARIOUS PARTS, HAS
MANY SOULS WHOSE NATURE IS DIVINE

The same Varro, then, still speaking by anticipation, says that he thinks that God is the soul of the world (which the Greeks call κοσμος) and that this world itself is God; but as a wise man, though he consists of body and mind, is nevertheless called wise on account of his mind, so the world is called God on account of mind, although it consists of mind and body. Here he seems, in some fashion at least, to acknowledge one God; but that he may introduce more, he adds that the world is divided into two parts, heaven and earth, which are again divided each into two parts, heaven into ether and air, earth into water and land, of all which the ether is the highest, the air second, the water third, and the earth the lowest. All these four parts, he says, are full of souls, those which are in the ether and air being immortal, and those which are in the water and on the earth mortal. From the highest part of the heavens to the orbit of the moon there are souls, namely, the stars and planets; and these are not only understood to be gods,

97

but are seen to be such. And between the orbit of the moon and the commencement of the region of clouds and winds there are aerial souls; but these are seen with the mind, not with the eyes, and are called Heroes, and Lares, and Genii. This is the natural theology which is briefly set forth in these anticipatory statements, and which satisfied not Varro only, but many philosophers besides. This I must discuss more carefully, when, with the help of God, I shall have completed what I have yet to say concerning the civil theology, as far as it concerns the select gods.

Book VII, Chapters 7-35

Summary

Chapter 7: Saint Augustine cannot find a real distinction between the deities, Janus and Terminus.

Chapter 8: Since Janus is the world, some of his worshippers conceive him to have two faces, some four.

Chapter 9: Jupiter and Janus, and their powers are compared.

Chapter 10: It seems very difficult to distinguish between Jupiter and Janus.

Chapter 11: Think of the many surnames given to the one god, all of them indicating different powers.

Chapter 12: They even call Jupiter Pecunia.

Chapter 13: When they talk about Saturn and Genius, they both are found to be Jupiter.

Chapter 14: Mercury and Mars both are supposed to have control over human works.

Chapter 15: The pagans have called certain stars after the names of their gods.

Chapter 16: Apollo is a diviner, a physician and the sun. Diana is the moon and the guardian of roads. Other parts of the world are assigned to the other select gods.

Chapter 17: Varro himself knew that his own opinions concerning the gods were ambiguous.

Chapter 18: Pagan error arose, it can be more credibly explained, from the theory that the gods were men.

Chapter 19: The legends concerning Saturn, and the seeding and ploughing of the earth, give the reason for his worship.

Chapter 20: The rites of Ceres have to do with the fertility of the earth.

Chapter 21: The rites in honor of Liber are abominably shameful.

Chapter 22: How can the silly stories of Neptune, Salacia, and Venilia be taken seriously.

Chapter 23: Varro affirms the earth to be a goddess, that the soul of the world which he thinks to be God pervades also this lowest part of his body and imparts to it a divine force.

Chapter 24: Tellus has many surnames. They indicate certain properties, but they are not ground for the opinion that there are a corresponding number of gods.

Chapter 25: There have been interpretations given by the Greeks of the mutilation of Atys.

Chapter 26: There is no evil to surpass the sacred rites of the great mother.

Chapter 27: The physical theologists neither worship the true Divinity nor worship in the way in which He should be served.

Chapter 28: Varro's theological doctrine is in no part self-consistent.

Chapter 29: All that which the physical theologists have referred to the world and its parts should have been referred to the one true God.

Chapter 30: The true religion distinguishes between Creator and creatures, and things are regarded as the works of one Author.

Chapter 31: God grants great benefits, in addition to His general bounty, to the followers of the truth.

Chapter 32: The mystery of Christ's redemption has been available at all times and has been declared in various forms.

Chapter 33: The Christian religion alone has revealed the deceit of evil spirits who rejoice in the errors of men.

Chapter 34: The senate ordered the books of Numa to be burned, so that no one could know the sources of the sacred rites therein assigned.

Chapter 35: Numa himself was fooled by hydromancy, by seeing images of demons in the water.

BOOK EIGHT

ARGUMENT

Augustine comes now to the third kind of Theology, that is, the natural, and takes up the question, whether the worship of the gods of the natural theology is of any avail towards securing blessedness in the life to come. This question he prefers to discuss with the Platonists, because the Platonic system is "facile princeps" among philosophies, and makes the nearest approximation to Christian truth. In pursuing this argument, he first refutes Apuleius, and all who maintain that the demons should be worshipped as messengers and mediators between gods and men; demonstrating that by no possibility can men be reconciled to good gods by demons, who are the slaves of vice, and who delight in and patronize what good and wise men abhor and condemn—the blasphemous fictions of poets, theatrical exhibitions, and magical arts.

CHAPTER I

THAT THE QUESTION OF NATURAL THEOLOGY IS TO BE DISCUSSED WITH THOSE PHILOSOPHERS WHO SOUGHT A MORE EXCELLENT WISDOM

WE SHALL require to apply our mind with far greater intensity to the present question than was requisite in the solution and unfolding of the questions handled in the preceding books; for it is not with ordinary men, but with philosophers that we must confer concerning the theology which they call natural. For it is not like the fabulous, that is, the theatrical; nor the civil, that is, the urban theology: the one of which displays the crimes of the gods, whilst the other manifests their criminal desires, which demonstrate them to be rather malign demons than gods. It is, we say, with philosophers we have to confer with respect to this theology—men whose very name, if rendered into Latin, signifies those who profess the love of wisdom. Now, if wisdom is God, who made all things, as is attested by the divine authority and truth,[1] then the philosopher is a lover of God. But since the thing itself, which is called by this name, exists not in all who glory in the name—for it does not follow, of course, that all who are called philosophers are lovers of true wisdom—we must select from the number of those with whose opinions we have been able to acquaint ourselves by reading, some with whom we may not unworthily engage in the treatment of this question. For I have not in this work undertaken to refute all the vain opinions of the philosophers, but only such as pertain to theology, which Greek word we

[1] Wisdom vii. 24-27

understand to mean an account or explanation of the divine nature. Nor, again, have I undertaken to refute all the vain theological opinions of all the philosophers, but only of such of them as, agreeing in the belief that there is a divine nature, and that this divine nature is concerned about human affairs, do nevertheless deny that the worship of the one unchangeable God is sufficient for the obtaining of a blessed life after death, as well as at the present time; and hold that, in order to obtain that life, many gods, created, indeed, and appointed to their several spheres by that one God, are to be worshipped. These approach nearer to the truth than even Varro; for, while he saw no difficulty in extending natural theology in its entirety even to the world and the soul of the world, these acknowledge God as existing above all that is of the nature of soul, and as the Creator not only of this visible world, which is often called heaven and earth, but also of every soul whatsoever, and as Him who gives blessedness to the rational soul—of which kind is the human soul—by participation in His own unchangeable and incorporeal light. There is no one, who has even a slender knowledge of these things, who does not know of the Platonic philosophers, who derive their name from their master Plato. Concerning this Plato, then, I will briefly state such things as I deem necessary to the present question, mentioning beforehand those who preceded him in time in the same department of literature.

CHAPTER II

CONCERNING THE TWO SCHOOLS OF PHILOSOPHERS, THAT IS, THE ITALIC AND IONIC, AND THEIR FOUNDERS

As far as concerns the literature of the Greeks, whose language holds a more illustrious place than any of the languages of the other nations, history mentions two schools of philosophers, the one called the Italic school, originating in that part of Italy which was formerly called Magna Graecia; the other called the Ionic school, having its origin in those regions which are still called by the name of Greece. The Italic school had for its founder Pythagoras of Samos, to whom also the term "philosophy" is said to owe its origin. For whereas formerly those who seemed to excel others by the laudable manner in which they regulated their lives were called sages, Pythagoras, on being asked what he professed, replied that he was a philosopher, that is, a student or lover of wisdom; for it seemed to him to be the height of arrogance to profess oneself a sage. The founder of the Ionic school, again, was Thales of Miletus, one of those seven who were styled the "seven sages," of whom six were distinguished by the kind of life they lived, and by certain maxims which they gave forth for the proper conduct of life. Thales was distinguished as an investigator into the nature of things; and, in order that he might have successors in his school, he committed his dissertations to writing. That, however, which especially rendered him eminent was his ability, by means of astronomical calculations, even to predict eclipses of the sun and moon. He thought, however, that water was the first principle of things, and that of it all the elements of the world, the world itself, and all things which are generated in it, ultimately consist. Over all this work, however, which, when we consider the world, appears so admirable, he set nothing of the nature of divine mind. To him succeeded Anaximander, his pupil, who held a different opinion concerning the nature of things; for he did not hold that all things spring from one principle, as Thales did, who held that principle to be water, but thought that each thing springs from its own proper principle. These principles of things he believed to be infinite in number, and thought that they generated innumerable worlds, and all the things which arise in them. He thought, also, that these worlds are subject to a perpetual process of alternate dissolution and regeneration, each one continuing for a longer or shorter period of time, according to the nature of the case; nor did he, any more than Thales, attribute anything to a divine mind in the production of all this activity of things. Anaximander left as his successor his disciple Anaximenes, who attributed all the causes of things to an infinite air. He neither denied nor ignored the existence of gods, but, so far from believing that the air was made by them, he held, on the contrary, that they sprang from the air. Anaxagoras, however, who was his pupil, perceived that a divine mind was the productive cause of all things which we see, and said that all the various kinds of things, according to their several modes and species, were produced out of an infinite matter consisting of homogeneous particles, but by the efficiency of a divine mind. Diogenes, also, another pupil of Anaximenes, said that a certain air was the original substance of things out of which all things were produced, but that it was possessed of a divine reason, without which nothing could be produced from it. Anaxagoras was succeeded by his disciple Archelaus, who also thought that all things consisted of homogeneous particles, of which each particular thing was made, but that those particles were pervaded by a divine mind, which perpetually energized all the eternal bodies, namely, those particles, so that they are alternately united and separated. Socrates, the master of Plato, is said to have been the disciple of Archelaus; and on Plato's account it is that I have given this brief historical sketch of the whole history of these schools.

CHAPTER III

OF THE SOCRATIC PHILOSOPHY

Socrates is said to have been the first who directed the entire effort of philosophy to the correction and regulation of morals, all who went before him having expended their greatest efforts in the investigation of physical, that is, natural phenomena. However, it seems to me that it cannot be certainly discovered whether Socrates did this because he was wearied of obscure and uncertain things, and so wished to direct his mind to the discovery of something manifest and certain, which was necessary in order to obtain a blessed life—that one great object toward which the labor, vigilance, and industry of all philosophers seem to have been directed—or whether (as some yet more favorable to him suppose) he did it because he was unwilling that minds defiled with earthly desires should essay to raise themselves upward to divine things. For he saw that the causes of things were sought for by them—which causes he believed to be ultimately reducible to nothing else than the will of the one true and supreme God—and on this account he thought they could only be comprehended by a purified mind; and therefore that all diligence ought to be given to the purification of the life by good morals, in order that the mind, delivered from the depressing weight of lusts, might raise itself upward by its native vigor to eternal things, and might, with purified understanding, contemplate that nature which is incorporeal and unchangeable light, where live the causes of all created natures. It is evident, however, that he hunted out and pursued, with a wonderful pleasantness of style and argument, and with a most pointed and insinuating urbanity, the foolishness of ignorant men, who thought that they knew this or that—sometimes confessing his own ignorance, and sometimes dissimulating his knowledge, even in those very moral questions to which he seems to have directed the whole force of his mind. And hence there arose hostility against him, which ended in his being calumniously impeached, and condemned to death. Afterwards, however, that very city of the Athenians, which had publicly condemned him, did publicly bewail him—the popular indignation having turned with such vehemence on his accusers, that one of them perished by the violence of the multitude, while the other only escaped a like punishment by voluntary and perpetual exile.

Illustrious, therefore, both in his life and in his death, Socrates left very many disciples of his philosophy, who vied with one another in desire for proficiency in handling those moral questions which concern the chief good (*summum bonum*), the possession of which can make a man blessed; and because, in the disputations of Socrates, where he raises all manner of questions, makes assertions, and then demolishes them, it did not evidently appear what he held to be the chief good, every one took from these disputations what pleased him best, and every one placed the final good in whatever it appeared to himself to consist. Now, that which is called the final good is that at which, when one has arrived, he is blessed. But so diverse were the opinions held by those followers of Socrates concerning this final good, that (a thing scarcely to be credited with respect to the followers of one master) some placed the chief good in pleasure, as Aristippus, others in virtue, as Antisthenes. Indeed, it is tedious to recount the various opinions of various disciples.

CHAPTER IV

But, among the disciples of Socrates, Plato was the one who shone with a glory which far excelled that of the others, and who not unjustly eclipsed them all. By birth, an Athenian of honorable parentage, he far surpassed his fellow-disciples in natural endowments, of which he was possessed in a wonderful degree. Yet, deeming himself and the Socratic discipline far from sufficient for bringing philosophy to perfection, he travelled as extensively as he was able, going to every place famed for the cultivation of any science of which he could make himself master. Thus he learned from the Egyptians whatever they held and taught as important; and from Egypt, passing into those parts of Italy which were filled with the fame of the Pythagoreans, he mastered, with the greatest facility, and under the most eminent teachers, all the Italic philosophy which was then in vogue. And, as he had a peculiar love for his master Socrates, he made him the speaker in all his dialogues, putting into his mouth whatever he had learned, either from others, or from the efforts of his own powerful intellect, tempering even his moral disputations with the grace and politeness of the Socratic style. And, as the study of wisdom consists in action and contemplation, so that one part of it may be called active, and the other contemplative—the active part having reference to the conduct of life, that is, to the regulation of morals, and the contemplative part to the investigation into the causes of nature and into pure truth—Socrates is said to have excelled in the active part of that study, while Pythagoras gave more attention to its contemplative part, on which he brought to bear all the force of his great intellect. To Plato is given the praise of having perfected philosophy by combining both parts into one. He then divides it into three parts—the first moral, which is chiefly occupied with action; the second natural, of which the object is contemplation; and the third rational, which discriminates between the true and the false. And though this last is necessary both to action and contemplation, it is contemplation, nevertheless, which lays peculiar claim to the office of investigating the nature of truth. Thus this tripartite division is not contrary to that which made the study of wisdom to consist in action and contemplation. Now, as to what Plato thought with respect to each of these parts—that is, what he believed to be the end of all actions, the cause of all natures, and the light of all intelligences—it would be a question too long to discuss, and about which we ought not to make any rash affirmation. For, as Plato liked and constantly affected the well-known method of his master Socrates, namely, that of dissimulating his knowledge or his opinions, it is not easy to discover clearly what he himself thought on various matters, any more than it is to discover what were the real opinions of

Socrates. We must, nevertheless, insert into our work certain of those opinions which he expresses in his writings, whether he himself uttered them,
or narrates them as expressed by others, and seems himself to approve of—
opinions sometimes favorable to the true religion, which our faith takes up
and defends, and sometimes contrary to it, as, for example, in the questions
concerning the existence of one God or of many, as it relates to the truly
blessed life which is to be after death. For those who are praised as having
most closely followed Plato, who is justly preferred to all the other philosophers of the Gentiles, and who are said to have manifested the greatest
acuteness in understanding him, do perhaps entertain such an idea of God
as to admit that in Him are to be found the cause of existence, the ultimate
reason for the understanding, and the end in reference to which the whole
life is to be regulated. Of these three things, the first is understood to pertain to the natural, the second to the rational, and the third to the moral
part of philosophy. For if man has been so created as to attain, through that
which is most excellent in him, to that which excels all things—that is, to
the one true and absolutely good God, without whom no nature exists, no
doctrine instructs, no exercise profits—let Him be sought in whom all things
are secure to us, let Him be discovered in whom all truth becomes certain
to us, let Him be loved in whom all becomes right to us.

CHAPTER V

THAT IT IS ESPECIALLY WITH THE PLATONISTS THAT WE MUST CARRY ON OUR DISPUTATIONS ON MATTERS OF THEOLOGY, THEIR OPINIONS BEING PREFERABLE TO THOSE OF ALL OTHER PHILOSOPHERS

If, then, Plato defined the wise man as one who imitates, knows, loves this
God, and who is rendered blessed through fellowship with Him in His own
blessedness, why discuss with the other philosophers? It is evident that none
come nearer to us than the Platonists. To them, therefore, let that fabulous
theology give place which delights the minds of men with the crimes of the
gods; and that civil theology also, in which impure demons, under the name
of gods, have seduced the peoples of the earth given up to earthly pleasures,
desiring to be honored by the errors of men, and by filling the minds of their
worshippers with impure desires, exciting them to make the representation
of their crimes one of the rites of their worship, whilst they themselves found
in the spectators of these exhibitions a most pleasing spectacle—a theology
in which, whatever was honorable in the temple, was defiled by its mixture
with the obscenity of the theatre, and whatever was base in the theatre was
vindicated by the abominations of the temples. To these philosophers also
the interpretations of Varro must give place, in which he explains the sacred
rites as having reference to heaven and earth, and to the seeds and operations
of perishable things; for, in the first place, those rites have not the signification which he would have men believe is attached to them, and therefore

truth does not follow him in his attempt so to interpret them; and even if they had this signification, still those things ought not to be worshipped by the rational soul as its god which are placed below it in the scale of nature, nor ought the soul to prefer to itself as gods things to which the true God has given it the preference. The same must be said of those writings pertaining to the sacred rites, which Numa Pompilius took care to conceal by causing them to be buried along with himself, and which, when they were afterwards turned up by the plough, were burned by order of the senate. And, to treat Numa with all honor, let us mention as belonging to the same rank as these writings that which Alexander of Macedon wrote to his mother as communicated to him by Leo, an Egyptian high priest. In this letter not only Picus and Faunus, and Aeneas and Romulus or even Hercules, and Aesculapius and Liber, born of Semele, and the twin sons of Tyndareus, or any other mortals who have been deified, but even the principal gods themselves, to whom Cicero, in his Tusculan questions,[2] alludes without mentioning their names, Jupiter, Juno, Saturn, Vulcan, Vesta, and many others whom Varro attempts to identify with the parts or the elements of the world, are shown to have been men. There is, as we have said, a similarity between this case and that of Numa; for the priest being afraid because he had revealed a mystery, earnestly begged of Alexander to command his mother to burn the letter which conveyed these communications to her. Let these two theologies, then, the fabulous and the civil, give place to the Platonic philosophers, who have recognized the true God as the author of all things, the source of the light of truth, and the bountiful bestower of all blessedness. And not these only, but to these great acknowledgers of so great a God, those philosophers must yield who, having their mind enslaved to their body, supposed the principles of all things to be material; as Thales, who held that the first principle of all things was water; Anaximenes, that it was air; the Stoics, that it was fire; Epicurus, who affirmed that it consisted of atoms, that is to say, of minute corpuscles; and many others whom it is needless to enumerate, but who believed that bodies, simple or compound, animate or inanimate, but nevertheless bodies, were the cause and principle of all things. For some of them—as, for instance, the Epicureans—believed that living things could originate from things without life; others held that all things living or without life spring from a living principle, but that, nevertheless, all things, being material, spring from a material principle. For the Stoics thought that fire, that is, one of the four material elements of which this visible world is composed, was both living and intelligent, the maker of the world and of all things contained in it— that it was in fact God. These and others like them have only been able to suppose that which their hearts enslaved to sense have vainly suggested to them. And yet they have within themselves something which they could not see: they represented to themselves inwardly things which they had seen

[2] i. 13

without, even when they were not seeing them, but only thinking of them. But this representation in thought is no longer a body, but only the similitude of a body; and that faculty of the mind by which this similitude of a body is seen is neither a body nor the similitude of a body; and the faculty which judges whether the representation is beautiful or ugly is without doubt superior to the object judged of. This principle is the understanding of man, the rational soul; and it is certainly not a body, since that similitude of a body which it beholds and judges of is itself not a body. The soul is neither earth, nor water, nor air, nor fire, of which four bodies, called the four elements, we see that this world is composed. And if the soul is not a body, how should God, its Creator, be a body? Let all those philosophers, then, give place, as we have said, to the Platonists, and those also who have been ashamed to say that God is a body, but yet have thought that our souls are of the same nature as God. They have not been staggered by the great changeableness of the soul—an attribute which it would be impious to ascribe to the divine nature—but they say it is the body which changes the soul, for in itself it is unchangeable. As well might they say, "Flesh is wounded by some body, for in itself it is invulnerable." In a word, that which is unchangeable can be changed by nothing, so that that which can be changed by the body cannot properly be said to be immutable.

CHAPTER VI

CONCERNING THE MEANING OF THE PLATONISTS IN THAT PART OF PHILOSOPHY CALLED PHYSICAL

These philosophers, then, whom we see not undeservedly exalted above the rest in fame and glory, have seen that no material body is God, and therefore they have transcended all bodies in seeking for God. They have seen that whatever is changeable is not the most high God, and therefore they have transcended every soul and all changeable spirits in seeking the supreme. They have seen also that, in every changeable thing, the form which makes it that which it is, whatever be its mode or nature, can only *be* through Him who truly *is*, because He is unchangeable. And therefore, whether we consider the whole body of the world, its figure, qualities, and orderly movement, and also all the bodies which are in it; or whether we consider all life, either that which nourishes and maintains, as the life of trees, or that which, besides this, has also sensation, as the life of beasts; or that which adds to all these intelligence, as the life of man; or that which does not need the support of nutriment, but only maintains, feels, understands, as the life of angels—all can only *be* through Him who absolutely *is*. For to Him it is not one thing to *be*, and another to live, as though He could *be*, not living; nor is it to Him one thing to live, and another thing to understand, as though He could live, not understanding; nor is it to Him one thing to understand, another thing to be blessed, as though He could understand and not be blessed. But to Him to live, to understand, to be blessed, are to *be*. They have understood, from this unchangeableness and this simplicity, that all things must have been made by Him, and that He could Himself have been made by none. For they have considered that whatever *is* is either body or life, and that life is something better than body, and that the nature of body is sensible, and that of life intelligible. Therefore they have preferred the intelligible nature to the sensible. We mean by sensible things such things as can be perceived by the sight and touch of the body; by intelligible things, such as can be understood by the sight of the mind. For there is no corporeal beauty, whether in the condition of a body, as figure, or in its movement, as in music, of which it is not the mind that judges. But this could never have been, had there not existed in the mind itself a superior form of these things, without bulk, without noise of voice, without space and time. But even in respect of these things, had the mind not been mutable, it would not have been possible for one to judge better than another with regard to sensible forms. He who is clever, judges better than he who is slow, he who is skilled than he who is unskillful, he who is practised than he who is un-practised; and the same person judges better after he has gained experience than he did before. But that which is capable of more and less is mutable; whence able men, who have thought deeply on these things, have gathered that the first form is not to be found in those things whose form is change-able. Since, therefore, they saw that body and mind might be more or less beautiful in form, and that, if they wanted form, they could have no exist-ence, they saw that there is some existence in which is the first form, un-changeable, and therefore not admitting of degrees of comparison, and in that they most rightly believed was the first principle of things which was not made, and by which all things were made. Therefore that which is known of God He manifested to them when His invisible things were seen by them, being understood by those things which have been made; also His eternal power and Godhead by whom all visible and temporal things have been created.[3] We have said enough upon that part of theology which they call physical, that is, natural.

CHAPTER VII

HOW MUCH THE PLATONISTS ARE TO BE HELD AS EXCELLING OTHER PHILOSOPHERS IN LOGIC, I.E. RATIONAL PHILOSOPHY

Then, again, as far as regards the doctrine which treats of that which they call logic, that is, rational philosophy, far be it from us to compare them with those who attributed to the bodily senses the faculty of discriminating truth, and thought, that all we learn is to be measured by their untrust-worthy and fallacious rules. Such were the Epicureans, and all of the same school. Such also were the Stoics, who ascribed to the bodily senses that

[3] Rom. i. 19, 20

expertness in disputation which they so ardently love, called by them dialectic, asserting that from the senses the mind conceives the notions (ἔννοιαι) of those things which they explicate by definition. And hence is developed the whole plan and connection of their learning and teaching. I often wonder, with respect to this, how they can say that none are beautiful but the wise; for by what bodily sense have they perceived that beauty, by what eyes of the flesh have they seen wisdom's comeliness of form? Those, however, whom we justly rank before all others, have distinguished those things which are conceived by the mind from those which are perceived by the senses, neither taking away from the senses anything to which they are competent, nor attributing to them anything beyond their competency. And the light of our understandings, by which all things are learned by us, they have affirmed to be that selfsame God by whom all things were made.

CHAPTER VIII

THAT THE PLATONISTS HOLD THE FIRST RANK IN MORAL PHILOSOPHY ALSO

The remaining part of philosophy is morals, or what is called by the Greeks ἠθική, in which is discussed the question concerning the chief good—that which will leave us nothing further to seek in order to be blessed, if only we make all our actions refer to it, and seek it not for the sake of something else, but for its own sake. Therefore it is called the end, because we wish other things on account of it, but itself only for its own sake. This beatific good, therefore, according to some, comes to a man from the body, according to others, from the mind, and, according to others, from both together. For they saw that man himself consists of soul and body; and therefore they believed that from either of these two, or from both together, their well-being must proceed, consisting in a certain final good, which could render them blessed, and to which they might refer all their actions, not requiring anything ulterior to which to refer that good itself. This is why those who have added a third kind of good things, which they call extrinsic —as honor, glory, wealth, and the like—have not regarded them as part of the final good, that is, to be sought after for their own sake, but as things which are to be sought for the sake of something else, affirming that this kind of good is good to the good, and evil to the evil. Wherefore, whether they have sought the good of man from the mind or from the body, or from both together, it is still only from man they have supposed that it must be sought. But they who have sought it from the body have sought it from the inferior part of man; they who have sought it from the mind, from the superior part; and they who have sought it from both, from the whole man. Whether, therefore, they have sought it from any part, or from the whole man, still they have only sought it from man; nor have these differences, being three, given rise only to three dissentient sects of philosophers, but to many. For diverse philosophers have held diverse opinions, both concerning the good of the body, and the good of the mind, and the good of both together. Let, therefore, all these give place to those philosophers who have not affirmed that a man is blessed by the enjoyment of the body, or by the enjoyment of the mind, but by the enjoyment of God—enjoying Him, however, not as the mind does the body or itself, or as one friend enjoys another, but as the eye enjoys light, if, indeed, we may draw any comparison between these things. But what the nature of this comparison is, will, if God help me, be shown in another place, to the best of my ability. At present, it is sufficient to mention that Plato determined the final good to be to live according to virtue, and affirmed that he only can attain to virtue who knows and imitates God—which knowledge and imitation are the only cause of blessedness. Therefore he did not doubt that to philosophize is to love God, whose nature is incorporeal. Whence it certainly follows that the student of wisdom, that is, the philosopher, will then become blessed when he shall have begun to enjoy God. For though he is not necessarily blessed who enjoys that which he loves (for many are miserable by loving that which ought not to be loved, and still more miserable when they enjoy it), nevertheless no one is blessed who does not enjoy that which he loves. For even they who love things which ought not to be loved do not count themselves blessed by loving merely, but by enjoying them. Who, then, but the most miserable will deny that he is blessed, who enjoys that which he loves, and loves the true and highest good? But the true and highest good, according to Plato, is God, and therefore he would call him a philosopher who loves God; for philosophy is directed to the obtaining of the blessed life, and he who loves God is blessed in the enjoyment of God.

CHAPTER IX

CONCERNING THAT PHILOSOPHY WHICH HAS COME NEAREST TO THE CHRISTIAN FAITH

Whatever philosophers, therefore, thought concerning the supreme God, that He is both the maker of all created things, the light by which things are known, and the good in reference to which things are to be done; that we have in Him the first principle of nature, the truth of doctrine, and the happiness of life—whether these philosophers may be more suitably called Platonists, or whether they may give some other name to their sect; whether, we say, that only the chief men of the Ionic school, such as Plato himself, and they who have well understood him, have thought thus; or whether we also include the Italic school, on account of Pythagoras and the Pythagoreans, and all who may have held like opinions; and, lastly, whether also we include all who have been held wise men and philosophers among all nations who are discovered to have seen and taught this, be they Atlantics, Libyans, Egyptians, Indians, Persians, Chaldeans, Scythians, Gauls, Spaniards, or of other nations—we prefer these to all other philosophers, and confess that they approach nearest to us.

CHAPTER X

THAT THE EXCELLENCY OF THE CHRISTIAN RELIGION IS ABOVE ALL THE SCIENCE OF PHILOSOPHERS

For although a Christian man instructed only in ecclesiastical literature may perhaps be ignorant of the very name of Platonists, and may not even know that there have existed two schools of philosophers speaking the Greek tongue, to wit, the Ionic and Italic, he is nevertheless not so deaf with respect to human affairs, as not to know that philosophers profess the study, and even the possession, of wisdom. He is on his guard, however, with respect to those who philosophize according to the elements of this world, not according to God, by whom the world itself was made; for he is warned by the precept of the apostle, and faithfully hears what has been said, "Beware that no one deceive you through philosophy and vain deceit, according to the elements of the world." [4] Then, that he may not suppose that all philosophers are such as do this, he hears the same apostle say concerning certain of them, "Because that which is known of God is manifest among them, for God has manifested it to them. For His invisible things from the creation of the world are clearly seen, being understood by the things which are made, also His eternal power and Godhead." [5] And, when speaking to the Athenians, after having spoken a mighty thing concerning God, which few are able to understand, "In Him we live, and move, and have our being," [6] he goes on to say, "As certain also of your own have said." He knows well, too, to be on his guard against even these philosophers in their errors. For where it has been said by him that God has manifested to them by those things which are made His invisible things, that they might be seen by the understanding, there it has also been said that they did not rightly worship God Himself, because they paid divine honors, which are due to Him alone, to other things also to which they ought not to have paid them—"because, knowing God, they glorified Him not as God: neither were thankful, but became vain in their imaginations, and their foolish heart was darkened. Professing themselves to be wise, they became fools, and changed the glory of the incorruptible God into the likeness of the image of corruptible man, and of birds, and fourfooted beasts, and creeping things" [7]—where the apostle would have us understand him as meaning the Romans, and Greeks, and Egyptians, who gloried in the name of wisdom; but concerning this we will dispute with them afterwards. With respect, however, to that wherein they agree with us we prefer them to all others, namely, concerning the one God, the author of this universe, who is not only above every body, being

[4] Col. ii. 8   [5] Rom. i. 19, 20   [6] Acts xvii. 28   [7] Rom. i. 21-23

incorporeal, but also above all souls, being incorruptible—our principle, our light, our good. And though the Christian man, being ignorant of their writings, does not use in disputation words which he has not learned—not calling that part of philosophy natural (which is the Latin term), or physical (which is the Greek one), which treats of the investigation of nature; or that part rational, or logical, which deals with the question how truth may be discovered; or that part moral, or ethical, which concerns morals, and shows how good is to be sought, and evil to be shunned—he is not, therefore, ignorant that it is from the one true and supremely good God that we have that nature in which we are made in the image of God, and that doctrine by which we know Him and ourselves, and that grace through which, by cleaving to Him, we are blessed. This, therefore, is the cause why we prefer these to all the others, because, while other philosophers have worn out their minds and powers in seeking the causes of things, and endeavoring to discover the right mode of learning and of living, these, by knowing God, have found where resides the cause by which the universe has been constituted, and the light by which truth is to be discovered, and the fountain at which felicity is to be drunk. All philosophers, then, who have had these thoughts concerning God, whether Platonists or others, agree with us. But we have thought it better to plead our cause with the Platonists, because their writings are better known. For the Greeks, whose tongue holds the highest place among the languages of the Gentiles, are loud in their praises of these writings; and the Latins, taken with their excellence, or their renown, have studied them more heartily than other writings, and, by translating them into our tongue, have given them greater celebrity and notoriety.

CHAPTER XI

HOW PLATO HAS BEEN ABLE TO APPROACH SO NEARLY TO CHRISTIAN KNOWLEDGE

Certain partakers with us in the grace of Christ wonder when they hear and read that Plato had conceptions concerning God, in which they recognize considerable agreement with the truth of our religion. Some have concluded from this, that when he went to Egypt he had heard the prophet Jeremiah, or, while travelling in the same country, had read the prophetic scriptures, which opinion I myself have expressed in certain of my writings.[8] But a careful calculation of dates, contained in chronological history, shows that Plato was born about a hundred years after the time in which Jeremiah prophesied, and, as he lived eighty-one years, there are found to have been about seventy years from his death to that time when Ptolemy, king of Egypt, requested the prophetic scriptures of the Hebrew people to be sent to him from Judea, and committed them to seventy Hebrews, who also knew the Greek tongue, to be translated and kept. Therefore, on that voy-

[8] *De Doctrina Christiana,* ii. 43

age of his, Plato could neither have seen Jeremiah, who was dead so long before, nor have read those same scriptures which had not yet been translated into the Greek language, of which he was a master, unless, indeed, we say that, as he was most earnest in the pursuit of knowledge, he also studied those writings through an interpreter, as he did those of the Egyptians— not, indeed, writing a translation of them (the facilities for doing which were only gained even by Ptolemy in return for munificent acts of kindness, though fear of his kingly authority might have seemed a sufficient motive), but learning as much as he possibly could concerning their contents by means of conversation. What warrants this supposition are the opening verses of Genesis: "In the beginning God made the heaven and earth. And the earth was invisible, and without order; and darkness was over the abyss: and the Spirit of God moved over the waters." [9] For in the *Timaeus*, when writing on the formation of the world, he says that God first united earth and fire; from which it is evident that he assigns to fire a place in heaven. This opinion bears a certain resemblance to the statement, "In the beginning God made heaven and earth." Plato next speaks of those two intermediary elements, water and air, by which the other two extremes, namely, earth and fire, were mutually united; from which circumstance he is thought to have so understood the words, "The Spirit of God moved over the waters." For, not paying sufficient attention to the designations given by those scriptures to the Spirit of God, he may have thought that the four elements are spoken of in that place, because the air also is called spirit. Then, as to Plato's saying that the philosopher is a lover of God, nothing shines forth more conspicuously in those sacred writings. But the most striking thing in this connection, and that which most of all inclines me almost to assent to the opinion that Plato was not ignorant of those writings, is the answer which was given to the question elicited from the holy Moses when the words of God were conveyed to him by the angel; for, when he asked what was the name of that God who was commanding him to go and deliver the Hebrew people out of Egypt, this answer was given: "I am who am; and thou shalt say to the children of Israel, He who *is* sent me unto you;" [10] as though compared with Him that truly *is*, because He is unchangeable, those things which have been created mutable *are* not—a truth which Plato zealously held, and most diligently commended. And I know not whether this sentiment is anywhere to be found in the books of those who were before Plato, unless in that book where it is said, "I am who am; and thou shalt say to the children of Israel, *who is* sent me unto you."

[9] Gen. i. 1, 2   [10] Ex. iii. 14

CHAPTER XII

THAT EVEN THE PLATONISTS, THOUGH THEY SAY THESE THINGS
CONCERNING THE ONE TRUE GOD, NEVERTHELESS THOUGHT
THAT SACRED RITES WERE TO BE PERFORMED IN HONOR
OF MANY GODS

But we need not determine from what source he learned these things—whether it was from the books of the ancients who preceded him, or, as is more likely, from the words of the apostle: "Because that which is known of God, has been manifested among them, for God hath manifested it to them. For His invisible things from the creation of the world are clearly seen, being understood by those things which have been made, also His eternal power and Godhead." [11] From whatever source he may have derived this knowledge, then, I think I have made it sufficiently plain that I have not chosen the Platonic philosophers undeservedly as the parties with whom to discuss; because the question we have just taken up concerns the natural theology—the question, namely, whether sacred rites are to be performed to one God, or to many, for the sake of the happiness which is to be after death. I have specially chosen them because their juster thoughts concerning the one God who made heaven and earth, have made them illustrious among philosophers. This has given them such superiority to all others in the judgment of posterity, that, though Aristotle, the disciple of Plato, a man of eminent abilities, inferior in eloquence to Plato, yet far superior to many in that respect, had founded the Peripatetic sect—so called because they were in the habit of walking about during their disputations—and though he had, through the greatness of his fame, gathered very many disciples into his school, even during the life of his master; and though Plato at his death was succeeded in his school, which was called the Academy, by Speusippus, his sister's son, and Xenocrates, his beloved disciple, who, together with their successors, were called from this name of the school, Academics; nevertheless the most illustrious recent philosophers, who have chosen to follow Plato, have been unwilling to be called Peripatetics, or Academics, but have preferred the name of Platonists. Among these were the renowned Plotinus, Iamblichus, and Porphyry, who were Greeks, and the African Apuleius, who was learned both in the Greek and Latin tongues. All these, however, and the rest who were of the same school, and also Plato himself, thought that sacred rites ought to be performed in honor of many gods.

[11] Rom. i. 20

CHAPTER XIII

CONCERNING THE OPINION OF PLATO, ACCORDING TO WHICH HE DEFINED THE GODS AS BEINGS ENTIRELY GOOD AND THE FRIENDS OF VIRTUE

Therefore, although in many other important respects they differ from us, nevertheless with respect to this particular point of difference, which I have just stated, as it is one of great moment, and the question on hand concerns it, I will first ask them to what gods they think that sacred rites are to be performed—to the good or to the bad, or to both the good and the bad? But we have the opinion of Plato affirming that all the gods are good, and that there is not one of the gods bad. It follows, therefore, that these are to be performed to the good, for then they are performed to gods; for if they are not good, neither are they gods. Now, if this be the case (for what else ought we to believe concerning the gods?), certainly it explodes the opinion that the bad gods are to be propitiated by sacred rites in order that they may not harm us, but the good gods are to be invoked in order that they may assist us. For there are no bad gods, and it is to the good that, as they say, the due honor of such rites is to be paid. Of what character, then, are those gods who love scenic displays, even demanding that a place be given them among divine things, and that they be exhibited in their honor? The power of these gods proves that they exist, but their liking such things proves that they are bad. For it is well-known what Plato's opinion was concerning scenic plays. He thinks that the poets themselves, because they have composed songs so unworthy of the majesty and goodness of the gods, ought to be banished from the state. Of what character, therefore, are those gods who contend with Plato himself about those scenic plays? He does not suffer the gods to be defamed by false crimes; the gods command those same crimes to be celebrated in their own honor.

In fine, when they ordered these plays to be inaugurated, they not only demanded base things, but also did cruel things, taking from Titus Latinius his son, and sending a disease upon him because he had refused to obey them, which they removed when he had fulfilled their commands. Plato, however, bad though they were, did not think they were to be feared; but, holding to his opinion with the utmost firmness and constancy, does not hesitate to remove from a well-ordered state all the sacrilegious follies of the poets, with which these gods are delighted because they themselves are impure. But Labeo places this same Plato (as I have mentioned already in the second book [12]) among the demi-gods. Now Labeo thinks that the bad deities are to be propitiated with bloody victims, and by fasts accompanied with the same, but the good deities with plays, and all other things which are associated with joyfulness. How comes it, then, that the demi-god Plato

[12] Ch. 14

so persistently dares to take away those pleasures, because he deems them base, not from the demi-gods but from the gods, and these the good gods? And, moreover, those very gods themselves do certainly refute the opinion of Labeo, for they showed themselves in the case of Latinius to be not only wanton and sportive, but also cruel and terrible. Let the Platonists, therefore, explain these things to us, since, following the opinion of their master, they think that all the gods are good and honorable, and friendly to the virtues of the wise, holding it unlawful to think otherwise concerning any of the gods. We will explain it, say they. Let us then attentively listen to them.

CHAPTER XIV

OF THE OPINION OF THOSE WHO HAVE SAID THAT RATIONAL SOULS ARE OF THREE KINDS, TO WIT, THOSE OF THE CELESTIAL GODS, THOSE OF THE AERIAL DEMONS, AND THOSE OF TERRESTRIAL MEN

There is, say they, a threefold division of all animals endowed with a rational soul, namely, into gods, men, and demons. The gods occupy the loftiest region, men the lowest, the demons the middle region. For the abode of the gods is heaven, that of men the earth, that of the demons the air. As the dignity of their regions is diverse, so also is that of their natures; therefore the gods are better than men and demons. Men have been placed below the gods and demons, both in respect of the order of the regions they inhabit, and the difference of their merits. The demons, therefore, who hold the middle place, as they are inferior to the gods, than whom they inhabit a lower region, so they are superior to men, than whom they inhabit a loftier one. For they have immortality of body in common with the gods, but passions of the mind in common with men. On which account, say they, it is not wonderful that they are delighted with the obscenities of the theatre, and the fictions of the poets, since they are also subject to human passions, from which the gods are far removed, and to which they are altogether strangers. Whence we conclude that it was not the gods, who are all good and highly exalted, that Plato deprived of the pleasure of theatric plays, by reprobating and prohibiting the fictions of the poets, but the demons.

Of these things many have written: among others Apuleius, the Platonist of Madaura, who composed a whole work on the subject, entitled, *Concerning the God of Socrates*. He there discusses and explains of what kind that deity was who attended on Socrates, a sort of familiar, by whom it is said he was admonished to desist from any action which would not turn out to his advantage. He asserts most distinctly, and proves at great length, that it was not a god but a demon; and he discusses with great diligence the opinion of Plato concerning the lofty estate of the gods, the lowly estate of men, and the middle estate of demons. These things being so, how did Plato dare to take away, if not from the gods, whom he removed from all human contagion, certainly from the demons, all the pleasures of the theatre, by expelling the poets from the state? Evidently in this way he wished to admonish the human soul, although still confined in these moribund members, to despise the shameful commands of the demons, and to detest their impurity, and to choose rather the splendor of virtue. But if Plato showed himself virtuous in answering and prohibiting these things, then certainly it was shameful of the demons to command them. Therefore either Apuleius is wrong, and Socrates' familiar did not belong to this class of deities, or Plato held contradictory opinions, now honoring the demons, now removing from the well-regulated state the things in which they delighted, or Socrates is not to be congratulated on the friendship of the demon, of which Apuleius was so ashamed that he entitled his book *On the God of Socrates*, while according to the tenor of his discussion, wherein he so diligently and at such length distinguishes gods from demons, he ought not to have entitled it, *Concerning the God*, but *Concerning the Demon of Socrates*. But he preferred to put this into the discussion itself rather than into the title of his book. For, through the sound doctrine which has illuminated human society, all, or almost all men have such a horror at the name of demons, that every one who before reading the dissertation of Apuleius, which sets forth the dignity of demons, should have read the title of the book, *On the Demon of Socrates*, would certainly have thought that the author was not a sane man. But what did even Apuleius find to praise in the demons, except subtlety and strength of body and a higher place of habitation? For when he spoke generally concerning their manners, he said nothing that was good, but very much that was bad. Finally, no one, when he has read that book, wonders that they desired to have even the obscenity of the stage among divine things, or that, wishing to be thought gods, they should be delighted with the crimes of the gods, or that all those sacred solemnities, whose obscenity occasions laughter, and whose shameful cruelty causes horror, should be in agreement with their passions.

CHAPTER XV

THAT THE DEMONS ARE NOT BETTER THAN MEN BECAUSE OF THEIR AERIAL BODIES, OR ON ACCOUNT OF THEIR SUPERIOR PLACE OF ABODE

Wherefore let not the mind truly religious, and submitted to the true God, suppose that demons are better than men, because they have better bodies. Otherwise it must put many beasts before itself which are superior to us both in acuteness of the senses, in ease and quickness of movement, in strength and in long-continued vigor of body. What man can equal the eagle or the vulture in strength of vision? Who can equal the dog in acuteness of smell? Who can equal the hare, the stag, and all the birds in swiftness? Who can equal in strength the lion or the elephant? Who can equal in length of life the serpents, which are affirmed to put off old age along with their skin, and to return to youth again? But as we are better than all these by the possession of reason and understanding, so we ought also to be better than the demons by living good and virtuous lives. For divine providence gave to them bodies of a better quality than ours, that that in which we excel them might in this way be commended to us as deserving to be far more cared for than the body, and that we should learn to despise the bodily excellence of the demons compared with goodness of life, in respect of which we are better than they, knowing that we too shall have immortality of body—not an immortality tortured by eternal punishment, but that which is consequent on purity of soul.

But now, as regards loftiness of place, it is altogether ridiculous to be so influenced by the fact that the demons inhabit the air, and we the earth, as to think that on that account they are to be put before us; for in this way we put all the birds before ourselves. But the birds, when they are weary with flying, or require to repair their bodies with food, come back to the earth to rest or to feed, which the demons, they say, do not. Are they, therefore, inclined to say that the birds are superior to us, and the demons superior to the birds? But if it be madness to think so, there is no reason why we should think that, on account of their inhabiting a loftier element, the demons have a claim to our religious submission. But as it is really the case that the birds of the air are not only not put before us who dwell on the earth, but are even subjected to us on account of the dignity of the rational soul which is in us, so also it is the case that the demons, though they are aerial, are not better than we who are terrestrial because the air is higher than the earth, but, on the contrary, men are to be put before demons because their despair is not to be compared to the hope of pious men. Even that law of Plato's, according to which he mutually orders and arranges the four elements, inserting between the two extreme elements—namely, fire, which is in the highest degree mobile, and the immoveable earth—the two middle ones, air and water, that by how much the air is higher up than the water, and the fire than the air, by so much also are the waters higher than the earth—this law, I say, sufficiently admonishes us not to estimate the merits of animated creatures according to the grades of the elements. And Apuleius himself says that man is a terrestrial animal in common with the rest, who is nevertheless to be put far before aquatic animals, though Plato puts the waters themselves before the land. By this he would have us understand that the same order is not to be observed when the question concerns the merits of animals, though it seems to be the true one in the gradation of bodies; for it appears to be possible that a soul of a higher order may inhabit a body of a lower, and a soul of a lower order a body of a higher.

CHAPTER XVI

WHAT APULEIUS THE PLATONIST THOUGHT CONCERNING THE MANNERS AND ACTIONS OF DEMONS

The same Apuleius, when speaking concerning the manners of demons, said that they are agitated with the same perturbations of mind as men; that they are provoked by injuries, propitiated by services and by gifts, rejoice in honors, are delighted with a variety of sacred rites, and are annoyed if any of them be neglected. Among other things, he also says that on them depend the divinations of augurs, soothsayers, and prophets, and the revelations of dreams, and that from them also are the miracles of the magicians. But, when giving a brief definition of them, he says, "Demons are of an animal nature, passive in soul, rational in mind, aerial in body, eternal in time." "Of which five things, the three first are common to them and us, the fourth peculiar to themselves, and the fifth common to them with the gods." [13] But I see that they have in common with the gods two of the first things, which they have in common with us. For he says that the gods also are animals; and when he is assigning to every order of beings its own element, he places us among the other terrestrial animals which live and feel upon the earth. Wherefore, if the demons are animals as to genus, this is common to them, not only with men, but also with the gods and with beasts; if they are rational as to their mind, this is common to them with the gods and with men; if they are eternal in time, this is common to them with the gods only; if they are passive as to their soul, this is common to them with men only; if they are aerial in body, in this they are alone. Therefore it is no great thing for them to be of an animal nature, for so also are the beasts; in being rational as to mind, they are not above ourselves, for so are we also; and as to their being eternal as to time, what is the advantage of that if they are not blessed? for better is temporal happiness than eternal misery. Again, as to their being passive in soul, how are they in this respect above us, since we also are so, but would not have been so had we not been miserable? Also, as to their being aerial in body, how much value is to be set on that, since a soul of any kind whatsoever is to be set above every body? and therefore religious worship, which ought to be rendered from the soul, is by no means due to that thing which is inferior to the soul. Moreover, if he had, among those things which he says belong to demons, enumerated virtue, wisdom, happiness, and affirmed that they have those things in common with the gods, and, like them, eternally, he would assuredly have attributed to them something greatly to be desired, and much to be prized. And even in that case it would not have been our duty to worship them like God on account of these things, but rather to worship Him from whom we

[13] *De Deo Socratis*

know they had received them. But how much less are they really worthy of divine honor—those aerial animals who are only rational that they may be capable of misery, passive that they may be actually miserable, and eternal that it may be impossible for them to end their misery!

CHAPTER XVII

WHETHER IT IS PROPER THAT MEN SHOULD WORSHIP THOSE SPIRITS FROM WHOSE VICES IT IS NECESSARY THAT THEY BE FREED

Wherefore, to omit other things, and confine our attention to that which he says is common to the demons with us, let us ask this question: If all the four elements are full of their own animals, the fire and the air of immortal, and the water and the earth of mortal ones, why are the souls of demons agitated by the whirlwinds and tempests of passions?—for the Greek word πάθος means perturbation, whence he chose to call the demons "passive in soul," because the word passion, which is derived from πάθος, signified a commotion of the mind contrary to reason. Why, then, are these things in the minds of demons which are not in beasts? For if anything of this kind appears in beasts, it is not perturbation, because it is not contrary to reason, of which they are devoid. Now it is foolishness or misery which is the cause of these perturbations in the case of men, for we are not yet blessed in the possession of that perfection of wisdom which is promised to us at last, when we shall be set free from our present mortality. But the gods, they say, are free from these perturbations, because they are not only eternal, but also blessed; for they also have the same kind of rational souls, but most pure from all spot and plague. Wherefore, if the gods are free from perturbation because they are blessed, not miserable animals, and the beasts are free from them because they are animals which are capable neither of blessedness nor misery, it remains that the demons, like men, are subject to perturbations because they are not blessed but miserable animals. What folly, therefore, or rather what madness, to submit ourselves through any sentiment of religion to demons, when it belongs to the true religion to deliver us from that depravity which makes us like to them! For Apuleius himself, although he is very sparing toward them, and thinks they are worthy of divine honors, is nevertheless compelled to confess that they are subject to anger; and the true religion commands us not to be moved with anger, but rather to resist it. The demons are won over by gifts; and the true religion commands us to favor no one on account of gifts received. The demons are flattered by honors; but the true religion commands us by no means to be moved by such things. The demons are haters of some men and lovers of others, not in consequence of a prudent and calm judgment, but because of what he calls their "passive soul;" whereas the true religion commands us to love even our enemies. Lastly, the true religion commands us to put away all disquietude of heart, and agitation of mind, and also all commotions and tempests of the soul, which Apuleius asserts to be continually swelling and surging in the souls of demons. Why, therefore, except through foolishness and miserable error, shouldst thou humble thyself to worship a being to whom thou desirest to be unlike in thy life? And why shouldst thou pay religious homage to him whom thou art unwilling to imitate, when it is the highest duty of religion to imitate Him whom thou worshippest?

CHAPTER XVIII

WHAT KIND OF RELIGION THAT IS WHICH TEACHES THAT MEN OUGHT TO EMPLOY THE ADVOCACY OF DEMONS IN ORDER TO BE RECOMMENDED TO THE FAVOR OF THE GOOD GODS

In vain, therefore, have Apuleius, and they who think with him, conferred on the demons the honor of placing them in the air, between the ethereal heavens and the earth, that they may carry to the gods the prayers of men, to men the answers of the gods: for Plato held, they say, that no god has intercourse with man. They who believe these things have thought it unbecoming that men should have intercourse with the gods, and the gods with men, but a befitting thing that the demons should have intercourse with both gods and men, presenting to the gods the petitions of men, and conveying to men what the gods have granted; so that a chaste man, and one who is a stranger to the crimes of the magic arts, must use as patrons, through whom the gods may be induced to hear him, demons who love these crimes, although the very fact of his not loving them ought to have recommended him to them as one who deserved to be listened to with greater readiness and willingness on their part. They love the abominations of the stage, which chastity does not love. They love, in the sorceries of the magicians, "a thousand arts of inflicting harm," [14] which innocence does not love. Yet both chastity and innocence, if they wish to obtain anything from the gods, will not be able to do so by their own merits, except their enemies act as mediators on their behalf. Apuleius need not attempt to justify the fictions of the poets, and the mockeries of the stage. If human modesty can act so faithlessly towards itself as not only to love shameful things, but even to think that they are pleasing to the divinity, we can cite on the other side their own highest authority and teacher, Plato.

CHAPTER XIX

OF THE IMPIETY OF THE MAGIC ART, WHICH IS DEPENDENT ON THE ASSISTANCE OF MALIGN SPIRITS

Moreover, against those magic arts, concerning which some men, exceedingly wretched and exceedingly impious, delight to boast, may not

---

[14] Virgil, *Aeneid*, 7, 338

public opinion itself be brought forward as a witness? For why are those arts so severely punished by the laws, if they are the works of deities who ought to be worshipped? Shall it be said that the Christians have ordained those laws by which magic arts are punished? With what other meaning, except that these sorceries are without doubt pernicious to the human race, did the most illustrious poet say,

> By heaven, I swear, and your dear life,
> Unwillingly these arms I wield,
> And take, to meet the coming strife,
> Enchantment's sword and shield.[15]

And that also which he says in another place concerning magic arts,

> I've seen him to another place transport the standing corn,[16]

has reference to the fact that the fruits of one field are said to be transferred to another by these arts which this pestiferous and accursed doctrine teaches. Does not Cicero inform us that, among the laws of the Twelve Tables, that is, the most ancient laws of the Romans, there was a law written which appointed a punishment to be inflicted on him who should do this? [17] Lastly, was it before Christian judges that Apuleius himself was accused of magic arts? Had he known these arts to be divine and pious, and congruous with the works of divine power, he ought not only to have confessed, but also to have professed them, rather blaming the laws by which these things were prohibited and pronounced worthy of condemnation, while they ought to have been held worthy of admiration and respect. For by so doing, either he would have persuaded the judges to adopt his own opinion, or, if they had shown their partiality for unjust laws, and condemned him to death notwithstanding his praising and commending such things, the demons would have bestowed on his soul such rewards as he deserved, who, in order to proclaim and set forth their divine works, had not feared the loss of his human life. As our martyrs, when that religion was charged on them as a crime, by which they knew they were made safe and most glorious throughout eternity, did not choose, by denying it, to escape temporal punishments, but rather by confessing, professing, and proclaiming it, by enduring all things for it with fidelity and fortitude, and by dying for it with pious calmness, put to shame the law by which that religion was prohibited, and caused its revocation. But there is extant a most copious and eloquent oration of this Platonic philosopher, in which he defends himself against the charge of practising these arts, affirming that he is wholly a stranger to them, and only wishing to show his innocence by denying such things as cannot be innocently committed. But all the miracles of the magicians, who he thinks are justly deserving of condemnation, are performed according to the teaching and by the power of demons. Why, then, does he think that they ought

[15] Virgil, *Aeneid*, 4, 492, 493   [16] Virgil, *Ec.* 8, 99   [17] Pliny, *Hist. Nat.* xxviii. 2

to be honored? For he asserts that they are necessary, in order to present our prayers to the gods, and yet their works are such as we must shun if we wish our prayers to reach the true God. Again, I ask, what kind of prayers of men does he suppose are presented to the good gods by the demons? If magical prayers, they will have none such; if lawful prayers, they will not receive them through such beings. But if a sinner who is penitent pour out prayers, especially if he has committed any crime of sorcery, does he receive pardon through the intercession of those demons by whose instigation and help he has fallen into the sin he mourns? or do the demons themselves, in order that they may merit pardon for the penitent, first become penitents because they have deceived them? This no one ever said concerning the demons; for had this been the case, they would never have dared to seek for themselves divine honors. For how should they do so who desired by penitence to obtain the grace of pardon, seeing that such detestable pride could not exist along with a humility worthy of pardon?

CHAPTER XX

WHETHER WE ARE TO BELIEVE THAT THE GOOD GODS ARE MORE WILLING TO HAVE INTERCOURSE WITH DEMONS THAN WITH MEN

But does any urgent and most pressing cause compel the demons to mediate between the gods and men, that they may offer the prayers of men, and bring back the answers from the gods? and if so, what, pray, is that cause, what is that so great necessity? Because, say they, no god has intercourse with man. Most admirable holiness of God, which has no intercourse with a supplicating man, and yet has intercourse with an arrogant demon! which has no intercourse with a penitent man, and yet has intercourse with a deceiving demon! which has no intercourse with a man fleeing for refuge to the divine nature, and yet has intercourse with a demon feigning divinity! which has no intercourse with a man seeking pardon, and yet has intercourse with a demon persuading to wickedness! which has no intercourse with a man expelling the poets by means of philosophical writings from a well-regulated state, and yet has intercourse with a demon requesting from the princes and priests of a state the theatrical performance of the mockeries of the poets! which has no intercourse with the man who prohibits the ascribing of crime to the gods, and yet has intercourse with a demon who takes delight in the fictitious representation of their crimes! which has no intercourse with a man punishing the crimes of the magicians by just laws, and yet has intercourse with a demon teaching and practising magical arts! which has no intercourse with a man shunning the imitation of a demon, and yet has intercourse with a demon lying in wait for the deception of a man!

CHAPTER XXI

WHETHER THE GODS USE THE DEMONS AS MESSENGERS AND INTERPRETERS, AND WHETHER THEY ARE DECEIVED BY THEM WILLINGLY, OR WITHOUT THEIR OWN KNOWLEDGE

But herein, no doubt, lies the great necessity for this absurdity, so unworthy of the gods, that the ethereal gods, who are concerned about human affairs, would not know what terrestrial men were doing unless the aerial demons should bring them intelligence, because the ether is suspended far away from the earth and far above it, but the air is contiguous both to the ether and to the earth. O admirable wisdom! what else do these men think concerning the gods who, they say, are all in the highest degree good, but that they are concerned about human affairs, lest they should seem unworthy of worship, while, on the other hand, from the distance between the elements, they are ignorant of terrestrial things? It is on this account that they have supposed the demons to be necessary as agents, through whom the gods may inform themselves with respect to human affairs, and through whom, when necessary, they may succor men; and it is on account of this office that the demons themselves have been held as deserving of worship. If this be the case, then a demon is better known by these good gods through nearness of body, than a man is by goodness of mind. O mournful necessity, or shall I not rather say detestable and vain error, that I may not impute vanity to the divine nature! For if the gods can, with their minds free from the hindrance of bodies, see our mind, they do not need the demons as messengers from our mind to them; but if the ethereal gods, by means of their bodies, perceive the corporeal indices of minds, as the countenance, speech, motion, and thence understand what the demons tell them, then it is also possible that they may be deceived by the falsehoods of demons. Moreover, if the divinity of the gods cannot be deceived by the demons, neither can it be ignorant of our actions. But I would they would tell me whether the demons have informed the gods that the fictions of the poets concerning the crimes of the gods displease Plato, concealing the pleasure which they themselves take in them; or whether they have concealed both, and have preferred that the gods should be ignorant with respect to this whole matter, or have told both, as well the pious prudence of Plato with respect to the gods as their own lust, which is injurious to the gods; or whether they have concealed Plato's opinion, according to which he was unwilling that the gods should be defamed with falsely alleged crimes through the impious license of the poets, while they have not been ashamed nor afraid to make known their own wickedness, which make them love theatrical plays, in which the infamous deeds of the gods are celebrated. Let them choose which they will of these four alternatives, and let them consider how much evil any one of them would require them to think of the gods. For if they choose the first, they must then confess that it was not possible for the good gods to dwell with the good Plato, though he sought to prohibit things injurious to them, while they dwelt with evil demons, who exulted in their injuries; and this because they suppose that the good gods can only know a good man, placed at so great a distance from them, through the mediation of evil demons, whom they could know on account of their nearness to themselves. If they shall choose the second, and shall say that both these things are concealed by the demons, so that the gods are wholly ignorant both of Plato's most religious law and the sacrilegious pleasure of the demons, what, in that case, can the gods know to any profit with respect to human affairs through these mediating demons, when they do not know those things which are decreed, through the piety of good men, for the honor of the good gods against the lust of evil demons? But if they shall choose the third, and reply that these intermediary demons have communicated, not only the opinion of Plato, which prohibited wrongs to be done to the gods, but also their own delight in these wrongs, I would ask if such a communication is not rather an insult? Now the gods, hearing both and knowing both, not only permit the approach of those malign demons, who desire and do things contrary to the dignity of the gods and the religion of Plato, but also, through these wicked demons, who are near to them, send good things to the good Plato, who is far away from them; for they inhabit such a place in the concatenated series of the elements, that they can come into contact with those by whom they are accused, but not with him by whom they are defended—knowing the truth on both sides, but not being able to change the weight of the air and the earth. There remains the fourth supposition; but it is worse than the rest. For who will suffer it to be said that the demons have made known the calumnious fictions of the poets concerning the immortal gods, and also the disgraceful mockeries of the theatres, and their own most ardent lust after, and most sweet pleasure in these things, whilst they have concealed from them that Plato, with the gravity of a philosopher, gave it as his opinion that all these things ought to be removed from a well-regulated republic; so that the good gods are now compelled, through such messengers, to know the evil doings of the most wicked beings, that is to say, of the messengers themselves, and are not allowed to know the good deeds of the philosophers, though the former are for the injury, but these latter for the honor of the gods themselves?

CHAPTER XXII

THAT WE MUST, NOTWITHSTANDING THE OPINION OF APULEIUS, REJECT THE WORSHIP OF DEMONS

None of these four alternatives, then, is to be chosen; for we dare not suppose such unbecoming things concerning the gods as the adoption of any one of them would lead us to think. It remains, therefore, that no credence whatever is to be given to the opinion of Apuleius and the other philosophers of the same school, namely, that the demons act as messengers and interpreters between the gods and men to carry our petitions from us to the gods, and to bring back to us the help of the gods. On the contrary, we must believe them to be spirits most eager to inflict harm, utterly alien from righteousness, swollen with pride, pale with envy, subtle in deceit; who dwell indeed in this air as in a prison, in keeping with their own character, because, cast down from the height of the higher heaven, they have been condemned to dwell in this element as the just reward of irretrievable transgression. But, though the air is situated above the earth and the waters, they are not on that account superior in merit to men, who, though they do not surpass them as far as their earthly bodies are concerned, do nevertheless far excel them through piety of mind—they having made choice of the true God as their helper. Over many, however, who are manifestly unworthy of participation in the true religion, they tyrannize as over captives whom they have subdued—the greatest part of whom they have persuaded of their divinity by wonderful and lying signs, consisting either of deeds or of predictions. Some, nevertheless, who have more attentively and diligently considered their vices, they have not been able to persuade that they are gods, and so have feigned themselves to be messengers between the gods and men. Some, indeed, have thought that not even this latter honor ought to be acknowledged as belonging to them, not believing that they were gods, because they saw that they were wicked, whereas the gods, according to their view, are all good. Nevertheless they dared not say that they were wholly unworthy of all divine honor, for fear of offending the multitude, by whom, through inveterate superstition, the demons were served by the performance of many rites, and the erection of many temples.

CHAPTER XXIII

WHAT HERMES TRISMEGISTUS THOUGHT CONCERNING IDOLATRY, AND FROM WHAT SOURCE HE KNEW THAT THE SUPERSTITIONS OF EGYPT WERE TO BE ABOLISHED

The Egyptian Hermes, whom they call Trismegistus, had a different opinion concerning those demons. Apuleius, indeed, denies that they are gods; but when he says that they hold a middle place between the gods and men, so that they seem to be necessary for men as mediators between them and the gods, he does not distinguish between the worship due to them and the religious homage due to the supernal gods. This Egyptian, however, says that there are some gods made by the supreme God, and some made by men. Any one who hears this, as I have stated it, no doubt supposes that it has reference to images, because they are the works of the hands of men; but he asserts that visible and tangible images are, as it were, only the bodies of the gods, and that there dwell in them certain spirits, which have been invited to come into them, and which have power to inflict harm, or to fulfil the desires of those by whom divine honors and services are rendered to them. To unite, therefore, by a certain art, those invisible spirits to visible and material things, so as to make, as it were, animated bodies, dedicated and given up to those spirits who inhabit them—this, he says, is to make gods, adding that men have received this great and wonderful power. I will give the words of this Egyptian as they have been translated into our tongue: "And, since we have undertaken to discourse concerning the relationship and fellowship between men and the gods, know, O Aesculapius, the power and strength of man. As the Lord and Father, or that which is highest, even God, is the maker of the celestial gods, so man is the maker of the gods who are in the temples, content to dwell near to men." And a little after he says, "Thus humanity, always mindful of its nature and origin, perseveres in the imitation of divinity; and as the Lord and Father made eternal gods, that they should be like Himself, so humanity fashioned its own gods according to the likeness of its own countenance." When this Aesculapius, to whom especially he was speaking, had answered him, and had said, "Dost thou mean the statues, O Trismegistus?"—"Yes, the statues," replied he, "however unbelieving thou art, O Aesculapius—the statues, animated, and full of sensation and spirit, and who do such great and wonderful things—the statues, prescient of future things, and foretelling them by lot, by prophet, by dreams, and many other things, who bring diseases on men and cure them again, giving them joy or sorrow according to their merits. Dost thou not know, O Aesculapius, that Egypt is an image of heaven, or, more truly, a translation and descent of all things which are ordered and transacted there, that it is, in truth, if we may say so, to be the temple of the whole world? And yet, as it becomes the prudent man to know all things beforehand, ye ought not to be ignorant of this, that there is a time coming when it shall appear that the Egyptians have all in vain, with pious mind, and with most scrupulous diligence, waited on the divinity, and when all their holy worship shall come to nought, and be found to be in vain."

Hermes then follows out at great length the statements of this passage, in which he seems to predict the present time, in which the Christian religion is overthrowing all lying figments with a vehemence and liberty proportioned to its superior truth and holiness, in order that the grace of the true Saviour may deliver men from those gods which man has made, and subject them to that God by whom man was made. But when Hermes predicts these things, he speaks as one who is a friend to these same mockeries of demons, and does not clearly express the name of Christ. On the contrary, he deplores, as if it had already taken place, the future abolition of those things by the observance of which there was maintained in Egypt a resemblance of heaven—he bears witness to Christianity by a kind of mournful prophecy. Now it was with reference to such that the apostle said, that "knowing

God, they glorified Him not as God, neither were thankful, but became vain in their imaginations, and their foolish heart was darkened; professing themselves to be wise, they became fools, and changed the glory of the incorruptible God into the likeness of the image of corruptible man," [18] and so on, for the whole passage is too long to quote. For Hermes makes many such statements agreeable to the truth concerning the one true God who fashioned this world. And I know not how he has become so bewildered by that darkening of the heart as to stumble into the expression of a desire that men should always continue in subjection to those gods which he confesses to be made by men, and to bewail their future removal; as if there could be anything more wretched than mankind tyrannized over by the work of his own hands, since man, by worshipping the works of his own hands, may more easily cease to be man, than the works of his hands can, through his worship of them, become gods. For it can sooner happen that man, who has received an honorable position, may, through lack of understanding, become comparable to the beasts, than that the works of man may become preferable to the work of God, made in His own image, that is, to man himself. Wherefore deservedly is man left to fall away from Him who made Him, when he prefers to himself that which he himself has made.

For these vain, deceitful, pernicious, sacrilegious things did the Egyptian Hermes sorrow, because he knew that the time was coming when they should be removed. But his sorrow was as impudently expressed as his knowledge was imprudently obtained; for it was not the Holy Spirit who revealed these things to him, as He had done to the holy prophets, who, foreseeing these things, said with exultation, "If a man shall make gods, lo, they are no gods;" [19] and in another place, "And it shall come to pass in that day, saith the Lord, that I will cut off the names of the idols out of the land, and they shall no more be remembered." [20] But the holy Isaiah prophesies expressly concerning Egypt in reference to this matter, saying, "And the idols of Egypt shall be moved at His presence, and their heart shall be overcome in them," [21] and other things to the same effect. And with the prophet are to be classed those who rejoiced that that which they knew was to come had actually come—as Simeon, or Anna, who immediately recognized Jesus when He was born, or Elizabeth, who in the Spirit recognized Him when He was conceived, or Peter, who said by the revelation of the Father, "Thou art Christ, the Son of the living God." [22] But to this Egyptian those spirits indicated the time of their own destruction, who also, when the Lord was present in the flesh, said with trembling, "Art Thou come hither to destroy us before the time?" [23] meaning by destruction before the time, either that very destruction which they expected to come, but which they did not think would come so suddenly as it appeared to have done, or only that destruction which consisted in their being brought into contempt by being

[18] Rom. i. 21   [19] Jer. xvi. 10   [20] Zech. xiii. 2   [21] Isa. xix. 1   [22] Matt. xvi. 16
[23] Matt. viii. 29

made known. And, indeed, this was a destruction before the time, that is, before the time of judgment, when they are to be punished with eternal damnation, together with all men who are implicated in their wickedness, as the true religion declares, which neither errs nor leads into error; for it is not like him who, blown hither and thither by every wind of doctrine, and mixing true things with things which are false, bewails as about to perish a religion which he afterwards confesses to be error.

CHAPTER XXIV

HOW HERMES OPENLY CONFESSED THE ERROR OF HIS FOREFATHERS, THE COMING DESTRUCTION OF WHICH HE NEVERTHELESS BEWAILED

After a long interval, Hermes again comes back to the subject of the gods which men have made, saying as follows: "But enough on this subject. Let us return to man and to reason, that divine gift on account of which man has been called a rational animal. For the things which have been said concerning man, wonderful though they are, are less wonderful than those which have been said concerning reason. For man to discover the divine nature, and to make it, surpasses the wonder of all other wonderful things. Because, therefore, our forefathers erred very far with respect to the knowledge of the gods, through incredulity and through want of attention to their worship and service, they invented this art of making gods; and this art once invented, they associated with it a suitable virtue borrowed from universal nature, and being incapable of making souls, they evoked those of demons or of angels, and united them with these holy images and divine mysteries, in order that through these souls the images might have power to do good or harm to men." I know not whether the demons themselves could have been made, even by adjuration, to confess as he has confessed in these words: "Because our forefathers erred very far with respect to the knowledge of the gods, through incredulity and through want of attention to their worship and service, they invented the art of making gods." Does he say that it was a moderate degree of error which resulted in their discovery of the art of making gods, or was he content to say "they erred?" No; he must needs add "very far," and say, *They erred very far.* It was this great error and incredulity, then, of their forefathers who did not attend to the worship and service of the gods, which was the origin of the art of making gods. And yet this wise man grieves over the ruin of this art at some future time, as if it were a divine religion. Is he not verily compelled by divine influence, on the one hand, to reveal the past error of his forefathers, and by a diabolical influence, on the other hand, to bewail the future punishment of demons? For if their forefathers, by erring very far with respect to the knowledge of the gods, through incredulity and aversion of mind from their worship and service, invented the art of making gods, what wonder is it that all that is done by this detestable art, which is opposed to the divine religion, should be taken away by that religion, when truth corrects error, faith refutes incredulity, and conversion rectifies aversion?

For if he had only said, without mentioning the cause, that his forefathers had discovered the art of making gods, it would have been our duty, if we paid any regard to what is right and pious, to consider and to see that they could never have attained to this art if they had not erred from the truth, if they had believed those things which are worthy of God, if they had attended to divine worship and service. However, if we alone should say that the causes of this art were to be found in the great error and incredulity of men, and aversion of the mind erring from and unfaithful to divine religion, the impudence of those who resist the truth were in some way to be borne with; but when he who admires in man, above all other things, this power which it has been granted him to practise, and sorrows because a time is coming when all those figments of gods invented by men shall even be commanded by the laws to be taken away—when even this man confesses nevertheless, and explains the causes which led to the discovery of this art, saying that their ancestors, through great error and incredulity, and through not attending to the worship and service of the gods, invented this art of making gods—what ought we to say, or rather to do, but to give to the Lord our God all the thanks we are able, because He has taken away those things by causes the contrary of those which led to their institution? For that which the prevalence of error instituted, the way of truth took away; that which incredulity instituted, faith took away; that which aversion from divine worship and service instituted, conversion to the one true and holy God took away. Nor was this the case only in Egypt, for which country alone the spirit of the demons lamented in Hermes, but in all the earth, which sings to the Lord a new song,[24] as the truly holy and truly prophetic Scriptures have predicted, in which it is written, "Sing unto the Lord a new song; sing unto the Lord, all the earth." For the title of this psalm is, "When the house was built after the captivity." For a house is being built to the Lord in all the earth, even the city of God, which is the holy Church, after that captivity in which demons held captive those men who, through faith in God, became living stones in the house. For although man made gods, it did not follow that he who made them was not held captive by them, when, by worshipping them, he was drawn into fellowship with them—into the fellowship not of stolid idols, but of cunning demons; for what are idols but what they are represented to be in the same Scriptures, "They have eyes, but they do not see,"[25] and, though artistically fashioned, are still without life and sensation? But unclean spirits, associated through that wicked art with these same idols, have miserably taken captive the souls of their worshippers, by bringing them down into fellowship with themselves. Whence the apostle says, "We know that an idol is nothing, but those things which the Gentiles sacrifice they sacrifice to demons, and not to God; and I would

[24] Ps. xcvi. 1   [25] Ps. cxv. 5

not ye should have fellowship with demons." [26] After this captivity, therefore, in which men were held by malign demons, the house of God is being built in all the earth; whence the title of that psalm in which it is said, "Sing unto the Lord a new song; sing unto the Lord, all the earth. Sing unto the Lord, bless His name; declare well His salvation from day to day. Declare His glory among the nations, among all people His wonderful things. For great is the Lord, and much to be praised: He is terrible above all gods. For all the gods of the nations are demons: but the Lord made the heavens." [27]

Wherefore he who sorrowed because a time was coming when the worship of idols should be abolished, and the domination of the demons over those who worshipped them, wished, under the influence of a demon, that that captivity should always continue, at the cessation of which that psalm celebrates the building of the house of the Lord in all the earth. Hermes foretold these things with grief, the prophet with joyfulness; and because the Spirit is victorious who sang these things through the ancient prophets, even Hermes himself was compelled in a wonderful manner to confess, that those very things which he wished not to be removed, and at the prospect of whose removal he was sorrowful, had been instituted, not by prudent, faithful, and religious, but by erring and unbelieving men, averse to the worship and service of the gods. And although he calls them gods, nevertheless, when he says that they were made by such men as we certainly ought not to be, he shows, whether he will or not, that they are not to be worshipped by those who do not resemble these image-makers, that is, by prudent, faithful, and religous men, at the same time also making it manifest that the very men who made them involved themselves in the worship of those as gods who were not gods. For true is the saying of the prophet, "If a man *make* gods, lo, they are no gods." [28] Such gods, therefore, acknowledged by such worshippers and made by such men, did Hermes call "gods made by men," that is to say, demons, through some art of I know not what description, bound by the chains of their own lusts to images. But, nevertheless, he did not agree with that opinion of the Platonic Apuleius, of which we have already shown the incongruity and absurdity, namely, that they were interpreters and intercessors between the gods whom God made, and men whom the same God made, bringing to God the prayers of men, and from God the gifts given in answer to these prayers. For it is exceedingly stupid to believe that gods whom men have made have more influence with gods whom God has made than men themselves have, whom the very same God has made. And consider, too, that it is a demon which, bound by a man to an image by means of an impious art, has been made a god, but a god to such a man only, not to every man. What kind of god, therefore, is that which no man would make but one erring, incredulous, and averse to the true God? Moreover, if the demons which are worshipped in the temples, being introduced by some kind of strange art into images, that is, into visible representations

[26] 1 Cor. x. 19, 20   [27] Ps. xcvi. 1-5   [28] Jer. xvi. 20

of themselves, by those men who by this art made gods when they were straying away from, and were averse to the worship and service of the gods —if, I say, those demons are neither mediators nor interpreters between men and the gods, both on account of their own most wicked and base manners, and because men, though erring, incredulous, and averse from the worship and service of the gods, are nevertheless beyond doubt better than the demons whom they themselves have evoked, then it remains to be affirmed that what power they possess they possess as demons, doing harm by bestowing pretended benefits—harm all the greater for the deception— or else openly and undisguisedly doing evil to men. They cannot, however, do anything of this kind unless where they are permitted by the deep and secret providence of God, and then only so far as they are permitted. When, however, they are permitted, it is not because they, being midway between men and the gods, have through the friendship of the gods great power over men; for these demons cannot possibly be friends to the good gods who dwell in the holy and heavenly habitation, by whom we mean holy angels and rational creatures, whether thrones, or dominations, or principalities, or powers, from whom they are as far separated in disposition and character as vice is distant from virtue, wickedness from goodness.

CHAPTER XXV

CONCERNING THOSE THINGS WHICH MAY BE COMMON TO THE HOLY ANGELS AND TO MEN

Wherefore we must by no means seek, through the supposed mediation of demons, to avail ourselves of the benevolence or beneficence of the gods, or rather of the good angels, but through resembling them in the possession of a good will, through which we are with them, and live with them, and worship with them the same God, although we cannot see them with the eyes of our flesh. But it is not in locality we are distant from them, but in merit of life, caused by our miserable unlikeness to them in will, and by the weakness of our character; for the mere fact of our dwelling on earth under the conditions of life in the flesh does not prevent our fellowship with them. It is only prevented when we, in the impurity of our hearts, mind earthly things. But in this present time, while we are being healed that we may eventually be as they are, we are brought near to them by faith, if by their assistance we believe that He who is their blessedness is also ours.

CHAPTER XXVI

THAT ALL THE RELIGION OF THE PAGANS HAS REFERENCE TO DEAD MEN

It is certainly a remarkable thing how this Egyptian, when expressing his grief that a time was coming when those things would be taken away from

Egypt, which he confesses to have been invented by men erring, incredulous, and averse to the service of divine religion, says, among other things, "Then shall that land, the most holy place of shrines and temples, be full of sepulchres and dead men," as if, in sooth, if these things were not taken away, men would not die! as if dead bodies could be buried elsewhere than in the ground! as if, as time advanced, the number of sepulchres must not necessarily increase in proportion to the increase of the number of the dead! But they who are of a perverse mind, and opposed to us, suppose that what he grieves for is that the memorials of our martyrs were to succeed to their temples and shrines, in order, forsooth, that they may have grounds for thinking that gods were worshipped by the pagans in temples, but that dead men are worshipped by us in sepulchres. For with such blindness do impious men, as it were, stumble over mountains, and will not see the things which strike their own eyes, that they do not attend to the fact that in all the literature of the pagans there are not found any, or scarcely any gods, who have not been men, to whom, when dead, divine honors have been paid. I will not enlarge on the fact that Varro says that all dead men are thought by them to be gods—Manes and proves it by those sacred rites which are performed in honor of almost all the dead, among which he mentions funeral games, considering this the very highest proof of divinity, because games are only wont to be celebrated in honor of divinities. Hermes himself, of whom we are now treating, in that same book in which, as if foretelling future things, he says with sorrow "Then shall that land, the most holy place of shrines and temples, be full of sepulchres and dead men," testifies that the gods of Egypt were dead men. For, having said that their forefathers, erring very far with respect to the knowledge of the gods, incredulous and inattentive to the divine worship and service, invented the art of making gods, with which art, when invented, they associated the appropriate virtue which is inherent in universal nature, and by mixing up that virtue with this art, they called forth the souls of demons or of angels (for they could not make souls), and caused them to take possession of, or associate themselves with holy images and divine mysteries, in order that through these souls the images might have power to do good or harm to men—having said this, he goes on, as it were, to prove it by illustrations, saying, "Thy grandsire, O Aesculapius, the first discoverer of medicine, to whom a temple was consecrated in a mountain of Libya, near to the shore of the crocodiles, in which temple lies his earthly man, that is, his body—for the better part of him, or rather the whole of him, if the whole man is in the intelligent life, went back to heaven—affords even now by his divinity all those helps to infirm men, which formerly he was wont to afford to them by the art of medicine." He says, therefore, that a dead man was worshipped as a god in that place where he had his sepulchre. He deceives men by a falsehood, for the man "went back to heaven." Then he adds, "Does not Hermes, who was my grandsire, and whose name I bear, abiding in the country which is called by his name, help and preserve all mortals who come to him from every quarter?" For this elder Hermes, that is, Mercury, who, he says, was his grandsire, is said to be buried in Hermopolis, that is, in the city called by his name; so here are two gods whom he affirms to have been men, Aesculapius and Mercury. Now concerning Aesculapius, both the Greeks and the Latins think the same thing; but as to Mercury, there are many who do not think that he was formerly a mortal, though Hermes testifies that he was his grandsire. But are these two different individuals who were called by the same name? I will not dispute much whether they are different individuals or not. It is sufficient to know that this Mercury of whom Hermes speaks is, as well as Aesculapius, a god who once was a man, according to the testimony of this same Trismegistus, esteemed so great by his countrymen, and also the grandson of Mercury himself.

Hermes goes on to say, "But do we know how many good things Isis, the wife of Osiris, bestows when she is propitious, and what great opposition she can offer when enraged?" Then, in order to show that there were gods made by men through this art, he goes on to say, "For it is easy for earthly and mundane gods to be angry, being made and composed by men out of either nature;" thus giving us to understand that he believed that demons were formerly the souls of dead men, which, as he says, by means of a certain art invented by men very far in error, incredulous, and irreligious, were caused to take possession of images, because they who made such gods were not able to make souls. When, therefore, he says "either nature," he means soul and body—the demon being the soul, and the image the body. What, then, becomes of that mournful complaint, that the land of Egypt, the most holy place of shrines and temples, was to be full of sepulchres and dead men? Verily, the fallacious spirit, by whose inspiration Hermes spoke these things, was compelled to confess through him that even already that land was full of sepulchres and of dead men, whom they were worshipping as gods. But it was the grief of the demons which was expressing itself through his mouth, who were sorrowing on account of the punishments which were about to fall upon them at the tombs of the martyrs. For in many such places they are tortured and compelled to confess, and are cast out of the bodies of men, of which they had taken possession.

CHAPTER XXVII

CONCERNING THE NATURE OF THE HONOR WHICH THE CHRISTIANS PAY TO THEIR MARTYRS

But, nevertheless, we do not build temples, and ordain priests, rites, and sacrifices for these same martyrs; for they are not our gods, but their God is our God. Certainly we honor their reliquaries, as the memorials of holy men of God who strove for the truth even to the death of their bodies, that the true religion might be made known, and false and fictitious religions exposed. For if there were some before them who thought that these religions were really false and fictitious, they were afraid to give expression to their convictions. But who ever heard a priest of the faithful, standing at an altar built for the honor and worship of God over the holy body of some martyr, say in the prayers, I offer to thee a sacrifice, O Peter, or O Paul, or O Cyprian? for it is to God that sacrifices are offered at their tombs—the God who made them both men and martyrs, and associated them with holy angels in celestial honor; and the reason why we pay such honors to their memory is, that by so doing we may both give thanks to the true God for their victories, and, by recalling them afresh to remembrance, may stir ourselves up to imitate them by seeking to obtain like crowns and palms, calling to our help that same God on whom they called. Therefore, whatever honors the religious may pay in the places of the martyrs, they are but honors rendered to their memory, not sacred rites or sacrifices offered to dead men as to gods. And even such as bring thither food—which, indeed, is not done by the better Christians, and in most places of the world is not done at all— do so in order that it may be sanctified to them through the merits of the martyrs, in the name of the Lord of the martyrs, first presenting the food and offering prayer, and thereafter taking it away to be eaten, or to be in part bestowed upon the needy.[29] But he who knows the one sacrifice of Christians, which is the sacrifice offered in those places, also knows that these are not sacrifices offered to the martyrs. It is, then, neither with divine honors nor with human crimes, by which they worship their gods, that we honor our martyrs; neither do we offer sacrifices to them, or convert the crimes of the gods into their sacred rites. For let those who will and can read the letter of Alexander to his mother Olympias, in which he tells the things which were revealed to him by the priest Leon, and let those who have read it recall to memory what it contains, that they may see what great abominations have been handed down to memory, not by poets, but by the mystic writings of the Egyptians, concerning the goddess Isis, the wife of Osiris, and the parents of both, all of whom, according to these writings, were royal personages. Isis, when sacrificing to her parents, is said to have discovered a crop of barley, of which she brought some ears to the king her husband, and his councillor Mercurius, and hence they identify her with Ceres. Those who read the letter may there see what was the character of those people to whom when dead sacred rites were instituted as to gods, and what those deeds of theirs were which furnished the occasion for these rites. Let them not once dare to compare in any respect those people, though they hold them to be gods, to our holy martyrs, though we do not hold them to be gods. For we do not ordain priests and offer sacrifices to our martyrs, as they do to their dead men, for that would be incongruous, undue, and unlawful, such being due only to God; and thus we do not delight them with their own crimes, or with such shameful plays as those in which the crimes

[29] Cf. *Confessions*, vi. 2

of the gods are celebrated, which are either real crimes committed by them at a time when they were men, or else, if they never were men, fictitious crimes invented for the pleasure of noxious demons. The god of Socrates, if he had a god, cannot have belonged to this class of demons. But perhaps they who wished to excel in this art of making gods, imposed a god of this sort on a man who was a stranger to, and innocent of any connection with that art. What need we say more? No one who is even moderately wise imagines that demons are to be worshipped on account of the blessed life which is to be after death. But perhaps they will say that all the gods are good, but that of the demons some are bad and some good, and that it is the good who are to be worshipped, in order that through them we may attain to the eternally blessed life. To the examination of this opinion we will devote the following book.

BOOK NINE

Book IX, Chapters 1-14

Summary

Chapter 1: Some have thought that there are both wicked and good gods, while others have maintained that there are only good gods. But the latter men are moved by demons to distinguish between gods and demons.

Chapter 2: It cannot be that among the demons there are any spirits through whom a soul could reach blessedness.

Chapter 3: Apuleius assigns reason to demons though he does not attribute virtue to them.

Chapter 4: Platonists and Peripatetics assert that wise men are subject to passions, while the Stoics do not. This controversy is one of words rather than of things.

Chapter 5: The passions which assail the souls of Christians do not seduce them to vice, but exercise their virtue.

Chapter 6: Apuleius maintains that certain passions agitate the demons who are supposed to mediate between gods and men.

Chapter 7: The Platonists hold that the poets wrong the gods by representing them as distracted by party feeling, to which the demons and not the gods are subject.

Chapter 8: Apuleius holds that the gods dwell in heaven, with the intermediate demons in the air, with men on earth with immortal souls and dull and corruptible bodies.

Chapter 9: It is clear that men cannot hope for a favorable introduction to the friendship of the gods through such mediators as the demons.

Chapter 10: Plotinus believed that the demons with their eternal bodies are more wretched than men with their mortal bodies.

Chapter 11: He further maintained that the souls of men become demons when disembodied.

Chapter 12: There are three qualities of the gods, according to the Platonists—sublimity of abode, perpetuity of life, and perfection of nature, to which men have three opposing qualities, viz., lowliness of habitation, mortality, and misery.

Chapter 13: It is difficult to see how the demons can be intermediate between gods and men, and can mediate between them.

Chapter 14: It is a great question whether men, though mortal, can enjoy true blessedness.

137

CHAPTER XV

OF THE MAN CHRIST JESUS, THE MEDIATOR BETWEEN GOD AND MEN

But if, as is much more probable and credible, it must needs be that all men, so long as they are mortal, are also miserable, we must seek an intermediate who is not only man, but also God, that, by the interposition of His blessed mortality, He may bring men out of their mortal misery to a blessed immortality. In this intermediate two things are requisite, that He become mortal, and that He do not continue mortal. He did become mortal, not rendering the divinity of the Word infirm, but assuming the infirmity of flesh. Neither did He continue mortal in the flesh, but raised it from the dead; for it is the very fruit of His mediation that those, for the sake of whose redemption He became the Mediator, should not abide eternally in bodily death. Wherefore it became the Mediator between us and God to have both a transient mortality and a permanent blessedness, that by that which is transient He might be assimilated to mortals, and might translate them from mortality to that which is permanent. Good angels, therefore, cannot mediate between miserable mortals and blessed immortals, for they themselves also are both blessed and immortal; but evil angels can mediate, because they are immortal like the one party, miserable like the other. To these is opposed the good Mediator, who, in opposition to their immortality and misery, has chosen to be mortal for a time, and has been able to continue blessed in eternity. It is thus He has destroyed, by the humility of His death and the benignity of His blessedness, those proud immortals and hurtful wretches, and has prevented them from seducing to misery by their boast of immortality those men whose hearts He has cleansed by faith, and whom He has thus freed from their impure dominion.

Man, then, mortal and miserable, and far removed from the immortal and the blessed, what medium shall he choose by which he may be united to immortality and blessedness? The immortality of the demons, which might have some charm for man, is miserable; the mortality of Christ, which might offend man, exists no longer. In the one there is the fear of an eternal misery; in the other, death, which could not be eternal, can no longer be feared, and blessedness, which is eternal, must be loved. For the immortal and miserable mediator interposes himself to prevent us from passing to a blessed immortality, because that which hinders such a passage, namely, misery, continues in him; but the mortal and blessed Mediator interposed Himself, in order that, having passed through mortality, He might of mortals make immortals (showing His power to do this in His own resurrection) and from being miserable to raise them to the blessed company from the number of whom He had Himself never departed. There is, then, a wicked mediator, who separates friends, and a good Mediator, who reconciles enemies. And those who separate are numerous, because the multitude of the blessed are blessed only by their participation in the one God; of which participation the evil angels being deprived, they are wretched, and interpose to hinder rather than to help to this blessedness, and by their very number prevent us from reaching that one beatific good, to obtain which we need not many but one Mediator, the uncreated Word of God, by whom all things were made, and in partaking of whom we are blessed. I do not say that He is Mediator because He is the Word, for as the Word He is supremely blessed and supremely immortal, and therefore far from miserable mortals; but He is Mediator as He is man, for by His humanity He shows us that, in order to obtain that blessed and beatific good, we need not seek other mediators to lead us through the successive steps of this attainment, but that the blessed and beatific God, having Himself become a partaker of our humanity, has afforded us ready access to the participation of His divinity. For in delivering us from our mortality and misery, He does not lead us to the immortal and blessed angels, so that we should become immortal and blessed by participating in their nature, but He leads us straight to that Trinity, by participating in which the angels themselves are blessed. Therefore, when He chose to be in the form of a servant, and lower than the angels, that He might be our Mediator, He remained higher than the angels, in the form of God—Himself at once the way of life on earth and life itself in heaven.

Book IX, Chapters 16-23

Summary

Chapter 16: The Platonist view is untenable that the gods, for fear of pollution, decline contact with earthly things and men, and hence require the mediation of demons.

Chapter 17: It is clear that to obtain the blessed life, the partaking in the supreme good, man needs the mediation not of demons but of Christ alone.

Chapter 18: The demons, in their deceit, promise to lead men to God, but really they intend to turn men away from the path of truth.

Chapter 19: We should remember that even to pagan worshippers the name "demon" never has a good connotation.

Chapter 20: The word demon comes from a Greek word meaning knowledge. The demons have knowledge without charity, and hence are puffed up with pride.

Chapter 21: To a certain extent the Lord let himself be known to the demons.

Chapter 22: Demons have knowledge of temporal things. Angels have such knowledge, hold it cheap, are never deceived as the demons frequently are, because the angels always see things in relation to the immutable.

Chapter 23: It is not correct to give the name gods to the gods of the gentiles, although Scripture uses the word to apply to holy angels and just men.

BOOK TEN

Book X, Chapter 1

Summary

Chapter 1: The Platonists maintain that God alone can bestow happiness either on angels or men. But when they wish us to worship those spirits, do those spirits wish us to sacrifice to themselves or to the one God only?

CHAPTER II

THE OPINION OF PLOTINUS THE PLATONIST REGARDING ENLIGHTENMENT FROM ABOVE

But with these more estimable philosophers we have no dispute in this matter. For they perceived, and in various forms abundantly expressed in their writings, that these spirits have the same source of happiness as ourselves—a certain intelligible light, which is their God, and is different from themselves, and illumines them that they may be penetrated with light, and enjoy perfect happiness in the participation of God. Plotinus, commenting on Plato, repeatedly and strongly asserts that not even the soul which they believe to be the soul of the world, derives its blessedness from any other source than we do, *viz.*, from that Light which is distinct from it and created it, and by whose intelligible illumination it enjoys light in things intelligible. He also compares those spiritual things to the vast and conspicuous heavenly bodies, as if God were the sun, and the soul the moon; for they suppose that the moon derives its light from the sun. That great Platonist, therefore, says that the rational soul, or rather the intellectual soul—in which class he comprehends the souls of the blessed immortals who inhabit heaven—has no nature superior to it save God, the Creator of the world and the soul itself, and that these heavenly spirits derive their blessed life, and the light of truth, from the same source as ourselves, agreeing with the gospel where we read, "There was a man sent from God whose name was John; the same came for a witness to bear witness of that Light, that through Him all might believe. He was not that Light, but that he might bear witness of the Light. That was the true Light which lighteth every man that cometh into the world;" a distinction which sufficiently proves that the rational or intellectual soul such as John had cannot be its own light, but needs to receive illumination from another, the true Light. This John himself avows when he delivers his witness: "We have all received of His fullness."[1]

[1] John, i, 6-9 and 16

140

Book X, Chapters 3-32

Summary

Chapter 3: If the Platonists had known and worshipped the one God, they would have acknowledged that only by worshipping Him can true blessedness be attained.

Chapter 4: Sacrifice is due only to the true God.

Chapter 5: There are certain sacrifices which God does not require, but rather wished to be observed to symbolize that which He does require.

Chapter 6: A true sacrifice is every work done that we may be united to God in holy fellowship. The sacrament at the altar is this type of sacrifice.

Chapter 7: The holy angels through their love want us to worship God, not themselves.

Chapter 8: The miracles which God works in attestation of His promises confirm the faith of the godly.

Chapter 9: Some of the illicit arts in demonolatry are accepted by Porphyry, and some discarded.

Chapter 10: Theurgy is supposed to provide purification of soul through the invocation of the demons.

Chapter 11: Porphyry has written an interesting letter to Anebo the Egyptian in which in a spirit of inquiry he asks for information about the differences among the demons.

Chapter 12: There are the great miracles, in distinction to whatever may be done by evil spirits, which are wrought by God through His angels.

Chapter 13: God, though invisible, has made himself visible, but in such form as the beholders could endure.

Chapter 14: The one God is to be worshipped for the sake of eternal blessings, and at the same time for temporal goods which His providence controls.

Chapter 15: It has pleased God that His worship involves the ministry of the angels.

Chapter 16: We must prefer those angels who bid us worship God and not themselves. They are to be trusted about the way to life eternal.

Chapter 17: For the worship of God, the law was deposited in the ark of the covenant. To authenticate the law and the promise, miraculous signs were given.

Chapter 18: The miracles on record in the books of the Church must be accepted. If they are not, one may as well deny that there are gods who care for human affairs.

Chapter 19: Visible sacrifice is reasonably offered to the invisible God, since it is itself a sign of the invisible.

Chapter 20: The true and supreme sacrifice was wrought by Jesus Christ, the Mediator between God and men.

Chapter 21: The power delegated to demons is useful to try and glorify the saints who conquer by their adherence to God.

Chapter 22: By true piety the saints meet and overcome these hostile spirits.

Chapter 23: Porphyry has insisted that we are not purified by sacrifices to sun or moon, but rather by what he as a Platonist calls "principles."

Chapter 24: The principle by which we are purified is God the Trinity.

Chapter 25: All the saints of old, under the law and before it, were purified by faith in the mystery of Christ's Incarnation.

Chapter 26: Porphyry somehow blushed for his friends the theurgists out of his belief in God, yet he could not frankly condemn polytheistic worship.

Chapter 27: Porphyry for this reason is even more impious than his Platonist cosectary, Apuleius, who acknowledged only a lower type of demon.

Chapter 28: If Porphyry had been a true lover of virtue and wisdom, he would have recognized Christ, the virtue of God and the wisdom of God.

Chapter 29: The Incarnation of Jesus Christ in its full meaning contains the answer to Porphyry and the Platonists.

Chapter 30: Porphyry made several important and good modifications of Platonism.

Chapter 31: The Platonists err in conceiving the soul to be co-eternal with God.

Chapter 32: Saint Augustine concludes by asserting that the universal way of delivering the soul, not found by Porphyry who did not rightly seek it, lies in the grace of Christ.

BOOK ELEVEN

ARGUMENT

Here begins the second part[1] of this work, which treats of the origin, history, and destinies of the two cities, the earthly and the heavenly. In the first place, Augustine shows in this book how the two cities were formed originally, by the separation of the good and bad angels; and takes occasion to treat of the creation of the world, as it is described in Holy Scripture in the beginning of the Book of Genesis.

CHAPTER I

OF THIS PART OF THE WORK, WHEREIN WE BEGIN TO EXPLAIN THE ORIGIN AND END OF THE TWO CITIES

THE city of God we speak of is the same to which testimony is borne by that Scripture, which excels all the writings of all nations by its divine authority, and has brought under its influence all kinds of minds, and this not by a casual intellectual movement, but obviously by an express providential arrangement. For there it is written, "Glorious things are spoken of thee, O city of God." [2] And in another psalm we read, "Great is the Lord, and greatly to be praised in the city of our God, in the mountain of His holiness, increasing the joy of the whole earth." [3] And, a little after, in the same psalm, "As we have heard, so have we seen in the city of the Lord of hosts, in the city of our God. God has established it for ever." And in another, "There is a river the streams whereof shall make glad the city of our God, the holy place of the tabernacles of the Most High. God is in the midst of her, she shall not be moved." [4] From these and similar testimonies, all of which it were tedious to cite, we have learned that there is a city of God, and its Founder has inspired us with a love which makes us covet its citizenship. To this Founder of the holy city the citizens of the earthly city prefer their own gods, not knowing that He is the God of gods, not of false, *i.e.*, of impious and proud gods, who, being deprived of His unchangeable and freely communicated light, and so reduced to a kind of poverty-stricken power, eagerly grasp at their own private privileges, and seek divine honors from their deluded subjects; but of the pious and holy gods, who are better pleased to submit themselves to one, than to subject many to themselves, and who would rather worship God than be worshipped as God. But to the enemies of this city we have replied in the ten preceding books, according

---

[1] Written in the year 416 or 417   [2] Ps. lxxxvii. 3   [3] Ps. xlviii. 1   [4] Ps. xlvi. 4

to our ability and help afforded by our Lord and King. Now, recognizing what is expected of me, and not unmindful of my promise, and relying, too, on the same succor, I will endeavor to treat of the origin, and progress, and deserved destinies of the two cities (the earthly and the heavenly, to wit), which, as we said, are in this present world commingled, and as it were entangled together. And, first, I will explain how the foundations of these two cities were originally laid, in the difference that arose among the angels.

CHAPTER II

OF THE KNOWLEDGE OF GOD, TO WHICH NO MAN CAN ATTAIN SAVE THROUGH THE MEDIATOR BETWEEN GOD AND MEN, THE MAN CHRIST JESUS

It is a great and very rare thing for a man, after he has contemplated the whole creation, corporeal and incorporeal, and has discerned its mutability, to pass beyond it, and, by the continued soaring of his mind, to attain to the unchangeable substance of God, and, in that height of contemplation, to learn from God Himself that none but He has made all that is not of the divine essence. For God speaks with a man not by means of some audible creature dinning in his ears, so that atmospheric vibrations connect Him that makes with him that hears the sound, nor even by means of a spiritual being with the semblance of a body, such as we see in dreams or similar states; for even in this case He speaks as if to the ears of the body, because it is by means of the semblance of a body He speaks, and with the appearance of a real interval of space—for visions are exact representations of bodily objects. Not by these, then, does God speak, but by the truth itself, if any one is prepared to hear with the mind rather than with the body. For He speaks to that part of man which is better than all else that is in him, and than which God Himself alone is better. For since man is most properly understood (or, if that cannot be, then, at least, *believed*) to be made in God's image, no doubt it is that part of him by which he rises above those lower parts he has in common with the beasts, which brings him nearer to the Supreme. But since the mind itself, though naturally capable of reason and intelligence, is disabled by besotting and inveterate vices not merely from delighting and abiding in, but even from tolerating His unchangeable light, until it has been gradually healed, and renewed, and made capable of such felicity, it had, in the first place, to be impregnated with faith, and so purified. And that in this faith it might advance the more confidently towards the truth, the truth itself, God, God's Son, assuming humanity without destroying His divinity, established and founded this faith, that there might be a way for man to man's God through a God-man. For this is the Mediator between God and men, the man Christ Jesus. For it is as man that He is the Mediator and the Way. Since, if the way lieth between him who goes, and the place whither he goes, there is hope of his reaching it;

but if there be no way, or if he know not where it is, what boots it to know whither he should go? Now the only way that is infallibly secured against all mistakes, is when the very same person is at once God and man, God our end, man our way.

CHAPTER III

OF THE AUTHORITY OF THE CANONICAL SCRIPTURES COMPOSED BY THE DIVINE SPIRIT

This Mediator, having spoken what He judged sufficient first by the prophets, then by His own lips, and afterwards by the apostles, has besides produced the Scripture which is called canonical, which has paramount authority, and to which we yield assent in all matters of which we ought not to be ignorant, and yet cannot know of ourselves. For if we attain the knowledge of present objects by the testimony of our own senses,[5] whether internal or external, then, regarding objects remote from our own senses, we need others to bring their testimony, since we cannot know them by our own, and we credit the persons to whom the objects have been or are sensibly present. Accordingly, as in the case of visible objects which we have not seen, we trust those who have (and likewise with all sensible objects), so in the case of things which are perceived[6] by the mind and spirit, i.e. which are remote from our own interior sense, it behoves us to trust those who have seen them set in that incorporeal light, or abidingly contemplate them.

CHAPTER IV

THAT THE WORLD IS NEITHER WITHOUT BEGINNING, NOR YET CREATED BY A NEW DECREE OF GOD, BY WHICH HE AFTERWARDS WILLED WHAT HE HAD NOT BEFORE WILLED

Of all visible things, the world is the greatest; of all invisible, the greatest is God. But, that the world is, we see; that God is, we believe. That God made the world, we can believe from no one more safely than from God Himself. But where have we heard Him? Nowhere more distinctly than in the Holy Scriptures, where His prophet said, "In the beginning God created the heavens and the earth." [7] Was the prophet present when God made the heavens and the earth? No; but the wisdom of God, by whom all things were made, was there,[8] and wisdom insinuates itself into holy souls, and makes them the friends of God and His prophets, and noiselessly informs them of His works. They are taught also by the angels of God, who always behold the face of the Father,[9] and announce His will to whom it befits. Of these prophets was he who said and wrote, "In the beginning God created

[5] A clause is here inserted to give the etymology of *praesentia* from *prae sensibus*
[6] Another derivation, *sententia* from *sensus,* the inward perception of the mind
[7] Gen. i. 1   [8] Prov. viii. 27   [9] Matt. xviii. 10

the heavens and the earth." And so fit a witness was he of God, that the same Spirit of God, who revealed these things to him, enabled him also so long before to predict that our faith also would be forthcoming.

(But why did God choose then to create the heavens and earth which up to that time He had not made? If they who put this question wish to make out that the world is eternal and without beginning, and that consequently it has not been made by God, they are strangely deceived, and rave in the incurable madness of impiety. For, though the voices of the prophets were silent, the world itself, by its well-ordered changes and movements, and by the fair appearance of all visible things, bears a testimony of its own, both that it has been created, and also that it could not have been created save by God, whose greatness and beauty are unutterable and invisible.) As for those[10] who own, indeed, that it was made by God, and yet ascribe to it not a temporal but only a creational beginning, so that in some scarcely intelligible way the world should always have existed a created world they make an assertion which seems to them to defend God from the charge of arbitrary hastiness, or of suddenly conceiving the idea of creating the world as a quite new idea, or of casually changing His will, though He be unchangeable. But I do not see how this supposition of theirs can stand in other respects, and chiefly in respect of the soul; for if they contend that it is coeternal with God, they will be quite at a loss to explain whence there has accrued to it new misery, which through a previous eternity had not existed. For if they said that its happiness and misery ceaselessly alternate, they must say, further, that this alternation will continue for ever; whence will result this absurdity, that, though the soul is called blessed, it is not so in this, that it foresees its own misery and disgrace. And yet, if it does not foresee it, and supposes that it will be neither disgraced nor wretched, but always blessed, then it is blessed because it is deceived; and a more foolish statement one cannot make. But if their idea is that the soul's misery has alternated with its bliss during the ages of the past eternity, but that now, when once the soul has been set free, it will return henceforth no more to misery, they are nevertheless of opinion that it has never been truly blessed before, but begins at last to enjoy a new and uncertain happiness; that is to say, they must acknowledge that some new thing, and that an important and signal thing, happens to the soul which never in a whole past eternity happened it before. And if they deny that God's eternal purpose included this new experience of the soul, they deny that He is the Author of its blessedness, which is unspeakable impiety. If, on the other hand, they say that the future blessedness of the soul is the result of a new decree of God, how will they show that God is not chargeable with that mutability which displeases them? Further, if they acknowledge that it was created in time, but will never perish in time—that it has, like number, a beginning but no end—and that, therefore, having once made trial of misery, and been de-

[10] The Neo-Platonists

livered from it, it will never again return thereto, they will certainly admit
that this takes place without any violation of the immutable counsel of God.
Let them, then, in like manner believe regarding the world that it too could
be made in time, and yet that God, in making it, did not alter His eternal
design.

CHAPTER V

THAT WE OUGHT NOT TO SEEK TO COMPREHEND THE INFINITE AGES
OF TIME BEFORE THE WORLD, NOR THE INFINITE REALMS OF
SPACE

Next, we must see what reply can be made to those who agree that God
is the Creator of the world, but have difficulties about the time of its creation, and what reply, also, they can make to difficulties we might raise
about the place of its creation. For, as they demand why the world was
created then and no sooner, we may ask why it was created just here where
it is, and not elsewhere. For if they imagine infinite spaces of time before
the world, during which God could not have been idle, in like manner they
may conceive outside the world infinite realms of space, in which, if any
one says that the Omnipotent cannot hold His hand from working, will it
not follow that they must adopt Epicurus' dream of innumerable worlds?
with this difference only, that he asserts that they are formed and destroyed
by the fortuitous movements of atoms, while they will hold that they are
made by God's hand, if they maintain that, throughout the boundless im-
mensity of space, stretching interminably in every direction round the world,
God cannot rest, and that the worlds which they suppose Him to make. cannot be destroyed. For here the question is with those who, with ourselves,
believe that God is spiritual, and the Creator of all existences but Himself.
As for others, it is a condescension to dispute with them on a religious question, for they have acquired a reputation only among men who pay divine
honors to a number of gods, and have become conspicuous among the other
philosophers for no other reason than that, though they are still far from
the truth, they are near it in comparison with the rest. While these, then,
neither confine in any place, nor limit, nor distribute the divine substance,
but, as is worthy of God, own it to be wholly though spiritually present
everywhere, will they perchance say that this substance is absent from such
immense spaces outside the world, and is occupied in one only (and that a
very little one compared with the infinity beyond) the one, namely, in which
is the world? I think they will not proceed to this absurdity. Since they
maintain that there is but one world, of vast material bulk, indeed, yet
finite, and in its own determinate position, and that this was made by the
working of God, let them give the same account of God's resting in the infinite times before the world as they give of His resting in the infinite spaces
outside of it. And as it does not follow that God set the world in the very

spot it occupies and no other by accident rather than by divine reason, although no human reason can comprehend why it was so set, and though there was no merit in the spot chosen to give it the precedence of infinite others, so neither does it follow that we should suppose that God was guided by chance when He created the world in that and no earlier time, although previous times had been running by during an infinite past, and though there was no difference by which one time could be chosen in preference to another. But if they say that the thoughts of men are idle when they conceive infinite places, since there is no place beside the world, we reply that, by the same showing, it is vain to conceive of the past times of God's rest, since there is no time before the world.

CHAPTER VI

THAT THE WORLD AND TIME HAD BOTH ONE BEGINNING, AND THE ONE DID NOT ANTICIPATE THE OTHER

For if eternity and time are rightly distinguished by this, that time does not exist without some movement and transition, while in eternity there is no change, who does not see that there could have been no time had not some creature been made, which by some motion could give birth to change —the various parts of which motion and change, as they cannot be simultaneous, succeed one another—and thus, in these shorter or longer intervals of duration, time would begin? Since then, God, in whose eternity is no change at all, is the Creator and Ordainer of time, I do not see how He can be said to have created the world after spaces of time had elapsed, unless it be said that prior to the world there was some creature by whose movement time could pass. And if the sacred and infallible Scriptures say that in the beginning God created the heavens and the earth, in order that it may be understood that He had made nothing previously—for if He had made anything before the rest, this thing would rather be said to have been made "in the beginning"—then assuredly the world was made, not in time, but simultaneously with time. For that which is made in time is made both after and before some time—after that which is past, before that which is future. But none could then be past, for there was no creature by whose movements its duration could be measured. But simultaneously with time the world was made, if in the world's creation change and motion were created, as seems evident from the order of the first six or seven days. For in these days the morning and evening are counted, until, on the sixth day, all things which God then made were finished, and on the seventh the rest of God was mysteriously and sublimely signalized. What kind of days these were it is extremely difficult, or perhaps impossible for us to conceive, and how much more to say!

CHAPTER VII

OF THE NATURE OF THE FIRST DAYS, WHICH ARE SAID TO HAVE
HAD MORNING AND EVENING, BEFORE THERE WAS A SUN

We see, indeed, that our ordinary days have no evening but by the setting, and no morning but by the rising, of the sun; but the first three days
of all were passed without sun, since it is reported to have been made on the
fourth day. And first of all, indeed, light was made by the word of God, and
God, we read, separated it from the darkness, and called the light Day, and
the darkness Night; but what kind of light that was, and by what periodic
movement it made evening and morning, is beyond the reach of our senses;
neither can we understand how it was, and yet must unhesitatingly believe
it. For either it was some material light, whether proceeding from the upper
parts of the world, far removed from our sight, or from the spot where the
sun was afterwards kindled; or under the name of light the holy city was
signified, composed of holy angels and blessed spirits, the city of which the
apostle says, "Jerusalem which is above is our eternal mother in heaven;"[11]
and in another place, "For ye are all the children of the light, and the children of the day; we are not of the night, nor of darkness." [12] Yet in some respects we may appropriately speak of a morning and evening of this day
also. For the knowledge of the creature is, in comparison of the knowledge
of the Creator, but a twilight; and so it dawns and breaks into morning when
the creature is drawn to the praise and love of the Creator; and night never
falls when the Creator is not forsaken through love of the creature. In fine,
Scripture, when it would recount those days in order, never mentions the
word night. It never says, "Night was," but "The evening and the morning
were the first day." So of the second and the rest. And, indeed, the knowledge of created things contemplated by themselves is, so to speak, more
colorless than when they are seen in the wisdom of God, as in the art by
which they were made. Therefore evening is a more suitable figure than
night; and yet, as I said, morning returns when the creature returns to the
praise and love of the Creator. When it does so in the knowledge of itself,
that is the first day; when in the knowledge of the firmament, which is the
name given to the sky between the waters above and those beneath, that
is the second day; when in the knowledge of the earth, and the sea, and all
things that grow out of the earth, that is the third day; when in the knowledge of the greater and less luminaries, and all the stars, that is the fourth
day; when in the knowledge of all animals that swim in the waters and that
fly in the air, that is the fifth day; when in the knowledge of all animals
that live on the earth, and of man himself, that is the sixth day.

[11] Gal. iv. 26   [12] I Thess. v. 5

CHAPTER VIII

WHAT WE ARE TO UNDERSTAND OF GOD'S RESTING ON THE SEVENTH DAY, AFTER THE SIX DAYS' WORK

When it is said that God rested on the seventh day from all His works, and hallowed it, we are not to conceive of this in a childish fashion, as if work were a toil to God, who "spake and it was done"—spake by the spiritual and eternal, not audible and transitory word. But God's rest signifies the rest of those who rest in God, as the joy of a house means the joy of those in the house who rejoice, though not the house, but something else, causes the joy. How much more intelligible is such phraseology, then, if the house itself, by its own beauty, makes the inhabitants joyful! For in this case we not only call it joyful by that figure of speech in which the thing containing is used for the thing contained (as when we say, "The theatres applaud," "The meadows low," meaning that the men in the one applaud, and the oxen in the other low), but also by that figure in which the cause is spoken of as if it were the effect, as when a letter is said to be joyful, because it makes its readers so. Most appropriately, therefore, the sacred narrative states that God rested, meaning thereby that those rest who are in Him, and whom He makes to rest. And this the prophetic narrative promises also to the men to whom it speaks, and for whom it was written, that they themselves, after those good works which God does in and by them, if they have managed by faith to get near to God in this life, shall enjoy in Him eternal rest. This was pre-figured to the ancient people of God by the rest enjoined in their sabbath law, of which, in its own place, I shall speak more at large.

CHAPTER IX

WHAT THE SCRIPTURES TEACH US TO BELIEVE CONCERNING THE CREATION OF THE ANGELS

At present, since I have undertaken to treat of the origin of the holy city, and first of the holy angels, who constitute a large part of this city, and indeed the more blessed part, since they have never been expatriated, I will give myself to the task of explaining, by God's help, and as far as seems suitable, the Scriptures which relate to this point. Where Scripture speaks of the world's creation, it is not plainly said whether or when the angels were created; but if mention of them is made, it is implicitly under the name of "heaven," when it is said, "In the beginning God created the heavens and the earth," or perhaps rather under the name of "light," of which presently. But that they were wholly omitted, I am unable to believe, because it is written that God on the seventh day rested from all His works which He made; and this very book itself begins, "In the beginning God created the heavens and the earth," so that before heaven and earth God seems to have made nothing. Since, therefore, He began with the heavens and the earth—and the earth itself, as Scripture adds, was at first invisible and formless, light not being as yet made, and darkness covering the face of the deep (that is to say, covering an undefined chaos of earth and sea, for where light is not, darkness must be)—and then when all things, which are recorded to have been completed in six days, were created and arranged, how should the angels be omitted, as if they were not among the works of God, from which on the seventh day He rested? Yet, though the fact that the angels are the work of God is not omitted here, it is indeed not explicitly mentioned; but elsewhere Holy Scripture asserts it in the clearest manner. For in the Hymn of the Three Children in the Furnace it was said, "O all ye works of the Lord, bless ye the Lord;" [13] and among these works mentioned afterwards in detail, the angels are named. And in the psalm it is said, "Praise ye the Lord from the heavens, praise Him in the heights. Praise ye Him, all His angels; praise ye Him, all His hosts. Praise ye Him, sun and moon; praise Him, all ye stars of light. Praise Him, ye heaven of heavens; and ye waters that be above the heavens. Let them praise the name of the Lord; for He commanded, and they were created." [14] Here the angels are most expressly and by divine authority said to have been made by God, for of them among the other heavenly things it is said, "He commanded, and they were created." Who, then, will be bold enough to suggest that the angels were made after the six days' creation? If any one is so foolish, his folly is disposed of by a scripture of like authority, where God says, "When the stars were made, the angels praised me with a loud voice." [15] The angels therefore existed before the stars; and the stars were made the fourth day. Shall we then say that they were made the third day? Far from it; for we know what was made that day. The earth was separated from the water, and each element took its own distinct form, and the earth produced all that grows on it. On the second day, then? Not even on this; for on it the firmament was made between the waters above and beneath, and was called "Heaven," in which firmament the stars were made on the fourth day. There is no question, then, that if the angels are included in the works of God during these six days, they are that light which was called "Day," and whose unity Scripture signalizes by calling that day not the "first day," but "one day." For the second day, the third, and the rest are not other days; but the same "one" day is repeated to complete the number six or seven, so that there should be knowledge both of God's works and of His rest. For when God said, "Let there be light, and there was light," if we are justified in understanding in this light the creation of the angels, then certainly they were created partakers of the eternal light which is the unchangeable Wisdom of God, by which all things were made, and whom we call the only-begotten Son of God; so that they, being illumined by the Light that created them, might

[13] 35   [14] Ps. cxlviii. 1-5   [15] Job xxxviii. 7

themselves become light and be called "Day," in participation of that unchangeable Light and Day which is the Word of God, by whom both themselves and all else were made. "The true Light, which lighteth every man that cometh into the world" [16]—this Light lighteth also every pure angel, that he may be light not in himself, but in God; from whom if an angel turn away, he becomes impure, as are all those who are called unclean spirits, and are no longer light in the Lord, but darkness in themselves, being deprived of the participation of Light eternal. For evil has no positive nature; but the loss of good has received the name "evil."

CHAPTER X

OF THE SIMPLE AND UNCHANGEABLE TRINITY, FATHER, SON, AND HOLY GHOST, ONE GOD, IN WHOM SUBSTANCE AND QUALITY ARE IDENTICAL

There is, accordingly, a good which is alone simple, and therefore alone unchangeable, and this is God. By this Good have all others been created, but not simple, and therefore not unchangeable. "Created," I say—that is, made, not begotten. For that which is begotten of the simple Good is simple as itself, and the same as itself. These two we call the Father and the Son; and both together with the Holy Spirit are one God; and to this Spirit the epithet Holy is in Scripture, as it were, appropriated. And He is another than the Father and the Son, for He is neither the Father nor the Son. I say "another," not "another thing," because He is equally with them the simple Good, unchangeable and co-eternal. And this Trinity is one God; and none the less simple because a Trinity. For we do not say that the nature of the good is simple, because the Father alone possesses it, or the Son alone, or the Holy Ghost alone; nor do we say, with the Sabellian heretics, that it is only nominally a Trinity, and has no real distinction of persons; but we say it is simple, because it is what it has, with the exception of the relation of the persons to one another. For, in regard to this relation, it is true that the Father has a Son, and yet is not Himself the Son; and the Son has a Father, and is not Himself the Father. But, as regards Himself, irrespective of relation to the other, each is what He has; thus, He is in Himself living, for He has life, and is Himself the Life which He has.

It is for this reason, then, that the nature of the Trinity is called simple, because it has not anything which it can lose, and because it is not one thing and its contents another, as a cup and the liquor, or a body and its color, or the air and the light or heat of it, or a mind and its wisdom. For none of these is what it has: the cup is not liquor, nor the body color, nor the air light and heat, nor the mind wisdom. And hence they can be deprived of what they have, and can be turned or changed into other qualities and

[16] John i. 9

states, so that the cup may be emptied of the liquid of which it is full, the body be discolored, the air darken, the mind grow silly. The incorruptible body which is promised to the saints in the resurrection cannot, indeed, lose its quality of incorruption, but the bodily substance and the quality of incorruption are not the same thing. For the quality of incorruption resides entire in each several part, not greater in one and less in another; for no part is more incorruptible than another. The body, indeed, is itself greater in whole than in part; and one part of it is larger, another smaller, yet is not the larger more incorruptible than the smaller. The body, then, which is not in each of its parts a whole body, is one thing; incorruptibility, which is throughout complete, is another thing—for every part of the incorruptible body, however unequal to the rest otherwise, is equally incorrupt. For the hand, e.g., is not more incorrupt than the finger because it is larger than the finger; so, though finger and hand are unequal, their incorruptibility is equal. Thus, although incorruptibility is inseparable from an incorruptible body, yet the substance of the body is one thing, the quality of incorruption another. And therefore the body is not what it has. The soul itself, too, though it be always wise (as it will be eternally when it is redeemed) will be so by participating in the unchangeable wisdom, which it is not; for though the air be never robbed of the light that is shed abroad in it, it is not on that account the same thing as the light. I do not mean that the soul is air, as has been supposed by some who could not conceive a spiritual nature;[17] but, with much dissimilarity, the two things have a kind of likeness, which makes it suitable to say that the immaterial soul is illumined with the immaterial light of the simple wisdom of God, as the material air is irradiated with material light, and that, as the air, when deprived of this light, grows dark (for material darkness is nothing else than air wanting light), so the soul, deprived of the light of wisdom, grows dark.

According to this, then, those things which are essentially and truly divine are called simple, because in them quality and substance are identical, and because they are divine, or wise, or blessed in themselves, and without extraneous supplement. In Holy Scripture, it is true, the Spirit of wisdom is called "manifold" [18] because it contains many things in it; but what it contains it also is, and it being one is all these things. For neither are there many wisdoms, but one, in which are untold and infinite treasures of things intellectual, wherein are all invisible and unchangeable reasons of things visible and changeable which were created by it.[19] For God made nothing unwittingly; not even a human workman can be said to do so. But if He

---

[17] Plutarch (De Plac. Phil. i. 3, and iv. 3) tells us that this opinion was held by Anaximenes of Miletus, the followers of Anaxagoras, and many of the Stoics. Diogenes the Cynic, as well as Diogenes of Appollonia, seems to have adopted the same opinion.

[18] Wisdom, vii. 22

[19] The strongly Platonic tinge of this language is perhaps best preserved in a bare literal translation.

knew all that He made, He made only those things which He had known. Whence flows a very striking but true conclusion, that this world could not be known to us unless it existed, but could not have existed unless it had been known to God.

CHAPTER XI

WHETHER THE ANGELS THAT FELL PARTOOK OF THE BLESSEDNESS WHICH THE HOLY ANGELS HAVE ALWAYS ENJOYED FROM THE TIME OF THEIR CREATION

And since these things are so, those spirits whom we call angels were never at any time or in any way darkness, but, as soon as they were made, were made light; yet they were not so created in order that they might exist and live in any way whatever, but were enlightened that they might live wisely and blessedly. Some of them, having turned away from this light, have not won this wise and blessed life, which is certainly eternal, and accompanied with the sure confidence of its eternity; but they have still the life of reason, though darkened with folly, and this they cannot lose even if they would. But who can determine to what extent they were partakers of that wisdom before they fell? And how shall we say that they participated in it equally with those who through it are truly and fully blessed, resting in a true certainty of eternal felicity? For if they had equally participated in this true knowledge, then the evil angels would have remained eternally blessed equally with the good, because they were equally expectant of it. For, though a life be never so long, it cannot be truly called eternal if it is destined to have an end; for it is called life inasmuch as it is lived, but eternal because it has no end. Wherefore, although everything eternal is not therefore blessed (for hell-fire is eternal), yet if no life can be truly and perfectly blessed except it be eternal, the life of these angels was not blessed, for it was doomed to end, and therefore not eternal, whether they knew it or not. In the one case fear, in the other ignorance, prevented them from being blessed. And even if their ignorance was not so great as to breed in them a wholly false expectation, but left them wavering in uncertainty whether their good would be eternal or would some time terminate, this very doubt concerning so grand a destiny was incompatible with the plenitude of blessedness which we believe the holy angels enjoyed. For we do not so narrow and restrict the application of the term "blessedness" as to apply it to God only, though doubtless He is so truly blessed that greater blessedness cannot be; and, in comparison of His blessedness, what is that of the angels, though, according to their capacity, they be perfectly blessed?

CHAPTER XII

A COMPARISON OF THE BLESSEDNESS OF THE RIGHTEOUS, WHO
HAVE NOT YET RECEIVED THE DIVINE REWARD, WITH THAT OF
OUR FIRST PARENTS IN PARADISE

And the angels are not the only members of the rational and intellectual creation whom we call blessed. For who will take upon him to deny that those first men in Paradise were blessed previously to sin, although they were uncertain how long their blessedness was to last, and whether it would be eternal (and eternal it would have been had they not sinned)—who, I say, will do so, seeing that even now we not unbecomingly call those blessed whom we see leading a righteous and holy life, in hope of immortality, who have no harrowing remorse of conscience, but obtain readily divine remission of the sins of their present infirmity? These, though they are certain that they shall be rewarded if they persevere, are not certain that they will persevere. For what man can know that he will persevere to the end in the exercise and increase of grace, unless he has been certified by some revelation from Him who, in His just and secret judgment, while He deceives none, informs few regarding this matter? Accordingly, so far as present comfort goes, the first man in Paradise was more blessed than any just man in this insecure state; but as regards the hope of future good, every man who not merely supposes, but certainly knows that he shall eternally enjoy the most high God in the company of angels, and beyond the reach of ill—this man, no matter what bodily torments afflict him, is more blessed than was he who, even in that great felicity of Paradise, was uncertain of his fate.

CHAPTER XIII

WHETHER ALL THE ANGELS WERE SO CREATED IN ONE COMMON
STATE OF FELICITY, THAT THOSE WHO FELL WERE NOT AWARE
THAT THEY WOULD FALL, AND THAT THOSE WHO STOOD
RECEIVED ASSURANCE OF THEIR OWN PERSEVERANCE
AFTER THE RUIN OF THE FALLEN

From all this, it will readily occur to any one that the blessedness which an intelligent being desires as its legitimate object results from a combination of these two things, namely, that it uninterruptedly enjoy the unchangeable good, which is God; and that it be delivered from all dubiety, and know certainly that it shall eternally abide in the same enjoyment. That it is so with the angels of light we piously believe; but that the fallen angels, who by their own default lost that light, did not enjoy this blessedness even before they sinned, reason bids us conclude. Yet if their life was of any duration before they fell, we must allow them a blessedness of some kind, though not that which is accompanied with foresight. Or, if it seems hard to believe that, when the angels were created, some were created in ignorance either of their perseverance or their fall, while others were most certainly assured of the eternity of their felicity—if it is hard to believe that they were not all from the beginning on an equal footing, until these who are now evil did of their own will fall away from the light of goodness, certainly it is much harder to believe that the holy angels are now uncertain of their eternal blessedness, and do not know regarding themselves as much as we have been able to gather regarding them from the Holy Scriptures. For what catholic Christian does not know that no new devil will ever arise among the good angels, as he knows that this present devil will never again return into the fellowship of the good? For the truth in the gospel promises to the saints and the faithful that they will be equal to the angels of God; and it is also promised them that they will "go away into life eternal." [20] But if we are certain that we shall never lapse from eternal felicity, while they are not certain, then we shall not be their equals, but their superiors. But as the truth never deceives, and as we shall be their equals, they must be certain of their blessedness. And because the evil angels could not be certain of that, since their blessedness was destined to come to an end, it follows either that the angels were unequal, or that, if equal, the good angels were assured of the eternity of their blessedness after the perdition of the others; unless, possibly, some one may say that the words of the Lord about the devil, "He was a murderer from the beginning, and abode not in the truth," [21] are to be understood as if he was not only a murderer from the beginning of the human race, when man, whom he could kill by his deceit, was made, but also that he did not abide in the truth from the time of his own creation, and was accordingly never blessed with the holy angels, but refused to submit to his Creator, and proudly exulted as if in a private lordship of his own, and was thus deceived and deceiving. For the dominion of the Almighty cannot be eluded; and he who will not piously submit himself to things as they are, proudly feigns, and mocks himself with a state of things that does not exist; so that what the blessed Apostle John says thus becomes intelligible: "The devil sinneth from the beginning" [22]—that is, from the time he was created he refused righteousness, which none but a will piously subject to God can enjoy. Whoever adopts this opinion at least disagrees with those heretics the Manichees, and with any other pestilential sect that may suppose that the devil has derived from some adverse evil principle a nature proper to himself. These persons are so befooled by error, that, although they acknowledge with ourselves the authority of the gospels, they do not notice that the Lord did not say, "The devil was naturally a stranger to the truth," but "The devil abode not in the truth," by which He meant us to understand that he had fallen from the truth, in which, if he had abode, he would have become a partaker of it, and have remained in blessedness along with the holy angels.

[20] Matt. xxv. 46   [21] John viii. 44   [22] 1 John iii. 8

CHAPTER XIV

AN EXPLANATION OF WHAT IS SAID OF THE DEVIL, THAT HE DID NOT ABIDE IN THE TRUTH, BECAUSE THE TRUTH WAS NOT IN HIM

Moreover, as if we had been inquiring why the devil did not abide in the truth, our Lord subjoins the reason, saying, "because the truth is not in him." Now, it would be in him had he abode in it. But the phraseology is unusual. For, as the words stand, "He abode not in the truth, because the truth is not in him," it seems as if the truth's not being in him were the cause of his not abiding in it; whereas his not abiding in the truth is rather the cause of its not being in him. The same form of speech is found in the psalm: "I have called upon Thee, for Thou hast heard me, O God," [23] where we should expect it to be said, Thou hast heard me, O God, for I have called upon Thee. But when he had said, "I have called," then, as if some one were seeking proof of this, he demonstrates the effectual earnestness of his prayer by the effect of God's hearing it; as if he had said, The proof that I have prayed is that Thou hast heard me.

CHAPTER XV

HOW WE ARE TO UNDERSTAND THE WORDS, "THE DEVIL SINNETH FROM THE BEGINNING"

As for what John says about the devil, "The devil sinneth from the beginning," [24] they[25] who suppose it is meant hereby that the devil was made with a sinful nature, misunderstand it; for if sin be natural, it is not sin at all. And how do they answer the prophetic proofs—either what Isaiah says when he represents the devil under the person of the king of Babylon, "How art thou fallen, O Lucifer, son of the morning!" [26] or what Ezekiel says, "Thou hast been in Eden, the garden of God; every precious stone was thy covering," [27] where it is meant that he was some time without sin; for a little after it is still more explicitly said, "Thou wast perfect in thy ways?" And if these passages cannot well be otherwise interpreted, we must understand by this one also, "He abode not in the truth," that he was once in the truth, but did not remain in it. And from this passage, "The devil sinneth from the beginning," it is not to be supposed that he sinned from the beginning of his created existence, but from the beginning of his sin, when by his pride he had once commenced to sin. There is a passage, too, in the Book of Job, of which the devil is the subject: "This is the beginning of the creation of God, which He made to be a sport to His angels," [28] which agrees with the psalm, where it is said, "There is that dragon which Thou hast made to be a sport

---

[23] Ps. xvii. 6   [24] 1 John iii. 8   [25] The Manichaeans   [26] Isa. xiv. 12   [27] Ezek. xxviii. 13   [28] Job xl. 14 (LXX)

therein." [29] But these passages are not to lead us to suppose that the devil was originally created to be the sport of the angels, but that he was doomed to this punishment after his sin. His beginning, then, is the handiwork of God; for there is no nature, even among the least, and lowest, and last of the beasts, which was not the work of Him from whom has proceeded all measure, all form, all order, without which nothing can be planned or conceived. How much more, then, is this angelic nature, which surpasses in dignity all else that He has made, the handiwork of the Most High!

CHAPTER XVI

OF THE RANKS AND DIFFERENCES OF THE CREATURES, ESTIMATED BY THEIR UTILITY, OR ACCORDING TO THE NATURAL GRADATIONS OF BEING

For, among those beings which exist, and which are not of God the Creator's essence, those which have life are ranked above those which have none; those that have the power of generation, or even of desiring, above those which want this faculty. And, among things that have life, the sentient are higher than those which have no sensation, as animals are ranked above trees. And, among the sentient, the intelligent are above those that have not intelligence—men, e.g., above cattle. And, among the intelligent, the immortal, such as the angels, above the mortal, such as men. These are the gradations according to the order of nature; but according to the utility each man finds in a thing, there are various standards of value, so that it happens that we prefer some things that have no sensation to some sentient beings. And so strong is this preference, that, had we the power, we would abolish the latter from nature altogether, whether in ignorance of the place they hold in nature, or, though we know it, sacrificing them to our own convenience. Who, e.g., would not rather have bread in his house than mice, gold than fleas? But there is little to wonder at in this, seeing that even when valued by men themselves (whose nature is certainly of the highest dignity), more is often given for a horse than for a slave, for a jewel than for a maid. Thus the reason of one contemplating nature prompts very different judgments from those dictated by the necessity of the needy, or the desire of the voluptuous; for the former considers what value a thing in itself has in the scale of creation, while necessity considers how it meets its need; reason looks for what the mental light will judge to be true, while pleasure looks for what pleasantly titilates the bodily sense. But of such consequence in rational natures is the weight, so to speak, of will and of love, that though in the order of nature angels rank above men, yet, by the scale of justice, good men are of greater value than bad angels.

[29] Ps. civ. 26

CHAPTER XVII

THAT THE FLAW OF WICKEDNESS IS NOT NATURE, BUT CONTRARY TO NATURE, AND HAS ITS ORIGIN, NOT IN THE CREATOR, BUT IN THE WILL

It is with reference to the nature, then, and not to the wickedness of the devil, that we are to understand these words, "This is the beginning of God's handiwork;" [30] for, without doubt, wickedness can be a flaw or vice only where the nature previously was not vitiated. Vice, too, is so contrary to nature, that it cannot but damage it. And therefore departure from God would be no vice, unless in a nature whose property it was to abide with God. So that even the wicked will is a strong proof of the goodness of the nature. But God, as He is the supremely good Creator of good natures, so is He of evil wills the most just Ruler; so that, while they make an ill use of good natures, He makes a good use even of evil wills. Accordingly, He caused the devil (good by God's creation, wicked by his own will) to be cast down from his high position, and to become the mockery of His angels—that is, He caused his temptations to benefit those whom he wishes to injure by them. And because God, when He created him, was certainly not ignorant of his future malignity, and foresaw the good which He Himself would bring out of his evil, therefore says the psalm, "This leviathan whom Thou hast made to be a sport therein," [31] that we may see that, even while God in His goodness created him good, He yet had already foreseen and arranged how He would make use of him when he became wicked.

CHAPTER XVIII

OF THE BEAUTY OF THE UNIVERSE, WHICH BECOMES, BY GOD'S ORDINANCE, MORE BRILLIANT BY THE OPPOSITION OF CONTRARIES

For God would never have created any, I do not say angel, but even man, whose future wickedness He foreknew, unless He had equally known to what uses in behalf of the good He could turn him, thus embellishing the course of the ages, as it were an exquisite poem set off with antitheses. For what are called antitheses are among the most elegant of the ornaments of speech. They might be called in Latin "oppositions," or, to speak more accurately, "contrapositions;" but this word is not in common use among us, though the Latin, and indeed the languages of all nations, avail themselves of the same ornaments of style. In the *Second Epistle to the Corinthians* the Apostle Paul also makes a graceful use of antithesis, in that place where he says, "By the armor of righteousness on the right hand and on the left, by honor and dishonor, by evil report and good report: as deceivers, and yet

[30] Job xl. 14 (LXX)   [31] Ps. civ. 26

true; as unknown, and yet well known; as dying, and, behold, we live; as chastened, and not killed; as sorrowful, yet always rejoicing; as poor, yet making many rich; as having nothing, and yet possessing all things." [32] As, then, these oppositions of contraries lend beauty to the language, so the beauty of the course of this world is achieved by the opposition of contraries, arranged, as it were, by an eloquence not of words, but of things. This is quite plainly stated in the *Book of Ecclesiasticus*, in this way: "Good is set against evil, and life against death: so is the sinner against the godly. So look upon all the works of the Most High, and these are two and two, one against another." [33]

CHAPTER XIX

WHAT, SEEMINGLY, WE ARE TO UNDERSTAND BY THE WORDS, "GOD DIVIDED THE LIGHT FROM THE DARKNESS"

Accordingly, though the obscurity of the divine word has certainly this advantage, that it causes many opinions about the truth to be started and discussed, each reader seeing some fresh meaning in it, yet, whatever is said to be meant by an obscure passage should be either confirmed by the testimony of obvious facts, or should be asserted in other and less ambiguous texts. This obscurity is beneficial, whether the sense of the author is at last reached after the discussion of many other interpretations, or whether, though that sense remain concealed, other truths are brought out by the discussion of the obscurity. To me it does not seem incongruous with the working of God, if we understand that the angels were created when that first light was made, and that a separation was made between the holy and the unclean angels, when, as is said, "God divided the light from the darkness; and God called the light Day, and the darkness He called Night." For He alone could make this discrimination, who was able also before they fell, to foreknow that they would fall, and that, being deprived of the light of truth, they would abide in the darkness of pride. For, so far as regards the day and night, with which we are familiar, He commanded those luminaries of heaven that are obvious to our senses to divide between the light and the darkness. "Let there be," He says, "lights in the firmament of the heaven, to divide the day from the night;" and shortly after He says, "And God made two great lights; the greater light to rule the day, and the lesser light to rule the night: the stars also. And God set them in the firmament of the heaven, to give light upon the earth, and to rule over the day and over the night, and to divide the light from the darkness." [34] But between that light, which is the holy company of the angels spiritually radiant with the illumination of the truth, and that opposing darkness, which is the noisome foulness of the spiritual condition of those angels who are turned away from

[32] 2 Cor. vi. 7-10   [33] Ecclus. xxxiii. 15   [34] Gen. i. 14-18

the light of righteousness, only He Himself could divide, from whom their wickedness (not of nature, but of will) while yet it was future, could not be hidden or uncertain.

CHAPTER XX

OF THE WORDS WHICH FOLLOW THE SEPARATION OF LIGHT AND DARKNESS, "AND GOD SAW THE LIGHT THAT IT WAS GOOD"

Then, we must not pass from this passage of Scripture without noticing that when God said, "Let there be light, and there was light," it was immediately added, "And God saw the light that it was good." No such expression followed the statement that He separated the light from the darkness, and called the light Day and the darkness Night, lest the seal of His approval might seem to be set on such darkness, as well as on the light. For when the darkness was not subject of disapprobation, as when it was divided by the heavenly bodies from this light which our eyes discern, the statement that God saw that it was good is inserted, not before, but after the division is recorded. "And God set them," so runs the passage, "in the firmament of the heaven, to give light upon the earth, and to rule over the day and over the night, and to divide the light from the darkness: and God saw that it was good." For He approved of both, because both were sinless. But where God said, "Let there be light, and there was light; and God saw the light that it was good;" and the narrative goes on, "and God divided the light from the darkness! and God called the light Day, and the darkness He called Night," there was not in this place subjoined the statement, "And God saw that it was good," lest both should be designated good, while one of them was evil, not by nature, but by its own fault. And therefore, in this case, the light alone received the approbation of the Creator, while the angelic darkness, though it had been ordained, was yet not approved.

CHAPTER XXI

OF GOD'S ETERNAL AND UNCHANGEABLE KNOWLEDGE AND WILL, WHEREBY ALL HE HAS MADE PLEASED HIM IN THE ETERNAL DESIGN AS WELL AS IN THE ACTUAL RESULT

For what else is to be understood by that invariable refrain, "And God saw that it was good," than the approval of the work in its design, which is the wisdom of God? For certainly God did not in the actual achievement of the work first learn that it was good, but, on the contrary, nothing would have been made had it not been first known by Him. While, therefore, He sees that that is good which, had He not seen it before it was made, would never have been made, it is plain that He is not discovering, but teaching that it is good. Plato, indeed, was bold enough to say that, when the universe was completed, God was, as it were, elated with joy.[35] And Plato was not so foolish as to mean by this that God was rendered more blessed by the novelty of His creation; but he wished thus to indicate that the work now completed met with its Maker's approval, as it had while yet in design. It is not as if the knowledge of God were of various kinds, knowing in different ways things which as yet are not, things which are, and things which have been. For not in our fashion does He look forward to what is future, nor at what is present, nor back upon what is past; but in a manner quite different and far and profoundly remote from our way of thinking. For He does not pass from this to that by transition of thought, but beholds all things with absolute unchangeableness; so that of those things which emerge in time, the future, indeed, are not yet, and the present are now, and the past no longer are; but all of these are by Him comprehended in His stable and eternal presence. Neither does He see in one fashion by the eye, in another by the mind, for He is not composed of mind and body; nor does His present knowledge differ from that which it ever was or shall be, for those variations of time, past, present, and future, though they alter our knowledge, do not affect His, "with whom is no variableness, neither shadow of turning."[36] Neither is there any growth from thought to thought in the conceptions of Him in whose spiritual vision all things which He knows are at once embraced. For as without any movement that time can measure, He Himself moves all temporal things, so He knows all times with a knowledge that time cannot measure. And therefore He saw that what He had made was good, when He saw that it was good to make it. And when He saw it made, He had not on that account a twofold nor any way increased knowledge of it; as if He had less knowledge before He made what He saw. For certainly He would not be the perfect worker He is, unless His knowledge were so perfect as to receive no addition from His finished works. Wherefore, if the only object had been to inform us who made the light, it had been enough to say, "God made the light;" and if further information regarding the means by which it was made had been intended, it would have sufficed to say, "And God said, Let there be light, and there was light," that we might know not only that God had made the world, but also that He had made it by the word. But because it was right that three leading truths regarding the creature be intimated to us, viz., who made it, by what means, and why, it is written, "God said, Let there be light, and there was light. And God saw the light that it was good." If, then, we ask who made it, it was "God." If, by what means, He said "Let it be," and it was. If we ask, why He made it, "it was good." Neither is there any author more excellent than God, nor any skill more efficacious than the word of God, nor any cause better than that good might be created by the good God. This also Plato has assigned as the most sufficient reason for the creation of the world, that good works might be made by a good God;[37] whether he read this passage, or, perhaps,

[35] Timaeus, 37 C   [36] Jas. i. 17   [37] Timaeus, 20 D

was informed of these things by those who had read them, or, by his quick-sighted genius, penetrated to things spiritual and invisible through the things that are created, or was instructed regarding them by those who had discerned them.

CHAPTER XXII

OF THOSE WHO DO NOT APPROVE OF CERTAIN THINGS WHICH ARE A PART OF THIS GOOD CREATION OF A GOOD CREATOR, AND WHO THINK THAT THERE IS SOME NATURAL EVIL

This cause, however, of a good creation, namely, the goodness of God—this cause, I say, so just and fit, which, when piously and carefully weighed, terminates all the controversies of those who inquire into the origin of the world, has not been recognized by some heretics,[38] because there are, forsooth, many things, such as fire, frost, wild beasts, and so forth, which do not suit but injure this thin-blooded and frail mortality of our flesh, which is at present under just punishment. They do not consider how admirable these things are in their own places, how excellent in their own natures, how beautifully adjusted to the rest of creation, and how much grace they contribute to the universe by their own contributions as it were to a commonwealth; and how serviceable they are even to ourselves, if we use them with a knowledge of their fit adaptations—so that even poisons, which are destructive when used injudiciously, become wholesome and medicinal when used in conformity with their qualities and design; just as, on the other hand, those things which give us pleasure, such as food, drink, and the light of the sun, are found to be hurtful when immoderately or unseasonably used. And thus divine providence admonishes us not foolishly to vituperate things, but to investigate their utility with care; and, where our mental capacity or infirmity is at fault, to believe that there is a utility, though hidden, as we have experienced that there were other things which we all but failed to discover. For this concealment of the use of things is itself either an exercise of our humility or a levelling of our pride; for no nature at all is evil, and this is a name for nothing but the want of good. But from things earthly to things heavenly, from the visible to the invisible, there are some things better than others; and for this purpose are they unequal, in order that they might all exist. Now God is in such sort a great worker in great things, that He is not less in little things—for these little things are to be measured not by their own greatness (which does not exist) but by the wisdom of their Designer; as, in the visible appearance of a man, if one eyebrow be shaved off, how nearly nothing is taken from the body, but how much from the beauty!—for that is not constituted by bulk, but by the proportion and arrangement of the members. But we do not greatly wonder

[38] The Manichaeans

that persons, who suppose that some evil nature has been generated and propagated by a kind of opposing principle proper to it, refuse to admit that the cause of the creation was this, that the good God produced a good creation. For they believe that He was driven to this enterprise of creation by the urgent necessity of repulsing the evil that warred against Him, and that He mixed His good nature with the evil for the sake of restraining and conquering it; and that this nature of His, being thus shamefully polluted, and most cruelly oppressed and held captive, He labors to cleanse and deliver it, and with all His pains does not wholly succeed; but such part of it as could not be cleansed from that defilement is to serve as a prison and chain of the conquered and incarcerated enemy. The Manichaeans would not drivel, or rather, rave in such a style as this, if they believed the nature of God to be, as it is, unchangeable and absolutely incorruptible, and subject to no injury; and if, moreover, they held in Christian sobriety, that the soul which has shown itself capable of being altered for the worse by its own will, and of being corrupted by sin, and so, of being deprived of the light of eternal truth—that this soul, I say, is not a part of God, nor of the same nature as God, but is created by Him, and is far different from its Creator.

CHAPTER XXIII

OF THE ERROR IN WHICH THE DOCTRINE OF ORIGEN IS INVOLVED

But it is much more surprising that some even of those who, with ourselves, believe that there is one only source of all things, and that no nature which is not divine can exist unless originated by that Creator, have yet refused to accept with a good and simple faith this so good and simple a reason of the world's creation, that a good God made it good; and that the things created, being different from God, were inferior to Him, and yet were good, being created by none other than He. But they say that souls, though not, indeed, parts of God, but created by Him, sinned by abandoning God; that, in proportion to their various sins, they merited different degrees of debasement from heaven to earth, and diverse bodies as prison-houses; and that this is the world, and this the cause of its creation, not the production of good things, but the restraining of evil. Origen is justly blamed for holding this opinion. For in the books which he entitles περὶ. ἀρχῶν, that is, *Of Origins*, this is his sentiment, this his utterance. And I cannot sufficiently express my astonishment, that a man so erudite and well versed in ecclesiastical literature, should not have observed, in the first place, how opposed this is to the meaning of this authoritative Scripture, which, in recounting all the works of God, regularly adds, "And God saw that it was good;" and, when all were completed, inserts the words, "And God saw everything that He had made, and, behold, it was very good." [39]

[39] Gen. i. 31

Was it not obviously meant to be understood that there was no other cause of the world's creation than that good creatures should be made by a good God? In this creation, had no one sinned, the world would have been filled and beautified with natures good without exception; and though there is sin, all things are not therefore full of sin, for the great majority of the heavenly inhabitants preserve their nature's integrity. And the sinful will, though it violated the order of its own nature, did not on that account escape the laws of God, who justly orders all things for good. For as the beauty of a picture is increased by well-managed shadows, so, to the eye that has skill to discern it, the universe is beautified even by sinners, though, considered by themselves, their deformity is a sad blemish.

In the second place, Origen, and all who think with him, ought to have seen that if it were the true opinion that the world was created in order that souls might, for their sins, be accommodated with bodies in which they should be shut up as in houses of correction, the more venial sinners receiving lighter and more ethereal bodies, while the grosser and graver sinners received bodies more crass and grovelling, then it would follow that the devils, who are deepest in wickedness, ought, rather than even wicked men, to have earthly bodies, since these are the grossest and least ethereal of all. But in point of fact, that we might see that the deserts of souls are not to be estimated by the qualities of bodies, the wickedest devil possesses an ethereal body, while man, wicked, it is true, but with a wickedness small and venial in comparison with his, received even before his sin a body of clay. And what more foolish assertion can be advanced than that God, by this sun of ours, did not design to benefit the material creation, or lend lustre to its loveliness, and therefore created one single sun for this single world, but that it so happened that one soul only had so sinned as to deserve to be enclosed in such a body as it is? On this principle, if it had chanced that not one, but two, yea, or ten, or a hundred had sinned similarly, and with a like degree of guilt, then this world would have one hundred suns. And that such is not the case, is due not to the considerate foresight of the Creator, contriving the safety and beauty of things material, but rather to the fact that so fine a quality of sinning was hit upon by only one soul, so that it alone has merited such a body. Manifestly persons holding such opinions should aim at confining, not souls of which they know not what they say, but themselves, lest they fall, and deservedly, far indeed from the truth. And as to these three answers which I formerly recommended when in the case of any creature the questions are put, Who made it? By what means? Why? that it should be replied, God, By the Word, Because it was good—as to these three answers, it is very questionable whether the Trinity itself is thus mystically indicated, that is, the Father, the Son, and the Holy Ghost, or whether there is some good reason for this acceptation in this passage of Scripture—this, I say, is questionable, and one can't be expected to explain everything in one volume.

CHAPTER XXIV

OF THE DIVINE TRINITY, AND THE INDICATIONS OF ITS PRESENCE SCATTERED EVERYWHERE AMONG ITS WORKS

We believe, we maintain, we faithfully preach, that the Father begat the Word, that is, Wisdom, by which all things were made, the only-begotten Son, one as the Father is one, eternal as the Father is eternal, and, equally with the Father, supremely good; and that the Holy Spirit is the Spirit alike of Father and of Son, and is Himself consubstantial and co-eternal with both; and that this whole is a Trinity by reason of the individuality of the persons, and one God by reason of the indivisible divine substance, as also one Almighty by reason of the indivisible omnipotence; yet so that, when we inquire regarding each singly, it is said that each is God and Almighty; and, when we speak of all together, it is said that there are not three Gods, nor three Almighties, but one God Almighty; so great is the indivisible unity of these Three, which requires that it be so stated. But, whether the Holy Spirit of the Father, and of the Son, who are both good, can be with propriety called the goodness of both, because He is common to both, I do not presume to determine hastily. Nevertheless, I would have less hesitation in saying that He is the holiness of both, not as if He were a divine attribute merely, but Himself also the divine substance, and the third person in the Trinity. I am the rather emboldened to make this statement, because, though the Father is a spirit, and the Son a spirit, and the Father holy, and the Son holy, yet the third person is distinctively called the Holy Spirit, as if He were the substantial holiness consubstantial with the other two. But if the divine goodness is nothing else than the divine holiness, then certainly it is a reasonable studiousness, and not presumptuous intrusion, to inquire whether the same Trinity be not hinted at in an enigmatical mode of speech, by which our inquiry is stimulated, when it is written who made each creature, and by what means, and why. For it is the Father of the Word who said, Let there be. And that which was made when He spoke was certainly made by means of the Word. And by the words, "God saw that it was good," it is sufficiently intimated that God made what was made not from any necessity, nor for the sake of supplying any want, but solely from His own goodness, i.e., because it was good. And this is stated after the creation had taken place, that there might be no doubt that the thing made satisfied the goodness on account of which it was made. And if we are right in understanding that this goodness is the Holy Spirit, then the whole Trinity is revealed to us in the creation. In this, too, is the origin, the enlightenment, the blessedness of the holy city which is above among the holy angels. For if we inquire whence it is, God created it; or whence its wisdom, God illumined it; or whence its blessedness, God is its bliss. It has its form by subsisting in Him; its enlightenment by contemplating Him; its joy by abiding in Him. It is; it sees; it loves. In God's eternity is its life; in God's truth its light; in God's goodness its joy.

CHAPTER XXV

OF THE DIVISION OF PHILOSOPHY INTO THREE PARTS

As far as one can judge, it is for the same reason that philosophers have aimed at a threefold division of science, or rather, were enabled to see that there was a threefold division (for they did not invent, but only discovered it) of which one part is called physical, another logical, the third ethical. The Latin equivalents of these names are now naturalized in the writings of many authors, so that these divisions are called natural, rational, and moral, on which I have touched slightly in the eighth book. Not that I would conclude that these philosophers, in this threefold division, had any thought of a trinity in God, although Plato is said to have been the first to discover and promulgate this distribution, and he saw that God alone could be the author of nature, the bestower of intelligence, and the kindler of love by which life becomes good and blessed. But certain it is that, though philosophers disagree both regarding the nature of things, and the mode of investigating truth, and of the good to which all our actions ought to tend, yet in these three great general questions all their intellectual energy is spent. And though there be a confusing diversity of opinion, every man striving to establish his own opinion in regard to each of these questions, yet no one of them all doubts that nature has some cause, science some method, life some end and aim. Then, again, there are three things which every artificer must possess if he is to effect anything—nature, education, practice. Nature is to be judged by capacity, education by knowledge, practice by its fruit. I am aware that, properly speaking, fruit is what one enjoys, use [practice] what one uses. And this seems to be the difference between them, that we are said to *enjoy* that which in itself, and irrespective of other ends, delights us; to *use* that which we seek for the sake of some end beyond. For which reason the things of time are to be used rather than enjoyed, that we may deserve to enjoy things eternal; and not as those perverse creatures who would fain enjoy money and use God—not spending money for God's sake, but worshipping God for money's sake. However, in common parlance, we both use fruits and enjoy uses. For we correctly speak of the "fruits of the field," which certainly we all use in the present life. And it was in accordance with this usage that I said that there were three things to be observed in a man, nature, education, practice. From these the philosophers have elaborated, as I said, the threefold division of that science by which a blessed life is attained: the natural having respect to nature, the rational to education, the moral to practice. If, then, we were ourselves the authors of our nature, we should have generated knowledge in ourselves, and should not require to reach it by education, *i.e.*, by learning it from others. Our love, too, proceeding from ourselves and returning to us, would suffice to make our life blessed, and would stand in need of no extraneous enjoyment. But now, since our nature has God as its requisite author, it is certain that we must have Him for our teacher that we may be wise; Him, too, to dispense to us spiritual sweetness that we may be blessed.

CHAPTER XXVI

OF THE IMAGE OF THE SUPREME TRINITY, WHICH WE FIND IN SOME SORT IN HUMAN NATURE EVEN IN ITS PRESENT STATE

And we indeed recognize in ourselves the image of God, that is, of the supreme Trinity, an image which, though it be not equal to God, or rather, though it be very far removed from Him—being neither co-eternal, nor, to say all in a word, consubstantial with Him—is yet nearer to Him in nature than any other of His works, and is destined to be yet restored, that it may bear a still closer resemblance. For we both are, and know that we are, and delight in our being, and our knowledge of it. Moreover, in these three things no true-seeming illusion disturbs us; for we do not come into contact with these by some bodily sense, as we perceive the things outside of us—colors, *e.g.*, by seeing, sounds by hearing, smells by smelling, tastes by tasting, hard and soft objects by touching—of all which sensible objects it is the images resembling them, but not themselves which we perceive in the mind and hold in the memory, and which excite us to desire the objects. But, without any delusive representation of images or phantasms, I am most certain that I am, and that I know and delight in this. In respect of these truths, I am not at all afraid of the arguments of the Academicians, who say, What if you are deceived? For if I am deceived, I am. For he who is not, cannot be deceived; and if I am deceived, by this same token I am. And since I am if I am deceived, how am I deceived in believing that I am? for it is certain that I am if I am deceived. Since, therefore, I, the person deceived, should be, even if I were deceived, certainly I am not deceived in this knowledge that I am. And, consequently, neither am I deceived in knowing that I know. For, as I know that I am, so I know this also, that I know. And when I love these two things, I add to them a certain third thing, namely, my love, which is of equal moment. For neither am I deceived in this, that I love, since in those things which I love I am not deceived; though even if these were false, it would still be true that I *loved* false things. For how could I justly be blamed and prohibited from loving false things, if it were false that I loved them? But, since they are true and real, who doubts that when they are loved, the love of them is itself true and real? Further, as there is no one who does not wish to be happy, so there is no one who does not wish to be. For how can he be happy, if he is nothing?

CHAPTER XXVII

OF EXISTENCE, AND KNOWLEDGE OF IT, AND THE LOVE OF BOTH

And truly the very fact of existing is by some natural spell so pleasant, that even the wretched are, for no other reason, unwilling to perish; and, when they feel that they are wretched, wish not that they themselves be annihilated, but that their misery be so. Take even those who, both in their own esteem, and in point of fact, are utterly wretched, and who are reckoned so, not only by wise men on account of their folly, but by those who count themselves blessed, and who think them wretched because they are poor and destitute—if any one should give these men an immortality, in which their misery should be deathless, and should offer the alternative, that if they shrank from existing eternally in the same misery they might be annihilated, and exist nowhere at all, nor in any condition, on the instant they would joyfully, nay exultantly, make election to exist always, even in such a condition, rather than not exist at all. The well-known feeling of such men witnesses to this. For when we see that they fear to die, and will rather live in such misfortune than end it by death, is it not obvious enough how nature shrinks from annihilation? And, accordingly, when they know that they must die, they seek, as a great boon, that this mercy be shown them, that they may a little longer live in the same misery, and delay to end it by death. And so they indubitably prove with what glad alacrity they would accept immortality, even though it secured to them endless destruction. What! do not even all irrational animals, to whom such calculations are unknown, from the huge dragons down to the least worms, all testify that they wish to exist, and therefore shun death by every movement in their power? Nay, the very plants and shrubs, which have no such life as enables them to shun destruction by movements we can see, do not they all seek in their own fashion to conserve their existence, by rooting themselves more and more deeply in the earth, that so they may draw nourishment, and throw out healthy branches towards the sky? In fine, even the lifeless bodies, which want not only sensation but seminal life, yet either seek the upper air or sink deep, or are balanced in an intermediate position, so that they may protect their existence in that situation where they can exist in most accordance with their nature.

And how much human nature loves the knowledge of its existence, and how it shrinks from being deceived, will be sufficiently understood from this fact, that every man prefers to grieve in a sane mind, rather than to be glad in madness. And this grand and wonderful instinct belongs to men alone of all animals; for, though some of them have keener eyesight than ourselves for this world's light, they cannot attain to that spiritual light with which our mind is somehow irradiated, so that we can form right judgments of all things. For our power to judge is proportioned to our acceptance of this light. Nevertheless, the irrational animals, though they have not knowledge, have certainly something resembling knowledge; whereas the other material things are said to be sensible, not because they have senses, but because they are the objects of our senses. Yet among plants, their nourishment and generation have some resemblance to sensible life. However, both these and all material things have their causes hidden in their nature; but their outward forms, which lend beauty to this visible structure of the world, are perceived by our senses, so that they seem to wish to compensate for their own want of knowledge by providing us with knowledge. But we perceive them by our bodily senses in such a way that we do not judge of them by these senses. For we have another and far superior sense, belonging to the inner man, by which we perceive what things are just, and what unjust— just by means of an intelligible idea, unjust by the want of it. This sense is aided in its functions neither by the eyesight, nor by the orifice of the ear, nor by the air-holes of the nostrils, nor by the palate's taste, nor by any bodily touch. By it I am assured both that I am, and that I know this; and these two I love, and in the same manner I am assured that I love them.

CHAPTER XXVIII

WHETHER WE OUGHT TO LOVE THE LOVE ITSELF WITH WHICH WE LOVE OUR EXISTENCE AND OUR KNOWLEDGE OF IT, THAT SO WE MAY MORE NEARLY RESEMBLE THE IMAGE OF THE DIVINE TRINITY

We have said as much as the scope of this work demands regarding these two things, to wit, our existence, and our knowledge of it, and how much they are loved by us, and how there is found even in the lower creatures a kind of likeness of these things, and yet with a difference. We have yet to speak of the love wherewith they are loved, to determine whether this love itself is loved. And doubtless it is; and this is the proof. Because in men who are justly loved, it is rather love itself that is loved; for he is not justly called a good man who knows what is good, but who loves it. Is it not then obvious that we love in ourselves the very love wherewith we love whatever good we love? For there is also a love wherewith we love that which we ought not to love; and this love is hated by him who loves that wherewith he loves what ought to be loved. For it is quite possible for both to exist in one man. And this co-existence is good for a man, to the end that this love which conduces to our living well may grow, and the other, which leads us to evil may decrease, until our whole life be perfectly healed and transmuted into good. For if we were beasts, we should love the fleshly and sensual life, and this would be our sufficient good; and when it was well with us in respect of it, we should seek nothing beyond. In like manner, if we were trees, we could not, indeed, in the strict sense of the word, love anything; nevertheless we should seem, as it were, to long for that by which we might become more abundantly and luxuriantly fruitful. If we were stones, or waves, or wind, or flame, or anything of that kind, we should want, indeed, both sensation and life, yet should possess a kind of attraction towards our own proper position and natural order. For the specific gravity of bodies is, as it were, their love, whether they are carried downwards by their weight, or upwards by their levity. For the body is borne by its gravity, as the spirit by love, whithersoever it is borne.[40] But we are men, created in the image of our Creator, whose eternity is true, and whose truth is eternal, whose love is eternal and true, and who Himself is the eternal, true, and adorable Trinity, without confusion, without separation; and, therefore, while, as we run over all the works which He has established, we may detect, as it were, His footprints, now more and now less distinct even in those things that are beneath us, since they could not so much as exist, or be bodied forth in any shape, or follow and observe any law, had they not been made by Him who supremely is, and is supremely good and supremely wise; yet in ourselves beholding His image, let us, like that younger son of the gospel, come to ourselves, and arise and return to Him from whom by our sin we had departed. There our being will have no death, our knowledge no error, our love no mishap. But now, though we are assured of our possession of these three things, not on the testimony of others, but by our own consciousness of their presence, and because we see them with our own most truthful interior vision, yet, as we cannot of ourselves know how long they are to continue, and whether they shall never cease to be, and what issue their good or bad use will lead to, we seek for others who can acquaint us of these things, if we have not already found them. Of the trustworthiness of these witnesses, there will, not now, but subsequently, be an opportunity of speaking. But in this book let us go on as we have begun, with God's help, to speak of the city of God, not in its state of pilgrimage and mortality, but as it exists ever immortal in the heavens—that is, let us speak of the holy angels who maintain their allegiance to God, who never were, nor ever shall be, apostate, between whom and those who forsook light eternal and became darkness, God, as we have already said, made at the first a separation.

CHAPTER XXIX

OF THE KNOWLEDGE BY WHICH THE HOLY ANGELS KNOW GOD IN HIS ESSENCE, AND BY WHICH THEY SEE THE CAUSES OF HIS WORKS IN THE ART OF THE WORKER, BEFORE THEY SEE THEM IN THE WORKS OF THE ARTIST

Those holy angels come to the knowledge of God not by audible words, but by the presence to their souls of immutable truth, i.e., of the only-begotten Word of God; and they know this Word Himself, and the Father,

[40] cf. *Confessions*, xiii. 9

and their Holy Spirit, and that this Trinity is indivisible, and that the three persons of it are one substance, and that there are not three Gods but one God; and this they so know, that it is better understood by them than we are by ourselves. Thus, too, they know the creature also, not in itself, but by this better way, in the wisdom of God, as if in the art by which it was created; and, consequently, they know themselves better in God than in themselves, though they have also this latter knowledge. For they were created, and are different from their Creator. In Him, therefore, they have, as it were, a noonday knowledge; in themselves, a twilight knowledge, according to our former explanations. For there is a great difference between knowing a thing in the design in conformity to which it was made, and knowing it in itself—e.g., the straightness of lines and correctness of figures is known in one way when mentally conceived, in another when described on paper; and justice is known in one way in the unchangeable truth, in another in the spirit of a just man. So is it with all other things—as, the firmament between the water above and below, which was called the heaven; the gathering of the waters beneath, and the laying bare of the dry land, and the production of plants and trees; the creation of sun, moon, and stars; and of the animals out of the waters, fowls, and fish, and monsters of the deep; and of everything that walks or creeps on the earth, and of man himself, who excels all that is on the earth—all these things are known in one way by the angels in the Word of God, in which they see the eternally abiding causes and reasons according to which they were made, and in another way in themselves: in the former, with a clearer knowledge; in the latter, with a knowledge dimmer, and rather of the bare works than of the design. Yet, when these works are referred to the praise and adoration of the Creator Himself, it is as if morning dawned in the minds of those who contemplate them.

CHAPTER XXX

OF THE PERFECTION OF THE NUMBER SIX, WHICH IS THE FIRST OF THE NUMBERS WHICH IS COMPOSED OF ITS OWN PARTS

These works are recorded to have been completed in six days (the same day being six times repeated), because six is a perfect number—not because God required a protracted time, as if He could not at once create all things, which then should mark the course of time by the movements proper to them, but because the perfection of the works was signified by the number six. For the number six is the first which is made up of its own parts, *i.e.*, of its sixth, third, and half, which are respectively one, two, and three, and which make a total of six. In this way of looking at a number, those are said to be its parts which exactly divide it, as a half, a third, a fourth, or a fraction with any denominator—*e.g.*, four is a part of nine, but not therefore an aliquot part; but one is, for it is the ninth part; and three is, for it is the third.

Yet these two parts, the ninth and the third, or one and three, are far from making its whole sum of nine. So again, in the number ten, four is a part, yet does not divide it; but one is an aliquot part, for it is a tenth; so it has a fifth, which is two; and a half, which is five. But these three parts, a tenth, a fifth, and a half, or one, two, and five, added together, do not make ten, but eight. Of the number twelve, again, the parts added together exceed the whole; for it has a twelfth, that is, one; a sixth, or two; a fourth, which is three; a third, which is four; and a half, which is six. But one, two, three, four, and six make up, not twelve, but more, viz., sixteen. So much I have thought fit to state for the sake of illustrating the perfection of the number six, which is, as I said, the first which is exactly made up of its own parts added together; and in this number of days God finished His work. And, therefore, we must not despise the science of numbers, which, in many passages of holy Scripture, is found to be of eminent service to the careful interpreter. Neither has it been without reason numbered among God's praises, "Thou hast ordered all things in number, and measure, and weight." [41]

CHAPTER XXXI

OF THE SEVENTH DAY, IN WHICH COMPLETENESS AND REPOSE ARE CELEBRATED

But, on the seventh day (*i.e.*, the same day repeated seven times, which number is also a perfect one, though for another reason), the rest of God is set forth, and then, too, we first hear of its being hallowed. So that God did not wish to hallow this day by His works, but by His rest, which has no evening, for it is not a creature; so that, being known in one way in the Word of God, and in another in itself, it should make a twofold knowledge, daylight and dusk (day and evening). Much more might be said about the perfection of the number seven, but this book is already too long, and I fear lest I should seem to catch at an opportunity of airing my little smattering of science more childishly than profitably. I must speak, therefore, in moderation and with dignity, lest, in too keenly following "number," I be accused of forgetting "weight" and "measure." Suffice it here to say, that three is the first whole number that is odd, four the first that is even, and of these two, seven is composed. On this account it is often put for all numbers together, as, "A just man falleth seven times, and riseth up again " [42] —that is, let him fall never so often, he will not perish (and this was meant to be understood not of sins, but of afflictions conducing to lowliness). Again, "Seven times a day will I praise Thee," [43] which elsewhere is expressed thus, "I will bless the Lord *at all times*." [44] And many such instances are found in the divine authorities, in which the number seven is, as I said, commonly

[41] Wisd. xi. 20   [42] Prov. xxiv. 16   [43] Ps. cxix. 164   [44] Ps. xxxiv. 1

used to express the whole, or the completeness of anything. And so the Holy Spirit, of whom the Lord says, "He will teach you all truth," [45] is signified by this number.[46] In it is the rest of God, the rest His people find in Him. For rest is in the whole, *i.e.*, in perfect completeness, while in the part there is labor. And thus we labor as long as we know in part; "but when that which is perfect is come, then that which is in part shall be done away." [47] It is even with toil we search into the Scriptures themselves. But the holy angels, towards whose society and assembly we sigh while in this our toilsome pilgrimage, as they already abide in their eternal home, so do they enjoy perfect facility of knowledge and felicity of rest. It is without difficulty that they help us; for their spiritual movements, pure and free, cost them no effort.

CHAPTER XXXII

OF THE OPINION THAT THE ANGELS WERE CREATED BEFORE THE WORLD

But if some one oppose our opinion, and say that the holy angels are not referred to when it is said, "Let there be light, and there was light;" if he suppose or teach that some material light, then first created, was meant, and that the angels were created, not only before the firmament dividing the waters and named "the heaven," but also before the time signified in the words, "In the beginning God created the heaven and the earth;" if he allege that this phrase, "In the beginning," does not mean that nothing was made before (for the angels were), but that God made all things by His Wisdom or Word, who is named in Scripture "the Beginning," as He Himself, in the gospel, replied to the Jews when they asked Him who He was, that He was the Beginning[48]—I will not contest the point, chiefly because it gives me the liveliest satisfaction to find the Trinity celebrated in the very beginning of the book of *Genesis*. For having said "In the Beginning God created the heaven and the earth," meaning that the Father made them in the Son (as the psalm testifies where it says, "How manifold are Thy works, O Lord! in Wisdom hast Thou made them all" [49]), a little afterwards mention is fitly made of the Holy Spirit also. For, when it had been told us what kind of earth God created at first, or what the mass or matter was which God, under the name of "heaven and earth," had provided for the construction of the world, as is told in the additional words, "And the earth was without form, and void; and darkness was upon the face of the deep," then, for the sake of completing the mention of the Trinity, it is immediately added, "And the Spirit of God moved upon the face of the waters." Let each one, then, take it as he pleases; for it is so profound a passage, that it

[45] John xvi. 13   [46] Isa. xi. 2   [47] 1 Cor. xiii. 10   [48] John viii. 25   [49] Ps. civ. 24

may well suggest, for the exercise of the reader's tact, many opinions, and none of them widely departing from the rule of faith. At the same time, let none doubt that the holy angels in their heavenly abodes are, though not, indeed, co-eternal with God, yet secure and certain of eternal and true felicity. To their company the Lord teaches that His little ones belong; and not only says, "They shall be equal to the angels of God," [50] but shows, too, what blessed contemplation the angels themselves enjoy, saying, "Take heed that ye despise not one of these little ones: for I say unto you, that in heaven their angels do always behold the face of my Father which is in heaven." [51]

CHAPTER XXXIII

OF THE TWO DIFFERENT AND DISSIMILAR COMMUNITIES OF ANGELS, WHICH ARE NOT INAPPROPRIATELY SIGNIFIED BY THE NAMES LIGHT AND DARKNESS

That certain angels sinned, and were thrust down to the lowest parts of this world, where they are, as it were, incarcerated till their final damnation in the day of judgment, the Apostle Peter very plainly declares, when he says that "God spared not the angels that sinned, but cast them down to hell, and delivered them into chains of darkness to be reserved into judgment." [52] Who, then, can doubt that God, either in foreknowledge or in act, separated between these and the rest? And who will dispute that the rest are justly called "light"? For even we who are yet living by faith, hoping only and not yet enjoying equality with them, are already called "light" by the apostle: "For ye were sometimes darkness, but now are ye light in the Lord." [53] But as for these apostate angels, all who understand or believe them to be worse than unbelieving men are well aware that they are called "darkness." Wherefore, though light and darkness are to be taken in their literal signification in these passages of *Genesis* in which it is said, "God said, Let there be light, and there was light," and "God divided the light from the darkness," yet, for our part, we understand these two societies of angels —the one enjoying God, the other swelling with pride; the one to whom it is said, "Praise ye Him, all His angels," [54] the other whose prince says, "All these things will I give Thee if Thou wilt fall down and worship me;" [55] the one blazing with the holy love of God, the other reeking with the unclean lust of self-advancement. And since, as it is written, "God resisteth the proud, but giveth grace unto the humble," [56] we may say, the one dwelling in the heaven of heavens, the other cast thence, and raging through the lower regions of the air; the one tranquil in the brightness of piety, the other tempest-tossed with beclouding desires; the one, at God's pleasure, tenderly succoring, justly avenging—the other, set on by its own pride, boiling with

[50] Matt. xxii. 30   [51] Matt. xviii. 10   [52] 2 Peter ii. 4   [53] Eph. v. 8   [54] Ps. cxlvii. 2   [55] Matt. iv. 9   [56] Jas. iv. 6

the lust of subduing and hurting; the one the minister of God's goodness to the utmost of their good pleasure, the other held in by God's power from doing the harm it would; the former laughing at the latter when it does good unwillingly by its persecutions, the latter envying the former when it gathers in its pilgrims. These two angelic communities, then, dissimilar and contrary to one another, the one both by nature good and by will upright, the other also good by nature but by will depraved, as they are exhibited in other and more explicit passages of holy writ, so I think they are spoken of in this book of *Genesis* under the names of light and darkness; and even if the author perhaps had a different meaning, yet our discussion of the obscure language has not been wasted time; for, though we have been unable to discover his meaning, yet we have adhered to the rule of faith, which is sufficiently ascertained by the faithful from other passages of equal authority. For, though it is the material works of God which are here spoken of, they have certainly a resemblance to the spiritual, so that Paul can say, "Ye are all the children of light, and the children of the day: we are not of the night, nor of darkness." [57] If, on the other hand, the author of *Genesis* saw in the words what we see, then our discussion reaches this more satisfactory conclusion, that the man of God, so eminently and divinely wise, or rather, that the Spirit of God who by him recorded God's works which were finished on the sixth day, may be supposed not to have omitted all mention of the angels whether he included them in the words "in the beginning," because He made them first, or, which seems most likely, because He made them in the only-begotten Word. And, under these names heaven and earth, the whole creation is signified, either as divided into spiritual and material, which seems the more likely, or into the two great parts of the world in which all created things are contained, so that, first of all, the creation is presented in sum, and then its parts are enumerated according to the mystic number of the days.

CHAPTER XXXIV

OF THE IDEA THAT THE ANGELS WERE MEANT WHERE THE SEPARATION OF THE WATERS BY THE FIRMAMENT IS SPOKEN OF, AND OF THAT OTHER IDEA THAT THE WATERS WERE NOT CREATED

Some, however, have supposed that the angelic hosts are somehow referred to under the name of waters, and that this is what is meant by "Let there be a firmament in the midst of the waters:" [58] that the waters above should be understood of the angels, and those below either of the visible waters, or of the multitude of bad angels, or of the nations of men. If this be so, then it does not here appear when the angels were created, but when they were separated. Though there have not been wanting men foolish and wicked enough to deny that the waters were made by God, because it is

---

[57] I Thess. v. 5   [58] Gen. i. 6

nowhere written, "God said, Let there be waters." With equal folly they might say the same of the earth, for nowhere do we read, "God said, Let the earth be." But, say they, it is written, "In the beginning God created the heaven and the earth." Yes, and there the water is meant, for both are included in one word. For "the sea is His," as the psalm says, "and He made it; and His hands formed the dry land." [59] But those who would understand the angels by the waters above the skies have a difficulty about the specific gravity of the elements, and fear that the waters, owing to their fluidity and weight, could not be set in the upper parts of the world. So that, if they were to construct a man upon their own principles, they would not put in his head any moist humors, or "phlegm" as the Greeks call it, and which acts the part of water among the elements of our body. But, in God's handiwork, the head is the seat of the phlegm, and surely most fitly; and yet, according to their supposition, so absurdly that if we were not aware of the fact, and were informed by this same record that God had put a moist and cold and therefore heavy humor in the uppermost part of man's body, these world-weighers would refuse belief. And if they were confronted with the authority of Scripture, they would maintain that something else must be meant by the words. But, were we to investigate and discover all the details which are written in this divine book regarding the creation of the world, we should have much to say, and should widely digress from the proposed aim of this work. Since, then, we have now said what seemed needful regarding these two diverse and contrary communities of angels, in which the origin of the two human communities (of which we intend to speak anon) is also found, let us at once bring this book also to a conclusion.

[59] Ps. xcv. 5

BOOK TWELVE

ARGUMENT

Augustine first institutes two inquiries regarding the angels; namely, whence is there in some a good, and in others an evil will? and, what is the reason of the blessedness of the good, and the misery of the evil? Afterwards he treats of the creation of man, and teaches that he is not from eternity, but was created, and by none other than God.

CHAPTER I

THAT THE NATURE OF THE ANGELS, BOTH GOOD AND BAD, IS ONE AND THE SAME

IT HAS already, in the preceding book, been shown how the two cities originated among the angels. Before I speak of the creation of man, and show how the cities took their rise, so far as regards the race of rational mortals, I see that I must first, so far as I can, adduce what may demonstrate that it is not incongruous and unsuitable to speak of a society composed of angels and men together; so that there are not four cities or societies—two, namely, of angels, and as many of men—but rather two in all, one composed of the good, the other of the wicked, angels or men indifferently.

That the contrary propensities in good and bad angels have arisen, not from a difference in their nature and origin, since God, the good Author and Creator of all essences, created them both, but from a difference in their wills and desires, it is impossible to doubt. While some steadfastly continued in that which was the common good of all, namely, in God Himself, and in His eternity, truth, and love; others, being enamored rather of their own power, as if they could be their own good, lapsed to this private good of their own, from that higher and beatific good which was common to all, and, bartering the lofty dignity of eternity for the inflation of pride, the most assured verity for the slyness of vanity, uniting love for factious partisanship, they became proud, deceived, envious. The cause, therefore, of the blessedness of the good is adherence to God. And so the cause of the others' misery will be found in the contrary, that is, in their not adhering to God. Wherefore, if when the question is asked, why are the former blessed, it is rightly answered, because they adhere to God; and when it is asked, why are the latter miserable, it is rightly answered, because they do not adhere to God—then there is no other good for the rational or intellectual creature save God only. Thus, though it is not every creature that can be blessed

178

(for beasts, trees, stones, and things of that kind have not this capacity) yet that creature which has the capacity cannot be blessed of itself, since it is created out of nothing, but only by Him by whom it has been created. For it is blessed by the possession of that whose loss makes it miserable. He, then, who is blessed not in another, but in himself, cannot be miserable, because he cannot lose himself.

Accordingly we say that there is no unchangeable good but the one, true, blessed God; that the things which He made are indeed good because from Him, yet mutable because made not out of Him, but out of nothing. Although, therefore, they are not the supreme good, for God is a greater good, yet those mutable things which can adhere to the immutable good, and so be blessed, are very good; for so completely is He their good, that without Him they cannot but be wretched. And the other created things in the universe are not better on this account, that they cannot be miserable. For no one would say that the other members of the body are superior to the eyes, because they cannot be blind. But as the sentient nature, even when it feels pain, is superior to the stony, which can feel none, so the rational nature, even when wretched, is more excellent than that which lacks reason or feeling, and can therefore experience no misery. And since this is so, then in this nature which has been created so excellent, that though it be mutable itself, it can yet secure its blessedness by adhering to the immutable good, the supreme God; and since it is not satisfied unless it be perfectly blessed, and cannot be thus blessed save in God—in this nature, I say, not to adhere to God, is manifestly a fault. Now every fault injures the nature, and is consequently contrary to the nature. The creature, therefore, which cleaves to God, differs from those who do not, not by nature, but by fault; and yet by this very fault the nature itself is proved to be very noble and admirable. For that nature is certainly praised, the fault of which is justly blamed. For we justly blame the fault because it mars the praiseworthy nature. As, then, when we say that blindness is a defect of the eyes, we prove that sight belongs to the nature of the eyes; and when we say that deafness is a defect of the ears, hearing is thereby proved to belong to their nature—so, when we say that it is a fault of the angelic creature that it does not cleave to God, we hereby most plainly declare that it pertained to its nature to cleave to God. And who can worthily conceive or express how great a glory that is, to cleave to God, so as to live to Him, to draw wisdom from Him, to delight in Him, and to enjoy this so great good, without death, error, or grief? And thus, since every vice is an injury of the nature, that very vice of the wicked angels, their departure from God, is sufficient proof that God created their nature so good, that it is an injury to it not to be with God.

CHAPTER II

THAT THERE IS NO ENTITY[1] CONTRARY TO THE DIVINE, BECAUSE
NONENTITY SEEMS TO BE THAT WHICH IS WHOLLY OPPOSITE
TO HIM WHO SUPREMELY AND ALWAYS IS

This may be enough to prevent any one from supposing, when we speak of the apostate angels, that they could have another nature, derived, as it were, from some different origin, and not from God. From the great impiety of this error we shall disentangle ourselves the more readily and easily, the more distinctly we understand that which God spoke by the angel when He sent Moses to the children of Israel: "I am that I am." [2] For since God is the supreme existence, that is to say, supremely is, and is therefore unchangeable, the things that He made He empowered to be, but not to be supremely like Himself. To some He communicated a more ample, to others a more limited existence, and thus arranged the natures of beings in ranks. For as from *sapere* comes *sapientia*, so from *esse* comes *essentia*—a new word indeed, which the old Latin writers did not use, but which is naturalized in our day, that our language may not want an equivalent for the Greek οὐσία. For this is expressed word for word by *essentia*. Consequently, to that nature which supremely is, and which created all else that exists, no nature is contrary save that which does not exist. For nonentity is the contrary of that which is. And thus there is no being contrary to God, the Supreme Being, and Author of all beings whatsoever.

CHAPTER III

THAT THE ENEMIES OF GOD ARE SO, NOT BY NATURE, BUT BY WILL,
WHICH, AS IT INJURES THEM, INJURES A GOOD NATURE; FOR IF
VICE DOES NOT INJURE, IT IS NOT VICE

In Scripture they are called God's enemies who oppose His rule, not by nature, but by vice; having no power to hurt Him, but only themselves. For they are His enemies, not through their power to hurt, but by their will to oppose Him. For God is unchangeable, and wholly proof against injury. Therefore the vice which makes those who are called His enemies resist Him, is an evil not to God, but to themselves. And to them it is an evil, solely because it corrupts the good of their nature. It is not nature, therefore, but vice, which is contrary to God. For that which is evil is contrary to the good. And who will deny that God is the supreme good? Vice, therefore, is contrary to God, as evil to good. Further, the nature it vitiates is a good, and therefore to this good also it is contrary. But while it is contrary to God only as evil to good, it is contrary to the nature it vitiates, both as evil and

[1] *Essentia* [2] Ex. iii. 14

as hurtful. For to God no evils are hurtful; but only to natures mutable and corruptible, though, by the testimony of the vices themselves, originally good. For were they not good, vices could not hurt them. For how do they hurt them but by depriving them of integrity, beauty, welfare, virtue, and, in short, whatever natural good vice is wont to diminish or destroy? But if there be no good to take away, then no injury can be done, and consequently there can be no vice. For it is impossible that there should be a harmless vice. Whence we gather, that though vice cannot injure the unchangeable good, it can injure nothing but good; because it does not exist where it does not injure. This, then, may be thus formulated: Vice cannot be in the highest good, and cannot be but in some good. Things solely good, therefore, can in some circumstances exist; things solely evil, never; for even those natures which are vitiated by an evil will, so far indeed as they are vitiated, are evil, but in so far as they are natures they are good. And when a vitiated nature is punished, besides the good it has in being a nature, it has this also, that it is not unpunished.[3] For this is just, and certainly everything just is a good. For no one is punished for natural, but for voluntary vices. For even the vice which by the force of habit and long continuance has become a second nature, had its origin in the will. For at present we are speaking of the vices of the nature, which has a mental capacity for that enlightenment which discriminates between what is just and what is unjust.

CHAPTER IV

OF THE NATURE OF IRRATIONAL AND LIFELESS CREATURES, WHICH IN THEIR OWN KIND AND ORDER DO NOT MAR THE BEAUTY OF THE UNIVERSE

But it is ridiculous to condemn the faults of beasts and trees, and other such mortal and mutable things as are void of intelligence, sensation, or life, even though these faults should destroy their corruptible nature; for these creatures received, at their Creator's will, an existence fitting them, by passing away and giving place to others, to secure that lowest form of beauty, the beauty of seasons, which in its own place is a requisite part of this world. For things earthly were neither to be made equal to things heavenly, nor were they, though inferior, to be quite omitted from the universe. Since, then, in those situations where such things are appropriate, some perish to make way for others that are born in their room, and the less succumb to the greater, and the things that are overcome are transformed into the quality of those that have the mastery, this is the appointed order of things transitory. Of this order the beauty does not strike us, because by our mortal frailty we are so involved in a part of it, that we cannot perceive the whole,

[3] With this may be compared the argument of Socrates in the *Gorgias,* in which it is shown that to escape punishment is worse than to suffer it, and that the greatest of evils is to do wrong and not be chastised.

in which these fragments that offend us are harmonized with the most accurate fitness and beauty. And therefore, where we are not so well able to perceive the wisdom of the Creator, we are very properly enjoined to believe it, lest in the vanity of human rashness we presume to find any fault with the work of so great an Artificer. At the same time, if we attentively consider even these faults of earthly things, which are neither voluntary nor penal, they seem to illustrate the excellence of the natures themselves, which are all originated and created by God; for it is that which pleases us in this nature which we are displeased to see removed by the fault—unless even the natures themselves displease men, as often happens when they become hurtful to them, and then men estimate them not by their nature, but by their utility; as in the case of those animals whose swarms scourged the pride of the Egyptians. But in this way of estimating, they may find fault with the sun itself; for certain criminals or debtors are sentenced by the judges to be set in the sun. Therefore it is not with respect to our convenience or discomfort, but with respect to their own nature, that the creatures are glorifying to their Artificer. Thus even the nature of the eternal fire, penal though it be to the condemned sinners, is most assuredly worthy of praise. For what is more beautiful than fire flaming, blazing, and shining? What more useful than fire for warming, restoring, cooking, though nothing is more destructive than fire burning and consuming? The same thing, then, when applied in one way, is destructive, but when applied suitably, is most beneficial. For who can find words to tell its uses throughout the whole world? We must not listen, then, to those who praise the light of fire but find fault with its heat, judging it not by its nature, but by their convenience or discomfort. For they wish to see, but not to be burnt. But they forget that this very light which is so pleasant to them, disagrees with and hurts weak eyes; and in that heat which is disagreeable to them, some animals find the most suitable conditions of a healthy life.

CHAPTER V

THAT IN ALL NATURES, OF EVERY KIND AND RANK, GOD IS GLORIFIED

All natures, then, inasmuch as they are, and have therefore a rank and species of their own, and a kind of internal harmony, are certainly good. And when they are in the places assigned to them by the order of their nature, they preserve such being as they have received. And those things which have not received everlasting being, are altered for better or for worse, so as to suit the wants and motions of those things to which the Creator's law has made them subservient; and thus they tend in the divine providence to that end which is embraced in the general scheme of the government of the universe. So that, though the corruption of transitory and perishable things brings them to utter destruction, it does not prevent their producing that which was designed to be their result. And this being so, God, who supremely is, and who therefore created every being which has not supreme existence (for that which was made of nothing could not be equal to Him, and indeed could not be at all had He not made it), is not to be found fault with on account of the creature's faults, but is to be praised in view of the natures He has made.

CHAPTER VI

WHAT THE CAUSE OF THE BLESSEDNESS OF THE GOOD ANGELS IS, AND WHAT THE CAUSE OF THE MISERY OF THE WICKED

Thus the true cause of the blessedness of the good angels is found to be this, that they cleave to Him who supremely is. And if we ask the cause of the misery of the bad, it occurs to us, and not unreasonably, that they are miserable because they have forsaken Him who supremely is, and have turned to themselves who have no such essence. And this vice, what else is it called than pride? For "pride is the beginning of sin." [4] They were unwilling, then, to preserve their strength for God; and as adherence to God was the condition of their enjoying an ampler being, they diminished it by preferring themselves to Him. This was the first defect, and the first impoverishment, and the first flaw of their nature, which was created, not indeed supremely existent, but finding its blessedness in the enjoyment of the Supreme Being; while by abandoning Him it should become, not indeed no nature at all, but a nature with a less ample existence, and therefore wretched.

If the further question be asked, What was the efficient cause of their evil will? there is none. For what is it which makes the will bad, when it is the will itself which makes the action bad? And consequently the bad will is the cause of the bad action, but nothing is the efficient cause of the bad will. For if anything is the cause, this thing either has or has not a will. If it has, the will is either good or bad. If good, who is so left to himself as to say that a good will makes a will bad? For in this case a good will would be the cause of sin; a most absurd supposition. On the other hand, if this hypothetical thing has a bad will, I wish to know what made it so; and that we may not go on forever, I ask at once, what made the *first* evil will bad? For that is not the first which was itself corrupted by an evil will, but that is the first which was made evil by no other will. For if it were preceded by that which made it evil, that will was first which made the other evil. But if it is replied, "Nothing made it evil; it always was evil," I ask if it has been existing in some nature. For if not, then it did not exist at all; and if it did exist in some nature, then it vitiated and corrupted it, and injured it, and consequently deprived it of good. And therefore the evil will could not exist

[4] Eccles. x. 13

in an evil nature, but in a nature at once good and mutable, which this vice could injure. For if it did no injury, it was no vice; and consequently the will in which it was, could not be called evil. But if it did injury, it did it by taking away or diminishing good. And therefore there could not be from eternity, as was suggested, an evil will in that thing in which there had been previously a natural good, which the evil will was able to diminish by corrupting it. If, then, it was not from eternity, who, I ask, made it? The only thing that can be suggested in reply is, that something which itself had no will, made the will evil. I ask, then, whether this thing was superior, inferior, or equal to it? If superior, then it is better. How, then, has it no will, and not rather a good will? The same reasoning applies if it was equal; for so long as two things have equally a good will, the one cannot produce in the other an evil will. Then remains the supposition that that which corrupted the will of the angelic nature which first sinned, was itself an inferior thing without a will. But that thing, be it of the lowest and most earthly kind, is certainly itself good, since it is a nature and being, with a form and rank of its own in its own kind and order. How, then, can a good thing be the efficient cause of an evil will? How, I say, can good be the cause of evil? For when the will abandons what is above itself, and turns to what is lower, it becomes evil—not because that is evil to which it turns, but because the turning itself is wicked. Therefore it is not an inferior thing which has made the will evil, but it is itself which has become so by wickedly and inordinately desiring an inferior thing. For if two men, alike in physical and moral constitution, see the same corporal beauty, and one of them is excited by the sight to desire an illicit enjoyment while the other steadfastly maintains a modest restraint of his will, what do we suppose brings it about, that there is an evil will in the one and not in the other? What produces it in the man in whom it exists? Not the bodily beauty, for that was presented equally to the gaze of both, and yet did not produce in both an evil will. Did the flesh of the one cause the desire as he looked? But why did not the flesh of the other? Or was it the disposition? But why not the disposition of both? For we are supposing that both were of a like temperament of body and soul. Must we, then, say that the one was tempted by a secret suggestion of the evil spirit? As if it was not by his own will that he consented to this suggestion and to any inducement whatever! This consent, then, this evil will which he presented to the evil suasive influence—what was the cause of it we ask? For, not to delay on such a difficulty as this, if both are tempted equally and one yields and consents to the temptation while the other remains unmoved by it, what other account can we give of the matter than this, that the one is willing, the other unwilling, to fall away from chastity? And what causes this but their own wills, in cases at least such as we are supposing, where the temperament is identical? The same beauty was equally obvious to the eyes of both; the same secret temptation pressed on both with equal violence. However minutely we examine the case, therefore we can discern nothing which caused the will of the one to be evil. For if we say that the man himself made his will evil, what was the man himself before his will was evil but a good nature created by God, the unchangeable good? Here are two men who, before the temptation, were alike in body and soul, and of whom one yielded to the tempter who persuaded him, while the other could not be persuaded to desire that lovely body which was equally before the eyes of both. Shall we say of the successfully tempted man that he corrupted his own will, since he was certainly good before his will became bad? Then, why did he do so? Was it because his will was a nature, or because it was made of nothing? We shall find that the latter is the case. For if a nature is the cause of an evil will, what else can we say than that evil arises from good or that good is the cause of evil? And how can it come to pass that a nature, good though mutable, should produce any evil—that is to say, should make the will itself wicked?

CHAPTER VII

THAT WE OUGHT NOT TO EXPECT TO FIND ANY EFFICIENT CAUSE OF THE EVIL WILL

Let no one, therefore, look for an efficient cause of the evil will; for it is not efficient, but deficient, as the will itself is not an effecting of something, but a defect. For defection from that which supremely is, to that which has less of being—this is to begin to have an evil will. Now, to seek to discover the causes of these defections—causes, as I have said, not efficient, but deficient—is as if some one sought to see darkness, or hear silence. Yet both of these are known by us, and the former by means only of the eye, the latter only by the ear; but not by their positive actuality, but by their want of it. Let no one, then seek to know from me what I know that I do not know; unless he perhaps wishes to learn to be ignorant of that of which all we know is, that it cannot be known. For those things which are known not by their actuality, but by their want of it, are known, if our expression may be allowed and understood, by not knowing them, that by knowing them they may be not known. For when the eyesight surveys objects that strike the sense, it nowhere sees darkness but where it begins not to see. And so no other sense but the ear can perceive silence, and yet it is only perceived by not hearing. Thus, too, our mind perceives intelligible forms by understanding them; but when they are deficient, it knows them by not knowing them; for who can understand defects? [5]

[5] Ps. xix. 12

CHAPTER VIII

OF THE MISDIRECTED LOVE WHEREBY THE WILL FELL AWAY FROM THE IMMUTABLE TO THE MUTABLE GOOD

This I do know, that the nature of God can never, nowhere, nowise be defective, and that natures made of nothing can. These latter, however, the more being they have, and the more good they do (for then they do something positive), the more they have efficient causes; but in so far as they are defective in being, and consequently do evil (for then what is their work but vanity?) they have deficient causes. And I know likewise, that the will could not become evil, were it unwilling to become so; and therefore its failings are justly punished, being not necessary, but voluntary. For its defections are not to evil things, but are themselves evil; that is to say, are not towards things that are naturally and in themselves evil, but the defection of the will is evil, because it is contrary to the order of nature, and an abandonment of that which has supreme being for that which has less. For avarice is not a fault inherent in gold, but in the man who inordinately loves gold, to the detriment of justice, which ought to be held in incomparably higher regard than gold. Neither is luxury the fault of lovely and charming objects, but of the heart that inordinately loves sensual pleasures, to the neglect of temperance, which attaches us to objects more lovely in their spirituality, and more delectable by their incorruptibility. Nor yet is boasting the fault of human praise, but of the soul that is inordinately fond of the applause of men, and that makes light of the voice of conscience. Pride, too, is not the fault of him who delegates power, nor of power itself, but of the soul that is inordinately enamored of its own power, and despises the more just dominion of a higher authority. Consequently he who inordinately loves the good which any nature possesses, even though he obtain it, himself becomes evil in the good, and wretched because deprived of a greater good.

CHAPTER IX

WHETHER THE ANGELS, BESIDES RECEIVING FROM GOD THEIR NATURE, RECEIVED FROM HIM ALSO THEIR GOOD WILL BY THE HOLY SPIRIT IMBUING THEM WITH LOVE

There is, then, no natural efficient cause, or, if I may be allowed the expression, no essential cause, of the evil will, since itself is the origin of evil in mutable spirits, by which the good of their nature is diminished and corrupted; and the will is made evil by nothing else than defection from God—a defection of which the cause, too, is certainly deficient. But as to the good will, if we should say that there is no efficient cause of it, we must beware of giving currency to the opinion that the good will of the good angels is not created, but is co-eternal with God. For if they themselves are created, how can we say that their good will was eternal? But if created, was it created along with themselves, or did they exist for a time without it? If along with themselves, then doubtless it was created by Him who created them, and, as soon as ever they were created, they attached themselves to Him who created them, with the love He created in them. And they are separated from the society of the rest, because they have continued in the same good will; while the others have fallen away to another will, which is an evil one, by the very fact of its being a falling away from the good; from which, we may add, they would not have fallen away had they been unwilling to do so. But if the good angels existed for a time without a good will, and produced it in themselves without God's interference, then it follows that they made themselves better than He made them. Away with such a thought! For without a good will, what were they but evil? Or if they were not evil, because they had not an evil will any more than a good one (for they had not fallen away from that which as yet they had not begun to enjoy), certainly they were not the same, not so good, as when they came to have a good will. Or if they could not make themselves better than they were made by Him who is surpassed by none in His work, then certainly, without His helpful operation, they could not come to possess that good will which made them better. And though their good will effected that they did not turn to themselves, who had a more stinted existence, but to Him who supremely is, and that, being united to Him, their own being was enlarged, and they lived a wise and blessed life by His communications to them, what does this prove but that the will, however good it might be, would have continued helplessly only to desire Him, had not He who had made their nature out of nothing, and yet capable of enjoying Him, first stimulated it to desire Him, and then filled it with Himself, and so made it better?

Besides, this too has to be inquired into, whether, if the good angels made their own will good, they did so with or without will? If without, then it was not their doing. If with, was the will good or bad? If bad, how could a bad will give birth to a good one? If good, then already they had a good will. And who made this will, which already they had, but He who created them with a good will, or with that chaste love by which they cleaved to Him, in one and the same act creating their nature, and endowing it with grace? And thus we are driven to believe that the holy angels never existed without a good will or the love of God. But the angels who, though created good, are yet evil now, became so by their own will. And this will was not made evil by their good nature, unless by its voluntary defection from good; for good is not the cause of evil, but a defection from good is. These angels, therefore, either received less of the grace of the divine love than those who persevered in the same; or if both were created equally good, then, while the one fell by their evil will, the others were more abundantly assisted, and attained to that pitch of blessedness at which they became certain they should never fall from it—as we have already shown in the preceding book.[6] We must therefore acknowledge, with the praise due to the Creator, that not only of holy men, but also of the holy angels, it can be said that "the love of God is shed abroad in their hearts by the Holy Ghost, which is given unto them."[7] And that not only of men, but primarily and principally of angels it is true, as it is written, "It is good to draw near to God."[8] And those who have this good in common, have, both with Him to whom they draw near, and with one another, a holy fellowship, and form one city of God—His living sacrifice, and His living temple. And I see that, as I have now spoken of the rise of this city among the angels, it is time to speak of the origin of that part of it which is hereafter to be united to the immortal angels, and which at present is being gathered from among mortal men, and is either sojourning on earth, or, in the persons of those who have passed through death, is resting in the secret receptacles and abodes of disembodied spirits. For from one man, whom God created as the first, the whole human race descended, according to the faith of Holy Scripture, which deservedly is of wonderful authority among all nations throughout the world; since, among its other true statements, it predicted, by its divine foresight, that all nations would give credit to it.

CHAPTER X

OF THE FALSENESS OF THE HISTORY WHICH ALLOTS MANY THOUSAND YEARS TO THE WORLD'S PAST

Let us, then, omit the conjectures of men who know not what they say, when they speak of the nature and origin of the human race. For some hold the same opinion regarding men that they hold regarding the world itself, that they have always been. Thus Apuleius says when he is describing our race, "Individually they are mortal, but collectively, and as a race, they are immortal."[9] And when they are asked, how, if the human race has always been, they vindicate the truth of their history, which narrates who were the inventors, and what they invented, and who first instituted the liberal studies and the other arts, and who first inhabited this or that region, and this or that island? they reply,[10] that most, if not all lands, were so desolated at intervals by fire and flood, that men were greatly reduced in numbers, and from these, again, the population was restored to its former numbers, and that thus there was at intervals a new beginning made, and though those things which had been interrupted and checked by the severe devastations were only renewed, yet they seemed to be originated then; but that man

[6] C. 13   [7] Rom. v. 5   [8] Ps. lxxiii. 28   [9] *De Deo Socrates*
[10] Augustine no doubt refers to the interesting account given by Critias, near the beginning of the *Timaeus*, of the conversation of Solon with the Egyptian priests.

could not exist at all save as produced by man. But they say what they think, not what they know.

They are deceived, too, by those highly mendacious documents which profess to give the history of many thousand years, though, reckoning by the sacred writings, we find that not 6000 years have yet passed. And, not to spend many words in exposing the baselessness of these documents, in which so many thousands of years are accounted for, nor in proving that their authorities are totally inadequate, let me cite only that letter which Alexander the Great wrote to his mother Olympias, giving her the narrative he had from an Egyptian priest, which he had extracted from their sacred archives, and which gave an account of kingdoms mentioned also by the Greek historians. In this letter of Alexander's a term of upwards of 5000 years is assigned to the kingdom of Assyria; while in the Greek history only 1300 years are reckoned from the reign of Bel himself, whom both Greek and Egyptian agree in counting the first king of Assyria. Then to the empire of the Persians and Macedonians this Egyptian assigned more than 8000 years, counting to the time of Alexander, to whom he was speaking; while among the Greeks, 485 years are assigned to the Macedonians down to the death of Alexander, and to the Persians 233 years, reckoning to the termination of his conquests. Thus these give a much smaller number of years than the Egyptians; and indeed, though multiplied three times, the Greek chronology would still be shorter. For the Egyptians are said to have formerly reckoned only four months to their year; so that one year, according to the fuller and truer computation now in use among them as well as among ourselves, would comprehend three of their old years. But not even thus, as I said, does the Greek history correspond with the Egyptian in its chronology. And therefore the former must receive the greater credit, because it does not exceed the true account of the duration of the world as it is given by our documents, which are truly sacred. Further, if this letter of Alexander, which has become so famous, differs widely in this matter of chronology from the probable credible account, how much less can we believe these documents which, though full of fabulous and fictitious antiquities, they would fain oppose to the authority of our well-known and divine books, which predicted that the whole world would believe them, and which the whole world accordingly has believed; which proved, too, that it had truly narrated past events by its prediction of future events, which have so exactly come to pass!

CHAPTER XI

OF THOSE WHO SUPPOSE THAT THIS WORLD INDEED IS NOT ETERNAL,
BUT THAT EITHER THERE ARE NUMBERLESS WORLDS, OR THAT
ONE AND THE SAME WORLD IS PERPETUALLY RESOLVED INTO
ITS ELEMENTS, AND RENEWED AT THE CONCLUSION
OF FIXED CYCLES

There are some, again, who, though they do not suppose that this world
is eternal, are of opinion either that this is not the only world, but that there
are numberless worlds, or that indeed it is the only one, but that it dies, and
is born again at fixed intervals, and this times without number;[11] but they
must acknowledge that the human race existed before there were other men
to beget them. For they cannot suppose that, if the whole world perish,
some men would be left alive in the world, as they might survive in floods
and conflagrations, which those other speculators suppose to be partial, and
from which they can therefore reasonably argue that a few men survived
whose posterity would renew the population; but as they believe that the
world itself is renewed out of its own material, so they must believe that out
of its elements the human race was produced, and then that the progeny
of mortals sprang like that of other animals from their parents.

CHAPTER XII

HOW THESE PERSONS ARE TO BE ANSWERED, WHO FIND FAULT
WITH THE CREATION OF MAN ON THE SCORE OF ITS RECENT
DATE

As to those who are always asking why man was not created during these
countless ages of the infinitely extended past, and came into being so lately
that, according to Scripture, less than 6000 years have elapsed since He
began to be, I would reply to them regarding the creation of man, just as I
replied regarding the origin of the world to those who will not believe that
it is not eternal, but had a beginning, which even Plato himself most plainly
declares, though some think his statement was not consistent with his real
opinion. If it offends them that the time that has elapsed since the creation
of man is so short, and his years so few according to our authorities, let them
take this into consideration, that nothing that has a limit is long, and that
all the ages of time being finite, are very little, or indeed nothing at all, when
compared to the interminable eternity. Consequently, if there had elapsed
since the creation of man, I do not say five or six, but even sixty or six hundred thousand years, or sixty times as many, or six hundred or six hundred

[11] The former opinion was held by Democritus and his disciple Epicurus; the latter
by Heraclitus, who supposed that "God amused Himself" by thus renewing worlds.

thousand times as many, or this sum multiplied until it could no longer be expressed in numbers, the same question could still be put, Why was he not made before? For the past and boundless eternity during which God abstained from creating man is so great, that, compare it with what vast and untold number of ages you please, so long as there is a definite conclusion of this term of time, it is not even as if you compared the minutest drop of water with the ocean that everywhere flows around the globe. For of these two, one indeed is very small, the other incomparably vast, yet both are finite; but that space of time which starts from some beginning, and is limited by some termination, be it of what extent it may, if you compare it with that which has no beginning, I know not whether to say we should count it the very minutest thing, or nothing at all. For, take this limited time, and deduct from the end of it, one by one, the briefest moments (as you might take day by day from a man's life, beginning at the day in which he now lives, back to that of his birth), and though the number of moments you must subtract in this backward movement be so great that no word can express it, yet this subtraction will sometime carry you to the beginning. But if you take away from a time which has no beginning, I do not say brief moments one by one, nor yet hours, or days, or months, or years even in quantities, but terms of years so vast that they cannot be named by the most skillful arithmeticians—take away terms of years as vast as that which we have supposed to be gradually consumed by the deduction of moments —and take them away not once and again repeatedly, but always, and what do you effect, what do you make by your deduction, since you never reach the beginning, which has no existence? Wherefore, that which we now demand after five thousand odd years our descendants might with like curiosity demand after six hundred thousand years, supposing these dying generations of men continue so long to decay and be renewed, and supposing posterity continues as weak and ignorant as ourselves. The same question might have been asked by those who have lived before us and while man was even newer upon earth. The first man himself in short might the day after or the very day of his creation have asked why he was created no sooner. And no matter at what earlier or later period he had been created, this controversy about the commencement of this world's history would have had precisely the same difficulties as it has now.

CHAPTER XIII

OF THE REVOLUTION OF THE AGES, WHICH SOME PHILOSOPHERS BELIEVE WILL BRING ALL THINGS ROUND AGAIN, AFTER A CERTAIN FIXED CYCLE, TO THE SAME ORDER AND FORM AS AT FIRST

This controversy some philosophers have seen no other approved means of solving than by introducing cycles of time, in which there should be a constant renewal and repetition of the order of nature;[12] and they have therefore asserted that these cycles will ceaselessly recur, one passing away and another coming, though they are not agreed as to whether one permanent world shall pass through all these cycles, or whether the world shall at fixed intervals die out, and be renewed so as to exhibit a recurrence of the same phenomena—the things which have been, and those which are to be, coinciding. And from this fantastic vicissitude they exempt not even the immortal soul that has attained wisdom, consigning it to a ceaseless transmigration between delusive blessedness and real misery. For how can that be truly called blessed which has no assurance of being so eternally, and is either in ignorance of the truth, and blind to the misery that is approaching, or, knowing it, is in misery and fear? Or if it passes to bliss, and leaves miseries forever, then there happens in time a new thing which time shall not end. Why not, then, the world also? Why may not man, too, be a similar thing? So that, by following the straight path of sound doctrine, we escape, I know not what circuitous paths, discovered by deceiving and deceived sages.

Some, too, in advocating these recurring cycles that restore all things to their original cite in favor of their supposition what Solomon says in the book of *Ecclesiastes:* "What is that which hath been? It is that which shall be. And what is that which is done? It is that which shall be done: and there is no new thing under the sun. Who can speak and say, See, this is new? It hath been already of old time, which was before us." [13] This he said either of those things of which he had just been speaking—the succession of generations, the orbit of the sun, the course of rivers—or else of all kinds of creatures that are born and die. For men were before us, are with us, and shall be after us; and so all living things and all plants. Even monstrous and irregular productions, though differing from one another, and though some are reported as solitary instances, yet resemble one another generally, in so far as they are miraculous and monstrous, and, in this sense, have been, and shall be, and are no new and recent things under the sun. However, some would understand these words as meaning that in the predestination of God all things have already existed, and that thus there is no new thing under the sun. At all events, far be it from any true believer to suppose that by these words of Solomon those cycles are meant, in which, according to those philosophers, the same periods and events of time are repeated; as if, for example, the philosopher Plato, having taught in the school at Athens which is called the Academy, so, numberless ages before, at long but certain intervals, this same Plato and the same school, and the same disciples existed, and so also are to be repeated during the countless cycles that are yet to be —far be it, I say, from us to believe this. For once Christ died for our sins; and, rising from the dead, He dieth no more. "Death hath no more dominion over Him;" [14] and we ourselves after the resurrection shall be ever with the

[12] *i.e.,* the orthodox Stoic position   [13] Eccles. i. 9, 10   [14] Rom. vi. 9

Lord,[15] to whom we now say, as the sacred Psalmist dictates, "Thou shalt keep us, O Lord, Thou shalt preserve us from this generation." [16] And that too which follows, is, I think, appropriate enough: "The wicked walk *in a circle;*" not because their life is to recur by means of these circles, which these philosophers imagine, but because the path in which their false doctrine now runs is circuitous.

CHAPTER XIV

OF THE CREATION OF THE HUMAN RACE IN TIME, AND HOW THIS WAS EFFECTED WITHOUT ANY NEW DESIGN OR CHANGE OF PURPOSE ON GOD'S PART

What wonder is it if, entangled in these circles, they find neither entrance nor egress? For they know not how the human race, and this mortal condition of ours, took its origin, nor how it will be brought to an end, since they cannot penetrate the inscrutable wisdom of God. For, though Himself eternal, and without beginning, yet He caused time to have a beginning; and man, whom He had not previously made He made in time, not from a new and sudden resolution, but by His unchangeable and eternal design. Who can search out the unsearchable depth of this purpose, who can scrutinize the inscrutable wisdom, wherewith God, without change of will, created man, who had never before been, and gave him an existence in time, and increased the human race from one individual? For the Psalmist himself, when he had first said, "Thou shalt keep us, O Lord, Thou shalt preserve us from this generation for ever," and had then rebuked those whose foolish and impious doctrine preserves for the soul no eternal deliverance and blessedness, adds immediately, "The wicked walk in a circle." Then, as if it were said to him, "What then do you believe, feel, know? Are we to believe that it suddenly occurred to God to create man, whom He had never before made in a past eternity—God, to whom nothing new can occur, and in whom is no changeableness?" the Psalmist goes on to reply, as if addressing God Himself, "According to the depth of Thy wisdom Thou hast multiplied the children of men." Let men, he seems to say, fancy what they please, let them conjecture and dispute as seems good to them, but Thou hast multiplied the children of men according to the depth of Thy wisdom, which no man can comprehend. For this is a depth indeed, that God always has been, and that man, whom He had never made before, He willed to make in time, and this without changing His design and will.

[15] 1 Thess. iv. 16   [16] Ps. xii. 7

CHAPTER XV

For my own part, indeed, as I dare not say that there ever was a time when the Lord God was not Lord,[17] so I ought not to doubt that man had no existence before time, and was first created in time. But when I consider what God could be the Lord of, if there was not always some creature, I shrink from making any assertion, remembering my own insignificance, and that it is written, "What man is he that can know the counsel of God? or who can think what the will of the Lord is? For the thoughts of mortal men are timid, and our devices are but uncertain. For the corruptible body presseth down the soul, and the earthly tabernacle weigheth down the mind that museth upon many things." [18] Many things certainly do I muse upon in this earthly tabernacle, because the one thing which is true among the many, or beyond the many, I cannot find. If, then, among these many thoughts, I say that there have always been creatures for Him to be Lord of, who is always and ever has been Lord, but that these creatures have not always been the same, but succeeded one another (for we would not seem to say that any is co-eternal with the Creator, an assertion condemned equally by faith and sound reason) I must take care lest I fall into the absurd and ignorant error of maintaining that by these successions and changes mortal creatures have always existed, whereas the immortal creatures had not begun to exist until the date of our own world, when the angels were created; if at least the angels are intended by that light which was first made, or, rather, by that heaven of which it is said, "In the beginning God created the heavens and the earth." [19] The angels, at least did not exist before they were created; for if we say that they have always existed, we shall seem to make them co-eternal with the Creator. Again, if I say that the angels were not created in time, but existed before all times, as those over whom God, who has ever been Sovereign, exercised His sovereignty, then I shall be asked whether, if they were created before all time, they, being creatures, could possibly always exist. It may perhaps be replied, Why not *always*, since that which is in all time may very properly be said to be "always"? Now so true is it that these angels have existed in all time that even before time was they were created; if at least time began with the heavens, and the angels existed before the heavens. And if time was even before the heavenly bodies, not indeed marked by hours, days,

---

[17] Cf. *de Trin.* v. 17   [18] Wisdom ix. 13-15   [19] Gen. i. 1

months, and years—for these measures of time's periods which are commonly and properly called times, did manifestly begin with the motion of the heavenly bodies, and so God said, when He appointed them, "Let them be for signs, and for seasons, and for days, and for years" [20]—if, I say, time was before these heavenly bodies by some changing movement, whose parts succeeded one another and could not exist simultaneously, and if there was some such movement among the angels which necessitated the existence of time, and that they from their very creation should be subject to these temporal changes, then they have existed in all time, for time came into being along with them. And who will say that what was in all time, was not always?

But if I make such a reply, it will be said to me, How, then, are they not co-eternal with the Creator, if He and they always have been? How even can they be said to have been created, if we are to understand that they have always existed? What shall we reply to this? Shall we say that both statements are true? that they always have been, since they have been in all time, they being created along with time, or time along with them, and yet that also they were created? For, similarly, we will not deny that time itself was created, though no one doubts that time has been in all time; for if it has not been in all time, then there was a time when there was no time. But the most foolish person could not make such an assertion. For we can reasonably say there was a time when Rome was not; there was a time when Jerusalem was not; there was a time when Abraham was not; there was a time when man was not, and so on: in fine, if the world was not made at the commencement of time, but after some time had elapsed, we can say there was a time when the world was not. But to say there was a time when time was not, is as absurd as to say there was a man when there was no man; or, this world was when this world was not. For if we are not referring to the same object, the form of expression may be used, as, there was another man when this man was not. Thus we can reasonably say there was another time when this time was not; but not the merest simpleton could say there was a time when there was no time. As, then, we say that time was created, though we also say that it always has been, since in all time time has been, so it does not follow that if the angels have always been, they were therefore not created. For we say that they have always been, because they have been in all time; and we say they have been in all time, because time itself could no wise be without them. For where there is no creature whose changing movements admits of succession, there cannot be time at all. And consequently, even if they have always existed, they were created; neither, if they have always existed, are they therefore co-eternal with the Creator. For He has always existed in unchangeable eternity; while they were created, and are said to have been always, because they have been in all time, time being impossible without the creature. But time passing away by its changeful-

[20] Gen. i. 14

ness, cannot be co-eternal with changeless eternity. And consequently, though the immortality of the angels does not pass in time, does not become past as if now it were not, nor has a future as if it were not yet, still their movements, which are the basis of time, do pass from future to past; and therefore they cannot be co-eternal with the Creator, in whose movement we cannot say that there has been that which now is not, or shall be that which is not yet. Wherefore, if God always has been Lord, He has always had creatures under His dominion—creatures, however, not begotten of Him, but created by Him out of nothing; nor co-eternal with Him, for He was before them though at no time without them, because He preceded them, not by the lapse of time, but by His abiding eternity. But if I make this reply to those who demand how He was always Creator, always Lord, if there were not always a subject creation; or how this was created, and not rather co-eternal with its Creator, if it always was, I fear I may be accused of recklessly affirming what I know not, instead of teaching what I know. I return, therefore, to that which our Creator has seen fit that we should know; and those things which He has allowed the abler men to know in this life, or has reserved to be known in the next by the perfected saints, I acknowledge to be beyond my capacity. But I have thought it right to discuss these matters without making positive assertions, that they who read may be warned to abstain from hazardous questions, and may not deem themselves fit for everything. Let them rather endeavor to obey the wholesome injunction of the apostle, when he says, "For I say, through the grace given unto me, to every man that is among you, not to think of himself more highly than he ought to think; but to think soberly, according as God hath dealt to every man the measure of faith." [21] For if an infant receive nourishment suited to its strength, it becomes capable, as it grows, of taking more; but if its strength and capacity be overtaxed, it dwindles away in place of growing.

CHAPTER XVI

HOW WE ARE TO UNDERSTAND GOD'S PROMISE OF LIFE ETERNAL, WHICH WAS UTTERED BEFORE THE "ETERNAL TIMES"

I own that I do not know what ages passed before the human race was created, yet I have no doubt that no created thing is co-eternal with the Creator. But even the apostle speaks of time as eternal, and this with reference, not to the future, but, which is more surprising, to the past. For he says, "In hope of eternal life, which God that cannot lie promised before the eternal times, but hath in due times manifested His word." [22] You see he says that in the past there have been eternal times, which, however, were not co-eternal with God. And since God before these eternal times not only

[21] Rom. xii. 3   [22] Titus i. 2, 3

existed, but also, "promised" life eternal, which He manifested in its own times (that is to say, in due times), what else is this than His word? For this is life eternal. But then, how did He promise; for the promise was made to men, and yet they had no existence before eternal times? Does this not mean that, in His own eternity, and in His co-eternal word, that which was to be in its own time was already predestined and fixed?

CHAPTER XVII

WHAT DEFENCE IS MADE BY SOUND FAITH REGARDING GOD'S UNCHANGEABLE COUNSEL AND WILL, AGAINST THE REASONINGS OF THOSE WHO HOLD THAT THE WORKS OF GOD ARE ETERNALLY REPEATED IN REVOLVING CYCLES THAT RESTORE ALL THINGS AS THEY WERE

Of this, too, I have no doubt, that before the first man was created, there never had been a man at all, neither this same man himself recurring by I know not what cycles, and having made I know not how many revolutions, nor any other of similar nature. From this belief I am not frightened by philosophical arguments, among which that is reckoned the most acute which is founded on the assertion that the infinite cannot be comprehended by any mode of knowledge. Consequently, they argue, God has in His own mind finite conceptions of all finite things which He makes. Now it cannot be supposed that His goodness was ever idle; for if it were, there should be ascribed to Him an awakening to activity in time, from a past eternity of inactivity, as if He repented of an idleness that had no beginning, and proceeded, therefore, to make a beginning of work. This being the case, they say it must be that the same things are always repeated, and that as they pass, so they are destined always to return, whether amidst all these changes the world remains the same—the world which has always been, and yet was created—or that the world in these revolutions is perpetually dying out and being renewed; otherwise, if we point to a time when the works of God were begun, it would be believed that He considered His past eternal leisure to be inert and indolent, and therefore condemned and altered it as displeasing to Himself. Now if God is supposed to have been indeed always making temporal things, but different from one another, and one after the other, so, that He thus came at last to make man, whom He had never made before, then it may seem that He made man not with knowledge (for they suppose no knowledge can comprehend the infinite succession of creatures) but at the dictate of the hour, as it struck Him at the moment, with a sudden and accidental change of mind. On the other hand, say they, if those cycles be admitted, and if we suppose that the same temporal things are repeated, while the world either remains identical through all these rotations, or else dies away and is renewed, then there is ascribed to God neither the slothful ease of a past eternity, nor a rash and unforeseen creation. And if the same things be not thus repeated in cycles, then they cannot by any science or prescience be comprehended in their endless diversity. Even though reason could not refute, faith would smile at these argumentations, with which the godless endeavor to turn our simple piety from the right way, that we may walk with them "in a circle." But by the help of the Lord our God, even reason, and that readily enough, shatters these revolving circles which conjecture frames. For that which specially leads these men astray to prefer their own circles to the straight path of truth, is, that they measure by their own human, changeable, and narrow intellect the divine mind, which is absolutely unchangeable, infinitely capacious, and without succession of thought, counting all things without number. So that saying of the apostle comes true of them, for, comparing themselves with themselves, they do not understand.[23] For because they do, in virtue of a new purpose, whatever new thing has occurred to them to be done (their minds being changeable), they conclude it is so with God; and thus compare, not God—for they cannot conceive God, but think of one like themselves when they think of Him—not God, but themselves, and not with Him, but with themselves. For our part, we dare not believe that God is affected in one way when He works, in another when He rests. Indeed, to say that He is affected at all, is an abuse of language, since it implies that there comes to be something in His nature which was not there before. For he who is affected is acted upon, and whatever is acted upon is changeable. His leisure, therefore, is no laziness, indolence, inactivity; as in His work is no labor, effort, industry. He can act while He reposes, and repose while He acts. He can begin a new work with (not a new, but) an eternal design; and what He has not made before, He does not now begin to make because He repents of His former repose. But when one speaks of His former repose and subsequent operation (and I know not how men can understand these things) this "former" and "subsequent" are applied only to the things created, which formerly did not exist, and subsequently came into existence. But in God the former purpose is not altered and obliterated by the subsequent and different purpose, but by one and the same eternal and unchangeable will He effected regarding the things He created, both that formerly, so long as they were not, they should not be, and that subsequently, when they began to be, they should come into existence. And thus, perhaps, He would show, in a very striking way, to those who have eyes for such things, how independent He is of what He makes, and how it is of His own gratuitous goodness He creates, since from eternity He dwelt without creatures in no less perfect a blessedness.

[23] 2 Cor. x. 12

CHAPTER XVIII

AGAINST THOSE WHO ASSERT THAT THINGS THAT ARE INFINITE CANNOT BE COMPREHENDED BY THE KNOWLEDGE OF GOD

As for their other assertion, that God's knowledge cannot comprehend things infinite, it only remains for them to affirm, in order that they may sound the depths of their impiety, that God does not know all numbers. For it is very certain that they are infinite; since, no matter of what number you suppose an end to be made, this number can be, I will not say, increased by the addition of one more, but however great it be, and however vast be the multitude of which it is the rational and scientific expression, it can still be not only doubled, but even multiplied. Moreover, each number is so defined by its own properties, that no two numbers are equal. They are therefore both unequal and different from one another; and while they are simply finite, collectively they are infinite. Does God, therefore, not know numbers on account of this infinity; and does His knowledge extend only to a certain height in numbers, while of the rest He is ignorant? Who is so left to himself as to say so? Yet they can hardly pretend to put numbers out of the question, or maintain that they have nothing to do with the knowledge of God; for Plato,[24] their great authority, represents God as framing the world on numerical principles: and in our books also it is said to God, "Thou hast ordered all things in number, and measure, and weight." [25] The prophet also says, "Who bringeth out their host by number." [26] And the Saviour says in the Gospel, "The very hairs of your head are all numbered." [27] Far be it, then, from us to doubt that all number is known to Him whose understanding, according to the Psalmist, is infinite.[28] The infinity of number, though there be no numbering of infinite numbers, is yet not incomprehensible by Him whose understanding is infinite. And thus, if everything which is comprehended is defined or made finite by the comprehension of him who knows it, then all infinity is in some ineffable way made finite to God, for it is comprehensible by His knowledge. Wherefore, if the infinity of numbers cannot be infinite to the knowledge of God, by which it is comprehended, what are we poor creatures that we should presume to fix limits to His knowledge, and say that unless the same temporal thing be repeated by the same periodic revolutions, God cannot either foreknow His creatures that He may make them, or know them when He has made them? God, whose knowledge is simply manifold, and uniform in its variety, comprehends all incomprehensibles with so incomprehensible a comprehension, that though He willed always to make His later works novel and unlike what went before them, He could not produce them without order and foresight, nor conceive them suddenly, but by His eternal foreknowledge.

---

[24] cf. *Timaeus*   [25] Wisdom xi. 20   [26] Isa. xl. 26   [27] Matt. x. 30   [28] Ps. cxlvii. 5

CHAPTER XIX

OF WORLDS WITHOUT END, OR AGES OF AGES

I do not presume to determine whether God does so, and whether these times which are called "ages of ages" are joined together in a continuous series, and succeed one another with a regulated diversity, and leave exempt from their vicissitudes only those who are freed from their misery, and abide without end in a blessed immortality; or whether these are called "ages of ages," that we may understand that the ages remain unchangeable in God's unwavering wisdom, and are the efficient causes, as it were, of those ages which are being spent in time. Possibly "ages" is used for "age," so that nothing else is meant by "ages of ages" than by "age of age," as nothing else is meant by "heavens of heavens" than by "heaven of heaven." For God called the firmament, above which are the waters, "Heaven," and yet the psalm says, "Let the waters that are above the *heavens* praise the name of the Lord." [29] Which of these two meanings we are to attach to "ages of ages," or whether there is not some other and better meaning still, is a very profound question; and the subject we are at present handling presents no obstacle to our meanwhile deferring the discussion of it, whether we may be able to determine anything about it, or may only be made more cautious by its further treatment, so as to be deterred from making any rash affirmations in a matter of such obscurity. For at present we are disputing the opinion that affirms the existence of those periodic revolutions by which the same things are always recurring at intervals of time. Now, whichever of these suppositions regarding the "ages of ages" be the true one, it avails nothing for the substantiating of those cycles; for whether the ages of ages be not a repetition of the same world, but different worlds succeeding one another in a regulated connection, the ransomed souls abiding in well-assured bliss without any recurrence of misery, or whether the ages of ages be the eternal causes which rule what shall be and is in time, it equally follows, that those cycles which bring round the same things have no existence; and nothing more thoroughly explodes them than the fact of the eternal life of the saints.

CHAPTER XX

OF THE IMPIETY OF THOSE WHO ASSERT THAT THE SOULS WHICH ENJOY TRUE AND PERFECT BLESSEDNESS, MUST YET AGAIN AND AGAIN IN THESE PERIODIC REVOLUTIONS RETURN TO LABOR AND MISERY

What pious ears could bear to hear that after a life spent in so many and severe distresses (if, indeed, that should be called a life at all which is rather

[29] Ps. cxlviii. 4

a death, so utter that the love of this present death makes us fear that death which delivers us from it) that after evils so disastrous, and miseries of all kinds have at length been expiated and finished by the help of true religion and wisdom, and when we have thus attained to the vision of God, and have entered into bliss by the contemplation of spiritual light and participation in His unchangeable immortality, which we burn to attain—that we must at some time lose all this, and that they who do lose it are cast down from that eternity, truth, and felicity to infernal mortality and shameful foolishness, and are involved in accursed woes, in which God is lost, truth held in detestation, and happiness sought in iniquitous impurities? and that this will happen endlessly again and again, recurring at fixed intervals, and in regularly returning periods? and that this everlasting and ceaseless revolution of definite cycles, which remove and restore true misery and deceitful bliss in turn, is contrived in order that God may be able to know His own works, since on the one hand He cannot rest from creating and on the other, cannot know the infinite number of His creatures, if He always makes creatures? Who, I say, can listen to such things? Who can accept or suffer them to be spoken? Were they true, it were not only more prudent to keep silence regarding them, but even (to express myself as best I can) it were the part of wisdom not to know them. For if in the future world we shall not remember these things, and by this oblivion be blessed, why should we now increase our misery, already burdensome enough, by the knowledge of them? If, on the other hand, the knowledge of them will be forced upon us hereafter, now at least let us remain in ignorance, that in the present expectation we may enjoy a blessedness which the future reality is not to bestow; since in this life we are expecting to obtain life everlasting, but in the world to come are to discover it to be blessed, but not everlasting.

And if they maintain that no one can attain to the blessedness of the world to come, unless in this life he has been indoctrinated in those cycles in which bliss and misery relieve one another, how do they avow that the more a man loves God, the more readily he attains to blessedness—they who teach what paralyzes love itself? For who would not be more remiss and lukewarm in his love for a person whom he thinks he shall be forced to abandon, and whose truth and wisdom he shall come to hate; and this, too, after he has quite attained to the utmost and most blissful knowledge of Him that he is capable of? Can any one be faithful in his love, even to a human friend, if he knows that he is destined to become his enemy? [30] God forbid that there be any truth in an opinion which threatens us with a real misery that is never to end, but is often and endlessly to be interrupted by intervals of fallacious happiness. For what happiness can be more fallacious and false than that in whose blaze of truth we yet remain ignorant that we shall be miserable, or in whose most secure citadel we yet fear that we shall be so? For if, on the one hand, we are to be ignorant of coming calamity,

[30] Cf. Cicero *de Amicitia,* 16

then our present misery is not so short-sighted for it is assured of coming bliss. If, on the other hand, the disaster that threatens is not concealed from us in the world to come, then the time of misery which is to be at last exchanged for a state of blessedness, is spent by the soul more happily than its time of happiness, which is to end in a return to misery. And thus our expectation of unhappiness is happy, but of happiness unhappy. And therefore, as we here suffer present ills, and hereafter fear ills that are imminent, it were truer to say that we shall always be miserable than that we can some time be happy.

But these things are declared to be false by the loud testimony of religion and truth; for religion truthfully promises a true blessedness, of which we shall be eternally assured, and which cannot be interrupted by any disaster. Let us therefore keep to the straight path, which is Christ, and, with Him as our Guide and Saviour, let us turn away in heart and mind from the unreal and futile cycles of the godless. Porphyry, Platonist though he was, abjured the opinion of his school, that in these cycles souls are ceaselessly passing away and returning, either being struck with the extravagance of the idea, or sobered by his knowledge of Christianity. As I mentioned in the tenth book, he preferred saying that the soul, as it had been sent into the world that it might know evil, and be purged and delivered from it, was never again exposed to such an experience after it had once returned to the Father. And if he abjured the tenets of his school, how much more ought we Christians to abominate and avoid an opinion so unfounded and hostile to our faith? But having disposed of these cycles and escaped out of them, no necessity compels us to suppose that the human race had no beginning in time, on the ground that there is nothing new in nature which, by I know not what cycles, has not at some previous period existed, and is not hereafter to exist again. For if the soul, once delivered, as it never was before, is never to return to misery, then there happens in its experience something which never happened before; and this, indeed, something of the greatest consequence, to wit, the secure entrance into eternal felicity. And if in an immortal nature there can occur a novelty, which never has been, nor ever shall be, reproduced by any cycle, why is it disputed that the same may occur in mortal natures? If they maintain that blessedness is no new experience to the soul, but only a return to that state in which it has been eternally, then at least its deliverance from misery is something new, since, by their own showing, the misery from which it is delivered is itself, too, a new experience. And if this new experience fell out by accident, and was not embraced in the order of things appointed by Divine Providence, then where are those determinate and measured cycles in which no new thing happens, but all things are reproduced as they were before? If, however, this new experience was embraced in that providential order of nature (whether the soul was exposed to the evil of this world for the sake of discipline, or fell into it by sin) then it is possible for new things to happen which never happened before, and which yet are not extraneous to the order of nature. And if the soul is able by its own imprudence to create for itself a new misery, which was not unforeseen by the Divine Providence, but was provided for in the order of nature along with the deliverance from it, how can we, even with all the rashness of human vanity, presume to deny that God can create new things—new to the world, but not to Him—which He never before created, but yet foresaw from all eternity? If they say that it is indeed true that ransomed souls return no more to misery, but that even so no new thing happens, since there always have been, now are, and ever shall be a succession of ransomed souls, they must at least grant that in this case there are new souls to whom the misery and the deliverance from it are new. For if they maintain that those souls out of which new men are daily being made (from whose bodies, if they have lived wisely, they are so delivered that they never return to misery) are not new, but have existed from eternity, they must logically admit that they are infinite. For however great a finite number of souls there were, that would not have sufficed to make perpetually new men from eternity—men whose souls were to be eternally freed from this mortal state, and never afterwards to return to it. And our philosophers will find it hard to explain how there is an infinite number of souls in an order of nature which they require shall be finite, that it may be known by God.

And now that we have exploded these cycles which were supposed to bring back the soul at fixed periods to the same miseries, what can seem more in accordance with godly reason than to believe that it is possible for God both to create new things never before created, and in doing so, to preserve His will unaltered? But whether the number of eternally redeemed souls can be continually increased or not, let the philosophers themselves decide, who are so subtle in determining where infinity cannot be admitted. For our own part, our reasoning holds in either case. For if the number of souls can be indefinitely increased, what reason is there to deny that what had never before been created, could be created? since the number of ransomed souls never existed before, and has yet not only been once made, but will never cease to be coming anew into being. If, on the other hand, it be more suitable that the number of eternally ransomed souls be definite, and that this number will never be increased, yet this number, whatever it be, did assuredly never exist before, and it cannot increase, and reach the amount it signifies, without having some beginning; and this beginning never before existed. That this beginning, therefore, might be, the first man was created.

CHAPTER XXI

THAT THERE WAS CREATED AT FIRST BUT ONE INDIVIDUAL, AND THAT THE HUMAN RACE WAS CREATED IN HIM

Now that we have solved, as well as we could, this very difficult question about the eternal God creating new things, without any novelty of will, it is easy to see how much better it is that God was pleased to produce the human race from the one individual whom He created, than if He had originated it in several men. For as to the other animals, He created some solitary, and naturally seeking lonely places—as the eagles, kites, lions, wolves, and such like; others gregarious, which herd together, and prefer to live in company —as pigeons, starlings, stags, and little fallow deer, and the like: but neither class did He cause to be propagated from individuals, but called into being several at once. Man, on the other hand, whose nature was to be a mean between the angelic and bestial, He created in such sort, that if he remained in subjection to His Creator as his rightful Lord, and piously kept His commandments, he should pass into the company of the angels, and obtain, without the intervention of death, a blessed and endless immortality; but if he offended the Lord his God by a proud and disobedient use of his free will, he should become subject to death, and live as the beasts do—the slave of appetite, and doomed to eternal punishment after death. And therefore God created only one single man, not, certainly, that he might be a solitary, bereft of all society, but that by this means the unity of society and the bond of concord might be more effectually commended to him, men being bound together not only by similarity of nature, but by family affection. And indeed He did not even create the woman that was to be given him as his wife, as he created the man, but created her out of the man, that the whole human race might derive from one man.

CHAPTER XXII

THAT GOD FOREKNEW THAT THE FIRST MAN WOULD SIN, AND THAT HE AT THE SAME TIME FORESAW HOW LARGE A MULTITUDE OF GODLY PERSONS WOULD BY HIS GRACE BE TRANSLATED TO THE FELLOWSHIP OF THE ANGELS

And God was not ignorant that man would sin, and that, being himself made subject now to death, he would propagate men doomed to die, and that these mortals would run to such enormities in sin, that even the beasts devoid of rational will, and who were created in numbers from the waters and the earth, would live more securely and peaceably with their own kind than men, who had been propagated from one individual for the very purpose of commending concord. For not even lions or dragons have ever waged with their kind such wars as men have waged with one another.[31] But God foresaw also that by His grace a people would be called to adoption, and that they, being justified by the remission of their sins, would be united by the Holy Ghost to the holy angels in eternal peace, the last enemy, death, being destroyed; and He knew that this people would derive profit from the consideration that God had caused all men to be derived from one, for the sake of showing how highly He prizes unity in a multitude.

[31] Cf. Juvenal, *Sat.* xv. 160-5

CHAPTER XXIII

OF THE NATURE OF THE HUMAN SOUL CREATED IN THE IMAGE OF GOD

God, then, made man in His own image. For He created for him a soul endowed with reason and intelligence, so that he might excel all the creatures of earth, air, and sea, which were not so gifted. And when He had formed the man out of the dust of the earth, and had willed that his soul should be such as I have said—whether He had already made it, and now by breathing imparted it to man, or rather made it by breathing, so that that breath which God made by breathing (for what else is "to breathe" than to make breath?) is the soul—He made also a wife for him, to aid him in the work of generating his kind, and her He formed of a bone taken out of the man's side, working in a divine manner. For we are not to conceive of this work in a carnal fashion, as if God wrought as we commonly see artisans, who use their hands, and material furnished to them, that by their artistic skill they may fashion some material object. God's hand is God's power; and He, working invisibly, effects visible results. But this seems fabulous rather than true to men, who measure by customary and everyday works the power and wisdom of God, whereby He understands and produces without seeds even seeds themselves; and because they cannot understand the things which at the beginning were created, they are sceptical regarding them—as if the very things which they do know about human propagation, conceptions and births, would seem less incredible if told to those who had no experience of them; though these very things, too, are attributed by many rather to physical and natural causes than to the work of the divine mind.

CHAPTER XXIV

WHETHER THE ANGELS CAN BE SAID TO BE THE CREATORS OF ANY, EVEN THE LEAST CREATURE

But in this book we have nothing to do with those who do not believe that the divine mind made or cares for this world. As for those who believe their own Plato, that all mortal animals—among whom man holds the pre-eminent place, and is near to the gods themselves—were created not by that most high God who made the world, but by other lesser gods created by the Supreme, and exercising a delegated power under His control—if only those persons be delivered from the superstition which prompts them to seek a plausible reason for paying divine honors and sacrificing to these gods as their creators, they will easily be disentangled also from this their error. For it is blasphemy to believe or to say (even before it can be understood) that any other than God is creator of any nature, be it never so small and mortal.

And as for the angels, whom those Platonists prefer to call gods, although they do, so far as they are permitted and commissioned, aid in the production of the things around us, yet not on that account are we to call them creators, any more than we call gardeners the creators of fruits and trees.

CHAPTER XXV

THAT GOD ALONE IS THE CREATOR OF EVERY KIND OF CREATURE, WHATEVER ITS NATURE OR FORM

For whereas there is one form which is given from without to every bodily substance—such as the form which is constructed by potters and smiths, and that class of artists who paint and fashion forms like the body of animals—but another and internal form which is not itself constructed, but, as the efficient cause, produces not only the natural bodily forms, but even the life itself of the living creatures, and which proceeds from the secret and hidden choice of an intelligent and living nature—let that first-mentioned form be attributed to every artificer, but this latter to one only, God, the Creator and Originator who made the world itself and the angels, without the help of world or angels. For the same divine and, so to speak, creative energy, which cannot be made, but makes, and which gave to the earth and sky their roundness—this same divine, effective, and creative energy gave their roundness to the eye and to the apple; and the other natural objects which we anywhere see, received also their form, not from without, but from the secret and profound might of the Creator, who said, "Do not I fill heaven and earth?" [32] and whose wisdom it is that reacheth from one end to another mightily; and sweetly doth she order all things.[33] Wherefore I know not what kind of aid the angels, themselves created first, afforded to the Creator in making other things. I cannot ascribe to them what perhaps they cannot do, neither ought I to deny them such faculty as they have. But, by their leave, I attribute the creating and originating work which gave being to all natures to God, to whom they themselves thankfully ascribe their existence. We do not call gardeners the creators of their fruits, for we read, "Neither is he that planteth anything, neither he that watereth, but God that giveth the increase." [34] Nay, not even the earth itself do we call a creator, though she seems to be the prolific mother of all things which she aids in germinating and bursting forth from the seed, and which she keeps rooted in her own breast; for we likewise read, "God giveth it a body, as it hath pleased Him, and to every seed his own body." [35] We ought not even to call a woman the creatress of her own offspring; for He rather is its Creator who said to His servant, "Before I formed thee in the womb, I knew thee." [36] And although the various mental emotions of a pregnant woman do produce in the fruit of her womb similar qualities—as Jacob with his

[32] Jer. xxiii. 24   [33] Wisdom viii. 1   [34] 1 Cor. iii. 7   [35] 1 Cor. xv. 38   [36] Jer. i. 5

peeled wands caused piebald sheep to be produced—yet the mother as little creates her offspring as she created herself. Whatever bodily or seminal causes, then, may be used for the production of things, either by the co-operation of angels, men, or the lower animals, or by sexual generation; and whatever power the desires and mental emotions of the mother have to produce in the tender and plastic foetus corresponding lineaments and colors; yet the natures themselves, which are thus variously affected, are the production of none but the most high God. It is His occult power which pervades all things, and is present in all without being contaminated, which gives being to all that is, and modifies and limits its existence; so that without Him it would not be thus, or thus, nor would have any being at all.[37] If, then, in regard to that outward form which the workman's hand imposes on his work, we do not say that Rome and Alexandria were built by masons and architects, but by the kings by whose will, plan, and resources they were built, so that the one has Romulus, the other Alexander, for its founder; with how much greater reason ought we to say that God alone is the Author of all natures, since He neither uses for His work any material which was not made by Him, nor any workmen who were not also made by Him, and since, if He were, so to speak, to withdraw from created things His creative power, they would straightway relapse into the nothingness in which they were before they were created? "Before," I mean, in respect of eternity, not of time. For what other creator could there be of time, than He who created those things whose movements make time? [38]

CHAPTER XXVI

OF THAT OPINION OF THE PLATONISTS, THAT THE ANGELS WERE THEMSELVES INDEED CREATED BY GOD, BUT THAT AFTERWARDS THEY CREATED MAN'S BODY

It is obvious, that in attributing the creation of the other animals to those inferior gods who were made by the Supreme, he meant it to be understood that the immortal part was taken from God Himself, and that these minor creators added the mortal part; that is to say, he meant them to be considered the creators of our bodies, but not of our souls. But since Porphyry maintains that if the soul is to be purified, all entanglement with a body must be escaped from; and at the same time agrees with Plato and the Platonists in thinking that those who have not spent a temperate and honorable life return to mortal bodies as their punishment (to bodies of brutes in Plato's opinion, to human bodies in Porphyry's); it follows that those whom they would have us worship as our parents and authors, that they may plausibly call them gods, are, after all, but the forgers of our fetters and chains—not our creators, but our jailers and turnkeys, who lock us up in

---

[37] Cf. *de Trin.* iii. 13-16   [38] Cf. Book xi. 5

the most bitter and melancholy house of correction. Let the Platonists, then, either cease menacing us with our bodies as the punishment of our souls, or preaching that we are to worship as gods those whose work upon us they exhort us by all means in our power to avoid and escape from. But, indeed, both opinions are quite false. It is false that souls return again to this life to be punished; and it is false that there is any other creator of anything in heaven or earth, than He who made the heaven and the earth. For if we live in a body only to expiate our sins, how says Plato in another place, that the world could not have been the most beautiful and good, had it not been filled with all kinds of creatures, mortal and immortal? [39] But if our creation even as mortals be a divine benefit, how is it a punishment to be restored to a body, that is, to a divine benefit? And if God, as Plato continually maintains, embraced in His eternal intelligence the ideas both of the universe and of all the animals, how, then, should He not with His own hand make them all? Could He be unwilling to be the constructor of works, the idea and plan of which called for His ineffable and ineffably to be praised intelligence?

CHAPTER XXVII

THAT THE WHOLE PLENITUDE OF THE HUMAN RACE WAS EMBRACED
IN THE FIRST MAN, AND THAT GOD THERE SAW THE PORTION
OF IT WHICH WAS TO BE HONORED AND REWARDED, AND
THAT WHICH WAS TO BE CONDEMNED AND PUNISHED

With good cause, therefore, does the true religion recognize and proclaim that the same God who created the universal cosmos, created also all the animals, souls as well as bodies. Among the terrestrial animals man was made by Him in His own image, and, for the reason I have given, was made one individual, though he was not left solitary. For there is nothing so social by nature, so unsocial by its corruption, as this race. And human nature has nothing more appropriate, either for the prevention of discord, or for the healing of it, where it exists, than the remembrance of that first parent of us all, whom God was pleased to create alone, that all men might be derived from one, and that they might thus be admonished to preserve unity among their whole multitude. But from the fact that the woman was made for him from his side, it was plainly meant that we should learn how dear the bond between man and wife should be. These works of God do certainly seem extraordinary, because they are the first works. They who do not believe them, ought not to believe any prodigies; for these would not be called prodigies did they not happen out of the ordinary course of nature. But, is it possible that anything should happen in vain, however hidden be its cause, in so grand a government of divine providence? One of the sacred Psalmists says, "Come, behold the works of the Lord, what prodigies He hath

[39] cf. *Timaeus,* 28 and 31.

wrought in the earth." [40] Why God made woman out of man's side, and what this first prodigy prefigured, I shall, with God's help, tell in another place. But at present, since this book must be concluded, let us merely say that in this first man, who was created in the beginning, there was laid the foundation, not indeed evidently, but in God's foreknowledge, of these two cities or societies, so far as regards the human race. For from that man all men were to be derived—some of them to be associated with the good angels in their reward, others with the wicked in punishment; all being ordered by the secret yet just judgment of God. For since it is written, "All the paths of the Lord are mercy and truth," [41] neither can His grace be unjust, nor His justice cruel.

[40] Ps. xlvi. 8   [41] Ps. xxv. 10

BOOK THIRTEEN

In this book it is taught that death is penal, and had its origin in Adam's sin.

CHAPTER I

OF THE FALL OF THE FIRST MAN, THROUGH WHICH MORTALITY HAS BEEN CONTRACTED

HAVING disposed of the very difficult questions concerning the origin of our world and the beginning of the human race, the natural order requires that we now discuss the fall of the first man (we may say of the first men) and of the origin and propagation of human death. For God had not made man like the angels, in such a condition that, even though they had sinned, they could none the more die. He had so made them, that if they discharged the obligations of obedience, an angelic immortality and a blessed eternity might ensue, without the intervention of death; but if they disobeyed, death should be visited on them with just sentence—which, too, has been spoken to in the preceding book.

CHAPTER II

OF THAT DEATH WHICH CAN AFFECT AN IMMORTAL SOUL, AND OF THAT TO WHICH THE BODY IS SUBJECT

But I see I must speak a little more carefully of the nature of death. For although the human soul is truly affirmed to be immortal, yet it also has a certain death of its own. For it is therefore called immortal, because, in a sense, it does not cease to live and to feel; while the body is called mortal, because it can be forsaken of all life, and cannot by itself live at all. The death, then, of the soul takes place when God forsakes it, as the death of the body when the soul forsakes it. Therefore the death of both—that is, of the whole man—occurs when the soul, forsaken by God, forsakes the body. For, in this case, neither is God the life of the soul, nor the soul the life of the body. And this death of the whole man is followed by that which, on the authority of the divine oracles, we call the second death. This the Saviour referred to when He said, "Fear Him which is able to destroy both soul and body in hell." [1] And since this does not happen before the soul is so joined

---

[1] Matt. x. 28

to its body that they cannot be separated at all, it may be matter of wonder how the body can be said to be killed by that death in which it is not forsaken by the soul, but, being animated and rendered sensitive by it, is tormented. For in that penal and everlasting punishment, of which in its own place we are to speak more at large, the soul is justly said to die, because it does not live in connection with God; but how can we say that the body is dead, seeing that it lives by the soul? For it could not otherwise feel the bodily torments which are to follow the resurrection. Is it because life of every kind is good, and pain an evil, that we decline to say that that body lives, in which the soul is the cause, not of life, but of pain? The soul, then, lives by God when it lives well, for it cannot live well unless by God working in it what is good; and the body lives by the soul when the soul lives in the body, whether itself be living by God or no. For the wicked man's life in the body is a life not of the soul, but of the body, which even dead souls—that is, souls forsaken of God—can confer upon bodies, how little soever of their own proper life, by which they are immortal, they retain. But in the last damnation, though man does not cease to feel, yet because this feeling of his is neither sweet with pleasure nor wholesome with repose, but painfully penal, it is not without reason called death rather than life. And it is called the second death because it follows the first, which sunders the two cohering essences, whether these be God and the soul, or the soul and the body. Of the first and bodily death, then, we may say that to the good it is good, and evil to the evil. But, doubtless, the second, as it happens to none of the good, so it can be good for none.

CHAPTER III

WHETHER DEATH, WHICH BY THE SIN OF OUR FIRST PARENTS HAS PASSED UPON ALL MEN, IS THE PUNISHMENT OF SIN, EVEN TO THE GOOD

But a question not to be shirked arises: Whether in very truth death, which separates soul and body, is good to the good? For if it be, how has it come to pass that such a thing should be the punishment of sin? For the first men would not have suffered death had they not sinned. How, then, can that be good to the good, which could not have happened except to the evil? Then, again, if it could only happen to the evil, to the good it ought not to be good, but non-existent. For why should there be any punishment where there is nothing to punish? Wherefore we must say that the first men were indeed so created, that if they had not sinned, they would not have experienced any kind of death; but that, having become sinners, they were so punished with death, that whatsoever sprang from their stock should also be punished with the same death. For nothing else could be born of them than that which they themselves had been. Their nature was deteriorated in pro- *doomed* portion to the greatness of the condemnation of their sin, so that what existed as punishment in those who first sinned, became a natural consequence in their children. For man is not produced by man, as he was from the dust. For dust was the material out of which man was made: man is the parent by whom man is begotten. Wherefore earth and flesh are not the same thing, though flesh be made of earth. But as man the parent is, such is man the offspring. In the first man, therefore, there existed the whole human nature, which was to be transmitted by the woman to posterity, when that conjugal union received the divine sentence of its own condemnation; and what man was made, not when created, but when he sinned and was punished, this he propagated, so far as the origin of sin and death are concerned. For neither by sin nor its punishment was he himself reduced to that infantine and helpless infirmity of body and mind which we see in children. For God ordained that infants should begin the world as the young of beasts begin it, since their parents had fallen to the level of the beasts in the fashion of their life and of their death; as it is written, "Man when he was in honor understood not; he became like the beasts that have no understanding." [2] Nay more, infants, we see, are even feebler in the use and movement of their limbs, and more infirm to choose and refuse, than the most tender offspring of other animals; as if the force that dwells in human nature were destined to surpass all other living things so much the more eminently, as its energy has been longer restrained, and the time of its exercise delayed, just as an arrow flies the higher the further back it has been drawn. To this infantine imbecility the first man did not fall by his lawless presumption and just sentence; but human nature was in his person vitiated and altered to such an extent, that he suffered in his members the warring of disobedient lust, and became subject to the necessity of dying. And what he himself had become by sin and punishment, such he generated those whom he begot; that is to say, subject to sin and death. And if infants are delivered from this bondage of sin by the Redeemer's grace, they can suffer only this death which separates soul and body; but being redeemed from the obligation of sin, they do not pass to that second endless and penal death.

CHAPTER IV

WHY DEATH, THE PUNISHMENT OF SIN, IS NOT WITHHELD FROM THOSE
WHO BY THE GRACE OF REGENERATION ARE ABSOLVED FROM SIN

If, moreover, any one is solicitous about this point, how, if death be the very punishment of sin, they whose guilt is cancelled by grace do yet suffer death, this difficulty has already been handled and solved in our other work which we have written on the baptism of infants.[3] There it was said that the

[2] Ps. xlix. 12

[3] *De Baptismo Parvulorum* is the second half of the title of the book, *de Peccatorum Meritis et Remissione.*

parting of soul and body was left, though its connection with sin was removed, for this reason, that if the immortality of the body followed immediately upon the sacrament of regeneration, faith itself would be thereby
enervated. For faith is then only faith when it waits in hope for what is not
yet seen in substance. And by the vigor and conflict of faith, at least in times
past, was the fear of death overcome. Specially was this conspicuous in the
holy martyrs, who could have had no victory, no glory, to whom there could
not even have been any conflict, if, after the laver of regeneration, saints
could not suffer bodily death. Who would not, then, in company with the
infants presented for baptism, run to the grace of Christ, that so he might
not be dismissed from the body? And thus faith would not be tested with an
unseen reward; and so would not even be faith, seeking and receiving an
immediate recompense of its works. But now, by the greater and more admirable grace of the Saviour, the punishment of sin is turned to the service of
righteousness. For then it was proclaimed to man, "If thou sinnest, thou
shalt die;" now it is said to the martyr, "Die, that thou sin not." Then it
was said, "If ye trangress the commandments, ye shall die;" now it is said,
"If ye decline death, ye transgress the commandment." That which was formerly set as an object of terror, that men might not sin, is now to be undergone if we would not sin. Thus, by the unutterable mercy of God, even the
very punishment of wickedness has become the armor of virtue, and the
penalty of the sinner becomes the reward of the righteous. For then death
was incurred by sinning, now righteousness is fulfilled by dying. In the case
of the holy martyrs it is so; for to them the persecutor proposes the alternative, apostasy or death. For the righteous prefer by believing to suffer what
the first transgressors suffered by not believing. For unless they had sinned,
they would not have died; but the martyrs sin if they do not die. The one
died because they sinned, the others do not sin because they die. By the guilt
of the first, punishment was incurred; by the punishment of the second,
guilt is prevented. Not that death, which was before an evil, has become
something good, but only that God has granted to faith this grace, that
death, which is the admitted opposite to life, should become the instrument
by which life is reached.

CHAPTER V

AS THE WICKED MAKE AN ILL USE OF THE LAW, WHICH IS GOOD,
SO THE GOOD MAKE A GOOD USE OF DEATH, WHICH IS AN ILL

The apostle, wishing to show how hurtful a thing sin is, when grace does
not aid us, has not hesitated to say that the strength of sin is that very law
by which sin is prohibited. "The sting of death is sin, and the strength of sin
is the law." [4] Most certainly true; for prohibition increases the desire of

4 I Cor. xv. 16

illicit action, if righteousness is not so loved that the desire of sin is conquered by that love. But unless divine grace aid us, we cannot love nor delight in true righteousness. But lest the law should be thought to be an evil, since it is called the strength of sin, the apostle, when treating a similar question in another place, says, "The law indeed is holy, and the commandment holy, and just, and good. Was then that which is holy made death unto me? God forbid. But sin, that it might appear sin, working death in me by that which is good; that sin by the commandment might become exceeding sinful." [5] *Exceeding*, he says, because the transgression is more heinous when through the increasing lust of sin the law itself also is despised. Why have we thought it worth while to mention this? For this reason, because, as the law is not an evil when it increases the lust of those who sin, so neither is death a good thing when it increases the glory of those who suffer it, since either the former is abandoned wickedly, and makes transgressors, or the latter is embraced for the truth's sake, and makes martyrs. And thus the law is indeed good, because it is prohibition of sin, and death is evil because it is the wages of sin; but as wicked men make an evil use not only of evil, but also of good things, so the righteous make a good use not only of good, but also of evil things. Whence it comes to pass that the wicked make an ill use of the law, though the law is good; and that the good die well, though death is an evil.

CHAPTER VI

OF THE EVIL OF DEATH IN GENERAL, CONSIDERED AS THE SEPARATION OF SOUL AND BODY

Wherefore, as regards bodily death, that is, the separation of the soul from the body, it is good to none while it is being endured by those whom we say are in the article of death. For the very violence with which body and soul are wrenched asunder, which in the living had been conjoined and closely intertwined, brings with it a harsh experience, jarring horridly on nature so long as it continues, till there comes a total loss of sensation, which arose from the very interpenetration of spirit and flesh. And all this anguish is sometimes forestalled by one stroke of the body or sudden flitting of the soul, the swiftness of which prevents it from being felt. But whatever that may be in the dying which with violently painful sensation robs of all sensation, yet, when it is piously and faithfully borne, it increases the merit of patience, but does not make the name of punishment inapplicable. Death, proceeding by ordinary generation from the first man, is the punishment of all who are born of him, yet, if it be endured for righteousness' sake, it becomes the glory of those who are born again; and though death be the award of sin, it sometimes secures that nothing be awarded to sin.

[5] Rom. vii. 12, 13

CHAPTER VII

OF THE DEATH WHICH THE UNBAPTIZED SUFFER FOR THE CONFESSION OF CHRIST

For whatever unbaptized persons die confessing Christ, this confession is of the same efficacy for the remission of sins as if they were washed in the sacred font of baptism. For He who said, "Except a man be born of water and of the Spirit, he cannot enter into the kingdom of God," [6] made also an exception in their favor, in that other sentence where He no less absolutely said, "Whosoever shall confess me before men, him will I confess also before my Father which is in heaven;" [7] and in another place, "Whosoever will lose his life for my sake, shall find it." [8] And this explains the verse, "Precious in the sight of the Lord is the death of His saints." [9] For what is more precious than a death by which a man's sins are all forgiven, and his merits increased an hundredfold? For those who have been baptized when they could no longer escape death, and have departed this life with all their sins blotted out, have not equal merit with those who did not defer death, though it was in their power to do so, but preferred to end their life by confessing Christ, rather than by denying Him to secure an opportunity of baptism. And even had they denied Him under pressure of the fear of death, this too would have been forgiven them in that baptism, in which was remitted even the enormous wickedness of those who had slain Christ. But how abundant in these men must have been the grace of the Spirit, who breathes where He listeth, seeing that they so dearly loved Christ as to be unable to deny Him even in so sore an emergency, and with so sure a hope of pardon! Precious, therefore, is the death of the saints, to whom the grace of Christ has been applied with such gracious effects, that they do not hesitate to meet death themselves, if so be they might meet Him. And precious is it, also, because it has proved that what was originally ordained for the punishment of the sinner, has been used for the production of a richer harvest of righteousness. But not on this account should we look upon death as a good thing, for it is diverted to such useful purposes, not by any virtue of its own, but by the divine interference. Death was originally proposed as an object of dread, that sin might not be committed; now it must be undergone that sin may not be committed, or, if committed, be remitted, and the award of righteousness bestowed on him whose victory has earned it.

CHAPTER VIII

THAT THE SAINTS, BY SUFFERING THE FIRST DEATH FOR THE TRUTH'S SAKE, ARE FREED FROM THE SECOND

For if we look at the matter a little more carefully, we shall see that even when a man dies faithfully and laudably for the truth's sake, it is still death

[6] John iii. 5   [7] Matt. x. 32   [8] Matt. xvi. 25   [9] Ps. cxvi. 15

he is avoiding. For he submits to some part of death, for the very purpose of avoiding the whole, and the second and eternal death over and above. He submits to the separation of soul and body, lest the soul be separated both from God and from the body, and so the whole first death be completed, and the second death receive him everlastingly. Wherefore death is indeed, as I said, good to none while it is being actually suffered, and while it is subduing the dying to its power; but it is meritoriously endured for the sake of retaining or winning what *is* good. And regarding what happens after death, it is no absurdity to say that death is good to the good, and evil to the evil. For the disembodied spirits of the just are at rest; but those of the wicked suffer punishment till their bodies rise again—those of the just to life everlasting, and of the others to death eternal, which is called the second death.

CHAPTER IX

WHETHER WE SHOULD SAY THAT THE MOMENT OF DEATH, IN WHICH SENSATION CEASES, OCCURS IN THE EXPERIENCE OF THE DYING OR IN THAT OF THE DEAD

The point of time in which the souls of the good and evil are separated from the body, are we to say it is after death, or in death rather? If it is after death, then it is not death which is good or evil, since death is done with and past, but it is the life which the soul has now entered on. Death was an evil when it was present, that is to say, when it was being suffered by the dying; for to them it brought with it a severe and grievous experience, which the good make a good use of. But when death is past, how can that which no longer is be either good or evil? Still further, if we examine the matter more closely, we shall see that even that sore and grievous pain which the dying experience is not death itself. For so long as they have any sensation, they are certainly still alive; and, if still alive, must rather be said to be in a state previous to death than in death. For when death actually comes, it robs us of all bodily sensation, which, while death is only approaching is painful. And thus it is difficult to explain how we speak of those who are not yet dead, but are agonized in their last and mortal extremity, as being in the article of death. Yet what else can we call them than dying persons? for when death which was imminent shall have actually come, we can no longer call them dying but dead. No one, therefore, is dying unless living; since even he who is in the last extremity of life, and, as we say, giving up the ghost, yet lives. The same person is therefore at once dying and living, but drawing near to death, departing from life; yet in life, because his spirit yet abides in the body; not yet in death, because not yet has his spirit forsaken the body. But if, when it has forsaken it, the man is not even then in death, but after death, who shall say when he is in death? On the one hand, no one can be called dying, if a man cannot be dying and living at the same time; and as long as the soul is in the body, we cannot deny that he is living. On the other hand, if the man who is approaching death be rather called dying, I know not who is living.

CHAPTER X

OF THE LIFE OF MORTALS, WHICH IS RATHER TO BE CALLED DEATH THAN LIFE

For no sooner do we begin to live in this dying body, than we begin to move ceaselessly towards death.[10] For in the whole course of this life (if life we must call it) its mutability tends towards death. Certainly there is no one who is not nearer it this year than last year, and to-morrow than to-day, and to-day than yesterday, and a short while hence than now, and now than a short while ago. For whatever time we live is deducted from our whole term of life, and that which remains is daily becoming less and less; so that our whole life is nothing but a race towards death, in which no one is allowed to stand still for a little space, or to go somewhat more slowly, but all are driven forwards with an impartial movement, and with equal rapidity. For he whose life is short spends a day no more swiftly than he whose life is longer. But while the equal moments are impartially snatched from both, the one has a nearer and the other a more remote goal to reach with this their equal speed. It is one thing to make a longer journey, and another to walk more slowly. He, therefore, who spends longer time on his way to death does not proceed at a more leisurely pace, but goes over more ground. Further, if every man begins to die, that is, is in death, as soon as death has begun to show itself in him (by taking away life, to wit; for when life is all taken away, the man will be then not in death, but after death) then he begins to die so soon as he begins to live. For what else is going on in all his days, hours, and moments, until this slow-working death is fully consummated? And then comes the time *after death*, instead of that in which life was being withdrawn, and which we called being *in death*. Man, then, is never in life from the moment he dwells in this dying rather than living body—if, at least, he cannot be in life and death at once. Or rather, shall we say, he is in both?—in life, namely, which he lives till all is consumed; but in death also, which he dies as his life is consumed? For if he is not in life, what is it which is consumed till all be gone? And if he is not in death, what is this consumption itself? For when the whole of life has been consumed, the expression "after death" would be meaningless, had that consumption not been death. And if, when it has all been consumed, a man is not in death but after death, when is he in death, unless when life is being consumed away?

[10] Much of this paradoxical statement about death is taken from Seneca.

CHAPTER XI

But if it is absurd to say that a man is in death before he reaches death (for to what is his course running as he passes through life, if already he is in death?) and if it outrage common usage to speak of a man being at once alive and dead, as much as it does so to speak of him as at once asleep and awake, it remains to be asked when a man is dying? For, before death comes, he is not dying but living; and when death has come, he is not dying but dead. The one is before, the other after death. When, then, is he in death so that we can say he is dying? For as there are three times, before death, in death, after death, so there are three states corresponding, living, dying, dead. And it is very hard to define when a man is in death or dying, when he is neither living, which is before death, nor dead, which is after death, but dying, which is in death. For so long as the soul is in the body, especially if consciousness remain, the man certainly lives; for body and soul constitute the man. And thus, before death, he cannot be said to be in death, but when, on the other hand, the soul has departed, and all bodily sensation is extinct, death is past, and the man is dead. Between these two states the dying condition finds no place; for if a man yet lives, death has not arrived; if he has ceased to live, death is past. Never, then, is he dying, that is, comprehended in the state of death. So also in the passing of time—you try to lay your finger on the present, and cannot find it, because the present occupies no space, but is only the transition of time from the future to the past. Must we then conclude that there is thus no death of the body at all? For if there is, where is it, since it is in no one, and no one can be in it? Since, indeed, if there is yet life, death is not yet; for this state is before death, not in death: and if life has already ceased, death is not present; for this state is after death, not in death. On the other hand, if there is no death before or after, what do we mean when we say "after death," or "before death"? This is a foolish way of speaking if there is no death. And would that we had lived so well in Paradise that in very truth there were now no death! But not only does it now exist, but so grievous a thing is it, that no skill is sufficient either to explain or to escape it.

Let us, then, speak in the customary way—no man ought to speak otherwise—and let us call the time before death come, "before death;" as it is written, "Praise no man before his death." [11] And when it has happened, let us say that "after death" this or that took place. And of the present time let us speak as best we can, as when we say, "He, when dying, made his will, and left this or that to such and such persons"—though, of course, he could not do so unless he were living, and did this rather before death than in

[11] Ecclus. xi. 28

death. And let us use the same phraseology as Scripture uses; for it makes no scruple of saying that the dead are not after but in death. So that verse, "For in death there is no remembrance of thee." [12] For until the resurrection men are justly said to be in death; as every one is said to be in sleep till he awakes. However, though we can say of persons in sleep that they are sleeping, we cannot speak in this way of the dead, and say they are dying. For, so far as regards the death of the body, of which we are now speaking, one cannot say that those who are already separated from their bodies continue dying. But this, you see, is just what I was saying—that no words can explain how either the dying are said to live, or how the dead are said, even after death, to be in death. For how can they be after death if they be in death, especially when we do not even call them dying, as we call those in sleep, sleeping; and those in languor, languishing; and those in grief, grieving; and those in life, living? And yet the dead, until they rise again, are said to be in death, but cannot be called dying.

And therefore I think it has not unsuitably nor inappropriately come to pass, though not by the intention of man, yet perhaps with divine purpose, that this Latin word *moritur* cannot be declined by the grammarians according to the rule followed by similar words. For *oritur* gives the form *ortus est* for the perfect; and all similar verbs form this tense from their perfect participles. But if we ask the perfect of *moritur*, we get the regular answer *mortuus est*, with a double *u*. For thus *mortuus* is pronounced, like *fatuus*, *arduus*, *conspicuus*, and similar words, which are not perfect participles but adjectives, and are declined without regard to tense. But *mortuus*, though in form an adjective, is used as perfect participle, as if that were to be declined which cannot be declined; and thus it has suitably come to pass that, as the thing itself cannot in point of fact be declined, so neither can the word significant of the act be declined. Yet, by the aid of our Redeemer's grace, we may manage at least to decline the second. For that is more grievous still, and, indeed, of all evils the worst, since it consists not in the separation of soul and body, but in the uniting of both in death eternal. And there, in striking contrast to our present conditions, men will not be before or after death, but always in death; and thus never living, never dead, but endlessly dying. And never can a man be more disastrously in death than when death itself shall be deathless.

CHAPTER XII

WHAT DEATH GOD INTENDED, WHEN HE THREATENED OUR FIRST PARENTS WITH DEATH IF THEY SHOULD DISOBEY HIS COMMANDMENT

When, therefore, it is asked what death it was with which God threatened our first parents if they should transgress the commandment they had re-

[12] Ps. vi. 5

ceived from Him, and should fail to preserve their obedience—whether it was the death of soul, or of body, or of the whole man, or that which is called second death—we must answer, It is all. For the first consists of two; the second is the complete death, which consists of all. For, as the whole earth consists of many lands, and the Church universal of many churches, so death universal consists of all deaths. The first consists of two, one of the body, and another of the soul. So that the first death is a death of the whole man, since the soul without God and without the body suffers punishment for a time; but the second is when the soul, without God but with the body, suffers punishment everlasting. When, therefore, God said to that first man whom he had placed in Paradise, referring to the forbidden fruit, "In the day that thou eatest thereof thou shalt surely die," [13] that threatening included not only the first part of the first death, by which the soul is deprived of God; nor only the subsequent part of the first death, by which the body is deprived of the soul; nor only the whole first death itself, by which the soul is punished in separation from God and from the body—but it includes whatever of death there is, even to that final death which is called second, and to which none is subsequent.

CHAPTER XIII

WHAT WAS THE FIRST PUNISHMENT OF THE TRANSGRESSION OF OUR FIRST PARENTS?

For, as soon as our first parents had transgressed the commandment, divine grace forsook them, and they were confounded at their own wickedness; and therefore they took fig-leaves (which were possibly the first that came to hand in their troubled state of mind) and covered their shame; for though their members remained the same, they had shame now where they had none before. They experienced a new motion of their flesh, which had become disobedient to them, in strict retribution of their own disobedience to God. For the soul, revelling in its own liberty, and scorning to serve God, was itself deprived of the command it had formerly maintained over the body. And because it had willfully deserted its superior Lord, it no longer held its own inferior servant; neither could it hold the flesh subject, as it would always have been able to do had it remained itself subject to God. Then began the flesh to lust against the Spirit, [14] in which strife we are born, deriving from the first transgression a seed of death, and bearing in our members, and in our vitiated nature, the contest or even victory of the flesh.

[13] Gen. ii. 17   [14] Gal. v. 17

CHAPTER XIV

IN WHAT STATE MAN WAS MADE BY GOD, AND INTO WHAT
ESTATE HE FELL BY THE CHOICE OF HIS OWN WILL

For God, the author of natures, not of vices, created man upright; but
man, being of his own will corrupted, and justly condemned, begot corrupted
and condemned children. For we all were in that one man, since we all were
that one man, who fell into sin by the woman who was made from him before
the sin. For not yet was the particular form created and distributed to us, in
which we as individuals were to live, but already the seminal nature was
there from which we were to be propagated; and this being vitiated by sin,
and bound by the chain of death, and justly condemned, man could not be
born of man in any other state. And thus, from the bad use of free will, there
originated the whole train of evil, which, with its concatenation of miseries,
convoys the human race from its depraved origin, as from a corrupt root, on
to the destruction of the second death, which has no end, those only being
excepted who are freed by the grace of God.

CHAPTER XV

THAT ADAM IN HIS SIN FORSOOK GOD ERE GOD FORSOOK HIM,
AND THAT HIS FALLING AWAY FROM GOD WAS THE FIRST
DEATH OF THE SOUL

It may perhaps be supposed that because God said, "Ye shall die the
death," [15] and not "deaths," we should understand only that death which
occurs when the soul is deserted by God, who is its life; for it was not deserted by God, and so deserted Him, but deserted Him, and so was deserted
by Him. For its own will was the originator of its evil, as God was the originator of its motions towards good, both in making it when it was not, and
in remaking it when it had fallen and perished. But though we suppose that
God meant only this death, and that the words, "In the day ye eat of it ye
shall die the death," should be understood as meaning, "In the day ye desert me in disobedience, I will desert you in justice," yet assuredly in this
death the other deaths also were threatened, which were its inevitable consequence. For in the first stirring of the disobedient motion which was felt in
the flesh of the disobedient soul, and which caused our first parents to cover
their shame, one death indeed is experienced, that, namely, which occurs
when God forsakes the soul. (This was intimated by the words He uttered,
when the man, stupefied by fear, had hid himself, "Adam, where art thou?" [16]
—words which He used not in ignorance of inquiry, but warning him to consider where he was, since God was not with him.) But when the soul itself

---

[15] Gen. ii. 17   [16] Gen. iii. 9

forsook the body, cor... ...decayed with age, the other death was experienced of which God h... ...n in pronouncing man's sentence, "Earth
thou art, and unto earth ...return." [17] And of these two deaths that
first death of the whole ...posed. And this first death is finally followed by the second, unle... ...freed by grace. For the body would not
...turn to the earth from whic... ...made, save only by the death proper
to itself, which occurs when it is forsaken of the soul, its life. And therefore
it is agreed among all Christ... who truthfully hold the Catholic faith, that
we are subject to the death... not by the law of nature, by which
God ordained no death for ma... but by His righteous infliction on account
of sin; for God, taking venge... on sin, said to the man, in whom we all
...en were, "Dust thou art, and unto dust shalt thou return."

VI

...E PHILOSOPHERS WHO THINK THAT THE SEPARATION
...ND BODY IS N...T PENAL, THOUGH PLATO REPRESENTS
T...PREME DEITY AS PROMISING TO THE INFERIOR GODS
THA... ...EY SHALL NEVER BE DISMISSED FROM THEIR BODIES

But the philosophers against whom we are defending the city of God, that
is, His Church, seem to themselves to have good cause to deride us, because
we...y that the separation of the soul from the body is to be held as part of
man's punishment. For they suppose that the blessedness of the soul then
only is complete, when it is quite denuded of the body, and returns to God
a pure and simple, and, as it were, naked soul. On this point, if I should find
nothing in their own literature to refute this opinion, I should be forced laboriously to demonstrate that it is not the body, but the corruptibility of
the body, which is a burden to the soul. Hence that sentence of Scripture we
quoted in a foregoing book, "For the corruptible body presseth down the
soul." [18] The word corruptible is added to show that the soul is burdened,
not by any body whatsoever, but by the body such as it has become in consequence of sin. And even though the word had not been added, we could
understand nothing else. But when Plato most expressly declares that the
gods who are made by the Supreme have immortal bodies, and when he introduces their Maker Himself, promising them as a great boon that they
should abide in their bodies eternally, and never by any death be loosed from
them, why do these adversaries of ours, for the sake of troubling the Christian faith, feign to be ignorant of what they quite well know, and even prefer
to contradict themselves rather than lose an opportunity of contradicting
us? Here are Plato's words, as Cicero has translated them,[19] in which he introduces the Supreme addressing the gods He had made, and saying, "Ye

[17] Gen. iii. 19　　[18] Wisdom ix. 15
[19] A translation of part of the *Timaeus,* given in a little book of Cicero's, *De Universo*

who are sprung from a divine stock, consider what works I am the parent and author. These (your bodies) are indissoluble so long as I will it; although all that is composed can be destroyed, yet it is wicked to dissolve what reason has compacted. But, seeing ye have been born, ye cannot indeed be immortal and indestructible, yet ye shall by no means be destroyed, nor shall any fates consign you to death, and prove superior to my will, which is a stronger assurance of your perpetuity than those bodies to which ye were joined when ye were born." Plato, you see, says that the gods are both mortal by the connection of the body and soul, and yet are rendered immortal by the will and decree of their maker. If, therefore, it is a punishment to the soul to be connected with any body whatever, why does God address them as if they were afraid of death, that is, of the separation of soul and body? Why does He seek to reassure them by promising them immortality, not in virtue of their nature, which is composite and not simple, but by virtue of His invincible will, whereby He can effect that neither things born die, nor things compounded be dissolved, but preserved eternally?

Whether this opinion of Plato's about the stars is true or not, is another question. For we cannot at once grant to him that these luminous bodies or globes, which by day and night shine on the earth with the light of their bodily substance, have also intellectual and blessed souls which animate each its own body, as he confidently affirms of the universe itself, as if it were one huge animal, in which all other animals were contained. But this, as I said, is another question, which we have not undertaken to discuss at present. This much only I deemed right to bring forward, in opposition to those who so pride themselves on being, or on being called Platonists, that they blush to be Christians, and who cannot brook to be called by a name which the common people also bear, lest they vulgarize the philosophers' coterie, which is proud in proportion to its exclusiveness. These men, seeking a weak point in the Christian doctrine, select for attack the eternity of the body, as if it were a contradiction to contend for the blessedness of the soul, and to wish it to be always resident in the body, bound, as it were, in a lamentable chain; and this although Plato, their own founder and master, affirms that it was granted by the Supreme as a boon to the gods He had made, that they should not die, that is, should not be separated from the bodies with which He had connected them.

CHAPTER XVII

AGAINST THOSE WHO AFFIRM THAT EARTHLY BODIES CANNOT BE MADE INCORRUPTIBLE AND ETERNAL

These same philosophers further contend that terrestrial bodies cannot be eternal, though they make no doubt that the whole earth, which is itself the central member of their god—not, indeed, of the greatest, but yet of a great god, that is, of this whole world—is eternal. Since, then, the Supreme made for them another god, that is, this world, superior to the other gods beneath Him; and since they suppose that this god is an animal, having, as they affirm, a rational or intellectual soul enclosed in the huge mass of its body, and having, as the fitly situated and adjusted members of its body, the four elements, whose union they wish to be indissoluble and eternal, lest perchance this great god of theirs might some day perish; what reason is there that the earth, which is the central member in the body of a greater creature, should be eternal, and the bodies of other terrestrial creatures should not possibly be eternal if God should so will it? But earth, say they, must return to earth, out of which the terrestrial bodies of the animals have been taken. For this, they say, is the reason of the necessity of their death and dissolution, and this the manner of their restoration to the solid and eternal earth whence they came. But if any one says the same thing of fire, holding that the bodies which are derived from it to make celestial beings must be restored to the universal fire, does not the immortality which Plato represents these gods as receiving from the Supreme evanesce in the heat of this dispute? Or does this not happen with those celestials because God, whose will, as Plato says, overpowers all powers, has willed it should not be so? What, then, hinders God from ordaining the same of terrestrial bodies? And since, indeed, Plato acknowledges that God can prevent things that are born from dying, and things that are joined from being sundered, and things that are composed from being dissolved, and can ordain that the souls once allotted to their bodies should never abandon them, but enjoy along with them immortality and everlasting bliss, why may He not also effect that terrestrial bodies die not? Is God powerless to do everything that is special to the Christian's creed, but powerful to effect everything the Platonists desire? The philosophers, forsooth, have been admitted to a knowledge of the divine purposes and power which has been denied to the prophets! The truth is, that the Spirit of God taught His prophets so much of His will as He thought fit to reveal, but the philosophers, in their efforts to discover it, were deceived by human conjecture.

But they should not have been so led astray, I will not say by their ignorance, but by their obstinacy, as to contradict themselves so frequently; for they maintain, with all their vaunted might, that in order to gain the happiness of the soul, it must abandon not only its earthly body, but every kind of body. And yet they hold that the gods, whose souls are most blessed, are bound to everlasting bodies, the celestials to fiery bodies, and the soul of Jove himself (or this world, as they would have us believe) to all the physical elements which compose this entire mass reaching from earth to heaven. For this soul Plato believes to be extended and diffused by musical numbers, from the middle of the inside of the earth, which geometricians call the centre, outwards through all its parts to the utmost heights and extremities of the heavens; so that this world is a very great and blessed immortal animal, whose soul has both the perfect blessedness of wisdom, and never leaves its own body, and whose body has life everlasting from the soul, and by no means clogs or hinders it, though itself be not a simple body, but compacted of so many and so huge materials. Since, therefore, they allow so much to their own conjectures, why do they refuse to believe that by the divine will and power immortality can be conferred on earthly bodies, in which the souls would be neither oppressed with the burden of them, nor separated from them by any death, but live eternally and blessedly? Do they not assert that their own gods so live in bodies of fire, and that Jove himself, their king, so lives in the physical elements? If, in order to gain its blessedness, the soul must quit every kind of body, let their gods flit from the starry spheres, and Jupiter from earth to sky; or, if they cannot do so, let them be pronounced miserable. But neither alternative will these men adopt. For, on the one hand, they dare not ascribe to their own gods a departure from the body, lest they should seem to worship mortals; on the other hand, they dare not deny their happiness, lest they should acknowledge wretches as gods. There-fore, to obtain blessedness, we need not quit every kind of body, but only the corruptible, cumbersome, painful, dying—not such bodies as the good-ness of God contrived for the first man, but such only as man's sin entailed.

CHAPTER XVIII

OF EARTHLY BODIES, WHICH THE PHILOSOPHERS AFFIRM CANNOT BE IN HEAVENLY PLACES, BECAUSE WHATEVER IS OF EARTH IS BY ITS NATURAL WEIGHT ATTRACTED TO EARTH

But it is necessary, they say, that the natural weight of earthly bodies either keeps them on earth or draws them to it; and therefore they cannot be in heaven. Our first parents were indeed on earth, in a well-wooded and fruitful spot, which has been named Paradise. But let our adversaries a little more carefully consider this subject of earthly weight, because it has impor-tant bearings, both on the ascension of the body of Christ, and also on the resurrection body of the saints. If human skill can by some contrivance fabri-cate vessels that float, out of metals which sink as soon as they are placed on the water, how much more credible is it that God, by some occult mode of operation, should even more certainly effect that these earthy masses be emancipated from the downward pressure of their weight? This cannot be impossible to that God by whose almighty will, according to Plato, neither things born perish, nor things composed dissolve, especially since it is much more wonderful that spiritual and bodily essences be conjoined than that bodies be adjusted to other material substances. Can we not also easily be-lieve that souls, being made perfectly blessed, should be endowed with the power of moving their earthy but incorruptible bodies as they please, with almost spontaneous movement, and of placing them where they please with the readiest action? If the angels transport whatever terrestrial creatures they please from any place they please, and convey them whither they please, is it to be believed that they cannot do so without toil and the feeling of burden? Why, then, may we not believe that the spirits of the saints, made perfect and blessed by divine grace, can carry their own bodies where they please, and set them where they will? For, though we have been accustomed to notice, in bearing weights, that the larger the quantity the greater the weight of earthly bodies is, and that the greater the weight the more burdensome it is, yet the soul carries the members of its own flesh with less difficulty when they are massive with health, than in sickness when they are wasted. And though the hale and strong man feels heavier to other men carrying him than the lank and sickly, yet the man himself moves and carries his own body with less feeling of burden when he has the greater bulk of vigorous health, than when his frame is reduced to a minimum by hunger or disease. Of such consequence, in estimating the weight of earthly bodies, even while yet corruptible and mortal, is the consideration not of dead weight, but of the healthy equilibrium of the parts. And what words can tell the difference between what we now call health and future immortality? Let not the philosophers, then, think to upset our faith with arguments from the weight of bodies; for I don't care to inquire why they cannot believe an earthly body can be in heaven, while the whole earth is suspended on nothing. For perhaps the world keeps its central place by the same law that attracts to its centre all heavy bodies. But this I say, if the lesser gods, to whom Plato committed the creation of man and the other terrestrial creatures, were able, as he affirms, to withdraw from the fire its quality of burning, while they left it that of lighting, so that it should shine through the eyes; and if to the supreme God Plato also concedes the power of preserving from death things that have been born, and of preserving from dissolution things that are composed of parts so different as body and spirit—are we to hesitate to concede to this same God the power to operate on the flesh of him whom He has endowed with immortality, so as to withdraw its corruption but leave its nature, remove its burdensome weight but retain its seemly form and members? But concerning our belief in the resurrection of the dead, and concerning their immortal bodies, we shall speak more at large, God willing, in the end of this work.

CHAPTER XIX

AGAINST THE OPINION OF THOSE WHO DO NOT BELIEVE THAT THE PRIMITIVE MEN WOULD HAVE BEEN IMMORTAL IF THEY HAD NOT SINNED

At present let us go on, as we have begun, to give some explanation regarding the bodies of our first parents. I say then, that, except as the just consequence of sin, they would not have been subjected even to this death, which is good to the good—this death, which is not exclusively known and believed in by a few, but is known to all, by which soul and body are separated, and by which the body of an animal which was but now visibly living is now visibly dead. For though there can be no manner of doubt that the souls of the just and holy dead live in peaceful rest, yet so much better would it be for them to be alive in healthy, well-conditioned bodies, that even those who hold the tenet that it is most blessed to be quit of every kind of body, condemn this opinion in spite of themselves. For no one will dare to set wise men, whether yet to die or already dead—in other words, whether already quit of the body, or shortly to be so—above the immortal gods, to whom the Supreme, in Plato, promises as a munificent gift life indissoluble, or in eternal union with their bodies. But this same Plato thinks that nothing better can happen to men than that they pass through life piously and justly, and, being separated from their bodies, be received into the bosom of the gods, who never abandon theirs; "that, oblivious of the past, they may revisit the upper air, and conceive the longing to return again to the body." [20] Virgil is applauded for borrowing this from the Platonic system. Assuredly Plato thinks that the souls of mortals cannot always be in their bodies, but must necessarily be dismissed by death; and, on the other hand, he thinks that without bodies they cannot endure for ever, but with ceaseless alternation pass from life to death, and from death to life. This difference, however, he sets between wise men and the rest, that they are carried after death to the stars, that each man may repose for a while in a star suitable for him, and may thence return to the labors and miseries of mortals when he has become oblivious of his former misery, and possessed with the desire of being embodied. Those, again, who have lived foolishly transmigrate into bodies fit for them, whether human or bestial. Thus he has appointed even the good and wise souls to a very hard lot indeed, since they do not receive such bodies as they might always and even immortally inhabit, but such only as they can neither permanently retain nor enjoy eternal purity without. Of this notion of Plato's, we have in a former book already said [21] that Porphyry was ashamed in the light of these Christian times, so that he not only emancipated human souls from a destiny in the bodies of beasts, but also contended for the liberation of the souls of the wise from all bodily ties, so that, escaping from all flesh, they might, as bare and blessed souls, dwell with the Father time without end. And that he might not seem to be outbid by Christ's promise of life everlasting to His saints, he also established purified souls in endless felicity, without return to their former woes; but, that he might contradict Christ, he denies the resurrection of incorruptible bodies, and maintains that these souls will live eternally, not only without earthly bodies, but without any bodies at all. And yet, whatever he meant by this teaching, he at least did not teach that these souls should offer no religious observance to the gods who dwelt in bodies. And why did he not, unless because he did not believe that the souls, even though separate from the body, were superior to those gods? Wherefore, if these philosophers will not dare

[20] Virgil, *Aeneid,* vi. 750, 751   [21] Book x. 30

(as I think they will not) to set human souls above the gods who are most blessed, and yet are tied eternally to their bodies, why do they find that absurd which the Christian faith preaches, namely, that our first parents were so created that, if they had not sinned, they would not have been dismissed from their bodies by any death, but would have been endowed with immortality as the reward of their obedience, and would have lived eternally with their bodies; and further, that the saints will in the resurrection inhabit those very bodies in which they have here toiled, but in such sort that neither shall any corruption or unwieldiness be suffered to attach to their flesh, nor any grief or trouble to cloud their felicity?

CHAPTER XX

THAT THE FLESH NOW RESTING IN PEACE SHALL BE RAISED TO A PERFECTION NOT ENJOYED BY THE FLESH OF OUR FIRST PARENTS

Thus the souls of departed saints are not affected by the death which dismisses them from their bodies, because their flesh rests in hope, no matter what indignities it receives after sensation is gone. For they do not desire that their bodies be forgotten, as Plato thinks fit, but rather, because they remember what has been promised by Him who deceives no man, and who gave them security for the safe keeping even of the hairs of their head, they with a longing patience wait in hope of the resurrection of their bodies, in which they have suffered many hardships, and are now to suffer never again. For if they did not "hate their own flesh," when it, with its native infirmity, opposed their will, and had to be constrained by the spiritual law, how much more shall they love it, when it shall even itself have become spiritual! For as, when the spirit serves the flesh, it is fitly called carnal, so, when the flesh serves the spirit, it will justly be called spiritual. Not that it is converted into spirit, as some fancy from the words, "It is sown in corruption, it is raised in incorruption," [22] but because it is subject to the spirit with a perfect and marvellous readiness of obedience, and responds in all things to the will that has entered on immortality—all reluctance, all corruption, and all slowness being removed. For the body will not only be better than it was here in its best estate of health, but it will surpass the bodies of our first parents ere they sinned. For, though they were not to die unless they should sin, yet they used food as men do now, their bodies not being as yet spiritual, but animal only. And though they decayed not with years, nor drew nearer to death—a condition secured to them in God's marvellous grace by the tree of life, which grew along with the forbidden tree in the midst of Paradise—yet they took other nourishment, though not of that one tree, which was interdicted not because it was itself bad, but for the sake of commending a pure and simple obedience, which is the great virtue of the rational creature set

[22] 1 Cor. xv. 42

under the Creator as his Lord. For, though no evil thing was touched, yet if a thing forbidden was touched, the very disobedience was sin. They were, then, nourished by other fruit, which they took that their animal bodies might not suffer the discomfort of hunger or thirst; but they tasted the tree of life, that death might not steal upon them from any quarter, and that they might not, spent with age, decay. Other fruits were, so to speak, their nourishment, but this their sacrament. So that the tree of life would seem to have been in the terrestrial Paradise what the wisdom of God is in the spiritual, of which it is written, "She is a tree of life to them that lay hold upon her." [23]

CHAPTER XXI

OF PARADISE, THAT IT CAN BE UNDERSTOOD IN A SPIRITUAL SENSE WITHOUT SACRIFICING THE HISTORIC TRUTH OF THE NARRATIVE REGARDING THE REAL PLACE

On this account some allegorize all that concerns Paradise itself, where the first men, the parents of the human race, are, according to the truth of holy Scripture, recorded to have been; and they understand all its trees and fruit-bearing plants as virtues and habits of life, as if they had no existence in the external world, but were only so spoken of or related for the sake of spiritual meanings. As if there could not be a real terrestrial Paradise! As if there never existed these two women, Sarah and Hagar, nor the two sons who were born to Abraham, the one of the bond woman, the other of the free, because the apostle says that in them the two covenants were prefigured; or as if water never flowed from the rock when Moses struck it, because therein Christ can be seen in a figure, as the same apostle says, "Now that rock was Christ!" [24] No one, then, denies that Paradise may signify the life of the blessed; its four rivers, the four virtues, prudence, fortitude, temperance, and justice; its trees, all useful knowledge; its fruits, the customs of the godly; its tree of life, wisdom herself, the mother of all good; and the tree of the knowledge of good and evil, the experience of a broken commandment. The punishment which God appointed was in itself, a just, and therefore a good thing; but man's experience of it is not good.

These things can also and more profitably be understood of the Church, so that they become prophetic foreshadowings of things to come. Thus Paradise is the Church, as it is called in the Canticles; [25] the four rivers of Paradise are the four gospels; the fruit-trees the saints, and the fruit their works; the tree of life is the holy of holies, Christ; the tree of the knowledge of good and evil, the will's free choice. For if man despise the will of God, he can only destroy himself; and so he learns the difference between consecrating himself to the common good and revelling in his own. For he who loves him-

[23] Prov. iii. 18   [24] 1 Cor. x. 4   [25] Cant. iv. 13

self is abandoned to himself, in order that, being overwhelmed with fears
and sorrows, he may cry, if there be yet soul in him to feel his ills, in the
words of the psalm, "My soul is cast down within me," [26] and when chastened, may say, "Because of his strength I will wait upon Thee." [27] These
and similar allegorical interpretations may be suitably put upon Paradise
without giving offence to any one, while yet we believe the strict truth of the
history, confirmed by its circumstantial narrative of facts.

CHAPTER XXII

THAT THE BODIES OF THE SAINTS SHALL AFTER THE RESURRECTION BE
SPIRITUAL, AND YET FLESH SHALL NOT BE CHANGED INTO SPIRIT

The bodies of the righteous, then, such as they shall be in the resurrection,
shall need neither any fruit to preserve them from dying of disease or the
wasting decay of old age, nor any other physical nourishment to allay the
cravings of hunger or of thirst; for they shall be invested with so sure and
every way inviolable an immortality, that they shall not eat save when they
choose, nor be under the necessity of eating, while they enjoy the power of
doing so. For so also was it with the angels who presented themselves to the
eye and touch of men, not because they could not do otherwise, but because
they were able and desirous to suit themselves to men by a kind of manhood
ministry. For neither are we to suppose, when men receive them as guest,
that the angels eat only in appearance, though to any who did not know
them to be angels they might seem to eat from the same necessity as ourselves. So these words spoken in the Book of Tobit, "You saw me eat, but
you saw it but in vision;" [28] that is, you thought I took food as you do for
the sake of refreshing my body. But if in the case of the angels another opinion seems more capable of defence, certainly our faith leaves no room to
doubt regarding our Lord Himself, that even after His resurrection, and
when now in spiritual but yet real flesh, He ate and drank with His disciples;
for not the power, but the need, of eating and drinking is taken from these
bodies. And so they will be spiritual, not because they shall cease to be
bodies, but because they shall subsist by the quickening spirit.

CHAPTER XXIII

WHAT WE ARE TO UNDERSTAND BY THE ANIMAL AND SPIRITUAL BODY;
OR OF THOSE WHO DIE IN ADAM, AND OF THOSE WHO ARE
MADE ALIVE IN CHRIST

For as those bodies of ours, that have a living soul, though not as yet a
quickening spirit, are called soul-informed bodies, and yet are not souls but
bodies, so also those bodies are called spiritual—yet God forbid we should

[26] Ps. xlii. 6   [27] Ps. lix. 9   [28] Tobit xii. 19

therefore suppose them to be spirits and not bodies—which, being quickened by the Spirit, have the substance, but not the unwieldiness and corruption of flesh. Man will then be not earthly but heavenly—not because the body will not be that very body which was made of earth, but because by its heavenly endowment it will be a fit inhabitant of heaven, and this not by losing its nature, but by changing its quality. The first man, of the earth earthy, was made a living soul, not a quickening spirit—which rank was reserved for him as the reward of obedience. And therefore his body, which required meat and drink to satisfy hunger and thirst, and which had no absolute and indestructible immortality, but by means of the tree of life warded off the necessity of dying, and was thus maintained in the flower of youth—this body, I say, was doubtless not spiritual, but animal; and yet it would not have died but that it provoked God's threatened vengeance by offending. And though sustenance was not denied him even outside Paradise, yet, being forbidden the tree of life, he was delivered over to the wasting of time, at least in respect of that life which, had he not sinned, he might have retained perpetually in Paradise, though only in an animal body, till such time as it became spiritual in acknowledgment of his obedience.

Wherefore, although we understand that this manifest death, which consists in the separation of soul and body, was also signified by God when He said, "In the day thou eatest thereof thou shalt surely die," [29] it ought not on that account to seem absurd that they were not dismissed from the body on that very day on which they took the forbidden and death-bringing fruit. For certainly on that very day their nature was altered for the worse and vitiated, and by their most just banishment from the tree of life they were involved in the necessity even of bodily death, in which necessity we are born. And therefore the apostle does not say, "The body indeed is doomed to die on account of sin," but he says, "The body indeed is dead because of sin." Then he adds, "But if the Spirit of Him that raised up Jesus from the dead dwell in you, He that raised up Christ from the dead shall also quicken your mortal bodies by His Spirit that dwelleth in you." [30] Then accordingly shall the body become a quickening spirit which is now a living soul; and yet the apostle calls it "dead," because already it lies under the necessity of dying. But in Paradise it was so made a living soul, though not a quickening spirit, that it could not properly be called dead, for, save through the commission of sin, it could not come under the power of death. Now, since God by the words, "Adam, where art thou?" pointed to the death of the soul, which results when He abandons it, and since in the words, "Earth thou art, and unto earth shalt thou return," [31] He signified the death of the body, which results when the soul departs from it, we are led, therefore, to believe that He said nothing of the second death, wishing it to be kept hidden, and reserving it for the New Testament dispensation, in which it is most plainly revealed. And this He did in order that, first of all, it might be evident that

[29] Gen. ii. 17   [30] Rom. viii. 10, 11   [31] Gen. iii. 19

this first death, which is common to all, was the result of that sin which in one man became common to all. But the second death is not common to all, those being excepted who were called according to His purpose. For whom He did foreknow, He also did predestinate to be conformed to the image of His Son, that He might be the first-born among many brethren.[32] Those the grace of God has, by a Mediator, delivered from the second death.

Thus the apostle states that the first man was made in an animal body. For, wishing to distinguish the animal body which now is from the spiritual, which is to be in the resurrection, he says, "It is sown in corruption, it is raised in incorruption: it is sown in dishonor, it is raised in glory: it is sown in weakness, it is raised in power: it is sown a natural body, it is raised a spiritual body." Then, to prove this, he goes on, "There is a natural body, and there is a spiritual body." And to show what the animated body is, he says, "Thus it was written, The first man Adam was made a living soul, the last Adam was made a quickening spirit." [33] He wished thus to show what the animated body is, though Scripture did not say of the first man Adam, when his soul was created by the breath of God, "Man was made in an animated body," but "Man was made a living soul." [34] By these words, therefore, "The first man was made a living soul," the apostle wishes man's animated body to be understood. But how he wishes the spiritual body to be understood he shows when he adds, "But the last Adam was made a quickening spirit," plainly referring to Christ, who has so risen from the dead that He cannot die any more. He then goes on to say, "But that was not first which is spiritual, but that which is natural; and afterward that which is spiritual." And here he much more clearly asserts that he referred to the animal body when he said that the first man was made a living soul, and to the spiritual when he said that the last man was made a quickening spirit. The animal body is the first, being such as the first Adam had, and which would not have died had he not sinned, being such also we now have, its nature being changed and vitiated by sin to the extent of bringing us under the necessity of death, and being such as even Christ condescended first of all to assume, not indeed of necessity, but of choice; but afterwards comes the spiritual body, which already is worn by anticipation by Christ as our head, and will be worn by His members in the resurrection of the dead.

Then the apostle subjoins a notable difference between these two men, saying, "The first man is of the earth, earthy; the second man is the Lord from heaven. As is the earthy, such are they also that are earthy, and as is the heavenly, such are they also that are heavenly. And as we have borne the image of the earthy, we shall also bear the image of the heavenly." [35] So he elsewhere says, "As many of you as have been baptized into Christ have put on Christ;" [36] but in very deed this shall be accomplished when that which is animal in us by our birth shall have become spiritual in our resur-

[32] Rom. viii. 28, 29   [33] 1 Cor. xv. 42-45   [34] Gen. ii. 7   [35] 1 Cor. xv. 47-49
[36] Gal. iii. 27

rection. For, to use his words again, "We are saved by hope." [37] Now we bear the image of the earthly man by the propagation of sin and death, which pass on us by ordinary generation; but we bear the image of the heavenly by the grace of pardon and life eternal, which regeneration confers upon us through the Mediator of God and men, the Man Christ Jesus. And He is the heavenly Man of Paul's passage, because He came from heaven to be clothed with a body of earthly mortality, that He might clothe it with heavenly immortality. And he calls others heavenly, because by grace they become His members, that, together with them, He may become one Christ, as head and body. In the same epistle he puts this yet more clearly: "Since by man came death, by Man came also the resurrection of the dead. For as in Adam all die, even so in Christ shall all be made alive" [38]—that is to say, in a spiritual body which shall be made a quickening spirit. Not that all who die in Adam shall be members of Christ—for the great majority shall be punished in eternal death—but he uses the word "all" in both clauses, because, as no one dies in an animal body except in Adam, so no one is quickened a spiritual body save in Christ. We are not, then, by any means to suppose that we shall in the resurrection have such a body as the first man had before he sinned, nor that the words, "As is the earthy such are they also that are earthy," are to be understood of that which was brought about by sin; for we are not to think that Adam had a spiritual body before he fell, and that, in punishment of his sin, it was changed into an animal body. If this be thought, small heed has been given to the words of so great a teacher, who says, "There is a natural body, there is also a spiritual body; as it is written, The first man Adam was made a living soul." Was it after sin he was made so? or was not this the primal condition of man from which the blessed apostle selects his testimony to show what the animal body is?

CHAPTER XXIV

HOW WE MUST UNDERSTAND THAT BREATHING OF GOD BY WHICH
"THE FIRST MAN WAS MADE A LIVING SOUL," AND THAT ALSO
BY WHICH THE LORD CONVEYED HIS SPIRIT TO HIS DISCIPLES
WHEN HE SAID, "RECEIVE YE THE HOLY GHOST"

Some have hastily supposed from the words, "God breathed into Adam's nostrils the breath of life, and man became a living soul," [39] that a soul was not then first given to man, but that the soul already given was quickened by the Holy Ghost. They are encouraged in this supposition by the fact that the Lord Jesus after His resurrection breathed on His disciples, and said, "Receive ye the Holy Spirit." [40] From this they suppose that the same thing was effected in either case, as if the evangelist had gone on to say, And they became living souls. But if he had made this addition, we should only understand that the Spirit is in some way the life of souls, and that without Him

[37] Rom. viii. 24   [38] 1 Cor. xv. 21, 22   [39] Gen. ii. 7   [40] John xx. 22

reasonable souls must be accounted dead, though their bodies seem to live before our eyes. But that this was not what happened when man was created, the very words of the narrative sufficiently show: "And God made man dust of the earth;" which some have thought to render more clearly by the words, "And God formed man of the clay of the earth." For it had before been said that there went up a mist from the earth, and watered the whole face of the ground,[41] in order that the reference to clay, formed of this moisture and dust, might be understood. For on this verse there immediately follows the announcement, "And God created man dust of the earth;" so those Greek manuscripts have it from which this passage has been translated into Latin. But whether one prefers to read "*created*" or "*formed,*" where the Greek reads ἔπλασεν, is of little importance; yet "*formed*" is the better rendering. But those who preferred "created" thought they thus avoided the ambiguity arising from the fact, that in the Latin language the usage obtains that those are said to form a thing who frame some feigned and fictitious thing. This man, then, who was created of the dust of the earth, or of the moistened dust or clay—this "dust of the earth" (that I may use the express words of Scripture) was made, as the apostle teaches, an animated body when he received a soul. This man, he says, "was made a living soul;" that is, this fashioned dust was made a living soul.

They say, Already he had a soul, else he would not be called a man; for man is not a body alone, nor a soul alone, but a being composed of both. This, indeed, is true, that the soul is not the whole man, but the better part of man; the body not the whole, but the inferior part of man; and that then, when both are joined, they receive the name of man—which, however, they do not severally lose even when we speak of them singly. For who is prohibited from saying, in colloquial usage, "That man is dead, and is now at rest or in torment," though this can be spoken only of the soul; or "He is buried in such and such a place," though this refers only to the body? Will they say that Scripture follows no such usage? On the contrary, it so thoroughly adopts it, that even while a man is alive, and body and soul are united, it calls each of them singly by the name "*man,*" speaking of the soul as the "inward man," and of the body as the "outward man," [42] as if there were two men, though both together are indeed but one. But we must understand in what sense man is said to be in the image of God, and is yet dust, and to return to the dust. The former is spoken of the rational soul, which God by His breathing, or, to speak more appropriately, by His inspiration, conveyed to man, that is, to his body; but the latter refers to his body, which God formed of the dust, and to which a soul was given, that it might become a living body, that is, that man might become a living soul.

Wherefore, when our Lord breathed on His disciples, and said, "Receive ye the Holy Ghost," He certainly wished it to be understood that the Holy Ghost was not only the Spirit of the Father, but of the only begotten Son

[41] Gen. ii. 6　　[42] 2 Cor. iv. 16

Himself. For the same Spirit is, indeed, the Spirit of the Father and of the Son, making with them the trinity of Father, Son, and Spirit, not a creature, but the Creator. For neither was that material breath which proceeded from the mouth of His flesh the very substance and nature of the Holy Spirit, but rather the intimation, as I said, that the Holy Spirit was common to the Father and to the Son; for they have not each a separate Spirit, but both one and the same. Now this Spirit is always spoken of in sacred Scripture by the Greek word πνεῦμα, as the Lord, too, named Him in the place cited when He gave Him to His disciples, and intimated the gift by the breathing of His lips; and there does not occur to me any place in the whole Scriptures where He is otherwise named. But in this passage where it is said, "And the Lord formed man dust of the earth, and breathed, or inspired, into his face the breath of life;" the Greek has not πνεῦμα, the usual word for the Holy Spirit, but πνοή, a word more frequently used of the creature than of the Creator; and for this reason some Latin interpreters have preferred to render it by "breath" rather than "spirit." For this word occurs also in the Greek in *Isaiah*,[43] where God says, "I have made all breath," meaning, doubtless, all souls. Accordingly, this word πνοή is sometimes rendered "breath," sometimes "spirit," sometimes "inspiration," sometimes "aspiration," sometimes "soul," even when it is used of God. Πνεῦμα, on the other hand, is uniformly rendered "spirit," whether of man, of whom the apostle says, "For what man knoweth the things of a man, save the spirit of man which is in him?" [44] or of beast, as in the book of Solomon, "Who knoweth the spirit of man that goeth upward, and the spirit of the beast that goeth downward to the earth?" [45] or of that physical spirit which is called wind, for so the Psalmist calls it: "Fire and hail; snow and vapors; stormy wind;" [46] or of the uncreated Creator Spirit, of whom the Lord said in the gospel, "Receive ye the Holy Ghost," indicating the gift by the breathing of His mouth; and when He says, "Go ye and baptize all nations in the name of the Father, of the Son, and of the Holy Ghost," [47] words which very expressly and excellently commend the Trinity; and where it is said, "God is a Spirit;" [48] and in very many other places of the sacred writings. In all these quotations from Scripture we do not find in the Greek the word πνοή used, but πνεῦμα, and in the Latin, not *flatus*, but *spiritus*. Wherefore, referring again to that place where it is written, "He inspired," or to speak more properly, "breathed into his face the breath of life," even though the Greek had not used πνοή (as it has) but πνεῦμα, it would not on that account necessarily follow that the Creator Spirit, who in the Trinity is distinctively called the Holy Ghost, was meant, since, as has been said, it is plain that πνεῦμα is used not only of the Creator, but also of the creature.

But, say they, when the Scripture used the word "spirit," it would not have added "of life" unless it meant us to understand the Holy Spirit; nor,

[43] lvii. 16   [44] I Cor. ii. 11   [45] Eccles. iii. 21   [46] Ps. cxlviii. 8   [47] Matt. xxviii. 19   [48] John iv. 24

when it said, "Man became a soul," would it also have inserted the word "living" unless that life of the soul were signified which is imparted to it from above by the gift of God. For, seeing that the soul by itself has a proper life of its own, what need, they ask, was there of adding "living," save only to show that the life which is given it by the Holy Spirit was meant? What is this but to fight strenuously for their own conjectures, while they carelessly neglect the teaching of Scripture? Without troubling themselves much, they might have found in a preceding page of this very book of *Genesis* the words, "Let the earth bring forth the living soul," [49] when all the terrestrial animals were created. Then at a slight interval, but still in the same book, was it impossible for them to notice this verse, "All in whose nostrils was the breath of life, of all that was in the dry land, died," by which it was signified that all the animals which lived on the earth had perished in the deluge? If, then, we find that Scripture is accustomed to speak both of the "living soul" and the "spirit of life" even in reference to beasts; and if in this place, where it is said, "All things which have the spirit of life," the word πνοή, not πνεῦμα, is used; why may we not say, What need was there to add "living," since the soul cannot exist without being alive? or, What need to add "of life" after the word spirit? But we understand that Scripture used these expressions in its ordinary style so long as it speaks of animals, that is, animated bodies, in which the soul serves as the residence of sensation; but when man is spoken of, we forget the ordinary and established usage of Scripture, whereby it signifies that man received a rational soul, which was not produced out of the waters and the earth like the other living creatures, but was created by the breath of God. Yet this creation was so ordered that the human soul should live in an animal body, like those other animals of which the Scripture said, "Let the earth produce every living soul," and regarding which it again says that in them is the breath of life, where the word πνοή and not πνεῦμα is used in the Greek, and where certainly not the Holy Spirit, but their spirit, is signified under that name.

But, again, they object that breath is understood to have been emitted from the mouth of God; and if we believe that is the soul, we must consequently acknowledge it to be of the same substance, and equal to that wisdom, which says, "I come out of the mouth of the Most High." [50] Wisdom, indeed, does not say it was breathed out of the mouth of God, but proceeded out of it. But as we are able, when we breathe, to make a breath, not of our own human nature, but of the surrounding air, which we inhale and exhale as we draw our breath and breathe again, so almighty God was able to make breath, not of His own nature, nor of the creature beneath Him, but even of nothing; and this breath, when He communicated it to man's body, He is most appropriately said to have breathed or inspired—the Immaterial breathing it also immaterial, but the Immutable not also the immutable;

[49] Gen. i. 24   [50] Ecclus. xxiv. 3

for it was created, He uncreated. Yet that these persons who wish to quote Scripture, and yet know not the usages of its language, may know that not only what is equal and consubstantial with God is said to proceed out of His mouth, let them hear or read what God says: "So then because thou art lukewarm, and neither cold nor hot, I will spue thee out of my mouth." [51]

There is no ground, then, for our objecting, when the apostle so expressly distinguishes the animal body from the spiritual—that is to say, the body in which we now are from that in which we are to be. He says, "It is sown a natural body, it is raised a spiritual body. There is a natural body, and there is a spiritual body. And so it is written, The first man Adam was made a living soul; the last Adam was made a quickening spirit. Howbeit that was not first which is spiritual, but that which is natural; and afterward that which is spiritual. The first man is of the earth, earthy; the second man is the Lord from heaven. As is the earthy, such are they also that are earthy; and as is the heavenly, such are they also that are heavenly. And as we have borne the image of the earthy, we shall also bear the image of the heavenly." [52] Of all these words of his we have previously spoken. The animal body, accordingly, in which the apostle says that the first man Adam was made, was not so made that it could not die at all, but so that it should not die unless he should have sinned. That body, indeed, which shall be made spiritual and immortal by the quickening Spirit shall not be able to die at all; as the soul has been created immortal, and therefore, although by sin it may be said to die, and does lose a certain life of its own, namely, the Spirit of God, by whom it was enabled to live wisely and blessedly, yet it does not cease living a kind of life, though a miserable one, because it is immortal by creation. So, too, the rebellious angels, though by sinning they did in a sense die, because they forsook God, the Fountain of life, which while they drank they were able to live wisely and well, yet they could not so die as utterly to cease living and feeling, for they are immortals by creation. And so, after the final judgment, they shall be hurled into the second death, and not even there be deprived of life or of sensation, but shall suffer torment. But those men who have been embraced by God's grace, and are become the fellow-citizens of the holy angels who have continued in bliss, shall never more either sin or die, being endued with spiritual bodies; yet, being clothed with immortality, such as the angels enjoy, of which they cannot be divested even by sinning, the nature of their flesh shall continue the same, but all carnal corruption and unwieldiness shall be removed.

There remains a question which must be discussed, and, by the help of the Lord God of truth, solved: If the motion of concupiscence in the unruly members of our first parents arose out of their sin, and only when the divine grace deserted them; and if it was on that occasion that their eyes were opened to see, or, more exactly, notice their nakedness, and that they cov-

[51] Rev. iii. 16   [52] 1 Cor. xv. 44-49

ered their shame because the shameless motion of their members was not subject to their will—how, then, would they have begotten children had they remained sinless as they were created? But as this book must be concluded, and so large a question cannot be summarily disposed of, we may relegate it to the following book, in which it will be more conveniently treated.

BOOK FOURTEEN

ARGUMENT

Augustine again treats of the sin of the first man, and teaches that it is the cause of the carnal life and vicious affections of man. Especially he proves that the shame which accompanies lust is the just punishment of that disobedience, and inquires how man, if he had not sinned, would have been able without lust to propagate his kind.

CHAPTER I

THAT THE DISOBEDIENCE OF THE FIRST MAN WOULD HAVE PLUNGED ALL MEN INTO THE ENDLESS MISERY OF THE SECOND DEATH, HAD NOT THE GRACE OF GOD RESCUED MANY

WE HAVE already stated in the preceding books that God, desiring not only that the human race might be able by their similarity of nature to associate with one another, but also that they might be bound together in harmony and peace by the ties of relationship, was pleased to derive all men from one individual, and created man with such a nature that the members of the race should not have died, had not the two first (of whom the one was created out of nothing, and the other out of him) merited this by their disobedience; for by them so great a sin was committed, that by it human nature was altered for the worse, and was transmitted also to their posterity, liable to sin and subject to death. And the kingdom of death so reigned over men, that the deserved penalty of sin would have hurled all headlong even into the second death, of which there is no end, had not the undeserved grace of God saved some therefrom. And thus it has come to pass, that though there are very many and great nations all over the earth, whose rites and customs, speech, arms, and dress, are distinguished by marked differences, yet there are no more than two kinds of human society, which we may justly call two cities, according to the language of our Scriptures. The one consists of those who wish to live after the flesh, the other of those who wish to live after the spirit; and when they severally achieve what they wish, they live in peace, each after their kind.

CHAPTER II

OF CARNAL LIFE, WHICH IS TO BE UNDERSTOOD NOT ONLY OF LIVING IN BODILY INDULGENCE, BUT ALSO OF LIVING IN THE VICES OF THE INNER MAN

First, we must see what it is to live after the flesh, and what to live after the spirit. For any one who either does not recollect, or does not sufficiently weigh, the language of sacred Scripture, may, on first hearing what we have said, suppose that the Epicurean philosophers live after the flesh, because they place man's highest good in bodily pleasure; and that those others do so who have been of opinion that in some form or other bodily good is man's supreme good; and that the mass of men do so who, without dogmatizing or philosophizing on the subject, are so prone to lust that they cannot delight in any pleasure save such as they receive from bodily sensations: and he may suppose that the Stoics, who place the supreme good of men in the soul, live after the spirit; for what is man's soul, if not spirit? But in the sense of the divine Scripture both are proved to live after the flesh. For by flesh it means not only the body of a terrestrial and mortal animal, as when it says, "All flesh is not the same flesh, but there is one kind of flesh of men, another flesh of beasts, another of fishes, another of birds," [1] but it uses this word in many other significations; and among these various usages, a frequent one is to use flesh for man himself, the nature of man taking the part for the whole, as in the words, "By the deeds of the law there shall no flesh be justified;" [2] for what does he mean here by "no flesh" but "no man"? And this, indeed, he shortly after says more plainly: "No man shall be justified by the law;" [3] and in the *Epistle to the Galatians*, "Knowing that man is not justified by the works of the law." And so we understand the words, "And the Word was made flesh" [4]—that is, man, which some not accepting in its right sense, have supposed that Christ had not a human soul.[5] For as the whole is used for the part in the words of Mary Magdalene in the Gospel, "They have taken away my Lord, and I know not where they have laid Him," [6] by which she meant only the flesh of Christ, which she supposed had been taken from the tomb where it had been buried, so the part is used for the whole, flesh being named, while man is referred to, as in the quotations above cited.

Since, then, Scripture uses the word flesh in many ways, which there is not time to collect and investigate, if we are to ascertain what it is to live after the flesh (which is certainly evil, though the nature of flesh is not itself evil), we must carefully examine that passage of the epistle which the Apostle Paul wrote to the Galatians, in which he says, "Now the works of the flesh are manifest, which are these: adultery, fornication, uncleanness, lasciviousness, idolatry, witchcraft, hatred, variance, emulations, wrath, strife, seditions, heresies, envyings, murders, drunkenness, revellings, and such like: of the which I tell you before, as I have also told you in time past, that they which do such things shall not inherit the kingdom of God." [7] This whole passage of the apostolic epistle being considered, so far as it bears on the matter in hand, will be sufficient to answer the question, what it is to live after the flesh. For among the works of the flesh which he said were manifest, and which he cited for condemnation, we find not only those which con-

---

[1] 1 Cor. xv. 39   [2] Rom. iii. 20   [3] Gal. iii. 11   [4] John i. 14   [5] The Apollinarians   [6] John xx. 13   [7] Gal. v. 19-21

cern the pleasure of the flesh, as fornications, uncleanness, lasciviousness, drunkenness, revellings, but also those which, though they be remote from fleshly pleasure, reveal the vices of the soul. For who does not see that idolatries, witchcrafts, hatreds, variance, emulations, wrath, strife, heresies, envyings, are vices rather of the soul than of the flesh? For it is quite possible for a man to abstain from fleshly pleasures for the sake of idolatry or some heretical error; and yet, even when he does so, he is proved by this apostolic authority to be living after the flesh; and in abstaining from fleshly pleasure, he is proved to be practising damnable works of the flesh. Who that has enmity has it not in his soul? or who would say to his enemy, or to the man he thinks his enemy, You have a bad flesh towards me, and not rather, You have a bad spirit towards me? In fine, if any one heard of what I may call "carnalities," he would not fail to attribute them to the carnal part of man; so no one doubts that "animosities" belong to the soul of man. Why then does the doctor of the Gentiles in faith and verity call all these and similar things works of the flesh, unless because, by that mode of speech whereby the part is used for the whole, he means us to understand by the word flesh the man himself?

CHAPTER III

THAT THE SIN IS CAUSED NOT BY THE FLESH, BUT BY THE SOUL, AND THAT THE CORRUPTION CONTRACTED FROM SIN IS NOT SIN BUT SIN'S PUNISHMENT

But if any one says that the flesh is the cause of all vices and ill conduct, inasmuch as the soul lives wickedly only because it is moved by the flesh, it is certain he has not carefully considered the whole nature of man. For "the corruptible body, indeed, weigheth down the soul." [8] Whence, too, the apostle, speaking of this corruptible body, of which he had shortly before said, "though our outward man perish," [9] says, "We know that if our earthly house of this tabernacle were dissolved, we have a building of God, an house not made with hands, eternal in the heavens. For in this we groan, earnestly desiring to be clothed upon with our house which is from heaven: if so be that being clothed we shall not be found naked. For we that are in this tabernacle do groan, being burdened: not for that we would be unclothed, but clothed upon, that mortality might be swallowed up in life." [10] We are then burdened with this corruptible body; but knowing that the cause of this burdensomeness is not the nature and substance of the body, but its corruption, we do not desire to be deprived of the body, but to be clothed with its immortality. For then, also, there will be a body, but it shall no longer be a burden, being no longer corruptible. At present, then, "the corruptible body presseth down the soul, and the earthly tabernacle weigheth

[8] Wisd. ix. 15　　[9] 2 Cor. iv. 16　　[10] 2 Cor. v. 1-4

down the mind that museth upon many things," nevertheless they are in error who suppose that all the evils of the soul proceed from the body.

Virgil, indeed, seems to express the sentiments of Plato in the beautiful lines, where he says—

> A fiery strength inspires their lives,
> An essence that from heaven derives,
> Though clogged in part by limbs of clay
> And the dull "vesture of decay;" [11]

but though he goes on to mention the four most common mental emotions—desire, fear, joy, sorrow—with the intention of showing that the body is the origin of all sins and vices, saying—

> Hence wild desires and grovelling fears,
> And human laughter, human tears,
> Immured in dungeon-seeming night,
> They look abroad, yet see no light,[12]

yet we believe quite otherwise. For the corruption of the body, which weighs down the soul, is not the cause but the punishment of the first sin; and it was not the corruptible flesh that made the soul sinful, but the sinful soul that made the flesh corruptible. And though from this corruption of the flesh there arise certain incitements to vice, and indeed vicious desires, yet we must not attribute to the flesh all the vices of a wicked life, in case we thereby clear the devil of all these, for he has no flesh. For though we cannot call the devil a fornicator or drunkard, or ascribe to him any sensual indulgence (though he is the secret instigator and prompter of those who sin in these ways) yet he is exceedingly proud and envious. And this viciousness has so possessed him, that on account of it he is reserved in chains of darkness to everlasting punishment. Now these vices, which have dominion over the devil, the apostle attributes to the flesh, which certainly the devil has not. For he says "hatred, variance, emulations, strife, envying" are the works of the flesh; and of all these evils pride is the origin and head, and it rules in the devil though he has no flesh. For who shows more hatred to the saints? who is more at variance with them? who more envious, bitter, and jealous? And since he exhibits all these works, though he has no flesh, how are they works of the flesh, unless because they are the works of man, who is, as I said, spoken of under the name of flesh? For it is not by having flesh, which the devil has not, but by living according to himself—that is, according to man—that man became like the devil. For the devil too, wished to live according to himself when he did not abide in the truth; so that when he lied, this was not of God, but of himself, who is not only a liar, but the father of lies, he being the first who lied, and the originator of lying as of sin.

[11] *Aeneid*, vi. 730-32   [12] *Ibid.* 733, 734

CHAPTER IV

WHAT IT IS TO LIVE ACCORDING TO MAN, AND WHAT TO LIVE
ACCORDING TO GOD

When, therefore, man lives according to man, not according to God, he is like the devil. Because not even an angel might live according to an angel, but only according to God, if he was to abide in the truth, and speak God's truth and not his own lie. And of man, too, the same apostle says in another place, "If the truth of God hath more abounded through my lie" [13]—"my lie," he said, and "God's truth." When, then, a man lives according to the truth, he lives not according to himself, but according to God; for He was God who said, "I am the truth." [14] When, therefore, man lives according to himself—that is, according to man, not according to God—assuredly he lives according to a lie; not that man himself is a lie, for God is his author and creator, who is certainly not the author and creator of a lie, but because man was made upright, that he might not live according to himself, but according to Him that made him—in other words, that he might do His will and not his own; and not to live as he was made to live, that is a lie. For he certainly desires to be blessed even by not living so that he may be blessed. And what is a lie if this desire be not? Wherefore it is not without meaning said that all sin is a lie. For no sin is committed save by that desire or will by which we desire that it be well with us, and shrink from it being ill with us. That, therefore, is a lie which we do in order that it may be well with us, but which makes us more miserable than we were. And why is this, but because the source of man's happiness lies only in God, whom he abandons when he sins, and not in himself, by living according to whom he sins?

In enunciating this proposition of ours, then, that because some live according to the flesh and others according to the spirit, there have arisen two diverse and conflicting cities, we might equally well have said, "because some live according to man, others according to God." For Paul says very plainly to the Corinthians, "For whereas there is among you envying and strife, are ye not carnal, and walk according to man?" [15] So that to walk according to man and to be carnal are the same; for by *flesh*, that is, by a part of man, man is meant. For before he said that those same persons were animal whom afterwards he calls carnal, saying, "For what man knoweth the things of a man, save the spirit of man which is in him? even so the things of God knoweth no man, but the Spirit of God. Now we have received not the spirit of this world, but the Spirit which is of God; that we might know the things which are freely given to us of God. Which things also we speak, not in the words which man's wisdom teacheth, but which the Holy Ghost teacheth; comparing spiritual things with spiritual. But the animal man per-

[13] Rom. iii. 7   [14] John xiv. 6   [15] I Cor. iii. 3

ceiveth not the things of the Spirit of God; for they are foolishness unto him." [16] It is to men of this kind, then, that is, to animal men, he shortly after says, "And I, brethren, could not speak unto you as unto spiritual, but as unto carnal." [17] And this is to be interpreted by the same usage, a part being taken for the whole. For both the soul and the flesh, the component parts of man, can be used to signify the whole man; and so the animal man and the carnal man are not two different things, but one and the same thing, viz., man living according to man. In the same way it is nothing else than men that are meant either in the words, "By the deeds of the law there shall no *flesh* be justified;" [18] or in the words, "Seventy-five *souls* went down into Egypt with Jacob." [19] In the one passage, "no flesh" signifies "no man;" and in the other, by "seventy-five souls" seventy-five men are meant. And the expression, "not in words which man's wisdom teacheth," might equally be "not in words which fleshly wisdom teacheth;" and the expression, "ye walk according to man," might be "according to the flesh." And this is still more apparent in the words which followed: "For while one saith, I am of Paul, and another, I am of Apollos, are ye not men?" The same thing which he had before expressed by "ye are animal," "ye are carnal," he now expresses by "ye are men;" that is, ye live according to man, not according to God, for if you lived according to Him, you should be gods.

CHAPTER V

THAT THE OPINION OF THE PLATONISTS REGARDING THE NATURE OF BODY AND SOUL IS NOT SO CENSURABLE AS THAT OF THE MANICHAEANS, BUT THAT EVEN IT IS OBJECTIONABLE, BECAUSE IT ASCRIBES THE ORIGIN OF VICES TO THE NATURE OF THE FLESH

There is no need, therefore, that in our sins and vices we accuse the nature of the flesh to the injury of the Creator, for in its own kind and degree the flesh is good; but to desert the Creator good, and live according to the created good, is not good, whether a man choose to live according to the flesh, or according to the soul, or according to the whole human nature, which is composed of flesh and soul, and which is therefore spoken of either by the name flesh alone, or by the name soul alone. For he who extols the nature of the soul as the chief good, and condemns the nature of the flesh as if it were evil, assuredly is fleshly both in his love of the soul and hatred of the flesh; for these his feelings arise from human fancy, not from divine truth. The Platonists, indeed, are not so foolish as, with the Manichaeans, to detest our present bodies as an evil nature; for they attribute all the elements of which this visible and tangible world is compacted, with all their qualities, to God their Creator. Nevertheless, from the death-infected members and earthly

---

[16] 1 Cor. ii. 11-14   [17] 1 Cor. iii. 1   [18] Rom. iii. 20   [19] Gen. xlvi. 27

construction of the body they believe the soul is so affected, that there are thus originated in it the diseases of desires, and fears, and joy, and sorrow, under which four perturbations, as Cicero[20] calls them, or passions, as most prefer to name them with the Greeks, is included the whole viciousness of human life. But if this be so, how is it that Aeneas in Virgil, when he had heard from his father in Hades that the souls should return to bodies, expresses surprise at this declaration, and exclaims:

> O father! and can thought conceive
> That happy souls this realm would leave,
>   And seek the upper sky,
> With sluggish clay to reunite?
> This direful longing for the light,
>   Whence comes it, say, and why? [21]

This direful longing, then, does it still exist even in that boasted purity of the disembodied spirits, and does it still proceed from the death-infected members and earthly limbs? Does he not assert that, when they begin to long to return to the body, they have already been delivered from all these so-called pestilences of the body? From which we gather that, were this endlessly alternating purification and defilement of departing and returning souls as true as it is most certainly false, yet it could not be averred that all culpable and vicious motions of the soul originate in the earthly body; for, on their own showing, "this direful longing," to use the words of their noble exponent, is so extraneous to the body, that it moves the soul that is purged of all bodily taint, and is existing apart from any body whatever, and moves it, moreover, to be embodied again. So that even they themselves acknowledge that the soul is not only moved to desire, fear, joy, sorrow, by the flesh, but that it can also be agitated with these emotions at its own instance.

CHAPTER VI

OF THE CHARACTER OF THE HUMAN WILL WHICH MAKES THE AFFECTIONS OF THE SOUL RIGHT OR WRONG

But the character of the human will is of moment; because, if it is wrong, these motions of the soul will be wrong, but if it is right, they will be not merely blameless, but even praiseworthy. For the will is in them all; indeed, none of them is anything else than will. For what are desire and joy but a volition of consent to the things we wish? And what are fear and sadness but a volition of aversion from the things which we do not wish? But when consent takes the form of seeking to possess the things we wish, this is called desire; and when consent takes the form of enjoying the things we wish, this is called joy. In like manner, when we turn with aversion from that which we do not wish to happen, this volition is termed fear; and when we turn away

[20] *Tusc. Quaest.* iv. 6   [21] *Aeneid*, vi. 719-21

from that which has happened against our will, this act of will is called sorrow. And generally in respect of all that we seek or shun, as a man's will is attracted or repelled, so it is changed and turned into these different affections. Wherefore the man who lives according to God, and not according to man, ought to be a lover of good, and therefore a hater of evil. And since no one is evil by nature, but whoever is evil is evil by vice, he who lives according to God ought to cherish towards evil men a perfect hatred, so that he shall neither hate the man because of his vice, nor love the vice because of the man, but hate the vice and love the man. For the vice being cursed, all that ought to be loved, and nothing that ought to be hated, will remain.

CHAPTER VII

THAT THE WORDS LOVE AND REGARD (AMOR AND DILECTIO) ARE IN SCRIPTURE USED INDIFFERENTLY OF GOOD AND EVIL AFFECTION

He who resolves to love God, and to love his neighbor as himself, not according to man but according to God, is on account of this love said to be of a good will; and this is in Scripture more commonly called charity, but it is also, even in the same books, called love. For the apostle says that the man to be elected as a ruler of the people must be a lover of good.[22] And when the Lord Himself had asked Peter, "Hast thou a regard for me (*diligis*) more than these?" Peter replied, "Lord, Thou knowest that I love (*amo*) Thee." And again a second time the Lord asked not whether Peter loved (*amaret*) Him, but whether he had a regard (*diligeret*) for Him, and he again answered, "Lord, Thou knowest that I love (*amo*) Thee." But on the third interrogation the Lord Himself no longer says, "Hast thou a regard (*diligis*) for me," but "Lovest thou (*amas*) me?" And then the evangelist adds, "Peter was grieved because He said unto him the third time, Lovest thou (*amas*) me?" though the Lord had not said three times but only once, "Lovest thou (*amas*) me?" and twice "*Diligis me?*" from which we gather that, even when the Lord said "*diligis*," He used an equivalent for "*amas*." Peter, too, throughout used one word for the one thing, and the third time also replied, "Lord, Thou knowest all things, Thou knowest that I love (*amo*) Thee."[23]

I have judged it right to mention this, because some are of opinion that charity or regard (*dilectio*) is one thing, love (*amor*) another. They say that *dilectio* is used of a good affection, *amor* of an evil love. But it is very certain that even secular literature knows no such distinction. However, it is for the philosophers to determine whether and how they differ, though their own writings sufficiently testify that they make great account of love (*amor*) placed on good objects, and even on God Himself. But we wished to show that the Scriptures of our religion, whose authority we prefer to all writings

[22] Tit. i. 8   [23] John xxi. 15-17

whatsoever, make no distinction between *amor*, *dilectio*, and *caritas;* and we have already shown that *amor* is used in a good connection. And if any one fancy that *amor* is no doubt used both of good and bad loves, but that *dilectio* is reserved for the good only, let him remember what the psalm says, "He that loveth (*diligit*) iniquity hateth his own soul;" [24] and the words of the Apostle John, "If any man love (*diligere*) the world, the love (*dilectio*) of the Father is not in him." [25] Here you have in one passage *dilectio* used both in a good and a bad sense. And if any one demands an instance of *amor* being used in a bad sense (for we have already shown its use in a good sense), let him read the words, "For men shall be lovers (*amantes*) of their own selves, lovers (*amatores*) of money." [26]

The right will is, therefore, well-directed love, and the wrong will is ill-directed love. Love, then, yearning to have what is loved, is desire; and having and enjoying it, is joy; fleeing what is opposed to it, it is fear; and feeling what is opposed to it, when it has befallen it, it is sadness. Now these motions are evil if the love is evil; good if the love is good. What we assert let us prove from Scripture. The apostle desires to depart, and to be with Christ.[27] And, "My soul desired to long for Thy judgments;" [28] or if it is more appropriate to say, "My soul longed to desire Thy judgments." And, "The desire of wisdom bringeth to a kingdom." [29] Yet there has always obtained the usage of understanding desire and concupiscence in a bad sense if the object be not defined. But joy is used in a good sense: "Be glad in the Lord, and rejoice, ye righteous." [30] And, "Thou hast put gladness in my heart." [31] And, "Thou wilt fill me with joy with Thy countenance." [32] Fear is used in a good sense by the apostle when he says, "Work out your salvation with fear and trembling." [33] And, "Be not high-minded, but fear." [34] And, "I fear, lest by any means, as the serpent beguiled Eve through his subtlety, so your minds should be corrupted from the simplicity that is in Christ." [35] But with respect to sadness, which Cicero prefers to call sickness (*aegritudo*), and Virgil pain (*dolor*) (as he says, "*Dolent gaudentque*" [36]) but which I prefer to call sorrow, because sickness and pain are more commonly used to express bodily suffering—with respect to this emotion, I say, the question whether it can be used in a good sense is more difficult.

CHAPTER VIII

OF THE THREE PERTURBATIONS, WHICH THE STOICS ADMITTED IN THE SOUL OF THE WISE MAN TO THE EXCLUSION OF GRIEF OR SADNESS, WHICH THE MANLY MIND OUGHT NOT TO EXPERIENCE

Those emotions which the Greeks call εὐπάθειαι, and which Cicero calls *constantiae*, the Stoics would restrict to three; and, instead of three "per-

[24] Ps. xi. 5   [25] 1 John ii. 15   [26] 2 Tim. iii. 2   [27] Phil. i. 23   [28] Ps. cxix. 20
[29] Wisd. vi. 20   [30] Ps. xxxii. 11   [31] Ps. iv. 7   [32] Ps. xvi. 11   [33] Phil. ii. 12
[34] Rom. xi. 20   [35] 2 Cor. xi. 3   [36] *Aeneid*, vi. 733

turbations" in the soul of the wise man, they substituted severally, in place of desire, will; in place of joy, contentment; and for fear, caution; and so to sickness or pain, which we, to avoid ambiguity, preferred to call sorrow, they denied that it could exist in the mind of a wise man. Will, they say, seeks the good, for this the wise man does. Contentment has its object in good that is possessed, and this the wise man continually possesses. Caution avoids evil, and this the wise man ought to avoid. But sorrow arises from evil that has already happened; and as they suppose that no evil can happen to the wise man, there can be no representative of sorrow in his mind. According to them, therefore, none but the wise man wills, is contented, uses caution; and that the fool can do no more than desire, rejoice, fear, be sad. The former three affections Cicero calls *constantiae*, the last four *perturbationes*. Many, however, call these last *passions;* and, as I have said, the Greeks call the former εὐπάθειαι, and the latter πάθη. And when I made a careful examination of Scripture to find whether this terminology was sanctioned by it, I came upon this saying of the prophet: "There is no contentment to the wicked, saith the Lord;" [37] as if the wicked might more properly rejoice than be contented regarding evils, for contentment is the property of the good and godly. I found also that verse in the Gospel: "Whatsoever ye would that men should do unto you, do ye even so unto them;" [38] which seems to imply that evil or shameful things may be the object of desire, but not of will. Indeed, some interpreters have added "good things," to make the expression more in conformity with customary usage, and have given this meaning, "Whatsoever good deeds that ye would that men should do unto you." For they thought that this would prevent any one from wishing other men to provide him with unseemly, not to say shameful gratifications—luxurious banquets, for example—on the supposition that if he returned the like to them he would be fulfilling this precept. In the Greek Gospel, however, from which the Latin is translated, "good" does not occur, but only, "All things whatsoever ye would that men should do unto you, do ye even so unto them," and, as I believe, because "good" is already included in the word "would;" for He does not say "desire."

Yet though we may sometimes avail ourselves of these precise proprieties of language, we are not to be always bridled by them; and when we read those writers against whose authority it is unlawful to reclaim, we must accept the meanings above mentioned in passages where a right sense can be educed by no other interpretation, as in those instances we adduced partly from the prophet, partly from the Gospel. For who does not know that the wicked exult with joy? Yet "there is no *contentment* for the wicked, saith the Lord." And how so, unless because contentment, when the word is used in its proper and distinctive significance, means something different from joy? In like manner, who would deny that it were wrong to enjoin upon men that whatever they desire others to do to them they should themselves do to

[37] Isa. lvii. 21   [38] Matt. vii. 12

others, lest they should mutually please one another by shameful and illicit pleasure? And yet the precept, "Whatsoever ye *would* that men should do unto you, do ye even so to them," is very wholesome and just. And how is this, unless because the will is in this place used strictly, and signifies that will which cannot have evil for its object? But ordinary phraseology would not have allowed the saying, "Be unwilling to make any manner of lie," [39] had there not been also an evil will, whose wickedness separates it from that which the angels celebrated, "Peace on earth, of good will to men." [40] For "good" is superfluous if there is no other kind of will but good will. And why should the apostle have mentioned it among the praises of charity as a great thing, that "it rejoices not in iniquity," unless because wickedness does so rejoice? For even with secular writers these words are used indifferently. For Cicero, that most fertile of orators, says, "I desire, conscript fathers, to be merciful." [41] And who would be so pedantic as to say that he should have said "I will" rather than "I desire," because the word is used in a good connection? Again, in Terence, the profligate youth, burning with wild lust, says, "I will nothing else than Philumena." [42] That this "will" was lust is sufficiently indicated by the answer of his old servant which is there introduced: "How much better were it to try and banish that love from your heart, than to speak so as uselessly to inflame your passion still more!" And that contentment was used by secular writers in a bad sense, that verse of Virgil testifies, in which he most succinctly comprehends these four perturbations—

Hence they fear and desire, grieve and are content.[43]

The same author had also used the expression, "the evil contentments of the mind." [44] So that good and bad men alike will, are cautious, and contented; or, to say the same thing in other words, good and bad men alike desire, fear, rejoice, but the former in a good, the latter in a bad fashion, according as the will is right or wrong. Sorrow itself, too, which the Stoics would not allow to be represented in the mind of the wise man, is used in a good sense, and especially in our writings. For the apostle praises the Corinthians because they had a godly sorrow. But possibly some one may say that the apostle congratulated them because they were penitently sorry, and that such sorrow can exist only in those who have sinned. For these are his words: "For I perceive that the same epistle hath made you sorry, though it were but for a season. Now I rejoice, not that ye were made sorry, but that ye sorrowed to repentance; for ye were made sorry after a godly manner, that ye might receive damage by us in nothing. For godly sorrow worketh repentance to salvation not to be repented of, but the sorrow of the world worketh death. For, behold, this selfsame thing that ye sorrowed after a godly sort, what carefulness it wrought in you!" [45] Consequently the Stoics

[39] Ecclus. vii. 13   [40] Luke ii. 14   [41] *Cat.* i. 2   [42] Ter. *Andr.* ii. 1, 6   [43] *Aeneid,* vi. 733   [44] *Aeneid,* v. 278   [45] 2 Cor. vii. 8-11

may defend themselves by replying,[46] that sorrow is indeed useful for repentance of sin, but that this can have no place in the mind of the wise man, inasmuch as no sin attaches to him of which he could sorrowfully repent, nor any other evil the endurance or experience of which could make him sorrowful. For they say that Alcibiades (if my memory does not deceive me), who believed himself happy, shed tears when Socrates argued with him, and demonstrated that he was miserable because he was foolish. In his case, therefore, folly was the cause of this useful and desirable sorrow, wherewith a man mourns that he is what he ought not to be. But the Stoics maintain not that the fool, but that the wise man, cannot be sorrowful.

CHAPTER IX

OF THE PERTURBATIONS OF THE SOUL WHICH APPEAR AS RIGHT AFFECTIONS IN THE LIFE OF THE RIGHTEOUS

But so far as regards this question of mental perturbations, we have answered these philosophers in the ninth book of this work, showing that it is rather a verbal than a real dispute, and that they seek contention rather than truth. Among ourselves, according to the sacred Scriptures and sound doctrine, the citizens of the holy city of God, who live according to God in the pilgrimage of this life, both fear and desire, and grieve and rejoice. And because their love is rightly placed, all these affections of theirs are right. They fear eternal punishment, they desire eternal life; they grieve because they themselves groan within themselves, waiting for the adoption, the redemption of their body;[47] they rejoice in hope, because there "shall be brought to pass the saying that is written, Death is swallowed up in victory."[48] In like manner they fear to sin, they desire to persevere; they grieve in sin, they rejoice in good works. They fear to sin, because they hear that "because iniquity shall abound, the love of many shall wax cold."[49] They desire to persevere, because they hear that it is written, "He that endureth to the end shall be saved."[50] They grieve for sin, hearing that "If we say that we have no sin, we deceive ourselves, and the truth is not in us."[51] They rejoice in good works, because they hear that "the Lord loveth a cheerful giver."[52] In like manner, according as they are strong or weak, they fear or desire to be tempted, grieve or rejoice in temptation. They fear to be tempted, because they hear the injunction, "If a man be overtaken in a fault, ye which are spiritual restore such an one in the spirit of meekness; considering thyself, lest thou also be tempted."[53] They desire to be tempted, because they hear one of the heroes of the city of God saying, "Examine me, O Lord, and tempt me: try my reins and my heart."[54] They grieve in temptations, because they see Peter weeping;[55] they rejoice in temptations, be-

[46] *Tusc. Quaest.* iii. 32   [47] Rom. viii. 23   [48] 1 Cor. xv. 54   [49] Matt. xxiv. 12
[50] Matt. x. 22   [51] 1 John i. 8   [52] 2 Cor. ix. 7   [53] Gal. vi. 1   [54] Ps. xxvi. 2
[55] Matt. xxvi. 75

cause they hear James saying, "My brethren, count it all joy when ye fall into divers temptations." [56]

And not only on their own account do they experience these emotions, but also on account of those whose deliverance they desire and whose perdition they fear, and whose loss or salvation affects them with grief or with joy. For if we who have come into the Church from among the Gentiles may suitably instance that noble and mighty hero who glories in his infirmities, the teacher (*doctor*) of the nations in faith and truth, who also labored more than all his fellow-apostles, and instructed the tribes of God's people by his epistles, which edified not only those of his own time, but all those who were to be gathered in—that hero, I say, and athlete of Christ, instructed by Him, anointed of His Spirit, crucified with Him, glorious in Him, lawfully maintaining a great conflict on the theatre of this world, and being made a spectacle to angels and men,[57] and pressing onwards for the prize of his high calling[58]—very joyfully do we with the eyes of faith behold him rejoicing with them that rejoice, and weeping with them that weep;[59] though hampered by fightings without and fears within;[60] desiring to depart and to be with Christ;[61] longing to see the Romans, that he might have some fruit among them as among other Gentiles;[62] being jealous over the Corinthians, and fearing in that jealousy lest their minds should be corrupted from the chastity that is in Christ;[63] having great heaviness and continual sorrow of heart for the Israelites,[64] because they, being ignorant of God's righteousness, and going about to establish their own righteousness, have not submitted themselves unto the righteousness of God;[65] and expressing not only his sorrow, but bitter lamentation over some who had formally sinned and had not repented of their uncleanness and fornications.[66]

If these emotions and affections, arising as they do from the love of what is good and from a holy charity, are to be called vices, then let us allow these emotions which are truly vices to pass under the name of virtues. But since these affections, when they are exercised in a becoming way, follow the guidance of right reason, who will dare to say that they are diseases or vicious passions? Wherefore even the Lord Himself, when He condescended to lead a human life in the form of a slave, had no sin whatever, and yet exercised these emotions where He judged they should be exercised. For as there was in Him a true human body and a true human soul, so was there also a true human emotion. When, therefore, we read in the Gospel that the hardheartedness of the Jews moved Him to sorrowful indignation,[67] that He said, "I am glad for your sakes, to the intent ye may believe,"[68] that when about to raise Lazarus He even shed tears,[69] that He earnestly desired to eat the passover with His disciples,[70] that as His passion drew near His soul was

[56] Jas. i. 2   [57] 1 Cor. iv. 9   [58] Phil. iii. 14   [59] Rom. xii. 15   [60] 2 Cor. vii. 5   [61] Phil. i. 23   [62] Rom. i. 11-13   [63] 2 Cor. xi. 1-3   [64] Rom. ix. 2   [65] Rom. x. 3   [66] 2 Cor. xii. 21   [67] Mark iii. 5   [68] John xi. 15   [69] John xi. 35   [70] Luke xxii. 15

sorrowful,[71] these emotions are certainly not falsely ascribed to Him. But as He became man when it pleased Him, so, in the grace of His definite purpose, when it pleased Him He experienced those emotions in His human soul.

But we must further make the admission, that even when these affections are well regulated, and according to God's will, they are peculiar to this life, not to that future life we look for, and that often we yield to them against our will. And thus sometimes we weep in spite of ourselves, being carried beyond ourselves, not indeed by culpable desire, but by praiseworthy charity. In us, therefore, these affections arise from human infirmity; but it was not so with the Lord Jesus, for even His infirmity was the consequence of His power. But so long as we wear the infirmity of this life, we are rather worse men than better if we have none of these emotions at all. For the apostle vituperated and abominated some who, as he said, were without natural affection.[72] The sacred Psalmist also found fault with those of whom he said, "I looked for some to lament with me, and there was none." [73] For to be quite free from pain while we are in this place of misery is only purchased, as one of this world's literati perceived and remarked,[74] at the price of blunted sensibilities both of mind and body. And therefore that which the Greeks called ἀπάθεια, and what the Latins would call, if their language would allow them, "impassibilitas," if it be taken to mean an impassibility of spirit and not of body, or, in other words, a freedom from those emotions which are contrary to reason and disturb the mind, then it is obviously a good and most desirable quality, but it is not one which is attainable in this life. For the words of the apostle are the confession, not of the common herd, but of the eminently pious, just, and holy men: "If we say we have no sin, we deceive ourselves, and the truth is not in us." [75] When there shall be no sin in a man, then there shall be this ἀπάθεια. At present it is enough if we live without crime; and he who thinks he lives without sin puts aside not sin, but pardon. And if that is to be called apathy, where the mind is the subject of no emotion, then who would not consider this insensibility to be worse than all vices? It may, indeed, reasonably be maintained that the perfect blessedness we hope for shall be free from all sting of fear or sadness; but who that is not quite lost to truth would say that neither love nor joy shall be experienced there? But if by apathy a condition be meant in which no fear terrifies nor any pain annoys, we must in this life renounce such a state if we would live according to God's will, but may hope to enjoy it in that blessedness which is promised as our eternal condition.

For that fear of which the Apostle John says, "There is no fear in love; but perfect love casteth out fear, because fear hath torment. He that feareth is not made perfect in love" [76]—that fear is not of the same kind as the Apostle Paul felt lest the Corinthians should be seduced by the subtlety of

[71] Matt. xxvi. 38   [72] Rom. i. 31   [73] Ps. lxix. 20
[74] Crantor, an Academic philosopher quoted by Cicero, *Tusc. Quaest.* iii. 6
[75] 1 John i. 8   [76] 1 John iv. 18

the serpent; for love is susceptible of this fear, yea, love alone is capable of it. But the fear which is not in love is of that kind of which Paul himself says, "For ye have not received the spirit of bondage again to fear." [77] But as for that clean fear which endureth for ever,[78] if it is to exist in the world to come (and how else can it be said to endure for ever?), it is not a fear deterring us from evil which may happen, but preserving us in the good which cannot be lost. For where the love of acquired good is unchangeable, there certainly the fear that avoids evil is, if I may say so, free from anxiety. For under the name of "clean fear" David signifies that will by which we shall necessarily shrink from sin, and guard against it, not with the anxiety of weakness, which fears that we may strongly sin, but with the tranquillity of perfect love. Or if no kind of fear at all shall exist in that most imperturbable security of perpetual and blissful delights, then the expression, "The fear of the Lord is clean, enduring for ever," must be taken in the same sense as that other, "The patience of the poor shall not perish for ever." [79] For patience, which is necessary only where ills are to be borne, shall not be eternal, but that which patience leads us to will be eternal. So perhaps this "clean fear" is said to endure for ever, because that to which fear leads shall endure.

And since this is so—since we must live a good life in order to attain to a blessed life—a good life has all these affections right, a bad life has them wrong. But in the blessed life eternal there will be love and joy, not only right, but also assured; but fear and grief there will be none. Whence it already appears in some sort what manner of persons the citizens of the city of God must be in this their pilgrimage, who live after the spirit, not after the flesh—that is to say, according to God, not according to man—and what manner of persons they shall be also in that immortality whither they are journeying. And the city or society of the wicked, who live not according to God, but according to man, and who accept the doctrines of men or devils in the worship of a false and contempt of the true divinity, is shaken with those wicked emotions as by diseases and disturbances. And if there be some of its citizens who seem to restrain and, as it were, temper those passions, they are so elated with ungodly pride, that their disease is as much greater as their pain is less. And if some, with a vanity monstrous in proportion to its rarity, have become enamored of themselves because they can be stimulated and excited by no emotion, moved or bent by no affection, such persons rather lose all humanity than obtain true tranquillity. For a thing is not necessarily right because it is inflexible, nor healthy because it is insensible.

[77] Rom. viii. 15   [78] Ps. xix. 9   [79] Ps. ix. 18

CHAPTER X

WHETHER IT IS TO BE BELIEVED THAT OUR FIRST PARENTS IN
PARADISE, BEFORE THEY SINNED, WERE FREE FROM ALL
PERTURBATION

But it is a fair question, whether our first parent or first parents (for there was a marriage of two), before they sinned, experienced in their animal body such emotions as we shall not experience in the spiritual body when sin has been purged and finally abolished. For if they did, then how were they blessed in that boasted place of bliss, Paradise? For who that is affected by fear or grief can be called absolutely blessed? And what could those persons fear or suffer in such affluence of blessings, where neither death nor ill-health was feared, and where nothing was wanting which a good will could desire, and nothing present which could interrupt man's mental or bodily enjoyment? Their love to God was unclouded, and their mutual affection was that of faithful and sincere marriage; and from this love flowed a wonderful delight, because they always enjoyed what was loved. Their avoidance of sin was tranquil; and, so long as it was maintained, no other ill at all could invade them and bring sorrow. Or did they perhaps desire to touch and eat the forbidden fruit, yet feared to die; and thus both fear and desire already, even in that blissful place, preyed upon those first of mankind? Away with the thought that such could be the case where there was no sin! And, indeed, this is already sin, to desire those things which the law of God forbids, and to abstain from them through fear of punishment, not through love of righteousness. Away, I say, with the thought, that before there was any sin, there should already have been committed regarding that fruit the very sin which our Lord warns us against regarding a woman: "Whosoever looketh on a woman to lust after her, hath committed adultery with her already in his heart." [80] As happy, then, as were these our first parents, who were agitated by no mental perturbations, and annoyed by no bodily discomforts, so happy should the whole human race have been, had they not introduced that evil which they have transmitted to their posterity, and had none of their descendants committed iniquity worthy of damnation; but this original blessedness continuing until, in virtue of that benediction which said, "Increase and multiply," [81] the number of the predestined saints should have been completed, there would then have been bestowed that higher felicity which is enjoyed by the most blessed angels—a blessedness in which there should have been a secure assurance that no one would sin, and no one die; and so should the saints have lived, after no taste of labor, pain, or death, as now they shall live in the resurrection, after they have endured all these things.

[80] Matt. v. 28   [81] Gen. i. 28

CHAPTER XI

OF THE FALL OF THE FIRST MAN, IN WHOM NATURE WAS CREATED GOOD, AND CAN BE RESTORED ONLY BY ITS AUTHOR

But because God foresaw all things, and was therefore not ignorant that man also would fall, we ought to consider this holy city in connection with what God foresaw and ordained, and not according to our own ideas, which do not embrace God's ordination. For man, by his sin, could not disturb the divine counsel, nor compel God to change what He had decreed; for God's foreknowledge had anticipated both—that is to say, both how evil the man whom He had created good should become, and what good He Himself should even thus derive from him. For though God is said to change His determinations (so that in a figurative sense the Holy Scripture says even that God repented [82]), this is said with reference to man's expectation, or the order of natural causes, and not with reference to that which the Almighty had foreknown that He would do. Accordingly God, as it is written, made man upright,[83] and consequently with a good will. For if he had not had a good will, he could not have been upright. The good will, then, is the work of God; for God created him with it. But the first evil will, which preceded all man's evil acts, was rather a kind of falling away from the work of God to its own works than any positive work. And therefore the acts resulting were evil, not having God, but the will itself for their end; so that the will or the man himself, so far as his will is bad, was as it were the evil tree bringing forth evil fruit. Moreover, the bad will, though it be not in harmony with, but opposed to nature, inasmuch as it is a vice or blemish, yet it is true of it as of all vice, that it cannot exist except in a nature, and only in a nature created out of nothing, and not in that which the Creator has begotten of Himself, as He begot the Word, by whom all things were made. For though God formed man of the dust of the earth, yet the earth itself, and every earthly material, is absolutely created out of nothing; and man's soul, too, God created out of nothing, and joined to the body, when He made man. But evils are so thoroughly overcome by good, that though they are permitted to exist, for the sake of demonstrating how the most righteous foresight of God can make a good use even of them, yet good can exist without evil, as in the true and supreme God Himself, and as in every invisible and visible celestial creature that exists above this murky atmosphere; but evil cannot exist without good, because the natures in which evil exists, in so far as they are natures, are good. And evil is removed, not by removing any nature, or part of a nature, which had been introduced by the evil, but by healing and correcting that which had been vitiated and depraved. The will, therefore, is then truly free, when it is not the slave of vices and sins. Such

---

[82] Gen. vi. 6, and 1 Sam. xv. 11   [83] Eccles. vii. 29

was it given us by God; and this being lost by its own fault, can only be re-stored by Him who was able at first to give it. And therefore the truth says, "If the Son shall make you free, ye shall be free indeed;" [84] which is equiva-lent to saying, If the Son shall save you, ye shall be saved indeed. For He is our Liberator, inasmuch as He is our Saviour.

Man then lived with God for his rule in a paradise at once physical and spiritual. For neither was it a paradise only physical for the advantage of the body, and not also spiritual for the advantage of the mind; nor was it only spiritual to afford enjoyment to man by his internal sensations, and not also physical to afford him enjoyment through his external senses. But ob-viously it was both for both ends. But after that proud and therefore envious angel (of whose fall I have said as much as I was able in the eleventh and twelfth books of this work, as well as that of his fellows, who, from being God's angels, became his angels), preferring to rule with a kind of pomp of empire rather than to be another's subject, fell from the spiritual Paradise, and essaying to insinuate his persuasive guile into the mind of man, whose unfallen condition provoked him to envy now that himself was fallen, he chose the serpent as his mouthpiece in that bodily Paradise in which it and all the other earthly animals were living with those two human beings, the man and his wife, subject to them, and harmless; and he chose the serpent because, being slippery, and moving in tortuous windings, it was suitable for his purpose. And this animal being subdued to his wicked ends by the pres-ence and superior force of his angelic nature, he abused as his instrument, and first tried his deceit upon the woman, making his assault upon the weaker part of that human alliance, that he might gradually gain the whole, and not supposing that the man would readily give ear to him, or be de-ceived, but that he might yield to the error of the woman. For as Aaron was not induced to agree with the people when they blindly wished him to make an idol, and yet yielded to constraint; and as it is not credible that Solomon was so blind as to suppose that idols should be worshipped, but was drawn over to such sacrilege by the blandishments of women; so we cannot believe that Adam was deceived, and supposed the devil's word to be truth, and therefore transgressed God's law, but that he by the drawings of kindred yielded to the woman, the husband to the wife, the one human being to the only other human being. For not without significance did the apostle say, "And Adam was not deceived, but the woman being deceived was in the transgression;" [85] but he speaks thus, because the woman accepted as true what the serpent told her, but the man could not bear to be severed from his only companion, even though this involved a partnership in sin. He was not on this account less culpable, but sinned with his eyes open. And so the apostle does not say, "He did not sin," but "He was not deceived." For he shows that he sinned when he says, "By one man sin entered into the world," [86] and immediately after more distinctly, "In the likeness of Adam's

[84] 1 John viii. 36   [85] 1 Tim. ii. 14   [86] Rom. v. 12

transgression." But he meant that those are deceived who do not judge that which they do to be sin; but he knew. Otherwise how were it true "Adam was not deceived"? But having as yet no experience of the divine severity, he was possibly deceived in so far as he thought his sin venial. And consequently he was not deceived as the woman was deceived, but he was deceived as to the judgment which would be passed on his apology: "The woman whom thou gavest to be with me, she gave me, and I did eat." [87] What need of saying more? Although they were not both deceived by credulity, yet both were entangled in the snares of the devil, and taken by sin.

CHAPTER XII

OF THE NATURE OF MAN'S FIRST SIN

If any one finds a difficulty in understanding why other sins do not alter human nature as it was altered by the transgression of those first human beings, so that on account of it this nature is subject to the great corruption we feel and see, and to death, and is distracted and tossed with so many furious and contending emotions, and is certainly far different from what it was before sin, even though it were then lodged in an animal body—if, I say, any one is moved by this, he ought not to think that that sin was a small and light one because it was committed about food, and that not bad nor noxious, except because it was forbidden; for in that spot of singular felicity God could not have created and planted any evil thing. But by the precept He gave, God commended obedience, which is, in a sort, the mother and guardian of all the virtues in the reasonable creature, which was so created that submission is advantageous to it, while the fulfillment of its own will in preference to the Creator's is destruction. And as this commandment enjoining abstinence from one kind of food in the midst of great abundance of other kinds was so easy to keep—so light a burden to the memory—and, above all, found no resistance to its observance in lust, which only afterwards sprung up as the penal consequence of sin, the iniquity of violating it was all the greater in proportion to the ease with which it might have been kept.

CHAPTER XIII

THAT IN ADAM'S SIN AN EVIL WILL PRECEDED THE EVIL ACT

Our first parents fell into open disobedience because already they were secretly corrupted; for the evil act had never been done had not an evil will preceded it. And what is the origin of our evil will but pride? For "pride is the beginning of sin." [88] And what is pride but the craving for undue exaltation? And this is undue exaltation, when the soul abandons Him to whom it ought to cleave as its end, and becomes a kind of end to itself. This happens

[87] Gen. iii. 12   [88] Ecclus. x. 13

when it becomes its own satisfaction. And it does so when it falls away from that unchangeable good which ought to satisfy it more than itself. This falling away is spontaneous; for if the will had remained steadfast in the love of that higher and changeless good by which it was illumined to intelligence and kindled into love, it would not have turned away to find satisfaction in itself, and so become frigid and benighted; the woman would not have believed the serpent spoke the truth, nor would the man have preferred the request of his wife to the command of God, nor have supposed that it was a venial transgression to cleave to the partner of his life even in a partnership of sin. The wicked deed, then—that is to say, the transgression of eating the forbidden fruit—was committed by persons who were already wicked. That evil fruit [89] could be brought forth only by a corrupt tree. But that the tree was evil was not the result of nature; for certainly it could become so only by the vice of the will, and vice is contrary to nature. Now, nature could not have been depraved by vice had it not been made out of nothing. Consequently, that it is a nature, this is because it is made by God; but that it falls away from Him, this is because it is made out of nothing. But man did not so fall away as to become absolutely nothing; but being turned towards himself, his being became more contracted than it was when he clung to Him who supremely is. Accordingly, to exist in himself, that is, to be his own satisfaction after abandoning God, is not quite to become a nonentity, but to approximate to that. And therefore the holy Scriptures designate the proud by another name, "self-pleasers." For it is good to have the heart lifted up, yet not to one's self, for this is proud, but to the Lord, for this is obedient, and can be the act only of the humble. There is, therefore, something in humility which, strangely enough, exalts the heart, and something in pride which debases it. This seems, indeed, to be contradictory, that loftiness should debase and lowliness exalt. But pious humility enables us to submit to what is above us; and nothing is more exalted above us than God; and therefore humility, by making us subject to God, exalts us. But pride, being a defect of nature, by the very act of refusing subjection and revolting from Him who is supreme, falls to a low condition; and then comes to pass what is written: "Thou castedst them down when they lifted up themselves." [90] For he does not say, "when they had been lifted up," as if first they were exalted, and then afterwards cast down; but "when they lifted up themselves" even then they were cast down—that is to say, the very lifting up was already a fall. And therefore it is that humility is specially recommended to the city of God as it sojourns in this world, and is specially exhibited in the city of God, and in the person of Christ its King; while the contrary vice of pride, according to the testimony of the sacred writings, specially rules his adversary the devil. And certainly this is the great difference which distinguishes the two cities of which we speak, the one being the society of the godly men, the other of the ungodly, each associated with the

[89] Matt. vii. 18   [90] Ps. lxxiii. 18

angels that adhere to their party, and the one guided and fashioned by love of self, the other by love of God.

The devil, then, would not have ensnared man in the open and manifest sin of doing what God had forbidden, had man not already begun to live for himself. It was this that made him listen with pleasure to the words, "Ye shall be as gods," [91] which they would much more readily have accomplished by obediently adhering to their supreme and true end than by proudly living to themselves. For created gods are gods not by virtue of what is in themselves, but by a participation of the true God. By craving to be more, man becomes less; and by aspiring to be self-sufficing, he fell away from Him who truly suffices him. Accordingly, this wicked desire which prompts man to please himself as if he were himself light, and which thus turns him away from that light by which, had he followed it, he would himself have become light—this wicked desire, I say, already secretly existed in him, and the open sin was but its consequence. For that is true which is written, "Pride goeth before destruction, and before honor is humility;" [92] that is to say, secret ruin precedes open ruin, while the former is not counted ruin. For who counts exaltation ruin, though no sooner is the Highest forsaken than a fall is begun? But who does not recognize it as ruin, when there occurs an evident and indubitable transgression of the commandment? And consequently, God's prohibition had reference to such an act as, when committed, could not be defended on any pretence of doing what was righteous. And I make bold to say that it is useful for the proud to fall into an open and indisputable transgression, and so displease themselves, as already, by pleasing themselves, they had fallen. For Peter was in a healthier condition when he wept and was dissatisfied with himself, than when he boldly presumed and satisfied himself. And this is averred by the sacred Psalmist when he says, "Fill their faces with shame, that they may seek Thy name, O Lord;" [93] that is, that they who have pleased themselves in seeking their own glory may be pleased and satisfied with Thee in seeking Thy glory.

CHAPTER XIV

OF THE PRIDE IN THE SIN, WHICH WAS WORSE THAN THE SIN ITSELF

But it is a worse and more damnable pride which casts about for the shelter of an excuse even in manifest sins, as these our first parents did, of whom the woman said, "The serpent beguiled me, and I did eat;" and the man said, "The woman whom Thou gavest to be with me, she gave me of the tree, and I did eat." [94] Here there is no word of begging pardon, no word of entreaty for healing. For though they do not, like Cain, deny that they have perpetrated the deed, yet their pride seeks to refer its wickedness to another—the woman's pride to the serpent, the man's to the woman. But

[91] Gen. iii. 5   [92] Prov. xviii. 12   [93] Ps. lxxxiii. 16   [94] Gen. iii. 12, 13

where there is a plain transgression of a divine commandment, this is rather to accuse than to excuse oneself. For the fact that the woman sinned on the serpent's persuasion, and the man at the woman's offer, did not make the transgression less, as if there were any one whom we ought rather to believe or yield to than God.

CHAPTER XV

OF THE JUSTICE OF THE PUNISHMENT WITH WHICH OUR FIRST PARENTS WERE VISITED FOR THEIR DISOBEDIENCE

Therefore, because the sin was a despising of the authority of God—who had created man; who had made him in His own image; who had set him above the other animals; who had placed him in Paradise; who had enriched him with abundance of every kind and of safety; who had laid upon him neither many, nor great, nor difficult commandments, but, in order to make a wholesome obedience easy to him, had given him a single very brief and very light precept by which He reminded that creature whose service was to be free that He was Lord—it was just that condemnation followed, and condemnation such that man, who by keeping the commandments should have been spiritual even in his flesh, became fleshly even in his spirit; and as in his pride he had sought to be his own satisfaction, God in His justice abandoned him to himself, not to live in the absolute independence he affected, but instead of the liberty he desired, to live dissatisfied with himself in a hard and miserable bondage to him to whom by sinning he had yielded himself, doomed in spite of himself to die in body as he had willingly become dead in spirit, condemned even to eternal death (had not the grace of God delivered him) because he had forsaken eternal life. Whoever thinks such punishment either excessive or unjust shows his inability to measure the great iniquity of sinning where sin might so easily have been avoided. For as Abraham's obedience is with justice pronounced to be great, because the thing commanded, to kill his son, was very difficult, so in Paradise the disobedience was the greater, because the difficulty of that which was commanded was imperceptible. And as the obedience of the second Man was the more laudable because He became obedient even unto death,[95] so the disobedience of the first man was the more detestable because he became disobedient even unto death. For where the penalty annexed to disobedience is great, and the thing commanded by the Creator is easy, who can sufficiently estimate how great a wickedness it is, in a matter so easy, not to obey the authority of so great a power, even when that power deters with so terrible a penalty?

In short, to say all in a word, what but disobedience was the punishment of disobedience in that sin? For what else is man's misery but his own dis-

[95] Phil. ii. 8

obedience to himself, so that in consequence of his not being willing to do what he could do, he now wills to do what he cannot? For though he could not do all things in Paradise before he sinned, yet he wished to do only what he could do, and therefore he could do all things he wished. But now, as we recognize in his offspring, and as divine Scripture testifies, "Man is like to vanity." [96] For who can count how many things he wishes which he cannot do, so long as he is disobedient to himself, that is, so long as his mind and his flesh do not obey his will? For in spite of himself his mind is both frequently disturbed, and his flesh suffers, and grows old, and dies; and in spite of ourselves we suffer whatever else we suffer, and which we would not suffer if our nature absolutely and in all its parts obeyed our will. But is it not the infirmities of the flesh which hamper it in its service? Yet what does it matter *how* its service is hampered, so long as the fact remains, that by the just retribution of the sovereign God whom we refused to be subject to and serve, our flesh, which was subjected to us, now torments us by insubordination, although our disobedience brought trouble on ourselves, not upon God? For He is not in need of our service as we of our body's; and therefore what we did was no punishment to Him, but what we receive is so to us. And the pains which are called bodily are pains of the soul in and from the body. For what pain or desire can the flesh feel by itself and without the soul? But when the flesh is said to desire or to suffer, it is meant, as we have explained, that the man does so, or some part of the soul which is affected by the sensation of the flesh, whether a harsh sensation causing pain, or gentle, causing pleasure. But pain in the flesh is only a discomfort of the soul arising from the flesh, and a kind of shrinking from its suffering, as the pain of the soul which is called sadness is a shrinking from those things which have happened to us in spite of ourselves. But sadness is frequently preceded by fear, which is itself in the soul, not in the flesh; while bodily pain is not preceded by any kind of fear of the flesh, which can be felt in the flesh before the pain. But pleasure is preceded by a certain appetite which is felt in the flesh like a craving, as hunger and thirst and that generative appetite which is most commonly identified with the name "lust," though this is the generic word for all desires. For anger itself was defined by the ancients as nothing else than the lust of revenge; [97] although sometimes a man is angry even at inanimate objects which cannot feel his vengeance, as when one breaks a pen, or crushes a quill that writes badly. Yet even this, though less reasonable, is in its way a lust of revenge, and is, so to speak, a mysterious kind of shadow of [the great law of] retribution, that they who do evil should suffer evil. There is therefore a lust for revenge, which is called anger; there is a lust of money, which goes by the name of avarice; there is a lust of conquering, no matter by what means, which is called opinionativeness; there is a lust of applause, which is named boasting. There are many and various lusts, of which some have names of their own, while others have not. For who could

[96] Ps. cxliv. 4   [97] Cicero, *Tusc. Quaest.* iii. 6 and iv. 9. So Aristotle, *Rhet.* ii. 2. 1

readily give a name to the lust of ruling, which yet has a powerful influence in the soul of tyrants, as civil wars bear witness?

CHAPTER XVI

OF THE EVIL OF LUST—A WORD WHICH, THOUGH APPLICABLE TO MANY VICES, IS SPECIALLY APPROPRIATED TO SEXUAL UNCLEANNESS

Although, therefore, lust may have many objects, yet when no object is specified, the word lust usually suggests to the mind the lustful excitement of the organs of generation. And this lust not only takes possession of the whole body and outward members, but also makes itself felt within, and moves the whole man with a passion in which mental emotion is mingled with bodily appetite, so that the pleasure which results is the greatest of all bodily pleasures. So possessing indeed is this pleasure, that at the moment of time in which it is consummated, all mental activity is suspended. What friend of wisdom and holy joys, who being married, but knowing, as the apostle says, "how to possess his vessel in sanctification and honor, not in the disease of desire, as the Gentiles who know not God," [98] would not prefer, if this were possible, to beget children without this lust, so that in this function of begetting offspring the members created for this purpose should not be stimulated by the heat of lust, but should be actuated by his volition, in the same way as his other members serve him for their respective ends? But even those who delight in this pleasure are not moved to it at their own will, whether they confine themselves to lawful or transgress to unlawful pleasures; but sometimes this lust importunes them in spite of themselves, and sometimes fails them when they desire to feel it, so that though lust rages in the mind, it stirs not in the body. Thus, strangely enough, this emotion not only fails to obey the legitimate desire to beget offspring, but also refuses to serve lascivious lust; and though it often opposes its whole combined energy to the soul that resists it, sometimes also it is divided against itself, and while it moves the soul, leaves the body unmoved.

CHAPTER XVII

OF THE NAKEDNESS OF OUR FIRST PARENTS, WHICH THEY SAW AFTER THEIR BASE AND SHAMEFUL SIN

Justly is shame very specially connected with this lust; justly, too, these members themselves, being moved and restrained not at our will, but by a certain independent autocracy, so to speak, are called "shameful." Their condition was different before sin. For as it is written, "They were naked and were not ashamed" [99]—not that their nakedness was unknown to them, but because nakedness was not yet shameful, because not yet did lust move

[98] 1 Thess. iv. 4   [99] Gen. ii. 25

those members without the will's consent; not yet did the flesh by its disobedience testify against the disobedience of man. For they were not created blind, as the unenlightened vulgar fancy; for Adam saw the animals to whom he gave names, and of Eve we read, "The woman saw that the tree was good for food, and that it was pleasant to the eyes." [100] Their eyes, therefore, were open, but were not open to this, that is to say, were not observant so as to recognize what was conferred upon them by the garment of grace, for they had no consciousness of their members warring against their will. But when they were stripped of this grace, that their disobedience might be punished by fit retribution, there began in the movement of their bodily members a shameless novelty which made nakedness indecent: it at once made them observant and made them ashamed. And therefore, after they violated God's command by open transgression, it is written: "And the eyes of them both were opened, and they knew that they were naked; and they sewed fig leaves together, and made themselves aprons." [101] "The eyes of them both were opened," not to see, for already they saw, but to discern between the good they had lost and the evil into which they had fallen. And therefore also the tree itself which they were forbidden to touch was called the tree of the knowledge of good and evil from this circumstance, that if they ate of it it would impart to them this knowledge. For the discomfort of sickness reveals the pleasure of health. "They knew," therefore, "that they were naked"—naked of that grace which prevented them from being ashamed of bodily nakedness while the law of sin offered no resistance to their mind. And thus they obtained a knowledge which they would have lived in blissful ignorance of, had they, in trustful obedience to God, declined to commit that offence which involved them in the experience of the hurtful effects of unfaithfulness and disobedience. And therefore, being ashamed of the disobedience of their own flesh, which witnessed to their disobedience while it punished it, "they sewed fig leaves together, and made themselves aprons," that is, cinctures for their privy parts; for some interpreters have rendered the word by *succinctoria*. *Campestria* is, indeed, a Latin word, but it is used of the drawers or aprons used for a similar purpose by the young men who stripped for exercise in the *campus;* hence those who were so girt were commonly called *campestrati*. Shame modestly covered that which lust disobediently moved in opposition to the will, which was thus punished for its own disobedience. Consequently all nations, being propagated from that one stock, have so strong an instinct to cover the shameful parts, that some barbarians do not uncover them even in the bath, but wash with their drawers on. In the dark solitudes of India also, though some philosophers go naked, and are therefore called gymnosophists, yet they make an exception in the case of these members, and cover them.

[100] Gen. iii. 6   [101] Gen. iii. 7

CHAPTER XVIII

OF THE SHAME WHICH ATTENDS ALL SEXUAL INTERCOURSE

Lust requires for its consummation darkness and secrecy; and this not only when unlawful intercourse is desired, but even such fornication as the earthly city has legalized. Where there is no fear of punishment, these permitted pleasures still shrink from the public eye. Even where provision is made for this lust, secrecy also is provided; and while lust found it easy to remove the prohibitions of law, shamelessness found it impossible to lay aside the veil of retirement. For even shameless men call this shameful; and though they love the pleasure, dare not display it. What! does not even conjugal intercourse, sanctioned as it is by law for the propagation of children, legitimate and honorable though it be, does it not seek retirement from every eye? Before the bridegroom fondles his bride, does he not exclude the attendants, and even the paranymphs, and such friends as the closest ties have admitted to the bridal chamber? The greatest master of Roman eloquence says, that all right actions wish to be set in the light, *i.e.*, desire to be known. This right action, however, has such a desire to be known, that yet it blushes to be seen. Who does not know what passes between husband and wife that children may be born? Is it not for this purpose that wives are married with such ceremony? And yet, when this well-understood act is gone about for the procreation of children, not even the children themselves, who may already have been born to them, are suffered to be witnesses. This right action seeks the light, in so far as it seeks to be known, but yet dreads being seen. And why so, if not because that which is by nature fitting and decent is so done as to be accompanied with a shame-begetting penalty of sin?

CHAPTER XIX

THAT IT IS NOW NECESSARY, AS IT WAS NOT BEFORE MAN SINNED, TO BRIDLE ANGER AND LUST BY THE RESTRAINING INFLUENCE OF WISDOM

Hence it is that even the philosophers who have approximated to the truth have avowed that anger and lust are vicious mental emotions, because, even when exercised towards objects which wisdom does not prohibit, they are moved in an ungoverned and inordinate manner, and consequently need the regulation of mind and reason. And they assert that this third part of the mind is posted as it were in a kind of citadel, to give rule to these other parts, so that, while it rules and they serve, man's righteousness is preserved without a breach. These parts, then, which they acknowledge to be vicious even in a wise and temperate man, so that the mind, by its composing and restraining influence, must bridle and recall them from those objects towards which they are unlawfully moved, and give them access to those which the law of wisdom sanctions—that anger, *e.g.*, may be allowed for the enforcement of a just authority, and lust for the duty of propagating offspring—these parts, I say, were not vicious in Paradise before sin, for they were never moved in opposition to a holy will towards any object from which it was necessary that they should be withheld by the restraining bridle of reason. For though now they are moved in this way, and are regulated by a bridling and restraining power, which those who live temperately, justly, and godly exercise, sometimes with ease, and sometimes with greater difficulty, this is not the sound health of nature, but the weakness which results from sin. And how is it that shame does not hide the acts and words dictated by anger or other emotions, as it covers the motions of lust, unless because the members of the body which we employ for accomplishing them are moved, not by the emotions themselves, but by the authority of the consenting will? For he who in his anger rails at or even strikes some one, could not do so were not his tongue and hand moved by the authority of the will, as also they are moved when there is no anger. But the organs of generation are so subjected to the rule of lust, that they have no motion but what it communicates. It is this we are ashamed of; it is this which blushingly hides from the eyes of onlookers. And rather will a man endure a crowd of witnesses when he is unjustly venting his anger on some one, than the eye of one man when he innocently copulates with his wife.

CHAPTER XX

OF THE FOOLISH BEASTLINESS OF THE CYNICS

It is this which those canine or cynic philosophers have overlooked, when they have, in violation of the modest instincts of men, boastfully proclaimed their unclean and shameless opinion, worthy indeed of dogs, *viz.*, that as the matrimonial act is legitimate, no one should be ashamed to perform it openly, in the street or in any public place. Instinctive shame has overborne this wild fancy. For though it is related [102] that Diogenes once dared to put his opinion in practice, under the impression that his sect would be all the more famous if his egregious shamelessness were deeply graven in the memory of mankind, yet this example was not afterwards followed. Shame had more influence with them, to make them blush before men, than error to make them affect a resemblance to dogs. And possibly, even in the case of Diogenes, and those who did imitate him, there was but an appearance and pretense of copulation, and not the reality. Even at this day there are still Cynic philosophers to be seen; for these are Cynics who are not content with being clad in the *pallium*, but also carry a club; yet no one of them dares to do this that we speak of. If they did, they would be spat upon, not to say stoned, by the mob. Human nature, then, is without doubt ashamed of this

---

[102] Cf. Diogenes Laertius, vi. 69, and Cicero, *De Offic.* i. 41

lust; and justly so, for the insubordination of these members, and their defiance of the will, are the clear testimony of the punishment of man's first sin. And it was fitting that this should appear specially in those parts by which is generated that nature which has been altered for the worse by that first and great sin—that sin from whose evil connection no one can escape, unless God's grace expiate in him individually that which was perpetrated to the destruction of all in common, when all were in one man, and which was avenged by God's justice.

CHAPTER XXI

THAT MAN'S TRANSGRESSION DID NOT ANNUL THE BLESSING OF FECUNDITY PRONOUNCED UPON MAN BEFORE HE SINNED, BUT INFECTED IT WITH THE DISEASE OF LUST

Far be it, then, from us to suppose that our first parents in Paradise felt that lust which caused them afterwards to blush and hide their nakedness, or that by its means they should have fulfilled the benediction of God, "Increase and multiply and replenish the earth;" [103] for it was after sin that lust began. It was after sin that our nature, having lost the power it had over the whole body, but not having lost all shame, perceived, noticed, blushed at, and covered it. But that blessing upon marriage, which encouraged them to increase and multiply and replenish the earth, though it continued even after they had sinned, was yet given before they sinned, in order that the procreation of children might be recognized as part of the glory of marriage, and not of the punishment of sin. But now, men being ignorant of the blessedness of Paradise, suppose that children could not have been begotten there in any other way than they know them to be begotten now, i.e., by lust, at which even honorable marriage blushes; some not simply rejecting, but sceptically deriding the divine Scriptures, in which we read that our first parents, after they sinned, were ashamed of their nakedness, and covered it; while others, though they accept and honor Scripture, yet conceive that this expression, "Increase and multiply," refers not to carnal fecundity, because a similar expression is used of the soul in the words, "Thou wilt multiply me with strength in my soul;" [104] and so, too, in the words which follow in *Genesis*, "And replenish the earth, and subdue it," they understand by the earth the body which the soul fills with its presence, and which it rules over when it is multiplied in strength. And they hold that children could no more then than now be begotten without lust, which, after sin, was kindled, observed, blushed for, and covered; and even that children would not have been born in Paradise, but only outside of it, as in fact it turned out. For it was after they were expelled from it that they came together to beget children, and begot them.

[103] Gen. i. 28   [104] Ps. cxxxviii. 3

CHAPTER XXII

OF THE CONJUGAL UNION AS IT WAS ORIGINALLY INSTITUTED AND BLESSED BY GOD

But we, for our part, have no manner of doubt that to increase and multiply and replenish the earth in virtue of the blessing of God, is a gift of marriage as God instituted it from the beginning before man sinned, when He created them male and female—in other words, two sexes manifestly distinct. And it was this work of God on which His blessing was pronounced. For no sooner had Scripture said, "Male and female created He them," [105] than it immediately continues, "And God blessed them, and God said unto them, Increase, and multiply, and replenish the earth, and subdue it," etc. And though all these things may not unsuitably be interpreted in a spiritual sense, yet "male and female" cannot be understood of two things in one man, as if there were in him one thing which rules, another which is ruled; but it is quite clear that they were created male and female, with bodies of different sexes, for the very purpose of begetting offspring, and so increasing, multiplying, and replenishing the earth; and it is great folly to oppose so plain a fact. It was not of the spirit which commands and the body which obeys, nor of the rational soul which rules and the irrational desire which is ruled, nor of the contemplative virtue which is supreme and the active which is subject, nor of the understanding of the mind and the sense of the body, but plainly of the matrimonial union by which the sexes are mutually bound together, that our Lord, when asked whether it were lawful for any cause to put away one's wife (for on account of the hardness of the hearts of the Israelites Moses permitted a bill of divorcement to be given), answered and said, "Have ye not read that He which made them at the beginning made them male and female, and said, For this cause shall a man leave father and mother, and shall cleave to his wife, and they twain shall be one flesh? Wherefore they are no more twain, but one flesh. What, therefore, God hath joined together, let not man put asunder." [106] It is certain, then, that from the first men were created, as we see and know them to be now, of two sexes, male and female, and that they are called one, either on account of the matrimonial union, or on account of the origin of the woman, who was created from the side of the man. And it is by this original example, which God Himself instituted, that the apostle admonishes all husbands to love their own wives in particular. [107]

[105] Gen. i. 27, 28   [106] Matt. xix. 4, 5   [107] Eph. v. 25

CHAPTER XXIII

WHETHER GENERATION SHOULD HAVE TAKEN PLACE EVEN IN PARADISE
HAD MAN NOT SINNED, OR WHETHER THERE SHOULD HAVE BEEN
ANY CONTENTION THERE BETWEEN CHASTITY AND LUST

But he who says that there should have been neither copulation nor generation but for sin, virtually says that man's sin was necessary to complete the number of the saints. For if these two by not sinning should have continued to live alone, because, as is supposed, they could not have begotten children had they not sinned, then certainly sin was necessary in order that there might be not only two but many righteous men. And if this cannot be maintained without absurdity, we must rather believe that the number of the saints fit to complete this most blessed city would have been as great though no one had sinned, as it is now that the grace of God gathers its citizens out of the multitude of sinners, so long as the children of this world generate and are generated.[108]

And therefore that marriage, worthy of the happiness of Paradise, should have had desirable fruit without the shame of lust, had there been no sin. But how that could be, there is now no example to teach us. Nevertheless, it ought not to seem incredible that one member might serve the will without lust then, since so many serve it now. Do we now move our feet and hands when we will to do the things we would by means of these members? do we meet with no resistance in them, but perceive that they are ready servants of the will, both in our own case and in that of others, and especially of artisans employed in mechanical operations, by which the weakness and clumsiness of nature become, through industrious exercise, wonderfully dexterous? and shall we not believe that, like as all those members obediently serve the will, so also should the members have discharged the function of generation, though lust, the award of disobedience, had been awanting? Did not Cicero, in discussing the difference of governments in his *De Republica*, adopt a simile from human nature, and say that we command our bodily members as children, they are so obedient; but that the vicious parts of the soul must be treated as slaves, and be coerced with a more stringent authority? And no doubt, in the order of nature, the soul is more excellent than the body; and yet the soul commands the body more easily than itself. Nevertheless this lust, of which we at present speak, is the more shameful on this account, because the soul is therein neither master of itself, so as not to lust at all, nor of the body, so as to keep the members under the control of the will; for if they were thus ruled, there should be no shame. But now the soul is ashamed that the body, which by nature is inferior and subject to it, should resist its authority. For in the resistance experienced by the soul in the other emotions there is less shame, because the resistance is from itself, and thus,

[108] Luke xx. 34

when it is conquered by itself, itself is the conqueror, although the conquest is inordinate and vicious, because accomplished by those parts of the soul which ought to be subject to reason, yet, being accomplished by its own parts and energies, the conquest is, as I say, its own. For when the soul conquers itself to a due subordination, so that its unreasonable motions are controlled by reason, while it again is subject to God, this is a conquest virtuous and praiseworthy. Yet there is less shame when the soul is resisted by its own vicious parts than when its will and order are resisted by the body, which is distinct from and inferior to it, and dependent on it for life itself.

But so long as the will retains under its authority the other members, without which the members excited by lust to resist the will cannot accomplish what they seek, chastity is preserved, and the delight of sin foregone. And certainly, had not culpable disobedience been visited with penal disobedience, the marriage of Paradise should have been ignorant of this struggle and rebellion, this quarrel between will and lust, that the will may be satisfied and lust restrained, but those members, like all the rest, should have obeyed the will. The field of generation[109] should have been sown by the organ created for this purpose, as the earth is sown by the hand. And whereas now, as we essay to investigate this subject more exactly, modesty hinders us, and compels us to ask pardon of chaste ears, there would have been no cause to do so, but we could have discoursed freely, and without fear of seeming obscene, upon all those points which occur to one who meditates on the subject. There would not have been even words which could be called obscene, but all that might be said of these members would have been as pure as what is said of the other parts of the body. Whoever, then, comes to the perusal of these pages with unchaste mind, let him blame his disposition, not his nature; let him brand the actings of his own impurity, not the words which necessity forces us to use, and for which every pure and pious reader or hearer will very readily pardon me, while I expose the folly of that scepticism which argues solely on the ground of its own experience, and has no faith in anything beyond. He who is not scandalized at the apostle's censure of the horrible wickedness of the women who changed the natural use into that which is against nature,[110] will read all this without being shocked, especially as we are not, like Paul, citing and censuring a damnable uncleanness, but are explaining, so far as we can, human generation, while with Paul we avoid all obscenity of language.

CHAPTER XXIV

THAT IF MEN HAD REMAINED INNOCENT AND OBEDIENT IN PARADISE,
THE GENERATIVE ORGANS SHOULD HAVE BEEN IN SUBJECTION
TO THE WILL AS THE OTHER MEMBERS ARE

The man, then, would have sown the seed, and the woman received it, as need required, the generative organs being moved by the will, not excited

[109] Cf. Virgil, *Georg.* iii. 136   [110] Rom. i. 26

by lust. For we move at will not only those members which are furnished with joints of solid bone, as the hands, feet, and fingers, but we move also at will those which are composed of slack and soft nerves: we can put them in motion, or stretch them out, or bend and twist them, or contract and stiffen them, as we do with the muscles of the mouth and face. The lungs, which are the very tenderest of the viscera except the brain, and are therefore carefully sheltered in the cavity of the chest, yet for all purposes of inhaling and exhaling the breath, and of uttering and modulating the voice, are obedient to the will when we breathe, exhale, speak, shout, or sing, just as the bellows obey the smith or the organist. I will not press the fact that some animals have a natural power to move a single spot of the skin with which their whole body is covered, if they have felt on it anything they wish to drive off—a power so great, that by this shivering tremor of the skin they can not only shake off flies that have settled on them, but even spears that have fixed in their flesh. Man, it is true, has not this power; but is this any reason for supposing that God could not give it to such creatures as He wished to possess it? And therefore man himself also might very well have enjoyed absolute power over his members had he not forfeited it by his disobedience; for it was not difficult for God to form him so that what is now moved in his body only by lust should have been moved only at will.

We know, too, that some men are differently constituted from others, and have some rare and remarkable faculty of doing with their body what other men can by no effort do, and, indeed, scarcely believe when they hear of others doing. There are persons who can move their ears, either one at a time, or both together. There are some who, without moving the head, can bring the hair down upon the forehead, and move the whole scalp backwards and forwards at pleasure. Some, by lightly pressing their stomach, bring up an incredible quantity and variety of things they have swallowed, and produce whatever they please, quite whole, as if out of a bag. Some so accurately mimic the voices of birds and beasts and other men, that, unless they are seen, the difference cannot be told. Some have such command of their bowels, that they can break wind continuously at pleasure, so as to produce the effect of singing. I myself have known a man who was accustomed to sweat whenever he wished. It is well known that some weep when they please, and shed a flood of tears. But far more incredible is that which some of our brethren saw quite recently. There was a presbyter called Restitutus, in the parish of the Calamensian Church, who, as often as he pleased (and he was asked to do this by those who desired to witness so remarkable a phenomenon), on some one imitating the wailings of mourners, became so insensible, and lay in a state so like death, that not only had he no feeling when they pinched and pricked him, but even when fire was applied to him, and he was burned by it, he had no sense of pain except afterwards from the wound. And that his body remained motionless, not by reason of his self-command, but because he was insensible, was proved by the fact that he breathed no more than a dead man; and yet he said that, when any one spoke with more than ordinary distinctness, he heard the voice, but as if it were a long way off. Seeing, then, that even in this mortal and miserable life the body serves some men by many remarkable movements and moods beyond the ordinary course of nature, what reason is there for doubting that, before man was involved by his sin in this weak and corruptible condition, his members might have served his will for the propagation of offspring without lust? Man has been given over to himself because he abandoned God, while he sought to be self-satisfying; and disobeying God, he could not obey even himself. Hence it is that he is involved in the obvious misery of being unable to live as he wishes. For if he lived as he wished, he would think himself blessed; but he could not be so if he lived wickedly.

CHAPTER XXV

OF TRUE BLESSEDNESS, WHICH THIS PRESENT LIFE CANNOT ENJOY

However, if we look at this a little more closely, we see that no one lives as he wishes but the blessed, and that no one is blessed but the righteous. But even the righteous himself does not live as he wishes, until he has arrived where he cannot die, be deceived, or injured, and until he is assured that this shall be his eternal condition. For this nature demands; and nature is not fully and perfectly blessed till it attains what it seeks. But what man is at present able to live as he wishes, when it is not in his power so much as to live? He wishes to live, he is compelled to die. How, then, does he live as he wishes who does not live as long as he wishes? or if he wishes to die, how can he live as he wishes, since he does not wish even to live? Or if he wishes to die, not because he dislikes life, but that after death he may live better, still he is not yet living as he wishes, but only has the prospect of so living when, through death, he reaches that which he wishes. But admit that he lives as he wishes, because he has done violence to himself, and forced himself not to wish what he cannot obtain, and to wish only what he can (as Terence has it, "Since you cannot do what you will, will what you can" [111]), is he therefore blessed because he is patiently wretched? For a blessed life is possessed only by the man who loves it. If it is loved and possessed, it must necessarily be more ardently loved than all besides; for whatever else is loved must be loved for the sake of the blessed life. And if it is loved as it deserves to be—and the man is not blessed who does not love the blessed life as it deserves—then he who so loves it cannot but wish it to be eternal. Therefore it shall then only be blessed when it is eternal.

CHAPTER XXVI

THAT WE ARE TO BELIEVE THAT IN PARADISE OUR FIRST PARENTS BEGAT OFFSPRING WITHOUT BLUSHING

In Paradise, then, man lived as he desired so long as he desired what God had commanded. He lived in the enjoyment of God, and was good by God's

[111] *Andr.* ii. 1, 5

goodness; he lived without any want, and had it in his power so to live eternally. He had food that he might not hunger, drink that he might not thirst, the tree of life that old age might not waste him. There was in his body no corruption, nor seed of corruption, which could produce in him any unpleasant sensation. He feared no inward disease, no outward accident. Soundest health blessed his body, absolute tranquillity his soul. As in Paradise there was no excessive heat or cold, so its inhabitants were exempt from the vicissitudes of fear and desire. No sadness of any kind was there, nor any foolish joy; true gladness ceaselessly flowed from the presence of God, who was loved out of a pure heart, and a good conscience, and faith unfeigned.[112] The honest love of husband and wife made a sure harmony between them. Body and spirit worked harmoniously together, and the commandment was kept without labor. No languor made their leisure wearisome; no sleepiness interrupted their desire to labor.

In such happy circumstances and general human well-being we should be far from suspecting that offspring could not have been begotten without the disease of lust, but those parts, like all the rest, would be set in motion at the command of the will; and without the seductive stimulus of passion, with calmness of mind and with no corrupting of the integrity of the body, the husband would lie upon the bosom of his wife. Nor ought we not to believe this because it cannot be proved by experiment. But rather, since no wild heat of passion would arouse those parts of the body, but a spontaneous power, according to the need, would be present, thus must we believe that the male semen could have been introduced into the womb of the wife with the integrity of the female genital organ being preserved, just as now, with that same integrity being safe, the menstrual flow of blood can be emitted from the womb of a virgin. To be sure, the seed could be introduced in the same way through which the menses can be emitted. In order that not the groans of labor-pain should relax the female organs for parturition, but rather the impulse of the fully developed foetus, thus not the eager desire of lust, but the normal exercise of the will, should join the male and female for breeding and conception.[b]

We speak of things which are now shameful, and although we try, as well as we are able, to conceive them as they were before they became shameful, yet necessity compels us rather to limit our discussion to the bounds set by modesty than to extend it as our moderate faculty of discourse might suggest. For since that which I have been speaking of was not experienced even by those who might have experienced it—I mean our first parents (for sin and its merited banishment from Paradise anticipated this passionless generation on their part)—when sexual intercourse is spoken of now, it suggests to men's thoughts not such a placid obedience to the will as is conceivable in our first parents, but such violent acting of lust as they themselves have experienced. And therefore modesty shuts my mouth, although my mind

[b] This paragraph appears in Latin in the original edition.—Ed.   [112] 1 Tim. i. 5

conceives the matter clearly. But Almighty God, the supreme and supremely good Creator of all natures, who aids and rewards good wills, while He abandons and condemns the bad, and rules both, was not destitute of a plan by which He might people His city with the fixed number of citizens which His wisdom had foreordained even out of the condemned human race, discriminating them not now by merits, since the whole mass was condemned as if in a vitiated root, but by grace, and showing, not only in the case of the redeemed, but also in those who were not delivered, how much grace He has bestowed upon them. For every one acknowledges that he has been rescued from evil, not by deserved, but by gratuitous goodness, when he is singled out from the company of those with whom he might justly have borne a common punishment, and is allowed to go scathless. Why, then, should God not have created those whom He foresaw would sin, since He was able to show in and by them both what their guilt merited, and what His grace bestowed, and since, under His creating and disposing hand, even the perverse disorder of the wicked could not pervert the right order of things?

CHAPTER XXVII

OF THE ANGELS AND MEN WHO SINNED, AND THAT THEIR WICKEDNESS DID NOT DISTURB THE ORDER OF GOD'S PROVIDENCE

The sins of men and angels do nothing to impede the great works of the Lord which accomplish His will.[113] For He who by His providence and omnipotence distributes to every one his own portion, is able to make good use not only of the good, but also of the wicked. And thus making a good use of the wicked angel, who, in punishment of his first wicked volition, was doomed to an obduracy that prevents him now from willing any good, why should not God have permitted him to tempt the first man, who had been created upright, that is to say, with a good will? For he had been so constituted, that if he looked to God for help, man's goodness should defeat the angel's wickedness; but if by proud self-pleasing he abandoned God, his Creator and Sustainer, he should be conquered. If his will remained upright, through leaning on God's help, he should be rewarded; if it became wicked, by forsaking God, he should be punished. But even this trusting in God's help could not itself be accomplished without God's help, although man had it in his own power to relinquish the benefits of divine grace by pleasing himself. For as it is not in our power to live in this world without sustaining ourselves by food, while it is in our power to refuse this nourishment and cease to live, as those do who kill themselves, so it was not in man's power, even in Paradise, to live as he ought without God's help; but it was in his power to live wickedly, though thus he should cut short his happiness, and incur very just punishment. Since, then, God was not ignorant that man would fall, why should He not have suffered him to be tempted by an angel

[113] Ps. cxi. 2

who hated and envied him? It was not, indeed, that He was unaware that he should be conquered, but because He foresaw that by the man's seed, aided by divine grace, this same devil himself should be conquered, to the greater glory of the saints. All was brought about in such a manner, that neither did any future event escape God's foreknowledge, nor did His foreknowledge compel any one to sin, and so as to demonstrate in the experience of the intelligent creation, human and angelic, how great a difference there is between the private presumption of the creature and the Creator's protection. For who will dare to believe or say that it was not in God's power to prevent both angels and men from sinning? But God preferred to leave this in their power, and thus to show both what evil could be wrought by their pride, and what good by His grace.

CHAPTER XXVIII

OF THE NATURE OF THE TWO CITIES, THE EARTHLY AND THE HEAVENLY

Accordingly, two cities have been formed by two loves: the earthly by the love of self, even to the contempt of God; the heavenly by the love of God, even to the contempt of self. The former, in a word, glories in itself, the latter in the Lord. For the one seeks glory from men; but the greatest glory of the other is God, the witness of conscience. The one lifts up its head in its own glory; the other says to its God, "Thou art my glory, and the lifter up of mine head." [114] In the one, the princes and the nations it subdues are ruled by the love of ruling; in the other, the princes and the subjects serve one another in love, the latter obeying, while the former take thought for all. The one delights in its own strength, represented in the persons of its rulers; the other says to its God, "I will love Thee, O Lord, my strength." [115] And therefore the wise men of the one city, living according to man, have sought for profit to their own bodies or souls, or both, and those who have known God "glorified Him not as God, neither were thankful, but became vain in their imaginations, and their foolish heart was darkened; professing themselves to be wise"—that is, glorying in their own wisdom, and being possessed by pride—"they became fools, and changed the glory of the incorruptible God into an image made like to corruptible man, and to birds, and four-footed beasts, and creeping things." For they were either leaders or followers of the people in adoring images, "and worshipped and served the creature more than the Creator, who is blessed for ever." [116] But in the other city there is no human wisdom, but only godliness, which offers due worship to the true God, and looks for its reward in the society of the saints, of holy angels as well as holy men, that God may be all in all. [117]

[114] Ps. iii. 3　[115] Ps. xviii. 1　[116] Rom. i. 21-25　[117] 1 Cor. xv. 28

BOOK FIFTEEN

ARGUMENT

Having treated in the four preceding books of the origin of the two cities, the earthly and the heavenly, Augustine explains their growth and progress in the four books which follow; and, in order to do so, he explains the chief passages of the sacred history which bear upon this subject. In this fifteenth book he opens this part of his work by explaining the events recorded in Genesis from the time of Cain and Abel to the Deluge.

CHAPTER I

OF THE TWO LINES OF THE HUMAN RACE WHICH FROM FIRST TO LAST DIVIDE IT

OF THE bliss of Paradise, of Paradise itself, and of the life of our first parents there, and of their sin and punishment, many have thought much, spoken much, written much. We ourselves, too, have spoken of these things in the foregoing books, and have written either what we read in the Holy Scriptures, or what we could reasonably deduce from them. And were we to enter into a more detailed investigation of these matters, an endless number of endless questions would arise, which would involve us in a larger work than the present occasion admits. We cannot be expected to find room for replying to every question that may be started by unoccupied and captious men, who are ever more ready to ask questions than capable of understanding the answer. Yet I trust we have already done justice to these great and difficult questions regarding the beginning of the world, or of the soul, or of the human race itself. This race we have distributed into two parts, the one consisting of those who live according to man, the other of those who live according to God. And these we also mystically call the two cities, or the two communities of men, of which the one is predestined to reign eternally with God, and the other to suffer eternal punishment with the devil. This, however, is their end, and of it we are to speak afterwards. At present, as we have said enough about their origin, whether among the angels, whose numbers we know not, or in the two first human beings, it seems suitable to attempt an account of their career, from the time when our two first parents began to propagate the race until all human generation shall cease. For this whole time or world-age, in which the dying give place and those who are born succeed, is the career of these two cities concerning which we treat.

Of these two first parents of the human race, then, Cain was the first-born, and he belonged to the city of men; after him was born Abel, who belonged to the city of God. For as in the individual the truth of the apostle's statement is discerned, "that is not first which is spiritual, but that which is

275

natural, and afterward that which is spiritual," [1] whence it comes to pass that each man, being derived from a condemned stock, is first of all born of Adam evil and carnal, and becomes good and spiritual only afterwards, when he is grafted into Christ by regeneration: so was it in the human race as a whole. When these two cities began to run their course by a series of deaths and births, the citizen of this world was the first-born, and after him the stranger in this world, the citizen of the city of God, predestinated by grace, elected by grace, by grace a stranger below, and by grace a citizen above. By grace—for so far as regards himself he is sprung from the same mass, all of which is condemned in its origin: but God, like a potter (for this comparison is introduced by the apostle judiciously, and not without thought) of the same lump made one vessel to honor, another to dishonor.[2] But first the vessel to dishonor was made, and after it another to honor. For in each individual, as I have already said, there is first of all that which is reprobate, that from which we must begin, but in which we need not necessarily remain; afterwards is that which is well-approved, to which we may by advancing attain, and in which, when we have reached it, we may abide. Not, indeed, that every wicked man shall be good, but that no one will be good who was not first of all wicked; but the sooner any one becomes a good man, the more speedily does he receive this title, and abolish the old name in the new. Accordingly, it is recorded of Cain that he built a city,[3] but Abel, being a sojourner, built none. For the city of the saints is above, although here below it begets citizens, in whom it sojourns till the time of its reign arrives, when it shall gather together all in the day of the resurrection; and then shall the promised kingdom be given to them, in which they shall reign with their Prince, the King of the ages, time without end.

CHAPTER II

OF THE CHILDREN OF THE FLESH AND THE CHILDREN OF THE PROMISE

There was indeed on earth, so long as it was needed, a symbol and foreshadowing image of this city, which served the purpose of reminding men that such a city was to be, rather than of making it present; and this image was itself called the holy city, as a symbol of the future city, though not itself the reality. Of this city which served as an image, and of that free city it typified, Paul writes to the Galatians in these terms: "Tell me, ye that desire to be under the law, do ye not hear the law? For it is written, that Abraham had two sons, the one by a bond maid, the other by a free woman. But he who was of the bond woman was born after the flesh, but he of the free woman was by promise. Which things are an allegory: for these are the two covenants; the one from the mount Sinai, which gendereth to bondage, which is Agar. For this Agar is mount Sinai in Arabia, and answereth to

[1] I Cor. xv. 46   [2] Rom. ix. 21   [3] Gen. iv. 17

Jerusalem which now is, and is in bondage with her children. But Jerusalem which is above is free, which is the mother of us all. For it is written, Rejoice, thou barren that bearest not; break forth and cry, thou that travailest not: for the desolate hath many more children than she which hath an husband. Now we, brethren, as Isaac was, are the children of promise. But as then he that was born after the flesh persecuted him that was born after the Spirit, even so it is now. Nevertheless, what saith the Scripture? Cast out the bond woman and her son: for the son of the bond woman shall not be heir with the son of the free woman. And we, brethren, are not children of the bond woman, but of the free, in the liberty wherewith Christ hath made us free." [4] This interpretation of the passage, handed down to us with apostolic authority, shows how we ought to understand the Scriptures of the two covenants—the old and the new. One portion of the earthly city became an image of the heavenly city, not having a significance of its own, but signifying another city, and therefore serving, or "being in bondage." For it was founded not for its own sake, but to prefigure another city; and this shadow of a city was also itself foreshadowed by another preceding figure. For Sarah's handmaid Agar, and her son, were an image of this image. And as the shadows were to pass away when the full light came, Sarah, the free woman, who prefigured the free city (which again was also prefigured in another way by that shadow of a city Jerusalem) therefore said, "Cast out the bond woman and her son; for the son of the bond woman shall not be heir with my son Isaac," or, as the apostle says, "with the son of the free woman." In the earthly city, then, we find two things—its own obvious presence, and its symbolic presentation of the heavenly city. Now citizens are begotten to the earthly city by nature vitiated by sin, but to the heavenly city by grace freeing nature from sin; whence the former are called "vessels of wrath," the latter "vessels of mercy." [5] And this was typified in the two sons of Abraham—Ishmael, the son of Agar the handmaid, being born according to the flesh, while Isaac was born of the free woman Sarah, according to the promise. Both, indeed, were of Abraham's seed; but the one was begotten by natural law, the other was given by gracious promise. In the one birth, human action is revealed; in the other, a divine kindness comes to light.

CHAPTER III

THAT SARAH'S BARRENNESS WAS MADE PRODUCTIVE BY GOD'S GRACE

Sarah, in fact, was barren; and, despairing of offspring, and being resolved that she would have at least through her handmaid that blessing she saw she could not in her own person procure, she gave her handmaid to her husband, to whom she herself had been unable to bear children. From him she required this conjugal duty, exercising her own right in another's womb. And thus Ishmael was born according to the common law of human gen-

[4] Gal. iv. 21-31   [5] Rom. ix. 22, 23

eration, by sexual intercourse. Therefore it is said that he was born "according to the flesh"—not because such births are not the gifts of God, nor His handiwork, whose creative wisdom "reaches," as it is written, "from one end to another mightily, and sweetly doth she order all things," [6] but because, in a case in which the gift of God, which was not due to men and was the gratuitous largess of grace, was to be conspicuous, it was requisite that a son be given in a way which no effort of nature could compass. Nature denies children to persons of the age which Abraham and Sarah had now reached; besides that, in Sarah's case, she was barren even in her prime. This nature, so constituted that offspring could not be looked for, symbolized the nature of the human race vitiated by sin and by just consequence condemned, which deserves no future felicity. Fitly, therefore, does Isaac, the child of promise, typify the children of grace, the citizens of the free city, who dwell together in everlasting peace, in which self-love and self-will have no place, but a ministering love that rejoices in the common joy of all, of many hearts makes one, that is to say, secures a perfect concord.

CHAPTER IV

OF THE CONFLICT AND PEACE OF THE EARTHLY CITY

But the earthly city, which shall not be everlasting (for it will no longer be a city when it has been committed to the extreme penalty), has its good in this world, and rejoices in it with such joy as such things can afford. But as this is not a good which can discharge its devotees of all distresses, this city is often divided against itself by litigations, wars, quarrels, and such victories as are either life-destroying or short-lived. For each part of it that arms against another part of it seeks to triumph over the nations though itself in bondage to vice. If, when it has conquered, it is inflated with pride, its victory is life-destroying; but if it turns its thoughts upon the common casualties of our mortal condition, and is rather anxious concerning the disasters that may befall it than elated with the successes already achieved, this victory, though of a higher kind, is still only short-lived; for it cannot abidingly rule over those whom it has victoriously subjugated. But the things which this city desires cannot justly be said to be evil, for it is itself, in its own kind, better than all other human good. For it desires earthly peace for the sake of enjoying earthly goods, and it makes war in order to attain to this peace; since, if it has conquered, and there remains no one to resist it, it enjoys a peace which it had not while there were opposing parties who contested for the enjoyment of those things which were too small to satisfy both. This peace is purchased by toilsome wars; it is obtained by what they style a glorious victory. Now, when victory remains with the party which had the juster cause, who hesitates to congratulate the victor, and style it a desirable peace? These things, then, are good things, and with-

[6] Wisd. viii. 1

out doubt the gifts of God. But if they neglect the better things of the heavenly city, which are secured by eternal victory and peace never-ending, and so inordinately covet these present good things that they believe them to be the only desirable things, or love them better than those things which are believed to be better—if this be so, then it is necessary that misery follow and ever increase.

CHAPTER V

OF THE FRATRICIDAL ACT OF THE FOUNDER OF THE EARTHLY CITY, AND THE CORRESPONDING CRIME OF THE FOUNDER OF ROME

Thus the founder of the earthly city was a fratricide. Overcome with envy, he slew his own brother, a citizen of the eternal city, and a sojourner on earth. So that we cannot be surprised that this first specimen, or, as the Greeks say, archetype of crime, should, long afterwards, find a corresponding crime at the foundation of that city which was destined to reign over so many nations, and be the head of this earthly city of which we speak. For of that city also, as one of their poets has mentioned, "the first walls were stained with a brother's blood," [7] or, as Roman history records, Remus was slain by his brother Romulus. And thus there is no difference between the foundation of this city and of the earthly city, unless it be that Romulus and Remus were both citizens of the earthly city. Both desired to have the glory of founding the Roman republic, but both could not have as much glory as if one only claimed it; for he who wished to have the glory of ruling would certainly rule less if his power were shared by a living consort. In order, therefore, that the whole glory might be enjoyed by one, his consort was removed; and by this crime the empire was made larger indeed, but inferior, while otherwise it would have been less, but better. Now these brothers, Cain and Abel, were not both animated by the same earthly desires, nor did the murderer envy the other because he feared that, by both ruling, his own dominion would be curtailed—for Abel was not solicitous to rule in that city which his brother built—he was moved by that diabolical, envious hatred with which the evil regard the good, for no other reason than because they are good while themselves are evil. For the possession of goodness is by no means diminished by being shared with a partner either permanent or temporarily assumed; on the contrary, the possession of goodness is increased in proportion to the concord and charity of each of those who share it. In short, he who is unwilling to share this possession cannot have it; and he who is most willing to admit others to a share of it will have the greatest abundance to himself. The quarrel, then, between Romulus and Remus shows how the earthly city is divided against itself; that which fell out between Cain and Abel illustrated the hatred that subsists between the two cities, that of God and that of men. The wicked war with the wicked; the good also war with the wicked. But with the good, good men, or at least

[7] Lucan, *Phar.* i. 95

perfectly good men, cannot war; though, while only going on towards perfection, they war to this extent, that every good man resists others in those points in which he resists himself. And in each individual "the flesh lusteth against the spirit, and the spirit against the flesh." [8] This spiritual lusting, therefore, can be at war with the carnal lust of another man; or carnal lust may be at war with the spiritual desires of another, in some such way as good and wicked men are at war; or, still more certainly, the carnal lusts of two men, good but not yet perfect, contend together, just as the wicked contend with the wicked, until the health of those who are under the treatment of grace attains final victory.

CHAPTER VI

OF THE WEAKNESSES WHICH EVEN THE CITIZENS OF THE CITY OF GOD SUFFER DURING THIS EARTHLY PILGRIMAGE IN PUNISHMENT OF SIN, AND OF WHICH THEY ARE HEALED BY GOD'S CARE

This sickliness—that is to say, that disobedience of which we spoke in the fourteenth book—is the punishment of the first disobedience. It is therefore not nature, but vice; and therefore it is said to the good who are growing in grace, and living in this pilgrimage by faith, "Bear ye one another's burdens, and so fulfill the law of Christ." [9] In like manner it is said elsewhere, "Warn them that are unruly, comfort the feeble-minded, support the weak, be patient toward all men. See that none render evil for evil unto any man." [10] And in another place, "If a man be overtaken in a fault, ye which are spiritual restore such an one in the spirit of meekness; considering thyself, lest thou also be tempted." [11] And elsewhere, "Let not the sun go down upon your wrath." [12] And in the Gospel, "If thy brother shall trespass against thee, go and tell him his fault between thee and him alone." [13] So too of sins which may create scandal the apostle says, "Them that sin rebuke before all, that others also may fear." [14] For this purpose, and that we may keep that peace without which no man can see the Lord,[15] many precepts are given which carefully inculcate mutual forgiveness; among which we may number that terrible word in which the servant is ordered to pay his formerly remitted debt of ten thousand talents, because he did not remit to his fellow-servant his debt of two hundred pence. To which parable the Lord Jesus added the words, "So likewise shall my heavenly Father do also unto you, if ye from your hearts forgive not every one his brother." [16] It is thus the citizens of the city of God are healed while still they sojourn in this earth and sigh for the peace of their heavenly country. The Holy Spirit, too, works within, that the medicine externally applied may have some good result. Otherwise, even though God Himself make use of the creatures that are subject to Him, and in some human form address our human senses, whether we receive those impressions in sleep or in some

[8] Gal. v. 17   [9] Gal. vi. 2   [10] 1 Thess. v. 14, 15   [11] Gal. vi. 1   [12] Eph. iv. 26
[13] Matt. xviii. 15   [14] 1 Tim. v. 20   [15] Heb. xii. 14   [16] Matt. xviii. 35

external appearance, still, if He does not by His own inward grace sway and act upon the mind, no preaching of the truth is of any avail. But this God does, distinguishing between the vessels of wrath and the vessels of mercy, by His own very secret but very just providence. When He Himself aids the soul in His own hidden and wonderful ways, and the sin which dwells in our members, and is, as the apostle teaches, rather the punishment of sin, does not reign in our mortal body to obey the lusts of it, and when we no longer yield our members as instruments of unrighteousness,[17] then the soul is converted from its own evil and selfish desires, and, God possessing it, it possesses itself in peace even in this life, and afterwards, with perfected health and endowed with immortality, will reign without sin in peace everlasting.

CHAPTER VII

OF THE CAUSE OF CAIN'S CRIME AND HIS OBSTINACY, WHICH NOT EVEN THE WORD OF GOD COULD SUBDUE

But though God made use of this very mode of address which we have been endeavoring to explain, and spoke to Cain in that form by which He was wont to accommodate Himself to our first parents and converse with them as a companion, what good influence had it on Cain? Did he not fulfill his wicked intention of killing his brother even after he was warned by God's voice? For when God had made a distinction between their sacrifices, neglecting Cain's, regarding Abel's, which was doubtless intimated by some visible sign to that effect; and when God had done so because the works of the one were evil but those of his brother good, Cain was very wroth, and his countenance fell. For thus it is written: "And the Lord said unto Cain, Why are thou wroth, and why is thy countenance fallen? If thou offerest rightly, but doest not rightly distinguish, hast thou not sinned? Fret not thyself, for unto thee shall be his turning, and thou shalt rule over him." [18] In this admonition administered by God to Cain, that clause indeed, "If thou offerest rightly, but dost not rightly distinguish, hast thou not sinned?" is obscure, inasmuch as it is not apparent for what reason or purpose it was spoken, and many meanings have been put upon it, as each one who discusses it attempts to interpret it according to the rule of faith. The truth is, that a sacrifice is "rightly offered" when it is offered to the true God, to whom alone we must sacrifice. And it is "not rightly distinguished" when we do not rightly distinguish the places or seasons or materials of the offering, or the person offering, or the person to whom it is presented, or those to whom it is distributed for food after the oblation. Distinguishing is here used for discriminating—whether when an offering is made in a place where it ought not or of a material which ought to be offered not there but elsewhere; or when an offering is made at a wrong time, or of a material suitable not then but at some other time; or when that is offered which in no place nor any time ought to be offered; or when a man keeps to himself choicer

[17] Rom. vi. 12, 13   [18] Gen. iv. 6, 7

specimens of the same kind than he offers to God; or when he or any other who may not lawfully partake profanely eats of the oblation. In which of these particulars Cain displeased God, it is difficult to determine. But the Apostle John, speaking of these brothers, says, "Not as Cain, who was of that wicked one, and slew his brother. And wherefore slew he him? Because his own works were evil, and his brother's righteous." [19] He thus gives us to understand that God did not respect his offering because it was not rightly "distinguished" in this, that he gave to God something of his own but kept himself to himself. For this all do who follow not God's will but their own, who live not with an upright but a crooked heart, and yet offer to God such gifts as they suppose will procure from Him that He aid them not by healing but by gratifying their evil passions. And this is the characteristic of the earthly city, that it worships God or gods who may aid it in reigning victoriously and peacefully on earth not through love of doing good, but through lust of rule. The good use the world that they may enjoy God: the wicked, on the contrary, that they may enjoy the world would fain use God —those of them, at least, who have attained to the belief that He is and takes an interest in human affairs. For they who have not yet attained even to this belief are still at a much lower level. Cain, then, when he saw that God had respect to his brother's sacrifice, but not to his own, should have humbly chosen his good brother as his example, and not proudly counted him his rival. But he was wroth, and his countenance fell. This angry regret for another person's goodness, even his brother's, was charged upon him by God as a great sin. And He accused him of it in the interrogation, "Why are thou wroth, and why is thy countenance fallen?" For God saw that he envied his brother, and of this He accused him. For to men, from whom the heart of their fellow is hid, it might be doubtful and quite uncertain whether that sadness bewailed his own wickedness by which, as he had learned, he had displeased God, or his brother's goodness, which had pleased God, and won His favorable regard to his sacrifice. But God, in giving the reason why He refused to accept Cain's offering and why Cain should rather have been displeased at himself than at his brother, shows him that though he was unjust in "not rightly distinguishing," that is, not rightly living and being unworthy to have his offering received, he was more unjust by far in hating his just brother without a cause.

Yet He does not dismiss him without counsel, holy, just, and good. "Fret not thyself," He says, "for unto thee shall be his turning, and thou shalt rule over him." Over his brother, does He mean? Most certainly not. Over what, then, but sin? For He had said, "Thou hast sinned," and then He added, "Fret not thyself, for to thee shall be its turning, and thou shalt rule over it." And the "turning" of sin to the man can be understood of his conviction that the guilt of sin can be laid at no other man's door but his own. For this is the health-giving medicine of penitence, and the fit plea for pardon; so that, when it is said, "To thee its turning," we must not supply

[19] 1 John iii. 12

"shall be," but we must read, "To thee let its turning be," understanding it as a command, not as a prediction. For then shall a man rule over his sin when he does not prefer it to himself and defend it, but subjects it by repentance; otherwise he that becomes protector of it shall surely become its prisoner. But if we understand this sin to be that carnal concupiscence of which the apostle says, "The flesh lusteth against the spirit," [20] among the fruits of which lust he names envy, by which assuredly Cain was stung and excited to destroy his brother, then we may properly supply the words "shall be," and read, "To thee shall be its turning, and thou shalt rule over it." For when the carnal part which the apostle calls sin, in that place where he says, "It is not I who do it, but sin that dwelleth in me," [21] that part which the philosophers also call vicious, and which ought not to lead the mind, but which the mind ought to rule and restrain by reason from illicit motions—when, then, this part has been moved to perpetrate any wickedness, if it be curbed and if it obey the word of the apostle, "Yield not your members instruments of unrighteousness unto sin," [22] it is turned towards the mind and subdued and conquered by it, so that reason rules over it as a subject. It was this which God enjoined on him who was kindled with the fire of envy against his brother, so that he sought to put out of the way him whom he should have set as an example. "Fret not thyself," or compose thyself, He says: withhold thy hand from crime; let not sin reign in your mortal body to fulfill it in the lusts thereof, nor yield your members instruments of unrighteousness unto sin. "For to thee shall be its turning," so long as you do not encourage it by giving it the rein, but bridle it by quenching its fire. "And thou shalt rule over it;" for when it is not allowed any external actings, it yields itself to the rule of the governing mind and righteous will, and ceases from even internal motions. There is something similar said in the same divine book of the woman, when God questioned and judged them after their sin, and pronounced sentence on them all—the devil in the form of the serpent, the woman and her husband in their own persons. For when He had said to her, "I will greatly multiply thy sorrow and thy conception; in sorrow shalt thou bring forth children," then He added, "and thy turning shall be to thy husband, and he shall rule over thee." [23] What is said to Cain about his sin, or about the vicious concupiscence of his flesh, is here said of the woman who had sinned; and we are to understand that the husband is to rule his wife as the soul rules the flesh. And therefore, says the apostle, "He that loveth his wife, loveth himself; for no man ever yet hated his own flesh." [24] This flesh, then, is to be healed, because it belongs to ourselves: is not to be abandoned to destruction as if it were alien to our nature. But Cain received that counsel of God in the spirit of one who did not wish to amend. In fact, the vice of envy grew stronger in him; and, having entrapped his brother, he slew him. Such was the founder of the earthly city. He was also a figure of the Jews who slew Christ the Shepherd of the

[20] Gal. v. 17   [21] Rom. vii. 17   [22] Rom. vi. 13   [23] Gen. iii. 16   [24] Eph. v. 28, 29

flock of men, prefigured by Abel the shepherd of sheep: but as this is an allegorical and prophetical matter, I forbear to explain it now; besides, I remember that I have made some remarks upon it in writing against Faustus the Manichaean.[25]

CHAPTER VIII

WHAT CAIN'S REASON WAS FOR BUILDING A CITY SO EARLY IN THE HISTORY OF THE HUMAN RACE

At present it is the history which I aim at defending, that Scripture may not be reckoned incredible when it relates that one man built a city at a time in which there seem to have been but four men upon earth, or rather indeed but three, after one brother slew the other—to wit, the first man the father of all, and Cain himself, and his son Enoch, by whose name the city was itself called. But they who are moved by this consideration forget to take into account that the writer of the sacred history does not necessarily mention all the men who might be alive at that time, but those only whom the scope of his work required him to name. The design of that writer (who in this matter was the instrument of the Holy Ghost) was to descend to Abraham through the successions of ascertained generations propagated from one man, and then to pass from Abraham's seed to the people of God, in whom, separated as they were from other nations, was prefigured and predicted all that relates to the city whose reign is eternal, and to its king and founder Christ, which things were foreseen in the Spirit as destined to come; yet neither is this object so effected as that nothing is said of the other society of men which we call the earthly city, but mention is made of it so far as seemed needful to enhance the glory of the heavenly city by contrast to its opposite. Accordingly, when the divine Scripture, in mentioning the number of years which those men lived, concludes its account of each man of whom it speaks, with the words, "And he begat sons and daughters, and all his days were so and so, and he died," are we to understand that, because it does not name those sons and daughters, therefore, during that long term of years over which one lifetime extended in those early days, there might not have been born very many men, by whose united numbers not one but several cities might have been built? But it suited the purpose of God, by whose inspiration these histories were composed, to arrange and distinguish from the first these two societies in their several generations—that on the one side the generations of men, that is to say, of those who live according to man, and on the other side the generations of the sons of God, that is to say, of men living according to God, might be traced down together and yet apart from one another as far as the deluge, at which point their dissociation and association are exhibited: their dissociation, inasmuch as the genera-

[25] *C. Faustum. Man.* xii. c. 9

tions of both lines are recorded in separate tables, the one line descending from the fratricide Cain, the other from Seth, who had been born to Adam instead of him whom his brother slew; their association, inasmuch as the good so deteriorated that the whole race became of such a character that it was swept away by the deluge, with the exception of one just man, whose name was Noah, and his wife and three sons and three daughters-in-law, which eight persons were alone deemed worthy to escape from that desolating visitation which destroyed all men.

Therefore, although it is written, "And Cain knew his wife, and she conceived and bare Enoch, and he builded a city and called the name of the city after the name of his son Enoch," [26] it does not follow that we are to believe this to have been his first-born; for we cannot suppose that this is proved by the expression "he knew his wife," as if then for the first time he had had intercourse with her. For in the case of Adam, the father of all, this expression is used not only when Cain, who seems to have been his first-born, was conceived, but also afterwards the same Scripture says, "Adam knew Eve his wife, and she conceived, and bare a son, and called his name Seth." [27] Whence it is obvious that Scripture employs this expression neither always when a birth is recorded nor then only when the birth of a first-born is mentioned. Neither is it necessary to suppose that Enoch was Cain's first-born because he named his city after him. For it is quite possible that though he had other sons, yet for some reason the father loved him more than the rest. Judah was not the first-born, though he gives his name to Judaea and the Jews. But even though Enoch was the first-born of the city's founder, that is no reason for supposing that the father named the city after him as soon as he was born; for at that time he, being but a solitary man, could not have founded a civic community, which is nothing else than a multitude of men bound together by some associating tie. But when his family increased to such numbers that he had quite a population, then it became possible to him both to build a city, and give it, when founded, the name of his son. For so long was the life of those antediluvians, that he who lived the shortest time of those whose years are mentioned in Scripture attained to the age of 753 years.[28] And though no one attained the age of a thousand years, several exceeded the age of nine hundred. Who then can doubt that during the lifetime of one man the human race might be so multiplied that there would be a population to build and occupy not one but several cities? And this might very readily be conjectured from the fact that from one man, Abraham, in not much more than four hundred years, the numbers of the Hebrew race so increased, that in the exodus of that people from Egypt there are recorded to have been six hundred thousand men capable of bearing arms,[29] and this over and above the Indumaeans, who, though not numbered with Israel's descendants, were yet sprung from his

[26] Gen. iv. 17   [27] Gen. iv. 25   [28] Lamech, according to the LXX   [29] Ex. xii. 37

brother, also a grandson of Abraham; and over and above the other nations which were of the same stock of Abraham, though not through Sarah—that is, his descendants by Hagar and Keturah, the Ishmaelites, Midianites, etc.

CHAPTER IX

OF THE LONG LIFE AND GREATER STATURE OF THE ANTEDILUVIANS

Wherefore no one who considerately weighs facts will doubt that Cain might have built a city, and that a large one, when it is observed how prolonged were the lives of men, unless perhaps some sceptic take exception to this very length of years which our authors ascribe to the antediluvians and deny that this is credible. And so, too, they do not believe that the size of men's bodies was larger then than now, though the most esteemed of their own poets, Virgil, asserts the same, when he speaks of that huge stone which had been fixed as a landmark, and which a strong man of those ancient times snatched up as he fought, and ran, and hurled, and cast it—

> Scarce twelve strong men of later mould
> That weight could on their necks uphold.[30]

thus declaring his opinion that the earth then produced mightier men. And if in the more recent times, how much more in the ages before the world-renowned deluge? But the large size of the primitive human body is often proved to the incredulous by the exposure of sepulchres, either through the wear of time or the violence of torrents or some accident, and in which bones of incredible size have been found or have rolled out. I myself, along with some others, saw on the shore at Utica a man's molar tooth of such a size, that if it were cut down into teeth such as we have, a hundred, I fancy, could have been made out of it. But that, I believe, belonged to some giant. For though the bodies of ordinary men were then larger than ours, the giants surpassed all in stature. And neither in our own age nor any other have there been altogether wanting instances of gigantic stature, though they may be few. The younger Pliny, a most learned man, maintains that the older the world becomes, the smaller will be the bodies of men.[31] And he mentions that Homer in his poems often lamented the same decline; and this he does not laugh at as a poetical figment, but in his character of a recorder of natural wonders accepts it as historically true. But, as I said, the bones which are from time to time discovered prove the size of the bodies of the ancients, and will do so to future ages, for they are slow to decay. But the length of an antediluvian's life cannot now be proved by any such monumental evidence. But we are not on this account to withhold our faith from the sacred history, whose statements of past fact we are the more inexcusable

[30] Virgil, *Aeneid*, xii. 899, 900. Compare the *Iliad*, v. 302, and Juvenal, xv. 65 *et seqq.*
[31] Plin. *Hist. Nat.* vii. 16

in discrediting, as we see the accuracy of its prediction of what was future. And even that same Pliny[32] tells us that there is still a nation in which men live 200 years. If, then, in places unknown to us, men are believed to have a length of days which is quite beyond our own experience, why should we not believe the same of times distant from our own? Or are we to believe that in other places there is what is not here, while we do not believe that in other times there has been anything but what is now?

CHAPTER X

OF THE DIFFERENT COMPUTATION OF THE AGES OF THE ANTEDILUVIANS, GIVEN BY THE HEBREW MANUSCRIPTS AND BY OUR OWN

Wherefore, although there is a discrepancy for which I cannot account between our manuscripts and the Hebrew, in the very number of years assigned to the antediluvians, yet the discrepancy is not so great that they do not agree about their longevity. For the very first man, Adam, before he begot his son Seth, is in our manuscripts found to have lived 230 years, but in the Hebrew MSS. 130. But after he begot Seth, our copies read that he lived 700 years, while the Hebrew give 800. And thus, when the two periods are taken together, the sum agrees. And so throughout the succeeding generations, the period before the father begets a son is always made shorter by 100 years in the Hebrew, but the period after his son is begotten is longer by 100 years in the Hebrew than in our copies. And thus, taking the two periods together, the result is the same in both. And in the sixth generation there is no discrepancy at all. In the seventh, however, of which Enoch is the representative, who is recorded to have been translated without death because he pleased God, there is the same discrepancy as in the first five generations, 100 years more being ascribed to him by our MSS. before he begat a son. But still the result agrees; for according to both documents he lived before he was translated 365 years. In the eighth generation the discrepancy is less than in the others, and of a different kind. For Methuselah, whom Enoch begat, lived, before he begat his successor, not 100 years less, but 100 years more, according to the Hebrew reading; and in our MSS. again these years are added to the period after he begat his son; so that in this case also the sum-total is the same. And it is only in the ninth generation, that is, in the age of Lamech, Methuselah's son and Noah's father, that there is a discrepancy in the sum total; and even in this case it is slight. For the Hebrew MSS. represent him as living twenty-four years more than ours assign to him. For before he begat his son, who was called Noah, six years fewer are given to him by the Hebrew MSS. than by ours; but after he begat

---

[32] Pliny, *Hist. Nat.* vii. 49, merely reports what he had read in Hellanicus about the Epirotes of Etolia

this son, they give him thirty years more than ours; so that, deducting the former six, there remains, as we said, a surplus of twenty-four.

CHAPTER XI

OF METHUSELAH'S AGE, WHICH SEEMS TO EXTEND FOURTEEN YEARS BEYOND THE DELUGE

From this discrepancy between the Hebrew books and our own arises the well-known question as to the age of Methuselah; for it is computed that he lived for fourteen years after the deluge, though Scripture relates that of all who were then upon the earth only the eight souls in the ark escaped destruction by the flood, and of these Methuselah was not one. For, according to our books, Methuselah, before he begat the son whom he called Lamech, lived 167 years; then Lamech himself, before his son Noah was born, lived 188 years which together make 355 years. Add to these the age of Noah at the date of the deluge, 600 years, and this gives a total of 955 from the birth of Methuselah to the year of the flood. Now all the years of the life of Methuselah are computed to be 969; for when he had lived 167 years, and had begotten his son Lamech, he then lived after this 802 years, which makes a total, as we said, of 969 years. From this, if we deduct 955 years from the birth of Methuselah to the flood, there remains fourteen years, which he is supposed to have lived after the flood. And therefore some suppose that, though he was not on earth (in which it is agreed that every living thing which could not naturally live in water perished), he was for a time with his father, who had been translated, and that he lived there till the flood had passed away. This hypothesis they adopt, that they may not cast a slight on the trustworthiness of versions which the Church has received into a position of high authority,[33] and because they believe that the Jewish MSS. rather than our own are in error. For they do not admit that this is a mistake of the translators, but maintain that there is a falsified statement in the original, from which, through the Greek, the Scripture has been translated into our own tongue. They say that it is not credible that the seventy translators, who simultaneously and unanimously produced one rendering, could have erred, or, in a case in which no interest of theirs was involved, could have falsified their translation; but that the Jews, envying us our translation of their Law and Prophets, have made alterations in their texts so as to undermine the authority of ours. This opinion or suspicion let each man adopt according to his own judgment. Certain it is that Methuselah did not survive the flood, but died in the very year it occurred, if the numbers given in the Hebrew MSS. are true. My own opinion regarding the seventy translators I will, with God's help, state more carefully in its own place, when I have come down (following the order which this work re-

[33] "Quos in auctoritatem celebriorum Ecclesia suscepit"

quires) to that period in which their translation was executed.[34] For the present question, it is enough that, according to our versions, the men of that age had lives so long as to make it quite possible that, during the life-time of the first-born of the two sole parents then on earth, the human race multiplied sufficiently to form a community,

CHAPTER XII

OF THE OPINION OF THOSE WHO DO NOT BELIEVE THAT IN THESE PRIMITIVE TIMES MEN LIVED SO LONG AS IS STATED

For they are by no means to be listened to who suppose that in those times years were differently reckoned, and were so short that one of our years may be supposed to be equal to ten of theirs. So that they say, when we read or hear that some man lived 900 years, we should understand ninety, ten of those years making but one of ours, and ten of ours equally 100 of theirs. Consequently, as they suppose, Adam was twenty-three years of age when he begat Seth, and Seth himself was twenty years and six months old when his son Enos was born, though the Scripture calls these months 205 years. For, on the hypothesis of those whose opinion we are explaining, it was customary to divide one such year as we have into ten parts, and to call each part a year. And each of these parts was composed of six days square; because God finished His works in six days, that He might rest the seventh. Of this I disputed according to my ability in the eleventh book.[35] Now six squared, or six times six, gives thirty-six days; and this multiplied by ten amounts to 360 days, or twelve lunar months. As for the five remaining days which are needed to complete the solar year, and for the fourth part of a day, which requires that into every fourth or leap-year a day be added, the ancients added such days as the Romans used to call "intercalary," in order to complete the number of the years. So that Enos, Seth's son, was nineteen years old when his son Cainan was born, though Scripture calls these years 190. And so through all the generations in which the ages of the antediluvians are given, we find in our versions that almost no one begat a son at the age of 100 or under, or even at the age of 120 or thereabouts; but the youngest fathers are recorded to have been 160 years old and upwards. And the reason of this, they say, is that no one can beget children when he is ten years old, the age spoken of by those men as 100, but that sixteen is the age of puberty, and competent now to propagate offspring; and this is the age called by them 160. And that it may not be thought incredible that in these days the year was differently computed from our own, they adduce what is recorded by several writers of history, that the Egyptians had a year of four months, the Acarnanians of six, and the Lavinians of thirteen months. The younger Pliny, after mentioning that

[34] cf. Book xviii. c. 42-44   [35] C. 8

some writers reported that one man had lived 152 years, another ten more, others 200, others 300, that some had even reached 500 and 600, and a few 800 years of age, gave it as his opinion that all must be ascribed to mistaken computation. For some, he says, make summer and winter each a year; others make each season a year, like the Arcadians, whose years, he says, were of three months. He added, too, that the Egyptians, of whose little years of four months we have spoken already, sometimes terminated their year at the wane of each moon; so that with them there are produced lifetimes of 1000 years.

By these plausible arguments certain persons, with no desire to weaken the credit of this sacred history, but rather to facilitate belief in it by removing the difficulty of such incredible longevity, have been themselves persuaded, and think they act wisely in persuading others, that in these days the year was so brief that ten of their years equal but one of ours, while ten of ours equal 100 of theirs. But there is the plainest evidence to show that this is quite false. Before producing this evidence, however, it seems right to mention a conjecture which is yet more plausible. From the Hebrew manuscripts we could at once refute this confident statement; for in them Adam is found to have lived not 230 but 130 years before he begat his third son. If, then, this mean thirteen years by our ordinary computation, then he must have begotten his first son when he was only twelve or thereabouts. Who can at this age beget children according to the ordinary and familiar course of nature? But not to mention him, since it is possible he may have been able to beget his like as soon as he was created—for it is not credible that he was created so little as our infants are—not to mention him, his son was not 205 years old when he begat Enos, as our versions have it, but 105, and consequently, according to this idea, was not eleven years old. But what shall I say of his son Cainan, who, though by our version 170 years old, was by the Hebrew text seventy when he begat Mahalaleel? If seventy years in those times meant only seven of our years, what man of seven years old begets children?

CHAPTER XIII

WHETHER, IN COMPUTING YEARS, WE OUGHT TO FOLLOW THE HEBREW OR THE SEPTUAGINT

But if I say this, I shall presently be answered, It is one of the Jews' lies. This, however, we have disposed of above, showing that it cannot be that men of so just a reputation as the seventy translators should have falsified their version. However, if I ask them which of the two is more credible, that the Jewish nation, scattered far and wide, could have unanimously conspired to forge this lie, and so, through envying others the authority of their Scriptures, have deprived themselves of their verity; or that seventy men, who were also themselves Jews, shut up in one place (for Ptolemy king of

Egypt had got them together for this work), should have envied foreign
nations that same truth, and by common consent inserted these errors: who
does not see which can be more naturally and readily believed? But far be
it from any prudent man to believe either that the Jews, however malicious
and wrong-headed, could have tampered with so many and so widely-
dispersed manuscripts; or that those renowned seventy individuals had any
common purpose to grudge the truth to the nations. One must therefore
more plausibly maintain, that when first their labors began to be transcribed
from the copy in Ptolemy's library, some such misstatement might find its
way into the first copy made, and from it might be disseminated far and
wide; and that this might arise from no fraud, but from a mere copyist's
error. This is a sufficiently plausible account of the difficulty regarding
Methuselah's life, and of that other case in which there is a difference in the
total of twenty-four years. But in those cases in which there is a methodical
resemblance in the falsification, so that uniformly the one version allots to
the period before a son and successor is born 100 years more than the other,
and to the period subsequent 100 years less, and *vice versa*, so that the totals
may agree—and this holds true of the first, second, third, fourth, fifth, and
seventh generations—in these cases error seems to have, if we may say so,
a certain kind of constancy, and savors not of accident, but of design.

Accordingly, that diversity of numbers which distinguishes the Hebrew
from the Greek and Latin copies of Scripture, and which consists of a uniform addition and deduction of 100 years in each lifetime for several consecutive generations, is to be attributed neither to the malice of the Jews
nor to men so diligent and prudent as the seventy translators, but to the
error of the copyist who was first allowed to transcribe the manuscript from
the library of the above-mentioned king. For even now, in cases where numbers contribute nothing to the easier comprehension or more satisfactory
knowledge of anything, they are both carelessly transcribed, and still more
carelessly emended. For who will trouble himself to learn how many thousand men the several tribes of Israel contained? He sees no resulting benefit
of such knowledge. Or how many men are there who are aware of the vast
advantage that lies hid in this knowledge? But in this case, in which during
so many consecutive generations 100 years are added in one manuscript
where they are not reckoned in the other, and then, after the birth of the
son and successor, the years which were wanting are added, it is obvious
that the copyist who contrived this arrangement designed to insinuate that
the antediluvians lived an excessive number of years only because each year
was excessively brief, and that he tried to draw the attention to this fact by
his statement of their age of puberty at which they became able to beget
children. For, lest the incredulous might stumble at the difficulty of so long
a lifetime, he insinuated that 100 of their years equalled but ten of ours;
and this insinuation he conveyed by adding 100 years whenever he found
the age below 160 years or thereabouts, deducting these years again from the

period after the son's birth, that the total might harmonize. By this means
he intended to ascribe the generation of offspring to a fit age, without diminishing the total sum of years ascribed to the lifetime of the individuals.
And the very fact that in the sixth generation he departed from this uniform practice, inclines us all rather to believe that when the circumstance
we have referred to required his alterations, he made them; seeing that when
this circumstance did not exist, he made no alteration. For in the same generation he found in the Hebrew MS., that Jared lived before he begat Enoch
162 years, which, according to the short year computation, is sixteen years
and somewhat less than two months, an age capable of procreation; and
therefore it was not necessary to add 100 short years, and so make the age
twenty-six years of the usual length; and of course it was not necessary to
deduct, after the son's birth, years which he had not added before it. And
thus it comes to pass that in this instance there is no variation between the
two manuscripts.

This is corroborated still further by the fact that in the eighth generation,
while the Hebrew books assign 182[36] years to Methuselah before Lamech's
birth, ours assign to him twenty less, though usually 100 years are added to
this period; then, after Lamech's birth, the twenty years are restored, so as
to equalize the total in the two books. For if his design was that these 170
years be understood as seventeen, so as to suit the age of puberty, as there
was no need for him adding anything, so there was none for his subtracting
anything; for in this case he found an age fit for the generation of children,
for the sake of which he was in the habit of adding those 100 years in cases
where he did not find the age already sufficient. This difference of twenty
years we might, indeed, have supposed had happened accidentally, had he
not taken care to restore them afterwards as he had deducted them from the
period before, so that there might be no deficiency in the total. Or are we
perhaps to suppose that there was the still more astute design of concealing
the deliberate and uniform addition of 100 years to the first period and their
deduction from the subsequent period—did he design to conceal this by
doing something similar, that is to say, adding and deducting, not indeed a
century, but some years, even in a case in which there was no need for his
doing so? But whatever may be thought of this, whether it be believed that
he did so or not, whether, in fine, it be so or not, I would have no manner of
doubt that when any diversity is found in the books, since both cannot be
true to fact, we do well to believe in preference that language out of which
the translation was made into another by translators. For there are three
Greek MSS., one Latin, and one Syriac, which agree with one another, and
in all of these Methuselah is said to have died six years before the deluge.

[36] One hundred and eighty-seven is the number given in the Hebrew, and one hundred
and sixty-seven in the Septuagint; but notwithstanding the confusion, the argument
of Augustine is easily followed

CHAPTER XIV

THAT THE YEARS IN THOSE ANCIENT TIMES WERE OF THE SAME LENGTH AS OUR OWN

Let us now see how it can be plainly made out that in the enormously protracted lives of those men the years were not so short that ten of their years were equal to only one of ours, but were of as great length as our own, which are measured by the course of the sun. It is proved by this, that Scripture states that the flood occurred in the six hundredth year of Noah's life. But why in the same place is it also written, "The waters of the flood were upon the earth in the six hundredth year of Noah's life, in the second month, the twenty-seventh day of the month," [37] if that very brief year (of which it took ten to make one of ours) consisted of thirty-six days? For so scant a year, if the ancient usage dignified it with the name of year, either has not months, or this month must be three days, so that it may have twelve of them. How then was it here said, "In the six hundredth year, the second month, the twenty-seventh day of the month," unless the months then were of the same length as the months now? For how else could it be said that the flood began on the twenty-seventh day of the second month? Then afterwards, at the end of the flood, it is thus written: "And the ark rested in the seventh month, on the twenty-seventh day of the month, on the mountains of Ararat. And the waters decreased continually until the eleventh month: on the first day of the month were the tops of the mountains seen." [38] But if the months were such as we have, then so were the years. And certainly months of three days each could not have a twenty-seventh day. Or if every measure of time was diminished in proportion, and a thirtieth part of three days was then called a day, then that great deluge, which is recorded to have lasted forty days and forty nights, was really over in less than four of our days. Who can away with such foolishness and absurdity? Far be this error from us—an error which seeks to build up our faith in the divine Scriptures on false conjecture only to demolish our faith at another point. It is plain that the day then was what it now is, a space of four-and-twenty hours, determined by the lapse of day and night; the month then equal to the month now, which is defined by the rise and completion of one moon; the year then equal to the year now, which is completed by twelve lunar months, with the addition of five days and a fourth to adjust it with the course of the sun. It was a year of this length which was reckoned the six hundredth of Noah's life, and in the second month, the twenty-seventh day of the month, the flood began—a flood which, as is recorded, was caused by heavy rains continuing for forty days, which days had not only two hours and a little more, but four-and-twenty hours, completing a night and a day.

[37] Gen. vii. 10, 11 (in our version the seventeenth day)   [38] Gen. viii. 4, 5

And consequently those antediluvians lived more than 900 years, which were years as long as those which afterwards Abraham lived 175 of, and after him his son Isaac 180, and his son Jacob nearly 150, and some time after, Moses 120, and men now seventy or eighty, or not much longer, of which years it is said, "their strength is labor and sorrow." [39]

But that discrepancy of numbers which is found to exist between our own and the Hebrew text does not touch the longevity of the ancients; and if there is any diversity so great that both versions cannot be true, we must take our ideas of the real facts from that text out of which our own version has been translated. However, though any one who pleases has it in his power to correct this version, yet it is not unimportant to observe that no one has presumed to emend the Septuagint from the Hebrew text in the many places where they seem to disagree. For this difference has not been reckoned a falsification; and for my own part I am persuaded it ought not to be reckoned so. But where the difference is not a mere copyist's error, and where the sense is agreeable to truth and illustrative of truth, we must believe that the divine Spirit prompted them to give a varying version, not in their function of translators, but in the liberty of prophesying. And therefore we find that the apostles justly sanction the Septuagint, by quoting it as well as the Hebrew when they adduce proofs from the Scriptures. But as I have promised to treat this subject more carefully, if God help me, in a more fitting place, I will now go on with the matter in hand. For there can be no doubt that, the lives of men being so long, the first-born of the first man could have built a city—a city, however, which was earthly, and not that which is called the city of God, to describe which we have taken in hand this great work.

CHAPTER XV

WHETHER IT IS CREDIBLE THAT THE MEN OF THE PRIMITIVE AGE ABSTAINED FROM SEXUAL INTERCOURSE UNTIL THAT DATE AT WHICH IT IS RECORDED THAT THEY BEGAT CHILDREN

Some one, then, will say, Is it to be believed that a man who intended to beget children, and had no intention of continence, abstained from sexual intercourse a hundred years and more, or even, according to the Hebrew version, only a little less, say eighty, seventy, or sixty years; or, if he did not abstain, was unable to beget offspring? This question admits of two solutions. For either puberty was so much later as the whole life was longer, or, which seems to me more likely, it is not the first-born sons that are here mentioned, but those whose names were required to fill up the series until Noah was reached, from whom again we see that the succession is continued to Abraham, and after him down to that point of time until which it was

[30] Ps. xc. 10

needful to mark by pedigree the course of the most glorious city, which sojourns as a stranger in this world, and seeks the heavenly country. That which is undeniable is that Cain was the first who was born of man and woman. For had he not been the first who was added by birth to the two unborn persons, Adam could not have said what he is recorded to have said, "I have gotten a man by the Lord." [40] He was followed by Abel, whom the elder brother slew, and who was the first to show, by a kind of foreshadowing of the sojourning city of God, what iniquitous persecutions that city would suffer at the hands of wicked and, as it were, earth-born men, who love their earthly origin, and delight in the earthly happiness of the earthly city. But how old Adam was when he begat these sons does not appear. After this the generations diverge, the one branch deriving from Cain, the other from him whom Adam begot in the room of Abel slain by his brother, and whom he called Seth, saying, as it is written, "For God hath raised me up another seed for Abel whom Cain slew." [41] These two series of generations accordingly, the one of Cain, the other of Seth, represent the two cities in their distinctive ranks, the one the heavenly city, which sojourns on earth, the other the earthly, which gapes after earthly joys, and grovels in them as if they were the only joys. But though eight generations, including Adam, are registered before the flood, no man of Cain's line has his age recorded at which the son who succeeded him was begotten. For the Spirit of God refused to mark the times before the flood in the generations of the earthly city, but preferred to do so in the heavenly line, as if it were more worthy of being remembered. Further, when Seth was born, the age of his father is mentioned; but already he had begotten other sons, and who will presume to say that Cain and Abel were the only ones previously begotten? For it does not follow that they alone had been begotten of Adam, because they alone were named in order to continue the series of generations which it was desirable to mention. For though the names of all the rest are buried in silence, yet it is said that Adam begot sons and daughters; and who that cares to be free from the charge of temerity will dare to say how many his offspring numbered? It was possible enough that Adam was divinely prompted to say, after Seth was born, "For God hath raised up to me another seed for Abel, "because that son was to be capable of representing Abel's holiness, not because he was born first after him in point of time. Then because it is written, "And Seth lived 205 years," or, according to the Hebrew reading, "105 years, and begat Enos," [42] who but a rash man could affirm that this was his first-born? Will any man do so to excite our wonder, and cause us to inquire how for so many years he remained free from sexual intercourse, though without any purpose of continuing so, or how, if he did not abstain, he yet had no children? Will any man do so when it is written of him, "And he begat sons and daughters, and all the days of Seth were 912 years, and he died?" [43] And similarly regarding those whose years are

[40] Gen. iv. 1   [41] Gen. iv. 25   [42] Gen. v. 6   [43] Gen. v. 8

afterwards mentioned, it is not disguised that they begat sons and daughters.

Consequently it does not at all appear whether he who is named as the son was himself the first begotten. Nay, since it is incredible that those fathers were either so long in attaining puberty, or could not get wives, or could not impregnate them, it is also incredible that those sons were their first-born. But as the writer of the sacred history designed to descend by well-marked intervals through a series of generations to the birth and life of Noah, in whose time the flood occurred, he mentioned not those sons who were first begotten, but those by whom the succession was handed down.

Let me make this clearer by here inserting an example, in regard to which no one can have any doubt that what I am asserting is true. The evangelist Matthew, where he designs to commit to our memories the generation of the Lord's flesh by a series of parents, beginning from Abraham and intending to reach David, says, "Abraham begat Isaac;" [44] why did he not say Ishmael, whom he first begat? Then "Isaac begat Jacob;" why did he not say Esau, who was the first-born? Simply because these sons would not have helped him to reach David. Then follows, "And Jacob begat Judah and his brethren:" was Judah the first begotten? "Judah," he says, "begat Pharez and Zara;" yet neither were these twins the first-born of Judah, but before them he had begotten three other sons. And so in the order of the generations he retained those by whom he might reach David, so as to proceed onwards to the end he had in view. And from this we may understand that the antediluvians who are mentioned were not the first-born, but those through whom the order of the succeeding generations might be carried on to the patriarch Noah. We need not, therefore, weary ourselves with discussing the needless and obscure question as to their lateness of reaching puberty.

CHAPTER XVI

OF MARRIAGE BETWEEN BLOOD-RELATIONS, IN REGARD TO WHICH THE PRESENT LAW COULD NOT BIND THE MEN OF THE EARLIEST AGES

As, therefore, the human race, subsequently to the first marriage of the man who was made of dust, and his wife who was made out of his side, required the union of males and females in order that it might multiply, and as there were no human beings except those who had been born of these two, men took their sisters for wives—an act which was as certainly dictated by necessity in these ancient days as afterwards it was condemned by the prohibitions of religion. For it is very reasonable and just that men, among whom concord is honorable and useful, should be bound together by various relationships; and that one man should not himself sustain many relation-

[44] Matt. i.

ships, but that the various relationships should be distributed among several, and should thus serve to bind together the greatest number in the same social interests. "Father" and "father-in-law" are the names of two relationships. When, therefore, a man has one person for his father, another for his father-in-law, friendship extends itself to a larger number. But Adam in his single person was obliged to hold both relations to his sons and daughters, for brothers and sisters were united in marriage. So too Eve his wife was both mother and mother-in-law to her children of both sexes; while, had there been two women, one the mother, the other the mother-in-law, the family affection would have had a wider field. Then the sister herself by becoming a wife sustained in her single person two relationships, which, had they been distributed among individuals, one being sister, and another being wife, the family tie would have embraced a greater number of persons. But there was then no material for effecting this, since there were no human beings but the brothers and sisters born of those two first parents. Therefore, when an abundant population made it possible, men ought to choose for wives women who were not already their sisters; for not only would there then be no necessity for marrying sisters, but, were it done, it would be most abominable. For if the grandchildren of the first pair, being now able to choose their cousins for wives, married their sisters, then it would no longer be only two but three relationships that were held by one man, while each of these relationships ought to have been held by a separate individual, so as to bind together by family affection a larger number. For one man would in that case be both father, and father-in-law, and uncle to his own children (brother and sister now man and wife); and his wife would be mother, aunt, and mother-in-law to them; and they themselves would be not only brother and sister, and man and wife, but cousins also, being the children of brother and sister. Now, all these relationships, which combined three men into one, would have embraced nine persons had each relationship been held by one individual, so that a man had one person for his sister, another his wife, another his cousin, another his father, another his uncle, another his father-in-law, another his mother, another his aunt, another his mother-in-law; and thus the social bond would not have been tightened to bind a few, but loosened to embrace a larger number of relations.

And we see that, since the human race has increased and multiplied, this is so strictly observed even among the profane worshippers of many and false gods, that though their laws perversely allow a brother to marry his sister,[45] yet custom, with a finer morality, prefers to forego this license; and though it was quite allowable in the earliest ages of the human race to marry one's sister, it is now abhorred as a thing which no circumstances could justify. For custom has very great power either to attract or to shock human feeling. And in this matter, while it restrains concupiscence within due bounds, the man who neglects and disobeys it is justly branded as abomi-

[45] This was allowed by the Egyptians and Athenians, never by the Romans

nable. For if it is iniquitous to plough beyond our own boundaries through the greed of gain, is it not much more iniquitous to transgress the recognized boundaries of morals through sexual lust? And with regard to marriage in the next degree of consanguinity, marriage between cousins, we have observed that in our own time the customary morality has prevented this from being frequent, though the law allows it. It was not prohibited by divine law, nor as yet had human law prohibited it; nevertheless, though legitimate, people shrank from it, because it lay so close to what was illegitimate, and in marrying a cousin seemed almost to marry a sister—for cousins are so closely related that they are called brothers and sisters,[46] and are almost really so. But the ancient fathers, fearing that near relationship might gradually in the course of generations diverge, and become distant relationship, or cease to be relationship at all, religiously endeavored to limit it by the bond of marriage before it became distant, and thus, as it were, to call it back when it was escaping them. And on this account, even when the world was full of people, though they did not choose wives from among their sisters or half-sisters, yet they preferred them to be of the same stock as themselves. But who doubts that the modern prohibition of the marriage even of cousins is the more seemly regulation—not merely on account of the reason we have been urging, the multiplying of relationships, so that one person might not absorb two, which might be distributed to two persons, and so increase the number of people bound together as a family, but also because there is in human nature I know not what natural and praiseworthy shamefacedness which restrains us from desiring that connection which, though for propagation, is yet lustful, and which even conjugal modesty blushes over, with any one to whom consanguinity bids us render respect?

The sexual intercourse of man and woman, then, is in the case of mortals a kind of seed-bed of the city; but while the earthly city needs for its population only generation, the heavenly needs also regeneration to rid it of the taint of generation. Whether before the deluge there was any bodily or visible sign of regeneration, such as was afterwards enjoined upon Abraham when he was circumcised, or what kind of sign it was, the sacred history does not inform us. But it does inform us that even these earliest of mankind sacrificed to God, as appeared also in the case of the two first brothers; Noah, too, is said to have offered sacrifices to God when he had come forth from the ark after the deluge. And concerning this subject we have already said in the foregoing books that the devils arrogate to themselves divinity, and require sacrifice that they may be esteemed gods, and delight in these honors on no other account than this, because they know that true sacrifice is due to the true God.

[46] Both in Hebrew, Greek, and Latin, though not uniformly, nor in Latin commonly

CHAPTER XVII

OF THE TWO FATHERS AND LEADERS WHO SPRANG FROM ONE PROGENITOR

Since, then, Adam was the father of both lines—the father, that is to say, both of the line which belonged to the earthly, and of that which belonged to the heavenly city—when Abel was slain, and by his death exhibited a marvellous mystery, there were henceforth two lines proceeding from two fathers, Cain and Seth, and in those sons of theirs, whom it behoved to register, the tokens of these two cities began to appear more distinctly. For Cain begat Enoch, in whose name he built a city, an earthly one, which was not from home in this world, but rested satisfied with its temporal peace and happiness. Cain, too, means "possession;" wherefore at his birth either his father or mother said, "I have gotten a man through God." Then Enoch means "dedication;" for the earthly city is dedicated in this world in which it is built, for in this world it finds the end towards which it aims and aspires. Further, Seth signifies "resurrection," and Enos his son signifies "man," not as Adam, which also signifies man, but is used in Hebrew indifferently for man and woman, as it is written, "Male and female created He them, and blessed them, and called their name Adam," [47] leaving no room to doubt that though the woman was distinctively called Eve, yet the name Adam, meaning man, was common to both. But Enos means man in so restricted a sense, that Hebrew linguists tell us it cannot be applied to woman: it is the equivalent of the "child of the resurrection," when they neither marry nor are given in marriage.[48] For there shall be no generation in that place to which regeneration shall have brought us. Wherefore I think it not immaterial to observe that in those generations which are propagated from him who is called Seth, although daughters as well as sons are said to have been begotten, no woman is expressly registered by name; but in those which sprang from Cain at the very termination to which the line runs, the last person named as begotten is a woman. For we read, "Methusael begat Lamech. And Lamech took unto him two wives: the name of the one was Adah, and the name of the other Zillah. And Adah bare Jabal: he was the father of the shepherds that dwell in tents. And his brother's name was Jubal: he was the father of all such as handle the harp and organ. And Zillah, she also bare Tubalcain, an instructor of every artificer in brass and iron: and the sister of Tubalcain was Naamah." [49] Here terminate all the generations of Cain, being eight in number, including Adam—to wit, seven from Adam to Lamech, who married two wives, and whose children, among whom a woman also is named, form the eighth generation. Whereby it is elegantly signified that the earthly city shall to its termination have carnal generations proceeding from the intercourse of males and females. And

[47] Gen. v. 2   [48] Luke xx. 35, 36   [49] Gen. iv. 18-22

therefore the wives themselves of the man who is the last named father of Cain's line, are registered in their own names—a practice nowhere followed before the deluge save in Eve's case. Now as Cain, signifying possession, the founder of the earthly city, and his son Enoch, meaning dedication, in whose name it was founded, indicate that this city is earthly both in its beginning and in its end—a city in which nothing more is hoped for than can be seen in this world—so Seth, meaning resurrection, and being the father of generations registered apart from the others, we must consider what this sacred history says of his son.

CHAPTER XVIII

THE SIGNIFICANCE OF ABEL, SETH, AND ENOS TO CHRIST AND HIS BODY THE CHURCH

"And to Seth," it is said, "there was born a son, and he called his name Enos: he hoped to call on the name of the Lord God." [50] Here we have a loud testimony to the truth. Man, then, the son of the resurrection, lives in hope: he lives in hope as long as the city of God, which is begotten by faith in the resurrection, sojourns in this world. For in these two men, Abel, signifying "grief," and his brother Seth, signifying "resurrection," the death of Christ and His life from the dead are prefigured. And by faith in these is begotten in this world the city of God, that is to say, the man who has hoped to call on the name of the Lord. "For by hope," says the apostle, "we are saved: but hope that is seen is not hope: for what a man seeth, why doth he yet hope for? But if we hope for that we see not, then do we with patience wait for it." [51] Who can avoid referring this to a profound mystery? For did not Abel hope to call upon the name of the Lord God when his sacrifice is mentioned in Scripture as having been accepted by God? Did not Seth himself hope to call on the name of the Lord God, of whom it was said, "For God hath appointed me another seed instead of Abel?" Why then is this which is found to be common to all the godly specially attributed to Enos, unless because it was fit that in him, who is mentioned as the first-born of the father of those generations which were separated to the better part of the heavenly city, there should be a type of the man, or society of men, who live not according to man in contentment with earthly felicity, but according to God in hope of everlasting felicity? And it was not said, "He hoped in the Lord God," nor "He called on the name of the Lord God," but "He hoped to call on the name of the Lord God." And what does this "hoped to call" mean, unless it is a prophecy that a people should arise who, according to the election of grace, would call on the name of the Lord God? It is this which has been said by another prophet, and which the apostle interprets of the people who belong to the grace of God: "And it shall be that whosoever shall

[50] Gen. iv. 26   [51] Rom. viii. 24, 25

call upon the name of the Lord shall be saved." [52] For these two expressions, "And he called his name Enos, which means man," and "He hoped to call on the name of the Lord God," are sufficient proof that man ought not to rest his hopes in himself; as it is elsewhere written, "Cursed is the man that trusteth in man." [53] Consequently no one ought to trust in himself that he shall become a citizen of that other city which is not dedicated in the name of Cain's son in this present time, that is to say, in the fleeting course of this mortal world, but in the immortality of perpetual blessedness.

CHAPTER XIX

THE SIGNIFICANCE OF ENOCH'S TRANSLATION

For that line also of which Seth is the father has the name "Dedication" in the seventh generation from Adam, counting Adam. For the seventh from him is Enoch, that is, Dedication. But this is that man who was translated because he pleased God, and who held in the order of the generations a remarkable place, being the seventh from Adam, a number signalized by the consecration of the Sabbath. But, counting from the diverging point of the two lines, or from Seth, he was the sixth. Now it was on the sixth day God made man, and consummated His works. But the translation of Enoch prefigured our deferred dedication; for though it is indeed already accomplished in Christ our Head, who so rose again that He shall die no more, and who was Himself also translated, yet there remains another dedication of the whole house, of which Christ Himself is the foundation, and this dedication is deferred till the end, when all shall rise again to die no more. And whether it is the house of God, or the temple of God, or the city of God, that is said to be dedicated, it is all the same, and equally in accordance with the usage of the Latin language. For Virgil himself calls the city of widest empire "the house of Assaracus," [54] meaning the Romans, who were descended through the Trojans from Assaracus. He also calls them the house of Aeneas, because Rome was built by those Trojans who had come to Italy under Aeneas. [55] For that poet imitated the sacred writings, in which the Hebrew nation, though so numerous, is called the house of Jacob.

CHAPTER XX

HOW IT IS THAT CAIN'S LINE TERMINATES IN THE EIGHTH GENERATION, WHILE NOAH, THOUGH DESCENDED FROM THE SAME FATHER, ADAM, IS FOUND TO BE THE TENTH FROM HIM

Some one will say, If the writer of this history intended, in enumerating the generations from Adam through his son Seth, to descend through them

[52] Rom. x. 13   [53] Jer. xvii. 5   [54] *Aeneid*, i. 288   [55] *Aeneid*, iii. 97

to Noah, in whose time the deluge occurred, and from him again to trace the connected generations down to Abraham, with whom Matthew begins the pedigree of Christ the eternal King of the city of God, what did he intend by enumerating the generations from Cain, and to what terminus did he mean to trace them? We reply, To the deluge, by which the whole stock of the earthly city was destroyed, but repaired by the sons of Noah. For the earthly city and community of men who live after the flesh will never fail until the end of this world, of which our Lord says, "The children of this world generate, and are generated." [56] But the city of God, which sojourns in this world, is conducted by regeneration to the world to come, of which the children neither generate nor are generated. In this world generation is common to both cities; though even now the city of God has many thousand citizens who abstain from the act of generation; yet the other city also has some citizens who imitate these, though erroneously. For to that city belong also those who have erred from the faith, and introduced divers heresies; for they live according to man, not according to God. And the Indian gymnosophists, who are said to philosophize in the solitudes of India in a state of nudity, are its citizens; and they abstain from marriage. For continence is not a good thing, except when it is practised in the faith of the highest good, that is, God. Yet no one is found to have practised it before the deluge; for indeed even Enoch himself, the seventh from Adam, who is said to have been translated without dying, begat sons and daughters before he was translated, and among these was Methuselah, by whom the succession of the recorded generations is maintained.

Why, then, is so small a number of Cain's generations registered, if it was proper to trace them to the deluge, and if there was no such delay of the date of puberty as to preclude the hope of offspring for a hundred or more years? For if the author of this book had not in view some one to whom he might rigidly trace the series of generations, as he designed in those which sprang from Seth's seed to descend to Noah, and thence to start again by a rigid order, what need was there of omitting the first-born sons for the sake of descending to Lamech, in whose sons that line terminates—that is to say, in the eighth generation from Adam, or the seventh from Cain—as if from this point he had wished to pass on to another series, by which he might reach either the Israelitish people, among whom the earthly Jerusalem presented a prophetic figure of the heavenly city, or to Jesus Christ, "according to the flesh, who is over all, God blessed for ever," [57] the Maker and Ruler of the heavenly city? What, I say, was the need of this, seeing that the whole of Cain's posterity were destroyed in the deluge? From this it is manifest that they are the first-born sons who are registered in this genealogy. Why, then, are there so few of them? Their numbers in the period before the deluge must have been greater, if the date of puberty bore no proportion to their longevity, and they had children before they were a

[56] Luke xx. 34   [57] Rom. ix. 5

hundred years old. For supposing they were on an average thirty years old
when they began to beget children, then, as there are eight generations, including Adam and Lamech's children, 8 times 30 gives 240 years; did they
then produce no more children in all the rest of the time before the deluge?
With what intention, then, did he who wrote this record make no mention of
subsequent generations? For from Adam to the deluge there are reckoned,
according to our copies of Scripture, 2262 years,[58] and according to the Hebrew text, 1656 years. Supposing, then, the smaller number to be the true
one, and subtracting from 1656 years 240, is it credible that during the remaining 1400 and odd years until the deluge the posterity of Cain begat no
children?

But let any one who is moved by this call to mind that when I discussed
the question, how it is credible that those primitive men could abstain for
so many years from begetting children, two modes of solution were found—
either a puberty late in proportion to their longevity, or that the sons registered in the genealogies were not the first-born, but those through whom the
author of the book intended to reach the point aimed at, as he intended to
reach Noah by the generations of Seth. So that, if in the generations of Cain
there occurs no one whom the writer could make it his object to reach by
omitting the first-born and inserting those who would serve such a purpose,
then we must have recourse to the supposition of late puberty, and say that
only at some age beyond a hundred years they became capable of begetting
children, so that the order of the generations ran through the first-born, and
filled up even the whole period before the deluge, long though it was. It is,
however, possible that, for some more secret reason which escapes me, this
city, which we say is earthly, is exhibited in all its generations down to
Lamech and his sons, and that then the writer withholds from recording the
rest which may have existed before the deluge. And without supposing so
late a puberty in these men, there might be another reason for tracing the
generations by sons who were not first-born, *viz.*, that the same city which
Cain built, and named after his son Enoch, may have had a widely extended
dominion and many kings, not reigning simultaneously, but successively, the
reigning king begetting always his successor. Cain himself would be the first
of these kings; his son Enoch, in whose name the city in which he reigned
was built, would be the second; the third Irad, whom Enoch begat; the
fourth Mehujael, whom Irad begat; the fifth Methusael, whom Mehujael
begat; the sixth Lamech, whom Methusael begat, and who is the seventh
from Adam through Cain. But it was not necessary that the first-born
should succeed their fathers in the kingdom, but those would succeed who
were recommended by the possession of some virtue useful to the earthly
city, or who were chosen by lot, or the son who was best liked by his father
would succeed by a kind of hereditary right to the throne. And the deluge

[58] Eusebius, Jerome, Bede, and others, who follow the Septuagint, reckon only 2242
years

may have happened during the lifetime and reign of Lamech, and may have destroyed him along with all other men, save those who were in the ark. For we cannot be surprised that, during so long a period from Adam to the deluge, and with the ages of individuals varying as they did, there should not be an equal number of generations in both lines, but seven in Cain's, and ten in Seth's; for as I have already said, Lamech is the seventh from Adam, Noah the tenth; and in Lamech's case not one son only is registered, as in the former instances, but more, because it was uncertain which of them would have succeeded when he died, if there had intervened any time to reign between his death and the deluge.

But in whatever manner the generations of Cain's line are traced downwards, whether it be by first-born sons or by the heirs to the throne, it seems to me that I must by no means omit to notice that, when Lamech had been set down as the seventh from Adam, there were named, in addition, as many of his children as made up this number to eleven, which is the number signifying sin; for three sons and one daughter are added. The wives of Lamech have another signification, different from that which I am now pressing. For at present I am speaking of the children, and not of those by whom the children were begotten. Since, then, the law is symbolized by the number ten—whence that memorable Decalogue—there is no doubt that the number eleven, which goes beyond ten, symbolizes the transgression of the law, and consequently sin. For this reason, eleven veils of goat's skin were ordered to be hung in the tabernacle of the testimony, which served in the wanderings of God's people as an ambulatory temple. And in that haircloth there was a reminder of sins, because the goats were to be set on the left hand of the Judge; and therefore, when we confess our sins, we prostrate ourselves in haircloth, as if we were saying what is written in the psalm, "My sin is ever before me." [59] The progeny of Adam, then, by Cain the murderer, is completed in the number eleven, which symbolizes sin; and this number itself is made up by a woman, as it was by the same sex that beginning was made of sin by which we all die. And it was committed that the pleasure of the flesh, which resists the spirit, might follow; and so Naamah, the daughter of Lamech, means "pleasure." But from Adam to Noah, in the line of Seth, there are ten generations. And to Noah three sons are added, of whom, while one fell into sin, two were blessed by their father; so that, if you deduct the reprobate and add the gracious sons to the number, you get twelve—a number signalized in the case of the patriarchs and of the apostles, and made up of the parts of the number seven multiplied into one another—for three times four, or four times three, give twelve. These things being so, I see that I must consider and mention how these two lines, which by their separate genealogies depict the two cities, one of earth-born, the other of regenerated persons, became afterwards so mixed and confused, that the whole human race, with the exception of eight persons, deserved to perish in the deluge.

[59] Ps. li. 3

CHAPTER XXI

We must first see why, in the enumeration of Cain's posterity, after Enoch, in whose name the city was built, has been first of all mentioned, the rest are at once enumerated down to that terminus of which I have spoken, and at which that race and the whole line was destroyed in the deluge; while, after Enos the son of Seth, has been mentioned, the rest are not at once named down to the deluge, but a clause is inserted to the following effect: "This is the book of the generations of Adam. In the day that God created man, in the likeness of God made He him; male and female created He them; and blessed them, and called their name Adam, in the day when they were created." [60] This seems to me to be inserted for this purpose, that here again the reckoning of the times may start from Adam himself— a purpose which the writer had not in view in speaking of the earthly city, as if God mentioned it, but did not take account of its duration. But why does he return to this recapitulation after mentioning the son of Seth, the man who hoped to call on the name of the Lord God, unless because it was fit thus to present these two cities, the one beginning with a murderer and ending in a murderer (for Lamech, too, acknowledges to his two wives that he had committed murder) the other built up by him who hoped to call upon the name of the Lord God? For the highest and complete terrestrial duty of the city of God, which is a stranger in this world, is that which was exemplified in the individual who was begotten by him who typified the resurrection of the murdered Abel. That one man is the unity of the whole heavenly city, not yet indeed complete, but to be completed, as this prophetic figure foreshows. The son of Cain, therefore, that is, the son of possession (and of what but an earthly possession?) may have a name in the earthly city which was built in his name. It is of such the Psalmist says, "They call their lands after their own names." [61] Wherefore they incur what is written in another psalm: "Thou, O Lord, in Thy city wilt despise their image." [62] But as for the son of Seth, the son of the resurrection, let him hope to call on the name of the Lord God. For he prefigures that society of men which says, "But I am like a green olive-tree in the house of God: I have trusted in the mercy of God." [63] But let him not seek the empty honors of a famous name upon earth, for "Blessed is the man that maketh the name of the Lord his trust, and respecteth not vanities nor lying follies." [64] After having presented the two cities, the one founded in the material good of this

[60] Gen. v. 1   [61] Ps. xlix. 11   [62] Ps. lxxiii. 20   [63] Ps. lii. 8   [64] Ps. xl. 4

world, the other in hope in God, but both starting from a common gate opened in Adam into this mortal state, and both running on and running out to their proper and merited ends, Scripture begins to reckon the times, and in this reckoning includes other generations, making a recapitulation from Adam, out of whose condemned seed, as out of one mass handed over to merited damnation, God made some vessels of wrath to dishonor and others vessels of mercy to honor; in punishment rendering to the former what is due, in grace giving to the latter what is not due: in order that by the very comparison of itself with the vessels of wrath, the heavenly city, which sojourns on earth, may learn not to put confidence in the liberty of its own will, but may hope to call on the name of the Lord God. For will, being a nature which was made good by the good God, but mutable by the immutable, because it was made out of nothing, can both decline from good to do evil, which takes place when it freely chooses, and can also escape the evil and do good, which takes place only by divine assistance.

CHAPTER XXII

OF THE FALL OF THE SONS OF GOD WHO WERE CAPTIVATED BY THE DAUGHTERS OF MEN, WHEREBY ALL, WITH THE EXCEPTION OF EIGHT PERSONS, DESERVEDLY PERISHED IN THE DELUGE

When the human race, in the exercise of this freedom of will, increased and advanced, there arose a mixture and confusion of the two cities by their participation in a common iniquity. And this calamity, as well as the first, was occasioned by woman, though not in the same way; for these women were not themselves betrayed, neither did they persuade the men to sin, but having belonged to the earthly city and society of the earthly, they had been of corrupt manners from the first, and were loved for their bodily beauty by the sons of God, or the citizens of the other city which sojourns in this world. Beauty is indeed a good gift of God; but that the good may not think it a great good, God dispenses it even to the wicked. And thus, when the good that is great and proper to the good was abandoned by the sons of God, they fell to a paltry good which is not peculiar to the good, but common to the good and the evil; and when they were captivated by the daughters of men, they adopted the manners of the earthly to win them as their brides, and forsook the godly ways they had followed in their own holy society. And thus beauty, which is indeed God's handiwork, but only a temporal, carnal, and lower kind of good, is not fitly loved in preference to God, the eternal, spiritual, and unchangeable good. When the miser prefers his gold to justice, it is through no fault of the gold, but of the man; and so with every created thing. For though it be good, it may be loved with an evil as well as with a good love: it is loved rightly when it is loved ordinately; evilly, when inordinately. It is this which some one has briefly said in these verses in praise of the Creator: "These are Thine, they are good, because

Thou art good who didst create them. There is in them nothing of ours, unless the sin we commit when we forget the order of things, and instead of
Thee love that which Thou hast made."

But if the Creator is truly loved, that is, if He Himself is loved and not
another thing in His stead, He cannot be evilly loved; for love itself is to be
ordinately loved, because we do well to love that which, when we love it,
makes us live well and virtuously. So that it seems to me that it is a brief
but true definition of virtue to say, it is the order of love; and on this account, in the *Canticles*, the bride of Christ, the city of God, sings, "Order
love within me." [65] It was the order of this love, then, this charity or attachment, which the sons of God disturbed when they forsook God, and were
enamored of the daughters of men. And by these two names (sons of God
and daughters of men) the two cities are sufficiently distinguished. For
though the former were by nature children of men, they had come into possession of another name by grace. For in the same Scripture in which the
sons of God are said to have loved the daughters of men, they are also called
angels of God; whence many suppose that they were not men but angels.

CHAPTER XXIII

WHETHER WE ARE TO BELIEVE THAT ANGELS, WHO ARE OF A SPIRITUAL SUBSTANCE, FELL IN LOVE WITH THE BEAUTY OF WOMEN, AND SOUGHT THEM IN MARRIAGE, AND THAT FROM THIS CONNECTION GIANTS WERE BORN

In the third book of this work (c. 5) we made a passing reference to this
question, but did not decide whether angels, inasmuch as they are spirits,
could have bodily intercourse with women. For it is written, "Who maketh
His angels spirits," [66] that is, He makes those who are by nature spirits His
angels by appointing them to the duty of bearing His messages. For the
Greek word ἄγγελος, which in Latin appears as "angelus," means a messenger. But whether the Psalmist speaks of their bodies when he adds, "and
His ministers a flaming fire," or means that God's ministers ought to blaze
with love as with a spiritual fire, is doubtful. However, the same trustworthy
Scripture testifies that angels have appeared to men in such bodies as could
not only be seen, but also touched. There is, too, a very general rumor, which
many have verified by their own experience, or which trustworthy persons
who have heard the experience of others corroborate, the sylvans and fauns,
who are commonly called "incubi," had often made wicked assaults upon
women, and satisfied their lust upon them; and that certain devils, called
Duses by the Gauls, are constantly attempting and effecting this impurity
is so generally affirmed, that it were impudent to deny it. From these assertions, indeed, I dare not determine whether there be some spirits embodied

---

[65] Cant. ii. 4   [66] Ps. civ. 4

in an aerial substance (for this element, even when agitated by a fan, is sensibly felt by the body) and who are capable of lust and of mingling sensibly with women; but certainly I could by no means believe that God's holy angels could at that time have so fallen, nor can I think that it is of them the Apostle Peter said, "For if God spared not the angels that sinned, but cast them down to hell, and delivered them into chains of darkness, to be reserved unto judgment." [67] I think he rather speaks of those who first apostatized from God, along with their chief the devil, who enviously deceived the first man under the form of a serpent. But the same holy Scripture affords the most ample testimony that even godly men have been called angels; for of John it is written: "Behold, I send my messenger (angel) before Thy face, who shall prepare Thy way." [68] And the prophet Malachi, by a peculiar grace specially communicated to him, was called an angel.[69]

But some are moved by the fact that we have read that the fruit of the connection between those who are called angels of God and the women they loved were not men like our own breed, but giants; just as if there were not born even in our own time (as I have mentioned above) men of much greater size than the ordinary stature. Was there not at Rome a few years ago, when the destruction of the city now accomplished by the Goths was drawing near, a woman, with her father and mother, who by her gigantic size overtopped all others? Surprising crowds from all quarters came to see her, and that which struck them most was the circumstance that neither of her parents were quite up to the tallest ordinary stature. Giants therefore might well be born, even before the sons of God, who are also called angels of God, formed a connection with the daughters of men, or of those living according to men, that is to say, before the sons of Seth formed a connection with the daughters of Cain. For thus speaks even the canonical Scripture itself in the book in which we read of this; its words are: "And it came to pass, when men began to multiply on the face of the earth, and daughters were born unto them, that the sons of God saw the daughters of men that they were fair [good]; and they took them wives of all which they chose. And the Lord God said, My Spirit shall not always strive with man, for that he also is flesh: yet his days shall be an hundred and twenty years. There were giants in the earth in those days; and also after that, when the sons of God came in unto the daughters of men, and they bare children to them, the same became the giants, men of renown." [70] These words of the divine book sufficiently indicate that already there were giants in the earth in those days, in which the sons of God took wives of the children of men, when they loved them because they were good, that is, fair. For it is the custom of this Scripture to call those who are beautiful in appearance "good." But after this connection had been formed, then too were giants born. For the words are: "There were giants in the earth in those days, *and also after that*, when the sons of God came in unto the daughters of men." Therefore there were giants

[67] 2 Pet. ii. 4   [68] Mark i. 2   [69] Mal. ii. 7   [70] Gen. vi. 1-4

both before, "in those days," and "also after that." And the words, "they bare children to them," show plainly enough that before the sons of God fell in this fashion they begat children to God, not to themselves—that is to say, not moved by the lust of sexual intercourse, but discharging the duty of propagation, intending to produce not a family to gratify their own pride, but citizens to people the city of God; and to these they as God's angels would bear the message, that they should place their hope in God, like him who was born of Seth, the son of resurrection, and who hoped to call on the name of the Lord God, in which hope they and their offspring would be co-heirs of eternal blessings, and brethren in the family of which God is the Father.

But that those angels were not angels in the sense of not being men, as some suppose, Scripture itself decides, which unambiguously declares that they were men. For when it had first been stated that "the angels of God saw the daughters of men that they were fair, and they took them wives of all which they chose," it was immediately added, "And the Lord God said, My Spirit shall not always strive with these men, for that they also are flesh." For by the Spirit of God they had been made angels of God, and sons of God; but declining towards lower things, they are called men, a name of nature, not of grace; and they are called flesh, as deserters of the Spirit, and by their desertion deserted [by Him]. The Septuagint indeed calls them both angels of God and sons of God, though all the copies do not show this, some having only the name "sons of God." And Aquila, whom the Jews prefer to the other interpreters,[71] has translated neither angels of God nor sons of God, but sons of gods. But both are correct. For they were both sons of God, and thus brothers of their own fathers, who were children of the same God; and they were sons of gods, because begotten by gods, together with whom they themselves also were gods, according to that expression of the psalm: "I have said, Ye are gods, and all of you are children of the Most High." [72] For the Septuagint translators are justly believed to have received the Spirit of prophecy; so that, if they made any alterations under His authority, and did not adhere to a strict translation, we could not doubt that this was divinely dictated. However, the Hebrew word may be said to be ambiguous, and to be susceptible of either translation, "sons of God," or "sons of gods."

Let us omit, then, the fables of those scriptures which are called apocryphal, because their obscure origin was unknown to the fathers from whom the authority of the true Scriptures has been transmitted to us by a most certain and well-ascertained succession. For though there is some truth in

[71] Aquila lived in the time of Hadrian, to whom he is said to have been related. He was excommunicated from the Church for the practice of astrology; and is best known by his translation of the Hebrew Scriptures into Greek, which he executed with great care and accuracy, though he has been charged with falsifying passages to support the Jews in their opposition to Christianity

[72] Ps. lxxxii. 6

these apocryphal writings, yet they contain so many false statements, that they have no canonical authority. We cannot deny that Enoch, the seventh from Adam, left some divine writings, for this is asserted by the Apostle Jude in his canonical epistle. But it is not without reason that these writings have no place in that canon of Scripture which was preserved in the temple of the Hebrew people by the diligence of successive priests; for their antiquity brought them under suspicion, and it was impossible to ascertain whether these were his genuine writings, and they were not brought forward as genuine by the persons who were found to have carefully preserved the canonical books by a successive transmission. So that the writings which are produced under his name, and which contain these fables about the giants, saying that their fathers were not men, are properly judged by prudent men to be not genuine; just as many writings are produced by heretics under the names both of other prophets, and, more recently, under the names of the apostles, all of which, after careful examination, have been set apart from canonical authority under the title of Apocrypha. There is therefore no doubt that, according to the Hebrew and Christian canonical Scriptures, there were many giants before the deluge, and that these were citizens of the earthly society of men, and that the sons of God, who were according to the flesh the sons of Seth, sunk into this community when they forsook righteousness. Nor need we wonder that giants should be born even from these. For all of their children were not giants; but there were more then than in the remaining periods since the deluge. And it pleased the Creator to produce them, that it might thus be demonstrated that neither beauty, nor yet size and strength, are of much moment to the wise man, whose blessedness lies in spiritual and immortal blessings, in far better and more enduring gifts, in the good things that are the peculiar property of the good, and are not shared by good and bad alike. It is this which another prophet confirms when he says, "These were the giants, famous from the beginning, that were of so great stature, and so expert in war. Those did not the Lord choose, neither gave He the way of knowledge unto them; but they were destroyed because they had no wisdom, and perished through their own foolishness." [73]

CHAPTER XXIV

HOW WE ARE TO UNDERSTAND THIS WHICH THE LORD SAID TO THOSE WHO WERE TO PERISH IN THE FLOOD: "THEIR DAYS SHALL BE 120 YEARS"

But that which God said, "Their days shall be an hundred and twenty years," is not to be understood as a prediction that henceforth men should not live longer than 120 years—for even after the deluge we find that they

[73] Baruch iii. 26-28

lived more than 500 years—but we are not to understand that God said this when Noah had nearly completed his fifth century, that is, had lived 480 years, which Scripture, as it frequently uses the name of the whole of the largest part, calls 500 years. Now the deluge came in the 600th year of Noah's life, the second month; and thus 120 years were predicted as being the remaining span of those who were doomed, which years being spent, they should be destroyed by the deluge. And it is not unreasonably believed that the deluge came as it did, because already there were not found upon earth any who were not worthy of sharing a death so manifestly judicial— not that a good man, who must die some time, would be a jot the worse of such a death after it was past. Nevertheless there died in the deluge none of those mentioned in the sacred Scripture as descended from Seth. But here is the divine account of the cause of the deluge: "The Lord God saw that the wickedness of man was great in the earth, and that every imagination of the thoughts of his heart was only evil continually. And it repented the Lord that He had made man on the earth, and it grieved Him at His heart. And the Lord said, I will destroy man, whom I have created, from the face of the earth; both man and beast, and the creeping thing, and the fowls of the air: for I am angry that I have made them." [74]

CHAPTER XXV

OF THE ANGER OF GOD, WHICH DOES NOT INFLAME HIS MIND, NOR DISTURB HIS UNCHANGEABLE TRANQUILLITY

The anger of God is not a disturbing emotion of His mind, but a judgment by which punishment is inflicted upon sin. His thought and reconsideration also are the unchangeable reason which changes things; for He does not, like man, repent of anything He has done, because in all matters His decision is as inflexible as His prescience is certain. But if Scripture were not to use such expressions as the above, it would not familiarly insinuate itself into the minds of all classes of men, whom it seeks access to for their good, that it may alarm the proud, arouse the careless, exercise the inquisitive, and satisfy the intelligent; and this it could not do, did it not first stoop, and in a manner descend, to them where they lie. But its denouncing death on all the animals of earth and air is a declaration of the vastness of the disaster that was approaching: not that it threatens destruction to the irrational animals as if they too had incurred it by sin.

[74] Gen. vi. 5-7

CHAPTER XXVI

THAT THE ARK WHICH NOAH WAS ORDERED TO MAKE FIGURES IN EVERY RESPECT CHRIST AND THE CHURCH

Moreover, inasmuch as God commanded Noah, a just man, and, as the truthful Scripture says, a man perfect in his generation—not indeed with the perfection of the citizens of the city of God in that immortal condition in which they equal the angels, but in so far as they can be perfect in their sojourn in this world—inasmuch as God commanded him, I say, to make an ark, in which he might be rescued from the destruction of the flood, along with his family, *i.e.*, his wife, sons, and daughters-in-law, and along with the animals who, in obedience to God's command, came to him into the ark: this is certainly a figure of the city of God sojourning in this world; that is to say, of the church, which is rescued by the wood on which hung the Mediator of God and men, the man Christ Jesus.[75] For even its very dimensions, in length, breadth, and height, represent the human body in which He came, as it had been foretold. For the length of the human body, from the crown of the head to the sole of the foot, is six times its breadth from side to side, and ten times its depth or thickness, measuring from back to front: that is to say, if you measure a man as he lies on his back or on his face, he is six times as long from head to foot as he is broad from side to side, and ten times as long as he is high from the ground. And therefore the ark was made 300 cubits in length, 50 in breadth, and 30 in height. And its having a door made in the side of it certainly signified the wound which was made when the side of the Crucified was pierced with the spear; for by this those who come to Him enter; for thence flowed the sacraments by which those who believe are initiated. And the fact that it was ordered to be made of squared timbers, signifies the immoveable steadiness of the life of the saints; for however you turn a cube, it still stands. And the other peculiarities of the ark's construction are signs of features of the church.

But we have not now time to pursue this subject; and, indeed, we have already dwelt upon it in the work we wrote against Faustus the Manichaean, who denies that there is anything prophesied of Christ in the Hebrew books. It may be that one man's exposition excels another's, and that ours is not the best; but all that is said must be referred to this city of God we speak of, which sojourns in this wicked world as in a deluge, at least if the expositor would not widely miss the meaning of the author. For example, the interpretation I have given in the work against Faustus, of the words, "with lower, second, and third stories shalt thou make it," is, that because the church is gathered out of all nations, it is said to have two stories, to represent the two kinds of men—the circumcision, to wit, and the uncir-

[75] I Tim. ii. 5

cumcision, or, as the apostle otherwise calls them, Jews and Gentiles; and to have three stories, because all the nations were replenished from the three sons of Noah. Now any one may object to this interpretation, and may give another which harmonizes with the rule of faith. For as the ark was to have rooms not only on the lower, but also on the upper stories, which were called "third stories," that there might be a habitable space on the third floor from the basement, some one may interpret these to mean the three graces commended by the apostle—faith, hope, and charity. Or even more suitably they may be supposed to represent those three harvests in the gospel, thirty-fold, sixty-fold, an hundred-fold—chaste marriage dwelling in the ground floor, chaste widowhood in the upper, and chaste virginity in the top story. Or any better interpretation may be given, so long as the reference to this city is maintained. And the same statement I would make of all the remaining particulars in this passage which require exposition, viz., that although different explanations are given, yet they must all agree with the one harmonious Catholic Faith.

CHAPTER XXVII

OF THE ARK AND THE DELUGE, AND THAT WE CANNOT AGREE WITH THOSE WHO RECEIVE THE BARE HISTORY, BUT REJECT THE ALLEGORICAL INTERPRETATION, NOR WITH THOSE WHO MAINTAIN THE FIGURATIVE AND NOT THE HISTORICAL MEANING

Yet no one ought to suppose either that these things were written for no purpose, or that we should study only the historical truth, apart from any allegorical meanings; or, on the contrary, that they are only allegories, and that there were no such facts at all, or that, whether it be so or no, there is here no prophecy of the church. For what right-minded man will contend that books so religiously preserved during thousands of years, and transmitted by so orderly a succession, were written without an object, or that only the bare historical facts are to be considered when we read them? For, not to mention other instances, if the number of the animals entailed the construction of an ark of great size, where was the necessity of sending into it two unclean and seven clean animals of each species, when both could have been preserved in equal numbers? Or could not God, who ordered them to be preserved in order to replenish the race, restore them in the same way He had created them?

But they who contend that these things never happened, but are only figures setting forth other things, in the first place suppose that there could not be a flood so great that the water should rise fifteen cubits above the highest mountains, because it is said that clouds cannot rise above the top of Mount Olympus, because it reaches the sky where there is none of that thicker atmosphere in which winds, clouds, and rains have their origin.

They do not reflect that the densest element of all, earth, can exist there; or perhaps they deny that the top of the mountain is earth. Why, then, do these measurers and weighers of the elements contend that earth can be raised to those aerial altitudes, and that water cannot, while they admit that water is lighter, and liker to ascend than earth? What reason do they adduce why earth, the heavier and lower element, has for so many ages scaled to the tranquil ether, while water, the lighter, and more likely to ascend, is not suffered to do the same even for a brief space of time?

They say, too, that the area of that ark could not contain so many kinds of animals of both sexes, two of the unclean and seven of the clean. But they seem to me to reckon only one area of 300 cubits long and 50 broad, and not to remember that there was another similar in the story above, and yet another as large in the story above that again; and that there was consequently an area of 900 cubits by 150. And if we accept what Origen[76] has with some appropriateness suggested, that Moses the man of God, being, as it is written, "learned in all the wisdom of the Egyptians," [77] who delighted in geometry, may have meant geometrical cubits, of which they say that one is equal to six of our cubits, then who does not see what a capacity these dimensions give to the ark? For as to their objection that an ark of such size could not be built, it is a very silly calumny; for they are aware that huge cities have been built, and they should remember that the ark was an hundred years in building. Or, perhaps, though stone can adhere to stone when cemented with nothing but lime, so that a wall of several miles may be constructed, yet plank cannot be riveted to plank by mortices, bolts, nails, and pitch-glue, so as to construct an ark which was not made with curved ribs but straight timbers, which was not to be launched by its builders, but to be lifted by the natural pressure of the water when it reached it, and which was to be preserved from shipwreck as it floated about rather by divine oversight than by human skill.

As to another customary inquiry of the scrupulous about the very minute creatures, not only such as mice and lizards, but also locusts, beetles, flies, fleas, and so forth, whether there were not in the ark a larger number of them than was determined by God in His command, those persons who are moved by this difficulty are to be reminded that the words "every creeping thing of the earth" only indicate that it was not needful to preserve in the ark the animals that can live in the water, whether the fishes that live submerged in it, or the sea-birds that swim on its surface. Then, when it is said "male and female," no doubt reference is made to the repairing of the races, and consequently there was no need for those creatures being in the ark which are born without the union of the sexes from inanimate things, or from their corruption; or if they were in the ark, they might be there as they commonly are in houses, not in any determinate numbers; or if it was necessary that

[76] In his second homily on *Genesis*   [77] Acts vii. 22

there should be a definite number of all those animals that cannot naturally live in the water, that so the most sacred mystery which was being enacted might be bodied forth and perfectly figured in actual realities, still this was not the care of Noah or his sons, but of God. For Noah did not catch the animals and put them into the ark, but gave them entrance as they came seeking it. For this is the force of the words, "They shall come unto thee"[78] —not, that is to say, by man's effort, but by God's will. But certainly we are not required to believe that those which have no sex also came; for it is expressly and definitely said, "They shall be male and female." [78] For there are some animals which are born out of corruption, but yet afterwards they themselves copulate and produce offspring, as flies; but others, which have no sex, like bees. Then, as to those animals which have sex, but without ability to propagate their kind, like mules and she-mules, it is probable that they were not in the ark, but that it was counted sufficient to preserve their parents, to wit, the horse and the ass; and this applies to all hybrids. Yet, if it was necessary for the completeness of the mystery, they were there; for even this species has "male and female."

Another question is commonly raised regarding the food of the carnivorous animals—whether, without transgressing the command which fixed the number to be preserved, there were necessarily others included in the ark for their sustenance; or, as is more probable, there might be some food which was not flesh, and which yet suited all. For we know how many animals whose food is flesh eat also vegetable products and fruits, especially figs and chestnuts. What wonder is it, therefore, if that wise and just man was instructed by God what would suit each, so that without flesh he prepared and stored provision fit for every species? And what is there which hunger would not make animals eat? Or what could not be made sweet and wholesome by God, who, with a divine facility, might have enabled them to do without food at all, had it not been requisite to the completeness of so great a mystery that they should be fed? But none but a contentious man can suppose that there was no prefiguring of the church in so manifold and circumstantial a detail. For the nations have already so filled the church, and are comprehended in the framework of its unity, the clean and unclean together, until the appointed end, that this one very manifest fulfillment leaves no doubt how we should interpret even those others which are somewhat more obscure, and which cannot so readily be discerned. And since this is so, if not even the most audacious will presume to assert that these things were written without a purpose, or that though the events really happened they mean nothing, or that they did not really happen, but are only allegory, or that at all events they are far from having any figurative reference to the church; if it has been made out that, on the other hand, we must rather believe that there was a wise purpose in their being committed

[78] Gen. vi. 19, 20

to memory and to writing, and that they did happen, and have a significance, and that this significance has a prophetic reference to the church, then this book, having served this purpose, may now be closed, that we may go on to trace in the history subsequent to the deluge the courses of the two cities—the earthly, that lives according to men, and the heavenly, that lives according to God.

BOOK SIXTEEN

ARGUMENT

In the former part of this book, from the first to the twelfth chapter, the progress of the two cities, the earthly and the heavenly, from Noah to Abraham, is exhibited from Holy Scripture: in the latter part, the progress of the heavenly alone, from Abraham to the kings of Israel, is the subject.

CHAPTER I

WHETHER, AFTER THE DELUGE, FROM NOAH TO ABRAHAM, ANY FAMILIES CAN BE FOUND WHO LIVED ACCORDING TO GOD

IT IS difficult to discover from Scripture, whether, after the deluge, traces of the holy city are continuous, or are so interrupted by intervening seasons of godlessness, that not a single worshipper of the one true God was found among men; because from Noah, who, with his wife, three sons, and as many daughters-in-law, achieved deliverance in the ark from the destruction of the deluge, down to Abraham, we do not find in the canonical books that the piety of any one is celebrated by express divine testimony, unless it be in the case of Noah, who commends with a prophetic benediction his two sons Shem and Japheth, while he beheld and foresaw what was long afterwards to happen. It was also by this prophetic spirit that, when his middle son— that is, the son who was younger than the first and older than the last born —had sinned against him, he cursed him not in his own person, but in his son's (his own grandson's), in the words, "Cursed be the lad Canaan; a servant shall he be unto his brethren."[1] Now Canaan was born of Ham, who, so far from covering his sleeping father's nakedness, had divulged it. For the same reason also he subjoins the blessing on his two other sons, the oldest and youngest, saying, "Blessed be the Lord God of Shem; and Canaan shall be his servant. God shall gladden Japheth, and he shall dwell in the houses of Shem."[2] And so, too, the planting of the vine by Noah, and his intoxication by its fruit, and his nakedness while he slept, and the other things done at that time, and recorded, are all of them pregnant with prophetic meanings, and veiled in mysteries.

[1] Gen. ix. 25   [2] Gen. ix. 26, 27

CHAPTER II

WHAT WAS PROPHETICALLY PREFIGURED IN THE SONS OF NOAH

The things which then were hidden are now sufficiently revealed by the actual events which have followed. For who can carefully and intelligently consider these things without recognizing them accomplished in Christ? Shem, of whom Christ was born in the flesh, means "named." And what is of greater name than Christ, the fragrance of whose name is now everywhere perceived, so that even prophecy sings of it beforehand, comparing it in the *Song of Songs*[a] to ointment poured forth? Is it not also in the houses of Christ, that is, in the churches, that the "enlargement" of the nations dwells? For Japheth means "enlargement." And Ham (*i.e.*, hot), who was the middle son of Noah, and, as it were, separated himself from both, and remained between them, neither belonging to the first-fruits of Israel nor to the fullness of the Gentiles, what does he signify but the tribe of heretics, hot with the spirit, not of patience, but of impatience, with which the breasts of heretics are wont to blaze, and with which they disturb the peace of the saints? But even the heretics yield an advantage to those that make proficiency, according to the apostle's saying, "There must also be heresies, that they which are approved may be made manifest among you." [4] Whence, too, it is elsewhere said, "The son that receives instruction will be wise, and he uses the foolish as his servant." [5] For while the hot restlessness of heretics stirs questions about many articles of the Catholic Faith, the necessity of defending them forces us both to investigate them more accurately, to understand them more clearly, and to proclaim them more earnestly; and the question mooted by an adversary becomes the occasion of instruction. However, not only those who are openly separated from the church, but also all who glory in the Christian name, and at the same time lead abandoned lives, may without absurdity seem to be figured by Noah's middle son: for the passion of Christ, which was signified by that man's nakedness, is at once proclaimed by their profession, and dishonored by their wicked conduct. Of such, therefore, it has been said, "By their fruits ye shall know them." [6] And therefore was Ham cursed in his son, he being, as it were, his fruit. So, too, this son of his, Canaan, is fitly interpreted "their movement," which is nothing else than their work. But Shem and Japheth, that is to say, the circumcision and uncircumcision, or, as the apostle otherwise calls them, the Jews and Greeks, but called and justified, having somehow discovered the nakedness of their father (which signifies the Saviour's passion) took a garment and laid it upon their backs, and entered backwards and covered their father's nakedness, without their seeing what their reverence hid. For we both honor the passion of Christ as accomplished for us, and we hate the

[a] Song of Solomon i. 3   [4] 1 Cor. xi. 19   [5] Prov. x. 5 (LXX.)   [6] Matt. vii. 20

crime of the Jews who crucified Him. The garment signifies the sacrament, their backs the memory of things past: for the church celebrates the passion of Christ as already accomplished, and no longer to be looked forward to, now that Japheth already dwells in the habitations of Shem, and their wicked brother between them.

But the wicked brother is, in the person of his son (*i.e.*, his work) the boy, or slave, of his good brothers, when good men make a skillful use of bad men, either for the exercise of their patience or for their advancement in wisdom. For the apostle testifies that there are some who preach Christ from no pure motives; "but," says he, "whether in pretence or in truth, Christ is preached; and I therein do rejoice, yea, and will rejoice." [7] For it is Christ Himself who planted the vine of which the prophet says, "The vine of the Lord of hosts is the house of Israel;" [8] and He drinks of its wine, whether we thus understand that cup of which He says, "Can ye drink of the cup that I shall drink of?" [9] and, "Father, if it be possible, let this cup pass from me," [10] by which He obviously means His passion. Or, as wine is the fruit of the vine, we may prefer to understand that from this vine, that is to say, from the race of Israel, He has assumed flesh and blood that He might suffer; "and he was drunken," that is, He suffered; "and was naked," that is, His weakness appeared in His suffering, as the apostle says, "though He was crucified through weakness." [11] Wherefore the same apostle says, "The weakness of God is stronger than men; and the foolishness of God is wiser than men." [12] And when to the expression "he was naked" Scripture adds "in his house," it elegantly intimates that Jesus was to suffer the cross and death at the hands of His own household, His own kith and kin, the Jews. This passion of Christ is only externally and verbally professed by the reprobate, for what they profess they do not understand. But the elect hold in the inner man this so great mystery, and honor inwardly in the heart this weakness and foolishness of God. And of this there is a figure in Ham going out to proclaim his father's nakedness; while Shem and Japheth, to cover or honor it, went in, that is to say, did it inwardly.

These secrets of divine Scripture we investigate as well as we can. All will not accept our interpretation with equal confidence, but all hold it certain that these things were neither done nor recorded without some foreshadowing of future events, and that they are to be referred only to Christ and His church, which is the city of God, proclaimed from the very beginning of human history by figures which we now see everywhere accomplished. From the blessing of the two sons of Noah, and the cursing of the middle son, down to Abraham, or for more than a thousand years, there is, as I have said, no mention of any righteous persons who worshipped God. I do not therefore conclude that there were none; but it had been tedious to mention every one, and would have displayed historical accuracy rather than pro-

[7] Phil. i. 18   [8] Isa. v. 7   [9] Matt. xx. 22   [10] Matt. xxvi. 39   [11] 2 Cor. xiii. 4
[12] 1 Cor. i. 25

phetic foresight. The object of the writer of these sacred books, or rather of the Spirit of God in him, is not only to record the past, but to depict the future, so far as it regards the city of God; for whatever is said of those who are not its citizens, is given either for her instruction, or as a foil to enhance her glory. Yet we are not to suppose that all that is recorded has some signification; but those things which have no signification of their own are interwoven for the sake of the things which are significant. It is only the ploughshare that cleaves the soil; but to effect this, other parts of the plough are requisite. It is only the strings in harps and other musical instruments which produce melodious sounds; but that they may do so, there are other parts of the instrument which are not indeed struck by those who sing, but are connected with the strings which are struck, and produce musical notes. So in this prophetic history some things are narrated which have no significance, but are, as it were, the framework to which the significant things are attached.

CHAPTER III

OF THE GENERATIONS OF THE THREE SONS OF NOAH

We must therefore introduce into this work an explanation of the generations of the three sons of Noah, in so far as that may illustrate the progress in time of the two cities. Scripture first mentions that of the youngest son, who is called Japheth: he had eight sons, and by two of these sons seven grandchildren, three by one son, four by the other; in all, fifteen descendants. Ham, Noah's middle son, had four sons, and by one of them five grandsons, and by one of these two great-grandsons; in all, eleven. After enumerating these, Scripture returns to the first of the sons, and says, "Cush begat Nimrod; he began to be a giant on the earth. He was a giant hunter against the Lord God: wherefore they say, As Nimrod the giant hunter against the Lord. And the beginning of his kingdom was Babylon, Erech, Accad, and Calneh, in the land of Shinar. Out of that land went forth Assur, and built Nineveh, and the city Rehoboth, and Calah, and Resen between Nineveh and Calah: this was a great city." Now this Cush, father of the giant Nimrod, is the first-named among the sons of Ham, to whom five sons and two grandsons are ascribed. But he either begat this giant after his grandsons were born, or, which is more credible, Scripture speaks of him separately on account of his eminence; for mention is also made of his kingdom, which began with that magnificent city Babylon, and the other places, whether cities or districts, mentioned along with it. But what is recorded of the land of Shinar which belonged to Nimrod's kingdom, to wit, that Assur went forth from it and built Nineveh and the other cities mentioned with it, happened long after; but he takes occasion to speak of it here on account of the grandeur of the Assyrian kingdom, which was wonderfully extended by Ninus son of Belus, and founder of the great city Nineveh, which was named after him, Nineveh, from Ninus. But Assur, father of the Assyrian, was not one of the sons of Ham, Noah's middle son, but is found among the sons of Shem, his eldest son. Whence it appears that among Shem's offspring there arose men who afterwards took possession of that giant's kingdom, and advancing from it, founded other cities, the first of which was called Nineveh, from Ninus. From him Scripture returns to Ham's other son, Mizraim; and his sons are enumerated, not as seven individuals, but as seven nations. And from the sixth, as if from the sixth son, the race called the Philistines are said to have sprung; so that there are in all eight. Then it returns again to Canaan, in whose person Ham was cursed; and his eleven sons are named. Then the territories they occupied, and some of the cities, are named. And thus, if we count sons and grandsons, there are thirty-one of Ham's descendants registered.

It remains to mention the sons of Shem, Noah's eldest son; for to him this genealogical narrative gradually ascends from the youngest. But in the commencement of the record of Shem's sons there is an obscurity which calls for explanation, since it is closely connected with the object of our investigation. For we read, "Unto Shem also, the father of all the children of Heber, the brother of Japheth the elder, were children born." [13] This is the order of the words: And to Shem was born Heber, even to himself, that is, to Shem himself was born Heber, and Shem is the father of all his children. We are intended to understand that Shem is the patriarch of all his posterity who were to be mentioned, whether sons, grandsons, great-grandsons, or descendants at any remove. For Shem did not beget Heber, who was indeed in the fifth generation from him. For Shem begat, among other sons, Arphaxad; Arphaxad begat Cainan, Cainan begat Salah, Salah begat Heber. And it was with good reason that he was named first among Shem's offspring, taking precedence even of his sons, though only a grandchild of the fifth generation; for from him, as tradition says, the Hebrews derived their name, though the other etymology which derives the name from Abraham (as if *Abrahews*) may possibly be correct. But there can be little doubt that the former is the right etymology, and that they were called after Heber, *Heberews*, and then, dropping a letter, Hebrews; and so was their language called Hebrew, which was spoken by none but the people of Israel among whom was the city of God, mysteriously prefigured in all the people, and truly present in the saints. Six of Shem's sons then are first named, then four grandsons born to one of these sons; then it mentions another son of Shem, who begat a grandson; and his son, again, or Shem's great-grandson, was Heber. And Heber begat two sons, and called the one Peleg, which means "dividing;" and Scripture subjoins the reason of this name, saying, "for in his days was the earth divided." What this means will afterwards appear. Heber's other son begat twelve sons; consequently all Shem's descendants are twenty-seven. The total number of the progeny of the three

[13] Gen. x. 21

sons of Noah is seventy-three, fifteen by Japheth, thirty-one by Ham, twenty-seven by Shem. Then Scripture adds, "These are the sons of Shem, after their families, after their tongues, in their lands, after their nations." And so of the whole number: "These are the families of the sons of Noah after their generations, in their nations; and by these were the isles of the nations dispersed through the earth after the flood." From which we gather that the seventy-three (or rather, as I shall presently show, seventy-two) were not individuals, but nations. For in a former passage, when the sons of Japheth were enumerated, it is said in conclusion, "By these were the isles of the nations divided in their lands, every one after his language, in their tribes, and in their nations."

But nations are expressly mentioned among the sons of Ham, as I showed above. "Mizraim begat those who are called Ludim;" and so also of the other seven nations. And after enumerating all of them, it concludes, "These are the sons of Ham, in their families, according to their languages, in their territories, and in their nations." The reason, then, why the children of several of them are not mentioned, is that they belonged by birth to other nations, and did not themselves become nations. Why else is it, that though eight sons are reckoned to Japheth, the sons of only two of these are mentioned; and though four are reckoned to Ham, only three are spoken of as having sons; and though six are reckoned to Shem, the descendants of only two of these are traced? Did the rest remain childless? We cannot suppose so; but they did not produce nations so great as to warrant their being mentioned, but were absorbed in the nations to which they belonged by birth.

CHAPTER IV

OF THE DIVERSITY OF LANGUAGES, AND OF THE FOUNDING OF BABYLON

But though these nations are said to have been dispersed according to their languages, yet the narrator recurs to that time when all had but one language, and explains how it came to pass that a diversity of languages was introduced. "The whole earth," he says, "was of one lip, and all had one speech. And it came to pass, as they journeyed from the east, that they found a plain in the land of Shinar, and dwelt there. And they said one to another, Come, and let us make bricks, and burn them thoroughly. And they had bricks for stone, and slime for mortar. And they said, Come, and let us build for ourselves a city, and a tower whose top shall reach the sky; and let us make us a name, before we be scattered abroad on the face of all the earth. And the Lord came down to see the city and the tower, which the children of men builded. And the Lord God said, Behold, the people is one, and they have all one language; and this they begin to do: and now nothing will be restrained from them, which they have imagined to do. Come, and let us go down, and confound there their language, that they may not understand one another's speech. And God scattered them thence on the face of all the earth: and they left off to build the city and the tower. Therefore the name of it is called Confusion; because the Lord did there confound the language of all the earth: and the Lord God scattered them thence on the face of all the earth." [14] This city, which was called Confusion, is the same as Babylon, whose wonderful construction Gentile history also notices. For Babylon means Confusion. Whence we conclude that the giant Nimrod was its founder, as had been hinted a little before, where Scripture, in speaking of him, says that the beginning of his kingdom was Babylon, that is, Babylon had a supremacy over the other cities as the metropolis and royal residence; although it did not rise to the grand dimensions designed by its proud and impious founder. The plan was to make it so high that it should reach the sky, whether this was meant of one tower which they intended to build higher than the others, or of all the towers, which might be signified by the singular number, as we speak of "the soldier," meaning the army, and of the frog or the locust, when we refer to the whole multitude of frogs and locusts in the plagues with which Moses smote the Egyptians. [15] But what did these vain and presumptuous men intend? How did they expect to raise this lofty mass against God, when they had built it above all the mountains and the clouds of the earth's atmosphere? What injury could any spiritual or material elevation do to God? The safe and true way to heaven is made by humility, which lifts up the heart to the Lord, not against Him; as this giant is said to have been a "hunter *against* the Lord." This has been misunderstood by some through the ambiguity of the Greek word, and they have translated it, not "against the Lord," but "before the Lord;" for ἐναντίον means both "before" and "against." In the Psalm this word is rendered, "Let us weep *before* the Lord our Maker." [16] The same word occurs in the book of Job, where it is written, "Thou hast broken into fury *against* the Lord." [17] And so this giant is to be recognized as a "hunter *against* the Lord." And what is meant by the term "hunter" but deceiver, oppressor, and destroyer of the animals of the earth? He and his people therefore, erected this tower against the Lord, and so gave expression to their impious pride; and justly was their wicked intention punished by God, even though it was unsuccessful. But what was the nature of the punishment? As the tongue is the instrument of domination, in it pride was punished; so that man, who would not understand God when He issued His commands, should be misunderstood when he himself gave orders. Thus was that conspiracy disbanded, for each man retired from those he could not understand, and associated with those whose speech was intelligible; and the nations were divided according to their languages, and scattered over the earth as seemed good to God, who accomplished this in ways hidden from and incomprehensible to us.

---

[14] Gen. xi. 1-9   [15] Ex. x.   [16] Ps. xcv. 6   [17] Job xv. 13

CHAPTER V

OF GOD'S COMING DOWN TO CONFOUND THE LANGUAGES OF THE BUILDERS OF THE CITY

We read, "The Lord came down to see the city and the tower which the sons of men builded:" it was not the sons of God, but that society which lived in a merely human way, and which we call the earthly city. God, who is always wholly everywhere, does not move locally; but He is said to descend when He does anything in the earth out of the usual course, which, as it were, makes His presence felt. And in the same way, He does not by "seeing" learn some new thing, for He cannot ever be ignorant of anything; but He is said to see and recognize, in time, that which He causes others to see and recognize. And therefore that city was not previously being seen as God made it be seen when He showed how offensive it was to Him. We might, indeed, interpret God's descending to the city of the descent of His angels in whom He dwells; so that the following words, "And the Lord God said, Behold, they are all one race and of one language," and also what follows, "Come, and let us go down and confound their speech," are a recapitulation, explaining how the previously intimated "descent of the Lord" was accomplished. For if He had already gone down, why does He say, "Come, and let us go down and confound?"—words which seem to be addressed to the angels, and to intimate that He who was in the angels descended in their descent. And the words most appropriately are, not, "Go ye down and confound," but, "Let us confound their speech;" showing that He so works by His servants, that they are themselves also fellow-laborers with God, as the apostle says, "For we are fellow-laborers with God." [18]

CHAPTER VI

WHAT WE ARE TO UNDERSTAND BY GOD'S SPEAKING TO THE ANGELS

We might have supposed that the words uttered at the creation of man, "Let us," and not Let me, "make man," were addressed to the angels, had He not added "in our image;" but as we cannot believe that man was made in the image of angels, or that the image of God is the same as that of angels, it is proper to refer this expression to the plurality of the Trinity. And yet this Trinity, being one God, even after saying "Let us make," goes on to say, "And God made man in His image," [19] and not "Gods made," or "in their image." And were there any difficulty in applying to the angels the words, "Come, and let us go down and confound their speech," we might refer the plural to the Trinity, as if the Father were addressing the Son and the Holy Spirit; but it rather belongs to the angels to approach God by holy movements, that is, by pious thoughts, and thereby to avail themselves of

[18] 1 Cor. iii. 9   [19] Gen. i. 26

the unchangeable truth which rules in the court of heaven as their eternal law. For they are not themselves the truth; but partaking in the creative truth, they are moved towards it as the fountain of life, that what they have not in themselves they may obtain in it. And this movement of theirs is steady, for they never go back from what they have reached. And to these angels God does not speak, as we speak to one another, or to God, or to angels, or as the angels speak to us, or as God speaks to us through them: He speaks to them in an ineffable manner of His own, and that which He says is conveyed to us in a manner suited to our capacity. For the speaking of God antecedent and superior to all His works, is the immutable reason of His work: it has no noisy and passing sound, but an energy eternally abiding and producing results in time. Thus He speaks to the holy angels; but to us, who are far off, He speaks otherwise. When, however, we hear with the inner ear some part of the speech of God, we approximate to the angels. But in this work I need not labor go give an account of the ways in which God speaks. For either the unchangeable Truth speaks directly to the mind of the rational creature in some indescribable way, or speaks through the changeable creature, either presenting spiritual images to our spirit, or bodily voices to our bodily sense.

The words, "Nothing will be restrained from them which they have imagined to do," [20] are assuredly not meant as an affirmation, but as an interrogation, such as is used by persons threatening, as *e.g.*, when Dido exclaims,

> They will not take arms and pursue? [21]

We are to understand the words as if it had been said, Shall nothing be restrained from them which they have imagined to do? [22] From these three men, therefore, the three sons of Noah we mean, 73, or rather, as the catalogue will show, 72 nations and as many languages were dispersed over the earth, and as they increased filled even the islands. But the nations multiplied much more than the languages. For even in Africa we know several barbarous nations which have but one language; and who can doubt that, as the human race increased, men contrived to pass to the islands in ships?

CHAPTER VII

WHETHER EVEN THE REMOTEST ISLANDS RECEIVED THEIR FAUNA
FROM THE ANIMALS WHICH WERE PRESERVED, THROUGH THE
DELUGE, IN THE ARK

There is a question raised about all those kinds of beasts which are not domesticated, nor are produced like frogs from the earth, but are propa-

---

[20] Gen. xi. 6   [21] *Aeneid,* iv. 592
[22] Here Augustine remarks on the addition of the particle *ne* to the word *non,* which he has made to bring out the sense

gated by male and female parents, such as wolves and animals of that kind; and it is asked how they could be found in the islands after the deluge, in which all the animals not in the ark perished, unless the breed was restored from those which were preserved in pairs in the ark. It might, indeed, be said that they crossed to the islands by swimming, but this could only be true of those very near the mainland; whereas there are some so distant, that we fancy no animal could swim to them. But if men caught them and took them across with themselves, and thus propagated these breeds in their new abodes, this would not imply an incredible fondness for the chase. At the same time, it cannot be denied that by the intervention of angels they might be transferred by God's order or permission. If, however, they were produced out of the earth as at their first creation, when God said, "Let the earth bring forth the living creature," [23] this makes it more evident that all kinds of animals were preserved in the ark, not so much for the sake of renewing the stock, as of prefiguring the various nations which were to be saved in the church; this, I say, is more evident, if the earth brought forth many animals in islands to which they could not cross over.

CHAPTER VIII

WHETHER CERTAIN MONSTROUS RACES OF MEN ARE DERIVED FROM THE STOCK OF ADAM OR NOAH'S SONS

It is also asked whether we are to believe that certain monstrous races of men, spoken of in secular history,[24] have sprung from Noah's sons, or rather, I should say, from that one man from whom they themselves were descended. For it is reported that some have one eye in the middle of the forehead; some, feet turned backwards from the heel; some, a double sex, the right breast like a man, the left like a woman, and that they alternately beget and bring forth: others are said to have no mouth, and to breathe only through the nostrils; others are but a cubit high, and are therefore called by the Greeks "Pigmies:" [25] they say that in some places the women conceive in their fifth year, and do not live beyond their eighth. So, too, they tell of a race who have two feet but only one leg, and are of marvellous swiftness, though they do not bend the knee: they are called Skiopodes, because in the hot weather they lie down on their backs and shade themselves with their feet. Others are said to have no head, and their eyes in their shoulders; and other human or quasi-human races are depicted in mosaic in the harbor esplanade of Carthage, on the faith of histories of rarities. What shall I say of the Cynocephali, whose doglike head and barking proclaim them beasts rather than men? But we are not bound to believe all we hear of these monstrosities. But whoever is anywhere born a man, that is, a

---

[23] Gen. i. 24   [24] Pliny, *Hist. Nat.* vii. 2; Aulus Gellius, *Noct. Att.* ix. 4   [25] From πυγμή, a cubit

rational, mortal animal, no matter what unusual appearance he presents in color, movement, sound, nor how peculiar he is in some power, part, or quality of his nature, no Christian can doubt that he springs from that one protoplast. We can distinguish the common human nature from that which is peculiar, and therefore wonderful.

The same account which is given of monstrous births in individual cases can be given of monstrous races. For God, the Creator of all, knows where and when each thing ought to be, or to have been created, because He sees the similarities and diversities which can contribute to the beauty of the whole. But He who cannot see the whole is offended by the deformity of the part, because he is blind to that which balances it, and to which it belongs. We know that men are born with more than four fingers on their hands or toes on their feet: this is a smaller matter; but far from us be the folly of supposing that the Creator mistook the number of a man's fingers, though we cannot account for the difference. And so in cases where the divergence from the rule is greater. He whose works no man justly finds fault with, knows what He has done. At Hippo-Diarrhytus there is a man whose hands are crescent-shaped, and have only two fingers each, and his feet similarly formed. If there were a race like him, it would be added to the history of the curious and wonderful. Shall we therefore deny that this man is descended from that one man who was first created? As for the Androgyn, or Hermaphrodites, as they are called, though they are rare, yet from time to time there appears persons of sex so doubtful, that it remains uncertain from which sex they take their name; though it is customary to give them a masculine name, as the more worthy. For no one ever called them Hermaphroditesses. Some years ago, quite within my own memory, a man was born in the East, double in his upper, but single in his lower half—having two heads, two chests, four hands, but one body and two feet like an ordinary man; and he lived so long that many had an opportunity of seeing him. But who could enumerate all the human births that have differed widely from their ascertained parents? As, therefore, no one will deny that these are all descended from that one man, so all the races which are reported to have diverged in bodily appearance from the usual course which nature generally or almost universally preserves, if they are embraced in that definition of man as rational and mortal animals, unquestionably trace their pedigree to that one first father of all. We are supposing these stories about various races who differ from one another and from us to be true; but possibly they are not: for if we were not aware that apes, and monkeys, and sphinxes are not men, but beasts, those historians would possibly describe them as races of men, and flaunt with impunity their false and vainglorious discoveries. But supposing they are men of whom these marvels are recorded, what if God has seen fit to create some races in this way, that we might not suppose that the monstrous births which appear among ourselves are the failures of that wisdom whereby He fashions the human nature, as we speak of the failure of a less perfect workman? Accordingly, it ought not to seem absurd to us, that as in individual races there are monstrous births, so in the whole race there are monstrous races. Wherefore, to conclude this question cautiously and guardedly, either these things which have been told of some races have no existence at all; or if they do exist, they are not human races; or if they are human, they are descended from Adam.

CHAPTER IX

WHETHER WE ARE TO BELIEVE IN THE ANTIPODES

But as to the fable that there are Antipodes, that is to say, men on the opposite side of the earth, where the sun rises when it sets to us, men who walk with their feet opposite ours, that is on no ground credible. And, indeed, it is not affirmed that this has been learned by historical knowledge, but by scientific conjecture, on the ground that the earth is suspended within the concavity of the sky, and that it has as much room on the one side of it as on the other: hence they say that the part which is beneath must also be inhabited. But they do not remark that, although it be supposed or scientifically demonstrated that the world is of a round and spherical form, yet it does not follow that the other side of the earth is bare of water; nor even, though it be bare, does it immediately follow that it is peopled. For Scripture, which proves the truth of its historical statements by the accomplishment of its prophecies, gives no false information; and it is too absurd to say, that some men might have taken ship and traversed the whole wide ocean, and crossed from this side of the world to the other, and that thus even the inhabitants of that distant region are descended from that one first man. Wherefore let us seek if we can find the city of God that sojourns on earth among those human races who are catalogued as having been divided into seventy-two nations and as many languages. For it continued down to the deluge and the ark, and is proved to have existed still among the sons of Noah by their blessings, and chiefly in the eldest son Shem; for Japheth received this blessing, that he should dwell in the tents of Shem.

CHAPTER X

OF THE GENEALOGY OF SHEM, IN WHOSE LINE THE CITY OF GOD IS PRESERVED TILL THE TIME OF ABRAHAM

It is necessary, therefore, to preserve the series of generations descending from Shem, for the sake of exhibiting the city of God after the flood; as before the flood it was exhibited in the series of generations descending from Seth. And therefore does divine Scripture, after exhibiting the earthly city as Babylon or "Confusion," revert to the patriarch Shem, and recapitulate the generations from him to Abraham, specifying besides, the year in which each father begat the son that belonged to this line, and how long he lived. And unquestionably it is this which fulfills the promise I made, that it should appear why it is said of the sons of Heber, "The name of the one was Peleg, for in his days the earth was divided." [26] For what can we understand by the division of the earth, if not the diversity of languages? And, therefore, omitting the other sons of Shem, who are not concerned in this matter, Scripture gives the genealogy of those by whom the line runs on to Abraham, as before the flood those are given who carried on the line to Noah from Seth. Accordingly this series of generations begins thus: "These are the generations of Shem: Shem was an hundred years old, and begat Arphaxad two years after the flood. And Shem lived after he begat Arphaxad five hundred years, and begat sons and daughters." In like manner it registers the rest, naming the year of his life in which each begat the son who belonged to that line which extends to Abraham. It specifies, too, how many years he lived thereafter, begetting sons and daughters, that we may not child-ishly suppose that the men named were the only men, but may understand how the population increased, and how regions and kingdoms so vast could be populated by the descendants of Shem; especially the kingdom of Assyria, from which Ninus subdued the surrounding nations, reigning with brilliant prosperity, and bequeathing to his descendants a vast but thoroughly con-solidated empire, which held together for many centuries.

But to avoid needless prolixity, we shall mention not the number of years each member of this series lived, but only the year of his life in which he begat his heir, that we may thus reckon the number of years from the flood to Abraham, and may at the same time leave room to touch briefly and cursorily upon some other matters necessary to our argument. In the second year, then, after the flood, Shem when he was a hundred years old begat Arphaxad; Arphaxad when he was 135 years old begat Cainan; Cainan when he was 130 years begat Salah. Salah himself, too, was the same age when he begat Eber. Eber lived 134 years, and begat Peleg, in whose days the earth was divided. Peleg himself lived 130 years, and begat Reu; and Reu lived 132 years, and begat Serug; Serug 130, and begat Nahor; and Nahor 79, and begat Terah; and Terah 70, and begat Abram, whose name God afterwards changed into *Abraham*. There are thus from the flood to Abraham 1072 years, according to the Vulgate or Septuagint versions. In the Hebrew copies far fewer years are given; and for this either no reason or a not very credible one is given.

When, therefore, we look for the city of God in these seventy-two nations, we cannot affirm that while they had but one lip, that is, one language, the human race had departed from the worship of the true God, and that gen-uine godliness had survived only in those generations which descend from Shem through Arphaxad and reach to Abraham; but from the time when

[26] Gen. x. 25

they proudly built a tower to heaven, a symbol of godless exaltation, the city or society of the wicked becomes apparent. Whether it was only disguised before, or non-existent; whether both cities remained after the flood—the godly in the two sons of Noah who were blessed, and in their posterity, and the ungodly in the cursed son and his descendants, from whom sprang that mighty hunter against the Lord—is not easily determined. For possibly—and certainly this is more credible—there were despisers of God among the descendants of the two sons, even before Babylon was founded, and worshippers of God among the descendants of Ham. Certainly neither race was ever obliterated from earth. For in both the Psalms in which it is said, "They are all gone aside, they are altogether become filthy; there is none that doeth good, no, not one," we read further, "Have all the workers of iniquity no knowledge? who eat up my people as they eat bread, and call not upon the Lord." [27] There was then a people of God even at that time. And therefore the words, "There is none that doeth good, no, not one," were said of the sons of men, not of the sons of God. For it had been previously said, "God looked down from heaven upon the sons of men, to see if any understood and sought after God;" and then follow the words which demonstrate that all the sons of men, that is, all who belong to the city which lives according to men, not according to God, are reprobate.

CHAPTER XI

THAT THE ORIGINAL LANGUAGE IN USE AMONG MEN WAS THAT WHICH WAS AFTERWARDS CALLED HEBREW, FROM HEBER, IN WHOSE FAMILY IT WAS PRESERVED WHEN THE CONCLUSION OF TONGUES OCCURRED

Wherefore, as the fact of all using one language did not secure the absence of sin-infected men from the race—for even before the deluge there was one language, and yet all but the single family of just Noah were found worthy of destruction by the flood—so when the nations, by a prouder godlessness, earned the punishment of the dispersion and the confusion of tongues, and the city of the godless was called Confusion or Babylon, there was still the house of Heber in which the primitive language of the race survived. And therefore, as I have already mentioned, when an enumeration is made of the sons of Shem, who each founded a nation, Heber is first mentioned, although he was of the fifth generation from Shem. And because, when the other races were divided by their own peculiar languages, his family preserved that language which is not unreasonably believed to have been the common language of the race, it was on this account thenceforth named Hebrew. For it then became necessary to distinguish this language from the rest by a proper name; though, while there was only one, it had

[27] Ps. xiv. 3, 4; liii. 3, 4

no other name than the language of man, or human speech, it alone being spoken by the whole human race. Some one will say: If the earth was divided by languages in the days of Peleg, Heber's son, that language, which was formerly common to all, should rather have been called after Peleg. But we are to understand that Heber himself gave to his son this name Peleg, which means Division; because he was born when the earth was divided, that is, at the very time of the division, and that this is the meaning of the words, "In his days the earth was divided." [28] For unless Heber had been still alive when the languages were multiplied, the language which was preserved in his house would not have been called after him. We are induced to believe that this was the primitive and common language, because the multiplication and change of languages was introduced as a punishment, and it is fit to ascribe to the people of God an immunity from this punishment. Nor is it without significance that this is the language which Abraham retained, and that he could not transmit it to all his descendants, but only to those of Jacob's line, who distinctively and eminently constituted God's people, and received His covenants, and were Christ's progenitors according to the flesh. In the same way, Heber himself did not transmit that language to all his posterity, but only to the line from which Abraham sprang. And thus, although it is not expressly stated, that when the wicked were building Babylon there was a godly seed remaining, this indistinctness is intended to stimulate research rather than to elude it. For when we see that originally there was one common language, and that Heber is mentioned before all Shem's sons, though he belonged to the fifth generation from him, and that the language which the patriarchs and prophets used, not only in their conversation, but in the authoritative language of Scripture, is called Hebrew, when we are asked where that primitive and common language was preserved after the confusion of tongues, certainly, as there can be no doubt that those among whom it was preserved were exempt from the punishment it embodied, what other suggestion can we make, than that it survived in the family of him whose name it took, and that this is no small proof of the righteousness of this family, that the punishment with which the other families were visited did not fall upon it?

But yet another question is mooted: How did Heber and his son Peleg each found a nation, if they had but one language? For no doubt the Hebrew nation propagated from Heber through Abraham, and becoming through him a great people, is one nation. How, then, are all the sons of the three branches of Noah's family enumerated as founding a nation each, if Heber and Peleg did not so? It is very probable that the giant Nimrod founded also his nation, and that Scripture has named him separately on account of the extraordinary dimensions of his empire and of his body, so that the number of seventy-two nations remains. But Peleg was mentioned, not because he founded a nation (for his race and language are Hebrew) but on account

[28] Gen. x. 25

of the critical time at which he was born, all the earth being then divided. Nor ought we to be surprised that the giant Nimrod lived to the time in which Babylon was founded and the confusion of tongues occurred, and the consequent division of the earth. For though Heber was in the sixth generation from Noah, and Nimrod in the fourth, it does not follow that they could not be alive at the same time. For when the generations are few, they live longer and are born later; but when they are many, they live a shorter time, and come into the world earlier. We are to understand that, when the earth was divided, the descendants of Noah who are registered as founders of nations were not only already born, but were of an age to have immense families, worthy to be called tribes or nations. And therefore we must by no means suppose that they were born in the order in which they were set down; otherwise, how could the twelve sons of Joktan, another son of Heber's, and brother of Peleg, have already founded nations, if Joktan was born, as he is registered, after his brother Peleg, since the earth was divided at Peleg's birth? We are therefore to understand that, though Peleg is named first, he was born long after Joktan, whose twelve sons had already families so large as to admit of their being divided by different languages. There is nothing extraordinary in the last born being first named: of the sons of Noah, the descendants of Japheth are first named; then the sons of Ham, who was the second son; and last the sons of Shem, who was the first and oldest. Of these nations the names have partly survived, so that at this day we can see from whom they have sprung, as the Assyrians from Assur, the Hebrews from Heber, but partly have been altered in the lapse of time, so that the most learned men, by profound research in ancient records, have scarcely been able to discover the origin, I do not say of all, but of some of these nations. There is, for example, nothing in the name Egyptians to show that they are descended from Misraim, Ham's son, nor in the name Ethiopians to show a connection with Cush, though such is said to be the origin of these nations. And if we take a general survey of the names, we shall find that more have been changed than have remained the same.

CHAPTER XII

OF THE ERA IN ABRAHAM'S LIFE FROM WHICH A NEW PERIOD IN THE HOLY SUCCESSION BEGINS

Let us now survey the progress of the city of God from the era of the patriarch Abraham, from whose time it begins to be more conspicuous, and the divine promises which are now fulfilled in Christ are more fully revealed. We learn, then, from the intimations of holy Scripture, that Abraham was born in the country of the Chaldeans, a land belonging to the Assyrian empire. Now, even at that time impious superstitions were rife with the Chaldeans, as with other nations. The family of Terah, to which Abraham belonged, was the only one in which the worship of the true God survived,

and the only one, we may suppose, in which the Hebrew language was preserved; although Joshua the son of Nun tells us that even this family served
other gods in Mesopotamia.[29] The other descendants of Heber gradually became absorbed in other races and other languages. And thus, as the single
family of Noah was preserved through the deluge of water to renew the
human race, so, in the deluge of superstition that flooded the whole world,
there remained but the one family of Terah in which the seed of God's city
was preserved. And as, when Scripture has enumerated the generations
prior to Noah, with their ages, and explained the cause of the flood before
God began to speak to Noah about the building of the ark, it is said, "These
are the generations of Noah;" so also now, after enumerating the generations
from Shem, Noah's son, down to Abraham, it then signalizes an era by saying, "These are the generations of Terah: Terah begat Abram, Nahor, and
Haran; and Haran begat Lot. And Haran died before his father Terah in the
land of his nativity, in Ur of the Chaldees. And Abram and Nahor took
them wives: the name of Abram's wife was Sarai; and the name of Nahor's
wife Milcah, the daughter of Haran, the father of Milcah, and the father of
Iscah." [30] This Iscah is supposed to be the same as Sarah, Abraham's wife.

CHAPTER XIII

WHY, IN THE ACCOUNT OF TERAH'S EMIGRATION, ON HIS FORSAKING THE CHALDEANS AND PASSING OVER INTO MESOPOTAMIA, NO MENTION IS MADE OF HIS SON NAHOR

Next it is related how Terah with his family left the region of the Chaldeans and came into Mesopotamia, and dwelt in Haran. But nothing is said
about one of his sons called Nahor, as if he had not taken him along with
him. For the narrative runs thus: "And Terah took Abram his son, and Lot
the son of Haran, his son's son, and Sarah his daughter-in-law, his son
Abram's wife, and led them forth out of the region of the Chaldeans to go
into the land of Canaan; and he came into Haran, and dwelt there." [31]
Nahor and Milcah his wife are nowhere named here. But afterwards, when
Abraham sent his servant to take a wife for his son Isaac, we find it thus
written: "And the servant took ten camels of the camels of his lord, and of
all the goods of his lord, with him; and arose, and went into Mesopotamia,
into the city of Nahor." [32] This and other testimonies of this sacred history
show that Nahor, Abraham's brother, had also left the region of the Chaldeans, and fixed his abode in Mesopotamia, where Abraham dwelt with his
father. Why, then, did the Scripture not mention him, when Terah with his
family went forth out of the Chaldean nation and dwelt in Haran, since it
mentions that he took with him not only Abraham his son, but also Sarah
his daughter-in-law, and Lot his grandson? The only reason we can think of

[29] Josh. xxiv. 2   [30] Gen. xi. 27-29   [31] Gen. xi. 31   [32] Gen. xxiv. 10

is, that perhaps he had lapsed from the piety of his father and brother, and adhered to the superstition of the Chaldeans, and had afterwards emigrated thence, either through penitence, or because he was persecuted as a suspected person. For in the book called *Judith, when Holofernes, the enemy of the Israelites,* inquired what kind of nation that might be, and whether war should be made against them, Achior, the leader of the Ammonites, answered him thus: "Let our lord now hear a word from the mouth of thy servant, and I will declare unto thee the truth concerning the people which dwelleth near thee in this hill country, and there shall no lie come out of the mouth of thy servant. For this people is descended from the Chaldeans, and they dwelt heretofore in Mesopotamia, because they would not follow the gods of their fathers, which were glorious in the land of the Chaldeans, but went out of the way of their ancestors, and adored the God of heaven, whom they knew; and they cast them out from the face of their gods, and they fled into Mesopotamia, and dwelt there many days. And their God said to them, that they should depart from their habitation, and go into the land of Canaan; and they dwelt," [33] etc., as Achior the Ammonite narrates. Whence it is manifest that the house of Terah had suffered persecution from the Chaldeans for the true piety with which they worshipped the one and true God.

CHAPTER XIV

OF THE YEARS OF TERAH, WHO COMPLETED HIS LIFETIME IN HARAN

On Terah's death in Mesopotamia, where he is said to have lived 205 years, the promises of God made to Abraham now begin to be pointed out; for thus it is written: "And the days of Terah in Haran were two hundred and five years, and he died in Haran." [34] This is not to be taken as if he had spent all his days there, but that he there completed the days of his life, which were two hundred and five years: otherwise it would not be known how many years Terah lived, since it is not said in what year of his life he came into Haran; and it is absurd to suppose that, in this series of generations, where it is carefully recorded how many years each one lived, his age was the only one not put on record. For although some whom the same Scripture mentions have not their age recorded, they are not in this series, in which the reckoning of time is continuously indicated by the death of the parents and the succession of the children. For this series, which is given in order from Adam to Noah, and from him down to Abraham, contains no one without the number of the years of his life.

[33] Judith v. 5-9   [34] Gen. xi. 32

CHAPTER XV

OF THE TIME OF THE MIGRATION OF ABRAHAM, WHEN, ACCORDING TO THE COMMANDMENT OF GOD, HE WENT OUT FROM HARAN

When, after the record of the death of Terah, the father of Abraham, we next read, "And the Lord said to Abram, Get thee out of thy country, and from thy kindred, and from thy father's house," [35] etc., it is not to be supposed, because this follows in the order of the narrative, that it also followed in the chronological order of events. For if it were so, there would be an insoluble difficulty. For after these words of God which were spoken to Abraham, the Scripture says: "And Abram departed, as the Lord had spoken unto him; and Lot went with him. Now Abraham was seventy-five years old when he departed out of Haran." [36] How can this be true if he departed from Haran after his father's death? For when Terah was seventy years old, as is intimated above, he begat Abraham; and if to this number we add the seventy-five years which Abraham reckoned when he went out of Haran, we get 145 years. Therefore that was the number of the years of Terah, when Abraham departed out of that city of Mesopotamia; for he had reached the seventy-fifth year of his life, and thus his father, who begat him in the seventieth year of his life, had reached, as was said, his 145th. Therefore he did not depart thence after his father's death, that is, after the 205 years his father lived; but the year of his departure from that place, seeing it was his seventy-fifth, is inferred beyond a doubt to have been the 145th of his father, who begat him in his seventieth year. And thus it is to be understood that the Scripture, according to its custom, has gone back to the time which had already been passed by the narrative; just as above, when it had mentioned the grandsons of Noah, it said that they were in their nations and tongues; and yet afterwards, as if this also had followed in order of time, it says, "And the whole earth was of one lip, and one speech for all." [37] How, then, could they be said to be in their own nations and according to their own tongues, if there was one for all; except because the narrative goes back to gather up what it had passed over? Here, too, in the same way, after saying, "And the days of Terah in Haran were 205 years, and Terah died in Haran," the Scripture, going back to what had been passed over in order to complete what had been begun about Terah, says, "And the Lord said to Abram, Get thee out of thy country," [38] etc. After which words of God it is added, "And Abram departed, as the Lord spake unto him; and Lot went with him. But Abram was seventy-five years old when he departed out of Haran." Therefore it was done when his father was in the 145th year of his age; for it was then the seventy-fifth of his own. But this question is also solved in another way, that the seventy-five years

---

[35] Gen. xii. 1   [36] Gen. xii. 4   [37] Gen. xi. 1   [38] Gen. xii. 1

of Abraham when he departed out of Haran are reckoned from the year in which he was delivered from the fire of the Chaldeans, not from that of his birth, as if he was rather to be held as having been born then.

Now the blessed Stephen, in narrating these things in the ~~Acts of the Apostles,~~ says: "The God of glory appeared unto our father Abraham, when he was in Mesopotamia, before he dwelt in Charran, and said unto him, Get thee out of thy country, and from thy kindred, and from thy father's house, and come into the land which I will show thee." [39] According to these words of Stephen, God spoke to Abraham, not after the death of his father, who certainly died in Haran, where his son also dwelt with him, but before he dwelt in that city, although he was already in Mesopotamia. Therefore he had already departed from the Chaldeans. So that when Stephen adds, "Then Abraham went out of the land of the Chaldeans, and dwelt in Charran," [40] this does not point out what took place after God spoke to him (for it was not after these words of God that he went out of the land of the Chaldeans, since he says that God spoke to him in Mesopotamia) but the word "*then*" which he uses refers to that whole period from his going out of the land of the Chaldeans and dwelling in Haran. Likewise in what follows, "And thenceforth, when his father was dead, he settled him in this land, wherein ye now dwell, and your fathers," he does not say, after his father was dead he went out from Haran; but thenceforth he settled him here, after his father was dead. It is to be understood, therefore, that God had spoken to Abraham when he was in Mesopotamia, before he dwelt in Haran; but that he came to Haran with his father, keeping in mind the precept of God, and that he went out thence in his own seventy-fifth year, which was his father's 145th. But he says that his settlement in the land of Canaan, not his going forth from Haran, took place after his father's death; because his father was already dead when he purchased the land, and personally entered on possession of it. But when, on his having already settled in Mesopotamia, that is, already gone out of the land of the Chaldeans, God says, "Get thee out of thy country, and from thy kindred, and from thy father's house," [41] this means, not that he should cast out his body from thence, for he had already done that, but that he should tear away his soul. For he had not gone out from thence in mind, if he was held by the hope and desire of returning —a hope and desire which was to be cut off by God's command and help, and by his own obedience. It would indeed be no incredible supposition that afterwards, when Nahor followed his father, Abraham then fulfilled the precept of the Lord, that he should depart out of Haran with Sarah his wife and Lot his brother's son.

[39] Acts vii. 2, 3   [40] Acts vii. 4   [41] Gen. xii. 1

CHAPTER XVI

OF THE ORDER AND NATURE OF THE PROMISES OF GOD WHICH WERE MADE TO ABRAHAM

God's promises made to Abraham are now to be considered; for in these the oracles of our God, that is, of the true God, began to appear more openly concerning the godly people, whom prophetic authority foretold. The first of these reads thus: "And the Lord said unto Abram, Get thee out of thy country, and from thy kindred, and from thy father's house, and go into a land that I will show thee: and I will make of thee a great nation, and I will bless thee, and magnify thy name; and thou shalt be blessed: and I will bless them that bless thee, and curse them that curse thee: and in thee shall all tribes of the earth be blessed."[42] Now it is to be observed that two things are promised to Abraham, the one, that his seed should possess the land of Canaan, which is intimated when it is said, "Go into a land that I will show thee, and I will make of thee a great nation;" but the other far more excellent, not about the carnal but the spiritual seed, through which he is the father, not of the one Israelite nation, but of all nations who follow the footprints of his faith, which was first promised in these words, "And in thee shall all tribes of the earth be blessed." Eusebius thought this promise was made in Abraham's seventy-fifth year, as if soon after it was made Abraham had departed out of Haran; because the Scripture cannot be contradicted, in which we read, "Abram was seventy and five years old when he departed out of Haran." But if this promise was made in that year, then of course Abraham was staying in Haran with his father; for he could not depart thence unless he had first dwelt there. Does this, then, contradict what Stephen says, "The God of glory appeared to our father Abraham, when he was in Mesopotamia, before he dwelt in Charran?"[43] But it is to be understood that the whole took place in the same year—both the promise of God before Abraham dwelt in Haran, and his dwelling in Haran, and his departure thence—not only because Eusebius in the Chronicles reckons from the year of this promise, and shows that after 430 years the exodus from Egypt took place, when the law was given but because the Apostle Paul also mentions it.

CHAPTER XVII

OF THE THREE MOST FAMOUS KINGDOMS OF THE NATIONS, OF WHICH ONE, THAT IS THE ASSYRIAN, WAS ALREADY VERY EMINENT WHEN ABRAHAM WAS BORN

During the same period there were three famous kingdoms of the nations, in which the city of the earth-born, that is, the society of men living accord-

[42] Gen. xii. 1-3   [43] Acts vii. 2

ing to man under the domination of the fallen angels, chiefly flourished, namely, the three kingdoms of Sicyon, Egypt, and Assyria. Of these, Assyria was much the most powerful and sublime; for that king Ninus, son of Belus, had subdued the people of all Asia except India. By Asia I now mean not that part which is one province of this greater Asia, but what is called Universal Asia, which some set down as the half, but most as the third part of the whole world—the three being Asia, Europe, and Africa, thereby making an unequal division. For the part called Asia stretches from the south through the east even to the north; Europe from the north even to the west; and Africa from the west even to the south. Thus we see that two, Europe and Africa, contain one half of the world, and Asia alone the other half. And these two parts are made by the circumstance, that there enters between them from the ocean all the Mediterranean water, which makes this great sea of ours. So that, if you divide the world into two parts, the east and the west, Asia will be in the one, and Europe and Africa in the other. So that of the three kingdoms then famous, one, namely Sicyon, was not under the Assyrians, because it was in Europe; but as for Egypt, how could it fail to be subject to the empire which ruled all Asia with the single exception of India? In Assyria, therefore, the dominion of the impious city had the pre-eminence. Its head was Babylon—an earth-born city, most fitly named, for it means confusion. There Ninus reigned after the death of his father Belus, who first had reigned there sixty-five years. His son Ninus, who, on his father's death, succeeded to the kingdom, reigned fifty-two years, and had been king forty-three years when Abraham was born, which was about the 1200th year before Rome was founded, as it were another Babylon in the west.

CHAPTER XVIII

OF THE REPEATED ADDRESS OF GOD TO ABRAHAM, IN WHICH HE PROMISED THE LAND OF CANAAN TO HIM AND TO HIS SEED

Abraham, then, having departed out of Haran in the seventy-fifth year of his own age, and in the hundred and forty-fifth of his father's, went with Lot, his brother's son, and Sarah his wife, into the land of Canaan, and came even to Sichem, where again he received the divine oracle, of which it is thus written: "And the Lord appeared unto Abram, and said unto him, Unto thy seed will I give this land." [44] Nothing is promised here about that seed in which he is made the father of all nations, but only about that by which he is the father of the one Israelite nation; for by this seed that land was possessed.

[44] Gen. xii. 7

CHAPTER XIX

OF THE DIVINE PRESERVATION OF SARAH'S CHASTITY IN EGYPT, WHEN
ABRAHAM HAD CALLED HER NOT HIS WIFE BUT HIS SISTER

Having built an altar there, and called upon God, Abraham proceeded thence and dwelt in the desert, and was compelled by pressure of famine to go on into Egypt. There he called his wife his sister, and told no lie. For she was this also, because she was near of blood; just as Lot, on account of the same nearness, being his brother's son, is called his brother. Now he did not deny that she was his wife, but held his peace about it, committing to God the defense of his wife's chastity, and providing as a man against human wiles; because if he had not provided against the danger as much as he could, he would have been tempting God rather than trusting in Him. We have said enough about this matter against the calumnies of Faustus the Manichaean. At last what Abraham had expected the Lord to do took place. For Pharaoh, king of Egypt, who had taken her to him as his wife, restored her to her husband on being severely plagued. And far be it from us to believe that she was defiled by lying with another; because it is much more credible that, by these great afflictions, Pharaoh was not permitted to do this.

CHAPTER XX

OF THE PARTING OF LOT AND ABRAHAM, WHICH THEY AGREED TO
WITHOUT BREACH OF CHARITY

On Abraham's return out of Egypt to the place he had left, Lot, his brother's son, departed from him into the land of Sodom, without breach of charity. For they had grown rich, and began to have many herdmen of cattle, and when these strove together, they avoided in this way the pugnacious discord of their families. Indeed, as human affairs go, this cause might even have given rise to some strife between themselves. Consequently these are the words of Abraham to Lot, when taking precaution against this evil, "Let there be no strife between me and thee, and between my herdmen and thy herdmen; for we be brethren. Behold, is not the whole land before thee? Separate thyself from me: if thou wilt go to the left hand, I will go to the right; or if thou wilt go to the right hand, I will go to the left." [45] From this, perhaps, has arisen a pacific custom among men, that when there is any partition of earthly things, the greater should make the division, the less the choice.

[45] Gen. xiii. 8, 9

CHAPTER XXI

OF THE THIRD PROMISE OF GOD, BY WHICH HE ASSURED THE LAND OF CANAAN TO ABRAHAM AND HIS SEED IN PERPETUITY

Now, when Abraham and Lot had separated, and dwelt apart, owing to the necessity of supporting their families, and not to vile discord, and Abraham was in the land of Canaan. [...] in Sodom, the Lord said to Abraham in a third oracle, "Lift up thine [...] and look from the place where thou now art, to the north, and to [...] and to the east, and to the sea; for all the land which thou seest, to thee will I give it, and to thy seed for ever. And I will make thy seed as the dust of the earth: if any one can number the dust of the earth, thy seed shall also be numbered. Arise, and walk through the [...], in the length of it, and in the breadth of it; for unto thee will I give [...] [46] It does not clearly appear whether in this promise that also is contained by which he is made the father of all nations. For the clause, "And I will make thy seed as the dust of the earth," may seem to refer to this, being spoken by that figure the Greeks call hyperbole, which indeed is figurative, not literal. But no person of understanding can doubt in what manner the Scripture uses this and other figures. For that figure (that is, way of speaking) is used when what is said is far larger than what is meant by it; for who does not see how incomparably larger the number of the dust must be than that of all men can be from Adam himself down to the end of the world? How much greater, then, must it be than the seed of Abraham—not only that pertaining to the nation of Israel, but also that which is and shall be according to the imitation of faith in all nations of the whole wide world! For that seed is indeed very small in comparison with the multitude of the wicked, although even those few of themselves make an innumerable multitude, which by a hyperbole is compared to the dust of the earth. Truly that multitude which was promised to Abraham is not innumerable to God, although to man; but to God not even the dust of the earth is so. Further, the promise here made may be understood not only of the nation of Israel, but of the whole seed of Abraham, which may be fitly compared to the dust for multitude, because regarding it also there is the promise of many children, not according to the flesh, but according to the spirit. But we have therefore said that this does not clearly appear, because the multitude even of that one nation, which was born according to the flesh of Abraham through his grandson Jacob, has increased so much as to fill almost all parts of the world. Consequently, even it might by hyperbole be compared to the dust for multitude, because even it alone is innumerable by man. Certainly no one questions that only that land is meant which is called Canaan. But that saying, "To thee will I give it, and to thy seed for ever," may move some, if by "for

[46] Gen. xiii. 14-17

ever" they understand "to eternity." But if in this passage they take "for
ever" thus, as we firmly hold it means, that the beginning of the world to
come is to be ordered from the end of the present, there is still no difficulty,
because, although the Israelites are expelled from Jerusalem, they still remain in other cities in the land of Canaan, and shall remain even to the end;
and when that whole land is inhabited by Christians, they also are the very
seed of Abraham.

CHAPTER XXII

OF ABRAHAM'S OVERCOMING THE ENEMIES OF SODOM, WHEN HE DELIVERED LOT FROM CAPTIVITY AND WAS BLESSED BY MELCHIZEDEK THE PRIEST.

Having received this oracle of promise, Abraham migrated, and remained
in another place of the same land, that is, beside the oak of Mamre, which
was Hebron. Then on the invasion of Sodom, when five kings carried on war
against four, and Lot was taken captive with the conquered Sodomites,
Abraham delivered him from the enemy, leading with him to battle three
hundred and eighteen of his home-born servants, and won the victory for
the kings of Sodom, but would take nothing of the spoils when offered by the
king for whom he had won them. He was then openly blessed by Melchizedek, who was priest of God Most High, about whom many and great things
are written in the epistle which is inscribed to the Hebrews, which most say
is by the Apostle Paul, though some deny this. For then first appeared the
sacrifice which is now offered to God by Christians in the whole wide world,
and that is fulfilled which long after the event was said by the prophet to
Christ, who was yet to come in the flesh, "Thou art a priest for ever after the
order of Melchizedek"[47]—that is to say, not after the order of Aaron, for
that order was to be taken away when the things shone forth which were
intimated beforehand by these shadows.

CHAPTER XXIII

OF THE WORD OF THE LORD TO ABRAHAM, BY WHICH IT WAS PROMISED TO HIM THAT HIS POSTERITY SHOULD BE MULTIPLIED ACCORDING TO THE MULTITUDE OF THE STARS; ON BELIEVING WHICH HE WAS DECLARED JUSTIFIED WHILE YET IN UNCIRCUMCISION

The word of the Lord came to Abraham in a vision also. For when God
promised him protection and exceeding great reward, he, being solicitous
about posterity, said that a certain Eliezer of Damascus, born in his house,
would be his heir. Immediately he was promised an heir, not that house-born
servant, but one who was to come forth of Abraham himself; and again a

[47] Ps. cx. 4

seed innumerable, not as the dust of the earth, but as the stars of heaven—
which rather seems to me a promise of a posterity exalted in celestial felicity.
For, so far as multitude is concerned, what are the stars of heaven to the dust
of the earth, unless one should say the comparison is like inasmuch as the
stars also cannot be numbered? For it is not to be believed that all of them
can be seen. For the more keenly one observes them, the more does he see.
So that it is to be supposed some remain concealed from the keenest observ-
ers, to say nothing of those stars which are said to rise and set in another
part of the world most remote from us. Finally, the authority of this book
condemns those like Aratus or Eudoxus, or any others who boast that they
have found out and written down the complete number of the stars. Here,
indeed, is set down that sentence which the apostle quotes in order to commend the grace of God, "Abraham believed God, and it was counted to him
for righteousness;" [48] lest the circumcision should glory, and be unwilling to
receive the uncircumcised nations to the faith of Christ. For at the time
when he believed, and his faith was counted to him for righteousness, Abraham had not yet been circumcised.

CHAPTER XXIV

OF THE MEANING OF THE SACRIFICE ABRAHAM WAS COMMANDED TO
OFFER WHEN HE SUPPLICATED TO BE TAUGHT ABOUT THOSE
THINGS HE HAD BELIEVED

In the same vision, God in speaking to him also says, "I am God that
brought thee out of the region of the Chaldees, to give thee this land to inherit it." [49] And when Abram asked whereby he might know that he should
inherit it, God said to him, "Take me an heifer of three years old, and a she-
goat of three years old, and a ram of three years old, and a turtle-dove, and
a pigeon. And he took unto him all these, and divided them in the midst, and
laid each piece one against another; but the birds divided he not. And the
fowls came down," as it is written, "on the carcasses, and Abram sat down
by them. But about the going down of the sun, great fear fell upon Abram;
and, lo, an horror of great darkness fell upon him. And He said unto Abram,
Know of a surety that thy seed shall be a stranger in a land not theirs, and
they shall reduce them to servitude and shall afflict them four hundred
years: but the nation whom they shall serve will I judge; and afterward shall
they come out hither with great substance. And thou shalt go to thy fathers
in peace; kept in a good old age. But in the fourth generation they shall come
hither again: for the iniquity of the Amorites is not yet full. And when the
sun was setting, there was a flame, and a smoking furnace, and lamps of fire,
that passed through between those pieces. In that day the Lord made a covenant with Abraham, saying, Unto thy seed will I give this land, from the

---

[48] Rom. iv. 3 ; Gen. xv. 6   [49] Gen. xv. 7

river of Egypt unto the great river Euphrates: the Kenites, and the Keniz-zites, and the Kadmonites, and the Hittites, and the Perizzites, and the Rephaims, and the Amorites, and the Canaanites, and the Hivites, and the Girgashites, and the Jebusites." [50]

All these things were said and done in a vision from God; but it would take long, and would exceed the scope of this work, to treat of them exactly in detail. It is enough that we should know that, after it was said Abram be-lieved in God, and it was counted to him for righteousness, he did not fail in faith in saying, "Lord God, whereby shall I know that I shall inherit it?" for the inheritance of that land was promised to him. Now he does not say, How shall I know, as if he did not yet believe; but he says, "Whereby shall I know," meaning that some sign might be given by which he might know the manner of those things which he had believed, just as it is not for lack of faith the Virgin Mary says, "How shall this be, seeing I know not a man?" [51] for she inquired as to the way in which that should take place which she was certain would come to pass. And when she asked this, she was told, "The Holy Ghost shall come upon thee, and the power of the Highest shall over-shadow thee." [52] Here also, in fine, a symbol was given, consisting of three animals, a heifer, a she-goat, and a ram and two birds, a turtle-dove and pigeon, that he might know that the things which he had not doubted should come to pass were to happen in accordance with this symbol. Whether, there-fore, the heifer was a sign that the people should be put under the law, the she-goat that the same people was to become sinful, the ram that they should reign (and these animals are said to be of three years old for this reason, that there are three remarkable divisions of time, from Adam to Noah, and from him to Abraham, and from him to David, who, on the rejection of Saul, was first established by the will of the Lord in the kingdom of the Israelite na-tion: in this third division, which extends from Abraham to David, that people grew up as if passing through the third age of life) or whether they had some other more suitable meaning, still I have no doubt whatever that spiritual things were prefigured by them as well as by the turtle-dove and pigeon. And it is said, "But the birds divided he not," because carnal men are divided among themselves, but the spiritual not at all, whether they se-clude themselves from the busy conversation of men, like the turtle-dove, or dwell among them, like the pigeon; for both birds are simple and harmless, signifying that even in the Israelite people, to which that land was to be given, there would be individuals who were children of the promise, and heirs of the kingdom that is to remain in eternal felicity. But the fowls coming down on the divided carcasses represent nothing good, but the spirits of this air, seeking some food for themselves in the division of carnal men. But that Abraham sat down with them, signifies that even amid these divisions of the carnal, true believers shall persevere to the end. And that about the going down of the sun great fear fell upon Abraham and a horror of great darkness,

[50] Gen. xv. 9-21   [51] Luke i. 34   [52] Luke i. 35

signifies that about the end of this world believers shall be in great perturbation and tribulation, of which the Lord said in the gospel, "For then shall be great tribulation, such as was not from the beginning." [53]

But what is said to Abraham, "Know of a surety that thy seed shall be a stranger in a land not theirs, and they shall reduce them to servitude, and shall afflict them 400 years," is most clearly a prophecy about the people of Israel which was to be in servitude in Egypt. Not that this people was to be in that servitude under the oppressive Egyptians for 400 years, but it is foretold that this should take place in the course of those 400 years. For as it is written of Terah the father of Abraham, "And the days of Terah in Haran were 205 years," [54] not because they were all spent there, but because they were completed there, so it is said here also, "And they shall reduce them to servitude, and shall afflict them 400 years," for this reason, because that number was completed, not because it was all spent in that affliction. The years are said to be 400 in round numbers, although they were a little more— whether you reckon from this time, when these things were promised to Abraham, or from the birth of Isaac, as the seed of Abraham, of which these things are predicted. For, as we have already said above, from the seventy-fifth year of Abraham, when the first promise was made to him, down to the exodus of Israel from Egypt, there are reckoned 430 years, which the apostle thus mentions: "And this I say, that the covenant confirmed by God, the law, which was made 430 years after, cannot disannul, that it should make the promise of none effect." [55] So then these 430 years might be called 400, because they are not much more, especially since part even of that number had already gone by when these things were shown and said to Abraham in vision, or when Isaac was born in his father's 100th year, twenty-five years after the first promise, when of these 430 years there now remained 405, which God was pleased to call 400. No one will doubt that the other things which follow in the prophetic words of God pertain to the people of Israel.

When it is added, "And when the sun was now setting there was a flame, and lo, a smoking furnace, and lamps of fire, which passed through between those pieces," this signifies that at the end of the world the carnal shall be judged by fire. For just as the affliction of the city of God, such as never was before, which is expected to take place under Antichrist, was signified by Abraham's horror of great darkness about the going down of the sun, that is, when the end of the world draws nigh—so at the going down of the sun, that is, at the very end of the world, there is signified by that fire the day of judgment, which separates the carnal who are to be saved by fire from those who are to be condemned in the fire. And then the covenant made with Abraham particularly sets forth the land of Canaan, and names eleven tribes in it from the river of Egypt even to the great river Euphrates. It is not then from the great river of Egypt, that is, the Nile, but from a small one which separates Egypt from Palestine, where the city of Rhinocorura is.

[53] Matt. xxiv. 21   [54] Gen. xi. 32   [55] Gal. iii. 17

CHAPTER XXV

OF SARAH'S HANDMAID, HAGAR, WHOM SHE HERSELF WISHED TO BE ABRAHAM'S CONCUBINE

And here follow the times of Abraham's sons, the one by Hagar the bond maid, the other by Sarah the free woman, about whom we have already spoken in the previous book. As regards this transaction, Abraham is in no way to be branded as guilty concerning this concubine, for he used her for the begetting of progeny, not for the gratification of lust; and not to insult, but rather to obey his wife, who supposed it would be a solace of her barren-ness if she could make use of the fruitful womb of her handmaid to supply the defect of her own nature, and by that law of which the apostle says, "Likewise also the husband hath not power of his own body, but the wife," [56] could, as a wife, make use of him for childbearing by another, when she could not do so in her own person. Here there is no wanton lust, no filthy lewdness. The handmaid is delivered to the husband by the wife for the sake of prog-eny, and is received by the husband for the sake of progeny, each seeking, not guilty excess, but natural fruit. And when the pregnant bond woman de-spised her barren mistress, and Sarah, with womanly jealousy, rather laid the blame of this on her husband, even then Abraham showed that he was not a slavish lover, but a free begetter of children, and that in using Hagar he had guarded the chastity of Sarah his wife, and had gratified her will and not his own—had received her without seeking, had gone in to her without being attached, had impregnated without loving her—for he says, "Behold thy maid is in thy hands: do to her as it pleaseth thee;" [57] a man able to use women as a man should—his wife temperately, his handmaid compliantly, neither intemperately!

CHAPTER XXVI

OF GOD'S ATTESTATION TO ABRAHAM, BY WHICH HE ASSURES HIM, WHEN NOW OLD, OF A SON BY THE BARREN SARAH, AND APPOINTS HIM THE FATHER OF THE NATIONS, AND SEALS HIS FAITH IN THE PROMISE BY THE SACRAMENT OF CIRCUMCISION

After these things Ishmael was born of Hagar; and Abraham might think that in him was fulfilled what God had promised him, saying, when he wished to adopt his home-born servant, "This shall not be thine heir; but he that shall come forth of thee, he shall be thine heir." [58] Therefore, lest he should think that what was promised was fulfilled in the handmaid's son, "when Abram was ninety years old and nine, God appeared to him, and said unto him, I am God; be well-pleasing in my sight, and be without complaint, and

I will make my covenant between me and thee, and will fill thee exceedingly." And Abram fell on his face: and God talked with him, saying, as for me, Behold, my covenant is with thee, and thou shalt be a father of many nations. Neither shall thy name any more be called Abram, but thy name shall be Abraham; for a father of many nations have I made thee. And I will make thee exceeding fruitful, and I will make nations of thee, and kings shall come out of thee. And I will establish my covenant between me and thee and thy seed after thee in their generations for an everlasting covenant, to be a God unto thee, and to thy seed after thee.

And I will give unto thee, and to thy seed after thee, the land wherein thou art a stranger, all the land of Canaan, for an everlasting possession; and I will be their God. And God said unto Abraham, Thou shalt keep my covenant therefore, thou, and thy seed after thee in their generations. This is my covenant, which ye shall keep, between me and you and thy seed after thee; Every man child among you shall be circumcised.

And ye shall circumcise the flesh of your foreskin; and it shall be a token of the covenant betwixt me and you. And he that is eight days old shall be circumcised among you, every man child in your generations, he that is born in the house, or bought with money of any stranger, which is not of thy seed. He that is born in thy house, and he that is bought with thy money, must needs be circumcised: and my covenant shall be in your flesh for an everlasting covenant. And the uncircumcised man child whose flesh or foreskin is not circumcised, that soul shall be cut off from his people; he hath broken my covenant.

And God said unto Abraham, As for Sarai thy wife, thou shalt not call her name Sarai, but Sarah shall her name be. And I will bless her, and give thee a son also of her: yea, I will bless her, and she shall be a mother of nations; kings of people shall be of her. Then Abraham fell upon his face, and laughed, and said in his heart, Shall a child be born unto him that is an hundred years old? and shall Sarah, that is ninety years old, bear?

And Abraham said unto God, O that Ishmael might live before thee! And God said, Sarah thy wife shall bear thee a son indeed; and thou shalt call his name Isaac: and I will establish my covenant with him for an everlasting covenant, and with his seed after him. And as for Ishmael, I have heard thee: Behold, I have blessed him, and will make him fruitful, and will multiply him exceedingly; twelve princes shall he beget, and I will make him a great nation. But my covenant will I establish with Isaac, which Sarah shall bear unto thee at this set time in the next year." [59]

Here there are more distinct promises about the calling of the nations in Isaac, that is, in the son of the promise, by which grace is signified, and not nature; for the son is promised from an old man and a barren old woman. For although God effects even the natural course of procreation, yet where the agency of God is manifest, through the decay or failure of nature, grace

[59] Gen. xvii. 1-21

is more plainly discerned. And because this was to be brought about, not by generation, but by regeneration, circumcision was enjoined now, when a son was promised of Sarah. And by ordering all, not only sons, but also home-born and purchased servants to be circumcised, he testifies that this grace pertains to all. For what else does circumcision signify than a nature renewed on the putting off of the old? And what else does the eighth day mean than Christ, who rose again when the week was completed, that is, after the Sabbath? The very names of the parents are changed: all things proclaim newness, and the new covenant is shadowed forth in the old. For what does the term old covenant imply but the concealing of the new? And what does the term new covenant imply but the revealing of the old? The laughter of Abraham is the exultation of one who rejoices, not the scornful laughter of one who mistrusts. And those words of his in his heart, "Shall a son be born to me that am an hundred years old? and shall Sarah, that is ninety years old, bear?" are not the words of doubt, but of wonder. And when it is said, "And I will give to thee, and to thy seed after thee, the land in which thou art a stranger, all the land of Canaan, for an everlasting possession," if it troubles any one whether this is to be held as fulfilled, or whether its fulfilment may still be looked for, since no kind of earthly possession can be ever-lasting for any nation whatever, let him know that the word translated everlasting by our writers is what the Greeks term αἰώνιον, which is derived from αἰών, the Greek for *saeculum*, an age. But the Latins have not ventured to translate this by *secular*, lest they should change the meaning into something widely different. For many things are called secular which so happen in this world as to pass away even in a short time; but what is termed αἰώνιον either has no end, or lasts to the very end of this world.

CHAPTER XXVII

OF THE MALE, WHO WAS TO LOSE HIS SOUL IF HE WAS NOT CIRCUMCISED ON THE EIGHTH DAY, BECAUSE HE HAD BROKEN GOD'S COVENANT

When it is said, "The male who is not circumcised in the flesh of his fore-skin, that soul shall be cut off from his people, because he hath broken my covenant," [60] some may be troubled how that ought to be understood, since it can be no fault of the infant whose life it is said must perish; nor has the covenant of God been broken by him, but by his parents, who have not taken care to circumcise him. But even the infants, not personally in their own life, but according to the common origin of the human race, have all broken God's covenant in that one in whom all have sinned. [61] Now there are many things called God's covenants besides those two great ones, the old and the new, which any one who pleases may read and know. For the first covenant, which was made with the first man, is just this: "In the day ye

---

[60] Gen. xvii. 14   [61] Rom. v. 12, 19

eat thereof, ye shall surely die." [62] Whence it is written in the book called *Ecclesiasticus*, "All flesh waxeth old as doth a garment. For the covenant from the beginning is, Thou shalt die the death." [63] Now, as the law was more plainly given afterward, and the apostle says, "Where no law is, there is no prevarication," [64] on what supposition is what is said in the psalm true, "I accounted all the sinners of the earth prevaricators," [65] except that all who are held liable for any sin are accused of dealing deceitfully (prevaricating) with some law? If on this account, then, even the infants are, according to the true belief, born in sin, not actual but original, so that we confess they have need of grace for the remission of sins, certainly it must be acknowledged that in the same sense in which they are sinners they are also prevaricators of that law which was given in Paradise, according to the truth of both scriptures, "I accounted all the sinners of the earth prevaricators," and "Where no law is, there is no prevarication." And thus, because circumcision was the sign of regeneration, and the infant, on account of the original sin by which God's covenant was first broken, was not undeservedly to lose his generation unless delivered by regeneration, these divine words are to be understood as if it had been said, Whoever is not born again, that soul shall perish from his people, because he hath broken my covenant, since he also has sinned in Adam with all others. For had He said, Because he hath broken this my covenant, He would have compelled us to understand by it only this of circumcision; but since He has not expressly said what covenant the infant has broken, we are free to understand Him as speaking of that covenant of which the breach can be ascribed to an infant. Yet if any one contends that it is said of nothing else than circumcision, that in it the infant has broken the covenant of God because, he is not circumcised, he must seek some method of explanation by which it may be understood without absurdity (such as this) that he has broken the covenant, because it has been broken in him although not by him. Yet in this case also it is to be observed that the soul of the infant, being guilty of no sin of neglect against itself, would perish unjustly, unless original sin rendered it obnoxious to punishment.

CHAPTER XXVIII

OF THE CHANGE OF NAME IN ABRAHAM AND SARAH, WHO RECEIVED THE GIFT OF FECUNDITY WHEN THEY WERE INCAPABLE OF REGENERATION OWING TO THE BARRENNESS OF ONE, AND THE OLD AGE OF BOTH

Now when a promise so great and clear was made to Abraham, in which it was so plainly said to him, "I have made thee a father of many nations, and I will increase thee exceedingly, and I will make nations of thee, and kings shall go forth of thee. And I will give thee a son of Sarah; and I will

---

[62] Gen. ii. 17　　[63] Ecclus. xv. 17　　[64] Rom. iv. 15　　[65] Ps. cxix. 119, LXX.

bless him, and he shall become nations, and kings of nations shall be of him" [66]—a promise which we now see fulfilled in Christ—from that time forward this couple are not called in Scripture, as formerly, Abram and Sarai, but Abraham and Sarah, as we have called them from the first, for every one does so now. The reason why the name of Abraham was changed is given: "For," He says, "I have made thee a father of many nations." This, then, is to be understood to be the meaning of *Abraham;* but *Abram,* as he was formerly called, means "exalted father." The reason of the change of Sarah's name is not given; but as those say who have written interpretations of the Hebrew names contained in these books, Sarah means "my princess," and Sarai "strength." Whence it is written in the *Epistle to the Hebrews,* "Through faith also Sarah herself received strength to conceive seed." [67] For both were old, as the Scripture testifies; but she was also barren, and had ceased to menstruate, so that she could no longer bear children even if she had not been barren. Further, if a woman is advanced in years, yet still retains the custom of women, she can bear children to a young man, but not to an old man, although that same old man can beget, but only of a young woman; as after Sarah's death Abraham could of Keturah, because he met with her in her lively age. This, then, is what the apostle mentions as wonderful, saying, besides, that Abraham's body was now dead;[68] because at that age he was no longer able to beget children of any woman who retained now only a small part of her natural vigor. Of course we must understand that his body was dead only to some purposes, not to all; for if it was so to all, it would no longer be the aged body of a living man, but the corpse of a dead one. Although that question, how Abraham begot children of Keturah, is usually solved in this way, that the gift of begetting which he received from the Lord, remained even after the death of his wife, yet I think that solution of the question which I have followed is preferable, because, although in our days an old man of a hundred years can beget children of no woman, it was not so then, when men still lived so long that a hundred years did not yet bring on them the decrepitude of old age.

CHAPTER XXIX

OF THE THREE MEN OR ANGELS, IN WHOM THE LORD IS RELATED TO HAVE APPEARED TO ABRAHAM AT THE OAK OF MAMRE

God appeared again to Abraham at the oak of Mamre in three men, who it is not to be doubted were angels, although some think that one of them was Christ, and assert that He was visible before He put on flesh. Now it belongs to the divine power, and invisible, incorporeal, and incommutable nature, without changing itself at all, to appear even to mortal men, not by what it is, but by what is subject to it. And what is not subject to it? Yet if

[66] Gen. xvii. 5, 6, 16   [67] Heb. xi. 11   [68] Heb. xi. 12

they try to establish that one of these three was Christ by the fact that, although he saw three, he addressed the Lord in the singular, as it is written, "And, lo, three men stood by him: and, when he saw them, he ran to meet them from the tent-door, and worshipped toward the ground, and said, Lord, if I have found favor before thee," [69] etc.; why do they not advert to this also, that when two of them came to destroy the Sodomites, while Abraham still spoke to one, calling him Lord, and interceding that he would not destroy the righteous along with the wicked in Sodom, Lot received these two in such a way that he too in his conversation with them addressed the Lord in the singular? For after saying to them in the plural, "Behold, my lords, turn aside into your servant's house," [70] etc., yet it is afterwards said, "And the angels laid hold upon his hand, and the hand of his wife, and the hands of his two daughters, because the Lord was merciful unto him. And it came to pass, whenever they had led him forth abroad, that they said, Save thy life; look not behind thee, neither stay thou in all this region: save thyself in the mountain, lest thou be caught. And Lot said unto them, I pray thee, Lord, since thy servant hath found grace in thy sight," [71] etc. And then after these words the Lord also answered him in the singular, although He was in two angels, saying, "See, I have accepted thy face," [72] etc. This makes it much more credible that both Abraham in the three men and Lot in the two recognized the Lord, addressing Him in the singular number, even when they were addressing men; for they received them as they did for no other reason than that they might minister human refreshment to them as men who needed it. Yet there was about them something so excellent, that those who showed them hospitality as men could not doubt that God was in them as He was wont to be in the prophets, and therefore sometimes addressed them in the plural, and sometimes God in them in the singular. But that they were angels the Scripture testifies, not only in this book of *Genesis*, in which these transactions are related, but also in the *Epistle to the Hebrews*, where in praising hospitality it is said, "For thereby some have entertained angels unawares." [73] By these three men, then, when a son Isaac was again promised to Abraham by Sarah, such a divine oracle was also given that it was said, "Abraham shall become a great and numerous nation, and all the nations of the earth shall be blessed in him." [74] And here these two things are promised with the utmost brevity and fullness—the nation of Israel according to the flesh, and all nations according to faith.

[69] Gen. xviii. 2, 3   [70] Gen. xix. 2   [71] Gen. xix. 16-19   [72] Gen. xix. 21   [73] Heb. xiii. 2   [74] Gen. xviii. 18

CHAPTER XXX

OF LOT'S DELIVERANCE FROM SODOM, AND ITS CONSUMPTION BY FIRE
FROM HEAVEN; AND OF ABIMELECH, WHOSE LUST COULD NOT HARM
SARAH'S CHASTITY

After this promise Lot was delivered out of Sodom, and a fiery rain from
heaven turned into ashes that whole region of the impious city, where custom had made sodomy as prevalent as laws have elsewhere made other kinds
of wickedness. But this punishment of theirs was a specimen of the divine
judgment to come. For what is meant by the angels forbidding those who
were delivered to look back, but that we are not to look back in heart to the
old life which, being regenerated through grace, we have put off, if we think
to escape the last judgment? Lot's wife, indeed, when she looked back, remained, and, being turned into salt, furnished to believing men a condiment
by which to savor somewhat the warning to be drawn from that example.
Then Abraham did again at Gerar, with Abimelech the king of that city,
what he had done in Egypt about his wife, and received her back untouched
in the same way. On this occasion, when the king rebuked Abraham for not
saying she was his wife, and calling her his sister, he explained what he had
been afraid of, and added this further, "And yet indeed she is my sister by
the father's side, but not by the mother's;" [75] for she was Abraham's sister
by his own father, and so near of kin. But her beauty was so great, that even
at that advanced age she could be fallen in love with.

CHAPTER XXXI

OF ISAAC, WHO WAS BORN ACCORDING TO THE PROMISE, WHOSE NAME
WAS GIVEN ON ACCOUNT OF THE LAUGHTER OF BOTH PARENTS

After these things a son was born to Abraham, according to God's promise,
of Sarah, and was called Isaac, which means *laughter*. For his father had
laughed when he was promised to him, in wondering delight, and his mother,
when he was again promised by those three men, had laughed, doubting for
joy; yet she was blamed by the angel because that laughter, although it was
for joy, yet was not full of faith. Afterwards she was confirmed in faith by
the same angel. From this, then, the boy got his name. For when Isaac was
born and called by that name, Sarah showed that her laughter was not that
of scornful reproach, but that of joyful praise; for she said, "God hath made
me to laugh, so that every one who hears will laugh with me." [76] Then in a
little while the bond maid was cast out of the house with her son; and, according to the apostle, these two women signify the old and new covenants—

[75] Gen. xx. 12   [76] Gen. xxi. 6

Sarah representing that of the Jerusalem which is above, that is, the city of God.[77]

CHAPTER XXXII

OF ABRAHAM'S OBEDIENCE AND FAITH, WHICH WERE PROVED BY THE
OFFERING UP OF HIS SON IN SACRIFICE, AND OF SARAH'S DEATH

Among other things, of which it would take too long time to mention the whole, Abraham was tempted about the offering up of his well-beloved son Isaac, to prove his pious obedience, and so make it known to the world, not to God. Now every temptation is not blame-worthy; it may even be praise-worthy, because it furnishes probation. And, for the most part, the human mind cannot attain to self-knowledge otherwise than by making trial of its powers through temptation, by some kind of experimental and not merely verbal self-interrogation; when, if it has acknowledged the gift of God, it is pious, and is consolidated by steadfast grace and not puffed up by vain boasting. Of course Abraham could never believe that God delighted in human sacrifices; yet when the divine commandment thundered, it was to be obeyed, not disputed. Yet Abraham is worthy of praise, because he all along believed that his son, on being offered up, would rise again; for God had said to him, when he was unwilling to fulfill his wife's pleasure by casting out the bond maid and her son, "In Isaac shall thy seed be called." No doubt He then goes on to say, "And as for the son of this bond woman, I will make him a great nation, because he is thy seed." [78] How then is it said, "In Isaac shall thy seed be called," when God calls Ishmael also his seed? The apostle, in explaining this, says, "In Isaac shall thy seed be called, that is, they which are the children of the flesh, these are not the children of God: but the children of the promise are counted for the seed." [79] In order, then, that the children of the promise may be the seed of Abraham, they are called in Isaac, that is, are gathered together in Christ by the call of grace. Therefore the father, holding fast from the first the promise which behoved to be fulfilled through this son whom God had ordered him to slay, did not doubt that he whom he once thought it hopeless he should ever receive would be restored to him when he had offered him up. It is in this way the passage in the *Epistle to the Hebrews* is also to be understood and explained. "By faith," he says, "Abraham overcame, when tempted about Isaac: and he who had received the promise offered up his only son, to whom it was said, In Isaac shall thy seed be called: thinking that God was able to raise him up, even from the dead;" therefore he has added, "from whence also he received him in a similitude." [80] In whose similitude but His of whom the apostle says, "He that spared not His own Son, but delivered Him up for us all?" [81] And on this ac-

---

[77] Gal. iv. 24-26   [78] Gen. xxi. 12, 13   [79] Rom. ix. 7, 8   [80] Heb. xi. 17-19
[81] Rom. viii. 32

count Isaac also himself carried to the place of sacrifice the wood on which he was to be offered up, just as the Lord Himself carried His own cross. Finally, since Isaac was not to be slain, after his father was forbidden to smite him, who was that ram by the offering of which that sacrifice was completed with typical blood? For when Abraham saw him, he was caught by the horns in a thicket. What, then, did he represent but Jesus, who, before He was offered up, was crowned with thorns by the Jews?

But let us rather hear the divine words spoken through the angel. For the Scripture says, "And Abraham stretched forth his hand to take the knife, that he might slay his son. And the Angel of the Lord called unto him from heaven, and said, Abraham. And he said, Here am I. And he said, Lay not thine hand upon the lad, neither do thou anything unto him: for now I know that thou fearest God, and hast not spared thy beloved son for my sake." [82] It is said, "Now I know," that is, Now I have made to be known; for God was not previously ignorant of this. Then, having offered up that ram instead of Isaac his son, "Abraham," as we read, "called the name of that place The Lord seeth: as they say this day, In the mount the Lord hath appeared." [83] As it is said, "Now I know," for Now I have made to be known, so here, "The Lord sees," for The Lord hath appeared, that is, made Himself to be seen. "And the Angel of the Lord called unto Abraham from heaven the second time, saying, By myself have I sworn, saith the Lord; because thou hast done this thing, and hast not spared thy beloved son for my sake; that in blessing I will bless thee, and in multiplying I will multiply thy seed as the stars of heaven, and as the sand which is upon the seashore; and thy seed shall possess by inheritance the cities of the adversaries: and in thy seed shall all the nations of the earth be blessed; because thou hast obeyed my voice." [84] In this manner is that promise concerning the calling of the nations in the seed of Abraham confirmed even by the oath of God, after that burnt-offering which typified Christ. For He had often promised, but never sworn. And what is the oath of God, the true and faithful, but a confirmation of the promise, and a certain reproof to the unbelieving?

After these things Sarah died, in the 127th year of her life, and the 137th of her husband; for he was ten years older than she, as he himself says, when a son is promised to him by her: "Shall a son be born to me that am an hundred years old? and shall Sarah, that is ninety years old, bear?" [85] Then Abraham bought a field, in which he buried his wife. And then, according to Stephen's account, he was settled in that land, entering then on actual possession of it—that is, after the death of his father, who is inferred to have died two years before.

---

[82] Gen. xxii. 10-12   [83] Gen. xxii. 14   [84] Gen. xxii. 15-18   [85] Gen. xvii. 17

CHAPTER XXXIII

OF REBECCA, THE GRAND-DAUGHTER OF NAHOR, WHOM ISAAC TOOK TO WIFE

Isaac married Rebecca, the grand-daughter of Nahor, his father's brother, when he was forty years old, that is, in the 140th year of his father's life, three years after his mother's death. Now when a servant was sent to Mesopotamia by his father to fetch her, and when Abraham said to that servant, "Put thy hand under my thigh, and I will make thee swear by the Lord, the God of heaven, and the Lord of the earth, that thou shalt not take a wife unto my son Isaac of the daughters of the Canaanites," [86] what else was pointed out by this, but that the Lord, the God of heaven, and the Lord of the earth, was to come in the flesh which was to be derived from that thigh? Are these small tokens of the foretold truth which we see fulfilled in Christ?

CHAPTER XXXIV

WHAT IS MEANT BY ABRAHAM'S MARRYING KETURAH AFTER SARAH'S DEATH

What did Abraham mean by marrying Keturah after Sarah's death? Far be it from us to suspect him of incontinence, especially when he had reached such an age and such sanctity of faith. Or was he still seeking to beget children, though he held fast, with most approved faith, the promise of God that his children should be multiplied out of Isaac as the stars of heaven and the dust of the earth? And yet, if Hagar and Ishmael, as the apostle teaches us, signified the carnal people of the old covenant, why may not Keturah and her sons also signify the carnal people who think they belong to the new covenant? For both are called both the wives and the concubines of Abraham; but Sarah is never called a concubine (but only a wife). For when Hagar is given to Abraham, it is written, "And Sarai, Abraham's wife, took Hagar the Egyptian, her handmaid, after Abraham had dwelt ten years in the land of Canaan, and gave her to her husband Abram to be his wife." [87] And of Keturah, whom he took after Sarah's departure, we read, "Then again Abraham took a wife, whose name was Keturah." [88] Lo! both are called wives, yet both are found to have been concubines; for the Scripture afterward says, "And Abraham gave his whole estate unto Isaac his son. But unto the sons of his concubines Abraham gave gifts, and sent them away from his son Isaac (while he yet lived), eastward, unto the east country." [89] Therefore the sons of the concubines, that is, the heretics and the carnal Jews, have some gifts, but do not attain the promised kingdom; "For they which are the children of the flesh, these are not the children of God: but the

[86] Gen. xxiv. 2, 3   [87] Gen. xvi. 3   [88] Gen. xxv. 1   [89] Gen. xxv. 5, 6

children of the promise are counted for the seed, of whom it was said, In Isaac shall thy seed be called." [90] For I do not see why Keturah, who was married after the wife's death, should be called a concubine, except on account of this mystery. But if any one is unwilling to put such meanings on these things, he need not calumniate Abraham. For what if even this was provided against the heretics who were to be the opponents of second marriages, so that it might be shown that it was no sin in the case of the father of many nations himself, when, after his wife's death, he married again? And Abraham died when he was 175 years old, so that he left his son Isaac seventy-five years old, having begotten him when 100 years old.

CHAPTER XXXV

WHAT WAS INDICATED BY THE DIVINE ANSWER ABOUT THE TWINS STILL SHUT UP IN THE WOMB OF REBECCA THEIR MOTHER

Let us now see how the times of the city of God run on from this point among Abraham's descendants. In the time from the first year of Isaac's life to the seventieth, when his sons were born, the only memorable thing is, that when he prayed God that his wife, who was barren, might bear, and the Lord granted what he sought, and she conceived, the twins leapt while still enclosed in her womb. And when she was troubled by this struggle, and inquired of the Lord, she received this answer: "Two nations are in thy womb, and two manner of people shall be separated from thy bowels; and the one people shall overcome the other people, and the elder shall serve the younger." [91] The Apostle Paul would have us understand this as a great instance of grace;[92] for the children being not yet born, neither having done any good or evil, the younger is chosen without any good desert, and the elder is rejected, when beyond doubt, as regards original sin, both were alike, and as regards actual sin, neither had any. But the plan of the work on hand does not permit me to speak more fully of this matter now, and I have said much about it in other works. Only that saying, "The elder shall serve the younger," is understood by our writers, almost without exception, to mean that the elder people, the Jews, shall serve the younger people, the Christians. And truly, although this might seem to be fulfilled in the Idumean nation, which was born of the elder (who had two names, being called both Esau and Edom, whence the name Idumeans) because it was afterwards to be overcome by the people which sprang from the younger, that is, by the Israelites, and was to become subject to them; yet it is more suitable to believe that, when it was said, "The one people shall overcome the other people, and the elder shall serve the younger," that prophecy meant some greater thing; and what is that except what is evidently fulfilled in the Jews and Christians?

[90] Rom. ix. 7, 8   [91] Gen. xxv. 23   [92] Rom. ix. 10-13

CHAPTER XXXVI

Isaac also received such an oracle as his father had often received. Of this oracle it is thus written: "And there was a famine over the land, beside the first famine that was in the days of Abraham. And Isaac went unto Abimelech king of the Philistines unto Gerar. And the Lord appeared unto him, and said, Go not down into Egypt; but dwell in the land which I shall tell thee of. And abide in this land, and I will be with thee, and will bless thee: unto thee and unto thy seed I will give all this land; and I will establish mine oath, which I sware unto Abraham thy father: and I will multiply thy seed as the stars of heaven, and will give unto thy seed all this land: and in thy seed shall all the nations of the earth be blessed; because that Abraham thy father obeyed my voice, and kept my precepts, my commandments, my righteousness, and my laws." [93] This patriarch neither had another wife, nor any concubine, but was content with the twin-children begotten by one act of generation. He also was afraid, when he lived among strangers, of being brought into danger owing to the beauty of his wife, and did like his father in calling her his sister, and not telling that she was his wife; for she was his near blood-relation by the father's and mother's side. She also remained untouched by the strangers, when it was known she was his wife. Yet we ought not to prefer him to his father because he knew no woman besides his one wife. For beyond doubt the merits of his father's faith and obedience were greater, inasmuch as God says it is for his sake He does Isaac good: "In thy seed," He says, "shall all the nations of the earth be blessed, because that Abraham thy father obeyed my voice, and kept my precepts, my commandments, my statutes, and my laws." And again in another oracle He says, "I am the God of Abraham thy father: fear not, for I am with thee, and will bless thee, and multiply thy seed for my servant Abraham's sake." [94] So that we must understand how chastely Abraham acted, because imprudent men, who seek some support for their own wickedness in the Holy Scriptures, think he acted through lust. We may also learn this, not to compare men by single good things, but to consider everything in each; for it may happen that one man has something in his life and character in which he excels another, and it may be far more excellent than that in which the other excels him. And thus, according to sound and true judgment, while continence is preferable to marriage, yet a believing married man is better than a continent unbeliever; for the unbeliever is not only less praiseworthy, but is even highly detestable. We must conclude, then, that both are good; yet so as to hold that the married man who is most faithful and most obedient is cer-

[93] Gen. xxvi. 1-5   [94] Gen. xxvi. 24

tainly better than the continent man whose faith and obedience are less. But
if equal in other things, who would hesitate to prefer the continent man to
the married?

CHAPTER XXXVII

OF THE THINGS MYSTICALLY PREFIGURED IN ESAU AND JACOB

Isaac's two sons, Esau and Jacob, grew up together. The primacy of the
elder was transferred to the younger by a bargain and agreement between
them, when the elder immoderately lusted after the lentiles the younger had
prepared for food, and for that price sold his birthright to him, confirming it
with an oath. We learn from this that a person is to be blamed, not for the
kind of food he eats, but for immoderate greed. Isaac grew old, and old age
deprived him of his eyesight. He wished to bless the elder son, and instead of
the elder, who was hairy, unwittingly blessed the younger, who put himself
under his father's hands, having covered himself with kid-skins, as if bearing
the sins of others. Lest we should think this guile of Jacob's was fraudulent
guile, instead of seeking in it the mystery of a great thing, the Scripture has
predicted in the words just before, "Esau was a cunning hunter, a man of the
field; and Jacob was a simple man, dwelling at home." [95] Some of our writers
have interpreted this, "without guile." But whether the Greek ἄπλαστος
means "without guile," or "simple," or rather "without feigning," in the receiving of that blessing what is the guile of the man without guile? What is
the guile of the simple, what the fiction of the man who does not lie, but a
profound mystery of the truth? But what is the blessing itself? "See," he
says, "the smell of my son is as the smell of a full field which the Lord hath
blessed: therefore God give thee of the dew of heaven, and of the fruitfulness
of the earth, and plenty of corn and wine: let nations serve thee, and princes
adore thee: and be lord of thy brethren, and let thy father's sons adore thee:
cursed be he that curseth thee, and blessed be he that blesseth thee." [96] The
blessing of Jacob is therefore a proclamation of Christ to all nations. It is this
which has come to pass, and is now being fulfilled. Isaac is the law and the
prophecy: even by the mouth of the Jews Christ is blessed by prophecy as by
one who knows not, because it is itself not understood. The world like a field
is filled with the odor of Christ's name: His is the blessing of the dew of
heaven, that is, of the showers of divine words; and of the fruitfulness of the
earth, that is, of the gathering together of the peoples: His is the plenty of
corn and wine, that is, the multitude that gathers bread and wine in the
sacrament of His body and blood. Him the nations serve, Him princes
adore. He is the Lord of His brethren, because His people rules over the
Jews. Him His Father's sons adore, that is, the sons of Abraham according
to faith; for He Himself is the son of Abraham according to the flesh. He is

[95] Gen. xxv. 27   [96] Gen. xxvii. 27-29

cursed that curseth Him, and he that blesseth Him is blessed. Christ, I say, who is ours is blessed, that is, truly spoken of out of the mouths of the Jews, when, although erring, they yet sing the law and the prophets, and think they are blessing another for whom they erringly hope. So, when the elder son claims the promised blessing, Isaac is greatly afraid, and wonders when he knows that he has blessed one instead of the other, and demands who he is; yet he does not complain that he has been deceived, yea, when the great mystery is revealed to him, in his secret heart he at once eschews anger, and confirms the blessing. "Who then," he says, "hath hunted me venison, and brought it me, and I have eaten of all before thou camest, and have blessed him, and he shall be blessed?" [97] Who would not rather have expected the curse of an angry man here, if these things had been done in an earthly manner, and not by inspiration from above? O things done, yet done prophetically; on the earth, yet celestially; by men, yet divinely! If everything that is fertile of so great mysteries should be examined carefully, many volumes would be filled; but the moderate compass fixed for this work compels us to hasten to other things.

CHAPTER XXXVIII

OF JACOB'S MISSION TO MESOPOTAMIA TO GET A WIFE, AND OF THE VISION WHICH HE SAW IN A DREAM BY THE WAY, AND OF HIS GETTING FOUR WOMEN WHEN HE SOUGHT ONE WIFE

Jacob was sent by his parents to Mesopotamia that he might take a wife there. These were his father's words on sending him: "Thou shalt not take a wife of the daughters of the Canaanites. Arise, fly to Mesopotamia, to the house of Bethuel, thy mother's father, and take thee a wife from thence of the daughters of Laban thy mother's brother. And my God bless thee, and increase thee, and multiply thee; and thou shalt be an assembly of peoples; and give to thee the blessing of Abraham thy father, and to thy seed after thee; that thou mayest inherit the land wherein thou dwellest, which God gave unto Abraham." [98] Now we understand here that the seed of Jacob is separated from Isaac's other seed which came through Esau. For when it is said, "In Isaac shall thy seed be called," [99] by this seed is meant solely the city of God; so that from it is separated Abraham's other seed, which was in the son of the bond woman, and which was to be in the sons of Keturah. But until now it had been uncertain regarding Isaac's twin-sons whether that blessing belonged to both or only to one of them; and if to one, which of them it was. This is now declared when Jacob is prophetically blessed by his father, and it is said to him, "And thou shalt be an assembly of peoples, and God give to thee the blessing of Abraham thy father."

When Jacob was going to Mesopotamia, he received in a dream an oracle,

[97] Gen. xxvii. 33   [98] Gen. xxviii. 1-4   [99] Gen. xxi. 12

of which it is thus written: "And Jacob went out from the well of the oath,[100] and went to Haran. And he came to a place, and slept there, for the sun was set; and he took of the stones of the place, and put them at his head, and slept in that place, and dreamed. And behold a ladder set up on the earth, and the top of it reached to heaven; and the angels of God ascended and descended by it. And the Lord stood above it, and said, I am the God of Abraham thy father, and the God of Isaac; fear not: the land whereon thou sleepest, to thee will I give it, and to thy seed; and thy seed shall be as the dust of the earth; and it shall be spread abroad to the sea, and to Africa, and to the north, and to the east: and all the tribes of the earth shall be blessed in thee and in thy seed. And, behold, I am with thee, to keep thee in all thy way wherever thou goest, and I will bring thee back into this land; for I will not leave thee, until I have done all which I have spoken to thee of. And Jacob awoke out of his sleep, and said, Surely the Lord is in this place, and I knew it not. And he was afraid, and said, How dreadful is this place! this is none other but the house of God, and this is the gate of heaven. And Jacob arose, and took the stone that he had put under his head there, and set it up for a memorial, and poured oil upon the top of it. And Jacob called the name of that place the house of God." [101] This is prophetic. For Jacob did not pour oil on the stone in an idolatrous way, as if making it a god; neither did he adore that stone, or sacrifice to it. But since the name of Christ comes from the chrism or anointing, something pertaining to the great mystery was certainly represented in this. And the Saviour Himself is understood to bring this latter to remembrance in the gospel, when He says of Nathanael, "Behold an Israelite indeed, in whom is no guile!" [102] because Israel who saw this vision is no other than Jacob. And in the same place He says, "Verily, verily, I say unto you, Ye shall see heaven open, and the angels of God ascending and descending upon the Son of man."

Jacob went on to Mesopotamia to take a wife from thence. And the divine Scripture points out how, without unlawfully desiring any of them, he came to have four women, of whom he begat twelve sons and one daughter; for he had come to take only one. But when one was falsely given him in place of the other, he did not send her away after unwittingly using her in the night, lest he should seem to have put her to shame; but as at that time, in order to multiply posterity, no law forbade a plurality of wives, he took her also to whom alone he had promised marriage. As she was barren, she gave her handmaid to her husband that she might have children by her; and her elder sister did the same thing in imitation of her, although she had borne, because she desired to multiply progeny. We do not read that Jacob sought any but one, or that he used many, except for the purpose of begetting offspring, saving conjugal rights; and he would not have done this, had not his wives, who had legitimate power over their own husband's body, urged him to do it. So he begat twelve sons and one daughter by four women. Then he en-

---

[100] Beer-sheba   [101] Gen. xxviii. 10-19   [102] John i. 47, 51

tered into Egypt by his son Joseph, who was sold by his brethren for envy, and carried there, and who was there exalted.

CHAPTER XXXIX

THE REASON WHY JACOB WAS ALSO CALLED ISRAEL

As I said a little ago, Jacob was also called Israel, the name which was most prevalent among the people descended from him. Now this name was given him by the angel who wrestled with him on the way back from Mesopotamia, and who was most evidently a type of Christ. For when Jacob overcame him, doubtless with his own consent, that the mystery might be represented, it signified Christ's passion, in which the Jews are seen overcoming Him. And yet he besought a blessing from the very angel he had overcome; and so the imposition of this name was the blessing. For Israel means *seeing God*,[103] which will at last be the reward of all the saints. The angel also touched him on the breadth of the thigh when he was overcoming him, and in that way made him lame. So that Jacob was at one and the same time blessed and lame: blessed in those among that people who believed in Christ, and lame in the unbelieving. For the breadth of the thigh is the multitude of the family. For there are many of that race of whom it was prophetically said beforehand, "And they have halted in their paths." [104]

CHAPTER XL

HOW IT IS SAID THAT JACOB WENT INTO EGYPT WITH SEVENTY-FIVE SOULS, WHEN MOST OF THOSE WHO ARE MENTIONED WERE BORN AT A LATER PERIOD

Seventy-five men are reported to have entered Egypt along with Jacob, counting him with his children. In this number only two women are mentioned, one a daughter, the other a grand-daughter. But when the thing is carefully considered, it does not appear that Jacob's offspring was so numerous on the day or year when he entered Egypt. There are also included among them the great-grandchildren of Joseph, who could not possibly be born already. For Jacob was then 130 years old, and his son Joseph thirty-nine; and as it is plain that he took a wife when he was thirty or more, how could he in nine years have great-grandchildren by the children whom he had by that wife? Now since, Ephraim and Manasseh, the sons of Joseph, could not even have children, for Jacob found them boys under nine years old when he entered Egypt, in what way are not only their sons but their grandsons reckoned among those seventy-five who then entered Egypt with Jacob? For there is reckoned there Machir the son of Manasseh, grandson of

---

[103] Gen. xxxii. 28: Israel = a prince of God; 30; Peniel = the face of God.
[104] Ps. xviii. 45

Joseph, and Machir's son, that is, Gilead, grandson of Manasseh, great-grandson of Joseph; there, too, is he whom Ephraim, Joseph's other son, begot, that is, Shuthelah, grandson of Joseph, and Shuthelah's son Ezer, grandson of Ephraim, and great-grandson of Joseph, who could not possibly be in existence when Jacob came into Egypt, and there found his grandsons, the sons of Joseph, their grandsires, still boys under nine years of age.[105] But doubtless, when the Scripture mentions Jacob's entrance into Egypt with seventy-five souls, it does not mean one day, or one year, but that whole time as long as Joseph lived, who was the cause of his entrance. For the same Scripture speaks thus of Joseph: "And Joseph dwelt in Egypt, he and his brethren, and all his father's house: and Joseph lived 110 years, and saw Ephraim's children of the third generation." [106] That is, his great-grandson, the third from Ephraim; for the third generation means son, grandson, great-grandson. Then it is added, "The children also of Machir, the son of Manasseh, were born upon Joseph's knees." [107] And this is that grandson of Manasseh, and great-grandson of Joseph. But the plural number is employed according to scriptural usage; for the one daughter of Jacob is spoken of as daughters, just as in the usage of the Latin tongue *liberi* is used in the plural for children even when there is only one. Now, when Joseph's own happiness is proclaimed, because he could see his great-grandchildren, it is by no means to be thought they already existed in the thirty-ninth year of their great-grandsire Joseph, when his father Jacob came to him in Egypt. But those who diligently look into these things will the less easily be mistaken, because it is written, "These are the names of the sons of Israel who entered into Egypt along with Jacob their father." [108] For this means that the seventy-five are reckoned along with him, not that they were all with him when he entered Egypt; for, as I have said, the whole period during which Joseph, who occasioned his entrance, lived, is held to be the time of that entrance.

CHAPTER XLI

OF THE BLESSING WHICH JACOB PROMISED IN JUDAH HIS SON

If, on account of the Christian people in whom the city of God sojourns in the earth, we look for the flesh of Christ in the seed of Abraham, setting aside the sons of the concubines, we have Isaac; if in the seed of Isaac, setting aside Esau, who is also Edom, we have Jacob, who also is Israel; if in the seed of Israel himself, setting aside the rest, we have Judah, because Christ sprang of the tribe of Judah. Let us hear, then, how Israel, when dying in Egypt, in blessing his sons, prophetically blessed Judah. He says: "Judah, thy brethren shall praise thee: thy hands shall be on the back of

[105] Augustine here follows the Septuagint, which at Gen. xlvi. 20 adds these names to those of Manasseh and Ephraim, and at ver. 27 gives the whole number as seventy-five   [106] Gen. l. 22, 23   [107] Gen. l. 23   [108] Gen. xlvi. 8

thine enemies; thy father's children shall adore thee. Judah is a lion's whelp: from the sprouting, my son, thou art gone up: lying down, thou hast slept as a lion, and as a lion's whelp; who shall awake him? A prince shall not be lacking out of Judah, and a leader from his thighs, until the things come that are laid up for him; and He shall be the expectation of the nations. Binding his foal unto the vine, and his ass's foal to the choice vine; he shall wash his robe in wine, and his clothes in the blood of the grape: his eyes are red with wine, and his teeth are whiter than milk." [109] I have expounded these words in disputing against Faustus the Manichaean; and I think it is enough to make the truth of this prophecy shine, to remark that the death of Christ is predicted by the word about his lying down, and not the necessity, but the voluntary character of His death, in the title of lion. That power He Himself proclaims in the gospel, saying, "I have the power of laying down my life, and I have the power of taking it again. No man taketh it from me; but I lay it down of myself, and take it again." [110] So the lion roared, so He fulfilled what He said. For to this power what is added about the resurrection refers, "Who shall awake him?" This means that no man but Himself has raised Him, who also said of His own body, "Destroy this temple, and in three days I will raise it up." [111] And the very nature of His death, that is, the height of the cross, is understood by the single word, "Thou are gone up." The evangelist explains what is added, "Lying down, thou hast slept," when he says, "He bowed His head, and gave up the ghost." [112] Or at least His burial is to be understood, in which He lay down sleeping, and whence no man raised Him, as the prophets did some, and as He Himself did others; but He Himself rose up as if from sleep. As for His robe which He washes in wine, that is, cleanses from sin in His own blood, of which blood those who are baptized know the mystery, so that he adds, "And his clothes in the blood of the grape," what is it but the Church? "And his eyes are red with wine," [these are] His spiritual people drunken with His cup, of which the psalm sings, "And thy cup that makes drunken, how excellent it is!" "And his teeth are whiter than milk" [113]—that is, the nutritive words which, according to the apostle, the babes drink, being as yet unfit for solid food.[114] And it is He in whom the promises of Judah were laid up, so that until they come, princes, that is, the kings of Israel, shall never be lacking out of Judah. "And He is the expectation of the nations." This is too plain to need exposition.

[109] Gen. xlix. 8-12   [110] John x. 18   [111] John ii. 19   [112] John xix. 30   [113] Gen. xlix. 12   [114] I Pet. ii. 2; I Cor. iii. 2

CHAPTER XLII

OF THE SONS OF JOSEPH, WHOM JACOB BLESSED, PROPHETICALLY CHANGING HIS HANDS

Now, as Isaac's two sons, Esau and Jacob, furnished a type of the two people, the Jews and the Christians (although as pertains to carnal descent it was not the Jews but the Idumeans who came of the seed of Esau, nor the Christian nations but rather the Jews who came of Jacob's; for the type holds only as regards the saying, "The elder shall serve the younger" [115]), so the same thing happened in Joseph's two sons; for the elder was a type of the Jews, and the younger of the Christians. For when Jacob was blessing them, and laid his right hand on the younger, who was at his left, and his left hand on the elder, who was at his right, this seemed wrong to their father, and he admonished his father by trying to correct his mistake and show him which was the elder. But he would not change his hands, but said, "I know, my son, I know. He also shall become a people, and he also shall be exalted; but his younger brother shall be greater than he, and his seed shall become a multitude of nations." [116] And these two promises show the same thing. For that one is to become "a people;" this one "a multitude of nations." And what can be more evident than that these two promises comprehend the people of Israel, and the whole world of Abraham's seed, the one according to the flesh, the other according to faith?

CHAPTER XLIII

OF THE TIMES OF MOSES AND JOSHUA THE SON OF NUN, OF THE JUDGES, AND THEREAFTER OF THE KINGS, OF WHOM SAUL WAS THE FIRST, BUT DAVID IS TO BE REGARDED AS THE CHIEF, BOTH BY THE OATH AND BY MERIT

Jacob being dead, and Joseph also, during the remaining 144 years until they went out of the land of Egypt, that nation increased to an incredible degree, even although wasted by so great persecutions, that at one time the male children were murdered at their birth, because the wondering Egyptians were terrified at the too great increase of that people. Then Moses, being stealthily kept from the murderers of the infants, was brought to the royal house, God preparing to do great things by him, and was nursed and adopted by the daughter of Pharaoh (that was the name of all the kings of Egypt), and became so great a man that he—yea, rather God, who had promised this to Abraham, by him—drew that nation, so wonderfully multiplied, out of the yoke of hardest and most grievous servitude it had borne there. At first, indeed, he fled thence (we are told he fled into the land of

[115] Gen. xxv. 23   [116] Gen. xlviii. 19

Midian), because, in defending an Israelite, he had slain an Egyptian, and was afraid. Afterward, being divinely commissioned in the power of the Spirit of God, he overcame the magi of Pharaoh who resisted him. Then, when the Egyptians would not let God's people go, ten memorable plagues were brought by Him upon them—the water turned into blood, the frogs and lice, the flies, the death of the cattle, the boils, the hail, the locusts, the darkness, the death of the first-born. At last the Egyptians were destroyed in the Red Sea while pursuing the Israelites, whom they had let go when at length they were broken by so many great plagues. The divided sea made a way for the Israelites who were departing, but, returning on itself, it overwhelmed their pursuers with its waves. Then for forty years the people of God went through the desert, under the leadership of Moses, when the tabernacle of testimony was dedicated, in which God was worshipped by sacrifices prophetic of things to come, and that was after the law had been very terribly given in the mount, for its divinity was most plainly attested by wonderful signs and voices. This took place soon after the exodus from Egypt, when the people had entered the desert, on the fiftieth day after the passover was celebrated by the offering up of a lamb, which is so completely a type of Christ, foretelling that through His sacrificial passion He should go from this world to the Father (for *pascha* in the Hebrew tongue means *transit*), that when the new covenant was revealed, after Christ our passover was offered up, the Holy Spirit came from heaven on the fiftieth day; and He is called in the gospel the Finger of God, because He recalls to our remembrance the things done before by way of types, and because the tables of that law are said to have been written by the finger of God.

On the death of Moses, Joshua the son of Nun ruled the people, and led them into the land of promise, and divided it among them. By these two wonderful leaders wars were also carried on most prosperously and wonderfully, God calling to witness that they had got these victories not so much on account of the merit of the Hebrew people as on account of the sins of the nations they subdued. After these leaders there were judges, when the people were settled in the land of promise, so that, in the meantime, the first promise made to Abraham began to be fulfilled about the one nation, that is, the Hebrew, and about the land of Canaan; but not as yet the promise about all nations, and the whole wide world, for that was to be fulfilled, not by the observances of the old law, but by the advent of Christ in the flesh, and by the faith of the gospel. And it was to prefigure this that it was not Moses, who received the law for the people on Mount Sinai, that led the people into the land of promise, but Joshua, whose name also was changed at God's command, so that he was called Jesus. But in the times of the judges prosperity alternated with adversity in war, according as the sins of the people and the mercy of God were displayed.

We come next to the times of the kings. The first who reigned was Saul; and when he was rejected and laid low in battle, and his offspring rejected so that no kings should arise out of it, David succeeded to the kingdom, whose son Christ is chiefly called. He was made a kind of starting-point and beginning of the advanced youth of God's people, who had passed a kind of age of puberty from Abraham to this David. And it is not in vain that the evangelist Matthew records the generations in such a way as to sum up this first period from Abraham to David in fourteen generations. For from the age of puberty man begins to be capable of generation; therefore he starts the list of generations from Abraham, who also was made the father of many nations when he got his name changed. So that previously this family of God's people was in its childhood, from Noah to Abraham; and for that reason the first language was then learned, that is, the Hebrew. For man begins to speak in childhood, the age succeeding infancy, which is so termed because then he cannot speak.[117] And that first age is quite drowned in oblivion, just as the first age of the human race was blotted out by the flood; for who is there that can remember his infancy? Wherefore in this progress of the city of God, as the previous book contained that first age, so this one ought to contain the second and third ages, in which third age, as was shown by the heifer of three years old, the she-goat of three years old, and the ram of three years old, the yoke of the law was imposed, and there appeared abundance of sins, and the beginning of the earthly kingdom arose, in which there were not lacking spiritual men, of whom the turtle-dove and pigeon represented the mystery.

[117] *Infans,* from *in,* not, and *fari,* to speak

BOOK SEVENTEEN

ARGUMENT

In this book the history of the City of God is traced during the period of the Kings and Prophets from Samuel to David, even to Christ; and the prophecies which are recorded in the books of Kings, Psalms, and those of Solomon, are interpreted of Christ and the Church.

CHAPTER I

OF THE PROPHETIC AGE

By THE favor of God we have treated distinctly of His promises made to Abraham, that both the nation of Israel according to the flesh, and all nations according to faith, should be his seed, and the City of God, proceeding according to the order of time, will point out how they were fulfilled. Having therefore in the previous book come down to the reign of David, we shall now treat of what remains, so far as may seem sufficient for the object of this work, beginning at the same reign. Now, from the time when holy Samuel began to prophesy, and ever onward until the people of Israel was led captive into Babylonia, and until, according to the prophecy of holy Jeremiah, on Israel's return thence after seventy years, the house of God was built anew, this whole period is the prophetic age. For although both the patriarch Noah himself, in whose days the whole earth was destroyed by the flood, and others before and after him down to this time when there began to be kings over the people of God, may not undeservedly be styled prophets, on account of certain things pertaining to the city of God and the kingdom of heaven, which they either predicted or in any way signified should come to pass, and especially since we read that some of them, as Abraham and Moses, were expressly so styled, yet those are most and chiefly called the days of the prophets from the time when Samuel began to prophesy, who at God's command first anointed Saul to be king, and, on his rejection, David himself, whom others of his issue should succeed as long as it was fitting they should do so. If, therefore, I wished to rehearse all that the prophets have predicted concerning Christ, while the city of God, with its members dying and being born in constant succession, ran its course through those times, this work would extend beyond all bounds. First, because the Scripture itself, even when, in treating in order of the kings and of their deeds and the events of their reigns, it seems to be occupied in narrating as

366

with historical diligence the affairs transacted, will be found, if the things handled by it are considered with the aid of the Spirit of God, either more, or certainly not less, intent on foretelling things to come than on relating things past. And who that thinks even a little about it does not know how laborious and prolix a work it would be, and how many volumes it would require to search this out by thorough investigation and demonstrate it by argument? And then, because of that which without dispute pertains to prophecy, there are so many things concerning Christ and the kingdom of heaven, which is the city of God, that to explain these a larger discussion would be necessary than the due proportion of this work admits of. Therefore I shall, if I can, so limit myself, that in carrying through this work, I may, with God's help, neither say what is superfluous nor omit what is necessary.

CHAPTER II

AT WHAT TIME THE PROMISE OF GOD WAS FULFILLED CONCERNING THE LAND OF CANAAN, WHICH EVEN CARNAL ISRAEL GOT IN POSSESSION

In the preceding book we said, that in the promise of God to Abraham two things were promised from the beginning, the one, namely, that his seed should possess the land of Canaan, which was intimated when it was said, "Go into a land that I will show thee, and I will make of thee a great nation;" [1] but the other far more excellent, concerning not the carnal but the spiritual seed, by which he is the father, not of the one nation of Israel, but of all nations who follow the footsteps of his faith, which began to be promised in these words, "And in thee shall all families of the earth be blessed." [2] And thereafter we showed by yet many other proofs that these two things were promised. Therefore the seed of Abraham, that is, the people of Israel according to the flesh, already was in the land of promise; and there, not only by holding and possessing the cities of the enemies, but also by having kings, had already begun to reign, the promises of God concerning that people being already in great part fulfilled: not only those that were made to those three fathers, Abraham, Isaac, and Jacob, and whatever others were made in their times, but those also that were made through Moses himself, by whom the same people was set free from servitude in Egypt, and by whom all bygone things were revealed in his times, when he led the people through the wilderness. But neither by the illustrious leader Jesus the son of Nun, who led that people into the land of promise, and, after driving out the nations, divided it among the twelve tribes according to God's command, and died; nor after him, in the whole time of the judges, was the promise of God concerning the land of Canaan fulfilled, that it should extend from

[1] Gen. xii. 1, 2   [2] Gen. xii. 3

some river of Egypt even to the great river Euphrates; nor yet was it still prophesied as to come, but its fulfillment was expected. And it was fulfilled through David, and Solomon his son, whose kingdom was extended over the whole promised space; for they subdued all those nations, and made them tributary. And thus, under those kings, the seed of Abraham was established in the land of promise according to the flesh, that is, in the land of Canaan, so that nothing yet remained to the complete fulfillment of that earthly promise of God, except that, so far as pertains to temporal prosperity, the Hebrew nation should remain in the same land by the succession of posterity in an unshaken state even to the end of this mortal age, if it obeyed the laws of the Lord its God. But since God knew it would not do this, He used His temporal punishments also for training His few faithful ones in it, and for giving needful warning to those who should afterwards be in all nations, in whom the other promise, revealed in the New Testament, was about to be fulfilled through the incarnation of Christ.

CHAPTER III

OF THE THREE-FOLD MEANING OF THE PROPHECIES, WHICH ARE TO BE REFERRED NOW TO THE EARTHLY, NOW TO THE HEAVENLY JERUSALEM, AND NOW AGAIN TO BOTH

Wherefore just as that divine oracle to Abraham, Isaac, and Jacob, and all the other prophetic signs or sayings which are given in the earlier sacred writings, so also the other prophecies from this time of the kings pertain partly to the nation of Abraham's flesh, and partly to that seed of his in which all nations are blessed as fellow-heirs of Christ by the New Testament, to the possessing of eternal life and the kingdom of the heavens. Therefore they pertain partly to the bond maid who gendereth to bondage, that is, the earthly Jerusalem, which is in bondage with her children; but partly to the free city of God, that is, the true Jerusalem eternal in the heavens, whose children are all those that live according to God in the earth: but there are some things among them which are understood to pertain to both—to the bond maid properly, to the free woman figuratively.[3]

Therefore prophetic utterances of three kinds are to be found; forasmuch as there are some relating to the earthly Jerusalem, some to the heavenly, and some to both. I think it proper to prove what I say by examples. The prophet Nathan was sent to convict king David of heinous sin, and predict to him what future evils should be consequent on it. Who can question that this and the like pertain to the terrestrial city, whether publicly, that is, for the safety or help of the people, or privately, when there are given forth for each one's private good divine utterances whereby something of the future may be known for the use of temporal life? But where we read, "Behold, the

[3] Gal. iv. 22-31

days come, saith the Lord, that I will make for the house of Israel, and for
the house of Judah, a new testament: not according to the testament that I
settled for their fathers in the day when I laid hold of their hand to lead them
out of the land of Egypt; because they continued not in my testament, and
I regarded them not, saith the Lord. For this is the testament that I will
make for the house of Israel: after those days, saith the Lord, I will give my
laws in their mind, and will write them upon their hearts, and I will see to
them; and I will be to them a God, and they shall be to me a people" [4]—
without doubt this is prophesied to the Jerusalem above, whose reward is
God Himself, and whose chief and entire good it is to have Him, and to be
His. But this pertains to both, that the city of God is called Jerusalem, and
that it is prophesied the house of God shall be in it; and this prophecy seems
to be fulfilled when king Solomon builds that most noble temple. For these
things both happened in the earthly Jerusalem, as history shows, and were
types of the heavenly Jerusalem. And this kind of prophecy, as it were compacted and commingled of both the others in the ancient canonical books,
containing historical narratives, is of very great significance, and has exercised and exercises greatly the wits of those who search holy writ. For example, what we read of historically as predicted and fulfilled in the seed of
Abraham according to the flesh, we must also inquire the allegorical meaning of, as it is to be fulfilled in the seed of Abraham according to faith. And
so much is this the case, that some have thought there is nothing in these
books either foretold and effected, or effected although not foretold, that
does not insinuate something else which is to be referred by figurative signification to the city of God on high, and to her children who are pilgrims in
this life. But if this be so, then the utterances of the prophets, or rather the
whole of those Scriptures that are reckoned under the title of the *Old Testament*, will be not of three, but of two different kinds. For there will be nothing there which pertains to the terrestrial Jerusalem only, if whatever is
there said and fulfilled of or concerning her signifies something which also
refers by allegorical prefiguration to the celestial Jerusalem; but there will
be only two kinds one that pertains to the free Jerusalem, the other to both.
But just as, I think, they err greatly who are of opinion that none of the
records of affairs in that kind of writings mean anything more than that they
so happened, so I think those very daring who contend that the whole gist
of their contents lies in allegorical significations. Therefore I have said they
are three-fold, not two-fold. Yet, in holding this opinion, I do not blame
those who may be able to draw out of everything there a spiritual meaning,
only saving, first of all, the historical truth. For the rest, what believer can
doubt that those things are spoken vainly which are such that, whether said
to have been done or to be yet to come, they do not beseem either human or
divine affairs? Who would not recall these to spiritual understanding if he
could, or confess that they should be recalled by him who is able?

[4] Heb. viii. 8-10

CHAPTER IV

ABOUT THE PREFIGURED CHANGE OF THE ISRAELITIC KINGDOM AND
PRIESTHOOD, AND ABOUT THE THINGS HANNAH THE MOTHER OF
SAMUEL PROPHESIED, PERSONATING THE CHURCH

Therefore the advance of the city of God, where it reached the times of
the kings, yielded a figure, when, on the rejection of Saul, David first obtained the kingdom on such a footing that thenceforth his descendants
should reign in the earthly Jerusalem in continual succession; for the course
of affairs signified and foretold, what is not to be passed by in silence, concerning the change of things to come, what belongs to both Testaments, the
Old and the New—where the priesthood and kingdom are changed by one
who is a priest, and at the same time a king, new and everlasting, even Christ
Jesus. For both the substitution in the ministry of God, on Eli's rejection as
priest, of Samuel, who executed at once the office of priest and judge, and
the establishment of David in the kingdom, when Saul was rejected, typified this of which I speak. And Hannah herself, the mother of Samuel, who
formerly was barren, and afterwards was gladdened with fertility, does not
seem to prophesy anything else, when she exultingly pours forth her thanksgiving to the Lord, on yielding up to God the same boy she had born and
weaned with the same piety with which she had vowed him. For she says,
"My heart is made strong in the Lord, and my horn is exalted in my God;
my mouth is enlarged over mine enemies; I am made glad in Thy salvation.
Because there is none holy as the Lord; and none is righteous as our God:
there is none holy save Thee. Do not glory so proudly, and do not speak lofty
things, neither let vaunting talk come out of your mouth; for a God of
knowledge is the Lord, and a God preparing His curious designs. The bow of
the mighty hath He made weak, and the weak are girded with strength.
They that were full of bread are diminished; and the hungry have passed
beyond the earth: for the barren hath born seven; and she that hath many
children is waxed feeble. The Lord killeth and maketh alive: He bringeth
down to hell, and bringeth up again. The Lord maketh poor and maketh
rich: He bringeth low and lifteth up. He raiseth up the poor out of the dust,
and lifteth up the beggar from the dunghill, that He may set him among the
mighty of [His] people, and maketh them inherit the throne of glory; giving
the vow to him that voweth, and He hath blessed the years of the just: for
man is not mighty in strength. The Lord shall make His adversary weak:
the Lord is holy. Let not the prudent glory in his prudence; and let not the
mighty glory in his might; and let not the rich glory in his riches: but let him
that glorieth glory in this, to understand and know the Lord, and to do judgment and justice in the midst of the earth. The Lord hath ascended into the
heavens, and hath thundered: He shall judge the ends of the earth, for He is

righteous: and He giveth strength to our kings, and shall exalt the horn of His Christ." [5]

Do you say that these are the words of a single weak woman giving thanks for the birth of a son? Can the mind of men be so much averse to the light of truth as not to perceive that the sayings this woman pours forth exceed her measure? Moreover, he who is suitably interested in these things which have already begun to be fulfilled even in this earthly pilgrimage also, does he not apply his mind, and perceive, and acknowledge, that through this woman—whose very name, which is Hannah, means "His grace"—the very Christian religion, the very city of God, whose king and founder is Christ, in fine, the very grace of God, hath thus spoken by the prophetic Spirit, whereby the proud are cut off so that they fall, and the humble are filled so that they rise, which that hymn chiefly celebrates? Unless perchance any one will say that this woman prophesied nothing, but only lauded God with exulting praise on account of the son whom she had obtained in answer to prayer. What then does she mean when she says, "The bow of the mighty hath He made weak, and the weak are girded with strength; they that were full of bread are diminished, and the hungry have gone beyond the earth; for the barren hath born seven, and she that hath many children is waxed feeble?" Had she herself born seven, although she had been barren? She had only one when she said that; neither did she bear seven afterwards, nor six, with whom Samuel himself might be the seventh, but three males and two females. And then, when as yet no one was king over that people, whence, if she did not prophesy, did she say what she puts at the end, "He giveth strength to our kings, and shall exalt the horn of His Christ?"

Therefore let the Church of Christ, the city of the great King,[6] full of grace, prolific of offspring, let her say what the prophecy uttered about her so long before by the mouth of this pious mother confesses, "My heart is made strong in the Lord, and my horn is exalted in my God." Her heart is truly made strong, and her horn is truly exalted, because not in herself, but in the Lord her God. "My mouth is enlarged over mine enemies;" because even in pressing straits the word of God is not bound, not even in preachers who are bound.[7] "I am made glad," she says, "in Thy salvation." This is Christ Jesus Himself, whom old Simeon, as we read in the Gospel, embracing as a little one, yet recognizing as great, said, "Lord, now lettest Thou Thy servant depart in peace, for mine eyes have seen Thy salvation." [8] Therefore may the Church say, "I am made glad in Thy salvation. For there is none holy as the Lord, and none is righteous as our God;" as holy and sanctifying, just and justifying.[9] "There is none holy beside Thee;" because no one becomes so except by reason of Thee. And then it follows, "Do not glory so proudly, and do not speak lofty things, neither let vaunting talk

[5] 1 Sam. ii. 1-10   [6] Ps. xlviii. 2   [7] 2 Tim. ii. 9; Eph. vi. 20   [8] Luke ii. 25-30
[9] Rom. iii. 26

come out of your mouth. For a God of knowledge is the Lord." He knows you even when no one knows; for "he who thinketh himself to be something when he is nothing deceiveth himself." [10] These things are said to the adversaries of the city of God who belong to Babylon, who presume in their own strength, and glory in themselves, not in the Lord; of whom are also the carnal Israelites, the earth-born inhabitants of the earthly Jerusalem, who, as saith the apostle, "being ignorant of the righteousness of God," [11] that is, which God, who alone is just, and the justifier, gives to man, "and wishing to establish their own," that is, which is as it were procured by their own selves, not bestowed by Him, "are not subject to the righteousness of God," just because they are proud, and think they are able to please God with their own, not with that which is of God, who is the God of knowledge, and therefore also takes the oversight of consciences, there beholding the thoughts of men that they are vain,[12] if they are of men, and are not from Him. "And preparing," she says, "His curious designs." What curious designs do we think these are, save that the proud must fall, and the humble rise? These curious designs she recounts, saying, "The bow of the mighty is made weak, and the weak are girded with strength." The bow is made weak, that is, the intention of those who think themselves so powerful, that without the gift and help of God they are able by human sufficiency to fulfill the divine commandments; and those are girded with strength whose inward cry is, "Have mercy upon me, O Lord, for I am weak." [13]

"They that were full of bread," she says, "are diminished, and the hungry have gone beyond the earth." Who are to be understood as full of bread except those same who were as if mighty, that is, the Israelites, to whom were committed the oracles of God? [14] But among that people the children of the bond maid were diminished—by which word *minus*, although it is Latin, the idea is well expressed that from being greater they were made less—because, even in the very bread, that is, the divine oracles, which the Israelites alone of all nations have received, they savor earthly things. But the nations to whom that law was not given, after they have come through the New Testament to these oracles, by thirsting much have gone beyond the earth, because in them they have savored not earthly, but heavenly things. And the reason why this is done is as it were sought; "for the barren," she says, "hath born seven, and she that hath many children is waxed feeble." Here all that had been prophesied hath shone forth to those who understood the number seven, which signifies the perfection of the universal Church. For which reason also the Apostle John writes to the seven churches,[15] showing in that way that he writes to the totality of the one Church; and in the *Proverbs* of Solomon it is said aforetime, prefiguring this, "Wisdom hath builded her house, she hath strengthened her seven pillars." [16] For the city of God was barren in all nations before that child arose whom we see. We also see that

---

[10] Gal. vi. 3   [11] Rom. x. 3   [12] Ps. xciv. 11; 1 Cor. iii. 20   [13] Ps. vi. 2   [14] Rom. iii. 2   [15] Rev. i. 4   [16] Prov. ix. 1

the temporal Jerusalem, who had many children, is now waxed feeble. Because, whoever in her were sons of the free woman were her strength; but now, forasmuch as the letter is there, and not the spirit, having lost her strength, she is waxed feeble.

"The Lord killeth and maketh alive:" He has killed her who had many children, and made this barren one alive, so that she has born seven. Although it may be more suitably understood that He has made those same alive whom He has killed. For she, as it were, repeats that by adding, "He bringeth down to hell, and bringeth up." To whom truly the apostle says, "If ye be dead with Christ, seek those things which are above, where Christ sitteth on the right hand of God." [17] Therefore they are killed by the Lord in a salutary way, so that he adds, "Savor things which are above, not things on the earth;" so that these are they who, hungering, have passed beyond the earth. "For ye are dead," he says: behold how God savingly kills! Then there follows, "And your life is hid with Christ in God:" behold how God makes the same alive! But does He bring them down to hell and bring them up again? It is without controversy among believers that we best see both parts of this work fulfilled in Him, to wit our Head, with whom the apostle has said our life is hid in God. "For when He spared not His own Son, but delivered Him up for us all," [18] in that way, certainly, He has killed Him. And forasmuch as He raised Him up again from the dead, He has made Him alive again. And since His voice is acknowledged in the prophecy, "Thou wilt not leave my soul in hell," [19] He has brought Him down to hell and brought Him up again. By this poverty of His we are made rich;[20] for "the Lord maketh poor and maketh rich." But that we may know what this is, let us hear what follows: "He bringeth low and lifteth up;" and truly He humbles the proud and exalts the humble. Which we also read elsewhere, "God resisteth the proud, but giveth grace to the humble." [21] This is the burden of the entire song of this woman whose name is interpreted "His grace."

Farther, what is added, "He raiseth up the poor from the earth," I understand of none better than of Him who, as was said a little ago, "was made poor for us, when He was rich, that by His poverty we might be made rich." For He raised Him from the earth so quickly that His flesh did not see corruption. Nor shall I divert from Him what is added, "And raiseth up the poor from the dunghill." For indeed he who is the poor man is also the beggar. But by the dunghill from which he is lifted up we are with the greatest reason to understand the persecuting Jews, of whom the apostle says, when telling that when he belonged to them he persecuted the Church, "What things were gain to me, those I counted loss for Christ; and I have counted them not only loss, but even dung, that I might win Christ." [22] Therefore that poor one is raised up from the earth above all the rich, and that beggar

[17] Col. iii. 1-3   [18] Rom. viii. 32   [19] Ps. xvi. 10; Acts ii. 27, 31   [20] 2 Cor. viii. 9
[21] Jas. iv. 6; 1 Pet. v. 5   [22] Phil. iii. 7, 8

is lifted up from that dunghill above all the wealthy, "that he may sit among the mighty of the people," to whom He says, "Ye shall sit upon twelve thrones," [23] "and to make them inherit the throne of glory." For these mighty ones had said, "Lo, we have forsaken all and followed Thee." They had most mightily vowed this vow.

But whence do they receive this, except from Him of whom it is here immediately said, "Giving the vow to him that voweth?" Otherwise they would be of those mighty ones whose bow is weakened. "Giving," she saith, "the vow to him that voweth." For no one could vow anything acceptable to God, unless he received from Him that which he might vow. There follows, "And He hath blessed the years of the just," to wit, that he may live for ever with Him to whom it is said, "And Thy years shall have no end." For there the years abide; but here they pass away, yea, they perish: for before they come they are not, and when they shall have come they shall not be, because they bring their own end with them. Now of these two, that is, "giving the vow to him that voweth," and "He hath blessed the years of the just," the one is what we do, the other what we receive. But this other is not received from God, the liberal giver, until He, the helper, Himself has enabled us for the former; "for man is not mighty in strength." "The Lord shall make his adversary weak," to wit, him who envies the man that vows, and resists him, lest he should fulfill what he has vowed. Owing to the ambiguity of the Greek, it may also be understood "his own adversary." For when God has begun to possess us, immediately he who had been our adversary becomes His, and is conquered by us; but not by our own strength, "for man is not mighty in strength." Therefore "the Lord shall make His own adversary weak, the Lord is holy," that he may be conquered by the saints, whom the Lord, the Holy of holies, hath made saints. For this reason, "let not the prudent glory in his prudence, and let not the mighty glory in his might, and let not the rich glory in his riches; but let him that glorieth glory in this—to understand and know the Lord, and to do judgment and justice in the midst of the earth." He in no small measure understands and knows the Lord who understands and knows that even this, that he can understand and know the Lord, is given to him by the Lord. "For what hast thou," saith the apostle, "that thou hast not received? But if thou hast received it, why dost thou glory as if thou hadst not received it?" [24] That is, as if thou hadst of thine own self whereof thou mightest glory. Now, he does judgment and justice who lives aright. But he lives aright who yields obedience to God when He commands. "The end of the commandment," that is, to which the commandment has reference, "is charity out of a pure heart, and a good conscience, and faith unfeigned." Moreover, this "charity," as the Apostle John testifies, "is of God." [25] Therefore to do justice and judgment is of God. But what is "in the midst of the earth"? For ought those who dwell in the ends of the earth not to do judgment and justice? Who

[23] Matt. xix. 27, 28   [24] 1 Cor. iv. 7   [25] 1 John iv. 7

would say so? Why, then, is it added, "In the midst of the earth?" For if this had not been added, and it had only been said, "To do judgment and justice," this commandment would rather have pertained to both kinds of men—both those dwelling inland and those on the sea-coast. But lest any one should think that, after the end of the life led in this body, there remains a time for doing judgment and justice which he has not done while he was in the flesh, and that the divine judgment can thus be escaped, "in the midst of the earth" appears to me to be said of the time when every one lives in the body; for in this life every one carries about his own earth, which, on a man's dying, the common earth takes back, to be surely returned to him on his rising again. Therefore "in the midst of the earth," that is, while our soul is shut up in this earthly body, judgment and justice are to be done, which shall be profitable for us hereafter, when "every one shall receive according to that he hath done in the body, whether good or bad." [26] For when the apostle there says "in the body," he means in the time he has lived in the body. Yet if any one blaspheme with malicious mind and impious thought, without any member of his body being employed in it, he shall not therefore be guiltless because he has not done it with bodily motion, for he will have done it in that time which he has spent in the body. In the same way we may suitably understand what we read in the psalm, "But God, our King before the worlds, hath wrought salvation in the midst of the earth;" [27] so that the Lord Jesus may be understood to be our God who is before the worlds, because by Him the worlds were made, working our salvation in the midst of the earth, for the Word was made flesh and dwelt in an earthly body.

Then after Hannah has prophesied in these words, that he who glorieth ought to glory not in himself at all, but in the Lord, she says, on account of the retribution which is to come on the day of judgment, "The Lord hath ascended into the heavens, and hath thundered: He shall judge the ends of the earth, for He is righteous." Throughout she holds to the order of the creed of Christians: For the Lord Christ has ascended into heaven, and is to come thence to judge the quick and dead. [28] For, as saith the apostle, "Who hath ascended but He who hath also descended into the lower parts of the earth? He that descended is the same also that ascended up above all heavens, that He might fill all things." [29] Therefore He hath thundered through His clouds, which He hath filled with His Holy Spirit when He ascended up. Concerning which the bond maid Jerusalem—that is, the unfruitful vineyard—is threatened in Isaiah the prophet that they shall rain no showers upon her. But "He shall judge the ends of the earth" is spoken as if it had been said, "even the extremes of the earth." For it does not mean that He shall not judge the other parts of the earth, who, without doubt; shall judge all men. But it is better to understand by the extremes of the earth the extremes of man, since those things shall not be judged which, in the middle time, are changed for the better or the worse, but the ending in which he

[26] 2 Cor. v. 10   [27] Ps. lxxiv. 12   [28] Acts x. 42   [29] Eph. iv. 9, 10

shall be found who is judged. For which reason it is said, "He that shall per-severe even unto the end, the same shall be saved." [30] He, therefore, who perseveringly does judgment and justice in the midst of the earth shall not be condemned when the extremes of the earth shall be judged. "And giveth," she saith, "strength to our kings," that He may not condemn them in judg-ing. He giveth them strength whereby as kings they rule the flesh, and con-quer the world in Him who hath poured out His blood for them. "And shall exalt the horn of His Christ." How shall Christ exalt the horn of His Christ? For He of whom it was said above, "The Lord hath ascended into the heav-ens," meaning the Lord Christ, Himself, as it is said here, "shall exalt the horn of His Christ." Who, therefore, is the Christ of His Christ? Does it mean that He shall exalt the horn of each one of His believing people, as she says in the beginning of this hymn, "Mine horn is exalted in my God?" For we can rightly call all those christs who are anointed with His chrism, foras-much as the whole body with its head is one Christ.[31] These things hath Hannah, the mother of Samuel, the holy and much-praised man, prophesied, in which, indeed, the change of the ancient priesthood was then figured and is now fulfilled, since she that had many children is waxed feeble, that the barren who hath born seven might have the new priesthood in Christ.

CHAPTER V

OF THOSE THINGS WHICH A MAN OF GOD SPAKE BY THE SPIRIT TO ELI THE PRIEST, SIGNIFYING THAT THE PRIESTHOOD WHICH HAD BEEN APPOINTED ACCORDING TO AARON WAS TO BE TAKEN AWAY

But this is said more plainly by a man of God sent to Eli the priest him-self, whose name indeed is not mentioned, but whose office and ministry show him to have been indubitably a prophet. For it is thus written: "And there came a man of God unto Eli, and said, Thus saith the Lord, I plainly revealed myself unto thy father's house, when they were in the land of Egypt slaves in Pharaoh's house; and I chose thy father's house out of all the sceptres of Israel to fill the office of priest for me, to go up to my altar, to burn incense and wear the ephod; and I gave thy father's house for food all the offerings made by fire of the children of Israel. Wherefore then hast thou looked at mine incense and at mine offerings with an impudent eye, and hast glorified thy sons above me, to bless the first-fruits of every sacri-fice in Israel before me? Therefore thus saith the Lord God of Israel, I said thy house and thy father's house should walk before me for ever: but now the Lord saith, Be it far from me; for them that honor me will I honor, and he that despiseth me shall be despised. Behold, the days come, that I will cut off thy seed, and the seed of thy father's house, and thou shalt never

[30] Matt. xxiv. 13   [31] i Cor. xii. 12

have an old man in my house. And I will cut off the man of thine from mine altar, so that his eyes shall be consumed, and his heart shall melt away; and every one of thy house that is left shall fall by the sword of men. And this shall be a sign unto thee that shall come upon these thy two sons, Hophni and Phinehas; in one day they shall die both of them. And I will raise me up a faithful priest, that shall do according to all that is in mine heart and in my soul; and I will build him a sure house, and he shall walk before my Christ for ever. And it shall come to pass that he who is left in thine house shall come to worship him with a piece of money, saying, Put me into one part of thy priesthood, that I may eat bread." [32]

We cannot say that this prophecy, in which the change of the ancient priesthood is foretold with so great plainness, was fulfilled in Samuel; for although Samuel was not of another tribe than that which had been appointed by God to serve at the altar, yet he was not of the sons of Aaron, whose offspring was set apart that the priests might be taken out of it. And thus by that transaction also the same change which should come to pass through Christ Jesus is shadowed forth, and the prophecy itself in deed, not in word, belonged to the Old Testament properly, but figuratively to the New, signifying by the fact just what was said by the word to Eli the priest through the prophet. For there were afterwards priests of Aaron's race, such as Zadok and Abiathar during David's reign, and others in succession, before the time came when those things which were predicted so long before about the changing of the priesthood behoved to be fulfilled by Christ. But who that now views these things with a believing eye does not see that they are fulfilled? Since, indeed, no tabernacle, no temple, no altar, no sacrifice, and therefore no priest either, has remained to the Jews, to whom it was commanded in the law of God that he should be ordained of the seed of Aaron; which is also mentioned here by the prophet, when he says, "Thus saith the Lord God of Israel, I said thy house and thy father's house shall walk before me for ever: but now the Lord saith, That be far from me; for them that honor me will I honor, and he that despiseth me shall be despised." For that in naming his father's house he does not mean that of his immediate father, but that of Aaron, who first was appointed priest, to be succeeded by others descended from him, is shown by the preceding words, when he says, "I was revealed unto thy father's house, when they were in the land of Egypt slaves in Pharaoh's house; and I chose thy father's house out of all the sceptres of Israel to fill the office of priest for me." Which of the fathers in that Egyptian slavery, but Aaron, was his father, who, when they were set free, was chosen to the priesthood? It was of his lineage, therefore, he has said in this passage it should come to pass that they should no longer be priests; which already we see fulfilled. If faith be watchful, the things are before us: they are discerned, they are grasped, and are forced on the eyes of the unwilling, so that they are seen: "Behold the days come," he says, "that I will cut off thy

[32] 1 Sam. ii. 27-36

seed, and the seed of thy father's house, and thou shalt never have an old man in mine house. And I will cut off the man of thine from mine altar, so that his eyes shall be consumed and his heart shall melt away." Behold the days which were foretold have already come. There is no priest after the order of Aaron; and whoever is a man of his lineage, when he sees the sacrifice of the Christians prevailing over the whole world, but that great honor taken away from himself, his eyes fail and his soul melts away consumed with grief.

But what follows belongs properly to the house of Eli, to whom these things were said: "And every one of thine house that is left shall fall by the sword of men. And this shall be a sign unto thee that shall come upon these thy two sons, Hophni and Phinehas; in one day they shall die both of them." This, therefore, is made a sign of the change of the priesthood from this man's house, by which it is signified that the priesthood of Aaron's house is to be changed. For the death of this man's sons signified the death not of the men, but of the priesthood itself of the sons of Aaron. But what follows pertains to that Priest whom Samuel typified by succeeding this one. Therefore the things which follow are said of Christ Jesus, the true Priest of the New Testament: "And I will raise me up a faithful Priest that shall do according to all that is in mine heart and in my soul; and I will build Him a sure house." The same is the eternal Jerusalem above. "And He shall walk," saith He, "before my Christ always." "He shall walk" means "he shall be conversant with," just as He had said before of Aaron's house, "I said that thine house and thy father's house shall walk before me for ever." But what He says, "He shall walk before my Christ," is to be understood entirely of the house itself, not of the priest, who is Christ Himself, the Mediator and Saviour. His house, therefore, shall walk before Him. "Shall walk" may also be understood to mean from death to life, all the time this mortality passes through, even to the end of this world. But where God says, "Who will do all that is in mine heart and in my soul," we must not think that God has a soul, for He is the Author of souls; but this is said of God figuratively, not properly, just as He is said to have hands and feet, and other corporal members. And, lest it should be supposed from such language that man in the form of this flesh is made in the image of God, wings also are ascribed to Him, which man has not at all; and it is said to God, "Hide me under the shadow of Thy wings," [33] that men may understand that such things are said of that ineffable nature not in proper but in figurative words.

But what is added, "And it shall come to pass that he who is left in thine house shall come to worship him," is not said properly of the house of this Eli, but of that Aaron, the men of which remained even to the advent of Jesus Christ, of which race there are not wanting men even to this present. For of that house of Eli it had already been said above, "And every one of thine house that is left shall fall by the sword of men." How, therefore,

[33] Ps. xvii. 8

could it be truly said here, "And it shall come to pass that every one that is left shall come to worship him," if that is true, that no one shall escape the avenging sword, unless he would have it understood of those who belong to the race of that whole priesthood after the order of Aaron? Therefore, if it is of these the predestinated remnant, about whom another prophet has said, "The remnant shall be saved;" [34] whence the apostle also says, "Even so then at this time also the remnant according to the election of grace is saved;" [35] since it is easily understood to be of such a remnant that it is said, "He that is left in thine house," assuredly he believes in Christ; just as in the time of the apostle very many of that nation believed; nor are there now wanting those, although very few, who yet believe, and in them is fulfilled what this man of God has here immediately added, "He shall come to worship him with a piece of money;" to worship whom, if not that Chief Priest, who is also God? For in that priesthood after the order of Aaron men did not come to the temple or altar of God for the purpose of worshipping the priest. But what is that he says, "With a piece of money," if not the short word of faith, about which the apostle quotes the saying, "A consummating and shortening word will the Lord make upon the earth?" [36] But that money is put for the word the psalm is a witness, where it is sung, "The words of the Lord are pure words, money tried with the fire." [37]

What then does he say who comes to worship the priest of God, even the Priest who is God? "Put me into one part of Thy priesthood, to eat bread." I do not wish to be set in the honor of my fathers, which is none; put me in a part of Thy priesthood. For "I have chosen to be mean in Thine house;" [38] I desire to be a member, no matter what, or how small, of Thy priesthood. By the priesthood he here means the people itself, of which He is the Priest who is the Mediator between God and men, the man Christ Jesus.[39] This people the Apostle Peter calls "a holy people, a royal priesthood." [40] But some have translated, "Of Thy sacrifice," not "Of Thy priesthood," which no less signifies the same Christian people. Whence the Apostle Paul says, "We being many are one bread, one body." What, therefore, he has added, to "eat bread," also elegantly expresses the very kind of sacrifice of which the Priest Himself says, "The bread which I will give is my flesh for the life of the world." [42] The same is the sacrifice not after the order of Aaron, but after the order of Melchisedec:[43] let him that readeth understand.[44] Therefore this short and salutarily humble confession, in which it is said, "Put me in a part of Thy priesthood, to eat bread," is itself the piece of money, for it is both brief, and it is the Word of God who dwells in the heart of one who believes. For because He had said above, that He had given for food to Aaron's house the sacrificial victims of the Old Testament, where He says, "I have given thy father's house for food all things which are offered by fire

[34] Isa. x. 21   [35] Rom. xi. 5   [36] Isa. xxxviii. 22; Rom. ix. 28   [37] Ps. xii. 6   [38] Ps. lxxxiv. 10   [39] 1 Tim. ii. 5   [40] 1 Pet. ii. 9   [41] 1 Cor. x. 17   [42] John vi. 51   [43] Heb. vii. 11, 27   [44] Matt. xxiv. 15

of the children of Israel," which indeed were the sacrifices of the Jews; therefore here He has said, "To eat bread," which is in the New Testament the sacrifice of the Christians.

CHAPTER VI

OF THE JEWISH PRIESTHOOD AND KINGDOM, WHICH, ALTHOUGH PROMISED TO BE ESTABLISHED FOR EVER, DID NOT CONTINUE; SO THAT OTHER THINGS ARE TO BE UNDERSTOOD TO WHICH ETERNITY IS ASSURED

While, therefore, these things now shine forth as clearly as they were loftily foretold, still some one may not vainly be moved to ask, How can we be confident that all things are to come to pass which are predicted in these books as about to come, if this very thing which is there divinely spoken, "Thine house and thy father's house shall walk before me for ever," could not have effect? For we see that priesthood has been changed; and there can be no hope that what was promised to that house may some time be fulfilled, because that which succeeds on its being rejected and changed is rather predicted as eternal. He who says this does not yet understand, or does not recollect, that this very priesthood after the order of Aaron was appointed as the shadow of a future eternal priesthood; and therefore, when eternity is promised to it, it is not promised to the mere shadow and figure, but to what is shadowed forth and prefigured by it. But lest it should be thought the shadow itself was to remain, therefore its mutation also behoved to be foretold.

In this way, too, the kingdom of Saul himself, who certainly was reprobated and rejected, was the shadow of a kingdom yet to come which should remain to eternity. For, indeed, the oil with which he was anointed, and from that chrism he is called Christ, is to be taken in a mystical sense, and is to be understood as a great mystery; which David himself venerated so much in him, that he trembled with smitten heart when, being hid in a dark cave, which Saul also entered when pressed by the necessity of nature, he had come secretly behind him and cut off a small piece of his robe, that he might be able to prove how he had spared him when he could have killed him, and might thus remove from his mind the suspicion through which he had vehemently persecuted the holy David, thinking him his enemy. Therefore he was much afraid lest he should be accused of violating so great a mystery in Saul, because he had thus meddled even his clothes. For thus it is written: "And David's heart smote him because he had taken away the skirt of his cloak." [45] But to the men with him, who advised him to destroy Saul thus delivered up into his hands, he saith, "The Lord forbid that I should do this thing to my lord, the Lord's christ, to lay my hand upon him, because he is the Lord's christ." Therefore he showed so great reverence to

[45] 1 Sam. xxiv. 5, 6

this shadow of what was to come, not for its own sake, but for the sake of what it prefigured. Whence also that which Samuel says to Saul, "Since thou hast not kept my commandment which the Lord commanded thee, whereas now the Lord would have prepared thy kingdom over Israel for ever, yet now thy kingdom shall not continue for thee; and the Lord will seek Him a man after His own heart, and the Lord will command him to be prince over His people, because thou hast not kept that which the Lord commanded thee," [46] is not to be taken as if God had settled that Saul himself should reign for ever, and afterwards, on his sinning, would not keep this promise; nor was He ignorant that he would sin, but He had established his kingdom that it might be a figure of the eternal kingdom. Therefore he added, "Yet now thy kingdom shall not continue *for thee*." Therefore what it signified has stood and shall stand; but it shall not stand for this man, because he himself was not to reign for ever, nor his offspring; so that at least that word "for ever" might seem to be fulfilled through his posterity one to another. "And the Lord," he saith, "will seek Him a man," meaning either David or the Mediator of the New Testament,[47] who was figured in the chrism with which David also and his offspring were anointed. But it is not as if He knew not where he was that God thus seeks Him a man, but, speaking through a man, He speaks as a man, and in this sense seeks us. For not only to God the Father, but also to His Only-begotten, who came to seek what was lost,[48] we had been known already even so far as to be chosen in Him before the foundation of the world.[49] "He will seek Him" therefore means, He will have His own (just as if He had said, Whom He already has known to be His own He will show to others to be His friend). Whence in Latin this word (*quaerit*) receives a preposition and becomes *acquirit* (acquires) the meaning of which is plain enough; although even without the addition of the preposition *quaerere* is understood as *acquirere*, whence gains are called *quaestus*.

CHAPTER VII

OF THE DISRUPTION OF THE KINGDOM OF ISRAEL, BY WHICH THE PERPETUAL DIVISION OF THE SPIRITUAL FROM THE CARNAL ISRAEL WAS PREFIGURED

Again Saul sinned through disobedience, and again Samuel says to him in the word of the Lord, "Because thou hast despised the word of the Lord, the Lord hath despised thee, that thou mayest not be king over Israel." [50] And again for the same sin, when Saul confessed it, and prayed for pardon, and besought Samuel to return with him to appease the Lord, he said, "I will not return with thee: for thou hast despised the word of the Lord, and the

[46] 1 Sam. xiii. 13, 14   [47] Heb. ix. 15   [48] Luke xix. 10   [49] Eph. i. 4   [50] 1 Sam. xv. 23

Lord will despise thee that thou mayest not be king over Israel. And Samuel turned his face to go away, and Saul laid hold upon the skirt of his mantle, and rent it. And Samuel said unto him, The Lord hath rent the kingdom from Israel out of thine hand this day, and will give it to thy neighbor, who is good above thee, and will divide Israel in twain. And He will not be changed, neither will He repent: for He is not as a man, that He should repent; who threatens and does not persist." [51] He to whom it is said, "The Lord will despise thee that thou mayest not be king over Israel," and "The Lord hath rent the kingdom from Israel out of thine hand this day," reigned forty years over Israel—that is, just as long a time as David himself—yet heard this in the first period of his reign, that we may understand it was said because none of his race was to reign, and that we may look to the race of David, whence also is sprung, according to the flesh,[52] the Mediator between God and men, the man Christ Jesus.[53]

But the Scripture has not what is read in most Latin copies, "The Lord hath rent the kingdom of Israel out of thine hand this day," but just as we have set it down it is found in the Greek copies, "The Lord hath rent the kingdom from Israel out of thine hand;" that the words "out of thine hand" may be understood to mean "from Israel." Therefore this man figuratively represented the people of Israel, which was to lose the kingdom, Christ Jesus our Lord being about to reign, not carnally, but spiritually. And when it is said of Him, "And will give it to thy neighbor," that is to be referred to the fleshly kinship, for Christ, according to the flesh, was of Israel, whence also Saul sprang. But what is added, "Good above thee," may indeed be understood, "Better than thee," and indeed some have thus translated it; but it is better taken thus, "Good above thee," as meaning that because He is good, therefore He must be above thee, according to that other prophetic saying, "Till I put all Thine enemies under Thy feet." [54] And among them is Israel, from whom, as His persecutor, Christ took away the kingdom; although the Israel in whom there was no guile may have been there too, a sort of grain, as it were, of that chaff. For certainly thence came the apostles, thence so many martyrs, of whom Stephen is the first, thence so many churches, which the Apostle Paul names, magnifying God in their conversion.

Of which thing I do not doubt what follows is to be understood, "And will divide Israel in twain," to wit, into Israel pertaining to the bond woman, and Israel pertaining to the free. For these two kinds were at first together, as Abraham still clave to the bond woman, until the barren, made fruitful by the grace of God, cried, "Cast out the bond woman and her son." [55] We know, indeed, that on account of the sin of Solomon, in the reign of his son Rehoboam, Israel was divided in two, and continued so, the separate parts having their own kings, until that whole nation was overthrown with a great destruction, and carried away by the Chaldeans. But what was this to Saul,

[51] 1 Sam. xv. 26-29   [52] Rom. i. 3   [53] 1 Tim. ii. 5   [54] Ps. cx. 1   [55] Gen. xxi. 10

when, if any such thing was threatened, it would be threatened against David himself, whose son Solomon was? Finally, the Hebrew nation is not now divided internally, but is dispersed through the earth indiscriminately, in the fellowship of the same error. But that division with which God threatened the kingdom and people in the person of Saul, who represented them, is shown to be eternal and unchangeable by this which is added, "And He will not be changed, neither will He repent: for He is not as a man, that He should repent; who threatens and does not persist"—that is, a man threatens and does not persist, but not God, who does not repent like man. For when we read that He repents, a change of circumstance is meant, flowing from the divine immutable foreknowledge. Therefore, when God is said not to repent, it is to be understood that He does not change.

We see that this sentence concerning this division of the people of Israel, divinely uttered in these words, has been altogether irremediable and quite perpetual. For whoever have turned, or are turning, or shall turn thence to Christ, it has been according to the foreknowledge of God, not according to the one and the same nature of the human race. Certainly none of the Israelites, who, cleaving to Christ, have continued in Him, shall ever be among those Israelites who persist in being His enemies even to the end of this life, but shall for ever remain in the separation which is here foretold. For the Old Testament, from the Mount Sinai, which gendereth to bondage,[56] profiteth nothing, unless because it bears witness to the New Testament. Otherwise, however long Moses is read, the veil is put over their heart; but when any one shall turn thence to Christ, the veil shall be taken away.[57] For the very desire of those who turn is changed from the old to the new, so that each no longer desires to obtain carnal but spiritual felicity. Wherefore that great prophet Samuel himself, before he had anointed Saul, when he had cried to the Lord for Israel, and He had heard him, and when he had offered a whole burnt-offering, as the aliens were coming to battle against the people of God, and the Lord thundered above them and they were confused, and fell before Israel and were overcome; [then] he took one stone and set it up between the old and new Massephat [Mizpeh], and called its name Ebenezer, which means "the stone of the helper," and said, "Hitherto hath the Lord helped us." [58] Massephat is interpreted "desire." That stone of the helper is the mediation of the Saviour, by which we go from the old Massephat to the new—that is, from the desire with which carnal happiness was expected in the carnal kingdom to the desire with which the truest spiritual happiness is expected in the kingdom of heaven; and since nothing is better than that, the Lord helpeth us hitherto.

[56] Gal. iv. 25   [57] 2 Cor. iii. 15, 16   [58] 1 Sam. vii. 9-12

CHAPTER VIII

OF THE PROMISES MADE TO DAVID IN HIS SON, WHICH ARE IN NO WISE
FULFILLED IN SOLOMON, BUT MOST FULLY IN CHRIST

And now I see I must show what, pertaining to the matter I treat of, God promised to David himself, who succeeded Saul in the kingdom, whose change prefigured that final change on account of which all things were divinely spoken, all things were committed to writing. When many things had gone prosperously with king David, he thought to make a house for God, even that temple of most excellent renown which was afterwards built by king Solomon his son. While he was thinking of this, the word of the Lord came to Nathan the prophet, which he brought to the king, in which, after God had said that a house should not be built unto Him by David himself, and that in all that long time He had never commanded any of His people to build Him a house of cedar, he says, "And now thus shalt thou say unto my servant David, Thus saith God Almighty, I took thee from the sheep-cote that thou mightest be for a ruler over my people in Israel: and I was with thee whithersoever thou wentest, and have cut off all thine enemies from before thy face, and have made thee a name, according to the name of the great ones who are over the earth. And I will appoint a place for my people Israel, and will plant him, and he shall dwell apart, and shall be troubled no more; and the son of wickedness shall not humble him any more, as from the beginning, from the days when I appointed judges over my people Israel. And I will give thee rest from all thine enemies, and the Lord will tell thee, because thou shalt build an house for Him. And it shall come to pass when thy days be fulfilled, and thou shalt sleep with thy fathers, that I will raise up thy seed after thee, which shall proceed out of thy bowels, and I will prepare his kingdom. He shall build me an house for my name; and I will order his throne even to eternity. I will be his Father, and he shall be my son. And if he commit iniquity, I will chasten him with the rod of men, and with the stripes of the sons of men: but my mercy I will not take away from him, as I took it away from those whom I put away from before my face. And his house shall be faithful, and his kingdom even for evermore before me, and his throne shall be set up even for evermore." [59]

He who thinks this grand promise was fulfilled in Solomon greatly errs: for he attends to the saying, "He shall build me an house," but he does not attend to the saying, "His house shall be faithful, and his kingdom for evermore before me." Let him therefore attend and behold the house of Solomon full of strange women worshipping false gods, and the king himself, aforetime wise, seduced by them, and cast down into the same idolatry: and let him not dare to think that God either promised this falsely, or was unable

[59] 2 Sam. vii. 8-16

to foreknow that Solomon and his house would become what they did. But we ought not to be in doubt here, or to see the fulfillment of these things save in Christ our Lord, who was made of the seed of David according to the flesh,[60] lest we should vainly and uselessly look for some other here, like the carnal Jews. For even they understand this much, that the son whom they read of in that place as promised to David was not Solomon; so that, with wonderful blindness to Him who was promised and is now declared with so great manifestation, they say they hope for another. Indeed, even in Solomon there appeared some image of the future event, in that he built the temple, and had peace according to his name (for Solomon means "pacific") and in the beginning of his reign was wonderfully praiseworthy; but while, as a shadow of Him that should come, he foreshowed Christ our Lord, he did not also in his own person resemble Him. Whence some things concerning him are so written as if they were prophesied of himself, while the Holy Scripture, prophesying even by events, somehow delineates in him the figure of things to come. For, besides the books of divine history, in which his reign is narrated, the 72d Psalm also is inscribed in the title with his name, in which so many things are said which cannot at all apply to him, but which apply to the Lord Christ with such evident fitness as makes it quite apparent that in the one the figure is in some way shadowed forth, but in the other the truth itself is presented. For it is known within what bounds the kingdom of Solomon was enclosed; and yet in that psalm, not to speak of other things, we read, "He shall have dominion from sea even to sea, and from the river to the ends of the earth," [61] which we see fulfilled in Christ. Truly he took the beginning of His reigning from the river where John baptized; for, when pointed out by him, He began to be acknowledged by the disciples, who called Him not only Master, but also Lord.

·Nor was it for any other reason that, while his father David was still living, Solomon began to reign, which happened to none other of their kings, except that from this also it might be clearly apparent that it was not himself this prophecy spoken to his father signified beforehand, saying, "And it shall come to pass when thy days be fulfilled, and thou shalt sleep with thy fathers, that I will raise up thy seed which shall proceed out of thy bowels, and I will prepare His kingdom." How, therefore, shall it be thought on account of what follows, "He shall build me an house," that this Solomon is prophesied, and not rather be understood on account of what precedes, "When thy days be fulfilled, and thou shalt sleep with thy fathers, I will raise up thy seed after thee," that another pacific One is promised, who is foretold as about to be raised up, not before David's death, as he was, but after it? For however long the interval of time might be before Jesus Christ came, beyond doubt it was after the death of king David, to whom He was so promised, that He behoved to come, who should build a house of God, not of wood and stone, but of men, such as we rejoice He does build. For to

[60] Rom. i. 3   [61] Ps. lxxii. 8

this house, that is, to believers, the apostle saith, "The temple of God is holy, which temple ye are." [62]

CHAPTER IX

HOW LIKE THE PROPHECY ABOUT CHRIST IN THE 89TH PSALM IS TO
THE THINGS PROMISED IN NATHAN'S PROPHECY IN THE BOOKS
OF SAMUEL

Wherefore also in the 89th Psalm, of which the title is, "An instruction for himself by Ethan the Israelite," mention is made of the promises God made to king David, and some things are there added similar to those found in the *Book of Samuel*, such as this, "I have sworn to David my servant that I will prepare his seed for ever." [63] And again, "Then thou spakest in vision to thy sons, and saidst, I have laid help upon the mighty One, and have exalted the chosen One out of my people. I have found David my servant, and with my holy oil I have anointed him. For mine hand shall help him, and mine arm shall strengthen him. The enemy shall not prevail against him, and the son of iniquity shall harm him no more. And I will beat down his foes from before his face, and those that hate him will I put to flight. And my truth and my mercy shall be with him, and in my name shall his horn be exalted. I will set his hand also in the sea, and his right hand in the rivers. He shall cry unto me, Thou art my Father, my God, and the undertaker of my salvation. Also I will make him my first-born, high among the kings of the earth. My mercy will I keep for him for evermore, and my covenant shall be faithful with him. His seed also will I set for ever and ever, and his throne as the days of heaven." [64] Which words, when rightly understood, are all understood to be about the Lord Jesus Christ, under the name of David, on account of the form of a servant, which the same Mediator assumed [65] from the virgin of the seed of David. [66] For immediately something is said about the sins of his children, such as is set down in the *Book of Samuel*, and is more readily taken as if of Solomon. For there, that is, in the *Book of Samuel*, he says, "And if he commit iniquity I will chasten him with the rod of men, and with the stripes of the sons of men; but my mercy will I not take away from him," [67] meaning by stripes the strokes of correction. Hence that saying, "Touch ye not my christs." [68] For what else is that than, Do not harm them? But in the psalm, when speaking as if of David, He says something of the same kind there too. "If his children," saith He, "forsake my law, and walk not in my judgments; if they profane my righteousnesses, and keep not my commandments; I will visit their iniquities with the rod, and their faults with stripes: but my mercy I will not make void from him." [69] He did not say "from them," although He spoke of his children, not of himself; but he said "from him," which means

[62] 1 Cor. iii. 27   [63] Ps. lxxxix. 3, 4   [64] Ps. lxxxix. 19-29   [65] Phil. ii. 7   [66] Matt. i. 1, 18; Luke i. 27   [67] 2 Sam. vii. 14, 15   [68] Ps. cv. 15   [69] Ps. lxxxix. 30-33

the same thing if rightly understood. For of Christ Himself, who is the head of the Church, there could not be found any sins which required to be divinely restrained by human correction, mercy being still continued; but they are found in His body and members, which is His people. Therefore in the *Book of Samuel* it is said, "iniquity of Him," but in the psalm, "of His children," that we may understand that what is said of His body is in some way said of Himself. Wherefore also, when Saul persecuted His body, that is, His believing people, He Himself saith from heaven, "Saul, Saul, why persecutest thou me?" [70] Then in the following words of the psalm He says, "Neither will I hurt in my truth, nor profane my covenant, and the things that proceed from my lips I will not disallow. Once have I sworn by my holiness, if I lie unto David" [71]—that is, I will in no wise lie unto David; for Scripture is wont to speak thus. But what that is in which He will not lie, He adds, saying, "His seed shall endure for ever, and his throne as the sun before me, and as the moon perfected for ever, and a faithful witness in heaven." [72]

CHAPTER X

HOW DIFFERENT THE ACTS IN THE KINGDOM OF THE EARTHLY JERUSALEM ARE FROM THOSE WHICH GOD HAD PROMISED, SO THAT THE TRUTH OF THE PROMISE SHOULD BE UNDERSTOOD TO PERTAIN TO THE GLORY OF THE OTHER KING AND KINGDOM

That it might not be supposed that a promise so strongly expressed and confirmed was fulfilled in Solomon, as if he hoped for, yet did not find it, he says, "But Thou hast cast off, and hast brought to nothing, O Lord." [73] This truly was done concerning the kingdom of Solomon among his posterity, even so the overthrow of the earthly Jerusalem itself, which was the seat of the kingdom, and especially the destruction of the very temple which had been built by Solomon. But lest on this account God should be thought to have done contrary to His promise, immediately he adds, "Thou hast delayed Thy Christ." [74] Therefore he is not Solomon, nor yet David himself, if the Christ of the Lord is delayed. For while all the kings are called His christs, who were consecrated with that mystical chrism, not only from king David downwards, but even from that Saul who first was anointed king of that same people, David himself indeed calling him the Lord's christ, yet there was one true Christ, whose figure they bore by the prophetic unction, who, according to the opinion of men, who thought he was to be understood as come in David or in Solomon, was long delayed, but who, according as God had disposed, was to come in His own time. The following part of this psalm goes on to say what in the meantime, while He was delayed, was to become of the kingdom of the earthly Jerusalem, where it was hoped He

[70] Acts ix. 4   [71] Ps. lxxxix. 34, 35   [72] Ps. lxxxix. 36, 37   [73] Ps. lxxxix. 38   [74] Ps. lxxxix. 38

would certainly reign: "Thou hast overthrown the covenant of Thy servant; Thou hast profaned in the earth his sanctuary. Thou hast broken down all his walls; Thou hast put his strong-holds in fear. All that pass by the way spoil him; he is made a reproach to his neighbors. Thou hast set up the right hand of his enemies; Thou hast made all his enemies to rejoice. Thou hast turned aside the help of his sword, and hast not helped him in war. Thou hast destroyed him from cleansing; Thou hast dashed down his seat to the ground. Thou hast shortened the days of his seat; Thou hast poured confusion over him." [75] All these things came upon Jerusalem the bond woman, in which some also reigned who were children of the free woman, holding that kingdom in temporary stewardship, but holding the kingdom of the heavenly Jerusalem, whose children they were, in true faith, and hoping in the true Christ. But how these things came upon that kingdom, the history of its affairs points out if it is read.

CHAPTER XI

OF THE SUBSTANCE OF THE PEOPLE OF GOD, WHICH THROUGH HIS ASSUMPTION OF FLESH IS IN CHRIST, WHO ALONE HAD POWER TO DELIVER HIS OWN SOUL FROM HELL

But after having prophesied these things, the prophet betakes him to praying to God; yet even the very prayer is prophecy: "How long, Lord, dost Thou turn away in the end?" [76] "Thy face" is understood, as it is elsewhere said, "How long dost Thou turn away Thy face from me?" [77] For therefore some copies have here not "dost," but "wilt Thou turn away;" although it could be understood, "Thou turnest away Thy mercy, which Thou didst promise to David." But when he says, "in the end," what does it mean, except even to the end? By which end is to be understood the last time, when even that nation is to believe in Christ Jesus, before which end what He has just sorrowfully bewailed must come to pass. On account of which it is also added here, "Thy wrath shall burn like fire. Remember what is my substance." [78] This cannot be better understood than of Jesus Himself, the substance of His people, of whose nature His flesh is. "For not in vain," he says, "hast Thou made all the sons of men." [79] For unless the one Son of man had been the substance of Israel, through which Son of man many sons of men should be set free, all the sons of men would have been made wholly in vain. But now, indeed, all mankind through the fall of the first man has fallen from the truth into vanity; for which reason another psalm says, "Man is like to vanity: his days pass away as a shadow;" [80] yet God has not made all the sons of men in vain, because He frees many from vanity through the Mediator Jesus, and those whom He did not foreknow as to be delivered, He

[75] Ps. lxxxix. 39-45   [76] Ps. lxxxix. 46   [77] Ps. xiii. 1   [78] Ps. lxxxix. 46, 47   [79] Ps. lxxxix. 47   [80] Ps. cxliv. 4

made not wholly in vain in the most beautiful and most just ordination of the whole rational creation, for the use of those who were to be delivered, and for the comparison of the two cities by mutual contrast. Thereafter it follows, "Who is the man that shall live, and shall not see death? shall he snatch his soul from the hand of hell?" [81] Who is this but that substance of Israel out of the seed of David, Christ Jesus, of whom the apostle says, that "rising from the dead He now dieth not, and death shall no more have dominion over Him?" [82] For He shall so live and not see death, that yet He shall have been dead; but shall have delivered His soul from the hand of hell, whither He had descended in order to loose some from the chains of hell; but He hath delivered it by that power of which He says in the Gospel, "I have the power of laying down my life, and I have the power of taking it again." [83]

CHAPTER XII

TO WHOSE PERSON THE ENTREATY FOR THE PROMISES IS TO BE UNDERSTOOD TO BELONG, WHEN HE SAYS IN THE PSALM, "WHERE ARE THINE ANCIENT COMPASSIONS, LORD?" ETC.

But the rest of this psalm runs thus: "Where are Thine ancient compassions, Lord, which Thou swarest unto David in Thy truth? Remember, Lord, the reproach of Thy servants, which I have borne in my bosom of many nations; wherewith Thine enemies have reproached, O Lord, wherewith they have reproached the change of Thy Christ." [84] Now it may with very good reason be asked whether this is spoken in the person of those Israelites who desired that the promise made to David might be fulfilled to them; or rather of the Christians, who are Israelites not after the flesh but after the Spirit.[85] This certainly was spoken or written in the time of Ethan, from whose name this psalm gets its title, and that was the same as the time of David's reign; and therefore it would not have been said, "Where are Thine ancient compassions, Lord, which Thou hast sworn unto David in Thy truth?" unless the prophet had assumed the person of those who should come long afterwards, to whom that time when these things were promised to David was ancient. But it may be understood thus, that many nations, when they persecuted the Christians, reproached them with the passion of Christ, which Scripture calls His change, because by dying He is made immortal. The change of Christ, according to this passage, may also be understood to be reproached by the Israelites, because, when they hoped He would be theirs, He was made the Saviour of the nations; and many nations who have believed in Him by the New Testament now reproach them who remain in the old with this: so that it is said, "Remember, Lord, the reproach of Thy servants;" because through the Lord's not forgetting, but rather pitying them, even they

[81] Ps. lxxxix. 48   [82] Rom. vi. 9   [83] John x. 18   [84] Ps. lxxxix. 49-51   [85] Rom. iii. 28, 29

after this reproach are to believe. But what I have put first seems to me the most suitable meaning. For to the enemies of Christ who are reproached with this, that Christ hath left them, turning to the Gentiles,[86] this speech is incongruously assigned, "Remember, Lord, the reproach of Thy servants," for such Jews are not to be styled the servants of God; but these words fit those who, if they suffered great humiliations through persecution for the name of Christ, could call to mind that an exalted kingdom had been promised to the seed of David, and in desire of it, could say not despairingly, but as asking, seeking, knocking,[87] "Where are Thine ancient compassions, Lord, which Thou swarest unto David in Thy truth? Remember, Lord, the reproach of Thy servants, that I have borne in my bosom of many nations;" that is, have patiently endured in my inward parts. "That Thine enemies have reproached, O Lord, wherewith they have reproached the change of Thy Christ," not thinking it a change, but a consumption. But what does "Remember, Lord," mean, but that Thou wouldst have compassion, and wouldst for my patiently borne humiliation reward me with the excellency which Thou swarest unto David in Thy truth? But if we assign these words to the Jews, those servants of God who, on the conquest of the earthly Jerusalem, before Jesus Christ was born after the manner of men, were led into captivity, could say such things, understanding the change of Christ, because indeed through Him was to be surely expected, not an earthly and carnal felicity, such as appeared during the few years of king Solomon, but a heavenly and spiritual felicity; and when the nations, then ignorant of this through unbelief, exulted over and insulted the people of God for being captives, what else was this than ignorantly to reproach with the change of Christ those who understand the change of Christ? And therefore what follows when this psalm is concluded, "Let the blessing of the Lord be for evermore, amen, amen," is suitable enough for the whole people of God belonging to the heavenly Jerusalem, whether for those things that lay hid in the Old Testament before the New was revealed, or for those that, being now revealed in the New Testament, are manifestly discerned to belong to Christ. For the blessing of the Lord in the seed of David does not belong to any particular time, such as appeared in the days of Solomon, but is for evermore to be hoped for, in which most certain hope it is said, "Amen, amen;" for this repetition of the word is the confirmation of that hope. Therefore David understanding this, says in the second *Book of Kings*, in the passage from which we digressed to this psalm,[88] "Thou hast spoken also for Thy servant's house for a great while to come." [89] Therefore also a little after he says, "Now begin, and bless the house of Thy servant for evermore," etc., because the son was then about to be born from whom his posterity should be continued to Christ, through whom his house should be eternal, and should also be the house of God. For it is called the house of David on account of David's race; but the selfsame is called the house of God on account of the temple of God, made of men, not of stones, where shall dwell for evermore the people with and in their God, and God with and in His people, so that God may fill His people, and the people be filled with their God, while God shall be all in all, Himself their reward in peace who is their strength in war. Therefore, when it is said in the words of Nathan, "And the Lord will tell thee what an house thou shalt build for Him," [90] it is afterwards said in the words of David, "For Thou, Lord Almighty, God of Israel, hast opened the ear of Thy servant, saying, I will build thee an house." [91] For this house is built both by us through living well, and by God through helping us to live well; for "except the Lord build the house, they labor in vain that build it." [92] And when the final dedication of this house shall take place, then what God here says by Nathan shall be fulfilled, "And I will appoint a place for my people Israel, and will plant him, and he shall dwell apart, and shall be troubled no more; and the son of iniquity shall not humble him any more, as from the beginning, from the days when I appointed judges over my people Israel." [93]

CHAPTER XIII

WHETHER THE TRUTH OF THIS PROMISED PEACE CAN BE ASCRIBED TO THOSE TIMES PASSED AWAY UNDER SOLOMON

Whoever hopes for this so great good in this world, and in this earth, his wisdom is but folly. Can any one think it was fulfilled in the peace of Solomon's reign? Scripture certainly commends that peace with excellent praise as a shadow of that which is to come. But this opinion is to be vigilantly opposed, since after it is said, "And the son of iniquity shall not humble him any more," it is immediately added, "as from the beginning, from the days in which I appointed judges over my people Israel." [94] For the judges were appointed over that people from the time when they received the land of promise, before kings had begun to be there. And certainly the son of iniquity, that is, the foreign enemy, humbled him through periods of time in which we read that peace alternated with wars; and in that period longer times of peace are found than Solomon had, who reigned forty years. For under that judge who is called Ehud there were eighty years of peace.[95] Be it far from us, therefore, that we should believe the times of Solomon are predicted in this promise, much less indeed those of any other king whatever. For none other of them reigned in such great peace as he; nor did that nation ever at all hold that kingdom so as to have no anxiety lest it should be subdued by enemies: for in the very great mutability of human affairs such great security is never given to any people, that it should not dread invasions hostile to this life. Therefore the place of this promised peaceful and secure habitation is eternal, and of right belongs eternally to Jerusalem the free mother, where the genuine people of Israel shall be: for this name is inter-

[90] 2 Sam. vii. 8   [91] 2 Sam. vii. 2   [92] Ps. cxxvii. 1   [93] 2 Sam. vii. 10, 11   [94] 2 Sam. vii. 10, 11   [95] Judg. iii. 30

preted "Seeing God;" in the desire of which reward a pious life is to be led through faith in this miserable pilgrimage.[96]

CHAPTER XIV

OF DAVID'S CONCERN IN THE WRITING OF THE PSALMS

In the progress of the city of God through the ages, therefore, David first reigned in the earthly Jerusalem as a shadow of that which was to come. Now David was a man skilled in songs, who dearly loved musical harmony, not with a vulgar delight, but with a believing disposition, and by it served his God, who is the true God, by the mystical representation of a great thing. For the rational and well-ordered concord of diverse sounds in harmonious variety suggests the compact unity of the well-ordered city. Then almost all his prophecy is in psalms, of which a hundred and fifty are contained in what we call the *Book of Psalms*, of which some will have it those only were made by David which are inscribed with his name. But there are also some who think none of them were made by him except those which are marked "Of David;" but those which have in the title "For David" have been made by others who assumed his person. Which opinion is refuted by the voice of the Saviour Himself in the Gospel, when He says that David himself by the Spirit said Christ was his Lord; for the 110th Psalm begins thus, "The Lord said unto my Lord, Sit Thou at my right hand, until I make Thine enemies Thy footstool." [97] And truly that very psalm, like many more, has in the title, not "of David," but "for David." But those seem to me to hold the more credible opinion, who ascribe to him the authorship of all these hundred and fifty psalms, and think that he prefixed to some of them the names even of other men, who prefigured something pertinent to the matter, but chose to have no man's name in the titles of the rest, just as God inspired him in the management of this variety, which, although dark, is not meaningless. Neither ought it to move one not to believe this that the names of some prophets who lived long after the times of king David are read in the inscriptions of certain psalms in that book, and that the things said there seem to be spoken as it were by them. Nor was the prophetic Spirit unable to reveal to king David, when he prophesied, even these names of future prophets, so that he might prophetically sing something which should suit their persons; just as it was revealed to a certain prophet that king Josiah should arise and reign after more than three hundred years, who predicted his future deeds also along with his name.[98]

[96] Israel—a prince of God; Peniel—the face of God (Gen. xxxii. 28-30)
[97] Ps. cx. 1, quoted in Matt. xxii. 44
[98] 1 Kings xiii. 2; fulfilled 2 Kings xxiii. 15-17

CHAPTER XV

WHETHER ALL THE THINGS PROPHESIED IN THE PSALMS CONCERNING
CHRIST AND HIS CHURCH SHOULD BE TAKEN UP IN THE TEXT
OF THIS WORK

And now I see it may be expected of me that I shall open up in this part of this book what David may have prophesied in the Psalms concerning the Lord Jesus Christ or His Church. But although I have already done so in one instance, I am prevented from doing as that expectation seems to demand, rather by the abundance than the scarcity of matter. For the necessity of shunning prolixity forbids my setting down all things; yet I fear lest if I select some I shall appear to many, who know these things, to have passed by the more necessary. Besides, the proof that is adduced ought to be supported by the context of the whole psalm, so that at least there may be nothing against it if everything does not support it; lest we should seem, after the fashion of the centos, to gather for the thing we wish, as it were, verses out of a grand poem, what shall be found to have been written not about it, but about some other and widely different thing. But ere this could be pointed out in each psalm, the whole of it must be expounded; and how great a work that would be, the volumes of others, as well as our own, in which we have done it, show well enough. Let him then who will, or can, read these volumes, and he will find out how many and great things David, at once king and prophet, has prophesied concerning Christ and His Church, to wit, concerning the King and the city which He has built.

CHAPTER XVI

OF THE THINGS PERTAINING TO CHRIST AND THE CHURCH, SAID
EITHER OPENLY OR FIGURATIVELY IN THE 45TH PSALM

For whatever direct and manifest prophetic utterances there may be about anything, it is necessary that those which are figurative should be mingled with them; which, chiefly on account of those of slower understanding, thrust upon the more learned the laborious task of clearing up and expounding them. Some of them, indeed, on the very first blush, as soon as they are spoken, exhibit Christ and the Church, although some things in them that are less intelligible remain to be expounded at leisure. We have an example of this in that same *Book of Psalms:* "My heart bubbled up a good matter: I utter my words to the king. My tongue is the pen of a scribe, writing swiftly. Thy form is beautiful beyond the sons of men; grace is poured out in Thy lips: therefore God hath blessed Thee for evermore. Gird Thy sword about Thy thigh, O Most Mighty. With Thy goodliness and Thy beauty go forward, proceed prosperously, and reign, because of Thy truth, and meekness, and righteousness; and Thy right hand shall lead Thee forth wonderfully. Thy sharp arrows are most powerful: in the heart of the king's enemies. The people shall fall under Thee. Thy throne, O God, is for ever and ever: a rod of direction is the rod of Thy kingdom. Thou hast loved righteousness, and hast hated iniquity: therefore God, Thy God, hath anointed Thee with the oil of exultation above Thy fellows. Myrrh and drops, and cassia from Thy vestments, from the houses of ivory: out of which the daughters of kings have delighted Thee in Thine honor." [99] Who is there, no matter how slow, but must here recognize Christ whom we preach, and in whom we believe, if he hears that He is God, whose throne is for ever and ever, and that He is anointed by God, as God indeed anoints, not with a visible, but with a spiritual and intelligible chrism? For who is so untaught in this religion, or so deaf to its far and wide spread fame, as not to know that Christ is named from this chrism, that is, from this anointing? But when it is acknowledged that this King is Christ, let each one who is already subject to Him who reigns because of truth, meekness, and righteousness, inquire at his leisure into these other things that are here said figuratively: how His form is beautiful beyond the sons of men, with a certain beauty that is the more to be loved and admired the less it is corporeal; and what His sword, arrows, and other things of that kind may be, which are set down, not properly, but figuratively.

Then let him look upon His Church, joined to her so great Husband in spiritual marriage and divine love, of which it is said in these words which follow, "The queen stood upon Thy right hand in gold-embroidered vestments, girded about with variety. Hearken, O daughter, and look, and incline thine ear; forget also thy people, and thy father's house. Because the King hath greatly desired thy beauty; for He is the Lord thy God. And the daughters of Tyre shall worship Him with gifts; the rich among the people shall entreat Thy face. The daughter of the King has all her glory within, in golden fringes, girded about with variety. The virgins shall be brought after her to the King: her neighbors shall be brought to Thee. They shall be brought with gladness and exultation: they shall be led into the temple of the King. Instead of thy fathers, sons shall be born to thee: thou shalt establish them as princes over all the earth. They shall be mindful of thy name in every generation and descent. Therefore shall the people acknowledge thee for evermore, even for ever and ever." [100] I do not think any one is so stupid as to believe that some poor woman is here praised and described, as the spouse, to wit, of Him to whom it is said, "Thy throne, O God, is for ever and ever: a rod of direction is the rod of Thy kingdom. Thou hast loved righteousness and hated iniquity: therefore God, Thy God, hath anointed Thee with the oil of exultation above Thy fellows;" [101] that is, plainly, Christ above Christians. For these are His fellows, out of the unity and concord of whom in all nations that queen is formed, as it is said of her in another psalm,

[99] Ps. xlv. 1-9   [100] Ps. xlv. 9-17   [101] Ps. xlv. 7

"The city of the great King." [102] The same is Sion spiritually, which name in Latin is interpreted *speculatio* (discovery); for she descries the great good of the world to come, because her attention is directed thither. In the same way she is also Jerusalem spiritually, of which we have already said many things. Her enemy is the city of the devil, Babylon, which is interpreted "confusion." Yet out of this Babylon this queen is in all nations set free by regeneration, and passes from the worst to the best King—that is, from the devil to Christ. Wherefore it is said to her, "Forget thy people and thy father's house." Of this impious city those also are a portion who are Israelites only in the flesh and not by faith, enemies also of this great King Himself, and of His queen. For Christ, having come to them, and been slain by them, has the more become the King of others, whom He did not see in the flesh. Whence our King Himself says through the prophecy of a certain psalm, "Thou wilt deliver me from the contradictions of the people; Thou wilt make me head of the nations. A people whom I have not known hath served me: in the hearing of the ear it hath obeyed me." [103] Therefore this people of the nations, which Christ did not know in His bodily presence, yet has believed in that Christ as announced to it; so that it might be said of it with good reason, "In the hearing of the ear it hath obeyed me," for "faith is by hearing." [104] This people, I say, added to those who are the true Israelites both by the flesh and by faith, is the city of God, which has brought forth Christ Himself according to the flesh, since He was in these Israelites only. For thence came the Virgin Mary, in whom Christ assumed flesh that He might be man. Of which city another psalm says, "Mother Sion, shall a man say, and the man is made in her, and the Highest Himself hath founded her." [105] Who is this Highest, save God? And thus Christ, who is God, before He became man through Mary in that city, Himself founded it by the patriarchs and prophets. As therefore was said by prophecy so long before to this queen, the city of God, what we already can see fulfilled, "Instead of thy fathers, sons are born to thee; thou shalt make them princes over all the earth;" [106] so out of her sons truly are set up even her fathers through all the earth, when the people, coming together to her, confess to her with the confession of eternal praise for ever and ever. Beyond doubt, whatever interpretation is put on what is here expressed somewhat darkly in figurative language, ought to be in agreement with these most manifest things.

CHAPTER XVII

OF THOSE THINGS IN THE 110TH PSALM WHICH RELATE TO THE PRIESTHOOD OF CHRIST, AND IN THE 22D TO HIS PASSION

Just as in that psalm also where Christ is most openly proclaimed as Priest, even as He is here as King, "The Lord said unto my Lord, Sit Thou

---

[102] Ps. xlviii. 2   [103] Ps. xviii. 43   [104] Rom. x. 5   [105] Ps. lxxxvii. 5   [106] Ps. xlv. 16

at my right hand, until I make Thine enemies Thy footstool." [107] That Christ
sits on the right hand of God the Father is believed, not seen; that His enemies also are put under His feet doth not yet appear; it is being done, it
will appear at last: yea, this is now believed, afterward it shall be seen. But
what follows, "The Lord will send forth the rod of Thy strength out of Sion,
and rule Thou in the midst of Thine enemies," [108] is so clear, that to deny it
would imply not merely unbelief and mistake, but downright impudence.
And even enemies must certainly confess that out of Sion has been sent the
law of Christ which we call the gospel, and acknowledge as the rod of His
strength. But that He rules in the midst of His enemies, these same enemies
among whom He rules themselves bear witness, gnashing their teeth and
consuming away, and having power to do nothing against Him. Then what
he says a little after, "The Lord hath sworn and will not repent," [109] by
which words He intimates that what He adds is immutable, "Thou art a
priest for ever after the order of Melchizedek," [110] who is permitted to doubt
of whom these things are said, seeing that now there is nowhere a priesthood
and sacrifice after the order of Aaron, and everywhere men offer under Christ
as the Priest, which Melchizedek showed when he blessed Abraham? Therefore to these manifest things are to be referred, when rightly understood,
those things in the same psalm that are set down a little more obscurely, and
we have already made known in our popular sermons how these things are
to be rightly understood. So also in that where Christ utters through prophecy the humiliation of His passion, saying, "They pierced my hands and
feet; they counted all my bones. Yea, they looked and stared at me." [111] By
which words he certainly meant His body stretched out on the cross, with
the hands and feet pierced and perforated by the striking through of the
nails, and that He had in that way made Himself a spectacle to those who
looked and stared. And he adds, "They parted my garments among them,
and over my vesture they cast lots." [112] How this prophecy has been fulfilled
the Gospel history narrates. Then, indeed, the other things also which are
said there less openly are rightly understood when they agree with those
which shine with so great clearness; especially because those things also
which we do not believe as past, but survey as present, are beheld by the
whole world, being now exhibited just as they are read of in this very psalm
as predicted so long before. For it is there said a little after, "All the ends of
the earth shall remember, and turn unto the Lord, and all the kindreds of
the nations shall worship before Him; for the kingdom is the Lord's, and He
shall rule the nations."

[107] Ps. cx. 1 [108] Ps. cx. 2 [109] Ps. cx. 4 [110] Ps. cx. 4 [111] Ps. xxii. 16, 17
[112] Ps. xxii. 18, 19

CHAPTER XVIII

OF THE 3D, 41ST, 15TH, AND 68TH PSALMS, IN WHICH THE DEATH AND RESURRECTION OF THE LORD ARE PROPHESIED

About His resurrection also the oracles of the Psalms are by no means silent. For what else is it that is sung in His person in the 3d Psalm, "I laid me down and took a sleep, I awaked, for the Lord shall sustain me"? [113] Is there perchance any one so stupid as to believe that the prophet chose to point it out to us as something great that He had slept and risen up, unless that sleep had been death, and that awaking the resurrection, which behoved to be thus prophesied concerning Christ? For in the 41st Psalm also it is shown much more clearly, where in the person of the Mediator, in the usual way, things are narrated as if past which were prophesied as yet to come, since these things which were yet to come were in the predestination and foreknowledge of God as if they were done, because they were certain. He says, "Mine enemies speak evil of me; When shall he die, and his name perish? And if he came in to see me, his heart spake vain things: he gathered iniquity to himself. He went out of doors, and uttered it all at once. Against me all mine enemies whisper together: against me do they devise evil. They have planned an unjust thing against me. Shall not he that sleeps also rise again?" [114] These words are certainly so set down here that he may be understood to say nothing else than if he said, Shall not He that died recover life again? The previous words clearly show that His enemies have meditated and planned His death, and that this was executed by him who came in to see, and went out to betray. But to whom does not Judas here occur, who, from being His disciple, became His betrayer? Therefore because they were about to do what they had plotted—that is, were about to kill Him—he, to show them that with useless malice they were about to kill Him who should rise again, so adds this verse, as if he said, What vain thing are you doing? What will be your crime will be my sleep. "Shall not He that sleeps also rise again?" And yet he indicates in the following verses that they should not commit so great an impiety with impunity, saying, "Yea, the man of my peace in whom I trusted, who ate my bread, hath enlarged the heel over me;" [115] that is, hath trampled me under foot. "But Thou," he saith, "O Lord, be merciful unto me, and raise me up, that I may requite them." [116] Who can now deny this who sees the Jews, after the passion and resurrection of Christ, utterly rooted up from their abodes by warlike slaughter and destruction? For, being slain by them, He has risen again, and has requited them meanwhile by temporary discipline, save that for those who are not corrected He keeps it in store for the time when He shall judge the quick and the dead.[117] For the Lord Jesus Himself, in pointing out that very

[113] Ps. iii. 5   [114] Ps. xli. 5-8   [115] Ps. xli. 9   [116] Ps. xli. 10   [117] 2 Tim. iv. 1; 2 Pet. iv. 5

man to the apostles as His betrayer, quoted this very verse of this psalm, and said it was fulfilled in Himself: "He that ate my bread enlarged the heel over me." But what he says, "In whom I trusted," does not suit the head but the body. For the Saviour Himself was not ignorant of him concerning whom He had already said before, "One of you is a devil." [118] But He is wont to assume the person of His members, and to ascribe to Himself what should be said of them, because the head and the body is one Christ;[119] whence that saying in the Gospel, "I was an hungered, and ye gave me to eat." [120] Expounding which, He says, "Since ye did it to one of the least of mine, ye did it to me." [121] Therefore He said that He had trusted, because his disciples then had trusted concerning Judas; for he was numbered with the apostles.[122]

But the Jews do not expect that the Christ whom they expect will die; therefore they do not think ours to be Him whom the law and the prophets announced, but feign to themselves I know not whom of their own, exempt from the suffering of death. Therefore, with wonderful emptiness and blindness, they contend that the words we have set down signify, not death and resurrection, but sleep and awaking again. But the 16th Psalm also cries to them, "Therefore my heart is jocund, and my tongue hath exulted; moreover, my flesh also shall rest in hope: for Thou wilt not leave my soul in hell; neither wilt Thou give Thine Holy One to see corruption." [123] Who but He that rose again the third day could say his flesh had rested in this hope; that His soul, not being left in hell, but speedily returning to it, should revive it, that it should not be corrupted as corpses are wont to be, which they can in no wise say of David the prophet and king? The 68th Psalm also cries out, "Our God is the God of salvation: even of the Lord the exit was by death." [124] What could be more openly said? For the God of salvation is the Lord Jesus, which is interpreted Saviour, or Healing One. For this reason this name was given, when it was said before He was born of the virgin: "Thou shalt bring forth a Son, and shalt call His name Jesus; for He shall save His people from their sins." [125] Because His blood was shed for the remission of their sins, it behoved Him to have no other exit from this life than death. Therefore, when it had been said, "Our God is the God of salvation," immediately it was added, "Even of the Lord the exit was by death," in order to show that we were to be saved by His dying. But that saying is marvellous, "Even of the Lord," as if it was said, Such is that life of mortals, that not even the Lord Himself could go out of it otherwise save through death.

[118] John vi. 70　　[119] 1 Cor. xii. 12　　[120] Matt. xxv. 35　　[121] Matt. xxv. 40　　[122] Acts i. 17　　[123] Ps. xvi. 9, 10　　[124] Ps. lxviii. 20　　[125] Matt. i. 21

CHAPTER XIX

OF THE 69TH PSALM, IN WHICH THE OBSTINATE UNBELIEF OF THE
JEWS IS DECLARED

But when the Jews will not in the least yield to the testimonies of this prophecy, which are so manifest, and are also brought by events to so clear and certain a completion, certainly that is fulfilled in them which is written in that psalm which here follows. For when the things which pertain to His passion are prophetically spoken there also in the person of Christ, that is mentioned which is unfolded in the Gospel: "They gave me gall for my meat; and in my thirst they gave me vinegar for drink." [126] And as it were after such a feast and dainties in this way given to Himself, presently He brings in these words: "Let their table become a trap before them, and a retribution, and an offence: let their eyes be dimmed that they see not, and their back be always bowed down," [127] etc. Which things are not spoken as wished for, but are predicted under the prophetic form of wishing. What wonder, then, if those whose eyes are dimmed that they see not do not see these manifest things? What wonder if those do not look up at heavenly things whose back is always bowed down that they may grovel among earthly things? For these words transferred from the body signify mental faults. Let these things which have been said about the Psalms, that is, about king David's prophecy, suffice, that we may keep within some bound. But let those readers excuse us who knew them all before; and let them not complain about those perhaps stronger proofs which they know or think I have passed by.

CHAPTER XX

OF DAVID'S REIGN AND MERIT; AND OF HIS SON SOLOMON, AND THAT
PROPHECY RELATING TO CHRIST WHICH IS FOUND EITHER IN THOSE
BOOKS WHICH ARE JOINED TO THOSE WRITTEN BY HIM,
OR IN THOSE WHICH ARE INDUBITABLY HIS

David therefore reigned in the earthly Jerusalem, a son of the heavenly Jerusalem, much praised by the divine testimony; for even his faults are overcome by great piety, through the most salutary humility of his repentance, that he is altogether one of those of whom he himself says, "Blessed are they whose iniquities are forgiven, and whose sins are covered." [128] After him Solomon his son reigned over the same whole people, who, as was said before, began to reign while his father was still alive. This man, after good beginnings, made a bad end. For indeed prosperity, which wears out the minds of the wise,[129] hurt him more than that wisdom profited him, which

[126] Ps. lxix. 21; Matt. xxvii. 34, 48   [127] Ps. lxix. 22, 23   [128] Ps. xxxii. 1   [129] Sallust, *Cat.* c. xi

even yet is and shall hereafter be renowned, and was then praised far and wide. He also is found to have prophesied in his books, of which three are received as of canonical authority, *Proverbs, Ecclesiastes*, and the *Song of Songs*. But it has been customary to ascribe to Solomon two others, of which one is called *Wisdom*, the other *Ecclesiasticus*, on account of some resemblance of style—but the more learned have no doubt that they are not his; yet of old the Church, especially the Western, received them into authority —in the one of which, called the *Wisdom of Solomon*, the passion of Christ is most openly prophesied. For indeed His impious murderers are quoted as saying, "Let us lie in wait for the righteous, for he is unpleasant to us, and contrary to our works; and he upbraideth us with our transgressions of the law, and objecteth to our disgrace the transgressions of our education. He professeth to have the knowledge of God, and he calleth himself the Son of God. He was made to reprove our thoughts. He is grievous for us even to behold; for his life is unlike other men's, and his ways are different. We are esteemed of him as counterfeits; and he abstaineth from our ways as from filthiness. He extols the latter end of the righteous; and glorieth that he hath God for his Father. Let us see, therefore, if his words be true; and let us try what shall happen to him, and we shall know what shall be the end of him. For if the righteous be the Son of God, He will undertake for him, and deliver him out of the hand of those that are against him. Let us put him to the question with contumely and torture, that we may know his reverence, and prove his patience. Let us condemn him to the most shameful death; for by His own sayings He shall be respected. These things did they imagine, and were mistaken; for their own malice hath quite blinded them." [130] But in *Ecclesiasticus* the future faith of the nations is predicted in this manner: "Have mercy upon us, O God, Ruler of all, and send Thy fear upon all the nations: lift up Thine hand over the strange nations, and let them see Thy power. As Thou wast sanctified in us before them, so be Thou sanctified in them before us, and let them acknowledge Thee, according as we also have acknowledged Thee; for there is not a God beside Thee, O Lord." [131] We see this prophecy in the form of a wish and prayer fulfilled through Jesus Christ. But the things which are not written in the canon of the Jews cannot be quoted against their contradictions with so great validity.

But as regards those three books which it is evident are Solomon's and held canonical by the Jews, to show what of this kind may be found in them pertaining to Christ and the Church demands a laborious discussion, which, if now entered on, would lengthen this work unduly. Yet what we read in the *Proverbs* of impious men saying, "Let us unrighteously hide in the earth the righteous man; yea, let us swallow him up alive as hell, and let us take away his memory from the earth: let us seize his precious possession," [132] is not so obscure that it may not be understood, without laborious exposition, of Christ and His possession the Church. Indeed, the gospel parable about

[130] Wisd. ii. 12-21   [131] Ecclus. xxxvi. 1-5   [132] Prov. i. 11-13

the wicked husbandmen shows that our Lord Jesus Himself said something like it: "This is the heir; come, let us kill him, and the inheritance shall be ours." [133] In like manner also that passage in this same book, on which we have already touched [134] when we were speaking of the barren woman who hath borne seven, must soon after it was uttered have come to be understood of only Christ and the Church by those who knew that Christ was the Wisdom of God. "Wisdom hath builded her an house, and hath set up seven pillars; she hath sacrificed her victims, she hath mingled her wine in the bowl; she hath also furnished her table. She hath sent her servants summoning to the bowl with excellent proclamation, saying, Who is simple, let him turn aside to me. And to the void of sense she hath said, Come, eat of my bread, and drink of the wine which I have mingled for you." [135] Here certainly we perceive that the Wisdom of God, that is, the Word co-eternal with the Father, hath builded Him an house, even a human body in the virgin womb, and hath subjoined the Church to it as members to a head, hath slain the martyrs as victims, hath furnished a table with wine and bread, where appears also the priesthood after the order of Melchizedek, and hath called the simple and the void of sense, because, as saith the apostle, "He hath chosen the weak things of this world that He might confound the things which are mighty." [136] Yet to these weak ones she saith what follows, "Forsake simplicity, that ye may live; and seek prudence, that ye may have life." [137] But to be made partakers of this table is itself to begin to have life. For when he says in another book, which is called *Ecclesiastes*, "There is no good for a man, except that he should eat and drink," [138] what can he be more credibly understood to say, than what belongs to the participation of this table which the Mediator of the New Testament Himself, the Priest after the order of Melchizedek, furnishes with His own body and blood? For that sacrifice has succeeded all the sacrifices of the Old Testament, which were slain as a shadow of that which was to come; wherefore also we recognize the voice in the 40th Psalm as that of the same Mediator speaking through prophecy, "Sacrifice and offering Thou didst not desire; but a body hast Thou perfected for me." [139] Because, instead of all these sacrifices and oblations, His body is offered, and is served up to the partakers of it. For that this *Ecclesiastes*, in this sentence about eating and drinking, which he often repeats, and very much commends, does not savor the dainties of carnal pleasures, is made plain enough when he says, "It is better to go into the house of mourning than to go into the house of feasting." [140] And a little after He says, "The heart of the wise is in the house of mourning, and the heart of the simple in the house of feasting." [141] But I think that more worthy of quotation from this book which relates to both cities, the one of the devil, the other of Christ, and to their kings, the devil and Christ: "Woe to thee, O land," he says,

---

[133] Matt. xxi. 38   [134] Ch. 4   [135] Prov. ix. 1-5 (ver. 1 is quoted above in ch. 4) [136] 1 Cor. i. 27   [137] Prov. ix. 6   [138] Eccles. ii. 24; iii. 13; v. 18; viii. 15   [139] Ps. xl. 6   [140] Eccles. vii. 2   [141] Eccles. vii. 4

"when thy king is a youth, and thy princes eat in the morning! Blessed art thou, O land, when thy king is the son of nobles, and thy princes eat in season, in fortitude, and not in confusion!" [142] He has called the devil a youth, because of the folly and pride, and rashness and unruliness, and other vices which are wont to abound at that age; but Christ is the Son of nobles, that is, of the holy patriarchs, of those belonging to the free city, of whom He was begotten in the flesh. The princes of that and other cities are eaters in the morning, that is, before the suitable hour, because they do not expect the seasonable felicity, which is the true, in the world to come, desiring to be speedily made happy with the renown of this world; but the princes of the city of Christ patiently wait for the time of a blessedness that is not fallacious. This is expressed by the words, "in fortitude, and not in confusion," because hope does not deceive them; of which the apostle says, "But hope maketh not ashamed." [143] A psalm also saith, "For they that hope in Thee shall not be put to shame." [144] But now the *Song of Songs* is a certain spiritual pleasure of holy minds, in the marriage of that King and Queen-city, that is, Christ and the Church. But this pleasure is wrapped up in allegorical veils, that the Bridegroom may be more ardently desired, and more joyfully unveiled, and may appear; to whom it is said in this same song, "Equity hath delighted Thee;" [145] and the bride who there hears, "Charity is in thy delights." [146] We pass over many things in silence, in our desire to finish this work.

CHAPTER XXI

OF THE KINGS AFTER SOLOMON, BOTH IN JUDAH AND ISRAEL

The other kings of the Hebrews after Solomon are scarcely found to have prophesied, through certain enigmatic words or actions of theirs, what may pertain to Christ and the Church, either in Judah or Israel; for so were the parts of that people styled, when, on account of Solomon's offence, from the time of Rehoboam his son, who succeeded him in the kingdom, it was divided by God as a punishment. The ten tribes, indeed, which Jeroboam the servant of Solomon received, being appointed the king in Samaria, were distinctively called Israel, although this had been the name of that whole people; but the two tribes, namely, of Judah and Benjamin, which for David's sake, lest the kingdom should be wholly wrenched from his race, remained subject to the city of Jerusalem, were called Judah, because that was the tribe whence David sprang. But Benjamin, the other tribe which, as was said, belonged to the same kingdom, was that whence Saul sprang before David. But these two tribes together, as was said, were called Judah, and were distinguished by this name from Israel, which was the distinctive title of the ten tribes under their own king. For the tribe of Levi, because it was the priestly one, bound to the servitude of God, not of the kings, was reckoned the thirteenth. For Joseph, one of the twelve sons of Israel, did not, like the others, form one tribe, but two, Ephraim and Manasseh. Yet the tribe of Levi also belonged more to the kingdom of Jerusalem, where was the temple of God whom it served. On the division of the people, therefore, Rehoboam, son of Solomon, reigned in Jerusalem as the first king of Judah, and Jeroboam, servant of Solomon, in Samaria as king of Israel. And when Rehoboam wished as a tyrant to pursue that separated part with war, the people were prohibited from fighting with their brethren by God, who told them through a prophet that He had done this; whence it appeared that in this matter there had been no sin either of the king or people of Israel, but the accomplished will of God the avenger. When this was known, both parts settled down peaceably, for the division made was not religious but political.

CHAPTER XXII

OF JEROBOAM, WHO PROFANED THE PEOPLE PUT UNDER HIM BY THE IMPIETY OF IDOLATRY, AMID WHICH, HOWEVER, GOD DID NOT CEASE TO INSPIRE THE PROPHETS, AND TO GUARD MANY FROM THE CRIME OF IDOLATRY

But Jeroboam king of Israel, with perverse mind, not believing in God, whom he had proved true in promising and giving him the kingdom, was afraid lest, by coming to the temple of God which was in Jerusalem, where, according to the divine law, that whole nation was to come in order to sacrifice, the people should be seduced from him, and return to David's line as the seed royal; and set up idolatry in his kingdom, and with horrible impiety beguiled the people, ensnaring them to the worship of idols with himself. Yet God did not altogether cease to reprove by the prophets, not only that king, but also his successors and imitators in his impiety, and the people too. For there the great and illustrious prophet Elijah and Elisha his disciple arose, who also did many wonderful works. Even there, when Elijah said, "O Lord, they have slain Thy prophets, they have digged down Thine altars; and I am left alone, and they seek my life," it was answered that seven thousand men were there who had not bowed the knee to Baal.[147]

CHAPTER XXIII

OF THE VARYING CONDITION OF BOTH THE HEBREW KINGDOMS, UNTIL THE PEOPLE OF BOTH WERE AT DIFFERENT TIMES LED INTO CAPTIVITY, JUDAH BEING AFTERWARDS RECALLED INTO HIS KINGDOM, WHICH FINALLY PASSED INTO THE POWER OF THE ROMANS

So also in the kingdom of Judah pertaining to Jerusalem prophets were not lacking even in the times of succeeding kings, just as it pleased God to send

[147] 1 Kings xix. 10, 14, 15

them, either for the prediction of what was needful, or for correction of sin and instruction in righteousness;[148] for there, too, although far less than in Israel, kings arose who grievously offended God by their impieties, and, along with their people, who were like them, were smitten with moderate scourges. The no small merits of the pious kings there are praised indeed. But we read that in Israel the kings were, some more, others less, yet all wicked. Each part, therefore, as the divine providence either ordered or permitted, was both lifted up by prosperity and weighed down by adversity of various kinds; and it was afflicted not only by foreign, but also by civil wars with each other, in order that by certain existing causes the mercy or anger of God might be manifested; until, by His growing indignation, that whole nation was by the conquering Chaldeans not only overthrown in its abode, but also for the most part transported to the lands of the Assyrians—first, that part of the thirteen tribes called Israel, but afterwards Judah also, when Jerusalem and that most noble temple was cast down—in which lands it rested seventy years in captivity. Being after that time sent forth thence, they rebuilt the overthrown temple. And although very many stayed in the lands of the strangers, yet the kingdom no longer had two separate parts, with different kings over each, but in Jerusalem there was one prince over them; and at certain times, from every direction wherever they were, and from whatever place they could, they all came to the temple of God which was there. Yet not even then were they without foreign enemies and conquerors; yea, Christ found them tributaries of the Romans.

CHAPTER XXIV

OF THE PROPHETS, WHO EITHER WERE THE LAST AMONG THE JEWS, OR WHOM THE GOSPEL HISTORY REPORTS ABOUT THE TIME OF CHRIST'S NATIVITY

But in that whole time after they returned from Babylon, after Malachi, Haggai, and Zechariah, who then prophesied, and Ezra, they had no prophets down to the time of the Saviour's advent except another Zechariah, the father of John, and Elisabeth his wife, when the nativity of Christ was already close at hand; and when He was already born, Simeon the aged, and Anna a widow, and now very old; and, last of all, John himself, who, being a young man, did not predict that Christ, now a young man, was to come, but by prophetic knowledge pointed Him out although unknown; for which reason the Lord Himself says, "The law and the prophets were until John." [149] But the prophesying of these five is made known to us in the gospel, where the virgin mother of our Lord herself is also found to have prophesied before John. But this prophecy of theirs the wicked Jews do not receive; but those innumerable persons received it who from them believed the gos-

[148] 2 Tim. iii. 16   [149] Matt. xi. 13

pel. For then truly Israel was divided in two, by that division which was foretold by Samuel the prophet to king Saul as immutable. But even the reprobate Jews hold Malachi, Haggai, Zechariah, and Ezra as the last received into canonical authority. For there are also writings of these, as of others, who being but a very few in the great multitude of prophets, have written those books which have obtained canonical authority, of whose predictions it seems good to me to put in this work some which pertain to Christ and His Church; and this, by the Lord's help, shall be done more conveniently in the following book, that we may not further burden this one, which is already too long.

BOOK EIGHTEEN

ARGUMENT

Augustine traces the parallel courses of the earthly and heavenly cities from the time of Abraham to the end of the world; and alludes to the oracles regarding Christ, both those uttered by the Sibyls, and those of the sacred prophets who wrote after the foundation of Rome, Hosea, Amos, Isaiah, Micah, and their successors.

CHAPTER I

OF THOSE THINGS DOWN TO THE TIMES OF THE SAVIOUR WHICH HAVE BEEN DISCUSSED IN THE SEVENTEEN BOOKS

I PROMISED to write of the rise, progress, and appointed end of the two cities, one of which is God's, the other this world's, in which, so far as mankind is concerned, the former is now a stranger. But first of all I undertook, so far as His grace should enable me, to refute the enemies of the city of God, who prefer their gods to Christ its founder, and fiercely hate Christians with the most deadly malice. And this I have done in the first ten books. Then, as regards my threefold promise which I have just mentioned, I have treated distinctly, in the four books which follow the tenth, of the rise of both cities. After that, I have proceeded from the first man down to the flood in one book, which is the fifteenth of this work; and from that again down to Abraham our work has followed both in chronological order. From the patriarch Abraham down to the time of the Israelite kings, at which we close our sixteenth book, and thence down to the advent of Christ Himself in the flesh, to which period the seventeenth book reaches, the city of God appears from my way of writing to have run its course alone; whereas it did not run its course alone in this age, for both cities, in their course amid mankind, certainly experienced chequered times together just as from the beginning. But I did this in order that, first of all, from the time when the promises of God began to be more clear, down to the virgin birth of Him in whom those things promised from the first were to be fulfilled, the course of that city which is God's might be made more distinctly apparent, without interpolation of foreign matter from the history of the other city, although down to the revelation of the new covenant it ran its course, not in light, but in shadow. Now, therefore, I think fit to do what I passed by, and show, so far as seems necessary, how that other city ran its course from the times of Abraham, so that attentive readers may compare the two.

CHAPTER II

OF THE KINGS AND TIMES OF THE EARTHLY CITY WHICH WERE SYNCHRONOUS WITH THE TIMES OF THE SAINTS, RECKONING FROM THE RISE OF ABRAHAM

The society of mortals spread abroad through the earth everywhere, and in the most diverse places, although bound together by a certain fellowship of our common nature, is yet for the most part divided against itself, and the strongest oppress the others, because all follow after their own interests and lusts, while what is longed for either suffices for none, or not for all, because it is not the very thing. For the vanquished succumb to the victorious, preferring any sort of peace and safety to freedom itself; so that they who chose to die rather than be slaves have been greatly wondered at. For in almost all nations the very voice of nature somehow proclaims, that those who happen to be conquered should choose rather to be subject to their conquerors than to be killed by all kinds of warlike destruction. This does not take place without the providence of God, in whose power it lies that any one either subdues or is subdued in war; that some are endowed with kingdoms, others made subject to kings. Now, among the very many kingdoms of the earth into which, by earthly interest or lust, society is divided (which we call by the general name of the city of this world) we see that two, settled and kept distinct from each other both in time and place, have grown far more famous than the rest, first that of the Assyrians, then that of the Romans. First came the one, then the other. The former arose in the east, and, immediately on its close, the latter in the west. I may speak of other kingdoms and other kings as appendages of these.

Ninus, then, who succeeded his father Belus, the first king of Assyria, was already the second king of that kingdom when Abraham was born in the land of the Chaldees. There was also at that time a very small kingdom of Sicyon, with which, as from an ancient date, that most universally learned man Marcus Varro begins, in writing of the Roman race. For from these kings of Sicyon he passes to the Athenians, from them to the Latins, and from these to the Romans. Yet very little is related about these kingdoms, before the foundation of Rome, in comparison with that of Assyria. For although even Sallust, the Roman historian, admits that the Athenians were very famous in Greece, yet he thinks they were greater in fame than in fact. For in speaking of them he says, "The deeds of the Athenians, as I think, were very great and magnificent, but yet somewhat less than reported by fame. But because writers of great genius arose among them, the deeds of the Athenians were celebrated throughout the world as very great. Thus the virtue of those who did them was held to be as great as men of transcendent genius could represent it to be by the power of laudatory words." [1] This city also derived no

[1] Sallust, *Cat*. c. 8

small glory from literature and philosophy, the study of which chiefly flourished there. But as regards empire, none in the earliest times was greater than the Assyrian, or so widely extended. For when Ninus the son of Belus was king, he is reported to have subdued the whole of Asia, even to the boundaries of Libya, which as to number is called the third part, but as to size is found to be the half of the whole world. The Indians in the eastern regions were the only people over whom he did not reign; but after his death Semiramis his wife made war on them. Thus it came to pass that all the people and kings in those countries were subject to the kingdom and authority of the Assyrians, and did whatever they were commanded. Now Abraham was born in that kingdom among the Chaldees, in the time of Ninus. But since Grecian affairs are much better known to us than Assyrian, and those who have diligently investigated the antiquity of the Roman nation's origin have followed the order of time through the Greeks to the Latins, and from them to the Romans, who themselves are Latins, we ought on this account, where it is needful, to mention the Assyrian kings, that it may appear how Babylon, like a first Rome, ran its course along with the city of God, which is a stranger in this world. But the things proper for insertion in this work in comparing the two cities, that is, the earthly and heavenly, ought to be taken mostly from the Greek and Latin kingdoms, where Rome herself is like a second Babylon.

At Abraham's birth, then, the second kings of Assyria and Sicyon respectively were Ninus and Europs, the first having been Belus and Aegialeus. But when God promised Abraham, on his departure from Babylonia, that he should become a great nation, and that in his seed all nations of the earth should be blessed, the Assyrians had their seventh king, the Sicyons their fifth; for the son of Ninus reigned among them after his mother Semiramis, who is said to have been put to death by him for attempting to defile him by incestuously lying with him. Some think that she founded Babylon, and indeed she may have founded it anew. But we have told, in the sixteenth book, when or by whom it was founded. Now the son of Ninus and Semiramis, who succeeded his mother in the kingdom, is also called Ninus by some, but by others Ninias, a patronymic word. Telexion then held the kingdom of the Sicyons. In his reign times were quiet and joyful to such a degree, that after his death they worshipped him as a god by offering sacrifices and by celebrating games, which are said to have been first instituted on this occasion.

CHAPTER III

WHAT KINGS REIGNED IN ASSYRIA AND SICYON WHEN, ACCORDING TO
THE PROMISE, ISAAC WAS BORN TO ABRAHAM IN HIS HUNDREDTH
YEAR, AND WHEN THE TWINS ESAU AND JACOB WERE BORN
OF REBECCA TO ISAAC IN HIS SIXTIETH YEAR

In his times also, by the promise of God, Isaac, the son of Abraham, was
born to his father when he was a hundred years old, of Sarah his wife, who,
being barren and old, had already lost hope of issue. Aralius was then the
fifth king of the Assyrians. To Isaac himself, in his sixtieth year, were born
twin-sons, Esau and Jacob, whom Rebecca his wife bore to him, their grandfather Abraham, who died on completing a hundred and seventy years, being
still alive, and reckoning his hundred and sixtieth year.[2] At that time there
reigned as the seventh kings—among the Assyrians, that more ancient
Xerxes, who was also called Balaeus; and among the Sicyons, Thuriachus,
or, as some write his name, Thurimachus. The kingdom of Argos, in which
Inachus reigned first, arose in the time of Abraham's grandchildren. And I
must not omit what Varro relates, that the Sicyons were also wont to sacrifice at the tomb of their seventh king Thuriachus. In the reign of Armamitres
in Assyria and Leucippus in Sicyon as the eighth kings, and of Inachus as
the first in Argos, God spoke to Isaac, and promised the same two things to
him as to his father—namely, the land of Canaan to his seed, and the blessing of all nations in his seed. These same things were promised to his son,
Abraham's grandson, who was at first called Jacob, afterwards Israel, when
Belocus was the ninth king of Assyria, and Phoroneus, the son of Inachus,
reigned as the second king of Argos, Leucippus still continuing king of Sicyon. In those times, under the Argive king Phoroneus, Greece was made
more famous by the institution of certain laws and judges. On the death of
Phoroneus, his younger brother Phegous built a temple at his tomb, in which
he was worshipped as God, and oxen were sacrificed to him. I believe they
thought him worthy of so great honor, because in his part of the kingdom
(for their father had divided his territories between them, in which they
reigned during his life) he had founded chapels for the worship of the gods,
and had taught them to measure time by months and years, and to that extent to keep count and reckoning of events. Men still uncultivated, admiring
him for these novelties, either fancied he was, or resolved that he should be
made, a god after his death. Io also is said to have been the daughter of
Inachus, who was afterwards called Isis, when she was worshipped in Egypt
as a great goddess; although others write that she came as a queen out of
Ethiopia, and because she ruled extensively and justly, and instituted for her
subjects letters and many useful things, such divine honor was given her

[2] In the Hebrew text, Gen. xxv. 7, a hundred and seventy-five years

there after she died, that if any one said she had been human, he was charged with a capital crime.

CHAPTER IV

OF THE TIMES OF JACOB AND HIS SON JOSEPH

In the reign of Balaeus, the ninth king of Assyria, and Mesappus, the eighth of Sicyon, who is said by some to have been also called Cephisos (if indeed the same man had both names, and those who put the other name in their writings have not rather confounded him with another man), while Apis was third king of Argos, Isaac died, a hundred and eighty years old, and left his twin-sons a hundred and twenty years old. Jacob, the younger of these, belonged to the city of God about which we write (the elder being wholly rejected) and had twelve sons, one of whom, called Joseph, was sold by his brothers to merchants going down to Egypt, while his grandfather Isaac was still alive. But when he was thirty years of age, Joseph stood before Pharaoh, being exalted out of the humiliation he endured, because, in divinely interpreting the king's dreams, he foretold that there would be seven years of plenty, the very rich abundance of which would be consumed by seven other years of famine that should follow. On this account the king made him ruler over Egypt, liberating him from prison, into which he had been thrown for keeping his chastity intact; for he bravely preserved it from his mistress, who wickedly loved him, and told lies to his weakly credulous master, and did not consent to commit adultery with her, but fled from her, leaving his garment in her hands when she laid hold of him. In the second of the seven years of famine Jacob came down into Egypt to his son with all he had, being a hundred and thirty years old, as he himself said in answer to the king's question. Joseph was then thirty-nine, if we add seven years of plenty and two of famine to the thirty he reckoned when honored by the king.

CHAPTER V

OF APIS KING OF ARGOS, WHOM THE EGYPTIANS CALLED SERAPIS, AND WORSHIPPED WITH DIVINE HONORS

In these times Apis king of Argos crossed over into Egypt in ships, and, on dying there, was made Serapis, the chief god of all the Egyptians. Now Varro gives this very ready reason why, after his death, he was called, not Apis, but Serapis. The ark in which he was placed when dead, which every one now calls a sarcophagus, was then called in Greek σορός, and they began to worship him when buried in it before his temple was built; and from Soros and Apis he was called first [Sorosapis, or] Sorapis, and then Serapis, by changing a letter, as easily happens. It was decreed regarding him also, that whoever should say he had been a man should be capitally punished.

And since in every temple where Isis and Serapis were worshipped there was also an image which, with finger pressed on the lips, seemed to warn men to keep silence, Varro thinks this signifies that it should be kept secret that they had been human. But that bull which, with wonderful folly, deluded Egypt nourished with abundant delicacies in honor of him, was not called Serapis, but Apis, because they worshipped him alive without a sarcophagus. On the death of that bull, when they sought and found a calf of the same color—that is, similarly marked with certain white spots—they believed it was something miraculous, and divinely provided for them. Yet it was no great thing for the demons, in order to deceive them, to show to a cow when she was conceiving and pregnant the image of such a bull, which she alone could see, and by it attract the breeding passion of the mother, so that it might appear in a bodily shape in her young, just as Jacob so managed with the spotted rods that the sheep and goats were born spotted. For what men can do with real colors and substances, the demons can very easily do by showing unreal forms to breeding animals.

CHAPTER VI

WHO WERE KINGS OF ARGOS, AND OF ASSYRIA, WHEN JACOB DIED IN EGYPT

Apis, then, who died in Egypt, was not the king of Egypt, but of Argos. He was succeeded by his son Argus, from whose name the land was called Argos and the people Argives, for under the earlier kings neither the place nor the nation as yet had this name. While he then reigned over Argos, and Eratus over Sicyon, and Balaeus still remained king of Assyria, Jacob died in Egypt a hundred and forty-seven years old, after he had, when dying, blessed his sons and his grandsons by Joseph, and prophesied most plainly of Christ, saying in the blessing of Judah, "A prince shall not fail out of Judah, nor a leader from his thighs, until those things come which are laid up for him; and He is the expectation of the nations." [3] In the reign of Argus, Greece began to use fruits, and to have crops of corn in cultivated fields, the seed having been brought from other countries. Argus also began to be accounted a god after his death, and was honored with a temple and sacrifices. This honor was conferred in his reign, before being given to him, on a private individual for being the first to yoke oxen in the plough. This was one Homogyrus, who was struck by lightning.

CHAPTER VII

WHO WERE KINGS WHEN JOSEPH DIED IN EGYPT

In the reign of Mamitus, the twelfth king of Assyria, and Plemnaeus, the eleventh of Sicyon, while Argus still reigned over the Argives, Joseph died in

[3] Gen. xlix. 10

Egypt a hundred and ten years old. After his death, the people of God,
increasing wonderfully, remained in Egypt a hundred and forty-five years,
in tranquillity at first, until those who knew Joseph were dead. Afterward,
through envy of their increase, and the suspicion that they would at length
gain their freedom, they were oppressed with persecutions and the labors of
intolerable servitude, amid which, however, they still grew, being multiplied
with God-given fertility. During this period the same kingdoms continued
in Assyria and Greece.

CHAPTER VIII

WHO WERE KINGS WHEN MOSES WAS BORN, AND WHAT GODS BEGAN TO BE WORSHIPPED THEN

When Saphrus reigned as the fourteenth king of Assyria, and Orthopolis
as the twelfth of Sicyon, and Criasus as the fifth of Argos, Moses was born
in Egypt, by whom the people of God were liberated from the Egyptian slavery, in which they behoved to be thus tried that they might desire the help
of their Creator. Some have thought that Prometheus lived during the reign
of the kings now named. He is reported to have formed men out of clay, because he was esteemed the best teacher of wisdom; yet it does not appear
what wise men there were in his days. His brother Atlas is said to have been
a great astrologer; and this gave occasion for the fable that he held up the
sky, although the vulgar opinion about his holding up the sky appears rather
to have been suggested by a high mountain named after him. Indeed, from
those times many other fabulous things began to be invented in Greece; yet,
down to Cecrops king of Athens, in whose reign that city received its name,
and in whose reign God brought His people out of Egypt by Moses, only a
few dead heroes are reported to have been deified according to the vain
superstition of the Greeks. Among these were Melantomice, the wife of king
Criasus, and Phorbas their son, who succeeded his father as sixth king of the
Argives, and Iasus, son of Triopas, their seventh king, and their ninth king,
Sthenelas, or Stheneleus, or Sthenelus—for his name is given differently by
different authors. In those times also, Mercury, the grandson of Atlas by his
daughter Maia, is said to have lived, according to the common report in
books. He was famous for his skill in many arts, and taught them to men,
for which they resolved to make him, and even believed that he deserved to
be, a god after death. Hercules is said to have been later, yet belonging to the
same period; although some, whom I think mistaken, assign him an earlier
date than Mercury. But at whatever time they were born, it is agreed among
grave historians, who have committed these ancient things to writing, that
both were men, and that they merited divine honors from mortals because
they conferred on them many benefits to make this life more pleasant to
them. Minerva was far more ancient than these; for she is reported to have
appeared in virgin age in the times of Ogyges at the lake called Triton, from

which she is also styled Tritonia, the inventress truly of many works, and the more readily believed to be a goddess because her origin was so little known. For what is sung about her having sprung from the head of Jupiter belongs to the region of poetry and fable, and not to that of history and real fact. And historical writers are not agreed when Ogyges flourished, in whose time also a great flood occurred—not that greatest one from which no man escaped except those who could get into the ark, for neither Greek nor Latin history knew of it, yet a greater flood than that which happened afterward in Deucalion's time. For Varro begins the book I have already mentioned at this date, and does not propose to himself, as the starting-point from which he may arrive at Roman affairs, anything more ancient than the flood of Ogyges, that is, which happened in the time of Ogyges. Now our writers of chronicles—first Eusebius, and afterwards Jerome, who entirely follow some earlier historians in this opinion—relate that the flood of Ogyges happened more than three hundred years after, during the reign of Phoroneus, the second king of Argos. But whenever he may have lived, Minerva was already worshipped as a goddess when Cecrops reigned in Athens, in whose reign the city itself is reported to have been rebuilt or founded.

CHAPTER IX

WHEN THE CITY OF ATHENS WAS FOUNDED, AND WHAT REASON VARRO ASSIGNS FOR ITS NAME

Athens certainly derived its name from Minerva, who in Greek is called Ἀθήνη, and Varro points out the following reason why it was so called. When an olive-tree suddenly appeared there, and water burst forth in another place, these prodigies moved the king to send to the Delphic Apollo to inquire what they meant and what he should do. He answered that the olive signified Minerva, the water Neptune, and that the citizens had it in their power to name their city as they chose, after either of these two gods whose signs these were. On receiving this oracle, Cecrops convoked all the citizens of either sex to give their vote, for it was then the custom in those parts for the women also to take part in public deliberations. When the multitude was consulted, the men gave their votes for Neptune, the women for Minerva; and as the women had a majority of one, Minerva conquered. Then Neptune, being enraged, laid waste the lands of the Athenians, by casting up the waves of the sea; for the demons have no difficulty in scattering any waters more widely. The same authority said, that to appease his wrath the women should be visited by the Athenians with the three-fold punishment—that they should no longer have any vote; that none of their children should be named after their mothers; and that no one should call them Athenians. Thus that city, the mother and nurse of liberal doctrines, and of so many and so great philosophers, than whom Greece had nothing more famous and noble, by the mockery of demons about the strife of their gods, a male and

female, and from the victory of the female one through the women, received
the name of Athens; and, on being damaged by the vanquished god, was
compelled to punish the very victory of the victress, fearing the waters of
Neptune more than the arms of Minerva. For in the women who were thus
punished, Minerva, who had conquered, was conquered too, and could not
even help her voters so far that, although the right of voting was henceforth
lost, and the mothers could not give their names to the children, they might
at least be allowed to be called Athenians, and to merit the name of that
goddess whom they had made victorious over a male god by giving her their
votes. What and how much could be said about this, if we had not to hasten
to other things in our discourse, is obvious.

CHAPTER X

WHAT VARRO REPORTS ABOUT THE TERM AREOPAGUS, AND ABOUT DEUCALION'S FLOOD

Marcus Varro, however, is not willing to credit lying fables against the
gods, lest he should find something dishonoring to their majesty; and therefore he will not admit that the Areopagus, the place where the Apostle Paul
disputed with the Athenians, got this name because Mars, who in Greek is
called Ἄρης, when he was charged with the crime of homicide, and was
judged by twelve gods in that field, was acquitted by the sentence of six;
because it was the custom, when the votes were equal, to acquit rather than
condemn. Against this opinion, which is much most widely published, he
tries, from the notices of obscure books, to support another reason for this
name, lest the Athenians should be thought to have called it Areopagus from
the words "Mars" and "field," [4] as if it were the field of Mars, to the dishonor of the gods, forsooth, from whom he thinks lawsuits and judgments
far removed. And he asserts that this which is said about Mars is not less
false than what is said about the three goddesses, to wit, Juno, Minerva, and
Venus, whose contest for the palm of beauty, before Paris as judge, in order
to obtain the golden apple, is not only related, but is celebrated in songs and
dances amid the applause of the theatres, in plays meant to please the gods
who take pleasure in these crimes of their own, whether real or fabled. Varro
does not believe these things, because they are incompatible with the nature
of the gods and of morality; and yet, in giving not a fabulous but a historic
reason for the name of Athens, he inserts in his books the strife between
Neptune and Minerva as to whose name should be given to that city, which
was so great that, when they contended by the display of prodigies, even
Apollo dared not judge between them when consulted; but, in order to end
the strife of the gods, just as Jupiter sent the three goddesses we have named
to Paris, so he sent them to men, when Minerva won by the vote, and yet

[4] Ἄρης and πάγος

was defeated by the punishment of her own voters, for she was unable to confer the title of Athenians on the women who were her friends, although she could impose it on the men who were her opponents. In these times, when Cranaos reigned at Athens as the successor of Cecrops, as Varro writes, but, according to our Eusebius and Jerome, while Cecrops himself still remained, the flood occurred which is called Deucalion's, because it occurred chiefly in those parts of the earth in which he reigned. But this flood did not at all reach Egypt or its vicinity.

CHAPTER XI

WHEN MOSES LED THE PEOPLE OUT OF EGYPT; AND WHO WERE KINGS WHEN HIS SUCCESSOR JOSHUA THE SON OF NUN DIED

Moses led the people out of Egypt in the last time of Cecrops king of Athens, when Ascatades reigned in Assyria, Marathus in Sicyon, Triopas in Argos; and having led forth the people, he gave them at Mount Sinai the law he received from God, which is called the Old Testament, because it has earthly promises, and because, through Jesus Christ, there was to be a New Testament, in which the kingdom of heaven should be promised. For the same order behoved to be observed in this as is observed in each man who prospers in God, according to the saying of the apostle, "That is not first which is spiritual, but that which is natural," since, as he says, and that truly, "The first man of the earth, is earthly; the second man, from heaven, is heavenly." [5] Now Moses ruled the people for forty years in the wilderness, and died a hundred and twenty years old, after he had prophesied of Christ by the types of carnal observances in the tabernacle, priesthood, and sacrifices, and many other mystic ordinances. Joshua the son of Nun succeeded Moses, and settled in the land of promise the people he had brought in, having by divine authority conquered the people by whom it was formerly possessed. He also died, after ruling the people twenty-seven years after the death of Moses, when Amyntas reigned in Assyria as the eighteenth king, Coracos as the sixteenth in Sicyon, Danaos as the tenth in Argos, Ericthonius as the fourth in Athens.

CHAPTER XII

OF THE RITUALS OF FALSE GODS INSTITUTED BY THE KINGS OF GREECE IN THE PERIOD FROM ISRAEL'S EXODUS FROM EGYPT DOWN TO THE DEATH OF JOSHUA THE SON OF NUN

During this period, that is, from Israel's exodus from Egypt down to the death of Joshua the son of Nun, through whom that people received the land of promise, rituals were instituted to the false gods by the kings of Greece,

[5] 1 Cor. xv. 46, 47

which, by stated celebration, recalled the memory of the flood, and of men's deliverance from it, and of that troublous life they then led in migrating to and fro between the heights and the plains. For even the Luperci,[6] when they ascend and descend the sacred path, are said to represent the men who sought the mountain summits because of the inundation of water, and returned to the lowlands on its subsidence. In those times, Dionysus, who was also called Father Liber, and was esteemed a god after death, is said to have shown the vine to his host in Attica. Then the musical games were instituted for the Delphic Apollo, to appease his anger, through which they thought the regions of Greece were afflicted with barrenness, because they had not defended his temple which Danaos burnt when he invaded those lands; for they were warned by his oracle to institute these games. But king Ericthonius first instituted games to him in Attica, and not to him only, but also to Minerva, in which games the olive was given as the prize to the victors, because they relate that Minerva was the discoverer of that fruit, as Liber was of the grape. In those years Europa is alleged to have been carried off by Xanthus king of Crete (to whom we find some give another name) and to have borne him Rhadamanthus, Sarpedon, and Minos, who are more commonly reported to have been the sons of Jupiter by the same woman. Now those who worship such gods regard what we have said about Xanthus king of Crete as true history; but this about Jupiter, which the poets sing, the theatres applaud, and the people celebrate, as empty fable got up as a reason for games to appease the deities, even with the false ascription of crimes to them. In those times Hercules was held in honor in Tyre, but that was not the same one as he whom we spoke of above. In the more secret history there are said to have been several who were called Father Liber and Hercules. This Hercules, whose great deeds are reckoned as twelve (not including the slaughter of Antaeus the African, because that affair pertains to another Hercules) is declared in their books to have burned himself on Mount Oeta, because he was not able, by that strength with which he had subdued monsters, to endure the disease under which he languished. At that time the king, or rather tyrant Busiris, who is alleged to have been the son of Neptune by Libya the daughter of Epaphus, is said to have offered up his guests in sacrifice to the gods. Now it must not be believed that Neptune committed this adultery, lest the gods should be criminated; yet such things must be ascribed to them by the poets and in the theatres, that they may be pleased with them. Vulcan and Minerva are said to have been the parents of Ericthonius king of Athens, in whose last years Joshua the son of Nun is found to have died. But since they will have it that Minerva is a virgin, they say that Vulcan, being disturbed in the struggle between them, poured out his seed into the earth, and on that account the man born of it received that name; for in the Greek language ἔρις is "strife," and χθών "earth," of which two words Ericthonius is a compound. Yet it must be admitted that

[6] The priests who officiated at the Lupercalia

the more learned disprove and disown such things concerning their gods, and declare that this fabulous belief originated in the fact that in the temple at Athens, which Vulcan and Minerva had in common, a boy who had been exposed was found wrapped up in the coils of a dragon, which signified that he would become great, and, as his parents were unknown, he was called the son of Vulcan and Minerva, because they had the temple in common. Yet that fable accounts for the origin of his name better than this history. But what does it matter to us? Let the one in books that speak the truth edify religious men, and the other in lying fables delight impure demons. Yet these religious men worship them as gods. Still, while they deny these things concerning them they cannot clear them of all crime, because at their demand they exhibit plays in which the very things they wisely deny are basely done, and the gods are appeased by these false and base things. Now, even although the play celebrates an unreal crime of the gods, yet to delight in the ascription of an unreal crime is a real one.

CHAPTER XIII

WHAT FABLES WERE INVENTED AT THE TIME WHEN JUDGES BEGAN TO RULE THE HEBREWS

After the death of Joshua the son of Nun, the people of God had judges, in whose times they were alternately humbled by afflictions on account of their sins, and consoled by prosperity through the compassion of God. In those times were invented the fables about Triptolemus, who, at the command of Ceres, borne by winged snakes, bestowed corn on the needy lands in flying over them; about that beast the Minotaur, which was shut up in the Labyrinth, from which men who entered its inextricable mazes could find no exit; about the Centaurs, whose form was a compound of horse and man; about Cerberus, the three-headed dog of hell; about Phryxus and his sister Hellas, who fled, borne by a winged ram; about the Gorgon, whose hair was composed of serpents, and who turned those who looked on her into stone; about Bellerophon, who was carried by a winged horse called Pegasus; about Amphion, who charmed and attracted the stones by the sweetness of his harp; about the artificer Daedalus and his son Icarus, who flew on wings they had fitted on; about Oedipus, who compelled a certain four-footed monster with a human face, called a sphinx, to destroy herself by casting herself headlong, having solved the riddle she was wont to propose as insoluble; about Antaeus, who was the son of the earth, for which reason, on falling on the earth, he was wont to rise up stronger, whom Hercules slew; and perhaps there are others which I have forgotten. These fables, easily found in histories containing a true account of events, bring us down to the Trojan war, at which Marcus Varro has closed his second book about the race of the Roman people; and they are so skillfully invented by men as to involve no scandal to the gods. But whoever have pretended as to Jupiter's rape of

Ganymede, a very beautiful boy, that king Tantalus committed the crime, and the fable ascribed it to Jupiter; or as to his impregnating Danae as a golden shower, that it means that the woman's virtue was corrupted by gold: whether these things were really done or only fabled in those days, or were really done by others and falsely ascribed to Jupiter, it is impossible to tell how much wickedness must have been taken for granted in men's hearts that they should be thought able to listen to such lies with patience. And yet they willingly accepted them, when, indeed, the more devotedly they worshipped Jupiter, they ought the more severely to have punished those who dared say such things of him. But they not only were not angry at those who invented these things, but were afraid that the gods would be angry at them if they did not act such fictions even in the theatres. In those times Latona bore Apollo, not him of whose oracle we have spoken above as so often consulted, but him who is said, along with Hercules, to have fed the flocks of king Admetus; yet he was so believed to be a god, that very many, indeed almost all, have believed him to be the self-same Apollo. Then also Father Liber made war in India, and led in his army many women called Bacchae, who were notable not so much for valor as for fury. Some, indeed, write that this Liber was both conquered and bound; and some that he was slain in Persia, even telling where he was buried; and yet in his name, as that of a god, the unclean demons have instituted the sacred, or rather the sacrilegious, Bacchanalia, of the outrageous vileness of which the senate, after many years, became so much ashamed as to prohibit them in the city of Rome. Men believed that in those times Perseus and his wife Andromeda were raised into heaven after their death, so that they were not ashamed or afraid to mark out their images by constellations, and call them by their names.

CHAPTER XIV

OF THE THEOLOGICAL POETS

During the same period of time arose the poets, who were also called *theologues*, because they made hymns about the gods; yet about such gods as, although great men, were yet but men, or the elements of this world which the true God made, or creatures who were ordained as principalities and powers according to the will of the Creator and their own merit. And if, among much that was vain and false, they sang anything of the one true God, yet, by worshipping Him along with others who are not gods, and showing them the service that is due to Him alone, they did not serve Him at all rightly; and even such poets as Orpheus, Musaeus, and Linus, were unable to abstain from dishonoring their gods by fables. But yet these theologues worshipped the gods, and were not worshipped as gods, although the city of the ungodly is wont, I know not how, to set Orpheus over the sacred, or rather sacrilegious, rites of hell. The wife of king Athamas, who was called Ino, and her son Melicertes, perished by throwing themselves into the sea, and were, according to popular belief, reckoned among the gods, like other men of the same times, [among whom were] Castor and Pollux. The Greeks, indeed, called her who was the mother of Melicertes, Leucothea, the Latins, Matuta; but both thought her a goddess.

CHAPTER XV

OF THE FALL OF THE KINGDOM OF ARGOS, WHEN PICUS THE SON OF SATURN FIRST RECEIVED HIS FATHER'S KINGDOM OF LAURENTUM

During those times the kingdom of Argos came to an end, being transferred to Mycene, from which Agamemnon came, and the kingdom of Laurentum arose, of which Picus son of Saturn was the first king, when the woman Deborah judged the Hebrews; but it was the Spirit of God who used her as His agent, for she was also a prophetess, although her prophecy is so obscure that we could not demonstrate, without a long discussion, that it was uttered concerning Christ. Now the Laurentes already reigned in Italy, from whom the origin of the Roman people is quite evidently derived after the Greeks; yet the kingdom of Assyria still lasted, in which Lampares was the twenty-third king when Picus first began to reign at Laurentum. The worshippers of such gods may see what they are to think of Saturn the father of Picus, who deny that he was a man; of whom some also have written that he himself reigned in Italy before Picus his son; and Virgil in his well-known book says,

> That race indocile, and through mountains high
> Dispersed, he settled, and endowed with laws,
> And named their country Latium, because
> Latent within their coasts he dwelt secure.
> Tradition says the golden ages pure
> Began when he was king.[7]

But they regard these as poetic fancies, and assert that the father of Picus was Sterces rather, and relate that, being a most skillful husbandman, he discovered that the fields could be fertilized by the dung of animals, which is called *stercus* from his name. Some say he was called Stercutius. But for whatever reason they chose to call him Saturn, it is yet certain they made this Sterces or Stercutius a god for his merit in agriculture; and they likewise received into the number of these gods Picus his son, whom they affirm to have been a famous augur and warrior. Picus begot Faunus, the second king of Laurentum; and he too is, or was, a god with them. These divine honors they gave to dead men before the Trojan war.

---

[7] *Aeneid,* viii. 321

CHAPTER XVI

OF DIOMEDE, WHO AFTER THE DESTRUCTION OF TROY WAS PLACED AMONG THE GODS, WHILE HIS COMPANIONS ARE SAID TO HAVE BEEN CHANGED INTO BIRDS

Troy was overthrown, and its destruction was everywhere sung and made well known even to boys; for it was signally published and spread abroad, both by its own greatness and by writers of excellent style. And this was done in the reign of Latinus the son of Faunus, from whom the kingdom began to be called Latium instead of Laurentum. The victorious Greeks, on leaving Troy destroyed and returning to their own countries, were torn and crushed by divers and horrible calamities. Yet even from among them they increased the number of their gods for they made Diomede a god. They allege that his return home was prevented by a divinely imposed punishment, and they prove, not by fabulous and poetic falsehood, but by historic attestation, that his companions were turned into birds. Yet they think that, even although he was made a god, he could neither restore them to the human form by his own power, nor yet obtain it from Jupiter his king, as a favor granted to a new inhabitant of heaven. They also say that his temple is in the island of Diomedaea, not far from Mount Garganus in Apulia, and that these birds fly round about this temple, and worship in it with such wonderful obedience, that they fill their beaks with water and sprinkle it; and if Greeks, or those born of the Greek race, come there, they are not only still, but fly to meet them; but if they are foreigners, they fly up at their heads, and wound them with such severe strokes as even to kill them. For they are said to be well enough armed for these combats with their hard and large beaks.

CHAPTER XVII

WHAT VARRO SAYS OF THE INCREDIBLE TRANSFORMATIONS OF MEN

In support of this story, Varro relates others no less incredible about that most famous sorceress Circe, who changed the companions of Ulysses into beasts, and about the Arcadians, who, by lot, swam across a certain pool, and were turned into wolves there, and lived in the deserts of that region with wild beasts like themselves. But if they never fed on human flesh for nine years, they were restored to the human form on swimming back again through the same pool. Finally, he expressly names one Demaenetus, who, on tasting a boy offered up in sacrifice by the Arcadians to their god Lycaeus according to their custom, was changed into a wolf, and, being restored to his proper form in the tenth year, trained himself as a pugilist, and was victorious at the Olympic games. And the same historian thinks that the epithet

Lycaeus was applied in Arcadia to Pan and Jupiter for no other reason than this metamorphosis of men into wolves, because it was thought it could not be wrought except by a divine power. For a wolf is called in Greek λύκος, from which the name Lycaeus appears to be formed. He says also that the Roman Luperci were as it were sprung of the seed of these mysteries.

CHAPTER XVIII

WHAT WE SHOULD BELIEVE CONCERNING THE TRANSFORMATIONS WHICH SEEM TO HAPPEN TO MEN THROUGH THE ART OF DEMONS

Perhaps our readers expect us to say something about this so great delusion wrought by the demons; and what shall we say but that men must fly out of the midst of Babylon? [8] For this prophetic precept is to be understood spiritually in this sense, that by going forward in the living God, by the steps of faith, which works by love, we must flee out of the city of this world, which is altogether a society of ungodly angels and men. Indeed, the greater we see the power of the demons to be in these depths, so much the more tenaciously must we cleave to the Mediator through whom we ascend from these lowest to the highest places. For if we should say these things are not to be credited, there are not wanting even now some who would affirm that they had either heard on the best authority, or even themselves experienced, something of that kind. Indeed we ourselves, when in Italy, heard such things about a certain region there, where landladies of inns, imbued with these wicked arts, were said to be in the habit of giving to such travellers as they chose, or could manage, something in a piece of cheese by which they were changed on the spot into beasts of burden, and carried whatever was necessary, and were restored to their own form when the work was done. Yet their mind did not become bestial, but remained rational and human, just as Apuleius, in the books he wrote with the title of *The Golden Ass*, has told, or feigned, that it happened to his own self that, on taking poison, he became an ass, while retaining his human mind.

These things are either false, or so extraordinary as to be with good reason disbelieved. But it is to be most firmly believed that Almighty God can do whatever He pleases, whether in punishing or favoring, and that the demons can accomplish nothing by their natural power (for their created being is itself angelic, although made malign by their own fault) except what He may permit, whose judgments are often hidden, but never unrighteous. And indeed the demons, if they really do such things as these on which this discussion turns, do not create real substances, but only change the appearance of things created by the true God so as to make them seem to be what they are not. I cannot therefore believe that even the body, much less the mind, can really be changed into bestial forms and lineaments by any reason, art,

[8] Isa. xlviii. 20

or power of the demons; but the phantasm of a man which even in thought or dreams goes through innumerable changes, may, when the man's senses are laid asleep or overpowered, be presented to the senses of others in a corporeal form, in some indescribable way unknown to me, so that men's bodies themselves may lie somewhere, alive, indeed, yet with their senses locked up much more heavily and firmly than by sleep, while that phantasm, as it were embodied in the shape of some animal, may appear to the senses of others, and may even seem to the man himself to be changed, just as he may seem to himself in sleep to be so changed, and to bear burdens; and these burdens, if they are real substances, are borne by the demons, that men may be deceived by beholding at the same time the real substance of the burdens and the simulated bodies of the beasts of burden. For a certain man called Praestantius used to tell that it had happened to his father in his own house, that he took that poison in a piece of cheese, and lay in his bed as if sleeping, yet could by no means be aroused. But he said that after a few days he as it were woke up and related the things he had suffered as if they had been dreams, namely, that he had been made a pack horse, and, along with other beasts of burden, had carried provisions for the soldiers of what is called the Rhoetian Legion, because it was sent to Rhoetia. And all this was found to have taken place just as he told, yet it had seemed to him to be his own dream. And another man declared that in his own house at night, before he slept, he saw a certain philosopher, whom he knew very well, come to him and explain to him some things in the Platonic philosophy which he had previously declined to explain when asked. And when he had asked this philosopher why he did in his house what he had refused to do at home, he said, "I did not do it, but I dreamed I had done it." And thus what the one saw when sleeping was shown to the other when awake by a phantasmal image.

These things have not come to us from persons we might deem unworthy of credit, but from informants we could not suppose to be deceiving us. Therefore what men say and have committed to writing about the Arcadians being often changed into wolves by the Arcadian gods, or demons rather, and what is told in song about Circe transforming the companions of Ulysses,[9] if they were really done, may, in my opinion, have been done in the way I have said. As for Diomede's birds, since their race is alleged to have been perpetuated by constant propagation, I believe they were not made through the metamorphosis of men, but were slyly substituted for them on their removal, just as the hind was for Iphigenia, the daughter of king Agamemnon. For juggleries of this kind could not be difficult for the demons if permitted by the judgment of God; and since that virgin was afterwards, found alive it is easy to see that a hind had been slyly substituted for her. But because the companions of Diomede were of a sudden nowhere to be seen, and afterwards could nowhere be found, being destroyed by bad avenging angels, they were believed to have been changed into those birds, which

[9] Virgil, *Eclogue* viii. 70

were secretly brought there from other places where such birds were, and suddenly substituted for them by fraud. But that they bring water in their beaks and sprinkle it on the temple of Diomede, and that they fawn on men of Greek race and persecute aliens, is no wonderful thing to be done by the inward influence of the demons, whose interest it is to persuade men that Diomede was made a god, and thus to beguile them into worshipping many false gods, to the great dishonor of the true God; and to serve dead men, who even in their lifetime did not truly live, with temples, altars, sacrifices, and priests, all which, when of the right kind, are due only to the one living and true God.

CHAPTER XIX

THAT AENEAS CAME INTO ITALY WHEN ABDON THE JUDGE RULED OVER THE HEBREWS

After the capture and destruction of Troy, Aeneas, with twenty ships laden with the Trojan relics, came into Italy, when Latinus reigned there, Menestheus in Athens, Polyphidos in Sicyon, and Tautanos in Assyria, and Abdon was judge of the Hebrews. On the death of Latinus, Aeneas reigned three years, the same kings continuing in the above-named places, except that Pelasgus was now king in Sicyon, and Samson was judge of the Hebrews, who is thought to be Hercules, because of his wonderful strength. Now the Latins made Aeneas one of their gods, because at his death he was nowhere to be found. The Sabines also placed among the gods their first king, Sancus, or Sanctus, as some call him. At that time Codrus king of Athens exposed himself *incognito* to be slain by the Peloponnesian foes of that city, and so was slain. In this way, they say, he delivered his country. For the Peloponnesians had received a response from the oracle, that they should overcome the Athenians only on condition that they did not slay their king. Therefore he deceived them by appearing in a poor man's dress, and provoking them, by quarrelling, to murder him. Whence Virgil says, "Or the quarrels of Codrus." [10] And the Athenians worshipped this man as a god with sacrificial honors. The fourth king of the Latins was Silvius the son of Aeneas, not by Creüsa, of whom Ascanius the third king was born, but by Lavinia the daughter of Latinus, and he is said to have been his posthumous child. Oneus was the twenty-ninth king of Assyria, Melanthus the sixteenth of the Athenians, and Eli the priest was judge of the Hebrews; and the kingdom of Sicyon then came to an end, after lasting, it is said, for nine hundred and fifty-nine years.

[10] Virgil, *Eclogue* v. 11

CHAPTER XX

OF THE SUCCESSION OF THE LINE OF KINGS AMONG THE ISRAELITES AFTER THE TIMES OF THE JUDGES

While these kings reigned in the places mentioned, the period of the judges being ended, the kingdom of Israel next began with king Saul, when Samuel the prophet lived. At that date those Latin kings began who were surnamed Silvii, having that surname, in addition to their proper name, from their predecessor, that son of Aeneas who was called Silvius; just as, long afterward, the successors of Caesar Augustus were surnamed Caesars. Saul being rejected, so that none of his issue should reign, on his death David succeeded him in the kingdom, after he had reigned forty years. Then the Athenians ceased to have kings after the death of Codrus, and began to have a magistracy to rule the republic. After David, who also reigned forty years, his son Solomon was king of Israel, who built that most noble temple of God at Jerusalem. In his time Alba was built among the Latins, from which thereafter the kings began to be styled kings not of the Latins, but of the Albans, although in the same Latium. Solomon was succeeded by his son Rehoboam, under whom that people was divided into two kingdoms, and its separate parts began to have separate kings.

CHAPTER XXI

OF THE KINGS OF LATIUM, THE FIRST AND TWELFTH OF WHOM, AENEAS AND AVENTINUS, WERE MADE GODS

After Aeneas, whom they deified, Latium had eleven kings, none of whom was deified. But Aventinus, who was the twelfth after Aeneas, having been laid low in war, and buried in that hill still called by his name, was added to the number of such gods as they made for themselves. Some, indeed, were unwilling to write that he was slain in battle, but said he was nowhere to be found, and that it was not from his name, but from the alighting of birds, that hill was called Aventinus.[11] After this no god was made in Latium except Romulus the founder of Rome. But two kings are found between these two, the first of whom I shall describe in the Virgilian verse:

Next came that Procas, glory of the Trojan race.[12]

That greatest of all kingdoms, the Assyrian, had its long duration brought to a close in his time, the time of Rome's birth drawing nigh. For the Assyrian empire was transferred to the Medes after nearly thirteen hundred and five years, if we include the reign of Belus, who begot Ninus, and, content with a small kingdom, was the first king there. Now Procas reigned before

[11] Varro, *De Lingua Latina*, v. 43   [12] *Aeneid*, vi. 767

Amulius. And Amulius had made his brother Numitor's daughter, Rhea by name, who was also called Ilia, a vestal virgin, who conceived twin sons by Mars, as they will have it, in that way honoring or excusing her adultery, adding as a proof that a she-wolf nursed the infants when exposed. For they think this kind of beast belongs to Mars, so that the she-wolf is believed to have given her teats to the infants, because she knew they were the sons of Mars her lord; although there are not wanting persons who say that when the crying babes lay exposed, they were first of all picked up by I know not what harlot, and sucked her breasts first (now harlots were called *lupae*, she-wolves, from which their vile abodes are even yet called *lupanaria*), and that afterwards they came into the hands of the shepherd Faustulus, and were nursed by Acca his wife. Yet what wonder is it, if, to rebuke the king who had cruelly ordered them to be thrown into the water, God was pleased, after divinely delivering them from the water, to succor, by means of a wild beast giving milk, these infants by whom so great a city was to be founded? Amulius was succeeded in the Latian kingdom by his brother Numitor, the grandfather of Romulus; and Rome was founded in the first year of this Numitor, who from that time reigned along with his grandson Romulus.

CHAPTER XXII

THAT ROME WAS FOUNDED WHEN THE ASSYRIAN KINGDOM PERISHED,
AT WHICH TIME HEZEKIAH REIGNED IN JUDAH

To be brief, the city of Rome was founded, like another Babylon, and as it were the daughter of the former Babylon, by which God was pleased to conquer the whole world, and subdue it far and wide by bringing it into one fellowship of government and laws. For there were already powerful and brave peoples and nations trained to arms, who did not easily yield, and whose subjugation necessarily involved great danger and destruction as well as great and horrible labor. For when the Assyrian kingdom subdued almost all Asia, although this was done by fighting, yet the wars could not be very fierce or difficult, because the nations were as yet untrained to resist, and neither so many nor so great as afterward; forasmuch as, after that greatest and indeed universal flood, when only eight men escaped in Noah's ark, not much more than a thousand years had passed when Ninus subdued all Asia with the exception of India. But Rome did not with the same thickness and facility wholly subdue all those nations of the east and west which we see brought under the Roman empire, because, in its gradual increase, in whatever direction it was extended, it found them strong and warlike. At the time when Rome was founded, then, the people of Israel had been in the land of promise seven hundred and eighteen years. Of these years twenty-seven belong to Joshua the son of Nun, and after that three hundred and twenty-nine to the period of the judges. But from the time when the kings began to reign there, three hundred and sixty-two years had passed. And at that time there was a king in Judah called Ahaz, or, as others compute, Hezekiah his successor, the best and most pious king, who it is admitted reigned in the times of Romulus. And in that part of the Hebrew nation called Israel, Hoshea had begun to reign.

CHAPTER XXIII

OF THE ERYTHRAEAN SIBYL, WHO IS KNOWN TO HAVE SUNG MANY THINGS ABOUT CHRIST MORE PLAINLY THAN THE OTHER SIBYLS [13]

Some say the Erythraean sibyl prophesied at this time. Now Varro declares there were many sibyls, and not merely one. This sibyl of Erythrae certainly wrote some things concerning Christ which are quite manifest, and we first read them in the Latin tongue in verses of bad Latin, and unrhythmical, through the unskillfulness, as we afterwards learned, of some interpreter unknown to me. For Flaccianus, a very famous man, who was also a proconsul, a man of most ready eloquence and much learning, when we were speaking about Christ, produced a Greek manuscript, saying that it was the prophecies of the Erythraean sibyl, in which he pointed out a certain passage which had the initial letters of the lines so arranged that these words could be read in them: Ἰησοῦς Χρειστὸς Θεοῦ υἱὸς σωτήρ, which means, "Jesus Christ the Son of God, the Saviour." And these verses, of which the initial letters yield that meaning, contain what follows as translated by some one into Latin in good rhythm:

Ι	Judgment shall moisten the earth with the sweat of its standard,
Η	Ever enduring, behold the King shall come through the ages,
Σ	Sent to be here in the flesh, and Judge at the last of the world.
Ο	O God, the believing and faithless alike shall behold Thee
Υ	Uplifted with saints, when at last the ages are ended.
Σ	Seated before Him are souls in the flesh for His judgment.

Χ	Hid in thick vapours, the while desolate lieth the earth.
Ρ	Rejected by men are the idols and long hidden treasures;
Ε	Earth is consumed by the fire, and it searcheth the ocean and heaven;
Ι	Issuing forth, it destroyeth the terrible portals of hell.
Σ	Saints in their body and soul freedom and light shall inherit;
Τ	Those who are guilty shall burn in fire and brimstone for ever.
Ο	Occult actions revealing, each one shall publish his secrets;
Σ	Secrets of every man's heart God shall reveal in the light.

[13] The *Sibylline Oracles* are a collection of prophecies and religious teachings in Greek hexameter under the assumed authority and inspiration of a Sibyl, *i.e.*, a female prophet. They are partly of heathen, partly of Jewish-Christian origin. They were used by the fathers against the heathen as genuine prophecies without critical discrimination, and they appear also in the famous *Dies irae* alongside with David, as witnesses of the future judgment ("*teste David cum Sibylla*").

Θ   Then shall be weeping and wailing, yea, and gnashing of teeth;
Ε   Eclipsed is the sun, and silenced the stars in their chorus.
Ο   Over and gone is the splendor of moonlight, melted the heaven.
ϒ   Uplifted by Him are the valleys, and cast down the mountains.

Σ   Utterly gone among men are distinctions of lofty and lowly.
Ι   Into the plains rush the hills, the skies and oceans are mingled.
Ο   Oh, what an end of all things! earth broken in pieces shall perish;
Ϲ   Swelling together at once shall the waters and flames flow in rivers.

Χ   Sounding the archangel's trumpet shall peal down from heaven,
Ρ   Over the wicked who groan in their guilt and their manifold sorrows.
Ε   Trembling, the earth shall be opened, revealing chaos and hell.
Ι   Every king before God shall stand in that day to be judged.
Ϲ   Rivers of fire and brimstone shall fall from the heavens.

In these Latin verses the meaning of the Greek is correctly given, although not in the exact order of the lines as connected with the initial letters; for in three of them, the fifth, eighteenth, and nineteenth, where the Greek letter Γ occurs, Latin words could not be found beginning with the corresponding letter, and yielding a suitable meaning. So that, if we note down together the initial letters of all the lines in our Latin translation except those three in which we retain the letter ϒ in the proper place, they will express in five Greek words this meaning, "Jesus Christ the Son of God, the Saviour." And the verses are twenty-seven, which is the cube of three. For three times three are nine; and nine itself, if tripled, so as to rise from the superficial square to the cube, comes to twenty-seven. But if you join the initial letters of these five Greek words, Ἰησοῦς Χρειστὸς Θεοῦ υἱὸς σωτήρ, which mean, "Jesus Christ the Son of God, the Saviour," they will make the word ἰχθύς, that is, "fish," in which word Christ is mystically understood, because He was able to live, that is, to exist, without sin in the abyss of this mortality as in the depth of waters.[14]

But this sibyl, whether she is the Erythraean, or, as some rather believe, the Cumaean, in her whole poem, of which this is a very small portion, not only has nothing that can relate to the worship of the false or feigned gods, but rather speaks against them and their worshippers in such a way that we might even think she ought to be reckoned among those who belong to the city of God. Lactantius also inserted in his work the prophecies about Christ of a certain sibyl, he does not say which. But I have thought fit to combine in a single extract, which may seem long, what he has set down in many short quotations. She says, "Afterward He shall come into the injurious hands of the unbelieving, and they will give God buffets with profane hands, and with impure mouth will spit out envenomed spittle; but He will with simplicity

---

[14] Hence the *fish* was a favorite symbol of the ancient Christians

yield His holy back to stripes. And He will hold His peace when struck with the fist, that no one may find out what word, or whence, He comes to speak to hell; and He shall be crowned with a crown of thorns. And they gave Him gall for meat, and vinegar for His thirst: they will spread this table of inhospitality. For thou thyself, being foolish, hast not understood thy God, deluding the minds of mortals, but hast both crowned Him with thorns and mingled for Him bitter gall. But the veil of the temple shall be rent; and at midday it shall be darker than night for three hours. And He shall die the death, taking sleep for three days; and then returning from hell, He first shall come to the light, the beginning of the resurrection being shown to the recalled." [15] Lactantius made use of these sibylline testimonies, introducing them bit by bit in the course of his discussion as the things he intended to prove seemed to require, and we have set them down in one connected series, uninterrupted by comment, only taking care to mark them by capitals, if only the transcribers do not neglect to preserve them hereafter. Some writers, indeed, say that the Erythraean sibyl was not in the time of Romulus, but of the Trojan war.

CHAPTER XXIV

THAT THE SEVEN SAGES FLOURISHED IN THE REIGN OF ROMULUS, WHEN THE TEN TRIBES WHICH WERE CALLED ISRAEL WERE LED INTO CAPTIVITY BY THE CHALDEANS, AND ROMULUS, WHEN DEAD, HAD DIVINE HONORS CONFERRED ON HIM

While Romulus reigned, Thales the Milesian is said to have lived, being one of the seven sages, who succeeded the theological poets, of whom Orpheus was the most renowned, and were called Σοφοί, that is, sages. During that time the ten tribes, which on the division of the people were called Israel, were conquered by the Chaldeans and led captive into their lands, while the two tribes which were called Judah, and had the seat of their kingdom in Jerusalem, remained in the land of Judea. As Romulus, when dead, could nowhere be found, the Romans, as is everywhere notorious, placed him among the gods—a thing which by that time had already ceased to be done, and which was not done afterwards till the time of the Caesars, and then not through error, but in flattery; so that Cicero ascribes great praises to Romulus, because he merited such honors not in rude and unlearned times, when men were easily deceived, but in times already polished and learned, although the subtle and acute loquacity of the philosophers had not yet culminated. But although the later times did not deify dead men, still they did not cease to hold and worship as gods those deified of old; nay, by images, which the ancients never had, they even increased the allurements of vain and impious superstition, the unclean demons effecting this in their

[15] *Instit.* iv. 18

heart, and also deceiving them by lying oracles, so that even the fabulous crimes of the gods, which were not once imagined by a more polite age, were yet basely acted in the plays in honor of these same false deities. Numa reigned after Romulus; and although he had thought that Rome would be better defended the more gods there were, yet on his death he himself was not counted worthy of a place among them, as if it were supposed that he had so crowded heaven that a place could not be found for him there. They report that the Samian sibyl lived while he reigned at Rome, and when Manasseh began to reign over the Hebrews—an impious king, by whom the prophet Isaiah is said to have been slain.

CHAPTER XXV

WHAT PHILOSOPHERS WERE FAMOUS WHEN TARQUINIUS PRISCUS
REIGNED OVER THE ROMANS, AND ZEDEKIAH OVER THE HEBREWS,
WHEN JERUSALEM WAS TAKEN AND THE TEMPLE OVERTHROWN

When Zedekiah reigned over the Hebrews, and Tarquinius Priscus, the successor of Ancus Martius, over the Romans, the Jewish people was led captive into Babylon, Jerusalem and the temple built by Solomon being overthrown. For the prophets, in chiding them for their iniquity and impiety, predicted that these things should come to pass, especially Jeremiah, who even stated the number of years. Pittacus of Mitylene, another of the sages, is reported to have lived at that time. And Eusebius writes that, while the people of God were held captive in Babylon, the five other sages lived, who must be added to Thales, whom we mentioned above, and Pittacus, in order to make up the seven. These are Solon of Athens, Chilo of Lacedaemon, Periander of Corinth, Cleobulus of Lindus, and Bias of Priene. These flourished after the theological poets, and were called sages, because they excelled other men in a certain laudable line of life, and summed up some moral precepts in epigrammatic sayings. But they left posterity no literary monuments, except that Solon is alleged to have given certain laws to the Athenians, and Thales was a natural philosopher, and left books of his doctrine in short proverbs. In that time of the Jewish captivity, Anaximander, Anaximenes, and Xenophanes, the natural philosophers, flourished. Pythagoras also lived then, and at this time the name philosopher was first used.

CHAPTER XXVI

THAT AT THE TIME WHEN THE CAPTIVITY OF THE JEWS WAS BROUGHT
TO AN END, ON THE COMPLETION OF SEVENTY YEARS, THE
ROMANS ALSO WERE FREED FROM KINGLY RULE

At this time, Cyrus king of Persia, who also ruled the Chaldeans and Assyrians, having somewhat relaxed the captivity of the Jews, made fifty thousand of them return in order to rebuild the temple. They only began the first foundations and built the altar; but, owing to hostile invasions, they were unable to go on, and the work was put off to the time of Darius. During the same time also those things were done which are written in the book of Judith, which, indeed, the Jews are said not to have received into the canon of the Scriptures. Under Darius king of Persia, then, on the completion of the seventy years predicted by Jeremiah the prophet, the captivity of the Jews was brought to an end, and they were restored to liberty. Tarquin then reigned as the seventh king of the Romans. On his expulsion, they also began to be free from the rule of their kings. Down to this time the people of Israel had prophets; but, although they were numerous, the canonical writings of only a few of them have been preserved among the Jews and among us. In closing the previous book, I promised to set down something in this one about them, and I shall now do so.

CHAPTER XXVII

OF THE TIMES OF THE PROPHETS WHOSE ORACLES ARE CONTAINED
IN BOOKS, AND WHO SANG MANY THINGS ABOUT THE CALL OF
THE GENTILES AT THE TIME WHEN THE ROMAN KINGDOM
BEGAN AND THE ASSYRIAN CAME TO AN END

In order that we may be able to consider these times, let us go back a little to earlier times. At the beginning of the book of the prophet Hosea, who is placed first of twelve, it is written, "The word of the Lord which came to Hosea in the days of Uzziah, Jotham, Ahaz, and Hezekiah, kings of Judah."[16] Amos also writes that he prophesied in the days of Uzziah, and adds the name of Jeroboam king of Israel, who lived at the same time.[17] Isaiah the son of Amos—either the above-named prophet, or, as is rather affirmed, another who was not a prophet, but was called by the same name—also puts at the head of his book these four kings named by Hosea, saying by way of preface that he prophesied in their days.[18] Micah also names the same times as those of his prophecy, after the days of Uzziah;[19] for he names the same three kings as Hosea named—Jotham, Ahaz, and Hezekiah. We find from their own writings that these men prophesied contemporaneously. To these are added Jonah in the reign of Uzziah, and Joel in that of Jotham, who succeeded Uzziah. But we can find the date of these two prophets in the chronicles,[20] not in their own writings, for they say nothing about it themselves. Now these days extend from Procas king of the Latins, or his predecessor Aventinus, down to Romulus king of the Romans, or even to the beginning of the reign of his successor Numa Pompilius. Hezekiah king of Judah certainly reigned till then. So that thus these fountains of prophecy,

---

[16] Hos. i. 1   [17] Amos i. 1   [18] Isa. i. 1. Isaiah's father was Amoz, a different name
[19] Mic. i. 1   [20] The chronicles of Eusebius and Jerome

as I may call them, burst forth at once during those times when the Assyrian kingdom failed and the Roman began; so that, just as in the first period of the Assyrian kingdom Abraham arose, to whom the most distinct promises were made that all nations should be blessed in his seed, so at the beginning of the western Babylon, in the time of whose government Christ was to come in whom these promises were to be fulfilled, the oracles of the prophets were given not only in spoken but in written words, for a testimony that so great a thing should come to pass. For although the people of Israel hardly ever lacked prophets from the time when they began to have kings, these were only for their own use, not for that of the nations. But when the more manifestly prophetic Scripture began to be formed, which was to benefit the nations too, it was fitting that it should begin when this city was founded which was to rule the nations.

CHAPTER XXVIII

OF THE THINGS PERTAINING TO THE GOSPEL OF CHRIST WHICH HOSEA AND AMOS PROPHESIED

The prophet Hosea speaks so very profoundly that it is laborious work to penetrate his meaning. But, according to promise, we must insert something from his book. He says, "And it shall come to pass that in the place where it was said unto them, Ye are not my people, there they shall be called the sons of the living God." [21] Even the apostles understood this as a prophetic testimony of the calling of the nations who did not formerly belong to God; and because this same people of the Gentiles is itself spiritually among the children of Abraham, and for that reason is rightly called Israel, therefore he goes on to say, "And the children of Judah and the children of Israel shall be gathered together in one, and shall appoint themselves one headship, and shall ascend from the earth." [22] We should but weaken the savor of this prophetic oracle if we set ourselves to expound it. Let the reader but call to mind that corner-stone and those two walls of partition, the one of the Jews, the other of the Gentiles,[23] and he will recognize them, the one under the term sons of Judah, the other as sons of Israel, supporting themselves by one and the same headship, and ascending from the earth. But that those carnal Israelites who are now unwilling to believe in Christ shall afterward believe, that is, their children shall (for they themselves, of course, shall go to their own place by dying) this same prophet testifies, saying, "For the children of Israel shall abide many days without a king, without a prince, without a sacrifice, without an altar, without a priesthood, without manifestations." [24] Who does not see that the Jews are now thus? But let us hear what he adds: "And afterward shall the children of Israel return, and seek the Lord their God, and David their king, and shall be amazed at the Lord

[21] Hos. i. 10   [22] Hos. i. 11   [23] Gal. ii. 14-20   [24] Hos. iii. 4

and at His goodness in the latter days." [25] Nothing is clearer than this prophecy, in which by David, as distinguished by the title of king, Christ is to be understood, "who is made," as the apostle says, "of the seed of David according to the flesh." [26] This prophet has also foretold the resurrection of Christ on the third day, as it behoved to be foretold, with prophetic loftiness, when he says, "He will heal us after two days, and in the third day we shall rise again." [27] In agreement with this the apostle says to us, "If ye be risen with Christ, seek those things which are above." [28] Amos also prophesies thus concerning such things: "Prepare thee, that thou mayst invoke thy God, O Israel; for lo, I am binding the thunder, and creating the spirit, and announcing to men their Christ." [29] And in another place he says, "In that day will I raise up the tabernacle of David that is fallen, and build up the breaches thereof: and I will raise up his ruins, and will build them up again as in the days of old: that the residue of men may inquire for me, and all the nations upon whom my name is invoked, saith the Lord that doeth this." [30]

CHAPTER XXIX

WHAT THINGS ARE PREDICTED BY ISAIAH CONCERNING CHRIST AND THE CHURCH

The prophecy of Isaiah is not in the book of the twelve prophets, who are called the minor from the brevity of their writings, as compared with those who are called the greater prophets because they published larger volumes. Isaiah belongs to the latter, yet I connect him with the two above named, because he prophesied at the same time. Isaiah, then, together with his rebukes of wickedness, precepts of righteousness, and predictions of evil, also prophesied much more than the rest about Christ and the Church, that is, about the King and that city which he founded; so that some say he should be called an evangelist rather than a prophet. But, in order to finish this work, I quote only one out of many in this place. Speaking in the person of the Father, he says, "Behold, my servant shall understand, and shall be exalted and glorified very much. As many shall be astonished at Thee. His visage was so marred more than any man, and his form more than the sons of men: so shall he sprinkle many nations; the kings shall shut their mouths at him: for that which had not been told them shall they see; and that which they had not heard shall they consider.

"Who hath believed our report? and to whom is the arm of the Lord revealed? For He shall grow up before Him as a tender plant, and as a root out of a dry ground: He hath no form nor comeliness; and when we shall see Him, there is no beauty that we should desire him. He is despised and rejected of men; a man of sorrows, and acquainted with grief: and we hid as it were our

[25] Hos. iii. 5   [26] Rom. i. 3   [27] Hos. vi. 2   [28] Col. iii. 1   [29] Amos iv. 12, 13
[30] Amos ix. 11, 12; Acts xv. 15-17

faces from Him; He was despised, and we esteemed Him not. Surely He hath borne our griefs, and carried our sorrows: yet we did esteem Him stricken, smitten of God, and afflicted.

"But He was wounded for our transgressions, He was bruised for our iniquities: the chastisement of our peace was upon Him; and with his stripes we are healed. All we like sheep have gone astray; we have turned every one to his own way and the Lord hath laid on Him the iniquity of us all. He was oppressed, and He was afflicted, yet He opened not His mouth: He is brought as a lamb to the slaughter, and as a sheep before her shearers is dumb, so He openeth not His mouth.

"He was taken from prison and from judgment: and who shall declare His generation? for He was cut off out of the land of the living: for the transgression of my people was He stricken. And He made his grave with the wicked, and with the rich in His death; because He had done no violence, neither was any deceit in His mouth.

"Yet it pleased the Lord to bruise Him; He hath put Him to grief: when thou shalt make His soul an offering for sin, He shall see His seed, He shall prolong His days, and the pleasure of the Lord shall prosper in His hand. He shall see the travail of His soul, and shall be satisfied: by His knowledge shall my righteous servant justify many; for He shall bear their iniquities. Therefore will I divide Him a portion with the great, and He shall divide the spoil with the strong; because He hath poured out His soul unto death: and He was numbered with the transgressors; and He bare the sin of many, and made intercession for the transgressors." [31] This is about Christ.

But let us now hear what follows about the Church. He says, "Rejoice, O barren, thou that barest not; break forth and cry, thou that didst not travail with child: for many more are the children of the desolate than of her that has an husband." [32] But these must suffice; and some things in them ought to be expounded; yet I think those parts sufficient which are so plain that even enemies must be compelled against their will to understand them.

CHAPTER XXX

WHAT MICAH, JONAH, AND JOEL PROPHESIED IN ACCORDANCE WITH THE NEW TESTAMENT

The prophet Micah, representing Christ under the figure of a great mountain, speaks thus: "It shall come to pass in the last days, that the manifested mountain of the Lord shall be prepared on the tops of the mountains, and it shall be exalted above the hills; and people shall hasten unto it. Many nations shall go, and shall say, Come, let us go up into the mountain of the Lord, and into the house of the God of Jacob; and He will show us His way, and we will go in His paths: for out of Zion shall proceed the law, and the word

[31] Isa. lii. 13-liii. 12   [32] Isa. liv. 1-5

of the Lord out of Jerusalem. And He shall judge among many people, and rebuke strong nations afar off." [33] This prophet predicts the very place in which Christ was born, saying, "And thou, Bethlehem, of the house of Ephratah, art the least that can be reckoned among the thousands of Judah; out of thee shall come forth unto me a leader, to be the prince in Israel; and His going forth is from the beginning, even from the days of eternity. Therefore will He give them [up] even until the time when she that travaileth shall bring forth; and the remnant of His brethren shall be converted to the sons of Israel. And He shall stand, and see, and feed His flock in the strength of the Lord, and in the dignity of the name of the Lord His God: for now shall He be magnified even to the utmost of the earth." [34]

The prophet Jonah, not so much by speech as by his own painful experience, prophesied Christ's death and resurrection much more clearly than if he had proclaimed them with his voice. For why was he taken into the whale's belly and restored on the third day, but that he might be a sign that Christ should return from the depths of hell on the third day?

I should be obliged to use many words in explaining all that Joel prophesies in order to make clear those that pertain to Christ and the Church. But there is one passage I must not pass by, which the apostles also quoted when the Holy Spirit came down from above on the assembled believers according to Christ's promise. He says, "and it shall come to pass after these things, that I will pour out my Spirit upon all flesh; and your sons and your daughters shall prophesy, and your old men shall dream, and your young men shall see visions: and even on my servants and mine handmaids in those days will I pour out my Spirit." [35]

CHAPTER XXXI

OF THE PREDICTIONS CONCERNING THE SALVATION OF THE WORLD IN CHRIST, IN OBADIAH, NAHUM, AND HABAKKUK

The date of three of the minor prophets, Obadiah, Nahum, and Habakkuk, is neither mentioned by themselves nor given in the chronicles of Eusebius and Jerome. For although they put Obadiah with Micah, yet when Micah prophesied does not appear from that part of their writings in which the dates are noted. And this, I think, has happened through their error in negligently copying the works of others. But we could not find the two others now mentioned in the copies of the chronicles which we have; yet because they are contained in the canon, we ought not to pass them by.

Obadiah, so far as his writings are concerned, the briefest of all the prophets, speaks against Idumea, that is, the nation of Esau, that reprobate elder of the twin sons of Isaac and grandsons of Abraham. Now if, by that form of speech in which a part is put for the whole, we take Idumea as put for

---

[33] Mic. iv. 1-3   [34] Mic. v. 2-4   [35] Joel ii. 28, 29

the nations, we may understand of Christ what he says among other things, "But upon Mount Sion shall be safety, and there shall be a Holy One." [36] And a little after, at the end of the same prophecy, he says, "and those who are saved again shall come up out of Mount Sion, that they may defend Mount Esau, and it shall be a kingdom to the Lord." [37] It is quite evident this was fulfilled when those saved again out cf Mount Sion—that is, the believers in Christ from Judea, of whom the apostles are chiefly to be acknowledged—went up to defend Mount Esau. How could they defend it except by making safe, through the preaching of the gospel, those who believe that they might be "delivered from the power of darkness and translated into the kingdom of God?" [38] This he expressed as an inference, adding, "And it shall be to the Lord a kingdom." For Mount Sion signifies Judea, where it is predicted there shall be safety, and a Holy One, that is, Christ Jesus. But Mount Esau is Idumea, which signifies the Church of the Gentiles, which, as I have expounded, those saved again out of Sion have defended that it should be a kingdom to the Lord. This was obscure before it took place; but what believer does not find it out now that it is done?

As for the prophet Nahum, through him God says, "I will exterminate the graven and the molten things: I will make thy burial. For lo, the feet of Him that bringeth good tidings and announceth peace are swift upon the mountains! O Judah, celebrate thy festival days, and perform thy vows; for now they shall not go on any more so as to become antiquated. It is completed, it is consumed, it is taken away. He ascendeth who breathes in thy face, delivering thee out of tribulation." [39] Let him that remembers the gospel call to mind who hath ascended from hell and breathed the Holy Spirit in the face of Judah, that is, of the Jewish disciples; for they belong to the New Testament, whose festival days are so spiritually renewed that they cannot become antiquated. Moreover, we already see the graven and molten things, that is, the idols of the false gods, exterminated through the gospel, and given up to oblivion as of the grave, and we know that this prophecy is fulfilled in this very thing.

Of what else than the advent of Christ, who was to come, is Habakkuk understood to say, "And the Lord answered me, and said, Write the vision openly on a tablet of boxwood, that he that readeth these things may understand. For the vision is yet for a time appointed, and it will arise in the end, and will not become void: if it tarry, wait for it; because it will surely come, and will not be delayed?" [49]

[36] Obad. 17   [37] Obad. 21   [38] Col. i. 13   [39] Nah. i. 14; ii. 1   [40] Hab. ii. 2, 3

CHAPTER XXXII

In his prayer, with a song, to whom but the Lord Christ does he say, "O Lord, I have heard Thy hearing, and was afraid: O Lord, I have considered Thy works, and was greatly afraid?" [41] What is this but the inexpressible admiration of the foreknown, new, and sudden salvation of men? "In the midst of two living creatures thou shalt be recognized." What is this but either between the two testaments, or between the two thieves, or between Moses and Elias talking with Him on the mount? "While the years draw nigh, Thou wilt be recognized; at the coming of the time Thou wilt be shown," does not even need exposition. "While my soul shall be troubled at Him, in wrath Thou wilt be mindful of mercy." What is this but that He puts Himself for the Jews, of whose nation He was, who were troubled with great anger and crucified Christ, when He, mindful of mercy, said, "Father, forgive them, for they know not what they do?" [42] "God shall come from Teman, and the Holy One from the shady and close mountain." [43] What is said here, "He shall come from Teman," some interpret "from the south," or "from the southwest," by which is signified the noonday, that is, the fervor of charity and the splendor of truth. "The shady and close mountain" might be understood in many ways, yet I prefer to take it as meaning the depth of the divine Scriptures, in which Christ is prophesied: for in the Scriptures there are many things shady and close which exercise the mind of the reader; and Christ comes thence when he who has understanding finds Him there. "His power covereth up the heavens, and the earth is full of His praise." What is this but what is also said in the psalm, "Be Thou exalted, O God, above the heavens; and Thy glory above all the earth?" [44] "His splendor shall be as the light." What is it but that the fame of Him shall illuminate believers? "Horns are in His hands." What is this but the trophy of the cross? "And He hath placed the firm charity of His strength" [45] needs no exposition. "Before His face shall go the word, and it shall go forth into the field after His feet." What is this but that He should both be announced before His coming hither and after His return hence? "He stood, and the earth was moved." What is this but that "He stood" for succor, "and the earth was moved" to believe? "He regarded, and the nations melted;" that is, He had compassion, and made the people penitent. "The mountains are broken with violence;" that is, through the power of those who work miracles the pride of the haughty is broken "The everlasting hills flowed down;" that is, they are humbled in time that they may be lifted up for eternity. "I saw His goings eternal for his labors;" that is, I beheld His labor of love not left without the reward of eternity. "The tents of Ethiopia

[41] Hab. iii. 2   [42] Luke xxiii. 34   [43] Hab. iii. 3   [44] Ps. lvii. 5, 11   [45] Hab. iii. 4

shall be greatly afraid, and the tents of the land of Midian;" that is, even those nations which are not under the Roman authority, being suddenly terrified by the news of Thy wonderful works, shall become a Christian people. "Wert Thou angry at the rivers, O Lord? or was Thy fury against the rivers? or was Thy rage against the sea? This is said because He does not now come to condemn the world, but that the world through Him might be saved.[46] "For Thou shalt mount upon Thy horses, and Thy riding shall be salvation;" that is, Thine evangelists shall carry Thee, for they are guided by Thee, and Thy gospel is salvation to them that believe in Thee. "Bending, Thou wilt bend Thy bow against the sceptres, saith the Lord;" that is, Thou wilt threaten even the kings of the earth with Thy judgment. "The earth shall be cleft with rivers;" that is, by the sermons of those who preach Thee flowing in upon them, men's hearts shall be opened to make confession, to whom it is said, "Rend your hearts and not your garments."[47] What does "The people shall see Thee and grieve" mean, but that in mourning they shall be blessed? [48] What is "Scattering the waters in marching," but that by walking in those who everywhere proclaim Thee, Thou wilt scatter hither and thither the streams of Thy doctrine? What is "The abyss uttered its voice?" Is it not that the depth of the human heart expressed what it perceived? The words, "The depth of its phantasy," are an explanation of the previous verse, for the depth is the abyss; and "Uttered its voice" is to be understood before them, that is, as we have said, it expressed what it perceived. Now the phantasy is the vision, which it did not hold or conceal, but poured forth in confession. "The sun was raised up, and the moon stood still in her course;" that is, Christ ascended into heaven, and the Church was established under her King. "Thy darts shall go in the light;" that is, Thy words shall not be sent in secret, but openly. For He had said to His own disciples, "What I tell you in darkness, that speak ye in the light." [49] "By threatening thou shalt diminish the earth;" that is, by that threatening Thou shalt humble men. "And in fury Thou shalt cast down the nations;" for in punishing those who exalt themselves Thou dashest them one against another. "Thou wentest forth for the salvation of Thy people, that Thou mightest save Thy Christ; Thou has sent death on the heads of the wicked." None of these words require exposition. "Thou hast lifted up the bonds, even to the neck." This may be understood even of the good bonds of wisdom, that the feet may be put into its fetters, and the neck into its collar. "Thou hast struck off in amazement of mind the bonds" must be understood for, He lifts up the good and strikes off the bad, about which it is said to Him, "Thou hast broken asunder my bonds,"[50] and that "in amazement of mind," that is, wonderfully. "The heads of the mighty shall be moved in it;" to wit, in that wonder. "They shall open their teeth like a poor man eating secretly." For some of the mighty among the Jews shall come to the Lord, admiring His works and words, and shall greedily eat the

---

[46] John iii. 17   [47] Joel ii. 13   [48] Matt. v. 4   [49] Matt. x. 27   [50] Ps. cxvi. 16

bread of His doctrine in secret for fear of the Jews, just as the Gospel has shown they did. "And Thou hast sent into the sea Thy horses, troubling many waters," which are nothing else than many people; for unless all were troubled, some would not be converted with fear, others pursued with fury: "I gave heed, and my belly trembled at the voice of the prayer of my lips; and trembling entered into my bones, and my habit of body was troubled under me." He gave heed to those things which he said, and was himself terrified at his own prayer, which he had poured forth prophetically, and in which he discerned things to come. For when many people are troubled, he saw the threatening tribulation of the Church, and at once acknowledged himself a member of it, and said, "I shall rest in the day of tribulation," as being one of those who are rejoicing in hope, patient in tribulation.[51] "That I may ascend," he says, "among the people of my pilgrimage," departing quite from the wicked people of his carnal kinship, who are not pilgrims in this earth, and do not seek the country above.[52] "Although the fig-tree," he says, "shall not blossom, neither shall fruit be in the vines; the labor of the olive shall lie, and the fields shall yield no meat; the sheep shall be cut off from the meat, and there shall be no oxen in the stalls." He sees that nation which was to slay Christ about to lose the abundance of spiritual supplies, which, in prophetic fashion, he has set forth by the figure of earthly plenty. And because that nation was to suffer such wrath of God, because, being ignorant of the righteousness of God, it wished to establish its own,[53] he immediately says, "Yet will I rejoice in the Lord; I will joy in God my salvation. The Lord God is my strength, and He will set my feet in completion; He will place me above the heights, that I may conquer in His song," to wit, in that song of which something similar is said in the psalm, "He set my feet upon a rock, and directed my goings, and put in my mouth a new song, a hymn to our God."[54] He therefore conquers in the song of the Lord, who takes pleasure in His praise, not in his own; that "He that glorieth, let him glory in the Lord."[55] But some copies have, "I will joy in God my Jesus," which seems to me better than the version of those who, wishing to put it in Latin, have not set down that very name which for us it is dearer and sweeter to name.

CHAPTER XXXIII

WHAT JEREMIAH AND ZEPHANIAH HAVE, BY THE PROPHETIC SPIRIT, SPOKEN BEFORE CONCERNING CHRIST AND THE CALLING OF THE NATIONS

Jeremiah, like Isaiah, is one of the greater prophets, not of the minor, like the others from whose writings I have just given extracts. He prophesied when Josiah reigned in Jerusalem, and Ancus Martius at Rome, when the

---

[51] Rom. xii. 12　[52] Heb. xi. 13, 16　[53] Rom. x. 3　[54] Ps. xl. 2, 3　[55] Jer. ix 23, 24, as in 1 Cor. i. 31

captivity of the Jews was already at hand; and he continued to prophesy down to the fifth month of the captivity, as we find from his writings. Zephaniah, one of the minor prophets, is put along with him, because he himself says that he prophesied in the days of Josiah; but he does not say till when. Jeremiah thus prophesied not only in the times of Ancus Martius, but also in those of Tarquinius Priscus, whom the Romans had for their fifth king. For he had already begun to reign when that captivity took place. Jeremiah, in prophesying of Christ says, "The breath of our mouth, the Lord Christ, was taken in our sins," [56] thus briefly showing both that Christ is our Lord and that He suffered for us. Also in another place he says, "This is my God, and there shall none other be accounted of in comparison of Him; who hath found out all the way of prudence, and hath given it to Jacob His servant, and to Israel His beloved: afterwards He was seen on the earth, and conversed with men." [57] Some attribute this testimony not to Jeremiah, but to his secretary, who was called Baruch; but it is more commonly ascribed to Jeremiah. Again the same prophet says concerning Him, "Behold the days come, saith the Lord, that I will raise up unto David a righteous shoot, and a King shall reign and shall be wise, and shall do judgment and justice in the earth. In those days Judah shall be saved, and Israel shall dwell confidently: and this is the name which they shall call Him, Our righteous Lord." [58] And of the calling of the nations which was to come to pass, and which we now see fulfilled, he thus spoke: "O Lord my God, and my refuge in the day of evils, to Thee shall the nations come from the utmost end of the earth, saying, Truly our fathers have worshipped lying images, wherein there is no profit." [59] But that the Jews, by whom He behoved even to be slain, were not going to acknowledge Him, this prophet thus intimates: "Heavy is the heart through all; and He is a man, and who shall know Him?" [60] That passage also is his which I have quoted in the seventeenth book concerning the *New Testament*, of which Christ is the Mediator. For Jeremiah himself says, "Behold, the days come, saith the Lord, that I will complete over the house of Jacob a new testament," and the rest, which may be read there.[61]

For the present I shall put down those predictions about Christ by the prophet Zephaniah, who prophesied with Jeremiah. "Wait ye upon me, saith the Lord, in the day of my resurrection, in the future; because it is my determination to assemble the nations, and gather together the kingdoms."[62] And again he says, "The Lord will be terrible upon them, and will exterminate all the gods of the earth; and they shall worship Him every man from his place, even all the isles of the nations." [63] And a little after he says, "Then will I turn to the people a tongue, and to His offspring, that they may call upon the name of the Lord, and serve Him under one yoke. From the borders of the rivers of Ethiopia shall they bring sacrifices unto me. In that day

[56] Lam. iv. 20   [57] Bar. iii. 35-37   [58] Jer. xxiii. 5, 6   [59] Jer. xvi. 19   [60] Jer. xvii. 9   [61] Jer. xxxi. 31; cf. Bk. xvii. 3   [62] Zeph. iii. 8   [63] Zeph. ii. 11

thou shalt not be confounded for all thy curious inventions, which thou hast done impiously against me: for then I will take away from thee the naughtiness of thy trespass; and thou shalt no more magnify thyself above thy holy mountain. And I will leave in thee a meek and humble people, and they who shall be left of Israel shall fear the name of the Lord." [64] These are the remnant of whom the apostle quotes that which is elsewhere prophesied: "Though the number of the children of Israel be as the sand of the sea, a remnant shall be saved." [65] These are the remnant of that nation who have believed in Christ.

CHAPTER XXXIV

OF THE PROPHECY OF DANIEL AND EZEKIEL, OTHER TWO OF THE GREATER PROPHETS

Daniel and Ezekiel, the other two of the greater prophets, also first prophesied in the very captivity of Babylon. Daniel even defined the time when Christ was to come and suffer by the exact date. It would take too long to show this by computation, and it has been done often by others before us. But of His power and glory he has thus spoken: "I saw in a night vision, and, behold, one like the Son of man was coming with the clouds of heaven, and He came even to the Ancient of days, and He was brought into His presence. And to Him there was given dominion, and honor, and a kingdom: and all people, tribes, and tongues shall serve Him. His power is an everlasting power, which shall not pass away, and His kingdom shall not be destroyed." [66]

Ezekiel also, speaking prophetically in the person of God the Father, thus foretells Christ, speaking of Him in the prophetic manner as David, because He assumed flesh of the seed of David, and on account of that form of a servant in which He was made man, He who is the Son of God is also called the servant of God. He says, "And I will set up over my sheep one Shepherd, who will feed them, even my servant David; and He shall feed them, and He shall be their shepherd. And I the Lord will be their God, and my servant David a prince in the midst of them. I the Lord have spoken." [67] And in another place he says, "And one King shall be over them all: and they shall no more be two nations, neither shall they be divided any more into two kingdoms: neither shall they defile themselves any more with their idols, and their abominations, and all their iniquities. And I will save them out of all their dwelling-places wherein they have sinned, and will cleanse them; and they shall be my people, and I will be their God. And my servant David shall be king over them, and there shall be one Shepherd for them all." [68]

[64] Zeph. iii. 9-12   [65] Isa. x. 22; Rom. ix. 27   [66] Dan. vii. 13, 14   [67] Ezek. xxxiv. 23   [68] Ezek. xxxvii. 22-24

CHAPTER XXXV

OF THE PROPHECY OF THE THREE PROPHETS, HAGGAI, ZECHARIAH, AND MALACHI

There remain three minor prophets, Haggai, Zechariah, and Malachi, who prophesied at the close of the captivity. Of these Haggai more openly prophesies of Christ and the Church thus briefly: "Thus saith the Lord of hosts, Yet one little while, and I will shake the heaven, and the earth, and the sea, and the dry land; and I will move all nations, and the desired of all nations shall come." [69] The fulfillment of this prophecy is in part already seen, and in part hoped for in the end. For He moved the heaven by the testimony of the angels and the stars, when Christ became incarnate. He moved the earth by the great miracle of His birth of the virgin. He moved the sea and the dry land, when Christ was proclaimed both in the isles and in the whole world. So we see all nations moved to the faith; and the fulfillment of what follows, "And the desired of all nations shall come," is looked for at His last coming. For ere men can desire and wait for Him, they must believe and love Him.

Zechariah says of Christ and the Church, "Rejoice greatly, O daughter of Sion; shout joyfully, O daughter of Jerusalem; behold, thy King shall come unto thee, just and the Saviour; Himself poor, and mounting an ass, and a colt the foal of an ass: and His dominion shall be from sea to sea, and from the river even to the ends of the earth." [70] How this was done, when the Lord Christ on His journey used a beast of burden of this kind, we read in the Gospel, where, also, as much of this prophecy is quoted as appears sufficient for the context. In another place, speaking in the Spirit of prophecy to Christ Himself of the remission of sins through His blood, he says, "Thou also, by the blood of Thy testament, has sent forth Thy prisoners from the lake wherein is no water." [71] Different opinions may be held, consistently with right belief, as to what he meant by this lake. Yet it seems to me that no meaning suits better than that of the depth of human misery, which is, as it were, dry and barren, where there are no streams of righteousness, but only the mire of iniquity. For it is said of it in the *Psalms*, "And He led me forth out of the lake of misery, and from the miry clay." [72]

Malachi, foretelling the Church which we now behold propagated through Christ, says most openly to the Jews, in the person of God, "I have no pleasure in you, and I will not accept a gift at your hand. For from the rising even to the going down of the sun, my name is great among the nations; and in every place sacrifice shall be made, and a pure oblation shall be offered unto my name: for my name shall be great among the nations, saith the Lord." [73] Since we can already see this sacrifice offered to God in every

---

[69] Hag. ii. 6   [70] Zech. ix. 9, 10   [71] Zech. ix. 11   [72] Ps. xi. 2   [73] Mal. i. 10, 11

place, from the rising of the sun to his going down, through Christ's priest-hood after the order of Melchisedec, while the Jews, to whom it was said, "I have no pleasure in you, neither will I accept a gift at your hand," can-not deny that their sacrifice has ceased, why do they still look for another Christ, when they read this in the prophecy, and see it fulfilled, which could not be fulfilled except through Him? And a little after he says of Him, in the person of God, "My covenant was with Him of life and peace: and I gave to Him that He might fear me with fear, and be afraid before my name. The law of truth was in His mouth: directing in peace He hath walked with me, and hath turned many away from iniquity. For the Priest's lips shall keep knowledge, and they shall seek the law at His mouth: for He is the Angel of the Lord Almighty." [74] Nor is it to be wondered at that Christ Jesus is called the Angel of the Almighty God. For just as He is called a serv-ant on account of the form of a servant in which He came to men, so He is called an angel on account of the *evangel* which He proclaimed to men. For if we interpret these Greek words, *evangel* is "good news," and *angel* is "messenger." Again he says of Him, "Behold I will send mine angel, and He will look out the way before my face: and the Lord, whom ye seek, shall suddenly come into His temple, even the Angel of the testament, whom ye desire. Behold, He cometh, saith the Lord Almighty, and who shall abide the day of His entry, or who shall stand at His appearing?" [75] In this place he has foretold both the first and second advent of Christ: the first, to wit, of which he says, "And He shall come suddenly into His temple;" that is, into His flesh, of which He said in the Gospel, "Destroy this temple, and in three days I will raise it up again." [76] And of the second advent he says, "Behold, He cometh, saith the Lord Almighty, and who shall abide the day of His entry, or who shall stand at His appearing?" But what he says, "The Lord whom ye seek, and the Angel of the testament whom ye desire," just means that even the Jews, according to the Scriptures which they read, shall seek and desire Christ. But many of them did not acknowledge that He whom they sought and desired had come, being blinded in their hearts, which were preoccupied with their own merits. Now what he here calls the testament, either above, where he says, "My testament had been with Him," or here, where he has called Him the Angel of the testament, we ought, beyond a doubt, to take to be the new testament, in which the things promised are eternal, and not the old, in which they are only temporal. Yet many who are weak are troubled when they see the wicked abound in such temporal things, because they value them greatly, and serve the true God to be rewarded with them. On this account, to distinguish the eternal blessedness of the new testament, which shall be given only to the good, from the earthly felicity of the old, which for the most part is given to the bad as well, the same prophet says, "Ye have made your words burdensome to me: yet ye have said, In what have we spoken ill of Thee? Ye have said,

[74] Mal. ii. 5-7   [75] Mal. iii. 1, 2   [76] John ii. 19

Foolish is every one who serves God; and what profit is it that we have kept His observances, and that we have walked as suppliants before the face of the Lord Almighty? And now we call the aliens blessed; yea, all that do wicked things are built up again; yea, they are opposed to God and are saved. They that feared the Lord uttered these reproaches every one to his neighbor: and the Lord hearkened and heard; and He wrote a book of remembrance before Him, for them that fear the Lord and that revere His name." [77] By that book is meant the New Testament. Finally, let us hear what follows: "And they shall be an acquisition for me, saith the Lord Almighty, in the day which I make; and I will choose them as a man chooseth his son that serveth him. And ye shall return, and shall discern between the just and the unjust, and between him that serveth God and him that serveth Him not. For, behold, the day cometh burning as an oven, and it shall burn them up; and all the aliens and all that do wickedly shall be stubble: and the day that shall come will set them on fire, saith the Lord Almighty, and shall leave neither root nor branch. And unto you that fear my name shall the Sun of Righteousness arise, and health shall be in His wings; and ye shall go forth, and exult as calves let loose from bonds. And ye shall tread down the wicked, and they shall be ashes under your feet, in the day in which I shall do this, saith the Lord Almighty." [78] This day is the day of judgment, of which, if God will, we shall speak more fully in its own place.

CHAPTER XXXVI

ABOUT ESDRAS AND THE BOOKS OF THE MACCABEES

After these three prophets, Haggai, Zechariah, and Malachi, during the same period of the liberation of the people from the Babylonian servitude Esdras also wrote, who is historical rather than prophetical, as is also the book called *Esther*, which is found to relate, for the praise of God, events not far from those times; unless, perhaps, Esdras is to be understood as prophesying of Christ in that passage where, on a question having arisen among certain young men as to what is the strongest thing, when one had said kings, another wine, the third women, who for the most part rule kings, yet that same third youth demonstrated that the truth is victorious over all.[79] For by consulting the Gospel we learn that Christ is the Truth. From this time, when the temple was rebuilt, down to the time of Aristobulus, the Jews had not kings but princes; and the reckoning of their dates is found, not in the Holy Scriptures which are called canonical, but in others, among which are also the books of the Maccabees. These are held as canonical, not by the Jews, but by the Church, on account of the extreme and wonderful sufferings of certain martyrs, who, before Christ had come in the flesh, con-

[77] Mal. iii. 13-16   [78] Mal. iii. 17: iv. 3   [79] Esdras iii. and iv.

tended for the law of God even unto death, and endured most grievous and horrible evils.

CHAPTER XXXVII

THAT PROPHETIC RECORDS ARE FOUND WHICH ARE MORE ANCIENT
THAN ANY FOUNTAIN OF THE GENTILE PHILOSOPHY

In the time of our prophets, then, whose writings had already come to the knowledge of almost all nations, the philosophers of the nations had not yet arisen—at least, not those who were called by that name, which originated with Pythagoras the Samian, who was becoming famous at the time when the Jewish captivity ended. Much more, then, are the other philosophers found to be later than the prophets. For even Socrates the Athenian, the master of all who were then most famous, holding the pre-eminence in that department that is called the moral or active, is found after Esdras in the chronicles. Plato also was born not much later, who far outwent the other disciples of Socrates. If, besides these, we take their predecessors, who had not yet been styled philosophers, to wit, the seven sages, and then the physicists, who succeeded Thales, and imitated his studious search into the nature of things, namely, Anaximander, Anaximenes, and Anaxagoras, and some others, before Pythagoras first professed himself a philosopher, even these did not precede the whole of our prophets in antiquity of time, since Thales, whom the others succeeded, is said to have flourished in the reign of Romulus, when the stream of prophecy burst forth from the fountains of Israel in those writings which spread over the whole world. So that only those theological poets, Orpheus, Linus, and Musaeus, and, it may be, some others among the Greeks, are found earlier in date than the Hebrew prophets whose writings we hold as authoritative. But not even these preceded in time our true divine, Moses, who authentically preached the one true God, and whose writings are first in the authoritative canon; and therefore the Greeks, in whose tongue the literature of this age chiefly appears, have no ground for boasting of their wisdom, in which our religion, wherein is true wisdom, is not evidently more ancient at least, if not superior. Yet it must be confessed that before Moses there had already been, not indeed among the Greeks, but among barbarous nations, as in Egypt, some doctrine which might be called their wisdom, else it would not have been written in the holy books that Moses was learned in all the wisdom of the Egyptians,[80] as he was, when, being born there, and adopted and nursed by Pharoah's daughter, he was also liberally educated. Yet not even the wisdom of the Egyptians could be antecedent in time to the wisdom of our prophets, because even Abraham was a prophet. And what wisdom could there be in Egypt before Isis had given them letters, whom they thought fit to worship

---

[80] Acts vii. 22

as a goddess after her death? Now Isis is declared to have been the daughter of Inachus, who first began to reign in Argos when the grandsons of Abraham are known to have been already born.

CHAPTER XXXVIII

THAT THE ECCLESIASTICAL CANON HAS NOT ADMITTED CERTAIN WRITINGS ON ACCOUNT OF THEIR TOO GREAT ANTIQUITY, LEST THROUGH THEM FALSE THINGS SHOULD BE INSERTED INSTEAD OF TRUE

If I may recall far more ancient times, our patriarch Noah was certainly even before that great deluge, and I might not undeservedly call him a prophet, forasmuch as the ark he made, in which he escaped with his family, was itself a prophecy of our times.[81] What of Enoch, the seventh from Adam? Does not the canonical epistle of the Apostle Jude declare that he prophesied?[82] But the writings of these men could not be held as authoritative either among the Jews or us, on account of their too great antiquity, which made it seem needful to regard them with suspicion, lest false things should be set forth instead of true. For some writings which are said to be theirs are quoted by those who, according to their own humor, loosely believe what they please. But the purity of the canon has not admitted these writings, not because the authority of these men who pleased God is rejected, but because they are not believed to be theirs. Nor ought it to appear strange if writings for which so great antiquity is claimed are held in suspicion, seeing that in the very history of the kings of Judah and Israel containing their acts, which we believe to belong to the canonical Scripture, very many things are mentioned which are not explained there, but are said to be found in other books which the prophets wrote, the very names of these prophets being sometimes given, and yet they are not found in the canon which the people of God received. Now I confess the reason of this is hidden from me; only I think that even those men, to whom certainly the Holy Spirit revealed those things which ought to be held as of religious authority, might write some things as men by historical diligence, and others as prophets by divine inspiration; and these things were so distinct, that it was judged that the former should be ascribed to themselves, but the latter to God speaking through them: and so the one pertained to the abundance of knowledge, the other to the authority of religion. In that authority the canon is guarded. So that, if any writings outside of it are now brought forward under the name of the ancient prophets, they cannot serve even as an aid to knowledge, because it is uncertain whether they are genuine; and on this account they are not trusted, especially those of them in which some things are found that are even contrary to the truth of the canonical books, so that it is quite apparent they do not belong to them.

[81] Heb. xi. 7; 1 Pet. iii. 20, 21   [82] Jude 14

CHAPTER XXXIX

Now we must not believe that Heber, from whose name the word Hebrew is derived, preserved and transmitted the Hebrew language to Abraham only as a spoken language, and that the Hebrew letters began with the giving of the law through Moses; but rather that this language, along with its letters, was preserved by that succession of fathers. Moses, indeed, appointed some among the people of God to teach letters, before they could know any letters of the divine law. The Scripture calls these men γραμματοεισαγωγούς, who may be called in Latin *inductores* or *introductores* of letters, because they, as it were, introduce them into the hearts of the learners, or rather lead those whom they teach into them. Therefore no nation could vaunt itself over our patriarchs and prophets by any wicked vanity for the antiquity of its wisdom; since not even Egypt, which is wont falsely and vainly to glory in the antiquity of her doctrines, is found to have preceded in time the wisdom of our patriarchs in her own wisdom, such as it is. Neither will any one dare to say that they were most skillful in wonderful sciences before they knew letters, that is, before Isis came and taught them there. Besides, what, for the most part, was that memorable doctrine of theirs which was called wisdom but astronomy, and it may be some other sciences of that kind, which usually have more power to exercise men's wit than to enlighten their minds with true wisdom? As regards philosophy, which professes to teach men something which shall make them happy, studies of that kind flourished in those lands about the times of Mercury, whom they called Trismegistus, long before the sages and philosophers of Greece, but yet after Abraham, Isaac, Jacob, and Joseph, and even after Moses himself. At that time, indeed, when Moses was born, Atlas is found to have lived, that great astronomer, the brother of Prometheus, and maternal grandson of the elder Mercury, of whom that Mercury Trismegistus was the grandson.

CHAPTER XL

In vain, then, do some babble with most empty presumption, saying that Egypt has understood the reckoning of the stars for more than a hundred thousand years. For in what books have they collected that number who learned letters from Isis their mistress, not much more than two thousand years ago? Varro, who has declared this, is no small authority in history, and it does not disagree with the truth of the divine books. For as it is not yet six thousand years since the first man, who is called Adam, are not those to be ridiculed rather than refuted who try to persuade us of anything regarding a space of time so different from, and contrary to, the ascertained truth? For what historian of the past should we credit more than him who has also predicted things to come which we now see fulfilled? And the very disagreement of the historians among themselves furnishes a good reason why we ought rather to believe him who does not contradict the divine history which we hold. But, on the other hand, the citizens of the impious city, scattered everywhere through the earth, when they read the most learned writers, none of whom seems to be of contemptible authority, and find them disagreeing among themselves about affairs most remote from the memory of our age, cannot find out whom they ought to trust. But we, being sustained by divine authority in the history of our religion, have no doubt that whatever is opposed to it is most false, whatever may be the case regarding other things in secular books, which, whether true or false, yield nothing of moment to our living rightly and happily.

CHAPTER XLI

ABOUT THE DISCORD OF PHILOSOPHIC OPINION, AND THE CONCORD OF THE SCRIPTURES THAT ARE HELD AS CANONICAL BY THE CHURCH

But let us omit further examination of history, and return to the philosophers from whom we digressed to these things. They seem to have labored in their studies for no other end than to find out how to live in a way proper for laying hold of blessedness. Why, then, have the disciples dissented from their masters, and the fellow-disciples from one another, except because as men they have sought after these things by human sense and human reasonings? Now, although there might be among them a desire of glory, so that each wished to be thought wiser and more acute than another, and in no way addicted to the judgment of others, but the inventor of his own dogma and opinion, yet I may grant that there were some, or even very many of them, whose love of truth severed them from their teachers or fellow-disciples, that they might strive for what they thought was the truth, whether it was so or not. But what can human misery do, or how or where can it reach forth, so as to attain blessedness, if divine authority does not lead it? Finally, let our authors, among whom the canon of the sacred books is fixed and bounded, be far from disagreeing in any respect. It is not without good reason, then, that not merely a few people prating in the schools and gymnasia in captious disputations, but so many and great people, both learned and unlearned, in countries and cities, have believed that God spoke to them or by them, *i.e.* the canonical writers, when they wrote these books. There ought, indeed, to be but few of them, lest on account of their multitude what ought to be religiously esteemed should grow cheap; and yet not so few that their agreement should not be wonderful. For among the multitude of philosophers, who in their works have left behind them the monuments of their dogmas, no one will easily find any who agree in all their opinions. But to show this is too long a task for this work.

But what author of any sect is so approved in this demon-worshipping city, that the rest who have differed from or opposed him in opinion have been disapproved? The Epicureans asserted that human affairs were not under the providence of the gods; and the Stoics, holding the opposite opinion, agreed that they were ruled and defended by favorable and tutelary gods. Yet were not both sects famous among the Athenians? I wonder, then, why Anaxagoras was accused of a crime for saying that the sun was a burning stone, and denying that it was a god at all; while in the same city Epicurus flourished gloriously and lived securely, although he not only did not believe that the sun or any star was a god, but contended that neither Jupiter nor any of the gods dwelt in the world at all, so that the prayers and supplications of men might reach them! Were not both Aristippus and Antisthenes there, two noble philosophers and both Socratic? yet they placed the chief end of life within bounds so diverse and contradictory, that the first made the delight of the body the chief good, while the other asserted that man was made happy mainly by the virtue of the mind. The one also said that the wise man should flee from the republic; the other, that he should administer its affairs. Yet did not each gather disciples to follow his own sect? Indeed, in the conspicuous and well-known porch, in gymnasia, in gardens, in places public and private, they openly strove in bands each for his own opinion, some asserting there was one world, others innumerable worlds; some that this world had a beginning, others that it had not; some that it would perish, others that it would exist always; some that it was governed by the divine mind, others by chance and accident; some that souls are immortal, others that they are mortal—and of those who asserted their immortality, some said they transmigrated through beasts, others that it was by no means so; while of those who asserted their mortality, some said they perished immediately after the body, others that they survived either a little while or a longer time, but not always; some fixing supreme good in the body, some in the mind, some in both; others adding to the mind and body external good things; some thinking that the bodily senses ought to be trusted always, some not always, others never. Now what people, senate, power, or public dignity of the impious city has ever taken care to judge between all these and other well-nigh innumerable dissensions of the philosophers, approving and accepting some, and disapproving and rejecting others? Has it not held in its bosom at random, without any judgment, and confusedly, so many controversies of men at variance, not about fields, houses, or anything of a pecuniary nature, but about those things which make life either miserable or happy? Even if some true things were said in it, yet falsehoods were uttered with the same licence; so that such a city has not amiss received the title of the mystic Babylon. For Babylon means confusion, as we remember we have already explained. Nor does it matter to the devil, its king, how they wrangle among themselves in contradictory errors, since all alike deservedly belong to him on account of their great and varied impiety.

But that nation, that people, that city, that republic, these Israelites, to whom the oracles of God were entrusted, by no means confounded with similar licence false prophets with the true prophets; but, agreeing together, and differing in nothing, acknowledged and upheld the authentic authors of their sacred books. These were their philosophers, these were their sages, divines, prophets, and teachers of probity and piety. Whoever was wise and lived according to them was wise and lived not according to men, but according to God who hath spoken by them. If sacrilege is forbidden there, God hath forbidden it. If it is said, "Honor thy father and thy mother," [83] God hath commanded it. If it is said, "Thou shalt not commit adultery, Thou shalt not kill, Thou shalt not steal," [84] and other similar commandments, not human lips but the divine oracles have brought them forth. Whatever truth certain philosophers, amid their false opinions, were able to see, and strove by laborious discussions to persuade men of—such as that God had made this world, and Himself most providently governs it, or of the nobility of the virtues, of the love of country, of fidelity in friendship, of good works and everything pertaining to virtuous manners, although they knew not to what end and what rule all these things were to be referred— all these, by words prophetic, that is, divine, although spoken by men, were commended to the people in that city, and not inculcated by contention in arguments, so that he who should know them might be afraid of contemning, not the wit of men, but the oracle of God.

CHAPTER XLII

BY WHAT DISPENSATION OF GOD'S PROVIDENCE THE SACRED SCRIPTURES OF THE OLD TESTAMENT WERE TRANSLATED OUT OF HEBREW INTO GREEK, THAT THEY MIGHT BE MADE KNOWN TO ALL THE NATIONS

One of the Ptolemies, kings of Egypt, desired to know and have these sacred books. For after Alexander of Macedon, who is also styled the Great, had by his most wonderful, but by no means enduring power, subdued the whole of Asia, indeed almost the whole world, partly by force of arms, partly by terror, and, among other kingdoms of the East, had entered and obtained Judea also, on his death his generals did not peaceably divide that most ample kingdom among them for a possession, but rather dissipated it, wasting all things by wars. Then Egypt began to have the Ptolemies as her

---

[83] Ex. xx. 12   [84] Ex. xx. 13-15, the order as in Mark x. 19

kings. The first of them, the son of Lagus, carried many captive out of Judea into Egypt. But another Ptolemy, called Philadelphus, who succeeded him, permitted all whom he had brought under the yoke to return free; and, more than that, sent kingly gifts to the temple of God, and begged Eleazar, who was the high priest, to give him the Scriptures, which he had heard by report were truly divine, and therefore greatly desired to have in that most noble library he had made. When the high priest had sent them to him in Hebrew, he afterwards demanded interpreters of him, and there were given him seventy-two, out of each of the twelve tribes six men, most learned in both languages, to wit, the Hebrew and Greek; and their translation is now by custom called the Septuagint. It is reported, indeed, that there was an agreement in their words so wonderful, stupendous, and plainly divine, that when they had sat at this work, each one apart (for so it pleased Ptolemy to test their fidelity) they differed from each other in no word which had the same meaning and force, or, in the order of the words; but, as if the translators had been one, so what all had translated was one, because in very deed the one Spirit had been in them all. And they received so wonderful a gift of God, in order that the authority of these Scriptures might be commended not as human but divine, as indeed it was, for the benefit of the nations who should at some time believe, as we now see them doing.

CHAPTER XLIII

OF THE AUTHORITY OF THE SEPTUAGINT TRANSLATION, WHICH, SAVING THE HONOR OF THE HEBREW ORIGINAL, IS TO BE PREFERRED TO ALL TRANSLATIONS

For while there were other interpreters who translated these sacred oracles out of the Hebrew tongue into Greek, as Aquila, Symmachus, and Theodotion, and also that translation which, as the name of the author is unknown, is quoted as the fifth edition, yet the Church has received this Septuagint translation just as if it were the only one; and it has been used by the Greek Christian people, most of whom are not aware that there is any other. From this translation there has also been made a translation in the Latin tongue, which the Latin churches use. Our times, however, have enjoyed the advantage of the presbyter Jerome, a man most learned, and skilled in all three languages, who translated these same Scriptures into the Latin speech, not from the Greek, but from the Hebrew.[85] But although the Jews acknowledge this very learned labor of his to be faithful, while they contend that the Septuagint translators have erred in many places, still the churches of Christ judge that no one should be preferred to the authority of

[85] Jerome was an older contemporary of Augustine, and next to him the most influential of the Latin fathers. He is the author of the Latin translation of the Scriptures, which under the name of the *Vulgate* is still the authorized Bible of the Roman church. He died at Bethlehem, 419, eleven years before Augustine

so many men, chosen for this very great work by Eleazar, who was then high priest; for even if there had not appeared in them one spirit, without doubt divine, and the seventy learned men had, after the manner of men, compared together the words of their translation, that what pleased them all might stand, no single translator ought to be preferred to them; but since so great a sign of divinity has appeared in them, certainly, if any other translator of their Scriptures from the Hebrew into any other tongue is faithful, in that case he agrees with these seventy translators, and if he is not found to agree with them, then we ought to believe that the prophetic gift is with them. For the same Spirit who was in the prophets when they spoke these things was also in the seventy men when they translated them, so that assuredly they could also say something else, just as if the prophet himself had said both, because it would be the same Spirit who said both; and could say the same thing differently, so that, although the words were not the same, yet the same meaning should shine forth to those of good understanding; and could omit or add something, so that even by this it might be shown that there was in that work not human bondage, which the translator owed to the words, but rather divine power, which filled and ruled the mind of the translator. Some, however, have thought that the Greek copies of the Septuagint version should be emended from the Hebrew copies; yet they did not dare to take away what the Hebrew lacked and the Septuagint had, but only added what was found in the Hebrew copies and was lacking in the Septuagint, and noted them by placing at the beginning of the verses certain marks in the form of stars which they call asterisks. And those things which the Hebrew copies have not, but the Septuagint have, they have in like manner marked at the beginning of the verses by horizontal spit-shaped marks like those by which we denote ounces; and many copies having these marks are circulated even in Latin. But we cannot, without inspecting both kinds of copies, find out those things which are neither omitted nor added, but expressed differently, whether they yield another meaning not in itself unsuitable, or can be shown to explain the same meaning in another way. If, then, as it behoves us, we behold nothing else in these Scriptures than what the Spirit of God has spoken through men, if anything is in the Hebrew copies and is not in the version of the Seventy, the Spirit of God did not choose to say it through them, but only through the prophets. But whatever is in the Septuagint and not in the Hebrew copies, the same Spirit chose rather to say through the latter, thus showing that both were prophets. For in that manner He spoke as He chose, some things through Isaiah, some through Jeremiah, some through several prophets, or else the same thing through this prophet and through that. Further, whatever is found in both editions, that one and the same Spirit willed to say through both, but so as that the former preceded in prophesying, and the latter followed in prophetically interpreting them; because, as the one Spirit of peace was in the former when they spoke true and concordant words, so the self-same one

Spirit hath appeared in the latter, when, without mutual conference, they yet interpreted all things as if with one mouth.

CHAPTER XLIV

HOW THE THREAT OF THE DESTRUCTION OF THE NINEVITES IS TO BE
UNDERSTOOD, WHICH IN THE HEBREW EXTENDS TO FORTY DAYS,
WHILE IN THE SEPTUAGINT IT IS CONTRACTED TO THREE

But some one may say, "How shall I know whether the prophet Jonah said to the Ninevites, 'Yet *three* days and Nineveh shall be overthrown,' or *forty* days?" [86] For who does not see that the prophet could not say both, when he was sent to terrify the city by the threat of imminent ruin? For if its destruction was to take place on the third day, it certainly could not be on the fortieth; but if on the fortieth, then certainly not on the third. If, then, I am asked which of these Jonah may have said, I rather think what is read in the Hebrew, "Yet forty days and Nineveh shall be overthrown." Yet the Seventy, interpreting long afterward, could say what was different and yet pertinent to the matter, and agree in the self-same meaning, although under a different signification. And this may admonish the reader not to despise the authority of either, but to raise himself above the history, and search for those things which the history itself was written to set forth. These things, indeed, took place in the city of Nineveh, but they also signified something else too great to apply to that city; just as, when it happened that the prophet himself was three days in the whale's belly, it signified besides, that He who is Lord of all the prophets should be three days in the depths of hell. Wherefore, if that city is rightly held as prophetically representing the Church of the Gentiles, to wit, as brought down by penitence, so as no longer to be what it had been, since this was done by Christ in the Church of the Gentiles, which Nineveh represented, Christ Himself was signified both by the forty and by the three days: by the forty, because he spent that number of days with His disciples after the resurrection, and then ascended into heaven, but by the three days, because He rose on the third day. So that, if the reader desires nothing else than to adhere to the history of events, he may be aroused from his sleep by the Septuagint interpreters, as well as the prophets, to search into the depth of the prophecy, as if they had said, In the forty days seek Him in whom thou mayest also find the three days—the one thou wilt find in His ascension, the other in His resurrection. Because that which could be most suitably signified by both numbers, of which one is used by Jonah the prophet, the other by the prophecy of the Septuagint version, the one and self-same Spirit has spoken. I dread prolixity, so that I must not demonstrate this by many instances in which the seventy interpreters may be thought to differ from the Hebrew, and yet,

[86] Jon. iii. 4

when well understood, are found to agree. For which reason I also, according to my capacity, following the footsteps of the apostles, who themselves have quoted prophetic testimonies from both, that is, from the Hebrew and the Septuagint, have thought that both should be used as authoritative, since both are one, and divine. But let us now follow out as we can what remains.

CHAPTER XLV

THAT THE JEWS CEASED TO HAVE PROPHETS AFTER THE REBUILDING
OF THE TEMPLE, AND FROM THAT TIME UNTIL THE BIRTH OF CHRIST
WERE AFFLICTED WITH CONTINUAL ADVERSITY, TO PROVE
THAT THE BUILDING OF ANOTHER TEMPLE HAD BEEN
PROMISED BY PROPHETIC VOICES

The Jewish nation no doubt became worse after it ceased to have prophets, just at the very time when, on the rebuilding of the temple after the captivity in Babylon, it hoped to become better. For so, indeed, did that carnal people understand what was foretold by Haggai the prophet, saying, "The glory of this latter house shall be greater than that of the former." [87] Now, that this is said of the New Testament, he showed a little above, where he says, evidently promising Christ, "And I will move all nations, and the desired One shall come to all nations." [88] In this passage the Septuagint translators giving another sense more suitable to the body than the Head, that is, to the Church than to Christ, have said by prophetic authority, "The things shall come that are chosen of the Lord from all nations," that is, *men*, of whom Jesus saith in the Gospel, "Many are called, but few are chosen." [89] For by such chosen ones of the nations there is built, through the New Testament, with living stones, a house of God far more glorious than that temple was which was constructed by king Solomon, and rebuilt after the captivity. For this reason, then, that nation had no prophets from that time, but was afflicted with many plagues by kings of alien race, and by the Romans themselves, lest they should fancy that this prophecy of Haggai was fulfilled by that rebuilding of the temple.

For not long after, on the arrival of Alexander, it was subdued, when, although there was no pillaging, because they dared not resist him, and thus, being very easily subdued, received him peaceably, yet the glory of that house was not so great as it was when under the free power of their own kings. Alexander, indeed, offered up sacrifices in the temple of God, not as a convert to His worship in true piety, but thinking, with impious folly, that He was to be worshipped along with false gods. Then Ptolemy son of Lagus, whom I have already mentioned, after Alexander's death carried them captive into Egypt. His successor, Ptolemy Philadelphus, most benevolently dismissed them; and by him it was brought about, as I have narrated a little

[87] Hag. ii. 9   [88] Hag. ii. 7   [89] Matt. xxii. 14

before, that we should have the Septuagint version of the Scriptures. Then they were crushed by the wars which are explained in the books of the Maccabees. Afterward they were taken captive by Ptolemy king of Alexandria, who was called Epiphanes. Then Antiochus king of Syria compelled them by many and most grievous evils to worship idols, and filled the temple itself with the sacrilegious superstitions of the Gentiles. Yet their most vigorous leader Judas, who is also called Maccabaeus, after beating the generals of Antiochus, cleansed it from all that defilement of idolatry.

But not long after, one Alcimus, although an alien from the sacerdotal tribe, was, through ambition, made pontiff, which was an impious thing. After almost fifty years, during which they never had peace, although they prospered in some affairs, Aristobulus first assumed the diadem among them, and was made both king and pontiff. Before that, indeed, from the time of their return from the Babylonian captivity and the rebuilding of the temple, they had not kings, but generals or *principes*. Although a king himself may be called a prince, from his principality in governing, and a leader, because he leads the army, but it does not follow that all who are princes and leaders may also be called kings, as that Aristobulus was. He was succeeded by Alexander, also both king and pontiff, who is reported to have reigned over them cruelly. After him his wife Alexandra was queen of the Jews, and from her time downwards more grievous evils pursued them; for this Alexandra's sons, Aristobulus and Hyrcanus, when contending with each other for the kingdom, called in the Roman forces against the nation of Israel. For Hyrcanus asked assistance from them against his brother. At that time Rome had already subdued Africa and Greece, and ruled extensively in other parts of the world also, and yet, as if unable to bear her own weight, had, in a manner, broken herself by her own size. For indeed she had come to grave domestic seditions, and from that to social wars, and by and by to civil wars, and had enfeebled and worn herself out so much, that the changed state of the republic, in which she should be governed by kings, was now imminent. Pompey then, a most illustrious prince of the Roman people, having entered Judea with an army, took the city, threw open the temple, not with the devotion of a suppliant, but with the authority of a conqueror, and went, not reverently, but profanely, into the holy of holies, where it was lawful for none but the pontiff to enter. Having established Hyrcanus in the pontificate, and set Antipater over the subjugated nation as guardian or procurator, as they were then called, he led Aristobulus with him bound. From that time the Jews also began to be Roman tributaries. After Cassius plundered the very temple. Then after a few years it was their desert to have Herod, a king of foreign birth, in whose reign Christ was born. For the time had now come signified by the prophetic Spirit through the mouth of the patriarch Jacob, when he says, "There shall not be lacking a prince out of Judah, nor a teacher from his loins, until He shall come for whom it is reserved; and He is the expectation of the nations." [90] There lacked not therefore a Jewish prince of the Jews until that Herod, who was the first king of a foreign race received by them. Therefore it was now the time when He should come for whom that was reserved which is promised in the New Testament, that He should be the expectation of the nations. But it was not possible that the nations should expect He would come, as we see they did, to do judgment in the splendor of power, unless they should first believe in Him when He came to suffer judgment in the humility of patience.

CHAPTER XLVI

OF THE BIRTH OF OUR SAVIOUR, WHEREBY THE WORD WAS MADE FLESH; AND OF THE DISPERSION OF THE JEWS AMONG ALL NATIONS, AS HAD BEEN PROPHESIED

While Herod, therefore, reigned in Judea, and Caesar Augustus was emperor at Rome, the state of the republic being already changed, and the world being set at peace by him, Christ was born in Bethlehem of Judah, man manifest out of a human virgin, God hidden out of God the Father. For so had the prophet foretold: "Behold, a virgin shall conceive in the womb, and bring forth a Son, and they shall call His name Immanuel, which, being interpreted, is, God with us." [91] He did many miracles that He might commend God in Himself, some of which, even as many as seemed sufficient to proclaim Him, are contained in the evangelic Scripture. The first of these is, that He was so wonderfully born, and the last, that with His body raised up again from the dead He ascended into heaven. But the Jews who slew Him, and would not believe in Him, because it behoved Him to die and rise again, were yet more miserably wasted by the Romans, and utterly rooted out from their kingdom, where aliens had already ruled over them, and were dispersed through the lands (so that indeed there is no place where they are not) and are thus by their own Scriptures a testimony to us that we have not forged the prophecies about Christ. And very many of them, considering this, even before His passion, but chiefly after His resurrection, believed on Him, of whom it was predicted, "Though the number of the children of Israel be as the sand of the sea, the remnant shall be saved." [92] But the rest are blinded, of whom it was predicted, "Let their table be made before them a trap, and a retribution, and a stumbling-block. Let their eyes be darkened lest they see, and bow down their back alway." [93] Therefore, when they do not believe our Scriptures, their own, which they blindly read, are fulfilled in them, lest perchance any one should say that the Christians have forged these prophecies about Christ which are quoted under the name of the sibyl, or of others, if such there be, who do not belong to the Jewish people. For us, indeed, those suffice which are quoted from the books of our

[90] Gen. xlix. 10   [91] Isa. vii. 14, as in Matt. i. 23   [92] Isa. x. 22, as in Rom. ix. 27, 28   [93] Ps. lxix. 22, 23; Rom. xi. 9, 10

enemies, to whom we make our acknowledgment, on account of this testimony which, in spite of themselves, they contribute by their possession of these books, while they themselves are dispersed among all nations, wherever the Church of Christ is spread abroad. For a prophecy about this thing was sent before in the Psalms, which they also read, where it is written, "My God, His mercy shall prevent me. My God hath shown me concerning mine enemies, that Thou shalt not slay them, lest they should at last forget Thy law: disperse them in Thy might." [94] Therefore God has shown the Church in her enemies the Jews the grace of His compassion, since, as saith the apostle, "their offence is the salvation of the Gentiles." [95] And therefore He has not slain them, that is, He has not let the knowledge that they are Jews be lost in them, although they have been conquered by the Romans, lest they should forget the law of God, and their testimony should be of no avail in this matter of which we treat. But it was not enough that he should say, "Slay them not, lest they should at last forget Thy law," unless he had also added, "Disperse them;" because if they had only been in their own land with that testimony of the Scriptures, and not everywhere, certainly the Church which is everywhere could not have had them as witnesses among all nations to the prophecies which were sent before concerning Christ.

CHAPTER XLVII

WHETHER BEFORE CHRISTIAN TIMES THERE WERE ANY OUTSIDE OF THE ISRAELITE RACE WHO BELONGED TO THE FELLOWSHIP OF THE HEAVENLY CITY

Wherefore if we read of any foreigner—that is, one neither born of Israel nor received by that people into the canon of the sacred books—having prophesied something about Christ, if it has come or shall come to our knowledge, we can refer to it over and above; not that this is necessary, even if wanting, but because it is not incongruous to believe that even in other nations there may have been men to whom this mystery was revealed, and who were also impelled to proclaim it, whether they were partakers of the same grace or had no experience of it, but were taught by bad angels, who, as we know, even confessed the present Christ, whom the Jews did not acknowledge. Nor do I think the Jews themselves dare contend that no one has belonged to God except the Israelites, since the increase of Israel began on the rejection of his elder brother. For in very deed there was no other people who were specially called the people of God; but they cannot deny that there have been certain men even of other nations who belonged, not to earthly but heavenly fellowship, to the true Israelites, the citizens of the country that is above. Because, if they deny this, they can be most easily

---

[94] Ps. lxix. 10, 11   [95] Rom. xi. 11

confuted by the case of the holy and wonderful man Job, who was neither a native nor a proselyte, that is, a stranger joining the people of Israel, but, being bred of the Idumean race, arose there and died there too, and who is so praised by the divine oracle, that no man of his times is put on a level with him as regards justice and piety. And although we do not find his date in the chronicles, yet from his book, which for its merit the Israelites have received as of canonical authority, we gather that he was in the third generation after Israel. And I doubt not it was divinely provided, that from this one case we might know that among other nations also there might be men pertaining to the spiritual Jerusalem who have lived according to God and have pleased Him. And it is not to be supposed that this was granted to any one, unless the one Mediator between God and men, the Man Christ Jesus,[96] was divinely revealed to him; who was pre-announced to the saints of old as yet to come in the flesh, even as He is announced to us as having come, that the self-same faith through Him may lead all to God who are predestinated to be the city of God, the house of God, and the temple of God. But whatever prophecies concerning the grace of God through Christ Jesus are quoted, they may be thought to have been forged by the Christians. So that there is nothing of more weight for confuting all sorts of aliens, if they contend about this matter, and for supporting our friends, if they are truly wise, than to quote those divine predictions about Christ which are written in the books of the Jews, who have been torn from their native abode and dispersed over the whole world in order to bear this testimony, so that the Church of Christ has everywhere increased.

CHAPTER XLVIII

THAT HAGGAI'S PROPHECY, IN WHICH HE SAID THAT THE GLORY OF THE
HOUSE OF GOD WOULD BE GREATER THAN THAT OF THE FIRST HAD
BEEN,[97] WAS REALLY FULFILLED, NOT IN THE REBUILDING
OF THE TEMPLE, BUT IN THE CHURCH OF CHRIST

This house of God is more glorious than that first one which was constructed of wood and stone, metals and other precious things. Therefore the prophecy of Haggai was not fulfilled in the rebuilding of that temple. For it can never be shown to have had so much glory after it was rebuilt as it had in the time of Solomon; yea, rather, the glory of that house is shown to have been diminished, first by the ceasing of prophecy, and then by the nation itself suffering so great calamities, even to the final destruction made by the Romans, as the things above-mentioned prove. But this house which pertains to the New Testament is just as much more glorious as the living stones, even believing, renewed men, of which it is constructed are better. But it was typified by the rebuilding of that temple for this reason, because

___

[96] 1 Tim. ii. 5   [97] Hag. ii. 9

the very renovation of that edifice typifies in the prophetic oracle another testament which is called the new. When, therefore, God said by the prophet just named, "And I will give peace in this place," [98] He is to be understood who is typified by that typical place; for since by that rebuilt place is typified the Church which was to be built by Christ, nothing else can be accepted as the meaning of the saying, "I will give peace in this place," except I will give peace in the place which that place signifies. For all typical things seem in some way to personate those whom they typify, as it is said by the apostle, "That Rock was Christ." [99] Therefore the glory of this New Testament house is greater than the glory of the Old Testament house; and it will show itself as greater when it shall be dedicated. For then "shall come the desired of all nations," [100] as we read in the Hebrew. For before His advent He had not yet been desired by all nations. For they knew not Him whom they ought to desire, in whom they had not believed. Then, also, according to the Septuagint interpretation (for it also is a prophetic meaning) "shall come those who are elected of the Lord out of all nations." For then indeed there shall come only those who are elected, whereof the apostle saith, "According as He hath chosen us in Him before the foundation of the world." [101] For the Master Builder who said, "Many are called, but few are chosen," [102] did not say this of those who, on being called, came in such a way as to be cast out from the feast, but would point out the house built up of the elect, which henceforth shall dread no ruin. Yet because the churches are also full of those who shall be separated by the winnowing as in the threshing-floor, the glory of this house is not so apparent now as it shall be when every one who is there shall be there always.

CHAPTER XLIX

OF THE INDISCRIMINATE INCREASE OF THE CHURCH, WHEREIN MANY REPROBATE ARE IN THIS WORLD MIXED WITH THE ELECT

In this wicked world, in these evil days, when the Church measures her future loftiness by her present humility, and is exercised by goading fears, tormenting sorrows, disquieting labors, and dangerous temptations, when she soberly rejoices, rejoicing only in hope, there are many reprobate mingled with the good, and both are gathered together by the gospel as in a drag net; [103] and in this world, as in a sea, both swim enclosed without distinction in the net, until it is brought ashore, when the wicked must be separated from the good, that in the good, as in His temple, God may be all in all. We acknowledge, indeed, that His word is now fulfilled who spoke in the psalm, and said, "I have announced and spoken; they are multiplied above number." [104] This takes place now, since He has spoken, first by the mouth of his

[98] Hag. ii. 9   [99] 1 Cor. x. 4; Ex. xvii. 6   [100] Hag. ii. 7   [101] Eph. i. 4   [102] Matt. xxii. 11-14   [103] Matt. xiii. 47-50   [104] Ps. xl. 5

forerunner John, and afterward by His own mouth, saying, "Repent: for the kingdom of heaven is at hand." [105] He chose disciples, whom He also called apostles,[106] of lowly birth, unhonored, and illiterate, so that whatever great thing they might be or do, He might be and do it in them. He had one among them whose wickedness He could use well in order to accomplish His appointed passion, and furnish His Church an example of bearing with the wicked. Having sown the holy gospel as much as that behoved to be done by His bodily presence, He suffered, died, and rose again, showing by His passion what we ought to suffer for the truth, and by His resurrection what we ought to hope for in adversity; saving always the mystery of the sacrament, by which His blood was shed for the remission of sins. He held converse on the earth forty days with His disciples, and in their sight ascended into heaven, and after ten days sent the promised Holy Spirit. It was given as the chief and most necessary sign of His coming on those who had believed, that every one of them spoke in the tongues of all nations; thus signifying that the unity of the Catholic Church would embrace all nations, and would in like manner speak in all tongues.

CHAPTER L

OF THE PREACHING OF THE GOSPEL, WHICH IS MADE MORE FAMOUS AND POWERFUL BY THE SUFFERINGS OF ITS PREACHERS

Then was fulfilled that prophecy, "Out of Sion shall go forth the law, and the word of the Lord out of Jerusalem;" [107] and the prediction of the Lord Christ Himself, when, after the resurrection, "He opened the understanding" of His amazed disciples "that they might understand the Scriptures, and said unto them, that thus it is written, and thus it behoved Christ to suffer, and to rise from the dead the third day, and that repentance and remission of sins should be preached in His name among all nations, beginning at Jerusalem." [108] And again, when, in reply to their questioning about the day of His last coming, He said, "It is not for you to know the times or the seasons which the Father hath put in His own power; but ye shall receive the power of the Holy Ghost coming upon you, and ye shall be witnesses unto me both in Jerusalem, and in all Judea, and Samaria, and even unto the ends of the earth." [109] First of all, the Church spread herself abroad from Jerusalem; and when very many in Judea and Samaria had believed, she also went into other nations by those who announced the gospel, whom, as lights, He Himself had both prepared by His word and kindled by His Holy Spirit. For He had said to them, "Fear ye not them which kill the body, but are not able to kill the soul." [110] And that they might not be frozen with fear, they burned with the fire of charity. Finally, the gospel of Christ was preached in the whole world, not only by those who had seen and heard Him

[105] Matt. iii. 2; iv. 17   [106] Luke vi. 13   [107] Isa. ii. 3   [108] Luke xxiv. 45-47
[109] Acts i. 7, 8   [110] Matt. x. 28

both before His passion and after His resurrection, but also after their death by their successors, amid the horrible persecutions, diverse torments and deaths of the martyrs, God also bearing them witness, both with signs and wonders, and divers miracles and gifts of the Holy Ghost,[111] that the people of the nations, believing in Him who was crucified for their redemption, might venerate with Christian love the blood of the martyrs which they had poured forth with devilish fury, and the very kings by whose laws the Church had been laid waste might become profitably subject to that name they had cruelly striven to take away from the earth, and might begin to persecute the false gods for whose sake the worshippers of the true God had formerly been persecuted.

CHAPTER LI

THAT THE CATHOLIC FAITH MAY BE CONFIRMED EVEN BY THE DISSENSIONS OF THE HERETICS

But the devil, seeing the temples of the demons deserted, and the human race running to the name of the liberating Mediator, has moved the heretics under the Christian name to resist the Christian doctrine, as if they could be kept in the city of God indifferently without any correction, just as the city of confusion indifferently held the philosophers who were of diverse and adverse opinions. Those, therefore, in the Church of Christ who savor anything morbid and depraved, and, on being corrected that they may savor what is wholesome and right, contumaciously resist, and will not amend their pestiferous and deadly dogmas, but persist in defending them, become heretics, and, going without, are to be reckoned as enemies who serve for her discipline. For even thus they profit by their wickedness those true catholic members of Christ, since God makes a good use even of the wicked, and all things work together for good to them that love Him.[112] For all the enemies of the Church, whatever error blinds or malice depraves them, exercise her patience if they receive the power to afflict her corporally; and if they only oppose her by wicked thought, they exercise her wisdom: but at the same time, if these enemies are loved, they exercise her benevolence, or even her beneficence, whether she deals with them by persuasive doctrine or by terrible discipline. And thus the devil, the prince of the impious city, when he stirs up his own vessels against the city of God that sojourns in this world, is permitted to do her no harm. For without doubt the divine providence procures for her both consolation through prosperity, that she may not be broken by adversity, and trial through adversity, that she may not be corrupted by prosperity; and thus each is tempered by the other, as we recognize in the *Psalms* that voice which arises from no other cause, "According to the multitude of my griefs in my heart, Thy consolations have

[111] Heb. ii. 4   [112] Rom. viii. 28

delighted my soul." [113] Hence also is that saying of the apostle, "Rejoicing in hope, patient in tribulation." [114]

For it is not to be thought that what the same teacher says can at any time fail, "Whoever will live piously in Christ shall suffer persecution." [115] Because even when those who are without do not rage, and thus there seems to be, and really is, tranquillity, which brings very much consolation, especially to the weak, yet there are not wanting, yea, there are many within who by their abandoned manners torment the hearts of those who live piously, since by them the Christian and Catholic name is blasphemed; and the dearer that name is to those who will live piously in Christ, the more do they grieve that through the wicked, who have a place within, it comes to be less loved than pious minds desire. The heretics themselves also, since they are thought to have the Christian name and sacraments, Scriptures, and profession, cause great grief in the hearts of the pious, both because many who wish to be Christians are compelled by their dissensions to hesitate, and many evil-speakers also find in them matter for blaspheming the Christian name, because they too are at any rate *called* Christians. By these and similar depraved manners and errors of men, those who will live piously in Christ suffer persecution, even when no one molests or vexes their body; for they suffer this persecution, not in their bodies, but in their hearts. Whence is that word, "According to the multitude of my griefs in my heart;" for he does not say, in my body. Yet, on the other hand, none of them can perish, because the immutable divine promises are thought of. And because the apostle says, "The Lord knoweth them that are His;[116] for whom He did foreknow, He also predestinated to be conformed to the image of His Son," [117] none of them can perish; therefore it follows in that psalm, "Thy consolations have delighted my soul." [118] But that grief which arises in the hearts of the pious, who are persecuted by the manners of bad or false Christians, is profitable to the sufferers, because it proceeds from the charity in which they do not wish them either to perish or to hinder the salvation of others. Finally, great consolations grow out of their chastisement, which imbue the souls of the pious with a fecundity as great as the pains with which they were troubled concerning their own perdition. Thus in this world, in these evil days, not only from the time of the bodily presence of Christ and His apostles, but even from that of Abel, whom first his wicked brother slew because he was righteous,[119] and thenceforth even to the end of this world, the Church has gone forward on pilgrimage amid the persecutions of the world and the consolations of God.

[113] Ps. xciv. 19   [114] Rom. xii. 12   [115] 2 Tim. iii. 12   [116] 2 Tim. ii. 19   [117] Rom. viii. 29   [118] Ps. xciv. 19   [119] 1 John iii. 12

CHAPTER LII

WHETHER WE SHOULD BELIEVE WHAT SOME THINK, THAT, AS THE TEN PERSECUTIONS WHICH ARE PAST HAVE BEEN FULFILLED, THERE REMAINS NO OTHER BEYOND THE ELEVENTH, WHICH MUST HAPPEN IN THE VERY TIME OF ANTICHRIST

I do not think, indeed, that what some have thought or may think is rashly said or believed, that until the time of Antichrist the Church of Christ is not to suffer any persecutions besides those she has already suffered—that is, *ten*—and that the eleventh and last shall be inflicted by Antichrist. They reckon as the first that made by Nero, the second by Domitian, the third by Trajan, the fourth by Antoninus, the fifth by Severus, the sixth by Maximin, the seventh by Decius, the eighth by Valerian, the ninth by Aurelian, the tenth by Diocletian and Maximian. For as there were ten plagues in Egypt before the people of God could begin to go out, they think this is to be referred to as showing that the last persecution by Antichrist must be like the eleventh plague, in which the Egyptians, while following the Hebrews with hostility, perished in the Red Sea when the people of God passed through on dry land. Yet I do not think persecutions were prophetically signified by what was done in Egypt, however nicely and ingeniously those who think so may seem to have compared the two in detail, not by the prophetic Spirit, but by the conjecture of the human mind, which sometimes hits the truth, and sometimes is deceived. But what can those who think this say of the persecution in which the Lord Himself was crucified? In which number will they put it? And if they think the reckoning is to be made exclusive of this one, as if those must be counted which pertain to the body, and not that in which the Head Himself was set upon and slain, what can they make of that one which, after Christ ascended into heaven, took place in Jerusalem, when the blessed Stephen was stoned; when James the brother of John was slaughtered with the sword; when the Apostle Peter was imprisoned to be killed, and was set free by the angel; when the brethren were driven away and scattered from Jerusalem; when Saul, who afterward became the Apostle Paul, wasted the Church; and when he himself, publishing the glad tidings of the faith he had persecuted, suffered such things as he had inflicted, either from the Jews or from other nations, where he most fervently preached Christ everywhere? Why, then, do they think fit to start with Nero, when the Church in her growth had reached the times of Nero amid the most cruel persecutions, about which it would be too long to say anything? But if they think that only the persecutions made by kings ought to be reckoned, it was king Herod who also made a most grievous one after the ascension of the Lord. And what account do they give of Julian, whom they do not number in the ten? Did not he persecute the Church, who forbade the Christians to teach or learn liberal letters?

Under him the elder Valentinian, who was the third emperor after him, stood forth as a confessor of the Christian faith, and was dismissed from his command in the army. I shall say nothing of what he did at Antioch, except to mention his being struck with wonder at the freedom and cheerfulness of one most faithful and steadfast young man, who, when many were seized to be tortured, was tortured during a whole day, and sang under the instrument of torture, until the emperor feared lest he should succumb under the continued cruelties and put him to shame at last, which made him dread and fear that he would be yet more dishonorably put to the blush by the rest. Lastly, within our own recollection, did not Valens the Arian, brother of the foresaid Valentinian, waste the Catholic Church by great persecution throughout the East? But how unreasonable it is not to consider that the Church, which bears fruit and grows through the whole world, may suffer persecution from kings in some nations even when she does not suffer it in others! Perhaps, however, it was not to be reckoned a persecution when the king of the Goths, in Gothia itself, persecuted the Christians with wonderful cruelty, when there were none but Catholics there, of whom very many were crowned with martyrdom, as we have heard from certain brethren who had been there at that time as boys, and unhesitatingly called to mind that they had seen these things? And what took place in Persia of late? Was not persecution so hot against the Christians (if even yet it is allayed) that some of the fugitives from it came even to Roman towns? When I think of these and the like things, it does not seem to me that the number of persecutions with which the Church is to be tried can be definitely stated. But, on the other hand, it is no less rash to affirm that there will be some persecutions by kings besides that last one, about which no Christian is in doubt. Therefore we leave this undecided, supporting or refuting neither side of this question, but only restraining men from the audacious presumption of affirming either of them.

CHAPTER LIII

OF THE HIDDEN TIME OF THE FINAL PERSECUTION

Truly Jesus Himself shall extinguish by His presence that last persecution which is to be made by Antichrist. For so it is written, that "He shall slay him with the breath of His mouth, and empty him with the brightness of His presence." [120] It is customary to ask, When shall that be? But this is quite unreasonable. For had it been profitable for us to know this, by whom could it better have been told than by God Himself, the Master, when the disciples questioned Him? For they were not silent when with Him, but inquired of Him, saying, "Lord, wilt Thou at this time present the kingdom to Israel, or when?" [121] But He said, "It is not for you to know the times, which the Father hath put in His own power." When they got that answer,

[120] Isa. xi. 4; 2 Thess. i. 9   [121] Acts i. 6, 7

they had not at all questioned Him about the hour, or day, or year, but about the time. In vain, then, do we attempt to compute definitely the years that may remain to this world, when we may hear from the mouth of the Truth that it is not for us to know this. Yet some have said that four hundred, some five hundred, others a thousand years, may be completed from the ascension of the Lord up to His final coming. But to point out how each of them supports his own opinion would take too long, and is not necessary; for indeed they use human conjectures, and bring forward nothing certain from the authority of the canonical Scriptures. But on this subject He puts aside the figures of the calculators, and orders silence, who says, "It is not for you to know the times, which the Father hath put in His own power."

But because this sentence is in the Gospel, it is no wonder that the worshippers of the many and false gods have been none the less restrained from feigning that by the responses of the demons, whom they worship as gods, it has been fixed how long the Christian religion is to last. For when they saw that it could not be consumed by so many and great persecutions, but rather drew from them wonderful enlargements, they invented I know not what Greek verses, as if poured forth by a divine oracle to some one consulting it, in which, indeed, they make Christ innocent of this, as it were, sacrilegious crime, but add that Peter by enchantments brought it about that the name of Christ should be worshipped for three hundred and sixty-five years, and, after the completion of that number of years, should at once take end. O the hearts of learned men! O, learned wits, meet to believe such things *about* Christ as you are not willing to believe *in* Christ, that His disciple Peter did not learn magic arts from Him, yet that, although He was innocent, His disciple was an enchanter, and chose that His name rather than his own should be worshipped through his magic arts, his great labors and perils, and at last even the shedding of his blood! If Peter the enchanter made the world so love Christ, what did Christ the innocent do to make Peter so love Him? Let them answer themselves then, and, if they can, let them understand that the world, for the sake of eternal life, was made to love Christ by that same supernal grace which made Peter also love Christ for the sake of the eternal life to be received from Him, and that even to the extent of suffering temporal death for Him. And then, what kind of gods are these who are able to predict such things, yet are not able to avert them, succumbing in such a way to a single enchanter and wicked magician (who, as they say, having slain a yearling boy and torn him to pieces, buried him with nefarious rites) that they permitted the sect hostile to themselves to gain strength for so great a time, and to surmount the horrid cruelties of so many great persecutions, not by resisting but by suffering, and to procure the overthrow of their own images, temples, rituals, and oracles? Finally, what god was it—not ours, certainly, but one of their own—who was either enticed or compelled by so great wickedness to perform these things? For those verses say that Peter bound, not any demon, but a god to do these things. Such a god have they who have not Christ.

CHAPTER LIV

OF THE VERY FOOLISH LIE OF THE PAGANS, IN FEIGNING THAT THE CHRISTIAN RELIGION WAS NOT TO LAST BEYOND THREE HUNDRED AND SIXTY-FIVE YEARS

I might collect these and many similar arguments, if that year had not already passed by which lying divination has promised, and deceived vanity has believed. But as a few years ago three hundred and sixty-five years were completed since the time when the worship of the name of Christ was established by His presence in the flesh, and by the apostles, what other proof need we seek to refute that falsehood? For, not to place the beginning of this period at the nativity of Christ, because as an infant and boy He had no disciples, yet, when He began to have them, beyond doubt the Christian doctrine and religion then became known through His bodily presence, that is, after He was baptized in the river Jordan by the ministry of John. For on this account that prophecy went before concerning Him: "He shall reign from sea even to sea, and from the river even to the ends of the earth." [122] But since, before He suffered and rose from the dead, the faith had not yet been defined to all, but was defined in the resurrection of Christ (for so the Apostle Paul speaks to the Athenians, saying, "But now He announces to men that all everywhere should repent, because He hath appointed a day in which to judge the world in equity, by the Man in whom He hath defined the faith to all men, raising Him from the dead" [123]), it is better that, in settling this question, we should start from that point, especially because the Holy Spirit was then given, just as He behoved to be given after the resurrection of Christ in that city from which the second law, that is, the new testament, ought to begin. For the first, which is called the Old Testament, was given from Mount Sinai through Moses. But concerning this which was to be given by Christ it was predicted, "Out of Sion shall go forth the law and the word of the Lord out of Jerusalem;" [124] whence He Himself said, that repentance in His name behoved to be preached among all nations, but yet beginning at Jerusalem.[125] There, therefore, the worship of this name took its rise, that Jesus should be believed in, who died and rose again. There this faith blazed up with such noble beginnings, that several thousand men, being converted to the name of Christ with wonderful alacrity, sold their goods for distribution among the needy, thus, by a holy resolution and most ardent charity, coming to voluntary poverty, and prepared themselves, amid the Jews who raged and thirsted for their blood, to contend for the truth even to death, not with armed power, but with more powerful

[122] Ps. lxxii. 8　　[123] Acts xvii. 30, 31　　[124] Isa. ii. 3　　[125] Luke xxiv. 47

patience. If this was accomplished by no magic arts, why do they hesitate to believe that the other could be done throughout the whole world by the same divine power by which this was done? But supposing Peter wrought that enchantment so that so great a multitude of men at Jerusalem was thus kindled to worship the name of Christ, who had either seized and fastened Him to the cross, or reviled Him when fastened there, we must still inquire when the three hundred and sixty-five years must be completed, counting from that year. Now Christ died when the Gemini were consuls, on the eighth day before the kalends of April. He rose the third day, as the apostles have proved by the evidence of their own senses. Then forty days after, He ascended into heaven. Ten days after, that is, on the fiftieth after his resurrection, He sent the Holy Spirit; then three thousand men believed when the apostles preached Him. Then, therefore, arose the worship of that name, as we believe, and according to the real truth, by the efficacy of the Holy Spirit, but, as impious vanity has feigned or thought, by the magic arts of Peter. A little afterward, too, on a wonderful sign being wrought, when at Peter's own word a certain beggar, so lame from his mother's womb that he was carried by others and laid down at the gate of the temple, where he begged alms, was made whole in the name of Jesus Christ, and leaped up, five thousand men believed, and thenceforth the Church grew by sundry accessions of believers. Thus we gather the very day with which that year began, namely, that on which the Holy Spirit was sent, that is, during the ides of May. And, on counting the consuls, the three hundred and sixty-five years are found completed on the same ides in the consulate of Honorius and Eutychianus. Now, in the following year, in the consulate of Mallius Theodorus, when, according to that oracle of the demons or figment of men, there ought already to have been no Christian religion, it was not necessary to inquire, what perchance was done in other parts of the earth. But, as we know, in the most noted and eminent city, Carthage, in Africa, Gaudentius and Jovius, officers of the Emperor Honorius, on the fourteenth day before the kalends of April, overthrew the temples and broke the images of the false gods. And from that time to the present, during almost thirty years, who does not see how much the worship of the name of Christ has increased, especially after many of those became Christians who had been kept back from the faith by thinking that divination true, but saw when that same number of years was completed that it was empty and ridiculous? We, therefore, who are called and *are* Christians, do not believe in Peter, but in Him whom Peter believed—being edified by Peter's sermons about Christ, not poisoned by his incantations; and not deceived by his enchantments, but aided by his good deeds. Christ Himself, who was Peter's Master in the doctrine which leads to eternal life, is our Master too.

But let us now at last finish this book, after thus far treating of, and showing as far as seemed sufficient, what is the mortal course of the two cities, the heavenly and the earthly, which are mingled together from the beginning down to the end. Of these, the earthly one has made to herself of whom she would, either from any other quarter, or even from among men, false gods whom she might serve by sacrifice; but she which is heavenly and is a pilgrim on the earth does not make false gods, but is herself made by the true God of whom she herself must be the true sacrifice. Yet both alike either enjoy temporal good things, or are afflicted with temporal evils, but with diverse faith, diverse hope, and diverse love, until they must be separated by the last judgment, and each must receive her own end, of which there is no end. About these ends of both we must next treat.

BOOK NINETEEN

ARGUMENT

In this book the end of the two cities, the earthly and the heavenly, is discussed. Augustine reviews the opinions of the philosophers regarding the supreme good, and their vain efforts to make for themselves a happiness in this life; and, while he refutes these, he takes occasion to show what the peace and happiness belonging to the heavenly city, or the people of Christ, are, both now and hereafter.

CHAPTER I

THAT VARRO HAS MADE OUT THAT TWO HUNDRED AND EIGHTY-EIGHT DIFFERENT SECTS OF PHILOSOPHY MIGHT BE FORMED BY THE VARIOUS OPINIONS REGARDING THE SUPREME GOOD

As I SEE that I have still to discuss the fit destinies of the two cities, the earthly and the heavenly, I must first explain, so far as the limits of this work allow me, the reasonings by which men have attempted to make for themselves a happiness in this unhappy life, in order that it may be evident, not only from divine authority, but also from such reasons as can be adduced to unbelievers, how the empty dreams of the philosophers differ from the hope which God gives to us, and from the substantial fulfillment of it which He will give us as our blessedness. Philosophers have expressed a great variety of diverse opinions regarding the ends of goods and of evils, and this question they have eagerly canvassed, that they might, if possible, discover what makes a man happy. For the end of our good is that for the sake of which other things are to be desired, while it is to be desired for its own sake; and the end of evil is that on account of which other things are to be shunned, while it is avoided on its own account. Thus, by the *end of good*, we at present mean, not that by which good is destroyed, so that it no longer exists, but that by which it is finished, so that it becomes complete; and by the *end of evil* we mean, not that which abolishes it, but that which completes its development. These two ends, therefore, are the supreme good and the supreme evil; and, as I have said, those who have in this vain life professed the study of wisdom have been at great pains to discover these ends, and to obtain the supreme good and avoid the supreme evil in this life. And although they erred in a variety of ways, yet natural insight has prevented them from wandering from the truth so far that they have not placed the supreme good and evil, some in the soul, some in the body, and some in both. From this tripartite distribution of the sects of philosophy, Marcus Varro, in his book *De Philosophia*,[1] has drawn so large a variety of opinions, that, by a subtle and minute analysis of distinctions, he numbers without difficulty as many as 288 sects—not that these have actually existed, but sects which are possible.

To illustrate briefly what he means, I must begin with his own introductory statement in the above-mentioned book, that there are four things which men desire, as it were by nature without a master, without the help of any instruction, without industry or the art of living which is called virtue, and which is certainly learned:[2] either pleasure, which is an agreeable stirring of the bodily sense; or repose, which excludes every bodily inconvenience; or both these, which Epicurus calls by the one name, pleasure; or the primary objects of nature,[3] which comprehend the things already named and other things, either bodily, such as health, and safety, and integrity of the members, or spiritual, such as the greater and less mental gifts that are found in men. Now these four things—pleasure, repose, the two combined, and the primary objects of nature—exist in us in such sort that we must either desire virtue on their account, or them for the sake of virtue, or both for their own sake; and consequently there arise from this distinction twelve sects, for each is by this consideration tripled. I will illustrate this in one instance, and, having done so, it will not be difficult to understand the others. According, then, as bodily pleasure is subjected, preferred, or united to virtue, there are three sects. It is subjected to virtue when it is chosen as subservient to virtue. Thus it is a duty of virtue to live for one's country, and for its sake to beget children, neither of which can be done without bodily pleasure. For there is pleasure in eating and drinking, pleasure also in sexual intercourse. But when it is preferred to virtue, it is desired for its own sake, and virtue is chosen only for its sake, and to effect nothing else than the attainment or preservation of bodily pleasure. And this, indeed, is to make life hideous; for where virtue is the slave of pleasure it no longer deserves the name of virtue. Yet even this disgraceful distortion has found some philosophers to patronize and defend it. Then virtue is united to pleasure when neither is desired for the other's sake, but both for their own. And therefore, as pleasure, according as it is subjected, preferred, or united to virtue, makes three sects, so also do repose, pleasure and repose combined, and the prime natural blessings, make their three sects each. For as men's opinions vary, and these four things are sometimes subjected, sometimes preferred, and sometimes united to virtue, there are produced twelve sects. But this number again is doubled by the addition of one difference, viz., the social life; for whoever attaches himself to any of these sects does so either for his own sake alone, or for the sake of a companion, for whom he ought to wish what he desires for himself. And thus there will be twelve of those who think some one of these opinions should be held for their own sakes, and twelve others who decide that they

[1] Not extant   [2] Alluding to the vexed question whether virtue could be taught
[3] The *prima naturae* or Τὰ πρῶτα κατὰ φύσιν of the Stoics

ought to follow this or that philosophy not for their own sakes only, but also for the sake of others whose good they desire as their own. These twenty-four sects again are doubled, and become forty-eight by adding a difference taken from the New Academy. For each of these four and twenty sects can hold and defend their opinion as certain, as the Stoics defended the position that the supreme good of man consisted solely in virtue; or they can be held as probable, but not certain, as the New Academics did. There are, therefore, twenty-four who hold their philosophy as certainly true, twenty-four others who hold their opinions as probable, but not certain. Again, as each person who attaches himself to any of these sects may adopt the mode of life either of the Cynics or of the other philosophers, this distinction will double the number, and so make ninety-six sects. Then, lastly, as each of these sects may be adhered to either by men who love a life of ease, as those who have through choice or necessity addicted themselves to study, or by men who love a busy life, as those who, while philosophizing, have been much occupied with state affairs and public business, or by men who choose a mixed life, in imitation of those who have apportioned their time partly to erudite leisure, partly to necessary business: by these differences the number of the sects is tripled, and becomes 288.

I have thus, as briefly and lucidly as I could, given in my own words the opinions which Varro expresses in his book. But how he refutes all the rest of these sects, and chooses one, the Old Academy, instituted by Plato, and continuing to Polemo, the fourth teacher of that school of philosophy which held that their system was certain; and how on this ground he distinguishes it from the New Academy,[4] which began with Polemo's successor Arcesilaus, and held that all things are uncertain; and how he seeks to establish that the Old Academy was as free from error as from doubt—all this, I say, were too long to enter upon in detail, and yet I must not altogether pass it by in silence. Varro then rejects, as a first step, all those differences which have multiplied the number of sects; and the ground on which he does so is that they are not differences about the supreme good. He maintains that in philosophy a sect is created only by its having an opinion of its own different from other schools on the point of the ends-in-chief. For man has no other reason for philosophizing than that he may be happy; but that which makes him happy is itself the supreme good. In other words, the supreme good is the reason of philosophizing; and therefore that cannot be called a sect of philosophy which pursues no way of its own towards the supreme good. Thus, when it is asked whether a wise man will adopt the social life, and desire and be interested in the supreme good of his friend as in his own, or will, on the contrary, do all that he does merely for his own sake, there is no question here about the supreme good, but only about the propriety of associating or not associating a friend in its participation: whether the wise man will do this not for his own sake, but for the sake of his friend in whose good

[4] Frequently called the Middle Academy; the New beginning with Carneades

he delights as in his own. So, too, when it is asked whether all things about which philosophy is concerned are to be considered uncertain, as by the New Academy, or certain, as the other philosophers maintain, the question here is not what end should be pursued, but whether or not we are to believe in the substantial existence of that end; or, to put it more plainly, whether he who pursues the supreme good must maintain that it is a true good, or only that it appears to him to be true, though possibly it may be delusive—both pursuing one and the same good. The distinction, too, which is founded on the dress and manners of the Cynics, does not touch the question of the chief good, but only the question whether he who pursues that good which seems to himself true should live as do the Cynics. There were, in fact, men who, though they pursued different things as the supreme good, some choosing pleasure, others virtue, yet adopted that mode of life which gave the Cynics their name. Thus, whatever it is which distinguishes the Cynics from other philosophers, this has no bearing on the choice and pursuit of that good which constitutes happiness. For if it had any such bearing, then the same habits of life would necessitate the pursuit of the same chief good, and diverse habits would necessitate the pursuit of different ends.

CHAPTER II

HOW VARRO, BY REMOVING ALL THE DIFFERENCES WHICH DO NOT FORM SECTS, BUT ARE MERELY SECONDARY QUESTIONS, REACHES THREE DEFINITIONS OF THE CHIEF GOOD, OF WHICH WE MUST CHOOSE ONE

The same may be said of those three kinds of life, the life of studious leisure and search after truth, the life of easy engagement in affairs, and the life in which both these are mingled. When it is asked, which of these should be adopted, this involves no controversy about the end of good, but inquires which of these three puts a man in the best position for finding and retaining the supreme good. For this good, as soon as a man finds it, makes him happy; but lettered leisure, or public business, or the alternation of these, do not necessarily constitute happiness. Many, in fact, find it possible to adopt one or other of these modes of life, and yet to miss what makes a man happy. The question, therefore, regarding the supreme good and the supreme evil, and which distinguishes sects of philosophy, is one; and these questions concerning the social life, the doubt of the Academy, the dress and food of the Cynics, the three modes of life—the active, the contemplative, and the mixed— these are different questions, into none of which the question of the chief good enters. And therefore, as Marcus Varro multiplied the sects to the number of 288 (or whatever larger number he chose) by introducing these four differences derived from the social life, the New Academy, the Cynics, and the threefold form of life, so, by removing these differences as having no bearing on the supreme good, and as therefore not constituting what can properly be called sects, he returns to those twelve schools which concern themselves with inquiring what that good is which makes man happy, and he shows that one of these is true, the rest false. In other words, he dismisses the distinction founded on the threefold mode of life, and so decreases the whole number by two-thirds, reducing the sects to ninety-six. Then, putting aside the Cynic peculiarities, the number decreases by a half, to forty-eight. Taking away next the distinction occasioned by the hesitancy of the New Academy, the number is again halved, and reduced to twenty-four. Treating in a similar way the diversity introduced by the consideration of the social life, there are left but twelve, which this difference had doubled to twenty-four. Regarding these twelve, no reason can be assigned why they should not be called sects. For in them the sole inquiry is regarding the supreme good and the ultimate evil—that is to say, regarding the supreme good, for this being found, the opposite evil is thereby found. Now, to make these twelve sects, he multiplies by three these four things—pleasure, repose, pleasure and repose combined, and the primary objects of nature which Varro calls *primigenia*. For as these four things are sometimes subordinated to virtue, so that they seem to be desired not for their own sake, but for virtue's sake; sometimes preferred to it, so that virtue seems to be necessary not on its own account, but in order to attain these things; sometimes joined with it, so that both they and virtue are desired for their own sakes—we must multiply the four by three, and thus we get twelve sects. But from those four things Varro eliminates three—pleasure, repose, pleasure and repose combined— not because he thinks these are not worthy of the place assigned them, but because they are included in the primary objects of nature. And what need is there, at any rate, to make a threefold division out of these two ends, pleasure and repose, taking them first severally and then conjunctly, since both they, and many other things besides, are comprehended in the primary objects of nature? Which of the three remaining sects must be chosen? This is the question that Varro dwells upon. For whether one of these three or some other be chosen, reason forbids that more than one be true. This we shall afterwards see; but meanwhile let us explain as briefly and distinctly as we can how Varro makes his selection from these three, that is, from the sects which severally hold that the primary objects of nature are to be desired for virtue's sake, that virtue is to be desired for their sake, and that virtue and these objects are to be desired each for their own sake.

CHAPTER III

WHICH OF THE THREE LEADING OPINIONS REGARDING THE CHIEF GOOD SHOULD BE PREFERRED, ACCORDING TO VARRO, WHO FOLLOWS ANTIOCHUS AND THE OLD ACADEMY

Which of these three is true and to be adopted he attempts to show in the following manner. As it is the supreme good, not of a tree, or of a beast, or of a god, but of man, that philosophy is in quest of, he thinks that, first of all, we must define man. He is of opinion that there are two parts in human nature, body and soul, and makes no doubt that of these two the soul is the better and by far the more worthy part. But whether the soul alone is the man, so that the body holds the same relation to it as a horse to the horseman, this he thinks has to be ascertained. The horseman is not a horse and a man, but only a man, yet he is called a horseman, because he is in some relation to the horse. Again, is the body alone the man, having a relation to the soul such as the cup has to the drink? For it is not the cup and the drink it contains which are called the cup, but the cup alone; yet it is so called because it is made to hold the drink. Or, lastly, is it neither the soul alone nor the body alone, but both together, which are man, the body and the soul being each a part, but the whole man being both together, as we call two horses yoked together a pair, of which pair the near and the off horse is each a part, but we do not call either of them, no matter how connected with the other, a pair, but only both together? Of these three alternatives, then, Varro chooses the third, that man is neither the body alone, nor the soul alone, but both together. And therefore the highest good, in which lies the happiness of man, is composed of goods of both kinds, both bodily and spiritual. And consequently he thinks that the primary objects of nature are to be sought for their own sake, and that virtue, which is the art of living, and can be communicated by instruction, is the most excellent of spiritual goods. This virtue, then, or art of regulating life, when it has received these primary objects of nature which existed independently of it, and prior to any instruction, seeks them all, and itself also, for its own sake; and it uses them, as it also uses itself, that from them all it may derive profit and enjoyment, greater or less, according as they are themselves greater or less; and while it takes pleasure in all of them, it despises the less that it may obtain or retain the greater when occasion demands. Now, of all goods, spiritual or bodily, there is none at all to compare with virtue. For virtue makes a good use both of itself and of all other goods in which lies man's happiness; and where it is absent, no matter how many good things a man has, they are not for his good, and consequently should not be called good things while they belong to one who makes them useless by using them badly. The life of man, then, is called happy when it enjoys virtue and these other spiritual and bodily good things without which virtue is impossible. It is called happier if it enjoys some or many other good things which are not essential to virtue; and happiest of all, if it lacks not one of the good things which pertain to the body and the soul. For life is not the same thing as virtue, since not every life, but a wisely regulated life, is virtue; and yet, while there can be life of some kind without virtue, there cannot be virtue without life. This I might apply to memory and reason, and such mental faculties; for these exist prior to instruction, and without them there cannot be any instruction, and consequently no virtue, since virtue is learned. But bodily advantages, such as swiftness of foot, beauty, or strength, are not essential to virtue, neither is virtue essential to them, and yet they are good things; and, according to our philosophers, even these advantages are desired by virtue for its own sake, and are used and enjoyed by it in a becoming manner.

They say that this happy life is also social, and loves the advantages of its friends as its own, and for their sake wishes for them what it desires for itself, whether these friends live in the same family, as a wife, children, domestics; or in the locality where one's home is, as the citizens of the same town; or in the world at large, as the nations bound in common human brotherhood; or in the universe itself, comprehended in the heavens and the earth, as those whom they call gods, and provide as friends for the wise man, and whom we more familiarly call angels. Moreover, they say that, regarding the supreme good and evil, there is no room for doubt, and that they therefore differ from the New Academy in this respect, and they are not concerned whether a philosopher pursues those ends which they think true in the Cynic dress and manner of life or in some other. And, lastly, in regard to the three modes of life, the contemplative, the active, and the composite, they declare in favor of the third. That these were the opinions and doctrines of the Old Academy, Varro asserts on the authority of Antiochus, Cicero's master and his own, though Cicero makes him out to have been more frequently in accordance with the Stoics than with the Old Academy. But of what importance is this to us, who ought to judge the matter on its own merits, rather than to understand accurately what different men have thought about it?

CHAPTER IV

WHAT THE CHRISTIANS BELIEVE REGARDING THE SUPREME GOOD AND EVIL, IN OPPOSITION TO THE PHILOSOPHERS, WHO HAVE MAINTAINED THAT THE SUPREME GOOD IS IN THEMSELVES

If, then, we be asked what the city of God has to say upon these points, and, in the first place, what its opinion regarding the supreme good and evil is, it will reply that life eternal is the supreme good, death eternal the supreme evil, and that to obtain the one and escape the other we must live rightly. And thus it is written, "The just lives by faith," [5] for we do not as yet see our good, and must therefore live by faith; neither have we in ourselves power to live rightly, but can do so only if He who has given us faith to believe in His help do help us when we believe and pray. As for those who have supposed that the sovereign good and evil are to be found in this life, and have placed it either in the soul or the body, or in both, or, to speak more explicitly, either in pleasure or in virtue, or in both; in repose or in virtue, or in both; in pleasure and repose, or in virtue, or in all combined; in the primary objects of nature, or in virtue, or in both—all these have, with

[5] Hab. ii. 4

a marvelous shallowness, sought to find their blessedness in this life and in themselves. Contempt has been poured upon such ideas by the Truth, saying by the prophet, "The Lord knoweth the thoughts of men" (or, as the Apostle Paul cites the passage, "The Lord knoweth the thoughts of the *wise*") "that they are vain." [6]

For what flood of eloquence can suffice to detail the miseries of this life? Cicero, in the *Consolation* on the death of his daughter, has spent all his ability in lamentation; but how inadequate was even his ability here? For when, where, how, in this life can these primary objects of nature be possessed so that they may not be assailed by unforeseen accidents? Is the body of the wise man exempt from any pain which may dispel pleasure, from any disquietude which may banish repose? The amputation or decay of the members of the body puts an end to its integrity, deformity blights its beauty, weakness its health, lassitude its vigor, sleepiness or sluggishness its activity —and which of these is it that may not assail the flesh of the wise man? Comely and fitting attitudes and movements of the body are numbered among the prime natural blessings; but what if some sickness makes the members tremble? what if a man suffers from curvature of the spine to such an extent that his hands reach the ground, and he goes upon all-fours like a quadruped? Does not this destroy all beauty and grace in the body, whether at rest or in motion? What shall I say of the fundamental blessings of the soul, sense and intellect, of which the one is given for the perception, and the other for the comprehension of truth? But what kind of sense is it that remains when a man becomes deaf and blind? where are reason and intellect when disease makes a man delirious? We can scarcely, or not at all, refrain from tears, when we think of or see the actions and words of such frantic persons, and consider how different from and even opposed to their own sober judgment and ordinary conduct their present demeanor is. And what shall I say of those who suffer from demoniacal possession? Where is their own intelligence hidden and buried while the malignant spirit is using their body and soul according to his own will? And who is quite sure that no such thing can happen to the wise man in this life? Then, as to the perception of truth, what can we hope for even in this way while in the body, as we read in the true book of Wisdom, "The corruptible body weigheth down the soul, and the earthly tabernacle presseth down the mind that museth upon many things?" [7] And eagerness, or desire of action, if this is the right meaning to put upon the Greek ὁρμή, is also reckoned among the primary advantages of nature; and yet is it not this which produces those pitiable movements of the insane, and those actions which we shudder to see, when sense is deceived and reason deranged?

In fine, virtue itself, which is not among the primary objects of nature, but succeeds to them as the result of learning, though it holds the highest place among human good things, what is its occupation save to wage per-

[6] Ps. xciv. 11, and 1 Cor. iii. 20   [7] Wisdom ix. 15

petual war with vices—not those that are outside of us, but within; not other men's, but our own—a war which is waged especially by that virtue which the Greeks call σωφροσύνη, and we temperance,[8] and which bridles carnal lusts, and prevents them from winning the consent of the spirit to wicked deeds? For we must not fancy that there is no vice in us, when, as the apostle says, "The flesh lusteth against the spirit;"[9] for to this vice there is a contrary virtue, when, as the same writer says, "The spirit lusteth against the flesh." "For these two," he says, "are contrary one to the other, so that you cannot do the things which you would." But what is it we wish to do when we seek to attain the supreme good, unless that the flesh should cease to lust against the spirit, and that there be no vice in us against which the spirit may lust? And as we cannot attain to this in the present life, however ardently we desire it, let us by God's help accomplish at least this, to preserve the soul from succumbing and yielding to the flesh that lusts against it, and to refuse our consent to the perpetration of sin. Far be it from us, then, to fancy that while we are still engaged in this intestine war, we have already found the happiness which we seek to reach by victory. And who is there so wise that he has no conflict at all to maintain against his vices?

What shall I say of that virtue which is called prudence? Is not all its vigilance spent in the discernment of good from evil things, so that no mistake may be admitted about what we should desire and what avoid? And thus it is itself a proof that we are in the midst of evils, or that evils are in us; for it teaches us that it is an evil to consent to sin, and a good to refuse this consent. And yet this evil, to which prudence teaches and temperance enables us not to consent, is removed from this life neither by prudence nor by temperance. And justice, whose office it is to render to every man his due, whereby there is in man himself a certain just order of nature, so that the soul is subjected to God, and the flesh to the soul, and consequently both soul and flesh to God—does not this virtue demonstrate that it is as yet rather laboring towards its end than resting in its finished work? For the soul is so much the less subjected to God as it is less occupied with the thought of God; and the flesh is so much the less subjected to the spirit as it lusts more vehemently against the spirit. So long, therefore, as we are beset by this weakness, this plague, this disease, how shall we dare to say that we are safe? and if not safe, then how can we be already enjoying our final beatitude? Then that virtue which goes by the name of fortitude is the plainest proof of the ills of life, for it is these ills which it is compelled to bear patiently. And this holds good, no matter though the ripest wisdom co-exists with it. And I am at a loss to understand how the Stoic philosophers can presume to say that these are no ills, though at the same time they allow the wise man to commit suicide and pass out of this life if they become so grievous that he cannot or ought not to endure them. But such is the stupid pride of these men who fancy that the supreme good can be found in this life, and

[8] Cicero, *Tusc. Quaest.* iii. 8   [9] Gal. v. 17

that they can become happy by their own resources, that their wise man, or at least the man whom they fancifully depict as such, is always happy, even though he become blind, deaf, dumb, mutilated, racked with pains, or suffer any conceivable calamity such as may compel him to make away with himself; and they are not ashamed to call the life that is beset with these evils happy. O happy life, which seeks the aid of death to end it? If it is happy, let the wise man remain in it; but if these ills drive him out of it, in what sense is it happy? Or how can they say that these are not evils which conquer the virtue of fortitude, and force it not only to yield, but so to rave that it in one breath calls life happy and recommends it to be given up? For who is so blind as not to see that if it were happy it would not be fled from? And if they say we should flee from it on account of the infirmities that beset it, why then do they not lower their pride and acknowledge that it is miserable? Was it, I would ask, fortitude or weakness which prompted Cato to kill himself? for he would not have done so had he not been too weak to endure Caesar's victory. Where, then, is his fortitude? It has yielded, it has succumbed, it has been so thoroughly overcome as to abandon, forsake, flee this happy life. Or was it no longer happy? Then it was miserable. How, then, were these not evils which made life miserable, and a thing to be escaped from?

And therefore those who admit that these are evils, as the Peripatetics do, and the Old Academy, the sect which Varro advocates, express a more intelligible doctrine; but theirs also is a surprising mistake, for they contend that this is a happy life which is beset by these evils, even though they be so great that he who endures them should commit suicide to escape them. "Pains and anguish of body," says Varro, "are evils, and so much the worse in proportion to their severity; and to escape them you must quit this life." What life, I pray? This life, he says, which is oppressed by such evils. Then it is happy in the midst of these very evils on account of which you say we must quit it? Or do you call it happy because you are at liberty to escape these evils by death? What, then, if by some secret judgment of God you were held fast and not permitted to die, nor suffered to live without these evils? In that case, at least, you would say that such a life was miserable. It is soon relinquished, no doubt, but this does not make it not miserable; for were it eternal, you yourself would pronounce it miserable. Its brevity, therefore, does not clear it of misery; neither ought it to be called happiness because it is a brief misery. Certainly there is a mighty force in these evils which compel a man—according to them, even a wise man—to cease to be a man that he may escape them, though they say, and say truly, that it is as it were the first and strongest demand of nature that a man cherish himself, and naturally therefore avoid death, and should so stand his own friend as to wish and vehemently aim at continuing to exist as a living creature, and subsisting in this union of soul and body. There is a mighty force in these evils to overcome this natural instinct by which death is by every means and with all a man's efforts avoided, and to overcome it so completely that what was avoided is desired, sought after, and if it cannot in any other way be obtained, is inflicted by the man on himself. There is a mighty force in these evils which make fortitude a homicide—if, indeed, that is to be called fortitude which is so thoroughly overcome by these evils, that it not only cannot preserve by patience the man whom it undertook to govern and defend, but is itself obliged to kill him. The wise man, I admit, ought to bear death with patience, but when it is inflicted by another. If, then, as these men maintain, he is obliged to inflict it on himself, certainly it must be owned that the ills, which compel him to this are not only evils, but intolerable evils. The life, then, which is either subject to accidents, or environed with evils so considerable and grievous, could never have been called happy, if the men who give it this name had condescended to yield to the truth, and to be conquered by valid arguments, when they inquired after the happy life, as they yield to unhappiness, and are overcome by overwhelming evils, when they put themselves to death, and if they had not fancied that the supreme good was to be found in this mortal life; for the very virtues of this life, which are certainly its best and most useful possessions, are all the more telling proofs of its miseries in proportion as they are helpful against the violence of its dangers, toils, and woes. For if these are true virtues—and such cannot exist save in those who have true piety—they do not profess to be able to deliver the men who possess them from all miseries; for true virtues tell no such lies, but they profess that by the hope of the future world this life, which is miserably involved in the many and great evils of this world, is happy as it is also safe. For if not yet safe, how could it be happy? And therefore the Apostle Paul, speaking not of men without prudence, temperance, fortitude, and justice, but of those whose lives were regulated by true piety, and whose virtues were therefore true, says, "For we are saved by hope: now hope which is seen is not hope; for what a man seeth, why doth he yet hope for? But if we hope for that we see not, then do we with patience wait for it." [10] As, therefore, we are saved, so we are made happy by hope. And as we do not as yet possess a present, but look for a future salvation, so is it with our happiness, and this "with patience;" for we are encompassed with evils, which we ought patiently to endure, until we come to the ineffable enjoyment of unmixed good; for there shall be no longer anything to endure. Salvation, such as it shall be in the world to come, shall itself be our final happiness. And this happiness these philosophers refuse to believe in, because they do not see it, and attempt to fabricate for themselves a happiness in this life, based upon a virtue which is as deceitful as it is proud.

[10] Rom. viii. 24

CHAPTER V

OF THE SOCIAL LIFE, WHICH, THOUGH MOST DESIRABLE, IS
FREQUENTLY DISTURBED BY MANY DISTRESSES

We give a much more unlimited approval to their idea that the life of the
wise man must be social. For how could the city of God (concerning which
we are already writing no less than the nineteenth book of this work) either
take a beginning or be developed, or attain its proper destiny, if the life of
the saints were not a social life? But who can enumerate all the great grievances with which human society abounds in the misery of this mortal state?
Who can weigh them? Hear how one of their comic writers makes one of his
characters express the common feelings of all men in this matter: "I am
married; this is one misery. Children are born to me; they are additional
cares." [11] What shall I say of the miseries of love which Terence also recounts
—"slights, suspicions, quarrels, war to-day, peace to-morrow?" [12] Is not
human life full of such things? Do they not often occur even in honorable
friendships? On all hands we experience these slights, suspicions, quarrels,
war, all of which are undoubted evils; while, on the other hand, peace is a
doubtful good, because we do not know the heart of our friend, and though
we did know it to-day, we should be as ignorant of what it might be to-morrow. Who ought to be, or who are more friendly than those who live in the
same family? And yet who can rely even upon this friendship, seeing that
secret treachery has often broken it up, and produced enmity as bitter as
the amity was sweet, or seemed sweet by the most perfect dissimulation? It
is on this account that the words of Cicero so move the heart of every one,
and provoke a sigh: "There are no snares more dangerous than those which
lurk under the guise of duty or the name of relationship. For the man who is
your declared foe you can easily baffle by precaution; but this hidden, intestine, and domestic danger not merely exists, but overwhelms you before you
can foresee and examine it." [13] It is also to this that allusion is made by the
divine saying, "A man's foes are those of his own household" [14]—words
which one cannot hear without pain; for though a man have sufficient fortitude to endure it with equanimity, and sufficient sagacity to baffle the malice
of a pretended friend, yet if he himself is a good man, he cannot but be
greatly pained at the discovery of the perfidy of wicked men, whether they
have always been wicked and merely feigned goodness, or have fallen from
a better to a malicious disposition. If, then, home, the natural refuge from
the ills of life, is itself not safe, what shall we say of the city, which, as it is
larger, is so much the more filled with lawsuits civil and criminal, and is
never free from the fear, if sometimes from the actual outbreak, of disturbing and bloody insurrections and civil wars?

[11] Terent. *Adelph.* .v. 4   [12] *Eunuch*, i. 1   [13] *In Verrem*, ii. 1. 15   [14] Matt. x. 36

CHAPTER VI

OF THE ERROR OF HUMAN JUDGMENTS WHEN THE TRUTH IS HIDDEN

What shall I say of these judgments which men pronounce on men, and which are necessary in communities, whatever outward peace they enjoy? Melancholy and lamentable judgments they are, since the judges are men who cannot discern the consciences of those at their bar, and are therefore frequently compelled to put innocent witnesses to the torture to ascertain the truth regarding the crimes of other men. What shall I say of torture applied to the accused himself? He is tortured to discover whether he is guilty, so that, though innocent, he suffers most undoubted punishment for crime that is still doubtful, not because it is proved that he committed it, but because it is not ascertained that he did not commit it. Thus the ignorance of the judge frequently involves an innocent person in suffering. And what is still more unendurable—a thing, indeed, to be bewailed, and, if that were possible, watered with fountains of tears—is this, that when the judge puts the accused to the question, that he may not unwittingly put an innocent man to death, the result of this lamentable ignorance is that this very person, whom he tortured that he might not condemn him if innocent, is condemned to death both tortured and innocent. For if he has chosen, in obedience to the philosophical instructions to the wise man, to quit this life rather than endure any longer such tortures, he declares that he has committed the crime which in fact he has not committed. And when he has been condemned and put to death, the judge is still in ignorance whether he has put to death an innocent or a guilty person, though he put the accused to the torture for the very purpose of saving himself from condemning the innocent; and consequently he has both tortured an innocent man to discover his innocence, and has put him to death without discovering it. If such darkness shrouds social life, will a wise judge take his seat on the bench or no? Beyond question he will. For human society, which he thinks it a wickedness to abandon, constrains him and compels him to this duty. And he thinks it no wickedness that innocent witnesses are tortured regarding the crimes of which other men are accused; or that the accused are put to the torture, so that they are often overcome with anguish, and, though innocent, make false confessions regarding themselves, and are punished; or that, though they be not condemned to die, they often die during, or in consequence of, the torture; or that sometimes the accusers, who perhaps have been prompted by a desire to benefit society by bringing criminals to justice, are themselves condemned through the ignorance of the judge, because they are unable to prove the truth of their accusations though they are true, and because the witnesses lie, and the accused endures the torture without being moved to confession. These numerous and important evils he does not consider sins; for the wise judge does these things, not with any intention of doing harm, but because his ignorance compels him, and because human society claims him as a judge. But though we therefore acquit the judge of malice, we must none the less condemn human life as miserable. And if he is compelled to torture and punish the innocent because his office and his ignorance constrain him, is he a happy as well as a guiltless man? Surely it were proof of more profound considerateness and finer feeling were he to recognize the misery of these necessities, and shrink from his own implication in that misery; and had he any piety about him, he would cry to God "From my necessities deliver Thou me." [15]

CHAPTER VII

OF THE DIVERSITY OF LANGUAGES, BY WHICH THE INTERCOURSE OF MEN IS PREVENTED; AND OF THE MISERY OF WARS, EVEN OF THOSE CALLED JUST

After the state or city comes the world, the third circle of human society—the first being the house, and the second the city. And the world, as it is larger, so it is fuller of dangers, as the greater sea is the more dangerous. And here, in the first place, man is separated from man by the difference of languages. For if two men, each ignorant of the other's language, meet, and are not compelled to pass, but, on the contrary, to remain in company, dumb animals, though of different species, would more easily hold intercourse than they, human beings though they be. For their common nature is no help to friendliness when they are prevented by diversity of language from conveying their sentiments to one another; so that a man would more readily hold intercourse with his dog than with a foreigner. But the imperial city has endeavored to impose on subject nations not only her yoke, but her language, as a bond of peace, so that interpreters, far from being scarce, are numberless. This is true; but how many great wars, how much slaughter and bloodshed, have provided this unity! And though these are past, the end of these miseries has not yet come. For though there have never been wanting, nor are yet wanting, hostile nations beyond the empire, against whom wars have been and are waged, yet, supposing there were no such nations, the very extent of the empire itself has produced wars of a more obnoxious description—social and civil wars—and with these the whole race has been agitated, either by the actual conflict or the fear of a renewed outbreak. If I attempted to give an adequate description of these manifold disasters, these stern and lasting necessities, though I am quite unequal to the task, what limit could I set? But, say they, the wise man will wage just wars. As if he would not all the rather lament the necessity of just wars, if he remembers that he is a man; for if they were not just he would not wage them, and would therefore be delivered from all wars. For it is the wrong-doing of the opposing party

[15] Ps. xxv. 17

which compels the wise man to wage just wars; and this wrong-doing, even though it gave rise to no war, would still be matter of grief to man because it is man's wrong-doing. Let every one, then, who thinks with pain on all these great evils, so horrible, so ruthless, acknowledge that this is misery. And if any one either endures or thinks of them without mental pain, this is a more miserable plight still, for he thinks himself happy because he has lost human feeling.

CHAPTER VIII

THAT THE FRIENDSHIP OF GOOD MEN CANNOT BE SECURELY RESTED IN, SO LONG AS THE DANGERS OF THIS LIFE FORCE US TO BE ANXIOUS

In our present wretched condition we frequently mistake a friend for an enemy, and an enemy for a friend. And if we escape this pitiable blindness, is not the unfeigned confidence and mutual love of true and good friends our one solace in human society, filled as it is with misunderstandings and calamities? And yet the more friends we have, and the more widely they are scattered, the more numerous are our fears that some portion of the vast masses of the disasters of life may light upon them. For we are not only anxious lest they suffer from famine, war, disease, captivity, or the inconceivable horrors of slavery, but we are also affected with the much more painful dread that their friendship may be changed into perfidy, malice, and injustice. And when these contingencies actually occur—as they do the more frequently the more friends we have, and the more widely they are scattered—and when they come to our knowledge, who but the man who has experienced it can tell with what pangs the heart is torn? We would, in fact, prefer to hear that they were dead, although we could not without anguish hear of even this. For if their life has solaced us with the charms of friendship, can it be that their death should affect us with no sadness? He who will have none of this sadness must, if possible, have no friendly intercourse. Let him interdict or extinguish friendly affection; let him burst with ruthless insensibility the bonds of every human relationship; or let him contrive so to use them that no sweetness shall distil into his spirit. But if this is utterly impossible, how shall we contrive to feel no bitterness in the death of those whose life has been sweet to us? Hence arises that grief which affects the tender heart like a wound or a bruise, and which is healed by the application of kindly consolation. For though the cure is affected all the more easily and rapidly the better condition the soul is in, we must not on this account suppose that there is nothing at all to heal. Although, then, our present life is afflicted, sometimes in a milder, sometimes in a more painful degree, by the death of those very dear to us, and especially of useful public men, yet we would prefer to hear that such men were dead rather than to hear or perceive that they had fallen from the faith, or from virtue—in other words, that they were spiritually dead. Of this vast material for misery the earth is full, and therefore it is written, "Is not human life upon earth a trial?" [16] And with the same reference the Lord says, "Woe to the world because of offenses!" [17] and again, "Because iniquity abounded, the love of many shall wax cold." [18] And hence we enjoy some gratification when our good friends die; for though their death leaves us in sorrow, we have the consolatory assurance that they are beyond the ills by which in this life even the best of men are broken down or corrupted, or are in danger of both results.

CHAPTER IX

OF THE FRIENDSHIP OF THE HOLY ANGELS, WHICH MEN CANNOT BE SURE OF IN THIS LIFE, OWING TO THE DECEIT OF THE DEMONS WHO HOLD IN BONDAGE THE WORSHIPPERS OF A PLURALITY OF GODS

The philosophers who wished us to have the gods for our friends rank the friendship of the holy angels in the fourth circle of society, advancing now from the three circles of society on earth to the universe, and embracing heaven itself. And in this friendship we have indeed no fear that the angels will grieve us by their death or deterioration. But as we cannot mingle with them as familiarly as with men (which itself is one of the grievances of this life), and as Satan, as we read,[19] sometimes transforms himself into an angel of light, to tempt those whom it is necessary to discipline, or just to deceive, there is great need of God's mercy to preserve us from making friends of demons in disguise, while we fancy we have good angels for our friends; for the astuteness and deceitfulness of these wicked spirits is equalled by their hurtfulness. And is this not a great misery of human life, that we are involved in such ignorance as, but for God's mercy, makes us a prey to these demons? And it is very certain that the philosophers of the godless city, who have maintained that the gods were their friends, had fallen a prey to the malignant demons who rule that city, and whose eternal punishment is to be shared by it. For the nature of these beings is sufficiently evinced by the sacred or rather sacrilegious observances which form their worship, and by the filthy games in which their crimes are celebrated, and which they themselves originated and exacted from their worshippers as a fit propitiation.

CHAPTER X

THE REWARD PREPARED FOR THE SAINTS AFTER THEY HAVE ENDURED THE TRIAL OF THIS LIFE

But not even the saints and faithful worshippers of the one true and most high God are safe from the manifold temptations and deceits of the demons. For in this abode of weakness, and in these wicked days, this state of anxiety

[16] Job vii. 1   [17] Matt. xvii. 7   [18] Matt. xxiv. 12   [19] 2 Cor. xi. 14

has also its use, stimulating us to seek with keener longing for that security where peace is complete and unassailable. There we shall enjoy the gifts of nature, that is to say, all that God the Creator of all natures has bestowed upon ours—gifts not only good, but eternal—not only of the spirit, healed now by wisdom, but also of the body renewed by the resurrection. There the virtues shall no longer be struggling against any vice or evil, but shall enjoy the reward of victory, the eternal peace which no adversary shall disturb. This is the final blessedness, this the ultimate consummation, the unending end. Here, indeed, we are said to be blessed when we have such peace as can be enjoyed in a good life; but such blessedness is mere misery compared to that final felicity. When we mortals possess such peace as this mortal life can afford, virtue, if we are living rightly, makes a right use of the advantages of this peaceful condition; and when we have it not, virtue makes a good use even of the evils a man suffers. But this is true virtue, when it refers all the advantages it makes a good use of, and all that it does in making good use of good and evil things, and itself also, to that end in which we shall enjoy the best and greatest peace possible.

CHAPTER XI

OF THE HAPPINESS OF THE ETERNAL PEACE, WHICH CONSTITUTES THE END OR TRUE PERFECTION OF THE SAINTS

And thus we may say of peace, as we have said of eternal life, that it is the end of our good; and the rather because the Psalmist says of the city of God, the subject of this laborious work, "Praise the Lord, O Jerusalem; praise thy God, O Zion: for He hath strengthened the bars of thy gates; He hath blessed thy children within thee; who hath made thy borders peace." [20] For when the bars of her gates shall be strengthened, none shall go in or come out from her; consequently we ought to understand the peace of her borders as that final peace we are wishing to declare. For even the mystical name of the city itself, that is, *Jerusalem*, means, as I have already said, "Vision of Peace." But as the word peace is employed in connection with things in this world in which certainly life eternal has no place, we have preferred to call the end or supreme good of this city life eternal rather than peace. Of this end the apostle says, "But now, being freed from sin, and become servants to God, ye have your fruit unto holiness, and the end life eternal." [21] But, on the other hand, as those who are not familiar with Scripture may suppose that the life of the wicked is eternal life, either because of the immortality of the soul, which some of the philosophers even have recognized, or because of the endless punishment of the wicked, which forms a part of our faith, and which seems impossible unless the wicked live for ever, it may therefore be advisable, in order that every one may readily understand what we mean, to say that the

[20] Ps. cxlvii. 12-14   [21] Rom. vi. 22

end or supreme good of this city is either peace in eternal life, or eternal life in peace. For peace is a good so great, that even in this earthly and mortal life there is no word we hear with such pleasure, nothing we desire with such zest, or find to be more thoroughly gratifying. So that if we dwell for a little longer on this subject, we shall not, in my opinion, be wearisome to our readers, who will attend both for the sake of understanding what is the end of this city of which we speak, and for the sake of the sweetness of peace which is dear to all.

CHAPTER XII

THAT EVEN THE FIERCENESS OF WAR AND ALL THE DISQUIETUDE OF MEN MAKE TOWARDS THIS ONE END OF PEACE, WHICH EVERY NATURE DESIRES

Whoever gives even moderate attention to human affairs and to our common nature, will recognize that if there is no man who does not wish to be joyful, neither is there any one who does not wish to have peace. For even they who make war desire nothing but victory—desire, that is to say, to attain to peace with glory. For what else is victory than the conquest of those who resist us? and when this is done there is peace. It is therefore with the desire for peace that wars are waged, even by those who take pleasure in exercising their warlike nature in command and battle. And hence it is obvious that peace is the end sought for by war. For every man seeks peace by waging war, but no man seeks war by making peace. For even they who intentionally interrupt the peace in which they are living have no hatred of peace, but only wish it changed into a peace that suits them better. They do not, therefore, wish to have no peace, but only one more to their mind. And in the case of sedition, when men have separated themselves from the community, they yet do not effect what they wish, unless they maintain some kind of peace with their fellow-conspirators. And therefore even robbers take care to maintain peace with their comrades, that they may with greater effect and greater safety invade the peace of other men. And if an individual happen to be of such unrivalled strength, and to be so jealous of partnership, that he trusts himself with no comrades, but makes his own plots, and commits depredations and murders on his own account, yet he maintains some shadow of peace with such persons as he is unable to kill, and from whom he wishes to conceal his deeds. In his own home, too, he makes it his aim to be at peace with his wife and children, and any other members of his household; for unquestionably their prompt obedience to his every look is a source of pleasure to him. And if this be not rendered, he is angry, he chides and punishes; and even by this storm he secures the calm peace of his own home, as occasion demands. For he sees that peace cannot be maintained unless all the members of the same domestic circle be subject to one head, such as he himself is in his own house. And therefore if a city or nation offered to submit itself to him, to serve him in the same style as he had made his household serve him, he would no longer lurk in a brigand's hiding-places, but lift his head in open day as a king, though the same covetousness and wickedness should remain in him. And thus all men desire to have peace with their own circle whom they wish to govern as suits themselves. For even those whom they make war against they wish to make their own, and impose on them the laws of their own peace.

But let us suppose a man such as poetry and mythology speak of—a man so insociable and savage as to be called rather a semi-man than a man.[22] Although, then, his kingdom was the solitude of a dreary cave, and he himself was so singularly bad-hearted that he was named Κακός, which is the Greek word for *bad;* though he had no wife to soothe him with endearing talk, no children to play with, no sons to do his bidding, no friend to enliven him with intercourse, not even his father Vulcan (though in one respect he was happier than his father, not having begotten a monster like himself); although he gave to no man, but took as he wished whatever he could, from whomsoever he could, when he could; yet in that solitary den, the floor of which, as Virgil [23] says, was always reeking with recent slaughter, there was nothing else than peace sought, a peace in which no one should molest him, or disquiet him with any assault or alarm. With his own body he desired to be at peace, and he was satisfied only in proportion as he had this peace. For he ruled his members, and they obeyed him; and for the sake of pacifying his mortal nature, which rebelled when it needed anything, and of allaying the sedition of hunger which threatened to banish the soul from the body, he made forays, slew, and devoured, but used the ferocity and savageness he displayed in these actions only for the preservation of his own life's peace. So that, had he been willing to make with other men the same peace which he made with himself in his own cave, he would neither have been called bad, nor a monster, nor a semi-man. Or if the appearance of his body and his vomiting smoky fires frightened men from having any dealings with him, perhaps his fierce ways arose not from a desire to do mischief, but from the necessity of finding a living. But he may have had no existence, or, at least, he was not such as the poets fancifully describe him, for they had to exalt Hercules, and did so at the expense of Cacus. It is better, then, to believe that such a man or semi-man never existed, and that this, in common with many other fancies of the poets, is mere fiction. For the most savage animals (and he is said to have been almost a wild beast) encompass their own species with a ring of protecting peace. They cohabit, beget, produce, suckle, and bring up their young, though very many of them are not gregarious, but solitary—not like sheep, deer, pigeons, starlings, bees, but such as lions, foxes, eagles, bats. For what tigress does not gently purr over her cubs, and lay aside her ferocity to fondle them? What kite, solitary as he is when circling over his prey, does not seek a mate, build a nest, hatch the eggs, bring

[22] He refers to the giant Cacus.   [23] *Aeneid,* viii. 195

up the young birds, and maintain with the mother of his family as peaceful a domestic alliance as he can? How much more powerfully do the laws of man's nature move him to hold fellowship and maintain peace with all men so far as in him lies, since even wicked men wage war to maintain the peace of their own circle, and wish that, if possible, all men belonged to them, that all men and things might serve but one head, and might, either through love or fear, yield themselves to peace with him! It is thus that pride in its perversity apes God. It abhors equality with other men under Him; but, instead of His rule, it seeks to impose a rule of its own upon its equals. It abhors, that is to say, the just peace of God, and loves its own unjust peace; but it cannot help loving peace of one kind or other. For there is no vice so clean contrary to nature that it obliterates even the faintest traces of nature.

He, then, who prefers what is right to what is wrong, and what is well-ordered to what is perverted, sees that the peace of unjust men is not worthy to be called peace in comparison with the peace of the just. And yet even what is perverted must of necessity be in harmony with, and in dependence on, and in some part of the order of things, for otherwise it would have no existence at all. Suppose a man hangs with his head downwards, this is certainly a perverted attitude of body and arrangement of its members; for that which nature requires to be above is beneath, and *vice versa*. This perversity disturbs the peace of the body, and is therefore painful. Nevertheless the spirit is at peace with its body, and labors for its preservation, and hence the suffering; but if it is banished from the body by its pains, then, so long as the bodily framework holds together, there is in the remains a kind of peace among the members, and hence the body remains suspended. And inasmuch as the earthly body tends towards the earth, and rests on the bond by which it is suspended, it tends thus to its natural peace, and the voice of its own weight demands a place for it to rest; and though now lifeless and without feeling, it does not fall from the peace that is natural to its place in creation, whether it already has it, or is tending towards it. For if you apply embalming preparations to prevent the bodily frame from mouldering and dissolving, a kind of peace still unites part to part, and keeps the whole body in a suitable place on the earth—in other words, in a place that is at peace with the body. If, on the other hand, the body receive no such care, but be left to the natural course, it is disturbed by exhalations that do not harmonize with one another, and that offend our senses; for it is this which is perceived in putrefaction until it is assimilated to the elements of the world, and particle by particle enters into peace with them. Yet throughout this process the laws of the most high Creator and Governor are strictly observed, for it is by Him the peace of the universe is administered. For although minute animals are produced from the carcass of a larger animal, all these little atoms, by the law of the same Creator, serve the animals they belong to in peace. And although the flesh of dead animals be eaten by others, no matter where it be carried, nor what it be brought into contact or what it be converted and changed into, it still is ruled by the same laws which pervade all things for the conservation of every mortal race, and which bring things that fit one another into harmony.

CHAPTER XIII

OF THE UNIVERSAL PEACE WHICH THE LAW OF NATURE PRESERVES THROUGH ALL DISTURBANCES, AND BY WHICH EVERY ONE REACHES HIS DESERT IN A WAY REGULATED BY THE JUST JUDGE

The peace of the body then consists in the duly proportioned arrangement of its parts. The peace of the irrational soul is the harmonious repose of the appetites, and that of the rational soul the harmony of knowledge and action. The peace of body and soul is the well-ordered and harmonious life and health of the living creature. Peace between man and God is the well-ordered obedience of faith to eternal law. Peace between man and man is well-ordered concord. Domestic peace is the well-ordered concord between those of the family who rule and those who obey. Civil peace is a similar concord among the citizens. The peace of the celestial city is the perfectly ordered and harmonious enjoyment of God, and of one another in God. The peace of all things is the tranquillity of order. Order is the distribution which allots things equal and unequal, each to its own place. And hence, though the miserable, in so far as they are such, do certainly not enjoy peace, but are severed from that tranquillity of order in which there is no disturbance, nevertheless, inasmuch as they are deservedly and justly miserable, they are by their very misery connected with order. They are not, indeed, conjoined with the blessed, but they are disjoined from them by the law of order. And though they are disquieted, their circumstances are notwithstanding adjusted to them, and consequently they have some tranquillity of order, and therefore some peace. But they are wretched because, although not wholly miserable, they are not in that place where any mixture of misery is impossible. They would, however, be more wretched if they had not that peace which arises from being in harmony with the natural order of things. When they suffer, their peace is in so far disturbed; but their peace continues in so far as they do not suffer, and in so far as their nature continues to exist. As, then, there may be life without pain, while there cannot be pain without some kind of life, so there may be peace without war, but there cannot be war without some kind of peace, because war supposes the existence of some natures to wage it, and these natures cannot exist without peace of one kind or other.

And therefore there is a nature in which evil does not or even cannot exist; but there cannot be a nature in which there is no good. Hence not even the nature of the devil himself is evil, in so far as it is nature, but it was made evil by being perverted. Thus he did not abide in the truth,[24] but could not

[24] John viii. 44

escape the judgment of the Truth; he did not abide in the tranquillity of order, but did not therefore escape the power of the Ordainer. The good imparted by God to his nature did not screen him from the justice of God by which order was preserved in his punishment; neither did God punish the good which He had created, but the evil which the devil had committed. God did not take back all He had imparted to his nature, but something He took and something He left, that there might remain enough to be sensible of the loss of what was taken. And this very sensibility to pain is evidence of the good which has been taken away and the good which has been left. For, were nothing good left, there could be no pain on account of the good which had been lost. For he who sins is still worse if he rejoices in his loss of righteousness. But he who is in pain, if he derives no benefit from it, mourns at least the loss of health. And as righteousness and health are both good things, and as the loss of any good thing is matter of grief, not of joy—if, at least, there is no compensation, as spiritual righteousness may compensate for the loss of bodily health—certainly it is more suitable for a wicked man to grieve in punishment than to rejoice in his fault. As, then, the joy of a sinner who has abandoned what is good is evidence of a bad will, so his grief for the good he has lost when he is punished is evidence of a good nature. For he who laments the peace his nature has lost is stirred to do so by some relics of peace which make his nature friendly to itself. And it is very just that in the final punishment the wicked and godless should in anguish bewail the loss of the natural advantages they enjoyed, and should perceive that they were most justly taken from them by that God whose benign liberality they had despised. God, then, the most wise Creator and most just Ordainer of all natures, who placed the human race upon earth as its greatest ornament, imparted to men some good things adapted to this life, to wit, temporal peace, such as we can enjoy in this life from health and safety and human fellowship, and all things needful for the preservation and recovery of this peace, such as the objects which are accommodated to our outward senses, light, night, the air, and waters suitable for us, and everything the body requires to sustain, shelter, heal, or beautify it: and all under this most equitable condition, that every man who made a good use of these advantages suited to the peace of this mortal condition, should receive ampler and better blessings, namely, the peace of immortality, accompanied by glory and honor in an endless life made fit for the enjoyment of God and of one another in God; but that he who used the present blessings badly should both lose them and should not receive the others.

CHAPTER XIV

OF THE ORDER AND LAW WHICH OBTAIN IN HEAVEN AND EARTH,
WHEREBY IT COMES TO PASS THAT HUMAN SOCIETY IS SERVED
BY THOSE WHO RULE IT

The whole use, then, of things temporal has a reference to this result of earthly peace in the earthly community, while in the city of God it is connected with eternal peace. And therefore, if we were irrational animals, we should desire nothing beyond the proper arrangement of the parts of the body and the satisfaction of the appetites—nothing, therefore, but bodily comfort and abundance of pleasures, that the peace of the body might contribute to the peace of the soul. For if bodily peace be wanting, a bar is put to the peace even of the irrational soul, since it cannot obtain the gratification of its appetites. And these two together help out the mutual peace of soul and body, the peace of harmonious life and health. For as animals, by shunning pain, show that they love bodily peace, and, by pursuing pleasure to gratify their appetites, show that they love peace of soul, so their shrinking from death is a sufficient indication of their intense love of that peace which binds soul and body in close alliance. But, as man has a rational soul, he subordinates all this which he has in common with the beasts to the peace of his rational soul, that his intellect may have free play and may regulate his actions, and that he may thus enjoy the well-ordered harmony of knowledge and action which constitutes, as we have said, the peace of the rational soul. And for this purpose he must desire to be neither molested by pain, nor disturbed by desire, nor extinguished by death, that he may arrive at some useful knowledge by which he may regulate his life and manners. But, owing to the liability of the human mind to fall into mistakes, this very pursuit of knowledge may be a snare to him unless he has a divine Master, whom he may obey without misgiving, and who may at the same time give him such help as to preserve his own freedom. And because, so long as he is in this mortal body, he is a stranger to God, he walks by faith, not by sight; and he therefore refers all peace, bodily or spiritual or both, to that peace which mortal man has with the immortal God, so that he exhibits the well-ordered obedience of faith to eternal law. But as this divine Master inculcates two precepts—the love of God and the love of our neighbor—and as in these precepts a man finds three things he has to love—God, himself, and his neighbor—and that he who loves God loves himself thereby, it follows that he must endeavor to get his neighbor to love God, since he is ordered to love his neighbor as himself. He ought to make this endeavor in behalf of his wife, his children, his household, all within his reach, even as he would wish his neighbor to do the same for him if he needed it; and consequently he will be at peace, or in well-ordered concord, with all men, as far as in him lies. And this is the order of this concord, that a man, in the first place, injure no one, and, in the second, do good to every one he can reach. Primarily, therefore, his own household are his care, for the law of nature and of society gives him readier access to them and greater opportunity of serving them. And hence the apostle says, "Now, if any provide not for his own, and specially for those of his own house, he hath denied the faith, and is worse than an infidel." [25] This is the origin of domestic peace, or the well-ordered concord of those in the family who rule and those who obey. For they who care for the rest rule—the husband the wife, the parents the children, the masters the servants; and they who are cared for obey—the women their husbands, the children their parents, the servants their masters. But in the family of the just man who lives by faith and is as yet a pilgrim journeying on to the celestial city, even those who rule serve those whom they seem to command; for they rule not from a love of power, but from a sense of the duty they owe to others—not because they are proud of authority, but because they love mercy.

CHAPTER XV

OF THE LIBERTY PROPER TO MAN'S NATURE, AND THE SERVITUDE INTRODUCED BY SIN—A SERVITUDE IN WHICH THE MAN WHOSE WILL IS WICKED IS THE SLAVE OF HIS OWN LUST, THOUGH HE IS FREE SO FAR AS REGARDS OTHER MEN

This is prescribed by the order of nature: it is thus that God has created man. For "let them," He says, "have dominion over the fish of the sea, and over the fowl of the air, and over every creeping thing which creepeth on the earth." [26] He did not intend that His rational creature, who was made in His image, should have dominion over anything but the irrational creation—not man over man, but man over the beasts. And hence the righteous men in primitive times were made shepherds of cattle rather than kings of men, God intending thus to teach us what the relative position of the creatures is, and what the desert of sin; for it is with justice, we believe, that the condition of slavery is the result of sin. And this is why we do not find the word "slave" in any part of Scripture until righteous Noah branded the sin of his son with this name. It is a name, therefore, introduced by sin and not by nature. The origin of the Latin word for slave is supposed to be found in the circumstance that those who by the law of war were liable to be killed were sometimes preserved by their victors, and were hence called servants.[c] And these circumstances could never have arisen save through sin. For even when we wage a just war, our adversaries must be sinning; and every victory, even though gained by wicked men, is a result of the first judgment of God, who humbles the vanquished either for the sake of removing or of punishing their sins. Witness that man of God, Daniel, who, when he was in captivity, con-

[25] 1 Tim. v. 8   [26] Gen. i. 26   [c] This is not a scientifically correct etymology.—Ed.

fessed to God his own sins and the sins of his people, and declared with pious grief that these were the cause of the captivity.[27] The prime cause, then, of slavery is sin, which brings man under the dominion of his fellow—that which does not happen save by the judgment of God, with whom is no unrighteousness, and who knows how to award fit punishments to every variety of offence. But our Master in heaven says, "Every one who doeth sin is the servant of sin." [28] And thus there are many wicked masters who have religious men as their slaves, and who are yet themselves in bondage; "for of whom a man is overcome, of the same is he brought in bondage." [29] And beyond question it is a happier thing to be the slave of a man than of a lust; for even this very lust of ruling, to mention no others, lays waste men's hearts with the most ruthless dominion. Moreover, when men are subjected to one another in a peaceful order, the lowly position does as much good to the servant as the proud position does harm to the master. But by nature, as God first created us, no one is the slave either of man or of sin. This servitude is, however, penal, and is appointed by that law which enjoins the preservation of the natural order and forbids its disturbance; for if nothing had been done in violation of that law, there would have been nothing to restrain by penal servitude. And therefore the apostle admonishes slaves to be subject to their masters, and to serve them heartily and with good-will, so that, if they cannot be freed by their masters, they may themselves make their slavery in some sort free, by serving not in crafty fear, but in faithful love, until all unrighteousness pass away, and all principality and every human power be brought to nothing, and God be all in all.

CHAPTER XVI

OF EQUITABLE RULE

And therefore, although our righteous fathers[30] had slaves, and administered their domestic affairs so as to distinguish between the condition of slaves and the heirship of sons in regard to the blessings of this life, yet in regard to the worship of God, in whom we hope for eternal blessings, they took an equally loving oversight of all the members of their household. And this is so much in accordance with the natural order, that the head of the household was called *paterfamilias;* and this name has been so generally accepted, that even those whose rule is unrighteous are glad to apply it to themselves. But those who are true fathers of their households desire and endeavor that all the members of their household, equally with their own children, should worship and win God, and should come to that heavenly home in which the duty of ruling men is no longer necessary, because the duty of caring for their everlasting happiness has also ceased; but, until they reach that home, masters ought to feel their position of authority

[27] Dan. ix.   [28] John viii. 34   [29] 2 Pet. ii. 19   [30] The patriarchs

a greater burden than servants their service. And if any member of the family interrupts the domestic peace by disobedience, he is corrected either by word or blow, or some kind of just and legitimate punishment, such as society permits, that he may himself be the better for it, and be readjusted to the family harmony from which he had dislocated himself. For as it is not benevolent to give a man help at the expense of some greater benefit he might receive, so it is not innocent to spare a man at the risk of his falling into graver sin. To be innocent, we must not only do harm to no man, but also restrain him from sin or punish his sin, so that either the man himself who is punished may profit by his experience, or others be warned by his example. Since, then, the house ought to be the beginning or element of the city, and every beginning bears reference to some end of its own kind, and every element to the integrity of the whole of which it is an element, it follows plainly enough that domestic peace has a relation to civic peace—in other words, that the well-ordered concord of domestic obedience and domestic rule has a relation to the well-ordered concord of civic obedience and civic rule. And therefore it follows, further, that the father of the family ought to frame his domestic rule in accordance with the law of the city, so that the household may be in harmony with the civic order.

CHAPTER XVII

WHAT PRODUCES PEACE, AND WHAT DISCORD, BETWEEN THE HEAVENLY AND EARTHLY CITIES

But the families which do not live by faith seek their peace in the earthly advantages of this life; while the families which live by faith look for those eternal blessings which are promised, and use as pilgrims such advantages of time and of earth as do not fascinate and divert them from God, but rather aid them to endure with greater ease, and to keep down the number of those burdens of the corruptible body which weigh upon the soul. Thus the things necessary for this mortal life are used by both kinds of men and families alike, but each has its own peculiar and widely different aim in using them. The earthly city, which does not live by faith, seeks an earthly peace, and the end it proposes, in the well-ordered concord of civic obedience and rule, is the combination of men's wills to attain the things which are helpful to this life. The heavenly city, or rather the part of it which sojourns on earth and lives by faith, makes use of this peace only because it must, until this mortal condition which necessitates it shall pass away. Consequently, so long as it lives like a captive and a stranger in the earthly city, though it has already received the promise of redemption, and the gift of the Spirit as the earnest of it, it makes no scruple to obey the laws of the earthly city, whereby the things necessary for the maintenance of this mortal life are administered; and thus, as this life is common to both cities, so there is a harmony between them in regard to what belongs to it. But, as the earthly city has had some philosophers whose doctrine is condemned by the divine teaching, and who, being deceived either by their own conjectures or by demons, supposed that many gods must be invited to take an interest in human affairs, and assigned to each a separate function and a separate department—to one the body, to another the soul; and in the body itself, to one the head, to another the neck, and each of the other members to one of the gods; and in like manner, in the soul, to one god the natural capacity was assigned, to another education, to another anger, to another lust; and so the various affairs of life were assigned —cattle to one, corn to another, wine to another, oil to another, the woods to another, money to another, navigation to another, wars and victories to another, marriages to another, births and fecundity to another, and other things to other gods: and as the celestial city, on the other hand, knew that one God only was to be worshipped, and that to Him alone was due that service which the Greeks call λατρεία, and which can be given only to a god, it has come to pass that the two cities could not have common laws of religion, and that the heavenly city has been compelled in this matter to dissent, and to become obnoxious to those who think differently, and to stand the brunt of their anger and hatred and persecutions, except in so far as the minds of their enemies have been alarmed by the multitude of the Christians and quelled by the manifest protection of God accorded to them. This heavenly city, then, while it sojourns on earth, calls citizens out of all nations, and gathers together a society of pilgrims of all languages, not scrupling about diversities in the manners, laws, and institutions whereby earthly peace is secured and maintained, but recognizing that, however various these are, they all tend to one and the same end of earthly peace. It therefore is so far from rescinding and abolishing these diversities, that it even preserves and adopts them, so long only as no hindrance to the worship of the one supreme and true God is thus introduced. Even the heavenly city, therefore, while in its state of pilgrimage, avails itself of the peace of earth, and, so far as it can without injuring faith and godliness, desires and maintains a common agreement among men regarding the acquisition of the necessaries of life, and makes this earthly peace bear upon the peace of heaven; for this alone can be truly called and esteemed the peace of the reasonable creatures, consisting as it does in the perfectly ordered and harmonious enjoyment of God and of one another in God. When we shall have reached that peace, this mortal life shall give place to one that is eternal, and our body shall be no more this animal body which by its corruption weighs down the soul, but a spiritual body feeling no want, and in all its members subjected to the will. In its pilgrim state the heavenly city possesses this peace by faith; and by this faith it lives righteously when it refers to the attainment of that peace every good action towards God and man; for the life of the city is a social life.

CHAPTER XVIII

HOW DIFFERENT THE UNCERTAINTY OF THE NEW ACADEMY IS FROM THE CERTAINTY OF THE CHRISTIAN FAITH

As regards the uncertainty about everything which Varro alleges to be the differentiating characteristic of the New Academy, the city of God thoroughly detests such doubt as madness. Regarding matters which it apprehends by the mind and reason it has most absolute certainty, although its knowledge is limited because of the corruptible body pressing down the mind, for, as the apostle says, "We know in part." [31] It believes also the evidence of the senses which the mind uses by aid of the body; for if one who trusts his senses is sometimes deceived, he is more wretchedly deceived who fancies he should never trust them. It believes also the Holy Scriptures, old and new, which we call canonical, and which are the source of the faith by which the just lives[32] and by which we walk without doubting whilst we are absent from the Lord.[33] So long as this faith remains inviolate and firm, we may without blame entertain doubts regarding some things which we have neither perceived by sense nor by reason, and which have not been revealed to us by the canonical Scriptures, nor come to our knowledge through witnesses whom it is absurd to disbelieve.

CHAPTER XIX

OF THE DRESS AND HABITS OF THE CHRISTIAN PEOPLE

It is a matter of no moment in the city of God whether he who adopts the faith that brings men to God adopts it in one dress and manner of life or another, so long only as he lives in conformity with the commandments of God. And hence, when philosophers themselves become Christians, they are compelled, indeed, to abandon their erroneous doctrines, but not their dress and mode of living, which are no obstacle to religion. So that we make no account of that distinction of sects which Varro adduced in connection with the Cynic school, provided always nothing indecent or self-indulgent is retained. As to these three modes of life, the contemplative, the active, and the composite, although, so long as a man's faith is preserved, he may choose any of them without detriment to his eternal interests, yet he must never overlook the claims of truth and duty. No man has a right to lead such a life of contemplation as to forget in his own ease the service due to his neighbor; nor has any man a right to be so immersed in active life as to neglect the contemplation of God. The charm of leisure must not be indolent vacancy of mind, but the investigation or discovery of truth, that thus every man may make solid attainments without grudging that others do the same. And, in

---

[31] 1 Cor. xiii. 9   [32] Hab. ii. 4   [33] 2 Cor. v. 6

active life, it is not the honors or power of this life we should covet, since all things under the sun are vanity, but we should aim at using our position and influence, if these have been honorably attained, for the welfare of those who are under us, in the way we have already explained.[34] It is to this the apostle refers when he says, "He that desireth the episcopate desireth a good work."[35] He wished to show that the episcopate is the title of a work, not of an honor. It is a Greek word, and signifies that he who governs superintends or takes care of those whom he governs: for ἐπί means *over*, and σκοπεῖν, *to see;* therefore ἐπίσκοπεῖν means "to oversee."[36] So that he who loves to govern rather than to do good is no bishop. Accordingly no one is prohibited from the search after truth, for in this leisure may most laudably be spent; but it is unseemly to covet the high position requisite for governing the people, even though that position be held and that government be administered in a seemly manner. And therefore holy leisure is longed for by the love of truth; but it is the necessity of love to undertake requisite business. If no one imposes this burden upon us, we are free to sift and contemplate truth; but if it be laid upon us, we are necessitated for love's sake to undertake it. And yet not even in this case are we obliged wholly to relinquish the sweets of contemplation; for were these to be withdrawn, the burden might prove more than we could bear.

CHAPTER XX

THAT THE SAINTS ARE IN THIS LIFE BLESSED IN HOPE

Since, then, the supreme good of the city of God is perfect and eternal peace, not such as mortals pass into and out of by birth and death, but the peace of freedom from all evil, in which the immortals ever abide, who can deny that that future life is most blessed, or that, in comparison with it, this life which now we live is most wretched, be it filled with all blessings of body and soul and external things? And yet, if any man uses this life with a reference to that other which he ardently loves and confidently hopes for, he may well be called even now blessed, though not in reality so much as in hope. But the actual possession of the happiness of this life, without the hope of what is beyond, is but a false happiness and profound misery. For the true blessings of the soul are not now enjoyed; for that is no true wisdom which does not direct all its prudent observations, manly actions, virtuous self-restraint, and just arrangements, to that end in which God shall be all and all in a secure eternity and perfect peace.

[34] Ch. 6   [35] 1 Tim. iii. 1

[36] Augustine's words are: ἐπί, *quippe, super:* σκοπός, *vero, intentio est: ergo* ἐπίσκοπεῖν, *si velimus, latine superintendere possumus dicere.*

CHAPTER XXI

WHETHER THERE EVER WAS A ROMAN REPUBLIC ANSWERING TO THE DEFINITIONS OF SCIPIO IN CICERO'S DIALOGUE

This, then, is the place where I should fulfill the promise I gave in the second book of this work,[37] and explain, as briefly and clearly as possible, that if we are to accept the definitions laid down by Scipio in Cicero's *De Republica*, there never was a Roman republic; for he briefly defines a republic as the weal of the people. And if this definition be true, there never was a Roman republic, for the people's weal was never attained among the Romans. For the people, according to his definition, is an assemblage associated by a common acknowledgment of right and by a community of interests. And what he means by a common acknowledgment of right he explains at large, showing that a republic cannot be administered without justice. Where, therefore, there is no true justice there can be no right. For that which is done by right is justly done, and what is unjustly done cannot be done by right. For the unjust inventions of men are neither to be considered nor spoken of as rights; for even they themselves say that right is that which flows from the fountain of justice, and deny the definition which is commonly given by those who misconceive the matter, that right is that which is useful to the stronger party. Thus, where there is not true justice there can be no assemblage of men associated by a common acknowledgment of right, and therefore there can be no people, as defined by Scipio or Cicero; and if no people, then no weal of the people, but only of some promiscuous multitude unworthy of the name of people. Consequently, if the republic is the weal of the people, and there is no people if it be not associated by a common acknowledgment of right, and if there is no right where there is no justice, then most certainly it follows that there is no republic where there is no justice. Further, justice is that virtue which gives every one his due. Where, then, is the justice of man, when he deserts the true God and yields himself to impure demons? Is this to give every one his due? Or is he who keeps back a piece of ground from the purchaser, and gives it to a man who has no right to it, unjust, while he who keeps back himself from the God who made him, and serves wicked spirits, is just?

This same book, *De Republica*, advocates the cause of justice against injustice with great force and keenness. The pleading for injustice against justice was first heard, and it was asserted that without injustice a republic could neither increase nor even subsist, for it was laid down as an absolutely unassailable position that it is unjust for some men to rule and some to serve; and yet the imperial city to which the republic belongs cannot rule her provinces without having recourse to this injustice. It was replied in behalf of justice, that this ruling of the provinces is just, because servitude may be

[37] Ch. 21

advantageous to the provincials, and is so when rightly administered—that is to say, when lawless men are prevented from doing harm. And further, as they became worse and worse so long as they were free, they will improve by subjection. To confirm this reasoning, there is added an eminent example drawn from nature: for "why," it is asked, "does God rule man, the soul the body, the reason the passions and other vicious parts of the soul?" This example leaves no doubt that, to some, servitude is useful; and, indeed, to serve God is useful to all. And it is when the soul serves God that it exercises a right control over the body; and in the soul itself the reason must be subject to God if it is to govern as it ought the passions and other vices. Hence, when a man does not serve God, what justice can we ascribe to him, since in this case his soul cannot exercise a just control over the body, nor his reason over his vices? And if there is no justice in such an individual, certainly there can be none in a community composed of such persons. Here, therefore, there is not that common acknowledgment of right which makes an assemblage of men a people whose affairs we call a republic. And why need I speak of the advantageousness, the common participation in which, according to the definition, makes a people? For although, if you choose to regard the matter attentively, you will see that there is nothing advantageous to those who live godlessly, as every one lives who does not serve God but demons, whose wickedness you may measure by their desire to receive the worship of men though they are most impure spirits, yet what I have said of the common acknowledgment of right is enough to demonstrate that, according to the above definition, there can be no people, and therefore no republic, where there is no justice. For if they assert that in their republic the Romans did not serve unclean spirits, but good and holy gods, must we therefore again reply to this evasion, though already we have said enough, and more than enough, to expose it? He must be an uncommonly stupid, or a shamelessly contentious person, who has read through the foregoing books to this point, and can yet question whether the Romans served wicked and impure demons. But, not to speak of their character, it is written in the law of the true God, "He that sacrificeth unto any god save unto the Lord only, he shall be utterly destroyed." [38] He, therefore, who uttered so menacing a commandment decreed that no worship should be given either to good or bad gods.

CHAPTER XXII

WHETHER THE GOD WHOM THE CHRISTIANS SERVE IS THE TRUE GOD TO WHOM ALONE SACRIFICE OUGHT TO BE PAID

But it may be replied, Who is this God, or what proof is there that He alone is worthy to receive sacrifice from the Romans? One must be very blind

[38] Ex. xxii. 20

to be still asking who this God is. He is the God whose prophets predicted the things we see accomplished. He is the God from whom Abraham received the assurance, "In thy seed shall all nations be blessed." [39] That this was fulfilled in Christ, who according to the flesh sprang from that seed, is recognized, whether they will or no, even by those who have continued to be the enemies of this name. He is the God whose divine Spirit spake by the men whose predictions I cited in the preceding books, and which are fulfilled in the Church which has extended over all the world. This is the God whom Varro, the most learned of the Romans, supposed to be Jupiter, though he knows not what he says; yet I think it right to note the circumstance that a man of such learning was unable to suppose that this God had no existence or was contemptible, but believed Him to be the same as the supreme God. In fine, He is the God whom Porphyry, the most learned of the philosophers, though the bitterest enemy of the Christians, confesses to be a great God, even according to the oracles of those whom he esteems gods.

CHAPTER XXIII

PORPHYRY'S ACCOUNT OF THE RESPONSES GIVEN BY THE ORACLES OF THE GODS CONCERNING CHRIST

For in his book called ἐκ λογίων φιλοσοφίας, in which he collects and comments upon the responses which he pretends were uttered by the gods concerning divine things, he says—I give his own words as they have been translated from the Greek: "To one who inquired what god he should propitiate in order to recall his wife from Christianity, Apollo replied in the following verses." Then the following words are given as those of Apollo: "You will probably find it easier to write lasting characters on the water, or lightly fly like a bird through the air, than to restore right feeling in your impious wife once she has polluted herself. Let her remain as she pleases in her foolish deception, and sing false laments to her dead God, who was condemned by right-minded judges, and perished ignominiously by a violent death." Then after these verses of Apollo (which we have given in a Latin version that does not preserve the metrical form), he goes on to say: "In these verses Apollo exposed the incurable corruption of the Christians, saying that the Jews, rather than the Christians, recognized God." See how he misrepresents Christ, giving the Jews the preference to the Christians in the recognition of God. This was his explanation of Apollo's verses, in which he says that Christ was put to death by right-minded or just judges—in other words, that He deserved to die. I leave the responsibility of this oracle regarding Christ on the lying interpreter of Apollo, or on this philosopher who believed it or possibly himself invented it; as to its agreement with Porphyry's opinions or with other oracles, we shall in a little have something to

---

[39] Gen. xxii. 18

say. In this passage, however, he says that the Jews, as the interpreters of God, judged justly in pronouncing Christ to be worthy of the most shameful death. He should have listened, then, to this God of the Jews to whom he bears this testimony, when that God says, "He that sacrificeth to any other god save to the Lord alone shall be utterly destroyed." But let us come to still plainer expressions, and hear how great a God Porphyry thinks the God of the Jews is. Apollo, he says, when asked whether word, *i.e.*, reason, or law is the better thing, replied in the following verses. Then he gives the verses of Apollo, from which I select the following as sufficient: "God, the Generator, and the King prior to all things, before whom heaven and earth, and the sea, and the hidden places of hell tremble, and the deities themselves are afraid, for their law is the Father whom the holy Hebrews honor." In this oracle of his god Apollo, Porphyry avowed that the God of the Hebrews is so great that the deities themselves are afraid before Him. I am surprised, therefore, that when God said, He that sacrificeth to other gods shall be utterly destroyed, Porphyry himself was not afraid lest he should be destroyed for sacrificing to other gods.

This philosopher, however, has also some good to say of Christ, oblivious, as it were, of that contumely of his of which we have just been speaking; or as if his gods spoke evil of Christ only while asleep, and recognized Him to be good, and gave Him His deserved praise, when they awoke. For, as if he were about to proclaim some marvellous thing passing belief, he says, "What we are going to say will certainly take some by surprise. For the gods have declared that Christ was very pious, and has become immortal, and that they cherish his memory: that the Christians, however, are polluted, contaminated, and involved in error. And many other such things," he says, "do the gods say against the Christians." Then he gives specimens of the accusations made, as he says, by the gods against them, and then goes on: "But to some who asked Hecate whether Christ were a God, she replied, You know the condition of the disembodied immortal soul, and that if it has been severed from wisdom it always errs. The soul you refer to is that of a man foremost in piety: they worship it because they mistake the truth." To this so-called oracular response he adds the following words of his own: "Of this very pious man, then, Hecate said that the soul, like the souls of other good men, was after death dowered with immortality, and that the Christians through ignorance worship it. And to those who asked why he was condemned to die, the oracle of the goddess replied, The body, indeed, is always exposed to torments, but the souls of the pious abide in heaven. And the soul you inquire about has been the fatal cause of error to other souls which were not fated to receive the gifts of the gods, and to have the knowledge of immortal Jove. Such souls are therefore hated by the gods; for they who were fated not to receive the gifts of the gods, and not to know God, were fated to be involved in error by means of him you speak of. He himself, however, was good, and heaven has been opened to him as to other good men. You are not, then, to speak evil of him, but to pity the folly of men: and through him men's danger is imminent."

Who is so foolish as not to see that these oracles were either composed by a clever man with a strong animus against the Christians, or were uttered as responses by impure demons with a similar design—that is to say, in order that their praise of Christ may win credence for their vituperation of Christians; and that thus they may, if possible, close the way of eternal salvation, which is identical with Christianity? For they believe that they are by no means counterworking their own hurtful craft by promoting belief in Christ, so long as their calumniation of Christians is also accepted; for they thus secure that even the man who thinks well of Christ declines to become a Christian, and is therefore not delivered from their own rule by the Christ he praises. Besides, their praise of Christ is so contrived that whosoever believes in Him as thus represented will not be a true Christian but a Photinian heretic, recognizing only the humanity, and not also the divinity of Christ, and will thus be precluded from salvation and from deliverance out of the meshes of these devilish lies. For our part, we are no better pleased with Hecate's praises of Christ than with Apollo's calumniation of Him. Apollo says that Christ was put to death by right-minded judges, implying that He was unrighteous. Hecate says that He was a most pious man, but no more. The intention of both is the same, to prevent men from becoming Christians, because if this be secured, men shall never be rescued from their power. But it is incumbent on our philosopher, or rather on those who believe in these pretended oracles against the Christians, first of all, if they can, to bring Apollo and Hecate to the same mind regarding Christ, so that either both may condemn or both praise Him. And even if they succeeded in this, we for our part would notwithstanding repudiate the testimony of demons, whether favorable or adverse to Christ. But when our adversaries find a god and goddess of their own at variance about Christ, the one praising, the other vituperating Him, they can certainly give no credence, if they have any judgment, to mere men who blaspheme the Christians.

When Porphyry or Hecate praises Christ, and adds that He gave Himself to the Christians as a fatal gift, that they might be involved in error, he exposes, as he thinks, the causes of this error. But before I cite his words to that purpose, I would ask, If Christ did thus give Himself to the Christians to involve them in error, did He do so willingly, or against His will? If willingly, how is He righteous? If against His will, how is He blessed? However, let us hear the causes of this error. "There are," he says, "in a certain place very small earthly spirits, subject to the power of evil demons. The wise men of the Hebrews, among whom was this Jesus, as you have heard from the oracles of Apollo cited above, turned religious persons from these very wicked demons and minor spirits, and taught them rather to worship the celestial gods, and especially to adore God the Father. This," he said, "the gods enjoin; and we have already shown how they admonish the soul to turn to God, and command it to worship Him. But the ignorant and the ungodly, who are not destined to receive favors from the gods, nor to know the immortal Jupiter, not listening to the gods and their messages, have turned away from all gods, and have not only refused to hate, but have venerated the prohibited demons. Professing to worship God, they refuse to do those things by which alone God is worshipped. For God, indeed, being the Father of all, is in need of nothing; but for us it is good to adore Him by means of justice, chastity, and other virtues, and thus to make life itself a prayer to Him, by inquiring into and imitating His nature. For inquiry," says he, "purifies and imitation deifies us, by moving us nearer to Him." He is right in so far as he proclaims God the Father, and the conduct by which we should worship Him. Of such precepts the prophetic books of the Hebrews are full, when they praise or blame the life of the saints. But in speaking of the Christians he is in error, and calumniates them as much as is desired by the demons whom he takes for gods, as if it were difficult for any man to recollect the disgraceful and shameful actions which used to be done in the theatres and temples to please the gods, and to compare with these things what is heard in our churches, and what is offered to the true God, and from this comparison to conclude where character is edified, and where it is ruined. But who but a diabolical spirit has told or suggested to this man so manifest and vain a lie, as that the Christians reverenced rather than hated the demons, whose worship the Hebrews prohibited? But that God, whom the Hebrew sages worshipped, forbids sacrifice to be offered even to the holy angels of heaven and divine powers, whom we, in this our pilgrimage, venerate and love as our most blessed fellow-citizens. For in the law which God gave to His Hebrew people He utters this menace, as in a voice of thunder: "He that sacrificeth unto any god, save unto the Lord only, he shall be utterly destroyed." [40] And that no one might suppose that this prohibition extends only to the very wicked demons and earthly spirits, whom this philosopher calls very small and inferior—for even these are in the Scripture called gods, not of the Hebrews, but of the nations, as the Septuagint translators have shown in the psalm where it is said, "For all the gods of the nations are demons" [41]—that no one might suppose, I say, that sacrifice to these demons was prohibited, but that sacrifice might be offered to all or some of the celestials, it was immediately added, "save unto the Lord alone," that is, only to the Lord, lest by chance in the phrase *Domino soli* some one may believe that the Lord is the Sun, to whom he thinks sacrifice should be made. That it is not to be thus understood is easily discoverable in the Greek version. The God of the Hebrews, then, to whom this renowned philosopher bears this signal testimony, gave to His Hebrew people a law, composed in the Hebrew language, and not obscure and unknown, but published now in every nation, and in this law it is written, "He that sacrificeth unto any god, save unto the Lord alone, he shall be utterly destroyed." What need is there

[40] Ex. xxii. 20   [41] Ps. xcvi. 5

to seek further proofs in the law or the prophets of this same thing? *Seek*, we need not say, for the passages are neither few nor difficult to find; but what need to collect and apply to my argument the proofs which are thickly sown and obvious, and by which it appears clear as day that sacrifice may be paid to none but the supreme and true God? Here is one brief but decided, even menacing, and certainly true utterance of that God whom the wisest of our adversaries so highly extol. Let this be listened to, feared, fulfilled, that there may be no disobedient soul cut off. "He that sacrifices," He says, not because He needs anything, but because it behoves us to be His possession. Hence the Psalmist in the Hebrew Scriptures sings, "I have said to the Lord, Thou art my God, for Thou needest not my good." [42] For we ourselves, who are His own city, are His most noble and worthy sacrifice, and it is this mystery we celebrate in our sacrifices, which are well known to the faithful, as we have explained in the preceding books. For through the prophets the oracles of God declared that the sacrifices which the Jews offered as a shadow of that which was to be would cease, and that the nations, from the rising to the setting of the sun, would offer one sacrifice. From these oracles, which we now see accomplished, we have made such selections as seemed suitable to our purpose in this work. And therefore, where there is not this righteousness whereby the one supreme God rules the obedient city according to His grace, so that it sacrifices to none but Him, and whereby, in all the citizens of this obedient city, the soul consequently rules the body and reason the vices in the rightful order, so that, as the individual just man, so also the community and people of the just, live by faith, which works by love, that love whereby man loves God as He ought to be loved, and his neighbor as himself—there, I say, there is not an assemblage associated by a common acknowledgment of right, and by a community of interests. But if there is not this, there is not a people, if our definition be true, and therefore there is no republic; for where there is no people there can be no republic.

CHAPTER XXIV

THE DEFINITION WHICH MUST BE GIVEN OF A PEOPLE AND A REPUBLIC, IN ORDER TO VINDICATE THE ASSUMPTION OF THESE TITLES BY THE ROMANS AND BY OTHER KINGDOMS

But if we discard this definition of a people, and, assuming another, say that a people is an assemblage of reasonable beings bound together by a common agreement as to the objects of their love, then, in order to discover the character of any people, we have only to observe what they love. Yet whatever it loves, if only it is an assemblage of reasonable beings and not of beasts, and is bound together by an agreement as to the objects of love, it is reasonably called a people; and it will be a superior people in proportion as it

---

[42] Ps. xvi. 2

is bound together by higher interests, inferior in proportion as it is bound together by lower. According to this definition of ours, the Roman people is a people, and its weal is without doubt a commonwealth or republic. But what its tastes were in its early and subsequent days, and how it declined into sanguinary seditions and then to social and civil wars, and so burst asunder or rotted off the bond of concord in which the health of a people consists, history shows, and in the preceding books I have related at large. And yet I would not on this account say either that it was not a people, or that its administration was not a republic, so long as there remains an assemblage of reasonable beings bound together by a common agreement as to the objects of love. But what I say of this people and of this republic I must be understood to think and say of the Athenians or any Greek state, of the Egyptians, of the early Assyrian Babylon, and of every other nation, great or small, which had a public government. For, in general, the city of the ungodly, which did not obey the command of God that it should offer no sacrifice save to Him alone, and which, therefore, could not give to the soul its proper command over the body, nor to the reason its just authority over the vices, is void of true justice.

CHAPTER XXV

THAT WHERE THERE IS NO TRUE RELIGION THERE ARE NO TRUE VIRTUES

For though the soul may seem to rule the body admirably, and the reason the vices, if the soul and reason do not themselves obey God, as God has commanded them to serve Him, they have no proper authority over the body and the vices. For what kind of mistress of the body and the vices can that mind be which is ignorant of the true God, and which, instead of being subject to His authority, is prostituted to the corrupting influences of the most vicious demons? It is for this reason that the virtues which it seems to itself to possess, and by which it restrains the body and the vices that it may obtain and keep what it desires, are rather vices than virtues so long as there is no reference to God in the matter. For although some suppose that virtues which have a reference only to themselves, and are desired only on their own account, are yet true and genuine virtues, the fact is that even then they are inflated with pride, and are therefore to be reckoned vices rather than virtues. For as that which gives life to the flesh is not derived from flesh, but is above it, so that which gives blessed life to man is not derived from man, but is something above him; and what I say of man is true of every celestial power and virtue whatsoever.

CHAPTER XXVI

OF THE PEACE WHICH IS ENJOYED BY THE PEOPLE THAT ARE ALIENATED
FROM GOD, AND THE USE MADE OF IT BY THE PEOPLE OF GOD
IN THE TIME OF ITS PILGRIMAGE

Wherefore, as the life of the flesh is the soul, so the blessed life of man is God, of whom the sacred writings of the Hebrews say, "Blessed is the people whose God is the Lord." [43] Miserable, therefore, is the people which is alienated from God. Yet even this people has a peace of its own which is not to be lightly esteemed, though, indeed, it shall not in the end enjoy it, because it makes no good use of it before the end. But it is our interest that it enjoy this peace meanwhile in this life; for as long as the two cities are commingled, we also enjoy the peace of Babylon. For from Babylon the people of God is so freed that it meanwhile sojourns in its company. And therefore the apostle also admonished the Church to pray for kings and those in authority, assigning as the reason, "that we may live a quiet and tranquil life in all godliness and love." [44] And the prophet Jeremiah, when predicting the captivity that was to befall the ancient people of God, and giving them the divine command to go obediently to Babylonia, and thus serve their God, counselled them also to pray for Babylonia, saying, "In the peace thereof shall ye have peace" [45]—the temporal peace which the good and the wicked together enjoy.

CHAPTER XXVII

THAT THE PEACE OF THOSE WHO SERVE GOD CANNOT IN THIS
MORTAL LIFE BE APPREHENDED IN ITS PERFECTION

But the peace which is peculiar to ourselves we enjoy now with God by faith, and shall hereafter enjoy eternally with Him by sight. But the peace which we enjoy in this life, whether common to all or peculiar to ourselves, is rather the solace of our misery than the positive enjoyment of felicity. Our very righteousness, too, though true in so far as it has respect to the true good, is yet in this life of such a kind that it consists rather in the remission of sins than in the perfecting of virtues. Witness the prayer of the whole city of God in its pilgrim state, for it cries to God by the mouth of all its members, "Forgive us our debts as we forgive our debtors." [46] And this prayer is efficacious not for those whose faith is without works and dead,[47] but for those whose faith worketh by love.[48] For as reason, though subjected to God, is yet pressed down by the corruptible body,[49] so long as it is in this mortal condition, it has not perfect authority over vice, and therefore this

[43] Ps. cxliv. 15   [44] 1 Tim. ii. 2   [45] Jer. xxix. 7   [46] Matt. vi. 12   [47] Jas. ii. 17
[48] Gal. v. 6   [49] Wisdom ix. 15

prayer is needed by the righteous. For though it exercises authority, the vices do not submit without a struggle. For however well one maintains the conflict, and however thoroughly he has subdued these enemies, there steals in some evil thing, which, if it do not find ready expression in act, slips out by the lips, or insinuates itself into the thought; and therefore his peace is not full so long as he is at war with his vices. For it is a doubtful conflict he wages with those that resist, and his victory over those that are defeated is not secure, but full of anxiety and effort. Amidst these temptations, therefore, of all which it has been summarily said in the divine oracles, "Is not human life upon earth a temptation?" [50] who but a proud man can presume that he so lives that he has no need to say to God, "Forgive us our debts?" And such a man is not great, but swollen and puffed up with vanity, and is justly resisted by Him who abundantly gives grace to the humble. Whence it is said, "God resisteth the proud, but giveth grace to the humble." [51] In this, then, consists the righteousness of a man, that he submit himself to God, his body to his soul, and his vices, even when they rebel, to his reason, which either defeats or at least resists them; and also that he beg from God grace to do his duty, and the pardon of his sins, and that he render to God thanks for all the blessings he receives. But, in that final peace to which all our righteousness has reference, and for the sake of which it is maintained, as our nature shall enjoy a sound immortality and incorruption, and shall have no more vices, and as we shall experience no resistance either from ourselves or from others, it will not be necessary that reason should rule vices which no longer exist, but God shall rule the man, and the soul shall rule the body, with a sweetness and facility suitable to the felicity of a life which is done with bondage. And this condition shall there be eternal, and we shall be assured of its eternity; and thus the peace of this blessedness and the blessedness of this peace shall be the supreme good.

CHAPTER XXVIII

THE END OF THE WICKED

But, on the other hand, they who do not belong to this city of God shall inherit eternal misery, which is also called the second death, because the soul shall then be separated from God its life, and therefore cannot be said to live, and the body shall be subjected to eternal pains. And consequently this second death shall be the more severe, because no death shall terminate it. But war being contrary to peace, as misery to happiness, and life to death, it is not without reason asked what kind of war can be found in the end of the wicked answering to the peace which is declared to be the end of the righteous? The person who puts this question has only to observe what it is in war that is hurtful and destructive, and he shall see that it is nothing else

[50] Job vii. 1   [51] Jas. iv. 6; 1 Pet. v. 5

than the mutual opposition and conflict of things. And can he conceive a more grievous and bitter war than that in which the will is so opposed to passion, and passion to the will, that their hostility can never be terminated by the victory of either, and in which the violence of pain so conflicts with the nature of the body, that neither yields to the other? For in this life, when this conflict has arisen, either pain conquers and death expels the feeling of it, or nature conquers and health expels the pain. But in the world to come the pain continues that it may torment, and the nature endures that it may be sensible of it; and neither ceases to exist, lest punishment also should cease. Now, as it is through the last judgment that men pass to these ends, the good to the supreme good, the evil to the supreme evil, I will treat of this judgment in the following book.

Best good is in contrast to evil
(all good would not be good)
what about evil? w/o good?

BOOK TWENTY

Concerning the last judgment, and the declarations regarding it in the Old and New Testaments.

CHAPTER I

THAT ALTHOUGH GOD IS ALWAYS JUDGING, IT IS NEVERTHELESS REASONABLE TO CONFINE OUR ATTENTION IN THIS BOOK TO HIS LAST JUDGMENT

INTENDING to speak, in dependence on God's grace, of the day of His final judgment, and to affirm it against the ungodly and incredulous, we must first of all lay, as it were, in the foundation of the edifice the divine declarations. Those persons who do not believe such declarations do their best to oppose to them false and illusive sophisms of their own, either contending that what is adduced from Scripture has another meaning, or altogether denying that it is an utterance of God's. For I suppose no man who understands what is written, and believes it to be communicated by the supreme and true God through holy men, refuses to yield and consent to these declarations, whether he orally confesses his consent, or is from some evil influence ashamed or afraid to do so; or even, with an obstinacy closely resembling madness, makes strenuous efforts to defend what he knows and believes to be false against what he knows and believes to be true.

That, therefore, which the whole Church of the true God holds and professes as its creed, that Christ shall come from heaven to judge quick and dead, this we call the last day, or last time, of the divine judgment. For we do not know how many days this judgment may occupy; but no one who reads the Scriptures, however negligently, need be told that in them "day" is customarily used for "time." And when we speak of the day of God's judgment, we add the word last or final for this reason, because even now God judges, and has judged from the beginning of human history, banishing from paradise, and excluding from the tree of life, those first men who perpetrated so great a sin. Yea, He was certainly exercising judgment also when He did not spare the angels who sinned, whose prince, overcome by envy, seduced men after being himself seduced. Neither is it without God's profound and just judgment that the life of demons and men, the one in the air, the other on earth, is filled with misery, calamities, and mistakes. And even though no one had sinned, it could only have been by the good and right judgment of God that the whole rational creation could have been maintained in eternal blessedness by a persevering adherence to its Lord. He judges, too, not only in the mass, condemning the race of devils and the race of men to be miserable on account of the original sin of these races, but He also judges the voluntary and personal acts of individuals. For even the devils pray that they may not be tormented,[1] which proves that without injustice they might either be spared or tormented according to their deserts. And men are punished by God for their sins often visibly, always secretly, either in this life or after death, although no man acts rightly save by the assistance of divine aid; and no man or devil acts unrighteously save by the permission of the divine and most just judgment. For, as the apostle says, "There is no unrighteousness with God;"[2] and as he elsewhere says, "His judgments are inscrutable, and His ways past finding out."[3] In this book, then, I shall speak, as God permits, not of those first judgments, nor of these intervening judgments of God, but of the last judgment, when Christ is to come from heaven to judge the quick and the dead. For that day is properly called the day of judgment, because in it there shall be no room left for the ignorant questioning why this wicked person is happy and that righteous man unhappy. In that day true and full happiness shall be the lot of none but the good, while deserved and supreme misery shall be the portion of the wicked, and of them only.

CHAPTER II

THAT IN THE MINGLED WEB OF HUMAN AFFAIRS GOD'S JUDGMENT IS PRESENT THOUGH IT CANNOT BE DISCERNED

In this present time we learn to bear with equanimity the ills to which even good men are subject, and to hold cheap the blessings which even the wicked enjoy. And consequently, even in those conditions of life in which the justice of God is not apparent, His teaching is salutary. For we do not know by what judgment of God this good man is poor and that bad man rich; why he who, in our opinion, ought to suffer acutely for his abandoned life enjoys himself, while sorrow pursues him whose praiseworthy life leads us to suppose he should be happy; why the innocent man is dismissed from the bar not only unavenged, but even condemned, being either wronged by the iniquity of the judge, or overwhelmed by false evidence, while his guilty adversary, on the other hand, is not only discharged with impunity, but even has his claims admitted; why the ungodly enjoys good health, while the godly pines in sickness; why ruffians are of the soundest constitution, while they who could not hurt any one even with a word are from infancy afflicted with complicated disorders; why he who

---

[1] Matt. viii. 29   [2] Rom. ix. 14   [3] Rom. xi. 33

is useful to society is cut off by premature death, while those who, as it might seem, ought never to have been so much as born have lives of unusual length; why he who is full of crimes is crowned with honors, while the blameless man is buried in the darkness of neglect. But who can collect or enumerate all the contrasts of this kind? But if this anomalous state of things were uniform in this life, in which, as the sacred Psalmist says, "Man is like to vanity, his days as a shadow that passeth away," [4]—so uniform that none but wicked men won the transitory prosperity of earth, while only the good suffered its ills—this could be referred to the just and even benign judgment of God. We might suppose that they who were not destined to obtain those everlasting benefits which constitute human blessedness were either deluded by transitory blessings as the just reward of their wickedness, or were, in God's mercy, consoled by them, and that they who were not destined to suffer eternal torments were afflicted with temporal chastisement for their sins, or were stimulated to greater attainment in virtue. But now, as it is, since we not only see good men involved in the ills of life, and bad men enjoying the good of it, which seems unjust, but also that evil often overtakes evil men, and good surprises the good, the rather on this account are God's judgments unsearchable, and His ways past finding out. Although, therefore, we do not know by what judgment these things are done or permitted to be done by God, with whom is the highest virtue, the highest wisdom, the highest justice, no infirmity, no rashness, no unrighteousness, yet it is salutary for us to learn to hold cheap such things, be they good or evil, as attach indifferently to good men and bad, and to covet those good things which belong only to good men, and flee those evils which belong only to evil men. But when we shall have come to that judgment, the date of which is called peculiarly the day of judgment, and sometimes the day of the Lord, we shall then recognize the justice of all God's judgments, not only of such as shall then be pronounced, but of all which take effect from the beginning, or may take effect before that time. And in that day we shall also recognize with what justice so many, or almost all, the just judgments of God in the present life defy the scrutiny of human sense or insight, though in this matter it is not concealed from pious minds that what is concealed is just.

CHAPTER III

WHAT SOLOMON, IN THE BOOK OF ECCLESIASTES, SAYS REGARDING THE THINGS WHICH HAPPEN ALIKE TO GOOD AND WICKED MEN

Solomon, the wisest king of Israel, who reigned in Jerusalem, thus commences the book called Ecclesiastes, which the Jews number among their canonical Scriptures. "Vanity of vanities, said Ecclesiastes, vanity of vanities; all is vanity. What profit hath a man of all his labor which he

[4] Ps. cxliv. 4

hath taken under the sun?" [5] And after going on to enumerate, with this as his text, the calamities and delusions of this life, and the shifting nature of the present time, in which there is nothing substantial, nothing lasting, he bewails, among the other vanities that are under the sun, this also, that though wisdom excelleth folly as light excelleth darkness, and though the eyes of the wise men are in his head, while the fool walketh in darkness,[6] yet one event happeneth to them all, that is to say, in this life under the sun, unquestionably alluding to those evils which we see befall good and bad men alike. He says, further, that the good suffer the ills of life as if they were evil doers, and the bad enjoy the good of life as if they were good. "There is a vanity which is done upon the earth; that there be just men unto whom it happeneth according to the work of the wicked: again, there be wicked men, to whom it happeneth according to the work of the righteous. I said, that this also is vanity." [7] This wisest man devoted this whole book to a full exposure of this vanity, evidently with no other object than that we might long for that life in which there is no vanity under the sun, but verity under Him who made the sun. In this vanity, then, was it not by the just and righteous judgment of God that man, made like to vanity, was destined to pass away? But in these days of vanity it makes an important difference whether he resists or yields to the truth, and whether he is destitute of true piety or a partaker of it—important not so far as regards the acquirement of the blessings or the evasion of the calamities of this transitory and vain life, but in connection with the future judgment which shall make over to good men good things, and to bad men bad things, in permanent, inalienable possession. In fine, this wise man concludes this book of his by saying, "Fear God, and keep His commandments: for this is every man. For God shall bring every work into judgment, with every despised person, whether it be good, or whether it be evil." [8] What truer, terser, more salutary enouncement could be made? "Fear God," he says, "and keep His commandments: for this is every man." For whosoever has real existence, is this, is a keeper of God's commandments; and he who is not this, is nothing. For so long as he remains in the likeness of vanity, he is not renewed in the image of the truth. "For God shall bring into judgment every work,"—that is, whatever man does in this life—"whether it be good or whether it be evil, with every despised person,"—that is, with every man who here seems despicable, and is therefore not considered; for God sees even him, and does not despise him nor pass him over in His judgment.

[5] Eccles. i. 2, 3   [6] Eccles. ii. 13, 14   [7] Eccles. viii. 14   [8] Eccles. xii. 13, 14

CHAPTER IV

THAT PROOFS OF THE LAST JUDGMENT WILL BE ADDUCED, FIRST FROM THE NEW TESTAMENT, AND THEN FROM THE OLD

The proofs, then, of this last judgment of God which I propose to adduce shall be drawn first from the New Testament, and then from the Old. For although the Old Testament is prior in point of time, the New has the precedence in intrinsic value; for the Old acts the part of herald to the New. We shall therefore first cite passages from the New Testament, and confirm them by quotations from the Old Testament. The Old contains the law and the prophets, the New the gospel and the apostolic epistles. Now the apostle says, "By the law is the knowledge of sin. But now the right-eousness of God without the law is manifested, being witnessed by the law and the prophet; now the righteousness of God is by faith of Jesus Christ upon all them that believe." [9] This righteousness of God belongs to the New Testament, and evidence for it exists in the old books, that is to say, in the law and the prophets. I shall first, then state the case, and then call the witnesses. This order Jesus Christ Himself directs us to observe, saying, "The scribe instructed in the kingdom of God is like a good householder, bringing out of his treasure things new and old." [10] He did not say "old and new," which He certainly would have said had He not wished to follow the order of merit rather than that of time.

CHAPTER V

THE PASSAGES IN WHICH THE SAVIOUR DECLARES THAT THERE SHALL BE A DIVINE JUDGMENT IN THE END OF THE WORLD

The Saviour Himself, while reproving the cities in which He had done great works, but which had not believed, and while setting them in unfavor-able comparison with foreign cities, says, "But I say unto you, It shall be more tolerable for Tyre and Sidon at the day of judgment than for you." [11] And a little after He says, "Verily, I say unto you, It shall be more toler-able for the land of Sodom in the day of judgment than for thee." [12] Here He most plainly predicts that a day of judgment is to come. And in another place He says, "The men of Nineveh shall rise in judgment with this generation, and shall condemn it: because they repented at the preaching of Jonas; and, behold, a greater than Jonas is here. The queen of the south shall rise up in the judgment with this generation, and shall con-demn it: for she came from the uttermost parts of the earth to hear the words of Solomon; and behold, a greater than Solomon is here." [13] Two things we learn from this passage, that a judgment is to take place, and

[9] Rom. iii. 20-22   [10] Matt. xiii. 52   [11] Matt. xi. 22   [12] Matt. xi. 24   [13] Matt. xii. 41, 42

that it is to take place at the resurrection of the dead. For when He spoke of the Ninevites and the queen of the south, He certainly spoke of dead persons, and yet He said that they should rise up in the day of judgment. He did not say, "They shall condemn," as if they themselves were to be the judges, but because, in comparison with them, the others shall be justly condemned.

Again, in another passage, in which He was speaking of the present intermingling and future separation of the good and bad—the separation which shall be made in the day of judgment—He adduced a comparison drawn from the sown wheat and tares sown among them, and gave this explanation of it to His disciples: "He that soweth the good seed is the Son of man; The field is the world; the good seed are the children of the kingdom; but the tares are the children of the wicked one; The enemy that sowed them is the devil; the harvest is the end of the world; and the reapers are the angels. As therefore the tares are gathered and burned in the fire; so shall it be in the end of this world.

"The Son of man shall send forth his angels, and they shall gather out of his kingdom all things that offend, and them which do iniquity; And shall cast them into a furnace of fire: there shall be wailing and gnashing of teeth. Then shall the righteous shine forth as the sun in the kingdom of their Father. Who hath ears to hear, let him hear." [13a] Here, indeed, He did not name the judgment or the day of judgment, but indicated it much more clearly by describing the circumstances, and foretold that it should take place in the end of the world.

In like manner He says to His disciples, "Verily I say unto you, That ye which have followed me, in the regeneration, when the Son of man shall sit on the throne of His glory, ye also shall sit upon twelve thrones, judging the twelve tribes of Israel." [14] Here we learn that Jesus shall judge with His disciples. And therefore He said elsewhere to the Jews, "If I by Beelzebub cast out devils, by whom do your sons cast them out? Therefore they shall be your judges." [15] Neither ought we to suppose that only twelve men shall judge along with Him, though He says that they shall sit upon twelve thrones; for by the number twelve is signified the completeness of the multitude of those who shall judge. For the two parts of the number seven (which commonly symbolizes totality), that is to say four and three, multiplied into one another, give twelve. For four times three, or three times four, are twelve. There are other meanings, too, in this number twelve. Were not this the right interpretation of the twelve thrones, then since we read that Matthias was ordained an apostle in the room of Judas the traitor, the Apostle Paul, though he labored more than them all,[16] should have no throne of judgment; but he unmistakeably considers himself to be included in the number of the judges when he says, "Know ye not that we

[13a] Matt. xiii. 37-43   [14] Matt. xix. 28   [15] Matt. xii. 27   [16] I Cor. xv. 10

shall judge angels?" [17] The same rule is to be observed in applying the number twelve to those who are to be judged. For though it was said, "judging the twelve tribes of Israel," the tribe of Levi, which is the thirteenth, shall not on this account be exempt from judgment, neither shall judgment be passed only on Israel and not on the other nations. And by the words "in the regeneration," He certainly meant the resurrection of the dead to be understood; for our flesh shall be regenerated by incorruption, as our soul is regenerated by faith.

Many passages I omit, because, though they seem to refer to the last judgment, yet on a closer examination they are found to be ambiguous, or to allude rather to some other event—whether to that of the coming of the Saviour which continually occurs in His Church, that is, in His members, in which He comes little by little, and piece by piece, since the whole Church is His body, or to the destruction of the earthly Jerusalem. For when He speaks even of this, He often uses language which is applicable to the end of the world and that last and great day of judgment, so that these two events cannot be distinguished unless all the corresponding passages bearing on the subject in the three evangelists, Matthew, Mark, and Luke, are compared with one another—for some things are put more obscurely by one evangelist and more plainly by another—so that it becomes apparent what things are meant to be referred to one event. It is this which I have been at pains to do in a letter which I wrote to Hesychius of blessed memory, bishop of Salon, and entitled, "Of the End of the World." [18]

I shall now cite from the Gospel according to Matthew the passage which speaks of the separation of the good from the wicked by the most efficacious and final judgment of Christ: "When the Son of man shall come in his glory, and all the holy angels with him, then shall he sit upon the throne of his glory: And before him shall be gathered all nations; and he shall separate them one from another, as a shepherd divideth his sheep from the goats: And he shall set the sheep on his right hand, but the goats on the left. Then shall the King say unto them on his right hand, Come, ye blessed of my Father, inherit the kingdom prepared for you from the foundation of the world:

For I was an hungred, and ye gave me meat: I was thirsty, and ye gave me drink: I was a stranger, and ye took me in: Naked, and ye clothed me: I was sick, and ye visited me: I was in prison, and ye came unto me. Then shall the righteous answer him, saying, Lord, when saw we thee an hungred, and fed thee? or thirsty, and gave thee drink? When saw we thee a stranger, and took thee in? or naked, and clothed thee? Or when saw we thee sick, or in prison, and came unto thee?

And the King shall answer and say unto them, Verily I say unto you, Inasmuch as ye have done it unto one of the least of these my brethren, ye

[17] 1 Cor. vi. 3   [18] Ep. 199

have done it unto me. Then shall he say also unto them on the left hand, Depart from me, ye cursed, into everlasting fire, prepared for the devil and his angels." [19] Then He in like manner recounts to the wicked the things they had not done, but which He had said those on the right hand had done. And when they ask when they had seen Him in need of these things, He replies that, inasmuch as they had not done it to the least of His brethren, they had not done it unto Him, and concludes His address in the words, "And these shall go away into everlasting punishment, but the righteous into life eternal." Moreover, the evangelist John most distinctly states that He had predicted that the judgment should be at the resurrection of the dead. For after saying, "The Father judgeth no man, but hath committed all judgment unto the Son; that all men should honor the Son, even as they honor the Father: he that honoreth not the Son, honoreth not the Father which hath sent Him;" He immediately adds, "Verily, verily, I say unto you, He that heareth my word and believeth on Him that sent me, hath everlasting life, and shall not come into judgment; but is passed from death to life." [20] Here He said that believers on Him should not come into judgment. How, then, shall they be separated from the wicked by judgment, and be set at His right hand, unless judgment be in this passage used for condemnation? For into judgment, in this sense, they shall not come who hear His word, and believe on Him that sent Him.

CHAPTER VI

WHAT IS THE FIRST RESURRECTION, AND WHAT IS THE SECOND

After that He adds the words, "Verily, verily, I say unto you, The hour is coming and now is, when the dead shall hear the voice of the Son of God; and they that hear shall live. For as the Father hath life in Himself; so hath He given to the Son to have life in Himself." [21] As yet He does not speak of the second resurrection, that is, the resurrection of the body, which shall be in the end, but of the first, which now is. It is for the sake of making this distinction that He says, "The hour is coming, and now is." Now this resurrection regards not the body, but the soul. For souls, too, have a death of their own in wickedness and sins, whereby they are the dead of whom the same lips say, "Suffer the dead to bury their dead," [22]—that is, let those who are dead in soul bury them that are dead in body. It is of these dead, then—the dead in ungodliness and wickedness—that He says, "The hour is coming, and now is, when the dead shall hear the voice of the Son of God; and they that hear shall live." "They that hear," that is, they who obey, believe, and persevere to the end. Here no difference is made between the good and the bad. For it is good for all men to hear His voice and live, by passing to the life of godliness from the death of ungodliness. Of

[19] Matt. xxv. 31-41   [20] John v. 22-24   [21] John v. 25, 26   [22] Matt. viii. 22

this death the Apostle Paul says, "Therefore all are dead, and He died for all, that they which live should not henceforth live unto themselves, but unto Him which died for them and rose again." [23] Thus all, without one exception, were dead in sins, whether original or voluntary sins, sins of ignorance, or sins committed against knowledge; and for all the dead there died the one only person who lived, that is, who had no sin whatever, in order that they who live by the remission of their sins should live, not to themselves, but to Him who died for all, for our sins, and rose again for our justification, that we, believing in Him who justifies the ungodly, and being justified from ungodliness or quickened from death, may be able to attain to the first resurrection which now is. For in this first resurrection none have a part save those who shall be eternally blessed; but in the second, of which He goes on to speak, all, as we shall learn, have a part, both the blessed and the wretched. The one is the resurrection of mercy, the other of judgment. And therefore it is written in the psalm, "I will sing of mercy and of judgment: unto Thee, O Lord, will I sing." [24]

And of this judgment He went on to say, "And hath given Him authority to execute judgment also, because He is the Son of man." Here He shows that He will come to judge in that flesh in which He had come to be judged. For it is to show this He says, "because He is the Son of man." And then follow the words for our purpose: "Marvel not at this: for the hour is coming, in the which all that are in the graves shall hear His voice, and shall come forth; they that have done good, unto the resurrection of life; and they that have done evil, unto the resurrection of judgment." [25] This judgment He uses here in the same sense as a little before, when He says, "He that heareth my word, and believeth on Him that sent me, hath everlasting life, and shall not come into *judgment,* but is passed from death to life;" *i.e.,* by having a part in the first resurrection, by which a transition from death to life is made in this present time, he shall not come into damnation, which He mentions by the name of judgment, as also in the place where He says, "but they that have done evil unto the resurrection of judgment," *i.e.,* of damnation. He, therefore, who would not be damned in the second resurrection, let him rise in the first. For "the hour is coming, and now is, when the dead shall hear the voice of the Son of God; and they that hear shall live," *i.e.,* shall not come into damnation, which is called the second death; into which death, after the second or bodily resurrection, they shall be hurled who do not rise in the first or spiritual resurrection. For the "hour is coming" (but here He does not say, "and now is," because it shall come in the end of the world in the last and greatest judgment of God) "when all that are in the graves shall hear His voice and shall come forth." He does not say, as in the first resurrection, "And they that hear shall live." For all shall not live, at least with such life as ought alone to be called life because

[23] 2 Cor. v. 14, 15   [24] Ps. ci. 1   [25] John v. 28, 29

it alone is blessed. For some kind of life they must have in order to hear, and come forth from the graves in their rising bodies. And why all shall not live He teaches in the words that follow: "They that have done good, to the resurrection of life"—these are they who shall live; "but they that have done evil, to the resurrection of judgment"—these are they who shall not live, for they shall die in the second death. They have done evil because their life has been evil; and their life has been evil because it has not been renewed in the first or spiritual resurrection which now is, or because they have not persevered to the end in their renewed life. As, then, there are two regenerations, of which I have already made mention—the one according to faith, and which takes place in the present life by means of baptism; the other according to the flesh, and which shall be accomplished in its incorruption and immortality by means of the great and final judgment—so are there also two resurrections—the one the first and spiritual resurrection, which has place in this life, and preserves us from coming into the second death; the other the second, which does not occur now, but in the end of the world, and which is of the body, not of the soul, and which by the last judgment shall dismiss some into the second death, others into that life which has no death.

CHAPTER VII

WHAT IS WRITTEN IN THE REVELATION OF JOHN REGARDING THE TWO RESURRECTIONS, AND THE THOUSAND YEARS, AND WHAT MAY REASONABLY BE HELD ON THESE POINTS

The evangelist John has spoken of these two resurrections in the book which is called the Apocalypse, but in such a way that some Christians do not understand the first of the two, and so construe the passage into ridiculous fancies. For the Apostle John says in the foresaid book, "And I saw an angel come down from heaven, having the key of the bottomless pit and a great chain in his hand. And he laid hold on the dragon, that old serpent, which is the Devil and Satan, and bound him a thousand years. And cast him into the bottomless pit, and shut him up, and set a seal upon him, that he should deceive the nations no more, till the thousand years should be fulfilled: and after that he must be loosed a little season.

And I saw thrones, and they sat upon them, and judgment was given unto them: and I saw the souls of them that were beheaded for the witness of Jesus, and for the word of God, and which had not worshipped the beast, neither his image, neither had received his mark upon their foreheads, or in their hands; and they lived and reigned with Christ a thousand years.

But the rest of the dead lived not again until the thousand years were finished. This is the first resurrection. Blessed and holy is he that hath part in the first resurrection: on such the second death hath no power, but they shall be priests of God and of Christ, and shall reign with him a thousand years." [26] Those who, on the strength of this passage, have suspected that the first resurrection is future and bodily, have been moved, among other things, specially by the number of a thousand years, as if it were a fit thing that the saints should thus enjoy a kind of Sabbath-rest during that period, a holy leisure after the labors of the six thousand years since man was created, and was on account of his great sin dismissed from the blessedness of paradise into the woes of this mortal life, so that thus, as it is written, "One day is with the Lord as a thousand years, and a thousand years as one day," [27] there should follow on the completion of six thousand years, as of six days, a kind of seventh-day Sabbath in the succeeding thousand years; and that it is for this purpose the saints rise, *viz.*, to celebrate this Sabbath. And this opinion would not be objectionable, if it were believed that the joys of the saints in that Sabbath shall be spiritual, and consequent on the presence of God; for myself, too, once held this opinion.[28] But, as they assert that those who then rise again shall enjoy the leisure of immoderate carnal banquets, furnished with an amount of meat and drink such as not only to shock the feeling of the temperate, but even to surpass the measure of credulity itself, such assertions can be believed only by the carnal. They who do believe them are called by the spiritual Chiliasts, which we may literally reproduce by the name Millenarians. It is a tedious process to refute these opinions point by point: we prefer proceeding to show how that passage of Scripture should be understood.

The Lord Jesus Christ Himself says, "No man can enter into a strong man's house, and spoil his goods, except he first bind the strong man" [29]— meaning by the strong man the devil, because he had power to take captive the human race; and meaning by his goods which he was to take, those who had been held by the devil in divers sins and iniquities, but were to become believers in Himself. It was then for the binding of this strong one that the apostle saw in the Apocalypse "an angel coming down from heaven, having the key of the abyss, and a chain in his hand. And he laid hold," he says, "on the dragon, that old serpent, which is called the devil and Satan, and bound him a thousand years"—that is, bridled and restained his power so that he could not seduce and gain possession of those who were to be freed. Now the thousand years may be understood in two ways, so far as occurs to me: either because these things happen in the sixth thousand of years or sixth millennium (the latter part of which is now passing), as if during the sixth day, which is to be followed by a Sabbath which has no evening, the endless rest of the saints, so that, speaking of a part under the name of the whole, he calls the last part of the millennium—the part, that is, which had yet to expire before the end of the world—a thousand years; or he used the thousand years as an equivalent for the whole duration of this world, employing the number of perfection to mark the fullness of time. For

[26] Rev. xx. 1-6   [27] 2 Pet. iii. 8   [28] *Serm.* 259   [29] Mark iii. 27

a thousand is the cube of ten. For ten times ten makes a hundred, that is, the square on a plane. But to give this height, and make it a cube, the hundred is again multiplied by ten, which gives a thousand. Besides, if a hundred is sometimes used for totality, as when the Lord said by way of promise to him that left all and followed Him, "He shall receive in this world an hundredfold;" [30] of which the apostle gives, as it were, an explanation when he says, "As having nothing, yet possessing all things," [31]—for even of old it had been said, The whole world is the wealth of a believer— with how much greater reason is a thousand put for totality since it is the cube, while the other is only the square? And for the same reason we cannot better interpret the words of the psalm, "He hath been mindful of His covenant for ever, the word which He commanded to a thousand generations," [32] than by understanding it to mean "to all generations."

"And he cast him into the abyss"—i.e., cast the devil into the abyss. By the *abyss* is meant the countless multitude of the wicked whose hearts are unfathomably deep in malignity against the Church of God—not that the devil was not there before, but he is said to be cast in thither, because, when prevented from harming believers, he takes more complete possession of the ungodly. For that man is more abundantly possessed by the devil who is not only alienated from God, but also gratuitously hates those who serve God. "And shut him up, and set a seal upon him, that he should deceive the nations no more till the thousand years should be fulfilled." "Shut him up" —i.e., prohibited him from going out, from doing what was forbidden. And the addition of "set a seal upon him" seems to me to mean that it was designed to keep it a secret who belonged to the devil's party and who did not. For in this world this is a secret, for we cannot tell whether even the man who seems to stand shall fall, or whether he who seems to lie shall rise again. But by the chain and prison-house of this interdict the devil is prohibited and restrained from seducing those nations which belong to Christ, but which he formerly seduced or held in subjection. For before the foundation of the world God chose to rescue these from the power of darkness, and to translate them into the kingdom of the Son of his Love, as the apostle says.[33] For what Christian is not aware that he seduces nations even now, and draws them with himself to eternal punishment, but not those predestined to eternal life? And let no one be dismayed by the circumstance that the devil often seduces even those who have been regenerated in Christ, and begun to walk in God's way. For "the Lord knoweth them that are His," [34] and of these the devil seduces none to eternal damnation. For it is as God, from whom nothing is hid even of things future, that the Lord knows them; not as a man, who sees a man at the present time (if he can be said to see one whose heart he does not see) but does not see even himself so far as to be able to know what kind of person he is to be. The devil, then, is bound and shut up in the abyss that he may not seduce the nations

[30] Matt. xix, 29   [31] 2 Cor. vi. 10   [32] Ps. cv. 8   [33] Col. i. 13   [34] 2 Tim. ii. 19

from which the Church is gathered, and which he formerly seduced before the Church existed. For it is not said "that he should not seduce any man," but "that he should not seduce the nations"—meaning, no doubt, those among which the Church exists—"till the thousand years should be fulfilled"—*i.e.*, either what remains of the sixth day which consists of a thousand years, or all the years which are to elapse till the end of the world.

The words, "that he should not seduce the nations till the thousand years should be fulfilled," are not to be understood as indicating that afterwards he is to seduce only those nations from which the predestined Church is composed, and from seducing whom he is restrained by that chain and imprisonment; but they are used in conformity with that usage frequently employed in Scripture and exemplified in the psalm, "So our eyes wait upon the Lord our God, until He have mercy upon us" [35]—not as if the eyes of His servants would no longer wait upon the Lord their God when He had mercy upon them. Or the order of the words is unquestionably this, "And he shut him up and set a seal upon him, till the thousand years should be fulfilled;" and the interposed clause, "that he should seduce the nations no more," is not to be understood in the connection in which it stands, but separately, and as if added afterwards, so that the whole sentence might be read, "And He shut him up and set a seal upon him till the thousand years should be fulfilled, that he should seduce the nations no more,"—*i.e.*, he is shut up till the thousand years be fulfilled, on this account, that he may no more deceive the nations.

CHAPTER VIII

OF THE BINDING AND LOOSING OF THE DEVIL

"After that," says John, "he must be loosed a little season." If the binding and shutting up of the devil means his being made unable to seduce the Church, must his loosing be the recovery of this ability? By no means. For the Church predestined and elected before the foundation of the world, the Church of which it is said, "The Lord knoweth them that are His," shall never be seduced by him. And yet there shall be a Church in this world even when the devil shall be loosed, as there has been since the beginning, and shall be always, the places of the dying being filled by new believers. For a little after John says that the devil, being loosed, shall draw the nations whom he has seduced in the whole world to make war against the Church, and that the number of these enemies shall be as the sand of the sea. "And they went up on the breadth of the earth, and compassed the camp of the saints about, and the beloved city: and fire came down from God out of heaven and devoured them. And the devil who seduced them was cast into the lake of fire and brimstone, where the beast and the false prophet are, and

[35] Ps. cxxiii. 2

shall be tormented day and night for ever and ever." [36] This relates to the last judgment, but I have thought fit to mention it now, lest any one might suppose that in that short time during which the devil shall be loose there shall be no Church upon earth, whether because the devil finds no Church, or destroys it by manifold persecutions. The devil, then, is not bound during the whole time which this book embraces—that is, from the first coming of Christ to the end of the world, when He shall come the second time—not bound in this sense, that during this interval, which goes by the name of a thousand years, he shall not seduce the Church, for not even when loosed shall he seduce it. For certainly if his being bound means that he is not able or not permitted to seduce the Church, what can the loosing of him mean but his being able or permitted to do so? But God forbid that such should be the case! But the binding of the devil is his being prevented from the exercise of his whole power to seduce men, either by violently forcing or fraudulently deceiving them into taking part with him. If he were during so long a period permitted to assail the weakness of men, very many persons, such as God would not wish to expose to such temptation, would have their faith overthrown, or would be prevented from believing; and that this might not happen, he is bound.

But when the short time comes he shall be loosed. For he shall rage with the whole force of himself and his angels for three years and six months; and those with whom he makes war shall have power to withstand all his violence and stratagems. And if he were never loosed, his malicious power would be less patent, and less proof would be given of the steadfast fortitude of the holy city: it would, in short, be less manifest what good use the Almighty makes of his great evil. For the Almighty does not absolutely seclude the saints from his temptation, but shelters only their inner man, where faith resides, that by outward temptation they may grow in grace. And He binds him that he may not, in the free and eager exercise of his malice, hinder or destroy the faith of those countless weak persons, already believing or yet to believe, from whom the Church must be increased and completed; and he will in the end loose him, that the city of God may see how mighty an adversary it has conquered, to the great glory of its Redeemer, Helper, Deliverer. And what are we in comparison with those believers and saints who shall then exist, seeing that they shall be tested by the loosing of an enemy with whom we make war at the greatest peril even when he is bound? Although it is also certain that even in this intervening period there have been and are some soldiers of Christ so wise and strong, that if they were to be alive in this mortal condition at the time of his loosing, they would both most wisely guard against, and most patiently endure, all his snares and assaults.

Now the devil was thus bound not only when the Church began to be more and more widely extended among the nations beyond Judea, but is

[36] Rev. xx. 9, 10

now and shall be bound till the end of the world, when he is to be loosed. Because even now men are, and doubtless to the end of the world shall be, converted to the faith from the unbelief in which he held them. And this strong one is bound in each instance in which he is spoiled of one of his goods; and the abyss in which he is shut up is not at an end when those die who were alive when first he was shut up in it, but these have been succeeded, and shall to the end of the world be succeeded, by others born after them with a like hate of the Christians, and in the depth of whose blind hearts he is continually shut up as in an abyss. But it is a question whether, during these three years and six months when he shall be loose, and raging with all his force, any one who has not previously believed shall attach himself to the faith. For how in that case would the words hold good, "Who entereth into the house of a strong one to spoil his goods, unless first he shall have bound the strong one?" Consequently this verse seems to compel us to believe that during that time, short as it is, no one will be added to the Christian community, but that the devil will make war with those who have previously become Christians, and that, though some of these may be conquered and desert to the devil, these do not belong to the predestined number of the sons of God. For it is not without reason that John, the same apostle as wrote this Apocalypse, says in his epistle regarding certain persons, "They went out from us, but they were not of us; for if they had been of us, they would no doubt have remained with us." [37] But what shall become of the little ones? For it is beyond all belief that in these days there shall not be found some Christian children born, but not yet baptized, and that there shall not also be some born during that very period; and if there be such, we cannot believe that their parents shall not find some way of bringing them to the laver of regeneration. But if this shall be the case, how shall these goods be snatched from the devil when he is loose, since into his house no man enters to spoil his goods unless he has first bound him? On the contrary, we are rather to believe that in these days there shall be no lack either of those who fall away from, or of those who attach themselves to the Church; but there shall be such resoluteness, both in parents to seek baptism for their little ones, and in those who shall then first believe, that they shall conquer that strong one, even though unbound—that is, shall both vigilantly comprehend, and patiently bear up against him, though employing such wiles and putting forth such force as he never before used; and thus they shall be snatched from him even though unbound. And yet the verse of the Gospel will not be untrue, "Who entereth into the house of the strong one to spoil his goods, unless he shall first have bound the strong one?" For in accordance with this true saying that order is observed —the strong one first bound, and then his goods spoiled; for the Church is so increased by the weak and strong from all nations far and near, that by its most robust faith in things divinely predicted and accomplished, it

[37] 1 John ii. 19

shall be able to spoil the goods of even the unbound devil. For as we must own that, "When iniquity abounds, the love of many waxes cold," [38] and that those who have not been written in the book of life shall in large numbers yield to the severe and unprecedented persecutions and stratagems of the devil now loosed, so we cannot but think that not only those whom that time shall find sound in the faith, but also some who till then shall be without, shall become firm in the faith they have hitherto rejected and mighty to conquer the devil even though unbound, God's grace aiding them to understand the Scriptures, in which, among other things, there is foretold that very end which they themselves see to be arriving. And if this shall be so, his binding is to be spoken of as preceding, that there might follow a spoiling of him both bound and loosed; for it is of this it is said, "Who shall enter into the house of the strong one to spoil his goods, unless he shall first have bound the strong one?"

CHAPTER IX

WHAT THE REIGN OF THE SAINTS WITH CHRIST FOR A THOUSAND YEARS IS, AND HOW IT DIFFERS FROM THE ETERNAL KINGDOM

But while the devil is bound, the saints reign with Christ during the same thousand years, understood in the same way, that is, of the time of His first coming.[39] For, leaving out of account that kingdom concerning which He shall say in the end, "Come, ye blessed of my Father, take possession of the kingdom prepared for you," [40] the Church could not now be called His kingdom or the kingdom of heaven unless His saints were even now reigning with Him, though in another and far different way; for to His saints He says, "Lo, I am with you always, even to the end of the world." [41] Certainly it is in this present time that the scribe well instructed in the kingdom of God, and of whom we have already spoken, brings forth from his treasure things new and old. And from the Church those reapers shall gather out the tares which He suffered to grow with the wheat till the harvest, as He explains in the words, "The harvest is the end of the world; and the reapers are the angels. As therefore the tares are gathered together and burned with fire, so shall it be in the end of the world. The Son of man shall send His angels, and they shall gather out of His kingdom all offenses." [42] Can He mean out of that kingdom in which are no offenses? Then it must be out of His present kingdom, the Church, that they are gathered. So He says, "He that breaketh one of the least of these commandments, and teacheth men so, shall be called least in the kingdom of heaven: but he that doeth and teacheth thus shall be called great in the kingdom of heaven." [43] He speaks of both as being in the kingdom of heaven, both the man who does not perform the commandments which He

[38] Matt. xxiv. 12   [39] Between His first and second coming   [40] Matt. xxv. 34
[41] Matt. xxviii. 20   [42] Matt. xiii. 39-41   [43] Matt. v. 19

teaches—for "to break" means not to keep, not to perform—and the man who does and teaches as He did; but the one He calls least, the other great. And He immediately adds, "For I say unto you, that except your righteousness exceed that of the scribes and Pharisees"—that is, the righteousness of those who break what they teach; for of the scribes and Pharisees He elsewhere says, "For they say and do not" [44]—unless, therefore, your righteousness exceed theirs, that is, so that you do not break but rather do what you teach, "ye shall not enter the kingdom of heaven." [45] We must understand in one sense the kingdom of heaven in which exist together both he who breaks what he teaches and he who does it, the one being least, the other great, and in another sense the kingdom of heaven into which only he who does what he teaches shall enter. Consequently, where both classes exist, it is the Church as it now is, but where only the one shall exist, it is the Church as it is destined to be when no wicked person shall be in her. Therefore the Church even now is the kingdom of Christ, and the kingdom of heaven. Accordingly, even now His saints reign with Him, though otherwise than as they shall reign hereafter; and yet, though the tares grow in the Church along with the wheat, they do not reign with Him. For they reign with Him who do what the apostle says, "If ye be risen with Christ, mind the things which are above, where Christ sitteth at the right hand of God. Seek those things which are above, not the things which are on the earth." [46] Of such persons he also says that their conversation is in heaven.[47] In fine, they reign with Him who are so in His kingdom that they themselves are His kingdom. But in what sense are those the kingdom of Christ who, to say no more, though they are in it until all offenses are gathered out of it at the end of the world, yet seek their own things in it, and not the things that are Christ's? [48]

It is then of this kingdom militant, in which conflict with the enemy is still maintained, and war carried on with warring lusts, or government laid upon them as they yield, until we come to that most peaceful kingdom in which we shall reign without an enemy, and it is of this first resurrection in the present life, that the Apocalypse speaks in the words just quoted. For, after saying that the devil is bound a thousand years and is afterwards loosed for a short season, it goes on to give a sketch of what the Church does or of what is done in the Church in those days, in the words, "And I saw seats and them that sat upon them, and judgment was given." It is not to be supposed that this refers to the last judgment, but to the seats of the rulers and to the rulers themselves by whom the Church is now governed. And no better interpretation of judgment being given can be produced than that which we have in the words, "What ye bind on earth shall be bound in heaven; and what ye loose on earth shall be loosed in heaven." [49] Whence the apostle says, "What have I to do with judging them that are without?

44 Matt. xxiii. 3   45 Matt. v. 20   46 Col. iii. 1, 2   47 Phil. iii. 20   48 Phil. ii. 21
49 Matt. xviii. 18

do not ye judge them that are within?" [50] "And the souls," says John, "of those who were slain for the testimony of Jesus and for the word of God" —understanding what he afterwards says, "reigned with Christ a thousand years" [51]—that is, the souls of the martyrs not yet restored to their bodies. For the souls of the pious dead are not separated from the Church, which even now is the kingdom of Christ; otherwise there would be no remembrance made of them at the altar of God in the partaking of the body of Christ, nor would it do any good in danger to run to His baptism, that we might not pass from this life without it; nor to reconciliation, if by penitence or a bad conscience any one may be severed from His body. For why are these things practised, if not because the faithful, even though dead, are His members? Therefore, while these thousand years run on, their souls reign with Him, though not as yet in conjunction with their bodies. And therefore in another part of this same book we read, "Blessed are the dead who die in the Lord from henceforth: and now, saith the Spirit, that they may rest from their labors; for their works do follow them." [52] The Church, then, begins its reign with Christ now in the living and in the dead. For, as the apostle says, "Christ died that He might be Lord both of the living and of the dead." [53] But he mentioned the souls of the martyrs only, because they who have contended even to death for the truth, themselves principally reign after death; but, taking the part for the whole, we understand the words of all others who belong to the Church, which is the kingdom of Christ.

As to the words following, "And if any have not worshipped the beast nor his image, nor have received his inscription on their forehead, or on their hand," we must take them of both the living and the dead. And what this beast is, though it requires a more careful investigation, yet it is not inconsistent with the true faith to understand it of the ungodly city itself, and the community of unbelievers set in opposition to the faithful people and the city of God. "His image" seems to me to mean his simulation, to wit, in those men who profess to believe, but live as unbelievers. For they pretend to be what they are not, and are called Christians, not from a true likeness, but from a deceitful image. For to this beast belong not only the avowed enemies of the name of Christ and His most glorious city, but also the tares which are to be gathered out of His kingdom, the Church, in the end of the world. And who are they who do not worship the beast and his image, if not those who do what the apostle says, "Be not yoked with unbelievers?" [54] For such do not worship, *i.e.*, do not consent, are not subjected; neither do they receive the inscription, the brand of crime, on their forehead by their profession, on their hand by their practice. They, then, who are free from these pollutions, whether they still live in this mortal flesh, or are dead, reign with Christ even now, through this whole interval which is indicated by the thousand years, in a fashion suited to this time.

[50] I Cor. v. 12   [51] Rev. xx. 4   [52] Rev. xiv. 13   [53] Rom. xiv. 9   [54] 2 Cor. vi. 14

"The rest of them" he says, "did not live." For now is the hour when the dead shall hear the voice of the Son of God, and they that hear shall live; and the rest of them shall not live. The words added, "until the thousand years are finished," mean that they did not live in the time in which they ought to have lived by passing from death to life. And therefore, when the day of the bodily resurrection arrives, they shall come out of their graves, not to life, but to judgment, namely, to damnation, which is called the second death. For whosoever has not lived until the thousand years be finished, *i.e.*, during this whole time in which the first resurrection is going on—whosoever has not heard the voice of the Son of God, and passed from death to life—that man shall certainly in the second resurrection, the resurrection of the flesh, pass with his flesh into the second death. For he goes on to say, "This is the first resurrection. Blessed and holy is he that hath part in the first resurrection," or who experiences it. Now he experiences it who not only revives from the death of sin, but continues in this renewed life. "In these the second death hath no power." Therefore it has power in the rest, of whom he said above, "The rest of them did not live until the thousand years were finished;" for in this whole intervening time called a thousand years, however lustily they lived in the body, they were not quickened to life out of that death in which their wickedness held them, so that by this revived life they should become partakers of the first resurrection, and so the second death should have no power over them.

CHAPTER X

WHAT IS TO BE REPLIED TO THOSE WHO THINK THAT RESURRECTION PERTAINS ONLY TO BODIES AND NOT TO SOULS

There are some who suppose that resurrection can be predicated only of the body, and therefore they contend that this first resurrection (of the Apocalypse) is a bodily resurrection. For, they say, "to rise again" can only be said of things that fall. Now, bodies fall in death, for they are called "corpses," *cadavera*, from *cadere*, "to fall." There cannot, therefore, be a resurrection of souls, but of bodies. But what do they say to the apostle who speaks of a resurrection of souls? For certainly it was in the inner and not the outer man that those had risen again to whom he says, "If ye have risen with Christ, mind the things that are above." [55] The same sense he elsewhere conveyed in other words, saying, "That as Christ has risen from the dead by the glory of the Father, so we also may walk in newness of life." [56] So, too, "Awake thou that sleepest, and arise from the dead, and Christ shall give thee light." [57] As to what they say about nothing being able to rise again but what falls, whence they conclude that resurrection pertains to bodies only, and not to souls, because bodies fall, why do they

[55] Col. iii. 1   [56] Rom. vi. 4   [57] Eph. v. 14

make nothing of the words, "Ye that fear the Lord, wait for his mercy; and go not aside lest ye fall;" [58] and "To his own Master he stands or falls;" [59] and "He that thinketh he standeth, let him take heed lest he fall?" [60] For I fancy this fall that we are to take heed against is a fall of the soul, not of the body. If, then, rising again belongs to things that fall, and souls fall, it must be owned that souls also rise again. To the words, "In them the second death hath no power," are added the words, "But they shall be priests of God and Christ, and shall reign with Him a thousand years;" and this refers not to the bishops alone, and presbyters, who are now specially called priests in the Church; but as we call all believers Christians on account of the mystical chrism, so we call all priests because they are members of the one Priest. Of them the Apostle Peter says, "A holy people, a royal priesthood." [61] Certainly he implied, though in a passing and incidental way, that Christ is God, saying priests of God and Christ, that is, of the Father and the Son, though it was in His servant-form and as Son of man that Christ was made a Priest for ever after the order of Melchisedec. But this we have already explained more than once.

CHAPTER XI

OF GOG AND MAGOG, WHO ARE TO BE ROUSED BY THE DEVIL TO PERSECUTE THE CHURCH, WHEN HE IS LOOSED IN THE END OF THE WORLD

"And when the thousand years are finished, Satan shall be loosed from his prison, and shall go out to seduce the nations which are in the four corners of the earth, Gog and Magog, and shall draw them to battle, whose number is as the sand of the sea." This, then, is his purpose in seducing them, to draw them to this battle. For even before this he was wont to use as many and various seductions as he could continue. And the words "he shall go out" mean, he shall burst forth from lurking hatred into open persecution. For this persecution, occurring while the final judgment is imminent, shall be the last which shall be endured by the holy Church throughout the world, the whole city of Christ being assailed by the whole city of the devil, as each exists on earth. For these nations which he names Gog and Magog are not to be understood of some barbarous nations in some part of the world, whether the Getae and Massagatae, as some conclude from the initial letters, or some other foreign nations not under the Roman government. For John marks that they are spread over the whole earth, when he says, "The nations which are in the four corners of the earth," and he added that these are Gog and Magog. The meaning of these names we find to be, Gog, "a roof," Magog, "from a roof"—a house, as it were, and he who comes out of the house. They are therefore the nations in which we found that the devil was shut up as in an abyss, and the devil himself coming out from them and

[58] Ecclus. ii. 7   [59] Rom. xiv. 4   [60] 1 Cor. x. 12   [61] 1 Peter ii. 9

going forth, so that they are the roof, he from the roof. Or if we refer both words to the nations, not one to them and one to the devil, then they are both the roof, because in them the old enemy is at present shut up, and as it were roofed in; and they shall be from the roof when they break forth from concealed to open hatred. The words, "And they went up on the breadth of the earth, and encompassed the camp of the saints and the beloved city," do not mean that they have come, or shall come, to one place, as if the camp of the saints and the beloved city should be in some one place; for this camp is nothing else than the Church of Christ extending over the whole world. And consequently wherever the Church shall be—and it shall be in all nations, as is signified by "the breadth of the earth"— there also shall be the camp of the saints and the beloved city, and there it shall be encompassed by the savage persecution of all its enemies; for they too shall exist along with it in all nations—that is, it shall be straitened, and hard pressed, and shut up in the straits of tribulation, but shall not desert its military duty, which is signified by the word "camp."

CHAPTER XII

WHETHER THE FIRE THAT CAME DOWN OUT OF HEAVEN AND DEVOURED THEM REFERS TO THE LAST PUNISHMENT OF THE WICKED

The words, "And fire came down out of heaven and devoured them," are not to be understood of the final punishment which shall be inflicted when it is said, "Depart from me, ye cursed, into everlasting fire;" [62] for then they shall be cast into the fire, not fire come down out of heaven upon them. In this place "fire out of heaven" is well understood of the firmness of the saints, wherewith they refuse to yield obedience to those who rage against them. For the firmament is "heaven," by whose firmness these assailants shall be pained with blazing zeal, for they shall be impotent to draw away the saints to the party of Antichrist. This is the fire which shall devour them, and this is "from God;" for it is by God's grace the saints become unconquerable, and so torment their enemies. For as in a good sense it is said, "The zeal of Thine house hath consumed me," [63] so in a bad sense it is said, "Zeal hath possessed the uninstructed people, and now fire shall consume the enemies." [64] "And now," that is to say, not the fire of the last judgment. Or if by this fire coming down out of heaven and consuming them, John meant that blow wherewith Christ in His coming is to strike those persecutors of the Church whom He shall then find alive upon earth, when He shall kill Antichrist with the breath of His mouth,[65] then even this is not the last judgment of the wicked; but the last judgment is that which they shall suffer when the bodily resurrection has taken place.

[62] Matt. xxv. 41   [63] Ps. lxix. 9   [64] Isa. xxvi. 11   [65] 2 Thess. ii. 8

CHAPTER XIII

WHETHER THE TIME OF THE PERSECUTION OF ANTICHRIST SHOULD BE RECKONED IN THE THOUSAND YEARS

This last persecution by Antichrist shall last for three years and six months, as we have already said, and as is affirmed both in the book of *Revelation* and by Daniel the prophet. Though this time is brief, yet not without reason is it questioned whether it is comprehended in the thousand years in which the devil is bound and the saints reign with Christ, or whether this little season should be added over and above to these years. For if we say that they are included in the thousand years, then the saints reign with Christ during a more protracted period than the devil is bound. For they shall reign with their King and Conqueror mightily even in that crowning persecution when the devil shall now be unbound and shall rage against them with all his might. How then does Scripture define both the binding of the devil and the reign of the saints by the same thousand years, if the binding of the devil ceases three years and six months before this reign of the saints with Christ? On the other hand, if we say that the brief space of this persecution is not to be reckoned as a part of the thousand years, but rather as an additional period, we shall indeed be able to interpret the words, "The priests of God and of Christ shall reign with Him a thousand years; and when the thousand years shall be finished, Satan shall be loosed out of his prison;" for thus they signify that the reign of the saints and the bondage of the devil shall cease simultaneously, so that the time of the persecution we speak of should be contemporaneous neither with the reign of the saints nor with the imprisonment of Satan, but should be reckoned over and above as a superadded portion of time. But then in this case we are forced to admit that the saints shall not reign with Christ during that persecution. But who can dare to say that His members shall not reign with Him at that very juncture when they shall most of all, and with the greatest fortitude, cleave to Him, and when the glory of resistance and the crown of martyrdom shall be more conspicuous in proportion to the hotness of the battle? Or if it is suggested that they may be said not to reign, because of the tribulations which they shall suffer, it will follow that all the saints who have formerly, during the thousand years, suffered tribulation, shall not be said to have reigned with Christ during the period of their tribulation, and consequently even those whose souls the author of this book says that he saw, and who were slain for the testimony of Jesus and the word of God, did not reign with Christ when they were suffering persecution, and they were not themselves the kingdom of Christ, though Christ was then pre-eminently possessing them. This is indeed perfectly absurd, and to be scouted. But assuredly the victorious souls of the glorious martyrs having overcome and finished all griefs and toils, and having laid down their mortal members, have reigned and do reign with Christ till the thousand years are finished, that they may afterwards reign with Him when they have received their immortal bodies. And therefore during these three years and a half the souls of those who were slain for His testimony, both those which formerly passed from the body and those which shall pass in that last persecution, shall reign with Him till the mortal world come to an end, and pass into that kingdom in which there shall be no death. And thus the reign of the saints with Christ shall last longer than the bonds and imprisonment of the devil, because they shall reign with their King the Son of God for these three years and a half during which the devil is no longer bound. It remains, therefore, that when we read that "the priests of God and of Christ shall reign with Him a thousand years; and when the thousand years are finished, the devil shall be loosed from his imprisonment," that we understand either that the thousand years of the reign of the saints does not terminate, though the imprisonment of the devil does—so that both parties have their thousand years, that is, their complete time, yet each with a different actual duration appropriate to itself, the kingdom of the saints being longer, the imprisonment of the devil shorter—or at least that, as three years and six months is a very short time, it is not reckoned as either deducted from the whole time of Satan's imprisonment, or as added to the whole duration of the reign of the saints, as we have shown above in the sixteenth book[66] regarding the round number of four hundred years, which were specified as four hundred, though actually somewhat more; and similar expressions are often found in the sacred writings, if one will mark them.

CHAPTER XIV

OF THE DAMNATION OF THE DEVIL AND HIS ADHERENTS; AND A SKETCH OF THE BODILY RESURRECTION OF ALL THE DEAD, AND OF THE FINAL RETRIBUTIVE JUDGMENT

After this mention of the closing persecution, he summarily indicates all that the devil, and the city of which he is the prince, shall suffer in the last judgment. For he says, "And the devil who seduced them is cast into the lake of fire and brimstone, in which are the beast and the false prophet, and they shall be tormented day and night, for ever and ever." We have already said that by the beast is well understood the wicked city. His false prophet is either Antichrist or that image or figment of which we have spoken in the same place. After this he gives a brief narrative of the last judgment itself, which shall take place at the second or bodily resurrection of the dead, as it had been revealed to him: "I saw a throne great and white, and One sitting on it from whose face the heaven and the earth fled away, and their place was not found." He does not say, "I saw a throne great and white, and One sitting on it, and from His face the heaven and the earth fled

[66] Ch. 24

away," for it had not happened then, *i.e.,* before the living and the dead were judged; but he says that he saw Him sitting on the throne from whose face heaven and earth fled away, but afterwards. For when the judgment is finished, this heaven and earth shall cease to be, and there will be a new heaven and a new earth. For this world shall pass away by transmutation, not by absolute destruction. And therefore the apostle says, "For the figure of this world passeth away. I would have you be without anxiety." [67] The figure, therefore, passes away, not the nature. After John had said that he had seen One sitting on the throne from whose face heaven and earth fled, though not till afterwards, he said, "And I saw the dead, great and small: and the books were opened; and another book was opened, which is the book of the life of each man: and the dead were judged out of those things which were written in the books, according to their deeds." He said that the books were opened, and a book; but he left us at a loss as to the nature of this book, "which is," he says, "the book of the life of each man." By those books, then, which he first mentioned, we are to understand the sacred books old and new, that out of them it might be shown what commandments God had enjoined; and that book of the life of each man is to show what commandments each man has done or omitted to do. If this book be materially considered, who can reckon its size or length, or the time it would take to read a book in which the whole life of every man is recorded? Shall there be present as many angels as men, and shall each man hear his life recited by the angel assigned to him? In that case there will be not one book containing all the lives, but a separate book for every life. But our passage requires us to think of one only. "And another book was opened," it says. We must therefore understand it of a certain divine power, by which it shall be brought about that every one shall recall to memory all his own works, whether good or evil, and shall mentally survey them with a marvellous rapidity, so that this knowledge will either accuse or excuse conscience, and thus all and each shall be simultaneously judged. And this divine power is called a book, because in it we shall as it were read all that it causes us to remember. That he may show who the dead, small and great, are who are to be judged, he recurs to this which he had omitted or rather deferred, and says, "And the sea presented the dead which were in it; and death and hell gave up the dead which were in them." This of course took place before the dead were judged, yet it is mentioned after. And so, I say, he returns again to what he had omitted. But now he preserves the order of events, and for the sake of exhibiting it repeats in its own proper place what he had already said regarding the dead who were judged. For after he had said, "And the sea presented the dead which were in it, and death and hell gave up the dead which were in them," he immediately subjoined what he had already said, "and they were judged every man according to their works."

[67] 1 Cor. vii. 31, 32

For this is just what he had said before, "And the dead were judged according to their works."

CHAPTER XV

WHO THE DEAD ARE WHO ARE GIVEN UP TO JUDGMENT
BY THE SEA, AND BY DEATH AND HELL

But who are the dead which were in the sea, and which the sea presented? For we cannot suppose that those who die in the sea are not in hell, nor that their bodies are preserved in the sea; nor yet, which is still more absurd, that the sea retained the good, while hell received the bad. Who could believe this? But some very sensibly suppose that in this place the sea is put for this world. When John then wished to signify that those whom Christ should find still alive in the body were to be judged along with those who should rise again, he called them dead, both the good to whom it is said, "For ye are dead, and your life is hid with Christ in God," [68] and the wicked of whom it is said, "Let the dead bury their dead." [69] They may also be called dead, because they wear mortal bodies, as the apostle says, "The body indeed is dead because of sin; but the spirit is life because of righteousness;" [70] proving that in a living man in the body there is both a body which is dead, and a spirit which is life. Yet he did not say that the body was mortal, but dead, although immediately after he speaks in the more usual way of mortal bodies. These, then, are the dead which were in the sea, and which the sea presented, to wit, the men who were in this world, because they had not yet died, and whom the world presented for judgment. "And death and hell," he says, "gave up the dead which were in them." The sea *presented* them because they had merely to be found in the place where they were; but death and hell *gave them up* or *restored* them, because they called them back to life, which they had already quitted. And perhaps it was not without reason that neither *death* nor *hell* were judged sufficient alone, and both were mentioned—death to indicate the good, who have suffered only death and not hell; hell to indicate the wicked, who suffer also the punishment of hell. For if it does not seem absurd to believe that the ancient saints who believed in Christ and His then future coming, were kept in places far removed indeed from the torments of the wicked, but yet in hell,[71] until Christ's blood and His descent into these places delivered them, certainly good Christians, redeemed by that precious price already paid, are quite unacquainted with hell while they wait for their restoration to the body, and the reception of their reward. After saying, "They were judged every man according to their works," he briefly added what the judgment was: "Death and hell were

[68] Col. iii. 3   [69] Matt. viii. 22   [70] Rom. viii. 10
[71] "Apud inferos," *i.e.* in hell, in the sense in which the word is used in the Psalms and in the Creed

cast into the lake of fire;" by these names designating the devil and the whole company of his angels, for he is the author of death and the pains of hell. For this is what he had already, by anticipation, said in clearer language: "The devil who seduced them was cast into a lake of fire and brimstone." The obscure addition he had made in the words, "in which were also the beast and the false prophet," he here explains, "They who were not ... the book of life were cast into the lake of fire." This book is not for reminding God, as if things might escape Him by forgetfulness, but it symbolizes His predestination of those to whom eternal life shall be given. For it is not that God is ignorant, and reads in the book to inform Himself, but rather His infallible prescience is the book of life in which they are written, that is to say, known beforehand.

CHAPTER XVI

OF THE NEW HEAVEN AND THE NEW EARTH

Having finished the prophecy of judgment, so far as the wicked are concerned, it remains that he speak also of the good. Having briefly explained the Lord's words, "These will go away into everlasting punishment," it remains that he explain the connected words, "but the righteous into life eternal." [72] "And I saw," he says, "a new heaven and a new earth: for the first heaven and the first earth have passed away; and there is no more sea." [73] This will take place in the order which he has by anticipation declared in the words, "I saw One sitting on the throne, from whose face heaven and earth fled." For as soon as those who are not written in the book of life have been judged and cast into eternal fire—the nature of which fire, or its position in the world or universe, I suppose is known to no man, unless perhaps the divine Spirit reveal it to some one—then shall the figure of this world pass away in a conflagration of universal fire, as once before the world was flooded with a deluge of universal water. And by this universal conflagration the qualities of the corruptible elements which suited our corruptible bodies shall utterly perish, and our substance shall receive such qualities as shall, by a wonderful transmutation, harmonize with our immortal bodies, so that, as the world itself is renewed to some better thing, it is fitly accommodated to men, themselves renewed in their flesh to some better thing. As for the statement, "And there shall be no more sea," I would not lightly say whether it is dried up with that excessive heat, or is itself also turned into some better thing. For we read that there shall be a new heaven and a new earth, but I do not remember to have anywhere read anything of a new sea, unless what I find in this same book, "As it were a sea of glass like crystal." [74] But he was not then speaking of this end of the world, neither does he seem to speak of a literal sea, but "as it were a

---

[72] Matt. xxv. 46   [73] Rev. xxi. 1   [74] Rev. xv. 2

sea." It is possible that, as prophetic diction delights in mingling figurative and real language, and thus in some sort veiling the sense, so the words "And there is no more sea" may be taken in the same sense as the previous phrase, "And the sea presented the dead which were in it." For then there shall be no more of this world, no more of the surgings and restlessness of human life, and it is this which is symbolized by the *sea*.

CHAPTER XVII

OF THE ENDLESS GLORY OF THE CHURCH

"And I saw," he says, "a great city, new Jerusalem, coming down from God out of heaven, prepared as a bride adorned for her husband. And I heard a great voice from the throne, saying, Behold, the tabernacle of God is with men, and He will dwell with them, and they shall be His people, and God Himself shall be with them. And God shall wipe away all tears from their eyes; and there shall be no more death, neither sorrow, nor crying, but neither shall there be any more pain: because the former things have passed away. And He that sat upon the throne said, Behold, I make all things new." [75] This city is said to come down out of heaven, because the grace with which God formed it is of heaven. Wherefore He says to it by Isaiah, "I am the Lord that formed thee." [76] It is indeed descended from heaven from its commencement, since its citizens during the course of this world grow by the grace of God, which cometh down from above through the laver of regeneration in the Holy Ghost sent down from heaven. But by God's final judgment, which shall be administered by His Son Jesus Christ, there shall by God's grace be manifested a glory so pervading and so new, that no vestige of what is old shall remain; for even our bodies shall pass from their old corruption and mortality to new incorruption and immortality. For to refer this promise to the present time, in which saints are reigning with their King a thousand years, seems to me excessively barefaced, when it is most distinctly said, "God shall wipe away all tears from their eyes; and there shall be no more death, neither sorrow, nor crying, but there shall be no more pain." And who is so absurd, and blinded by contentious opinionativeness, as to be audacious enough to affirm that in the midst of the calamities of this mortal state, God's people, or even one single saint, does live, or has ever lived, or shall ever live, without tears or pain—the fact being that the holier a man is, and the fuller of holy desire, so much the more abundant is the tearfulness of his supplication? Are not these the utterances of a citizen of the heavenly Jerusalem: "My tears have been my meat day and night;" [77] and "Every night shall I make my bed to swim; with my tears shall I water my couch;[78] and "My groaning is not hid from Thee;" [79] and "My sorrow was renewed?" [80] Or are

[75] Rev. xxi. 2-5   [76] Isa. xlv. 8   [77] Ps. xlii. 3   [78] Ps. vi. 6   [79] Ps. xxxviii. 9
[80] Ps. xxxix. 2

not those God's children who groan, being burdened, not that they wish to be unclothed, but clothed upon, that mortality may be swallowed up of life? [81] Do not they even who have the first-fruits of the Spirit groan within themselves, waiting for the adoption, the redemption of their body? [82] Was not the Apostle Paul himself a citizen of the heavenly Jerusalem, and was he not so all the more when he had heaviness and continual sorrow of heart for his Israelitish brethren? [83] But when shall there be no more death in that city, except when it shall be said, "O death, where is thy contention? [84] O death, where is thy sting? The sting of death is sin." [85] Obviously there shall be no sin when it can be said, "Where is"— But as for the present it is not some poor weak citizen of this city, but this same Apostle John himself who says, "If we say that we have no sin, we deceive ourselves, and the truth is not in us." [86] No doubt, though this book is called the Apocalypse, there are in it many obscure passages to exercise the mind of the reader, and there are few passages so plain as to assist us in the interpretation of the others, even though we take pains; and this difficulty is increased by the repetition of the same things, in forms so different, that the things referred to seem to be different, although in fact they are only differently stated. But in the words, "God shall wipe away all tears from their eyes; and there shall be no more death, neither sorrow, nor crying, but there shall be no more pain," there is so manifest a reference to the future world and the immortality and eternity of the saints—for only then and only there shall such a condition be realized—that if we think this obscure, we need not expect to find anything plain in any part of Scripture.

CHAPTER XVIII

WHAT THE APOSTLE PETER PREDICTED REGARDING THE LAST JUDGMENT

Let us now see what the Apostle Peter predicted concerning this judgment. "There shall come," he says, "in the last days scoffers, walking after their own lusts, and saying, Where is the promise of his coming? for since the fathers fell asleep, all things continue as they were from the beginnings of the creation.

For this they willingly are ignorant of, that by the word of God the heavens were of old, and the earth standing out of the water and in the water: whereby the world that then was, being overflowed with water, perished: but the heavens and the earth, which are now, by the same word are kept in store, reserved unto fire against the day of judgment and perdition of ungodly men. But, beloved, be not ignorant of this one thing, that

---

[81] 2 Cor. v. 4   [82] Rom. viii. 23   [83] Rom. ix. 2
[84] Augustine, therefore read νεῖκος, and not with the Vulgate νίκη. The correct reading is τὸ νῖκος, later form for νίκη, *victory*   [85] I Cor. xv. 55   [86] I John i. 8

one day is with the Lord as a thousand years, and a thousand years as one day. The Lord is not slack concerning his promise, as some men count slackness; but is longsuffering to usward, not willing that any should perish, but that all should come to repentance.

But the day of the Lord will come as a thief in the night; in the which the heavens shall pass away with a great noise, and the elements shall melt with fervent heat, the earth also and the works that are therein shall be burned up. Seeing then that all these things shall be dissolved, what manner of persons ought ye to be in all holy conversation and godliness, Looking for and hasting unto the coming of the day of God, wherein the heavens being on fire shall be dissolved, and the elements shall melt with fervent heat? Nevertheless, we, according to his promise, look for new heavens and a new earth, wherein dwelleth righteousness." [87] There is nothing said here about the resurrection of the dead, but enough certainly regarding the destruction of this world. And by his reference to the deluge he seems as it were to suggest to us how far we should believe the ruin of the world will extend in the end of the world. For he says that the world which then was perished, and not only the earth itself, but also the heavens, by which we understand the air, the place and room of which was occupied by the water. Therefore the whole, or almost the whole, of the gusty atmosphere (which he calls heaven, or rather the heavens, meaning the earth's atmosphere, and not the upper air in which sun, moon, and stars are set) was turned into moisture, and in this way perished together with the earth, whose former appearance had been destroyed by the deluge. "But the heavens and the earth which are now, by the same word are kept in store, reserved unto fire against the day of judgment and perdition of ungodly men." Therefore the heavens and the earth, or the world which was preserved from the water to stand in place of that world which perished in the flood, is itself reserved to fire at last in the day of the judgment and perdition of ungodly men. He does not hesitate to affirm that in this great change men also shall perish: their nature, however, shall notwithstanding continue, though in eternal punishments. Some one will perhaps put the question, If after judgment is pronounced the world itself is to burn, where shall the saints be during the conflagration, and before it is replaced by a new heavens and a new earth, since somewhere they must be, because they have material bodies? We may reply that they shall be in the upper regions into which the flame of that conflagration shall not ascend, as neither did the water of the flood; for they shall have such bodies that they shall be wherever they wish. Moreover, when they have become immortal and incorruptible, they shall not greatly dread the blaze of that conflagration, as the corruptible and mortal bodies of the three men were able to live unhurt in the blazing furnace.

[87] 2 Pet. iii. 3-13

CHAPTER XIX

WHAT THE APOSTLE PAUL WROTE TO THE THESSALONIANS ABOUT THE MANIFESTATION OF ANTICHRIST WHICH SHALL PRECEDE THE DAY OF THE LORD

I see that I must omit many of the statements of the gospels and epistles about this last judgment, that this volume may not become unduly long; but I can on no account omit what the Apostle Paul says, in writing to the Thessalonians, "Now we beseech you, brethren, by the coming of our Lord Jesus Christ, and by our gathering together unto him. That ye be not soon shaken in mind, or be troubled, neither by spirit, nor by word, nor by letter as from us, as that the day of Christ is at hand. Let no man deceive you by any means: for that day shall not come, except there come a falling away first, and that man of sin be revealed the son of perdition; who opposeth and exalteth himself above all that is called God, or that is worshipped; so that he as God sitteth in the temple of God, shewing himself that he is God.

Remember ye not, that, when I was yet with you, I told you these things? And now ye know what withholdeth that he might be revealed in his time. For the mystery of iniquity does already work: only he who now letteth will let, until he be taken out of the way. And then shall that Wicked be revealed, whom the Lord shall consume with the spirit of his mouth, and shall destroy with the brightness of his coming: even him, whose coming is after the working of Satan with all power and signs and lying wonders, and with all deceivableness of unrighteousness in them that perish; because they received not the love of the truth, that they might be saved. And for this cause God shall send them strong delusion, that they should believe a lie.[88]

No one can doubt that he wrote this of Antichrist and of the day of judgment, which he here calls the day of the Lord, nor that he declared that this day should not come unless he first came who is called the apostate —apostate, to wit, from the Lord God. And if this may justly be said of all the ungodly, how much more of him? But it is uncertain in what temple he shall sit, whether in that ruin of the temple which was built by Solomon, or in the Church; for the apostle would not call the temple of any idol or demon the temple of God. And on this account some think that in this passage Antichrist means not the prince himself alone, but his whole body, that is, the mass of men who adhere to him, along with him their prince; and they also think that we should render the Greek more exactly were we to read, not "in the temple of God," but "for" or "as the temple of God," as if he himself were the temple of God, the Church; just as we say, "he

---

[88] 2 Thess. ii. 1-11

sits 'in a friend,' " that is, "as a friend," or anything similar which is customarily used in this type of discourse. Then as for the words, "And now ye know what withholdeth," *i.e.*, ye know what hindrance or cause of delay there is, "that he might be revealed in his own time;" they show that he was unwilling to make an explicit statement, because he said that they knew. And thus we who have not their knowledge wish and are not able even with pains to understand what the apostle referred to, especially as his meaning is made still more obscure by what he adds. For what does he mean by "For the mystery of iniquity doth already work: only he who now holdeth, let him hold until he be taken out of the way: and then shall the wicked be revealed?" I frankly confess I do not know what he means. I will nevertheless mention such conjectures as I have heard or read.

Some think that the Apostle Paul referred to the Roman empire, and that he was unwilling to use language more explicit, lest he should incur the calumnious charge of wishing ill to the empire which it was hoped would be eternal; so that in saying, "For the mystery of iniquity doth already work," he alluded to Nero, whose deeds already seemed to be as the deeds of Antichrist. And hence some suppose that he shall rise again and be Antichrist. Others, again, suppose that he is not even dead, but that he was concealed that he might be supposed to have been killed, and that he now lives in concealment in the vigor of that same age which he had reached when he was believed to have perished, and will live until he is revealed in his own time and restored to his kingdom.[89] But I wonder that men can be so audacious in their conjectures. However, it is not absurd to believe that these words of the apostle, "Only he who now holdeth, let him hold until he be taken out of the way," refer to the Roman empire, as if it were said, "Only he who now reigneth, let him reign until he be taken out of the way." "And then shall the wicked be revealed:" no one doubts that this means Antichrist. But others think that the words, "Ye know what withholdeth," and "The mystery of iniquity worketh," refer only to the wicked and the hypocrites who are in the Church, until they reach a number so great as to furnish Antichrist with a great people, and that this is the *mystery* of iniquity, because it seems hidden; also that the apostle is exhorting the faithful tenaciously to hold the faith they hold when he says, "Only he who now holdeth, let him hold until he be taken out of the way," that is, until the mystery of iniquity which now is hidden departs from the Church. For they suppose that it is to this same mystery John alludes when in his epistle he says, "Little children, it is the last time: and as ye have heard that Antichrist shall come, even now are there many antichrists; whereby we know that it is the last time. They went out from us, but they were not of us; for if they had been of us, they would no doubt have continued with us." [90] As therefore there went out from the Church many heretics, whom John calls "many antichrists," at that time prior to the

[89] Suetonius, *Nero*, c. 57   [90] 1 John ii. 18, 19

end, and which John calls "the last time," so in the end they shall go out who do not belong to Christ, but to that last Antichrist, and then he shall be revealed.

Thus various, then, are the conjectural explanations of the obscure words of the apostle. That which there is no doubt he said is this, that Christ will not come to judge quick and dead unless Antichrist, His adversary, first come to seduce those who are dead in soul; although their seduction is a result of God's secret judgment already passed. For, as it is said "his presence shall be after the working of Satan, with all power, and signs, and lying wonders, and with all seduction of unrighteousness in them that perish." For then shall Satan be loosed, and by means of that Antichrist shall work with all power in a lying though a wonderful manner. It is commonly questioned whether these works are called "signs and lying wonders" because he is to deceive men's senses by false appearances, or because the things he does, though they be true prodigies, shall be a lie to those who shall believe that such things could be done only by God, being ignorant of the devil's power, and especially of such unexampled power as he shall then for the first time put forth. For when he fell from heaven as fire, and at a stroke swept away from the holy Job his numerous household and his vast flocks, and then as a whirlwind rushed upon and smote the house and killed his children, these were not deceitful appearances, and yet they were the works of Satan to whom God had given this power. Why they are called signs and lying wonders, we shall then be more likely to know when the time itself arrives. But whatever be the reason of the name, they shall be such signs and wonders as shall seduce those who shall deserve to be seduced, "because they received not the love of the truth that they might be saved." Neither did the apostle scruple to go on to say, "For this cause God shall send upon them the working of error that they should believe a lie." For God shall *send,* because God shall permit the devil to do these things, the permission being by His own just judgment, though the doing of them is in pursuance of the devil's unrighteous and malignant purpose, "that they all might be judged who believed not the truth, but had pleasure in unrighteousness." Therefore, being judged, they shall be seduced, and, being seduced, they shall be judged. But, being judged, they shall be seduced by those secretly just and justly secret judgments of God, with which He has never ceased to judge since the first sin of the rational creatures; and, being seduced, they shall be judged in that last and manifest judgment administered by Jesus Christ, who was Himself most unjustly judged and shall most justly judge.

CHAPTER XX

But the apostle has said nothing here regarding the resurrection of the dead; but in his first *Epistle to the Thessalonians* he says, "But I would not have you to be ignorant, brethren, concerning them which are asleep, that ye sorrow not, even as others which have no hope. For if we believe that Jesus died and rose again, even so them also which sleep in Jesus will God bring with him.

For this we say unto you by the word of the Lord, that we which are alive and remain unto the coming of the Lord shall not prevent them which are asleep. For the Lord himself shall descend from heaven with a shout, with the voice of the archangel, and with the trump of God; and the dead in Christ shall rise first." [91] These words of the apostle most distinctly proclaim the future resurrection of the dead, when the Lord Christ shall come to judge the quick and the dead.

But it is commonly asked whether those whom our Lord shall find alive upon earth, personated in this passage by the apostle and those who were alive with him, shall never die at all, or shall pass with incomprehensible swiftness through death to immortality in the very moment during which they shall be caught up along with those who rise again to meet the Lord in the air? For we cannot say that it is impossible that they should both die and revive again while they are carried aloft through the air. For the words, "And so shall we ever be with the Lord," are not to be understood as if he meant that we shall always remain in the air with the Lord; for He Himself shall not remain there, but shall only pass through it as He comes. For we shall go to meet Him as He comes, not where He remains; but "so shall we be with the Lord," that is, we shall be with Him possessed of immortal bodies wherever we shall be with Him. We seem compelled to take the words in this sense, and to suppose that those whom the Lord shall find alive upon earth shall in that brief space both suffer death and receive immortality; for this same apostle says, "In Christ shall all be made alive;" [92] while, speaking of the same resurrection of the body, he elsewhere says, "That which thou sowest is not quickened, except it die." [93] How, then, shall those whom Christ shall find alive upon earth be made alive to immortality in Him if they die not, since on this very account it is said, "That which thou sowest is not quickened, except it die?" Or if we cannot properly speak of human bodies as sown, unless in so far as by dying they do in some sort return to the earth, as also the sentence pronounced by God against the sinning father of the human race runs, "Earth

[91] 1 Thess. iv. 13-16   [92] 1 Cor. xv. 22   [93] 1 Cor. xv. 36

thou art, and unto earth shalt thou return," [94] we must acknowledge that those whom Christ at His coming shall find still in the body are not included in these words of the apostle nor in those of *Genesis;* for, being caught up into the clouds, they are certainly not sown, neither going nor returning to the earth, whether they experience no death at all or die for a moment in the air.

But, on the other hand, there meets us the saying of the same apostle when he was speaking to the Corinthians about the resurrection of the body, "We shall all rise," or as other MSS. read, "We shall all sleep." [95] Since, then, there can be no resurrection unless death has preceded, and since we can in this passage understand by sleep nothing else than death, how shall *all* either sleep or rise again if so many persons whom Christ shall find in the body shall neither sleep nor rise again? If, then, we believe that the saints who shall be found alive at Christ's coming, and shall be caught up to meet Him, shall in that same ascent pass from mortal to immortal bodies, we shall find no difficulty in the words of the apostle, either when he says, "That which thou sowest is not quickened, except it die," or when he says, "We shall all rise," or "all sleep," for not even the saints shall be quickened to immortality unless they first die, however briefly; and consequently they shall not be exempt from resurrection which is preceded by sleep, however brief. And why should it seem to us incredible that that multitude of bodies should be, as it were, sown in the air, and should in the air forthwith revive immortal and incorruptible, when we believe, on the testimony of the same apostle, that the resurrection shall take place in the twinkling of an eye, and that the dust of bodies long dead shall return with incomprehensible facility and swiftness to those members that are now to live endlessly? Neither do we suppose that in the case of these saints the sentence, "Earth thou art, and unto earth shalt thou return," is null, though their bodies do not, on dying, fall to earth, but both die and rise again at once while caught up into the air. For "Thou shalt return to earth" means, Thou shalt at death return to that which thou wert before life began. Thou shalt, when deprived of life, be that which thou wert before thou wast animate. For it was into a face of earth that God breathed the breath of life when man was made a living soul; as if it were said, Thou art earth with a soul, which thou wast not; thou shalt be earth without a soul, as thou wast. And this is what all bodies of the dead are before they rot; and what the bodies of those saints shall be if they die, no matter where they die, as soon as they shall give up that life which they are immediately to receive back again. In this way, then, they return or go to earth, inasmuch as from being living men they shall be earth, as that which becomes cinder is said to go to cinder; that which decays, to go to decay; and so of six hundred other things. But the manner in which this shall take place we can now only feebly conjecture, and shall understand it only when it comes to pass. For that there shall be a bodily resurrection of the dead when Christ comes to judge quick and dead, we must believe if we would be Christians. But if we are unable perfectly to comprehend the manner in which it shall take place, our faith is not on this account vain. Now, however, we ought, as we formerly promised, to show, as far as seems necessary, what the ancient prophetic books predicted concerning this final judgment of God; and I fancy no great time need be spent in discussing and explaining these predictions, if the reader has been careful to avail himself of the help we have already furnished.

CHAPTER XXI

UTTERANCES OF THE PROPHET ISAIAH REGARDING THE RESURRECTION OF THE DEAD AND THE RETRIBUTIVE JUDGMENT

The prophet Isaiah says, "The dead shall rise again, and all who were in the graves shall rise again; and all who are in the earth shall rejoice: for the dew which is from Thee is their health, and the earth of the wicked shall fall." [96] All the former part of this passage relates to the resurrection of the blessed; but the words, "the earth of the wicked shall fall," is rightly understood as meaning that the bodies of the wicked shall fall into the ruin of damnation. And if we would more exactly and carefully scrutinize the words which refer to the resurrection of the good, we may refer to the first resurrection the words, "the dead shall rise again," and to the second the following words, "and all who were in the graves shall rise again." And if we ask what relates to those saints whom the Lord at His coming shall find alive upon earth, the following clause may suitably be referred to them; "All who are in the earth shall rejoice: for the dew which is from Thee is their health." By "health" in this place it is best to understand immortality. For that is the most perfect health which is not repaired by nourishment as by a daily remedy. In like manner the same prophet, affording hope to the good and terrifying the wicked regarding the day of judgment, says, "Thus saith the Lord, Behold, I will flow down upon them as a river of peace, and upon the glory of the Gentiles as a rushing torrent; their sons shall be carried on the shoulders, and shall be comforted on the knees. As one whom his mother comforteth, so shall I comfort you; and ye shall be comforted in Jerusalem. And ye shall see, and your heart shall rejoice, and your bones shall rise up like a herb; and the hand of the Lord shall be known by His worshippers, and He shall threaten the contumacious. For, behold, the Lord shall come as a fire, and as a whirlwind His chariots, to execute vengeance with indignation, and wasting with a flame of fire. For with fire of the Lord shall all the earth be judged, and all flesh with His sword: many shall be wounded by the Lord." [97] In His promise

[96] Isa. xxvi. 19   [97] Isa. lxvi. 12-16

to the good he says that He will flow down as a river of peace, that is to say, in the greatest possible abundance of peace. With this peace we shall in the end be refreshed; but of this we have spoken abundantly in the preceding book. It is this river in which he says He shall flow down upon those to whom He promises so great happiness, that we may understand that in the region of that felicity, which is in heaven, all things are satisfied from this river. But because there shall thence flow, even upon earthly bodies, the peace of incorruption and immortality, therefore he says that He shall flow down as this river, that He may as it were pour Himself from things above to things beneath, and make men the equals of the angels. By "Jerusalem," too, we should understand not that which serves with her children, but that which, according to the apostle, is our free mother, eternal in the heavens.[98] In her we shall be comforted as we pass toilworn from earth's cares and calamities, and be taken up as her children on her knees and shoulders. Inexperienced and new to such blandishments, we shall be received into unwonted bliss. There we shall see, and our heart shall rejoice. He does not say what we shall see; but what but God, that the promise in the Gospel may be fulfilled in us, "Blessed are the pure in heart, for they shall see God?"[99] What shall we see but all those things which now we see not, but believe in, and of which the idea we form, according to our feeble capacity, is incomparably less than the reality? "And ye shall see," he says, "and your heart shall rejoice." Here ye believe, there ye shall see.

But because he said, "Your heart shall rejoice," lest we should suppose that the blessings of that Jerusalem are only spiritual, he adds, "And your bones shall rise up like a herb," alluding to the resurrection of the body, and as it were supplying an omission he had made. For it will not take place when we have seen; but we shall see when it has taken place. For he had already spoken of the new heavens and the new earth, speaking repeatedly, and under many figures, of the things promised to the saints, and saying, "There shall be new heavens, and a new earth: and the former shall not be remembered nor come into mind; but they shall find in it gladness and exultation. Behold, I will make Jerusalem an exultation, and my people a joy. And I will exult in Jerusalem, and joy in my people; and the voice of weeping shall be no more heard in her;"[100] and other promises, which some endeavor to refer to carnal enjoyment during the thousand years. For, in the manner of prophecy, figurative and literal expressions are mingled, so that a serious mind may, by useful and salutary effort, reach the spiritual sense; but carnal sluggishness, or the slowness of an uneducated and undisciplined mind, rests in the superficial letter, and thinks there is nothing beneath to be looked for. But let this be enough regarding the style of those prophetic expressions just quoted. And now, to return to their interpretation. When he had said, "And your bones shall rise up

[98] Gal. iv. 26   [99] Matt. v. 8   [100] Isa. lxv. 17-19

like a herb," in order to show that it was the resurrection of the good, though a bodily resurrection, to which he alluded, he added, "And the hand of the Lord shall be known by His worshippers." What is this but the hand of Him who distinguishes those who worship from those who despise Him? Regarding these the context immediately adds, "And He shall threaten the contumacious," or, as another translator has it, "the unbelieving." He shall not actually threaten then, but the threats which are now uttered shall then be fulfilled in effect. "For behold," he says, "the Lord shall come as a fire, and as a whirlwind His chariots, to execute vengeance with indignation, and wasting with a flame of fire. For with fire of the Lord shall all the earth be judged, and all flesh with His sword: many shall be wounded by the Lord." By *fire, whirlwind, sword,* he means the judicial punishment of God. For he says that the Lord Himself shall come as a fire, to those, that is to say, to whom His coming shall be penal. By His *chariots* (for the word is plural) we suitably understand the ministration of angels. And when he says that all flesh and all the earth shall be judged with His fire and sword, we do not understand the spiritual and holy to be included, but the earthly and carnal, of whom it is said that they "mind earthly things," [101] and "to be carnally minded is death," [102] and whom the Lord calls simply flesh when He says, "My Spirit shall not always remain in these men, for they are flesh." [103] As to the words, "Many shall be wounded by the Lord," this wounding shall produce the second death. It is possible, indeed, to understand *fire, sword,* and *wound* in a good sense. For the Lord said, that He wished to send fire on the earth.[104] And the cloven tongues appeared to them as fire when the Holy Spirit came.[105] And our Lord says, "I am not come to send peace on earth, but a sword." [106] And Scripture says that the word of God is a doubly sharp sword,[107] on account of the two edges, the two Testaments. And in the *Song of Songs* the holy Church says that she is wounded with love[108]—pierced, as it were, with the arrow of love. But here, where we read or hear that the Lord shall come to execute vengeance, it is obvious in what sense we are to understand these expressions.

After briefly mentioning those who shall be consumed in this judgment, speaking of the wicked and sinners under the figure of the meats forbidden by the old law, from which they had not abstained, he summarily recounts the grace of the new testament, from the first coming of the Saviour to the last judgment, of which we now speak; and herewith he concludes his prophecy. For he relates that the Lord declares that He is coming to gather all nations, that they may come and witness His glory.[109] For, as the apostle says, "All have sinned and are in want of the glory of God." [110] And he says that He will do wonders among them, at which they shall mar-

---

[101] Phil. iii. 19   [102] Rom. viii. 6   [103] Gen. vi. 3   [104] Luke xii. 49   [105] Acts ii. 3
[106] Matt. x. 34   [107] Heb. iv. 12   [108] Song of Sol. ii. 5   [109] Isa. lxvi. 18   [110] Rom. iii. 23

vel and believe in Him; and that from them He will send forth those that
are saved into various nations, and distant islands which have not heard His
name nor seen His glory, and that they shall declare His glory among the
nations, and shall *bring* the brethren of those to whom the prophet was
speaking, *i.e.*, shall bring to the faith under God the Father the brethren
of the elect Israelites; and that they shall bring from all nations an offering
to the Lord on beasts of burden and waggons (which are understood to
mean the aids furnished by God in the shape of angelic or human ministry), to the holy city Jerusalem, which at present is scattered over the
earth, in the faithful saints. For where divine aid is given, men believe, and
where they believe, they come. And the Lord compared them, in a figure,
to the children of Israel offering sacrifice to Him in His house with psalms,
which is already everywhere done by the Church; and He promised that
from among them He would choose for Himself priests and Levites, which
also we see already accomplished. For we see that priests and Levites are
now chosen, not from a certain family and blood, as was originally the rule
in the priesthood according to the order of Aaron, but as befits the new
testament, under which Christ is the High Priest after the order of
Melchisedec, in consideration of the merit which is bestowed upon each
man by divine grace. And these priests are not to be judged by their mere
title, which is often borne by unworthy men, but by that holiness which is
not common to good men and bad.

After having thus spoken of this mercy of God which is now experienced
by the Church, and is very evident and familiar to us, he foretells also the
ends to which men shall come when the last judgment has separated the
good and the bad, saying by the prophet, or the prophet himself speaking
for God, "For as the new heavens and the new earth shall remain before
me, said the Lord, so shall your seed and your name remain, and there
shall be to them month after month, and Sabbath after Sabbath. All flesh
shall come to worship before me in Jerusalem, said the Lord. And they shall
go out, and shall see the members of the men who have sinned against me:
their worm shall not die, neither shall their fire be quenched; and they shall
be for a spectacle to all flesh." [111] At this point the prophet closed his book,
as at this point the world shall come to an end. Some, indeed, have translated "carcases" instead of "members of the men," meaning by *carcases*
the manifest punishment of the body, although *carcase* is commonly used
only of dead flesh, while the bodies here spoken of shall be animated, else
they could not be sensible of any pain; but perhaps they may, without
absurdity, be called carcases, as being the bodies of those who are to fall
into the second death. And for the same reason it is said, as I have already
quoted, by this same prophet, "The earth of the wicked shall fall." Who
does not see that *cadavera* (carcases) are so called from *cadendo* (falling)?
It is obvious that those translators who use a different word for *men* do

[111] Isa. lxvi. 22-24

not mean to include only males, for no one will say that the women who sinned shall not appear in that judgment; but the male sex, being the more worthy, and that from which the woman was derived, is intended to include both sexes. But that which is especially pertinent to our subject is this, that since the words "All flesh shall come," apply to the good, for the people of God shall be composed of every race of men—for all men shall not be present, since the greater part shall be in punishment—but, as I was saying, since *flesh* is used of the good, and *members* or *carcases* of the bad, certainly it is thus put beyond a doubt that that judgment in which the good and the bad shall be allotted to their destinies shall take place after the resurrection of the body, our faith in which is thoroughly established by the use of these words.

CHAPTER XXII

WHAT IS MEANT BY THE GOOD GOING OUT TO SEE THE PUNISHMENT OF THE WICKED

But in what way shall the good go out to see the punishment of the wicked? Are they to leave their happy abodes by a bodily movement, and proceed to the places of punishment, so as to witness the torments of the wicked in their bodily presence? Certainly not; but they shall go out by knowledge. For this expression, *go out*, signifies that those who shall be punished shall be without. And thus the Lord also calls these places "the outer darkness," [112] to which is opposed that entrance concerning which it is said to the good servant, "Enter into the joy of thy Lord," that it may not be supposed that the wicked can enter thither and be known, but rather that the good by their knowledge go out to them, because the good are to know that which is without. For those who shall be in torment shall not know what is going on within in the joy of the Lord; but they who shall enter into that joy shall know what is going on outside in the outer darkness. Therefore it is said, "They shall go out," because they shall know what is done by those who are without. For if the prophets were able to know things that had not yet happened, by means of that indwelling of God in their minds, limited though it was, shall not the immortal saints know things that have already happened, when God shall be all in all? [113] The seed, then, and the name of the saints shall remain in that blessedness— the seed, to wit, of which John says, "And his seed remaineth in him;" [114] and the name, of which it was said through Isaiah himself, "I will give them an everlasting name." [115] "And there shall be to them month after month, and Sabbath after Sabbath," as if it were said, Moon after moon, and rest upon rest, both of which they shall themselves be when they shall pass from the old shadows of time into the new lights of eternity. The worm

[112] Matt. xxv. 30   [113] I Cor. xv. 28   [114] I John iii. 9   [115] Isa. lvi. 5

that dieth not, and the fire that is not quenched, which constitute the punishment of the wicked, are differently interpreted by different people. For some refer both to the body, others refer both to the soul; while others again refer the fire literally to the body, and the worm figuratively to the soul, which seems the more credible idea. But the present is not the time to discuss this difference, for we have undertaken to occupy this book with the last judgment, in which the good and the bad are separated: their rewards and punishments we shall more carefully discuss elsewhere.

CHAPTER XXIII

WHAT DANIEL PREDICTED REGARDING THE PERSECUTION OF ANTICHRIST, THE JUDGMENT OF GOD, AND THE KINGDOM OF THE SAINTS

Daniel prophesies of the last judgment in such a way as to indicate that Antichrist shall first come, and to carry on his description to the eternal reign of the saints. For when in prophetic vision he had seen four beasts, signifying four kingdoms, and the fourth conquered by a certain king, who is recognized as Antichrist, and after this the eternal kingdom of the Son of man, that is to say, of Christ, he says, "I Daniel was grieved in my spirit in the midst of my body, and the visions of my head troubled me. I came near unto one of them that stood by, and asked him the truth of all this. So he told me, and made me know the interpretation of the things. These great beasts, which are four, are four kings, which shall arise out of the earth. But the saints of the most High shall take the kingdom, and possess the kingdom for ever, even for ever and ever.

Then I would know the truth of the fourth beast, which was diverse from all others, exceeding dreadful, whose teeth were of iron, and his nails of brass; which devoured, brake in pieces, and stamped the residue with his feet; And of the ten horns that were in his head, and of the other which came up, and before whom three fell; even of that horn that had eyes, and a mouth that spake very great things, whose look was more stout than his fellows.

I beheld, and the same horn made war with the saints, and prevailed against them; Until the Ancient of days came, and judgment was given to the saints of the most High; and the time came that the saints possessed the kingdom. Thus he said, The fourth beast shall be the fourth kingdom upon earth, which shall be diverse from all kingdoms, and shall devour the whole earth, and shall tread it down, and break it in pieces. And the ten horns out of this kingdom are ten kings that shall arise; and another shall rise after them; and he shall be diverse from the first, and he shall subdue three kings.

And he shall speak great words against the most High, and shall wear out the saints of the most High, and think to change times and laws: and they shall be given into his hand until a time and times and the dividing of time. But the judgment shall sit, and they shall take away his dominion, to consume and destroy it unto the end. And the kingdom and dominion, and the greatness of the kingdom under the whole heaven, shall be given to the people of the saints of the most High, whose kingdom is an everlasting kingdom, and all dominions shall serve and obey him.

Hitherto is the end of the matter. As for me Daniel, my cogitations much troubled me, and my countenance changed in me: but I kept the matter in my heart." [116] Some have interpreted these four kingdoms as signifying those of the Assyrians, Persians, Macedonians, and Romans. They who desire to understand the fitness of this interpretation may read Jerome's book on Daniel, which is written with a sufficiency of care and erudition. But he who reads this passage, even half asleep, cannot fail to see that the kingdom of Antichrist shall fiercely, though for a short time, assail the Church before the last judgment of God shall introduce the eternal reign of the saints. For it is patent from the context that the *time, times, and half a time*, means a year, and two years, and half a year, that is to say, three years and a half. Sometimes in Scripture the same thing is indicated by months. For though the word *times* seems to be used here in the Latin indefinitely, that is only because the Latins have no dual, as the Greeks have, and as the Hebrews also are said to have. Times, therefore, is used for two times. As for the ten kings, whom, as it seems, Antichrist is to find in the person of ten individuals when he comes, I own I am afraid we may be deceived in this, and that he may come unexpectedly while there are not ten kings living in the Roman world. For what if this number ten signifies the whole number of kings who are to precede his coming, as totality is frequently symbolized by a thousand, or a hundred, or seven, or other numbers, which it is not necessary to recount?

In another place the same Daniel says, "And there shall be a time of trouble, such as was not since there was born a nation upon earth until that time: and in that time all Thy people which shall be found written in the book shall be delivered. And many of them that sleep in the mound of earth shall arise, some to everlasting life, and some to shame and everlasting confusion. And they that be wise shall shine as the brightness of the firmament; and many of the just as the stars for ever." [117] This passage is very similar to the one we have quoted from the Gospel,[118] at least so far as regards the resurrection of dead bodies. For those who are there said to be "in the graves" are here spoken of as "sleeping in the mound of earth," or, as others translate, "in the dust of earth." There it is said, "They shall come forth;" so here, "They shall arise." There, "They that have done good, to the resurrection of life; and they that have done evil, to the resurrection of judgment;" here, "Some to everlasting life, and some to shame and everlasting confusion." Neither is it to be supposed a difference, though in place

[116] Dan. vii. 15-28   [117] Dan. xii. 1-3   [118] John v. 28

of the expression in the Gospel, "All who are in their graves," the prophet does not say "all," but "many of them that sleep in the mound of earth." For *many* is sometimes used in Scripture for *all*. Thus it was said to Abraham, "I have set thee as the father of many nations," though in another place it was said to him, "In thy seed shall all nations be blessed." [119] Of such a resurrection it is said a little afterwards to the prophet himself, "And come thou and rest: for there is yet a day till the completion of the consummation; and thou shalt rest, and rise in thy lot in the end of the days." [120]

CHAPTER XXIV

PASSAGES FROM THE PSALMS OF DAVID WHICH PREDICT THE END OF THE
WORLD AND THE LAST JUDGMENT

There are many allusions to the last judgment in the Psalms, but for the most part only casual and slight. I cannot, however, omit to mention what is said there in express terms of the end of this world: "In the beginning hast Thou laid the foundations of the earth, O Lord; and the heavens are the work of Thy hands. They shall perish, but Thou shalt endure; yea, all of them shall wax old like a garment; and as a vesture Thou shalt change them, and they shall be changed: but Thou art the same, and Thy years shall not fail." [121] Why is it that Porphyry, while he lauds the piety of the Hebrews in worshipping a God great and true, and terrible to the gods themselves, follows the oracles of these gods in accusing the Christians of extreme folly because they say that this world shall perish? For here we find it said in the sacred books of the Hebrews, to that God whom this great philosopher acknowledges to be terrible even to the gods themselves, "The heavens are the work of Thy hands; they shall perish." When the heavens, the higher and more secure part of the world, perish, shall the world itself be preserved? If this idea is not relished by Jupiter, whose oracle is quoted by this philosopher as an unquestionable authority in rebuke of the credulity of the Christians, why does he not similarly rebuke the wisdom of the Hebrews as folly, seeing that the prediction is found in their most holy books? But if this Hebrew wisdom, with which Porphyry is so captivated that he extols it through the utterances of his own gods, proclaims that the heavens are to perish, how is he so infatuated as to detest the faith of the Christians partly, if not chiefly, on this account, that they believe the world is to perish?—though how the heavens are to perish if the world does not is not easy to see. And, indeed, in the sacred writings which are peculiar to ourselves, and not common to the Hebrews and us—I mean the evangelic and apostolic books—the following expressions are used: "The figure of this world passeth away;" [122] "The world passeth away;" [123] "Heaven and earth shall pass away" [124]—expressions which are, I fancy, somewhat milder

[119] Gen. xvii. 5, and xxii. 18   [120] Dan. xii. 13   [121] Ps. cii. 25-27   [122] 1 Cor. vii. 31
[123] 1 John ii. 17   [124] Matt. xxiv. 35

than "They shall *perish*." In the Epistle of the Apostle Peter, too, where the world which then was is said to have perished, being overflowed with water, it is sufficiently obvious what part of the world is signified by the whole, and in what sense the word *perished* is to be taken, and what heavens were kept in store, reserved unto fire against the day of judgment and perdition of ungodly men.[125] And when he says a little afterwards, "The day of the Lord will come as a thief; in the which the heavens shall pass away with a great rush, and the elements shall melt with burning heat, and the earth and the works which are in it shall be burned up and then adds, "Seeing, then, that all these things shall be dissolved, what manner of persons ought ye to be?" [126]—these heavens which are to perish may be understood to be the same which he said were kept in store reserved for fire; and the elements which are to be burned are those which are full of storm and disturbance in this lowest part of the world in which he said that these heavens were kept in store; for the higher heavens in whose firmament are set the stars are safe, and remain in their integrity. For even the expression of Scripture, that "the stars shall fall from heaven," [127] not to mention that a different interpretation is much preferable, rather shows that the heavens themselves shall remain, if the stars are to fall from them. This expression, then, is either figurative, as is more credible, or this phenomenon will take place in this lowest heaven, like that mentioned by Virgil—

> A meteor with a train of light
> Athwart the sky gleamed dazzling bright,
> Then in Idaean woods was lost.[128]

But the passage I have quoted from the psalm seems to except none of the heavens from the destiny of destruction; for he says, "The heavens are the works of Thy hands: they shall perish;" so that, as none of them are excepted from the category of God's works, none of them are excepted from destruction. For our opponents will not condescend to defend the Hebrew piety, which has won the approbation of their gods, by the words of the Apostle Peter, whom they vehemently detest; nor will they argue that, as the apostle in his epistle understands a part when he speaks of the whole world perishing in the flood, though only the lowest part of it, and the corresponding heavens were destroyed, so in the psalm the whole is used for a part, and it is said "They shall perish," though only the lowest heavens are to perish. But since, as I said, they will not condescend to reason thus, lest they should seem to approve of Peter's meaning, or ascribe as much importance to the final conflagration as we ascribe to the deluge, whereas they contend that no waters or flames could destroy the whole human race, it only remains to them to maintain that their gods lauded the wisdom of the Hebrews because they had not read this psalm.

[125] 2 Pet. iii. 6   [126] 2 Pet. iii. 10, 11   [127] Matt. xxiv. 29   [128] *Aeneid,* ii. 694

It is the last judgment of God which is referred to also in the 50th Psalm in the words, "God shall come manifestly, our God, and shall not keep silence: fire shall devour before Him, and it shall be very tempestuous round about Him. He shall call the heaven above, and the earth, to judge His people. Gather His saints together to Him; they who make a covenant with Him over sacrifices."[129] This we understand of our Lord Jesus Christ, whom we look for from heaven to judge the quick and the dead. For He shall come manifestly to judge justly the just and the unjust, who before came hiddenly to be unjustly judged by the unjust. He, I say, shall come manifestly, and shall not keep silence, that is, shall make Himself known by His voice of judgment, who before, when He came hiddenly, was silent before His judge when He was led as a sheep to the slaughter, and, as a lamb before the shearer, opened not His mouth, as we read that it was prophesied of Him by Isaiah,[130] and as we see it fulfilled in the Gospel.[131] As for the *fire* and *tempest*, we have already said how these are to be interpreted when we were explaining a similar passage in Isaiah.[132] As to the expression, "He shall call the heaven above," as the saints and the righteous are rightly called *heaven*, no doubt this means what the apostle says, "We shall be caught up together with them in the clouds, to meet the Lord in the air."[133] For if we take the bare literal sense, how is it possible to call the heaven above, as if the heaven could be anywhere else than above? And the following expression, "And the earth to judge His people," if we supply only the words, "He shall call," that is to say, "He shall call the earth also," and do not supply "above," seems to give us a meaning in accordance with sound doctrine, the heaven symbolizing those who will judge along with Christ, and the earth those who shall be judged; and thus the words, "He shall call the heaven above," would not mean, "He shall catch up into the air," but "He shall lift up to seats of judgment." Possibly, too, "He shall call the heaven," may mean, He shall call the angels in the high and lofty places, that He may descend with them to do judgment; and "He shall call the earth also" would then mean, He shall call the men on the earth to judgment. But if with the words "and the earth" we understand not only "He shall call," but also "above," so as to make the full sense be, He shall call the heaven above, and He shall call the earth above, then I think it is best understood of the men who shall be caught up to meet Christ in the air, and that they are called *the heaven* with reference to their souls, and *the earth* with reference to their bodies. Then what is "to judge His people," but to separate by judgment the good from the bad, as the sheep from the goats? Then he turns to address the angels: "Gather His saints together unto Him." For certainly a matter so important must be accomplished by the ministry of angels. And if we ask who the saints are who are gathered unto Him by the angels, we are told, "They who make a covenant with Him over sacrifices." This is the whole life of the saints, to make a covenant

---

[129] Ps. l. 3-5   [130] Isa. liii. 7   [131] Matt. xxvi. 63   [132] Ch. 21   [133] 1 Thess. iv. 17

with God over sacrifices. For "over sacrifices" either refers to works of mercy, which are preferable to sacrifices in the judgment of God, who says, "I desire mercy more than sacrifices," [134] or if "over sacrifices" means in sacrifices, then these very works of mercy are the sacrifices with which God is pleased, as I remember to have stated in the tenth book of this work; [135] and in these works the saints make a covenant with God, because they do them for the sake of the promises which are contained in His new testament or covenant. And hence, when His saints have been gathered to Him and set at His right hand in the last judgment, Christ shall say, "Come, ye blessed of my Father, take possession of the kingdom prepared for you from the foundation of the world. For I was hungry, and ye gave me to eat," [136] and so on, mentioning the good works of the good, and their eternal rewards assigned by the last sentence of the Judge.

CHAPTER XXV

OF MALACHI'S PROPHECY, IN WHICH HE SPEAKS OF THE LAST JUDGMENT, AND OF A CLEANSING WHICH SOME ARE TO UNDERGO BY PURIFYING PUNISHMENTS

The prophet Malachi or Malachias, who is also called Angel, and is by some (for Jerome[137] tells us that this is the opinion of the Hebrews) identified with Ezra the priest, others of whose writings have been received into the canon, predicts the last judgment, saying, "Behold, He shall come, saith the Lord of hosts. But who may abide the day of His coming? and who shall stand when He appeareth? for He is like a refiner's fire, and like fullers' soap: And He shall sit as a refiner and purifier of silver: and He shall purify the sons of Levi, and purge them as gold and silver, that they may offer unto the Lord an offering in righteousness.

Then shall the offering of Judah and Jerusalem be pleasant unto the Lord, as in the primitive days, and as in former years. And I will come near to you to judgment; and I will be a swift witness against the sorcerers, and against the adulterers, and against false swearers, and against those that oppress the hireling in his wages, the widow, and the fatherless, and that turn aside the stranger from his right, and fear not me, saith the Lord of hosts. For I am the Lord your God, and I change not." [138] From these words it more evidently appears that some shall in the last judgment suffer some kind of purgatorial punishments; for what else can be understood by the word, "Who shall abide the day of His entrance, or who shall be able to look upon Him? for He enters as a moulder's fire, and as the herb of fullers: and He shall sit fusing and purifying as if over gold and silver: and He shall purify the sons of Levi, and pour them out like gold and silver?" Similarly Isaiah says, "The Lord shall wash the filthiness of the sons and

[134] Hos. vi. 6   [135] Ch. 6   [136] Matt. xxv. 34   [137] In his *Proem. ad Mal*   [138] Mal. iii. 1-6

daughters of Zion, and shall cleanse away the blood from their midst, by the spirit of judgment and by the spirit of burning." [139] Unless perhaps we should say that they are cleansed from filthiness and in a manner clarified, when the wicked are separated from them by penal judgment, so that the elimination and damnation of the one party is the purgation of the others, because they shall henceforth live free from the contamination of such men. But when he says, "And he shall purify the sons of Levi, and pour them out like gold and silver, and they shall offer to the Lord sacrifices in righteousness; and the sacrifices of Judah and Jerusalem shall be pleasing to the Lord," he declares that those who shall be purified shall then please the Lord with sacrifices of righteousness, and consequently they themselves shall be purified from their own unrighteousness which made them displeasing to God. Now they themselves, when they have been purified, shall be sacrifices of complete and perfect righteousness; for what more acceptable offering can such persons make to God than themselves? But this question of purgatorial punishments we must defer to another time, to give it a more adequate treatment. By the sons of Levi and Judah and Jerusalem we ought to understand the Church herself, gathered not from the Hebrews only, but from other nations as well; nor such a Church as she now is, when "if we say that we have no sin, we deceive ourselves, and the truth is not in us," [140] but as she shall then be, purged by the last judgment as a threshing-floor by a winnowing wind, and those of her members who need it being cleansed by fire, so that there remains absolutely not one who offers sacrifice for his sins. For all who make such offerings are assuredly in their sins, for the remission of which they make offerings, that having made to God an acceptable offering, they may then be absolved.

CHAPTER XXVI

OF THE SACRIFICES OFFERED TO GOD BY THE SAINTS, WHICH ARE TO BE PLEASING TO HIM, AS IN THE PRIMITIVE DAYS AND FORMER YEARS

And it was with the design of showing that His city shall not then follow this custom, that God said that the sons of Levi should offer sacrifices in righteousness—not therefore in sin, and consequently not for sin. And hence we see how vainly the Jews promise themselves a return of the old times of sacrificing according to the law of the old testament, grounding on the words which follow, "And the sacrifice of Judah and Jerusalem shall be pleasing to the Lord, as in the primitive days, and as in former years." For in the times of the law they offered sacrifices not in righteousness but in sins, offering especially and primarily for sins, so much so that even the priest himself, whom we must suppose to have been their most righteous man, was accustomed to offer, according to God's commandments,

[139] Isa. iv. 4   [140] 1 John i. 8

first for his own sins, and then for the sins of the people. And therefore we must explain how we are to understand the words, "as in the primitive days, and as in former years;" for perhaps he alludes to the time in which our first parents were in paradise. Then, indeed, intact and pure from all stain and blemish of sin, they offered themselves to God as the purest sacrifices. But since they were banished thence on account of their transgression, and human nature was condemned in them, with the exception of the one Mediator and those who have been baptized, and are as yet infants, "there is none clean from stain, not even the babe whose life has been but for a day upon the earth." [141] But if it be replied that those who offer in faith may be said to offer in righteousness, because the righteous lives by faith[142] —he deceives himself, however, if he says that he has no sin, and therefore he does not say so, because he lives by faith—will any man say this time of faith can be placed on an equal footing with that consummation when they who offer sacrifices in righteousness shall be purified by the fire of the last judgment? And consequently, since it must be believed that after such a cleansing the righteous shall retain no sin, assuredly that time, so far as regards its freedom from sin, can be compared to no other period, unless to that during which our first parents lived in paradise in the most innocent happiness before their transgression. It is this period, then, which is properly understood when it is said, "as in the primitive days, and as in former years." For in Isaiah, too, after the new heavens and the new earth have been promised, among other elements in the blessedness of the saints which are there depicted by allegories and figures, from giving an adequate explanation of which I am prevented by a desire to avoid prolixity, it is said, "According to the days of the tree of life shall be the days of my people." [143] And who that has looked at Scripture does not know where God planted the tree of life, from whose fruit He excluded our first parents when their own iniquity ejected them from paradise, and round which a terrible and fiery fence was set?

But if any one contends that those days of the tree of life mentioned by the prophet Isaiah are the present times of the Church of Christ, and that Christ Himself is prophetically called the Tree of Life, because He is Wisdom, and of wisdom Solomon says, "It is a tree of life to all who embrace it;" [144] and if they maintain that our first parents did not pass *years* in paradise, but were driven from it so soon that none of their children were begotten there, and that therefore that time cannot be alluded to in words which run, "as in the primitive days, and as in former years," I forbear entering on this question, lest by discussing everything I become prolix, and leave the whole subject in uncertainty. For I see another meaning, which should keep us from believing that a restoration of the primitive days and former years of the legal sacrifices could have been promised to us by the prophet as a great boon. For the animals selected as victims under the old

[141] Job xiv. 4   [142] Rom. i. 17   [143] Isa. lxv. 22   [144] Prov. iii. 18

law were required to be immaculate, and free from all blemish whatever, and symbolized holy men free from all sin, the only instance of which character was found in Christ. As, therefore, after the judgment those who are worthy of such purification shall be purified even by fire, and shall be rendered thoroughly sinless, and shall offer themselves to God in righteousness, and be indeed victims immaculate and free from all blemish whatever, they shall then certainly be, "as in the primitive days, and as in former years," when the purest victims were offered, the shadow of this future reality. For there shall then be in the body and soul of the saints the purity which was symbolized in the bodies of these victims.

Then, with reference to those who are worthy not of cleansing but of damnation, He says, "And I will draw near to you to judgment, and I will be a swift witness against evildoers and against adulterers;" and after enumerating other damnable crimes, He adds, "For I am the Lord your God, and I am not changed." It is as if He said, Though your fault has changed you for the worse, and my grace has changed you for the better, I am not changed. And He says that He Himself will be a witness, because in His judgment He needs no witnesses; and that He will be "swift," either because He is to come suddenly, and the judgment which seemed to lag shall be very swift by His unexpected arrival, or because He will convince the consciences of men directly and without any prolix harangue. "For," as it is written, "in the thoughts of the wicked His examination shall be conducted." [145] And the apostle says, "The thoughts accusing or else excusing, in the day in which God shall judge the hidden things of men, according to my gospel in Jesus Christ." [146] Thus, then, shall the Lord be a swift witness, when He shall suddenly bring back into the memory that which shall convince and punish the conscience.

CHAPTER XXVII

OF THE SEPARATION OF THE GOOD AND THE BAD, WHICH PROCLAIM THE DISCRIMINATING INFLUENCE OF THE LAST JUDGMENT

The passage also which I formerly quoted for another purpose from this prophet refers to the last judgment, in which he says, "And they shall be mine, saith the Lord of hosts, in that day when I make up my jewels; and I will spare them, as a man spareth his own son that serveth him. Then shall ye return, and discern between the righteous and the wicked, between him that serveth God and him that serveth him not.

For, behold, the day cometh, that shall burn as an oven; and all the proud, yea, and all that do wickedly, shall be stubble: and the day that cometh shall burn them up, saith the Lord of hosts, that it shall leave them neither root nor branch. But unto you that fear my name shall the Sun

[145] Wisd. i. 9   [146] Rom. ii. 15, 16

of righteousness arise with healing in his wings; and ye shall go forth, and grow up as calves of the stall. And ye shall tread down the wicked; for they shall be ashes under the soles of your feet in the day that I shall do this, saith the Lord of hosts." [147] When this diversity between the rewards and punishments which distinguish the righteous from the wicked shall appear under that Sun of righteousness in the brightness of life eternal—a diversity which is not discerned under this sun which shines on the vanity of this life—there shall then be such a judgment as has never before been.

CHAPTER XXVIII

THAT THE LAW OF MOSES MUST BE SPIRITUALLY UNDERSTOOD TO PRECLUDE THE DAMNABLE MURMURS OF A CARNAL INTERPRETATION

In the succeeding words, "Remember the law of Moses my servant, which I commanded to him in Horeb for all Israel," [148] the prophet opportunely mentions precepts and statutes, after declaring the important distinction hereafter to be made between those who observe and those who despise the law. He intends also that they learn to interpret the law spiritually, and find Christ in it, by whose judgment that separation between the good and the bad is to be made. For it is not without reason that the Lord Himself says to the Jews, "Had ye believed Moses, ye would have believed me; for he wrote of me." [149] For by receiving the law carnally without perceiving that its earthly promises were figures of things spiritual, they fell into such murmurings as audaciously to say, "It is vain to serve God; and what profit is it that we have kept His ordinance, and that we have walked suppliantly before the face of the Lord Almighty? And now we call aliens happy; yea, they that work wickedness are set up." [150] It was these words of theirs which in a manner compelled the prophet to announce the last judgment, in which the wicked shall not even in appearance be happy, but shall manifestly be most miserable; and in which the good shall be oppressed with not even a transitory wretchedness, but shall enjoy unsullied and eternal felicity. For he had previously cited some similar expressions of those who said, "Every one that doeth evil is good in the sight of the Lord, and such are pleasing to Him." [151] It was, I say, by understanding the law of Moses carnally that they had come to murmur thus against God. And hence, too, the writer of the 73d Psalm says that his feet were almost gone, his steps had well-nigh slipped, because he was envious of sinners while he considered their prosperity, so that he said among other things, How doth God know, and is there knowledge in the Most High? and again, Have I sanctified my heart in vain, and washed my hands in innocency? He goes on to say that his efforts to solve this most difficult problem, which arises

[147] Mal. iii. 17; iv. 3   [148] Mal. iv. 4   [149] John v. 46   [150] Mal. iii. 14, 15
[151] Mal. ii. 17

when the good seem to be wretched and the wicked happy, were in vain until he went into the sanctuary of God, and understood the last things.[152] For in the last judgment things shall not be so; but in the manifest felicity of the righteous and manifest misery of the wicked quite another state of things shall appear.

CHAPTER XXIX

OF THE COMING OF ELIAS BEFORE THE JUDGMENT, THAT THE JEWS MAY BE CONVERTED TO CHRIST BY HIS PREACHING AND EXPLANATION OF SCRIPTURE

After admonishing them to give heed to the law of Moses, as he foresaw that for a long time to come they would not understand it spiritually and rightly, he went on to say, "And, behold, I will send to you Elias the Tishbite before the great and signal day of the Lord come: and he shall turn the heart of the father to the son, and the heart of a man to his next of kin, lest I come and utterly smite the earth." [153] It is a familiar theme in the conversation and heart of the faithful, that in the last days before the judgment the Jews shall believe in the true Christ, that is, our Christ, by means of this great and admirable prophet Elias who shall expound the law to them. For not without reason do we hope that before the coming of our Judge and Saviour Elias shall come, because we have good reason to believe that he is now alive; for, as Scripture most distinctly informs us,[154] he was taken up from this life in a chariot of fire. When, therefore, he is come, he shall give a spiritual explanation of the law which the Jews at present understand carnally, and shall thus "turn the heart of the father to the son," that is, the heart of fathers to their children; for the Septuagint translators have frequently put the singular for the plural number. And the meaning is, that the sons, that is, the Jews, shall understand the law as the fathers, that is, the prophets, and among them Moses himself, understood it. For the heart of the fathers shall be turned to their children when the children understand the law as their fathers did; and the heart of the children shall be turned to their fathers when they have the same sentiments as the fathers. The Septuagint used the expression, "and the heart of a man to his next of kin," because fathers and children are eminently neighbors to one another. Another and a preferable sense can be found in the words of the Septuagint translators, who have translated Scripture with an eye to prophecy, the sense, *viz.*, that Elias shall turn the heart of God the Father to the Son, not certainly as if he should bring about this love of the Father for the Son, but meaning that he should make it known, and that the Jews also, who had previously hated, should then love the Son who is our Christ. For so far as regards the Jews, God has His heart turned away from our

[152] Ps. lxxiii.   [153] Mal. iv. 5, 6   [154] 2 Kings ii. 11

Christ, this being their conception about God and Christ. But in their case the heart of God shall be turned to the Son when they themselves shall turn in heart, and learn the love of the Father towards the Son. The words following, "and the heart of a man to his next of kin"—that is, Elias shall also turn the heart of a man to his next of kin—how can we understand this better than as the heart of a man to the man Christ? For though in the form of God He is our God, yet, taking the form of a servant, He condescended to become also our next of kin. It is this, then, which Elias will do, "lest," he says, "I come and smite the earth utterly." For they who mind earthly things are the earth. Such are the carnal Jews until this day; and hence these murmurs of theirs against God, "The wicked are pleasing to Him," and "It is a vain thing to serve God." [155]

CHAPTER XXX

THAT IN THE BOOKS OF THE OLD TESTAMENT, WHERE IT IS SAID THAT GOD SHALL JUDGE THE WORLD, THE PERSON OF CHRIST IS NOT EXPLICITLY INDICATED, BUT IT PLAINLY APPEARS FROM SOME PASSAGES IN WHICH THE LORD GOD SPEAKS THAT CHRIST IS MEANT

There are many other passages of Scripture bearing on the last judgment of God—so many, indeed, that to cite them all would swell this book to an unpardonable size. Suffice it to have proved that both Old and New Testament enounce the judgment. But in the Old it is not so definitely declared as in the New that the judgment shall be administered by Christ, that is, that Christ shall descend from heaven as the Judge; for when it is therein stated by the Lord God or His prophet that the Lord God shall come, we do not necessarily understand this of Christ. For both the Father, and the Son, and the Holy Ghost are the Lord God. We must not, however, leave this without proof. And therefore we must first show how Jesus Christ speaks in the prophetical books under the title of the Lord God, while yet there can be no doubt that it is Jesus Christ who speaks; so that in other passages where this is not at once apparent, and where nevertheless it is said that the Lord God will come to that last judgment, we may understand that Jesus Christ is meant. There is a passage in the prophet Isaiah which illustrates what I mean. For God says by the prophet, "Hear me, Jacob and Israel, whom I call. I am the first, and I am for ever: and my hand has founded the earth, and my right hand has established the heaven. I will call them, and they shall stand together, and be gathered, and hear. Who has declared to them these things? In love of thee I have done thy pleasure upon Babylon, that I might take away the seed of the Chaldeans. I have spoken, and I have called: I have brought him, and have made his way prosperous. Come ye near unto me, and hear this. I have not spoken in

[155] Mal. ii. 17; iii. 14

secret from the beginning; when they were made, there was I. And now the Lord God and His Spirit hath sent me." [156] It was Himself who was speaking as the Lord God; and yet we should not have understood that it was Jesus Christ had He not added, "And now the Lord God and His Spirit hath sent me." For He said this with reference to the form of a servant, speaking of a future event as if it were past, as in the same prophet we read, "He was led as a sheep to the slaughter," [157] not "He shall be led;" but the past tense is used to express the future. And prophecy constantly speaks in this way.

There is also another passage in Zechariah which plainly declares that the Almighty sent the Almighty; and of what persons can this be understood but of God the Father and God the Son? For it is written, "Thus saith the Lord Almighty, After the glory hath He sent me unto the nations which spoiled you; for he that toucheth you toucheth the apple of His eye. Behold, I will bring mine hand upon them, and they shall be a spoil to their servants: and ye shall know that the Lord Almighty hath sent me." [158] Observe, the Lord Almighty saith that the Lord Almighty sent Him. Who can presume to understand these words of any other than Christ, who is speaking to the lost sheep of the house of Israel? For He says in the Gospel, "I am not sent save to the lost sheep of the house of Israel," [159] which He here compared to the pupil of God's eye, to signify the profoundest love. And to this class of sheep the apostles themselves belonged. But after the glory, to wit, of His resurrection—for before it happened the evangelist said that "Jesus was not yet glorified" [160]—He was sent unto the nations in the persons of His apostles; and thus the saying of the psalm was fulfilled, "Thou wilt deliver me from the contradictions of the people; Thou wilt set me as the head of the nations," [161] so that those who had spoiled the Israelites, and whom the Israelites had served when they were subdued by them, were not themselves to be spoiled in the same fashion, but were in their own persons to become the spoil of the Israelites. For this had been promised to the apostles when the Lord said, "I will make you fishers of men." [162] And to one of them He says, "From henceforth thou shalt catch men." [163] They were then to become a spoil, but in a good sense, as those who are snatched from that strong one when he is bound by a stronger.[164]

In like manner the Lord, speaking by the same prophet, says, "And it shall come to pass in that day, that I will seek to destroy all the nations that come against Jerusalem. And I will pour upon the house of David, and upon the inhabitants of Jerusalem, the spirit of grace and mercy; and they shall look upon me because they have insulted me, and they shall mourn for Him as for one very dear, and shall be in bitterness as for an only-begotten." [165] To whom but to God does it belong to destroy all the nations

[156] Isa. xlviii. 12-16   [157] Isa. liii. 7   [158] Zech. ii. 8, 9   [159] Matt. xv. 24   [160] John vii. 39   [161] Ps. xviii. 43   [162] Matt. iv. 19   [163] Luke v. 10   [164] Matt. xii. 29   [165] Zech. xii. 9, 10

that are hostile to the holy city Jerusalem, which "come against it," that is, are opposed to it, or, as some translate, "come upon it," as if putting it down under them; or to pour out upon the house of David and the Inhabitants of Jerusalem the spirit of grace and mercy? This belongs doubtless to God, and it is to God the prophet ascribes the words; and yet Christ shows that He is the God who does these so great and divine things, when He goes on to say, "And they shall look upon me because they have insulted me, and they shall mourn for Him as if for one very dear (or beloved), and shall be in bitterness for Him as for an only-begotten." For in that day the Jews—those of them, at least, who shall receive the spirit of grace and mercy—when they see Him coming in His majesty, and recognize that it is He whom they, in the person of their parents, insulted when He came before in His humiliation, shall repent of insulting Him in His passion: and their parents themselves, who were the perpetrators of this huge impiety, shall see Him when they rise; but this will be only for their punishment, and not for their correction. It is not of them we are to understand the words, "And I will pour upon the house of David, and upon the inhabitants of Jerusalem, the spirit of grace and mercy, and they shall look upon me because they have insulted me;" but we are to understand the words of their descendants, who shall at that time believe through Elias. But as we say to the Jews, You killed Christ, although it was their parents who did so, so these persons shall grieve that they in some sort did what their progenitors did. Although, therefore, those that receive the spirit of mercy and grace, and believe, shall not be condemned with their impious parents, yet they shall mourn as if they themselves had done what their parents did. Their grief shall arise not so much from guilt as from pious affection. Certainly the words which the Septuagint have translated, "They shall look upon me because they insulted me," stand in the Hebrew, "They shall look upon me whom they pierced." [166] And by this word the crucifixion of Christ is certainly more plainly indicated. But the Septuagint translators preferred to allude to the insult which was involved in His whole passion. For in point of fact they insulted Him both when He was arrested and when He was bound, when He was judged, when He was mocked by the robe they put on Him and the homage they did on bended knee, when He was crowned with thorns and struck with a rod on the head, when He bore His cross, and when at last He hung upon the tree. And therefore we recognize more fully the Lord's passion when we do not confine ourselves to one interpretation, but combine both, and read both "insulted" and "pierced."

When, therefore, we read in the prophetical books that God is to come to do judgment at the last, from the mere mention of the judgment, and although there is nothing else to determine the meaning, we must gather that Christ is meant; for though the Father will judge, He will judge by the

[166] So the Vulgate

coming of the Son. For He Himself, by His own manifested presence, "judges no man, but has committed all judgment to the Son;" [167] for as the Son was judged as a man, He shall also judge in human form. For it is none but He of whom God speaks by Isaiah under the name of Jacob and Israel, of whose seed Christ took a body, as it is written, "Jacob is my servant, I will uphold Him; Israel is mine elect, my Spirit has assumed Him: I have put my Spirit upon Him; He shall bring forth judgment to the Gentiles. He shall not cry, nor cease, neither shall His voice be heard without. A bruised reed shall He not break, and the smoking flax shall He not quench: but in truth shall He bring forth judgment. He shall shine and shall not be broken, until He sets judgment in the earth: and the nations shall hope in His name." [168] The Hebrew has not "Jacob" and "Israel;" but the Septuagint translators, wishing to show the significance of the expression "my servant," and that it refers to the form of a servant in which the Most High humbled Himself, inserted the name of that man from whose stock He took the form of a servant. The Holy Spirit was given to Him, and was manifested, as the evangelist testifies, in the form of a dove.[169] He brought forth judgment to the Gentiles, because He predicted what was hidden from them. In His meekness He did not cry, nor did He cease to proclaim the truth. But His voice was not heard, nor is it heard, without, because He is not obeyed by those who are outside of His body. And the Jews themselves, who persecuted Him, He did not break, though as a bruised reed they had lost their integrity, and as smoking flax their light was quenched; for He spared them, having come to be judged and not yet to judge. He brought forth judgment in truth, declaring that they should be punished did they persist in their wickedness. His face shone on the Mount,[170] His fame in the world. He is not broken nor overcome, because neither in Himself nor in His Church has persecution prevailed to annihilate Him. And therefore that has not, and shall not, be brought about which His enemies said or say, "When shall He die, and His name perish?" [171] "until He set judgment in the earth." Behold, the hidden thing which we were seeking is discovered. For this is the last judgment, which He will set in the earth when He comes from heaven. And it is in Him, too, we already see the concluding expression of the prophecy fulfilled: "In His name shall the nations hope." And by this fulfillment, which no one can deny, men are encouraged to believe in that which is most impudently denied. For who could have hoped for that which even those who do not yet believe in Christ now see fulfilled among us, and which is so undeniable that they can but gnash their teeth and pine away? Who, I say, could have hoped that the nations would hope in the name of Christ, when He was arrested, bound, scourged, mocked, crucified, when even the disciples themselves had lost the hope which they had begun to have in Him? The hope

[167] John v. 22 [168] Isa. xlii. 1-4 [169] John i. 32 [170] Matt. xvii. 1, 2 [171] Ps. xli. 5

which was then entertained scarcely by the one thief on the cross, is now cherished by nations everywhere on the earth, who are marked with the sign of the cross on which He died that they may not die eternally.

That the last judgment, then, shall be administered by Jesus Christ in the manner predicted in the sacred writings is denied or doubted by no one, unless by those who, through some incredible animosity or blindness, decline to believe these writings, though already their truth is demonstrated to all the world. And at or in connection with that judgment the following events shall come to pass, as we have learned: Elias the Tishbite shall come; the Jews shall believe; Antichrist shall persecute; Christ shall judge; the dead shall rise; the good and the wicked shall be separated; the world shall be burned and renewed. All these things, we believe, shall come to pass; but how, or in what order, human understanding cannot perfectly teach us, but only the experience of the events themselves. My opinion, however, is, that they will happen in the order in which I have related them.

Two books yet remain to be written by me, in order to complete, by God's help, what I promised. One of these will explain the punishment of the wicked, the other the happiness of the righteous; and in them I shall be at special pains to refute, by God's grace, the arguments by which some unhappy creatures seem to themselves to undermine the divine promises and threatenings, and to ridicule as empty words statements which are the most salutary nutriment of faith. But they who are instructed in divine things hold the truth and omnipotence of God to be the strongest arguments in favor of those things which, however incredible they seem to men, are yet contained in the Scriptures, whose truth has already in many ways been proved; for they are sure that God can in no wise lie, and that He can do what is impossible to the unbelieving.

BOOK TWENTY-ONE

ARGUMENT

Of the end reserved for the city of the devil, namely, the eternal punishment of the damned; and of the arguments which unbelief brings against it.

CHAPTER I

OF THE ORDER OF THE DISCUSSION, WHICH REQUIRES THAT WE FIRST SPEAK OF THE ETERNAL PUNISHMENT OF THE LOST IN COMPANY WITH THE DEVIL, AND THEN OF THE ETERNAL HAPPINESS OF THE SAINTS

I PROPOSE, with such ability as God may grant me, to discuss in this book more thoroughly the nature of the punishment which shall be assigned to the devil and all his retainers, when the two cities, the one of God, the other of the devil, shall have reached their proper ends through Jesus Christ our Lord, the Judge of quick and dead. And I have adopted this order, and preferred to speak, first of the punishment of the devils, and afterwards of the blessedness of the saints, because the *body* partakes of either destiny; and it seems to be more incredible that bodies endure in everlasting torments than that they continue to exist without any pain in everlasting felicity. Consequently, when I shall have demonstrated that that punishment ought not to be incredible, this will materially aid me in proving that which is much more credible, *viz.*, the immortality of the bodies of the saints which are delivered from all pain. Neither is this order out of harmony with the divine writings, in which sometimes, indeed, the blessedness of the good is placed first, as in the words, "They that have done good, unto the resurrection of life; and they that have done evil, unto the resurrection of judgment;" [1] but sometimes also last, as, "The Son of man shall send forth His angels, and they shall gather out of His kingdom all things which offend, and shall cast them into a furnace of fire: there shall be wailing and gnashing of teeth. Then shall the righteous shine forth as the sun in the kingdom of His Father;" [2] and that, "These shall go away into eternal punishment, but the righteous into life eternal." [3] And though we have not room to cite instances, any one who examines the prophets will find that they adopt now the one arrangement and now the other. My own reason for following the latter order I have given.

[1] John v. 29   [2] Matt. xiii. 41-43   [3] Matt. xxv. 46

CHAPTER II

WHETHER IT IS POSSIBLE FOR BODIES TO LAST FOR EVER IN BURNING FIRE

What, then, can I adduce to convince those who refuse to believe that human bodies, animated and living, can not only survive death, but also last in the torments of everlasting fires? They will not allow us to refer this simply to the power of the Almighty, but demand that we persuade them by some example. If, then, we reply to them, that there are animals which certainly are corruptible, because they are mortal, and which yet live in the midst of flames; and likewise, that in springs of water so hot that no one can put his hand in it with impunity a species of worm is found, which not only lives there, but cannot live elsewhere; they either refuse to believe these facts unless we can show them, or, if we are in circumstances to prove them by ocular demonstration or by adequate testimony, they contend, with the same scepticism, that these facts are not examples of what we seek to prove, inasmuch as these animals do not live for ever, and besides, they live in that blaze of heat without pain, the element of fire being congenial to their nature, and causing it to thrive and not to suffer— just as if it were not more incredible that it should thrive than that it should suffer in such circumstances. It is strange that anything should suffer in fire and yet live, but stranger that it should live in fire and not suffer. If, then, the latter be believed, why not also the former?

CHAPTER III

WHETHER BODILY SUFFERING NECESSARILY TERMINATES IN THE
DESTRUCTION OF THE FLESH

But, say they, there is no body which can suffer and cannot also die. How do we know this? For who can say with certainty that the devils do not suffer in their bodies, when they own that they are grievously tormented? And if it is replied that there is no earthly body—that is to say, no solid and perceptible body, or, in one word, no flesh—which can suffer and cannot die, is not this to tell us only what men have gathered from experience and their bodily senses? For they indeed have no acquaintance with any flesh but that which is mortal; and this is their whole argument, that what they have had no experience of they judge quite impossible. For we cannot call it reasoning to make pain a presumption of death, while, in fact, it is rather a sign of life. For though it be a question whether that which suffers can continue to live for ever, yet it is certain that everything which suffers pain does live, and that pain can exist only in a living subject. It is necessary, therefore, that he who is pained be living, not necessary that pain kill him; for every pain does not kill even those mortal bodies of ours which are destined to die. And that any pain kills them is caused by the circumstance that the soul is so connected with the body that it succumbs to great pain and withdraws; for the structure of our members and vital parts is so infirm that it cannot bear up against that violence which causes great or extreme agony. But in the life to come this connection of soul and body is of such a kind, that as it is dissolved by no lapse of time, so neither is it burst asunder by any pain. And so, although it be true that in this world there is no flesh which can suffer pain and yet cannot die, yet in the world to come there shall be flesh such as now there is not, as there will also be death such as now there is not. For death will not be abolished, but will be eternal, since the soul will neither be able to enjoy God and live, nor to die and escape the pains of the body. The first death drives the soul from the body against her will: the second death holds the soul in the body against her will. The two have this in common, that the soul suffers against her will what her own body inflicts.

Our opponents, too, make much of this, that in this world there is no flesh which can suffer pain and cannot die; while they make nothing of the fact that there is something which is greater than the body. For the spirit, whose presence animates and rules the body, can both suffer pain and cannot die. Here then is something which, though it can feel pain, is immortal. And this capacity, which we now see in the spirit of all, shall be hereafter in the bodies of the damned. Moreover, if we attend to the matter a little more closely, we see that what is called bodily pain is rather to be referred to the soul. For it is the soul not the body, which is pained, even when the pain originates with the body—the soul feeling pain at the point where the body is hurt. As then we speak of bodies feeling and living, though the feeling and life of the body are from the soul, so also we speak of bodies being pained, though no pain can be suffered by the body apart from the soul. The soul, then, is pained with the body in that part where something occurs to hurt it; and it is pained alone, though it be in the body, when some invisible cause distresses it, while the body is safe and sound. Even when not associated with the body it is pained; for certainly that rich man was suffering in hell when he cried, "I am tormented in this flame." [4] But as for the body, it suffers no pain when it is soulless; and even when animate it can suffer only by the soul's suffering. If, therefore, we might draw a just presumption from the existence of pain to that of death, and conclude that where pain can be felt death can occur, death would rather be the property of the soul, for to it pain more peculiarly belongs. But, seeing that that which suffers most cannot die, what ground is there for supposing that those bodies, because destined to suffer, are therefore, destined to die? The Platonists indeed maintained that these earthly bodies and dying members

[4] Luke xvi. 24

gave rise to the fears, desires, griefs, and joys of the soul. "Hence," says Virgil (*i.e.*, from these earthly bodies and dying members),

> Hence wild desires and grovelling fears,
> And human laughter, human tears.[5]

But in the fourteenth book of this work[6] we have proved that, according to the Platonists' own theory, souls, even when purged from all pollution of the body, are yet possessed by a monstrous desire to return again into their bodies. But where desire can exist, certainly pain also can exist; for desire frustrated, either by missing what it aims at or losing what it had attained, is turned into pain. And therefore, if the soul, which is either the only or the chief sufferer, has yet a kind of immortality of its own, it is inconsequent to say that because the bodies of the damned shall suffer pain, therefore they shall die. In fine, if the body causes the soul to suffer, why can the body not cause death as well as suffering, unless because it does not follow that what causes pain causes death as well? And why then is it incredible that these fires can cause pain but not death to those bodies we speak of, just as the bodies themselves cause pain, but not therefore death, to the souls? Pain is therefore no necessary presumption of death.

CHAPTER IV

EXAMPLES FROM NATURE PROVING THAT BODIES MAY REMAIN UNCONSUMED AND ALIVE IN FIRE

If, therefore, the salamander lives in fire, as naturalists have recorded, and if certain famous mountains of Sicily have been continually on fire from the remotest antiquity until now, and yet remain entire, these are sufficiently convincing examples that everything which burns is not consumed. As the soul, too, is a proof that not everything which can suffer pain can also die, why then do they yet demand that we produce real examples to prove that it is not incredible that the bodies of men condemned to everlasting punishment may retain their soul in the fire, may burn without being consumed,·and may suffer without perishing? For suitable properties will be communicated to the substance of the flesh by Him who has endowed the things we see with so marvellous and diverse properties, that their very multitude prevents our wonder. For who but God the Creator of all things has given to the flesh of the peacock its antiseptic property? This property, when I first heard of it, seemed to me incredible; but it happened at Carthage that a bird of this kind was cooked and served up to me, and, taking a suitable slice of flesh from its breast, I ordered it to be kept, and when it had been kept as many days as make any other flesh

[5] *Aeneid*, vi. 733   [6] Ch. 3, 5, 6

stinking, it was produced and set before me, and emitted no offensive smell. And after it had been laid by for thirty days and more, it was still in the same state; and a year after, the same still, except that it was a little more shrivelled, and drier. Who gave to chaff such power to freeze that it preserves snow buried under it, and such power to warm that it ripens green fruit?

But who can explain the strange properties of fire itself, which blackens everything it burns, though itself bright; and which, though of the most beautiful colors, discolors almost all it touches and feeds upon, and turns blazing fuel into grimy cinders? Still this is not laid down as an absolutely uniform law; for, on the contrary, stones baked in glowing fire themselves also glow, and though the fire be rather of a red hue, and they white, yet white is congruous with light, and black with darkness. Thus, though the fire burns the wood in calcining the stones, these contrary effects do not result from the contrariety of the materials. For though wood and stone differ, they are not contraries, like black and white, the one of which colors is produced in the stones, while the other is produced in the wood by the same action of fire, which imparts its own brightness to the former, while it begrimes the latter, and which could have no effect on the one were it not fed by the other. Then what wonderful properties do we find in charcoal, which is so brittle that a light tap breaks it and a slight pressure pulverizes it, and yet is so strong that no moisture rots it, nor any time causes it to decay? So enduring is it, that it is customary in laying down landmarks to put charcoal underneath them, so that if, after the longest interval, any one raises an action, and pleads that there is no boundary stone, he may be convicted by the charcoal below. What then has enabled it to last so long without rotting, though buried in the damp earth in which its original wood rots, except this same fire which consumes all things?

Again, let us consider the wonders of lime; for besides growing white in fire, which makes other things black, and of which I have already said enough, it has also a mysterious property of conceiving fire within it. Itself cold to the touch, it yet has a hidden store of fire, which is not at once apparent to our senses, but which experience teaches us, lies as it were slumbering within it even while unseen. And it is for this reason called "quick lime," as if the fire were the invisible soul quickening the visible substance or body. But the marvellous thing is, that this fire is kindled when it is extinguished. For to disengage the hidden fire the lime is moistened or drenched with water, and then, though it be cold before, it becomes hot by that very application which cools what is hot. As if the fire were departing from the lime and breathing its last, it no longer lies hid, but appears; and then the lime lying in the coldness of death cannot be requickened, and what we before called "quick," we now call "slaked." What can be stranger than this? Yet there is a greater marvel still. For if you treat the lime, not with water, but with oil, which is as fuel to fire, no amount of oil will heat it. Now if this marvel had been told us of some Indian mineral which we had no opportunity of experimenting upon, we should either have forthwith pronounced it a falsehood, or certainly should have been greatly astonished. But things that daily present themselves to our own observation we despise, not because they are really less marvellous, but because they are common; so that even some products of India itself, remote as it is from ourselves, cease to excite our admiration as soon as we can admire them at our leisure.

The diamond is a stone possessed by many among ourselves, especially by jewellers and lapidaries, and the stone is so hard that it can be wrought neither by iron nor fire, nor, they say, by anything at all except goat's blood. But do you suppose it is as much admired by those who own it and are familiar with its properties as by those to whom it is shown for the first time? Persons who have not seen it perhaps do not believe what is said of it, or if they do, they wonder as at a thing beyond their experience; and if they happen to see it, still they marvel because they are unused to it, but gradually familiar experience of it dulls their admiration. We know that the loadstone has a wonderful power of attracting iron. When I first saw it I was thunderstruck, for I saw an iron ring attracted and suspended by the stone; and then, as if it had communicated its own property to the iron it attracted, and had made it a substance like itself, this ring was put near another, and lifted it up; and as the first ring clung to the magnet, so did the second ring to the first. A third and a fourth were similarly added, so that there hung from the stone a kind of chain of rings, with their hoops connected, not interlinking, but attached together by their outer surface. Who would not be amazed at this virtue of the stone, subsisting as it does not only in itself, but transmitted through so many suspended rings, and binding them together by invisible links? Yet far more astonishing is what I heard about this stone from my brother in the episcopate, Severus bishop of Milevis. He told me that Bathanarius, once count of Africa, when the bishop was dining with him, produced a magnet, and held it under a silver plate on which he placed a bit of iron; then as he moved his hand with the magnet underneath the plate, the iron upon the plate moved about accordingly. The intervening silver was not affected at all, but precisely as the magnet was moved backwards and forwards below it, no matter how quickly, so was the iron attracted above. I have related what I myself have witnessed; I have related what I was told by one whom I trust as I trust my own eyes. Let me further say what I have read about this magnet. When a diamond is laid near it, it does not lift iron; or if it has already lifted it, as soon as the diamond approaches, it drops it. These stones come from India. But if we cease to admire them because they are now familiar, how much less must they admire them who procure them very easily and send them to us? Perhaps they are held as cheap as we hold lime, which, because it is common, we think nothing of, though it has the strange property of burning when water, which is wont to quench fire, is poured on it, and of remaining cool when mixed with oil, which ordinarily feeds fire.

CHAPTER V

THAT THERE ARE MANY THINGS WHICH REASON CANNOT ACCOUNT FOR, AND WHICH ARE NEVERTHELESS TRUE

Nevertheless, when we declare the miracles which God has wrought, or will yet work, and which we cannot bring under the very eyes of men, sceptics keep demanding that we shall explain these marvels to reason. And because we cannot do so, inasmuch as they are above human comprehension, they suppose we are speaking falsely. These persons themselves, therefore, ought to account for all these marvels which we either can or do see. And if they perceive that this is impossible for man to do, they should acknowledge that it cannot be concluded that a thing has not been or shall not be because it cannot be reconciled to reason, since there are things now in existence of which the same is true. I will not, then, detail the multitude of marvels which are related in books, and which refer not to things that happened once and passed away, but that are permanent in certain places, where, if any one has the desire and opportunity, he may ascertain their truth; but a few only I recount. The following are some of the marvels men tell us:—The salt of Agrigentum in Sicily, when thrown into the fire, becomes fluid as if it were in water, but in the water it crackles as if it were in the fire. The Garamantae have a fountain so cold by day that no one can drink it, so hot by night no one can touch it. In Epirus, too, there is a fountain which, like all others, quenches lighted torches, but, unlike all others, lights quenched torches. There is a stone found in Arcadia, and called asbestos, because once lit it cannot be put out. The wood of a certain kind of Egyptian fig-tree sinks in water, and does not float like other wood; and, stranger still, when it has been sunk to the bottom for some time, it rises again to the surface, though nature requires that when soaked in water it should be heavier than ever. Then there are the apples of Sodom, which grow indeed to an appearance of ripeness, but, when you touch them with hand or tooth, the peel cracks, and they crumble into dust and ashes. The Persian stone pyrites burns the hand when it is tightly held in it, and so gets its name from fire. In Persia, too, there is found another stone called selenite, because its interior brilliancy waxes and wanes with the moon. Then in Cappadocia the mares are impregnated by the wind, and their foals live only three years. Tilon, an Indian island, has this advantage over all other lands, that no tree which grows in it ever loses its foliage.

These and numberless other marvels recorded in the history, not of past events, but of permanent localities, I have no time to enlarge upon and diverge from my main object; but let those sceptics who refuse to credit the divine writings give me, if they can, a rational account of them. For their only ground of unbelief in the Scriptures is, that they contain incredible things, just such as I have been recounting. For, say they, reason cannot admit that flesh burn and remain unconsumed, suffer without dying. Mighty reasoners, indeed, who are competent to give the reason of all the marvels that exist! Let them then give us the reason of the few things we have cited, and which, if they did not know they existed, and were only assured by us they would at some future time occur, they would believe still less than that which they now refuse to credit on our word. For which of them would believe us if, instead of saying that the living bodies of men hereafter will be such as to endure everlasting pain and fire without ever dying, we were to say that in the world to come there will be salt which becomes liquid in fire as if it were in water, and crackles in water as if it were in fire; or that there will be a fountain whose water in the chill air of night is so hot that it cannot be touched, while in the heat of day it is so cold that it cannot be drunk; or that there will be a stone which by its own heat burns the hand when tightly held, or a stone which cannot be extinguished if it has been lit in any part; or any of those wonders I have cited, while omitting numberless others? If we were to say that these things would be found in the world to come, and our sceptics were to reply, "If you wish us to believe these things, satisfy our reason about each of them," we should confess that we could not, because the frail comprehension of man cannot master these and such-like wonders of God's working; and that yet our reason was thoroughly convinced that the Almighty does nothing without reason, though the frail mind of man cannot explain the reason; and that while we are in many instances uncertain what He intends, yet that it is always most certain that nothing which He intends is impossible to Him; and that when He declares His mind, we believe Him whom we cannot believe to be either powerless or false. Nevertheless these cavillers at faith and exactors of reason, how do they dispose of those things of which a reason cannot be given, and which yet exist, though in apparent contrariety to the nature of things? If we had announced that these things were to be, these sceptics would have demanded from us the reason of them, as they do in the case of those things which we are announcing as destined to be. And consequently, as these present marvels are not non-existent, though human reason and discourse are lost in such works of God, so those things we speak of are not impossible because inexplicable; for in this particular they are in the same predicament as the marvels of earth.

CHAPTER VI

THAT ALL MARVELS ARE NOT OF NATURE'S PRODUCTION, BUT THAT SOME ARE DUE TO HUMAN INGENUITY AND OTHERS TO DIABOLIC CONTRIVANCE

At this point they will perhaps reply, "These things have no existence; we don't believe one of them; they are travellers' tales and fictitious romances;" and they may add what has the appearance of argument, and say, "If you believe such things as these, believe what is recorded in the same books, that there was or is a temple of Venus in which a candelabrum set in the open air holds a lamp, which burns so strongly that no storm or rain extinguishes it, and which is therefore called, like the stone mentioned above, the asbestos or inextinguishable lamp." They may say this with the intention of putting us into a dilemma: for if we say this is incredible, then we shall impugn the truth of the other recorded marvels; if, on the other hand, we admit that this is credible, we shall avouch the pagan deities. But, as I have already said in the eighteenth book of this work, we do not hold it necessary to believe all that profane history contains, since, as Varro says, even historians themselves disagree on so many points, that one would think they intended and were at pains to do so; but we believe, if we are disposed, those things which are not contradicted by these books, which we do not hesitate to say we *are* bound to believe. But as to those permanent miracles of nature, whereby we wish to persuade the sceptical of the miracles of the world to come, those are quite sufficient for our purpose which we ourselves can observe, or of which it is not difficult to find trustworthy witnesses. Moreover, that temple of Venus, with its inextinguishable lamp, so far from hemming us into a corner, opens an advantageous field to our argument. For to this inextinguishable lamp we add a host of marvels wrought by men, or by magic—that is, by men under the influence of devils, or by the devils directly—for such marvels we cannot deny without impugning the truth of the sacred Scriptures we believe. That lamp, therefore, was either by some mechanical and human device fitted with asbestos, or it was arranged by magical art in order that the worshippers might be astonished, or some devil under the name of Venus so signally manifested himself that this prodigy both began and became permanent. Now devils are attracted to dwell in certain temples by means of the creatures (God's creatures, not theirs), who present to them what suits their various tastes. They are attracted not by food like animals, but, like spirits, by such symbols as suit their taste, various kinds of stones, woods, plants, animals, songs, rites. And that men may provide these attractions, the devils first of all cunningly seduce them, either by imbuing their hearts with a secret poison, or by revealing themselves under a friendly guise, and thus make a few of them their disciples, who become the instructors of the multitude. For unless they first instructed men, it were impossible to know what each of them desires, what they shrink from, by what name they should be invoked or constrained to be present. Hence the origin of magic and magicians. But, above all, they possess the hearts of men, and are chiefly proud of this possession when they transform themselves into angels of light. Very many things that occur, therefore, are their doing; and these deeds of theirs we ought all the more carefully to shun as we acknowledge them to be very surprising. And yet these very deeds forward my present arguments. For if such marvels are wrought by unclean devils, how much mightier are the holy angels! and what can not that God do who made the angels themselves capable of working miracles!

If, then, very many effects can be contrived by human art, of so surprising a kind that the uninitiated think them divine, as when, *e.g.*, in a certain temple two magnets have been adjusted, one in the roof, another in the floor, so that an iron image is suspended in mid-air between them, one would suppose by the power of the divinity, were he ignorant of the magnets above and beneath; or, as in the case of that lamp of Venus which we already mentioned as being a skillful adaptation of asbestos; if, again, by the help of magicians, who Scripture calls sorcerers and enchanters, the devils could gain such power that the noble poet Virgil should consider himself justified in describing a very powerful magician in these lines:

> Her charms can cure what souls she please,
> Rob other hearts of healthful ease,
> Turn rivers backward to their source,
> And make the stars forget their course,
>   And call up ghosts from night:
> The ground shall bellow 'neath your feet:
> The mountain-ash shall quit its seat,
>   And travel down the height;[7]

if this be so, how much more able is God to do those thing which to sceptics are incredible, but to His power easy, since it is He who has given to stones and all other things their virtue, and to men their skill to use them in wonderful ways; He who has given to the angels a nature more mighty than that of all that lives on earth; He whose power surpasses all marvels, and whose wisdom in working, ordaining, and permitting is no less marvellous in its governance of all things than in its creation of all!

[7] *Aeneid,* iv. 487-491

CHAPTER VII

THAT THE ULTIMATE REASON FOR BELIEVING MIRACLES
IS THE OMNIPOTENCE OF THE CREATOR

Why, then, cannot God effect both that the bodies of the dead shall rise, and that the bodies of the damned shall be tormented in everlasting fire— God, who made the world full of countless miracles in sky, earth, air, and waters, while itself is a miracle unquestionably greater and more admirable than all the marvels it is filled with? But those with whom or against whom we are arguing, who believe both that there is a God who made the world, and that there are gods created by Him who administer the world's laws as His viceregents—our adversaries, I say, who, so far from denying emphatically, assert that there are powers in the world which effect marvellous results (whether of their own accord, or because they are invoked by some rite or prayer, or in some magical way) when we lay before them the wonderful properties of other things which are neither rational animals nor rational spirits, but such material objects as those we have just cited, are in the habit of replying, This is their natural property, their nature; these are the powers naturally belonging to them. Thus the whole reason why Agrigentine salt dissolves in fire and crackles in water is that this is its nature. Yet this seems rather contrary to nature, which has given not to fire but to water the power of melting salt, and the power of scorching it not to water but to fire. But this, they say, is the natural property of *this* salt, to show effects contrary to these. The same reason, therefore, is assigned to account for that Garamantian fountain, of which one and the same runlet is chill by day and boiling by night, so that in either extreme it cannot be touched. So also of that other fountain which, though it is cold to the touch, and though it, like other fountains, extinguishes a lighted torch, yet, unlike other fountains, and in a surprising manner, kindles an extinguished torch. So of the asbestos stone, which, though it has no heat of its own, yet when kindled by fire applied to it, cannot be extinguished. And so of the rest, which I am weary of reciting, and in which, though there seems to be an extraordinary property contrary to nature, yet no other reason is given for them than this, that this is their nature—a brief reason truly, and, I own, a satisfactory reply. But since God is the author of all natures, how is it that our adversaries, when they refuse to believe what we affirm, on the ground that it is impossible, are unwilling to accept from us a better explanation than their own, *viz.*, that this is the will of Almighty God—for certainly He is called Almighty only because He is mighty to do all He will—He who was able to create so many marvels, not only unknown, but very well ascertained, as I have been showing, and which, were they not under our own observation, or reported by recent and credible witnesses, would certainly be pronounced impossible? For as for those marvels which have no other testimony than the writers in whose books we read them, and who wrote without being divinely instructed, and are therefore liable to human error, we cannot justly blame any one who declines to believe them.

For my own part, I do not wish all the marvels I have cited to be rashly accepted, for I do not myself believe them implicitly, save those which have either come under my own observation, or which any one can readily verify, such as the lime which is heated by water and cooled by oil; the magnet which by its mysterious and insensible suction attracts the iron, but has no effect on a straw; the peacock's flesh which triumphs over the corruption from which not the flesh of Plato is exempt; the chaff so chilling that it prevents snow from melting, so heating that it forces apples to ripen; the glowing fire, which, in accordance with its glowing appearance, whitens the stones it bakes, while, contrary to its glowing appearance, it begrimes most things it burns (just as dirty stains are made by oil, however pure it be, and as the lines drawn by white silver are black); the charcoal, too, which by the action of fire is so completely changed from its original, that a finely marked piece of wood becomes hideous, the tough becomes brittle, the decaying incorruptible. Some of these things I know in common with many other persons, some of them in common with all men; and there are many others which I have not room to insert in this book. But of those which I have cited, though I have not myself seen, but only read about them, I have been unable to find trustworthy witnesses from whom I could ascertain whether they are facts, except in the case of that fountain in which burning torches are extinguished and extinguished torches lit, and of the apples of Sodom, which are ripe to appearance, but are filled with dust. And indeed I have not met with any who said they had seen that fountain in Epirus, but with some who knew there was a similar fountain in Gaul not far from Grenoble. The fruit of the trees of Sodom, however, is not only spoken of in books worthy of credit, but so many persons say that they have seen it that I cannot doubt the fact. But the rest of the prodigies I receive without definitely affirming or denying them; and I have cited them because I read them in the authors of our adversaries, and that I might prove how many things many among themselves believe, because they are written in the works of their own literary men, though no rational explanation of them is given, and yet they scorn to believe us when we assert that Almighty God will do what is beyond their experience and observation; and this they do even though we assign a reason for His work. For what better and stronger reason for such things can be given than to say that the Almighty is able to bring them to pass, and will bring them to pass, having predicted them in those books in which many other marvels which have already come to pass were predicted? Those things which are regarded as impossible will be accomplished according to the word, and by the power of that God who predicted and effected that the incredulous nations should believe incredible wonders.

CHAPTER VIII

THAT IT IS NOT CONTRARY TO NATURE THAT, IN AN OBJECT WHOSE NATURE IS KNOWN, THERE SHOULD BE DISCOVERED AN ALTERATION OF THE PROPERTIES WHICH HAVE BEEN KNOWN AS ITS NATURAL PROPERTIES

But if they reply that their reason for not believing us when we say that human bodies will always burn and yet never die, is that the nature of human bodies is known to be quite otherwise constituted; if they say that for this miracle we cannot give the reason which was valid in the case of those natural miracles, viz., that this is the natural property, the nature of the thing—for we know that this is not the nature of human flesh—we find our answer in the sacred writings, that even this human flesh was constituted in one fashion before there was sin—was constituted, in fact, so that it could not die—and in another fashion after sin, being made such as we see it in this miserable state of mortality, unable to retain enduring life. And so in the resurrection of the dead shall it be constituted differently from its present well-known condition. But as they do not believe these writings of ours, in which we read what nature man had in paradise, and how remote he was from the necessity of death—and indeed, if they did believe them, we should of course have little trouble in debating with them the future punishment of the damned—we must produce from the writings of their own most learned authorities some instances to show that it is possible for a thing to become different from what it was formerly known characteristically to be.

From the book of Marcus Varro, entitled, *Of the Race of the Roman People*, I cite word for word the following instance: "There occurred a remarkable celestial portent; for Castor records that, in the brilliant star Venus, called Vesperugo by Plautus, and the lovely Hesperus by Homer, there occurred so strange a prodigy, that it changed its color, size, form, course, which never happened before nor since. Adrastus of Cyzicus, and Dion of Naples, famous mathematicians, said that this occurred in the reign of Ogyges." So great an author as Varro would certainly not have called this a portent had it not seemed to be contrary to nature. For we say that all portents are contrary to nature; but they are not so. For how is that contrary to nature which happens by the will of God, since the will of so mighty a Creator is certainly the nature of each created thing? A portent, therefore, happens not contrary to nature, but contrary to what we know as nature. But who can number the multitude of portents recorded in profane histories? Let us then at present fix our attention on this one only which concerns the matter in hand. What is there so arranged by the Author of the nature of heaven and earth as the exactly ordered course of the stars? What is there established by laws so sure and inflexible? And yet, when it pleased Him who with sovereignty and supreme power regulates all He has created, a star conspicuous among the rest by its size and splendor changed its color, size, form, and, most wonderful of all, the order and law of its course! Certainly that phenomenon disturbed the canons of the astronomers, if there were any then, by which they tabulate, as by unerring computation, the past and future movements of the stars, so as to take upon them to affirm that this which happened to the morning star (Venus) never happened before nor since. But we read in the divine books that even the sun itself stood still when a holy man, Joshua the son of Nun, had begged this from God until victory should finish the battle he had begun; and that it even went back, that the promise of fifteen years added to the life of king Hezekiah might be sealed by this additional prodigy. But these miracles, which were vouchsafed to the merits of holy men, even when our adversaries believe them, they attribute to magical arts; so Virgil, in the lines I quoted above, ascribes to magic the power to

> Turn rivers backward to their source,
> And make the stars forget their course.

For in our sacred books we read that this also happened, that a river "turned backward," was stayed above while the lower part flowed on, when the people passed over under the above-mentioned leader, Joshua the son of Nun; and also when Elias the prophet crossed; and afterwards, when his disciple Elisha passed through it: and we have just mentioned how, in the case of king Hezekiah, the greatest of the "stars forgot its course." But what happened to Venus, according to Varro, was not said by him to have happened in answer to any man's prayer.

Let not the sceptics then benight themselves in this knowledge of the nature of things, as if divine power cannot bring to pass in an object anything else than what their own experience has shown them to be in its nature. Even the very things which are most commonly known as natural would not be less wonderful nor less effectual to excite surprise in all who beheld them, if men were not accustomed to admire nothing but what is rare. For who that thoughtfully observes the countless multitude of men, and their similarity of nature, can fail to remark with surprise and admiration the individuality of each man's appearance, suggesting to us, as it does, that unless men were like one another, they would not be distinguished from the rest of the animals; while unless, on the other hand, they were unlike, they could not be distinguished from one another, so that those whom we declare to be like, we also find to be unlike? And the unlikeness is the more wonderful consideration of the two; for a common nature seems rather to require similarity. And yet, because the very rarity of things is that which makes them wonderful, we are filled with much greater wonder when we are introduced to two men so like, that we either always or frequently mistake in endeavoring to distinguish between them.

But possibly, though Varro is a heathen historian, and a very learned one, they may disbelieve that what I have cited from him truly occurred; or they may say the example is invalid, because the star did not for any length of time continue to follow its new course, but returned to its ordinary orbit. There is, then, another phenomenon at present open to their observation, and which, in my opinion, ought to be sufficient to convince them that, though they have observed and ascertained some natural law, they ought not on that account to prescribe to God, as if He could not change and turn it into something very different from what they have observed. The land of Sodom was not always as it now is; but once it had the appearance of other lands, and enjoyed equal if not richer fertility; for, in the divine narrative, it was compared to the paradise of God. But after it was touched by fire from heaven, as even pagan history testifies, and as is now witnessed by those who visit the spot, it became unnaturally and horribly sooty in appearance; and its apples, under a deceitful appearance of ripeness, contain ashes within. Here is a thing which was of one kind, and is of another. You see how its nature was converted by the wonderful transmutation wrought by the Creator of all natures into so very disgusting a diversity—an alteration which after so long a time took place, and after so long a time still continues. As therefore it was not impossible to God to create such natures as He pleased, so it is not impossible to Him to change these natures of His own creation into whatever He pleases, and thus spread abroad a multitude of those marvels which are called monsters, portents, prodigies, phenomena, and which if I were minded to cite and record, what end would there be to this work? They say that they are called "monsters," because they *demonstrate* or signify something; "portents," because they *portend* something, that is, *show before; prodigies*, because they *speak before*, that is foretell the future. But let their diviners see how they are either deceived, or even when they do predict true things, it is because they are inspired by spirits, who are intent upon entangling the minds of men (worthy, indeed, of such a fate) in the meshes of a hurtful curiosity, or how they light now and then upon some truth, because they make so many predictions. Yet, for our part, these things which happen contrary to nature, and are said to be contrary to nature (as the apostle, speaking after the manner of men, says, that to graft the wild olive into the good olive, and to partake of its fatness, is contrary to nature), and are called monsters, phenomena, portents, prodigies, ought to demonstrate, portend, predict that God will bring to pass what He has foretold regarding the bodies of men, no difficulty preventing Him, no law of nature prescribing to Him His limit. How He has foretold what He is to do, I think I have sufficiently shown in the preceding book, culling from the sacred Scriptures, both of the New and Old Testaments, not, indeed, all the passages that relate to this, but as many as I judged to suffice for this work.

CHAPTER IX

OF HELL, AND THE NATURE OF ETERNAL PUNISHMENTS

So then what God by His prophet has said of the everlasting punishment of the damned shall come to pass—shall without fail come to pass—"their worm shall not die, neither shall their fire be quenched." [8] In order to impress this upon us most forcibly, the Lord Jesus Himself, when ordering us to cut off our members, meaning thereby those persons whom a man loves as the most useful members of his body, says, "It is better for thee to enter into life maimed, than having two hands to go into hell, into the fire that never shall be quenched; where their worm dieth not, and their fire is not quenched." Similarly of the foot: "It is better for thee to enter halt into life, than having two feet to be cast into hell, into the fire that never shall be quenched; where their worm dieth not, and the fire is not quenched." So, too, of the eye: "It is better for thee to enter into the kingdom of God with one eye, than having two eyes to be cast into hell fire; where their worm dieth not, and the fire is not quenched." [9] He did not shrink from using the same words three times over in one passage. And who is not terrified by this repetition, and by the threat of that punishment uttered so vehemently by the lips of the Lord Himself?

Now they who would refer both the fire and the worm to the spirit, and not to the body, affirm that the wicked, who are separated from the kingdom of God, shall be burned, as it were, by the anguish of a spirit repenting too late and fruitlessly; and they contend that fire is therefore not inappropriately used to express this burning torment, as when the apostle exclaims "Who is offended, and I burn not?" [10] The worm, too, they think, is to be similarly understood. For it is written, they say, "As the moth consumes the garment, and the worm the wood, so does grief consume the heart of a man." [11] But they who make no doubt that in that future punishment both body and soul shall suffer, affirm that the body shall be burned with fire, while the soul shall be, as it were, gnawed by a worm of anguish. Though this view is more reasonable—for it is absurd to suppose that either body or soul will escape pain in the future punishment—yet, for my own part, I find it easier to understand both as referring to the body than to suppose that neither does; and I think that Scripture is silent regarding the spiritual pain of the damned, because, though not expressed, it is necessarily understood that in a body thus tormented the soul also is tortured with a fruitless repentance. For we read in the ancient Scriptures, "The vengeance of the flesh of the ungodly is fire and worms." [12] It might have been more briefly said, "The vengeance of the ungodly." Why, then, was it said, "The flesh of the ungodly," unless because both the fire and the worm are to be the pun-

[8] Isa. lxvi. 24   [9] Mark ix. 43-48   [10] 2 Cor. xi. 29   [11] Isa. li. 8   [12] Ecclus. vii. 17

ishment of the flesh? Or if the object of the writer in saying, "The vengeance of the flesh," was to indicate that this shall be the punishment of those who live after the flesh (for this leads to the second death, as the apostle intimated when he said, "For if ye live after the flesh, ye shall die" [13]) let each one make his own choice, either assigning the fire to the body and the worm to the soul—the one figuratively, the other really—or assigning both really to the body. For I have already sufficiently made out that animals can live in the fire, in burning without being consumed, in pain without dying, by a miracle of the most omnipotent Creator, to whom no one can deny that this is possible, if he be not ignorant by whom has been made all that is wonderful in all nature. For it is God Himself who has wrought all these miracles, great and small, in this world which I have mentioned, and incomparably more which I have omitted, and who has enclosed these marvels in this world, itself the greatest miracle of all. Let each man, then, choose which he will, whether he thinks that the worm is real and pertains to the body, or that spiritual things are meant by bodily representations, and that it belongs to the soul. But which of these is true will be more readily discovered by the facts themselves, when there shall be in the saints such knowledge as shall not require that their own experience teach them the nature of these punishments, but as shall, by its own fullness and perfection, suffice to instruct them in this matter. For "now we know in part, until that which is perfect is come;" [14] only, this we believe about those future bodies, that they shall be such as shall certainly be pained by the fire.

CHAPTER X

WHETHER THE FIRE OF HELL, IF IT BE MATERIAL FIRE, CAN BURN THE WICKED SPIRITS, THAT IS TO SAY, DEVILS, WHO ARE IMMATERIAL

Here arises the question: If the fire is not to be immaterial, analogous to the pain of the soul, but material, burning by contact, so that bodies may be tormented in it, how can evil spirits be punished in it? For it is undoubtedly the same fire which is to serve for the punishment of men and of devils, according to the words of Christ: "Depart from me, ye cursed, into everlasting fire, prepared for the devil and his angels;" [15] unless, perhaps, as learned men have thought, the devils have a kind of body made of that dense and humid air which we feel strikes us when the wind is blowing. And if this kind of substance could not be affected by fire, it could not burn when heated in the baths. For in order to burn, it is first burned, and affects other things as itself is affected. But if any one maintains that the devils have no bodies, this is not a matter either to be laboriously investigated, or to be debated with keenness. For why may we not assert that even immaterial spirits may, in some extraordinary way, yet really be pained by

---

[13] Rom. viii. 13   [14] 1 Cor. xiii. 9, 10   [15] Matt. xxv. 41

the punishment of material fire, if the spirits of men, which also are certainly immaterial, are both now contained in material members of the body, and in the world to come shall be indissolubly united to their own bodies? Therefore, though the devils have no bodies, yet their spirits, that is, the devils themselves, shall be brought into thorough contact with the material fires, to be tormented by them; not that the fires themselves with which they are brought into contact shall be animated by their connection with these spirits, and become animals composed of body and spirit, but, as I said, this junction will be effected in a wonderful and ineffable way, so that they shall receive pain from the fires, but give no life to them. And, in truth, this other mode of union, by which bodies and spirits are bound together and become animals, is thoroughly marvellous, and beyond the comprehension of man, though this it is which is man.

I would indeed say that these spirits will burn without any body of their own, as that rich man was burning in hell when he exclaimed, "I am tormented in this flame," [16] were I not aware that it is aptly said in reply, that that flame was of the same nature as the eyes he raised and fixed on Lazarus, as the tongue on which he entreated that a little cooling water might be dropped, or as the finger of Lazarus, with which he asked that this might be done—all of which took place where souls exist without bodies. Thus, therefore, both that flame in which he burned and that drop he begged were immaterial, and resembled the visions of sleepers or persons in an ecstasy, to whom immaterial objects appear in a bodily form. For the man himself who is in such a state, though it be in spirit only, not in body, yet sees himself so like to his own body that he cannot discern any difference whatever. But that hell, which also is called a lake of fire and brimstone,[17] will be material fire, and will torment the bodies of the damned, whether men or devils—the solid bodies of the one, aerial bodies of the others; or if only men have bodies as well as souls, yet the evil spirits, though without bodies, shall be so connected with the bodily fires as to receive pain without imparting life. One fire certainly shall be the lot of both, for thus the truth has declared.

CHAPTER XI

WHETHER IT IS JUST THAT THE PUNISHMENTS OF SINS LAST LONGER THAN THE SINS THEMSELVES LASTED

Some, however, of those against whom we are defending the city of God, think it unjust that any man be doomed to an eternal punishment for sins which, no matter how great they were, were perpetrated in a brief space of time; as if any law ever regulated the duration of the punishment by the duration of the offence punished! Cicero tells us that the laws recognize

---

[16] Luke xvi. 24   [17] Rev. xx. 10

eight kinds of penalty—damages, imprisonment, scourging, reparation,[18] disgrace, exile, death, slavery. Is there any one of these which may be compressed into a brevity proportioned to the rapid commission of the offence, so that no longer time may be spent in its punishment than in its perpetration, unless, perhaps, reparation? For this requires that the offender suffer what he did, as that clause of the law says, "Eye for eye, tooth for tooth." [19] For certainly it is possible for an offender to lose his eye by the severity of legal retaliation in as brief a time as he deprived another of his eye by the cruelty of his own lawlessness. But if scourging be a reasonable penalty for kissing another man's wife, is not the fault of an instant visited with long hours of atonement, and the momentary delight punished with lasting pain? What shall we say of imprisonment? Must the criminal be confined only for so long a time as he spent on the offence for which he is committed? or is not a penalty of many years' confinement imposed on the slave who has provoked his master with a word, or has struck him a blow that is quickly over? And as to damages, disgrace, exile, slavery, which are commonly inflicted so as to admit of no relaxation or pardon, do not these resemble eternal punishments in so far as this short life allows a resemblance? For they are not eternal only because the life in which they are endured is not eternal; and yet the crimes which are punished with these most protracted sufferings are perpetrated in a very brief space of time. Nor is there any one who would suppose that the pains of punishment should occupy as short a time as the offence; or that murder, adultery, sacrilege, or any other crime, should be measured, not by the enormity of the injury or wickedness, but by the length of time spent in its perpetration. Then as to the award of death for any great crime, do the laws reckon the punishment to consist in the brief moment in which death is inflicted, or in this, that the offender is eternally banished from the society of the living? And just as the punishment of the first death cuts men off from this present mortal city, so does the punishment of the second death cut men off from that future immortal city. For as the laws of this present city do not provide for the executed criminal's return to it, so neither is he who is condemned to the second death recalled again to life everlasting. But if temporal sin is visited with eternal punishment, how, then, they say, is that true which your Christ says, "With the same measure that ye mete withal it shall be measured to you again?" [20] and they do not observe that "the same measure" refers, not to an equal space of time, but to the retribution of evil, or, in other words, to the law by which he who has done evil suffers evil. Besides, these words could be appropriately understood as referring to the matter of which our Lord was speaking when He used them, viz., judgments and condemnation. Thus, if he who unjustly judges and condemns is himself justly judged and condemned, he receives "with the same measure" though not the same thing

[18] "Talio," i.e., the rendering of like for like, the punishment being exactly similar to the injury sustained   [19] Ex. xxi. 24   [20] Luke vi. 38

as he gave. For judgment he gave, and judgment he receives, though the judgment he gave was unjust, the judgment he receives just.

CHAPTER XII

OF THE GREATNESS OF THE FIRST TRANSGRESSION, ON ACCOUNT OF WHICH ETERNAL PUNISHMENT IS DUE TO ALL WHO ARE NOT WITHIN THE PALE OF THE SAVIOUR'S GRACE

But eternal punishment seems hard and unjust to human perceptions, because in the weakness of our mortal condition there is wanting that highest and purest wisdom by which it can be perceived how great a wickedness was committed in that first transgression. The more enjoyment man found in God, the greater was his wickedness in abandoning Him; and he who destroyed in himself a good which might have been eternal, became worthy of eternal evil. Hence the whole mass of the human race is condemned; for he who at first gave entrance to sin has been punished with all his posterity who were in him as in a root, so that no one is exempt from this just and due punishment, unless delivered by mercy and undeserved grace; and the human race is so apportioned that in some is displayed the efficacy of merciful grace, in the rest the efficacy of just retribution. For both could not be displayed in all; for if all had remained under the punishment of just condemnation, there would have been seen in no one the mercy of redeeming grace. And, on the other hand, if all had been transferred from darkness to light, the severity of retribution would have been manifested in none. But many more are left under punishment than are delivered from it, in order that it may thus be shown what was due to all. And had it been inflicted on all, no one could justly have found fault with the justice of Him who taketh vengeance; whereas, in the deliverance of so many from that just award, there is cause to render the most cordial thanks to the gratuitous bounty of Him who delivers.

CHAPTER XIII

AGAINST THE OPINION OF THOSE WHO THINK THAT THE PUNISHMENTS OF THE WICKED AFTER DEATH ARE PURGATORIAL

The Platonists, indeed, while they maintain that no sins are unpunished, suppose that all punishment is administered for remedial purposes, be it inflicted by human or divine law, in this life or after death; for a man may be scathless here, or, though punished, may yet not amend. Hence that passage of Virgil, where, when he had said of our earthly bodies and mortal members, that our souls derive—

> Hence wild desires and grovelling fears,
> And human laughter, human tears;

> Immured in dungeon-seeming night,
> They look abroad, yet see no light,

goes on to say:

> Nay, when at last the life has fled,
> And left the body cold and dead,
> Ee'n then there passes not away
> The painful heritage of clay;
> Full many a long-contracted stain
> Perforce must linger deep in grain.
> So penal sufferings they endure
> For ancient crime, to make them pure;
> Some hang aloft in open view,
> For winds to pierce them through and through,
> While others purge their guilt deep-dyed
> In burning fire or whelming tide.[21]

They who are of this opinion would have all punishments after death to be purgatorial; and as the elements of air, fire, and water are superior to earth, one or other of these may be the instrument of expiating and purging away the stain contracted by the contagion of earth. So Virgil hints at the air in the words, "Some hang aloft for winds to pierce;" at the water in "whelming tide;" and at fire in the expression "in burning fire." For our part, we recognize that even in this life some punishments are purgatorial—not, indeed, to those whose life is none the better, but rather the worse for them, but to those who are constrained by them to amend their life. All other punishments, whether temporal or eternal, inflicted as they are on every one by divine providence, are sent either on account of past sins, or of sins presently allowed in the life, or to exercise and reveal a man's graces. They may be inflicted by the instrumentality of bad men and angels as well as of the good. For even if any one suffers some hurt through another's wickedness or mistake, the man indeed sins whose ignorance or injustice does the harm; but God, who by His just though hidden judgment permits it to be done, sins not. But temporary punishments are suffered by some in this life only, by others after death, by others both now and then; but all of them before that last and strictest judgment. But of those who suffer temporary punishments after death, all are not doomed to those everlasting pains which are to follow that judgment; for to some, as we have already said, what is not remitted in this world is remitted in the next, that is, they are not punished with the eternal punishment of the world to come.

[21] *Aeneid*, vi. 733

CHAPTER XIV

OF THE TEMPORARY PUNISHMENTS OF THIS LIFE TO WHICH THE HUMAN CONDITION IS SUBJECT

Quite exceptional are those who are not punished in this life, but only afterwards. Yet that there have been some who have reached the decrepitude of age without experiencing even the slightest sickness, and who have had uninterrupted enjoyment of life, I know both from report and from my own observation. However, the very life we mortals lead is itself all punishment, for it is all temptation, as the Scriptures declare, where it is written, "Is not the life of man upon earth a temptation?" [22] For ignorance is itself no slight punishment, or want of culture, which it is with justice thought so necessary to escape, that boys are compelled, under pain of severe punishment, to learn trades or letters; and the learning to which they are driven by punishment is itself so much of a punishment to them, that they sometimes prefer the pain that drives them to the pain to which they are driven by it. And who would not shrink from the alternative, and elect to die, if it were proposed to him either to suffer death or to be again an infant? Our infancy, indeed, introducing us to this life not with laughter but with tears, seems unconsciously to predict the ills we are to encounter. Zoroaster alone is said to have laughed when he was born, and that unnatural omen portended no good to him. For he is said to have been the inventor of magical arts, though indeed they were unable to secure to him even the poor felicity of this present life against the assaults of his enemies. For, himself king of the Bactrians, he was conquered by Ninus king of the Assyrians. In short, the words of Scripture, "An heavy yoke is upon the sons of Adam, from the day that they go out of their mother's womb till the day that they return to the mother of all things" [23]—these words so infallibly find fulfillment, that even the little ones, who by the laver of regeneration have been freed from the bond of original sin in which alone they were held, yet suffer many ills, and in some instances are even exposed to the assaults of evil spirits. But let us not for a moment suppose that this suffering is prejudicial to their future happiness, even though it has so increased as to sever soul from body, and to terminate their life in that early age.

[22] Job vii. 1   [23] Ecclus. xl. 1

CHAPTER XV

THAT EVERYTHING WHICH THE GRACE OF GOD DOES IN THE WAY OF
RESCUING US FROM THE INVETERATE EVILS IN WHICH WE ARE
SUNK, PERTAINS TO THE FUTURE WORLD, IN WHICH ALL
THINGS ARE MADE NEW

Nevertheless, in the "heavy yoke that is laid upon the sons of Adam, from the day that they go out of their mother's womb to the day that they return to the mother of all things," there is found an admirable though painful monitor teaching us to be sober-minded, and convincing us that this life has become penal in consequence of that outrageous wickedness which was perpetrated in Paradise, and that all to which the New Testament invites belongs to that future inheritance which awaits us in the world to come, and is offered for our acceptance, as the earnest that we may, in its own due time, obtain that of which it is the pledge. Now, therefore, let us walk in hope, and let us by the spirit mortify the deeds of the flesh, and so make progress from day to day. For "the Lord knoweth them that are His;" [24] and "as many as are led by the Spirit of God, they are sons of God," [25] but by grace, not by nature. For there is but one Son of God by nature, who in His compassion became Son of man for our sakes, that we, by nature sons of men, might by grace become through Him sons of God. For He, abiding unchangeable, took upon Him our nature, that thereby He might take us to Himself; and, holding fast His own divinity, He became partaker of our infirmity, that we, being changed into some better thing, might, by participating in His righteousness and immortality, lose our own properties of sin and mortality, and preserve whatever good quality He had implanted in our nature, perfected now by sharing in the goodness of His nature. For as by the sin of one man we have fallen into a misery so deplorable, so by the righteousness of one Man, who also is God, shall we come to a blessedness inconceivably exalted. Nor ought any one to trust that he has passed from the one man to the other until he shall have reached that place where there is no temptation, and have entered into the peace which he seeks in the many and various conflicts of this war, in which "the flesh lusteth against the spirit, and the spirit against the flesh." [26] Now, such a war as this would have had no existence, if human nature had, in the exercise of free will, continued steadfast in the uprightness in which it was created. But now in its misery it makes war upon itself, because in its blessedness it would not continue at peace with God; and this, though it be a miserable calamity, is better than the earlier stages of this life, which do not recognize that a war is to be maintained. For better is it to contend with vices than without conflict to be subdued by them. Better, I say, is war with the hope of peace

[24] 2 Tim. ii. 19   [25] Rom. viii. 14   [26] Gal. v. 17

everlasting than captivity without any thought of deliverance. We long, indeed, for the cessation of this war, and, kindled by the flame of divine love, we burn for entrance on that well-ordered peace in which whatever is inferior is for ever subordinated to what is above it. But if (which God forbid) there had been no hope of so blessed a consummation, we should still have preferred to endure the hardness of this conflict, rather than, by our non-resistance, to yield ourselves to the dominion of vice.

CHAPTER XVI

THE LAWS OF GRACE, WHICH EXTEND TO ALL THE EPOCHS OF THE LIFE OF THE REGENERATE

But such is God's mercy towards the vessels of mercy which He has prepared for glory, that even the first age of man, that is, infancy, which submits without any resistance to the flesh, and the second age, which is called boyhood, and which has not yet understanding enough to undertake this warfare, and therefore yields to almost every vicious pleasure (because though this age has the power of speech, and may therefore seem to have passed infancy, the mind is still too weak to comprehend the commandment), yet if either of these ages has received the sacraments of the Mediator, then, although the present life be immediately brought to an end, the child, having been translated from the power of darkness to the kingdom of Christ, shall not only be saved from eternal punishments, but shall not even suffer purgatorial torments after death. For spiritual regeneration of itself suffices to prevent any evil consequences resulting after death from the connection with death which carnal generation forms.[27] But when we reach that age which can now comprehend the commandment, and submit to the dominion of law, we must declare war upon vices, and wage this war keenly, lest we be landed in damnable sins. And if vices have not gathered strength, by habitual victory they are more easily overcome and subdued; but if they have been used to conquer and rule, it is only with difficulty and labor they are mastered. And indeed this victory cannot be sincerely and truly gained but by delighting in true righteousness, and it is faith in Christ that gives this. For if the law be present with its command, and the Spirit be absent with His help, the presence of the prohibition serves only to increase the desire to sin, and adds the guilt of transgression. Sometimes, indeed, patent vices are overcome by other and hidden vices, which are reckoned virtues, though pride and a kind of ruinous self-sufficiency are their informing principles. Accordingly vices are then only to be considered overcome when they are conquered by the love of God, which God Himself alone gives, and which He gives only through the Mediator between God and men, the man Christ Jesus, who became a partaker of our mortality that He might make

[27] Cf. *Ep.* 98, *ad Bonifacium*

us partakers of His divinity. But few indeed are they who are so happy as to have passed their youth without committing any damnable sins, either by dissolute or violent conduct, or by following some godless and unlawful opinions, but have subdued by their greatness of soul everything in them which could make them the slaves of carnal pleasures. The greater number having first become transgressors of the law that they have received, and having allowed vice to have the ascendency in them, then flee to grace for help, and so, by a penitence more bitter, and a struggle more violent than it would otherwise have been, they subdue the soul to God, and thus give it its lawful authority over the flesh, and become victors. Whoever, therefore, desires to escape eternal punishment, let him not only be baptized, but also justified in Christ, and so let him in truth pass from the devil to Christ. And let him not fancy that there are any purgatorial pains except before that final and dreadful judgment. We must not, however, deny that even the eternal fire will be proportioned to the deserts of the wicked, so that to some it will be more, and to others less painful, whether this result be accomplished by a variation in the temperature of the fire itself, graduated according to every one's merit, or whether it be that the heat remains the same, but that all do not feel it with equal intensity of torment.

CHAPTER XVII

OF THOSE WHO FANCY THAT NO MEN SHALL BE PUNISHED ETERNALLY

I must now, I see, enter the lists of amicable controversy with those tender-hearted Christians who decline to believe that any, or that all of those whom the infallibly just Judge may pronounce worthy of the punishment of hell, shall suffer eternally, and who suppose that they shall be delivered after a fixed term of punishment, longer or shorter according to the amount of each man's sin. In respect of this matter, Origen was even more indulgent; for he believed that even the devil himself and his angels, after suffering those more severe and prolonged pains which their sins deserved, should be delivered from their torments, and associated with the holy angels. But the Church, not without reason, condemned him for this and other errors, especially for his theory of the ceaseless alternation of happiness and misery, and the interminable transitions from the one state to the other at fixed periods of ages; for in this theory he lost even the credit of being merciful, by allotting to the saints real miseries for the expiation of their sins, and false happiness, which brought them no true and secure joy, that is, no fearless assurance of eternal blessedness. Very different, however, is the error we speak of, which is dictated by the tenderness of these Christians who suppose that the sufferings of those who are condemned in the judgment will be temporary, while the blessedness of all who are sooner or later set free will be eternal. Which opinion, if it is good and true because it is merciful, will be so much the better and truer in proportion as it becomes more merciful. Let, then, this fountain of mercy be extended, and flow forth even to the lost angels, and let them also be set free, at least after as many and long ages as seem fit! Why does this stream of mercy flow to all the human race, and dry up as soon as it reaches the angelic? And yet they dare not extend their pity further, and propose the deliverance of the devil himself. Or if any one is bold enough to do so, he does indeed put to shame their charity, but is himself convicted of error that is more unsightly, and a wresting of God's truth that is more perverse, in proportion as his clemency of sentiment seems to be greater.

CHAPTER XVIII

OF THOSE WHO FANCY THAT, ON ACCOUNT OF THE SAINTS' INTERCESSION, NO MAN SHALL BE DAMNED IN THE LAST JUDGMENT

There are others, again, with whose opinions I have become acquainted in conversation, who, though they seem to reverence the holy Scriptures, are yet of reprehensible life, and who accordingly, in their own interest, attribute to God a still greater compassion towards men. For they acknowledge that it is truly predicted in the divine word that the wicked and unbelieving are worthy of punishment, but they assert that, when the judgment comes, mercy will prevail. For, say they, God, having compassion on them, will give them up to the prayers and intercessions of His saints. For if the saints used to pray for them when they suffered from their cruel hatred, how much more will they do so when they see them prostrate and humble suppliants? For we cannot, they say, believe that the saints shall lose their bowels of compassion when they have attained the most perfect and complete holiness; so that they who, when still sinners, prayed for their enemies, should now, when they are freed from sin, withhold from interceding for their suppliants. Or shall God refuse to listen to so many of His beloved children, when their holiness has purged their prayers of all hindrance to His answering them? And the passage of the psalm which is cited by those who admit that wicked men and infidels shall be punished for a long time, though in the end delivered from all sufferings, is claimed also by the persons we are now speaking of as making much more for them. The verse runs: "Shall God forget to be gracious? Shall He in anger shut up His tender mercies?" [28] His anger, they say, would condemn all that are unworthy of everlasting happiness to endless punishment. But if He suffer them to be punished for a long time, or even at all, must He not shut up His tender mercies, which the Psalmist implies He will not do? For he does not

[28] Ps. lxxvii. 9

say, Shall He in anger shut up His tender mercies for a long period? but he implies that He will not shut them up at all.

And they deny that thus God's threat of judgment is proved to be false even though He condemn no man, any more than we can say that His threat to overthrow Nineveh was false, though the destruction which was absolutely predicted was not accomplished. For He did not say, "Nineveh shall be overthrown if they do not repent and amend their ways," but without any such condition He foretold that the city should be overthrown. And this prediction, they maintain, was true because God predicted the punishment which they deserved, although He was not to inflict it. For though He spared them on their repentance, yet He was certainly aware that they would repent, and, notwithstanding, absolutely and definitely predicted that the city should be overthrown. This was true, they say, in the truth of severity, because they were worthy of it; but in respect of the compassion which checked His anger, so that He spared the suppliants from the punishment with which He had threatened the rebellious, it was not true. If, then, He spared those whom His own holy prophet was provoked at His sparing, how much more shall He spare those more wretched suppliants for whom all His saints shall intercede? And they suppose that this conjecture of theirs is not hinted at in Scripture, for the sake of stimulating many to reformation of life through fear of very protracted or eternal sufferings, and of stimulating others to pray for those who have not reformed. However, they think that the divine oracles are not altogether silent on this point; for they ask to what purpose is it said, "How great is Thy goodness which Thou hast hidden for them that fear Thee," [29] if it be not to teach us that the great and hidden sweetness of God's mercy is concealed in order that men may fear? To the same purpose they think the apostle said, "For God hath concluded all men in unbelief, that He may have mercy upon all," [30] signifying that no one should be condemned by God. And yet they who hold this opinion do not extend it to the acquittal or liberation of the devil and his angels. Their human tenderness is moved only towards men, and they plead chiefly their own cause, holding out false hopes of impunity to their own depraved lives by means of this quasi-compassion of God to the whole race. Consequently they who promise this impunity even to the prince of the devils and his satellites make a still fuller exhibition of the mercy of God.

CHAPTER XIX

OF THOSE WHO PROMISE IMPUNITY FROM ALL SINS EVEN TO HERETICS, THROUGH VIRTUE OF THEIR PARTICIPATION OF THE BODY OF CHRIST

So, too, there are others who promise this deliverance from eternal punishment, not, indeed, to all men, but only to those who have been washed

[29] Ps. xxxi. 19   [30] Rom. xi. 32

in Christian baptism, and who become partakers of the body of Christ, no matter how they have lived, or what heresy or impiety they have fallen into. They ground this opinion on the saying of Jesus, "This is the bread which cometh down from heaven, that if any man eat thereof, he shall not die. I am the living bread which came down from heaven. If a man eat of this bread, he shall live for ever." [31] Therefore, say they, it follows that these persons must be delivered from death eternal, and at one time or other be introduced to everlasting life.

CHAPTER XX

OF THOSE WHO PROMISE THIS INDULGENCE NOT TO ALL, BUT ONLY TO THOSE WHO HAVE BEEN BAPTIZED AS CATHOLICS, THOUGH AFTERWARDS THEY HAVE BROKEN OUT INTO MANY CRIMES AND HERESIES

There are others still who make this promise not even to all who have received the sacraments of the baptism of Christ and of His body, but only to the catholics, however badly they have lived. For these have eaten the body of Christ, not only sacramentally but really, being incorporated in His body, as the apostle says, "We, being many, are one bread, one body;" [32] so that, though they have afterwards lapsed into some heresy, or even into heathenism and idolatry, yet by virtue of this one thing, that they have received the baptism of Christ, and eaten the body of Christ, in the body of Christ, that is to say, in the catholic Church, they shall not die eternally, but at one time or other obtain eternal life; and all that wickedness of theirs shall not avail to make their punishment eternal, but only proportionately long and severe.

CHAPTER XXI

OF THOSE WHO ASSERT THAT ALL CATHOLICS WHO CONTINUE IN THE FAITH, EVEN THOUGH BY THE DEPRAVITY OF THEIR LIVES THEY HAVE MERITED HELL FIRE, SHALL BE SAVED ON ACCOUNT OF THE "FOUNDATION" OF THEIR FAITH

There are some, too, who found upon the expression of Scripture, "He that endureth to the end shall be saved," [33] and who promise salvation only to those who continue in the Church catholic; and though such persons have lived badly, yet, say they, they shall be saved as by fire through virtue of the foundation of which the apostle says, "For other foundation hath no man laid than that which is laid, which is Christ Jesus. Now if any man build upon this foundation gold, silver, precious stones, wood, hay, stubble; every man's work shall be made manifest: for the day of the Lord shall

[31] John vi. 50, 51   [32] I Cor. x. 17   [33] Matt. xxiv. 13

declare it, for it shall be revealed by fire; and each man's work shall be proved of what sort it is. If any man's work shall endure which he hath built thereupon, he shall receive a reward. But if any man's work shall be burned, he shall suffer loss: but he himself shall be saved; yet so as through fire." [34] They say, accordingly, that the catholic Christian, no matter what his life be, has Christ as his foundation, while this foundation is not possessed by any heresy which is separated from the unity of His body. And therefore, through virtue of this foundation, even though the catholic Christian by the inconsistency of his life has been as one building up wood, hay, stubble, upon it, they believe that he shall be saved by fire, in other words, that he shall be delivered after tasting the pain of that fire to which the wicked shall be condemned at the last judgment.

CHAPTER XXII

OF THOSE WHO FANCY THAT THE SINS WHICH ARE INTERMINGLED WITH ALMS-DEEDS SHALL NOT BE CHARGED AT THE DAY OF JUDGMENT

I have also met with some who are of opinion that such only as neglect to cover their sins with alms-deeds shall be punished in everlasting fire; and they cite the words of the Apostle James, "He shall have judgment without mercy who hath shown no mercy." [35] Therefore, say they, he who has not amended his ways, but yet has intermingled his profligate and wicked actions with works of mercy, shall receive mercy in the judgment, so that he shall either quite escape condemnation, or shall be liberated from his doom after some time shorter or longer. They suppose that this was the reason why the Judge Himself of quick and dead declined to mention anything else than works of mercy done or omitted, when awarding to those on His right hand life eternal, and to those on His left everlasting punishment.[36] To the same purpose, they say, is the daily petition we make in the Lord's prayer, "Forgive us our debts, as we forgive our debtors." [37] For, no doubt, whoever pardons the person who has wronged him does a charitable action. And this has been so highly commended by the Lord Himself, that He says, "For if ye forgive men their trespasses, your heavenly Father will also forgive you: but if ye forgive not men their trespasses, neither will your Father forgive your trespasses." [38] And so it is to this kind of alms-deeds that the saying of the Apostle James refers, "He shall have judgment without mercy that hath shown no mercy." And our Lord, they say, made no distinction of great and small sins, but "Your Father will forgive your sins, if ye forgive men theirs." Consequently they conclude that, though a man has led an abandoned life up to the last day of it, yet whatsoever his sins have been, they are all remitted by virtue of this daily prayer, if only he has been

[34] I Cor. iii. 11-15   [35] Jas. ii. 13   [36] Matt. xxv. 33   [37] Matt. vi. 12   [38] Matt. vi. 14, 15

mindful to attend to this one thing, that when they who have done him any injury ask his pardon, he forgive them from his heart.

When, by God's help, I have replied to all these errors, I shall conclude this (twenty-first) book.

CHAPTER XXIII

AGAINST THOSE WHO ARE OF OPINION THAT THE PUNISHMENT NEITHER OF THE DEVIL NOR OF WICKED MEN SHALL BE ETERNAL

First of all, it behoves us to inquire and to recognize why the Church has not been able to tolerate the idea that promises cleansing or indulgence to the devil even after the most severe and protracted punishment. For so many holy men, imbued with the spirit of the Old and New Testament, did not grudge to angels of any rank or character that they should enjoy the blessedness of the heavenly kingdom after being cleansed by suffering, but rather they perceived that they could not invalidate nor evacuate the divine sentence which the Lord predicted that He would pronounce in the judgment, saying, "Depart from me, ye cursed, into everlasting fire, prepared for the devil and his angels." [39] For here it is evident that the devil and his angels shall burn in everlasting fire. And there is also that declaration in the Apocalypse, "The devil their deceiver was cast into the lake of fire and brimstone, where also are the beast and the false prophet. And they shall be tormented day and night for ever." [40] In the former passage "everlasting" is used, in the latter "for ever;" and by these words Scripture is wont to mean nothing else than endless duration. And therefore no other reason, no reason more obvious and just, can be found for holding it as the fixed and immovable belief of the truest piety, that the devil and his angels shall never return to the justice and life of the saints, than that Scripture, which deceives no man, says that God spared them not, and that they were condemned beforehand by Him, and cast into prisons of darkness in hell,[41] being reserved to the judgment of the last day, when eternal fire shall receive them, in which they shall be tormented world without end. And if this be so, how can it be believed that all men, or even some, shall be withdrawn from the endurance of punishment after some time has been spent in it? how can this be believed without enervating our faith in the eternal punishment of the devils? For if all or some of those to whom it shall be said, "Depart from me, ye cursed, into everlasting fire, prepared for the devil and his angels," [42] are not to be always in that fire, then what reason is there for believing that the devil and his angels shall always be there? Or is perhaps the sentence of God, which is to be pronounced on wicked men and angels alike, to be true in the case of the angels, false in that of men? Plainly it

[39] Matt. xxv. 41   [40] Rev. xx. 10   [41] 2 Pet. ii. 4   [42] Matt. xxv. 41

will be so if the conjectures of men are to weigh more than the word of God. But because this is absurd, they who desire to be rid of eternal punishment ought to abstain from arguing against God, and rather, while yet there is opportunity, obey the divine commands. Then what a fond fancy is it to suppose that eternal punishment means long continued punishment, while eternal life means life without end, since Christ in the very same passage spoke of both in similar terms in one and the same sentence, "These shall go away into eternal punishment, but the righteous into life eternal!" [43] If both destinies are "eternal," then we must either understand both as long-continued but at last terminating, or both as endless. For they are correlative—on the one hand, punishment eternal, on the other hand, life eternal. And to say in one and the same sense, life eternal shall be endless, punishment eternal shall come to an end, is the height of absurdity. Wherefore, as the eternal life of the saints shall be endless, so too the eternal punishment of those who are doomed to it shall have no end.

CHAPTER XXIV

AGAINST THOSE WHO FANCY THAT IN THE JUDGMENT OF GOD ALL THE
ACCUSED WILL BE SPARED IN VIRTUE OF THE PRAYERS OF THE
SAINTS

And this reasoning is equally conclusive against those who, in their own interest, but under the guise of a greater tenderness of spirit, attempt to invalidate the words of God, and who assert that these words are true, not because men shall suffer those things which are threatened by God, but because they deserve to suffer them. For God, they say, will yield them to the prayers of His saints, who will then the more earnestly pray for their enemies, as they shall be more perfect in holiness, and whose prayers will be the more efficacious and the more worthy of God's ear, because now purged from all sin whatsoever. Why, then, if in that perfected holiness their prayers be so pure and all-availing, will they not use them in behalf of the angels for whom eternal fire is prepared, that God may mitigate His sentence and alter it, and extricate them from that fire? Or will there, perhaps, be some one hardy enough to affirm that even the holy angels will make common cause with holy men (then become the equals of God's angels), and will intercede for the guilty, both men and angels, that mercy may spare them the punishment which truth has pronounced them to deserve? But this has been asserted by no one sound in the faith, nor will be. Otherwise there is no reason why the Church should not even now pray for the devil and his angels, since God her Master has ordered her to pray for her enemies. The reason, then, which prevents the Church from now praying for the wicked angels, whom she knows to be her enemies, is the identical reason which

[43] Matt. xxv. 46

shall prevent her, however perfected in holiness, from praying at the last judgment for those men who are to be punished in eternal fire. At present she prays for her enemies among men, because they have yet opportunity for fruitful repentance. For what does she especially beg for them but that "God would grant them repentance," as the apostle says, "that they may return to soberness out of the snare of the devil, by whom they are held captive according to his will?" [44] But if the Church were certified who those are, who, though they are still abiding in this life, are yet predestinated to go with the devil into eternal fire, then for them she could no more pray than for him. But since she has this certainty regarding no man, she prays for all her enemies who yet live in this world; and yet she is not heard in behalf of all. But she is heard in the case of those only who, though they oppose the Church, are yet predestinated to become her sons through her intercession. But if any retain an impenitent heart until death, and are not converted from enemies into sons, does the Church continue to pray for them, for the spirits, *i.e.*, of such persons deceased? And why does she cease to pray for them, unless because the man who was not translated into Christ's kingdom while he was in the body, is now judged to be of Satan's following?

It is then, I say, the same reason which prevents the Church at any time from praying for the wicked angels, which prevents her from praying hereafter for those men who are to be punished in eternal fire; and this also is the reason why, though she prays even for the wicked so long as they live, she yet does not even in this world pray for the unbelieving and godless who are dead. For some of the dead, indeed, the prayer of the Church or of pious individuals is heard; but it is for those who, having been regenerated in Christ, did not spend their life so wickedly that they can be judged unworthy of such compassion, nor so well that they can be considered to have no need of it.[45] As also, after the resurrection, there will be some of the dead to whom, after they have endured the pains proper to the spirits of the dead, mercy shall be accorded, and acquittal from the punishment of the eternal fire. For were there not some whose sins, though not remitted in this life, shall be remitted in that which is to come, it could not be truly said, "They shall not be forgiven, neither in this world, neither in that which is to come." [46] But when the Judge of quick and dead has said, "Come, ye blessed of my Father, inherit the kingdom prepared for you from the foundation of the world," and to those on the other side, "Depart from me, ye cursed, into the eternal fire, which is prepared for the devil and his angels," and "These shall go away into eternal punishment, but the righteous into eternal

---

[44] 2 Tim. ii. 25, 26

[45] This contains the germ of the doctrine of purgatory, which was afterwards more fully developed by Pope Gregory I., and adopted by the Roman church, but rejected by the Reformers, as unfounded in Scripture, though Matt. xii. 32, and 1 Cor. iii. 15 are quoted in support of it   [46] Matt. xii. 32

life," [47] it were excessively presumptuous to say that the punishment of any of those whom God has said shall go away into eternal punishment shall not be eternal, and so bring either despair or doubt upon the corresponding promise of life eternal.

Let no man then so understand the words of the Psalmist, "Shall God forget to be gracious? shall He shut up in His anger His tender mercies" [48] as if the sentence of God were true of good men, false of bad men, or true of good men and wicked angels, but false of bad men. For the Psalmist's words refer to the vessels of mercy and the children of the promise, of whom the prophet himself was one; for when he had said, "Shall God forget to be gracious? shall He shut up in His anger His tender mercies?" and then immediately subjoins, "And I said, Now I begin: this is the change wrought by the right hand of the Most High," [49] he manifestly explained what he meant by the words, "Shall he shut up in His anger His tender mercies?" For God's anger is this mortal life, in which man is made like to vanity, and his days pass as a shadow.[50] Yet in this anger God does not forget to be gracious, causing His sun to shine and His rain to descend on the just and the unjust;[51] and thus He does not in His anger cut short His tender mercies, and especially in what the Psalmist speaks of in the words, "Now I begin: this change is from the right hand of the Most High;" for He changes for the better the vessels of mercy, even while they are still in this most wretched life, which is God's anger, and even while His anger is manifesting itself in this miserable corruption; for "in His anger He does not shut up His tender mercies." And since the truth of this divine canticle is quite satisfied by this application of it, there is no need to give it a reference to that place in which those who do not belong to the city of God are punished in eternal fire. But if any persist in extending its application to the torments of the wicked, let them at least understand it so that the anger of God, which has threatened the wicked with eternal punishment, shall abide, but shall be mixed with mercy to the extent of alleviating the torments which might justly be inflicted; so that the wicked shall neither wholly escape, nor only for a time endure these threatened pains, but that they shall be less severe and more endurable than they deserve. Thus the anger of God shall continue, and at the same time He will not in this anger shut up His tender mercies. But even this hypothesis I am not to be supposed to affirm because I do not positively oppose it.

As for those who find an empty threat rather than a truth in such passages as these: "Depart from me, ye cursed, into everlasting fire;" and "These shall go away into eternal punishment;" [52] and "They shall be tormented for ever and ever;" [53] and "Their worm shall not die, and their fire shall not be quenched" [54]—such persons, I say, are most emphatically and abundantly refuted, not by me so much as by the divine Scripture itself. For the

[47] Matt. xxv. 34, 41, 46   [48] Ps. lxxvii. 9   [49] Ps. lxxvii. 10   [50] Ps. cxliv. 4
[51] Matt. v. 45   [52] Matt. xxv. 41, 46   [53] Rev. xx. 10   [54] Isa. lxvi. 24

men of Nineveh repented in this life, and therefore their repentance was fruitful, inasmuch as they sowed in that field which the Lord meant to be sown in tears that it might afterwards be reaped in joy. And yet who will deny that God's prediction was fulfilled in their case, if at least he observes that God destroys sinners not only in anger but also in compassion? For sinners are destroyed in two ways—either, like the Sodomites, the men themselves are punished for their sins, or, like the Ninevites, the men's sins are destroyed by repentance. God's prediction, therefore, was fulfilled—the wicked Nineveh was overthrown, and a good Nineveh built up. For its walls and houses remained standing; the city was overthrown in its depraved manners. And thus, though the prophet was provoked that the destruction which the inhabitants dreaded, because of his prediction, did not take place, yet that which God's foreknowledge had predicted did take place, for He who foretold the destruction knew how it should be fulfilled in a less calamitous sense.

But that these perversely compassionate persons may see what is the purport of these words, "How great is the abundance of Thy sweetness, Lord, which Thou hast hidden for them that fear Thee," [55] let them read what follows:" "And Thou hast perfected it for them that hope in Thee." For what means, "Thou hast hidden it for them that fear Thee," "Thou hast perfected it for them that hope in Thee," unless this, that to those who through fear of punishment seek to establish their own righteousness by the law, the righteousness of God is not sweet, because they are ignorant of it? They have not tasted it. For they hope in themselves, not in Him; and therefore God's abundant sweetness is hidden from them. They fear God, indeed, but it is with that servile fear "which is not in love; for perfect love casteth out fear." [56] Therefore to them that hope in Him He perfecteth His sweetness, inspiring them with His own love, so that with a holy fear, which love does not cast out, but which endureth for ever, they may, when they glory, glory in the Lord. For the righteousness of God is Christ, "who is of God made unto us," as the apostle says, "wisdom, and righteousness, and sanctification, and redemption: as it is written, He that glorieth, let him glory in the Lord." [57] This righteousness of God, which is the gift of grace without merits, is not known by those who go about to establish their own righteousness, and are therefore not subject to the righteousness of God, which is Christ.[58] But it is in this righteousness that we find the great abundance of God's sweetness, of which the psalm says, "Taste and see how sweet the Lord is." [59] And this we rather taste than partake of to satiety in this our pilgrimage. We hunger and thirst for it now, that hereafter we may be satisfied with it when we see Him as He is, and that is fulfilled which is written, "I shall be satisfied when Thy glory shall be manifested." [60] It is thus that Christ perfects the great abundance of His sweetness to them that

[55] Ps. xxxi. 19   [56] 1 John iv. 18   [57] 1 Cor. i. 30, 31   [58] Rom. x. 3   [59] Ps. xxxiv. 8   [60] Ps. xvii. 15

hope in Him. But if God conceals His sweetness from them that fear Him in the sense that these our objectors fancy, so that men's ignorance of His purpose of mercy towards the wicked may lead them to fear Him and live better, and so that there may be prayer made for those who are not living as they ought, how then does He perfect His sweetness to them that hope in Him, since, if their dreams be true, it is this very sweetness which will prevent Him from punishing those who do not hope in Him? Let us then seek that sweetness of His, which He perfects to them that hope in Him, not that which He is supposed to perfect to those who despise and blaspheme Him; for in vain, after this life, does a man seek for what he has neglected to provide while in this life.

Then, as to that saying of the apostle, "For God hath concluded all in unbelief, that He may have mercy upon all," [61] it does not mean that He will condemn no one; but the foregoing context shows what is meant. The apostle composed the epistle for the Gentiles who were already believers; and when he was speaking to them of the Jews who were yet to believe, he says, "For as ye in times past believed not God, yet have now obtained mercy through their unbelief; even so have these also now not believed, that through your mercy they also may obtain mercy." Then he added the words in question with which these persons beguile themselves: "For God concluded all in unbelief, that He might have mercy upon all." All whom, if not all those of whom he was speaking, just as if he had said, "Both you and them?" God then concluded all those in unbelief, both Jews and Gentiles, whom He foreknew and predestinated to be conformed to the image of His Son, in order that they might be confounded by the bitterness of unbelief, and might repent and believingly turn to the sweetness of God's mercy, and might take up that exclamation of the psalm, "How great is the abundance of Thy sweetness, O Lord, which Thou hast hidden for them that fear Thee, but hast perfected to them that hope," not in themselves, but "in Thee." He has mercy, then, on all the vessels of mercy. And what means "all?" Both those of the Gentiles and those of the Jews whom He predestinated, called, justified, glorified: none of these will be condemned by Him; but we cannot say none of all men whatever.

[61] Rom. xi. 32

CHAPTER XXV

WHETHER THOSE WHO RECEIVED HERETICAL BAPTISM, AND HAVE
AFTERWARDS FALLEN AWAY TO WICKEDNESS OF LIFE; OR THOSE
WHO HAVE RECEIVED CATHOLIC BAPTISM, BUT HAVE
AFTERWARDS PASSED OVER TO HERESY AND SCHISM;
OR THOSE WHO HAVE REMAINED IN THE CATHOLIC
CHURCH IN WHICH THEY WERE BAPTIZED, BUT
HAVE CONTINUED TO LIVE IMMORALLY—MAY
HOPE THROUGH THE VIRTUE OF THE SACRAMENTS
FOR THE REMISSION OF ETERNAL PUNISHMENT

But let us now reply to those who promise deliverance from eternal fire, not to the devil and his angels (as neither do they of whom we have been speaking), nor even to all men whatever, but only to those who have been washed by the baptism of Christ, and have become partakers of His body and blood, no matter how they have lived, no matter what heresy or impiety they have fallen into. But they are contradicted by the apostle, where he says, "Now the works of the flesh are manifest, which are these; fornication, uncleanness, lasciviousness, idolatry, witchcraft, hatred, variances, emulations, wrath, strife, heresies, envyings, drunkenness, revellings, and the like: of the which I tell you before, as I have also told you in time past, for they which do such things shall not inherit the kingdom of God." [62] Certainly this sentence of the apostle is false, if such persons shall be delivered after any lapse of time, and shall then inherit the kingdom of God. But as it is not false, they shall certainly never inherit the kingdom of God. And if they shall never enter that kingdom, then they shall always be retained in eternal punishment; for there is no middle place where he may live unpunished who has not been admitted into that kingdom.

And therefore we may reasonably inquire how we are to understand these words of the Lord Jesus: "This is the bread which cometh down from heaven, that a man may eat thereof, and not die. I am the living bread which came down from heaven. If any man eat of this bread, he shall live for ever." [63] And those, indeed, whom we are now answering, are refuted in their interpretation of this passage by those whom we are shortly to answer, and who do not promise this deliverance to all who have received the sacraments of baptism and the Lord's body, but only to the catholics, however wickedly they live; for these, say they, have eaten the Lord's body not only sacramentally, but really, being constituted members of His body, of which the apostle says, "We being many are one bread, one body." [64] He then who is in the unity of Christ's body (that is to say, in the Christian membership), of which body the faithful have been wont to receive the sacrament at the

[62] Gal. v. 19-21   [63] John vi. 50, 51   [64] 1 Cor. x. 17

altar, that man is truly said to eat the body and drink the blood of Christ. And consequently heretics and schismatics being separate from the unity of this body, are able to receive the same sacrament, but with no profit to themselves—nay, rather to their own hurt, so that they are rather more severely judged than liberated after some time. For they are not in that bond of peace which is symbolized by that sacrament.

But again, even those who sufficiently understand that he who is not in the body of Christ cannot be said to eat the body of Christ, are in error when they promise liberation from the fire of eternal punishment to persons who fall away from the unity of that body into heresy, or even into heathenish superstition. For, in the first place, they ought to consider how intolerable it is, and how discordant with sound doctrine, to suppose that many, indeed, or almost all, who have forsaken the Church catholic, and have originated impious heresies and become heresiarchs, should enjoy a destiny superior to those who never were catholics, but have fallen into the snares of these others; that is to say, if the fact of their catholic baptism and original reception of the sacrament of the body of Christ in the true body of Christ is sufficient to deliver these heresiarchs from eternal punishment. For certainly he who deserts the faith, and from a deserter becomes an assailant, is worse than he who has not deserted the faith he never held. And, in the second place, they are contradicted by the apostle, who, after enumerating the works of the flesh, says with reference to heresies, "They who do such things shall not inherit the kingdom of God."

And therefore neither ought such persons as lead an abandoned and damnable life to be confident of salvation, though they persevere to the end in the communion of the Church catholic, and comfort themselves with the words, "He that endureth to the end shall be saved." By the iniquity of their life they abandon that very righteousness of life which Christ is to them, whether it be by fornication, or by perpetrating in their body the other uncleannesses which the apostle would not so much as mention, or by a dissolute luxury, or by doing any one of those things of which he says, "They who do such things shall not inherit the kingdom of God." Consequently, they who do such things shall not exist anywhere but in eternal punishment, since they cannot be in the kingdom of God. For, while they continue in such things to the very end of life, they cannot be said to abide in Christ to the end; for to abide in Him is to abide in the faith of Christ. And this faith, according to the apostle's definition of it, "worketh by love." [65] And "love," as he elsewhere says, "worketh no evil." [66] Neither can these persons be said to eat the body of Christ, for they cannot even be reckoned among His members. For, not to mention other reasons, they cannot be at once the members of Christ and the members of a harlot. In fine, He Himself, when He says, "He that eateth my flesh and drinketh my blood, dwelleth in me, and I in him," [67] shows what it is in reality, and not

[65] Gal. v. 6　　[66] Rom. xiii. 10　　[67] John vi. 56

sacramentally, to eat His body and drink His blood; for this is to dwell in Christ, that He also may dwell in us. So that it is as if He said, He that dwelleth not in me, and in whom I do not dwell, let him not say or think that he eateth my body or drinketh my blood. Accordingly, they who are not Christ's members do not dwell in Him. And they who make themselves members of a harlot, are not members of Christ unless they have penitently abandoned that evil, and have returned to this good to be reconciled to it.

CHAPTER XXVI

WHAT IT IS TO HAVE CHRIST FOR A FOUNDATION, AND WHO THEY ARE TO WHOM SALVATION AS BY FIRE IS PROMISED

But, say they, the catholic Christians have Christ for a foundation, and they have not fallen away from union with Him, no matter how depraved a life they have built on this foundation, as wood, hay, stubble; and accordingly the well-directed faith by which Christ is their foundation will suffice to deliver them some time from the continuance of that fire, though it be with loss, since those things they have built on it shall be burned. Let the Apostle James summarily reply to them: "If any man say he has faith, and have not works, can faith save him?" [68] And who then is it, they ask, of whom the Apostle Paul says, "But he himself shall be saved, yet so as by fire?" [69] Let us join them in their inquiry; and one thing is very certain, that it is not he of whom James speaks, else we should make the two apostles contradict one another, if the one says, "Though a man's works be evil, his faith will save him as by fire," while the other says, "If he have not good works, can his faith save him?"

We shall then ascertain who it is who can be saved by fire, if we first discover what it is to have Christ for a foundation. And this we may very readily learn from the image itself. In a building the foundation is first. Whoever, then, has Christ in his heart, so that no earthly or temporal things— not even those that are legitimate and allowed—are preferred to Him, has Christ as a foundation. But if these things be preferred, then even though a man seem to have faith in Christ, yet Christ is not the foundation to that man; and much more if he, in contempt of wholesome precepts, seek forbidden gratifications, is he clearly convicted of putting Christ not first but last, since he has despised Him as his ruler, and has preferred to fulfill his own wicked lusts, in contempt of Christ's commands and allowances. Accordingly, if any Christian man loves a harlot, and, attaching himself to her, becomes one body, he has not now Christ for a foundation. But if any one loves his own wife, and loves her as Christ would have him love her, who can doubt that he has Christ for a foundation? But if he loves her in

---

[68] Jas. ii. 14   [69] I Cor. iii. 15. This is the chief passage quoted in favor of purgatory

the world's fashion, carnally, as the disease of lust prompts him, and as the Gentiles love who know not God, even this the apostle, or rather Christ by the apostle, allows as a venial fault. And therefore even such a man may have Christ for a foundation. For so long as he does not prefer such an affection or pleasure to Christ, Christ is his foundation, though on it he builds wood, hay, stubble; and therefore he shall be saved as by fire. For the fire of affliction shall burn such luxurious pleasures and earthly loves, though they be not damnable, because enjoyed in lawful wedlock. And of this fire the fuel is bereavement, and all those calamities which consume these joys. Consequently the superstructure will be loss to him who has built it, for he shall not retain it, but shall be agonized by the loss of those things in the enjoyment of which he found pleasure. But by this fire he shall be saved through virtue of the foundation, because even if a persecutor demanded whether he would retain Christ or these things, he would prefer Christ. Would you hear, in the apostle's own words, who he is who builds on the foundation gold, silver, precious stones? "He that is unmarried," he says, "careth for the things that belong to the Lord, how he may please the Lord." [70] Would you hear who he is that buildeth wood, hay, stubble? "But he that is married careth for the things that are of the world, how he may please his wife." [71] "Every man's work shall be made manifest: for the day shall declare it"—the day, no doubt, of tribulation—"because," says he, "it shall be revealed by fire." [72] He calls tribulation fire, just as it is elsewhere said, "The furnace proves the vessels of the potter, and the trial of affliction righteous men." [73] And "The fire shall try every man's work of what sort it is. If any man's work abide"—for a man's care for the things of the Lord, how he may please the Lord, abides—"which he hath built thereupon, he shall receive a reward"—that is, he shall reap the fruit of his care. "But if any man's work shall be burned, he shall suffer loss"—for what he loved he shall not retain—"but he himself shall be saved"—for no tribulation shall have moved him from that stable foundation—"yet so as by fire;" [74] for that which he possessed with the sweetness of love he does not lose without the sharp sting of pain. Here, then, as seems to me, we have a fire which destroys neither, but enriches the one, brings loss to the other, proves both.

But if this passage of *Corinthians* is to interpret that fire of which the Lord shall say to those on His left hand, "Depart from me, ye cursed, into everlasting fire," [75] so that among these we are to believe there are those who build on the foundation wood, hay, stubble, and that they, through virtue of the good foundation, shall after a time be liberated from the fire that is the award of their evil deserts, what then shall we think of those on the right hand, to whom it shall be said, "Come, ye blessed of my Father, inherit the kingdom prepared for you," [76] unless that they are those who

[70] 1 Cor. vii. 32   [71] 1 Cor. vii. 33   [72] 1 Cor. iii. 13   [73] Ecclus. xxvii. 5   [74] 1 Cor. iii. 14, 15   [75] Matt. xxv. 41   [76] Matt. xxv. 34

have built on the foundation gold, silver, precious stones? But if the fire of which our Lord speaks is the same as that of which the apostle says, "Yet so as by fire," then both—that is to say, both those on the right as well as those on the left—are to be cast into it. For that fire is to try both, since it is said, "For the day of the Lord shall declare it, because it shall be revealed by fire; and the fire shall try every man's work of what sort it is." [77] If, therefore, the fire shall try both, in order that if any man's work abide— *i.e.*, if the superstructure be not consumed by the fire—he may receive a reward, and that if his work is burned he may suffer loss, certainly that fire is not the eternal fire itself. For into this latter fire only those on the left hand shall be cast, and that with final and everlasting doom; but that former fire proves those on the right hand. But some of them it so proves that it does not burn and consume the structure which is found to have been built by them on Christ as the foundation; while others of them it proves in another fashion, so as to burn what they have built up, and thus cause them to suffer loss, while they themselves are saved because they have retained Christ, who was laid as their sure foundation, and have loved Him above all. But if they are saved, then certainly they shall stand at the right hand, and shall with the rest hear the sentence, "Come, ye blessed of my Father, inherit the kingdom prepared for you;" and not at the left hand, where those shall be who shall not be saved, and shall therefore hear the doom, "Depart from me, ye cursed, into everlasting fire." For from that fire no man shall be saved, because they all shall go away into eternal punishment, where their worms shall not die, nor their fire be quenched, in which they shall be tormented day and night for ever.

But if it be said that in the interval of time between the death of this body and that last day of judgment and retribution which shall follow the resurrection, the bodies of the dead shall be exposed to a fire of such a nature that it shall not affect those who have not in this life indulged in such pleasures and pursuits as shall be consumed like wood, hay, stubble, but shall affect those others who have carried with them structures of that kind; if it be said that such worldliness, being venial, shall be consumed in the fire of tribulation either here only, or here and hereafter both, or here that it may not be hereafter—this I do not contradict, because possibly it is true. For perhaps even the death of the body is itself a part of this tribulation, for it results from the first transgression, so that the time which follows death takes its color in each case from the nature of the man's building. The persecutions, too, which have crowned the martyrs, and which Christians of all kinds suffer, try both buildings like a fire, consuming some, along with the builders themselves, if Christ is not found in them as their foundation, while others they consume without the builders, because Christ is found in them, and they are saved, though with loss; and other buildings still they do not consume, because such materials as abide for ever are found

[77] 1 Cor. iii. 13

in them. In the end of the world there shall be in the time of Antichrist tribulation such as has never before been. How many edifices there shall then be, of gold or of hay, built on the best foundation, Christ Jesus, which that fire shall prove, bringing joy to some, loss to others, but without destroying either sort, because of this stable foundation! But whosoever prefers, I do not say his wife, with whom he lives for carnal pleasure, but any of those relatives who afford no delight of such a kind, and whom it is right to love—whosoever prefers these to Christ, and loves them after a human and carnal fashion, has not Christ as a foundation, and will therefore not be saved by fire, nor indeed at all; for he shall not possibly dwell with the Saviour, who says very explicitly concerning this very matter, "He that loveth father or mother more than me is not worthy of me; and he that loveth son or daughter more than me is not worthy of me." [78] But he who loves his relations carnally, and yet so that he does not prefer them to Christ, but would rather want them than Christ if he were put to the proof, shall be saved by fire, because it is necessary that by the loss of these relations he suffer pain in proportion to his love. And he who loves father, mother, sons, daughters, according to Christ, so that he aids them in obtaining His kingdom and cleaving to Him, or loves them because they are members of Christ, God forbid that this love should be consumed as wood, hay, stubble, and not rather be reckoned a structure of gold, silver, precious stones. For how can a man love those more than Christ whom he loves only for Christ's sake?

CHAPTER XXVII

AGAINST THE BELIEF OF THOSE WHO THINK THAT THE SINS WHICH HAVE BEEN ACCOMPANIED WITH ALMSGIVING WILL DO THEM NO HARM

It remains to reply to those who maintain that those only shall burn in eternal fire who neglect alms-deeds proportioned to their sins, resting this opinion on the words of the Apostle James, "He shall have judgment without mercy that hath showed no mercy." [79] Therefore, they say, he that hath showed mercy, though he has not reformed his dissolute conduct, but has lived wickedly and iniquitously even while abounding in alms, shall have a merciful judgment, so that he shall either be not condemned at all, or shall be delivered from final judgment after a time. And for the same reason they suppose that Christ will discriminate between those on the right hand and those on the left, and will send the one party into His kingdom, the other into eternal punishment, on the sole ground of their attention to or neglect of works of charity. Moreover, they endeavor to use the prayer which the Lord Himself taught as a proof and bulwark of their opinion, that daily sins

---

[78] Matt. x. 37   [79] Jas. ii. 13

which are never abandoned can be expiated through alms-deeds, no matter how offensive or of what sort they be. For, say they, as there is no day on which Christians ought not to use this prayer, so there is no sin of any kind which, though committed every day, is not remitted when we say, "Forgive us our debts," if we take care to fulfill what follows, "as we forgive our debtors." [80] For, they go on to say, the Lord does not say, "If ye forgive men their trespasses, your heavenly Father will forgive you your little daily sins," but "will forgive you your sins." Therefore, be they of any kind or magnitude whatever, be they perpetrated daily and never abandoned or subdued in this life, they can be pardoned, they presume, through alms-deeds.

But they are right to inculcate the giving of alms proportioned to past sins; for if they said that any kind of alms could obtain the divine pardon of great sins committed daily and with habitual enormity, if they said that such sins could thus be daily remitted, they would see that their doctrine was absurd and ridiculous. For they would thus be driven to acknowledge that it were possible for a very wealthy man to buy absolution from murders, adulteries, and all manner of wickedness, by paying a daily alms of ten paltry coins. And if it be most absurd and insane to make such an acknowledgment, and if we still ask what are those fitting alms of which even the forerunner of Christ said, "Bring forth therefore fruits meet for repentance," [81] undoubtedly it will be found that they are not such as are done by men who undermine their life by daily enormities even to the very end. For they suppose that by giving to the poor a small fraction of the wealth they acquire by extortion and spoliation they can propitiate Christ, so that they may with impunity commit the most damnable sins, in the persuasion that they have bought from Him a license to transgress, or rather do buy a daily indulgence. And if they for one crime have distributed all their goods to Christ's needy members, that could profit them nothing unless they desisted from all similar actions, and attained charity which worketh no evil. He therefore who does alms-deeds proportioned to his sins must first begin with himself. For it is not reasonable that a man who exercises charity towards his neighbor should not do so towards himself, since he hears the Lord saying, "Thou shalt love thy neighbor as thyself," [82] and again, "Have compassion on thy soul, and please God." [83] He then who has not compassion on his own soul that he may please God, how can he be said to do alms-deeds proportioned to his sins? To the same purpose is that written, "He who is bad to himself, to whom can he be good?" [84] We ought therefore to do alms that we may be heard when we pray that our past sins may be forgiven, not that while we continue in them we may think to provide ourselves with a license for wickedness by alms-deeds.

The reason, therefore, of our predicting that He will impute to those on

[80] Matt. vi. 12   [81] Matt. iii. 8   [82] Matt. xxii. 39   [83] Ecclus. xxx. 24   [84] Ecclus. xxi. 1

His right hand the alms-deeds they have done, and charge those on His left with omitting the same, is that He may thus show the efficacy of charity for the deletion of past sins, not for impunity in their perpetual commission. And such persons, indeed, as decline to abandon their evil habits of life for a better course cannot be said to do charitable deeds. For this is the purport of the saying, "Inasmuch as ye did it not to one of the least of these, ye did it not to me." [85] He shows them that they do not perform charitable actions even when they think they are doing so. For if they gave bread to a hungering Christian because he is a Christian, assuredly they would not deny to themselves the bread of righteousness, that is, Christ Himself; for God considers not the person to whom the gift is made, but the spirit in which it is made. He therefore who loves Christ in a Christian extends alms to him in the same spirit in which he draws near to Christ, not in that spirit which would abandon Christ if it could do so with impunity. For in proportion as a man loves what Christ disapproves does he himself abandon Christ. For what does it profit a man that he is baptized, if he is not justified? Did not He who said, "Except a man be born of water and of the Spirit, he shall not enter into the kingdom of God," [86] say also, "Except your righteousness shall exceed the righteousness of the scribes and Pharisees, ye shall not enter into the kingdom of heaven?" [87] Why do many through fear of the first saying run to baptism, while few through fear of the second seek to be justified? As therefore it is not to his brother a man says, "Thou fool," if when he says it he is indignant not at the brotherhood, but at the sin of the offender—for otherwise he were guilty of hell fire—so he who extends charity to a Christian does not extend it to a Christian if he does not love Christ in him. Now he does not love Christ who refuses to be justified in Him. Or, again, if a man has been guilty of this sin of calling his brother Fool, unjustly reviling him without any desire to remove his sin, his alms-deeds go a small way towards expiating this fault, unless he adds to this the remedy of reconciliation which the same passage enjoins. For it is there said, "Therefore, if thou bring thy gift to the altar, and there rememberest that thy brother hath aught against thee; leave there thy gift before the altar, and go thy way; first be reconciled to thy brother, and then come and offer thy gift." [88] Just so it is a small matter to do alms-deeds, no matter how great they be, for any sin, so long as the offender continues in the practice of sin.

Then as to the daily prayer which the Lord Himself taught, and which is therefore called the Lord's prayer, it obliterates indeed the sins of the day, when day by day we say, "Forgive us our debts," and when we not only say but act out that which follows, "as we forgive our debtors;" [89] but we utter this petition because sins have been committed, and not that they may be. For by it our Saviour designed to teach us that, however righteously we live in this life of infirmity and darkness, we still commit sins for the remission of

[85] Matt. xxv. 45   [86] John iii. 5   [87] Matt. v. 20   [88] Matt. v. 23, 24   [89] Matt. vi. 12

which we ought to pray, while we must pardon those who sin against us that we ourselves also may be pardoned. The Lord then did not utter the words, "If ye forgive men their trespasses, your Father will also forgive you your trespasses," [90] in order that we might contract from this petition such confidence as should enable us to sin securely from day to day, either putting ourselves above the fear of human laws, or craftily deceiving men concerning our conduct, but in order that we might thus learn not to suppose that we are without sins, even though we should be free from crimes; as also God admonished the priests of the old law to this same effect regarding their sacrifices, which He commanded them to offer first for their own sins, and then for the sins of the people. For even the very words of so great a Master and Lord are to be intently considered. For He does not say, If ye forgive men their sins, your Father will also forgive you your sins, no matter of what sort they be, but He says, your sins; for it was a daily prayer He was teaching, and it was certainly to disciples already justified He was speaking. What, then, does He mean by "your sins," but those sins from which not even you who are justified and sanctified can be free? While, then, those who seek occasion from this petition to indulge in habitual sin maintain that the Lord meant to include great sins, because He did not say, He will forgive you your small sins, but "your sins," we, on the other hand, taking into account the character of the persons He was addressing, cannot see our way to interpret the expression "your sins" of anything but small sins, because such persons are no longer guilty of great sins. Nevertheless not even great sins themselves—sins from which we must flee with a total reformation of life—are forgiven to those who pray, unless they observe the appended precept, "as ye also forgive your debtors." For if the very small sins which attach even to the life of the righteous be not remitted without that condition, how much further from obtaining indulgence shall those be who are involved in many great crimes, if, while they cease from perpetrating such enormities, they still inexorably refuse to remit any debt incurred to themselves, since the Lord says, "But if ye forgive not men their trespasses, neither will your Father forgive your trespasses?" [91] For this is the purport of the saying of the Apostle James also, "He shall have judgment without mercy that hath showed no mercy." [92] For we should remember that servant whose debt of ten thousand talents his lord cancelled, but afterwards ordered him to pay up, because the servant himself had no pity for his fellow-servant who owed him an hundred pence.[93] The words which the Apostle James subjoins, "And mercy rejoiceth against judgment," [94] find their application among those who are the children of the promise and vessels of mercy. For even those righteous men, who have lived with such holiness that they receive into the eternal habitations others also who have won their friendship with the mammon of unrighteousness,[95] became such

[90] Matt. vi. 14   [91] Matt. vi. 15   [92] Jas. ii. 13   [93] Matt. xviii. 23   [94] Jas. ii. 13
[95] Luke xvi. 9

only through the merciful deliverance of Him who justifies the ungodly, imputing to him a reward according to grace, not according to debt. For among this number is the apostle, who says, "I obtained mercy to be faithful." [96]

But it must be admitted, that those who are thus received into the eternal habitations are not of such a character that their own life would suffice to rescue them without the aid of the saints, and consequently in their case especially does mercy rejoice against judgment. And yet we are not on this account to suppose that every abandoned profligate, who has made no amendment of his life, is to be received into the eternal habitations if only he has assisted the saints with the mammon of unrighteousness—that is to say, with money or wealth which has been unjustly acquired, or, if rightfully acquired, is yet not the true riches, but only what iniquity counts riches, because it knows not the true riches in which those persons abound, who even receive others also into eternal habitations. There is then a certain kind of life, which is neither, on the one hand, so bad that those who adopt it are not helped towards the kingdom of heaven by any bountiful alms-giving by which they may relieve the wants of the saints, and make friends who could receive them into eternal habitations, nor, on the other hand, so good that it of itself suffices to win for them that great blessedness, if they do not obtain mercy through the merits of those whom they have made their friends. And I frequently wonder that even Virgil should give expression to this sentence of the Lord, in which He says, "Make to yourselves friends of the mammon of unrighteousness, that they may receive you into everlasting habitations;" [97] and this very similar saying, "He that receiveth a prophet, in the name of a prophet, shall receive a prophet's reward; and he that receiveth a righteous man, in the name of a righteous man, shall receive a righteous man's reward." [98] For when that poet described the Elysian fields, in which they suppose that the souls of the blessed dwell, he placed there not only those who had been able by their own merit to reach that abode, but added—

> And they who grateful memory won
> By services to others done,[99]

that is, they who had served others, and thereby merited to be remembered by them. Just as if they used the expression so common in Christian lips, where some humble person commends himself to one of the saints, and says, Remember me, and secures that he do so by deserving well at his hand. But what that kind of life we have been speaking of is, and what those sins are which prevent a man from winning the kingdom of God by himself, but yet permit him to avail himself of the merits of the saints, it is very difficult to ascertain, very perilous to define. For my own part, in spite of all investi-

---

[96] 1 Cor. vii. 25   [97] Luke xvi. 9   [98] Matt. x. 41   [99] *Aen.* vi. 664

gation, I have been up to the present hour unable to discover this. And possibly it is hidden from us, lest we should become careless in avoiding such sins, and so cease to make progress. For if it were known what these are, which, though they continue, and be not abandoned for a higher do yet not prevent us from seeking and hoping for the intercession of saints, human sloth would presumptuously wrap itself in these sins, and would take no steps to be disentangled from such wrappings by the deft energy of any virtue, but would only desire to be rescued by the merits of other people, whose friendship had been won by a bountiful use of the mammon of unrighteousness. But now that we are left in ignorance of the precise nature of that iniquity which is venial, even though it be persevered in, certainly we are both more vigilant in our prayers and efforts for progress, and more careful to secure with the mammon of unrighteousness friends for ourselves among the saints.

But this deliverance, which is effected by one's own prayers, or the intercession of holy men, secures that a man be not cast into eternal fire, but not that, when once he has been cast into it, he should after a time be rescued from it. For even those who fancy that what is said of the good ground bringing forth abundant fruit, some thirty, some sixty, some an hundred fold, is to be referred to the saints, so that in proportion to their merits some of them shall deliver thirty men, some sixty, some an hundred —even those who maintain this are yet commonly inclined to suppose that this deliverance will take place at, and not after the day of judgment. Under this impression, some one who observed the unseemly folly with which men promise themselves impunity on the ground that all will be included in this method of deliverance, is reported to have very happily remarked that we should rather endeavor to live so well that we shall be all found among the number of those who are to intercede for the liberation of others, lest these should be so few in number, that, after they have delivered one thirty, another sixty, another a hundred, there should still remain many who could not be delivered from punishment by their intercessions, and among them every one who has vainly and rashly promised himself the fruit of another's labor. But enough has been said in reply to those who acknowledge the authority of the same sacred Scriptures as ourselves, but who, by a mistaken interpretation of them, conceive of the future rather as they themselves wish, than as the Scriptures teach. And having given this reply, I now, according to promise, close this book.

BOOK TWENTY-TWO

ARGUMENT

This book treats of the end of the City of God, that is to say, of the eternal happiness of the saints; the faith of the resurrection of the body is established and explained; and the work concludes by showing how the saints, clothed in immortal and spiritual bodies, shall be employed.

CHAPTER I

OF THE CREATION OF ANGELS AND MEN

As WE promised in the immediately preceding book, this, the last of the whole work, shall contain a discussion of the eternal blessedness of the city of God. This blessedness is named eternal, not because it shall endure for many ages, though at last it shall come to an end, but because, according to the words of the gospel, "of His kingdom there shall be no end." [1] Neither shall it enjoy the mere appearance of perpetuity which is maintained by the rise of fresh generations to occupy the place of those that have died out, as in an evergreen the same freshness seems to continue permanently, and the same appearance of dense foliage is preserved by the growth of fresh leaves in the room of those that have withered and fallen; but in that city all the citizens shall be immortal, men now for the first time enjoying what the holy angels have never lost. And this shall be accomplished by God, the most almighty Founder of the city. For He has promised it, and cannot lie, and has already performed many of His promises, and has done many unpromised kindnesses to those whom He now asks to believe that He will do this also.

For it is He who in the beginning created the world full of all visible and intelligible beings, among which He created nothing better than those spirits whom He endowed with intelligence, and made capable of contemplating and enjoying Him, and united in our society, which we call the holy and heavenly city, and in which the material of their sustenance and blessedness is God Himself, as it were their common food and nourishment. It is He who gave to this intellectual nature free-will of such a kind, that if he wished to forsake God, *i.e.*, his blessedness, misery should forthwith result. It is He who, when He foreknew that certain angels would in their pride desire to suffice for their own blessedness, and would forsake their great good, did not deprive them of this power, deeming it to be more befitting His power and

---

[1] Luke i. 33

goodness to bring good out of evil than to prevent the evil from coming into existence. And indeed evil had never been, had not the mutable nature— mutable, though good, and created by the most high God and immutable Good, who created all things good—brought evil upon itself by sin. And this its sin is itself proof that its nature was originally good. For had it not been very good, though not equal to its Creator, the desertion of God as its light could not have been an evil to it. For as blindness is a vice of the eye, and this very fact indicates that the eye was created to see the light, and as, consequently, vice itself proves that the eye is more excellent than the other members, because it is capable of light (for on no other supposition would it be a vice of the eye to want light) so the nature which once enjoyed God teaches, even by its very vice, that it was created the best of all, since it is now miserable because it does not enjoy God. It is He who with very just punishment doomed the angels who voluntarily fell to everlasting misery, and rewarded those who continued in their attachment to the supreme good with the assurance of endless stability as the meed of their fidelity. It is He who made also man himself upright, with the same freedom of will—an earthly animal, indeed, but fit for heaven if he remained faithful to his Creator, but destined to the misery appropriate to such a nature if he forsook Him. It is He who, when He foreknew that man would in his turn sin by abandoning God and breaking His law, did not deprive him of the power of freewill, because He at the same time foresaw what good He Himself would bring out of the evil, and how from this mortal race, deservedly and justly condemned, He would by His grace collect, as now He does, a people so numerous, that He thus fills up and repairs the blank made by the fallen angels, and that thus that beloved and heavenly city is not defrauded of the full number of its citizens, but perhaps may even rejoice in a still more overflowing population.

CHAPTER II

OF THE ETERNAL AND UNCHANGEABLE WILL OF GOD

It is true that wicked men do many things contrary to God's will; but so great is His wisdom and power, that all things which seem adverse to His purpose do still tend towards those just and good ends and issues which He Himself has foreknown. And consequently, when God is said to change His will, as when, *e.g.*, He becomes angry with those to whom He was gentle, it is rather they than He who are changed, and they find Him changed in so far as their experience of suffering at His hand is new, as the sun is changed to injured eyes, and becomes as it were fierce from being mild, and hurtful from being delightful, though in itself it remains the same as it was. That also is called the will of God which He does in the hearts of those who obey His commandments; and of this the apostle says, "For it is God that worketh in you both to will." [2] As God's "righteousness" is used not only of the righteousness wherewith He Himself is righteous, but also of that which He produces in the man whom He justifies, so also that is called His law, which, though given by God, is rather the law of men. For certainly they were men to whom Jesus said, "It is written in your law," [3] though in another place we read, "The law of his God is in his heart." [4] According to this will which God works in men, He is said also to will what He Himself does not will, but causes His people to will; as He is said to know what He has caused those to know who were ignorant of it. For when the apostle says, "But now, after that ye have known God, or rather are known of God," [5] we cannot suppose that God there for the first time knew those who were foreknown by Him before the foundation of the world; but He is said to have known them then, because then He caused them to know. But I remember that I discussed these modes of expression in the preceding books. According to this will, then, by which we say that God wills what He causes to be willed by others, from whom the future is hidden, He wills many things which He does not perform.

Thus His saints, inspired by His holy will, desire many things which never happen. They pray, *e.g.*, for certain individuals—they pray in a pious and holy manner—but what they request He does not perform, though He Himself by His own Holy Spirit has wrought in them this will to pray. And consequently, when the saints, in conformity with God's mind, will and pray that all men be saved, we can use this mode of expression: God wills and does not perform—meaning that He who causes them to will these things Himself wills them. But if we speak of that will of His which is eternal as His foreknowledge, certainly He has already done all things in heaven and on earth that He has willed—not only past and present things, but even things still future. But before the arrival of that time in which He has willed the occurrence of what He foreknew and arranged before all time, we say, It will happen when God wills. But if we are ignorant not only of the time in which it is to be, but even whether it shall be at all, we say, It will happen if God wills—not because God will then have a new will which He had not before, but because that event, which from eternity has been prepared in His unchangeable will, shall then come to pass.

CHAPTER III

OF THE PROMISE OF ETERNAL BLESSEDNESS TO THE SAINTS, AND EVERLASTING PUNISHMENT TO THE WICKED

Wherefore, not to mention many other instances besides, as we now see in Christ the fulfillment of that which God promised to Abraham when He said, "In thy seed shall all nations be blessed," [6] so this also shall be fulfilled

[2] Phil. ii. 13   [3] John viii. 17   [4] Ps. xxxvii. 31   [5] Gal. iv. 9   [6] Gen. xxii. 18

which He promised to the same race, when He said by the prophet, "They that are in their sepulchres shall rise again," [7] and also, "There shall be a new heaven and a new earth: and the former shall not be mentioned, nor come into mind; but they shall find joy and rejoicing in it: for I will make Jerusalem a rejoicing, and my people a joy. And I will rejoice in Jerusalem, and joy in my people, and the voice of weeping shall be no more heard in her." [8] And by another prophet He uttered the same prediction: "At that time thy people shall be delivered, every one that shall be found written in the book. And many of them that sleep in the dust" (or, as some interpret it, "in the mound") "of the earth shall awake, some to everlasting life, and some to shame and everlasting contempt." [9] And in another place by the same prophet: "The saints of the Most High shall take the kingdom, and shall possess the kingdom for ever, even for ever and ever." [10] And a little after he says, "His kingdom is an everlasting kingdom." [11] Other prophecies referring to the same subject I have advanced in the twentieth book, and others still which I have not advanced are found written in the same Scriptures; and these predictions shall be fulfilled, as those also have been which unbelieving men supposed would not happen. For it is the same God who promised both, and predicted that both would come to pass—the God whom the pagan deities tremble before, as even Porphyry, the noblest of pagan philosophers, testifies.

CHAPTER IV

AGAINST THE WISE MEN OF THE WORLD, WHO FANCY THAT THE EARTHLY BODIES OF MEN CANNOT BE TRANSFERRED TO A HEAVENLY HABITATION

But men who use their learning and intellectual ability to resist the force of that great authority which, in fulfillment of what was so long before predicted, has converted all races of men to faith and hope in its promises, seem to themselves to argue acutely against the resurrection of the body while they cite what Cicero mentions in the third book of his *De Republica*. For when he was asserting the apotheosis of Hercules and Romulus, he says: "Whose bodies were not taken up into heaven; for nature would not permit a body of earth to exist anywhere except upon earth." This, forsooth, is the profound reasoning of the wise men, whose thoughts God knows that they are vain. For if we were only souls, that is, spirits without any body, and if we dwelt in heaven and had no knowledge of earthly animals, and were told that we should be bound to earthly bodies by some wonderful bond of union, and should animate them, should we not much more vigorously refuse to believe this, and maintain that nature would not permit an incorporeal substance to be held by a corporeal bond? And yet the earth is full of living

[7] Isa. xxvi. 19   [8] Isa. lxv. 17-19   [9] Dan. xii. 1, 2   [10] Dan. vii. 18   [11] Dan. vii. 27

spirits, to which terrestrial bodies are bound, and with which they are in a wonderful way implicated. If, then, the same God who has created such beings wills this also, what is to hinder the earthly body from being raised to a heavenly body, since a spirit, which is more excellent than all bodies, and consequently than even a heavenly body, has been tied to an earthly body? If so small an earthly particle has been able to hold in union with itself something better than a heavenly body, so as to receive sensation and life, will heaven disdain to receive, or at least to retain, this sentient and living particle, which derives its life and sensation from a substance more excellent than any heavenly body? If this does not happen now, it is because the time is not yet come which has been determined by Him who has already done a much more marvellous thing than that which these men refuse to believe. For why do we not more intensely wonder that incorporeal souls, which are of higher rank than heavenly bodies, are bound to earthly bodies, rather than that bodies, although earthly, are exalted to an abode which, though heavenly, is yet corporeal, except because we have been accustomed to see this, and indeed are this, while we are not as yet that other marvel, nor have as yet ever seen it? Certainly, if we consult sober reason, the more wonderful of the two divine works is found to be to attach somehow corporeal things to incorporeal, and not to connect earthly things with heavenly, which, though diverse, are yet both of them corporeal.

CHAPTER V

OF THE RESURRECTION OF THE FLESH, WHICH SOME REFUSE TO BELIEVE, THOUGH THE WORLD AT LARGE BELIEVES IT

But granting that this was once incredible, behold, now, the world has come to the belief that the earthly body of Christ was received up into heaven. Already both the learned and unlearned have believed in the resurrection of the flesh and its ascension to the heavenly places, while only a very few either of the educated or uneducated are still staggered by it. If this is a credible thing which is believed, then let those who do not believe see how stolid they are; and if it is incredible, then this also is an incredible thing, that what is incredible should have received such credit. Here then we have two incredibles—to wit, the resurrection of our body to eternity, and that the world should believe so incredible a thing; and both these incredibles the same God predicted should come to pass before either had as yet occurred. We see that already one of the two has come to pass, for the world has believed what was incredible; why should we despair that the remaining one shall also come to pass, and that this which the world believed, though it was incredible, shall itself occur? For already that which was equally incredible has come to pass, in the world's believing an incredible thing. Both were incredible: the one we see accomplished, the other we believe shall be; for both were predicted in those same Scriptures by means of which the world believed. And the very manner in which the world's faith was won is found to be even more incredible, if we consider it. Men uninstructed in any branch of a liberal education, without any of the refinement of heathen learning, unskilled in grammar, not armed with dialectic, not adorned with rhetoric, but plain fishermen, and very few in number—these were the men whom Christ sent with the nets of faith to the sea of this world, and thus took out of every race so many fishes, and even the philosophers themselves, wonderful as they are rare. Let us add, if you please, or because you ought to be pleased, this third incredible thing to the two former. And now we have three incredibles, all of which have yet come to pass. It is incredible that Jesus Christ should have risen in the flesh and ascended with flesh into heaven; it is incredible that the world should have believed so incredible a thing; it is incredible that a very few men, of mean birth and the lowest rank, and no education, should have been able so effectually to persuade the world, and even its learned men, of so incredible a thing. Of these three incredibles, the parties with whom we are debating refuse to believe the first; they cannot refuse to see the second, which they are unable to account for if they do not believe the third. It is indubitable that the resurrection of Christ, and His ascension into heaven with the flesh in which He rose, is already preached and believed in the whole world. If it is not credible, how is it that it has already received credence in the whole world? If a number of noble, exalted, and learned men had said that they had witnessed it, and had been at pains to publish what they had witnessed, it is not wonderful that the world should have believed it, but it is very stubborn to refuse credence; but if, as is true, the world has believed a few obscure, inconsiderable, uneducated persons, who state and write that they witnessed it, is it not unreasonable that a handful of wrong-headed men should oppose themselves to the creed of the whole world, and refuse their belief? And if the world has put faith in a small number of men, of mean birth and the lowest rank, and no education, it is because the divinity of the thing itself appeared all the more manifestly in such contemptible witnesses. The eloquence, indeed, which lent persuasion to their message, consisted of wonderful works, not words. For they who had not seen Christ risen in the flesh, nor ascending into heaven with His risen body, believed those who related how they had seen these things, and who testified not only with words but wonderful signs. For men whom they knew to be acquainted with only one, or at most two languages, they marvelled to hear speaking in the tongues of all nations. They saw a man, lame from his mother's womb, after forty years stand up sound at their word in the name of Christ; that handkerchiefs taken from their bodies had virtue to heal the sick; that countless persons, sick of various diseases, were laid in a row in the road where they were to pass, that their shadow might fall on them as they walked, and that they forthwith received health; that many other stupendous miracles were wrought by them in the name of Christ; and, finally, that they even raised the dead. If it be admitted that these things occurred as they are related, then we have a multitude of incredible things to add to those three incredibles. That the one incredibility of the resurrection and ascension of Jesus Christ may be believed, we accumulate the testimonies of countless incredible miracles, but even so we do not bend the frightful obstinacy of these sceptics. But if they do not believe that these miracles were wrought by Christ's apostles to gain credence to their preaching of His resurrection and ascension, this one grand miracle suffices for us, that the whole world has believed without any miracles.

CHAPTER VI

THAT ROME MADE ITS FOUNDER ROMULUS A GOD BECAUSE IT LOVED HIM; BUT THE CHURCH LOVED CHRIST BECAUSE IT BELIEVED HIM TO BE GOD

Let us here recite the passage in which Tully expresses his astonishment that the apotheosis of Romulus should have been credited. I shall insert his words as they stand: "It is most worthy of remark in Romulus, that other men who are said to have become gods lived in less educated ages, when there was a greater propensity to the fabulous, and when the uninstructed were easily persuaded to believe anything. But the age of Romulus was barely six hundred years ago, and already literature and science had dispelled the errors that attach to an uncultured age." And a little after he says of the same Romulus words to this effect: "From this we may perceive that Homer had flourished long before Romulus, and that there was now so much learning in individuals, and so generally diffused an enlightenment, that scarcely any room was left for fable. For antiquity admitted fables, and sometimes even very clumsy ones; but this age of Romulus was sufficiently enlightened to reject whatever had not the air of truth." Thus one of the most learned men, and certainly the most eloquent, M. Tullius Cicero, says that it is surprising that the divinity of Romulus was believed in, because the times were already so enlightened that they would not accept a fabulous fiction. But who believed that Romulus was a god except Rome, which was itself small and in its infancy? Then afterwards it was necessary that succeeding generations should preserve the tradition of their ancestors; that, drinking in this superstition with their mother's milk, the state might grow and come to such power that it might dictate this belief, as from a point of vantage, to all the nations over whom its sway extended. And these nations, though they might not believe that Romulus was a god, at least said so, that they might not give offence to their sovereign state by refusing to give its founder that title which was given him by Rome, which had adopted this belief, not by a love of error, but an error of love. But though Christ is the founder of the heavenly and eternal city, yet it did not believe Him to be God because it was founded by Him, but rather it is founded by Him, in virtue of its belief. Rome, after it had been built and dedicated, worshipped its founder in a temple as a god; but this Jerusalem laid Christ, its God, as its foundation, that the building and dedication might proceed. The former city loved its founder, and therefore believed him to be a god; the latter believed Christ to be God, and therefore loved Him. There was an antecedent cause for the love of the former city, and for its believing that even a false dignity attached to the object of its love; so there was an antecedent cause for the belief of the latter, and for its loving the true dignity which a proper faith, not a rash surmise, ascribed to its object. For, not to mention the multitude of very striking miracles which proved that Christ is God, there were also divine prophecies heralding Him, prophecies most worthy of belief, which being already accomplished, we have not, like the fathers, to wait for their verification. Of Romulus, on the other hand, and of his building Rome and reigning in it, we read or hear the narrative of what did take place, not prediction which beforehand said that such things should be. And so far as his reception among the gods is concerned, history only records that this was believed, and does not state it as a fact; for no miraculous signs testified to the truth of this. For as to that wolf which is said to have nursed the twin-brothers, and which is considered a great marvel, how does this prove him to have been divine? For even supposing that this nurse was a real wolf and not a mere courtesan, yet she nursed both brothers, and Remus is not reckoned a god. Besides, what was there to hinder any one from asserting that Romulus or Hercules, or any such man, was a god? Or who would rather choose to die than profess belief in his divinity? And did a single nation worship Romulus among its gods, unless it were forced through fear of the Roman name? But who can number the multitudes who have chosen death in the most cruel shapes rather than deny the divinity of Christ? And thus the dread of some slight indignation, which it was supposed, perhaps groundlessly, might exist in the minds of the Romans, constrained some states who were subject to Rome to worship Romulus as a god; whereas the dread, not of a slight mental shock, but of severe and various punishments, and of death itself, the most formidable of all, could not prevent an immense multitude of martyrs throughout the world from not merely worshipping but also confessing Christ as God. The city of Christ, which, although as yet a stranger upon earth, had countless hosts of citizens, did not make war upon its godless persecutors for the sake of temporal security, but preferred to win eternal salvation by abstaining from war. They were bound, imprisoned, beaten, tortured, burned, torn in pieces, massacred, and yet they multiplied. It was not given to them to fight for their eternal salvation except by despising their temporal salvation for their Saviour's sake.

I am aware that Cicero, in the third book of his *De Republica*, if I mistake not, argues that a first-rate power will not engage in war except either for honor or for safety. What he has to say about the question of safety, and what he means by safety, he explains in another place, saying, "Private persons frequently evade, by a speedy death, destitution, exile, bonds, the scourge, and the other pains which even the most insensible feel. But to states, death, which seems to emancipate individuals from all punishments, is itself a punishment; for a state should be so constituted as to be eternal. And thus death is not natural to a republic as to a man, to whom death is not only necessary, but often even desirable. But when a state is destroyed, obliterated, annihilated, it is as if (to compare great things with small) this whole world perished and collapsed." Cicero said this because he, with the Platonists, believed that the world would not perish. It is therefore agreed that, according to Cicero, a state should engage in war for the safety which preserves the state permanently in existence, though its citizens change; as the foliage of an olive or laurel, or any tree of this kind, is perennial, the old leaves being replaced by fresh ones. For death, as he says, is no punishment to individuals, but rather delivers them from all other punishments, but it is a punishment to the state. And therefore it is reasonably asked whether the Saguntines did right when they chose that their whole state should perish rather than that they should break faith with the Roman republic; for this deed of theirs is applauded by the citizens of the earthly republic. But I do not see how they could follow the advice of Cicero, who tell us that no war is to be undertaken save for safety or for honor; neither does he say which of these two is to be preferred, if a case should occur in which the one could not be preserved without the loss of the other. For manifestly, if the Saguntines chose safety, they must break faith; if they kept faith, they must reject safety; as also it fell out. But the safety of the city of God is such that it can be retained, or rather acquired, by faith and with faith; but if faith be abandoned, no one can attain it. It is this thought of a most steadfast and patient spirit that has made so many noble martyrs, while Romulus has not had, and could not have, so much as one to die for his divinity.

CHAPTER VII

THAT THE WORLD'S BELIEF IN CHRIST IS THE RESULT OF DIVINE POWER, NOT OF HUMAN PERSUASION

But it is thoroughly ridiculous to make mention of the false divinity of Romulus as any way comparable to that of Christ. Nevertheless, if Romulus lived about six hundred years before Cicero, in an age which already was so enlightened that it rejected all impossibilities, how much more, in an age which certainly was more enlightened, being six hundred years later, the age of Cicero himself, and of the emperors Augustus and Tiberius, would the human mind have refused to listen to or believe in the resurrection of Christ's body and its ascension into heaven, and have scouted it as an impossibility, had not the divinity of the truth itself, or the truth of the divinity, and corroborating miraculous signs, proved that it could happen and had happened? Through virtue of these testimonies, and notwithstanding the opposition and terror of so many cruel persecutions, the resurrection and immortality of the flesh, first in Christ, and subsequently in all in the new world, was believed, was intrepidly proclaimed, and was sown over the whole world, to be fertilized richly with the blood of the martyrs. For the predictions of the prophets that had preceded the events were read, they were corroborated by powerful signs, and the truth was seen to be not contradictory to reason, but only different from customary ideas, so that at length the world embraced the faith it had furiously persecuted.

CHAPTER VIII

OF MIRACLES WHICH WERE WROUGHT THAT THE WORLD MIGHT BELIEVE IN CHRIST, AND WHICH HAVE NOT CEASED SINCE THE WORLD BELIEVED

Why, they say, are those miracles, which you affirm were wrought formerly, wrought no longer? I might, indeed, reply that miracles were necessary before the world believed, in order that it might believe. And whoever now-a-days demands to see prodigies that he may believe, is himself a great prodigy, because he does not believe, though the whole world does. But they make these objections for the sole purpose of insinuating that even those former miracles were never wrought. How, then, is it that everywhere Christ is celebrated with such firm belief in His resurrection and ascension? How is it that in enlightened times, in which every impossibility is rejected, the world has, without any miracles, believed things marvellously incredible? Or will they say that these things were credible, and therefore were credited? Why then do they themselves not believe? Our argument, therefore, is a summary one—either incredible things which were not witnessed have caused the world to believe other incredible things which both occurred and were witnessed, or this matter was so credible that it needed no miracles in proof of it, and therefore convicts these unbelievers of unpardonable scepticism. This I might say for the sake of refuting these most frivolous objectors. But we cannot deny that many miracles were wrought to confirm that one grand and health-giving miracle of Christ's ascension to heaven with the flesh in which He rose. For these most trustworthy books of ours contain in one narrative both the miracles that were wrought and the creed which they were wrought to confirm. The miracles were published that they might produce faith, and the faith which they produced brought them into greater prominence. For they are read in congregations that they may be believed, and yet they would not be so read unless they were believed. For even now miracles are wrought in the name of Christ, whether by His sacraments or by the prayers or relics of His saints; but they are not so brilliant and conspicuous as to cause them to be published with such glory as accompanied the former miracles. For the canon of the sacred writings, which must be authoritative, causes those to be everywhere recited, and to sink into the memory of all the congregations; but these modern miracles are scarcely known even to the whole population in the midst of which they are wrought, and at the best are confined to one spot. For frequently they are known only to a very few persons, while all the rest are ignorant of them, especially if the state is a large one; and when they are reported to other persons in other localities, there is no sufficient authority to give them prompt and unwavering credence, although they are reported to the faithful by the faithful.

The miracle which was wrought at Milan when I was there, and by which a blind man was restored to sight, could come to the knowledge of many; for not only is the city a large one, but also the emperor was there at the time, and the occurrence was witnessed by an immense concourse of people that had gathered to the bodies of the martyrs Protasius and Gervasius, which had long lain concealed and unknown, but were now made known to the bishop Ambrose in a dream, and discovered by him. By virtue of these remains the darkness of that blind man was scattered, and he saw the light of day.[12]

But who but a very small number are aware of the cure which was wrought upon Innocentius, ex-advocate of the deputy prefecture, a cure wrought at Carthage, in my presence, and under my own eyes? For when I and my brother Alypius,[13] who were not yet clergymen, though already servants of God, came from abroad, this man received us, and made us live with him, for he and all his household were devotedly pious. He was being treated by medical men for fistulae, of which he had a large number intricately seated in the rectum. He had already undergone an operation, and the surgeons were using every means at their command for his relief. In that operation he had suffered long-continued and acute pain; yet, among the many folds of the gut, one had escaped the operators so entirely, that, though they ought to have laid it open with the knife, they never touched it. And thus, though all those that had been opened were cured, this one remained as it was, and frustrated all their labor. The patient, having his suspicions awakened by the delay thus occasioned, and fearing greatly a second operation, which another medical man—one of his own domestics—had told him he must undergo, though this man had not even been allowed to witness the first operation, and had been banished from the house, and with difficulty allowed to come back to his enraged master's presence—the patient, I say, broke out to the surgeons, saying, "Are you going to cut me again? Are you, after all, to fulfill the prediction of that man whom you would not allow even to be present?" The surgeons laughed at the unskillful doctor, and soothed their patient's fears with fair words and promises. So several days passed, and yet nothing they tried did him good. Still they persisted in promising that they

---

[12] A somewhat fuller account of this miracle is given by Augustine in the *Confessions*, ix. 16. See also *Serm*. 286, and Ambrose, *Ep.* 22

[13] Alypius was a countryman of Augustine, and one of his most attached friends. See the *Confessions*, passim

would cure that fistula by drugs, without the knife. They called in also another old practitioner of great repute in that department, Ammonius (for he was still alive at that time); and he, after examining the part, promised the same result as themselves from their care and skill. On this great authority, the patient became confident, and, as if already well, vented his good spirits in facetious remarks at the expense of his domestic physician, who had predicted a second operation. To make a long story short, after a number of days had thus uselessly elapsed, the surgeons, wearied and confused, had at last to confess that he could only be cured by the knife. Agitated with excessive fear, he was terrified, and grew pale with dread; and when he collected himself and was able to speak, he ordered them to go away and never to return. Worn out with weeping, and driven by necessity, it occurred to him to call in an Alexandrian, who was at that time esteemed a wonderfully skillful operator, that he might perform the operation his rage would not suffer them to do. But when he had come, and examined with a professional eye the traces of their careful work, he acted the part of a good man, and persuaded his patient to allow those same hands the satisfaction of finishing his cure which had begun it with a skill that excited his admiration, adding that there was no doubt his only hope of a cure was by an operation, but that it was thoroughly inconsistent with his nature to win the credit of the cure by doing the little that remained to be done, and rob of their reward men whose consummate skill, care, and diligence he could not but admire when he saw the traces of their work. They were therefore again received to favor; and it was agreed that, in the presence of the Alexandrian, they should operate on the fistula, which, by the consent of all, could now only be cured by the knife. The operation was deferred till the following day. But when they had left, there arose in the house such a wailing, in sympathy with the excessive despondency of the master, that it seemed to us like the mourning at a funeral, and we could scarcely repress it. Holy men were in the habit of visiting him daily; Saturninus of blessed memory, at that time bishop of Uzali, and the presbyter Gelosus, and the deacons of the church of Carthage; and among these was the bishop Aurelius, who alone of them all survives—a man to be named by us with due reverence—and with him I have often spoken of this affair, as we conversed together about the wonderful works of God, and I have found that he distinctly remembers what I am now relating. When these persons visited him that evening according to their custom, he besought them, with pitiable tears, that they would do him the honor of being present next day at what he judged his funeral rather than his suffering. For such was the terror his former pains had produced, that he made no doubt he would die in the hands of the surgeons. They comforted him, and exhorted him to put his trust in God, and nerve his will like a man. Then we went to prayer; but while we, in the usual way, were kneeling and bending to the ground, he cast himself down, as if some one were hurling him violently to the earth, and began to pray; but in what a manner, with what earnestness and emotion, with what a flood of tears, with what groans and sobs, that shook his whole body, and almost prevented him speaking, who can describe! Whether the others prayed, and had not their attention wholly diverted by this conduct, I do not know. For myself, I could not pray at all. This only I briefly said in my heart: "O Lord, what prayers of Thy people dost Thou hear if Thou hearest not these?" For it seemed to me that nothing could be added to this prayer, unless he expired in praying. We rose from our knees, and, receiving the blessing of the bishop, departed, the patient beseeching his visitors to be present next morning, they exhorting him to keep up his heart. The dreaded day dawned. The servants of God were present, as they had promised to be; the surgeons arrived; all that the circumstances required was ready; the frightful instruments are produced; all look on in wonder and suspense. While those who have most influence with the patient are cheering his fainting spirit, his limbs are arranged on the couch so as to suit the hand of the operator; the knots of the bandages are untied; the part is bared; the surgeon examines it, and, with knife in hand, eagerly looks for the sinus that is to be cut. He searches for it with his eyes; he feels for it with his finger; he applies every kind of scrutiny: he finds a perfectly firm cicatrix! No words of mine can describe the joy, and praise, and thanksgiving to the merciful and almighty God which was poured from the lips of all, with tears of gladness. Let the scene be imagined rather than described!

In the same city of Carthage lived Innocentia, a very devout woman of the highest rank in the state. She had cancer in one of her breasts, a disease which, as physicians say, is incurable. Ordinarily, therefore, they either amputate, and so separate from the body the member on which the disease has seized, or, that the patient's life may be prolonged a little, though death is inevitable even if somewhat delayed, they abandon all remedies, following, as they say, the advice of Hippocrates. This the lady we speak of had been advised to by a skillful physician, who was intimate with her family; and she betook herself to God alone by prayer. On the approach of Easter, she was instructed in a dream to wait for the first woman that came out from the baptistery after being baptized, and to ask her to make the sign of Christ upon her sore. She did so, and was immediately cured. The physician who had advised her to apply no remedy if she wished to live a little longer, when he had examined her after this, and found that she who, on his former examination, was afflicted with that disease was now perfectly cured, eagerly asked her what remedy she had used, anxious, as we may well believe, to discover the drug which should defeat the decision of Hippocrates. But when she told him what had happened, he is said to have replied, with religious politeness, though with a contemptuous tone, and an expression which made her fear he would utter some blasphemy against Christ, "I thought you would make some great discovery to me." She, shuddering at his indifference, quickly replied, "What great thing was it for Christ to heal a cancer, who raised one who had been four days dead?" When, therefore, I had heard this,

I was extremely indignant that so great a miracle, wrought in that well-known city, and on a person who was certainly not obscure, should not be divulged, and I considered that she should be spoken to, if not reprimanded on this score. And when she replied to me that she had not kept silence on the subject, I asked the women with whom she was best acquainted whether they had ever heard of this before. They told me they knew nothing of it. "See," I said, "what your not keeping silence amounts to, since not even those who are so familiar with you know of it." And as I had only briefly heard the story, I made her tell how the whole thing happened, from beginning to end, while the other women listened in great astonishment, and glorified God.

A gouty doctor of the same city, when he had given in his name for baptism, and had been prohibited the day before his baptism from being baptized that year, by black woolly-haired boys who appeared to him in his dreams, and whom he understood to be devils, and when, though they trod on his feet, and inflicted the acutest pain he had ever yet experienced, he refused to obey them, but overcame them, and would not defer being washed in the laver of regeneration, was relieved in the very act of baptism, not only of the extraordinary pain he was tortured with, but also of the disease itself, so that, though he lived a long time afterwards, he never suffered from gout; and yet who knows of this miracle? We, however, do know it, and so, too, do the small number of brethren who were in the neighborhood, and to whose ears it might come.

An old comedian of Curubis[14] was cured at baptism not only of paralysis, but also of hernia, and, being delivered from both afflictions, came up out of the font of regeneration as if he had had nothing wrong with his body. Who outside of Curubis knows of this, or who but a very few who might hear it elsewhere? But we, when we heard of it, made the man come to Carthage, by order of the holy bishop Aurelius, although we had already ascertained the fact on the information of persons whose word we could not doubt.

Hesperius, of a tribunician family, and a neighbor of our own, has a farm called Zubedi in the Fussalian district,[15] and, finding that his family, his cattle, and his servants were suffering from the malice of evil spirits, he asked our presbyters, during my absence, that one of them would go with him and banish the spirits by his prayers. One went, offered there the sacrifice of the body of Christ, praying with all his might that that vexation might cease. It did cease forthwith, through God's mercy. Now he had received from a friend of his own some holy earth brought from Jerusalem, where Christ, having been buried, rose again the third day. This earth he had hung up in his bedroom to preserve himself from harm. But when his house was purged of that demoniacal invasion, he began to consider what should be done with the earth; for his reverence for it made him unwilling to have it any longer in his bedroom. It so happened that I and Maximinus bishop of Synita, and

[14] A town near Carthage   [15] Near Hippo

then my colleague, were in the neighborhood. Hesperius asked us to visit him, and we did so. When he had related all the circumstances, he begged that the earth might be buried somewhere, and that the spot should be made a place of prayer where Christians might assemble for the worship of God. We made no objection: it was done as he desired. There was in that neighborhood a young countryman who was paralytic, who, when he heard of this, begged his parents to take him without delay to that holy place. When he had been brought there, he prayed, and forthwith went away on his own feet perfectly cured.

There is a country-seat called Victoriana, less than thirty miles from Hippo-regius. At it there is a monument to the Milanese martyrs, Protasius and Gervasius. Thither a young man was carried, who, when he was watering his horse one summer day at noon in a pool of a river, had been taken possession of by a devil. As he lay at the monument, near death, or even quite like a dead person, the lady of the manor, with her maids and religious attendants, entered the place for evening prayer and praise, as her custom was, and they began to sing hymns. At this sound the young man, as if electrified, was thoroughly aroused, and with frightful screaming seized the altar, and held it as if he did not dare or were not able to let it go, and as if he were fixed or tied to it; and the devil in him, with loud lamentation, besought that he might be spared, and confessed where and when and how he took possession of the youth. At last, declaring that he would go out of him, he named one by one the parts of his body which he threatened to mutilate as he went out and with these words he departed from the man. But his eye, falling out on his cheek, hung by a slender vein as by a root, and the whole of the pupil which had been black became white. When this was witnessed by those present (others too had now gathered to his cries, and had all joined in prayer for him), although they were delighted that he had recovered his sanity of mind, yet, on the other hand, they were grieved about his eye, and said he should seek medical advice. But his sister's husband, who had brought him there, said, "God, who has banished the devil, is able to restore his eye at the prayers of His saints." Therewith he replaced the eye that was fallen out and hanging, and bound it in its place with his handkerchief as well as he could, and advised him not to loose the bandage for seven days. When he did so, he found it quite healthy. Others also were cured there, but of them it is tedious to speak.

I know that a young woman of Hippo was immediately dispossessed of a devil, on anointing herself with oil, mixed with the tears of the presbyter who had been praying for her. I know also that a bishop once prayed for a demoniac young man whom he never saw, and that he was cured on the spot.

There was a fellow-townsman of ours at Hippo, Florentius, an old man, religious and poor, who supported himself as a tailor. Having lost his coat, and not having means to buy another, he prayed to the Twenty Martyrs,[16]

[16] Augustine's 325th sermon is in honor of these martyrs

who have a very celebrated memorial shrine in our town, begging in a distinct voice that he might be clothed. Some scoffing young men, who happened to be present, heard him, and followed him with their sarcasm as he went away, as if he had asked the martyrs for fifty pence to buy a coat. But he, walking on in silence, saw on the shore a great fish, gasping as if just cast up, and having secured it with the good-natured assistance of the youths, he sold it for curing to a cook of the name of Catosus, a good Christian man, telling him how he had come by it, and receiving for it three hundred pence, which he laid out in wool, that his wife might exercise her skill upon, and make into a coat for him. But, on cutting up the fish, the cook found a gold ring in its belly; and forthwith, moved with compassion, and influenced, too, by religious fear, gave it up to the man, saying, "See how the Twenty Martyrs have clothed you."

When the bishop Projectus was bringing the relics of the most glorious martyr Stephen to the waters of Tibilis, a great concourse of people came to meet him at the shrine. There a blind woman entreated that she might be led to the bishop who was carrying the relics. He gave her the flowers he was carrying. She took them, applied them to her eyes, and forthwith saw. Those who were present were astounded, while she, with every expression of joy, preceded them, pursuing her way without further need of a guide.

Lucillus bishop of Sinita, in the neighborhood of the colonial town of Hippo, was carrying in procession some relics of the same martyr, which had been deposited in the castle of Sinita. A fistula under which he had long labored, and which his private physician was watching an opportunity to cut, was suddenly cured by the mere carrying of that sacred burden—at least, afterwards there was no trace of it in his body.

Eucharius, a Spanish priest, residing at Calama, was for a long time a sufferer from stone. By the relics of the same martyr, which the bishop Possidius brought him, he was cured. Afterwards the same priest, sinking under another disease, was lying dead, and already they were binding his hands. By the succor of the same martyr he was raised to life, the priest's cloak having been brought from the oratory and laid upon the corpse.

There was there an old nobleman named Martial, who had a great aversion to the Christian religion, but whose daughter was a Christian, while her husband had been baptized that same year. When he was ill, they besought him with tears and prayers to become a Christian, but he positively refused, and dismissed them from his presence in a storm of indignation. It occurred to the son-in-law to go to the oratory of St. Stephen, and there pray for him with all earnestness that God might give him a right mind, so that he should not delay believing in Christ. This he did with great groaning and tears, and the burning fervor of sincere piety; then, as he left the place, he took some of the flowers that were lying there, and, as it was already night, laid them by his father's head, who so slept. And lo! before dawn, he cries out for some one to run for the bishop; but he happened at that time to be with me at

Hippo. So when he had heard that he was from home, he asked the presbyters to come. They came. To the joy and amazement of all, he declared that he believed, and he was baptized. As long as he remained in life, these words were ever on his lips: "Christ, receive my spirit," though he was not aware that these were the last words of the most blessed Stephen when he was stoned by the Jews. They were his last words also, for not long after he himself also gave up the ghost.

There, too, by the same martyr, two men, one a citizen, the other a stranger, were cured of gout; but while the citizen was absolutely cured, the stranger was only informed what he should apply when the pain returned; and when he followed this advice, the pain was at once relieved.

Audurus is the name of an estate, where there is a church that contains a memorial shrine of the martyr Stephen. It happened that, as a little boy was playing in the court, the oxen drawing a wagon went out of the track and crushed him with the wheel, so that immediately he seemed at his last gasp. His mother snatched him up, and laid him at the shrine, and not only did he revive, but also appeared uninjured.

A religious female, who lived at Caspalium, a neighboring estate, when she was so ill as to be despaired of, had her dress brought to this shrine, but before it was brought back she was gone. However, her parents wrapped her corpse in the dress, and, her breath returning, she became quite well.

At Hippo a Syrian called Bassus was praying at the relics of the same martyr for his daughter, who was dangerously ill. He too had brought her dress with him to the shrine. But as he prayed, behold, his servants ran from the house to tell him she was dead. His friends, however, intercepted them, and forbade them to tell him, lest he should bewail her in public. And when he had returned to his house, which was already ringing with the lamentations of his family, and had thrown on his daughter's body the dress he was carrying, she was restored to life.

There, too, the son of a man, Irenaeus, one of our tax-gatherers, took ill and died. And while his body was lying lifeless, and the last rites were being prepared, amidst the weeping and mourning of all, one of the friends who were consoling the father suggested that the body should be anointed with the oil of the same martyr. It was done, and he revived.

Likewise Eleusinus, a man of tribunitian rank among us, laid his infant son, who had died, on the shrine of the martyr, which is in the suburb where he lived, and, after prayer, which he poured out there with many tears, he took up his child alive.

What am I to do? I am so pressed by the promise of finishing this work, that I cannot record all the miracles I know; and doubtless several of our adherents, when they read what I have narrated, will regret that I have omitted so many which they, as well as I, certainly know. Even now I beg these persons to excuse me, and to consider how long it would take me to relate all those miracles, which the necessity of finishing the work I have undertaken forces me to omit. For were I to be silent of all others, and to record exclusively the miracles of healing which were wrought in the district of Calama and of Hippo by means of this martyr—I mean the most glorious Stephen—they would fill many volumes; and yet all even of these could not be collected, but only those of which narratives have been written for public recital. For when I saw, in our own times, frequent signs of the presence of divine powers similar to those which had been given of old, I desired that narratives might be written, judging that the multitude should not remain ignorant of these things. It is not yet two years since these relics were first brought to Hippo-regius, and though many of the miracles which have been wrought by it have not, as I have the most certain means of knowing, been recorded, those which have been published amount to almost seventy at the hour at which I write. But at Calama, where these relics have been for a longer time, and where more of the miracles were narrated for public information, there are incomparably more.

At Uzali, too, a colony near Utica, many signal miracles were, to my knowledge, wrought by the same martyr, whose relics had found a place there by direction of the bishop Evodius, long before we had them at Hippo. But there the custom of publishing narratives does not obtain, or, I should say, did not obtain, for possibly it may now have been begun. For, when I was there recently, a woman of rank, Petronia, had been miraculously cured of a serious illness of long standing, in which all medical appliances had failed, and, with the consent of the above-named bishop of the place, I exhorted her to publish an account of it that might be read to the people. She most promptly obeyed, and inserted in her narrative a circumstance which I cannot omit to mention, though I am compelled to hasten on to the subjects which this work requires me to treat. She said that she had been persuaded by a Jew to wear next her skin, under all her clothes, a hair girdle, and on this girdle a ring, which, instead of a gem, had a stone which had been found in the kidneys of an ox. Girt with this charm, she was making her way to the threshold of the holy martyr. But, after leaving Carthage, and when she had been lodging in her own demesne on the river Bagrada, and was now rising to continue her journey, she saw her ring lying before her feet. In great surprise she examined the hair girdle, and when she found it bound, as it had been, quite firmly with knots, she conjectured that the ring had been worn through and dropped off; but when she found that the ring was itself also perfectly whole, she presumed that by this great miracle she had received somehow a pledge of her cure, whereupon she untied the girdle, and cast it into the river, and the ring along with it. This is not credited by those who do not believe either that the Lord Jesus Christ came forth from His mother's womb without destroying her virginity, and entered among His disciples when the doors were shut; but let them make strict inquiry into this miracle, and if they find it true, let them believe those others. The lady is of distinction, nobly born, married to a nobleman. She resides at Carthage. The city is distinguished, the person is distinguished, so that they who make inquiries cannot fail to find satisfaction. Certainly the martyr himself, by whose prayers she was healed, believed on the Son of her who remained a virgin; on Him who came in among the disciples when the doors were shut; in fine—and to this tends all that we have been retailing—on Him who ascended into heaven with the flesh in which He had risen; and it is because he laid down his life for this faith that such miracles were done by his means.

Even now, therefore, many miracles are wrought, the same God who wrought those we read of still performing them, by whom He will and as He will; but they are not as well known, nor are they beaten into the memory, like gravel, by frequent reading, so that they cannot fall out of mind. For even where, as is now done among ourselves, care is taken that the pamphlets of those who receive benefit be read publicly, yet those who are present hear the narrative but once, and many are absent; and so it comes to pass that even those who are present forget in a few days what they heard, and scarcely one of them can be found who will tell what he heard to one who he knows was not present.

One miracle was wrought among ourselves, which, though no greater than those I have mentioned, was yet so signal and conspicuous, that I suppose there is no inhabitant of Hippo who did not either see or hear of it, none who could possibly forget it. There were seven brothers and three sisters of a noble family of the Cappadocian Caesarea, who were cursed by their mother, a new-made widow, on account of some wrong they had done her, and which she bitterly resented, and who were visited with so severe a punishment from Heaven, that all of them were seized with a hideous shaking in all their limbs. Unable, while presenting this loathsome appearance, to endure the eyes of their fellow-citizens, they wandered over almost the whole Roman world, each following his own direction. Two of them came to Hippo, a brother and a sister, Paulus and Palladia, already known in many other places by the fame of their wretched lot. Now it was about fifteen days before Easter when they came, and they came daily to church, and specially to the relics of the most glorious Stephen, praying that God might now be appeased, and restore their former health. There, and wherever they went, they attracted the attention of every one. Some who had seen them elsewhere, and knew the cause of their trembling, told others as occasion offered. Easter arrived, and on the Lord's day, in the morning, when there was now a large crowd present, and the young man was holding the bars of the holy place where the relics were, and praying, suddenly he fell down, and lay precisely as if asleep, but not trembling as he was wont to do even in sleep. All present were astonished. Some were alarmed, some were moved with pity; and while some were for lifting him up, others prevented them, and said they should rather wait and see what would result. And behold! he rose up, and trembled no more, for he was healed, and stood quite well, scanning those who were scanning him. Who then refrained himself from praising

God? The whole church was filled with the voices of those who were shouting and congratulating him. Then they came running to me, where I was sitting ready to come into the church. One after another they throng in, the last comer telling me as news what the first had told me already; and while I rejoiced and inwardly gave God thanks, the young man himself also enters, with a number of others, falls at my knees, is raised up to receive my kiss. We go in to the congregation: the church was full, and ringing with the shouts of joy, "Thanks to God! Praised be God!" every one joining and shouting on all sides, "I have healed the people," and then with still louder voice shouting again. Silence being at last obtained, the customary lessons of the divine Scriptures were read. And when I came to my sermon, I made a few remarks suitable to the occasion and the happy and joyful feeling, not desiring them to listen to me, but rather to consider the eloquence of God in this divine work. The man dined with us, and gave us a careful account of his own, his mother's, and his family's calamity. Accordingly, on the following day, after delivering my sermon, I promised that next day I would read his narrative to the people.[17] And when I did so, the third day after Easter Sunday, I made the brother and sister both stand on the steps of the raised place from which I used to speak; and while they stood there their pamphlet was read.[18] The whole congregation, men and women alike, saw the one standing without any unnatural movement, the other trembling in all her limbs; so that those who had not before seen the man himself saw in his sister what the divine compassion had removed from him. In him they saw matter of congratulation, in her subject for prayer. Meanwhile, their pamphlet being finished, I instructed them to withdraw from the gaze of the people; and I had begun to discuss the whole matter somewhat more carefully, when lo! as I was proceeding, other voices are heard from the tomb of the martyr, shouting new congratulations. My audience turned round, and began to run to the tomb. The young woman, when she had come down from the steps where she had been standing, went to pray at the holy relics, and no sooner had she touched the bars than she, in the same way as her brother, collapsed, as if falling asleep, and rose up cured. While, then, we were asking what had happened, and what occasioned this noise of joy, they came into the basilica where we were, leading her from the martyr's tomb in perfect health. Then, indeed, such a shout of wonder rose from men and women together, that the exclamations and the tears seemed like never to come to an end. She was led to the place where she had a little before stood trembling. They now rejoiced that she was like her brother, as before they had mourned that she remained unlike him; and as they had not yet uttered their prayers in her behalf, they perceived that their intention of doing so had been speedily heard. They shouted God's praises without words, but with such a noise that our ears could scarcely bear it. What was there in the hearts of these exultant people but the faith of Christ, for which Stephen had shed his blood?

[17] cf. Augustine's *Sermons*, 321   [18] *Sermon* 322

CHAPTER IX

THAT ALL THE MIRACLES WHICH ARE DONE BY MEANS OF THE MARTYRS IN THE NAME OF CHRIST TESTIFY TO THAT FAITH WHICH THE MARTYRS HAD IN CHRIST

To what do these miracles witness, but to this faith which preaches Christ risen in the flesh, and ascended with the same into heaven? For the martyrs themselves were martyrs, that is to say, witnesses of this faith, drawing upon themselves by their testimony the hatred of the world, and conquering the world not by resisting it, but by dying. For this faith they died, and can now ask these benefits from the Lord in whose name they were slain. For this faith their marvellous constancy was exercised, so that in these miracles great power was manifested as the result. For if the resurrection of the flesh to eternal life had not taken place in Christ, and were not to be accomplished in His people, as predicted by Christ, or by the prophets who foretold that Christ was to come, why do the martyrs who were slain for this faith which proclaims the resurrection possess such power? For whether God Himself wrought these miracles by that wonderful manner of working by which, though Himself eternal, He produces effects in time; or whether He wrought them by servants, and if so, whether He made use of the spirits of martyrs as He uses men who are still in the body, or effects all these marvels by means of angels, over whom He exerts an invisible, immutable, incorporeal sway, so that what is said to be done by the martyrs is done not by their operation, but only by their prayer and request; or whether, finally, some things are done in one way, others in another, and so that man cannot at all comprehend them—nevertheless these miracles attest this faith which preaches the resurrection of the flesh to eternal life.

CHAPTER X

THAT THE MARTYRS WHO OBTAIN MANY MIRACLES IN ORDER THAT THE TRUE GOD MAY BE WORSHIPPED, ARE WORTHY OF MUCH GREATER HONOR THAN THE DEMONS, WHO DO SOME MARVELS THAT THEY THEMSELVES MAY BE SUPPOSED TO BE GOD

Here perhaps our adversaries will say that their gods also have done some wonderful things, if now they begin to compare their gods to our dead men. Or will they also say that they have gods taken from among dead men, such as Hercules, Romulus, and many others whom they fancy to have been received into the number of the gods? But our martyrs are not our gods; for we know that the martyrs and we have both but one God, and that the same. Nor yet are the miracles which they maintain to have been done by means of their temples at all comparable to those which are done by the tombs of our martyrs. If they seem similar, their gods have been defeated by our martyrs as Pharaoh's magi were by Moses. In reality, the demons wrought these marvels with the same impure pride with which they aspired to be the gods of the nations; but the martyrs do these wonders, or rather God does them while they pray and assist, in order that an impulse may be given to the faith by which we believe that they are not our gods, but have, together with ourselves, one God. In fine, they built temples to these gods of theirs, and set up altars, and ordained priests, and appointed sacrifices; but to our martyrs we build, not temples as if they were gods, but monuments as to dead men whose spirits live with God. Neither do we erect altars at these monuments that we may sacrifice to the martyrs, but to the one God of the martyrs and of ourselves; and in this sacrifice they are named in their own place and rank as men of God who conquered the world by confessing Him, but they are not invoked by the sacrificing priest. For it is to God, not to them, he sacrifices, though he sacrifices at their monument; for he is God's priest, not theirs. The sacrifice itself, too, is the body of Christ, which is not offered to them, because they themselves are this body. Which then can more readily be believed to work miracles? They who wish themselves to be reckoned gods by those on whom they work miracles, or those whose sole object in working any miracle is to induce faith in God, and in Christ also as God? They who wished to turn even their crimes into sacred rites, or those who are unwilling that even their own praises be consecrated, and seek that everything for which they are justly praised be ascribed to the glory of Him in whom they are praised? For in the Lord their souls are praised. Let us therefore believe those who both speak the truth and work wonders. For by speaking the truth they suffered, and so won the power of working wonders. And the leading truth they professed is that Christ rose from the dead, and first showed in His own flesh the immortality of the resurrection which He promised should be ours, either in the beginning of the world to come, or in the end of this world.

CHAPTER XI

AGAINST THE PLATONISTS, WHO ARGUE FROM THE PHYSICAL WEIGHT OF THE ELEMENTS THAT AN EARTHLY BODY CANNOT INHABIT HEAVEN

But against this great gift of God, these reasoners, whose thoughts the Lord knows that they are vain,[19] bring arguments from the weights of the elements; for they have been taught by their master Plato[20] that the two greatest elements of the world, and the furthest removed from one another, are coupled and united by the two intermediate, air and water. And conse-

---

[19] Ps. xciv. 11   [20] *Timaeus,* 32a

quently they say, since the earth is the first of the elements, beginning from the base of the series, the second the water above the earth, the third the air above the water, the fourth the heaven above the air, it follows that a body of earth cannot live in the heaven; for each element is poised by its own weight so as to preserve its own place and rank. Behold with what arguments human infirmity, possessed with vanity, contradicts the omnipotence of God! What, then, do so many earthly bodies do in the air, since the air is the third element from the earth? Unless perhaps He who has granted to the earthly bodies of birds that they be carried through the air by the lightness of feathers and wings, has not been able to confer upon the bodies of men made immortal the power to abide in the highest heaven. The earthly animals, too, which cannot fly, among which are men, ought on these terms to live under the earth, as fishes, which are the animals of the water, live under the water. Why, then, can an animal of earth not live in the second element, that is, in water, while it can in the third? Why, though it belongs to the earth, is it forthwith suffocated if it is forced to live in the second element next above earth, while it lives in the third, and cannot live out of it? Is there a mistake here in the order of the elements, or is not the mistake rather in their reasonings, and not in the nature of things? I will not repeat what I said in the thirteenth book,[21] that many earthly bodies, though heavy like lead, receive from the workman's hand a form which enables them to swim in water; and yet it is denied that the omnipotent Worker can confer on the human body a property which shall enable it to pass into heaven and dwell there.

But against what I have formerly said they can find nothing to say, even though they introduce and make the most of this order of the elements in which they confide. For if the order be that the earth is first, the water second, the air third, the heaven fourth, then the soul is above all. For Aristotle said that the soul was a fifth body, while Plato denied that it was a body at all. If it were a fifth body, then certainly it would be above the rest; and if it is not a body at all, so much the more does it rise above all. What, then, does it do in an earthly body? What does this soul, which is finer than all else, do in such a mass of matter as this? What does the lightest of substances do in this ponderosity? this swiftest substance in such sluggishness? Will not the body be raised to heaven by virtue of so excellent a nature as this? and if now earthly bodies can retain the souls below, shall not the souls be one day able to raise the earthly bodies above?

If we pass now to their miracles which they oppose to our martyrs as wrought by their gods, shall not even these be found to make for us, and help out our argument? For if any of the miracles of their gods are great, certainly that is a great one which Varro mentions of a vestal virgin, who, when she was endangered by a false accusation of unchastity, filled a sieve with water from the Tiber, and carried it to her judges without any part of

[21] Ch. 18

it leaking. Who kept the weight of water in the sieve? Who prevented any drop from falling from it through so many open holes? They will answer, Some god or some demon. If a god, is he greater than the God who made the world? If a demon, is he mightier than an angel who serves the God by whom the world was made? If, then, a lesser god, angel, or demon could so sustain the weight of this liquid element that the water might seem to have changed its nature, shall not Almighty God, who Himself created all the elements, be able to eliminate from the earthly body its heaviness, so that the quickened body shall dwell in whatever element the quickening spirit pleases?

Then, again, since they give the air a middle place between the fire above and the water beneath, how is it that we often find it between water and water, and between the water and the earth? For what do they make of those watery clouds, between which and the seas air is constantly found intervening? I should like to know by what weight and order of the elements it comes to pass that very violent and stormy torrents are suspended in the clouds above the earth before they rush along upon the earth under the air. In fine, why is it that throughout the whole globe the air is between the highest heaven and the earth, if its place is between the sky and the water, as the place of the water is between the sky and the earth?

Finally, if the order of the elements is so disposed that, as Plato thinks, the two extremes, fire and earth, are united by the two means, air and water, and that the fire occupies the highest part of the sky, and the earth the lowest part, or as it were the foundation of the world, and that therefore earth cannot be in the heavens, how is fire in the earth? For, according to this reasoning, these two elements, earth and fire, ought to be so restricted to their own places, the highest and the lowest, that neither the lowest can rise to the place of the highest, nor the highest sink to that of the lowest. Thus, they think that no particle of earth is or shall ever be in the sky so we ought to see no particle of fire on the earth. But the fact is that it exists to such an extent, not only on but even under the earth, that the tops of mountains vomit it forth; besides that we see it to exist on earth for human uses, and even to be produced from the earth, since it is kindled from wood and stones, which are without doubt earthly bodies. But that upper fire, they say, is tranquil, pure, harmless, eternal; but this earthly fire is turbid, smoky, corruptible, and corrupting. But it does not corrupt the mountains and caverns of the earth in which it rages continually. But grant that the earthly fire is so unlike the other as to suit its earthly position, why then do they object to our believing that the nature of earthly bodies shall some day be made incorruptible and fit for the sky, even as now fire is corruptible and suited to the earth? They therefore adduce from their weights and order of the elements nothing from which they can prove that it is impossible for Almighty God to make our bodies such that they can dwell in the skies.

CHAPTER XII

AGAINST THE CALUMNIES WITH WHICH UNBELIEVERS THROW RIDICULE UPON THE CHRISTIAN FAITH IN THE RESURRECTION OF THE FLESH

But their way is to feign a scrupulous anxiety in investigating this question, and to cast ridicule on our faith in the resurrection of the body, by asking, Whether abortions shall rise? And as the Lord says, "Verily I say unto you, not a hair of your head shall perish," [22] shall all bodies have an equal stature and strength, or shall there be differences in size? For if there is to be equality, where shall those abortions, supposing that they rise again, get that bulk which they had not here? Or if they shall not rise because they were not born but cast out, they raise the same question about children who have died in childhood, asking us whence they get the stature which we see they had not here; for we will not say that those who have been not only born, but born again, shall not rise again. Then, further, they ask of what size these equal bodies shall be. For if all shall be as tall and large as were the tallest and largest in this world, they ask us how it is that not only children but many full-grown persons shall receive what they here did not possess, if each one is to receive what he had here. And if the saying of the apostle, that we are all to come to the "measure of the age of the fullness of Christ," [23] or that other saying, "Whom He predestinated to be conformed to the image of His Son," [24] is to be understood to mean that the stature and size of Christ's body shall be the measure of the bodies of all those who shall be in His kingdom, then, say they, the size and height of many must be diminished; and if so much of the bodily frame itself be lost, what becomes of the saying, "Not a hair of your head shall perish?" Besides, it might be asked regarding the hair itself, whether all that the barber has cut off shall be restored? And if it is to be restored, who would not shrink from such deformity? For as the same restoration will be made of what has been pared off the nails, much will be replaced on the body which a regard for its appearance had cut off. And where, then, will be its beauty, which assuredly ought to be much greater in that immortal condition than it could be in this corruptible state? On the other hand, if such things are not restored to the body, they must perish; how, then, they say, shall not a hair of the head perish? In like manner they reason about fatness and leanness; for if all are to be equal, then certainly there shall not be some fat, others lean. Some, therefore, shall gain, others lose something. Consequently there will not be a simple restoration of what formerly existed, but, on the one hand, an addition of what had no existence, and, on the other, a loss of what did before exist.

[22] Luke xxi. 18   [23] Eph. iv. 13   [24] Rom. viii. 29

The difficulties, too, about the corruption and dissolution of dead bodies —that one is turned into dust, while another evaporates into the air; that some are devoured by beasts, some by fire, while some perish by shipwreck or by drowning in one shape or other, so that their bodies decay into liquid— these difficulties give them immoderate alarm, and they believe that all those dissolved elements cannot be gathered again and reconstructed into a body. They also make eager use of all the deformities and blemishes which either accident or birth has produced, and accordingly, with horror and derision, cite monstrous births, and ask if every deformity will be preserved in the resurrection. For if we say that no such thing shall be reproduced in the body of a man, they suppose that they confute us by citing the marks of the wounds which we assert were found in the risen body of the Lord Christ. But of all these, the most difficult question is, into whose body that flesh shall return which has been eaten and assimilated by another man constrained by hunger to use it so; for it has been converted into the flesh of the man who used it as his nutriment, and it filled up those losses of flesh which famine had produced. For the sake, then, of ridiculing the resurrection, they ask, Shall this return to the man whose flesh it first was, or to him whose flesh it afterwards became? And thus, too, they seek to give promise to the human soul of alternations of true misery and false happiness, in accordance with Plato's theory; or, in accordance with Porphyry's, that, after many transmigrations into different bodies, it ends its miseries, and never more returns to them, not, however, by obtaining an immortal body, but by escaping from every kind of body.

CHAPTER XIII

WHETHER ABORTIONS, IF THEY ARE NUMBERED AMONG THE DEAD, SHALL NOT ALSO HAVE A PART IN THE RESURRECTION

To these objections, then, of our adversaries which I have thus detailed, I will now reply, trusting that God will mercifully assist my endeavors. That abortions, which, even supposing they were alive in the womb, did also die there, shall rise again, I make bold neither to affirm nor to deny, although I fail to see why, if they are not excluded from the number of the dead, they should not attain to the resurrection of the dead. For either all the dead shall not rise, and there will be to all eternity some souls without bodies though they once had them—only in their mother's womb, indeed; or, if all human souls shall receive again the bodies which they had wherever they lived, and which they left when they died, then I do not see how I can say that even those who died in their mother's womb shall have no resurrection. But whichever of these opinions any one may adopt concerning them, we must at least apply to them, if they rise again, all that we have to say of infants who have been born.

CHAPTER XIV

WHETHER INFANTS SHALL RISE IN THAT BODY WHICH THEY WOULD HAVE HAD HAD THEY GROWN UP

What, then, are we to say of infants, if not that they will not rise in that diminutive body in which they died, but shall receive by the marvellous and rapid operation of God that body which time by a slower process would have given them? For in the Lord's words, where He says, "Not a hair of your head shall perish," [25] it is asserted that nothing which was possessed shall be wanting; but it is not said that nothing which was not possessed shall be given. To the dead infant there was wanting the perfect stature of its body; for even the perfect infant lacks the perfection of bodily size, being capable of further growth. This perfect stature is, in a sense, so possessed by all that they are conceived and born with it—that is, they have it potentially, though not yet in actual bulk; just as all the members of the body are potentially in the seed, though, even after the child is born, some of them, the teeth for example, may be wanting. In this seminal principle of every substance, there seems to be, as it were, the beginning of everything which does not yet exist, or rather does not appear, but which in process of time will come into being, or rather into sight. In this, therefore, the child who is to be tall or short is already tall or short. And in the resurrection of the body, we need, for the same reason, fear no bodily loss; for though all should be of equal size, and reach gigantic proportions, lest the men who were largest here should lose anything of their bulk and it should perish, in contradiction to the words of Christ, who said that not a hair of their head should perish, yet why should there lack the means by which that wonderful Worker should make such additions, seeing that He is the Creator, who Himself created all things out of nothing?

CHAPTER XV

WHETHER THE BODIES OF ALL THE DEAD SHALL RISE THE SAME SIZE AS THE LORD'S BODY

It is certain that Christ rose in the same bodily stature in which He died, and that it is wrong to say that, when the general resurrection shall have arrived, His body shall, for the sake of equalling the tallest, assume proportions which it had not when He appeared to the disciples in the figure with which they were familiar. But if we say that even the bodies of taller men are to be reduced to the size of the Lord's body, there will be a great loss in many bodies, though He promised that not a hair of their head should perish. It remains, therefore, that we conclude that every man shall receive his own

[25] Luke xxi. 18

size which he had in youth, though he died an old man, or which he would have had, supposing he died before his prime. As for what the apostle said of the measure of the age of the fullness of Christ, we must either understand him to refer to something else, *viz.*, to the fact that the measure of Christ will be completed when all the members among the Christian communities are added to the Head; or if we are to refer it to the resurrection of the body, the meaning is that all shall rise neither beyond nor under youth, but in that vigor and age to which we know that Christ had arrived. For even the world's wisest men have fixed the bloom of youth at about the age of thirty; and when this period has been passed, the man begins to decline towards the defective and duller period of old age. And therefore the apostle did not speak of the measure of the body, nor of the measure of the stature, but of "the measure of the age of the fullness of Christ."

CHAPTER XVI

WHAT IS MEANT BY THE CONFORMING OF THE SAINTS TO THE IMAGE OF THE SON OF GOD

Then, again, these words, "Predestinate to be conformed to the image of the Son of God," [26] may be understood of the inner man. So in another place He says to us, "Be not conformed to this world, but be ye transformed in the renewing of your mind." [27] In so far, then, as we are transformed so as not to be conformed to the world, we are conformed to the Son of God. It may also be understood thus, that as He was conformed to us by assuming mortality, we shall be conformed to Him by immortality; and this indeed is connected with the resurrection of the body. But if we are also taught in these words what form our bodies shall rise in, as the measure we spoke of before, so also this conformity is to be understood not of size, but of age. Accordingly all shall rise in the stature they either had attained or would have attained had they lived to their prime, although it will be no great disadvantage even if the form of the body be infantine or aged, while no infirmity shall remain in the mind nor in the body itself. So that even if any one contends that every person will rise again in the same bodily form in which he died, we need not spend much labor in disputing with him.

CHAPTER XVII

WHETHER THE BODIES OF WOMEN SHALL RETAIN THEIR OWN SEX IN THE RESURRECTION

From the words, "Till we all come to a perfect man, to the measure of the age of the fullness of Christ," [28] and from the words, "Conformed to the image of the Son of God," [29] some conclude that women shall not rise

[26] Rom. viii. 29   [27] Rom. xii. 2   [28] Eph. iv. 13   [29] Rom. viii. 29

women, but that all shall be men, because God made man only of earth, and woman of the man. For my part, they seem to be wiser who make no doubt that both sexes shall rise. For there shall be no lust, which is now the cause of confusion. For before they sinned, the man and the woman were naked, and were not ashamed. From those bodies, then, vice shall be withdrawn, while nature shall be preserved. And the sex of woman is not a vice, but nature. It shall then indeed be superior to carnal intercourse and child-bearing; nevertheless the female members shall remain adapted not to the old uses, but to a new beauty, which, so far from provoking lust, now extinct, shall excite praise to the wisdom and clemency of God, who both made what was not and delivered from corruption what He made. For at the beginning of the human race the woman was made of a rib taken from the side of the man while he slept; for it seemed fit that even then Christ and His Church should be foreshadowed in this event. For that sleep of the man was the death of Christ, whose side, as He hung lifeless upon the cross, was pierced with a spear, and there flowed from it blood and water, and these we know to be the sacraments by which the Church is "built up." For Scripture used this very word, not saying "He formed" or "framed," but "built her up into a woman;"[30] whence also the apostle speaks of the *edification* of the body of Christ,[31] which is the Church. The woman, therefore, is a creature of God even as the man; but by her creation from man unity is commended; and the manner of her creation prefigured, as has been said, Christ and the Church. He, then, who created both sexes will restore both. Jesus Himself also, when asked by the Sadducees, who denied the resurrection, which of the seven brothers should have to wife the woman whom all in succession had taken to raise up seed to their brother, as the law enjoined, says, "Ye do err, not knowing the Scriptures nor the power of God." [32] And though it was a fit opportunity for His saying, She about whom you make inquiries shall herself be a man, and not a woman, He said nothing of the kind; but "In the resurrection they neither marry nor are given in marriage, but are as the angels of God in heaven." [33] They shall be equal to the angels in immortality and happiness, not in flesh, nor in resurrection, which the angels did not need, because they could not die. The Lord then denied that there would be in the resurrection, not women, but marriages; and He uttered his denial in circumstances in which the question mooted would have been more easily and speedily solved by denying that the female sex would exist, if this had in truth been foreknown by Him. But, indeed, He even affirmed that the sex should exist by saying, "They shall not be given in marriage," which can only apply to females; "Neither shall they marry," which applies to males. There shall therefore be those who are in this world accustomed to marry and be given in marriage, only they shall there make no such marriages.

[30] Gen. ii. 22   [31] Eph. iv. 12   [32] Matt. xxii. 29   [33] Matt. xxii. 30

CHAPTER XVIII

OF THE PERFECT MAN, THAT IS, CHRIST; AND OF HIS BODY, THAT IS, THE CHURCH, WHICH IS HIS FULLNESS

To understand what the apostle means when he says that we shall all come to a perfect man, we must consider the connection of the whole passage, which runs thus: "He that descended is the same also that ascended up far above all heavens, that He might fill all things. And He gave some, apostles; and some, prophets; and some, evangelists; and some, pastors and teachers; for the perfecting of the saints, for the work of the ministry, for the edifying of the body of Christ: till we all come to the unity of the faith and knowledge of the Son of God, to a perfect man, to the measure of the age of the fullness of Christ; that we henceforth be no more children, tossed and carried about with every wind of doctrine, by the sleight of men, and cunning craftiness, whereby they lie in wait to deceive; but, speaking the truth in love, may grow up in Him in all things, which is the Head, even Christ: from whom the whole body fitly joined together and compacted by that which every joint supplieth, according to the effectual working in the measure of every part, maketh increase of the body, unto the edifying of itself in love." [34] Behold what the perfect man is—the head and the body, which is made up of all the members, which in their own time shall be perfected. But new additions are daily being made to this body while the Church is being built up, to which it is said, "Ye are the body of Christ and His members;" [35] and again, "For His body's sake," he says, "which is the Church;" [36] and again, "We being many are one head, one body." [37] It is of the edification of this body that it is here, too, said, "For the perfecting of the saints, for the work of the ministry, for the edification of the body of Christ;" and then that passage of which we are now speaking is added, "Till we all come to the unity of the faith and knowledge of the Son of God, to a perfect man, to the measure of the age of the fullness of Christ," and so on. And he shows of what body we are to understand this to be the measure, when he says, "That we may grow up into Him in all things, which is the Head, even Christ: from whom the whole body fitly joined together and compacted by that which every joint supplieth, according to the effectual working in the measure of every part." As, therefore, there is a measure of every part, so there is a measure of the fullness of the whole body which is made up of all its parts, and it is of this measure it is said, "To the measure of the age of the fullness of Christ." This fullness he spoke of also in the place where he says of Christ, "And gave Him to be the Head over all things to the Church, which is His body, the fullness of Him that filleth all in all." [38] But even if this should be

---

[34] Eph. iv. 10-16   [35] 1 Cor. xii. 27   [36] Col. i. 24   [37] 1 Cor. x. 17   [38] Eph. i. 22, 23

referred to the form in which each one shall rise, what should hinder us from applying to the woman what is expressly said of the man, understanding both sexes to be included under the general term "man"? For certainly in the saying, "Blessed is he who feareth the Lord," [39] women also who fear the Lord are included.

CHAPTER XIX

THAT ALL BODILY BLEMISHES WHICH MAR HUMAN BEAUTY IN THIS LIFE SHALL BE REMOVED IN THE RESURRECTION, THE NATURAL SUBSTANCE OF THE BODY REMAINING, BUT THE QUALITY AND QUANTITY OF IT BEING ALTERED SO AS TO PRODUCE BEAUTY

What am I to say now about the hair and nails? Once it is understood that no part of the body shall so perish as to produce deformity in the body, it is at the same time understood that such things as would have produced a deformity by their excessive proportions shall be added to the total bulk of the body, not to parts in which the beauty of the proportion would thus be marred. Just as if, after making a vessel of clay, one wished to make it over again of the same clay, it would not be necessary that the same portion of the clay which had formed the handle should again form the new handle, or that what had formed the bottom should again do so, but only that the whole clay should go to make up the whole new vessel, and that no part of it should be left unused. Wherefore, if the hair that has been cropped and the nails that have been cut would cause a deformity were they to be restored to their places, they shall not be restored; and yet no one will lose these parts at the resurrection, for they shall be changed into the same flesh, their substance being so altered as to preserve the proportion of the various parts of the body. However, what our Lord said, "Not a hair of your head shall perish," might more suitably be interpreted of the number, and not of the length of the hairs, as He elsewhere says, "The hairs of your head are all numbered." [40] Nor would I say this because I suppose that any part naturally belonging to the body can perish, but that whatever deformity was in it, and served to exhibit the penal condition in which we mortals are, should be restored in such a way that, while the substance is entirely preserved, the deformity shall perish. For if even a human workman, who has, for some reason, made a deformed statue, can recast it and make it very beautiful, and this without suffering any part of the substance, but only the deformity to be lost—if he can, for example, remove some unbecoming or disproportionate part, not by cutting off and separating this part from the whole, but by so breaking down and mixing up the whole as to get rid of the blemish without diminishing the quantity of his material—shall we not think as highly of the almighty Worker? Shall He not be able to remove and abolish all deformities of the human body, whether common ones or rare and monstrous, which, though in keeping with this miserable life, are yet not to be thought of in connection with that future blessedness; and shall He not be able so to remove them that, while the natural but unseemly blemishes are put an end to, the natural substance shall suffer no diminution?

And consequently overgrown and emaciated persons need not fear that they shall be in heaven of such a figure as they would not be even in this world if they could help it. For all bodily beauty consists in the proportion of the parts, together with a certain agreeableness of color. Where there is no proportion, the eye is offended, either because there is something awanting, or too small, or too large. And thus there shall be no deformity resulting from want of proportion in that state in which all that is wrong is corrected, and all that is defective supplied from resources the Creator knows, and all that is excessive removed without destroying the integrity of the substance. And as for the pleasant color, how conspicuous shall it be where "the just shall shine forth as the sun in the kingdom of their Father!" [41] This brightness we must rather believe to have been concealed from the eyes of the disciples when Christ rose, than to have been awanting. For weak human eyesight could not bear it, and it was necessary that they should so look upon Him as to be able to recognize Him. For this purpose also He allowed them to touch the marks of His wounds, and also ate and drank—not because He needed nourishment, but because He could take it if He wished. Now, when an object, though present, is invisible to persons who see other things which are present, as we say that that brightness was present but invisible by those who saw other things, this is called in Greek ἀορασία; and our Latin translators, for want of a better word, have rendered this caecitas (blindness) in the book of Genesis. This blindness the men of Sodom suffered when they sought the just Lot's gate and could not find it. But if it had been blindness, that is to say, if they could see nothing, then they would not have asked for the gate by which they might enter the house, but for guides who might lead them away.

But the love we bear to the blessed martyrs causes us, I know not how, to desire to see in the heavenly kingdom the marks of the wounds which they received for the name of Christ, and possibly we shall see them. For this will not be a deformity, but a mark of honor, and will add lustre to their appearance, and a spiritual, if not a bodily beauty. And yet we need not believe that they to whom it has been said, "Not a hair of your head shall perish," shall, in the resurrection, want such of their members as they have been deprived of in their martyrdom. But if it will be seemly in that new kingdom to have some marks of these wounds still visible in that immortal flesh, the places where they have been wounded or mutilated shall retain the scars without any of the members being lost. While, therefore, it is quite true that

[41] Matt. xiii. 43

no blemishes which the body has sustained shall appear in the resurrection, yet we are not to reckon or name these marks of virtue blemishes.

CHAPTER XX

THAT, IN THE RESURRECTION, THE SUBSTANCE OF OUR BODIES, HOWEVER DISINTEGRATED, SHALL BE ENTIRELY REUNITED

Far be it from us to fear that the omnipotence of the Creator cannot, for the resuscitation and reanimation of our bodies, recall all the portions which have been consumed by beasts or fire, or have been dissolved into dust or ashes, or have decomposed into water, or evaporated into the air. Far from us be the thought, that anything which escapes our observation in any most hidden recess of nature either evades the knowledge or transcends the power of the Creator of all things. Cicero, the great authority of our adversaries, wishing to define God as accurately as possible, says, "God is a mind free and independent, without materiality, perceiving and moving all things, and itself endowed with eternal movement." [42] This he found in the systems of the greatest philosophers. Let me ask, then, in their own language, how anything can either lie hid from Him who perceives all things, or irrevocably escape Him who moves all things?

This leads me to reply to that question which seems the most difficult of all—To whom, in the resurrection, will belong the flesh of a dead man which has become the flesh of a living man? For if some one, famishing for want and pressed with hunger, use human flesh as food—an extremity not unknown, as both ancient history and the unhappy experience of our own days have taught us—can it be contended, with any show of reason, that all the flesh eaten has been evacuated, and that none of it has been assimilated to the substance of the eater though the very emaciation which existed before, and has now disappeared, sufficiently indicates what large deficiencies have been filled up with this food? But I have already made some remarks which will suffice for the solution of this difficulty also. For all the flesh which hunger has consumed finds its way into the air by evaporation, whence, as we have said, God Almighty can recall it. That flesh, therefore, shall be restored to the man in whom it first became human flesh. For it must be looked upon as borrowed by the other person, and, like a pecuniary loan, must be returned to the lender. His own flesh, however, which he lost by famine, shall be restored to him by Him who can recover even what has evaporated. And though it had been absolutely annihilated, so that no part of its substance remained in any secret spot of nature, the Almighty could restore it by such means as He saw fit. For this sentence, uttered by the Truth, "Not a hair of your head shall perish," forbids us to suppose that, though no hair of a man's

[42] Cic. *Tusc. Quaest.* i. 27

head can perish, yet the large portions of his flesh eaten and consumed by the famishing can perish.

From all that we have thus considered, and discussed with such poor ability as we can command, we gather this conclusion, that in the resurrection of the flesh the body shall be of that size which it either had attained or should have attained in the flower of its youth, and shall enjoy the beauty that arises from preserving symmetry and proportion in all its members. And it is reasonable to suppose that, for the preservation of this beauty, any part of the body's substance, which, if placed in one spot, would produce a deformity, shall be distributed through the whole of it, so that neither any part, nor the symmetry of the whole, may be lost, but only the general stature of the body somewhat increased by the distribution in all the parts of that which, in one place, would have been unsightly. Or if it is contended that each will rise with the same stature as that of the body he died in, we shall not obstinately dispute this, provided only there be no deformity, no infirmity, no languor, no corruption—nothing of any kind which would ill become that kingdom in which the children of the resurrection and of the promise shall be equal to the angels of God, if not in body and age, at least in happiness.

CHAPTER XXI

OF THE NEW SPIRITUAL BODY INTO WHICH THE FLESH
OF THE SAINTS SHALL BE TRANSFORMED

Whatever, therefore, has been taken from the body, either during life or after death, shall be restored to it, and, in conjunction with what has remained in the grave, shall rise again, transformed from the oldness of the animal body into the newness of the spiritual body, and clothed in incorruption and immortality. But even though the body has been all quite ground to powder by some severe accident, or by the ruthlessness of enemies, and though it has been so diligently scattered to the winds, or into the water, that there is no trace of it left, yet it shall not be beyond the omnipotence of the Creator—no, not a hair of its head shall perish. The flesh shall then be spiritual, and subject to the spirit, but still flesh, not spirit, as the spirit itself, when subject to the flesh, was fleshly, but still spirit and not flesh. And of this we have experimental proof in the deformity of our penal condition. For those persons were carnal, not in a fleshly, but in a spiritual way, to whom the apostle said, "I could not speak to you as unto spiritual, but as unto carnal." [43] And a man is in this life spiritual in such a way, that he is yet carnal with respect to his body, and sees another law in his members warring against the law of his mind; but even in his body he will be spiritual when the same flesh shall have had that resurrection of which these words

[43] 1 Cor. iii. 1

speak, "It is sown an animal body, it shall rise a spiritual body." [44] But what this spiritual body shall be and how great its grace, I fear it were but rash to pronounce, seeing that we have as yet no experience of it. Nevertheless, since it is fit that the joyfulness of our hope should utter itself, and so show forth God's praise, and since it was from the profoundest sentiment of ardent and holy love that the Psalmist cried, "O Lord, I have loved the beauty of Thy house," [45] we may, with God's help, speak of the gifts He lavishes on men, good and bad alike, in this most wretched life, and may do our best to conjecture the great glory of that state which we cannot worthily speak of, because we have not yet experienced it. For I say nothing of the time when God made man upright; I say nothing of the happy life of "the man and his wife" in the fruitful garden, since it was so short that none of their children experienced it: I speak only of this life which we know, and in which we now are, from the temptations of which we cannot escape so long as we are in it, no matter what progress we make, for it is all temptation, and I ask, Who can describe the tokens of God's goodness that are extended to the human race even in this life?

CHAPTER XXII

OF THE MISERIES AND ILLS TO WHICH THE HUMAN RACE IS JUSTLY EXPOSED THROUGH THE FIRST SIN, AND FROM WHICH NONE CAN BE DELIVERED SAVE BY CHRIST'S GRACE

That the whole human race has been condemned in its first origin, this life itself, if life it is to be called, bears witness by the host of cruel ills with which it is filled. Is not this proved by the profound and dreadful ignorance which produces all the errors that enfold the children of Adam, and from which no man can be delivered without toil, pain, and fear? Is it not proved by his love of so many vain and hurtful things, which produces gnawing cares, disquiet, griefs, fears, wild joys, quarrels, law-suits, wars, treasons, angers, hatreds, deceit, flattery, fraud, theft, robbery, perfidy, pride, ambition, envy, murders, parricides, cruelty, ferocity, wickedness, luxury, insolence, impudence, shamelessness, fornications, adulteries, incests, and the numberless uncleannesses and unnatural acts of both sexes, which it is shameful so much as to mention; sacrileges, heresies, blasphemies, perjuries, oppression of the innocent, calumnies, plots, falsehoods, false witnessings, unrighteous judgments, violent deeds, plunderings, and whatever similar wickedness has found its way into the lives of men, though it cannot find its way into the conception of pure minds? These are indeed the crimes of wicked men, yet they spring from that root of error and misplaced love which is born with every son of Adam. For who is there that has not observed with what profound ignorance, manifesting itself even in infancy, and with what

[44] I Cor. xv. 44   [45] Ps. xxvi. 8

superfluity of foolish desires, beginning to appear in boyhood, man comes
into this life, so that, were he left to live as he pleased, and to do whatever
he pleased, he would plunge into all, or certainly into many of those crimes
~~and iniquities which I mentioned, and could not mention?~~

But because God does not wholly desert those whom He condemns, nor
shuts up in His anger His tender mercies, the human race is restrained by
law and instruction, which keep guard against the ignorance that besets us,
and oppose the assaults of vice, but are themselves full of labor and sorrow.
For what mean those multifarious threats which are used to restrain the
folly of children? What mean pedagogues, masters, the birch, the strap, the
cane, the schooling which Scripture says must be given a child, "beating him
on the sides lest he wax stubborn," [46] and it be hardly possible or not possible
at all to subdue him? Why all these punishments, save to overcome ignorance and bridle evil desires—these evils with which we come into the world?
For why is it that we remember with difficulty, and without difficulty forget?
learn with difficulty, and without difficulty remain ignorant? are diligent
with difficulty, and without difficulty are indolent? Does not this show what
vitiated nature inclines and tends to by its own weight, and what succor it
needs if it is to be delivered? Inactivity, sloth, laziness, negligence, are vices
which shun labor, since labor, though useful, is itself a punishment.

But, besides the punishments of childhood, without which there would be
no learning of what the parents wish—and the parents rarely wish anything
useful to be taught—who can describe, who can conceive the number and
severity of the punishments which afflict the human race—pains which are
not only the accompaniment of the wickedness of godless men, but are a part
of the human condition and the common misery—what fear and what grief
are caused by bereavement and mourning, by losses and condemnations, by
fraud and falsehood, by false suspicions, and all the crimes and wicked deeds
of other men? For at their hands we suffer robbery, captivity, chains, imprisonment, exile, torture, mutilation, loss of sight, the violation of chastity
to satisfy the lust of the oppressor, and many other dreadful evils. What
numberless casualties threaten our bodies from without—extremes of heat
and cold, storms, floods, inundations, lightning, thunder, hail, earthquakes,
houses falling; or from the stumbling, or shying, or vice of horses; from
countless poisons in fruits, water, air, animals; from the painful or even
deadly bites of wild animals; from the madness which a mad dog communicates, so that even the animal which of all others is most gentle and friendly
to its own master, becomes an object of intenser fear than a lion or dragon,
and the man whom it has by chance infected with this pestilential contagion
becomes so rabid, that his parents, wife, children, dread him more than any
wild beast. What disasters are suffered by those who travel by land or sea!
What man can go out of his own house without being exposed on all hands
to unforeseen accidents? Returning home sound in limb, he slips on his own

[46] Ecclus. xxx. 12

doorstep, breaks his leg, and never recovers. What can seem safer than a man sitting in his chair? Eli the priest fell from his, and broke his neck. How many accidents do farmers, or rather all men, fear that the crops may suffer from the weather, or the soil, or the ravages of destructive animals? Commonly they feel safe when the crops are gathered and housed. Yet, to my certain knowledge, sudden floods have driven the laborers away, and swept the barns clean of the finest harvest. Is innocence a sufficient protection against the various assaults of demons? That no man might think so, even baptized infants, who are certainly unsurpassed in innocence, are sometimes so tormented, that God, who permits it, teaches us hereby to bewail the calamities of this life, and to desire the felicity of the life to come. As to bodily diseases, they are so numerous that they cannot all be contained even in medical books. And in very many, or almost all of them, the cures and remedies are themselves tortures, so that men are delivered from a pain that destroys by a cure that pains. Has not the madness of thirst driven men to drink human urine, and even their own? Has not hunger driven men to eat human flesh, and that the flesh not of bodies found dead, but of bodies slain for the purpose? Have not the fierce pangs of famine driven mothers to eat their own children, incredibly savage as it seems? In fine, sleep itself, which is justly called repose, how little of repose there sometimes is in it when disturbed with dreams and visions; and with what terror is the wretched mind overwhelmed by the appearances of things which are so presented, and which, as it were, so stand out before the senses, that we can not distinguish them from realities! How wretchedly do false appearances distract men in certain diseases! With what astonishing variety of appearances are even healthy men sometimes deceived by evil spirits, who produce these delusions for the sake of perplexing the senses of their victims, if they cannot succeed in seducing them to their side!

From this hell upon earth there is no escape, save through the grace of the Saviour Christ, our God and Lord. The very name Jesus shows this, for it means Saviour; and He saves us especially from passing out of this life into a more wretched and eternal state, which is rather a death than a life. For in this life, though holy men and holy pursuits afford us great consolations, yet the blessings which men crave are not invariably bestowed upon them, lest religion should be cultivated for the sake of these temporal advantages, while it ought rather to be cultivated for the sake of that other life from which all evil is excluded. Therefore, also, does grace aid good men in the midst of present calamities, so that they are enabled to endure them with a constancy proportioned to their faith. The world's sages affirm that philosophy contributes something to this—that philosophy which, according to Cicero, the gods have bestowed in its purity only on a few men. They have never given, he says, nor can ever give, a greater gift to men. So that even those against whom we are disputing have been compelled to acknowledge, in some fashion, that the grace of God is necessary for the acquisition, not, indeed, of any philosophy, but of the true philosophy. And if the true philosophy—this sole support against the miseries of this life—has been given by Heaven only to a few, it sufficiently appears from this that the human race has been condemned to pay this penalty of wretchedness. And as, according to their acknowledgment, no greater gift has been bestowed by God, so it must be believed that it could be given only by that God whom they themselves recognize as greater than all the gods they worship.

CHAPTER XXIII

OF THE MISERIES OF THIS LIFE WHICH ATTACH PECULIARLY TO THE TOIL OF GOOD MEN, IRRESPECTIVE OF THOSE WHICH ARE COMMON TO THE GOOD AND BAD

But, irrespective of the miseries which in this life are common to the good and bad, the righteous undergo labors peculiar to themselves, in so far as they make war upon their vices, and are involved in the temptations and perils of such a contest. For though sometimes more violent and at other times slacker, yet without intermission does the flesh lust against the spirit and the spirit against the flesh, so that we cannot do the things we would,[47] and extirpate all lust, but can only refuse consent to it, as God gives us ability, and so keep it under, vigilantly keeping watch lest a semblance of truth deceive us, lest a subtle discourse blind us, lest error involve us in darkness, lest we should take good for evil or evil for good, lest fear should hinder us from doing what we ought, or desire precipitate us into doing what we ought not, lest the sun go down upon our wrath, lest hatred provoke us to render evil for evil, lest unseemly or immoderate grief consume us, lest an ungrateful disposition make us slow to recognize benefits received, lest calumnies fret our conscience, lest rash suspicion on our part deceive us regarding a friend, or false suspicion of us on the part of others give us too much uneasiness, lest sin reign in our mortal body to obey its desires, lest our members be used as the instruments of unrighteousness, lest the eye follow lust, lest thirst for revenge carry us away, lest sight or thought dwell too long on some evil thing which gives us pleasure, lest wicked or indecent language be willingly listened to, lest we do what is pleasant but unlawful, and lest in this warfare, filled so abundantly with toil and peril, we either hope to secure victory by our own strength, or attribute it when secured to our own strength, and not to His grace of whom the apostle says, "Thanks be unto God, who giveth us the victory through our Lord Jesus Christ;"[48] and in another place he says, "In all these things we are more than conquerors through Him that loved us."[49] But yet we are to know this, that however valorously we resist our vices, and however successful we are in overcoming them, yet as long as we are in this body we have always reason to say to God, "Forgive us our

[47] Gal. v. 17   [48] 1 Cor. xv. 57   [49] Rom. viii. 37

debts." [50] But in that kingdom where we shall dwell for ever, clothed in immortal bodies, we shall no longer have either conflicts or debts—as indeed we should not have had at any time or in any condition, had our nature continued upright as it was created. Consequently even this conflict of ours, in which we are exposed to peril, and from which we hope to be delivered by a final victory, belongs to the ills of this life, which is proved by the witness of so many grave evils to be a life under condemnation.

CHAPTER XXIV

OF THE BLESSINGS WITH WHICH THE CREATOR HAS FILLED THIS LIFE, OBNOXIOUS THOUGH IT BE TO THE CURSE

But we must now contemplate the rich and countless blessings with which the goodness of God, who cares for all He has created, has filled this very misery of the human race, which reflects His retributive justice. That first blessing which He pronounced before the fall, when He said, "Increase, and multiply, and replenish the earth," [51] He did not inhibit after man had sinned, but the fecundity originally bestowed remained in the condemned stock; and the vice of sin, which has involved us in the necessity of dying, has yet not deprived us of that wonderful power of seed, or rather of that still more marvellous power by which seed is produced, and which seems to be as it were inwrought and inwoven in the human body. But in this river, as I may call it, or torrent of the human race, both elements are carried along together—both the evil which is derived from him who begets, and the good which is bestowed by Him who creates us. In the original evil there are two things, sin and punishment; in the original good, there are two other things, propagation and conformation. But of the evils, of which the one, sin, arose from our audacity, and the other, punishment, from God's judgment, we have already said as much as suits our present purpose. I mean now to speak of the blessings which God has conferred or still confers upon our nature, vitiated and condemned as it is. For in condemning it He did not withdraw all that He had given it, else it had been annihilated; neither did He, in penally subjecting it to the devil, remove it beyond His own power; for not even the devil himself is outside of God's government, since the devil's nature subsists only by the supreme Creator, who gives being to all that in any form exists.

Of these two blessings, then, which we have said flow from God's goodness, as from a fountain, towards our nature, vitiated by sin and condemned to punishment, the one, propagation, was conferred by God's benediction when He made those first works, from which He rested on the seventh day. But the other, conformation, is conferred in that work of His wherein "He worketh hitherto." [52] For were He to withdraw His efficacious power from

[50] Matt. vi. 12   [51] Gen. i. 28   [52] John v. 17

things, they should neither be able to go on and complete the periods assigned to their measured movements, nor should they even continue in possession of that nature they were created in. God, then, so created man that He gave him what we may call fertility, whereby he might propagate other men, giving them a congenital capacity to propagate their kind, but not imposing on them any necessity to do so. This capacity God withdraws at pleasure from individuals, making them barren; but from the whole race He has not withdrawn the blessing of propagation once conferred. But though not withdrawn on account of sin, this power of propagation is not what it would have been had there been no sin. For since "man placed in honor fell, he has become like the beasts," [53] and generates as they do, though the little spark of reason, which was the image of God in him, has not been quite quenched. But if conformation were not added to propagation, there would be no reproduction of one's kind. For even though there were no such thing as copulation, and God wished to fill the earth with human inhabitants, He might create all these as He created one without the help of human generation. And, indeed, even as it is, those who copulate can generate nothing save by the creative energy of God. As, therefore, in respect of that spiritual growth whereby a man is formed to piety and righteousness, the apostle says, "Neither is he that planteth anything, neither he that watereth, but God that giveth the increase," [54] so also it must be said that it is not he that generates that is anything, but God that giveth the essential form; that it is not the mother who carries and nurses the fruit of her womb that is anything, but God that giveth the increase. For He alone, by that energy wherewith "He worketh hitherto," causes the seed to develop, and to evolve from certain secret and invisible folds into the visible forms of beauty which we see. He alone, coupling and connecting in some wonderful fashion the spiritual and corporeal natures, the one to command, the other to obey, makes a living being. And this work of His is so great and wonderful, that not only man, who is a rational animal, and consequently more excellent than all other animals of the earth, but even the most diminutive insect, cannot be considered attentively without astonishment and without praising the Creator.

It is He, then, who has given to the human soul a mind, in which reason and understanding lie as it were asleep during infancy, and as if they were not, destined, however, to be awakened and exercised as years increase, so as to become capable of knowledge and of receiving instruction, fit to understand what is true and to love what is good. It is by this capacity the soul drinks in wisdom, and becomes endowed with those virtues by which, in prudence, fortitude, temperance, and righteousness, it makes war upon error and the other inborn vices, and conquers them by fixing its desires upon no other object than the supreme and unchangeable Good. And even though this be not uniformly the result, yet who can competently utter or even con-

[53] Ps. xlix. 20   [54] 1 Cor. iii. 7

ceive the grandeur of this work of the Almighty, and the unspeakable boon He has conferred upon our rational nature, by giving us even the capacity of such attainment? For over and above those arts which are called virtues, and which teach us how we may spend our life well, and attain to endless happiness—arts which are given to the children of the promise and the kingdom by the sole grace of God which is in Christ—has not the genius of man invented and applied countless astonishing arts, partly the result of necessity, partly the result of exuberant invention, so that this vigor of mind, which is so active in the discovery not merely of superfluous but even of dangerous and destructive things, betokens an inexhaustible wealth in the nature which can invent, learn, or employ such arts? What wonderful—one might say stupefying—advances has human industry made in the arts of weaving and building, of agriculture and navigation! With what endless variety are designs in pottery, painting, and sculpture produced, and with what skill executed! What wonderful spectacles are exhibited in the theatres, which those who have not seen them cannot credit! How skillful the contrivances for catching, killing, or taming wild beasts! And for the injury of men, also, how many kinds of poisons, weapons, engines of destruction, have been invented, while for the preservation or restoration of health the appliances and remedies are infinite! To provoke appetite and please the palate, what a variety of seasonings have been concocted! To express and gain entrance for thoughts, what a multitude and variety of signs there are, among which speaking and writing hold the first place! what ornaments has eloquence at command to delight the mind! what wealth of song is there to captivate the ear! how many musical instruments and strains of harmony have been devised! What skill has been attained in measures and numbers! with what sagacity have the movements and connections of the stars been discovered! Who could tell the thought that has been spent upon nature, even though, despairing of recounting it in detail, he endeavored only to give a general view of it? In fine, even the defence of errors and misapprehensions, which has illustrated the genius of heretics and philosophers, cannot be sufficiently declared. For at present it is the nature of the human mind which adorns this mortal life which we are extolling, and not the faith and the way of truth which lead to immortality. And since this great nature has certainly been created by the true and supreme God, who administers all things He has made with absolute power and justice, it could never have fallen into these miseries, nor have gone out of them to miseries eternal— saving only those who are redeemed—had not an exceeding great sin been found in the first man from whom the rest have sprung.

Moreover, even in the body, though it dies like that of the beasts, and is in many ways weaker than theirs, what goodness of God, what providence of the great Creator, is apparent! The organs of sense and the rest of the members, are not they so placed, the appearance, and form, and stature of the body as a whole, is it not so fashioned, as to indicate that it was made for the service of a reasonable soul? Man has not been created stooping towards the earth, like the irrational animals; but his bodily form, erect and looking heavenwards, admonishes him to mind the things that are above. Then the marvellous nimbleness which has been given to the tongue and the hands, fitting them to speak, and write, and execute so many duties, and practise so many arts, does it not prove the excellence of the soul for which such an assistant was provided? And even apart from its adaptation to the work required of it, there is such a symmetry in its various parts, and so beautiful a proportion maintained, that one is at a loss to decide whether, in creating the body, greater regard was paid to utility or to beauty. Assuredly no part of the body has been created for the sake of utility which does not also contribute something to its beauty. And this would be all the more apparent, if we knew more precisely how all its parts are connected and adapted to one another, and were not limited in our observations to what appears on the surface; for as to what is covered up and hidden from our view, the intricate web of veins and nerves, the vital parts of all that lies under the skin, no one can discover it. For although, with a cruel zeal for science, some medical men, who are called anatomists, have dissected the bodies of the dead, and sometimes even of sick persons who died under their knives, and have inhumanly pried into the secrets of the human body to learn the nature of the disease and its exact seat, and how it might be cured, yet those relations of which I speak, and which form the concord,[55] or, as the Greeks call it, "harmony," of the whole body outside and in, as of some instrument, no one has been able to discover, because no one has been audacious enough to seek for them. But if these could be known, then even the inward parts, which seem to have no beauty, would so delight us with their exquisite fitness, as to afford a profounder satisfaction to the mind—and the eyes are but its ministers—than the obvious beauty which gratifies the eye. There are some things, too, which have such a place in the body, that they obviously serve no useful purpose, but are solely for beauty, as *e.g.* the teats on a man's breast, or the beard on his face; for that this is for ornament, and not for protection, is proved by the bare faces of women, who ought rather, as the weaker sex, to enjoy such a defence. If, therefore, of all those members which are exposed to our view, there is certainly not one in which beauty is sacrificed to utility, while there are some which serve no purpose but only beauty, I think it can readily be concluded that in the creation of the human body comeliness was more regarded than necessity. In truth, necessity is a transitory thing; and the time is coming when we shall enjoy one another's beauty without any lust—a condition which will specially redound to the praise of the Creator, who, as it is said in the psalm, has "put on praise and comeliness,"[56]

How can I tell of the rest of creation, with all its beauty and utility, which

[55] *Coaptatio*, a word coined by Augustine, and used by him again in the *De Trin*. iv. 2
[56] Ps. civ. 1

the divine goodness has given to man to please his eye and serve his purposes, condemned though he is, and hurled into these labors and miseries? Shall I speak of the manifold and various loveliness of sky, and earth, and sea; of the plentiful supply and wonderful qualities of the light; of sun, moon, and stars; of the shade of trees; of the colors and perfume of flowers; of the multitude of birds, all differing in plumage and in song; of the variety of animals, of which the smallest in size are often the most wonderful—the works of ants and bees astonishing us more than the huge bodies of whales? Shall I speak of the sea, which itself is so grand a spectacle, when it arrays itself as it were in vestures of various colors, now running through every shade of green, and again becoming purple or blue? Is it not delightful to look at it in storm, and experience the soothing complacency which it inspires, by suggesting that we ourselves are not tossed and shipwrecked?[57] What shall I say of the numberless kinds of food to alleviate hunger, and the variety of seasonings to stimulate appetite which are scattered everywhere by nature, and for which we are not indebted to the art of cookery? How many natural appliances are there for preserving and restoring health! How grateful is the alternation of day and night! how pleasant the breezes that cool the air! how abundant the supply of clothing furnished us by trees and animals! Who can enumerate all the blessings we enjoy? If I were to attempt to detail and unfold only these few which I had indicated in the mass, such an enumeration would fill a volume. And all these are but the solace of the wretched and condemned, not the rewards of the blessed. What then shall these rewards be, if such be the blessings of a condemned state? What will He give to those whom He has predestined to life, who has given such things even to those whom He has predestined to death? What blessings will He in the blessed life shower upon those for whom, even in this state of misery, He has been willing that His only-begotten Son should endure such sufferings even to death? Thus the apostle reasons concerning those who are predestined to that kingdom: "He that spared not His own Son, but delivered Him up for us all, how shall He not with Him also give us all things?" [58] When this promise is fulfilled, what shall we be? What blessings shall we receive in that kingdom, since already we have received as the pledge of them Christ's dying? In what condition shall the spirit of man be, when it has no longer any vice at all; when it neither yields to any, nor is in bondage to any, nor has to make war against any, but is perfected, and enjoys undisturbed peace with itself? Shall it not then know all things with certainty, and without any labor or error, when unhindered and joyfully it drinks the wisdom of God at the fountain-head? What shall the body be, when it is in every respect subject to the spirit, from which it shall draw a life so sufficient, as to stand in need of no other nutriment? For it shall no longer be animal, but spiritual, having indeed the substance of flesh, but without any fleshly corruption.

[57] He apparently has in view the celebrated passage in the opening of the second book of Lucretius.   [58] Rom. viii. 32

CHAPTER XXV

OF THE OBSTINACY OF THOSE INDIVIDUALS WHO IMPUGN THE RESUR-
RECTION OF THE BODY, THOUGH, AS WAS PREDICTED, THE WHOLE
WORLD BELIEVES IT

The foremost of the philosophers agree with us about the spiritual felicity enjoyed by the blessed in the life to come; it is only the resurrection of the flesh they call in question, and with all their might deny. But the mass of men, learned and unlearned, the world's wise men and its fools, have believed, and have left in meagre isolation the unbelievers, and have turned to Christ, who in His own resurrection demonstrated the reality of that which seems to our adversaries absurd. For the world has believed this which God predicted, as it was also predicted that the world would believe—a prediction not due to the sorceries of Peter,[59] since it was uttered so long before. He who has predicted these things, as I have already said, and am not ashamed to repeat, is the God before whom all other divinities tremble, as Porphyry himself owns, and seeks to prove, by testimonies from the oracles of these gods, and goes so far as to call Him God the Father and King. Far be it from us to interpret these predictions as they do who have not believed, along with the whole world, in that which it was predicted the world would believe in. For why should we not rather understand them as the world does, whose belief was predicted, and leave that handful of unbelievers to their idle talk and obstinate and solitary infidelity? For if they maintain that they interpret them differently only to avoid charging Scripture with folly, and so doing an injury to that God to whom they bear so notable a testimony, is it not a much greater injury they do Him when they say that His predictions must be understood otherwise than the world believed them, though He Himself praised, promised, accomplished this belief on the world's part? And why cannot He cause the body to rise again, and live for ever? or is it not to be believed that He will do this, because it is an undesirable thing, and unworthy of God? Of His omnipotence, which effects so many great miracles, we have already said enough. If they wish to know what the Almighty cannot do, I shall tell them He cannot lie. Let us therefore believe what He can do, by refusing to believe what He cannot do. Refusing to believe that He can lie, let them believe that He will do what He has promised to do; and let them believe it as the world has believed it, whose faith He predicted, whose faith He praised, whose faith He promised, whose faith He now points to. But how do they prove that the resurrection is an undesirable thing? There shall then be no corruption, which is the only evil thing about the body. I have already said enough about the order of the elements, and the other fanciful objections men raise; and in the thirteenth book I have,

[59] Cf. Book xviii. c. 53

in my own judgment, sufficiently illustrated the facility of movement which the incorruptible body shall enjoy, judging from the ease and vigor we experience even now, when the body is in good health. Those who have either not read the former books, or wish to refresh their memory, may read them for themselves.

CHAPTER XXVI

THAT THE OPINION OF PORPHYRY, THAT THE SOUL, IN ORDER TO BE
BLESSED, MUST BE SEPARATED FROM EVERY KIND OF BODY, IS
DEMOLISHED BY PLATO, WHO SAYS THAT THE SUPREME GOD
PROMISED THE GODS THAT THEY SHOULD NEVER BE
OUSTED FROM THEIR BODIES

But, they say, Porphyry tells us that the soul, in order to be blessed, must escape connection with every kind of body. It does not avail, therefore, to say that the future body shall be incorruptible, if the soul cannot be blessed till delivered from every kind of body. But in the book above mentioned I have already sufficiently discussed this. This one thing only will I repeat— let Plato, their master, correct his writings, and say that their gods, in order to be blessed, must quit their bodies, or, in other words, die; for he said that they were shut up in celestial bodies, and that, nevertheless, the God who made them promised them immortality—that is to say, an eternal tenure of these same bodies, such as was not provided for them naturally, but only by the further intervention of His will, that thus they might be assured of felicity. In this he obviously overturns their assertion that the resurrection of the body cannot be believed because it is impossible; for, according to him, when the uncreated God promised immortality to the created gods, He expressly said that He would do what was impossible. For Plato tells us that He said, "As ye have had a beginning, so you cannot be immortal and incorruptible; yet ye shall not decay, nor shall any fate destroy you or prove stronger than my will, which more effectually binds you to immortality than the bond of your nature keeps you from it." [60] If they who hear these words have, we do not say understanding, but ears, they cannot doubt that Plato believed that God promised to the gods He had made that He would effect an impossibility. For He who says, "Ye cannot be immortal, but by my will ye shall be immortal," what else does He say than this, "I shall make you what ye cannot be?" The body, therefore, shall be raised incorruptible, immortal, spiritual, by Him who, according to Plato, has promised to do that which is impossible. Why then do they still exclaim that this which God has promised, which the world has believed on God's promise as was predicted, is an impossibility? For what we say is, that the God who, even according to Plato, does impossible things, will do this. It is not, then, necessary to the

---

[60] *Timaeus*, 41b

blessedness of the soul that it be detached from a body of any kind whatever, but that it receive an incorruptible body. And in what incorruptible body will they more suitably rejoice than in that in which they groaned when it was corruptible? For thus they shall not feel that dire craving which Virgil, in imitation of Plato, has ascribed to them when he says that they wish to return again to their bodies.[61] They shall not, I say, feel this desire to return to their bodies, since they shall have those bodies to which a return was desired, and shall, indeed, be in such thorough possession of them, that they shall never lose them even for the briefest moment, nor ever lay them down in death.

CHAPTER XXVII

OF THE APPARENTLY CONFLICTING OPINIONS OF PLATO AND PORPHYRY, WHICH WOULD HAVE CONDUCTED THEM BOTH TO THE TRUTH IF THEY COULD HAVE YIELDED TO ONE ANOTHER

Statements were made by Plato and Porphyry singly, which if they could have seen their way to hold in common, they might possibly have become Christians. Plato said that souls could not exist eternally without bodies; for it was on this account, he said, that the souls even of wise men must some time or other return to their bodies. Porphyry, again, said that the purified soul, when it has returned to the Father, shall never return to the ills of this world. Consequently, if Plato had communicated to Porphyry that which he saw to be true, that souls, though perfectly purified, and belonging to the wise and righteous, must return to human bodies; and if Porphyry, again, had imparted to Plato the truth which he saw, that the holy soul shall never return to the miseries of a corruptible body, so that they should not each have held only his own opinion, but should both have held both truths, I think they would have seen that it follows that the souls return to their bodies, and also that these bodies shall be such as to afford them a blessed and immortal life. For, according to Plato, even holy souls shall return to the body; according to Porphyry, holy souls shall not return to the ills of this world. Let Porphyry then say with Plato, they shall return to the body; let Plato say with Porphyry, they shall not return to their old misery: and they will agree that they return to bodies in which they shall suffer no more. And this is nothing else than what God has promised—that He will give eternal felicity to souls joined to their own bodies. For this, I presume, both of them would readily concede, that if the souls of the saints are to be reunited to bodies, it shall be to their own bodies, in which they have endured the miseries of this life, and in which, to escape these miseries, they served God with piety and fidelity.

[61] Virg. *Aen.* vi. 751

CHAPTER XXVIII

WHAT PLATO OR LABEO, OR EVEN VARRO, MIGHT HAVE CONTRIBUTED
TO THE TRUE FAITH OF THE RESURRECTION, IF THEY HAD
ADOPTED ONE ANOTHER'S OPINIONS INTO ONE SCHEME

Some Christians, who have a liking for Plato on account of his magnificent style and the truths which he now and then uttered, say that he even held an opinion similar to our own regarding the resurrection of the dead. Cicero, however, alluding to this in his *Republic*, asserts that Plato meant it rather as a playful fancy than as a reality; for he introduces a man [62] who had come to life again, and gave a narrative of his experience in corroboration of the doctrines of Plato. Labeo, too, says that two men died on one day, and met at a cross-road, and that, being afterwards ordered to return to their bodies, they agreed to be friends for life, and were so till they died again. But the resurrection which these writers instance resembles that of those persons whom we have ourselves known to rise again, and who came back indeed to this life, but not so as never to die again. Marcus Varro, however, in his work *On the Origin of the Roman People*, records something more remarkable; I think his own words should be given. "Certain astrologers," he says, "have written that men are destined to a new birth, which the Greeks call *palingenesy*. This will take place after four hundred and forty years have elapsed; and then the same soul and the same body, which were formerly united in the person, shall again be reunited." This Varro, indeed, or those nameless astrologers—for he does not give us the names of the men whose statement he cites—have affirmed what is indeed not altogether true; for once the souls have returned to the bodies they wore, they shall never afterwards leave them. Yet what they say upsets and demolishes much of that idle talk of our adversaries about the impossibility of the resurrection. For those who have been or are of this opinion, have not thought it possible that bodies which have dissolved into air, or dust, or ashes, or water, or into the bodies of the beasts or even of the men that fed on them, should be restored again to that which they formerly were. And therefore, if Plato and Porphyry, or rather, if their disciples now living, agree with us that holy souls shall return to the body, as Plato says, and that, nevertheless, they shall not return to misery, as Porphyry maintains—if they accept the consequence of these two propositions which is taught by the Christian faith, that they shall receive bodies in which they may live eternally without suffering any misery—let them also adopt from Varro the opinion that they shall return to the same bodies as they were formerly in, and thus the whole question of the eternal resurrection of the body shall be resolved out of their own mouths.

[62] In the *Republic*, x.

CHAPTER XXIX

And now let us consider, with such ability as God may vouchsafe, how the saints shall be employed when they are clothed in immortal and spiritual bodies, and when the flesh shall live no longer in a fleshly but a spiritual fashion. And indeed, to tell the truth, I am at a loss to understand the nature of that employment, or, shall I rather say, repose and ease, for it has never come within the range of my bodily senses. And if I should speak of my mind or understanding, what is our understanding in comparison of its excellence? For then shall be that "peace of God which," as the apostle says, "passeth all understanding" [63]—that is to say, all human, and perhaps all angelic understanding, but certainly not the divine. That it passeth ours there is no doubt; but if it passeth that of the angels—and he who says *all* understanding" seems to make no exception in their favor—then we must understand him to mean that neither we nor the angels can understand, as God understands, the peace which God Himself enjoys. Doubtless this passeth all understanding but His own. But as we shall one day be made to participate, according to our slender capacity, in His peace, both in ourselves, and with our neighbor, and with God our chief good, in this respect the angels understand the peace of God in their own measure, and men too, though now far behind them, whatever spiritual advance they have made. For we must remember how great a man he was who said, "We know in part, and we prophesy in part, until that which is perfect is come;" [64] and "Now we see through a glass, darkly; but then face to face." [65] Such also is now the vision of the holy angels, who are also called our angels, because we, being rescued out of the power of darkness, and receiving the earnest of the Spirit, are translated into the kingdom of Christ, and already begin to belong to those angels with whom we shall enjoy that holy and most delightful city of God of which we have now written so much. Thus, then, the angels of God are our angels, as Christ is God's and also ours. They are God's, because they have not abandoned Him; they are ours, because we are their fellow-citizens. The Lord Jesus also said, "See that ye despise not one of these little ones: for I say unto you, That in heaven their angels do always see the face of my Father which is in heaven." [66] As, then, they see, so shall we also see; but not yet do we thus see. Wherefore the apostle uses the words cited a little ago, "Now we see through a glass, darkly; but then face to face." This vision is reserved as the reward of our faith; and of it the Apostle John also says, "When He shall appear, we shall be like Him, for we shall see Him as He is." [67] By "the face" of God we are to understand His manifestation, and

[63] Phil. iv. 7   [64] 1 Cor. xiii. 9, 10   [65] 1 Cor. xiii. 12   [66] Matt. xviii. 10   [67] 1 John iii. 2

not a part of the body similar to that which in our bodies we call by that name.

And so, when I am asked how the saints shall be employed in that spiritual body, I do not say what I see, but I say what I believe, according to that which I read in the psalm, "I believed, therefore have I spoken." [68] I say, then, they shall in the body see God; but whether they shall see Him by means of the body, as now we see the sun, moon, stars, sea, earth, and all that is in it, that is a difficult question. For it is hard to say that the saints shall then have such bodies that they shall not be able to shut and open their eyes as they please; while it is harder still to say that every one who shuts his eyes shall lose the vision of God. For if the prophet Elisha, though at a distance, saw his servant Gehazi, who thought that his wickedness would escape his master's observation and accepted gifts from Naaman the Syrian, whom the prophet had cleansed from his foul leprosy, how much more shall the saints in the spiritual body see all things, not only though their eyes be shut, but though they themselves be at a great distance? For then shall be "that which is perfect," of which the apostle says, "We know in part, and we prophesy in part; but when that which is perfect is come, then that which is in part shall be done away." Then, that he may illustrate as well as possible, by a simile, how superior the future life is to the life now lived, not only by ordinary men, but even by the foremost of the saints, he says, "When I was a child, I understood as a child, I spake as a child, I thought as a child; but when I became a man, I put away childish things. Now we see through a glass, darkly; but then face to face: now I know in part; but then shall I know even as also I am known." [69] If, then, even in this life, in which the prophetic power of remarkable men is no more worthy to be compared to the vision of the future life than childhood is to manhood, Elisha, though distant from his servant, saw him accepting gifts, shall we say that when that which is perfect is come, and the corruptible body no longer oppresses the soul, but is incorruptible and offers no impediment to it, the saints shall need bodily eyes to see, though Elisha had no need of them to see his servant? For, following the Septuagint version, these are the prophet's words: "Did not my heart go with thee, when the man came out of his chariot to meet thee, and thou tookedst his gifts?" [70] Or, as the presbyter Jerome rendered it from the Hebrew, "Was not my heart present when the man turned from his chariot to meet thee?" The prophet said that he saw this with his heart, miraculously aided by God, as no one can doubt. But how much more abundantly shall the saints enjoy this gift when God shall be all in all? Nevertheless the bodily eyes also shall have their office and their place, and shall be used by the spirit through the spiritual body. For the prophet did not forego the use of his eyes for seeing what was before them, though he did not need them to see his absent servant, and though he could have seen these present objects in spirit, and with his eyes shut, as he saw things far distant

[68] Ps. cxvi. 10   [69] 1 Cor. xiii. 11, 12   [70] 2 Kings v. 26

in a place where he himself was not. Far be it, then, from us to say that in the life to come the saints shall not see God when their eyes are shut, since they shall always see Him with the spirit.

But the question arises, whether, when their eyes are open, they shall see Him with the bodily eye? If the eyes of the spiritual body have no more power than the eyes which we now possess, manifestly God cannot be seen with them. They must be of a very different power if they can look upon that incorporeal nature which is not contained in any place, but is all in every place. For though we say that God is in heaven and on earth, as He Himself says by the prophet, "I fill heaven and earth," [71] we do not mean that there is one part of God in heaven and another part on earth; but He is all in heaven and all on earth, not at alternate intervals of time, but both at once, as no bodily nature can be. The eye, then, shall have a vastly superior power —the power not of keen sight, such as is ascribed to serpents or eagles, for however keenly these animals see, they can discern nothing but bodily substances—but the power of seeing things incorporeal. Possibly it was this great power of vision which was temporarily communicated to the eyes of the holy Job while yet in this mortal body, when he says to God, "I have heard of Thee by the hearing of the ear; but now mine eye seeth Thee: wherefore I abhor myself, and melt away, and count myself dust and ashes;" [72] although there is no reason why we should not understand this of the eye of the heart, of which the apostle says, "Having the eyes of your heart illuminated." [73] But that God shall be seen with these eyes no Christian doubts who believingly accepts what our God and Master says, "Blessed are the pure in heart: for they shall see God." [74] But whether in the future life God shall also be seen with the bodily eye, this is now our question.

The expression of Scripture, "And all flesh shall see the salvation of God," [75] may without difficulty be understood as if it were said, "And every man shall see the Christ of God." And He certainly was seen in the body, and shall be seen in the body when He judges quick and dead. And that Christ is the salvation of God, many other passages of Scripture witness, but especially the words of the venerable Simeon, who, when he had received into his hands the infant Christ, said, "Now lettest Thou Thy servant depart in peace, according to Thy word: for mine eyes have seen Thy salvation." [76] As for the words of the above-mentioned Job, as they are found in the Hebrew manuscripts, "And in my flesh I shall see God," [77] no doubt they were a prophecy of the resurrection of the flesh; yet he does not say "by the flesh." And indeed, if he had said this, it would still be possible that Christ was meant by "God;" for Christ shall be seen by the flesh in the flesh. But even understanding it of God, it is only equivalent to saying, I shall be in the flesh when I see God. Then the apostle's expression, "face to face," [78] does not oblige us to believe that we shall see God by the bodily face in

[71] Jer. xxiii. 24 [72] Job xlii. 5, 6 [73] Eph. i. 18 [74] Matt. v. 8 [75] Luke iii. 6 [76] Luke ii. 29, 30 [77] Job xix. 26 [78] 1 Cor. xiii. 12

which are the eyes of the body, for we shall see Him without intermission in spirit. And if the apostle had not referred to the face of the inner man, he would not have said, "But we, with unveiled face beholding as in a glass the glory of the Lord, are transformed into the same image, from glory to glory, as by the spirit of the Lord." [79] In the same sense we understand what the Psalmist sings, "Draw near unto Him, and be enlightened; and your faces shall not be ashamed." [80] For it is by faith we draw near to God, and faith is an act of the spirit, not of the body. But as we do not know what degree of perfection the spiritual body shall attain—for here we speak of a matter of which we have no experience, and upon which the authority of Scripture does not definitely pronounce—it is necessary that the words of the *Book of Wisdom* be illustrated in us: "The thoughts of mortal men are timid, and our fore-castings uncertain." [81]

For if that reasoning of the philosophers, by which they attempt to make out that intelligible or mental objects are so seen by the mind, and sensible or bodily objects so seen by the body, that the former cannot be discerned by the mind through the body, nor the latter by the mind itself without the body—if this reasoning were trustworthy, then it would certainly follow that God could not be seen by the eye even of a spiritual body. But this reasoning is exploded both by true reason and by prophetic authority. For who is so little acquainted with the truth as to say that God has no cognisance of sensible objects? Has He therefore a body, the eyes of which give Him this knowledge? Moreover, what we have just been. relating of the prophet Elisha, does this not sufficiently show that bodily things can be discerned by the spirit without the help of the body? For when that servant received the gifts, certainly this was a bodily or material transaction, yet the prophet saw it not by the body, but by the spirit. As, therefore, it is agreed that bodies are seen by the spirit, what if the power of the spiritual body shall be so great that spirit also is seen by the body? For God is a spirit. Besides, each man recognizes his own life—that life by which he now lives in the body, and which vivifies these earthly members and causes them to grow— by an interior sense, and not by his bodily eye; but the life of other men, though it is invisible, he sees with the bodily eye. For how do we distinguish between living and dead bodies, except by seeing at once both the body and the life which we cannot see save by the eye? But a life without a body we cannot see thus.

Wherefore it may very well be, and it is thoroughly credible, that we shall in the future world see the material forms of the new heavens and the new earth in such a way that we shall most distinctly recognize God everywhere present and governing all things, material as well as spiritual, and shall see Him, not as now we understand the invisible things of God, by the things which are made,[82] and see Him darkly, as in a mirror, and in part, and rather by faith than by bodily vision of material appearances, but by means of the

---

[79] 2 Cor. iii. 18   [80] Ps. xxxiv. 5   [81] Wisd. ix. 14   [82] Rom. i. 20

bodies we shall wear and which we shall see wherever we turn our eyes. As we do not believe, but see that the living men around us who are exercising vital functions are alive, though we cannot see their life without their bodies, but see it most distinctly by means of their bodies, so, wherever we shall look with those spiritual eyes of our future bodies, we shall then, too, by means of bodily substances behold God, though a spirit, ruling all things. Either, therefore, the eyes shall possess some quality similar to that of the mind, by which they may be able to discern spiritual things, and among these God—a supposition for which it is difficult or even impossible to find any support in Scripture—or, which is more easy to comprehend, God will be so known by us, and shall be so much before us, that we shall see Him by the spirit in ourselves, in one another, in Himself, in the new heavens and the new earth, in every created thing which shall then exist; and also by the body we shall see Him in every body which the keen vision of the eye of the spiritual body shall reach. Our thoughts also shall be visible to all, for then shall be fulfilled the words of the apostle, "Judge nothing before the time, until the Lord come, who both will bring to light the hidden things of darkness, and will make manifest the thoughts of the heart, and then shall every one have praise of God." [83]

CHAPTER XXX

OF THE ETERNAL FELICITY OF THE CITY OF GOD, AND OF THE PERPETUAL SABBATH

How great shall be that felicity, which shall be tainted with no evil, which shall lack no good, and which shall afford leisure for the praises of God, who shall be all in all! For I know not what other employment there can be where no lassitude shall slacken activity, nor any want stimulate to labor. I am admonished also by the sacred song, in which I read or hear the words, "Blessed are they that dwell in Thy house, O Lord; they will be still praising Thee." [84] All the members and organs of the incorruptible body, which now we see to be suited to various necessary uses, shall contribute to the praises of God; for in that life necessity shall have no place, but full, certain, secure, everlasting felicity. For all those parts of the bodily harmony, which are distributed through the whole body, within and without, and of which I have just been saying that they at present elude our observation, shall then be discerned; and, along with the other great and marvellous discoveries which shall then kindle rational minds in praise of the great Artificer, there shall be the enjoyment of a beauty which appeals to the reason. What power of movement such bodies shall possess, I have not the audacity rashly to define, as I have not the ability to conceive. Nevertheless I will say that in any case, both in motion and at rest, they shall be, as in their appearance,

[83] I Cor. iv. 5   [84] Ps. lxxxiv. 4

seemly; for into that state nothing which is unseemly shall be admitted. One thing is certain, the body shall forthwith be wherever the spirit wills, and the spirit shall will nothing which is unbecoming either to the spirit or to the body. True honor shall be there, for it shall be denied to none who is worthy, nor yielded to any unworthy; neither shall any unworthy person so much as sue for it, for none but the worthy shall be there. True peace shall be there, where no one shall suffer opposition either from himself or any other. God Himself, who is the Author of virtue, shall there be its reward; for, as there is nothing greater or better, He has promised Himself. What else was meant by His word through the prophet, "I will be your God, and ye shall be my people," [85] than, I shall be their satisfaction, I shall be all that men honorably desire—life, and health, and nourishment, and plenty, and glory, and honor, and peace, and all good things? This, too, is the right interpretation of the saying of the apostle, "That God may be all in all." [86] He shall be the end of our desires who shall be seen without end, loved without cloy, praised without weariness. This outgoing of affection, this employment, shall certainly be, like eternal life itself, common to all.

But who can conceive, not to say describe, what degrees of honor and glory shall be awarded to the various degrees of merit? Yet it cannot be doubted that there shall be degrees. And in that blessed city there shall be this great blessing, that no inferior shall envy any superior, as now the archangels are not envied by the angels, because no one will wish to be what he has not received, though bound in strictest concord with him who has received; as in the body the finger does not seek to be the eye, though both members are harmoniously included in the complete structure of the body. And thus, along with his gift, greater or less, each shall receive this further gift of contentment to desire no more than he has.

Neither are we to suppose that because sin shall have no power to delight them, free will must be withdrawn. It will, on the contrary, be all the more truly free, because set free from delight in sinning to take unfailing delight in not sinning. For the first freedom of will which man received when he was created upright consisted in an ability not to sin, but also in an ability to sin; whereas this last freedom of will shall be superior, inasmuch as it shall not be able to sin. This, indeed, shall not be a natural ability, but the gift of God. For it is one thing to be God, another thing to be a partaker of God. God by nature cannot sin, but the partaker of God receives this inability from God. And in this divine gift there was to be observed this gradation, that man should first receive a free will by which he was able not to sin, and at last a free will by which he was not able to sin—the former being adapted to the acquiring of merit, the latter to the enjoying of the reward. But the nature thus constituted, having sinned when it had the ability to do so, it is by a more abundant grace that it is delivered so as to reach that freedom in which it cannot sin. For as the first immortality which Adam lost by sinning

[85] Lev. xxvi. 12   [86] 1 Cor. xv. 28

consisted in his being able not to die, while the last shall consist in his not being able to die; so the first free will consisted in his being able not to sin, the last in his not being able to sin. And thus piety and justice shall be as indefeasible as happiness. For certainly by sinning we lost both piety and happiness; but when we lost happiness, we did not lose the love of it. Are we to say that God Himself is not free because He cannot sin? In that city, then, there shall be free will, one in all the citizens, and indivisible in each, delivered from all ill, filled with all good, enjoying indefeasibly the delights of eternal joys, oblivious of sins, oblivious of sufferings, and yet not so oblivious of its deliverance as to be ungrateful to its Deliverer.

The soul, then, shall have an intellectual remembrance of its past ills; but, so far as regards sensible experience, they shall be quite forgotten. For a skillful physician knows, indeed, professionally almost all diseases; but experimentally he is ignorant of a great number which he himself has never suffered from. As, therefore, there are two ways of knowing evil things—one by mental insight, the other by sensible experience, for it is one thing to understand all vices by the wisdom of a cultivated mind, another to understand them by the foolishness of an abandoned life—so also there are two ways of forgetting evils. For a well-instructed and learned man forgets them one way, and he who has experimentally suffered from them forgets them another—the former by neglecting what he has learned, the latter by escaping what he has suffered. And in this latter way the saints shall forget their past ills, for they shall have so thoroughly escaped them all, that they shall be quite blotted out of their experience. But their intellectual knowledge, which shall be great, shall keep them acquainted not only with their own past woes, but with the eternal sufferings of the lost. For if they were not to know that they had been miserable, how could they, as the Psalmist says, for ever sing the mercies of God? Certainly that city shall have no greater joy than the celebration of the grace of Christ, who redeemed us by His blood. There shall be accomplished the words of the psalm, "Be still, and know that I am God." [87] There shall be the great Sabbath which has no evening, which God celebrated among His first works, as it is written, "And God rested on the seventh day from all His works which He had made. And God blessed the seventh day, and sanctified it; because that in it He had rested from all His work which God began to make." [88] For we shall ourselves be the seventh day, when we shall be filled and replenished with God's blessing and sanctification. There shall we be still, and know that He is God; that He is that which we ourselves aspired to be when we fell away from Him, and listened to the voice of the seducer, "Ye shall be as gods," [89] and so abandoned God, who would have made us as gods, not by deserting Him, but by participating in Him. For without Him what have we accomplished, save to perish in His anger? But when we are restored by Him, and perfected with greater grace, we shall have eternal leisure to see that He is God,

[87] Ps. xlvi. 10   [88] Gen. ii. 2, 3   [89] Gen. iii. 5

for we shall be full of Him when He shall be all in all. For even our good works, when they are understood to be rather His than ours, are imputed to us that we may enjoy this Sabbath rest. For if we attribute them to ourselves, they shall be servile; for it is said of the Sabbath, "Ye shall do no servile work in it." [90] Wherefore also it is said by Ezekiel the prophet, "And I gave them my Sabbaths to be a sign between me and them, that they might know that I am the Lord who sanctify them." [91] This knowledge shall be perfected when we shall be perfectly at rest, and shall perfectly know that He is God.

This Sabbath shall appear still more clearly if we count the ages as days, in accordance with the periods of time defined in Scripture, for that period will be found to be the seventh. The first age, as the first day, extends from Adam to the deluge; the second from the deluge to Abraham, equalling the first, not in length of time, but in the number of generations, there being ten in each. From Abraham to the advent of Christ there are, as the evangelist Matthew calculates, three periods, in each of which are fourteen generations —one period from Abraham to David, a second from David to the captivity, a third from the captivity to the birth of Christ in the flesh. There are thus five ages in all. The sixth is now passing, and cannot be measured by any number of generations, as it has been said, "It is not for you to know the times, which the Father hath put in His own power." [92] After this period God shall rest as on the seventh day, when He shall give us (who shall be the seventh day) rest in Himself. But there is not now space to treat of these ages; suffice it to say that the seventh shall be our Sabbath, which shall be brought to a close, not by an evening, but by the Lord's day, as an eighth and eternal day, consecrated by the resurrection of Christ, and prefiguring the eternal repose not only of the spirit, but also of the body. There we shall rest and see, see and love, love and praise. This is what shall be in the end without end. For what other end do we propose to ourselves than to attain to the kingdom of which there is no end?

I think I have now, by God's help, discharged my obligation in writing this large work. Let those who think I have said too little, or those who think I have said too much, forgive me; and let those who think I have said just enough give thanks, not to me, but rather join me in giving thanks to God. Amen.

[90] Deut. v. 14   [91] Ezek. xx. 12   [92] Acts i. 7

ON THE TRINITY

ON THE TRINITY

Introductory Note

The fifteen books of the great treatise *On the Trinity* were composed over a long period of years from 400 to 416 A.D. The work was not written against any antagonist, nor indeed was it precipitated, as were so many of his works, by the heat of controversy. Rather, it was composed in the lulls between the ecclesiastical disputes of the early years of the fourth century. There are two distinct parts to the work. The first seven books are exegetical in character, and through them Saint Augustine in masterly fashion marshals and weaves together the scriptural evidence for the doctrine of the Trinity. The last eight books are speculative and philosophical. Here he seeks via his reason evidences for the doctrine and searches out at various levels of experience anything which in view of its trinal character might reasonably be considered to adumbrate the nature of God as Trinity. In the architecture of the whole treatise and through its two divisions Saint Augustine has incorporated his central theme of faith seeking understanding.

ON THE TRINITY

BOOK ONE

In which the unity and equality of the Supreme Trinity is established from the sacred Scriptures, and some texts alleged against the equality of the Son are explained.

CHAPTER I

THIS WORK IS WRITTEN AGAINST THOSE WHO SOPHISTICALLY ASSAIL
THE FAITH OF THE TRINITY, THROUGH MISUSE OF REASON. THEY
WHO DISPUTE CONCERNING GOD ERR FROM A THREEFOLD CAUSE.
HOLY SCRIPTURE, REMOVING WHAT IS FALSE, LEADS US ON BY
DEGREES TO THINGS DIVINE. WHAT TRUE IMMORTALITY
IS. WE ARE NOURISHED BY FAITH, THAT WE
MAY BE ENABLED TO APPREHEND THINGS DIVINE

THE following dissertation concerning the Trinity, as the reader ought to be informed, has been written in order to guard against the sophistries of those who disdain to begin with faith, and are deceived by a crude and perverse love of reason. Now one class of such men endeavor to transfer to things incorporeal and spiritual the ideas they have formed, whether through experience of the bodily senses, or by natural human wit and diligent quickness, or by the aid of art, from things corporeal; so as to seek to measure and conceive of the former by the latter. Others, again, frame whatever sentiments they may have concerning God according to the nature or affections of the human mind; and through this error they govern their discourse, in disputing concerning God, by distorted and fallacious rules. While yet a third class strive indeed to transcend the whole creation, which doubtless is changeable, in order to raise their thought to the unchangeable substance, which is God; but being weighed down by the burden of mortality, while they both would seem to know what they do not, and cannot know what they would, preclude themselves from entering the very path of understanding, by an over-bold affirmation of their own presumptuous judgments; choosing rather not to correct their own opinion when it is perverse, than to change that which they have once defended. And, indeed, this is the common disease of all the three classes which I have mentioned—*viz.*, both of those who frame their thoughts of God according to things corporeal, and of those who do so according to the spiritual creature, such as is the soul; and of those who neither regard the body nor the spiritual creature, and yet think falsely about God; and are indeed so much the further from the truth, that nothing can be found answering to their conceptions, either in the body, or in the made or created spirit, or in the Creator Himself. For he who thinks, for instance, that God is white or red, is in error; and yet these things are found in the body. Again, he who thinks of God as now forgetting and now remembering, or anything of the same kind, is none the less in error; and yet these things are found in the mind. But he who thinks that God is of such power as to have generated Himself, is so much the more in error, because not only does God not so exist, but neither does the spiritual nor the bodily creature; for there is nothing whatever that generates its own existence.

In order, therefore, that the human mind might be purged from falsities of this kind, Holy Scripture, which suits itself to babes, has not avoided words drawn from any class of things really existing, through which, as by nourishment, our understanding might rise gradually to things divine and transcendent. For, in speaking of God, it has both used words taken from things corporeal, as when it says, "Hide me under the shadow of Thy wings;" [1] and it has borrowed many things from the spiritual creature, whereby to signify that which indeed is not so, but must needs so be said: as, for instance, "I the Lord thy God am a jealous God;" [2] and, "It repenteth me that I have made man." [3] But it has drawn no words whatever, whereby to frame either figures of speech or enigmatic sayings, from things which do not exist at all. And hence it is that they who are shut out from the truth by that third kind of error are more mischievously and emptily vain than their fellows; in that they surmise respecting God, what can neither be found in Himself nor in any creature. For divine Scripture is wont to frame, as it were, allurements for children from the things which are found in the creature; whereby, according to their measure, and as it were by steps, the affections of the weak may be moved to seek those things that are above, and to leave those things that are below. But the same Scripture rarely employs those things which are spoken properly of God, and are not found in any creature; as, for instance, that which was said to Moses, "I am that I am;" and, "I Am hath sent me to you." [4] For since both body and soul also are said in some sense to *be*, Holy Scripture certainly would not so express itself unless it meant to be understood in some special sense of the term. So, too, that which the Apostle says, "Who only hath immortality." [5] Since the soul also both is said to be, and is, in a certain manner immortal, Scripture would not say "only hath," unless because true immortality is unchangeableness; which no creature can possess, since it belongs to the creator alone. So also James says, "Every good gift and every perfect gift is from above, and cometh down from the Father of Lights, with whom is no variableness, neither shadow of turning." [6] So also

[1] Ps. xvii. 8   [2] Ex. xx. 5   [3] Gen. vi. 7   [4] Ex. iii. 14   [5] 1 Tim. vi. 16   [6] Jas. i. 17

David, "Thou shalt change them, and they shall be changed; but Thou art the same." [7]

Further, it is difficult to contemplate and fully know the substance of God; who fashions things changeable, yet without any change in Himself, and creates things temporal, yet without any temporal movement in Himself. And it is necessary, therefore, to purge our minds, in order to be able to see ineffably that which is ineffable; whereto not having yet attained, we are to be nourished by faith, and led by such ways as are more suited to our capacity, that we may be rendered apt and able to comprehend it. And hence the Apostle says, that "in Christ indeed are hid all the treasures of wisdom and knowledge;" [8] and yet has commended Him to us, as to babes in Christ, who, although already born again by His grace, yet are still carnal and psychical, not by that divine virtue wherein He is equal to the Father, but by that human infirmity whereby He was crucified. For he says, "I determined not to know anything among you, save Jesus Christ and Him crucified;" [9] and then he continues, "And I was with you in weakness, and in fear, and in much trembling." And a little after he says to them, "And I, brethren, could not speak unto you as unto spiritual, but as unto carnal, even as unto babes in Christ. I have fed you with milk, and not with meat: for hitherto ye were not able to bear it, neither yet now are ye able." [10] There are some who are angry at language of this kind, and think it is used in slight to themselves, and for the most part prefer rather to believe that they who so speak to them have nothing to say, than that they themselves cannot understand what they have said. And sometimes, indeed, we do allege to them, not certainly that account of the case which they seek in their inquiries about God—because neither can they themselves receive it, nor can we perhaps either apprehend or express it—but such an account of it as to demonstrate to them how incapable and utterly unfit they are to understand that which they require of us. But they, on their parts, because they do not hear what they desire, think that we are either playing them false in order to conceal our own ignorance, or speaking in malice because we grudge them knowledge; and so go away indignant and perturbed.

CHAPTER II

IN WHAT MANNER THIS WORK PROPOSES TO DISCOURSE CONCERNING THE TRINITY

Wherefore, our Lord God helping, we will undertake to render, as far as we are able, that very account which they so importunately demand: *viz.*, that the Trinity is the one and only and true God, and also how the Father, the Son, and the Holy Spirit are rightly said, believed, understood, to be of one and the same substance or essence; in such wise that they may not fancy

---

[7] Ps. cii. 26, 27   [8] Col. ii. 3   [9] 1 Cor. ii. 2, 3   [10] 1 Cor. iii. 1, 2

themselves mocked by excuses on our part, but may find by actual trial, both that the highest good is that which is discerned by the most purified minds, and that for this reason it cannot be discerned or understood by themselves, because the eye of the human mind, being weak, is dazzled in that so transcendent light, unless it be invigorated by the nourishment of the righteousness of faith. First, however, we must demonstrate, according to the authority of the Holy Scriptures, whether the faith be so. Then, if God be willing and aid us, we may perhaps at least so far serve these talkative arguers—more puffed up than capable, and therefore laboring under the more dangerous disease—as to enable them to find something which they are not able to doubt, that so, in that case where they cannot find the like, they may be led to lay the fault to their own minds, rather than to the truth itself or to our reasonings; and thus, if there be anything in them of either love or fear towards God, they may return and begin from faith in due order: perceiving at length how healthful a medicine has been provided for the faithful in the holy Church, whereby a heedful piety, healing the feebleness of the mind, may render it able to perceive the unchangeable truth, and hinder it from falling headlong, through disorderly rashness, into pestilent and false opinion. Neither will I myself shrink from inquiry, if I am anywhere in doubt; nor be ashamed to learn, if I am anywhere in error.

CHAPTER III

WHAT AUGUSTINE REQUESTS FROM HIS READERS. THE ERRORS OF READERS DULL OF COMPREHENSION NOT TO BE ASCRIBED TO THE AUTHOR

Further let me ask of my reader, wherever, alike with myself, he is certain, there to go on with me; wherever, alike with myself, he hesitates, there to join with me in inquiring; wherever he recognizes himself to be in error, there to return to me; wherever he recognizes me to be so, there to call me back: so that we may enter together upon the path of charity, and advance towards Him of whom it is said, "Seek His face evermore." [11] And I would make this pious and safe agreement, in the presence of our Lord God, with all who read my writings, as well in all other cases as, above all, in the case of those which inquire into the unity of the Trinity, of the Father and the Son and the Holy Spirit; because in no other subject is error more dangerous, or inquiry more laborious, or the discovery of truth more profitable. If, then, any reader shall say, This is not well said, because I do not understand it; such a one finds fault with my language, not with my faith: and it might perhaps in very truth have been put more clearly; yet no man ever so spoke as to be understood in all things by all men. Let him, therefore, who finds this fault with my discourse, see whether he can understand other men

[11] Ps. cv. 4

who have handled similar subjects and questions, when he does not understand me: and if he can, let him put down my book, or even, if he pleases, throw it away; and let him spend labor and time rather on those whom he understands. Yet let him not think on that account that I ought to have been silent, because I have not been able to express myself so smoothly and clearly to him as those do whom he understands. For neither do all things, which all men have written, come into the hands of all. And possibly some, who are capable of understanding even our writings, may not find those more lucid works, and may meet with ours only. And therefore it is useful that many persons should write many books, differing in style but not in faith, concerning even the same questions, that the matter itself may reach the greatest number—some in one way, some in another. But if he who complains that he has not understood these things has never been able to comprehend any careful and exact reasonings at all upon such subjects, let him in that case deal with himself by resolution and study, that he may know better; not with me by quarrellings and wranglings, that I may hold my peace. Let him, again, who says, when he reads my book, Certainly I understand what is said, but it is not true, assert, if he pleases, his own opinion, and refute mine if he is able. And if he do this with charity and truth, and take the pains to make it known to me (if I am still alive), I shall then receive the most abundant fruit of this my labor. And if he cannot inform myself, most willing and glad should I be that he should inform those whom he can. Yet, for my part, "I meditate in the law of the Lord," [12] if not "day and night," at least such short times as I can; and I commit my meditations to writing, lest they should escape me through forgetfulness; hoping by the mercy of God that He will make me hold steadfastly all truths of which I feel certain; "but if in anything I be otherwise minded, that He will himself reveal even this to me," [13] whether through secret inspiration and admonition, or through His own plain utterances, or through the reasonings of my brethren. This I pray for, and this my trust and desire I commit to Him, who is sufficiently able to keep those things which He has given me, and to render those which He has promised.

I expect, indeed, that some, who are more dull of understanding, will imagine that in some parts of my books I have held sentiments which I have not held, or have not held those which I have. But their error, as none can be ignorant, ought not to be attributed to me, if they have deviated into false doctrine through following my steps without apprehending me, while I am compelled to pick my way through a hard and obscure subject: seeing that neither can any one, in any way, rightly ascribe the numerous and various errors of heretics to the holy testimonies themselves of the divine books; although all of them endeavor to defend out of those same Scriptures their own false and erroneous opinions. The law of Christ, that is, charity, admonishes me clearly, and commands me with a sweet constraint, that

[12] Ps. i. 2   [13] Phil. iii. 15

when men think that I have held in my books something false which I have not held, and that same falsehood displeases one and pleases another, I should prefer to be blamed by him who reprehends the falsehood, rather than praised by him who praises it. For although I, who never held the error, am not rightly blamed by the former, yet the error itself is rightly censured; while by the latter neither am I rightly praised, who am thought to have held that which the truth censures, nor the sentiment itself, which the truth also censures. Let us therefore essay the work which we have undertaken in the name of the Lord.

CHAPTER IV

WHAT THE DOCTRINE OF THE CATHOLIC FAITH IS CONCERNING THE TRINITY

All those Catholic expounders of the divine Scriptures, both Old and New, whom I have been able to read, who have written before me concerning the Trinity, Who is God, have purposed to teach, according to the Scriptures, this doctrine, that the Father, and the Son, and the Holy Spirit intimate a divine unity of one and the same substance in an indivisible equality; and therefore that they are not three Gods, but one God: although the Father hath begotten the Son, and so He who is the Father is not the Son; and the Son is begotten by the Father, and so He who is the Son is not the Father; and the Holy Spirit is neither the Father nor the Son, but only the Spirit of the Father and of the Son, Himself also co-equal with the Father and the Son, and pertaining to the unity of the Trinity. Yet not that this Trinity was born of the Virgin Mary, and crucified under Pontius Pilate, and buried, and rose again the third day, and ascended into heaven, but only the Son. Nor, again, that this Trinity descended in the form of a dove upon Jesus when He was baptized;[14] nor that, on the day of Pentecost, after the ascension of the Lord, when "there came a sound from heaven, as of a rushing mighty wind," [15] the same Trinity "sat upon each of them with cloven tongues like as of fire," but only the Holy Spirit. Nor yet that this Trinity said from heaven, "Thou art my Son," [16] whether when He was baptized by John, or when the three disciples were with Him in the mount,[17] or when the voice sounded, saying, "I have both glorified it, and will glorify it again;" [18] but that it was a word of the Father only, spoken to the Son; although the Father, and the Son, and the Holy Spirit, as they are indivisible, so work indivisibly.[19] This is also my faith, since it is the Catholic faith.

[14] Matt. iii. 16   [15] Acts ii. 2, 4   [16] Mark i. 11   [17] Matt. xvii. 5   [18] John xii. 28
[19] The term Trinity denotes the Divine essence in all three modes. The term Father (or Son, or Spirit) denotes the essence in only one mode. Consequently, there is something in the Trinity that cannot be attributed to any one of the Persons, as such; and something in a Person that cannot be attributed to the Trinity, as such. Trinality cannot be ascribed to the first Person; paternity cannot be ascribed to the Trinity.— W. G. T. S.

CHAPTER V

OF DIFFICULTIES CONCERNING THE TRINITY: IN WHAT MANNER THREE ARE ONE GOD, AND HOW, WORKING INDIVISIBLY, THEY YET PERFORM SOME THINGS SEVERALLY

Some persons, however, find a difficulty in this faith; when they hear that the Father is God, and the Son God, and the Holy Spirit God, and yet that this Trinity is not three Gods, but one God; and they ask how they are to understand this: especially when it is said that the Trinity works indivisibly in everything that God works, and yet that a certain voice of the Father spoke, which is not the voice of the Son; and that none except the Son was born in the flesh, and suffered, and rose again, and ascended into heaven; and that none except the Holy Spirit came in the form of a dove. They wish to understand how the Trinity uttered that voice which was only of the Father; and how the same Trinity created that flesh in which the Son only was born of the Virgin; and how the very same Trinity itself wrought that form of a dove, in which the Holy Spirit only appeared. Yet, otherwise, the Trinity does not work indivisibly, but the Father does some things, the Son other things, and the Holy Spirit yet others: or else, if they do some things together, some severally, then the Trinity is not indivisible. It is a difficulty, too, to them, in what manner the Holy Spirit is in the Trinity, whom neither the Father nor the Son, nor both, have begotten, although He is the Spirit both of the Father and of the Son. Since, then, men weary us with asking such questions, let us unfold to them, as we are able, whatever wisdom God's gift has bestowed upon our weakness on this subject; neither "let us go on our way with consuming envy."[20] Should we say that we are not accustomed to think about such things, it would not be true; yet if we acknowledge that such subjects commonly dwell in our thoughts, carried away as we are by the love of investigating the truth, then they require of us, by the law of charity, to make known to them what we have herein been able to find out. "Not as though I had already attained, either were already perfect" (for, if the Apostle Paul, how much more must I, who lie far beneath his feet, count myself not to have apprehended!); but, according to my measure, "if I forget those things that are behind, and reach forth unto those things which are before, and press towards the mark for the prize of the high calling,"[21] I am requested to disclose so much of the road as I have already passed, and the point to which I have reached, whence the course yet remains to bring me to the end. And those make the request, whom a generous charity compels me to serve. Needs must compel me too, and God will grant that, in supplying them with matter to read, I shall profit myself also; and that, in seeking to reply to their inquiries, I shall myself

[20] Wisd. vi. 23   [21] Phil. iii. 12-14

likewise find that for which I was inquiring. Accordingly I have undertaken the task, by the bidding and help of the Lord my God, not so much of discoursing with authority respecting things I know already, as of learning those things by piously discoursing of them.

CHAPTER VI

THAT THE SON IS VERY GOD, OF THE SAME SUBSTANCE WITH THE
FATHER. NOT ONLY THE FATHER, BUT THE TRINITY, IS AFFIRMED
TO BE IMMORTAL. ALL THINGS ARE NOT FROM THE FATHER
ALONE, BUT ALSO FROM THE SON. THAT THE HOLY
SPIRIT IS VERY GOD, EQUAL WITH THE FATHER
AND THE SON

They who have said that our Lord Jesus Christ is not God, or not very God, or not with the Father the One and only God, or not truly immortal because changeable, are proved wrong by the most plain and unanimous voice of divine testimonies; as, for instance, "In the beginning was the Word, and the Word was with God, and the Word was God." For it is plain that we are to take the Word of God to be the only Son of God, of whom it is afterwards said, "And the Word was made flesh, and dwelt among us," on account of that birth of His incarnation, which was wrought in time of the Virgin. But herein is declared, not only that He is God, but also that He is of the same substance with the Father; because, after saying, "And the Word was God," it is said also, "The same was in the beginning with God: all things were made by Him, and without Him was not anything made." [22] Not simply "all things;" but only all things that were *made*, that is, the whole creature. From which it appears clearly, that He Himself was not made, by whom all things were made. And if He was not made, then He is not a creature; but if He is not a creature, then He is of the same substance with the Father. For all substance that is not God is creature; and all that is not creature is God. And if the Son is not of the same substance with the Father, then He is a substance that was made: and if He is a substance that was made, then all things were not made by Him; but "all things were made by Him," therefore He is of one and the same substance with the Father. And so He is not only God, but also very God. And the same John most expressly affirms this in his epistle: "For we know that the Son of God is come, and hath given us an understanding, that we may know the true God, and that we may be in His true Son Jesus Christ. This is the true God, and eternal life." [23]

Hence also it follows by consequence, that the Apostle Paul did not say, "Who alone has immortality," of the Father merely; but of the One and only God, which is the Trinity itself. For that which is itself eternal life is

[22] John i. 1, 14, 2, 3   [23] 1 John v. 20

not mortal according to any changeableness; and hence the Son of God, because "He is Eternal Life," is also Himself understood with the Father, where it is said, "Who only hath immortality." For we, too, are made partakers of this eternal life, and become, in our own measure, immortal. But the eternal life itself, of which we are made partakers, is one thing; we ourselves, who, by partaking of it, shall live eternally, are another. For if He had said, "Whom in His own time the Father will show, who is the blessed and only Potentate, the King of kings, and Lord of lords; who only hath immortality;" not even so would it be necessarily understood that the Son is excluded. For neither has the Son separated the Father from Himself, because He Himself, speaking elsewhere with the voice of wisdom (for He Himself is the Wisdom of God),[24] says, "I alone compassed the circuit of heaven."[25] And therefore so much the more is it not necessary that the words, "Who hath immortality," should be understood of the Father alone, omitting the Son; when they are said thus: "That thou keep this commandment without spot, unrebukeable, until the appearing of our Lord Jesus Christ: whom in His own time He will show, who is the blessed and only Potentate, the King of kings, and Lord of lords; who only hath immortality, dwelling in the light which no man can approach unto; whom no man hath seen, nor can see: to whom be honor and power everlasting. Amen."[26] In these words neither is the Father specially named, nor the Son, nor the Holy Spirit; but the blessed and only Potentate, the King of kings, and Lord of lords; that is, the One and only and true God, the Trinity itself.

But perhaps what follows may interfere with this meaning; because it is said, "Whom no man hath seen, nor can see:" although this may also be taken as belonging to Christ according to His divinity, which the Jews did not see, who yet saw and crucified Him in the flesh; whereas His divinity can in no wise be seen by human sight, but is seen with that sight with which they who see are no longer men, but beyond men. Rightly, therefore, is God Himself, the Trinity, understood to be the "blessed and only Potentate," who "shows the coming of our Lord Jesus Christ in His own time." For the words, "Who only hath immortality," are said in the same way as it is said, "Who only doeth wondrous things."[27] And I should be glad to know of whom they take these words to be said. If only of the Father, how then is that true which the Son Himself says, "For what things soever the Father doeth, these also doeth the Son likewise?" Is there any, among wonderful works, more wonderful than to raise up and quicken the dead? Yet the same Son saith, "As the Father raiseth up the dead, and quickeneth them, even so the Son quickeneth whom He will."[28] How, then, does the Father alone "do wondrous things," when these words allow us to understand neither the Father only, nor the Son only, but assuredly the one only true God, that is, the Father, and the Son, and the Holy Spirit?

[24] 1 Cor. i. 24   [25] Ecclus. xxiv. 5   [26] 1 Tim. vi. 14-16   [27] Ps. lxxii. 18   [28] John v. 19, 21

Also, when the same apostle says, "But to us there is but one God, the Father, of whom are all things, and we in Him: and one Lord Jesus Christ, by whom are all things, and we by Him," [29] who can doubt that he speaks of all things which are created; as does John, when he says, "All things were made by Him"? I ask, therefore, of whom he speaks in another place: "For of Him, and through Him, and in Him, are all things: to whom be glory for ever. Amen." [30] For if of the Father, and the Son, and the Holy Spirit, so as to assign each clause severally to each person: of Him, that is to say, of the Father; through Him, that is to say, through the Son; in Him, that is to say, in the Holy Spirit—it is manifest that the Father, and the Son, and the Holy Spirit is one God, inasmuch as the words continue in the singular number, "To whom[31] be glory for ever." For at the beginning of the passage he does not say, "O the depth of the riches both of the wisdom and knowledge" of the Father, or of the Son, or of the Holy Spirit, but "of the wisdom and knowledge of God!" "How unsearchable are His judgments, and His ways past finding out! For who hath known the mind of the Lord? or who hath been His counsellor? Or who hath first given to Him and it shall be recompensed unto him again? For of Him, and through Him, and in Him, are all things: to whom be glory for ever. Amen." [32] But if they will have this to be understood only of the Father, then in what way are all things by the Father, as is said here; and all things by the Son, as where it is said to the Corinthians, "And one Lord Jesus Christ, by whom are all things," [33] and as in the Gospel of John, "All things were made by Him?" For if some things were made by the Father, and some by the Son, then all things were not made by the Father, nor all things by the Son; but if all things were made by the Father, and all things by the Son, then the same things were made by the Father and by the Son. The Son, therefore, is equal with the Father, and the working of the Father and the Son is indivisible. Because if the Father made even the Son, whom certainly the Son Himself did not make, then all things were not made by the Son; but all things *were* made by the Son: therefore He Himself was not made, that with the Father He might make all things that were made. And the apostle has not refrained from using the very word itself, but has said most expressly, "Who, being in the form of God, thought it not robbery to be equal with God;" [34] using here the name of God specially of the Father; as elsewhere, "But the head of Christ is God." [35]

Similar evidence has been collected also concerning the Holy Spirit, of which those who have discussed the subject before ourselves have most fully availed themselves, that He too is God, and not a creature. But if not a creature, then not only God (for men likewise are called gods[36]), but also very God; and therefore absolutely equal with the Father and the Son, and in the unity of the Trinity consubstantial and co-eternal. But that the Holy

[29] I Cor. viii. 6   [30] Rom. xi. 36   [31] Ipsi   [32] Rom. xi. 33-36   [33] I Cor. viii. 6
[34] Phil. ii. 6   [35] I Cor. xi. 3   [36] Ps. lxxxii. 6

Spirit is not a creature is made quite plain by that passage above all others, where we are commanded not to serve the creature, but the Creator;[37] not in the sense in which we are commanded to "serve" one another by love,[38] which is in Greek δουλεύειν, but in that in which God alone is served, which is in Greek λατρεύειν. From whence they are called idolaters who tender that service to images which is due to God. For it is this service concerning which it is said, "Thou shalt worship the Lord thy God, and Him only shalt thou serve." [39] For this is found also more distinctly in the Greek Scriptures, which have λατρεύσεις. Now if we are forbidden to serve the creature with such a service, seeing that it is written, "Thou shalt worship the Lord thy God, and Him only shalt thou serve" (and hence, too, the apostle repudiates those who worship and serve the creature more than the Creator), then assuredly the Holy Spirit is not a creature, to whom such a service is paid by all the saints; as says the apostle, "For we are the circumcision, which serve the Spirit of God," [40] which is in the Greek λατρεύοντες. For even most Latin copies also have it thus, "We who serve the Spirit of God;" but all Greek ones, or almost all, have it so. Although in some Latin copies we find, not "We worship the Spirit of God," but, "We worship God in the Spirit." But let those who err in this case, and refuse to give up to the more weighty authority, tell us whether they find this text also varied in the mss.: "Know ye not that your body is the temple of the Holy Ghost, which is in you, which ye have of God?" Yet what can be more senseless or more profane, than that any one should dare to say that the members of Christ are the temple of one who, in their opinion, is a creature inferior to Christ? For the apostle says in another place, "Your bodies are members of Christ." But if the members of Christ are also the temple of the Holy Spirit, then the Holy Spirit is not a creature; because we must owe to Him, of whom our body is the temple, that service wherewith God only is to be served, which in Greek is called λατρεια. And accordingly the apostle says, "Therefore glorify God in your body." [41]

CHAPTER VII

IN WHAT MANNER THE SON IS LESS THAN THE FATHER, AND THAN HIMSELF

In these and like testimonies of the divine Scriptures, by free use of which, as I have said, our predecessors exploded such sophistries or errors of the heretics, the unity and equality of the Trinity are intimated to our faith. But because, on account of the incarnation of the Word of God for the working out of our salvation, that the man Christ Jesus might be the Mediator between God and men,[42] many things are so said in the sacred

---

[37] Rom. i. 25   [38] Gal. v. 13   [39] Deut. vi. 13   [40] Phil. iii. 3   [41] 1 Cor. vi. 19, 15, 20   [42] 1 Tim. ii. 5

books as to signify, or even most expressly declare, the Father to be greater than the Son; men have erred through a want of careful examination or consideration of the whole tenor of the Scriptures, and have endeavored to transfer those things which are said of Jesus Christ according to the flesh, to that substance of His which was eternal before the incarnation, and is eternal. They say, for instance, that the Son is less than the Father, because it is written that the Lord Himself said, "My Father is greater than I." [43] But the truth shows that after the same sense the Son is less also than Himself; for how was He not made less also than Himself, who "emptied Himself, and took upon Him the form of a servant?" For He did not so take the form of a servant as that He should lose the form of God, in which He was equal to the Father. If, then, the form of a servant was so taken that the form of God was not lost, since both in the form of a servant and in the form of God He Himself is the same only-begotten Son of God the Father, in the form of God equal to the Father, in the form of a servant the Mediator between God and men, the man Christ Jesus; is there any one who cannot perceive that He Himself in the form of God is also greater than Himself, but yet likewise in the form of a servant less than Himself? And not, therefore, without cause the Scripture says both the one and the other, both that the Son is equal to the Father, and that the Father is greater than the Son. For there is no confusion when the former is understood as on account of the form of God, and the latter as on account of the form of a servant. And, in truth, this rule for clearing the question through all the sacred Scriptures is set forth in one chapter of an epistle of the Apostle Paul, where this distinction is commended to us plainly enough. For he says, "Who, being in the form of God, thought it not robbery to be equal with God; but emptied Himself, and took upon Him the form of a servant, and was made in the likeness of men: and was found in fashion as a man." [44] The Son of God, then, is equal to God the Father in nature, but less in "fashion." For in the form of a servant which He took He is less than the Father; but in the form of God, in which also He was before He took the form of a servant, He is equal to the Father. In the form of God He is the Word, "by whom all things are made;" [45] but in the form of a servant He was "made of a woman, made under the law, to redeem them that were under the law." [46] In like manner, in the form of God He made man; in the form of a servant He was made man. For if the Father alone had made man without the Son, it would not have been written, "Let us make man in *our* image, after *our* likeness." [47] Therefore, because the form of God took the form of a servant, both is God and both is man; but both God, on account of God who takes; and both man, on account of man who is taken. For neither by that taking is the one of them turned and changed into the other: the Divinity is not changed into the creature, so as to cease to be Divinity nor the creature into Divinity, so as to cease to be creature.

[43] John xiv. 28   [44] Phil. ii. 6, 7   [45] John i. 3   [46] Gal. iv. 4, 5   [47] Gen. i. 26

CHAPTER VIII

THE TEXTS OF SCRIPTURE EXPLAINED RESPECTING THE SUBJECTION
OF THE SON TO THE FATHER, WHICH HAVE BEEN MISUNDER-
STOOD. CHRIST WILL NOT SO GIVE UP THE KINGDOM TO
THE FATHER, AS TO TAKE IT AWAY FROM HIMSELF.
THE BEHOLDING HIM IS THE PROMISED END OF
ALL ACTIONS. THE HOLY SPIRIT IS SUFFI-
CIENT TO OUR BLESSEDNESS EQUALLY
WITH THE FATHER

As for that which the apostle says, "And when all things shall be subdued unto Him, then shall the Son also Himself be subject unto Him that
put all things under Him:" either the text has been so turned, lest any one
should think that the "fashion" of Christ, which He took according to the
human creature, was to be transformed hereafter into the Divinity, or (to
express it more precisely) the Godhead itself, who is not a creature, but is
the unity of the Trinity—a nature incorporeal, and unchangeable, and
consubstantial, and co-eternal with itself; or if any one contends, as some
have thought, that the text, "Then shall the Son also Himself be subject
unto Him that put all things under Him," is so turned in order that one may
believe that very "subjection" to be a change and conversion hereafter of
the creature into the substance or essence itself of the Creator, that is, that
that which had been the substance of a creature shall become the substance
of the Creator—such an one at any rate admits this, of which in truth there
is no possible doubt, that this had not yet taken place, when the Lord said,
"My Father is greater than I." For He said this not only before He ascended
into heaven, but also before He had suffered, and had risen from the dead.
But they who think that the human nature in Him is to be changed and
converted into the substance of the Godhead, and that it was so said,
"Then shall the Son also Himself be subject unto Him that put all things
under Him"—as if to say, Then also the Son of man Himself, and the human nature taken by the Word of God, shall be changed into the nature of
Him who put all things under Him—must also think that this will then take
place, when, after the day of judgment, "He shall have delivered up the
kingdom to God, even the Father." And hence even still, according to this
opinion, the Father is greater than that form of a servant which was taken
of the Virgin. But if some affirm even further, that the man Christ Jesus
has already been changed into the substance of God, at least they cannot
deny that the human nature still remained, when He said before His passion,
"For my Father is greater than I;" whence there is no question that it was
said in this sense, that the Father is greater than the form of a servant, to
whom in the form of God the Son is equal. Nor let any one, hearing what the
apostle says, "But when He saith all things are put under Him, it is mani-

fest that He is excepted which did put all things under Him," [48] think the words, that He hath put all things under the Son, to be so understood of the Father, as that He should not think that the Son Himself put all things under Himself. For this the apostle plainly declares, when he says to the Philippians, "For our conversation is in heaven; from whence also we look for the Saviour, the Lord Jesus Christ: who shall change our vile body, that it may be fashioned like unto His glorious body, according to the working whereby He is able even to subdue all things unto Himself." [49] For the working of the Father and of the Son is indivisible. Otherwise, neither hath the Father Himself put all things under Himself, but the Son hath put all things under Him, who delivers the kingdom to Him, and puts down all rule and all authority and power. For these words are spoken of the Son: "When He shall have delivered up," says the apostle, "the kingdom to God, even the Father; when He shall have put down all rule, and all authority, and all power." For the same that puts down, also makes subject.

Neither may we think that Christ shall so give up the kingdom to God, even the Father, as that He shall take it away from Himself. For some vain talkers have thought even this. For when it is said, "He shall have delivered up the kingdom to God, even the Father," He Himself is not excluded; because He is one God together with the Father. But that word "until" deceives those who are careless readers of the divine Scriptures, but eager for controversies. For the text continues, "For He must reign, until He hath put all enemies under His feet;" [50] as though, when He had so put them, He would no more reign. Neither do they perceive that this is said in the same way as that other text, "His heart is established: He shall not be afraid, until He see His desire upon His enemies." [51] For He will not then be afraid when He has seen it. What then means, "When He shall have delivered up the kingdom to God, even the |Father," as though God the Father has not the kingdom now? But because He is hereafter to bring all the just, over whom now, living by faith, the Mediator between God and men, the man Christ Jesus, reigns, to that sight which the same apostle calls "face to face;" [52] therefore the words, "When He shall have delivered up the kingdom to God, even the Father," are as much as to say, When He shall have brought believers to the contemplation of God, even the Father. For He says, "All things are delivered unto me of my Father: and no man knoweth the Son, but the Father; neither knoweth any man the Father, save the Son, and he to whomsoever the Son will reveal Him." [53] The Father will then be revealed by the Son, "when He shall have put down all rule, and all authority, and all power;" that is, in such wise that there shall be no more need of any economy of similitudes, by means of angelic rulers, and authorities, and powers. Of whom that is not unfitly understood, which is said in the *Song of Songs* to the bride, "We will make thee borders of gold,

[48] I Cor. xv. 28, 24, 27   [49] Phil. iii. 20, 21   [50] I Cor. xv. 24, 25   [51] Ps. cxii. 8
[52] I Cor. xiii. 12   [53] Matt. xi. 27

with studs of silver, while the King sitteth at His table;"[54] that is, as long as Christ is in His secret place: since "your life is hid with Christ in God; when Christ, who is our life, shall appear, then shall ye also appear with Him in glory." [55] Before which time, "we see now through a glass, in an enigma," that is, in similitudes, "but then face to face." [56]

For this contemplation is held forth to us as the end of all actions, and the everlasting fullness of joy. For "we are the sons of God; and it doth not yet appear what we shall be: but we know that, when He shall appear, we shall be like Him; for we shall see Him as He is." [57] For that which He said to His servant Moses, "I am that I am; thus shalt thou say to the children of Israel, I Am hath sent me to you;" [58] this it is which we shall contemplate when we shall live in eternity. For so it is said, "And this is life eternal, that they might know Thee, the only true God, and Jesus Christ, whom Thou hast sent." [59] This shall be when the Lord shall have come, and "shall have brought to light the hidden things of darkness;" [60] when the darkness of this present mortality and corruption shall have passed away. Then will be our morning, which is spoken of in the Psalm, "In the morning will I direct my prayer unto Thee, and will contemplate Thee." [61] Of this contemplation I understand it to be said, "When He shall have delivered up the kingdom to God, even the Father;" that is, when He shall have brought the just, over whom now, living by faith, the Mediator between God and man, the man Christ Jesus, reigns, to the contemplation of God, even the Father. If herein I am foolish, let him who knows better correct me; to me at least the case seems as I have said. For we shall not seek anything else, when we shall have come to the contemplation of Him. But that contemplation is not yet, so long as our joy is in hope. For "hope that is seen is not hope: for what a man seeth, why doth he yet hope for? But if we hope for that we see not, then do we with patience wait for it," [62] *viz.* "as long as the King sitteth at His table." [63] Then will take place that which is written, "In Thy presence is fullness of joy." [64] Nothing more than that joy will be required; because there will be nothing more than can be required. For the Father will be manifested to us, and that will suffice for us. And this much Philip had well understood, so that he said to the Lord, "Show us the Father, and it sufficeth us." But he had not yet understood that he himself was able to say this very same thing in this way also: Lord, show Thyself to us, and it sufficeth us. For, that he might understand this, the Lord replied to him, "Have I been so long time with you, and yet hast thou not known me, Philip? he that hath seen me hath seen the Father." But because He intended him, before he could see this, to live by faith, He went on to say, "Believest thou not that I am in the Father, and the Father in me?" [65] For "while we are at home in the body, we are absent from the Lord: for we

[54] Cant. i. 11   [55] Col. iii. 3, 4   [56] 1 Cor. xiii. 12   [57] 1 John iii. 2   [58] Ex. iii. 14   [59] John xvii. 3   [60] 1 Cor. iv. 5   [61] Ps. v. 5   [62] Rom. viii. 24, 25   [63] Cant. i. 12   [64] Ps. xvi. 11   [65] John xiv. 8, 10

walk by faith, not by sight." [66] For contemplation is the recompense of faith, for which recompense our hearts are purified by faith; as it is written, "Purifying their hearts by faith." [67] And that our hearts are to be purified for this contemplation, is proved above all by this text, "Blessed are the pure in heart, for they shall see God." [68] And that this is life eternal, God says in the Psalm, "With long life will I satisfy him, and show him my salvation." [69] Whether, therefore, we hear, Show us the Son; or whether we hear, Show us the Father; it is even all one, since neither can be manifested without the other. For they are one, as He also Himself says, "My Father and I are one." [70] Finally, on account of this very indivisibility, it suffices that sometimes the Father alone, or the Son alone, should be named, as hereafter to fill us with the joy of His countenance.

Neither is the Spirit of either thence excluded, that is, the Spirit of the Father and of the Son; which Holy Spirit is specially called "the Spirit of truth, whom the world cannot receive." [71] For to have the fruition of God the Trinity, after whose image we are made, is indeed the fullness of our joy, than which there is no greater. On this account the Holy Spirit is some-times spoken of as if He alone sufficed to our blessedness: and He does alone so suffice, because He cannot be divided from the Father and the Son; as the Father alone is sufficient, because He cannot be divided from the Son and the Holy Spirit; and the Son alone is sufficient because He cannot be divided from the Father and the Holy Spirit. For what does He mean by saying, "If ye love me, keep my commandments; and I will pray the Father, and He shall give you another Comforter, that He may abide with you for ever; even the Spirit of truth, whom the world cannot receive," [72] that is, the lovers of the world? For "the natural man receiveth not the things of the Spirit of God." [73] But it may perhaps seem, further, as if the words, "And I will pray the Father, and He shall give you another Comforter," were so said as if the Son alone were not sufficient. And that place so speaks of the Spirit, as if He alone were altogether sufficient: "When He, the Spirit of truth, is come, He will guide you into all truth." [74] Pray, therefore, is the Son here excluded, as if He did not teach all truth, or as if the Holy Spirit were to fill up that which the Son could not fully teach? Let them say then, if it pleases them, that the Holy Spirit is greater than the Son, whom they are wont to call less. Or is it, forsooth, because it is not said, He alone—or, No one else except Himself—will guide you into all truth, that they allow that the Son also may be believed to teach together with Him? In that case the apostle has excluded the Son from knowing those things which are of God, where he says, "Even so the things of God knoweth no one, but the Spirit of God:" [75] so that these perverse men might, upon this ground, go on to say that none but the Holy Spirit teaches even the Son the things of

[66] 2 Cor. v. 6, 7   [67] Acts xv. 9   [68] Matt. v. 8   [69] Ps. xci. 16   [70] John x. 30
[71] John xiv. 17   [72] John xiv. 15-17   [73] 1 Cor. ii. 14   [74] John xvi. 13   [75] 1 Cor. ii. 11

God, as the greater teaches the less; to whom the Son Himself ascribes so much as to say, "But because I have said these things unto you, sorrow hath filled your heart. Nevertheless I tell you the truth; it is expedient for you that I go away: for if I go not away, the Comforter will not come unto you." [76]

CHAPTER IX

ALL ARE SOMETIMES UNDERSTOOD IN ONE PERSON

But this is said, not on account of any inequality of the Word of God and of the Holy Spirit, but as though the presence of the Son of man with them would be a hindrance to the coming of Him, who was not less, because He did not "empty Himself, taking upon Him the form of a servant," [77] as the Son did. It was necessary, then, that the form of a servant should be taken away from their eyes, because, through gazing upon it, they thought that alone which they saw to be Christ. Hence also is that which is said, "If ye loved me, ye would rejoice because I said, "I go unto the Father; for my Father is greater than I:" [78] that is, on that account it is necessary for me to go to the Father, because, while you see me thus, you hold me to be less than the Father through that which you see; and so, being taken up with the creature and the "fashion" which I have taken upon me, you do not perceive the equality which I have with the Father. Hence, too, is this: "Touch me not; for I am not yet ascended to my Father." [79] For touch, as it were, puts a limit to their conception, and He therefore would not have the thought of the heart, directed towards Himself, to be so limited as that He should be held to be only that which He seemed to be. But the "ascension to the Father" meant, so to appear as He is equal to the Father, that the limit of the sight which sufficeth us might be attained there. Sometimes also it is said of the Son alone, that He himself sufficeth, and the whole reward of our love and longing is held forth as in the sight of Him. For so it is said, "He that hath my commandments, and keepeth them, he it is that loveth me; and he that loveth me shall be loved of my Father; and I will love him, and will manifest myself to him." [80] Pray, because He has not here said, And I will show the Father also to him, has He therefore excluded the Father? On the contrary, because it is true, "I and my Father are one," when the Father is manifested, the Son also, who is in Him, is manifested; and when the Son is manifested, the Father also, who is in Him, is manifested. As, therefore, when it is said, "And I will manifest myself to him," it is understood that He manifests also the Father; so likewise in that which is said, "When He shall have delivered up the kingdom to God, even the Father," it is understood that He does not take it away from Himself; since, when He shall bring believers to the contemplation of God, even the

<hr>

[76] John xvi. 6, 7   [77] Phil. ii. 7   [78] John xiv. 28   [79] John xx. 17   [80] John xiv. 21

Father, doubtless He will bring them to the contemplation of Himself, who has said, "And I will manifest myself to him." And so, consequently, when Judas had said to Him, "Lord, how is it that Thou wilt manifest Thyself unto us, and not unto the world?" Jesus answered and said to him, "If a man love me, he will keep my words: and my Father will love him, and we will come unto him, and make our abode with him." [81] Behold, that He manifests not only Himself to him by whom He is loved, because He comes to him together with the Father, and abides with him. ·

Will it perhaps be thought, that when the Father and the Son make their abode with him who loves them, the Holy Spirit is excluded from that abode? What, then, is that which is said above of the Holy Spirit: "Whom the world cannot receive, because it seeth Him not: but ye know Him; for He abideth with you, and is in you"? He, therefore, is not excluded from that abode, of whom it is said, "He abideth with you, and is in you;" unless, perhaps, any one be so senseless as to think, that when the Father and the Son have come that they may make their abode with him who loves them, the Holy Spirit will depart thence, and (as it were) give place to those who are greater. But the Scripture itself meets this carnal idea; for it says a little above: "I will pray the Father, and He shall give you another Comforter, that He may abide with you for ever." [82] He will not therefore depart when the Father and the Son come, but will be in the same abode with them eternally; because neither will He come without them, nor they without Him. But in order to intimate the Trinity, some things are separately affirmed, the Persons being also each severally named; and yet are not to be understood as though the other Persons were excluded, on account of the unity of the same Trinity and the One substance and Godhead of the Father and of the Son and of the Holy Spirit.

CHAPTER X

IN WHAT MANNER CHRIST SHALL DELIVER UP THE KINGDOM TO GOD, EVEN THE FATHER. THE KINGDOM HAVING BEEN DELIVERED TO GOD, EVEN THE FATHER, CHRIST WILL NOT THEN MAKE INTERCESSION FOR US

Our Lord Jesus Christ, therefore, will so deliver up the kingdom to God, even the Father, Himself not being thence excluded, nor the Holy Spirit, when He shall bring believers to the contemplation of God, wherein is the end of all good actions, and everlasting rest, and joy which never will be taken from us. For He signifies this in that which He says: "I will see you again, and your heart shall rejoice; and your joy no man taketh from you." [83] Mary, sitting at the feet of the Lord, and earnestly listening to His word, foreshowed a similitude of this joy; resting as she did from all business, and

---

[81] John xiv. 22, 23　　[82] John xiv. 16-23　　[83] John xvi. 22

intent upon the truth, according to that manner of which this life is capable, by which, however, to prefigure that which shall be for eternity. For while Martha, her sister, was cumbered about necessary business, which, although good and useful, yet, when rest shall have succeeded, is to pass away, she herself was resting in the word of the Lord. And so the Lord replied to Martha, when she complained that her sister did not help her: "Mary hath chosen the best part, which shall not be taken away from her." [84] He did not say that Martha was acting a bad part; but He called that part the best which shall not be taken away. For that part which is occupied in the ministering to a need shall be "taken away" when the need itself has passed away. Indeed, the reward of a good work that will pass away is rest that will not pass away. In that contemplation, therefore, God will be all in all; because nothing else but Himself will be required, but it will be sufficient to be enlightened by and to enjoy Him alone. And so he in whom "the Spirit maketh intercession with groanings which cannot be uttered," [85] says, "One thing have I desired of the Lord, that I will seek after; that I may dwell in the house of the Lord all the days of my life, to contemplate the beauty of the Lord." [86] For we shall then contemplate God, the Father and the Son and the Holy Spirit, when the Mediator between God and men, the man Christ Jesus, shall have delivered up the kingdom to God, even the Father, so as no longer to make intercession for us, as our Mediator and Priest, Son of God and Son of man; but that He Himself too, in so far as He is a Priest that has taken the form of a servant for us, shall be put under Him who has put all things under Him, and under whom He has put all things: so that, in so far as He is God, He with Him will have put us under Himself; in so far as He is a Priest, He with us will be put under Him.[87] And therefore as the [incarnate] Son is both God and man, it is rather to be said that the manhood in the Son is another substance [from the Son], than that the Son in the Father [is another substance from the Father]; just as the carnal nature of my soul is more another substance in relation to my soul itself, although in one and the same man, than the soul of another man is in relation to my soul.

When, therefore, He "shall have delivered up the kingdom to God, even the Father"—that is, when He shall have brought those who believe and live by faith, for whom now as Mediator He maketh intercession, to that contemplation, for the obtaining of which we sigh and groan, and when labor and groaning shall have passed away—then, since the kingdom will have been delivered up to God, even the Father, He will no more make intercession for us. And this He signifies, when He says: "These things have I spoken unto you in similitudes;[88] but the time cometh when I shall no more speak unto you in similitudes, but I shall declare to you plainly of the Father:" that is, they will not then be "similitudes," when the sight shall be "face to face." For this it is which He says, "But I will declare to you plainly

[84] Luke x. 30-42   [85] Rom. viii. 26   [86] Ps. xxvii. 4   [87] 1 Cor. xv. 24-28   [88] Proverbs—A. V.

of the Father;" as if He said, I will plainly show you the Father. For He says, I will "declare" to you, because He is His word. For He goes on to say, "At that day ye shall ask in my name; and I say not unto you, that I will pray the Father for you: for the Father Himself loveth you, because ye have loved me, and have believed that I came out from God. I came forth from the Father, and am come into the world: again, I leave the world, and go to the Father." [89] What is meant by "I came forth from the Father," unless this, that I have not appeared in that form in which I am equal to the Father, but otherwise, that is, as less than the Father, in the creature which I have taken upon me? And what is meant by "I am come into the world," unless this, that I have manifested to the eyes even of sinners who love this world, the form of a servant which I took, making myself of no reputation? And what is meant by "Again, I leave the world," unless this, that I take away from the sight of the lovers of this world that which they have seen? And what is meant by "I go to the Father," unless this, that I teach those who are my faithful ones to understand me in that being in which I am equal to the Father? Those who believe this will be thought worthy of being brought by faith to sight, that is, to that very sight, in bringing them to which He is said to "deliver up the kingdom to God, even the Father." For His faithful ones, whom He has redeemed with His blood, are called His kingdom, for whom He now intercedes; but then, making them to abide in Himself there, where He is equal to the Father, He will no longer pray the Father for them. "For," He says, "the Father Himself loveth you." For indeed He "prays," in so far as He is less than the Father; but as He is equal with the Father, He with the Father grants. Wherefore He certainly does not exclude Himself from that which He says, "The Father Himself loveth you;" but He means it to be understood after that manner which I have above spoken of, and sufficiently intimated—namely, that for the most part each Person of the Trinity is so named, that the other Persons also may be understood. Accordingly, "For the Father Himself loveth you," is so said that by consequence both the Son and the Holy Spirit also may be understood: not that He does not now love us, who spared not His own Son, but delivered Him up for us all; [90] but God loves us, such as we shall be, not such as we are, for such as they are whom He loves, such are they whom He keeps eternally; which shall then be, when He who now maketh intercession for us shall have "delivered up the kingdom to God, even the Father," so as no longer to ask the Father, because the Father Himself loveth us. But for what deserving, except of faith, by which we believe before we see that which is promised? For by this faith we shall arrive at sight; so that He may love us, being such, as He loves us in order that we may become; and not such, as He hates us because we are, and exhorts and enables us to wish not to be always.

[89] John xvi. 25-28   [90] Rom. viii. 32

CHAPTER XI

BY WHAT RULE IN THE SCRIPTURES IT IS UNDERSTOOD THAT THE SON IS NOW EQUAL AND NOW LESS

Wherefore, having mastered this rule for interpreting the Scriptures concerning the Son of God, that we are to distinguish in them what relates to the form of God, in which He is equal to the Father, and what to the form of a servant which He took, in which He is less than the Father; we shall not be disquieted by apparently contrary and mutually repugnant sayings of the sacred books. For both the Son and the Holy Spirit, according to the form of God, are equal to the Father, because neither of them is a creature, as we have already shown: but according to the form of a servant He is less than the Father, because He Himself has said, "My Father is greater than I;" [91] and He is less than Himself, because it is said of Him, He emptied Himself;" [92] and He is less than the Holy Spirit, because He Himself says, "Whosoever speaketh a word against the Son of man, it shall be forgiven him; but whosoever speaketh against the Holy Ghost, it shall not be forgiven Him." [93] And in the Spirit too He wrought miracles, saying: "But if I with the Spirit of God cast out devils, no doubt the kingdom of God is come upon you." [94] And in *Isaiah* He says—in the lesson which He Himself read in the synagogue, and showed without a scruple of doubt to be fulfilled concerning Himself—"The Spirit of the Lord God," He says, "is upon me: because He hath anointed me to preach good tidings unto the meek He hath sent me to proclaim liberty to the captives," [95] etc.: for the doing of these things He therefore declares Himself to be "sent," because the Spirit of God is upon Him. According to the form of God, all things were made by Him; [96] according to the form of a servant, He was Himself made of a woman, made under the law.[97] According to the form of God, He and the Father are one; [98] according to the form of a servant, He came not to do His own will, but the will of Him that sent Him.[99] According to the form of God, "As the Father hath life in Himself, so hath He given to the Son to have life in Himself;" [100] according to the form of a servant, His "soul is sorrowful even unto death;" and, "O my Father," He says, "if it be possible, let this cup pass from me." [101] According to the form of God, "He is the True God, and eternal life;" [102] according to the form of a servant, "He became obedient unto death, even the death of the cross." [103] According to the form of God, all things that the Father hath are His,[104] and "All mine," He says, "are Thine, and Thine are mine;" [105] according to the form of a servant, the doctrine is not His own, but His that sent Him.[106]

[91] John xiv. 28   [92] Phil. ii. 7   [93] Matt. xii. 32   [94] Matt. xii. 28   [95] Isa. lxi. 1; Luke iv. 18, 19   [96] John i. 3   [97] Gal. iv. 4   [98] John. x. 30   [99] John vi. 38 [100] John v. 26   [101] Matt. xxvi. 38, 39   [102] 1 John v. 20   [103] Phil. ii. 8   [104] John xvii. 15   [105] John xvii. 10   [106] John vii. 16

CHAPTER XII

IN WHAT MANNER THE SON IS SAID NOT TO KNOW THE DAY AND THE
HOUR WHICH THE FATHER KNOWS. SOME THINGS SAID OF CHRIST
ACCORDING TO THE FORM OF GOD, OTHER THINGS ACCORDING TO
THE FORM OF A SERVANT. IN WHAT WAY IT IS OF CHRIST
TO GIVE THE KINGDOM, IN WHAT NOT OF CHRIST.
CHRIST WILL BOTH JUDGE AND NOT JUDGE

Again, "Of that day and that hour knoweth no man, no, not the angels which are in heaven; neither the Son, but the Father." [107] For He is ignorant of this, as *making others ignorant;* that is, in that He did not so know as at that time to show His disciples: as it was said to Abraham, "Now I know that thou fearest God," [108] that is, now I have caused thee to know it; because he himself, being tried in that temptation, became known to himself. For He was certainly going to tell this same thing to His disciples at the fitting time; speaking of which yet future as if past, He says, "Henceforth I call you not servants, but friends; for the servant knoweth not what his Lord doeth: but I have called you friends; for all things that I have heard of my Father I have made known unto you;" [109] which He had not yet done, but spoke as though He had already done it, because He certainly would do it. For He says to the disciples themselves, "I have yet many things to say unto you; but ye cannot bear them now." [110] Among which is to be understood also, "Of the day and hour." For the apostle also says, "I determined not to know anything among you, save Jesus Christ, and Him crucified;" [111] because he was speaking to those who were not able to receive higher things concerning the Godhead of Christ. To whom also a little while after he says, "I could not speak unto you as unto spiritual, but as unto carnal." [112] He was "ignorant," therefore, among them of that which they were not able to know from him. And that only he said that he knew, which it was fitting that they should know from him. In short, he knew among the perfect what he knew not among babes; for he there says: "We speak wisdom among them that are perfect." [113] For a man is said not to know what he hides, after that kind of speech, after which a ditch is called blind which is hidden. For the Scriptures do not use any other kind of speech than may be found in use among men, because they speak to men.

According to the form of God, it is said, "Before all the hills He begat me," [114] that is, before all the loftinesses of things created; and, "Before the dawn I begat Thee," [115] that is, before all times and temporal things: but according to the form of a servant, it is said, "The Lord created me in the beginning of His ways." [116] Because, according to the form of God, He said,

[107] Mark xiii. 32   [108] Gen. xxii. 12   [109] John xv. 15   [110] John xvi. 12   [111] I Cor. ii. 2   [112] I Cor. iii. 1   [113] I Cor. ii. 6   [114] Prov. viii. 25   [115] Ps. cx. 3, *Vulgate*   [116] Prov. viii. 22

"I am the truth;" and according to the form of a servant, "I am the way." [117]
For, because He Himself, being the first-begotten of the dead,[118] made a passage to the kingdom of God to life eternal for His Church, to which He is so the Head as to make the body also immortal, therefore He was "created in the beginning of the ways" of God in His work. For, according to the form of God, He is the beginning,[119] that also speaketh unto us, in which "beginning" God created the heaven and the earth; [120] but according to the form of a servant, "He is a bridegroom coming out of His chamber." [121] According to the form of God, "He is the first-born of every creature, and He is before all things and by him all things consist;" according to the form of a servant, "He is the head of the body, the Church." [122] According to the form of God, "He is the Lord of glory." [123] From which it is evident that He Himself glorifies His saints: for, "Whom He did predestinate, them He also called; and whom He called, them He also justified; and whom He justified, them He also glorified." [124] Of Him accordingly it is said, that He justifieth the ungodly; [125] of Him it is said, that He is just and a justifier.[126] If, therefore, He has also glorified those whom He has justified, He who justifies, Himself also glorifies; who is, as I have said, the Lord of glory. Yet, according to the form of a servant, He replied to His disciples, when inquiring about their own glorification: "To sit on my right hand and on my left is not mine to give, but it shall be given to them for whom it is prepared by my Father." [127]

But that which is prepared by His Father is prepared also by the Son Himself, because He and the Father are one.[128] For we have already shown, by many modes of speech in the divine Scriptures, that, in this Trinity, what is said of each is also said of all, on account of the indivisible working of the one and same substance. As He also says of the Holy Spirit, "If I depart, I will send Him unto you." [129] He did not say, *We* will send; but in such way as if the Son only should send Him, and not the Father; while yet He says in another place, "These things have I spoken unto you, being yet present with you; but the Comforter, which is the Holy Ghost, whom the Father will send in my name, He shall teach you all things." [130] Here again it is so said as if the Son also would not send Him, but the Father only. As therefore in these texts, so also where He says, "But for them for whom it is prepared by my Father," He meant it to be understood that He Himself, with the Father, prepares seats of glory for those for whom He will. But some one may say: There, when He spoke of the Holy Spirit, He so says that He Himself will send Him, as not to deny that the Father will send Him; and in the other place, He so says that the Father will send Him, as not to deny that He will do so Himself; but here He expressly says, "It is not mine to give," and so goes on to say that these things are prepared by the Father.

[117] John xiv. 6   [118] Apoc. i. 5   [119] John viii. 25   [120] Gen. i. 1   [121] Ps. xix. 5
[122] Col. i. 15, 17, 18   [123] 1 Cor. ii. 8   [124] Rom. viii. 30   [125] Rom. iv. 5   [126] Rom.
iii. 26   [127] Matt. xx. 23   [128] John x. 30   [129] John xvi. 7   [130] John xiv. 25, 26

But this is the very thing which we have already laid down to be said according to the form of a servant: *viz.*, that we are so to understand "It is not mine to give," as if it were said, This is not in the power of man to give; that so He may be understood to give it through that wherein He is God equal to the Father. "It is not mine," He says, "to give;" that is, I do not give these things by human power, but "to those for whom it is prepared by my Father;" but then take care you understand also, that if "all things which the Father hath are mine," [131] then this certainly is mine also, and I with the Father have prepared these things.

For I ask again, in what manner this is said, "If any man hear not my words, I will not judge him"? [132] For perhaps He has said here, "I will not judge him," in the same sense as there, "It is not mine to give." But what follows here? "I came not," He says, "to judge the world, but to save the world;" and then He adds, "He that rejecteth me, and receiveth not my words, hath one that judgeth him." Now here we should understand the Father, unless He had added, "The word that I have spoken, the same shall judge him in the last day." Well, then, will neither the Son judge, because He says, "I will not judge him," nor the Father, but the word which the Son hath spoken? Nay, but hear what yet follows: "For I," He says, "have not spoken of myself; but the Father which sent me, He gave me a commandment, what I should say, and what I should speak; and I know that His commandment is life everlasting: whatsoever I speak therefore, even as the Father said unto me, so I speak." If therefore the Son judges not, but "the word which the Son hath spoken;" and the word which the Son hath spoken therefore judges, because the Son "hath not spoken of Himself, but the Father who sent Him gave Him a commandment what He should say, and what He should speak:" then the Father assuredly judges, whose word it is which the Son hath spoken; and the same Son Himself is the very Word of the Father. For the commandment of the Father is not one thing, and the word of the Father another; for He hath called it both a word and a commandment. Let us see, therefore, whether perchance, when He says, "I have not spoken of myself," He meant to be understood thus—I am not born of myself. For if He speaks the word of the Father, then He speaks Himself, because He is Himself the Word of the Father. For ordinarily He says, "The Father gave to me;" by which He means it to be understood that the Father begat Him: not that He gave anything to Him, already existing and not possessing it; but that the very meaning of, To have given that He might have, is, To have begotten that He might be. For it is not, as with the creature, so with the Son of God before the incarnation and before He took upon Him our flesh, the Only-begotten by whom all things were made; that He *is* one thing, and *has* another: but He *is* in such way as to *be* what He *has*. And this is said more plainly, if any one is fit to receive it, in that place where He says: "For as the Father hath life in Himself, so hath He given to the Son

[131] John xvi. 15   [132] John xii. 47-50

to have life in Himself."[133] For He did not give to Him, already existing and not having life, that He should have life in Himself; inasmuch as, in that He *is*, He is life. Therefore "He gave to the Son to have life in Himself" means, He begat the Son to be unchangeable life, which is life eternal. Since, therefore, the Word of God is the Son of God, and the Son of God is "the true God and eternal life," [134] as John says in his *Epistle;* so here, what else are we to acknowledge when the Lord says, "The word which I have spoken, the same shall judge him at the last day," [135] and calls that very word the word of the Father and the commandment of the Father, and that very commandment everlasting life?" "And I know," He says, "that His commandment is life everlasting."

I ask, therefore, how we are to understand, "I will not judge him; but the Word which I have spoken shall judge him:" which appears from what follows to be so said, as if He would say, I will not judge; but the Word of the Father will judge. But the Word of the Father is the Son of God Himself. Is it to be so understood: I will not judge, but I will judge? How can this be true, unless in this way: *viz.*, I will not judge by human power, because I am the Son of man; but I will judge by the power of the Word, because I am the Son of God? Or if it still seems contradictory and inconsistent to say, I will not judge, but I will judge; what shall we say of that place where He says, "My doctrine is not mine?" How "mine," when "not mine?" For He did not say, *This* doctrine is not mine, but "*My* doctrine is not mine:" that which He called His own, the same He called not His own. How can this be true, unless He has called it His own in one relation; not His own, in another? According to the form of God, His own; according to the form of a servant, not His own. For when He says, "It is not mine, but His that sent me," [136] He makes us recur to the Word itself. For the doctrine of the Father is the Word of the Father, which is the Only Son. And what, too, does that mean, "He that believeth on me, believeth not on me?" [137] How believe on Him, yet not believe on Him? How can so opposite and inconsistent a thing be understood—"Whoso believeth on me," He says, "believeth not on me, but on Him that sent me"—unless you so understand it, Whoso believeth on me believeth not on that· which he sees, lest our hope should be in the creature; but on Him who took the creature, whereby He might appear to human eyes, and so might cleanse our hearts by faith, to contemplate Himself as equal to the Father? So that in turning the attention of believers to the Father, and saying, "Believeth not on me, but on Him that sent me," He certainly did not mean Himself to be separated from the Father, that is, from Him that sent Him; but that men might so believe on Himself, as they believe on the Father, to whom He is equal. And this He says in express terms in another place, "Ye believe in God, believe also in me:" [138] that is, in the same way as you believe in God, so also believe in me; because I and

[133] John v. 26   [134] 1 John v. 20   [135] John xii. 48   [136] John vii. 16   [137] John xii. 44   [138] John xiv. 1

the Father are One God. As therefore, here, He has as it were withdrawn the faith of men from Himself, and transferred it to the Father, by saying, "Believeth not on me, but on Him that sent me," from whom nevertheless He certainly did not separate Himself; so also, when He says, "It is not mine to give, but [it shall be given to them] for whom it is prepared by my Father," it is I think plain in what relation both are to be taken. For that other also is of the same kind, "I will not judge;" whereas He Himself shall judge the quick and dead.[139] But because He will not do so by human power, therefore, reverting to the Godhead, He raises the hearts of men upwards; which to lift up, He Himself came down.

CHAPTER XIII

DIVERSE THINGS ARE SPOKEN CONCERNING THE SAME CHRIST, ON ACCOUNT OF THE DIVERSE NATURES OF THE ONE HYPOSTASIS [THEANTHROPIC PERSON]. WHY IT IS SAID THAT THE FATHER WILL NOT JUDGE, BUT HAS GIVEN JUDGMENT TO THE SON

Yet unless the very same were the Son of man on account of the form of a servant which He took, who is the Son of God on account of the form of God in which He is; Paul the apostle would not say of the princes of this world, "For had they known it, they would not have crucified the Lord of glory." [140] For He was crucified after the form of a servant, and yet "the Lord of glory" was crucified. For that "taking" was such as to make God man, and man God. Yet what is said on account of what, and what according to what, the thoughtful, diligent, and pious reader discerns for himself, the Lord being his helper. For instance, we have said that He glorifies His own, as being God, and certainly then as being the Lord of glory; and yet the Lord of glory was crucified, because even God is rightly said to have been crucified, not after the power of the divinity, but after the weakness of the flesh:[141] just as we say, that He judges as God, that is, by divine power, not by human; and yet the man Himself will judge, just as the Lord of glory was crucified: for so He expressly says, "When the Son of man shall come in His glory, and all the holy angels with Him, and before Him shall be gathered all nations;" [142] and the rest that is foretold of the future judgment in that place even to the last sentence. And the Jews, inasmuch as they will be punished in that judgment for persisting in their wickedness, as it is elsewhere written, "shall look upon Him whom they have pierced." [143] For whereas both good and bad shall see the Judge of the quick and dead, without doubt the bad will not be able to see Him, except after the form in which He is the Son of man; but yet in the glory wherein He will judge, not in the lowliness wherein He was judged. But the ungodly without doubt will not see that form of God in which He is equal to the Father. For they are not

[139] 2 Tim. iv. 1   [140] 1 Cor. ii. 8   [141] 2 Cor. xiii. 4   [142] Matt. xxv. 31, 32   [143] Zech. xii. 10

pure in heart; and "Blessed are the pure in heart: for they shall see God." [144] And that sight is face to face,[145] the very sight that is promised as the highest reward to the just, and which will then take place when He "shall have delivered up the kingdom to God, even the Father;" and in this "kingdom" He means the sight of His own form also to be understood, the whole creature being made subject to God, including that wherein the Son of God was made the Son of man. Because, according to this creature, "The Son also Himself shall be subject unto Him, that put all things under Him, that God may be all in all." [146] Otherwise if the Son of God, judging in the form in which He is equal to the Father, shall appear when He judges to the ungodly also; what becomes of that which He promises, as some great thing, to him who loves Him, saying, "And I will love him, and will manifest myself to him?" [147] Wherefore He will judge as the Son of man, yet not by human power, but by that whereby He is the Son of God; and on the other hand, He will judge as the Son of God, yet not appearing in that [unincarnate] form in which He is God equal to the Father, but in that [incarnate form] in which He is the Son of man.

Therefore both ways of speaking may be used; the Son of man will judge, and, the Son of man will not judge: since the Son of man will judge, that the text may be true which says, "When the Son of man shall come, then before Him shall be gathered all nations;" and the Son of man will not judge, that the text may be true which says, "I will not judge him;" [148] and, "I seek not mine own glory: there is One that seeketh and judgeth." [149] For in respect to this, that in the judgment, not the form of God, but the form of the Son of man will appear, the Father Himself will not judge; for according to this it is said, "For the Father judgeth no man, but hath committed all judgment unto the Son." Whether this is said after that mode of speech which we have mentioned above, where it is said, "So hath He given to the Son to have life in Himself," [150] that it should signify that so He begat the Son; or, whether after that of which the apostle speaks, saying, "Wherefore God also hath highly exalted Him, and given Him a name which is above every name:"— (For this is said of the Son of man, in respect to whom the Son of God was raised from the dead; since He, being in the form of God equal to the Father, wherefrom He "emptied" Himself by taking the form of a servant, both acts and suffers, and receives, in that same form of a servant, what the apostle goes on to mention: "He humbled Himself, and became obedient unto death, even the death of the cross; wherefore God also hath highly exalted Him, and given Him a name which is above every name; that at the name of Jesus every knee should bow, of things in heaven, and things in earth, and things under the earth; and that every tongue should confess that Jesus Christ is Lord, in the Glory of God the Father:" [151])—whether then the words, "He hath committed all judgment unto the Son," are said ac-

---

[144] Matt. v. 8   [145] 1 Cor. xiii. 12   [146] 1 Cor. xv. 24-28   [147] John xiv. 21
[148] John xii. 47   [149] John viii. 50   [150] John v. 22, 26   [151] Phil. ii. 8-11

cording to this or that mode of speech; it sufficiently appears from this place, that if they were said according to that sense in which it is said, "He hath given to the Son to have life in Himself," it certainly would not be said, "The Father judgeth no man." For in respect to this, that the Father hath begotten the Son equal to Himself, He judges with Him. Therefore it is in respect to this that it is said, that in the judgment, not the form of God, but the form of the Son of man will appear. Not that He will not judge, who hath committed all judgment unto the Son, since the Son saith of Him, "There is One that seeketh and judgeth:" but it is so said, "The Father judgeth no man, but hath committed all judgment unto the Son;" as if it were said, No one will see the Father in the judgment of the quick and the dead, but all will see the Son: because He is also the Son of man, so that He can be seen even by the ungodly, since they too shall see Him whom they have pierced.

Lest, however, we may seem to conjecture this rather than to prove it clearly, let us produce a certain and plain sentence of the Lord Himself, by which we may show that this was the cause why He said, "The Father judgeth no man, but hath committed all judgment unto the Son," *viz.* because He will appear as Judge in the form of the Son of man, which is not the form of the Father, but of the Son; nor yet that form of the Son in which He is equal to the Father, but that in which He is less than the Father; in order that, in the judgment, He may be visible both to the good and to the bad. For a little while after He says, "Verily, verily, I say unto you, He that heareth my word, and believeth on Him that sent me, hath everlasting life, and shall not come into condemnation; but shall pass from death unto life." Now this life eternal is that sight which does not belong to the bad. Then follows, "Verily, verily, I say unto you, The hour is coming, and now is, when the dead shall hear the voice of the Son of God, and they that hear shall live." [152] And this is proper to the godly, who so hear of His incarnation, as to believe that He is the Son of God, that is, who so receive Him, as made for their sakes less than the Father, in the form of a servant, that they believe Him equal to the Father, in the form of God. And thereupon He continues, enforcing this very point, "For as the Father hath life in Himself, so hath He given to the Son to have life in Himself." And then He comes to the sight of His own glory, in which He shall come to judgment; which sight will be common to the ungodly and to the just. For He goes on to say, "And hath given Him authority to execute judgment also, because He is the Son of man." [153] I think nothing can be more clear. For inasmuch as the Son of God is equal to the Father, He does not receive this power of executing judgment, but He has it with the Father in secret; but He receives it, so that the good and the bad may see Him judging, inasmuch as He is the Son of man. Since the sight of the Son of man will be shown to the bad also: for the sight of the form of God will not be shown except to the pure in heart,

[152] John v. 24, 25   [153] John v. 25, 26

for they shall see God; that is, to the godly only, to whose love He promises this very thing, that He will show Himself to them. And see, accordingly, what follows: "Marvel not at this," He says. Why does He forbid us to marvel, unless it be that, in truth, every one marvels who does not understand, that therefore He said the Father gave Him power also to execute judgment, because He is the Son of man; whereas, it might rather have been anticipated that He would say, since He is the Son of God? But because the wicked are not able to see the Son of God as He is in the form of God equal to the Father, but yet it is necessary that both the just and the wicked should see the Judge of the quick and dead, when they will be judged in His presence; 'Marvel not at this," He says, "for the hour is coming, in the which all that are in the graves shall hear His voice, and shall come forth; they that have done good, unto the resurrection of life; and they that have done evil, unto the resurrection of damnation." [154] For this purpose, then, it was necessary that He should therefore receive that power, because He is the Son of man, in order that all in rising again might see Him in the form in which He can be seen by all, but by some to damnation, by others to life eternal. And what is life eternal, unless that sight which is not granted to the ungodly? "That they might know Thee," He says, "the One true God, and Jesus Christ, whom Thou hast sent." [155] And how are they to know Jesus Christ Himself also, unless as the One true God, who will show Himself to them; not as He will show Himself, in the form of the Son of man, to those also that shall be punished?

He is "good," according to that sight, according to which God appears to the pure in heart; for "truly God is good unto Israel, even to such as are of a clean heart." [156] But when the wicked shall see the Judge, He will not seem good to them; because they will not rejoice in their heart to see Him, but all "kindreds of the earth shall then wail because of Him," [157] namely, as being reckoned in the number of all the wicked and unbelievers. On this account also He replied to him, who had called Him Good Master, when seeking advice of Him how he might attain eternal life, "Why askest thou me about good? there is none good but One, that is, God." [158] And yet the Lord Himself, in another place, calls man good: "A good man," He says, "out of the good treasure of his heart, bringeth forth good things: and an evil man, out of the evil treasure of his heart, bringeth forth evil things." [159] But because that man was seeking eternal life, and eternal life consists in that contemplation in which God is seen, not for punishment, but for everlasting joy; and because he did not understand with whom he was speaking, and thought Him to be only the Son of man: Why, He says, askest thou me about good? that is, with respect to that form which thou seest, why askest thou about good, and callest me, according to what thou seest, Good Master? This is the form of the Son of man, the form which has been taken, the form that

[154] John v. 22-29   [155] John xvii. 3   [156] Ps. lxxiii. 1   [157] Apoc. i. 7   [158] Matt. xix. 17   [159] Matt. xii. 35

will appear in judgment, not only to the righteous, but also to the ungodly; and the sight of this form will not be for good to those who are wicked. But there is a sight of that form of mine, in which when I was, I thought it not robbery to be equal with God: but in order to take this form I emptied myself.[160] That one God, therefore, the Father and the Son and the Holy Spirit, who will not appear, except for joy which cannot be taken away from the just; for which future joy he sighs, who says, "One thing have I desired of the Lord, that will I seek after; that I may dwell in the house of the Lord all the days of my life, to behold the beauty of the Lord:" [161] that one God, therefore, Himself, I say, is alone good, for this reason, that no one sees Him for sorrow and wailing, but only for salvation and true joy. If you understand me after this latter form, then I am good; but if according to that former only, then why askest thou me about good? If thou art among those who "shall look upon Him whom they have pierced," [162] that very sight itself will be evil to them, because it will be penal. That after this meaning, then, the Lord said, "Why askest thou me about good? there is none good but One, that is, God," is probable upon those proofs which I have alleged, because that sight of God, whereby we shall contemplate the substance of God unchangeable and invisible to human eyes (which is promised to the saints alone; which the Apostle Paul speaks of, as "face to face;" [163] and of which the Apostle John says, "We shall be like Him, for we shall see Him as He is;" [164] and of which it is said, "One thing have I desired of the Lord, that I may behold the beauty of the Lord," and of which the Lord Himself says, "I will both love him, and will manifest myself to him;" [165] and on account of which alone we cleanse our hearts by faith, that we may be those "pure in heart who are blessed for they shall see God:" [166] and whatever else is spoken of that sight: which whosoever turns the eye of love to seek it, may find most copiously scattered through all the Scriptures)—that sight alone, I say, is our chief good, for the attaining of which we are directed to do whatever we do aright. But that sight of the Son of man which is foretold, when all nations shall be gathered before Him, and shall say to Him, "Lord, when saw we Thee an hungered, or thirsty, etc.?" will neither be a good to the ungodly, who shall be sent into everlasting fire, nor the chief good to the righteous. For He still goes on to call these to the kingdom which has been prepared for them from the foundation of the world. For, as He will say to those, "Depart into everlasting fire;" so to these, "Come, ye blessed of my Father, inherit the kingdom prepared for you." And as those will go into everlasting burning; so the righteous will go into life eternal. But what is life eternal, except "that they may know Thee," He says, "the One true God, and Jesus Christ, whom Thou hast sent"? [167] but know Him now in that glory of which He says to the Father, "Which I had with Thee before the world was." [168] For then He will deliver up the kingdom to God, even the

[160] Phil. ii. 6, 7   [161] Ps. xxvii. 4   [162] Zech. xii. 10   [163] 1 Cor. xiii. 12   [164] 1 John iii. 2   [165] John xiv. 21   [166] Matt. v. 8   [167] Matt. xxv. 37, 41, 34   [168] John xvii. 3-5

Father,[169] that the good servant may enter into the joy of his Lord,[170] and that He may hide those whom God keeps in the hiding of His countenance from the confusion of men, namely, of those men who shall then be confounded by hearing this sentence; of which evil hearing "the righteous man shall not be afraid" [171] if only he be kept in "the tabernacle," that is, in the true faith of the Catholic Church, from "the strife of tongues," [172] that is, from the sophistries of heretics. But if there is any other explanation of the words of the Lord, where He says, "Why asketh thou me about good? there is none good; but One, that is, God;" provided only that the substance of the Father be not therefore believed to be of greater goodness than that of the Son, according to which He is the Word by whom all things were made; and if there is nothing in it abhorrent from sound doctrine; let us securely use it, and not one explanation only, but as many as we are able to find. For so much the more powerfully are the heretics proved wrong, the more outlets are open for avoiding their snares. But let us now start afresh, and address ourselves to the consideration of that which still remains.

[169] 1 Cor. xv. 24   [170] Matt. xxv. 21, 23   [171] Ps. cxii. 7   [172] Ps. xxxi. 21

BOOK TWO

Augustine pursues his defense of the equality of the Trinity; and in treating of the sending of the Son and of the Holy Spirit, and of the various appearances of God, demonstrates that He who is sent is not therefore less than He who sends, because the One has sent, the Other has been sent; but that the Trinity, being in all things equal, and alike in its own nature unchangeable and invisible and omnipresent, works indivisibly in each sending or appearance.

PREFACE

WHEN men seek to know God, and bend their minds according to the capacity of human weakness to the understanding of the Trinity; learning, as they must, by experience, the wearisome difficulties of the task, whether from the sight itself of the mind striving to gaze upon light unapproachable, or, indeed, from the manifold and various modes of speech employed in the sacred writings (wherein, as it seems to me, the mind is nothing else but roughly exercised, in order that it may find sweetness when glorified by the grace of Christ);—such men, I say, when they have dispelled every ambiguity, and arrived at something certain, ought of all others most easily to make allowance for those who err in the investigation of so deep a secret. But there are two things most hard to bear with, in the case of those who are in error: hasty assumption before the truth is made plain; and, when it has been made plain, defense of the falsehood thus hastily assumed. From which two faults, inimical as they are to the finding out of the truth, and to the handling of the divine and sacred books, should God, as I pray and hope, defend and protect me with the shield of His good will,[1] and with the grace of His mercy, I will not be slow to search out the substance of God, whether through His Scripture or through the creature. For both of these are set forth for our contemplation to this end, that He may Himself be sought, and Himself be loved, who inspired the one, and created the other. Nor shall I be afraid of giving my opinion, in which I shall more desire to be examined by the upright, than fear to be carped at by the perverse. For charity, most excellent and unassuming, gratefully accepts the dovelike eye; but for the dog's tooth nothing remains, save either to shun it by the most cautious humility, or to blunt it by the most solid truth; and far rather would I be censured by any one whatsoever, than be praised by either the erring or the flatterer. For the lover of truth need fear no one's censure. For he that censures must be either enemy or friend. And if an enemy reviles, he must be borne with:

[1] Ps. v. 12

but a friend, if he errs, must be taught; if he teaches, listened to. But if one who errs praises you, he confirms your error; if one who flatters, he seduces you into error. "Let the righteous," therefore, "smite me, it shall be a kindness; and let him reprove me; but the oil of the sinner shall not anoint my head." [2]

CHAPTER I

THERE IS A DOUBLE RULE FOR UNDERSTANDING THE SCRIPTURAL MODES OF SPEECH CONCERNING THE SON OF GOD. THESE MODES OF SPEECH ARE OF A THREEFOLD KIND

Wherefore, although we hold most firmly, concerning our Lord Jesus Christ, what may be called the canonical rule, as it is both disseminated through the Scriptures, and has been demonstrated by learned and Catholic handlers of the same Scriptures, namely, that the Son of God is both understood to be equal to the Father according to the form of God in which He is, and less than the Father according to the form of a servant which He took; [3] in which form He was found to be not only less than the Father, but also less than the Holy Spirit; and not only so, but less even than Himself— not than Himself who was, but than Himself who is; because, by taking the form of a servant, He did not lose the form of God, as the testimonies of the Scriptures taught us, to which we have referred in the former book: yet there are some things in the sacred text so put as to leave it ambiguous to which rule they are rather to be referred; whether to that by which we understand the Son as less, in that He has taken upon Him the creature, or to that by which we understand that the Son is not indeed less than, but equal to the Father, but yet that He is from Him, God of God, Light of light. For we call the Son God *of* God; but the Father, God only; not *of* God. Whence it is plain that the Son has another *of* whom He is, and to whom He is Son; but that the Father has not a Son *of* whom He is, but only to whom He is father. For every son is what he is, *of* his father, and is son to his father; but no father is what he is, *of* his son, but is father to his son.

Some things, then, are so put in the Scriptures concerning the Father and the Son, as to intimate the unity and equality of their substance; as, for instance, "I and the Father are one;" [4] and, "Who, being in the form of God, thought it not robbery to be equal with God;" [5] and whatever other texts there are of the kind. And some, again, are so put that they show the Son as less on account of the form of a servant, that is, of His having taken upon Him the creature of a changeable and human substance; as, for instance, that which says, "For my Father is greater than I;" [6] and, "The Father judgeth no man, but hath committed all judgment unto the Son." For a little after he goes on to say, "And hath given Him authority to execute

---

[2] Ps. cxli. 5   [3] Phil. ii. 6, 7   [4] John x. 30   [5] Phil. ii. 6   [6] John xiv. 28

judgment also, because He is the Son of man." And further, some are so put as to show Him at that time neither as less nor as equal, but only to intimate that He is of the Father; as, for instance, that which says, "For as the Father hath life in Himself, so hath He given to the Son to have life in Himself;" and that other: "The Son can do nothing of Himself, but what He seeth the Father do."[7] For if we shall take this to be therefore so said, because the Son is less in the form taken from the creature, it will follow that the Father must have walked on the water, or opened the eyes with clay and spittle of some other one born blind, and have done the other things which the Son appearing in the flesh did among men, before the Son did them;[8] in order that He might be able to do those things, who said that the Son was not able to do anything of Himself, except what He hath seen the Father do. Yet who, even though he were mad, would think this? It remains, therefore, that these texts are so expressed, because the life of the Son is unchangeable as that of the Father is, and yet He is of the Father; and the working of the Father and of the Son is indivisible, and yet so to work is given to the Son from Him of whom He Himself is, that is, from the Father; and the Son so sees the Father, as that He is the Son in the very seeing Him. For to be of the Father, that is, to be born of the Father, is to Him nothing else than to see the Father; and to see Him working, is nothing else than to work with Him: but therefore not from Himself, because He is not from Himself. And, therefore, those things which "He sees the Father do, these also doeth the Son likewise," because He is of the Father. For He neither does other things in like manner, as a painter paints other pictures, in the same way as he sees others to have been painted by another man; nor the same things in a different manner, as the body expresses the same letters, which the mind has thought; but "whatsoever things," saith He, "the Father doeth, these same things also doeth the Son likewise."[9] He has said both "these same things," and "likewise;" and hence the working of both the Father and the Son is indivisible and equal, but it is from the Father to the Son. Therefore the Son cannot do anything of Himself, except what He seeth the Father do. From this rule, then, whereby the Scriptures so speak as to mean, not to set forth one as less than another, but only to show which is of which, some have drawn this meaning, as if the Son were said to be less. And some among ourselves who are more unlearned and least instructed in these things, endeavoring to take these texts according to the form of a servant, and so misinterpreting them, are troubled. And to prevent this, the rule in question is to be observed, whereby the Son is not less, but it is simply intimated that He is of the Father, in which words not His inequality but His birth is declared.

[7] John v. 22, 27, 26, 19   [8] Matt. xiv. 26, and John ix. 6, 7   [9] John v. 19

CHAPTER II

THAT SOME WAYS OF SPEAKING CONCERNING THE SON ARE TO BE UNDERSTOOD ACCORDING TO EITHER RULE

There are, then, some things in the sacred books, as I began by saying, so put, that it is doubtful to which they are to be referred: whether to that rule whereby the Son is less on account of His having taken the creature; or whether to that whereby it is intimated that although equal, yet He is of the Father. And in my opinion, if this is in such way doubtful, that which it really is can neither be explained nor discerned, then such passages may without danger be understood according to either rule, as that, for instance, "My doctrine is not mine, but His that sent me." [10] For this may both be taken according to the form of a servant, as we have already treated it in the former book; [11] or according to the form of God, in which He is in such way equal to the Father, that He is yet of the Father. For according to the form of God, as the Son is not one and His life another, but the life itself is the Son; so the Son is not one and His doctrine another, but the doctrine itself is the Son. And hence, as the text, "He hath given life to the Son," is no otherwise to be understood than, He hath begotten the Son, who is life; so also when it is said, He hath given doctrine to the Son, it may be rightly understood to mean, He hath begotten the Son, who is doctrine; so that, when it is said, "My doctrine is not mine, but His who sent me," it is so to be understood as if it were, I am not from myself, but from Him who sent me.

CHAPTER III

SOME THINGS CONCERNING THE HOLY SPIRIT ARE TO BE UNDERSTOOD ACCORDING TO THE ONE RULE ONLY

For even of the Holy Spirit, of whom it is not said, "He emptied Himself, and took upon Him the form of a servant;" yet the Lord Himself says, "Howbeit, when He the Spirit of Truth is come, He will guide you into all truth. For He shall not speak of Himself, but whatsoever He shall hear that shall He speak; and He will show you things to come. He shall glorify me; for He shall receive of mine, and shall show it unto you." And except He had immediately gone on to say after this, "All things that the Father hath are mine; therefore said I, that He shall take of mine, and shall show it unto you;" [12] it might, perhaps, have been believed that the Holy Spirit was so born of Christ, as Christ is of the Father. Since He had said of Himself, "My doctrine is not mine, but His that sent me;" but of the Holy Spirit, "For He shall not speak of Himself, but whatsoever he shall hear, that shall

[10] John vii. 16   [11] See above, Book I. c. 12   [12] John xvi. 13-15

He speak;" and, "For He shall receive of mine, and shall show it unto you." But because He has rendered the reason why He said, "He shall receive of mine" (for He says, "All things that the Father hath are mine; therefore said I, that He shall take of mine"); it remains that the Holy Spirit be understood to have of that which is the Father's, as the Son also hath. And how can this be, unless according to that which we have said above, "But when the Comforter is come, whom I will send unto you from the Father, even the Spirit of truth which proceedeth from the Father, He shall testify of me"? [13] He is said, therefore, not to speak of Himself, in that He proceedeth from the Father; and as it does not follow that the Son is less because He said, "The Son can do nothing of Himself, but what He seeth the Father do" (for He has not said this according to the form of a servant, but according to the form of God, as we have already shown, and these words do not set Him forth as less than, but as of the Father), so it is not brought to pass that the Holy Spirit is less, because it is said of Him, "For He shall not speak of Himself, but whatsoever He shall hear, that shall He speak;" for the words belong to Him as *proceeding* from the Father. But whereas both the Son is of the Father, and the Holy Spirit proceeds from the Father, why both are not called sons, and both not said to be begotten, but the former is called the one only-begotten Son, and the latter, *viz.* the Holy Spirit, neither son nor begotten, because if begotten, then certainly a son, we will discuss in another place, if God shall grant, and so far as He shall grant. [14]

CHAPTER IV

THE GLORIFICATION OF THE SON BY THE FATHER DOES NOT PROVE INEQUALITY

But here also let them wake up if they can, who have thought this, too, to be a testimony on their side, to show that the Father is greater than the Son, because the Son hath said, "Father, glorify me." Why, the Holy Spirit also glorifies Him. Pray, is the Spirit, too, greater than He? Moreover, if on that account the Holy Spirit glorifies the Son, because He shall receive of that which is the Son's, and shall therefore receive of that which is the Son's because all things that the Father has are the Son's also; it is evident that when the Holy Spirit glorifies the Son, the Father glorifies the Son. Whence it may be perceived that all things that the Father hath are not only of the Son, but also of the Holy Spirit, because the Holy Spirit is able to glorify the Son, whom the Father glorifies. But if he who glorifies is greater than he whom he glorifies, let them allow that those are equal who mutually glorify each other. But it is written, also, that the Son glorifies the Father; for He says, "I have glorified Thee on the earth." [15] Truly let them beware lest the Holy Spirit be thought greater than both, because He glorifies the Son whom

[13] John xv. 26   [14] Below, Bk. XV. c. 25   [15] John xvii. 1, 4

the Father glorifies, while it is not written that He Himself is glorified either by the Father or by the Son.

CHAPTER V

But being proved wrong so far, men betake themselves to saying, that he who sends is greater than he who is sent: therefore the Father is greater than the Son, because the Son continually speaks of Himself as being sent by the Father; and the Father is also greater than the Holy Spirit, because Jesus has said of the Spirit, "Whom the Father will send in my name;" [16] and the Holy Spirit is less than both, because both the Father sends Him, as we have said, and the Son, when He says, "But if I depart, I will send Him unto you." I first ask, then, in this inquiry, whence and whither the Son was sent. "I," He says, "came forth from the Father, and am come into the world." [17] Therefore, to be sent, is to come forth from the Father, and to come into the world. What, then, is that which the same evangelist says concerning Him, "He was in the world, and the world was made by Him, and the world knew Him not;" and then he adds, "He came unto His own?" [18] Certainly He was sent thither, whither He came; but if He was sent into the world, because He came forth from the Father, then He both came into the world and was in the world. He was sent therefore thither, where He already was. For consider that, too, which is written in the prophet, that God said, "Do not I fill heaven and earth?" [19] If this is said of the Son (for some will have it understood that the Son Himself spoke either by the prophets or in the prophets), whither was He sent except to the place where He already was? For He who says, "I fill heaven and earth," was everywhere. But if it is said of the Father, where could He be without His own word and without His own wisdom, which "reacheth from one end to another mightily, and sweetly ordereth all things?" [20] But He cannot be anywhere without His own Spirit. Therefore, if God is everywhere, His Spirit also is everywhere. Therefore, the Holy Spirit, too, was sent thither, where He already was. For he, too, who finds no place to which he might go from the presence of God, and who says, "If I ascend up into heaven, Thou art there; if I shall go down into hell, behold, Thou art there;" wishing it to be understood that God is present everywhere, named in the previous verse His Spirit; for He says, "Whither shall I go from Thy Spirit? or whither shall I flee from Thy presence?" [21]

For this reason, then, if both the Son and the Holy Spirit are sent thither

---

[16] John xiv. 26   [17] John xvi. 7, 28   [18] John i. 10, 11   [19] Jer. xxiii. 24   [20] Wisd. viii. 1   [21] Ps. cxxxix. 8, 7

where they were, we must inpuire, how that sending, whether of the Son or of the Holy Spirit, is to be understood; for of the Father alone, we nowhere read that He is sent. Now, of the Son, the apostle writes thus: "But when the fullness of the time was come, God sent forth His Son, made of a woman, made under the law, to redeem them that were under the law." [22] "He sent," he says, "His Son, made of a woman." And by this term, woman,[23] what Catholic does not know that he did not wish to signify the privation of virginity; but, according to a Hebraism, the difference of sex? When, therefore, he says, "God sent His Son, made of a woman," he sufficiently shows that the Son was "sent" in this very way, in that He was "made of a woman." Therefore, in that He was born of God, He was in the world; but in that He was born of Mary, He was sent and came into the world. Moreover, He could not be sent by the Father without the Holy Spirit, not only because the Father, when He sent Him, that is, when He made Him of a woman, is certainly understood not to have so made Him without His own Spirit; but also because it is most plainly and expressly said in the Gospel in answer to the Virgin Mary, when she asked of the angel, "How shall this be?" "The Holy Ghost shall come upon thee, and the power of the Highest shall overshadow thee." [24] And Matthew says, "She was found with child of the Holy Ghost." [25] Although, too, in the prophet Isaiah, Christ Himself is understood to say of His own future advent, "And now the Lord God, and His Spirit, hath sent me." [26]

Perhaps some one may wish to drive us to say, that the Son is sent also by Himself, because the conception and childbirth of Mary is the working of the Trinity, by whose act of creating all things are created. And how, he will go on to say, has the Father sent Him, if He sent Himself? To whom I answer first, by asking him to tell me, if he can, in what manner the Father hath sanctified Him, if He hath sanctified Himself? For the same Lord says both; "Say ye of Him," He says, "whom the Father hath sanctified and sent into the world, Thou blasphemest, because I said, I am the Son of God;" [27] while in another place He says, "And for their sake I sanctify myself." [28] I ask, also, in what manner the Father delivered Him, if He delivered Himself? For the Apostle Paul says both: "Who," he says, "spared not His own Son, but delivered Him up for us all;" [29] while elsewhere he says of the Saviour Himself, "Who loved me, and delivered Himself for me." [30] He will reply, I suppose, if he has a right sense in these things, Because the will of the Father and the Son is one, and their working indivisible. In like manner, then, let him understand the incarnation and nativity of the Virgin, wherein the Son is understood as sent, to have been wrought by one and the same operation of the Father and of the Son indivisibly; the Holy Spirit certainly not being thence excluded, of whom it is expressly said, "She was found with child by the Holy Ghost." For perhaps our meaning will be more plainly

[22] Gal. iv. 4, 5　　[23] *Mulier*　　[24] Luke i. 34, 35　　[25] Matt. i. 18　　[26] Isa. xlviii. 16　　[27] John x. 36　　[28] John xvii. 19　　[29] Rom. viii. 32　　[30] Gal. ii. 20

unfolded, if we ask in what manner God sent His Son. He commanded that He should come, and He, complying with the commandment, came. Did He then request, or did He only suggest? But whichever of these it was, certainly it was done by a word, and the Word of God is the Son of God Himself. Wherefore, since the Father sent Him by a word, His being sent was the work of both the Father and His Word; therefore the same Son was sent by the Father and the Son, because the Son Himself is the Word of the Father. For who would embrace so impious an opinion as to think the Father to have uttered a word in time, in order that the eternal Son might thereby be sent and might appear in the flesh in the fullness of time? But assuredly it was in that Word of God itself which was in the beginning with God and was God, namely, in the wisdom itself of God, apart from time, at what time that wisdom must appear in the flesh. Therefore, since without any commencement of time, the Word was in the beginning, and the Word was with God, and the Word was God, it was in the Word itself without any time, at what time the Word was to be made flesh and dwell among us.[31] And when this fullness of time had come, "God sent His Son, made of a woman," [32] that is, made in time, that the Incarnate Word might appear to men; while it was in that Word Himself, apart from time, at what time this was to be done; for the order of times is in the eternal wisdom of God without time. Since, then, that the Son should appear in the flesh was wrought by both the Father and the Son, it is fitly said that He who appeared in that flesh was sent, and that He who did not appear in it, sent Him; because those things which are transacted outwardly before the bodily eyes have their existence from the inward structure of the spiritual nature, and on that account are fitly said to be sent. Further, that form of man which He took is the person of the Son, not also of the Father; on which account the invisible Father, together with the Son, who with the Father is invisible, is said to have sent the same Son by making Him visible. But if He became visible in such way as to cease to be invisible with the Father, that is, if the substance of the invisible Word were turned by a change and transition into a visible creature, then the Son would be so understood to be sent by the Father, that He would be found to be only sent; not also, with the Father, sending. But since He so took the form of a servant, as that the unchangeable form of God remained, it is clear that that which became apparent in the Son was done by the Father and the Son not being apparent; that is, that by the invisible Father, with the invisible Son, the same Son Himself was sent so as to be visible. Why, therefore, does He say, "Neither came I of myself?" This, we may now say, is said according to the form of a servant, in the same way as it is said, "I judge no man." [33]

If, therefore, He is said to be sent, in so far as He appeared outwardly in the bodily creature, who inwardly in His spiritual nature is always hidden from the eyes of mortals, it is now easy to understand also of the Holy Spirit

[31] John i. 1, 2, 14   [32] Gal. iv. 4   [33] John viii. 42, 15

why He too is said to be sent. For in due time a certain outward appearance of the creature was wrought, wherein the Holy Spirit might be visibly shown; whether when He descended upon the Lord Himself in a bodily shape as a dove,[34] or when, ten days having passed since His ascension, on the day of Pentecost a sound came suddenly from heaven as of a rushing mighty wind, and cloven tongues like as of fire were seen upon them, and it sat upon each of them.[35] This operation, visibly exhibited, and presented to mortal eyes, is called the sending of the Holy Spirit; not that His very substance appeared, in which He himself also is invisible and unchangeable, like the Father and the Son, but that the hearts of men, touched by things seen outwardly, might be turned from the manifestation in time of Him as coming to His hidden eternity as ever present.

CHAPTER VI

THE CREATURE IS NOT SO TAKEN BY THE HOLY SPIRIT AS FLESH IS BY THE WORD

It is, then, for this reason nowhere written, that the Father is greater than the Holy Spirit, or that the Holy Spirit is less than God the Father, because the creature in which the Holy Spirit was to appear was not taken in the same way as the Son of man was taken, as the form in which the person of the Word of God Himself should be set forth; not that He might possess the word of God, as other holy and wise men have possessed it, but "above His fellows;"[36] not certainly that He possessed the word more than they, so as to be of more surpassing wisdom than the rest were, but that He was the very Word Himself. For the word in the flesh is one thing, and the Word made flesh is another; i.e. the word in man is one thing, the Word that is man is another. For flesh is put for man, where it is said, "The Word was made flesh;"[37] and again, "And all flesh shall see the salvation of God."[38] For it does not mean flesh without soul and without mind; but "all flesh," is the same as if it were said, every man. The creature, then, in which the Holy Spirit should appear, was not so taken, as that flesh and human form were taken, of the Virgin Mary. For the Spirit did not beatify the dove, or the wind, or the fire, and join them for ever to Himself and to His person in unity and "fashion." Nor, again, is the nature of the Holy Spirit mutable and changeable; so that these things were not made of the creature, but He himself was turned and changed first into one and then into another, as water is changed into ice. But these things appeared at the seasons at which they ought to have appeared, the creature serving the Creator, and being changed and converted at the command of Him who remains immutably in Himself, in order to signify and manifest Him in such way as it was fit He should be signified and manifested to mortal men. Accordingly, although

[34] Matt. iii. 16　　[35] Acts ii. 2-4　　[36] Heb. i. 9　　[37] John i. 14　　[38] Luke iii. 6

that dove is called the Spirit:[39] and in speaking of that fire, "There appeared unto them," he says, "cloven tongues, like as of fire, and it sat upon each of them; and they began to speak with other tongues, as the Spirit gave them utterance;"[40] in order to show that the Spirit was manifested by that fire, as by the dove; yet we cannot call the Holy Spirit both God and a dove, or both God and fire, in the same way as we call the Son both God and man; nor as we call the Son the Lamb of God; which not only John the Baptist says, "Behold the Lamb of God,"[41] but also John the Evangelist sees the Lamb slain in the Apocalypse.[42] For that prophetic vision was not shown to bodily eyes through bodily forms, but in the spirit through spiritual images of bodily things. But whosoever saw that dove and that fire, saw them with their eyes. Although it may perhaps be disputed concerning the fire, whether it was seen by the eyes or in the spirit, on account of the form of the sentence. For the text does not say, They saw cloven tongues like fire, but, "There appeared to them." But we are not wont to say with the same meaning, It appeared to me; as we say, I saw. And in those spiritual visions of corporeal images the usual expressions are, both, It appeared to me; and, I saw: but in those things which are shown to the eyes through express corporeal forms, the common expression is not, It appeared to me; but, I saw. There may, therefore, be a question raised respecting that fire, how it was seen; whether within in the spirit as it were outwardly, or really outwardly before the eyes of the flesh. But of that dove, which is said to have descended in a bodily form, no one ever doubted that it was seen by the eyes. Nor, again, as we call the Son a Rock (for it is written, "And that Rock was Christ"[43]), can we so call the Spirit a dove or fire. For that rock was a thing already created, and after the mode of its action was called by the name of Christ, whom it signified; like the stone placed under Jacob's head, and also anointed, which he took in order to signify the Lord;[44] or as Isaac was Christ, when he carried the wood for the sacrifice of himself.[45] A particular significative action was added to those already existing things; they did not, as that dove and fire, suddenly come into being in order simply so to signify. The dove and the fire, indeed, seem to me more like that flame which appeared to Moses in the bush,[46] or that pillar which the people followed in the wilderness,[47] or the thunders and lightnings which came when the Law was given in the mount.[48] For the corporeal form of these things came into being for the very purpose, that it might signify something, and then pass away.

[39] Matt. iii. 16   [40] Acts ii. 3, 4   [41] John i. 29   [42] Apoc. v. 6   [43] 1 Cor. x. 4
[44] Gen. xxviii. 18   [45] Gen. xxii. 6   [46] Ex. iii. 2   [47] Ex. xiii. 21, 22   [48] Ex. xix. 16

CHAPTER VII

A DOUBT RAISED ABOUT DIVINE APPEARANCES

The Holy Spirit, then, is also said to be sent, on account of these corporeal forms which came into existence in time, in order to signify and manifest Him, as He must needs be manifested, to human senses; yet He is not said to be less than the Father, as the Son, because He was in the form of a servant, is said to be; because that form of a servant inhered in the unity of the person of the Son, but those corporeal forms appeared for a time, in order to show what was necessary to be shown, and then ceased to be. Why, then, is not the Father also said to be sent, through those corporeal forms, the fire of the bush, and the pillar of cloud or of fire, and the lightnings in the mount, and whatever other things of the kind appeared at that time, when (as we have learned from Scripture testimony) He spake face to face with the fathers, if He Himself was manifested by those modes and forms of the creature, as exhibited and presented corporeally to human sight? But if the Son was manifested by them, why is He said to be sent so long after, when He was made of a woman, as the apostle says, "But when the fullness of time was come, God sent forth His Son, made of a woman," [49] seeing that He was sent also before, when He appeared to the fathers by those changeable forms of the creature? Or if He cannot rightly be said to be sent, unless when the Word was made flesh, why is the Holy Spirit said to be sent, of whom no such incarnation was ever wrought? But if by those visible things, which are put before us in the Law and in the prophets, neither the Father nor the Son but the Holy Spirit was manifested, why also is He said to be sent now, when He was sent also before after these modes?

In the perplexity of this inquiry, the Lord helping us, we must ask, first, whether the Father, or the Son, or the Holy Spirit; or whether, sometimes the Father, sometimes the Son, sometimes the Holy Spirit; or whether it was without any distinction of persons, in such way as the one and only God is spoken of, that is, that the Trinity itself appeared to the Fathers by those forms of the creature. Next, whichever of these alternatives shall have been found or thought true, whether for this purpose only the creature was fashioned, wherein God, as He judged it suitable at that time, should be shown to human sight; or whether angels, who already existed, were so sent, as to speak in the person of God, taking a corporeal form from the corporeal creature, for the purpose of their ministry, as each had need; or else, according to the power the Creator has given them, changing and converting their own body itself, to which they are not subject, but govern it as subject to themselves, into whatever appearances they would that were suited and apt to their several actions. Lastly, we shall discern that which it was our purpose to ask, viz. whether the Son and the Holy Spirit were also sent before; and,

[49] Gal. iv. 4

if they were so sent, what difference there is between that sending, and the one which we read of in the Gospel; or whether in truth neither of them was sent, except when either the Son was made of the Virgin Mary, or the Holy Spirit appeared in a visible form, whether in the dove or in tongues of fire.

CHAPTER VIII

THE ENTIRE TRINITY INVISIBLE

Let us therefore say nothing of those who, with an over carnal mind, have thought the nature of the Word of God, and the Wisdom, which, "remaining in herself, maketh all things new," [50] whom we call the only Son of God, not only to be changeable, but also to be visible. For these, with more audacity than religion, bring a very dull heart to the inquiry into divine things. For whereas the soul is a spiritual substance, and whereas itself also was made, yet could not be made by any other than by Him by whom all things were made, and without whom nothing is made, [51] it, although changeable, is yet not visible; and this they have believed to be the case with the Word Himself and with the Wisdom of God itself, by which the soul was made; whereas this Wisdom is not only invisible, as the soul also is, but likewise unchangeable, which the soul is not. It is in truth the same unchangeableness in it, which is referred to when it was said, "Remaining in herself she maketh all things new." Yet these people, endeavoring, as it were, to prop up their error in its fall by testimonies of the divine Scriptures, adduce the words of the Apostle Paul; and take that, which is said of the one only God, in whom the Trinity itself is understood, to be said only of the Father, and neither of the Son nor of the Holy Spirit: "Now unto the King eternal, immortal, invisible, the only wise God, be honor and glory for ever and ever;" [52] and that other passage, "The blessed and only Potentate, the King of kings, and Lord of lords; who only hath immortality, dwelling in the light which no man can approach unto; whom no man hath seen, nor can see." [53] How these passages are to be understood, I think we have already discoursed sufficiently.

CHAPTER IX

AGAINST THOSE WHO BELIEVED THE FATHER ONLY TO BE IMMORTAL AND INVISIBLE. THE TRUTH TO BE SOUGHT BY PEACEFUL STUDY

But they who will have these texts understood only of the Father, and not of the Son or the Holy Spirit, declare the Son to be visible, not by having taken flesh of the Virgin, but aforetime also in Himself. For He Himself, they say, appeared to the eyes of the Fathers. And if you say to them, In whatever manner, then, the Son is visible in Himself, in that manner also He is

[50] Wisd. vii. 27   [51] John i. 3   [52] 1 Tim. i. 17   [53] 1 Tim. vi. 15, 16

mortal in Himself; so that it plainly follows that you would have this saying also understood only of the Father, *viz.*, "Who only hath immortality;" for if the Son is mortal from having taken upon Him our flesh, then allow that it is on account of this flesh that He is also visible: they reply, that it is not on account of this flesh that they say that the Son is mortal; but that, just as He was also before visible, so He was also before mortal. For if they say the Son is mortal from having taken our flesh, then it is not the Father alone without the Son who hath immortality; because His Word also has immortality, by which all things were made. For He did not therefore lose His immortality, because He took mortal flesh; seeing that it could not happen even to the human soul, that it should die with the body, when the Lord Himself says, "Fear not them which kill the body, but are not able to kill the soul." [54] Or, forsooth, also the Holy Spirit took flesh: concerning whom certainly they will, without doubt, be troubled to say—if the Son is mortal on account of taking our flesh—in what manner they understand that the Father only has immortality without the Son and the Holy Spirit, since, indeed, the Holy Spirit did not take our flesh; and if He has not immortality, then the Son is not mortal on account of taking our flesh; but if the Holy Spirit has immortality, then it is not said only of the Father, "Who only hath immortality." And therefore they think they are able to prove that the Son in Himself was mortal also before the incarnation, because changeableness itself is not unfitly called mortality, according to which the soul also is said to die; not because it is changed and turned into body, or into some substance other than itself, but because, whatever in its own self-same substance is now after another mode than it once was, is discovered to be mortal, in so far as it has ceased to be what it was. Because then, they say, before the Son of God was born of the Virgin Mary, He Himself appeared to our fathers, not in one and the same form only, but in many forms; first, in one form, then in another; He is both visible in Himself, because His substance was visible to mortal eyes, when He had not yet taken our flesh, and mortal, inasmuch as He is changeable. And so also the Holy Spirit, who appeared at one time as a dove, and another time as fire. Whence, they say, the following texts do not belong to the Trinity, but singularly and properly to the Father only: "Now unto the King eternal, immortal, and invisible, the only wise God;" and, "Who only hath immortality, dwelling in the light which no man can approach unto; whom no man hath seen, nor can see."

Passing by, then, these reasoners, who are unable to know the substance even of the soul, which is invisible, and therefore are very far indeed from knowing that the substance of the one and only God, that is, the Father and the Son and the Holy Spirit, remains ever not only invisible, but also unchangeable, and that hence it possesses true and real immortality; let us, who deny that God, whether the Father, or the Son, or the Holy Spirit, ever appeared to bodily eyes, unless through the corporeal creature made subject

[54] Matt. x. 28

to His own power; let us, I say—ready to be corrected, if we are reproved in a fraternal and upright spirit, ready to be so, even if carped at by an enemy, so that he speak the truth—in catholic peace and with peaceful study inquire, whether God indiscriminately appeared to our fathers before Christ came in the flesh, or whether it was any one person of the Trinity, or whether severally, as it were by turns.

CHAPTER X

WHETHER GOD THE TRINITY INDISCRIMINATELY APPEARED TO THE FATHERS, OR ANY ONE PERSON OF THE TRINITY. THE APPEARING OF GOD TO ADAM. OF THE SAME APPEARANCE. THE VISION TO ABRAHAM

And first, in that which is written in *Genesis, viz.,* that God spake with man whom He had formed out of the dust; if we set apart the figurative meaning, and treat it so as to place faith in the narrative even in the letter, it should appear that God then spake with man in the appearance of a man. This is not indeed expressly laid down in the book, but the general tenor of its reading sounds in this sense, especially in that which is written, that Adam heard the voice of the Lord God, walking in the garden in the cool of the evening, and hid himself among the trees of the garden; and when God said, "Adam, where art thou?" [55] replied, "I heard Thy voice, and I was afraid because I was naked, and I hid myself from Thy face." For I do not see how such a walking and conversation of God can be understood literally, except He appeared as a man. For it can neither be said that a voice only of God was framed, when God is said to have walked, or that He who was walking in a place was not visible; while Adam, too, says that he hid himself from the face of God. Who then was He? Whether the Father, or the Son, or the Holy Spirit? Whether altogether indiscriminately did God the Trinity Himself speak to man in the form of man? The context, indeed, itself of the Scripture nowhere, it should seem, indicates a change from person to person; but He seems still to speak to the first man, who said, "Let there be light," and, "Let there be a firmament," and so on through each of those days; whom we usually take to be God the Father, making by a word whatever He willed to make. For He made all things by His word, which Word we know, by the right rule of faith, to be His only Son. If, therefore, God the Father spake to the first man, and Himself was walking in the garden in the cool of the evening, and if it was from His face that the sinner hid himself amongst the trees of the garden, why are we not to go on to understand that it was He also who appeared to Abraham and to Moses, and to whom He would, and how He would, through the changeable and visible creature, subjected to Himself, while He Himself remains in Himself and in His own sub-

[55] Gen. iii. 8-10

stance, in which He is unchangeable and invisible? But, possibly, it might be that the Scripture passed over in a hidden way from person to person, and while it had related that the Father said "Let there be light," and the rest which it mentioned Him to have done by the Word, went on to indicate the Son as speaking to the first man; not unfolding this openly, but intimating it to be understood by those who could understand it.

Let him, then, who has the strength whereby he can penetrate this secret with his mind's eye, so that to him it appears clearly, either that the Father also is able, or that only the Son and Holy Spirit are able, to appear to human eyes through a visible creature; let him, I say, proceed to examine these things if he can, or even to express and handle them in words; but the thing itself, so far as concerns this testimony of Scripture, where God spake with man, is, in my judgment, not discoverable, because it does not evidently appear even whether Adam usually saw God with the eyes of his body; especially as it is a great question what manner of eyes it was that were opened when they tasted the forbidden fruit; [56] for before they had tasted, these eyes were closed. Yet I would not rashly assert, even if that scripture implies Paradise to have been a material place, that God could not have walked there in any way except in some bodily form. For it might be said, that only words were framed for the man to hear, without seeing any form. Neither, because it is written, "Adam hid himself from the face of God," does it follow forthwith that he usually saw His face. For what if he himself indeed could not see, but feared to be himself seen by Him whose voice he had heard, and had felt His presence as he walked? For Cain, too, said to God, "From Thy face I will hide myself;" [57] yet we are not therefore compelled to admit that he was wont to behold the face of God with his bodily eyes in any visible form, although he had heard the voice of God questioning and speaking with him of his sin. But what manner of speech it was that God then uttered to the outward ears of men, especially in speaking to the first man, it is both difficult to discover, and we have not undertaken to say in this discourse. But if words alone and sounds were wrought, by which to bring about some sensible presence of God to those first men, I do not know why I should not there understand the person of God the Father, seeing that His person is manifested also in that voice, when Jesus appeared in glory on the mount before the three disciples; [58] and in that when the dove descended upon Him at His baptism; [59] and in that where He cried to the Father concerning His own glorification, and it was answered Him, "I have both glorified, and will glorify again." [60] Not that the voice could be wrought without the work of the Son and of the Holy Spirit (since the Trinity works indivisibly), but that such a voice was wrought as to manifest the person of the Father only; just as the Trinity wrought that human form from the Virgin Mary, yet it is the person of the Son alone; for the invisible Trinity wrought the visible person of the Son alone. Neither does anything forbid us, not only

[56] Gen. iii. 7   [57] Gen. iv. 14   [58] Matt. xvii. 5   [59] Matt. iii. 17   [60] John xii. 28

to understand those words spoken to Adam as spoken by the Trinity, but also to take them as manifesting the person of that Trinity. For we are compelled to understand of the Father only, that which is said, "This is my beloved Son." [61] For Jesus can neither be believed nor understood to be the Son of the Holy Spirit, or even His own Son. And where the voice uttered, "I have both glorified, and will glorify again," we confess it was only the person of the Father; since it is the answer to that word of the Lord, in which He had said, "Father, glorify thy Son," which He could not say except to God the Father only, and not also to the Holy Spirit, whose Son He was not. But here, where it is written, "And the Lord God said to Adam," no reason can be given why the Trinity itself should not be understood.

Likewise, also, in that which is written, "Now the Lord had said unto Abraham, Get thee out of thy country, and from thy kindred, and thy father's house," it is not clear whether a voice alone came to the ears of Abraham, or whether anything also appeared to his eyes. But a little while after, it is somewhat more clearly said, "And the Lord appeared unto Abraham, and said, Unto thy seed will I give this land." [62] But neither there is it expressly said in what form God appeared to him, or whether the Father, or the Son, or the Holy Spirit appeared to him. Unless, perhaps, they think that it was the Son who appeared to Abraham, because it is not written, God appeared to him, but "the Lord appeared to him." For the Son seems to be called the Lord as though the name was appropriated to Him; as e.g. the apostle says, "For though there be that are called gods, whether in heaven or in earth (as there be gods many and lords many), but to us there is but one God, the Father, of whom are all things, and we in Him; and one Lord Jesus Christ, by whom are all things, and we by Him." [63] But since it is found that God the Father also is called Lord in many places—for instance, "The Lord hath said unto me, Thou art my Son; this day have I begotten Thee;" [64] and again, "The Lord said unto my Lord, Sit Thou at my right hand;" [65] since also the Holy Spirit is found to be called Lord, as where the apostle says, "Now the Lord is that Spirit;" and then, lest any one should think the Son to be signified, and to be called the Spirit on account of His incorporeal substance, has gone on to say, "And where the Spirit of the Lord is, there is liberty;" [66] and no one ever doubted the Spirit of the Lord to be the Holy Spirit: therefore, neither here does it appear plainly whether it was any person of the Trinity that appeared to Abraham, or God Himself the Trinity, of which one God it is said, "Thou shalt fear the Lord thy God, and Him only shalt thou serve." [67] But under the oak at Mamre he saw three men, whom he invited, and hospitably received, and ministered to them as they feasted. Yet Scripture at the beginning of that narrative does not say, three men appeared to him, but, "The Lord appeared to him." And then, setting forth in due order after what manner the Lord

[61] Matt. iii. 17   [62] Gen. xii. 1, 7   [63] 1 Cor. viii. 5, 6   [64] Ps. ii. 7   [65] Ps. cx. 1
[66] 2 Cor. iii. 17   [67] Deut. vi. 13

appeared to him, it has added the account of the three men, whom Abraham invites to his hospitality in the plural number, and afterwards speaks to them in the singular number as one; and as one He promises him a son by Sara, *viz.* the one whom the Scripture calls Lord, as in the beginning of the same narrative, "The Lord," it says, "appeared to Abraham." He invites them then, and washes their feet, and leads them forth at their departure, as though they were men; but he speaks as with the Lord God, whether when a son is promised to him, or when the destruction is shown to him that was impending over Sodom.[68]

CHAPTER XI

OF THE SAME APPEARANCE

That place of Scripture demands neither a slight nor a passing consideration. For if one man had appeared, what else would those at once cry out, who say that the Son was visible also in His own substance before He was born of the Virgin, but that it was Himself? since it is said, they say, of the Father, "To the only invisible God." [69] And yet, I could still go on to demand, in what manner "He was found in fashion as a man," before He had taken our flesh, seeing that his feet were washed, and that He fed upon earthly food? How could that be, when He was still "in the form of God, and thought it not robbery to be equal with God?" [70] For, pray, had He already "emptied Himself, taking upon Him the form of a servant, and made in the likeness of men, and found in fashion as a man?" when we know when it was that He did this through His birth of the Virgin. How, then, before He had done this, did He appear as one man to Abraham? or, was not that form a reality? I could put these questions, if it had been one man that appeared to Abraham, and if that one were believed to be the Son of God. But since three men appeared, and no one of them is said to be greater than the rest either in form, or age, or power, why should we not here understand, as visibly intimated by the visible creature, the equality of the Trinity, and one and the same substance in three persons?

For, lest any one should think that one among the three is in this way intimated to have been the greater, and that this one is to be understood to have been the Lord, the Son of God, while the other two were His angels; because, whereas three appeared, Abraham there speaks to one as the Lord: Holy Scripture has not forgotten to anticipate, by a contradiction, such future cogitations and opinions, when a little while after it says that two angels came to Lot, among whom that just man also, who deserved to be freed from the burning of Sodom, speaks to one as to the Lord. For so Scripture goes on to say, "And the Lord went His way, as soon as He left communing with Abraham; and Abraham returned to his place." [71]

[68] Gen. xviii.   [69] 1 Tim. i. 17   [70] Phil. ii. 6, 7   [71] Gen. xviii. 33

themselves that they were sent, which is that which we say of the Son and of the Holy Spirit. For .... Scripture that the Father was sent.

CHAPTER XII

THE APPEARANCE TO LOT IS EXAMINED

"But there came two angels to Sodom at even." Here, what I have begun to set forth must be considered more attentively. Certainly Abraham was speaking with three, and called that one, in the singular number, the Lord. Perhaps, some one may say, he recognized one of the three to be the Lord, but the other two His angels. What, then, does that mean which Scripture goes on to say, "And the Lord went His way, as soon as He had left communing with Abraham; and Abraham returned to his place: and there came two angels to Sodom at even?" Are we to suppose that the one who, among the three, was recognized as the Lord, had departed, and had sent the two angels that were with Him to destroy Sodom? Let us see, then, what follows. "There came," it is said, "two angels to Sodom at even; and Lot sat in the gate of Sodom: and Lot seeing them, rose up to meet them; and he bowed himself with his face toward the ground; and he said, Behold now, my lords, turn in, I pray you, into your servant's house." Here it is clear, both that there were two angels, and that in the plural number they were invited to partake of hospitality, and that they were honorably designated lords, when they perchance were thought to be men.

Yet, again, it is objected that except they were known to be angels of God, Lot would not have bowed himself with his face to the ground. Why, then, is both hospitality and food offered to them, as though they wanted such human succor? But whatever may here lie hid, let us now pursue that which we have undertaken. Two appear; both are called angels; they are invited plurally; he speaks as with two plurally, until the departure from Sodom. And then Scripture goes on to say, "And it came to pass, when they had brought them forth abroad, that they said, Escape for thy life; look not behind thee, neither stay thou in all the plain; escape to the mountain, and there thou shalt be saved,[72] lest thou be consumed. And Lot said unto them, Oh! not so, my lord: behold now, thy servant hath found grace in thy sight,"[73] etc. What is meant by his saying to them, "Oh! not so, my lord," if He who was the Lord had already departed, and had sent the angels? Why is it said, "Oh! not so, my lord," and not, "Oh! not so, my lords?" Or if he wished to speak to one of them, why does Scripture say, "But Lot said to them, Oh! not so, my lord: behold now, thy servant hath found grace in thy sight,"? Are we here, too, to understand two persons in the plural number, but when the two are addressed as one, then the one Lord God of one substance? But which two persons do we here understand?—of the Father and of the Son, or of the Father and of the Holy Spirit, or of the Son and of the Holy Spirit? The last, perhaps, is the most suitable; for they said of

[72] This clause is not in the Hebrew   [73] Gen. xix. 1-19

themselves that they were sent, which is that which we say of the Son and of the Holy Spirit. For we find nowhere in the Scriptures that the Father was sent.

CHAPTER XIII

THE APPEARANCE IN THE BUSH

But when Moses was sent to lead the children of Israel out of Egypt, it is written that the Lord appeared to him thus: "Now Moses kept the flock of Jethro his father-in-law, the priest of Midian: and he led the flock to the back side of the desert, and came to the mountain of God, even to Horeb. And the Angel of the Lord appeared unto him in a flame of fire, out of the midst of a bush; and he looked, and, behold, the bush burned with fire, and the bush was not consumed. And Moses said, I will now turn aside, and see this great sight, why the bush is not burnt. And when the Lord saw that he turned aside to see, God called unto him out of the midst of the bush, and said, I am the God of thy father, the God of Abraham, the God of Isaac, and the God of Jacob." [74] He is here also first called the Angel of the Lord, and then God. Was an angel, then, the God of Abraham, and the God of Isaac, and the God of Jacob? Therefore He may be rightly understood to be the Saviour Himself, of whom the apostle says, "Whose are the fathers, and of whom as concerning the flesh Christ came, who is over all, God blessed for ever." [75] He, therefore, "who is over all, God blessed for ever," is not unreasonably here understood also to be Himself the God of Abraham, the God of Isaac, and the God of Jacob. But why is He previously called the Angel of the Lord, when He appeared in a flame of fire out of the bush? Was it because it was one of many angels, who by an economy [or arrangement] bare the person of his Lord? or was something of the creature assumed by Him in order to bring about a visible appearance for the business in hand, and that words might thence be audibly uttered, whereby the presence of the Lord might be shown, in such way as was fitting, to the corporeal senses of man, by means of the creature made subject? For if he was one of the angels, who could easily affirm whether it was the person of the Son which was imposed upon him to announce, or that of the Holy Spirit, or that of God the Father, or altogether of the Trinity itself, who is the one and only God, in order that he might say, "I am the God of Abraham, and the God of Isaac, and the God of Jacob?" For we cannot say that the Son of God is the God of Abraham, and the God of Isaac, and the God of Jacob, and that the Father is not; nor will any one dare to deny that either the Holy Spirit, or the Trinity itself, whom we believe and understand to be the one God, is the God of Abraham, and the God of Isaac, and the God of Jacob. For he who is not God, is not the God of those fathers. Furthermore, if not only the Father is

[74] Ex. iii. 1-6   [75] Rom. ix. 5

God, as all, even heretics, admit; but also the Son, which, whether they will or not, they are compelled to acknowledge, since the apostle says, "Who is over all, God blessed for ever;" and the Holy Spirit, since the same apostle says, "Therefore glorify God in your body;" when he had said above, "Know ye not that your body is the temple of the Holy Ghost, which is in you, which ye have of God?" [76] and these three are one God, as catholic soundness believes: it is not sufficiently apparent which person of the Trinity that angel bare, if he was one of the rest of the angels, and whether any person, and not rather that of the Trinity itself. But if the creature was assumed for the purpose of the business in hand, whereby both to appear to human eyes, and to sound in human ears, and to be called the Angel of the Lord, and the Lord, and God; then God cannot here be understood to be the Father, but either the Son or the Holy Spirit. Although I cannot call to mind that the Holy Spirit is anywhere else called an angel, which yet may be understood from His work; for it is said of Him, "And He will show you things to come;" [77] and "angel" in Greek is certainly equivalent to "messenger" [78] in Latin: but we read most evidently of the Lord Jesus Christ in the prophet, that He is called "the Angel of Great Counsel," [79] while both the Holy Spirit and the Son of God is God and Lord of the angels.

CHAPTER XIV

OF THE APPEARANCE IN THE PILLAR OF CLOUD AND OF FIRE

Also in the going forth of the children of Israel from Egypt it is written, "And the Lord went before them, by day in a pillar of cloud to lead them the way, and by night in a pillar of fire. He took not away the pillar of the cloud by day, nor the pillar of fire by night, from before the people." [80] Who here, too, would doubt that God appeared to the eyes of mortal men by the corporeal creature made subject to Him, and not by His own substance? But it is not similarly apparent whether it was the Father, or the Son, or the Holy Spirit, or the Trinity itself, the one God. Nor is this distinguished there either, in my judgment, where it is written, "The glory of the Lord appeared in the cloud, and the Lord spake unto Moses, saying, I have heard the murmurings of the children of Israel," [81] etc.

CHAPTER XV

OF THE APPEARANCE ON SINAI. WHETHER THE TRINITY SPAKE IN THAT APPEARANCE OR SOME ONE PERSON SPECIALLY

But now of the clouds, and voices, and lightnings, and the trumpet, and the smoke on Mount Sinai, when it was said, "And Mount Sinai was alto-

[76] 1 Cor. vi. 20, 19   [77] John xvi. 13   [78] *Nuntius*   [79] Isa. ix. 6   [80] Ex. iii. 21, 22
[81] Ex. xvi. 10-12

gether on a smoke, because the Lord descended upon it in fire, and the smoke thereof ascended as the smoke of a furnace; and all the people that was in the camp trembled; and when the voice of the trumpet sounded long and waxed louder and louder, Moses spake, and God answered him by a voice." [82] And a little after, when the Law had been given in the ten commandments, it follows in the text, "And all the people saw the thunderings, and the lightnings, and the noise of the trumpet, and the mountain smoking." And a little after, "And [when the people saw it,] they removed and stood afar off, and Moses drew near unto the thick darkness where God was, and the Lord said unto Moses," [83] etc. What shall I say about this, save that no one can be so insane as to believe the smoke, and the fire, and the cloud, and the darkness, and whatever there was of the kind, to be the substance of the word and wisdom of God which is Christ, or of the Holy Spirit? For not even the Arians ever dared to say that they were the substance of God the Father. All these things, then, were wrought through the creature serving the Creator, and were presented in a suitable economy to human senses; unless, perhaps, because it is said, "And Moses drew near to the cloud where God was," carnal thoughts must suppose that the cloud was indeed seen by the people, but that within the cloud Moses with the eyes of the flesh saw the Son of God, whom doting heretics will have to be seen in His own substance. Forsooth, Moses may have seen Him with the eyes of the flesh, if not only the wisdom of God which is Christ, but even that of any man you please and howsoever wise, can be seen with the eyes of the flesh; or if, because it is written of the elders of Israel, that "they saw the place where the God of Israel had stood," and that "there was under His feet as it were a paved work of a sapphire stone, and as it were the body of heaven in his clearness," [84] therefore we are to believe that the word and wisdom of God in His own substance stood within the space of an earthly place, who indeed "reacheth firmly from end to end, and sweetly ordereth all things;" [85] and that the Word of God, by whom all things were made,[86] is in such wise changeable, as now to contract, now to expand Himself; (may the Lord cleanse the hearts of His faithful ones from such thoughts!) But indeed all these visible and sensible things are, as we have often said, exhibited through the creature made subject in order to signify the invisible and intelligible God, not only the Father, but also the Son and the Holy Spirit, "of whom are all things, and through whom are all things, and in whom are all things;" [87] although "the invisible things of God, from the creation of the world, are clearly seen, being understood by the things that are made, even His eternal power and Godhead." [88]

But as far as concerns our present undertaking; neither on Mount Sinai do I see how it appears, by all those things which were fearfully displayed to the senses of mortal men, whether God the Trinity spake, or the Father,

[82] Ex. xix. 18, 19   [83] Ex. xx. 18, 21   [84] Ex. xxiv. 10   [85] Wisd. viii. 1   [86] John i. 3   [87] Rom. xi. 36   [88] Rom. i. 20

or the Son, or the Holy Spirit severally. But if it is allowable, without rash assertion, to venture upon a modest and hesitating conjecture from this passage, if it is possible to understand it of one person of the Trinity, why do we not rather understand the Holy Spirit to be spoken of, since the Law itself also, which was given there, is said to have been written upon tables of stone with the finger of God,[89] by which name we know the Holy Spirit to be signified in the Gospel.[90] And fifty days are numbered from the slaying of the lamb and the celebration of the Passover until the day in which these things began to be done in Mount Sinai; just as after the passion of our Lord fifty days are numbered from His resurrection, and then came the Holy Spirit which the Son of God had promised. And in that very coming of His, which we read of in the *Acts of the Apostles*, there appeared cloven tongues like as of fire, and it sat upon each of them:[91] which agrees with *Exodus*, where it is written, "And Mount Sinai was altogether on a smoke, because the Lord descended upon it in fire;" and a little after, "And the sight of the glory of the Lord," he says, "was like devouring fire on the top of the mount in the eyes of the children of Israel."[92] Or if these things were therefore wrought because neither the Father nor the Son could be there presented in that mode without the Holy Spirit, by whom the Law itself must needs be written; then we know doubtless that God appeared there, not by His own substance, which remains invisible and unchangeable, but by the appearance above mentioned of the creature; but that some special person of the Trinity appeared, distinguished by a proper mark, as far as my capacity of understanding reaches, we do not see.

CHAPTER XVI

IN WHAT MANNER MOSES SAW GOD

There is yet another difficulty which troubles most people, *viz.* that it is written, "And the Lord spake unto Moses face to face, as a man speaketh unto his friend;" whereas a little after, the same Moses says, "Now therefore, I pray Thee, if I have found grace in Thy sight, show me now Thyself plainly, that I may see Thee, that I may find grace in Thy sight, and that I may consider that this nation is Thy people;" and a little after Moses again said to the Lord, "Show me Thy glory." What means this then, that in everything which was done, as above said, God was thought to have appeared by His own substance; whence the Son of God has been believed by these miserable people to be visible not by the creature, but by Himself; and that Moses, entering into the cloud, appeared to have had this very object in entering, that a cloudy darkness indeed might be shown to the eyes of the people, but that Moses within might hear the words of God, as though he beheld His face; and, as it is said, "And the Lord spake unto Moses face

---

[89] Ex. xxi. 18   [90] Luke. xi. 20   [91] Acts ii. 1-4   [92] Ex. xxiv. 17

to face, as a man speaketh unto his friend;" and yet, behold, the same Moses says, "If I have found grace in Thy sight, show me Thyself plainly"? Assuredly he knew that he saw corporeally, and he sought the true sight of God spiritually. And that mode of speech accordingly which was wrought in words, was so modified, as if it were of a friend speaking to a friend. Yet who sees God the Father with the eyes of the body? And that Word, which was in the beginning, the Word which was with God, the Word which was God, by which all things were made[93]—who sees Him with the eyes of the body? And the spirit of wisdom, again, who sees with the eyes of the body? Yet what is, "Show me now Thyself plainly, that I may see Thee," unless, Show me Thy substance? But if Moses had not said this, we must indeed have borne with those foolish people as we could, who think that the substance of God was made visible to his eyes through those things which, as above mentioned, were said or done. But when it is here demonstrated most evidently that this was *not granted* to him, even though he desired it; who will dare to say, that by the like forms which had appeared visibly to him also, not the creature serving God, but that itself which is God, appeared to the eyes of a mortal man?

Add, too, that which the Lord afterward said to Moses, "Thou canst not see my face: for there shall no man see my face, and live. And the Lord said, Behold, there is a place by me, and thou shall stand upon a rock: and it shall come to pass, while my glory passeth by, that I will put thee into a watch-tower of the rock, and will cover thee with my hand while I pass by: and I will take away my hand, and thou shalt see my back parts; but my face shall not be seen."[94]

CHAPTER XVII

HOW THE BACK PARTS OF GOD WERE SEEN. THE FAITH OF THE
RESURRECTION OF CHRIST. THE CATHOLIC CHURCH ONLY IS THE
PLACE FROM WHENCE THE BACK PARTS OF GOD ARE SEEN.
THE BACK PARTS OF GOD WERE SEEN BY THE ISRAELITES.
IT IS A RASH OPINION TO THINK THAT GOD THE FATHER
ONLY WAS NEVER SEEN BY THE FATHERS

Not unfitly is it commonly understood to be prefigured from the person of our Lord Jesus Christ, that His "back parts" are to be taken to be His flesh, in which He was born of the Virgin, and died, and rose again; whether they are called back parts[95] on account of the posteriority of mortality, or because it was almost in the end of the world, that is, at a late period,[96] that He deigned to take it: but that His "face" was that form of God, in which He "thought it not robbery to be equal with God,"[97] which no one certainly can see and live; whether because after this life, in which we are absent from

---

[93] John i. 1, 3   [94] Ex. xxxiii. 11-23   [95] *Posteriora*   [96] *Posterius*   [97] Phil. ii. 6

the Lord,[98] and where the corruptible body presseth down the soul,[99] we shall see "face to face," [100] as the apostle says—(for it is said in the *Psalms*, of this life, "Verily every man living is altogether vanity;" [101] and again, "For in Thy sight shall no man living be justified;" [102] and in this life also, according to John, "It doth not yet appear what we shall be, but we know," he says, "that when He shall appear, we shall be like Him, for we shall see Him as He is," [103] which he certainly intended to be understood as after this life, when we shall have paid the debt of death, and shall have received the promise of the resurrection)—or whether that even now, in whatever degree we spiritually understand the wisdom of God, by which all things were made, in that same degree we die to carnal affections, so that, considering this world dead to us, we also ourselves die to this world, and say what the apostle says, "The world is crucified unto me, and I unto the world." [104] For it was of this death that he also says, "Wherefore, if ye be dead with Christ, why as though living in the world are ye subject to ordinances?" [105] Not therefore without cause will no one be able to see the "face," that is, the manifestation itself of the wisdom of God, and live. For it is this very appearance, for the contemplation of which every one sighs who strives to love God with all his heart, and with all his soul, and with all his mind; to the contemplation of which, he who loves his neighbor, too, as himself builds up his neighbor also as far as he may; on which two commandments hang all the law and the prophets.[106] And this is signified also in Moses himself. For when he had said, on account of the love of God with which he was specially inflamed, "If I have found grace in thy sight, show me now Thyself plainly, that I may find grace in Thy sight;" he immediately subjoined, on account of the love also of his neighbor, "And that I may know that this nation is Thy people." It is therefore that "appearance" which hurries away every rational soul with the desire of it, and the more ardently the more pure that soul is; and it is the more pure the more it rises to spiritual things; and it rises the more to spiritual things the more it dies to carnal things. But while we are absent from the Lord, and walk by faith, not by sight,[107] we ought to see the "back parts" of Christ, that is His flesh, by that very faith, that is, standing on the solid foundation of faith, which the rock signifies, [108] and beholding it from such a safe watch-tower, namely in the Catholic Church, of which it is said, "And upon this rock I will build my Church." [109] For so much the more certainly we love that face of Christ, which we earnestly desire to see, as we recognize in His back parts how much first Christ loved us.

But in the flesh itself, the faith in His resurrection saves and justifies us. For, "If thou shalt believe," he says, "in thine heart, that God hath raised

---

[98] 2 Cor. v. 6   [99] Wisd. ix. 15   [100] 1 Cor. xiii. 12   [101] Ps. xxxix. 5   [102] Ps. cxliii. 2   [103] 1 John iii. 2   [104] Gal. vi. 14   [105] Col. ii. 20   [106] Matt. xxii. 37-40   [107] 2 Cor. v. 6, 7

[108] Augustine here gives the Protestant interpretation of the word "rock," in the passage "on this rock I will build my church."—W.G.T.S.   [109] Matt. xvi. 18

Him from the dead, thou shalt be saved;" [110] and again, "Who was delivered," he says, "for our offenses, and was raised again for our justification." [111] So that the reward of our faith is the resurrection of the body of our Lord. For even His enemies believe that that flesh died on the cross of His passion, but they do not believe it to have risen again. Which we believing most firmly, gaze upon it as from the solidity of a rock: whence we wait with certain hope for the adoption, to wit, the redemption of our body; [112] because we hope for that in the members of Christ, that is, in ourselves, which by a sound faith we acknowledge to be perfect in Him as in our Head. Thence it is that He would not have His back parts seen, unless as He passed by, that His resurrection may be believed. For that which is Pascha in Hebrew, is translated Passover. Whence John the Evangelist also says, "Before the feast of the Passover, when Jesus knew that His hour was come, that He should pass out of this world unto the Father." [113]

But they who believe this, but believe it not in the Catholic Church, but in some schism or in heresy, do not see the back parts of the Lord from "the place that is by Him." For what does that mean which the Lord says, "Behold, there is a place by me, and thou shalt stand upon a rock?" What earthly place is "by" the Lord, unless that is "by Him" which touches Him spiritually? For what place is not "by" the Lord, who "reacheth from one end to another mightily, and sweetly doth order all things," [114] and of whom it is said, "Heaven is His throne, and earth is His footstool;" and who said, "Where is the house that ye build unto me, and where is the place of my rest? For has not my hand made all those things?" [115] But manifestly the Catholic Church itself is understood to be "the place by Him," wherein one stands upon a rock, where he healthfully sees the "Pascha Domini," that is, the "Passing by" of the Lord, and His back parts, that is, His body, who believes in His resurrection. "And thou shalt stand," He says, "upon a rock while my glory passeth by." For in reality, immediately after the majesty of the Lord had passed by in the glorification of the Lord, in which He rose again and ascended to the Father, we stood firm upon the rock. And Peter himself then stood firm, so that he preached Him with confidence, whom, before he stood firm, he had thrice from fear denied; [116] although, indeed, already before placed in predestination upon the watch-tower of the rock, but with the hand of the Lord still held over him that he might not see. For he was to see His back parts, and the Lord had not yet "passed by," namely, from death to life; He had not yet been glorified by the resurrection.

For as to that, too, which follows in *Exodus*, "I will cover thee with mine hand while I pass by, and I will take away my hand and thou shalt see my back parts;" many Israelites, of whom Moses was then a figure, believed in the Lord after His resurrection, as if His hand had been taken off from their eyes, and they now saw His back parts. And hence the evangelist also men-

[110] Rom. x. 9   [111] Rom. iv. 25   [112] Rom. viii. 23   [113] John xiii. 1   [114] Wisd. viii. 1   [115] Isa. lxvi. 1, 2   [116] Matt. xxvi. 70-74

tions that prophecy of Isaiah, "Make the heart of this people fat, and make their ears heavy, and shut their eyes." [117] Lastly, in the *Psalm*, that is not unreasonably understood to be said in their person, "For day and night Thy hand was heavy upon me." "By day," perhaps, when He performed manifest miracles, yet was not acknowledged by them; but "by night," when He died in suffering, when they thought still more certainly that, like any one among men, He was cut off and brought to an end. But since, when He had already passed by, so that His back parts were seen, upon the preaching to them by the Apostle Peter that it behoved Christ to suffer and rise again, they were pricked in their hearts with the grief of repentance,[118] that that might come to pass among the baptized which is said in the beginning of that *Psalm*, "Blessed are they whose transgressions are forgiven, and whose sins are covered;" therefore, after it had been said, "Thy hand is heavy upon me," the Lord, as it were, passing by, so that now He removed His hand, and His back parts were seen, there follows the voice of one who grieves and confesses and receives remission of sins by faith in the resurrection of the Lord: "My moisture," he says, "is turned into the drought of summer. I acknowledged my sin unto Thee, and mine iniquity have I not hid. I said, I will confess my transgressions unto the Lord, and Thou forgavest the iniquity of my sin." [119] For we ought not to be so wrapped up in the darkness of the flesh, as to think the face indeed of God to be invisible, but His back visible, since both appeared visibly in the form of a servant; but far be it from us to think anything of the kind in the form of God; far be it from us to think that the Word of God, the Wisdom of God, has a face on one side, and on the other a back, as a human body has, or is at all changed either in place or time by any appearance or motion.

Wherefore, if in those words which were spoken in *Exodus*, and in all those corporeal appearances, the Lord Jesus Christ was manifested; or if in some cases Christ was manifested, as the consideration of this passage persuades us, in others the Holy Spirit, as that which we have said above admonishes us; at any rate no such result follows, as that God the Father never appeared in any such form to the fathers. For many such appearances happened in those times, without either the Father, or the Son, or the Holy Spirit being expressly named and designated in them; but yet with some intimations given through certain very probable interpretations, so that it would be too rash to say that God the Father never appeared by any visible forms to the fathers or the prophets. For they gave birth to this opinion who were not able to understand in respect to the unity of the Trinity such texts as, "Now unto the King eternal, immortal, invisible, the only wise God;" [120] and, "Whom no man hath seen, nor can see." [121] These texts are understood by a sound faith in that substance itself, the highest, and in the highest degree divine and unchangeable, whereby the Father and the Son and the Holy

---

[117] Isa. vi. 10; Matt. xiii. 15   [118] Acts ii. 37, 41   [119] Ps. xxxii. 4, 5   [120] 1 Tim. i. 17   [121] 1 Tim. vi. 16

Spirit are the one and only God. But those visions were wrought through the changeable creature, made subject to the unchangeable God, and did not manifest God properly as He is, but by intimations such as suited the causes and times of the several circumstances.

CHAPTER XVIII

THE VISION OF DANIEL

I do not know in what manner these men understand that the Ancient of Days appeared to Daniel, from whom the Son of man, which He deigned to be for our sakes, is understood to have received the kingdom; namely, from Him who says to Him in the *Psalms*, "Thou art my Son; this day have I begotten Thee; ask of me, and I shall give Thee the heathen for Thine inheritance;" [122] and who has "put all things under His feet." [123] If, however, both the Father giving the kingdom, and the Son receiving it, appeared to Daniel in bodily form, how can those men say that the Father never appeared to the prophets, and, therefore, that He only ought to be understood to be invisible whom no man has seen, nor can see? For Daniel has told us thus: "I beheld," he says, "till the thrones were set, and the Ancient of Days did sit, whose garment was white as snow, and the hair of His head like the pure wool: His throne was like the fiery flame, and His wheels as burning fire; a fiery stream issued and came forth from before Him: thousand thousands ministered unto Him, and ten thousand times ten thousand stood before Him: the judgment was set, and the books were opened," etc. And a little after, "I saw," he says, "in the night visions, and behold, one like the Son of man came with the clouds of heaven, and came to the Ancient of Days, and they brought Him near before Him. And there was given Him dominion, and glory, and a kingdom, that all peoples, nations, and languages should serve Him: His dominion is an everlasting dominion, which shall not pass away, and His kingdom that which shall not be destroyed." [124] Behold the Father giving, and the Son receiving, an eternal kingdom; and both are in the sight of him who prophesies, in a visible form. It is not, therefore, unsuitably believed that God the Father also was wont to appear in that manner to mortals.

Unless, perhaps, some one shall say, that the Father is therefore not visible, because He appeared within the sight of one who was dreaming; but that therefore the Son and the Holy Spirit are visible, because Moses saw all those things being awake; as if, forsooth, Moses saw the Word and the Wisdom of God with fleshly eyes, or that even the human spirit which quickens that flesh can be seen, or even that corporeal thing which is called wind—how much less can that Spirit of God be seen, who transcends the minds of all men, and of angels, by the ineffable excellence of the divine sub-

[122] Ps. ii. 7, 8   [123] Ps. viii. 8   [124] Dan. vii. 9-14

stance? Or can any one fall headlong into such an error as to dare to say that the Son and the Holy Spirit are visible also to men who are awake, but that the Father is not visible except to those who dream? How, then, do they understand that of the Father alone, "Whom no man hath seen, nor can see."? When men sleep, are they then not men? Or cannot He, who can fashion the likeness of a body to signify Himself through the visions of dreamers, also fashion that same bodily creature to signify Himself to the eyes of those who are awake? Whereas His own very substance, whereby He Himself is that which He is, cannot be shown by any bodily likeness to one who sleeps, or by any bodily appearance to one who is awake; but this not of the Father only, but also of the Son and of the Holy Spirit. And certainly, as to those who are moved by the visions of waking men to believe that not the Father, but only the Son, or the Holy Spirit, appeared to the corporeal sight of men—to omit the great extent of the sacred pages, and their manifold interpretation, such that no one of sound reason ought to affirm that the person of the Father was nowhere shown to the eyes of waking men by any corporeal appearance—but, as I said, to omit this, what do they say of our father Abraham, who was certainly awake and ministering, when, after Scripture had premised, "The Lord appeared unto Abraham," not one, or two, but three men appeared to him; no one of whom is said to have stood prominently above the others, no one more than the others to have shone with greater glory, or to have acted more authoritatively? [125]

Wherefore, since in our threefold division we determined to inquire, first, whether the Father, or the Son, or the Holy Spirit; or whether sometimes the Father, sometimes the Son, sometimes the Holy Spirit; or whether, without any distinction of persons, as it is said, the one and only God, that is, the Trinity itself, appeared to the fathers through those forms of the creature: now that we have examined, so far as appeared to be sufficient, what places of the Holy Scriptures we could, a modest and cautious consideration of divine mysteries leads, as far as I can judge, to no other conclusion, unless that we may not rashly affirm which person of the Trinity appeared to this or that of the fathers or the prophets in some body or likeness of body, unless when the context attaches to the narrative some probable intimations on the subject. For the nature itself, or substance, or essence, or by whatever other name that very thing, which is God, whatever it be, is to be called, cannot be seen corporeally: but we must believe that by means of the creature made subject to Him, not only the Son, or the Holy Spirit, but also the Father, may have given intimations of Himself to mortal senses by a corporeal form or likeness. And since the case stands thus, that this second book may not extend to an immoderate length, let us consider what remains in those which follow.

[125] Gen. xviii. 1, 2

ON THE TRINITY

BOOK THREE

Summary

Preface: Saint Augustine is compelled to write out of his religious zeal, since, in his opinion, not enough has been written about the Trinity, or is not easily available. Nor is he competent enough in Greek to be able to study the works on the subject in that tongue. He also begs his reader to be critical of what he writes.

Chapter 1: He proposes now to discuss the ways in which God is manifested to human sight, and the question whether the Son and the Holy Spirit were also "sent" before the occasions reported in the Gospel. Are the angels the agents of God's appearances?

Chapter 2: The will of God is the first cause of all corporeal change. As an example of this truth, one can see the human body which is subject to change, and yet has a soul which can partake of that unchangeable good, God.

Chapter 3: The illness of a wise man, who has worn out his body through an act of mercy, is cited as another illustration that the will of God is the first cause.

Chapter 4: God uses all things as He wills to use them. As the soul moves the body, so God moves the soul. The Apostle Paul, even while bearing the burden of the body, was able to see in part, and could preach Christ by tongue, epistle, and the sacrament in which visibly God is made manifest.

Chapter 5: God's power is manifest in the usual events of the universe. When His power is shown in an unusual manner, it is a miracle, as, for example, on Mount Sinai.

Chapter 6: When life is created by God in each new body, it is called natural. But when such a thing happens unusually, it is called a miracle.

Chapter 7: Miracles were wrought by the magic art of Pharaoh's wise men. But they failed. Whence we can understand that no power comes except from above. By such a miracle, Job lost his goods and manifested the patience of the righteous.

Chapter 8: God has created the things which even wicked men by magic arts have changed. They work through their own evil wills.

Chapter 9: God is the supreme turning-point of causation, though there are, of course, many proximate causes.

Chapter 10: Miracles and signs are brought within reach of our senses in order to announce something from God. Sometimes this occurs through an angel, or through men, or through the bread of the sacrament. Sometimes a rod is used, as in the case of

Moses, or a stone as in the case of Jacob. The sacrament in a supreme way signifies God.

Chapter 11: The essence of God cannot in its proper self be visible. God has used the ministry of angels, as we know on the authority of the Holy Scriptures. The Lord speaks through the prophets. Through an angel, He appeared to Abraham and Moses. The Lord Christ is the one supreme Mediator between God and man.

BOOK FOUR

Explains for what the Son of God was sent, viz. that by Christ's dying for sinners, we were to be convinced how great is God's love for us, and also what manner of men we are whom He loved. That the word came in the flesh, to the purpose also of enabling us to be so cleansed as to contemplate and cleave to God. That our double death was abolished by His death, being one and single. And hereupon is discussed, how the single of our Saviour harmonizes to salvation with our double; and the perfection is treated at length of the senary number, to which the ratio itself of single to double is reducible. That all are gathered together from many into one by the one Mediator of life, viz. Christ, through whom alone is wrought the true cleansing of the soul. Further it is demonstrated that the Son of God, although made less by being sent, on account of the form of a servant which He took, is not therefore less than the Father according to the form of God, because He was sent by Himself: and that the same account is to be given of the sending of the Holy Spirit.

PREFACE

THE KNOWLEDGE OF GOD IS TO BE SOUGHT FROM GOD

THE knowledge of things terrestrial and celestial is commonly thought much of by men. Yet those doubtless judge better who prefer to that knowledge, the knowledge of themselves; and that mind is more praiseworthy which knows even its own weakness, than that which, without regard to this, searches out, and even comes to know, the ways of the stars, or which holds fast such knowledge already acquired, while ignorant of the way by which itself to enter into its own proper health and strength. But if any one has already become awake towards God, kindled by the warmth of the Holy Spirit, and in the love of God has become vile in his own eyes; and through wishing, yet not having strength to come in unto Him, and through the light He gives, has given heed to himself, and has found himself, and has learned that his own filthiness cannot mingle with His purity; and feels it sweet to weep and to entreat Him, that again and again He will have compassion, until he have put off all his wretchedness; and to pray confidently, as having already received of free gift the pledge of salvation through his only Saviour and Enlightener of man—such an one, so acting, and so lamenting, knowledge does not puff up, because charity edifieth;[1] for he has preferred knowledge to knowledge, he has preferred to know his own weakness, rather than to know the walls of the world, the foundations of the earth, and the pinnacles of heaven. And by obtaining this knowledge, he has obtained also sorrow;[2] but sorrow for straying away from the desire of reaching his own

[2] Eccles. i. 18   [1] 1 Cor. viii. 1

728

proper country, and the Creator of it, his own blessed God. And if among men such as these, in the family of Thy Christ, O Lord my God, I groan among Thy poor, give me out of Thy bread to answer men who do not hunger and thirst after righteousness, but are sated and abound.[3] But it is the vain image of those things that has sated them, not Thy truth, which they have repelled and shrunk from, and so fall into their own vanity. I certainly know how many figments the human heart gives birth to. And what is my own heart but a human heart? But I pray the God of my heart, that I may not vomit forth into these writings any of these figments for solid truths, but that there may pass into them only what the breath of His truth has breathed into me; cast out though I am from the sight of His eyes,[4] and striving from afar to return by the way which the divinity of His only-begotten Son has made by His humanity. And this truth, changeable though I am, I so far drink in, as far as in it I see nothing changeable: neither in place and time, as is the case with bodies; nor in time alone, and in a certain sense place, as with the thoughts of our own spirits; nor in time alone, and not even in any semblance of place, as with some of the reasonings of our own minds. For the essence of God, whereby He is, has altogether nothing changeable, neither in eternity, nor in truth, nor in will; since there truth is eternal, love eternal; and there love is true, eternity true; and there eternity is loved, and truth is loved.

CHAPTER I

WE ARE MADE PERFECT BY ACKNOWLEDGMENT OF OUR OWN WEAKNESS. THE INCARNATE WORD DISPELS OUR DARKNESS

But since we are exiled from the unchangeable joy, yet neither cut off nor torn away from it so that we should not seek eternity, truth, blessedness, even in those changeable and temporal things (for we wish neither to die, nor to be deceived, nor to be troubled); visions have been sent to us from heaven suitable to our state of pilgrimage, in order to remind us that what we seek is not here, but that from this pilgrimage we must return thither, whence unless we originated we should not here seek these things. And first we have had to be persuaded how much God loved us, lest from despair we should not dare to look up to Him. And we needed to be shown also what manner of men we are whom He loved, lest being proud, as if of our own merits, we should recede the more from Him, and fail the more in our own strength. And hence He so dealt with us, that we might the rather profit by His strength, and that so in the weakness of humility the virtue of charity might be perfected. And this is intimated in the *Psalm*, where it is said, "Thou, O God, didst send a spontaneous rain, whereby Thou didst make Thine inheritance perfect, when it was weary." [5] For by "spontaneous rain" nothing else is meant than grace, not rendered to merit, but given freely,[6] whence also it is called grace; for He gave it, not because we were worthy, but because He willed. And knowing this, we shall not trust in ourselves; and this is to be made "weak." But He Himself makes us perfect, who says also to the Apostle Paul, "My grace is sufficient for thee, for my strength is made perfect in weakness." [7] Man, then, was to be persuaded how much God loved us, and what manner of men we were whom He loved; the former, lest we should despair; the latter, lest we should be proud. And this most necessary topic the apostle thus explains: "But God commendeth," he says, "His love towards us, in that, while we were yet sinners, Christ died for us. Much more then, being now justified by His blood, we shall be saved from wrath through Him. For if, when we were enemies, we were reconciled to God by the death of His Son; much more, being reconciled, we shall be saved by His life." [8] Also in another place: "What," he says, "shall we then say to these things? If God be for us, who can be against us? He that spared not His own Son, but delivered Him up for us all, how has He not with Him also freely given us all things?" [9] Now that which is declared to us as already done, was shown also to the ancient righteous as about to be done; that through the same faith they themselves also might be humbled, and so made weak; and might be made weak, and so perfected.

Because therefore the Word of God is One, by which all things were made, which is the unchangeable truth, all things are simultaneously therein, potentially and unchangeably; not only those things which are now in this whole creation, but also those which have been and those which shall be. And therein they neither have been, nor shall be, but only *are;* and all things are life, and all things are one; or rather it is one being and one life. For all things were so made by Him, that whatsoever was made in them was not made in Him, but was life in Him. Since, "in the beginning," the Word was not made, but "the Word was with God, and the Word was God, and all things were made by Him;" neither had all things been made by Him, unless He had Himself been before all things and not made. But in those things which were made by Him, even body, which is not life, would not have been made by Him, except it had been life in Him before it was made. For "that which was made was already life in Him;" and not life of any kind soever: for the soul also is the life of the body, but this too is made, for it is changeable; and by what was it made, except by the unchangeable Word of God? For "all things were made by Him; and without Him was not anything made that was made." "What, therefore, was made was already life in Him;" and not any kind of life, but "the life [which] was the light of men;" the light certainly of rational minds, by which men differ from beasts, and therefore are men. Therefore not corporeal light, which is the light of the flesh, whether it shine from heaven, or whether it be lighted by earthly fires; nor that of human flesh only, but also that of beasts, and down even to the

---

[6] Gratis   [7] 2 Cor. xii. 9   [8] Rom. v. 8-10   [9] Rom. viii. 31, 32

minutest of worms. For all these things see that light: but that life was the light of men; nor is it far from any one of us, for in it "we live, and move, and have our being." [10]

CHAPTER II

HOW WE ARE RENDERED APT FOR THE PERCEPTION OF TRUTH THROUGH THE INCARNATE WORD

But "the light shineth in darkness, and the darkness comprehended it not." Now the "darkness" is the foolish minds of men, made blind by vicious desires and unbelief. And that the Word, by whom all things were made, might care for these and heal them, "The Word was made flesh, and dwelt among us." For our enlightening is the partaking of the Word, namely, of that life which is the light of men. But for this partaking we were utterly unfit, and fell short of it, on account of the uncleanness of sins. Therefore we were to be cleansed. And further, the one cleansing of the unrighteous and of the proud is the blood of the Righteous One, and the humbling of God Himself;[11] that we might be cleansed through Him, made as He was what we are by nature, and what we are not by sin, that we might contemplate God, which by nature we are not. For by nature we are not God: by nature we are men, by sin we are not righteous. Wherefore God, made a righteous man, interceded with God for man the sinner. For the sinner is not congruous to the righteous, but man is congruous to man. By joining therefore to us the likeness of His humanity, He took away the unlikeness of our unrighteousness; and by being made partaker of our mortality, He made us partakers of His divinity. For the death of the sinner springing from the necessity of condemnation is deservedly abolished by the death of the Righteous One springing from the free choice of His compassion, while His single [death and resurrection] answers to our double [death and resurrection]. For this congruity, or suitableness, or concord, or consonance, or whatever more appropriate word there may be, whereby one is [united] to two, is of great weight in all compacting, or better, perhaps, co-adaptation, of the creature. For (as it just occurs to me) what I mean is precisely that co-adaptation which the Greeks call ἁρμονία. However this is not the place to set forth the power of that consonance of single to double which is found especially in us, and which is naturally so implanted in us (and by whom, except by Him who created us?) that not even the ignorant can fail to perceive it, whether when singing themselves or hearing others. For by this it is that treble and bass voices are in harmony, so that any one who in his note departs from it, offends extremely, not only trained skill, of which the most part of men are devoid, but the very sense of hearing. To demonstrate this, needs no doubt a long discourse; but any one who knows it, may make it plain to the very ear in a rightly ordered monochord.

[10] Acts xvii. 27, 28   [11] John i. 1, 14

CHAPTER III

THE ONE DEATH AND RESURRECTION OF THE BODY OF CHRIST HARMONIZES WITH OUR DOUBLE DEATH AND RESURRECTION OF BODY AND SOUL, TO THE EFFECT OF SALVATION. IN WHAT WAY THE SINGLE DEATH OF CHRIST IS BESTOWED UPON OUR DOUBLE DEATH

But for our present need we must discuss, so far as God gives us power, in what manner the single of our Lord and Saviour Jesus Christ answers to, and is, so to say, in harmony with our double to the effect of salvation. We certainly, as no Christian doubts, are dead both in soul and body: in soul, because of sin; in body, because of the punishment of sin, and through this also in body because of sin. And to both these parts of ourselves, that is, both to soul and to body, there was need both of a medicine and of resurrection, that what had been changed for the worse might be renewed for the better. Now the death of the soul is ungodliness, and the death of the body is corruptibility, through which comes also a departure of the soul from the body. For as the soul dies when God leaves it, so the body dies when the soul leaves it; whereby the former becomes foolish, the latter lifeless. For the soul is raised up again by repentance, and the renewing of life is begun in the body still mortal by faith, by which men believe on Him who justifies the ungodly;[12] and it is increased and strengthened by good habits from day to day, as the inner man is renewed more and more.[13] But the body, being as it were the outward man, the longer this life lasts is so much the more corrupted, either by age or by disease, or by various afflictions, until it come to that last affliction which all call death. And its resurrection is delayed until the end; when also our justification itself shall be perfected ineffably. For then we shall be like Him, for we shall see Him as He is.[14] But now, so long as the corruptible body presseth down the soul,[15] and human life upon earth is all temptation,[16] in His sight shall no man living be justified,[17] in comparison of the righteousness in which we shall be made equal with the angels, and of the glory which shall be revealed in us. But why mention more proofs respecting the difference between the death of the soul and the death of the body, when the Lord in one sentence of the Gospel has made either death easily distinguishable by any one from the other, where He says, "Let the dead bury their dead"?[18] For burial was the fitting disposal of a dead body. But by those who were to bury it He meant those who were dead in soul by the impiety of unbelief, such, namely, as are awakened when it is said, "Awake thou that sleepest, and arise from the dead, and Christ shall give thee light."[19] And there is a death which the apostle denounces, saying of

---

[12] Rom. iv. 5   [13] 2 Cor. iv. 16   [14] 1 John iii. 1   [15] Wisd. ix. 15   [16] Job vii. 1
[17] Ps. cxliii. 2   [18] Matt. viii. 22   [19] Eph. v. 14

the widow, "But she that liveth in pleasure is dead while she liveth." [20] Therefore the soul, which was before ungodly and is now godly, is said to have come alive again from the dead and to live, on account of the righteousness of faith. But the body is not only said to be about to die, on account of that departure of the soul which will be; but on account of the great infirmity of flesh and blood it is even said to be now dead, in a certain place in the Scriptures, namely, where the apostle says, that "the body is dead because of sin, but the spirit is life because of righteousness." [21] Now this life is wrought by faith, "since the just shall live by faith." [22] But what follows? "But if the spirit of Him that raised up Jesus from the dead dwell in you, He that raised up Christ from the dead shall also quicken your mortal bodies by His Spirit which dwelleth in you." [23]

Therefore on this double death of ours our Saviour bestowed His own single death; and to cause both our resurrections, He appointed beforehand and set forth in mystery and type His own one resurrection. For He was not a sinner or ungodly, that, as though dead in spirit, He should need to be renewed in the inner man, and to be recalled as it were to the life of righteousness by repentance; but being clothed in mortal flesh, and in that alone dying, in that alone rising again, in that alone did He answer to both for us; since in it was wrought a mystery as regards the inner man, and a type as regards the outer. For it was in a mystery as regards our inner man, so as to signify the death of our soul, that those words were uttered, not only in the Psalm, but also on the cross: "My God, my God, why hast Thou forsaken me?" [24] To which words the apostle agrees, saying, "Knowing this, that our old man is crucified with Him, that the body of sin might be destroyed, that henceforth we should not serve sin;" since by the crucifixion of the inner man are understood the pains of repentance, and a certain wholesome agony of self-control, by which death the death of ungodliness is destroyed, and in which death God has left us. And so the body of sin is destroyed through such a cross, that now we should not yield our members as instruments of unrighteousness unto sin. [25] Because, if even the inner man certainly is renewed day by day, [26] yet undoubtedly it is old before it is renewed. For that is done inwardly of which the same apostle speaks: "Put off the old man, and put on the new;" which he goes on to explain by saying, "Wherefore, putting away lying, speak every man truth." [27] But where is lying put away, unless inwardly, that he who speaketh the truth from his heart may inhabit the holy hill of God? [28] But the resurrection of the body of the Lord is shown to belong to the mystery of our own inner resurrection, where, after He had risen, He says to the woman, "Touch me not, for I am not yet ascended to my Father;" [29] with which mystery the apostle's words agree, where he says, "If ye then be risen with Christ, seek those things which are above, where

[20] I Tim. v. 6   [21] Rom. viii. 10   [22] Rom. i. 17   [23] Rom. viii. 10, 11   [24] Ps. xxii. 1, and Matt. xxvii. 46   [25] Rom. vi. 6, 13   [26] 2 Cor. iv. 16   [27] Eph. iv. 22-25   [28] Ps. xv. 1, 3   [29] John xx. 17

Christ sitteth on the right hand of God; set your thoughts on things above." [30] For not to touch Christ, unless when He had ascended to the Father, means not to have thoughts of Christ after a fleshly manner. Again, the death of the flesh of our Lord contains a type of the death of our outer man, since it is by such suffering most of all that He exhorts His servants that they should not fear those who kill the body, but are not able to kill the soul.[31] Wherefore the apostle says, "That I may fill up that which is behind of the afflictions of Christ in my flesh." [32] And the resurrection of the body of the Lord is found to contain a type of the resurrection of our outward man, because He says to His disciples, "Handle me, and see; for a spirit hath not flesh and bones, as ye see me have." [33] And one of the disciples also, handling His scars, exclaimed, "My Lord and my God!" [34] And whereas the entire integrity of that flesh was apparent, this was shown in that which He had said when exhorting His disciples: "There shall not a hair of your head perish." [35] For how comes it that first is said, "Touch me not, for I am not yet ascended to my Father;" [36] and how comes it that before He ascends to the Father, He actually is touched by the disciples; unless because in the former the mystery of the inner man was intimated, in the latter a type was given of the outer man? Or can any one possibly be so without understanding, and so turned away from the truth, as to dare to say that He was touched by men before He ascended, but by women when He had ascended? It was on account of this type, which went before in the Lord, of our future resurrection in the body, that the apostle says, "Christ the first-fruits; afterward they that are Christ's." [37] For it was the resurrection of the body to which this place refers, on account of which he also says, "Who has changed our vile body, that it may be fashioned like unto His glorious body." [38] The one death therefore of our Saviour brought salvation to our double death, and His one resurrection wrought for us two resurrections; since His body in both cases, that is, both in His death and in His resurrection, was ministered to us by a kind of healing suitableness, both as a mystery of the inner man, and as a type of the outer.

CHAPTER IV

THE RATIO OF THE SINGLE TO THE DOUBLE COMES FROM THE PERFECTION OF THE SENARY NUMBER. THE PERFECTION OF THE SENARY NUMBER IS COMMENDED IN THE SCRIPTURES. THE YEAR ABOUNDS IN THE SENARY NUMBER

Now this ratio of the single to the double arises, no doubt, from the ternary number, since one added to two makes three; but the whole which these make reaches to the senary, for one and two and three make six. And

[30] Col. iii. 1, 2   [31] Matt. x. 28   [32] Col. i. 24   [33] Luke xxiv. 39   [34] John xx. 28
[35] Luke xxi. 18   [36] John xx. 17   [37] 1 Cor. xv. 23   [38] Phil. iii. 21

this number is on that account called perfect, because it is completed in its own parts: for it has these three, sixth, third, and half; nor is there any other part found in it, which we can call an aliquot part. The sixth part of it, then, is one; the third part, two; the half, three. But one and two and three complete the same six. And Holy Scripture commends to us the perfection of this number, especially in this, that God finished His works in six days, and on the sixth day man was made in the image of God.[39] And the Son of God came and was made the Son of man, that He might re-create us after the image of God, in the sixth age of the human race. For that is now the present age, whether a thousand years apiece are assigned to each age, or whether we trace out memorable and remarkable epochs or turning-points of time in the divine Scriptures, so that the first age is to be found from Adam until Noah, and the second thence onwards to Abraham, and then next, after the division of Matthew the evangelist, from Abraham to David, from David to the carrying away to Babylon, and from thence to the travail of the Virgin,[40] which three ages joined to those other two make five. Accordingly, the nativity of the Lord began the sixth, which is now going onwards until the hidden end of time. We recognize also in this senary number a kind of figure of time, in that threefold mode of division, by which we compute one portion of time before the Law; a second, under the Law; a third, under grace. In which last time we have received the sacrament of renewal, that we may be renewed also in the end of time, in every part, by the resurrection of the flesh, and so may be made whole from our entire infirmity, not only of soul, but also of body. And thence that woman is understood to be a type of the church, who was made whole and upright by the Lord, after she had been bowed by infirmity through the binding of Satan. For those words of the *Psalm* lament such hidden enemies: "They bowed down my soul." [41] And this woman had her infirmity eighteen years, which is thrice six. And the months of eighteen years are found in number to be the cube of six, *viz.* six times six times six. Nearly, too, in the same place in the Gospel is that fig tree, which was convicted also by the third year of its miserable barrenness. But intercession was made for it, that it might be let alone that year, that if it bore fruit, well; if otherwise, it should be cut down.[42] For both three years belong to the same threefold division, and the months of three years make the square of six, which is six times six.

A single year also, if the whole twelve months are taken into account, which are made up of thirty days each (for the month that has been kept from of old is that which the revolution of the moon determines), abounds in the number six. For that which six is, in the first order of numbers, which consists of units up to ten, that sixty is in the second order, which consists of tens up to a hundred. Sixty days, then, are a sixth part of the year. Further, if that which stands as the sixth of the second order is multiplied by the sixth of the first order, then we make six times sixty, *i.e.* three hundred and

[39] Gen. i. 27   [40] Matt. i. 17   [41] Ps. lvii. 6   [42] Luke xiii. 6-17

sixty days, which are the whole twelve months. But since, as the revolution of the moon determines the month for men, so the year is marked by the revolution of the sun; and five days and a quarter of a day remain, that the sun may fulfill its course and end the year; for four quarters make one day, which must be intercalated in every fourth year, which they call bissextile, that the order of time may not be disturbed: if we consider, also, these five days and a quarter themselves, the number six prevails in them. First, because, as it is usual to compute the whole from a part, we must not call it five days, but rather six, taking the quarter day for one day. Next, because five days themselves are the sixth part of a month; while the quarter of a day contains six hours. For the entire day, *i.e.* including its night, is twenty-four hours, of which the fourth part, which is a quarter of a day, is found to be six hours. So much in the course of the year does the sixth number prevail.

CHAPTER V

THE NUMBER SIX IS ALSO COMMENDED IN THE BUILDING UP OF THE BODY OF CHRIST AND OF THE TEMPLE AT JERUSALEM

And not without reason is the number six understood to be put for a year in the building up of the body of the Lord, as a figure of which He said that He would raise up in three days the temple destroyed by the Jews. For they said, "Forty and six years was this temple in building." [43] And six times forty-six makes two hundred and seventy-six. And this number of days completes nine months and six days, which are reckoned, as it were, ten months for the travail of women; not because all come to the sixth day after the ninth month, but because the perfection itself of the body of the Lord is found to have been brought in so many days to the birth, as the authority of the church maintains upon the tradition of the elders. For He is believed to have been conceived on the 25th of March, upon which day also He suffered; so the womb of the Virgin, in which He was conceived, where no one of mortals was begotten, corresponds to the new grave in which He was buried, wherein was never man laid,[44] neither before nor since. But He was born, according to tradition, upon December the 25th. If, then you reckon from that day to this you find two hundred and seventy-six days which is forty-six times six. And in this number of years the temple was built, because in that number of sixes the body of the Lord was perfected; which being destroyed by the suffering of death, He raised again on the third day. For "He spake this of the temple of His body," [45] as is declared by the most clear and solid testimony of the Gospel; where He said, "For as Jonas was three days and three nights in the whale's belly, so shall the Son of man be three days and three nights in the heart of the earth." [46]

[43] John ii. 20   [44] John xix. 41, 42   [45] John ii. 19-21   [46] Matt. xii. 40

CHAPTER VI

THE THREE DAYS OF THE RESURRECTION, IN WHICH ALSO
THE RATIO OF SINGLE TO DOUBLE IS APPARENT

Scripture again witnesses that the space of those three days themselves was not whole and entire, but the first day is counted as a whole from its last part, and the third day is itself also counted as a whole from its first part; but the intervening day, *i.e.* the second day, was absolutely a whole with its twenty-four hours, twelve of the day and twelve of the night. For He was crucified first by the voices of the Jews in the third hour, when it was the sixth day of the week. Then He hung on the cross itself at the sixth hour, and yielded up His spirit at the ninth hour.[47] But He was buried, "now when the even was come," as the words of the evangelist express it;[48] which means, at the end of the day. Wheresoever then you begin—even if some other explanation can be given, so as not to contradict the *Gospel of John*,[49] but to understand that He was suspended on the cross at the third hour—still you cannot make the first day an entire day. It will be reckoned then an entire day from its last part, as the third from its first part. For the night up to the dawn, when the resurrection of the Lord was made known, belongs to the third day; because God (who commanded the light to shine out of darkness,[50] that through the grace of the New Testament and the partaking of the resurrection of Christ the words might be spoken to us "For ye were sometimes darkness, but now are ye light in the Lord" [51]) intimates to us in some way that the day takes its beginning from the night. For as the first days of all were reckoned from light to night, on account of the future fall of man;[52] so these on account of the restoration of man, are reckoned from darkness to light. From the hour, then, of His death to the dawn of the resurrection are forty hours, counting in also the ninth hour itself. And with this number agrees also His life upon earth of forty days after His resurrection. And this number is most frequently used in Scripture to express the mystery of perfection in the fourfold world. For the number ten has a certain perfection, and that multiplied by four makes forty. But from the evening of the burial to the dawn of the resurrection are thirty-six hours which is six squared. And this is referred to that ratio of the single to the double wherein there is the greatest consonance of co-adaptation. For twelve added to twenty-four suits the ratio of single added to double and makes thirty-six: namely a whole night with a whole day and a whole night, and this not without the mystery which I have noticed above. For not unfitly do we liken the spirit to the day and the body to the night. For the body of the Lord in His death and resurrection was a figure of our spirit and a type of our body. In this way, then, also that ratio of the single to the double is apparent in the thirty-six hours,

[47] Matt. xxvii. 23-50   [48] Mark xv. 42-46   [49] John xix. 14   [50] 2 Cor. iv. 6
[51] Eph. v. 8   [52] Gen. i. 4, 5

when twelve are added to twenty-four. As to the reasons, indeed, why these numbers are so put in the Holy Scriptures, other people may trace out other reasons, either such that those which I have given are to be preferred to them, or such as are equally probable with mine, or even more probable than they are; but there is no one surely so foolish or so absurd as to contend that they are so put in the Scriptures for no purpose at all, and that there are no mystical reasons why those numbers are there mentioned. But those reasons which I have here given, I have either gathered from the authority of the church, according to the tradition of our forefathers, or from the testimony of the divine Scriptures, or from the nature itself of numbers and of similitudes. No sober person will decide against reason, no Christian against the Scriptures, no peaceable person against the church.

CHAPTER VII

IN WHAT MANNER WE ARE GATHERED FROM MANY INTO ONE THROUGH ONE MEDIATOR

This mystery, this sacrifice, this priest, this God, before He was sent and came, being made of a woman—of Him, all those things which appeared to our fathers in a sacred and mystical way by angelical miracles, or which were done by the fathers themselves, were similitudes; in order that every creature by its acts might speak in some way of that One who was to be, in whom there was to be salvation in the recovery of all from death. For because by the wickedness of ungodliness we had recoiled and fallen away in discord from the one true and supreme God, and had in many things become vain, being distracted through many things and cleaving fast to many things; it was needful, by the decree and command of God in His mercy, that those same many things should join in proclaiming the One that should come, and that One should come so proclaimed by these many things, and that these many things should join in witnessing that this One had come; and that so, freed from the burden of these many things, we should come to that One, and dead as we were in our souls by many sins, and destined to die in the flesh on account of sin, that we should love that One who, without sin, died in the flesh for us; and by believing in Him now raised again, and by rising again with Him in the spirit through faith, that we should be justified by being made one in the one righteous One; and that we should not despair of our own resurrection in the flesh itself, when we consider that the one Head had gone before us the many members; in whom, being now cleansed through faith, and then renewed by sight, and through Him as Mediator reconciled to God, we are to cleave to the One, to feast upon the One, to continue one.

CHAPTER VIII

IN WHAT MANNER CHRIST WILLS THAT ALL SHALL BE ONE IN HIMSELF

So the Son of God Himself, the Word of God, Himself also the Mediator between God and men, the Son of man,[53] equal to the Father through the unity of the Godhead, and partaker with us by the taking upon Him of humanity, interceding for us with the Father in that He was man,[54] yet not concealing that He was God, one with the Father, among other things speaks thus: "Neither pray I for these alone," He says, "but for them also which shall believe on me through their word; that they all may be one; as Thou, Father, art in me, and I in Thee, that they also may be one in us: that the world may believe that Thou hast sent me. And the glory which Thou gavest me I have given them; that they may be one, even as we are one." [55]

CHAPTER IX

THE SAME ARGUMENT CONTINUED

He did not say, I and they are one thing; although, in that He is the head of the church, which is His body,[56] He might have said, I and they are, not one thing, but one person, because the head and the body is one Christ; but in order to show His own Godhead consubstantial with the Father (for which reason He says in another place, "I and my Father are one" [57]), in His own kind, that is, in the consubstantial parity of the same nature, He wills His own to be one, but in Himself; since they could not be so in themselves, separated as they are one from another by divers pleasures and desires and uncleannesses of sin; whence they are cleansed through the Mediator, that they may be one in Him, not only through the same nature in which all become from mortal men equal to the angels, but also through the same will most harmoniously conspiring to the same blessedness, and fused in some way by the fire of charity into one spirit. For to this His words come, "That they may be one, even as we are one;" namely, that as the Father and Son are one, not only in equality of substance, but also in will, so those also may be one, between whom and God the Son is Mediator, not only in that they are of the same nature, but also through the same union of love. And then He goes on thus to intimate the truth itself, that He is the Mediator, through whom we are reconciled to God, by saying, "I in them, and Thou in me, that they may be made perfect in one." [58]

[53] 1 Tim. ii. 5   [54] Rom. viii. 34   [55] John xvii. 20-22   [56] Eph. i. 22, 23   [57] John x. 30   [58] John xvii. 23

CHAPTER X

AS CHRIST IS THE MEDIATOR OF LIFE, SO THE DEVIL IS THE MEDIATOR OF DEATH

Therein is our true peace and firm bond of union with our Creator, that we should be purified and reconciled through the Mediator of life, as we had been polluted and alienated, and so had departed from Him, through the mediator of death. For as the devil through pride led man through pride to death; so Christ through lowliness led back man through obedience to life. Since, as the one fell through being lifted up, and cast down man also who consented to him; so the other was raised up through being abased, and lifted up man also who believed in Him. For because the devil had not himself come thither whither he had led the way (inasmuch as he bare indeed in his ungodliness the death of the spirit, but had not undergone the death of the flesh, because he had not assumed the covering of the flesh), he appeared to man to be a mighty chief among the legions of devils, through whom he exercises his reign of deceits; so puffing up man the more, who is eager for power more than righteousness, through the pride of elation, or through false philosophy; or else entangling him through sacrilegious rites, in which, while casting down headlong by deceit and illusion the minds of the more curious and prouder sort, he holds him captive also to magical trickery; promising too the cleansing of the soul, through those initiations which they call τελεταί, by transforming himself into an angel of light,[59] through divers machinations in signs and prodigies of lying.

CHAPTER XI

MIRACLES WHICH ARE DONE BY DEMONS ARE TO BE SPURNED

For it is easy for the most worthless spirits to do many things by means of aerial bodies, such as to cause wonder to souls which are weighed down by earthly bodies, even though they be of the better inclined. For if earthly bodies themselves, when trained by a certain skill and practice, exhibit to men so great marvels in theatrical spectacles, that they who never saw such things scarcely believe them when told; why should it be hard for the devil and his angels to make out of corporeal elements, through their own aerial bodies, things at which the flesh marvels; or even by hidden inspirations to contrive fantastic appearances to the deluding of men's senses, whereby to deceive them, whether awake or asleep, or to drive them into frenzy? But just as it may happen that one who is better than they in life and character may gaze at the most worthless of men, either walking on a rope, or doing by various motions of the body many things difficult of belief, and yet he

[59] 2 Cor. xi. 14

may not at all desire to do such things, nor think those men on that account to be preferred to himself; so the faithful and pious soul, not only if it sees, but even if on account of the frailty of the flesh it shudders at, the miracles of demons, yet will not for that either deploer its own want of power to do such things, or judge them on this account to be better than itself; especially since it is in the company of the holy, who, whether they are men or good angels, accomplish, through the power of God, to whom all things are subject, wonders which are far greater and the very reverse of deceptive.

CHAPTER XII

THE DEVIL THE MEDIATOR OF DEATH, CHRIST OF LIFE

In no wise therefore are souls cleansed and reconciled to God by sacrilegious imitations, or curious arts that are impious, or magical incantations; since the false mediator does not translate them to higher things, but rather blocks and cuts off the way thither through the affections, malignant in proportion as they are proud, which he inspires into those of his own company; which are not able to nourish the wings of virtues so as to fly upwards, but rather to heap up the weight of vices so as to press downwards; since the soul will fall down the more heavily, the more it seems to itself to have been carried upwards. Accordingly, as the Magi did when warned of God,[60] whom the star led to adore the low estate of the Lord; so we also ought to return to our country, not by the way by which we came, but by another way which the lowly King has taught, and which the proud king, the adversary of that lowly King, cannot block up. For to us, too, that we may adore the lowly Christ, the "heavens have declared the glory of God, when their sound went into all the earth, and their words to the ends of the world." [61] A way was made for us to death through sin in Adam. For, "By one man sin entered into the world, and death by sin; and so death passed upon all men, in whom all have sinned." [62] Of this way the devil was the mediator, the persuader to sin, and the caster down into death. For he, too, applied his one death to work out our double death. Since he indeed died in the spirit through ungodliness, but certainly did not die in the flesh: yet both persuaded us to ungodliness, and thereby brought it to pass that we deserved to come into the death of the flesh. We desired therefore the one through wicked persuasion, the other followed us by a just condemnation; and therefore it is written, "God made not death," [63] since He was not Himself the cause of death; but yet death was inflicted on the sinner, through His most just retribution. Just as the judge inflicts punishment on the guilty; yet it is not the justice of the judge, but the desert of the crime, which is the cause of the punishment. Whither, then, the mediator of death caused us to pass, yet did not come himself, that is, to the death of the flesh, there our Lord God introduced for

[60] Matt. ii. 12   [61] Ps. xix. 1, 4   [62] Rom. v. 12   [63] Wisd. i. 13

us the medicine of correction, which He deserved not, by a hidden and exceeding mysterious decree of divine and profound justice. In order, therefore, that as by one man came death, so by one man might come also the resurrection of the dead;[64] because men strove more to shun that which they could not shun, *viz.* the death of the flesh, than the death of the spirit, *i.e.* punishment more than the desert of punishment (for not to sin is a thing about which either men are not solicitous or are too little solicitous; but not to die, although it be not within reach of attainment, is yet eagerly sought after); the Mediator of life, making it plain that death is not to be feared, which by the condition of humanity cannot now be escaped, but rather ungodliness, which can be guarded against through faith, meets us at the end to which we have come, but not by the way by which we came. For we, indeed, came to death through sin; He through righteousness: and, therefore, as our death is the punishment of sin, so His death was made a sacrifice for sin.

CHAPTER XIII

THE DEATH OF CHRIST VOLUNTARY. HOW THE MEDIATOR OF LIFE SUBDUED THE MEDIATOR OF DEATH. HOW THE DEVIL LEADS HIS OWN TO DESPISE THE DEATH OF CHRIST

Wherefore, since the spirit is to be preferred to the body, and the death of the spirit means that God has left it, but the death of the body that the spirit has left it; and since herein lies the punishment in the death of the body, that the spirit leaves the body against its will, because it left God willingly; so that, whereas the spirit left God because it would, it leaves the body although it would not; nor leaves it when it would, unless it has offered violence to itself, whereby the body itself is slain: the spirit of the Mediator showed how it was through no punishment of sin that He came to the death of the flesh, because He did not leave it against His will, but because He willed, when He willed, as He willed. For because He is so commingled [with the flesh] by the Word of God as to be one, He says: "I have power to lay down my life, and I have power to take it again. No man taketh it from me, but I lay down my life that I might take it again." [65] And, as the *Gospel* tells us, they who were present were most astonished at this, that after that last word, in which He set forth the figure of our sin, He immediately gave up His spirit. For they who are hung on the cross are commonly tortured by a prolonged death. Whence it was that the legs of the thieves were broken, in order that they might die directly, and be taken down from the cross before the Sabbath. And that He was found to be dead already, caused wonder. And it was this also, at which, as we read, Pilate marvelled, when the body of the Lord was asked of him for burial.[66]

[64] 1 Cor. xv. 21, 22   [65] John x. 17, 18   [66] Mark xv. 37, 39, 43, 44, and John xix. 30-34

Because that deceiver then—who was a mediator to death for man, and feignedly puts himself forward as to life, under the name of cleansing by sacrilegious rites and sacrifices, by which the proud are led away—can neither share in our death, nor rise again from his own: he has indeed been able to apply his single death to our double one; but he certainly has not been able to apply a single resurrection, which should be at once a mystery of our renewal, and a type of that waking up which is to be in the end. He then who being alive in the spirit raised again His own flesh that was dead, the true Mediator of life, has cast out him, who is dead in the spirit and the mediator of death, from the spirits of those who believe in Himself, so that he should not reign within, but should assault from without, and yet not prevail. And to him, too, He offered Himself to be tempted, in order that He might be also a mediator to overcome his temptations, not only by succor, but also by example. But when the devil, from the first, although striving through every entrance to creep into His inward parts, was thrust out, having finished all his alluring temptation in the wilderness after the baptism;[67] because, being dead in the spirit, he forced no entrance into Him who was alive in the spirit, he betook himself, through eagerness for the death of man in any way whatsoever, to effecting that death which he could, and was permitted to effect it upon that mortal element which the living Mediator had received from us. And where he could do anything, there in every respect he was conquered; and wherein he received outwardly the power of slaying the Lord in the flesh, therein his inward power, by which he held ourselves, was slain. For it was brought to pass that the bonds of many sins in many deaths were loosed, through the one death of One which no sin had preceded. Which death, though not due, the Lord therefore rendered for us, that the death which was due might work us no hurt. For He was not stripped of the flesh by obligation of any authority, but He stripped Himself. For doubtless He who was able not to die, if He would not, did die because He would: and so He made a show of principalities and powers, openly triumphing over them in Himself.[68] For whereas by His death the one and most real sacrifice was offered up for us, whatever fault there was, whence principalities and powers held us fast as of right to pay its penalty, He cleansed, abolished, extinguished; and by His own resurrection He also called us whom He predestinated to a new life; and whom He called, them He justified; and whom He justified, them He glorified.[69] And so the devil, in that very death of the flesh, lost man, whom he was possessing as by an absolute right, seduced as he was by his own consent, and over whom he ruled, himself impeded by no corruption of flesh and blood, through that frailty of man's mortal body, whence he was both too poor and too weak; he who was proud in proportion as he was, as it were, both richer and stronger, ruling over him who was, as it were, both clothed in rags and full of troubles. For whither he drove the sinner to fall, himself not following, there by following he compelled the

[67] Matt. iv. 1-11   [68] Col. ii. 15   [69] Rom. viii. 30

Redeemer to descend. And so the Son of God deigned to become our friend in the fellowship of death, to which because he came not, the enemy thought himself to be better and greater than ourselves. For our Redeemer says, "Greater love hath no man than this, that a man lay down his life for his friends." [70] Wherefore also the devil thought himself superior to the Lord Himself, inasmuch as the Lord in His sufferings yielded to him; for of Him, too, is understood what is read in the *Psalm*, "For Thou hast made Him a little lower than the angels;" [71] so that He, being Himself put to death, although innocent, by the unjust one acting against us as it were by just right, might by a most just right overcome him, and so might lead captive the captivity wrought through sin,[72] and free us from a captivity that was just on account of sin, by blotting out the handwriting, and redeeming us who were to be justified although sinners, through His own righteous blood unrighteously poured out.

Hence also the devil mocks those who are his own until this very day, to whom he presents himself as a false mediator, as though they would be cleansed or rather entangled and drowned by his rites, in that he very easily persuades the proud to ridicule and despise the death of Christ, from which the more he himself is estranged, the more is he believed by them to be the holier and more divine. Yet those who have remained with him are very few, since the nations acknowledge and with pious humility imbibe the price paid for themselves, and in trust upon it abandon their enemy, and gather together to their Redeemer. For the devil does not know how the most excellent wisdom of God makes use of both his snares and his fury to bring about the salvation of His own faithful ones, beginning from the former end, which is the beginning of the spiritual creature, even to the latter end, which is the death of the body, and so "reaching from the one end to the other, mightily and sweetly ordering all things." [73] For wisdom "passeth and goeth through all things by reason of her pureness, and no defiled thing can fall into her." [74] And since the devil has nothing to do with the death of the flesh, whence comes his exceeding pride, a death of another kind is prepared in the eternal fire of hell, by which not only the spirits that have earthly, but also those who have aerial bodies, can be tormented. But proud men, by whom Christ is despised, because He died, wherein He bought us with so great a price,[75] both bring back the former death, and also men, to that miserable condition of nature, which is derived from the first sin, and will be cast down into the latter death with the devil. And they on this account preferred the devil to Christ, because the former cast them into that former death, whither he himself fell not through the difference of his nature, and whither on account of them Christ descended through His great mercy: and yet they do not hesitate to believe themselves better than the devils, and do not cease to assail and denounce them with every sort of malediction, while they know

[70] John xv. 13   [71] Ps. viii. 5   [72] Eph. iv. 8   [73] Wisd. viii. 1   [74] Wisd. vii. 24, 25
[75] I Cor. vi. 20

them at any rate to have nothing to do with the suffering of this kind of death, on account of which they despise Christ. Neither will they take into account that the case may possibly be, that the Word of God, remaining in Himself, and in Himself in no way changeable, may yet, through the taking upon Him of a lower nature, be able to suffer somewhat of a lower kind, which the unclean spirit cannot suffer, because he has not an earthly body. And so, whereas they themselves are better than the devils, yet, because they bear a body of flesh, they can so die, as the devils certainly cannot die, who do not bear such a body. They presume much on the deaths of their own sacrifices, which they do not perceive that they sacrifice to deceitful and proud spirits; or if they have come to perceive it, think their friendship to be of some good to themselves, treacherous and envious although they are, whose purpose is bent upon nothing else except to hinder our return.

CHAPTER XIV

CHRIST THE MOST PERFECT VICTIM FOR CLEANSING OUR FAULTS. IN EVERY SACRIFICE FOUR THINGS ARE TO BE CONSIDERED

They do not understand, that not even the proudest of spirits themselves could rejoice in the honor of sacrifices, unless a true sacrifice was due to the one true God, in whose stead they desire to be worshipped: and that this cannot be rightly offered except by a holy and righteous priest; nor unless that which is offered be received from those for whom it is offered; and unless also it be without fault, so that it may be offered for cleansing the faulty. This at least all desire who wish sacrifice to be offered for themselves to God. Who then is so righteous and holy a priest as the only Son of God, who had no need to purge His own sins by sacrifice,[76] neither original sins, nor those which are added by human life? And what could be so fitly chosen by men to be offered for them as human flesh? And what so fit for this immolation as mortal flesh? And what so clean for cleansing the faults of mortal men as the flesh born in and from the womb of a virgin, without any infection of carnal concupiscence? And what could be so acceptably offered and taken, as the flesh of our sacrifice, made the body of our priest? In such wise that, whereas four things are to be considered in every sacrifice—to whom it is offered, by whom it is offered, what is offered, for whom it is offered—the same One and true Mediator Himself, reconciling us to God by the sacrifice of peace, might remain one with Him to whom He offered, might make those one in Himself for whom He offered, Himself might be in one both the offerer and the offering.

[76] Heb. vii

CHAPTER XV

THEY ARE PROUD WHO THINK THEY ARE ABLE, BY THEIR OWN
RIGHTEOUSNESS, TO BE CLEANSED SO AS TO SEE GOD

There are, however, some who think themselves capable of being cleansed by their own righteousness, so as to contemplate God, and to dwell in God; whom their very pride itself stains above all others. For there is no sin to which the divine law is more opposed, and over which that proudest of spirits, who is a mediator to things below, but a barrier against things above, receives a greater right of mastery: unless either his secret snares be avoided by going another way, or if he rage openly by means of a sinful people (which Amalek, being interpreted, means), and forbid by fighting the passage to the land of promise, he be overcome by the cross of the Lord, which is prefigured by the holding out of the hands of Moses.[77] For these persons promise themselves cleansing by their own righteousness for this reason, because some of them have been able to penetrate with the eye of the mind beyond the whole creature, and to touch, though it be in ever so small a part, the light of the unchangeable truth; a thing which they deride many Christians for being not yet able to do, who, in the meantime, live by faith alone. But of what use is it for the proud man, who on that account is ashamed to embark upon the ship of wood,[78] to behold from afar his country beyond the sea? Or how can it hurt the humble man not to behold it from so great a distance, when he is actually coming to it by that wood upon which the other disdains to be borne?

CHAPTER XVI

THE OLD PHILOSOPHERS ARE NOT TO BE CONSULTED CONCERNING
THE RESURRECTION AND CONCERNING THINGS TO COME

These people also blame us for believing the resurrection of the flesh, and rather wish us to believe themselves concerning these things. As though, because they have been able to understand the high and unchangeable substance by the things which are made,[79] for this reason they had a claim to be consulted concerning the revolutions of mutable things, or concerning the connected order of the ages. For pray, because they dispute most truly, and persuade us by most certain proofs, that all things temporal are made after a science that is eternal, are they therefore able to see clearly in the matter of this science itself, or to collect from it, how many kinds of animals there are, what are the seeds of each in their beginnings, what measure in their

[77] Ex. xvii. 8-16
[78] The wood of the cross is meant. One of the ancient symbols of the church was a ship.   [79] Rom. i. 20

increase, what numbers run through their conceptions, births, ages, settings; what motions in desiring things according to their nature, and in avoiding the contrary? Have they not sought out all these things, not through that unchangeable wisdom, but through the actual history of places and times, or have trusted the written experience of others? Wherefore it is the less to be wondered at, that they have utterly failed in searching out the succession of more lengthened ages, and in finding any goal of that course, down which, as though down a river, the human race is sailing, and the transition thence of each to its own appropriate end. For these are subjects which historians could not describe, inasmuch as they are far in the future, and have been experienced and related by no one. Nor have those philosophers, who have profited better than others in that high and eternal science, been able to grasp such subjects with the understanding; otherwise they would not be inquiring as they could into past things of the kind, such as are in the province of historians, but rather would foreknow also things future; and those who are able to do this are called by them soothsayers, but by us prophets.

CHAPTER XVII

IN HOW MANY WAYS THINGS FUTURE ARE FOREKNOWN. NEITHER PHILOSOPHERS, NOR THOSE WHO WERE DISTINGUISHED AMONG THE ANCIENTS, ARE TO BE CONSULTED CONCERNING THE RESURRECTION OF THE DEAD

And yet the name of prophets, too, is not altogether foreign to their writings. But it makes the greatest possible difference, whether things future are conjectured by experience of things past (as physicians also have committed many things to writing in the way of foresight, which they themselves have noted by experience; or as again husbandmen, or sailors, too, foretell many things; for if such predictions are made a long while before, they are thought to be divinations), or whether such things have already started on their road to come to us, and being seen coming far off, are announced in proportion to the acuteness of the sense of those who see them, by doing which the aerial powers are thought to divine (just as if a person from the top of a mountain were to see far off some one coming, and were to announce it beforehand to those who dwelt close by in the plain); or whether they are either fore-announced to certain men, or are heard by them and again transmitted to other men, by means of holy angels, to whom God shows those things by His Word and His Wisdom, wherein both things future and things past consist; or whether the minds of certain men themselves are so far borne upwards by the Holy Spirit, as to behold, not through the angels, but of themselves, the immovable causes of things future, in that very highest pinnacle of the universe itself. For the aerial powers, too, hear these things, either by message through angels, or through men; and hear only so much as He judges to be fitting, to whom all things are subject. Many things, too, are foretold by a kind of instinct and inward impulse of such as know them not: as Caiaphas did not know what he said, but being the high priest, he prophesied.[80]

Therefore, neither concerning the successions of ages, nor concerning the resurrection of the dead, ought we to consult those philosophers, who have understood as much as they could the eternity of the Creator, in whom "we live, and move, and have our being." [81] Since, knowing God through those things which are made, they have not glorified Him as God, neither were thankful; but professing themselves wise, they became fools.[82] And whereas they were not fit to fix the eye of the mind so firmly upon the eternity of the spiritual and unchangeable nature, as to be able to see, in the wisdom itself of the Creator and Governor of the universe, those revolutions of the ages, which in that wisdom were already and were always, but here were about to be so that as yet they were not; or, again, to see therein those changes for the better, not of the souls only, but also of the bodies of men, even to the perfection of their proper measure; whereas then, I say, they were in no way fit to see these things therein, they were not even judged worthy of receiving any announcement of them by the holy angels; whether externally through the senses of the body, or by interior revelations exhibited in the spirit; as these things actually were manifested to our fathers, who were gifted with true piety, and who by foretelling them, obtaining credence either by present signs, or by events close at hand, which turned out as they had foretold, earned authority to be believed respecting things remotely future, even to the end of the world. But the proud and deceitful powers of the air, even if they are found to have said through their soothsayers some things of the fellowship and citizenship of the saints, and of the true Mediator, which they heard from the holy prophets or the angels, did so with the purpose of seducing even the faithful ones of God, if they could, by these alien truths, to revolt to their own proper falsehoods. But God did this by those who knew not what they said, in order that the truth might sound abroad from all sides, to aid the faithful, to be a witness against the ungodly.

CHAPTER XVIII

THE SON OF GOD BECAME INCARNATE IN ORDER THAT WE BEING CLEANSED BY FAITH MAY BE RAISED TO THE UNCHANGEABLE . TRUTH

Since, then, we were not fit to take hold of things eternal, and since the foulness of sins weighed us down, which we had contracted by the love of temporal things, and which were implanted in us as it were naturally, from the root of mortality, it was needful that we should be cleansed. But cleansed we could not be, so as to be tempered together with things eternal, except it

[80] John xi. 51   [81] Acts xvii. 28   [82] Rom. i. 21, 22

were through things temporal, wherewith we were already tempered together and held fast. For health is at the opposite extreme from disease; but the intermediate process of healing does not lead us to perfect health, unless it has some congruity with the disease. Things temporal that are useless merely deceive the sick; things temporal that are useful take up those that need healing, and pass them on healed, to things eternal. And the rational mind, as when cleansed it owes contemplation to things eternal; so, when needing cleansing, owes faith to things temporal. One even of those who were formerly esteemed wise men among the Greeks has said, The truth stands to faith in the same relation in which eternity stands to that which has a beginning. And he is no doubt right in saying so. For what we call temporal, he describes as having had a beginning. And we also ourselves come under this kind, not only in respect to the body, but also in respect to the changeableness of the soul. For that is not properly called eternal which undergoes any degree of change. Therefore, in so far as we are changeable, in so far we stand apart from eternity. But life eternal is promised to us through the truth, from the clear knowledge of which, again, our faith stands as far apart as mortality does from eternity. We then now put faith in things done in time on our account, and by that faith itself we are cleansed; in order that when we have come to sight, as truth follows faith, so eternity may follow upon mortality. And therefore, since our faith will become truth, when we have attained to that which is promised to us who believe: and that which is promised us is eternal life; and the Truth (not that which shall come to be according as our faith shall be, but that truth which is always, because in it is eternity—the Truth then) has said, "And this is life eternal, that they might know Thee the only true God, and Jesus Christ, whom Thou hast sent:" [83] when our faith by seeing shall come to be truth, then eternity shall possess our now changed mortality. And until this shall take place, and in order that it may take place—because we adapt the faith of belief to things which have a beginning, as in things eternal we hope for the truth of contemplation, lest the faith of mortal life should be at discord with the truth of eternal life—the Truth itself, co-eternal with the Father, took a beginning from earth,[84] when the Son of God so came as to become the Son of man, and to take to Himself our faith, that He might thereby lead us on to His own truth, who so undertook our mortality, as not to lose His own eternity. For truth stands to faith in the relation in which eternity stands to that which has a beginning. Therefore, we must needs so be cleansed, that we may come to have such a beginning as remains eternal, that we may not have one beginning in faith, and another in truth. Neither could we pass to things eternal from the condition of having a beginning, unless we were transferred, by union of the eternal to ourselves through our own beginning, to His own eternity. Therefore our faith has, in some measure, now followed thither, whither He in whom we have believed has ascended; born, dead, risen again,

[83] John xvii. 3   [84] Ps. lxxxv. 11

taken up. Of these four things, we knew the first two in ourselves. For we know that men both have a beginning and die. But the remaining two, that is, to be raised, and to be taken up, we rightly hope will be in us, because we have believed them done in Him. Since, therefore, in Him that, too, which had a beginning has passed over to eternity, in ourselves also it will so pass over, when faith shall have arrived at truth. For to those who thus believe, in order that they might remain in the word of faith, and being thence led on to the truth, and through that to eternity, might be freed from death, He speaks thus: "If ye continue in my word, then are ye my disciples indeed." And as though they would ask, With what fruit? He proceeds to say, "And ye shall know the truth." And again, as though they would say, Of what good is truth to mortal men? "And the truth," He says, "shall make you free." [85] From what, except from death, from corruption, from changeableness? Since truth remains immortal, incorrupt, unchangeable. But true immortality, true incorruptibility, true unchangeableness, is eternity itself.

CHAPTER XIX

IN WHAT MANNER THE SON WAS SENT AND PROCLAIMED BEFOREHAND. HOW IN THE SENDING OF HIS BIRTH IN THE FLESH HE WAS MADE LESS WITHOUT DETRIMENT TO HIS EQUALITY WITH THE FATHER

Behold, then, why the Son of God was sent; nay, rather behold what it is for the Son of God to be sent. Whatever things they were which were wrought in time, with a view to produce faith, whereby we might be cleansed so as to contemplate truth, in things that have a beginning, which have been put forth from eternity, and are referred back to eternity: these were either testimonies of this mission, or they were the mission itself of the Son of God. But some of these testimonies announced Him beforehand as to come, some testified that He had come already. For that He was made a creature by whom the whole creation was made, must needs find a witness in the whole creation. For except one were preached by the sending of many [witnesses] one would not be bound to the sending away of many. And unless there were such testimonies as should seem to be great to those who are lowly, it would not be believed, that He being great should make men great, who as lowly was sent to the lowly. For the heaven and the earth and all things in them are incomparably greater works of the Son of God, since all things were made by Him, than the signs and the portents which broke forth in testimony of Him. But yet men, in order that, being lowly, they might believe these great things to have been wrought by Him, trembled at those lowly things, as if they had been great.

"When, therefore, the fullness of time was come, God sent forth His Son,

[85] John viii. 31, 32

made of a woman, made under the Law;" [86] to such a degree lowly, that He was "made;" in this way therefore sent, in that He was made. If, therefore, the greater sends the less, we too, acknowledge Him to have been made less; and in so far less, in so far as made; and in so far made, in so far as sent. For "He sent forth His Son made of a woman." And yet, because all things were made by Him, not only before He was made and sent, but before all things were at all, we confess the same to be equal to the sender, whom we call less, as having been sent. In what way, then, could He be seen by the fathers, when certain angelical visions were shown to them, before that fullness of time at which it was fitting He should be sent, and so before He was sent, at a time when not yet sent He was seen as He is equal with the Father? For how does He say to Philip, by whom He was certainly seen as by all the rest, and even by those by whom He was crucified in the flesh, "Have I been so long time with you, and yet hast thou not known me, Philip? he that hath seen me, hath seen the Father also;" unless because He was both seen and yet not seen? He was seen, as He had been made in being sent; He was not seen, as by Him all things were made. Or how does He say this too, "He that hath my commandments, and keepeth them, he it is that loveth me; and he that loveth me shall be loved of my Father, and I will love him, and will manifest myself to him," [87] at a time when He was manifest before the eyes of men; unless because He was offering that flesh, which the Word was made in the fullness of time, to be accepted by our faith; but was keeping back the Word itself, by whom all things were made, to be contemplated in eternity by the mind when cleansed by faith?

CHAPTER XX

THE SENDER AND THE SENT EQUAL. WHY THE SON IS SAID TO BE
SENT BY THE FATHER. OF THE MISSION OF THE HOLY SPIRIT.
HOW AND BY WHOM HE WAS SENT. THE FATHER THE BE-
GINNING OF THE WHOLE GODHEAD

But if the Son is said to be sent by the Father on this account, that the one is the Father, and the other the Son, this does not in any manner hinder us from believing the Son to be equal, and consubstantial, and co-eternal with the Father, and yet to have been sent as Son by the Father. Not because the one is greater, the other less; but because the one is Father, the other Son; the one begetter, the other begotten; the one, He from whom He is who is sent; the other, He who is from Him who sends. For the Son is from the Father, not the Father from the Son. And according to this manner we can now understand that the Son is not only said to have been sent because "the Word was made flesh," [88] but therefore sent that the Word might be made flesh, and that He might perform through His bodily presence those

[86] Gal. iv. 4   [87] John xiv. 9, 21   [88] John i. 3, 18, 14

things which were written; that is, that not only is He understood to have been sent as man, which the Word was made but the Word, too, was sent that it might be made man; because He was not sent in respect to any in-equality of power, or substance, or anything that in Him was not equal to the Father; but in respect to this, that the Son is from the Father, not the Father from the Son; for the Son is the Word of the Father, which is also called His wisdom. What wonder, therefore, if He is sent, not because He is unequal with the Father, but because He is "a pure emanation issuing from the glory of the Almighty God?" For there, that which issues, and that from which it issues, is of one and the same substance. For it does not issue as water issues from an aperture of earth or of stone, but as light issues from light. For the words, "For she is the brightness of the everlasting light," what else are they than, she is light of everlasting light? For what is the brightness of light, except light itself? and so co-eternal with the light, from which the light is. But it is preferable to say, "the brightness of light," rather than "the light of light;" lest that which issues should be thought to be darker than that from which it issues. For when one hears of the brightness of light as being light itself, it is more easy to believe that the former shines by means of the latter, than that the latter shines less. But because there was no need of warning men not to think that light to be less, which begat the other (for no heretic ever dared say this, neither is it to be believed that any one will dare to do so), Scripture meets that other thought, whereby that light which issues might seem darker than that from which it issues; and it has removed this surmise by saying, "It is the brightness of that light," namely, of eternal light, and so shows it to be equal. For if it were less, then it would be its darkness, not its brightness; but if it were greater, then it could not issue from it, for it could not surpass that from which it is educed. Therefore, because it issues from it, it is not greater than it is; and because it is not its darkness, but its brightness, it is not less than it is: there-fore it is equal. Nor ought this to trouble us, that it is called a pure emana-tion issuing from the glory of the Almighty God, as if itself were not omnip-otent, but an emanation from the Omnipotent; for soon after it is said of it, "And being but one, she can do all things." [89] But who is omnipotent, unless He who can do all things? It is sent, therefore, by Him from whom it issues; for so she is sought after by him who loved and desired her. "Send her," he says, "out of Thy holy heavens, and from the throne of Thy glory, that, being present, she may labor with me;" [90] that is, may teach me to labor [heartily] in order that I may not labor [irksomely]. For her labors are vir-tues. But she is sent in one way that she may be with man; she has been sent in another way that she herself may be man. For, "entering into holy souls, she maketh them friends of God and prophets;" [91] so she also fills the holy angels, and works all things fitting for such ministries by them. But when the fullness of time was come, she was sent,[92] not to fill angels, nor to be an

[89] Wisd. vii. 25-27   [90] Wisd. ix. 10   [91] Wisd. vii. 27   [92] Gal. iv. 4

angel, except in so far as she announced the counsel of the Father, which was her own also; nor, again, to be with men or in men, for this too took place before, both in the fathers and in the prophets; but that the Word itself should be made flesh, that is, should be made man. In which future mystery, when revealed, was to be the salvation of those wise and holy men also, who, before He was born of the Virgin, were born of women; and in which, when done and made known, is the salvation of all who believe, and hope, and love. For this is "the great mystery of godliness, which was manifest in the flesh, justified in the Spirit, seen of angels, preached unto the Gentiles, believed on in the world, received up into glory." [93]

Therefore the Word of God is sent by Him, of whom He is the Word; He is sent by Him, from whom He was begotten; He sends who begot, That is sent which is begotten. And He is then sent to each one, when He is apprehended and perceived by each, in so far as He can be apprehended and perceived, in proportion to the comprehension of the rational soul, either advancing towards God, or already perfect in God. The Son, therefore, is not properly said to have been sent in that He is begotten of the Father; but either in that the Word made flesh appeared to the world, whence He says, "I came forth from the Father, and am come into the world;" [94] or in that from time to time, He is perceived by the mind of each, according to the saying, "Send her, that, being present with me, she may labor with me." [95] What then is born from eternity is eternal, "for it is the brightness of the everlasting light;" but what is sent from time to time, is that which is apprehended by each. But when the Son of God was made manifest in the flesh, He was sent into this world in the fullness of time, made of a woman. "For after that, in the wisdom of God, the world by wisdom knew not God" (since "the light shineth in darkness, and the darkness comprehended it not"), it "pleased God by the foolishness of preaching to save them that believe," [96] and that the Word should be made flesh, and dwell among us.[97] But when from time to time He comes forth and is perceived by the mind of each, He is said indeed to be sent, but not into this world; for He does not appear sensibly, that is, He does not present Himself to the corporeal senses. For we ourselves, too, are not in this world, in respect to our grasping with the mind as far as we can that which is eternal; and the spirits of all the righteous are not in this world, even of those who are still living in the flesh, in so far as they have discernment in things divine. But the Father is not said to be sent, when from time to time He is apprehended by any one, for He has no one of whom to be, or from whom to proceed; since Wisdom says, "I came out of the mouth of the Most High," [98] and it is said of the Holy Spirit, "He proceedeth from the Father," [99] but the Father is from no one.

As, therefore, the Father begat, the Son is begotten; so the Father sent, the Son was sent. But in like manner as He who begat and He who was be-

[93] 1 Tim. iii. 16 [94] John xvi. 28 [95] Wisd. ix. 10 [96] 1 Cor. i. 21 [97] John i. 5, 14 [98] Ecclus. xxiv. 3 [99] John xv. 26

gotten, so both He who sent and He who was sent, are one, since the Father and the Son are one.[100] So also the Holy Spirit is one with them, since these three are one. For as to be born, in respect to the Son, means to be from the Father; so to be sent, in respect to the Son, means to be known to be from the Father. And as to be the gift of God in respect to the Holy Spirit, means to proceed from the Father; so to be sent, is to be known to proceed from the Father. Neither can we say that the Holy Spirit does not also proceed from the Son, for the same Spirit is not without reason said to be the Spirit both of the Father and of the Son. Nor do I see what else He intended to signify, when He breathed on the face of the disciples, and said, "Receive ye the Holy Ghost." [101] For that bodily breathing, proceeding from the body with the feeling of bodily touching, was not the substance of the Holy Spirit, but a declaration by a fitting sign, that the Holy Spirit proceeds not only from the Father, but also from the Son. For the veriest of madmen would not say, that it was one Spirit which He gave when He breathed on them, and another which He sent after His ascension.[102] For the Spirit of God is one, the Spirit of the Father and of the Son, the Holy Spirit, who worketh all in all.[103] But that He was given twice was certainly a significant economy, which we will discuss in its place, as far as the Lord may grant. That then which the Lord says—"Whom I will send unto you from the Father" [104]—shows the Spirit to be both of the Father and of the Son; because, also, when He had said, "Whom the Father will send," He added also, "in my name." [105] Yet He did not say, Whom the Father will send from *me*, as He said, "Whom *I* will send unto you from the Father"—showing, namely, that the Father is the beginning of the whole divinity, or if it is better so expressed, deity. He, therefore, who proceeds from the Father and from the Son, is referred back to Him from whom the Son was born. And that which the evangelist says, "For the Holy Ghost was not yet given, because that Jesus was not yet glorified;" [106] how is this to be understood, unless because the special giving or sending of the Holy Spirit after the glorification of Christ was to be such as it had never been before? For it was not previously none at all, but it had not been such as this. For if the Holy Spirit was not given before, wherewith were the prophets who spoke filled? Whereas the Scripture plainly says, and shows in many places, that they spake by the Holy Spirit. Whereas, also, it is said of John the Baptist, "And he shall be filled with the Holy Ghost, even from his mother's womb." And his father Zacharias is found to have been filled with the Holy Ghost, so as to say such things of him. And Mary, too, was filled with the Holy Ghost, so as to foretell such things of the Lord, whom she was bearing in her womb.[107] And Simeon and Anna were filled with the Holy Spirit, so as to acknowledge the greatness of the little child Christ.[108] How, then, was "the Spirit not yet given, since Jesus was not yet glorified," unless because that giving, or granting, or mission of the Holy

[100] John x. 30   [101] John xx. 22   [102] Acts ii. 1-4   [103] 1 Cor. xii. 6   [104] John xv. 26   [105] John xiv. 26   [106] John vii. 39   [107] Luke i. 15, 41-79   [108] Luke ii. 25-38

Spirit was to have a certain speciality of its own in its very advent, such as never was before? For we read nowhere that men spoke in tongues which they did not know, through the Holy Spirit coming upon them; as happened then, when it was needful that His coming should be made plain by visible signs, in order to show that the whole world, and all nations constituted with different tongues, should believe in Christ through the gift of the Holy Spirit, to fulfill that which is sung in the *Psalm*, "There is no speech nor language where their voice is not heard; their sound is gone out through all the earth, and their words to the end of the world." [109]

Therefore man was united, and in some sense commingled, with the Word of God, so as to be One Person, when the fullness of time was come, and the Son of God, made of a woman, was sent into this world, that He might be also the Son of man for the sake of the sons of men. And this person angelic nature could prefigure beforehand, so as to pre-announce, but could not appropriate, so as to be that person itself.

CHAPTER XXI

OF THE SENSIBLE SHOWING OF THE HOLY SPIRIT, AND OF THE CO-ETERNITY OF THE TRINITY. WHAT HAS BEEN SAID, AND WHAT REMAINS TO BE SAID

But with respect to the sensible showing of the Holy Spirit, whether by the shape of a dove,[110] or by fiery tongues,[111] when the subjected and subservient creature by temporal motions and forms manifested His substance co-eternal with the Father and the Son, and alike with them unchangeable, while it was not united so as to be one person with Him, as the flesh was which the Word was made;[112] I do not dare to say that nothing of the kind was done aforetime. But I would boldly say, that the Father, Son, and Holy Spirit, of one and the same substance, God the Creator, the Omnipotent Trinity, work indivisibly; but that this cannot be indivisibly manifested by the creature, which is far inferior, and least of all by the bodily creature: just as the Father, Son, and Holy Spirit cannot be named by our words, which certainly are bodily sounds, except in their own proper intervals of time, divided by a distinct separation, which intervals the proper syllables of each word occupy. Since in their proper substance wherein they are, the three are one, the Father, and the Son, and the Holy Spirit, the very same, by no temporal motion, above the whole creature, without any interval of time and place, and at once one and the same from eternity to eternity, as it were eternity itself, which is not without truth and charity. But, in my words, the Father, Son, and Holy Spirit are separated, and cannot be named at once, and occupy their own proper places separately in visible letters. And as, when I name my memory, and intellect, and will, each name refers to

[109] Ps. xix. 3, 4   [110] Matt. iii. 16   [111] Acts ii. 3   [112] John i. 14

each severally, but yet each is uttered by all three; for there is no one of these three names that is not uttered by both my memory and my intellect and my will together [by the so i as a whole]; so the Trinity together wrought the voice of the Father, and the flesh of the Son, and the dove of the Holy Spirit, while each of these things is referred severally to each person. And by this similitude it is in some degree discernible, that the Trinity, which is inseparable in itself, is manifested separably by the appearance of the visible creature; and that the operation of the Trinity is also inseparable in each severally of those things which are said to pertain properly to the manifesting of either the Father, or the Son, or the Holy Spirit.

If then I am asked, in what manner either words or sensible forms and appearances were wrought before the incarnation of the Word of God, which should prefigure it as about to come, I reply that God wrought those things by the angels; and this I have also shown sufficiently, as I think, by testimonies of the Holy Scriptures. And if I am asked how the incarnation itself was brought to pass, I reply that the Word of God itself was made flesh, that is, was made man, yet not turned and changed into that which was made; but so made, that there should be there not only the Word of God and the flesh of man, but also the rational soul of man, and that this whole should both be called God on account of God, and man on account of man. And if this is understood with difficulty, the mind must be purged by faith, by more and more abstaining from sins, and by doing good works, and by praying with the groaning of holy desires; that by profiting through the divine help, it may both understand and love. And if I am asked, how, after the incarnation of the Word, either a voice of the Father was produced, or a corporeal appearance by which the Holy Spirit was manifested: I do not doubt indeed that this was done through the creature; but whether only corporeal and sensible, or whether by the employment also of the spirit rational or intellectual (for this is the term by which some choose to call what the Greeks name νοερόν), not certainly so as to form one person (for who could possibly say that whatever creature it was by which the voice of the Father sounded, is in such sense God the Father; or whatever creature it was by which the Holy Spirit was manifested in the form of a dove, or in fiery tongues, is in such sense the Holy Spirit, as the Son of God is that man who was made of a virgin?), but only to the ministry of bringing about such intimations as God judged needful; or whether anything else is to be understood: is difficult to discover, and not expedient rashly to affirm. Yet I see not how those things could have been brought to pass without the rational or intellectual creature. But it is not yet the proper place to explain, as the Lord may give me strength, why I so think; for the arguments of heretics must first be discussed and refuted, which they do not produce from the divine books, but from their own reasons, and by which, as they think, they forcibly compel us so to understand the testimonies of the Scriptures which treat of the Father, and the Son, and the Holy Spirit, as they themselves will.

But now, as I think, it has been sufficiently shown, that the Son is not therefore less because He is sent by the Father, nor the Holy Spirit less because both the Father sent Him and the Son. For these things are perceived to be laid down in the Scriptures, either on account of the visible creature; or rather on account of commending to our thoughts the emanation [within the Godhead]; but not on account of inequality, or imparity, or unlikeness of substance; since, even if God the Father had willed to appear visibly through the subject creature, yet it would be most absurd to say that He was sent either by the Son, whom He begot, or by the Holy Spirit, who proceeds from Him. Let this, therefore, be the limit of the present book. Henceforth in the rest we shall see, the Lord helping, of what sort are those crafty arguments of the heretics, and in what manner they may be confuted.

BOOK FIVE

Summary

Chapter 1: Human understanding always falls far short of God the Trinity. Saint Augustine prays for help for his understanding and also pardon for any offence. He also begs the indulgence of the reader. God must be conceived as unchangeable, and He must never be measured after the custom of things changeable, visible, and mortal. We must try to understand that God is "good without quality, great without quantity, a creator though He lacks nothing, ruling but from no position, sustaining all things without 'having' them, in His wholeness everywhere, yet without place, eternal without time, making things that are changeable, without change of Himself, and without passion."

Chapter 2: God is the only unchangeable essence, to whom being most truly belongs, and without accidents.

Chapter 3: Saint Augustine refutes the argument of the Arians that since "unbegotten" is predicated of the Father according to substance, and "begotten" is predicated of the Son according to substance, therefore the substance of the Father and the substance of the Son are different, because "unbegotten" is different from "begotten." After all, there are the words of Jesus, "I and the Father are one." (John x. 30)

Chapter 4: An accident always implies change in the thing of which it is an accident. Since God is unchangeable, there can be nothing accidental in God.

Chapter 5: Nothing is said of God according to accident, but only according to substance or according to relation, as in His relation to the Son.

Chapter 6: The heretical argument from the terms "unbegotten" and "begotten" is not compelling. Father and Son are equal. What is said according to relation is not affirmed according to substance.

Chapter 7: Begotten and unbegotten are terms which are asserted relatively and therefore do not denote substance.

Chapter 8: Whatever is spoken of God according to substance is spoken of each person severally, and together of the Trinity itself. In the Greek language God is called one essence and three hypostases; in Latin one essence and three substances.

Chapter 9: But in Latin usage, since essence and substance have come to have the same meaning, it is customary to say one essence or substance and three persons, though "person" itself is not a completely satisfactory word.

Chapter 10: Such things as being and greatness belong absolutely to God as an essence, and are spoken of the Trinity in the singular, not in the plural.

Chapter 11: The Trinity cannot be called the Father, except perhaps metaphorically, nor can it be called the Son. But the Trinity can be called the Holy Spirit, because the Holy Spirit is a certain unutterable communion of the Father and the Son. The Father is a spirit; the Son is a spirit, and They are both holy. The Holy Spirit is called the gift of both, and is given a name which suitably signifies the communion of both.

Chapter 12: Terms are wanting to express accurately the relations within the Trinity.

Chapter 13: The term beginning is used relatively in the Trinity, yet the Trinity as one God, Father, Son, and Holy Spirit, is the Beginning, the Creator with respect to the creature.

Chapter 14: In the Trinity, the Father is the beginning (principium) of the Son, and the Father and the Son are a Beginning of the Holy Spirit. But the Trinity is one Beginning in respect to the creature.

Chapter 15: The Holy Spirit existed as a gift even before He was given.

Chapter 16: Since nothing can be spoken of God accidentally, all that is said of Him in time is said relatively, not accidentally.

BOOK SIX

The question is proposed, how the apostle calls Christ "The power of God, and the wisdom of God." And an argument is raised, whether the Father is not wisdom Himself, but only the father of wisdom; or whether wisdom begat wisdom. But the answer to this is deferred for a little, while the unity and equality of the Father, and of the Son, and of the Holy Ghost, are proved; and that we ought to believe in a Trinity, not in a threefold (triplicem) God. Lastly, that saying of Hilary is explained, eternity in the Father, appearance in the image, use in the gift.

CHAPTER I

THE SON, ACCORDING TO THE APOSTLE, IS THE POWER AND WISDOM OF THE FATHER. HENCE THE REASONING OF THE CATHOLICS AGAINST THE EARLIER ARIANS. A DIFFICULTY IS RAISED, WHETHER THE FATHER IS NOT WISDOM HIMSELF, BUT ONLY THE FATHER OF WISDOM

SOME think themselves hindered from admitting the equality of the Father, Son, and Holy Spirit, because it is written, "Christ, the power of God, and the wisdom of God;" in that, on this ground, there does not appear to be equality; because the Father is not Himself power and wisdom, but the begetter of power and wisdom. And, in truth, the question is usually asked with no common earnestness, in what way God can be called the Father of power and wisdom. For the apostle says, "Christ the power of God, and the wisdom of God." [1] And hence some on our side have reasoned in this way against the Arians, at least against those who at first set themselves up against the Catholic faith. For Arius himself is reported to have said, that if He is a Son, then He was born; if He was born, there was a time when the Son was not: not understanding that even to be born is, to God, from all eternity; so that the Son is co-eternal with the Father, as the brightness which is produced and is spread around by fire is co-eval with it, and would be co-eternal, if fire were eternal. And therefore some of the later Arians have abandoned that opinion, and have confessed that the Son of God did not begin to be in time. But among the arguments which those on our side used to hold against them who said that there was a time when the Son was not, some were wont to introduce such an argument as this: If the Son of God is the power and wisdom of God, and God was never without power and wisdom, then the Son is co-eternal with God the Father; but the apostle

[1] 1 Cor. i. 24

says, "Christ the power of God, and the wisdom of God;" and a man must be senseless to say that God at any time had not power or wisdom; therefore there was no time when the Son was not.

Now this argument compels us to say that God the Father is not wise, except by having the wisdom which He begat, not by the Father in Himself being wisdom itself. Further, if it be so, just as the Son also Himself is called God of God, Light of Light, we must consider whether He can be called wisdom of wisdom, if God the Father is not wisdom itself, but only the begetter of wisdom. And if we hold this, why is He not the begetter also of His own greatness, and of His own goodness, and of His own eternity, and of His own omnipotence; so that He is not Himself His own greatness, and His own goodness, and His own eternity, and His own omnipotence; but is great with that greatness which He begat, and good with that goodness, and eternal with that eternity, and omnipotent with that omnipotence, which was born of Him; just as He Himself is not His own wisdom, but is wise with that wisdom which was born of Him? For we need not be afraid of being compelled to say that there are many sons of God, over and above the adoption of the creature, co-eternal with the Father, if He be the begetter of His own greatness, and goodness, and eternity, and omnipotence. Because it is easy to reply to this cavil, that it does not at all follow, because many things are named, that He should be the Father of many co-eternal *sons;* just as it does not follow that He is the Father of two sons, because Christ is said to be the power of God, and the wisdom of God. For that certainly is the power which is the wisdom, and that is the wisdom which is the power; and in like manner, therefore, of the rest also; so that that is the greatness which is the power, or any other of those things which either have been mentioned above, or may hereafter be mentioned.

CHAPTER II

WHAT IS SAID OF THE FATHER AND SON TOGETHER, AND WHAT NOT

But if nothing is spoken of the Father as such, except that which is spoken of Him in relation to the Son, that is, that He is His father, or begetter, or beginning; and if also the begetter is by consequence a beginning to that which he begets of himself; but whatever else is spoken of Him is so spoken as *with* the Son, or rather *in* the Son; whether that He is great with that greatness which He begat, or just with that justice which He begat, or good with that goodness which He begat, or powerful with that force or power which He begat, or wise with that wisdom which He begat: yet the Father is not said to be greatness itself, but the begetter of greatness; but the Son, as He is called the Son as such, is not so called *with* the Father but in relation *to* the Father, so is not great in and by himself, but *with* the Father, of whom He is the greatness; and so also is called wise *with* the Father, of whom He Himself is the wisdom; just as the Father is called wise *with* the Son, because

He is wise with that wisdom which He begat; therefore the one is not called without the other, whatever they are called in respect to themselves; that is, whatever they are called that manifests their essential nature, both are so called together—if these things are so, then the Father is not God without the Son, nor the Son God without the Father, but both together are God. And that which is said, "In the beginning was the Word," means that the Word was in the Father. Or if "In the beginning" is intended to mean, Before all things; then in that which follows, "And the Word was with God," the Son alone is understood to be the Word, not the Father and Son together, as though both were one Word (for He is the Word in the same way as He is the Image, but the Father and Son are not both together the Image, but the Son alone is the Image of the Father: just as He is also the Son of the Father, for both together are not the Son). But in that which is added, "And the Word was with God," there is much reason to understand thus: "The Word," which is the Son alone, "was with God," which is not the Father alone, but God the Father and the Son together. But what wonder is there, if this can be said in the case of some twofold things widely different from each other? For what are so different as soul and body? Yet we can say the soul was with a man, that is, in a man; although the soul is not the body, and man is both soul and body together. So that what follows in the Scripture, "And the Word was God," [2] may be understood thus: The Word, which is not the Father, was God together with the Father. Are we then to say thus, that the Father is the begetter of His own greatness, that is, the begetter of His own power, or the begetter of His own wisdom; and that the Son is greatness, and power, and wisdom; but that the great, omnipotent, and wise God, is both together? How then God *of* God, Light of Light? For not both together are God of God, but only the Son is of God, that is to say, of the Father; nor are both together Light of Light, but the Son only is of Light, that is, of the Father. Unless, perhaps, it was in order to intimate and inculcate briefly that the Son is co-eternal with the Father, that it is said, God of God, and Light of Light, or anything else of the like kind: as if to say, This which is not the Son without the Father, *of* this which is not the Father without the Son; that is, this Light which is not Light without the Father, *of* that Light, *viz.* the Father, which is not Light without the Son; so that, when it is said, God which is not the Son without the Father, and *of* God which is not the Father without the Son, it may be perfectly understood that the Begetter did not precede that which He begot. And if this be so, then this alone cannot be said of them, namely, this or that of this or that, which they are not both together. Just as the Word cannot be said to be *of* the Word, because both are not the Word together, but only the Son; nor image *of* image, since they are not both together the image; nor Son *of* Son, since both together are not the Son, according to that which is said, "I and my Father are one." [3] For "we are one" means, what He is, that am I also; according to essence, not according to relation.

[2] John i. 1   [3] John x. 30

CHAPTER III

And I know not whether the words, "They are one," are ever found in Scripture as spoken of things of which the nature is different. But if there are more things than one of the same nature, and they differ in sentiment, they are not one, and that so far as they differ in sentiment. For if the disciples were already one by the fact of being men, He would not say, "That they may be one, as we are one," [4] when commending them to the Father. But because Paul and Apollos were both alike men, and also of like sentiments, "He that planteth," he says, "and he that watereth are one." [5] When, therefore, anything is so called one, that it is not added in what it is one, and yet more things than one are called one, then the same essence and nature is signified, not differing nor disagreeing. But when it is added in what it is one, it may be meant that something is made one out of things more than one, though they are different in nature. As soul and body are assuredly not one; for what are so different? unless there be added or understood in what they are one, that is, one man, or one animal [person]. Thence the apostle says, "He who is joined to a harlot, is one body;" he does not say, they are one or he is one; but he has added "body," as though it were one body composed by being joined together of two different bodies, masculine and feminine.[6] And, "He that is joined unto the Lord," he says, "is one spirit;" he did not say, he that is joined unto the Lord is one, or they are one; but he added, "spirit." For the spirit of man and the Spirit of God are different in nature; but by being joined they become one spirit of two different spirits, so that the Spirit of God is blessed and perfect without the human spirit, but the spirit of man cannot be blessed without God. Nor is it without cause, I think, that when the Lord said so much in the Gospel according to John, and so often, of unity itself, whether of His own with the Father, or of ours interchangeably with ourselves; He has nowhere said, that we are also one with Himself, but, "that they may be one as we also are one." [7] Therefore the Father and the Son are one, undoubtedly according to unity of substance; and there is one God, and one great, and one wise, as we have argued.

Whence then is the Father greater? For if greater, He is greater by greatness; but whereas the Son is His greatness, neither assuredly is the Son greater than He who begat Him, nor is the Father greater than that greatness, whereby He is great; therefore they are equal. For whence is He equal, if not in that which He is, to whom it is not one thing to be, and another to

---

[4] John xvii. 11   [5] 1 Cor. iii. 8   [6] 1 Cor. vi. 16, 17   [7] John xvii. 11

be great? Or if the Father is greater in eternity, the Son is not equal in anything whatsoever. For whence equal? If you say in greatness, that greatness
is not equal which is less eternal, and so of all things else. Or is He perhaps
equal in power, but not equal in wisdom? But how is that power which is less
wise, equal? Or is He equal in wisdom, but not equal in power? But how is
that wisdom equal which is less powerful? It remains, therefore, that if He
is not equal in anything, He is not equal in all. But Scripture proclaims, that
"He thought it not robbery to be equal with God." [8] Therefore any adversary of the truth whatever, provided he feels bound by apostolical authority,
must needs confess that the Son is equal with God in each one thing whatsoever. Let him choose that which he will; from it he will be shown, that He
is equal in all things which are said of His substance.

CHAPTER IV

THE SAME ARGUMENT CONTINUED

For in like manner the virtues which are in the human mind, although
each has its own several and different meaning, yet are in no way mutually
separable; so that, for instance, whosoever were equal in courage, are equal
also in prudence, and temperance, and justice. For if you say that such and
such men are equal in courage, but that one of them is greater in prudence,
it follows that the courage of the other is less prudent, and so neither are
they equal in courage, since the courage of the former is more prudent. And
so you will find it to be the case with the other virtues, if you consider them
one by one. For the question is not of the strength of the body, but of the
courage of the mind. How much more therefore is this the case in that unchangeable and eternal substance, which is incomparably more simple than
the human mind is? Since, in the human mind, to be is not the same as to be
strong, or prudent, or just, or temperate; for a mind can exist, and yet have
none of these virtues. But in God to be is the same as to be strong, or to be
just, or to be wise, or whatever is said of that simple multiplicity, or multi-
fold simplicity, whereby to signify His substance. Wherefore, whether we
say God of God in such way that this name belongs to each, yet not so that
both together are two Gods, but one God; for they are in such way united
with each other, as according to the apostle's testimony may take place even
in diverse and differing substances; for both the Lord alone is a Spirit, and
the spirit of a man alone is assuredly a spirit; yet, if it cleave to the Lord,
"it is one spirit:" how much more there, where there is an absolutely inseparable and eternal union, so that He may not seem absurdly to be called as
it were the Son of both, when He is called the Son of God, if that which is
called God is only said of both together. Or perhaps it is, that whatever is
said of God so as to indicate His substance, is not said except of both to-

[8] Phil. ii. 6

gether, nay of the Trinity itself together? Whether therefore it be this or
that (which needs a closer inquiry), it is enough for the present to see from
what has been said, that the Son is in no respect equal with the Father, if He
is found to be unequal in anything which has to do with signifying His substance, as we have already shown. But the apostle has said that He is equal.
Therefore the Son is equal with the Father in all things, and is of one and
the same substance.

CHAPTER V

THE HOLY SPIRIT ALSO IS EQUAL TO THE FATHER AND THE SON IN ALL THINGS

Wherefore also the Holy Spirit consists in the same unity of substance,
and in the same equality. For whether He is the unity of both, or the holiness, or the love, or therefore the unity because the love, and therefore the
love because the holiness, it is manifest that He is not one of the two, through
whom the two are joined, through whom the Begotten is loved by the Begetter, and loves Him that begat Him, and through whom, not by participation, but by their own essence, neither by the gift of any superior, but by
their own, they are "keeping the unity of the Spirit in the bond of peace;" [9]
which we are commanded to imitate by grace, both towards God and towards ourselves. "On which two commandments hang all the law and the
prophets." [10] So those three are God, one, alone, great, wise, holy, blessed.
But we are blessed from Him, and through Him, and in Him; because we
ourselves are one by His gift, and one spirit with Him, because our soul
cleaves to Him so as to follow Him. And it is good for us to cleave to God,
since He will destroy every man who is estranged from Him.[11] Therefore the
Holy Spirit, whatever it is, is something common both to the Father and
Son. But that communion itself is consubstantial and co-eternal; and if it
may fitly be called friendship, let it be so called; but it is more aptly called
love. And this is also a substance, since God is a substance, and "God is
love," as it is written.[12] But as He is a substance together with the Father
and the Son, so that substance is together with them great, and together
with them good, and together with them holy, and whatsoever else is said in
reference to substance; since it is not one thing to God to be, and another to
be great or to be good, and the rest, as we have shown above. For if love is
less great therein [*i.e.* in God] than wisdom, then wisdom is loved in less degree than according to what it is; love is therefore equal, in order that wisdom may be loved according to its being; but wisdom is equal with the Father, as we have proved above; therefore also the Holy Spirit is equal; and
if equal, equal in all things, on account of the absolute simplicity which is in
that substance. And therefore they are not more than three: One who loves

---

[9] Eph. iv. 3   [10] Matt. xxii. 37-40   [11] Ps. lxxvii. 28, 27   [12] 1 John iv. 16

Him who is from Himself, and One who loves Him from whom He is, and Love itself. And if this last is nothing, how is "God love"? If it is not substance, how is God substance?

CHAPTER VI

HOW GOD IS A SUBSTANCE BOTH SIMPLE AND MANIFOLD

But if it is asked how that substance is both simple and manifold: consider, first, why the creature is manifold, but in no way really simple. And first, all that is body is composed certainly of parts; so that therein one part is greater, another less, and the whole is greater than any part whatever or how great soever. For the heaven and the earth are parts of the whole bulk of the world; and the earth alone, and the heaven alone, is composed of innumerable parts; and its third part is less than the remainder, and the half of it is less than the whole; and the whole body of the world, which is usually called by its two parts, *viz.* the heaven and the earth, is certainly greater than the heaven alone or the earth alone. And in each several body, size is one thing, color another, shape another; for the same color and the same shape may remain with diminished size; and the same shape and the same size may remain with the color changed; and the same shape not remaining, yet the thing may be just as great, and of the same color. And whatever other things are predicated together of body can be changed either all together, or the larger part of them without the rest. And hence the nature of body is conclusively proved to be manifold, and in no respect simple. The spiritual creature also, that is, the soul, is indeed the more simple of the two if compared with the body; but if we omit the comparison with the body, it is manifold, and itself also not simple. For it is on this account more simple than the body, because it is not diffused in bulk through extension of place, but in each body, it is both whole in the whole, and whole in each several part of it; and, therefore, when anything takes place in any small particle whatever of the body, such as the soul can feel, although it does not take place in the whole body, yet the whole soul feels it, since the whole soul is not unconscious of it. But, nevertheless, since in the soul also it is one thing to be skillful, another to be indolent, another to be intelligent, another to be of retentive memory; since cupidity is one thing, fear another, joy another, sadness another; and since things innumerable, and in innumerable ways, are to be found in the nature of the soul, some without others, and some more, some less; it is manifest that its nature is not simple, but manifold. For nothing simple is changeable, but every creature is changeable.

CHAPTER VII

GOD IS A TRINITY, BUT NOT TRIPLE (TRIPLEX)

But God is truly called in manifold ways, great, good, wise, blessed, true, and whatsoever other thing seems to be said of Him not unworthily: but His greatness is the same as His wisdom; for He is not great by bulk, but by power; and His goodness is the same as His wisdom and greatness, and His truth the same as all those things; and in Him it is not one thing to be blessed, and another to be great, or wise, or true, or good, or in a word to be Himself.

Neither, since He is a Trinity, is He therefore to be thought triple (*triplex*), otherwise the Father alone, or the Son alone, will be less than the Father and Son together. Although, indeed, it is hard to see how we can say, either the Father alone, or the Son alone; since both the Father is with the Son, and the Son with the Father, always and inseparably: not that both are the Father, or both are the Son; but because they are always one in relation to the other, and neither the one nor the other alone. But because we call even the Trinity itself God alone, although He is always with holy spirits and souls, but say that He only is God, because they are not also God with Him; so we call the Father the Father alone, not because He is separate from the Son, but because they are not both together the Father.

CHAPTER VIII

NO ADDITION CAN BE MADE TO THE NATURE OF GOD

Since, therefore, the Father alone, or the Son alone, or the Holy Spirit alone, is as great as is the Father and the Son and the Holy Spirit together, in no manner is He to be called threefold. Forasmuch as bodies increase by union of themselves. For although he who cleaves to his wife is one body; yet it is a greater body than if it were that of the husband alone, or of the wife alone. But in spiritual things, when the less adheres to the greater, as the creature to the Creator, the former becomes greater than it was, not the latter. For in those things which are not great by bulk, to be greater is to be better. And the spirit of any creature becomes better, when it cleaves to the Creator, than if it did not so cleave; and therefore also greater because better. "He," then, "that is joined unto the Lord is one spirit:" [13] but yet the Lord does not therefore become greater, although he who is joined to the Lord does so. In God Himself, therefore, when the equal Son, or the Holy Spirit equal to the Father and the Son, is joined to the equal Father, God does not become greater than each of them severally; because that perfectness cannot increase. But whether it be the Father, or the Son, or the Holy

[13] Cor. vi. 17

Spirit, He is perfect, and God the Father the Son and the Holy Spirit is perfect; and therefore He is a Trinity rather than triple.

CHAPTER IX

WHETHER ONE OR THE THREE PERSONS TOGETHER ARE CALLED THE ONLY GOD

And since we are showing how we can say the Father alone, because there is no Father in the Godhead except Himself, we must consider also the opinion which holds that the only true God is not the Father alone, but the Father and the Son and the Holy Spirit. For if any one should ask whether the Father alone is God, how can it be replied that He is not, unless perhaps we were to say that the Father indeed is God, but that He is not God alone, but that the Father, Son, and Holy Spirit are God alone? But then what shall we do with that testimony of the Lord? For He was speaking to the Father, and had named the Father as Him to whom He was speaking, when He says, "And this is life eternal, that they may know Thee the one true God." [14] And this the Arians indeed usually take, as if the Son were not true God. Passing them by, however, we must see whether, when it is said to the Father, "That they may know Thee the one true God," we are forced to understand it as if He wished to intimate that the Father alone is the true God; lest we should not understand any to be God, except the three together, the Father, Son, and Holy Spirit. Are we therefore, from the testimony of the Lord, both to call the Father the one true God, and the Son the one true God, and the Holy Spirit the one true God, and the Father, the Son, and the Holy Spirit together, that is, the Trinity itself together, not three true Gods but one true God? Or because He added, "And Jesus Christ whom Thou hast sent," are we to supply "the one true God:" so that the order of the words is this, "That they may know Thee, and Jesus Christ whom Thou hast sent, the one true God?" Why then did He omit to mention the Holy Spirit? Is it because it follows, that whenever we name One who cleaves to One by a harmony so great that through this harmony both are one, this harmony itself must be understood, although it is not mentioned? For in that place, too, the apostle seems as it were to pass over the Holy Spirit; and yet there, too, He is understood, where he says, "All are yours, and ye are Christ's, and Christ is God's" [15] And again, "The head of the woman is the man, the head of the man is Christ, and the head of Christ is God." [16] But again, if God is only all three together, how can God be the head of Christ, that is, the Trinity the head of Christ, since Christ is in the Trinity in order that it may be the Trinity? Is that which is the Father with the Son, the head of that which is the Son alone? For the Father with the Son is God, but the Son alone is Christ: especially since it is the Word already made flesh that speaks; and

[14] John xvii. 3   [15] 1 Cor. iii. 22, 23   [16] 1 Cor. xi. 3

according to this His humiliation also, the Father is greater than He, as He says, "for my Father is greater than I;" [17] so that the very being of God, which is one to Him with the Father, is itself the head of the man who is Mediator, which He is alone.[18] For if we rightly call the mind the chief thing of man, that is, as it were the head of the human substance, although the man himself together with the mind is man; why is not the Word with the Father, which together is God, much more suitably and much more the head of Christ, although Christ as man cannot be understood except with the Word which was made flesh? But this, as we have already said, we shall consider somewhat more carefully hereafter. At present the equality and one and the same substance of the Trinity has been demonstrated as briefly as possible, that in whatever way that other question be determined, the more rigorous discussion of which we have deferred, nothing may hinder us from confessing the absolute equality of the Father, Son, and Holy Spirit.

CHAPTER X

OF THE ATTRIBUTES ASSIGNED BY HILARY TO EACH PERSON. THE TRINITY IS REPRESENTED IN THINGS THAT ARE MADE

A certain writer, when he would briefly intimate the special attributes of each of the persons in the Trinity, tells us that "Eternity is in the Father, form in the Image, use in the Gift." And since he was a man of no mean authority in handling the Scriptures, and in the assertion of the faith, for it is Hilary who put this in his book (*On the Trinity*, ii.); I have searched into the hidden meaning of these words as far as I can, that is, of the Father, and the Image, and the Gift, of eternity, and of form, and of use. And I do not think that he intended more by the word eternity, than that the Father has not a father from whom He is; but the Son is from the Father, so as to be, and so as to be co-eternal with Him. For if an image perfectly fills the measure of that of which it is the image, then the image is made equal to that of which it is the image, not the latter to its own image. And in respect to this image he has named form, I believe on account of the quality of beauty, where there is at once such great fitness, and prime equality, and prime likeness, differing in nothing, and unequal in no respect, and in no part unlike, but answering exactly to Him whose image it is: where there is prime and absolute life, to whom it is not one thing to live, and another to be, but the same thing to be and to live; and prime and absolute intellect, to whom it is not one thing to live, another to understand, but to understand is to live, and is to be, and all things are one: as though a perfect Word, to which nothing is wanting, and a certain skill of the omnipotent and wise God, full of all living, unchangeable sciences, and all one in it, as itself is one from one, with whom it is one. Therein God knew all things which he made by it; and therefore,

[17] John xiv. 28   [18] 1 Tim. ii. 5

while times pass away and succeed, nothing passes away or succeeds to the knowledge of God. For things which are created are not therefore known by God, because they have been made; and not rather have been therefore made, even although changeable, because they are known unchangeably by Him. Therefore that unspeakable conjunction of the Father and His image is not without fruition, without love, without joy. Therefore that love, delight, felicity, or blessedness, if indeed it can be worthily expressed by any human word, is called by him, in short, Use; and is the Holy Spirit in the Trinity, not begotten, but the sweetness of the begetter and of the begotten, filling all creatures according to their capacity with abundant bountifulness and copiousness, that they may keep their proper order and rest satisfied in their proper place.

Therefore all these things which are made by divine skill, show in themselves a certain unity, and form, and order; for each of them is both some one thing, as are the several natures of bodies and dispositions of souls; and is fashioned in some form, as are the figures or qualities of bodies, and the various learning or skill of souls; and seeks or preserves a certain order, as are the several weights or combinations of bodies and the loves or delights of souls. When therefore we regard the Creator, who is understood by the things that are made[19] we must needs understand the Trinity of whom there appear traces in the creature, as is fitting. For in that Trinity is the supreme source of all things, and the most perfect beauty, and the most blessed delight. Those three, therefore, both seem to be mutually determined to each other, and are in themselves infinite. But here in corporeal things, one thing alone is not as much as three together, and two are something more than one; but in that highest Trinity one is as much as the three together, nor are two anything more than one. And They are infinite in themselves. So each is in each, and all in each, and each in all, and all in all, and all are one. Let him who sees this, whether in part, or "through a glass and in an enigma," [20] rejoice in knowing God; and let him honor Him as God, and give thanks; but let him who does not see it, strive to see it through piety, not to cavil at it through blindness. Since God is one, but yet is a Trinity. Neither are we to take the words, "of whom, and through whom, and to whom are all things," as used indiscriminately [*i.e.*, to denote a unity without distinctions]; nor yet to denote many gods, for "to *Him*, be glory for ever and ever. Amen." [21]

[19] Rom. i. 20   [20] 1 Cor. xiii. 12   [21] Rom. xi. 36

BOOK SEVEN

Summary

Chapter 1: Can each person in the Trinity, not with the other two, be called God, or wise, or true, or great? They are all one essence, and since in the Divine simplicity to be is to be wise or to be great, wisdom or greatness is the same as essence.

Chapter 2: The Father and the Son are one essence, one greatness, one truth and one wisdom. But both are not the Word or the Son, which are relative terms, for to be is not to be the Word or the Son.

Chapter 3: Christ as the Word is intimated in the Holy Scriptures by the name of Wisdom, while both the Father and the Holy Spirit are Wisdom. The Father is wisdom, the Son is wisdom, and the Holy Spirit is wisdom, and together not three wisdoms, but one wisdom.

Chapter 4: The Greeks speak of one essence and three substances; the Latins of one essence or substance and three persons. The three in the Trinity have one essence in common. The term person is chosen, though the Scriptures do not speak of three persons, because Scripture does not contradict the usage. We have to use terms for speaking, particularly because heretical error has to be opposed. Speech is weak to express that which can be grasped in the secret places of the mind.

Chapter 5: Since the term substance implies a subject, and there can be something in it to make it complex, to be absolutely precise, and to preserve the conception of God's simplicity, the term essence should be used.

Chapter 6: Person seems to be the most desirable term for the constituents of the Trinity. To try to discover appropriate terms by an analysis into genus and species is not satisfactory. We must remember that the three "persons" together are equal to each singly. They are one essence. Man is made "after the image" of God, but there is an inequality of likeness. In the Trinity, there is no bulk, or interval, or unlikeness, or inequality. If we cannot understand this, we must hold it by faith.

771

BOOK EIGHT

Explains and proves that not only the Father is not greater than the Son, but neither are both together anything greater than the Holy Spirit, nor any two together in the same Trinity anything greater than one, nor all three together anything greater than each severally. It is then shown how the nature itself of God may be understood from our understanding of truth, and from our knowledge of the supreme good, and from the innate love of righteousness, whereby a righteous soul is loved even by a soul that is itself not yet righteous. But it is urged above all, that the knowledge of God is to be sought by love, which God is said to be in the Scriptures; and in this love is also pointed out the existence of some trace of a Trinity.

PREFACE

THE CONCLUSION OF WHAT HAS BEEN SAID ABOVE. THE RULE TO BE OBSERVED IN THE MORE DIFFICULT QUESTIONS OF THE FAITH

WE HAVE said elsewhere that those things are predicated specially in the Trinity as belonging severally to each person, which are predicated relatively the one to the other, as Father and Son, and the gift of both, the Holy Spirit; for the Father is not the Trinity, nor the Son the Trinity, nor the gift the Trinity: but what whenever each is singly spoken of in respect to themselves, then they are not spoken of as three in the plural number, but one, the Trinity itself, as the Father God, the Son God, and the Holy Spirit God; the Father good, the Son good, and the Holy Spirit good; and the Father omnipotent, the Son omnipotent, and the Holy Spirit omnipotent: yet neither three Gods, nor three goods, nor three omnipotents, but one God, good, omnipotent, the Trinity itself; and whatsoever else is said of them not relatively in respect to each other, but individually in respect to themselves. For they are thus spoken of according to essence, since in them to be is the same as to be great, as to be good, as to be wise, and whatever else is said of each person individually therein, or of the Trinity itself, in respect to themselves. And that therefore they are called three persons, or three substances, not in order that any difference of essence may be understood, but that we may be able to answer by some one word, should any one ask what three, or what three things? And that there is so great an equality in that Trinity, that not only the Father is not greater than the Son, as regards divinity, but neither are the Father and Son together greater than the Holy Spirit; nor is each individual person, whichever it be of the three, less than the Trinity itself. This is what we have said; and if it is handled and repeated frequently, it becomes, no doubt, more familiarly known: yet some limit, too, must be put to the discussion, and we must supplicate God with most devout piety, that He will open our understanding, and take away the inclination of disputing, in order that our minds may discern the essence of the truth, that has neither bulk nor moveableness. Now, therefore, so far as the Creator Himself aids us in His marvellous mercy, let us consider these subjects, into which we will enter more deeply than we entered into those which preceded, although they are in truth the same; preserving the while this rule, that what has not yet been made clear to our intellect, be nevertheless not loosened from the firmness of our faith.

CHAPTER I

IT IS SHOWN BY REASON THAT IN GOD THREE ARE NOT ANYTHING GREATER THAN ONE PERSON

For we say that in this Trinity two or three persons are not anything greater than one of them; which carnal perception does not receive, for no other reason except because it perceives as it can the true things which are created, but cannot discern the truth itself by which they are created; for if it could, then the very corporeal light would in no way be more clear than this which we have said. For in respect to the substance of truth, since it alone truly is, nothing is greater, unless because it more truly is.[1] But in respect to whatsoever is intelligible and unchangeable, no one thing is more truly than another, since all alike are unchangeably eternal; and that which therein is called great, is not great from any other source than from that by which it truly is. Wherefore, where magnitude itself is truth, whatsoever has more of magnitude must needs have more of truth; whatsoever therefore has not more of truth, has not also more of magnitude. Further, whatsoever has more of truth is certainly more true, just as that is greater which has more of magnitude; therefore in respect to the substance of truth that is more great which is more true. But the Father and the Son together are not more truly than the Father singly, or the Son singly. Both together, therefore, are not anything greater than each of them singly. And since also the Holy Spirit equally is truly, the Father and Son together are not anything greater than He, since neither are they more truly. The Father also and the Holy Spirit together, since they do not surpass the Son in truth (for they are not more truly), do not surpass Him either in magnitude. And so the Son and the Holy Spirit together are just as great as the Father alone, since they are as truly. So also the Trinity itself is as great as each several person therein. For

[1] [In this and the following chapter, the meaning of Augustine will be clearer, if the Latin *"veritas," "vera,"* and *"vere,"* are rendered, occasionally, by "reality," "real," and "really." He is endeavoring to prove the equality of the three persons, by the fact that they are equally real (true), and the degree of their reality (truth) is the same. Real being is true being; reality is truth. In common phraseology, truth and reality are synonymous.—W. G. T. S.]

where truth itself is magnitude, that is not more great which is not more true: since in regard to the essence of truth, to be true is the same as to be, and to be is the same as to be great; therefore to be great is the same as to be true. And in regard to it, therefore, what is equally true must needs also be equally great.

CHAPTER II

EVERY CORPOREAL CONCEPTION MUST BE REJECTED, IN ORDER THAT IT MAY BE UNDERSTOOD HOW GOD IS TRUTH

But in respect to bodies, it may be the case that this gold and that gold may be equally true [real], but this may be greater than that, since magnitude is not the same thing in this case as truth; and it is one thing for it to be gold, another to be great. So also in the nature of the soul; a soul is not called great in the same respect in which it is called true. For he, too, has a true [real] soul who has not a great soul; since the essence of body and soul is not the essence of the truth [reality] itself; as is the Trinity, one God, alone, great, true, truthful, the truth. Of whom if we endeavor to think, so far as He Himself permits and grants, let us not think of any touch or embrace in local space, as if of three bodies, or of any compactness of conjunction, as fables tell of three-bodied Geryon; but let whatsoever may occur to the mind, that is of such sort as to be greater in three than in each singly, and less in one than in two, be rejected without any doubt; for so everything corporeal is rejected. But also in spiritual things let nothing changeable that may have occurred to the mind be thought of God. For when we aspire from this depth to that height, it is a step towards no small knowledge, if, before we can know what God is, we can already know what He is not. For certainly He is neither earth nor heaven; nor, as it were, earth and heaven; nor any such thing as we see in the heaven; nor any such thing as we do not see, but which perhaps is in heaven. Neither if you were to magnify in the imagination of your thought the light of the sun as much as you are able, either that it may be greater, or that it may be brighter, a thousand times as much, or times without number; neither is this God. Neither as we think of the pure angels as spirits animating celestial bodies, and changing and dealing with them after the will by which they serve God; not even if all, and there are "thousands of thousands," [2] were brought together into one, and became one; neither is any such thing God. Neither if you were to think of the same spirits as without bodies—a thing indeed most difficult for carnal thought to do. Behold and see, if thou canst, O soul pressed down by the corruptible body, and weighed down by earthly thoughts, many and various; behold and see, if thou canst, that God is truth.[3] For it is written that "God is light;" [4] not in such way as these eyes see, but in such way as the heart sees,

[2] Apoc. v. 11   [3] Wisd. ix. 15   [4] 1 John i. 5

when it is said, He is truth [reality]. Ask not what is truth [reality]; for immediately the darkness of corporeal images and the clouds of phantasms will put themselves in the way, and will disturb that calm which at the first twinkling shone forth to thee, when I said truth [reality]. See that thou remainest, if thou canst, in that first twinkling with which thou art dazzled, as it were, by a flash, when it is said to thee, Truth [Reality]. But thou canst not; thou wilt glide back into those usual and earthly things. And what weight, pray, is it that will cause thee so to glide back, unless it be the bird-lime of the stains of appetite thou hast contracted, and the errors of thy wandering from the right path?

CHAPTER III

HOW GOD MAY BE KNOWN TO BE THE CHIEF GOOD. THE MIND DOES NOT BECOME GOOD UNLESS BY TURNING TO GOD

Behold again, and see if thou canst. Thou certainly dost not love anything except what is good, since good is the earth, with the loftiness of its mountains, and the due measure of its hills, and the level surface of its plains; and good is an estate that is pleasant and fertile; and good is a house that is arranged in due proportions, and is spacious and bright; and good are animal and animate bodies; and good is air that is temperate and salubrious; and good is food that is agreeable and fit for health; and good is health, without pains or lassitude; and good is the countenance of man that is disposed in fit proportions, and is cheerful in look, and bright in color; and good is the mind of a friend, with the sweetness of agreement, and with the confidence of love; and good is a righteous man; and good are riches, since they are readily useful; and good is the heaven, with its sun, and moon, and stars; and good are the angels, by their holy obedience; and good is discourse that sweetly teaches and suitably admonishes the hearer; and good is a poem that is harmonious in its numbers and weighty in its sense. And why add yet more and more? This thing is good and that good, but take away this and that, and regard good itself if thou canst; so wilt thou see God, not good by a good that is other than Himself, but the good of all good. For in all these good things, whether those which I have mentioned, or any else that are to be discerned or thought, we could not say that one was better than another, when we judge truly, unless a conception of the good itself had been impressed upon us, such that according to it we might both approve some things as good, and prefer one good to another. So God is to be loved, not this and that good, but the good itself. For the good that must be sought for the soul is not one above which it is to fly by judging, but to which it is to cleave by loving; and what can this be except God? Not a good mind, or a good angel, or the good heaven, but the good good. For perhaps what I wish to say may be more easily perceived in this way. For when, for instance, a mind is called good, as there are two words, so from these words I understand two things—one whereby it is mind, and another whereby it is good. And itself had no share in making itself a mind, for there was nothing as yet to make itself to be anything; but to make itself to be a good mind, I see, must be brought about by the will: not because that by which it is mind is not itself anything good— for how else is it already called, and most truly called, better than the body? —but it is not yet called a good mind, for this reason, that the action of the will still is wanted, by which it is to become more excellent; and if it has neglected this, then it is justly blamed, and is rightly called not a good mind. For it then differs from the mind which does perform this; and since the latter is praiseworthy, the former doubtless, which does not perform it, is blameable. But when it does this of set purpose, and becomes a good mind, it yet cannot attain to being so unless it turn itself to something which itself is not. And to what can it turn itself that it may become a good mind, except to the good which it loves, and seeks, and obtains? And if it turns itself back again from this, and becomes not good, then by the very act of turning away from the good, unless that good remain in it from which it turns away, it cannot again turn itself back thither if it should wish to amend.

Wherefore there would be no changeable goods, unless there were the unchangeable good. Whenever then thou art told of this good thing and that good thing, which things can also in other respects be called not good, if thou canst put aside those things which are good by the participation of the good, and discern that good itself by the participation of which they are good (for when this or that good thing is spoken of, thou understandest together with them the good itself also): if, then, I say thou canst remove these things, and canst discern the good in itself, then thou wilt have discerned God. And if thou shalt cleave to Him with love, thou shalt be forthwith blessed. But whereas other things are not loved, except because they are good, be ashamed, in cleaving to them, not to love the good itself whence they are good. That also, which is a mind, only because it is a mind, while it is not yet also good by the turning itself to the unchangeable good, but, as I said, is only a mind; whenever it so pleases us, as that we prefer it even, if we understand aright, to all corporeal light, does not please us in itself, but in that skill by which it was made. For it is thence approved as made, wherein it is seen to have been to be made. This is truth, and simple good: for it is nothing else than the good itself, and for this reason also the chief good. For no good can be diminished or increased, except that which is good from some other good. Therefore the mind turns itself, in order to be good, to that by which it comes to be a mind. Therefore the will is then in harmony with nature, so that the mind may be perfected in good, when that good is loved by the turning of the will to it, whence that other good also comes which is not lost by the turning away of the will from it. For by turning itself from the chief good, the mind loses the being a good mind; but it does not lose the being a mind. And this, too, is a good already, and one better than the body. The will, therefore, loses that which the will obtains. For the mind already was, that could wish to be turned to that from which it was: but that as yet was not, that could wish to be before it was. And herein is our [supreme] good, when we see whether the thing ought to be or to have been, respecting which we comprehend that it ought to be or to have been, and when we see that the thing could not have been unless it ought to have been, of which we also do not comprehend in what manner it ought to have been. This good then is not far from every one of us: for in it we live, and move, and have our being.[5]

CHAPTER IV

GOD MUST FIRST BE KNOWN BY AN UNERRING FAITH, THAT HE MAY BE LOVED

But it is by love that we must stand firm to this and cleave to this, in order that we may enjoy the presence of that by which we are, and in the absence of which we could not be at all. For as "we walk as yet by faith, and not by sight," [6] we certainly do not yet see God, as the same apostle saith, "face to face:" [7] whom however we shall never see, unless now already we love. But who loves what he does not know? For it is possible something may be known and not loved: but I ask whether it is possible that what is not known can be loved; since if it cannot, then no one loves God before he knows Him. And what is it to know God except to behold Him and steadfastly perceive Him with the mind? For He is not a body to be searched out by carnal eyes. But before also that we have power to behold and to perceive God, as He can be beheld and perceived, which is permitted to the pure in heart; for "blessed are the pure in heart, for they shall see God;" [8] except He is loved by faith, it will not be possible for the heart to be cleansed, in order that it may be apt and meet to see Him. For where are there those three, in order to build up which in the mind the whole apparatus of the divine Scriptures has been raised up, namely Faith, Hope, and Charity,[9] except in a mind believing what it does not yet see, and hoping and loving what it believes? Even He therefore who is not known, but yet is believed, can be loved. But indisputably we must take care, lest the mind believing that which it does not see, feign to itself something which is not, and hope for and love that which is false. For in that case, it will not be charity out of a pure heart, and of a good conscience, and of faith unfeigned, which is the end of the commandment, as the same apostle says.[10]

But it must needs be, that, when by reading or hearing of them we believe in any corporeal things which we have not seen, the mind frames for itself something under bodily features and forms, just as it may occur to our thoughts; which either is not true, or even if it be true, which can most rarely happen, yet this is of no benefit to us to believe in by faith, but it is useful for some other purpose, which is intimated by means of it. For who is there

[5] Acts xvii. 27, 28   [6] 2 Cor. v. 7   [7] 1 Cor. xiii. 12   [8] Matt. v. 8   [9] 1 Cor. xiii. 13   [10] 1 Tim. i. 5

that reads or hears what the Apostle Paul has written, or what has been written of him, that does not imagine to himself the countenance both of the apostle himself, and of all those whose names are there mentioned? And whereas, among such a multitude of men to whom these books are known, each imagines in a different way those bodily features and forms, it is assuredly uncertain which it is that imagines them more nearly and more like the reality. Nor, indeed, is our faith busied therein with the bodily countenance of those men; but only that by the grace of God they so lived and so acted as that Scripture witnesses: this it is which it is both useful to believe, and which must not be despaired of, and must be sought. For even the countenance of our Lord Himself in the flesh is variously fancied by the diversity of countless imaginations, which yet was one, whatever it was. Nor in our faith which we have of our Lord Jesus Christ, is that wholesome which the mind imagines for itself, perhaps far other than the reality, but that which we think of man according to his kind: for we have a notion of human nature implanted in us, as it were by rule, according to which we know forthwith, that whatever such thing we see is a man or the form of a man.

CHAPTER V

HOW THE TRINITY MAY BE LOVED THOUGH UNKNOWN

Our conception is framed according to this notion, when we believe that God was made man for us, as an example of humility, and to show the love of God towards us. For this it is which it is good for us to believe, and to retain firmly and unshakenly in our heart, that the humility by which God was born of a woman, and was led to death through contumelies so great by mortal men, is the chiefest remedy by which. the swelling of our pride may be cured, and the profound mystery by which the bond of sin may be loosed. So also, because we know what omnipotence is, we believe concerning the omnipotent God in the power of His miracles and of His resurrection, and we frame conceptions respecting actions of this kind, according to the species and genera of things that are either ingrafted in us by nature, or gathered by experience, that our faith may not be feigned. For neither do we know the countenance of the Virgin Mary; from whom, untouched by a husband, nor tainted in the birth itself, He was wonderfully born. Neither have we seen what were the lineaments of the body of Lazarus; nor yet Bethany; nor the sepulchre, and that stone which He commanded to be removed when He raised Him from the dead; nor the new tomb cut out in the rock, whence He Himself arose; nor the Mount of Olives, from whence He ascended into heaven. And, in short, whoever of us have not seen these things, know not whether they are as we conceive them to be, nay judge them more probably not to be so. For when the aspect either of a place, or a man, or of any other body, which we happened to imagine before we saw it, turns out to be the same when it occurs to our sight as it was when it occurred to our mind, we are moved with no little wonder, so scarcely and hardly ever does it happen. And yet we believe those things most steadfastly, because we imagine them according to a special and general notion, of which we are certain. For we believe our Lord Jesus Christ to be born of a virgin who was called Mary. But what a virgin is, or what it is to be born, and what is a proper name, we do not believe, but certainly know. And whether that was the countenance of Mary which occurred to the mind in speaking of those things or recollecting them, we neither know at all, nor believe. It is allowable, then, in this case to say without violation of the faith, perhaps she had such or such a countenance, perhaps she had not: but no one could say without violation of the Christian faith, that perhaps Christ was born of a virgin.

Wherefore, since we desire to understand the eternity, and equality, and unity of the Trinity, as much as is permitted us, but ought to believe before we understand; and since we must watch carefully, that our faith be not feigned; since we must have the fruition of the same Trinity, that we may live blessedly; but if we have believed anything false of it, our hope would be worthless, and our charity not pure: how then can we love, by believing, that Trinity which we do not know? Is it according to the special or general notion, according to which we love the Apostle Paul? In whose case, even if he was not of that countenance which occurs to us when we think of him (and this we do not know at all), yet we know what a man is. For not to go far away, this *we* are; and it is manifest he, too, was this, and that his soul joined to his body lived after the manner of mortals. Therefore we believe this of him, which we find in ourselves, according to the species or genus under which all human nature alike is comprised. What then do we know, whether specially or generally, of that most excellent Trinity, as if there were many such trinities, some of which we had learned by experience, so that we may believe that Trinity, too, to have been such as they, through the rule of similitude, impressed upon us, whether a special or a general notion; and thus love also that thing which we believe and do not yet know, from the parity of the thing which we do know? But this certainly is not so. Or is it that, as we love in our Lord Jesus Christ, that He rose from the dead, although we never saw any one rise from thence, so we can believe in and love the Trinity which we do not see, and the like of which we never have seen? But we certainly know what it is to die, and what it is to live; because we both live, and from time to time have seen and experienced both dead and dying persons. And what else is it to rise again, except to live again, that is, to return to life from death? When, therefore, we say and believe that there is a Trinity, we know what a Trinity is, because we know what three are; but this is not what we love. For we can easily have this whenever we will, to pass over other things, by just holding up three fingers. Or do we indeed love, not every trinity, but *the* Trinity, that is God? We love then in the Trinity, that it is God: but we never saw or knew any other God, because God is One; He alone whom we have not yet seen, and whom we love by believing.

But the question is, from what likeness or comparison of known things can we believe, in order that we may love God, whom we do not yet know?

CHAPTER VI

HOW THE MAN NOT YET RIGHTEOUS CAN KNOW THE RIGHTEOUS MAN WHOM HE LOVES

Return then with me, and let us consider why we love the apostle. Is it at all on account of his human kind, which we know right well, in that we believe him to have been a man? Assuredly not; for if it were so, he now is not him whom we love, since he is no longer that man, for his soul is separated from his body. But we believe that which we love in him to be still living, for we love his righteous mind. From what general or special rule then, except that we know both what a mind is, and what it is to be righteous? And we say, indeed, not unfitly, that we therefore know what a mind is, because we too have a mind. For neither did we ever see it with our eyes, and gather a special or general notion from the resemblance of more minds than one, which we had seen; but rather, as I have said before, because we too have it. For what is known so intimately, and so perceives itself to be itself, as that by which also all other things are perceived, that is, the mind itself? For we recognize the movements of bodies also, by which we perceive that others live besides ourselves, from the resemblance of ourselves; since we also so move our body in living as we observe those bodies to be moved. For even when a living body is moved, there is no way opened to our eyes to see the mind, a thing which cannot be seen by the eyes; but we perceive something to be contained in that bulk, such as is contained in ourselves, so as to move in like manner our own bulk, which is the life and the soul. Neither is this, as it were, the property of human foresight and reason, since brute animals also perceive that not only they themselves live, but also other brute animals interchangeably, and the one the other, and that we ourselves do so. Neither do they see our souls, save from the movements of the body, and that immediately and most easily by some natural agreement. Therefore we both know the mind of any one from our own, and believe also from our own of him whom we do not know. For not only do we perceive that there is a mind, but we can also know what a mind is, by reflecting upon our own: for we have a mind. But whence do we know what a righteous man is? For we said above that we love the apostle for no other reason except that he is a righteous mind. We know, then, what a righteous man also is, just as we know what a mind is. But what a mind is, as has been said, we know from ourselves, for there is a mind in us. But whence do we know what a righteous man is, if we are not righteous? But if no one but he who is righteous knows what is a righteous man, no one but a righteous man loves a righteous man; for one cannot love him whom one believes to be righteous, for this very reason that one does believe him to be righteous, if one does not know what it is to be righteous; according to that which we have shown above, that no one loves what he believes and does not see, except by some rule of a general or special notion. And if for this reason no one but a righteous man loves a righteous man, how will any one wish to be a righteous man who is not yet so? For no one wishes to be that which he does not love. But, certainly, that he who is not righteous may be so, it is necessary that he should wish to be righteous; and in order that he may wish to be righteous, he loves the righteous man. Therefore, even he who is not yet righteous, loves the righteous man. But he cannot love the righteous man, who is ignorant what a righteous man is. Accordingly, even he who is not yet righteous, knows what a righteous man is. Whence then does he know this? Does he see it with his eyes? Is any corporeal thing righteous, as it is white, or black, or square, or round? Who could say this? Yet with one's eyes one has seen nothing except corporeal things. But there is nothing righteous in a man except the mind; and when a man is called a righteous man, he is called so from the mind, not from the body. For righteousness is in some sort the beauty of the mind, by which men are beautiful; very many too who are misshapen and deformed in body. And as the mind is not seen with the eyes, so neither is its beauty. From whence then does he who is not yet righteous know what a righteous man is, and love the righteous man that he may become righteous? Do certain signs shine forth by the motion of the body, by which this or that man is manifested to be righteous? But whence does any one know that these are the signs of a righteous mind, when he is wholly ignorant what it is to be righteous? Therefore he does know. But whence do we know what it is to be righteous, even when we are not yet righteous? If we know from without ourselves, we know it by some bodily thing. But this is not a thing of the body. Therefore we know in ourselves what it is to be righteous. For I find this nowhere else when I seek to utter it, except within myself; and if I ask another what it is to be righteous, he seeks within himself what to answer; and whosoever hence can answer truly, he has found within himself what to answer. And when indeed I wish to speak of Carthage, I seek within myself what to speak, and I find within myself a notion or image of Carthage; but I have received this through the body, that is, through the perception of the body, since I have been present in that city in the body, and I saw and perceived it, and retained it in my memory, that I might find within myself a word concerning it, whenever I might wish to speak of it. For its word is the image itself of it in my memory, not that sound of two syllables when Carthage is named, or even when that name itself is thought of silently from time to time, but that which I discern in my mind, when I utter that dissyllable with my voice, or even before I utter it. So also, when I wish to speak of Alexandria, which I never saw, an image of it is present with me. For whereas I had heard from many and had believed that city to be great, in such way as it could be told me, I formed an image of it in my mind as I was able; and this is with me its word when I wish to speak of it, before I utter with my voice the five syllables which make the name that almost every one knows. And yet if I could bring forth that image from my mind to the eyes of men who know Alexandria, certainly all either would say, It is not it; or if they said, It is, I should greatly wonder; and as I gazed at it in my mind, that is, at the image which was as it were its picture, I should yet not know it to be it, but should believe those who retained an image they had seen. But I do not so ask what it is to be righteous, nor do I so find it, nor do I so gaze upon it, when I utter it; neither am I so approved when I am heard, nor do I so approve when I hear; as though I have seen such a thing with my eyes, or learned it by some perception of the body, or heard it from those who had so learned it. For when I say, and say knowingly, that mind is righteous which knowingly and of purpose assigns to every one his due in life and behavior, I do not think of anything absent, as Carthage, or imagine it as I am able, as Alexandria, whether it be so or not; but I discern something present, and I discern it within myself, though I myself am not that which I discern; and many if they hear will approve it. And whoever hears me and knowingly approves, he too discerns this same thing within himself, even though he himself be not what he discerns. But when a righteous man says this, he discerns and says that which he himself is. And whence also does he discern it, except within himself? But this is not to be wondered at; for whence should he discern himself except within himself? The wonderful thing is, that the mind should see within itself that which it has seen nowhere else, and should see truly, and should see the very true righteous mind, and should itself be a mind, and yet not a righteous mind, which nevertheless it sees within itself. Is there another mind that is righteous in a mind that is not yet righteous? Or if there is not, what does it there see when it sees and says what is a righteous mind, nor sees it anywhere else but in itself, when itself is not a righteous mind? Is that which it sees an inner truth present to the mind which has power to behold it? Yet all have not that power; and they who have power to behold it, are not all also that which they behold, that is, they are not also righteous minds themselves, just as they are able to see and to say what is a righteous mind. And whence will they be able to be so, except by cleaving to that very same form itself which they behold, so that from thence they may be formed and may be righteous minds; not only discerning and saying that the mind is righteous which knowingly and of purpose assigns to every one that which is his due in life and behavior, but so likewise that they themselves may live righteously and be righteous in character, by assigning to every one that which is his due, so as to owe no man anything, but to love one another.[11] And whence can any one cleave to that form but by loving it? Why then do we love another whom we believe to be righteous, and do not love that form itself wherein we see what is a righteous mind, that we also may be able to be righteous? Is it that unless we loved that also, we should not love him at all, whom through it we love: but whilst we are not righteous,

[11] Rom. xiii. 8

we love that form too little to allow of our being able to be righteous? The man therefore who is believed to be righteous, is loved through that form and truth which he who loves discerns and understands within himself; but that very form and truth itself cannot be loved from any other source than itself. For we do not find any other such thing besides itself, so that by believing we might love it when it is unknown, in that we here already know another such thing. For whatsoever of such a kind one may have seen, is itself; and there is not any other such thing, since itself alone is such as itself is. He therefore who loves men, ought to love them either because they are righteous, or that they may become righteous. For so also he ought to love himself, either because he is righteous, or that he may become righteous; for in this way he loves his neighbor as himself without any risk. For he who loves himself otherwise, loves himself wrongfully, since he loves himself to this end that he may be unrighteous; therefore to this end that he may be wicked; and hence it follows next that he does not love himself; for, "He who loveth iniquity, hateth his own soul." [12]

CHAPTER VII

OF TRUE LOVE, BY WHICH WE ARRIVE AT THE KNOWLEDGE OF THE
TRINITY. GOD IS TO BE SOUGHT, NOT OUTWARDLY, BY SEEKING
TO DO WONDERFUL THINGS WITH THE ANGELS, BUT INWARDLY,
BY IMITATING THE PIETY OF GOOD ANGELS

No other thing, then, is chiefly to be regarded in this inquiry, which we make concerning the Trinity and concerning knowing God, except what is true love, nay, rather what is love. For that is to be called love which is true, otherwise it is desire; and so those who desire are said improperly to love, just as they who love are said improperly to desire. But this is true love, that cleaving to the truth we may live righteously, and so may despise all mortal things in comparison with the love of men, whereby we wish them to live righteously. For so we should be prepared also to die profitably for our brethren, as our Lord Jesus Christ taught us by His example. For as there are two commandments on which hang all the Law and the prophets, love of God and love of our neighbor;[13] not without cause the Scripture mostly puts one for both: whether it be of God only, as is that text, "For we know that all things work together for good to them that love God;" [14] and again, "But if any man love God, the same is known of Him;" [15] and that, "Because the love of God is shed abroad in our hearts by the Holy Ghost which is given unto us;" [16] and many other passages; because he who loves God must both needs do what God has commanded, and loves Him just in such proportion as he does so; therefore he must needs also love his neighbor, because God has commanded it: or whether it be that Scripture only mentions the love of

[12] Ps. xi. 6   [13] Matt. xxii. 37-40   [14] Rom. viii. 28   [15] 1 Cor. viii. 3   [16] Rom.
v. 5

our neighbor, as in that text, "Bear ye one another's burdens, and so fulfill the law of Christ;" [17] and again, "For all the law is fulfilled in one word, even in this, Thou shalt love thy neighbor as thyself;" [18] and in the Gospel, "All things whatsoever ye would that men should do to you, do ye even so to them; for this is the Law and the prophets." [19] And many other passages occur in the sacred writings, in which only the love of our neighbor seems to be commanded for perfection, while the love of God is passed over in silence; whereas the Law and the prophets hang on both precepts. But this, too, is because he who loves his neighbor must needs also love above all else love itself. But "God is love; and he that dwelleth in love, dwelleth in God." [20] Therefore he must needs above all else love God.

Wherefore they who seek God through those Powers which rule over the world, or parts of the world, are removed and cast away far from Him; not by intervals of space, but by difference of affections: for they endeavor to find a path outwardly, and forsake their own inward things, within which is God. Therefore, even although they may either have heard some holy heavenly Power, or in some way or another may have thought of it, yet they rather covet its deeds at which human weakness marvels, but do not imitate the piety by which divine rest is acquired. For they prefer, through pride, to be able to do that which an angel does, more than, through devotion, to be that which an angel is. For no holy being rejoices in his own power, but in His from whom he has the power which he fitly can have; and he knows it to be more a mark of power to be united to the Omnipotent by a pious will, than to be able, by his own power and will, to do what they may tremble at who are not able to do such things. Therefore the Lord Jesus Christ Himself, in doing such things, in order that He might teach better things to those who marvelled at them, and might turn those who were intent and in doubt about unusual temporal things to eternal and inner things, says, "Come unto me, all ye that labor and are heavy laden, and I will give you rest. Take my yoke upon you." And He does not say, Learn of me, because I raise those who have been dead four days; but He says, "Learn of me; for I am meek and lowly in heart." For humility, which is most solid, is more powerful and safer than pride, that is most inflated. And so He goes on to say, "And ye shall find rest unto your souls," [21] for "Love is not puffed up;" [22] and "God is Love;" [23] and "such as be faithful in love shall rest in Him," [24] called back from the din which is without to silent joys. Behold, "God is Love:" why do we go forth and run to the heights of the heavens and the lowest parts of the earth, seeking Him who is within us, if we wish to be with Him?

[17] Gal. vi. 2   [18] Gal. v. 14   [19] Matt. vii. 12   [20] 1 John iv. 6   [21] Matt. xi. 28, 29   [22] 1 Cor. xiii. 4   [23] 1 John iv. 8   [24] Wisd. iii. 9

CHAPTER VIII

THAT HE WHO LOVES HIS BROTHER, LOVES GOD; BECAUSE HE LOVES
LOVE ITSELF, WHICH IS OF GOD, AND IS GOD

Let no one say, I do not know what I love. Let him love his brother, and he will love the same love. For he knows the love with which he loves, more than the brother whom he loves. So now he can know God more than he knows his brother: clearly known more, because more present; known more, because more within him; known more, because more certain. Embrace the love of God, and by love embrace God. That is love itself, which associates together all good angels and all the servants of God by the bond of sanctity, and joins together us and them mutually with ourselves, and joins us subordinately to Himself. In proportion, therefore, as we are healed from the swelling of pride, in such proportion are we more filled with love; and with what is he full, who is full of love, except with God? Well, but you will say, I see love, and, as far as I am able, I gaze upon it with my mind, and I believe the Scripture, saying, that "God is love; and he that dwelleth in love, dwelleth in God;" [25] but when I see love, I do not see in it the Trinity. Nay, but thou dost see the Trinity if thou seest love. But if I can I will put you in mind, that thou mayest see that thou seest it; only let itself be present, that we may be moved by love to something good. Since, when we love love, we love one who loves something, and that on account of this very thing, that he does love something; therefore what does love love, that love itself also may be loved? For that is not love which loves nothing. But if it loves itself it must love something, that it may love itself as love. For as a word indicates something, and indicates also itself, but does not indicate itself to be a word, unless it indicates that it does indicate something; so love also loves indeed itself, but except it love itself as loving something, it loves itself not as love. What therefore does love love, except that which we love with love? But this, to begin from that which is nearest to us, is our brother. And listen how greatly the Apostle John commends brotherly love: "He that loveth his brother abideth in the light, and there is none occasion of stumbling in him." [26] It is manifest that he placed the perfection of righteousness in the love of our brother; for he certainly is perfect in whom "there is no occasion of stumbling." And yet he seems to have passed by the love of God in silence; which he never would have done, unless because he intends God to be understood in brotherly love itself. For in this same epistle, a little further on, he says most plainly thus: "Beloved, let us love one another: for love is of God; and every one that loveth is born of God, and knoweth God. He that loveth not, knoweth not God; for God is love." And this passage declares sufficiently and plainly, that this same brotherly love itself (for that is brotherly

[25] 1 John iv. 16   [26] 1 John ii. 10

love by which we love each other) is set forth by so great authority, not only to be from God, but also to be God. When, therefore, we love our brother from love, we love our brother from God; neither can it be that we do not love above all else that same love by which we love our brother: whence it may be gathered that these two commandments cannot exist unless interchangeably. For since "God is love," he who loves love certainly loves God; but he must needs love love, who loves his brother. And so a little after he says, "For he that loveth not his brother whom he hath seen, how can he love God whom he hath not seen"? [27] because the reason that he does not see God is, that he does not love his brother. For he who does not love his brother, abideth not in love; and he who abideth not in love, abideth not in God, because God is love. Further, he who abideth not in God, abideth not in light; for "God is light, and in Him is no darkness at all." [28] He therefore who abideth not in light, what wonder is it if he does not see light, that is, does not see God, because he is in darkness? But he sees his brother with human sight, with which God cannot be seen. But if he loved with spiritual love him whom he sees with human sight, he would see God, who is love itself, with the inner sight by which He can be seen. Therefore he who does not love his brother whom he sees, how can he love God, whom on that account he does not see, because God is love, which he has not who does not love his brother? Neither let that further question disturb us, how much of love we ought to spend upon our brother, and how much upon God: incomparably more upon God than upon ourselves, but upon our brother as much as upon ourselves; and we love ourselves so much the more, the more we love God. Therefore we love God and our neighbor from one and the same love; but we love God for the sake of God, and ourselves and our neighbors for the sake of God.

CHAPTER IX

OUR LOVE OF THE RIGHTEOUS IS KINDLED FROM LOVE ITSELF OF THE UNCHANGEABLE FORM OF RIGHTEOUSNESS

For why is it, pray, that we burn when we hear and read, "Behold, now is the accepted time; behold, now is the day of salvation: giving no offense in anything, that the ministry be not blamed: but in all things approving ourselves as the ministers of God, in much patience, in afflictions, in necessities, in distresses, in stripes, in imprisonments, in tumults, in labors, in watchings, in fastings; by pureness, by knowledge, by long-suffering, by kindness, by the Holy Ghost, by love unfeigned, by the word of truth, by the power of God, by the armor of righteousness on the right hand and on the left, by honor and dishonor, by evil report and good report: as deceivers, and yet true; as unknown, and yet well known; as dying, and, behold, we live; as

[27] 1 John iv. 7, 8, 20   [28] 1 John i. 5

chastened, and not killed; as sorrowful, yet alway rejoicing; as poor, yet making many rich; as having nothing, and yet possessing all things?" [29] Why is it that we are inflamed with love of the Apostle Paul, when we read these things, unless that we believe him so to have lived? But we do not believe that the ministers of God ought so to live because we have heard it from any one, but because we behold it inwardly within ourselves, or rather above ourselves, in the truth itself. Him, therefore, whom we believe to have so lived, we love for that which we see. And except we loved above all else that form which we discern as always steadfast and unchangeable, we should not for that reason love him, because we hold fast in our belief that his life, when he was living in the flesh, was adapted to, and in harmony with, this form. But somehow we are stirred up the more to the love of this form itself, through the belief by which we believe some one to have so lived; and to the hope by which we no more at all despair, that we, too, are able so to live; we who are men, from this fact itself, that some men have so lived, so that we both desire this more ardently, and pray for it more confidently. So both the love of that form, according to which they are believed to have lived, makes the life of these men themselves to be loved by us; and their life thus believed stirs up a more burning love towards that same form; so that the more ardently we love God, the more certainly and the more calmly do we see Him, because we behold in God the unchangeable form of righteousness, according to which we judge that man ought to live. Therefore faith avails to the knowledge and to the love of God, not as though of one altogether unknown, or altogether not loved; but so that thereby He may be known more clearly, and loved more steadfastly.

CHAPTER X

THERE ARE THREE THINGS IN LOVE, AS IT WERE A TRACE OF THE TRINITY

But what is love or charity, which divine Scripture so greatly praises and proclaims, except the love of good? But love is *of* some one that loves, and *with* love something *is* loved. Behold, then, there are three things: he that loves, and that which is loved, and love. What, then, is love, except a certain life which couples or seeks to couple together some two things, namely, him that loves, and that which is loved? And this is so even in outward and carnal loves. But that we may drink in something more pure and clear, let us tread down the flesh and ascend to the mind. What does the mind love in a friend except the mind? There, then, also are three things: he that loves, and that which is loved, and love. It remains to ascend also from hence, and to seek those things which are above, as far as is given to man. But here for a little while let our purpose rest, not that it may think itself to have found al-

[29] 2 Cor. vi. 2-10

ready what it seeks; but just as usually the place has first to be found where anything is to be sought, while the thing itself is not yet found, but we have only found already where to look for it; so let it suffice to have said thus much, that we may have, as it were, the hinge of some starting-point, whence to weave the rest of our discourse.

BOOK NINE

That a kind of trinity exists in man, who is the image of God, viz. the mind, and the knowledge wherewith the mind knows itself, and the love wherewith it loves both itself and its own knowledge; and these three are shown to be mutually equal, and of one essence.

CHAPTER I

IN WHAT WAY WE MUST INQUIRE CONCERNING THE TRINITY

WE CERTAINLY seek a trinity—not any trinity, but that Trinity which is God, and the true and supreme and only God. Let my hearers then wait, for we are still seeking. And no one justly finds fault with such a search, if at least he who seeks that which either to know or to utter is most difficult, is steadfast in the faith. But whosoever either sees or teaches better, finds fault quickly and justly with any one who confidently affirms concerning it. "Seek God," he says, "and your heart shall live;" [1] and lest any one should rashly rejoice that he has, as it were, apprehended it, "Seek," he says, "His face evermore." [2] And the apostle: "If any man," he says, "think that he knoweth anything, he knoweth nothing yet as he ought to know. But if any man love God, the same is known of Him." [3] He has not said, has known Him, which is dangerous presumption, but "is known of Him." So also in another place, when he had said, "But now after that ye have known God;" immediately correcting himself, he says, "or rather are known of God." [4] And above all in that other place, "Brethren," he says, "I count not myself to have apprehended: but this one thing I do, forgetting those things which are behind, and reaching forth unto those things which are before, I press in purpose toward the mark, for the prize of the high calling of God in Christ Jesus. Let us therefore, as many as be perfect, be thus minded." [5] Perfection in this life, he tells us, is nothing else than to forget those things which are behind, and to reach forth and press in purpose toward those things which are before. For he that seeks has the safest purpose, [who seeks] until that is taken hold of whither we are tending, and for which we are reaching forth. But that is the right purpose which starts from faith. For a certain faith is in some way the starting-point of knowledge; but a certain knowledge will not be made perfect, except after this life, when we shall see face to face.[6] Let us therefore be thus minded, so as to know that the disposition to seek the truth is more

[1] Ps. lxix. 32   [2] Ps. cv. 4   [3] 1 Cor. viii. 2   [4] Gal. iv. 19   [5] Phil. iii. 13-15
[6] 1 Cor. xiii. 12

safe than that which presumes things unknown to be known. Let us therefore so seek as if we should find, and so find as if we were about to seek: For "when a man hath done, then he beginneth." [7] Let us doubt without unbelief of things to be believed; let us affirm without rashness of things to be understood: authority must be held fast in the former, truth sought out in the latter. As regards this question, then, let us believe that the Father, and the Son, and the Holy Spirit is one God, the Creator and Ruler of the whole creature; and that the Father is not the Son, nor the Holy Spirit either the Father or the Son, but a trinity of persons mutually interrelated, and a unity of an equal essence. And let us seek to understand this, praying for help from Himself, whom we wish to understand; and as much as He grants, desiring to explain what we understand with so much pious care and anxiety, that even if in any case we say one thing for another, we may at least say nothing unworthy. As, for the sake of example, if we say anything concerning the Father that does not properly belong to the Father, or does belong to the Son, or to the Holy Spirit, or to the Trinity itself; and if anything of the Son which does not properly suit with the Son, or at all events which does suit with the Father, or with the Holy Spirit, or with the Trinity; or if, again, anything concerning the Holy Spirit, which is not fitly a property of the Holy Spirit, yet is not alien from the Father, or from the Son, or from the one God the Trinity itself. Even as now our wish is to see whether the Holy Spirit is properly that love which is most excellent; which if He is not, either the Father is love, or the Son, or the Trinity itself; since we cannot withstand the most certain faith and weighty authority of Scripture, saying, "God is love." [8] And yet we ought not to deviate into profane error, so as to say anything of the Trinity which does not suit the Creator, but rather the creature, or which is feigned outright by mere empty thought.

CHAPTER II

THE THREE THINGS WHICH ARE FOUND IN LOVE MUST BE CONSIDERED

And this being so, let us direct our attention to those three things which we fancy we have found. We are not yet speaking of heavenly things, nor yet of God the Father, and Son, and Holy Spirit, but of that inadequate image, which yet is an image, that is, man; for our feeble mind perhaps can gaze upon this more familiarly and more easily. Well then, when I, who make this inquiry, love anything, there are three things concerned—myself, and that which I love, and love itself. For I do not love love, except I love a lover; for there is no love where nothing is loved. Therefore there are three things—he who loves, and that which is loved, and love. But what if I love none except myself? Will there not then be two things—that which I love, and love? For

[7] Ecclus. xviii. 7   [8] 1 John iv. 16

which is loved are the same when any one loves him—just as to love and to be loved, in the same way, is the very same thing any one loves himself. Since the same thing is said, when it is said, he lov himself, and he is loved by himself. For in that case to love and to be loved are not two different things: just as he who loves and he who is loved are not two different persons. But yet, even so, love and what is loved are still two things. For there is no love when any one loves himself, except when love itself is loved. But it is one thing to love one's self, another to love one's own love. For love is not loved, unless as already loving something; since where nothing is loved there is no love. Therefore there are two things when any one loves himself—love, and that which is loved. For then he that loves and that which is loved are one. Whence it seems that it does not follow that three things are to be understood wherever love is. For let us put aside from the inquiry all the other many things of which a man consists; and in order that we may discover clearly what we are now seeking, as far as in such a subject is possible, let us treat of the mind alone. The mind, then, when it loves itself, discloses two things—mind and love. But what is to love one's self, except to wish to help one's self to the enjoyment of self? And when any one wishes himself to be just as much as he is, then the will is on a par with the mind, and the love is equal to him who loves. And if love is a substance, it is certainly not body, but spirit; and the mind also is not body, but spirit. Yet love and mind are not two spirits, but one spirit; nor yet two essences, but one: and yet here are two things that are one, he that loves and love; or, if you like so to put it, that which is loved and love. And these two, indeed, are mutually said relatively. Since he who loves is referred to love, and love to him who loves. For he who loves, loves with some love, and love is the love of some one who loves. But mind and spirit are not said relatively, but express essence. For mind and spirit do not exist because the mind and spirit of some particular man exist. For if we subtract the body from that which is man, which is so called with the conjunction of body, the mind and spirit remain. But if we subtract him that loves, then there is no love; and if we subtract love, then there is no one that loves. And therefore, in so far as they are mutually referred to one another, they are two; but whereas they are spoken in respect to themselves, each is spirit, and both together also are one spirit; and each is mind, and both together one mind. Where, then, is the trinity? Let us attend as much as we can, and let us invoke the everlasting light, that He may illuminate our darkness, and that we may see in ourselves, as much as we are permitted, the image of God.

CHAPTER III

THE IMAGE OF THE TRINITY IN THE MIND OF MAN WHO KNOWS
HIMSELF AND LOVES HIMSELF. THE MIND KNOWS ITSELF
THROUGH ITSELF

For the mind cannot love itself, except also it know itself; for how can it love what it does not know? Or if any body says that the mind, from either general or special knowledge, believes itself of such a character as it has by experience found others to be, and therefore loves itself, he speaks most foolishly. For whence does a mind know another mind, if it does not know itself? For the mind does not know other minds and not know itself, as the eye of the body sees other eyes and does not see itself; for we see bodies through the eyes of the body, because, unless we are looking into a mirror, we cannot refract and reflect the rays into themselves, which shine forth through those eyes, and touch whatever we discern—a subject, indeed, which is treated of most subtlely and obscurely, until it be clearly demonstrated whether the fact be so, or whether it be not. But whatever is the nature of the power by which we discern through the eyes, certainly, whether it be rays or anything else, we cannot discern with the eyes that power itself; but we inquire into it with the mind, and if possible, understand even this with the mind. As the mind, then, itself gathers the knowledge of corporeal things through the senses of the body, so of incorporeal things through itself. Therefore it knows itself also through itself, since it is incorporeal; for if it does not know itself, it does not love itself.

CHAPTER IV

THE THREE ARE ONE, AND ALSO EQUAL, VIZ. THE MIND ITSELF, AND
THE LOVE, AND THE KNOWLEDGE OF IT. THAT THE SAME THREE
EXIST SUBSTANTIALLY, AND ARE PREDICATED RELATIVELY.
THAT THE SAME THREE ARE INSEPARABLE. THAT THE
SAME THREE ARE NOT JOINED AND COMMINGLED
LIKE PARTS, BUT THAT THEY ARE OF ONE
ESSENCE, AND ARE RELATIVES

But as there are two things, the mind and the love of it, when it loves itself; so there are two things, the mind and the knowledge of it, when it knows itself. Therefore the mind itself, and the love of it, and the knowledge of it, are three things, and these three are one; and when they are perfect they are equal. For if one loves himself less than as he is—as for example, suppose that the mind of a man only loves itself as much as the body of a man ought to be loved, whereas the mind is more than the body—then it is in fault, and its love is not perfect. Again, if it loves itself more than as it is—as if, for instance, it loves itself as much as God is to be loved, whereas the mind is incomparably less than God—here also it is exceedingly in fault, and its love of self is not perfect. But it is in fault more perversely and wrongly still, when it loves the body as much as God is to be loved. Also, if knowledge is less than that thing which is known, and which can be fully known, then knowledge is not perfect; but if it is greater, then the nature which knows is above that which is known, as the knowledge of the body is greater than the body itself, which is known by that knowledge. For knowledge is a kind of life in the reason of the knower, but the body is not life; and any life is greater than any body, not in bulk, but in power. But when the mind knows itself, its own knowledge does not rise above itself, because itself knows, and itself is known. When, therefore, it knows itself entirely, and no other thing with itself, then its knowledge is equal to itself; because its knowledge is not from another nature, since it knows itself. And when it perceives itself entirely, and nothing more, then it is neither less nor greater. We said therefore rightly, that these three things, [mind, love, and knowledge], when they are perfect, are by consequence equal.

Similar reasoning suggests to us, if indeed we can any way understand the matter, that these things [*i.e.* love and knowledge] exist in the soul, and that, being as it were involved in it, they are so evolved from it as to be perceived and reckoned up substantially, or, so to say, essentially. Not as though in a subject; as color, or shape, or any other quality or quantity, are in the body. For anything of this [material] kind does not go beyond the subject in which it is; for the color or shape of this particular body cannot be also those of another body. But the mind can also love something besides itself, with that love with which it loves itself. And further, the mind does not know itself only, but also many other things. Wherefore love and knowledge are not contained in the mind as in a subject, but these also exist *substantially, as the mind itself does;* because, even if they are mutually predicated relatively, yet they exist each severally in their own substance. Nor are they so mutually predicated relatively as color and the colored subject are; so that color is in the colored subject, but has not any proper substance in itself, since colored body is a substance, but color is in a substance; but as two friends are also two men, which are substances, while they are said to be men not relatively, but friends relatively.

But, further, although one who loves or one who knows is a substance, and *knowledge is a substance,* and *love is a substance,* but he that loves and love, or, he that knows and knowledge, are spoken of relatively to each other, as are friends: yet mind or spirit are not relatives, as neither are men relatives: nevertheless he that loves and love, or he that knows and knowledge, cannot exist separately from each other, as men can that are friends. Although it would seem that friends, too, can be separated in body, not in mind, in as far as they are friends: nay, it can even happen that a friend may even also begin to hate a friend, and on this account cease to be a friend, while the other does not know it, and still loves him. But if the love with which the mind loves itself ceases to be, then the mind also will at the same time cease to love. Likewise, if the knowledge by which the mind knows itself ceases to be, then the mind will also at the same time cease to know itself. Just as the head of anything that has a head is certainly a head, and they are predicated relatively to each other, although they are also substances: for both a head is a body, and so is that which has a head; and if there be no head, then neither will there be that which has a head. Only these things can be separated from each other by cutting off, those cannot.

And even if there are some bodies which cannot be wholly separated and divided, yet they would not be bodies unless they consisted of their own proper parts. A part then is predicated relatively to a whole, since every part is a part of some whole, and a whole is a whole by having all its parts. But since both part and whole are bodies, these things are not only predicated relatively, but exist also substantially. Perhaps, then, the mind is a whole, and the love with which it loves itself, and the knowledge with which it knows itself, are as it were its parts, of which two parts that whole consists. Or are there three equal parts which make up the one whole? But no part embraces the whole, of which it is a part; whereas, when the mind knows itself as a whole, that is, knows itself perfectly, then the knowledge of it extends through the whole of it; and when it loves itself perfectly, then it loves itself as a whole, and the love of it extends through the whole of it. Is it, then, as one drink is made from wine and water and honey, and each single part extends through the whole, and yet they are three things (for there is no part of the drink which does not contain these three things; for they are not joined as if they were water and oil, but are entirely commingled: and they are all substances, and the whole of that liquor which is composed of the three is one substance)—is it, I say, in some such way as this we are to think these three to be together, mind, love, and knowledge? But water, wine, and honey are not of one substance, although one substance results in the drink made from the commingling of them. And I cannot see how those other three are not of the same substance, since the mind itself loves itself, and itself knows itself; and these three so exist, as that the mind is neither loved nor known by any other thing at all. These three, therefore, must needs be of one and the same essence; and for that reason, if they were confounded together as it were by a commingling, they could not be in any way three, neither could they be mutually referred to each other. Just as if you were to make from one and the same gold three similar rings, although connected with each other, they are mutually referred to each other, because they are similar. For everything similar is similar to something, and there is a trinity of rings, and one gold. But if they are blended with each other, and each mingled with the other through the whole of their own bulk, then that trinity will fall through, and it will not exist at all; and not only will it be called one gold, as it was called in the case of those three rings, but now it will not be called three things of gold at all.

CHAPTER V

THAT THESE THREE ARE SEVERAL IN THEMSELVES, AND MUTUALLY ALL IN ALL

But in these three, when the mind knows itself and loves itself, there remains a trinity: mind, love, knowledge; and this trinity is not confounded together by any commingling: although they are each severally in themselves and mutually all in all, or each severally in each two, or each two in each. Therefore all are in all. For certainly the mind is in itself, since it is called mind in respect to itself: although it is said to be knowing, or known, or knowable, relatively to its own knowledge; and although also as loving, and loved, or lovable, it is referred to love, by which it loves itself. And knowledge, although it is referred to the mind that knows or is known, nevertheless is also predicated both as known and knowing in respect to itself: for the knowledge by which the mind knows itself is not unknown to itself. And although love is referred to the mind that loves, whose love it is; nevertheless it is also love in respect to itself, so as to exist also in itself: since love too is loved, yet cannot be loved with anything except with love, that is with itself. So these things are severally in themselves. But so are they in each other; because both the mind that loves is *in* love, and love is *in* the knowledge of him that loves, and knowledge is *in* the mind that knows. And each severally is in like manner in each two, because the mind which knows and loves itself, is in its own love and knowledge: and the love of the mind that loves and knows itself, is in the mind and in its knowledge: and the knowledge of the mind that knows and loves itself is in the mind and in its love, because it loves itself that knows, and knows itself that loves. And hence also each two is in each severally, since the mind which knows and loves itself, is together with its own knowledge in love, and together with its own love in knowledge; and love too itself and knowledge are together in the mind, which loves and knows itself. But in what way all are in all, we have already shown above; since the mind loves itself as a whole, and knows itself as a whole, and knows its own love wholly, and loves its own knowledge wholly, when these three things are perfect in respect to themselves. Therefore these three things are marvellously inseparable from each other, and yet each of them is severally a substance, and all together are one substance or essence, whilst they are mutually predicated relatively.

CHAPTER VI

THERE IS ONE KNOWLEDGE OF THE THING IN THE THING ITSELF.
AND ANOTHER IN ETERNAL TRUTH ITSELF. THAT CORPOREAL
THINGS, TOO, ARE TO BE JUDGED BY THE RULES OF
ETERNAL TRUTH

But when the human mind knows itself and loves itself, it does not know
and love anything unchangeable: and each individual man declares his own
particular mind by one manner of speech, when he considers what takes
place in himself; but defines the human mind abstractly by special or general
knowledge. And so, when he speaks to me of his own individual mind, as to
whether he understands this or that, or does not understand it, or whether
he wishes or does not wish this or that, I believe; but when he speaks the
truth of the mind of man generally or specially, I recognize and approve.
Whence it is manifest, that each sees a thing in himself, in such way that
another person may believe what he says of it, yet may not see it; but another [sees a thing] in the truth itself, in such way that another person also
can gaze upon it; of which the former undergoes changes at successive times,
the latter consists in an unchangeable eternity. For we do not gather a
generic or specific knowledge of the human mind by means of resemblance
by seeing many minds with the eyes of the body: but we gaze upon indestructible truth, from which to define perfectly, as far as we can, not of what
sort is the mind of any one particular man, but of what sort it ought to be
upon the eternal plan.

Whence also, even in the case of the images of things corporeal which are
drawn in through the bodily sense, and in some way infused into the memory, from which also those things which have not been seen are thought under a fancied image, whether otherwise than they really are, or even perchance as they are—even here too, we are proved either to accept or reject,
within ourselves, by other rules which remain altogether unchangeable
above our mind, when we approve or reject anything rightly. For both when
I recall the walls of Carthage which I have seen, and imagine to myself the
walls of Alexandria which I have not seen, and, in preferring this to that
among forms which in both cases are imaginary, make that preference upon
grounds of reason; the judgment of truth from above is still strong and clear,
and rests firmly upon the utterly indestructible rules of its own right; and if
it is covered as it were by cloudiness of corporeal images, yet is not wrapt up
and confounded in them.

But it makes a difference, whether, under that or in that darkness, I am
shut off as it were from the clear heaven; or whether (as usually happens on
lofty mountains), enjoying the free air between both, I at once look up above
to the calmest light, and down below upon the densest clouds. For whence

is the ardor of brotherly love kindled in me, when I hear that some man has borne bitter torments for the excellence and steadfastness of faith? And if that man is shown to me with the finger, I am eager to join myself to him, to become acquainted with him, to bind him to myself in friendship. And accordingly, if opportunity offers, I draw near, I address him, I converse with him, I express my goodwill towards him in what words I can, and wish that in him too in turn should be brought to pass and expressed goodwill towards me; and I endeavor after a spiritual embrace in the way of belief, since I cannot search out so quickly and discern altogether his innermost heart. I love therefore the faithful and courageous man with a pure and genuine love. But if he were to confess to me in the course of conversation, or were through unguardedness to show in any way, that either he believes something unseemly of God, and desires also something carnal in Him, and that he bore these torments on behalf of such an error, or from the desire of money for which he hoped, or from empty greediness of human praise: immediately it follows that the love with which I was borne towards him, displeased, and as it were repelled, and taken away from an unworthy man, remains in that form, after which, believing him such as I did, I had loved him; unless perhaps I have come to love him to this end, that he may become such, while I have found him not to be such in fact. And in that man, too, nothing is changed: although it can be changed, so that he may become that which I had believed him to be already. But in my mind there certainly is something changed, *viz.*, the estimate I had formed of him, which was before of one sort, and now is of another: and the same love, at the bidding from above of unchangeable righteousness, is turned aside from the purpose of enjoying, to the purpose of taking counsel. But the form itself of unshaken and stable truth, wherein I should have enjoyed the fruition of the man, believing him to be good, and wherein likewise I take counsel that he may be good, sheds in an immoveable eternity the same light of incorruptible and most sound reason, both upon the sight of my mind, and upon that cloud of images, which I discern from above, when I think of the same man whom I had seen. Again, when I call back to my mind some arch, turned beautifully and symmetrically, which, let us say, I saw at Carthage; a certain reality that had been made known to the mind through the eyes, and transferred to the memory, causes the imaginary view. But I behold in my mind yet another thing, according to which that work of art pleases me; and whence also, if it displeased me, I should correct it. We judge therefore of those particular things according to that [form of eternal truth], and discern that form by the intuition of the rational mind. But those things themselves we either touch if present by the bodily sense, or if absent remember their images as fixed in our memory, or picture, in the way of likeness to them, such things as we ourselves also, if we wished and were able, would laboriously build up: figuring in the mind after one fashion the images of bodies, or seeing bodies through the body; but after another, grasping by simple intelligence what is above the eye of the mind, *viz.*, the reasons and the unspeakably beautiful skill of such forms.

CHAPTER VII

WE CONCEIVE AND BEGET THE WORD WITHIN, FROM THE THINGS WE HAVE BEHELD IN THE ETERNAL TRUTH. THE WORD, WHETHER OF THE CREATURE OR OF THE CREATOR, IS CONCEIVED BY LOVE

We behold, then, by the sight of the mind, in that eternal truth from which all things temporal are made, the form according to which we are, and according to which we do anything by true and right reason, either in ourselves, or in things corporeal; and we have the true knowledge of things, thence conceived, as it were as a word within us, and by speaking we beget it from within; nor by being born does it depart from us. And when we speak to others, we apply to the word, remaining within us, the ministry of the voice or of some bodily sign, that by some kind of sensible remembrance some similar thing may be wrought also in the mind of him that hears— similar, I say, to that which does not depart from the mind of him that speaks. We do nothing, therefore, through the members of the body in our words and actions, by which the behavior of men is either approved or blamed, which we do not anticipate by a word uttered within ourselves. For no one willingly does anything, which he has not first said in his heart.

And this word is conceived by love, either of the creature or of the Creator, that is, either of changeable nature or of unchangeable truth.

CHAPTER VIII

IN WHAT DESIRE AND LOVE DIFFER

[Conceived] therefore, either by desire or by love: not that the creature ought not to be loved; but if that love [of the creature] is referred to the Creator, then it will not be desire (*cupiditas*), but love (*charitas*). For it is desire when the creature is loved for itself. And then it does not help a man through making use of it, but corrupts him in the enjoying it. When, therefore, the creature is either equal to us or inferior, we must use the inferior to reach God, but we must enjoy the equal only in God. For as thou oughtest to enjoy thyself, not in thyself, but in Him who made thee, so also him whom thou lovest as thyself. Let us enjoy, therefore, both ourselves and our brethren in the Lord; and hence let us not dare to yield, and as it were to relax, ourselves to ourselves in the direction downwards. Now a word is born, when, being thought out, it pleases us either to the effect of sinning, or to that of doing right. Therefore love, as it were a mean, conjoins our word and the mind from which it is conceived, and without any confusion binds itself as a third with them, in an incorporeal embrace.

CHAPTER IX

IN THE LOVE OF SPIRITUAL THINGS THE WORD BORN IS THE SAME AS THE WORD CONCEIVED. IT IS OTHERWISE IN THE LOVE OF CARNAL THINGS

But the word conceived and the word born are the very same when the will finds rest in knowledge itself, as is the case in the love of spiritual things. For instance, he who knows righteousness perfectly, and loves it perfectly, is already righteous; even if no necessity exist of working according to it outwardly through the members of the body. But in the love of carnal and temporal things, as in the offspring of animals, the conception of the word is one thing, the bringing forth another. For here what is conceived by desiring is born by attaining. Since it does not suffice to avarice to know and to love gold, except it also have it; nor to know and love to eat, or to lie with any one, unless also one does it; nor to know and love honors and power, unless they actually come to pass. Nay, all these things, even if obtained, do not suffice. "Whosoever drinketh of this water," He says, "shall thirst again." [9] And so also the Psalmist, "He hath conceived pain and brought forth iniquity." [10] And he speaks of pain or labor as conceived, when those things are conceived which it is not sufficient to know and will, and when the mind burns and grows sick with want, until it arrives at those things, and, as it were, brings them forth. Whence in the Latin language we have the word "*parta*" used elegantly for both "*reperta*" and "*comperta*," which words sound as if derived from bringing forth.[11] Since "lust, when it hath conceived, bringeth forth sin." [12] Wherefore the Lord proclaims, "Come unto me all ye that labor and are heavy laden;" [13] and in another place "Woe unto them that are with child, and to them that give suck, in those days!" [14] And when therefore He referred all either right actions or sins to the bringing forth of the word, "By thy mouth," He says, "thou shalt be justified, and by thy mouth thou shalt be condemned," [15] intending thereby not the visible mouth, but that which is within and invisible, of the thought and of the heart.

CHAPTER X

WHETHER ONLY KNOWLEDGE THAT IS LOVED IS THE WORD OF THE MIND

It is rightly asked then, whether all knowledge is a word, or only knowledge that is loved. For we also know the things which we hate; but what we do not like, cannot be said to be either conceived or brought forth by the mind. For not all things which in any way touch it, are conceived by it; but

---

[9] John iv. 13   [10] Ps. vii. 14   [11] *Partus*   [12] Jas. i. 15   [13] Matt. xi. 28
[14] Matt. xxiv. 19   [15] Matt. xii. 37

some only reach the point of being known, but yet are not spoken as words, as for instance those of which we speak now. For those are called words in one way, which occupy spaces of time by their syllables, whether they are pronounced or only thought; and in another way, all that is known is called a word imprinted on the mind, as long as it can be brought forth from the memory and defined, even though we dislike the thing itself; and in another way still, when we like that which is conceived in the mind. And that which the apostle says, must be taken according to this last kind of word, "No man can say that Jesus is the Lord, but by the Holy Ghost;" [16] since those also say this, but according to another meaning of the term "word," of whom the Lord Himself says, "Not every one that saith unto me, Lord, Lord, shall enter into the kingdom of heaven." [17] Nay, even in the case of things which we hate, when we rightly dislike and rightly censure them, we approve and like the censure bestowed upon them, and it becomes a word. Nor is it the knowledge of vices that displeases us, but the vices themselves. For I like to know and define what intemperance is; and this is its word. Just as there are known faults in art, and the knowledge of them is rightly approved, when a connoisseur discerns the species or the privation of excellence, as to affirm and deny that it is or that it is not; yet to be without excellence and to fall away into fault, is worthy of condemnation. And to define intemperance, and to say its word, belongs to the art of morals; but to be intemperate belongs to that which that art censures. Just as to know and define what a solecism is, belongs to the art of speaking; but to be guilty of one, is a fault which the same art reprehends. A word, then, which is the point we wish now to discern and intimate, is knowledge together with love. Whenever, then, the mind knows and loves itself, its word is joined to it by love. And since it loves knowledge and knows love, both the word is in love and love is in the word, and both are in him who loves and speaks.

CHAPTER XI

THAT THE IMAGE OR BEGOTTEN WORD OF THE MIND THAT KNOWS ITSELF IS EQUAL TO THE MIND ITSELF

But all knowledge according to species is like the thing which it knows. For there is another knowledge according to privation, according to which we speak a word only when we condemn. And this condemnation of a privation is equivalent to praise of the species, and so is approved. The mind, then, contains some likeness to a known species, whether when liking that species or when disliking its privation. And hence, in so far as we know God, we are like Him, but not like to the point of equality, since we do not know Him to the extent of His own being. And as, when we speak of bodies by means of the bodily sense, there arises in our mind some likeness of them,

[16] I Cor. xii. 3   [17] Matt. vii. 21

which is a phantasm of the memory; for the bodies themselves are not at all in the mind, when we think them, but only the likenesses of those bodies; therefore, when we approve the latter for the former, we err, for the approving of one thing for another is an error; yet the image of the body in the mind is a thing of a better sort than the species of the body itself, inasmuch as the former is in a better nature, *viz.* in a living substance, as the mind is: so when we know God, although we are made better than we were before we knew Him, and above all when the same knowledge being also liked and worthily loved becomes a word, and so that knowledge becomes a kind of likeness of God; yet that knowledge is of a lower kind, since it is in a lower nature; for the mind is creature, but God is Creator. And from this it may be inferred, that when the mind knows and approves itself, this same knowledge is in such way its word, as that it is altogether on a par and equal with it, and the same; because it is neither the knowledge of a lower essence, as of the body, nor of a higher, as of God. And whereas knowledge bears a likeness to that which it knows, that is, of which it is the knowledge; in this case it has perfect and equal likeness, when the mind itself, which knows, is known. And so it is both image and word; because it is uttered concerning that mind to which it is equalled in knowing, and that which is begotten is equal to the begetter.

CHAPTER XII

WHY LOVE IS NOT THE OFFSPRING OF THE MIND, AS KNOWLEDGE IS SO. THE SOLUTION OF THE QUESTION. THE MIND WITH THE KNOWLEDGE OF ITSELF AND THE LOVE OF ITSELF IS THE IMAGE OF THE TRINITY

What then is love? Will it not be an image? Will it not be a word? Will it not be begotten? For why does the mind beget its knowledge when it knows itself, and not beget its love when it loves itself? For if it is the cause of its own knowing, for the reason that it is knowable, it is also the cause of its own love because it is lovable. It is hard, then, to say why it does not beget both. For there is a further question also respecting the supreme Trinity itself, the omnipotent God the Creator, after whose image man is made which troubles men, whom the truth of God invites to the faith by human speech; *viz.* why the Holy Spirit is not also to be either believed or understood to be begotten by God the Father, so that He also may be called a Son. And this question we are endeavoring in some way to investigate in the human mind, in order that from a lower image, in which our own nature itself as it were answers, upon being questioned, in a way more familiar to ourselves, we may be able to direct a more practised mental vision from the enlightened creature to the unchangeable light; assuming, however, that the truth itself has persuaded us, that as no Christian doubts the Word of God to be the Son, so that the Holy Spirit is love. Let us return, then, to a more careful questioning and consideration upon this subject of that image which is the creature, that is, of the rational mind; wherein the knowledge of some things coming into existence in time, but which did not exist before, and the love of some things which were not loved before, opens to us more clearly what to say: because to speech also itself, which must be disposed in time, that thing is easier of explanation which is comprehended in the order of time.

First, therefore, it is clear that a thing may possibly be knowable, that is, such as can be known, and yet that it may be unknown; but that it is not possible for that to be known which is not knowable. Wherefore it must be clearly held that everything whatsoever that we know begets at the same time in us the knowledge of itself; for knowledge is brought forth from both, from the knower and from the thing known. When, therefore, the mind knows itself, it alone is the parent of its own knowledge; for it is itself both the thing known and the knower of it. But it was knowable to itself also before it knew itself, only the knowledge of itself was not in itself so long as it did not know itself. In knowing itself, then, it begets a knowledge of itself equal to itself; since it does not know itself as less than itself is, nor is its knowledge the knowledge of the essence of some one else, not only because itself knows, but also because it knows itself, as we have said above. What then is to be said of love; why, when the mind loves itself, it should not seem also to have begotten the love of itself? For it was lovable to itself even before it loved itself, since it could love itself; just as it was knowable to itself even before it knew itself, since it could know itself. For if it were not knowable to itself, it never could have known itself; and so, if it were not lovable to itself, it never could have loved itself. Why therefore may it not be said by loving itself to have begotten its own love, as by knowing itself it has begotten its own knowledge? Is it because it is thereby indeed plainly shown that this is the principle of love, whence it proceeds? for it proceeds from the mind itself, which is lovable to itself before it loves itself, and so is the principle of its own love by which it loves itself: but that this love is not therefore rightly said to be begotten by the mind, as is the knowledge of itself by which the mind knows itself, because in the case of knowledge the thing has been found already, which is what we call brought forth or discovered; and this is commonly preceded by an inquiry such as to find rest when that end is attained. For inquiry is the desire of finding, or, what is the same thing, of discovering. But those things which are discovered are as it were brought forth, whence they are like offspring; but wherein, except in the case itself of knowledge? For in that case they are as it were uttered and fashioned. For although the things existed already which we found by seeking, yet the knowledge of them did not exist, which knowledge we regard as an offspring that is born. Further, the desire (*appetitus*) which there is in seeking proceeds from him who seeks, and is in some way in suspense, and does not rest in the end whither it is directed, except that which is sought be found and conjoined with him who seeks. And this desire, that is, inquiry—although it does not seem to be love, by which that which is known is loved, for in this case we are still striving to know—yet it is something of the same kind. For it can be called will (*voluntas*), since every one who seeks wills (*vult*) to find; and if that is sought which belongs to knowledge, every one who seeks wills to know. But if he wills ardently and earnestly, he is said to study (*studere*): a word that is most commonly employed in the case of pursuing and obtaining any branches of learning. Therefore, the bringing forth of the mind is preceded by some desire, by which, through seeking and finding what we wish to know, the offspring, *viz.* knowledge itself, is born. And for this reason, that desire by which knowledge is conceived and brought forth, cannot rightly be called the bringing forth and the offspring; and the same desire which led us to long for the knowing of the thing, becomes the love of the thing when known, while it holds and embraces its accepted offspring, that is, knowledge, and unites it to its begetter. And so there is a kind of image of the Trinity in the mind itself, and the knowledge of it, which is its offspring and its word concerning itself, and love as a third, and these three are one, and one substance. Neither is the offspring less, since the mind knows itself according to the measure of its own being; nor is the love less, since it loves itself according to the measure both of its own knowledge and of its own being.

BOOK TEN

Summary

Chapter 1: The love of a mind that is desirous to know is not directed towards a thing of which it is wholly ignorant. We may love something which we do not know but the genus of which we do know, so that actually we cannot be said to be ignorant of it.

Chapter 2: It is absolutely impossible for one to love things completely unknown.

Chapter 3: Next it is demonstrated that the mind loves itself, and by the very fact of seeking itself, is more known to itself than unknown.

Chapter 4: The mind knows itself as a whole. As a mind is a whole mind, so it lives as a whole. It knows that it lives. Therefore it knows itself as a whole.

Chapter 5: The mind is enjoined to know itself, in order to live according to its own nature, "under Him by whom it ought to be ruled, above those things which it ought to rule." By not knowing itself in this way comes what the mind does through vicious desires.

Chapter 6: The mind errs when it connects itself with corporeal images and conceives itself to be something of the same kind.

Chapter 7: Philosophers err when they hold that the mind is corporeal and the soul mortal. Mind is at once substance and incorporeal. The error comes from conceiving that substance must be corporeal and hence these thinkers associate with mind qualities that are appropriate to that which is corporeal. The mind "finds out" those things which it seeks by directing a carnal sense towards them. It also "finds out" other things, not by the bodily senses, but through itself, when it "comes into" them. In this way, it "finds out" God.

Chapter 8: The mind seeks itself, and is in itself, but in itself are also images of corporeal things. It is difficult to separate out these images of corporeal things, and to see itself by itself. This is a source of shameful error.

Chapter 9: If one really understands *the injunction, "know thyself," the mind will know itself.*

Chapter 10: When a mind is bidden to know itself, it knows that this is said to itself, to a self that is, lives, and understands. Further, men know that they will, and they know that no one can will who does not exist and does not live. Also they know they have memory. All these come to mind quite apart from the knowledge that is received from without. Even if a man doubts, he knows he lives. All this operation cannot be explained on the hypothesis that the mind is corporeal.

804

Chapter 11: The mind then has memory, understanding, and will. In them we should note ability, learning, and use. Memory, understanding, and will are not three minds, but one mind—one essence, though they are three relatively. "And, therefore, while all are mutually comprehended by each, and as wholes, each as a whole is equal to each as a whole, and each as a whole at the same time to all as wholes; and these three are one, one life, one mind, one essence."

Chapter 12: Thus, the mind is an image of the Trinity in its own memory, understanding, and will.

BOOK ELEVEN

Summary

Chapter 1: Let us see if we can find a trace of the Trinity in the outer man and let us begin with the sense of sight.

Chapter 2: In sight, three things can be distinguished: the visible object, the act of seeing, and the attention of the mind. These three, though different, are tempered together into a kind of unity.

Chapter 3: The rational soul lives in a degenerate fashion if it lives according to a trinity of the outer man, employing a base desire instead of a praiseworthy will. The presentation of an external sensation is combined into a conception by memory, internal vision, and will.

Chapter 4: The combining takes place entirely within the mind.

Chapter 5: The vision of external things may attract the will and render it unclean. Thus one lives badly if one lives according to the trinity of the outer man. This trinity is not an image of God, but yet is not altogether dissimilar, since all things created by God bear a certain likeness to Him. In vision, the form of the sense object is, as it were, the parent, and vision itself the offspring, though not a true parent nor true offspring since the sense of the one who sees is applied to the bodily thing, in order for it to be formed. The will which unites them is more spiritual. The vision, to be sure, is spiritual to some extent. But the will as more spiritual begins to suggest the person of the Spirit in the Trinity.

Chapter 6: The end and rest of the will may be used to express the state in which it is when a particular act of vision has been accomplished, but all the several wills are bound together by orientation of the whole will.

Chapter 7: Another trinity, which is more inward, occurs in the recollection of something that has been seen.

Chapter 8: This trinity is innumerably numerous, according to the number of things stored in the memory. But the mind can conceive of more than it has seen. For example, this happens when one hears a narration. This comes from remembering generically the things narrated. The will and its attention also play their part in such a transaction.

Chapter 9: There are four species which arise in succession: the species of the bodily object, the species in the sense of the percipient, the species which comes to be in the memory, and the species which comes to be in the mind's eye of the concipient. The will acts to combine these successive species. Two trinities are suggested: one when the vision of sensuous perception is formed from the bodily object, the other when the vision of conception is formed from the memory. A third and intermediate type is not suggested, because we do not commonly call it vision, when the form which comes to be in the sense of him who perceives is entrusted to the memory.

Chapter 10: We can conceive what is false by combining things from parts of our memory.

Chapter 11: Measure appears in the memory of things, number in the vision. Measure, number, and weight are to be perceived in all things. But it is important to remember that the will is the uniter of the visible thing and of the vision.

BOOK TWELVE

Commencing with a distinction between wisdom and knowledge, points out a kind of trinity, of a peculiar sort, in that which is properly called knowledge, and which is the lower of the two; and that trinity, although it certainly pertains to the inner man, is still not yet to be called or thought an image of God.

CHAPTER I

OF WHAT KIND ARE THE OUTER AND THE INNER MAN

COME now, and let us see where lies, as it were, the boundary line between the outer and inner man. For whatever we have in the mind common with the beasts, thus much is rightly said to belong to the outer man. For the outer man is not to be considered to be the body only, but with the addition also of a certain peculiar life of the body, whence the structure of the body derives its vigor, and all the senses with which he is equipped for the perception of outward things; and when the images of these outward things already perceived, that have been fixed in the memory, are seen again by recollection, it is still a matter pertaining to the outer man. And in all these things we do not differ from the beasts, except that in shape of body we are not prone, but upright. And we are admonished through this, by Him who made us, not to be like the beasts in that which is our better part—that is, the mind—while we differ from them by the uprightness of the body. Not that we are to throw our mind into those bodily things which are exalted; for to seek rest for the will, even in such things, is to prostrate the mind. But as the body is naturally raised upright to those bodily things which are most elevated, that is, to things celestial; so the mind, which is a spiritual substance, must be raised upright to those things which are most elevated in spiritual things, not by the elation of pride, but by the dutifulness of righteousness.

CHAPTER II

MAN ALONE OF ANIMATE CREATURES PERCEIVES THE ETERNAL REASONS OF THINGS PERTAINING TO THE BODY

And the beasts, too, are able both to perceive things corporeal from without, through the senses of the body, and to fix them in the memory, and remember them, and in them to seek after things suitable, and shun things inconvenient. But to note these things, and to retain them not only as caught up naturally but also as deliberately committed to memory, and to imprint them again by recollection and conception when now just slipping away into forgetfulness; in order that as conception is formed from that which the memory contains, so also the contents themselves of the memory may be fixed firmly by thought: to combine again imaginary objects of sight, by taking this or that of what the memory remembers, and, as it were, tacking them to one another: to examine after what manner it is that in this kind things like the true are to be distinguished from the true, and this not in things spiritual, but in corporeal things themselves—these acts, and the like, although performed in reference to things sensible, and those which the mind has deduced through the bodily senses, yet, as they are combined with reason, so are not common to men and beasts. But it is the part of the higher reason to judge of these corporeal things according to incorporeal and eternal reasons; which, unless they were above the human mind, would certainly not be unchangeable; and yet, unless something of our own were subjoined to them, we should not be able to employ them as our measures by which to judge of corporeal things. But we judge of corporeal things from the rule of dimensions and figures, which the mind knows to remain unchangeably.

CHAPTER III

THE HIGHER REASON WHICH BELONGS TO CONTEMPLATION, AND THE LOWER WHICH BELONGS TO ACTION, ARE IN ONE MIND

But that of our own which thus has to do with the handling of corporeal and temporal things, is indeed rational, in that it is not common to us with the beasts; but it is drawn, as it were, out of that rational substance of our mind, by which we depend upon and cleave to the intelligible and unchangeable truth, and which is deputed to handle and direct the inferior things. For as among all the beasts there was not found for the man a help like unto him, unless one were taken from himself, and formed to be his consort: so for that mind, by which we consult the supernal and inward truth, there is no like help for such employment as man's nature requires among things corporeal out of those parts of the soul which we have in common with the beasts. And so a certain part of our reason, not separated so as to sever unity, but, as it were, diverted so as to be a help to fellowship, is parted off for the performing of its proper work. And as the twain is one flesh in the case of male and female, so in the mind one nature embraces our intellect and action, or our counsel and performance, or our reason and rational appetite, or whatever other more significant terms there may be by which to express them; so that, as it was said of the former, "And they two shall be in one flesh," [1] it may be said of these, they two are in one mind.

[1] Gen. ii. 24

CHAPTER IV

THE TRINITY AND THE IMAGE OF GOD IS IN THAT PART OF THE
MIND ALONE WHICH BELONGS TO THE CONTEMPLATION OF
ETERNAL THINGS

When, therefore, we discuss the nature of the human mind, we discuss a single subject, and do not double it into those two which I have mentioned, except in respect to its functions. Therefore, when we seek the trinity in the mind, we seek it in the whole mind, without separating the action of the reason in things temporal from the contemplation of things eternal, so as to have further to seek some third thing, by which a trinity may be completed. But this trinity must needs be so discovered in the whole nature of the mind, as that even if action upon temporal things were to be withdrawn, for which work that help is necessary, with a view to which some part of the mind is diverted in order to deal with these inferior things, yet a trinity would still be found in the one mind that is no where parted off; and that when this distribution has been already made, not only a trinity may be found, but also an image of God, in that alone which belongs to the contemplation of eternal things; while in that other which is diverted from it in the dealing with temporal things, although there may be a trinity, yet there cannot be found an image of God.

CHAPTER V

THE OPINION WHICH DEVISES AN IMAGE OF THE TRINITY IN THE
MARRIAGE OF MALE AND FEMALE, AND IN THEIR OFFSPRING

Accordingly they do not seem to me to advance a probable opinion, who lay it down that a trinity of the image of God in three persons, so far as regards human nature, can so be discovered as to be completed in the marriage of male and female and in their offspring; in that the man himself, as it were, indicates the person of the Father, but that which has so proceeded from him as to be born, that of the Son; and so the third person as of the Spirit, is, they say, the woman, who has so proceeded from the man as not herself to be either son or daughter,[2] although it was by her conception that the offspring was born. For the Lord hath said of the Holy Spirit that He proceedeth from the Father,[3] and yet he is not a son. In this erroneous opinion, then, the only point probably alleged, and indeed sufficiently shown according to the faith of the Holy Scripture, is this—in the account of the original creation of the woman—that what so comes into existence from some person as to make another person, cannot in every case be called a son; since the person of the woman came into existence from the person of the man, and yet

[2] Gen. ii. 22   [3] John xv. 26

she is not called his daughter. All the rest of this opinion is in truth so absurd, nay indeed so false, that it is most easy to refute it. For I pass over such a thing, as to think the Holy Spirit to be the mother of the Son of God, and the wife of the Father; since perhaps it may be answered that these things offend us in carnal things, because we think of bodily conceptions and births. Although these very things themselves are most chastely thought of by the pure, to whom all things are pure; but to the defiled and unbelieving, of whom both the mind and conscience are polluted, nothing is pure;[4] so that even Christ, born of a virgin according to the flesh, is a stumbling-block to some of them. But yet in the case of those supreme spiritual things, after the likeness of which those kinds of the inferior creature also are made although most remotely, and where there is nothing that can be injured and nothing corruptible, nothing born in time, nothing formed from that which is formless, or whatever like expressions there may be; yet they ought not to disturb the sober prudence of any one, lest in avoiding empty disgust he run into pernicious error. Let him accustom himself so to find in corporeal things the traces of things spiritual, that when he begins to ascend upwards from thence, under the guidance of reason, in order to attain to the unchangeable truth itself through which these things were made, he may not draw with himself to things above what he despises in things below. For no one ever blushed to choose for himself wisdom as a wife, because the name of wife puts into a man's thoughts the corruptible connection which consists in begetting children; or because in truth wisdom itself is a woman in sex, since it is expressed in both Greek and Latin tongues by a word of the feminine gender.

CHAPTER VI

WHY THIS OPINION IS TO BE REJECTED

We do not therefore reject this opinion, because we fear to think of that holy and inviolable and unchangeable Love, as the spouse of God the Father, existing as it does from Him, but not as an offspring in order to beget the Word by which all things are made; but because divine Scripture evidently shows it to be false. For God said, "Let us make man in our image, after our likeness;" and a little after it is said, "So God created man in the image of God." [5] Certainly, in that it is of the plural number, the word "our" would not be rightly used if man were made in the image of one person, whether of the Father, or of the Son, or of the Holy Spirit; but because he was made in the image of the Trinity, on that account it is said, "After our image." But again, lest we should think that three Gods were to be believed in the Trinity, whereas the same Trinity is one God, it is said, "So God created man in the image of God," instead of saying, "In His own image."

[4] Tit. i. 15   [5] Gen. i. 26, 27

For such expressions are customary in the Scriptures; and yet some persons, while maintaining the Catholic faith, do not carefully attend to them, in such wise that they think the words, "God made man in the image of God," to mean that the Father made man after the image of the Son; and they thus desire to assert that the Son also is called God in the divine Scriptures, as if there were not other most true and clear proofs wherein the Son is called not only God, but also the true God. For whilst they aim at explaining another difficulty in this text, they become so entangled that they cannot extricate themselves. For if the Father made man after the image of the Son, so that he is not the image of the Father, but of the Son, then the Son is unlike the Father. But if a pious faith teaches us, as it does, that the Son is like the Father after an equality of essence, then that which is made in the likeness of the Son must needs also be made in the likeness of the Father. Further, if the Father made man not in His own image, but in the image of His son, why does He not say, "Let us make man after Thy image and likeness," whereas He does say, "our;" unless it be because the image of the Trinity was made in man, that in this way man should be the image of the one true God, because the Trinity itself is the one true God? Such expressions are innumerable in the Scriptures, but it will suffice to have produced these. It is so said in the *Psalms*, "Salvation belongeth unto the Lord; Thy blessing is upon Thy people;" [6] as if the words were spoken to some one else, not to Him of whom it had been said, "Salvation belongeth unto the Lord." And again, "For by Thee," he says, "I shall be delivered from temptation, and by hoping in my God I shall leap over the wall;" [7] as if he said to some one else, "By Thee I shall be delivered from temptation." And again, "In the heart of the king's enemies; whereby the people fall under Thee;" [8] as if he were to say, in the heart of Thy enemies. For he had said to that King, that is, to our Lord Jesus Christ, "The people fall under Thee," whom he intended by the word King, when he said, "In the heart of the king's enemies." Things of this kind are found more rarely in the New Testament. But yet the apostle says to the Romans, "Concerning His Son who was made to Him of the seed of David according to the flesh, and declared to be the Son of God with power, according to the spirit of holiness, by the resurrection of the dead of Jesus Christ our Lord;" [9] as though he were speaking above of some one else. For what is meant by the Son of God declared by the resurrection of the dead of Jesus Christ, except of the same Jesus Christ who was declared to be Son of God with power? And as then in this passage, when we are told, "the Son of God with power of Jesus Christ," or "the Son of God according to the spirit of holiness of Jesus Christ," or "the Son of God by the resurrection of the dead of Jesus Christ," whereas it might have been expressed in the ordinary way, In His own power, or according to the spirit of His own holiness, or by the resurrection of His dead, or of their dead: as, I say, we are not compelled to understand another person, but one and the

[6] Ps. iii. 8   [7] Ps. xviii. 29   [8] Ps. xlv. 5   [9] Rom. i. 3, 4

same, that is, the person of the Son of God our Lord Jesus Christ; so, when we are told that "God made man in the image of God," although it might have been more usual to say, after His own image, yet we are not compelled to understand any other person in the Trinity, but the one and self-same Trinity itself, who is one God, and after whose image man is made.

And since the case stands thus, if we are to accept the same image of the Trinity, as not in one, but in three human beings, father and mother and son, then the man was not made after the image of God before a wife was made for him, and before they procreated a son; because there was not yet a trinity. Will any one say there was already a trinity, because, although not yet in their proper form, yet in their original nature, both the woman was already in the side of the man, and the son in the loins of his father? Why then, when Scripture had said, "God made man after the image of God," did it go on to say, "God created him; male and female created He them: and God blessed them"? [10] (Or if it is to be so divided, "And God created man," so that thereupon is to be added, "in the image of God created He him," and then subjoined in the third place, "male and female created He them;" for some have feared to say, He made him male and female, lest something monstrous, as it were, should be understood, as are those whom they call hermaphrodites, although even so both might be understood not falsely in the singular number, on account of that which is said, "Two in one flesh.") Why then, as I began by saying, in regard to the nature of man made after the image of God, does Scripture specify nothing except male and female? Certainly, in order to complete the image of the Trinity, it ought to have added also son, although still placed in the loins of his father, as the woman was in his side. Or was it perhaps that the woman also had been already made, and that Scripture had combined in a short and comprehensive statement, that of which it was going to explain afterwards more carefully, how it was done; and that therefore a son could not be mentioned, because no son was yet born? As if the Holy Spirit could not have comprehended this, too, in that brief statement, while about to narrate the birth of the son afterwards in its own place; as it narrated afterwards in its own place, that the woman was taken from the side of the man,[11] and yet has not omitted here to name her.

[10] Gen. i. 27, 28 [11] Gen. ii. 24, 22

CHAPTER VII

We ought not therefore so to understand that man is made in the image of the supreme Trinity, that is, in the image of God, as that the same image should be understood to be in three human beings; especially when the apostle says that the man is the image of God, and on that account removes the covering from his head, which he warns the woman to use, speaking thus: "For a man indeed ought not to cover his head, forasmuch as he is the image and glory of God; but the woman is the glory of the man." What then shall we say to this? If the woman fills up the image of the trinity after the measure of her own person, why is the man still called that image after she has been taken out of his side? Or if even one person of a human being out of three can be called the image of God, as each person also is God in the supreme Trinity itself, why is the woman also not the image of God? For she is instructed for this very reason to cover her head, which he is forbidden to do because he is the image of God.[12]

But we must notice how that which the apostle says, that not the woman but the man is the image of God, is not contrary to that which is written in Genesis, "God created man: in the image of God created He him; male and female created He them: and He blessed them." For this text says that human nature itself, which is complete [only] in both sexes, was made in the image of God; and it does not separate the woman from the image of God which it signifies. For after saying that God made man in the image of God, "He created him," it says, "male and female;" or at any rate, punctuating the words otherwise, "male and female created He them." How then did the apostle tell us that the man is the image of God, and therefore he is forbidden to cover his head; but that the woman is not so, and therefore is commanded to cover hers? Unless, forsooth, according to that which I have said already, when I was treating of the nature of the human mind, that the woman together with her own husband is the image of God, so that that whole substance may be one image; but when she is referred separately to her quality of *help-meet*, which regards the woman herself alone, then she is not the image of God; but as regards the man alone, he is the image of God as fully and completely as when the woman too is joined with him in one. As we said of the nature of the human mind, that both in the case when as a whole it contemplates the truth it is the image of God; and in the case when anything is

---

[12] 1 Cor. xi. 7, 5

divided from it, and diverted to the cognition of temporal things; never-theless on that side on which it beholds and consults truth, here also it is the image of God, but on that side whereby it is directed to the cognition of the lower things, it is not the image of God. And since it is so much the more formed after the image of God, the more it has extended itself to that which is eternal, and is on that account not to be restrained, so as to with-hold and refrain itself from thence; therefore the man ought not to cover his head. But because too great a progression towards inferior things is danger-ous to that rational cognition that is conversant with things corporeal and temporal; this ought to have power on its head, which the covering indicates, by which it is signified that it ought to be restrained. For a holy and pious meaning is pleasing to the holy angels.[13] For God sees not after the way of time, neither does anything new take place in His vision and knowledge, when anything is done in time and transitorily, after the way in which such things affect the senses, whether the carnal senses of animals and men, or even the heavenly senses of the angels.

For that the Apostle Paul, when speaking outwardly of the sex of male and female, figured the mystery of some more hidden truth, may be understood from this, that when he says in another place that she is a widow indeed who is desolate, without children and nephews, and yet that she ought to trust in God, and to continue in prayers night and day,[14] he here indicates, that the woman having been brought into the transgression by being deceived, is brought to salvation by child-bearing; and then he has added, "If they con-tinue in faith, and charity, and holiness, with sobriety." [15] As if it could pos-sibly hurt a good widow, if either she had not sons, or if those whom she had did not choose to continue in good works. But because those things which are called good works are, as it were, the sons of our life, according to that sense of life in which it answers to the question, What is a man's life? that is, How does he act in these temporal things? which life the Greeks do not call ζωή but βίος; and because these good works are chiefly performed in the way of offices of mercy, while works of mercy are of no profit, either to Pagans, or to Jews who do not believe in Christ, or to any heretics or schismatics whatso-ever in whom faith and charity and sober holiness are not found: what the apostle meant to signify is plain, and in so far figuratively and mystically, because he was speaking of covering the head of the woman, which will re-main mere empty words, unless referred to some hidden sacrament.

For, as not only most true reason but also the authority of the apostle himself declares, man was not made in the image of God according to the shape of his body, but according to his rational mind. For the thought is a debased and empty one, which holds God to be circumscribed and limited by the lineaments of bodily members. But further, does not the same blessed apostle say, "Be renewed in the spirit of your mind, and put on the new man, which is created after God;" [16] and in another place more clearly, "Putting

[13] 1 Cor. xi. 10   [14] 1 Tim. v. 5   [15] 1 Tim. ii. 15   [16] Eph. iv. 23, 24

off the old man," he says, "with his deeds; put on the new man, which is renewed to the knowledge of God after the image of Him that created him?" [17] If, then, we are renewed in the spirit of our mind, and he is the new man who is renewed to the knowledge of God after the image of Him that created him; no one can doubt, that man was made after the image of Him that created him, not according to the body, nor indiscriminately according to any part of the mind, but according to the rational mind, wherein the knowledge of God can exist. And it is according to this renewal, also, that we are made sons of God by the baptism of Christ; and putting on the new man, certainly put on Christ through faith. Who is there, then, who will hold women to be alien from this fellowship, whereas they are fellow-heirs of grace with us; and whereas in another place the same apostle says, "For ye are all the children of God by faith in Christ Jesus; for as many as have been baptized into Christ have put on Christ: there is neither Jew nor Greek, there is neither bond nor free, there is neither male nor female; for ye are all one in Christ Jesus?" [18] Pray, have faithful women then lost their bodily sex? But because they are there renewed after the image of God, where there is no sex; man is there made after the image of God, where there is no sex, that is, in the spirit of his mind. Why, then, is the man on that account not bound to cover his head, because he is the image and glory of God, while the woman is bound to do so, because she is the glory of the man; as though the woman were not renewed in the spirit of her mind, which spirit is renewed to the knowledge of God after the image of Him who created him? But because she differs from the man in bodily sex, it was possible rightly to represent under her bodily covering that part of the reason which is diverted to the government of temporal things; so that the image of God may remain on that side of the mind of man on which it cleaves to the beholding or the consulting of the eternal reasons of things; and this, it is clear, not men only, but also women have.

CHAPTER VIII

TURNING ASIDE FROM THE IMAGE OF GOD

A common nature, therefore, is recognized in their minds, but in their bodies a division of that one mind itself is figured. As we ascend, then, by certain steps of thought within, along the succession of the parts of the mind, there where something first meets us which is not common to ourselves with the beasts reason begins, so that here the inner man can now be recognized. And if this inner man himself, through that reason to which the administering of things temporal has been delegated, slips on too far by over-much progress into outward things, that which is his head moreover consenting, that is, the (so to call it) masculine part which presides in the watch-tower of counsel not restraining or bridling it: then he waxeth old because of all his

---

[17] Col. iii. 9, 10   [18] Gal. iii. 26-28

enemies,[19] *viz.* the demons with their prince the devil, who are envious of virtue; and that vision of eternal things is withdrawn also from the head himself, eating with his spouse that which was forbidden, so that the light of his eyes is gone from him;[20] and so both being naked from that enlightenment of truth, and with the eyes of their conscience opened to behold how they were left shameful and unseemly, like the leaves of sweet fruits, but without the fruits themselves, they so weave together good words without the fruit of good works, as while living wickedly to cover over their disgrace as it were by speaking well.[21]

CHAPTER IX

THE SAME ARGUMENT IS CONTINUED

For the soul loving its own power, slips onwards from the whole which is common, to a part, which belongs especially to itself. And that apostatizing pride, which is called "the beginning of sin," [22] whereas it might have been most excellently governed by the laws of God, if it had followed Him as its ruler in the universal creature, by seeking something more than the whole, and struggling to govern this by a law of its own, is thrust on, since nothing is more than the whole, into caring for a part; and thus by lusting after something more, is made less; whence also covetousness is called "the root of all evil." [23] And it administers that whole, wherein it strives to do something of its own against the laws by which the whole is governed, by its own body, which it possesses only in part; and so being delighted by corporeal forms and motions, because it has not the things themselves within itself, and because it is wrapped up in their images, which it has fixed in the memory, and is foully polluted by fornication of the phantasy, while it refers all its functions to those ends, for which it curiously seeks corporeal and temporal things through the senses of the body, either it affects with swelling arrogance to be more excellent than other souls that are given up to the corporeal senses, or it is plunged into a foul whirlpool of carnal pleasure.

CHAPTER X

THE LOWEST DEGRADATION IS REACHED BY DEGREES

When the soul then consults either for itself or for others with a good will towards perceiving the inner and higher things, such as are possessed in a chaste embrace, without any narrowness or envy, not individually, but in common by all who love such things; then even if it be deceived in anything, through ignorance of things temporal (for its action in this case is a temporal one), and if it does not hold fast to that mode of acting which it ought, the temptation is but one common to man. And it is a great thing so to pass

[19] Ps. vi. 7   [20] Ps. xxxviii. 10   [21] Gen. iii. 4   [22] Ecclus. x. 15   [23] 1 Tim. vi. 10

through this life, on which we travel, as it were, like a road on our return home, that no temptation may take us, but what is common to man.[24] For this is a sin without the body, and must not be reckoned fornication, and on that account is very easily pardoned. But when the soul does anything in order to attain those things which are perceived through the body, through lust of proving or of surpassing or of handling them, in order that it may place in them its final good, then whatever it does, it does wickedly, and commits fornication, sinning against its own body:[25] and while snatching from within the deceitful images of corporeal things, and combining them by vain thought, so that nothing seems to it to be divine, unless it be of such a kind as this; by selfish greediness it is made fruitful in errors, and by selfish prodigality it is emptied of strength. Yet it would not leap on at once from the commencement to such shameless and miserable fornication, but, as it is written, "He that contemneth small things, shall fall by little and little." [26]

CHAPTER XI

THE IMAGE OF THE BEAST IN MAN

For as a snake does not creep on with open steps, but advances by the very minutest efforts of its several scales; so the slippery motion of falling away [from what is good] takes possession of the negligent only gradually, and beginning from a perverse desire for the likeness of God, arrives in the end at the likeness of beasts. Hence it is that being naked of their first garment, they earned by mortality coats of skins.[27] For the true honor of man is the image and likeness of God, which is not preserved except it be in relation to Him by whom it is impressed. The less therefore that one loves what is one's own, the more one cleaves to God. But through the desire of making trial of his own power, man by his own bidding falls down to himself as to a sort of intermediate grade. And so, while he wishes to be as God is, that is, under no one, he is thrust on, even from his own middle grade, by way of punishment, to that which is lowest, that is, to those things in which beasts delight: and thus, while his honor is the likeness of God, but his dishonor is the likeness of the beast, "Man being in honor abideth not: he is compared to the beasts that are foolish, and is made like to them." [28] By what path, then, could he pass so great a distance from the highest to the lowest, except through his own intermediate grade? For when he neglects the love of wisdom, which remains always after the same fashion, and lusts after knowledge by experiment upon things temporal and mutable, that knowledge puffeth up, it does not edify:[29] so the mind is overweighed and thrust out, as it were, by its own weight from blessedness; and learns by its own punishment, through that trial of its own intermediateness, what the difference is between the good it has abandoned and the bad to which it has committed itself; and

[24] 1 Cor. x. 13   [25] 1 Cor. vi. 18   [26] Ecclus. xix. 1   [27] Gen. iii. 21   [28] Ps. xlix. 12   [29] 1 Cor. viii. 1

having thrown away and destroyed its strength, it cannot return, unless by the grace of its Maker calling it to repentance, and forgiving its sins. For who will deliver the unhappy soul from the body of this death, unless the grace of God through Jesus Christ our Lord? [30] Of which grace we will discourse in its place, so far as He Himself enables us.

CHAPTER XII

THERE IS A KIND OF HIDDEN WEDLOCK IN THE INNER MAN. UNLAWFUL PLEASURES OF THE THOUGHTS

Let us now complete, so far as the Lord helps us, the discussion which we have undertaken, respecting that part of reason to which knowledge belongs, that is, the cognizance of things temporal and changeable, which is necessary for managing the affairs of this life. For as in the case of that visible wedlock of the two human beings who were made first, the serpent did not eat of the forbidden tree, but only persuaded them to eat of it; and the woman did not eat alone, but gave to her husband, and they ate together; although she alone spoke with the serpent, and she alone was led away by him:[31] so also in the case of that hidden and secret kind of wedlock, which is transacted and discerned in a single human being, the carnal, or as I may say, since it is directed to the senses of the body, the sensuous movement of the soul, which is common to us with beasts, is shut off from the reason of wisdom. For certainly bodily things are perceived by the sense of the body; but spiritual things, which are eternal and unchangeable, are understood by the reason of wisdom. But the reason of knowledge has appetite very near to it: seeing that what is called the science or knowledge of actions reasons concerning the bodily things which are perceived by the bodily sense; if well, in order that it may refer that knowledge to the end of the chief good; but if ill, in order that it may enjoy them as being such good things as those wherein it reposes with a false blessedness. Whenever, then, that carnal or animal sense introduces into this purpose of the mind which is conversant about things temporal and corporeal, with a view to the offices of a man's actions, by the living force of reason, some inducement to enjoy itself, that is, to enjoy itself as if it were some private good of its own, not as the public and common, which is the unchangeable, good; then, as it were, the serpent discourses with the woman. And to consent to this allurement, is to eat of the forbidden tree. But if that consent is satisfied by the pleasure of thought alone, but the members are so restrained by the authority of higher counsel that they are not yielded as instruments of unrighteousness unto sin;[32] this, I think, is to be considered as if the woman alone should have eaten the forbidden food. But if, in this consent to use wickedly the things which are perceived through the senses of the body, any sin at all is so determined upon, that if there is

[30] Rom. vii. 24, 25   [31] Gen. iii. 1-6   [32] Rom. vi. 13

the power it is also fulfilled by the body; then that woman must be understood to have given the unlawful food to her husband with her, to be eaten together. For it is not possible for the mind to determine that a sin is not only to be thought of with pleasure, but also to be effectually committed, unless also that intention of the mind yields, and serves the bad action, with which rests the chief power of applying the members to an outward act, or of restraining them from one.

And yet, certainly, when the mind is pleased in thought alone with unlawful things, while not indeed determining that they are to be done, but yet holding and pondering gladly things which ought to have been rejected the very moment they touched the mind, it cannot be denied to be a sin, but far less than if it were also determined to accomplish it in outward act. And therefore pardon must be sought for such thoughts too, and the breast must be smitten, and it must be said, "Forgive us our debts;" and what follows must be done, and must be joined in our prayer, "As we also forgive our debtors." [33] For it is not as it was with those two first human beings, of which each one bare his own person; and so, if the woman alone had eaten the forbidden food, she certainly alone would have been smitten with the punishment of death: it cannot, I say, be so said also in the case of a single human being now, that if the thought, remaining alone, be gladly fed with unlawful pleasures, from which it ought to turn away directly, while yet there is no determination that the bad actions are to be done, but only that they are retained with pleasure in remembrance, the woman as it were can be condemned without the man. Far be it from us to believe this. For here is one person, one human being, and he as a whole will be condemned, unless those things which, as lacking the will to do, and yet having the will to please the mind with them, are perceived to be sins of thought alone, are pardoned through the grace of the Mediator.

This reasoning, then, whereby we have sought in the mind of each several human being a certain rational wedlock of contemplation and action, with functions distributed through each severally, yet with the unity of the mind preserved in both; saving meanwhile the truth of that history which divine testimony hands down respecting the first two human beings, that is, the man and his wife, from whom the human species is propagated—this reasoning, I say, must be listened to only thus far, that the apostle may be understood to have intended to signify something to be sought in one individual man, by assigning the image of God to the man only, and not also to the woman, although in the merely different sex of two human beings.

[33] Matt. vi. 12

CHAPTER XIII

THE OPINION OF THOSE WHO HAVE THOUGHT THAT THE MIND WAS SIGNIFIED BY THE MAN, THE BODILY SENSE BY THE WOMAN

Nor does it escape me, that some who before us were eminent defenders of the Catholic faith and expounders of the word of God, while they looked for these two things in one human being, whose entire soul they perceived to be a sort of excellent paradise, asserted that the man was the mind, but that the woman was the bodily sense. And according to this distribution, by which the man is assumed to be the mind, but the woman the bodily sense, all things seem aptly to agree together if they are handled with due attention: unless that it is written, that in all the beasts and flying things there was not found for man an helpmate like to himself; and then the woman was made out of his side.[34] And on this account I, for my part, have not thought that the bodily sense should be taken for the woman, which we see to be common to ourselves and to the beasts; but I have desired to find something which the beasts had not; and I have rather thought the bodily sense should be understood to be the serpent, whom we read to have been more subtle than all beasts of the field.[35] For in those natural good things which we see are common to ourselves and to the irrational animals, the sense excels by a kind of living power; not the sense of which it is written in the epistle addressed to the Hebrews, where we read, that "strong meat belongeth to them that are of full age, even those who by reason of use have their senses exercised to discern both good and evil;" [36] for these "senses" belong to the rational nature and pertain to the understanding; but that sense which is divided into five parts in the body, through which corporeal species and motion is perceived not only by ourselves, but also by the beasts.

But whether that the apostle calls the man the image and glory of God, but the woman the glory of the man,[37] is to be received in this, or that, or in any other way; yet it is clear, that when we live according to God, our mind which is intent on the invisible things of Him ought to be fashioned with proficiency from His eternity, truth, charity; but that something of our own rational purpose, that is, of the same mind, must be directed to the using of changeable and corporeal things, without which this life does not go on; not that we may be conformed to this world,[38] by placing our end in such good things, and by forcing the desire of blessedness towards them, but that whatever we do rationally in the using of temporal things, we may do it with the contemplation of attaining eternal things, passing through the former, but cleaving to the latter.

[34] Gen. ii. 20-22   [35] Gen. iii. 1   [36] Heb. v. 14   [37] 1 Cor. xi. 7   [38] Rom. xii. 2

CHAPTER XIV

For knowledge also has its own good measure, if that in it which puffs up, or is wont to puff up, is conquered by love of eternal things, which does not puff up but, as we know, edifieth.[39] Certainly without knowledge the virtues themselves, by which one lives rightly, cannot be possessed, by which this miserable life may be so governed, that we may attain to that eternal life which is truly blessed.

Yet action, by which we use temporal things well, differs from contemplation of eternal things; and the latter is reckoned to wisdom, the former to knowledge. For although that which is wisdom can also be called knowledge, as the apostle too speaks, where he says, "Now I know in part, but then shall I know even as also I am known;"[40] when doubtless he meant his words to be understood of the knowledge of the contemplation of God, which will be the highest reward of the saints; yet where he says, "For to one is given by the Spirit the word of wisdom, to another the word of knowledge by the same Spirit,"[41] certainly he distinguishes without doubt these two things, although he does not there explain the difference, nor in what way one may be discerned from the other. But having examined a great number of passages from the Holy Scriptures, I find it written in the *Book of Job*, that holy man being the speaker, "Behold, piety, that is wisdom; but to depart from evil is knowledge."[42] In thus distinguishing, it must be understood that wisdom belongs to contemplation, knowledge to action. For in this place he meant by piety the worship of God, which in Greek is called θεοσέβεια. For the sentence in the Greek MSS. has that word. And what is there in eternal things more excellent than God, of whom alone the nature is unchangeable? And what is the worship of Him except the love of Him, by which we now desire to see Him, and we believe and hope that we shall see Him; and in proportion as we make progress, see now through a glass in an enigma, but then in clearness? For this is what the Apostle Paul means by "face to face."[43] This is also what John says, "Beloved, now we are the sons of God, and it doth not yet appear what we shall be; but we know that, when He shall appear, we shall be like Him; for we shall see Him as He is."[44] Discourse about these and the like subjects seems to me to be the discourse itself of wisdom. But to depart from evil, which Job says is knowledge, is without doubt of temporal things. Since it is in reference to time [and this world] that we are in evil,

---

[39] 1 Cor. viii. 1   [40] 1 Cor. xiii. 12   [41] 1 Cor. xii. 8   [42] Job xxviii. 8   [43] 1 Cor. xiii. 12   [44] 1 John iii. 2

Wisdom is contemplating the eternal truth of God.

from which we ought to abstain that we may come to those good eternal things. And therefore, whatsoever we do prudently, boldly, temperately, and justly, belongs to that knowledge or discipline wherewith our action is conversant in avoiding evil and desiring good; and so also, whatsoever we gather by the knowledge that comes from inquiry, in the way of examples either to be guarded against or to be imitated, and in the way of necessary proofs respecting any subject, accommodated to our use.

When a discourse then relates to these things, I hold it to be a discourse belonging to knowledge, and to be distinguished from a discourse belonging to wisdom, to which those things belong, which neither have been, nor shall be, but are; and on account of that eternity in which they are, are said to have been, and to be, and to be about to be, without any changeableness of times. For neither have they been in such way as that they should cease to be, nor are they about to be in such way as if they were not now; but they have always had and always will have that very absolute being. And they abide, but not as if fixed in some place as are bodies; but as intelligible things in incorporeal nature, they are so at hand to the glance of the mind, as things visible or tangible in place are to the sense of the body. And not only in the case of sensible things posited in place, there abide also intelligible and incorporeal reasons of them apart from local space; but also of motions that pass by in successive times, apart from any transit in time, there stand also like reasons, themselves certainly intelligible, and not sensible. And to attain to these with the eye of the mind is the lot of few; and when they are attained as much as they can be, he himself who attains to them does not abide in them, but is as it were repelled by the rebounding of the eye itself of the mind, and so there comes to be a transitory thought of a thing not transitory. And yet this transient thought is committed to the memory through the instructions by which the mind is taught; that the mind which is compelled to pass from thence, may be able to return thither again; although, if the thought should not return to the memory and find there what it had committed to it, it would be led thereto like an uninstructed person, as it had been led before, and would find it where it had first found it, that is to say, in that incorporeal truth, whence yet once more it may be as it were written down and fixed in the mind. For the thought of man, for example, does not so abide in that incorporeal and unchangeable reason of a square body, as that reason itself abides: if, to be sure, it could attain to it at all without the phantasy of local space. Or if one were to apprehend the rhythm of any artificial or musical sound, passing through certain intervals of time, as it rested without time in some secret and deep silence, it could at least be thought as long as that song could be heard; yet what the glance of the mind, transient though it was, caught from thence, and, absorbing as it were into a belly, so laid up in the memory, over this it will be able to ruminate in some measure by recollection, and to transfer what it has thus learned into systematic knowledge. But if this has been blotted out by absolute forgetfulness, yet once again, under the guidance of teaching, one will come to that which had altogether dropped away, and it will be found such as it was.

CHAPTER XV

IN OPPOSITION TO THE REMINISCENCE OF PLATO AND PYTHAGORAS. PYTHAGORAS THE SAMIAN. OF THE DIFFERENCE BETWEEN WISDOM AND KNOWLEDGE, AND OF SEEKING THE TRINITY IN THE KNOWLEDGE OF TEMPORAL THINGS

And hence that noble philosopher Plato endeavored to persuade us that the souls of men lived even before they bare these bodies; and that hence those things which are learnt are rather remembered, as having been known already, than taken into knowledge as things new. For he has told us that a boy, when questioned I know not what respecting geometry, replied as if he were perfectly skilled in that branch of learning. For being questioned step by step and skillfully, he saw what was to be seen, and said that which he saw.[45] But if this had been a recollecting of things previously known, then certainly every one, or almost every one, would not have been able so to answer when questioned. For not every one was a geometrician in the former life, since geometricians are so few among men that scarcely one can be found anywhere. But we ought rather to believe, that the intellectual mind is so formed in its nature as to see those things, which by the disposition of the Creator are subjoined to things intelligible in a natural order, by a sort of incorporeal light of an unique kind; as the eye of the flesh sees things adjacent to itself in this bodily light, of which light it is made to be receptive, and adapted to it. For none the more does this fleshly eye, too, distinguish black things from white without a teacher, because it had already known them before it was created in this flesh. Why, lastly, is it possible only in intelligible things that any one properly questioned should answer according to any branch of learning, although ignorant of it? Why can no one do this with things sensible, except those which he has seen in this his present body, or has believed the information of others who knew them, whether somebody's writings or words? For we must not acquiesce in their story, who assert that the Samian Pythagoras recollected some things of this kind, which he had experienced when he was previously here in another body; and others tell yet of others, that they experienced something of the same sort in their minds: but it may be conjectured that these were untrue recollections, such as we commonly experience in sleep, when we fancy we remember, as though we had done or seen it, what we never did or saw at all; and that the minds of these persons, even though awake, were affected in this way at the suggestion of malignant and deceitful spirits, whose care it is to confirm or to sow some false belief concerning the changes of souls, in order to deceive

[45] Cf. Plato, *Meno.*

men. This, I say, may be conjectured from this, that if they really remembered those things which they had seen here before, while occupying other bodies, the same thing would happen to many, nay to almost all; since they suppose that as the dead from the living, so, without cessation and continually, the living are coming into existence from the dead; as sleepers from those that are awake, and those that are awake from them that sleep.

If therefore this is the right distinction between wisdom and knowledge, that the intellectual cognizance of eternal things belongs to wisdom, but the rational cognizance of temporal things to knowledge, it is not difficult to judge which is to be preferred or postponed to which. But if we must employ some other distinction by which to know these two apart, which without doubt the apostle teaches us are different, saying, "To one is given by the Spirit the word of wisdom; to another the word of knowledge, by the same Spirit;" still the difference between those two which we have laid down is a most evident one, in that the intellectual cognizance of eternal things is one thing, the rational cognizance of temporal things another; and no one doubts but that the former is to be preferred to the latter. As then we leave behind those things which belong to the outer man, and desire to ascend within from those things which we have in common with beasts, before we come to the cognizance of things intelligible and supreme, which are eternal, the rational cognizance of temporal things presents itself. Let us then find a trinity in this also, if we can, as we found one in the senses of the body, and in those things which through them entered in the way of images into our soul or spirit; so that instead of corporeal things which we touch by corporeal sense, placed as they are without us, we might have resemblances of bodies impressed within on the memory from which thought might be formed, while the will as a third united them; just as the sight of the eyes was formed from without, which the will applied to the visible thing in order to produce vision, and united both, while itself also added itself thereto as a third. But this subject must not be compressed into this book; so that in that which follows, if God help, it may be suitably examined, and the conclusions to which we come may be unfolded.

BOOK FOURTEEN

Summary

826

Chapter 12: By the justice of God in some sense, the human race was delivered into the power of the devil. The sin of Adam has been passed to his progeny. God did not command this deliverance into the power of the devil, but He permitted it, and justly. The remission of sins through the mercy of God rescues man from the devil.

Chapter 13: The devil is overcome, and man rescued from him, not by the power of God, but by His righteousness.

Chapter 14: The righteousness by which the devil was conquered is the righteousness of Jesus Christ. To deal with the devil it was necessary that Christ be both God and man. As man in humility he died. He could have conquered the devil by power, but He conquered him by righteousness. Christ was crucified, not through immortal power, but through the weakness which He took upon Him in mortal flesh, but "the weakness of God is stronger than men." (I Cor. i. 25)

Chapter 15: The devil was conquered by Christ's death. His sinless blood was poured out for the remission of our sins.

Chapter 16: The death of the flesh, which came originally from the sin of the first man, has been used well by the glorious martyrs. Death and the evils of this world are turned to good for those who are saved. God took upon Him a temporal death to free men from an eternal death. The wrath of God is not as human anger, but is just retribution.

Chapter 17: The Incarnation shows man his place among the things which God has created. The grace of God is commended to us in the man Christ without any precedent merits. The greatest sin of man, pride, can be healed, as is shown by the Incarnation, through the great humility of God.

Chapter 18: God took upon Him man from the race of Adam to conquer the enemy of the human race, and from a virgin without lust but in faith. He therefore became man without sin.

Chapter 19: All that the Word did for us belongs to knowledge, and not to wisdom. If any one can speak truly concerning the Word, this belongs to wisdom. The word made flesh has the treasures both of wisdom and of knowledge. Grace belongs to knowledge, truth to wisdom. Christ gives us faith concerning temporal things and truth concerning eternal things. Through Christ we stretch through knowledge to wisdom. However, in a less precise mode of speech, we can be said to have both knowledge and wisdom concerning things human and things divine.

Chapter 20: All will blessedness. Faith is necessary. The Incarnation shows direction to faith. A certain trinity can be found in practical knowledge and true faith.

BOOK FOURTEEN

Summary

Chapter 1: We will now speak not of the wisdom of God, but of the true wisdom of man which is according to God. The wisdom of man is the "worship of God." Wise men, philosophers, "lovers of wisdom," dispute of wisdom. They define it as "knowledge of things human and divine." Whereas, we precisely should refer knowledge to things human, and wisdom to things divine. Faith should strengthen knowledge—and should lead on to things eternal.

Chapter 2: A kind of trinity is found in the remembering, contemplating, and loving of temporal faith. If this is an image of God it must be reckoned among things transient.

Chapter 3: But this trinity, since it is in an immortal soul, will be different, when the faith which is remembered, contemplated, and loved, will exist always.

Chapter 4: The image of God is to be sought in the immortality of the rational soul. It is the image of God, because it can use reason and intellect to understand God. In seeking for a trinity in this image of God, we must remember that the mind knows itself, as we demonstrated in the tenth book.

Chapter 5: We really cannot know whether the mind of the infant knows itself.

Chapter 6: A kind of trinity is found in the mind understanding and cognizing itself. The trinity is intimated by memory, intelligence, and will.

Chapter 7: Just as we remember, understand, and love things of which we may not happen to be thinking, so it is with the mind in relation to itself.

Chapter 8: The trinity which is the image of God is sought in the noblest part of the mind.

Chapter 9: Some have maintained that the virtues, justice, prudence, temperance, and fortitude will cease with mortal life. Justice will be perfected in blessedness, and, perhaps, the other three. They will make a different trinity for us as we look at acts of virtue as things past.

Chapter 10: A trinity is produced by the mind remembering, understanding, and loving itself.

Chapter 11: Memory may be said to be of things present.

Chapter 12: The trinity in the mind is an image of God, because it can remember, understand, and love God, and in so doing is made wise.

Chapter 13: Man can forget God, but if he has not altogether forgotten Him, he can remember Him again.

Chapter 14: The mind loves God in rightly loving itself. And if the mind does not love God, it may be rightly said to hate itself. Even a weak mind does not lose its natural memory, love, and understanding of itself. It should turn to God, the Trinity, whose image it is, and reach blessedness by remembering, understanding, and loving Him.

Chapter 15: Although the soul hopes for blessedness, yet it cannot remember lost blessedness, but it does remember God and His eternal laws. Even the unchanging rules of right living are known to the unrighteous.

Chapter 16: Those who are turned to the Lord are formed anew, and in the mind this is wrought after God, or after the image of God.

Chapter 17: This renewal takes place by gradually making progress in the renewal of that image—in the knowledge of God. The likeness of God will finally be perfected, when in blessedness the sight of God will be perfected.

Chapter 18: The full likeness of God is to take place in that image of God at that time when it shall receive the full sight of God. And this will be in the immortality of the body.

Chapter 19: Man is made after the image of the Trinity, and its perfect likeness will be in eternal life. This contemplative wisdom is in seeing Him as He is perfected in happiness.

BOOK FIFTEEN

Begins by setting forth briefly and in sum the contents of the previous fourteen books. The argument is then shown to have reached so far as to allow of our now inquiring concerning the Trinity, which is God, in those eternal, incorporeal, and unchangeable things themselves, in the perfect contemplation of which a blessed life is promised to us. But this Trinity, as he shows, is here seen by us as by a mirror and in an enigma, in that it is seen by means of the image of God, which we are, as in a likeness that is obscure and hard of discernment. In like manner, it is shown that some kind of conjecture and explanation may be gathered respecting the generation of the divine word, from the word of our own mind, but only with difficulty, on account of the exceeding disparity which is discernible between the two words; and, again, respecting the procession of the Holy Spirit, from the love that is joined thereto by the will.

CHAPTER I

GOD IS ABOVE THE MIND

DESIRING to exercise the reader in the things that are made, in order that he may know Him by whom they are made, we have now advanced so far as to His image, which is man, in that wherein he excels the other animals, *i.e.* in reason or intelligence, and whatever else can be said of the rational or intellectual soul that pertains to what is called the mind.[1] For by this name some Latin writers, after their own peculiar mode of speech, distinguish that which excels in man, and is not in the beast, from the soul,[2] which is in the beast as well. If, then, we seek anything that is above this nature, and seek truly, it is God—namely, a nature not created, but creating. And whether this is the Trinity, it is now our business to demonstrate not only to believers, by authority of divine Scripture, but also to such as understand, by some kind of reason, if we can. And why I say, if we can, the thing itself will show better when we have begun to argue about it in our inquiry.

CHAPTER II

GOD, ALTHOUGH INCOMPREHENSIBLE, IS EVER TO BE SOUGHT. THE TRACES OF THE TRINITY ARE NOT VAINLY SOUGHT IN THE CREATURE

For God Himself, whom we seek, will, as I hope, help our labors, that they may not be unfruitful, and that we may understand how it is said in the

[1] *Mens* or *animus*   [2] *Anima*

holy *Psalm,* "Let the heart of them rejoice that seek the Lord. Seek the Lord,
and be strengthened: seek His face evermore." [3] For that which is always
being sought seems as though it were never found; and how then will the
heart of them that seek rejoice, and not rather be made sad, if they cannot
find what they seek? For it is not said, The heart shall rejoice of them that
find, but of them that seek, the Lord. And yet the prophet Isaiah testifies,
that the Lord God can be found when He is sought, when he says: "Seek ye
the Lord; and as soon as ye have found Him, call upon Him: and when He
has drawn near to you, let the wicked man forsake his ways, and the unrighteous man his thoughts." [4] If, then, when sought, He can be found, why
is it said, "Seek ye His face evermore?" Is He perhaps to be sought even
when found? For things incomprehensible must so be investigated, as that
no one may think he has found nothing, when he has been able to find how
incomprehensible that is which he was seeking. Why then does he so seek,
if he comprehends that which he seeks to be incomprehensible, unless because he may not give over seeking so long as he makes progress in the inquiry itself into things incomprehensible, and becomes ever better and better
while seeking so great a good, which is both sought in order to be found, and
found in order to be sought? For it is both sought in order that it may be
found more sweetly, and found in order that it may be sought more eagerly.
The words of Wisdom in the book of *Ecclesiasticus* may be taken in this
meaning: "They who eat me shall still be hungry, and they who drink me
shall still be thirsty." [5] For they eat and drink because they find; and they
still continue seeking because they are hungry and thirst. Faith seeks, understanding finds; whence the prophet says, "Unless ye believe, ye shall not
understand." [6] And yet, again, understanding still seeks Him, whom it finds;
for "God looked down upon the sons of men," as it is sung in the holy Psalm,
"to see if there were any that would understand, and seek after God." [7] And
man, therefore, ought for this purpose to have understanding, that he may
seek after God.

We shall have tarried then long enough among those things that God has
made, in order that by them He Himself may be known that made them.
"For the invisible things of Him from the creation of the world are clearly
seen, being understood by the things that are made." [8] And hence they are
rebuked in the book of *Wisdom,* "who could not out of the good things that
are seen know Him that is: neither by considering the works, did they acknowledge the workmaster; but deemed either fire, or wind, or the swift air,
or the circle of the stars, or the violent water, or the lights of heaven, to be
the gods which govern the world: with whose beauty if they, being delighted,
took them to be gods, let them know how much better the Lord of them is;
for the first Author of beauty hath created them. But if they were astonished
at their power and virtue, let them understand by them how much mightier

[3] Ps. cv. 3, 4   [4] Isa. lv. 6, 7   [5] Ecclus. xxiv. 29   [6] Isa. vii. 9   [7] Ps. xiv. 2
[8] Rom. i. 20

He is that made them. For by the greatness and beauty of the creatures proportionably the Maker of them is seen." [9] I have quoted these words from
the book of *Wisdom* for this reason, that no one of the faithful may think me
vainly and emptily to have sought first in the creature, step by step through
certain trinities, each of their own appropriate kind, until I came at last to
the mind of man, traces of that highest Trinity which we seek when we seek
God.

CHAPTER III

A BRIEF RECAPITULATION OF ALL THE PREVIOUS BOOKS

But since the necessities of our discussion and argument have compelled
us to say a great many things in the course of fourteen books, which we cannot view at once in one glance, so as to be able to refer them quickly in
thought to that which we desire to grasp, I will attempt, by the help of God,
to the best of my power, to put briefly together, without arguing, whatever
I have established in the several books by argument as known, and to place,
as it were, under one mental view, not the way in which we have been convinced of each point, but the points themselves of which we have been convinced; in order that what follows may not be so far separated from that
which precedes, as that the perusal of the former shall produce forgetfulness
of the latter; or at any rate, if it have produced such forgetfulness, that what
has escaped the memory may be speedily recalled by reperusal.

In the first book, the unity and equality of that highest Trinity is shown
from Holy Scripture. In the second, and third, and fourth, the same: but a
careful handling of the question respecting the sending of the Son and of the
Holy Spirit has resulted in three books; and we have demonstrated, that He
who is sent is not therefore less than He who sends because the one sent, the
other was sent; since the Trinity, which is in all things equal, being also
equally in its own nature unchangeable, and invisible, and everywhere present, works indivisibly. In the fifth—with a view to those who think that the
substance of the Father and of the Son is therefore not the same, because
they suppose everything that is predicated of God to be predicated according
to substance, and therefore contend that to beget and to be begotten, or to
be begotten and unbegotten, as being diverse, are diverse substances—it is
demonstrated that not everything that is predicated of God is predicated
according to substance, as He is called good and great according to substance, or anything else that is predicated of Him in respect to Himself, but
that some things also are predicated relatively, *i.e.* not in respect to Himself,
but in respect to something which is not Himself; as He is called the Father
in respect to the Son, or the Lord in respect to the creature that serves Him;
and that here, if anything thus relatively predicated, *i.e.* predicated in re-

---

[9] Wisd. xiii. 1-5

spect to something that is not Himself, is predicated also as in time, as, e.g., "Lord, Thou hast become our refuge," [10] then nothing happens to Him so as to work a change in Him, but He Himself continues altogether unchangeable in His own nature or essence. In the sixth, the question how Christ is called by the mouth of the apostle "the power of God and the wisdom of God," [11] is so far argued that the more careful handling of that question is deferred, viz. whether He from whom Christ is begotten is not wisdom Himself, but only the father of His own wisdom, or whether wisdom begat wisdom. But be it which it may, the equality of the Trinity became apparent in this book also, and that God was not triple, but a Trinity; and that the Father and the Son are not, as it were, a double as opposed to the single Holy Spirit: for therein three are not anything more than one. We considered, too, how to understand the words of Bishop Hilary, "Eternity in the Father, form in the Image, use in the Gift." In the seventh, the question is explained which had been deferred: in what way that God who begat the Son is not only Father of His own power and wisdom, but is Himself also power and wisdom; so, too, the Holy Spirit; and yet that they are not three powers or three wisdoms, but one power and one wisdom, as one God and one essence. It was next inquired, in what way they are called one essence, three persons, or by some Greeks one essence, three substances; and we found that the words were so used through the needs of speech, that there might be one term by which to answer, when it is asked what the three are, whom we truly confess to be three, viz. Father, and Son, and Holy Spirit. In the eighth, it is made plain by reason also to those who understand, that not only the Father is not greater than the Son in the substance of truth, but that both together are not anything greater than the Holy Spirit alone, nor that any two at all in the same Trinity are anything greater than one, nor all three together anything greater than each severally. Next, I have pointed out, that by means of the truth, which is beheld by the understanding, and by means of the highest good, from which is all good, and by means of the righteousness for which a righteous mind is loved even by a mind not yet righteous, we might understand, so far as it is possible to understand, that not only incorporeal but also unchangeable nature which is God; and by means, too, of love, which in the Holy Scriptures is called God,[12] by which, first of all, those who have understanding begin also, however feebly, to discern the Trinity, to wit, one that loves, and that which is loved, and love. In the ninth, the argument advances as far as to the image of God, viz. man in respect to his mind; and in this we found a kind of trinity, i.e. the mind, and the knowledge whereby the mind knows itself, and the love whereby it loves both itself and its knowledge of itself; and these three are shown to be mutually equal, and of one essence. In the tenth, the same subject is more carefully and subtly handled, and is brought to this point, that we found in the mind a still more manifest trinity of the mind, viz. in memory, and understanding, and will.

[10] Ps. xc. 1   [11] 1 Cor. i. 24   [12] 1 John iv. 16

But since it turned out also, that the mind could never be in such a case as not to remember, understand, and love itself, although it did not always think of itself; but that when it did think of itself, it did not in the same act of thought distinguish itself from things corporeal; the argument respecting the Trinity, of which this is an image, was deferred, in order to find a trinity also in the things themselves that are seen with the body, and to exercise the reader's attention more distinctly in that. Accordingly, in the eleventh, we chose the sense of sight, wherein that which should have been there found to hold good might be recognized also in the other four bodily senses, although not expressly mentioned; and so a trinity of the outer man first showed itself in those things which are discerned from without, to wit, from the bodily object which is seen, and from the form which is thence impressed upon the eye of the beholder, and from the purpose of the will combining the two. But these three things, as was patent, were not mutually equal and of one substance. Next, we found yet another trinity in the mind itself, introduced into it, as it were, by the things perceived from without; wherein the same three things, as it appeared, were of one substance: the image of the bodily object which is in the memory, and the form thence impressed when the mind's eye of the thinker is turned to it, and the purpose of the will combining the two. But we found this trinity to pertain to the outer man, on this account, that it was introduced into the mind from bodily objects which are perceived from without. In the twelfth, we thought good to distinguish wisdom from knowledge, and to seek first, as being the lower of the two, a kind of appropriate and special trinity in that which is specially called knowledge; but that although we have got now in this to something pertaining to the inner man, yet it is not yet to be either called or thought an image of God. And this is discussed in the thirteenth book by the commendation of Christian faith. In the fourteenth we discuss the true wisdom of man, *viz.* that which is granted him by God's gift in the partaking of that very God Himself, which is distinct from knowledge; and the discussion reached this point, that a trinity is discovered in the image of God, which is man in respect to his mind, which mind is "renewed in the knowledge" of God, "after the image of Him that created" man;[13] "after His own image;" [14] and so obtains wisdom, wherein is the contemplation of things eternal.

CHAPTER IV

WHAT UNIVERSAL NATURE TEACHES US CONCERNING GOD

Let us, then, now seek the Trinity which is God, in the things themselves that are eternal, incorporeal, and unchangeable; in the perfect contemplation of which a blessed life is promised us, which cannot be other than eternal. For not only does the authority of the divine books declare that God is;

---

[13] Col. iii. 10   [14] Gen. i. 27

but the whole nature of the universe itself which surrounds us, and to which we also belong, proclaims that it has a most excellent Creator, who has given to us a mind and natural reason, whereby to see that things living are to be preferred to things that are not living; things that have sense to things that have not; things that have understanding to things that have not; things immortal to things mortal; things powerful to things impotent; things righteous to things unrighteous; things beautiful to things deformed; things good to things evil; things incorruptible to things corruptible; things unchangeable to things changeable; things invisible to things visible; things incorporeal to things corporeal; things blessed to things miserable. And hence, since without doubt we place the Creator above things created, we must needs confess that the Creator both lives in the highest sense, and perceives and understands all things, and that He cannot die, or suffer decay, or be changed; and that He is not a body, but a spirit, of all the most powerful, most righteous, most beautiful, most good, most blessed.

CHAPTER V

HOW DIFFICULT IT IS TO DEMONSTRATE THE TRINITY BY NATURAL REASON

But all that I have said, and whatever else seems to be worthily said of God after the like fashion of human speech, applies to the whole Trinity, which is one God, and to the several Persons in that Trinity. For who would dare to say either of the one God, which is the Trinity itself, or of the Father, or Son, or Holy Spirit, either that He is not living, or is without sense or intelligence; or that, in that nature in which they are affirmed to be mutually equal, any one of them is mortal, or corruptible, or changeable, or corporeal? Or is there any one who would deny that any one in the Trinity is most powerful, most righteous, most beautiful, most good, most blessed? If, then, these things, and all others of the kind, can be predicated both of the Trinity itself, and of each several one in that Trinity, where or how shall the Trinity manifest itself? Let us therefore first reduce these numerous predicates to some limited number. For that which is called life in God, is itself His essence and nature. God, therefore, does not live, unless by the life which He is to Himself. And this life is not such as that which is in a tree, wherein is neither understanding nor sense; nor such as is in a beast, for the life of a beast possesses the fivefold sense, but has no understanding. But the life which is God perceives and understands all things, and perceives by mind, not by body, because "God is a spirit." [15] And God does not perceive through a body, as animals do, which have bodies, for He does not consist of soul and body. And hence that single nature perceives as it understands, and understands as it perceives, and its sense and understanding are one and the same.

[15] John iv. 24

Nor yet so, that at any time He should either cease or begin to be; for He is immortal. And it is not said of Him in vain, that "He only hath immortality." [16] For immortality is true immortality in His case whose nature admits no change. That is also true eternity by which God is unchangeable, without beginning, without end; consequently also incorruptible. It is one and the same thing, therefore, to call God eternal, or immortal, or incorruptible, or unchangeable; and it is likewise one and the same thing to say that He is living, and that He is intelligent, that is, in truth, wise. For He did not receive wisdom whereby to be wise, but He is Himself wisdom. And this is life, and again is power or might, and yet again beauty, whereby He is called powerful and beautiful. For what is more powerful and more beautiful than wisdom, "which reaches from end to end mightily, and sweetly disposes all things"? [17] Or do goodness, again, and righteousness, differ from each other in the nature of God, as they differ in His works, as though they were two diverse qualities of God—goodness one, and righteousness another? Certainly not; but that which is righteousness is also itself goodness; and that which is goodness is also itself blessedness. And God is therefore called incorporeal, that He may be believed and understood to be a spirit, not a body.

Further, if we say, Eternal, immortal, incorruptible, unchangeable, living, wise, powerful, beautiful, righteous, good, blessed, spirit; only the last of this list as it were seems to signify substance, but the rest to signify qualities of that substance; but it is not so in that ineffable and simple nature. For whatever seems to be predicated therein according to quality, is to be understood according to substance or essence. For far be it from us to predicate spirit of God according to substance, and good according to quality; but both according to substance. And so in like manner of all those we have mentioned, of which we have already spoken at length in the former books. Let us choose, then, one of the first four of those in our enumeration and arrangement, i.e. eternal, immortal, incorruptible, unchangeable; since these four, as I have argued already, have one meaning; in order that our aim may not be distracted by a multiplicity of objects. And let it be rather that which was placed first, viz. eternal. Let us follow the same course with the four that come next, viz. living, wise, powerful, beautiful. And since life of some sort belongs also to the beast, which has not wisdom; while the next two, viz. wisdom and might, are so compared to one another in the case of man, as that Scripture says, "Better is he that is wise than he that is strong;" [18] and beauty, again, is commonly attributed to bodily objects also: out of these four that we have chosen, let Wise be the one we take. Although these four are not to be called unequal in speaking of God; for they are four names, but one thing. But of the third and last four—although it is the same thing in God to be righteous that it is to be good or to be blessed; and the same thing to be a spirit that it is to be righteous, and good, and blessed; yet, because in men there can be a spirit that is not blessed, and there can be one both

[16] 1 Tim. vi. 16   [17] Wisd. viii. 1   [18] Wisd. vi. 1

righteous and good, but not yet blessed; but that which is blessed is doubtless both just, and good, and a spirit—let us rather choose that one which cannot exist even in men without the three others, *viz.* blessed.

CHAPTER VI

HOW THERE IS A TRINITY IN THE VERY SIMPLICITY OF GOD.
WHETHER AND HOW THE TRINITY THAT IS GOD IS MANI-
FESTED FROM THE TRINITIES WHICH HAVE BEEN SHOWN
TO BE IN MEN

When, then, we say, Eternal, wise, blessed, are these three the Trinity that is called God? We reduce, indeed, those twelve to this small number of three; but perhaps we can go further, and reduce these three also to one of them. For if wisdom and might, or life and wisdom, can be one and the same thing in the nature of God, why cannot eternity and wisdom, or blessedness and wisdom, be one and the same thing in the nature of God? And hence, as it made no difference whether we spoke of these twelve or of those three when we reduced the many to the small number; so does it make no difference whether we speak of those three, or of that one, to the singularity of which we have shown that the other two of the three may be reduced. What fashion, then, of argument, what possible force and might of understanding, what liveliness of reason, what sharp-sightedness of thought, will set forth how (to pass over now the others) this one thing, that God is called wisdom, is a trinity? For God does not receive wisdom from any one as we receive it from Him, but He is Himself His own wisdom; because His wisdom is not one thing, and His essence another, seeing that to Him to be wise is to be. Christ, indeed, is called in the Holy Scriptures, "the power of God, and the wisdom of God." [19] But we have discussed in the seventh book how this is to be understood, so that the Son may not seem to make the Father wise; and our explanation came to this, that the Son is wisdom of wisdom, in the same way as He is light of light, God of God. Nor could we find the Holy Spirit to be in any other way than that He Himself also is wisdom, and altogether one wisdom, as one God, one essence. How, then, do we understand this wisdom, which is God, to be a trinity? I do not say, How do we believe this? For among the faithful this ought to admit no question. But supposing there is any way by which we can see with the understanding what we believe, what is that way?

For if we recall where it was in these books that a trinity first began to show itself to our understanding, the eighth book is that which occurs to us; since it was there that to the best of our power we tried to raise the aim of the mind to understand that most excellent and unchangeable nature, which our mind is not. And we so contemplated this nature as to think of it as not

[19] I Cor. i. 24

far from us, and as above us, not in place, but by its own awful and wonderful excellence, and in such wise that it appeared to be with us by its own present light. Yet in this no trinity was yet manifest to us, because in that blaze of light we did not keep the eye of the mind steadfastly bent upon seeking it; only we discerned it in a sense, because there was no bulk wherein we must needs think the magnitude of two or three to be more than that of one. But when we came to treat of love, which in the Holy Scriptures is called God,[20] then a trinity began to dawn upon us a little, *i.e.* one that loves, and that which is loved, and love. But because that ineffable light beat back our gaze, and it became in some degree plain that the weakness of our mind could not as yet be tempered to it, we turned back in the midst of the course we had begun, and planned according to the (as it were) more familiar consideration of our own mind, according to which man is made after the image of God,[21] in order to relieve our overstrained attention; and thereupon we dwelt from the ninth to the fourteenth book upon the consideration of the creature, which we are, that we might be able to understand and behold the invisible things of God by those things which are made. And now that we have exercised the understanding, as far as was needful, or perhaps more than was needful, in lower things, lo! we wish, but have not strength, to raise ourselves to behold that highest Trinity which is God. For in such manner as we see most undoubted trinities, whether those which are wrought from without by corporeal things, or when these same things are thought of which were perceived from without; or when those things which take their rise in the mind, and do not pertain to the senses of the body, as faith, or as the virtues which comprise the art of living, are discerned by manifest reason, and held fast by knowledge; or when the mind itself, by which we know whatever we truly say that we know, is known to itself, or thinks of itself; or when that mind beholds anything eternal and unchangeable, which itself is not—in such way, then, I say, as we see in all these instances most undoubted trinities, because they are wrought in ourselves, or are in ourselves, when we remember, look at, or desire these things—do we, I say, in such manner also see the Trinity that is God; because there also, by the understanding, we behold both Him as it were speaking, and His Word, *i.e.* the Father and the Son; and then, proceeding thence, the love common to both, namely, the Holy Spirit? These trinities that pertain to our senses or to our mind, do we rather see than believe them, but rather believe than see that God is a trinity? But if this is so, then doubtless we either do not at all understand and behold the invisible things of God by those things that are made, or if we behold them at all, we do not behold the Trinity in them; and there is therein somewhat to behold, and somewhat also which we ought to believe, even though not beheld. And as the eighth book showed that we behold the unchangeable good which we are not, so the fourteenth reminded us thereof, when we spoke of the wisdom that man has from God. Why, then,

[20] 1 John iv. 16   [21] Gen. i. 27

do we not recognize the Trinity therein? Does that wisdom which God is said to be, not perceive itself, and not love itself? Who would say this? Or who is there that does not see, that where there is no knowledge, there in no way is there wisdom? Or are we, in truth, to think that the Wisdom which is God knows other things, and does not know itself; or loves other things, and does not love itself? But if this is a foolish and impious thing to say or believe, then behold we have a trinity—to wit, wisdom, and the knowledge wisdom has of itself, and its love of itself. For so, too, we find a trinity in man also, *i.e.* mind, and the knowledge wherewith mind knows itself, and the love wherewith it loves itself.

CHAPTER VII

THAT IT IS NOT EASY TO DISCOVER THE TRINITY THAT IS GOD FROM THE TRINITIES WE HAVE SPOKEN OF

But these three are in such way in man, that they are not themselves man. For man, as the ancients defined him, is a rational mortal animal. These things, therefore, are the chief things in man, but are not man themselves. And any one person, *i.e.* each individual man, has these three things in his mind. But if, again, we were so to define man as to say, Man is a rational substance consisting of mind and body, then without doubt man has a soul that is not body, and a body that is not soul. And hence these three things are not man, but belong to man, or are in man. If, again, we put aside the body, and think of the soul by itself, the mind is somewhat belonging to the soul, as though its head, or eye, or countenance; but these things are not to be regarded as bodies. It is not then the soul, but that which is chief in the soul, that is called the mind. But can we say that the Trinity is in such way in God, as to be somewhat belonging to God, and not itself God? And hence each individual man, who is called the image of God, not according to all things that pertain to his nature, but according to his mind alone, is one person, and is an image of the Trinity in his mind. But that Trinity of which he is the image is nothing else in its totality than God, is nothing else in its totality than the Trinity. Nor does anything pertain to the nature of God so as not to pertain to that Trinity; and the Three Persons are of one essence, not as each individual man is one person.

There is, again, a wide difference in this point likewise, that whether we speak of the mind in a man, and of its knowledge and love; or of memory, understanding, will—we remember nothing of the mind except by memory, nor understand anything except by understanding, nor love anything except by will. But in that Trinity, who would dare to say that the Father understands neither Himself, nor the Son, nor the Holy Spirit, except by the Son, or loves them except by the Holy Spirit; and that He remembers only by Himself either Himself, or the Son, or the Holy Spirit; and in the same way that the Son remembers neither Himself nor the Father, except by the Father, nor loves them except by the Holy Spirit; but that by Himself He only understands the Father and Son and Holy Spirit: and in like manner, that the Holy Spirit by the Father remembers the Father and the Son and Himself, and by the Son understands the Father and the Son and Himself; but by Himself only loves Himself and the Father and the Son —as though the Father were both His own memory, and that of the Son and of the Holy Spirit; and the Son were the understanding of both Himself, and the Father and the Holy Spirit; but the Holy Spirit were the love both of Himself, and of the Father and of the Son? Who would presume to think or affirm this of that Trinity? For if therein the Son alone understands both for Himself and for the Father and for the Holy Spirit, we have returned to the old absurdity, that the Father is not wise from Himself, but from the Son, and that wisdom has not begotten wisdom, but that the Father is said to be wise by that wisdom which He begat. For where there is no understanding there can be no wisdom; and hence, if the Father does not understand Himself for Himself, but the Son understands for the Father, assuredly the Son makes the Father wise. But if to God to be is to be wise, and essence is to Him the same as wisdom, then it is not the Son that has His essence from the Father, which is the truth, but rather the Father from the Son, which is a most absurd falsehood. And this absurdity, beyond all doubt, we have discussed, disproved, and rejected, in the seventh book. Therefore God the Father is wise by that wisdom by which He is His own wisdom, and the Son is the wisdom of the Father from the wisdom which is the Father, from whom the Son is begotten; whence it follows that the Father understands also by that understanding by which He is His own understanding (for he could not be wise that did not understand); and that the Son is the understanding of the Father, begotten of the understanding which is the Father. And this same may not be unfitly said of memory also. For how is he wise, that re-members nothing, or does not remember himself? Accordingly, since the Father is wisdom, and the Son is wisdom, therefore, as the Father remembers Himself, so does the Son also remember Himself; and as the Father remembers both Himself and the Son, not by the memory of the Son, but by His own, so does the Son remember both Himself and the Father, not by the memory of the Father, but by His own. Where, again, there is no love, who would say there was any wisdom? And hence we must infer that the Father is in such way His own love, as He is His own understanding and memory. And therefore these three, *i.e.* memory, understanding, love or will, in that highest and unchangeable essence which is God, are, we see, not the Father and the Son and the Holy Spirit, but the Father alone. And because the Son too is wisdom begotten of wisdom, as neither the Father nor the Holy Spirit understands for Him, but He understands for Himself; so neither does the Father remember for Him, nor the Holy Spirit love for Him, but He remembers and loves for Himself: for He is Himself also His own memory, His own understanding, and His own love. But that He is so comes to Him from the

Father, of whom He is born. And because the Holy Spirit also is wisdom proceeding from wisdom, He too has not the Father for a memory, and the Son for an understanding, and Himself for love: for He would not be wisdom if another remembered for Him, and yet another understood for Him, and He only loved for Himself; but Himself has all three things, and has them in such way that they are Himself. But that He is so comes to Him thence, whence He proceeds.

What man, then, is there who can comprehend that wisdom by which God knows all things, in such wise that neither what we call things past are past therein, nor what we call things future are therein waited for as coming, as though they were absent, but both past and future with things present are all present; nor yet are things thought severally, so that thought passes from one to another but all things simultaneously are at hand in one glance— what man, I say, is there that comprehends that wisdom, and the like prudence, and the like knowledge, since in truth even our own wisdom is beyond our comprehension? For somehow we are able to behold the things that are present to our senses or to our understanding; but the things that are absent, and yet have once been present, we know by memory, if we have not forgotten them. And we conjecture, too, not the past from the future, but the future from the past, yet by an unstable knowledge. For there are some of our thoughts to which, although future, we, as it were, look onward with greater plainness and certainty as being very near; and we do this by the means of memory when we are able to do it, as much as we ever are able, although memory seems to belong not to the future, but to the past. And this may be tried in the case of any words or songs, the due order of which we are rendering by memory; for we certainly should not utter each in succession, unless we foresaw in thought what came next. And yet it is not foresight, but memory, that enables us to foresee it; for up to the very end of the words or the song, nothing is uttered except as foreseen and looked forward to. And yet in doing this, we are not said to speak or sing by foresight, but by memory; and if any one is more than commonly capable of uttering many pieces in this way, he is usually praised, not for his foresight, but for his memory. We know, and are absolutely certain, that all this takes place in our mind or by our mind; but how it takes place, the more attentively we desire to scrutinize, the more do both our very words break down, and our purpose itself fails, when by our understanding, if not our tongue, we would reach to something of clearness. And do such as we are, think, that in so great infirmity of mind we can comprehend whether the foresight of God is the same as His memory and His understanding, who does not regard in thought each several thing, but embraces all that He knows in one eternal and unchangeable and ineffable vision? In this difficulty, then, and strait, we may well cry out to the living God, "Such knowledge is too wonderful for me: it is high, I cannot attain unto it." [22] For I understand by myself how wonderful and incompre-

[22] Ps. cxxxix. 6

hensible is Thy knowledge, by which Thou madest me, when I cannot even comprehend myself whom Thou hast made! And yet, "while I was musing, the fire burned," [23] so that "I seek Thy face evermore." [24]

CHAPTER VIII

HOW THE APOSTLE SAYS THAT GOD IS NOW SEEN BY US THROUGH A GLASS

I know that wisdom is an incorporeal substance, and that it is the light by which those things are seen that are not seen by carnal eyes; and yet a man so great and so spiritual [as Paul] says, "We see now through a glass, in an enigma, but then face to face." [25] If we ask what and of what sort is this "glass," this assuredly occurs to our minds, that in a glass nothing is discerned but an image. We have endeavored, then, so to do; in order that we might see in some way or other by this image which we are, Him by whom we are made, as by a glass. And this is intimated also in the words of the same apostle: "But we with open face, beholding as in a glass the glory of the Lord, are transformed into the same image, from glory to glory, even as by the Spirit of the Lord." [26] "Beholding as in a glass," [27] he has said, *i.e.* seeing by means of a glass, not looking from a watch-tower: an ambiguity that does not exist in the Greek language, whence the apostolic epistles have been rendered into Latin. For in Greek, a glass,[28] in which the images of things are visible, is wholly distinct in the sound of the word also from a watch-tower,[29] from the height of which we command a more distant view. And it is quite plain that the apostle, in using the word *speculantes* in respect to the glory of the Lord, meant it to come from *speculum*, not from *specula*. But where he says, "We are transformed into the same image," he assuredly means to speak of the image of God; and by calling it "the same," he means that very image which we see in the glass, because that same image is also the glory of the Lord; as he says elsewhere, "For a man indeed ought not to cover his head, forasmuch as he is the image and glory of God," [30]—a text already discussed in the twelfth book. He means, then, by "We are transformed," that we are changed from one form to another, and that we pass from a form that is obscure to a form that is bright: since the obscure form, too, is the image of God; and if an image, then assuredly also "glory," in which we are created as men, being better than the other animals. For it is said of human nature in itself, "The man ought not to cover his head, because he is the image and glory of God." And this nature, being the most excellent among things created, is transformed from a form that is defaced into a form that is beautiful, when it is justified by its own Creator from ungodliness. Since even in ungodliness itself, the more the faultiness is to be con-

---

[23] Ps. xxxix. 3   [24] Ps. cv. 4   [25] 1 Cor. xiii. 12   [26] 2 Cor. iii. 18   [27] *Speculantes*   [28] *Speculum*   [29] *Specula*   [30] 1 Cor. xi. 7

demned, the more certainly is the nature to be praised. And therefore he has added, "from glory to glory:" from the glory of creation to the glory of justification. Although these words, "from glory to glory," may be understood also in other ways—from the glory of faith to the glory of sight, from the glory whereby we are sons of God to the glory whereby we shall be like Him, because "we shall see Him as He is." [31] But in that he has added, "as from the Spirit of the Lord," he declares, that the blessing of so desirable a transformation is conferred upon us by the grace of God.

CHAPTER IX

OF THE TERM "ENIGMA," AND OF TROPICAL MODES OF SPEECH

What has been said relates to the words of the apostle, that "we see now through a glass;" but whereas he has added, "in an enigma," the meaning of this addition is unknown to any who are unacquainted with the books that contain the doctrine of those modes of speech, which the Greeks call Tropes, which Greek word we also use in Latin. For as we more commonly speak of *schemata* than of figures, so we more commonly speak of tropes than of modes. And it is a very difficult and uncommon thing to express the names of the several modes or tropes in Latin, so as to refer its appropriate name to each. And hence some Latin translators, through unwillingness to employ a Greek word, where the apostle says, "Which things are an allegory," [32] have rendered it by a circumlocution—Which things signify one thing by another. But there are several species of this kind of trope that is called allegory, and one of them is that which is called enigma. Now the definition of the generic term must necessarily embrace also all its species; and hence, as every horse is an animal, but not every animal is a horse, so every enigma is an allegory, but every allegory is not an enigma. What then is an allegory, but a trope wherein one thing is understood from another? as in the *Epistle to the Thessalonians*, "Let us not therefore sleep, as do others; but let us watch and be sober: for they who sleep, sleep in the night; and they who are drunken, are drunken in the night: but let us who are of the day, be sober." [33] But this allegory is not an enigma, for here the meaning is patent to all but the very dull; but an enigma is, to explain it briefly, an obscure allegory, as *e.g.*, "The horseleech had three daughters," [34] and other like instances. But when the apostle spoke of an allegory, he does not find it in the words, but in the fact; since he has shown that the two Testaments are to be understood by the two sons of Abraham, one by a bondmaid, and the other by a free woman, which was a thing not only said, but also done. And before this was explained, it was obscure; and accordingly such an allegory, which is the generic name, could be specifically called an enigma.

But because it is not only those that are ignorant of the books that contain the doctrine of tropes, who inquire the apostle's meaning, when he said that

[31] 1 John iii. 2   [32] Gal. iv. 24   [33] 1 Thess. v. 6-8   [34] Prov. xxx. 15

we "see now in an enigma," but those, too, who are acquainted with the doctrine, but yet desire to know what that enigma is in which "we now see;" we must find a single meaning for the two phrases, *viz*. for that which says, "we see now through a glass," and for that which adds, "in an enigma." For it makes but one sentence, when the whole is so uttered, "We see now through a glass in an enigma." Accordingly, as far as my judgment goes, as by the word glass he meant to signify an image, so by that of enigma any likeness you will, but yet one obscure, and difficult to see through. While, therefore, any likenesses whatever may be understood as signified by the apostle when he speaks of a glass and an enigma, so that they are adapted to the understanding of God, in such way as He can be understood; yet nothing is better adapted to this purpose than that which is not vainly called His image. Let no one, then, wonder, that we labor to see in any way at all, even in that fashion of seeing which is granted to us in this life, *viz*. through a glass, in an enigma. For we should not hear of an enigma in this place if sight were easy. And this is a yet greater enigma, that we do not see what we cannot but see. For who does not see his own thought? And yet who does see his own thought, I do not say with the eye of the flesh, but with the inner sight itself? Who does not see it, and who does see it? Since thought is a kind of sight of the mind; whether those things are present which are seen also by the bodily eyes, or perceived by the other senses; or whether they are not present, but their likenesses are discerned by thought; or whether neither of these is the case, but things are thought of that are neither bodily things nor likenesses of bodily things, as the virtues and vices; or as, indeed, thought itself is thought of; or whether it be those things which are the subjects of instruction and of liberal sciences; or whether the higher causes and reasons themselves of all these things in the unchangeable nature are thought of; or whether it be even evil, and vain, and false things that we are thinking of, with either the sense not consenting, or erring in its consent.

CHAPTER X

CONCERNING THE WORD OF THE MIND, IN WHICH WE SEE THE WORD OF GOD, AS IN A GLASS AND AN ENIGMA

But let us now speak of those things of which we think as known, and have in our knowledge even if we do not think of them; whether they belong to the contemplative knowledge, which, as I have argued, is properly to be called wisdom, or to the active, which is properly to be called knowledge. For both together belong to one mind, and are one image of God. But when we treat of the lower of the two distinctly and separately, then it is not to be called an image of God, although even then, too, some likeness of that Trinity may be found in it; as we showed in the thirteenth book. We speak now, therefore, of the entire knowledge of man altogether, in which whatever is known to us is known; that, at any rate, which is true; otherwise it would not be known. For no one knows what is false, except when he knows it to be false; and if he knows this, then he knows what is true: for it is true that that is false. We treat, therefore, now of those things which we think as known, and which are known to us even if they are not being thought of. But certainly, if we would utter them in words, we can only do so by thinking them. For although there were no words spoken, at any rate, he who thinks speaks in his heart. And hence that passage in the book of *Wisdom:* "They said within themselves, thinking not aright." [35] For the words, "They said within themselves," are explained by the addition of "thinking." A like passage to this is that in the *Gospel*—that certain scribes, when they heard the Lord's words to the paralytic man, "Be of good cheer, my son, thy sins are forgiven thee," said within themselves, "This man blasphemeth." For how did they "say within themselves," except by thinking? Then follows, "And when Jesus saw their thoughts, He said, Why think ye evil in your thoughts?" [36] So far Matthew. But Luke narrates the same thing thus: "The scribes and Pharisees began to think, saying, Who is this that speaketh blasphemies? Who can forgive sins but God alone? But when Jesus perceived their thoughts, He, answering, said unto them, What think ye in your hearts?" [37] That which in the book of Wisdom is, "They said, thinking," is the same here with, "They thought, saying." For both there and here it is declared that they spake within themselves, and in their own heart, *i.e.* spake by thinking. For they "spake within themselves," and it was said to them, "What think ye?" And the Lord Himself says of that rich man whose ground brought forth plentifully, "And he thought within himself, saying." [38]

Some thoughts, then, are speeches of the heart, wherein the Lord also shows that there is a mouth, when He says, "Not that which entereth into the mouth defileth a man; but that which proceedeth out of the mouth, that defileth a man." In one sentence He has comprised two diverse mouths of the man, one of the body, one of the heart. For assuredly, that from which they thought the man to be defiled, enters into the mouth of the body; but that from which the Lord said the man was defiled, proceedeth out of the mouth of the heart. So certainly He Himself explained what He had said. For a little after, He says also to His disciples concerning the same thing: "Are ye also yet without understanding? Do ye not understand, that whatsoever entereth in at the mouth goeth into the belly, and is cast out into the draught?" Here He most certainly pointed to the mouth of the body. But in that which follows He plainly speaks of the mouth of the heart, where He says, "But those things which proceed out of the mouth come forth from the heart; and they defile the man. For out of the heart proceed evil thoughts," [39] etc. What is clearer than this explanation? And yet, when we call thoughts speeches of the heart, it does not follow that they are not also acts of sight,

[35] Wisd. ii. 1   [36] Matt. ix. 2-4   [37] Luke v. 21, 22   [38] Luke xii. 17   [39] Matt. xv. 10-20

arising from the sight of knowledge, when they are true. For when these things are done outwardly by means of the body, then speech and sight are different things; but when we think inwardly, the two are one—just as sight and hearing are two things mutually distinct in the bodily senses, but to see and hear are the same thing in the mind; and hence, while speech is not seen but rather heard outwardly, yet the inward speeches, *i.e.* thoughts, are said by the holy *Gospel* to have been seen, not heard, by the Lord. "They said within themselves, This man blasphemeth," says the *Gospel;* and then subjoined, "And when Jesus saw their thoughts." Therefore He saw what they said. For by His own thought He saw their thoughts, which they supposed no one saw but themselves.

Whoever, then, is able to understand a word, not only before it is uttered in sound, but also before the images of its sounds are considered in thought —for this it is which belongs to no tongue, to wit, of those which are called the tongues of nations, of which our Latin tongue is one—whoever, I say, is able to understand this, is able now to see through this glass and in this enigma some likeness of that Word of whom it is said, "In the beginning was the Word, and the Word was with God, and the Word was God." [40] For of necessity, when we speak what is true, *i.e.* speak what we know, there is born from the knowledge itself which the memory retains, a word that is altogether of the same kind with that knowledge from which it is born. For the thought that is formed by the thing which we know, is the word which we speak in the heart: which word is neither Greek nor Latin, nor of any other tongue. But when it is needful to convey this to the knowledge of those to whom we speak, then some sign is assumed whereby to signify it. And generally a sound, sometimes a nod, is exhibited, the former to the ears, the latter to the eyes, that the word which we bear in our mind may become known also by bodily signs to the bodily senses. For what is to nod or beckon, except to speak in some way to the sight? And Holy Scripture gives its testimony to this; for we read in the *Gospel according to John:* "Verily, verily, I say unto you, that one of you shall betray me. Then the disciples looked one upon another, doubting of whom He spake. Now there was leaning on Jesus' breast one of His disciples whom Jesus loved. Simon Peter therefore beckons to him, and says to him, Who is it of whom He speaks?" [41] Here he spoke by beckoning what he did not venture to speak by sounds. But whereas we exhibit these and the like bodily signs either to ears or eyes of persons present to whom we speak, letters have been invented that we might be able to converse also with the absent; but these are signs of words, as words themselves are signs in our conversation of those things which we think.

[40] John i. 1　　[41] John xiii. 21-24

CHAPTER XI

THE LIKENESS OF THE DIVINE WORD, SUCH AS IT IS, IS TO BE SOUGHT,
NOT IN OUR OWN OUTER AND SENSIBLE WORD, BUT IN THE INNER
AND MENTAL ONE. THERE IS THE GREATEST POSSIBLE UNLIKE-
NESS BETWEEN OUR WORD AND KNOWLEDGE AND THE DIVINE
WORD AND KNOWLEDGE

Accordingly, the word that sounds outwardly is the sign of the word that gives light inwardly; which latter has the greater claim to be called a word. For that which is uttered with the mouth of the flesh is the articulate sound of a word; and is itself also called a word, on account of that to make which outwardly apparent it is itself assumed. For our word is so made in some way into an articulate sound of the body, by assuming that articulate sound by which it may be manifested to men's senses, as the Word of God was made flesh, by assuming that flesh in which itself also might be manifested to men's senses. And as our word becomes an articulate sound, yet is not changed into one; so the Word of God became flesh, but far be it from us to say He was changed into flesh. For both that word of ours became an articulate sound, and that other Word became flesh, by assuming it, not by consuming itself so as to be changed into it. And therefore whoever desires to arrive at any likeness, be it of what sort it may, of the Word of God, however in many respects unlike, must not regard the word of ours that sounds in the ears, either when it is uttered in an articulate sound or when it is silently thought. For the words of all tongues that are uttered in sound are also silently thought, and the mind runs over verses while the bodily mouth is silent. And not only the numbers of syllables, but the tunes also of songs, since they are corporeal, and pertain to that sense of the body which is called hearing, are at hand by certain incorporeal images appropriate to them, to those who think of them, and who silently revolve all these things. But we must pass by this, in order to arrive at that word of man, by the likeness of which, be it of what sort it may, the Word of God may be somehow seen as in an enigma. Not that word which was spoken to this or that prophet, and of which it is said, "Now the word of God grew and multiplied;" [42] and again, "Faith then cometh by hearing, and hearing by the word of Christ;" [43] and again, "When ye received the word of God which ye heard of us, ye received it not as the word of men, but, as it is in truth, the word of God" [44] (and there are countless other like sayings in the Scriptures respecting the word of God, which is disseminated in the sounds of many and diverse languages through the hearts and mouths of men; and which is therefore called the word of God, because the doctrine that is delivered is not human, but divine) —but we are now seeking to see, in whatsoever way we can, by means of this

[42] Acts vi. 7   [43] Rom. x. 17   [44] 1 Thess. ii. 13

likeness, that Word of God of which it is said, "The Word was God;" of which it is said, "All things were made by Him;" of which it is said, "The Word became flesh;" of which it is said, "The Word of God on high is the fountain of wisdom." [45] We must go on, then, to that word of man, to the word of the rational animal, to the word of that image of God, that is not born of God, but made by God; which is neither utterable in sound nor capable of being thought under the likeness of sound, such as must needs be with the word of any tongue; but which precedes all the signs by which it is signified, and is begotten from the knowledge that continues in the mind, when that same knowledge is spoken inwardly according as it really is. For the sight of thinking is exceedingly like the sight of knowledge. For when it is uttered by sound, or by any bodily sign, it is not uttered according as it really is, but as it can be seen or heard by the body. When, therefore, that is in the word which is in the knowledge, then there is a true word, and truth, such as is looked for from man; such that what is in the knowledge is also in the word, and what is not in the knowledge is also not in the word. Here may be recognized, "Yea, yea; nay, nay." [46] And so this likeness of the image that is made, approaches as nearly as is possible to that likeness of the image that is born, by which God the Son is declared to be in all things like in substance to the Father. We must notice in this enigma also another likeness of the word of God; *viz.* that, as it is said of that Word, "All things were made by Him," where God is declared to have made the universe by His only-begotten Son, so there are no works of man that are not first spoken in his heart: whence it is written, "A word is the beginning of every work." [47] But here also, it is when the word is true, that then it is the beginning of a good work. And a word is true when it is begotten from the knowledge of working good works, so that there too may be preserved the "yea yea, nay nay;" in order that whatever is in that knowledge by which we are to live, may be also in the word by which we are to work, and whatever is not in the one may not be in the other. Otherwise such a word will be a lie, not truth; and what comes thence will be a sin, and not a good work. There is yet this other likeness of the Word of God in this likeness of our word, that there can be a word of ours with no work following it, but there cannot be any work unless a word precedes; just as the Word of God could have existed though no creature existed, but no creature could exist unless by that Word by which all things are made. And therefore not God the Father, not the Holy Spirit, not the Trinity itself, but the Son only, which is the Word of God, was made flesh; although the Trinity was the maker: in order that we might live rightly through our word following and imitating His example, *i.e.* by having no lie in either the thought or the work of our word. But this perfection of this image is one to be at some time hereafter. It is in order to attain this that the good master teaches us by Christian faith, and by pious doctrine, that "with face unveiled" from the veil of the law, which is the shadow of things

[45] Ecclus. i. 5   [46] Matt. v. 37   [47] Ecclus. xxxvii. 20

to come, "beholding as in a glass the glory of the Lord," *i.e.* gazing at it through a glass, "we may be transformed into the same image from glory to glory, as by the Spirit of the Lord;" [48] as we explained above.

When, therefore, this image shall have been renewed to perfection by this transformation, then we shall be like God, because we shall see Him, not through a glass, but "as He is;" [49] which the Apostle Paul expresses by "face to face." [50] But now, who can explain how great is the unlikeness also, in this glass, in this enigma, in this likeness such as it is? Yet I will touch upon some points, as I can, by which to indicate it.

CHAPTER XII

THE ACADEMIC PHILOSOPHY

Knowledge

First, of what sort and how great is the very knowledge itself that a man can attain, be he ever so skillful and learned, by which our thought is formed with truth, when we speak what we know? For to pass by those things that come into the mind from the bodily senses, among which so many are otherwise than they seem to be, that he who is overmuch pressed down by their resemblance to truth, seems sane to himself, but really is not sane—whence it is that the Academic philosophy has so prevailed as to be still more wretchedly insane by doubting all things—passing by, then, those things that come into the mind by the bodily senses, how large a proportion is left of things which we know in such manner as we know that we live? In regard to this, indeed, we are absolutely without any fear lest perchance we are being deceived by some resemblance of the truth; since it is certain, that he who is deceived, yet lives. And this again is not reckoned among those objects of sight that are presented from without, so that the eye may be deceived in it; in such way as it is when an oar in the water looks bent, and towers seem to move as you sail past them, and a thousand other things that are otherwise than they seem to be: for this is not a thing that is discerned by the eye of the flesh. The knowledge by which we know that we live is the most inward of all knowledge, of which even the Academic cannot insinuate: Perhaps you are asleep, and do not know it, and you see things in your sleep. For who does not know that what people see in dreams is precisely like what they see when awake? But he who is certain of the knowledge of his own life, does not therein say, I know I am awake, but, I know I am alive; therefore, whether he be asleep or awake, he is alive. Nor can he be deceived in that knowledge by dreams; since it belongs to a living man both to sleep and to see in sleep. Nor can the Academic again say, in confutation of this knowledge: Perhaps you are mad, and do not know it: for what madmen see is precisely like what they also see who are sane; but he who is mad is alive. Nor does he answer the Academic by saying, I know I am not mad, but, I

[48] 2 Cor. iii. 17   [49] 1 John iii. 4   [50] 1 Cor. xiii. 12

know I am alive. Therefore he who says he knows he is alive, can neither be deceived nor lie. Let a thousand kinds, then, of deceitful objects of sight be presented to him who says, I know I am alive; yet he will fear none of them, for he who is deceived yet is alive. But if such things alone pertain to human knowledge, they are very few indeed; unless that they can be so multiplied in each kind, as not only not to be few, but to reach in the result to infinity. For he who says, I know I am alive, says that he knows one single thing. Further, if he says, I know that I know I am alive, now there are two; but that he knows these two is a third thing to know. And so he can add a fourth and a fifth, and innumerable others, if he holds out. But since he cannot either comprehend an innumerable number by additions of units, or say a thing innumerable times, he comprehends this at least, and with perfect certainty, viz. that this is both true and so innumerable that he cannot truly comprehend and say its infinite number. This same thing may be noticed also in the case of a will that is certain. For it would be an impudent answer to make to any one who should say, I will to be happy, that perhaps you are deceived. And if he should say, I know that I will this, and I know that I know it, he can add yet a third to these two, viz. that he knows these two; and a fourth, that he knows that he knows these two; and so on ad infinitum. Likewise, if any one were to say, I will not to be mistaken; will it not be true, whether he is mistaken or whether he is not, that nevertheless he does will not to be mistaken? Would it not be most impudent to say to him, Perhaps you are deceived? when beyond doubt, wheresoever he may be deceived, he is nevertheless not deceived in thinking that he wills not to be deceived. And if he says he knows this, he adds any number he chooses of things known, and perceives that number to be infinite. For he who says, I will not to be deceived, and I know that I will not to be so, and I know that I know it, is able now to set forth an infinite number here also, however awkward may be the expression of it. And other things too are to be found capable of refuting the Academics, who contend that man can know nothing. But we must restrict ourselves, especially as this is not the subject we have undertaken in the present work. There are three books of ours on that subject,[51] written in the early time of our conversion, which he who can and will read, and who understands them, will doubtless not be much moved by any of the many arguments which they have found out against the discovery of truth. For whereas there are two kinds of knowable things—one, of those things which the mind perceives by the bodily senses; the other, of those which it perceives by itself—these philosophers have babbled much against the bodily senses, but have never been able to throw doubt upon those most certain perceptions of things true, which the mind knows by itself, such as is that which I have mentioned, I know that I am alive. But far be it from us to doubt the truth of what we have learned by the bodily senses; since by them we have learned to know the heaven and the earth, and those things in them which

[51] *Libri Tres contra Academicos*

are known to us, so far as He who created both us and them has willed them to be within our knowledge. Far be it from us, too, to deny that we know what we have learned by the testimony of others: otherwise we know not that there is an ocean; we know not that the lands and cities exist which most copious report commends to us; we know not that those men were, and their works, which we have learned by reading history; we know not the news that is daily brought us from this quarter or that, and confirmed by consistent and conspiring evidence; lastly, we know not at what place or from whom we have been born: since in all these things we have believed the testimony of others. And if it is most absurd to say this, then we must confess, that not only our own senses, but those of other persons also, have added very much indeed to our knowledge.

All these things, then, both those which the human mind knows by itself, and those which it knows by the bodily senses, and those which it has received and knows by the testimony of others, are laid up and retained in the storehouse of the memory; and from these is begotten a word that is true, when we speak what we know, but a word that is before all sound, before all thought of a sound. For the word is then most like to the thing known, from which also its image is begotten, since the sight of thinking arises from the sight of knowledge; when it is a word belonging to no tongue, but is a true word concerning a true thing, having nothing of its own, but wholly derived from that knowledge from which it is born. Nor does it signify when he learned it, who speaks what he knows; for sometimes he says it immediately upon learning it; provided only that the word is true, *i.e.* sprung from things that are known.

CHAPTER XIII

STILL FURTHER OF THE DIFFERENCE BETWEEN THE KNOWLEDGE AND WORD OF OUR MIND, AND THE KNOWLEDGE AND WORD OF GOD

But is it so, that God the Father, from whom is born the Word that is God of God—is it so, then, that God the Father, in respect to that wisdom which He is to Himself, has learned some things by His bodily senses, and others by Himself? Who could say this, who thinks of God, not as a rational animal, but as One above the rational soul? So far at least as He can be thought of, by those who place Him above all animals and all souls, although they see Him by conjecture through a glass and in an enigma, not yet face to face as He is. Is it that God the Father has learned those very things which He knows, not by the body, for He has none, but by Himself, from elsewhere from some one? or has stood in need of messengers or witnesses that He might know them? Certainly not; since His own perfection enables Him to know all things that He knows. No doubt He has messengers, *viz.* the angels; but not to announce to Him things that He knows not, for there is nothing

He does not know. But their good lies in consulting the truth about their own works. And this it is which is meant by saying that they bring Him word of some things, not that He may learn of them, but they of Him by His word without bodily sound. They bring Him word, too, of that which He wills, being sent by Him to whomever He wills, and hearing all from Him by that word of His, *i.e.* finding in His truth what themselves are to do: what, to whom, and when, they are to bring word. For we too pray to Him, yet do not inform Him what our necessities are. "For your Father knoweth," says His Word, "what things ye have need of, before you ask Him." [52] Nor did He become acquainted with them, so as to know them, at any definite time; but He knew beforehand, without any beginning, all things to come in time, and among them also both what we should ask of Him, and when; and to whom He would either listen or not listen, and on what subjects. And with respect to all His creatures, both spiritual and corporeal, He does not know them because they are, but they are because He knows them. For He was not ignorant of what He was about to create; therefore He created because He knew; He did not know because He created. Nor did He know them when created in any other way than He knew them when still to be created, for nothing accrued to His wisdom from them; but that wisdom remained as it was, while they came into existence as it was fitting and when it was fitting. So, too, it is written in the book of *Ecclesiasticus:* "All things are known to Him ere ever they were created: so also after they were perfected." [53] "So," he says, not otherwise; so were they known to Him, both ere ever they were created, and after they were perfected. This knowledge, therefore, is far unlike our knowledge. And the knowledge of God is itself also His wisdom, and His wisdom is itself His essence or substance. Because in the marvellous simplicity of that nature, it is not one thing to be wise and another to be, but to be wise is to be; as we have often said already also in the earlier books. But our knowledge is in most things capable both of being lost and of being recovered, because to us to be is not the same as to know or to be wise; since it is possible for us to be, even although we know not, neither are wise in that which we have learned from elsewhere. Therefore, as our knowledge is unlike that knowledge of God, so is our word, also, which is born from our knowledge, unlike that Word of God which is born from the essence of the Father. And this is as if I should say, born from the Father's knowledge, from the Father's wisdom; or still more exactly, from the Father who is knowledge, from the Father who is wisdom.

[52] Matt. vi. 8   [53] Ecclus. xxiii. 20

CHAPTER XIV

THE WORD OF GOD IS IN ALL THINGS EQUAL TO THE FATHER,
FROM WHOM IT IS

The Word of God, then, the only-begotten Son of the Father, in all things like and equal to the Father, God of God, Light of Light, Wisdom of Wisdom, Essence of Essence, is altogether that which the Father is, yet is not the Father, because the one is Son, the other is Father. And hence He knows all that the Father knows; but to Him to know, as to be, is from the Father, for to know and to be is there one. And therefore, as to be is not to the Father from the Son, so neither is to know. Accordingly, as though uttering Himself, the Father begat the Word equal to Himself in all things; for He would not have uttered Himself wholly and perfectly, if there were in His Word anything more or less than in Himself. And here that is recognized in the highest sense, "Yea, yea; nay, nay." [54] And therefore this Word is truly truth, since whatever is in that knowledge from which it is born is also in itself, and whatever is not in that knowledge is not in the Word. And this Word can never have anything false, because it is unchangeable, as He is from whom it is. For "the Son can do nothing of Himself, but what He seeth the Father do." [55] Through power He cannot do this; nor is it infirmity, but strength, by which truth cannot be false. Therefore God the Father knows all things in Himself, knows all things in the Son; but in Himself as though Himself, in the Son as though His own Word which Word is spoken concerning all those things that are in Himself. Similarly the Son knows all things, *viz.* in Himself, as things which are born of those which the Father knows in Himself, and in the Father, as those of which they are born, which the Son Himself knows in Himself. The Father, then, and the Son know mutually; but the one by begetting, the other by being born. And each of them sees simultaneously all things that are in their knowledge, in their wisdom, in their essence: not by parts or singly, as though by alternately looking from this side to that, and from that side to this, and again from this or that object to this or that object, so as not to be able to see some things without at the same time not seeing others; but, as I said, sees all things simultaneously, whereof there is not one that He does not always see.

And that word, then, of ours which has neither sound nor thought of sound, but is of that thing in seeing which we speak inwardly, and which therefore belongs to no tongue; and hence is in some sort like, in this enigma, to that Word of God which is also God; since this too is born of our knowledge, in such manner as that also is born of the knowledge of the Father: such a word, I say, of ours, which we find to be in some way like that Word, let us not be slow to consider how unlike also it is, as it may be in our power to utter it.

[54] Matt. v. 37   [55] John v. 19

CHAPTER XV

~~HOW GREAT IS THE UNLIKENESS BETWEEN OUR WORD AND THE~~
DIVINE WORD. OUR WORD CANNOT BE OR BE CALLED ETERNAL

Is our word, then, born of our knowledge only? Do we not say many things also that we do not know? And say them not with doubt, but thinking them to be true; while if perchance they are true in respect to the things themselves of which we speak, they are yet not true in respect to our word, because a word is not true unless it is born of a thing that is known. In this sense, then, our word is false, not when we lie, but when we are deceived. And when we doubt, our word is not yet of the thing of which we doubt, but it is a word concerning the doubt itself. For although we do not know whether that is true of which we doubt, yet we do know that we doubt; and hence, when we say we doubt, we say a word that is true, for we say what we know. And what, too, of its being possible for us to lie? And when we do, certainly we both willingly and knowingly have a word that is false, wherein there is a word that is true, *viz.* that we lie, for this we know. And when we confess that we have lied, we speak that which is true; for we say what we know, for we know that we lied. But that Word which is God, and can do more than we, cannot do this. For it "can do nothing except what it sees the Father do;" and it "speaks not of itself," but it has from the Father all that it speaks, since the Father speaks it in a special way; and the great might of that Word is that it cannot lie, because there cannot be there "yea and nay," [56] but "yea yea, nay nay." Well, but that is not even to be called a word, which is not true. I willingly assent, if so it be. What, then, if our word is true, and therefore is rightly called a word? Is it the case that, as we can speak of sight of sight, and knowledge of knowledge, so we can speak of essence of essence, as that Word of God is especially spoken of, and is especially to be spoken of? Why so? Because to us, to be is not the same as to know; since we know many things which in some sense live by memory, and so in some sense die by being forgotten; and so, when those things are no longer in our knowledge, yet we still are; and while our knowledge has slipped away and perished out of our mind, we are still alive.

In respect to those things also which are so known that they can never escape the memory, because they are present, and belong to the nature of the mind itself—as, *e.g.*, the knowing that we are alive (for this continues so long as the mind continues; and because the mind continues always, this also continues always)—I say, in respect to this and to any other like instances, in which we are the rather to contemplate the image of God, it is difficult to make out in what way, although they are always known, yet because they are not always also thought of, an eternal word can be spoken respecting

[56] 2 Cor. i. 19

them, when our word is spoken in our thought. For it is eternal to the soul to live; it is eternal to know that it lives. Yet it is not eternal to it to be thinking of its own life, or to be thinking of its own knowledge of its own life; since, in entering upon this or that occupation, it will cease to think of this, although it does not cease from knowing it. And hence it comes to pass, that if there can be in the mind any knowledge that is eternal, while the thought of that knowledge cannot be eternal, and any inner and true word of ours is only said by our thought, then God alone can be understood to have a Word that is eternal, and co-eternal with Himself. Unless, perhaps, we are to say that the very possibility of thought—since that which is known is capable of being truly thought, even at the time when it is not being thought—constitutes a word as perpetual as the knowledge itself is perpetual. But how is that a word which is not yet formed in the vision of the thought? How will it be like the knowledge of which it is born, if it has not the form of that knowledge, and is only now called a word because it can have it? For it is much as if one were to say that a word is to be so called because it can be a word. But what is this that can be a word, and is therefore already held worthy of the name of a word? What, I say, is this thing that is formable, but not yet formed, except a something in our mind, which we toss to and fro by revolving it this way or that, while we think of first one thing and then another, according as they are found by or occur to us? And the true word then comes into being, when, as I said, that which we toss to and fro by revolving it arrives at that which we know, and is formed by that, in taking its entire likeness; so that in what manner each thing is known, in that manner also it is thought, *i.e.* is said in this manner in the heart, without articulate sound, without thought of articulate sound, such as no doubt belongs to some particular tongue. And hence if we even admit, in order not to dispute laboriously about a name, that this something of our mind, which can be formed from our knowledge, is to be already called a word, even before it is so formed, because it is, so to say, already formable, who would not see how great would be the unlikeness between it and that Word of God, which is so in the form of God, as not to have been formable before it was formed, or to have been capable at any time of being formless, but is a simple form, and simply equal to Him from whom it is, and with whom it is wonderfully co-eternal?

CHAPTER XVI

OUR WORD IS NEVER TO BE EQUALLED TO THE DIVINE WORD, NOT EVEN WHEN WE SHALL BE LIKE GOD

Wherefore that Word of God is in such wise so called, as not to be called a thought of God, lest we believe that there is anything in God which can be revolved, so that it at one time receives and at another recovers a form, so as to be a word, and again can lose that form and be revolved in some sense formlessly. Certainly that excellent master of speech knew well the force of words, and had looked into the nature of thought, who said in his poem, "And revolves with himself the varying issues of war," [57] *i.e.* thinks of them. That Son of God, then, is not called the Thought of God, but the Word of God. For our own thought, attaining to what we know, and formed thereby, is our true word. And so the Word of God ought to be understood without any thought on the part of God, so that it be understood as the simple form itself, but containing nothing formable that can be also unformed. There are, indeed, passages of Holy Scripture that speak of God's thoughts; but this is after the same mode of speech by which the forgetfulness of God is also there spoken of, whereas in strict propriety of language there is in Him certainly no forgetfulness.

Wherefore, since we have found now in this enigma so great an unlikeness to God and the Word of God, wherein yet there was found before some likeness, this, too, must be admitted, that even when we shall be like Him, when "we shall see Him as He is" [58] (and certainly he who said this was aware beyond doubt of our present unlikeness), not even then shall we be equal to Him in nature. For that nature which is made is ever less than that which makes. And at that time our word will not indeed be false, because we shall neither lie nor be deceived. Perhaps, too, our thoughts will no longer revolve by passing and repassing from one thing to another, but we shall see all our knowledge at once, and at one glance. Still, when even this shall have come to pass, if indeed it shall come to pass, the creature which was formable will indeed have been formed, so that nothing will be wanting of that form to which it ought to attain; yet nevertheless it will not be to be equalled to that simplicity wherein there is not anything formable, which has been formed or re-formed, but only form; and which being neither formless nor formed, itself is eternal and unchangeable substance.

CHAPTER XVII

HOW THE HOLY SPIRIT IS CALLED LOVE, AND WHETHER HE ALONE IS SO CALLED. THAT THE HOLY SPIRIT IS IN THE SCRIPTURES PROPERLY CALLED BY THE NAME OF LOVE

We have sufficiently spoken of the Father and of the Son, so far as was possible for us to see through this glass and in this enigma. We must now treat of the Holy Spirit, so far as by God's gift it is permitted to see Him. And the Holy Spirit, according to the Holy Scriptures, is neither of the Father alone, nor of the Son alone, but of both; and so intimates to us a mutual love, wherewith the Father and the Son reciprocally love one another. But the language of the Word of God, in order to exercise us, has caused those things to be sought into with the greater zeal, which do not lie on the surface,

[57] *Aen.* x. 159, 160   [58] 1 John iii. 2

but are to be scrutinized in hidden depths, and to be drawn out from thence. The Scriptures, accordingly, have not said, The Holy Spirit is Love. If they had said so, they would have done away with no small part of this inquiry. But they have said, "God is love;" [59] so that it is uncertain and remains to be inquired whether God the Father is love, or God the Son, or God the Holy Ghost, or the Trinity itself which is God. For we are not going to say that God is called Love because love itself is a substance worthy of the name of God, but because it is a gift of God, as it is said to God, "Thou art my patience." [60] For this is not said because our patience is God's substance, but in that He Himself gives it to us; as it is elsewhere read, "Since from Him is my patience." [61] For the usage of words itself in Scripture sufficiently refutes this interpretation; for "Thou art my patience" is of the same kind as "Thou, Lord, art my hope," [62] and "The Lord my God is my mercy," [63] and many like texts. And it is not said, O Lord my love, or, Thou art my love, or, God my love; but it is said thus, "God is love," as it is said, "God is a Spirit." [64] And he who does not discern this, must ask understanding from the Lord, not an explanation from us; for we cannot say anything more clearly.

"God," then, "is love;" but the question is, whether the Father, or the Son, or the Holy Spirit, or the Trinity itself: because the Trinity is not three Gods, but one God. But I have already argued above in this book, that the Trinity, which is God, is not so to be understood from those three things which have been set forth in the trinity of our mind, as that the Father should be the memory of all three, and the Son the understanding of all three, and the Holy Spirit the love of all three; as though the Father should neither understand nor love for Himself, but the Son should understand for Him, and the Holy Spirit love for Him, but He Himself should remember only both for Himself and for them; nor the Son remember nor love for Himself, but the Father should remember for Him, and the Holy Spirit love for Him, but He Himself understand only both for Himself and them; nor likewise that the Holy Spirit should neither remember nor understand for Himself, but the Father should remember for Him, and the Son understand for Him, while He Himself should love only both for Himself and for them; but rather in this way, that both all and each have all three each in His own nature. Nor that these things should differ in them, as in us memory is one thing, understanding another, love or charity another, but should be some one thing that is equivalent to all, as wisdom itself; and should be so contained in the nature of each, as that He who has it is that which He has, as being an unchangeable and simple substance. If all this, then, has been understood, and so far as is granted to us to see or conjecture in things so great, has been made patently true, I know not why the Father and the Son and the Holy Spirit should not be called Love, and all together one love, just as the Father and the Son and the Holy Spirit are called Wisdom, and all

[59] 1 John iv. 16   [60] Ps. lxxi. 5   [61] Ps. lxii. 5   [62] Ps. xci. 9   [63] Ps. lix. 17
[64] John iv. 24

together not three, but one wisdom. For so also the Father is God, and the Son God, and the Holy Ghost God, and all three together one God.

And yet it is not to no purpose that in this Trinity the Son and none other is called the Word of God, and the Holy Spirit and none other the Gift of God, and God the Father alone is He from whom the Word is born, and from whom the Holy Spirit principally proceeds. And therefore I have added the word principally, because we find that the Holy Spirit proceeds from the Son also. But the Father gave Him this too, not as to one already existing, and not yet having it; but whatever He gave to the only-begotten Word, He gave by begetting Him. Therefore He so begat Him as that the common Gift should proceed from Him also, and the Holy Spirit should be the Spirit of both. This distinction, then, of the inseparable Trinity is not to be merely accepted in passing, but to be carefully considered; for hence it was that the Word of God was specially called also the Wisdom of God, although both Father and Holy Spirit are wisdom. If, then, any one of the three is to be specially called Love, what more fitting than that it should be the Holy Spirit?—namely, that in that simple and highest nature, substance should not be one thing and love another, but that substance itself should be love, and love itself should be substance, whether in the Father, or in the Son, or in the Holy Spirit; and yet that the Holy Spirit should be specially called Love.

Just as sometimes all the utterances of the Old Testament together in the Holy Scriptures are signified by the name of the Law. For the apostle, in citing a text from the prophet Isaiah, where he says, "With divers tongues and with divers lips will I speak to this people," yet prefaced it by, "It is written in the Law." [65] And the Lord Himself says, "It is written in their Law, They hated me without a cause," [66] whereas this is read in the *Psalm.*[67] And sometimes that which was given by Moses is specially called the Law: as it is said, "The Law and the Prophets were until John;" [68] and, "On these two commandments hang all the Law and the Prophets." [69] Here, certainly, that is specially called the Law which was from Mount Sinai. And the Psalms, too, are signified under the name of the Prophets; and yet in another place the Saviour Himself says, "All things must needs be fulfilled, which are written in the Law, and the Prophets, and the Psalms concerning me." [70] Here, on the other side, He meant the name of Prophets to be taken as not including the Psalms. Therefore the Law with the Prophets and the Psalms taken together is called the Law universally, and the Law is also specially so called which was given by Moses. Likewise the Prophets are so called in common together with the Psalms, and they are also specially so called exclusive of the Psalms. And many other instances might be adduced to teach us, that many names of things are both put universally, and also specially applied to particular things, were it not that a long discourse is to be avoided in a plain

[65] Isa. xxviii, 11 and 1 Cor. xiv. 21   [66] John xv. 25   [67] Ps. xxxv. 19   [68] Matt. xi. 13   [69] Matt. xxii. 40   [70] Luke xxiv. 44

case. I have said so much, lest any one should think that it was therefore unsuitable for us to call the Holy Spirit Love, because both God the Father and God the Son can be called Love.

As, then, we call the only Word of God specially by the name of Wisdom, although universally both the Holy Spirit and the Father Himself are wisdom; so the Holy Spirit is specially called by the name of Love, although universally both the Father and the Son are love. But the Word of God, *i.e.* the only-begotten Son of God, is expressly called the Wisdom of God by the mouth of the apostle, where he says, "Christ the power of God, and the wisdom of God." [71] But where the Holy Spirit is called Love, is to be found by careful scrutiny of the language of John the apostle, who, after saying, "Beloved, let us love one another, for love is of God," has gone on to say, "And every one that loveth is born of God, and knoweth God. He that loveth not, knoweth not God; for God is love." Here, manifestly, he has called that love God, which he said was of God; therefore God of God is love. But because both the Son is born of God the Father, and the Holy Spirit proceeds from God the Father, it is rightly asked which of them we ought here to think is the rather called the love that is God. For the Father only is so God as not to be of God; and hence the love that is so God as to be of God, is either the Son or the Holy Spirit. But when, in what follows, the apostle had mentioned the love of God, not that by which we love Him, but that by which He "loved us, and sent His Son to be a propitiator for our sins," [72] and thereupon had exhorted us also to love one another, and that so God would abide in us —because, namely, he had called God Love; immediately, in his wish to speak yet more expressly on the subject, "Hereby," he says, "know we that we dwell in Him, and He in us, because He hath given us of His Spirit." Therefore the Holy Spirit, of whom He hath given us, makes us to abide in God, and Him in us; and this it is that love does. Therefore He is the God that is love. Lastly, a little after, when he had repeated the same thing, and had said "God is love," he immediately subjoined, "And he who abideth in love, abideth in God, and God abideth in him;" whence he had said above, "Hereby we know that we abide in Him, and He in us, because He hath given us of His Spirit." He therefore is signified, where we read that God is love. Therefore God the Holy Spirit, who proceedeth from the Father, when He has been given to man, inflames him to the love of God and of his neighbor, and is Himself love. For man has not whence to love God, unless from God; and therefore he says a little after, "Let us love Him, because He first loved us." [73] The Apostle Paul, too, says, "The love of God is shed abroad in our hearts by the Holy Ghost, which is given unto us." [74]

[71] 1 Cor. i. 24   [72] John iv. 10   [73] 1 John iv. 7-19   [74] Rom. v. 5

CHAPTER XVIII

NO GIFT OF GOD IS MORE EXCELLENT THAN LOVE

There is no gift of God more excellent than this. It alone distinguishes the sons of the eternal kingdom and the sons of eternal perdition. Other gifts, too, are given by the Holy Spirit; but without love they profit nothing. Unless, therefore, the Holy Spirit is so far imparted to each, as to make him one who loves God and his neighbor, he is not removed from the left hand to the right. Nor is the Spirit specially called the Gift, unless on account of love. And he who has not this love, "though he speak with the tongues of men and angels, is sounding brass and a tinkling cymbal; and though he have the gift of prophecy, and know all mysteries and all knowledge, and though he have all faith, so that he can remove mountains, he is nothing; and though he bestow all his goods to feed the poor, and though he give his body to be burned, it profiteth him nothing." [75] How great a good, then, is that without which goods so great bring no one to eternal life! But love or charity itself—for they are two names for one thing—if he have it that does not speak with tongues, nor has the gift of prophecy, nor knows all mysteries and all knowledge, nor gives all his goods to the poor, either because he has none to give or because some necessity hinders, nor delivers his body to be burned, if no trial of such a suffering overtakes him, brings that man to the kingdom, so that faith itself is only rendered profitable by love, since faith without love can indeed exist, but cannot profit. And therefore also the Apostle Paul says, "In Christ Jesus neither circumcision availeth anything, nor uncircumcision, but faith that worketh by love:" [76] so distinguishing it from that faith by which even "the devils believe and tremble." [77] Love, therefore, which is of God and is God, is specially the Holy Spirit, by whom the love of God is shed abroad in our hearts, by which love the whole Trinity dwells in us. And therefore most rightly is the Holy Spirit, although He is God, called also the gift of God. [78] And by that gift what else can properly be understood except love, which brings to God, and without which any other gift of God whatsoever does not bring to God?

CHAPTER XIX

THE HOLY SPIRIT IS CALLED THE GIFT OF GOD IN THE SCRIPTURES. BY THE GIFT OF THE HOLY SPIRIT IS MEANT THE GIFT WHICH IS THE HOLY SPIRIT. THE HOLY SPIRIT IS SPECIALLY CALLED LOVE, ALTHOUGH NOT ONLY THE HOLY SPIRIT IN THE TRINITY IS LOVE

Is this too to be proved, that the Holy Spirit is called in the sacred books the gift of God? If people look for this too, we have in the *Gospel according to*

[75] I Cor. xiii. 1-3   [76] Gal. v. 6   [77] Jas. ii. 19   [78] Acts viii. 20

John the words of our Lord Jesus Christ, who says, "If any one thirst, let him come to me and drink: he that believeth on me, as the Scripture saith, out of his belly shall flow rivers of living water." And the evangelist has gone on further to add, "And this He spake of the Spirit, which they should receive who believe in Him." [79] And hence Paul the apostle also says, "And we have all been made to drink into one Spirit." [80] The question then is, whether that water is called the gift of God which is the Holy Spirit. But as we find here that this water is the Holy Spirit, so we find elsewhere in the Gospel itself that this water is called the gift of God. For when the same Lord was talking with the woman of Samaria at the well, to whom He had said, "Give me to drink," and she had answered that the Jews "have no dealings" with the Samaritans, Jesus answered and said unto her, "If thou hadst known the gift of God, and who it is that says to thee, Give me to drink, thou wouldest have asked of Him, and He would have given thee living water. The woman saith unto Him, Sir, thou hast nothing to draw with, and the well is deep: whence then hast thou this living water, etc.? Jesus answered and said unto her, Every one that drinketh of this water shall thirst again; but whoso shall drink of the water that I shall give him, shall never thirst; but the water that I shall give him, shall be in him a fountain of water springing up unto eternal life." [81] Because this living water, then, as the evangelist has explained to us, is the Holy Spirit, without doubt the Spirit is the gift of God, of which the Lord says here, "If thou hadst known the gift of God, and who it is that saith unto thee, Give me to drink, thou wouldest have asked of Him, and He would have given thee living water." For that which is in the one passage, "Out of his belly shall flow rivers of living water," is in the other, "shall be in him a fountain of water springing up unto eternal life."

Paul the apostle also says, "To each of us is given grace according to the measure of the gift of Christ;" and then, that he might show that by the gift of Christ he meant the Holy Spirit, he has gone on to add, "Wherefore He saith, He hath ascended up on high, He hath led captivity captive, and hath given gifts to men." [82] And every one knows that the Lord Jesus, when He had ascended into heaven after the resurrection from the dead, gave the Holy Spirit, with whom they who believed were filled, and spake with the tongues of all nations. And let no one object that he says *gifts*, not *gift:* for he quoted the text from the *Psalm*. And in the *Psalm* it is read thus, "Thou hast ascended up on high, Thou hast led captivity captive, Thou hast received gifts in men." [83] For so it stands in many MSS., especially in the Greek MSS., and so we have it translated from the Hebrew. The apostle therefore said *gifts*, as the prophet did, not *gift*. But whereas the prophet said, "Thou hast received gifts in men," the apostle has preferred saying, "He gave gifts to men:" and this in order that the fullest sense may be gathered from both expressions, the one prophetic, the other apostolic; because both possess the

[79] John vii. 37-39   [80] 1 Cor. xii. 13   [81] John iv. 7-14   [82] Eph. iv. 7, 8   [83] Ps. lxviii. 18

authority of a divine utterance. For both are true, as well that He gave to men, as that He received in men. He gave to men, as the head to His own members: He Himself that gave, received in men, no doubt as in His own members; on account of which, namely, His own members, He cried from heaven, "Saul, Saul, why persecutest thou me?" [84] And of which, namely, His own members, He says, "Since ye have done it to one of the least of these that are mine, ye have done it unto me." [85] Christ Himself, therefore, both gave from heaven and received on earth. And further, both prophet and apostle have said *gifts* for this reason, because many gifts, which are proper to each, are divided in common to all the members of Christ, by the Gift, which is the Holy Spirit. For each severally has not all, but some have these and some have those; although all have the Gift itself by which that which is proper to each is divided to Him, *i.e.* the Holy Spirit. For elsewhere also, when he had mentioned many gifts, "All these," he says, "worketh that one and the self-same Spirit, dividing to each severally as He will." [86] And this word is found also in the *Epistle to the Hebrews*, where it is written, "God also bearing witness both with signs and wonders, and with divers miracles, and gifts of the Holy Ghost." [87] And so here, when he had said, "He ascended up on high, He led captivity captive, He gave gifts to men," he says further, "But that He ascended, what is it but that He also first descended into the lower parts of the earth? He who descended is the same also that ascended up far above all heavens, that He might fill all things. And He gave some apostles, some prophets, and some evangelists, and some pastors and doctors." (This we see is the reason why gifts are spoken of; because, as he says elsewhere, "Are all apostles? are all prophets?" [88] etc.) And here he has added, "For the perfecting of the saints, for the work of the ministry, for the building up of the body of Christ." [89] This is the house which, as the *Psalm* sings, is built up after the captivity;[90] since the house of Christ, which house is called His Church, is built up of those who have been rescued from the devil, by whom they were held captive. But He Himself led this captivity captive, who conquered the devil. And that he might not draw with him into eternal punishment those who were to become the members of the Holy Head, He bound him first by the bonds of righteousness, and then by those of might. The devil himself, therefore, is called captivity, which He led captive who ascended up on high, and gave gifts to men, or received gifts in men.

And Peter the apostle, as we read in that canonical book, wherein the Acts of the Apostles are recorded—when the hearts of the Jews were troubled as he spake of Christ, and they said, "Brethren, what shall we do? tell us"—said to them, "Repent, and be baptized every one of you in the name of the Lord Jesus Christ, for the remission of sins: and ye shall receive the gift of the Holy Spirit." [91] And we read likewise in the same book, that Simon

[84] Acts ix. 4   [85] Matt. xxv. 40   [86] 1 Cor. xii. 11   [87] Heb. ii. 4   [88] 1 Cor. xii. 29
[89] Eph. iv. 7-12   [90] Ps. cxxvi. 1   [91] Acts ii. 37, 38

Magus desired to give money to the apostles, that he might receive power from them, whereby the Holy Spirit might be given by the laying on of his hands. And the same Peter said to him, "Thy money perish with thee: because thou hast thought to purchase for money the gift of God." [92] And in another place of the same book, when Peter was speaking to Cornelius, and to those who were with him, and was announcing and preaching Christ, the Scripture says, "While Peter was still speaking these words, the Holy Spirit fell upon all them that heard the word; and they of the circumcision that believed, as many as came with Peter, were astonished, because that upon the Gentiles also the gift of the Holy Spirit was poured out. For they heard them speak with tongues, and magnify God." [93] And when Peter afterwards was giving an account to the brethren that were at Jerusalem of this act of his, that he had baptized those who were not circumcised, because the Holy Spirit, to cut the knot of the question, had come upon them before they were baptized, and the brethren at Jerusalem were moved when they heard it, he says; after the rest of his words, "And when I began to speak to them, the Holy Spirit fell upon them, as upon us in the beginning. And I remembered the word of the Lord, how He said, that John indeed baptized with water, but ye shall be baptized with the Holy Spirit. If, therefore, He gave a like gift to them, as also to us who believed in the Lord Jesus Christ, who was I, that I could hinder God from giving to them the Holy Spirit?" [94] And there are many other testimonies of the Scriptures, which unanimously attest that the Holy Spirit is the gift of God, in so far as He is given to those who by Him love God. But it is too long a task to collect them all. And what is enough to satisfy those who are not satisfied with those we have alleged?

Certainly they must be warned, since they now see that the Holy Spirit is called the gift of God, that when they hear of "the gift of the Holy Spirit," they should recognize therein that mode of speech which is found in the words, "In the spoiling of the body of the flesh." [95] For as the body of the flesh is nothing else but the flesh, so the gift of the Holy Spirit is nothing else but the Holy Spirit. He is then the gift of God, so far as He is given to those to whom He is given. But in Himself He is God, although He were given to no one, because He was God co-eternal with the Father and the Son before He was given to any one. Nor is He less than they, because they give, and He is given. For He is given as a gift of God in such way that He Himself also gives Himself as being God. For He cannot be said not to be in His own power, of whom it is said, "The Spirit bloweth where it listeth;" [96] and the apostle says, as I have already mentioned above, "All these things worketh that self-same Spirit, dividing to every man severally as He will." We have not here the creating of Him that is given, and the rule of them that give, but the concord of the given and the givers.

Wherefore, if Holy Scripture proclaims that God is love, and that love is

---

[92] Acts viii. 18-20   [93] Acts x. 44, 46   [94] Acts xi. 15-17   [95] Col. ii. 11   [96] John iii. 6

of God, and works this in us that we abide in God and He in us, and that hereby we know this, because He has given us of His Spirit, then the Spirit Himself is God, who is love. Next, if there be among the gifts of God none greater than love, and there is no greater gift of God than the Holy Spirit, what follows more naturally than that He is Himself love, who is called both God and of God? And if the love by which the Father loves the Son, and the Son loves the Father, ineffably demonstrates the communion of both, what is more suitable than that He should be specially called love, who is the Spirit common to both? For this is the sounder thing both to believe and to understand, that the Holy Spirit is not alone love in that Trinity, yet is not specially called love to no purpose, for the reasons we have alleged; just as He is not alone in that Trinity either a Spirit or holy, since both the Father is a Spirit, and the Son is a Spirit; and both the Father is holy, and the Son is holy—as piety doubts not. And yet it is not to no purpose that He is specially called the Holy Spirit; for because He is common to both, He is specially called that which both are in common. Otherwise, if in that Trinity the Holy Spirit alone is love, then doubtless the Son too turns out to be the Son, not of the Father only, but also of the Holy Spirit. For He is both said and read in countless places to be so—the only-begotten Son of God the Father; as that what the apostle says of God the Father is true too: "Who hath delivered us from the power of darkness, and hath translated us into the kingdom of the Son of His own love." [97] He did not say, "of His own Son." If He had so said, He would have said it most truly, just as He did say it most truly, because He has often said it; but He says, "the Son of His own love." Therefore He is the Son also of the Holy Spirit, if there is in that Trinity no love in God except the Holy Spirit. And if this is most absurd, it remains that the Holy Spirit is not alone therein love, but is specially so called for the reasons I have sufficiently set forth; and that the words, "Son of His own love," mean nothing else than His own beloved Son—the Son, in short, of His own substance. For the love in the Father, which is in His ineffably simple nature, is nothing else than His very nature and substance itself—as we have already often said, and are not ashamed of often repeating. And hence the "Son of His love," is none other than He who is born of His substance.

CHAPTER XX

AGAINST EUNOMIUS, SAYING THAT THE SON OF GOD IS THE SON, NOT OF HIS NATURE, BUT OF HIS WILL. EPILOGUE TO WHAT HAS BEEN SAID ALREADY

Wherefore the logic of Eunomius, from whom the Eunomian heretics sprang, is ridiculous. For when he could not understand, and would not believe, that the only-begotten Word of God, by which all things were made, is

[97] Col. i. 13

the Son of God by nature—*i.e.* born of the substance of the Father—he alleged that He was not the Son of His own nature or substance or essence, but the Son of the will of God; so as to mean to assert that the will by which he begat the Son was something accidental [and optional] to God—to wit, in that way that we ourselves sometimes will something which before we did not will, as though it was not for these very things that our nature is perceived to be changeable—a thing which far be it from us to believe of God. For it is written, "Many are the thoughts in the heart of man, but the counsel of the Lord abideth for ever," [98] for no other reason except that we may understand or believe that as God is eternal, so is His counsel for eternity, and therefore unchangeable, as He himself is. And what is said of thoughts can most truly be said also of the will: there are many wills in the heart of man, but the will of the Lord abideth for ever. Some, again, to escape saying that the only-begotten Word is the Son of the counsel or will of God, have affirmed the same Word to be the counsel or will itself of the Father. But it is better in my judgment to say counsel of counsel, and will of will, as substance of substance, wisdom of wisdom, that we may not be led into that absurdity, which we have refuted already, and say that the Son makes the Father wise or willing, if the Father has not in His own substance either counsel or will. It was certainly a sharp answer that somebody gave to the heretic, who most subtly asked him whether God begat the Son willingly or unwillingly, in order that if he said unwillingly, it would follow most absurdly that God was miserable; but if willingly, he would forthwith infer, as though by an invincible reason, that at which he was aiming, *viz.* that He was the Son, not of His nature, but of His will. But that other, with great wakefulness, demanded of him in turn, whether God the Father was God willingly or unwillingly; in order that if he answered unwillingly, that misery would follow, which to believe of God is sheer madness; and if he said willingly, it would be replied to him, Then He is God too by His own will, not by His nature. What remained, then, except that he should hold his peace, and discern that he was himself bound by his own question in an insoluble bond? But if any person in the Trinity is also to be specially called the will of God, this name, like love, is better suited to the Holy Spirit; for what else is love, except will?

I see that my argument in this book respecting the Holy Spirit, according to the Holy Scripture, is quite enough for faithful men who know already that the Holy Spirit is God, and not of another substance, nor less than the Father and the Son—as we have shown to be true in the former books, according to the same Scriptures. We have reasoned also from the creature which God made, and, as far as we could, have warned those who demand a reason on such subjects to behold and understand His invisible things, so far as they could, by those things which are made, [99] and especially by the rational or intellectual creature which is made after the image of God; through which glass, so to say, they might discern as far as they could, if they could,

[98] Prov. xix. 21   [99] Rom. i. 20

the Trinity which is God, in our own memory, understanding, will. Which three things, if any one intelligently regards as by nature divinely appointed in his own mind, and remembers by memory, contemplates by understanding, embraces by love, how great a thing that is in the mind, whereby even the eternal and unchangeable nature can be recollected, beheld, desired, doubtless that man finds an image of that highest Trinity. And he ought to refer the whole of his life to the remembering, seeing, loving that highest Trinity, in order that he may recollect, contemplate, be delighted by it. But I have warned him, so far as seemed sufficient, that he must not so compare this image thus wrought by that Trinity, and by his own fault changed for the worse, to that same Trinity as to think it in all points like to it, but rather that he should discern in that likeness, of whatever sort it be, a great unlikeness also.

CHAPTER XXI

OF THE LIKENESS OF THE FATHER AND OF THE SON ALLEGED TO BE IN OUR MEMORY AND UNDERSTANDING. OF THE LIKENESS OF THE HOLY SPIRIT IN OUR WILL OR LOVE

I have undoubtedly taken pains so far as I could, not indeed so that the thing might be seen face to face, but that it might be seen by this likeness in an enigma,[100] in how small a degree soever, by conjecture, in our memory and understanding, to intimate God the Father and God the Son: *i.e.* God the begetter, who has in some way spoken by His own co-eternal Word all things that He has in His substance; and God His Word Himself, who Himself has nothing either more or less in substance than is in Him, who, not lyingly but truly, hath begotten the Word; and I have assigned to memory everything that we know, even if we were not thinking of it, but to understanding the formation after a certain special mode of the thought. For we are usually said to understand what, by thinking of it, we have found to be true; and this it is again that we leave in the memory. But that is a still more hidden depth of our memory, wherein we found this also first when we thought of it, and wherein an inner word is begotten such as belongs to no tongue—as it were, knowledge of knowledge, vision of vision, and understanding which appears in [reflective] thought; of understanding which had indeed existed before in the memory, but was latent there, although, unless the thought itself had also some sort of memory of its own, it would not return to those things which it had left in the memory while it turned to think of other things.

But I have shown nothing in this enigma respecting the Holy Spirit such as might appear to be like Him, except our own will, or love, or affection, which is a stronger will, since our will which we have naturally is variously

[100] I Cor. xiii. 12

affected, according as various objects are adjacent or occur to it, by which we are attracted or offended. What, then, is this? Are we to say that our will, when it is right, knows not what to desire, what to avoid? Further, if it knows, doubtless then it has a kind of knowledge of its own, such as cannot be without memory and understanding. Or are we to listen to any one who should say that love knows not what it does, which does not do wrongly? As, then, there are both understanding and love in that primary memory wherein we find provided and stored up that to which we can come in thought, because we find also those two things there, when we find by thinking that we both understand and love anything; which things were there too when we were not thinking of them: and as there are memory and love in that understanding, which is formed by thought, which true word we say inwardly without the tongue of any nation when we say what we know; for the gaze of our thought does not return to anything except by remembering it, and does not care to return unless by loving it: so love, which combines the vision brought about in the memory, and the vision of the thought formed thereby, as if parent and offspring, would not know what to love rightly unless it had a knowledge of what it desired, which it cannot have without memory and understanding.

CHAPTER XXII

HOW GREAT THE UNLIKENESS IS BETWEEN THE IMAGE OF THE TRINITY WHICH WE HAVE FOUND IN OURSELVES, AND THE TRINITY ITSELF

But since these are in one person, as man is, some one may say to us, These three things, memory, understanding, and love, are mine, not their own; neither do they do that which they do for themselves, but for me, or rather I do it by them. For it is I who remember by memory, and understand by understanding, and love by love: and when I direct the mind's eye to my memory, and so say in my heart the thing I know, and a true word is begotten of my knowledge, both are mine, both the knowledge certainly and the word. For it is I who know, and it is I who say in my heart the thing I know. And when I come to find in my memory by thinking that I understand and love anything, which understanding and love were there also before I thought thereon, it is my own understanding and my own love that I find in my own memory, whereby it is I that understand, and I that love, not those things themselves. Likewise, when my thought is mindful, and wills to return to those things which it had left in the memory, and to understand and behold them, and say them inwardly, it is my own memory that is mindful, and it is my own, not its will, wherewith it wills. When my very love itself, too, remembers and understands what it ought to desire and what to avoid, it remembers by my, not by its own memory; and understands that which it intelligently loves by my, not by its own, understanding. In brief, by all these three things, it is I that remember, I that understand, I that love, who am neither memory, nor understanding, nor love, but who have them. These things, then, can be said by a single person, which has these three, but is not these three. But in the simplicity of that Highest Nature, which is God, although there is one God, there are three persons, the Father, the Son, and the Holy Spirit.

CHAPTER XXIII

AUGUSTINE DWELLS STILL FURTHER ON THE DISPARITY BETWEEN
THE TRINITY WHICH IS IN MAN, AND THE TRINITY WHICH IS
GOD. THE TRINITY IS NOW SEEN THROUGH A GLASS BY THE
HELP OF FAITH, THAT IT MAY HEREAFTER BE MORE CLEARLY
SEEN IN THE PROMISED SIGHT FACE TO FACE

A thing itself, then, which is a trinity is different from the image of a trinity in some other thing; by reason of which image, at the same time that also in which these three things are is called an image; just as both the panel, and the picture painted on it, are at the same time called an image; but by reason of the picture painted on it, the panel also is called by the name of image. But in that Highest Trinity, which is incomparably above all things, there is so great an indivisibility, that whereas a trinity of men cannot be called one man, in that, there both is said to be and is one God, nor is that Trinity in one God, but it is one God. Nor, again, as that image in the case of man has these three things but is one person, so is it with the Trinity; but therein are three persons, the Father of the Son, and the Son of the Father, and the Spirit of both Father and Son. For although the memory in the case of man, and especially that memory which beasts have not—*viz.* the memory by which things intelligible are so contained as that they have not entered that memory through the bodily senses—has in this image of the Trinity, in proportion to its own small measure, a likeness of the Father, incomparably unequal, yet of some sort, whatever it be: and likewise the understanding in the case of man, which by the purpose of the thought is formed thereby, when that which is known is said, and there is a word of the heart belonging to no tongue, has in its own great disparity some likeness of the Son; and love in the case of man proceeding from knowledge, and combining memory and understanding, as though common to parent and offspring, whereby it is understood to be neither parent nor offspring, has in that image, some, however exceedingly unequal, likeness of the Holy Spirit: it is nevertheless not the case, that, as in that image of the Trinity, these three are not one man, but belong to one man, so in the Highest Trinity itself, of which this is an image, these three belong to one God, but they are one God, and these are three persons, not one. A thing certainly wonderfully ineffable, or ineffably wonderful, that while this image of the Trinity is ône person, but the Highest

Trinity itself is three persons, yet that Trinity of three persons is more indivisible than this of one. For that [Trinity], in the nature of the Divinity, or perhaps better Deity, is that which it is, and is mutually and always unchangeably equal: and there was no time when it was not, or when it was otherwise; and there will be no time when it will not be, or when it will be otherwise. But these three that are in the inadequate image, although they are not separate in place, for they are not bodies, yet are now in this life mutually separate in magnitude. For that there are therein no several bulks, does not hinder our seeing that memory is greater than understanding in one man, but the contrary in another; and that in yet another these two are overpassed by the greatness of love; and this whether the two themselves are or are not equal to one another. And so each two by each one, and each one by each two, and each one by each one: the less are surpassed by the greater. And when they have been healed of all infirmity, and are mutually equal, not even then will that thing which by grace will not be changed, be made equal to that which by nature cannot change, because the creature cannot be equalled to the Creator, and when it shall be healed from all infirmity, will be changed.

But when the sight shall have come which is promised anew to us face to face, we shall see this not only incorporeal but also absolutely indivisible and truly unchangeable Trinity far more clearly and certainly than we now see its image which we ourselves are: and yet they who see through this glass and in this enigma, as it is permitted in this life to see, are not those who behold in their own mind the things which we have set in order and pressed upon them; but those who see this as if an image, so as to be able to refer what they see, in some way be it what it may, to Him whose image it is, and to see that also by conjecturing, which they see through the image by beholding, since they cannot yet see face to face. For the apostle does not say, We see now a glass, but, We see now through a glass.[101]

CHAPTER XXIV

THE INFIRMITY OF THE HUMAN MIND

They, then, who see their own mind, in whatever way that is possible, and in it that Trinity of which I have treated as I could in many ways, and yet do not believe or understand it to be an image of God, see indeed a glass, but do not so far see through the glass Him who is now to be seen through the glass, that they do not even know the glass itself which they see to be a glass, *i.e.* an image. And if they knew this, perhaps they would feel that He too whose glass this is, should by it be sought, and somehow provisionally be seen, an unfeigned faith purging their hearts,[102] that He who is now seen through a glass may be able to be seen face to face. And if they despise this

[101] Cor. xiii. 12   [102] 1 Tim. i. 5

faith that purifies the heart, what do they accomplish by understanding the most subtle disputes concerning the nature of the human mind, unless that they be condemned also by the witness of their own understanding? And they would certainly not so fail in understanding, and hardly arrive at anything certain, were they not involved in penal darkness, and burdened with the corruptible body that presses down the soul.[103] And for what demerit save that of sin is this evil inflicted on them? Wherefore, being warned by the magnitude of so great an evil, they ought to follow the Lamb that taketh away the sins of the world.[104]

CHAPTER XXV

THE QUESTION WHY THE HOLY SPIRIT IS NOT BEGOTTEN, AND HOW HE PROCEEDS FROM THE FATHER AND THE SON, WILL ONLY BE UNDERSTOOD WHEN WE ARE IN BLISS

For if any belong to Him, although far duller in intellect than those, yet when they are freed from the body at the end of this life, the envious powers have no right to hold them. For that Lamb that was slain by them without any debt of sin has conquered them; but not by the might of power before He had done so by the righteousness of blood. And free accordingly from the power of the devil, they are borne up by holy angels, being set free from all evils by the Mediator of God and men, the man Christ Jesus.[105] Since by the harmonious testimony of the Divine Scriptures, both Old and New, both those by which Christ was foretold, and those by which He was announced, there is no other name under heaven whereby men must be saved.[106] And when purged from all contagion of corruption, they are placed in peaceful abodes until they take their bodies again, their own, but now incorruptible, to adorn, not to burden them. For this is the will of the best and most wise Creator, that the spirit of a man, when piously subject to God, should have a body happily subject, and that this happiness should last for ever.

There we shall see the truth without any difficulty, and shall enjoy it to the full, most clear and most certain. Nor shall we be inquiring into anything by a mind that reasons, but shall discern by a mind that contemplates, why the Holy Spirit is not a Son, although He proceeds from the Father. In that light there will be no place for inquiry: but here, by experience itself it has appeared to me so difficult—as beyond doubt it will likewise appear to them also who shall carefully and intelligently read what I have written—that although in the second book[107] I promised that I would speak thereof in another place, yet as often as I have desired to illustrate it by the creaturely image of it which we ourselves are, so often, let my meaning be of what sort it might, did adequate utterance entirely fail me; nay, even in my very meaning I felt that I had attained to endeavor rather than accomplishment. I had

---

[103] Wisd. ix. 15   [104] John i. 29   [105] I Tim. ii. 5   [106] Acts iv. 12   [107] Ch. 3

indeed found in one person, such as is a man, an image of that Highest Trinity, and had desired, especially in the ninth book, to illustrate and render more intelligible the relation of the Three Persons by that which is subject to time and change. But three things belonging to one person cannot suit those Three Persons, as man's purpose demands; and this we have demonstrated in this fifteenth book.

CHAPTER XXVI

THE HOLY SPIRIT TWICE GIVEN BY CHRIST. THE PROCESSION OF THE HOLY SPIRIT FROM THE FATHER AND FROM THE SON IS APART FROM TIME, NOR CAN HE BE CALLED THE SON OF BOTH

Further, in that Highest Trinity which is God, there are no intervals of time, by which it could be shown, or at least inquired, whether the Son was born of the Father first, and then afterwards the Holy Spirit proceeded from both; since Holy Scripture calls Him the Spirit of both. For it is He of whom the apostle says, "But because ye are sons, God hath sent forth the Spirit of His Son into your hearts:" [108] and it is He of whom the same Son says, "For it is not ye who speak, but the Spirit of your Father who speaketh in you." [109] And it is proved by many other testimonies of the Divine Word, that the Spirit, who is specially called in the Trinity the Holy Spirit, is of the Father and of the Son: of whom likewise the Son Himself says, "Whom I will send unto you from the Father;" [110] and in another place, "Whom the Father will send in my name." [111] And we are so taught that He proceeds from both, because the Son Himself says, He proceeds from the Father. And when He had risen from the dead, and had appeared to His disciples, "He breathed upon them, and said, Receive the Holy Ghost," [112] so as to show that He proceeded also from Himself. And Itself is that very "power that went out from Him," as we read in the *Gospel*, "and healed them all." [113]

But the reason why, after His resurrection, He both gave the Holy Spirit, first on earth,[114] and afterwards sent Him from heaven,[115] is in my judgment this: that "love is shed abroad in our hearts," [116] by that Gift itself, whereby we love God and our neighbors, according to those two commandments, "on which hang all the law and the prophets." [117] And Jesus Christ, in order to signify this, gave to them the Holy Spirit, once upon earth, on account of the love of our neighbor, and a second time from heaven, on account of the love of God. And if some other reason may perhaps be given for this double gift of the Holy Spirit, at any rate we ought not to doubt that the same Holy Spirit was given when Jesus breathed upon them, of whom He by and by says, "Go, baptize all nations in the name of the Father, and of the Son, and of the Holy Spirit," where this Trinity is especially commended to us. It is

[108] Gal. iv. 6   [109] Matt. x. 20   [110] John xv. 26   [111] John xiv. 26   [112] John xx. 23   [113] Luke vi. 19   [114] John xx. 22   [115] Acts ii. 4   [116] Rom. v. 5   [117] Matt. xxii. 37-40

therefore He who was also given from heaven on the day of Pentecost, *i.e.* ten days after the Lord ascended into heaven. How, therefore, is He not God, who gives the Holy Spirit? Nay, how great a God is He who gives God! For no one of His disciples gave the Holy Spirit, since they prayed that He might come upon those upon whom they laid their hands: they did not give Him themselves. And the Church preserves this custom even now in the case of her rulers. Lastly, Simon Magus also, when he offered the apostles money, does not say, "Give me also this power, that I may give" the Holy Spirit; but, "that on whomsoever I may lay my hands, he may receive the Holy Spirit." Because neither had the Scriptures said before, And Simon, seeing that the apostles gave the Holy Spirit; but it had said, "And Simon, seeing that the Holy Spirit was given by the laying on of the apostles' hands." [118] Therefore also the Lord Jesus Christ Himself not only gave the Holy Spirit as God, but also received it as man, and therefore He is said to be full of grace,[119] and of the Holy Spirit.[120] And in the *Acts of the Apostles* it is more plainly written of Him, "Because God anointed Him with the Holy Spirit." [121] Certainly not with visible oil but with the gift of grace which is signified by the visible ointment wherewith the Church anoints the baptized. And Christ was certainly not then anointed with the Holy Spirit, when He, as a dove, descended upon Him at His baptism.[122] For at that time He deigned to prefigure His body, *i.e.* His Church, in which especially the baptized receive the Holy Spirit. But He is to be understood to have been then anointed with that mystical and invisible unction, when the Word of God was made flesh,[123] *i.e.* when human nature, without any precedent merits of good works, was joined to God the Word in the womb of the Virgin, so that with it it became one person. Therefore it is that we confess Him to have been born of the Holy Spirit and of the Virgin Mary. For it is most absurd to believe Him to have received the Holy Spirit when He was near thirty years old: for at that age He was baptized by John;[124] but that He came to baptism as without any sin at all, so not without the Holy Spirit. For if it was written of His servant and forerunner John himself, "He shall be filled with the Holy Spirit, even from his mother's womb," [125] because, although generated by his father, yet he received the Holy Spirit when formed in the womb; what must be understood and believed of the man Christ, of whose flesh the very conception was not carnal, but spiritual? Both natures, too, as well the human as the divine, are shown in that also that is written of Him, that He received of the Father the promise of the Holy Spirit, and shed forth the Holy Spirit.[126] seeing that He received as man, and shed forth as God. And we indeed can receive that gift according to our small measure, but assuredly we cannot shed it forth upon others; but, that this may be done, we invoke over them God, by whom this is accomplished.

[118] Acts viii. 18, 19   [119] John i. 14   [120] Luke ii. 52 and iv. 1   [121] Acts x. 38
[122] Matt. iii. 16   [123] John i. 14   [124] Luke iii. 21-23   [125] Luke i. 15   [126] Acts ii. 33

Are we therefore able to ask whether the Holy Spirit had already proceeded from the Father when the Son was born, or had not yet proceeded, and when He was born, proceeded from both, wherein there is no such thing as distinct times: just as we have been able to ask, in a case where we do find times, that the will proceeds from the human mind first, in order that that may be sought which, when found, may be called offspring; which offspring being already brought forth or born, that will is made perfect, resting in this end, so that what had been its desire when seeking, is its love when enjoying; which love now proceeds from both, *i.e.* from the mind that begets, and from the notion that is begotten, as if from parent and offspring? These things it is absolutely impossible to ask in this case, where nothing is begun in time, so as to be perfected in a time following. Wherefore let him who can understand the generation of the Son from the Father without time, understand also the procession of the Holy Spirit from both without time. And let him who can understand, in that which the Son says, "As the Father hath life in Himself, so hath He given to the Son to have life in Himself," [127] not that the Father gave life to the Son already existing without life, but that He so begat Him apart from time, that the life which the Father gave to the Son by begetting Him is co-eternal with the life of the Father who gave it: let him, I say, understand, that as the Father has in Himself that the Holy Spirit should proceed from Him, so has He given to the Son that the same Holy Spirit should proceed from Him, and be both apart from time: and that the Holy Spirit is so said to proceed from the Father as that it be understood that His proceeding also from the Son, is a property derived by the Son from the Father. For if the Son has of the Father whatever He has, then certainly He has of the Father, that the Holy Spirit proceeds also from Him. But let no one think of any times therein which imply a sooner and a later; because these things are not there at all. How, then, would it not be most absurd to call Him the Son of both: when, just as generation from the Father, without any changeableness of nature, gives to the Son essence, without beginning of time; so procession from both, without any changeableness of nature, gives to the Holy Spirit essence without beginning of time? For while we do not say that the Holy Spirit is begotten, yet we do not therefore dare to say that He is unbegotten, lest any one suspect in this word either two Fathers in that Trinity, or two who are not from another. For the Father alone is not from another, and therefore He alone is called unbegotten, not indeed in the Scriptures, but in the usage of disputants, who employ such language as they can on so great a subject. And the Son is born of the Father; and the Holy Spirit proceeds from the Father principally, the Father giving the procession without any interval of time, yet in common from both [Father and Son]. But He would be called the Son of the Father and of the Son, if—a thing abhorrent to the feeling of all sound minds—both had *begotten* Him. Therefore the Spirit of both is not begotten of both, but proceeds from both.

[127] John v. 26

CHAPTER XXVII

WHAT IT IS THAT SUFFICES HERE TO SOLVE THE QUESTION WHY
THE SPIRIT IS NOT SAID TO BE BEGOTTEN, AND WHY THE
FATHER ALONE IS UNBEGOTTEN. WHAT THEY OUGHT TO
DO WHO DO NOT UNDERSTAND THESE THINGS

But because it is most difficult to distinguish generation from procession
in that co-eternal, and equal, and incorporeal, and ineffably unchangeable
and indivisible Trinity, let it suffice meanwhile to put before those who are
not able to be drawn on further, what we said upon this subject in a sermon
to be delivered in the ears of Christian people, and after saying wrote it
down. For when, among other things, I had taught them by testimonies of
the Holy Scriptures that the Holy Spirit proceeds from both, I continue:
"If, then, the Holy Spirit proceeds both from the Father and from the Son,
why did the Son say, 'He proceedeth from the Father?' " [128] Why, think you,
except as He is wont to refer to Him, that also which is His own, from whom
also He Himself is? Whence also is that which He saith, "My doctrine is not
mine own, but His that sent me?" [129] If, therefore, it is His doctrine that is
here understood, which yet He said was not His own, but His that sent Him,
how much more is it there to be understood that the Holy Spirit proceeds
also from Himself, where He so says, He proceedeth from the Father, as not
to say, He proceedeth not from me? From Him, certainly, from whom the
Son had his Divine nature, for He is God of God, He has also, that from Him
too proceeds the Holy Spirit; and hence the Holy Spirit has from the Father
Himself, that He should proceed from the Son also, as He proceeds from the
Father. Here, too, in some way may this also be understood, so far as it can
be understood by such as we are, why the Holy Spirit is not said to be born,
but rather to proceed; since if He, too, was called a Son, He would certainly
be called the Son of both, which is most absurd, since no one is son of two,
save of father and mother. But far be it from us to surmise any such thing as
this between God the Father and God the Son. Because not even the son of
men proceeds at the same time from both father and mother; but when he
proceeds from the father into the mother, he does not at that time proceed
from the mother; and when he proceeds from the mother into this present
light, he does not at that time proceed from the father. But the Holy Spirit
does not proceed from the Father into the Son, and from the Son proceed to
sanctify the creature, but proceeds at once from both; although the Father
has given this to the Son, that He should proceed, as from Himself, so also
from Him. For we cannot say that the Holy Spirit is not life, while the Father is life, and the Son is life: and hence as the Father, while He has life in
Himself, has given also to the Son to have life in Himself; so has He given

[128] John xv. 26   [129] John vii. 16

also to Him that life should proceed from Him, as it also proceeds from Himself." [130] I have transferred this from that sermon into this book, but I was speaking to believers, not to unbelievers.

But if they are not competent to gaze upon this image, and to see how true these things are which are in their mind, and yet which are not so three as to be three persons, but all three belong to a man who is one person; why do they not believe what they find in the sacred books respecting that highest Trinity which is God, rather than insist on the clearest reason being rendered them, which cannot be comprehended by the human mind, dull and infirm as it is? And to be sure, when they have steadfastly believed the Holy Scriptures as most true witnesses, let them strive, by praying and seeking and living well, that they may understand, *i.e.* that so far as it can be seen, that may be seen by the mind which is held fast by faith. Who would forbid this? Nay, who would not rather exhort them to it? But if they think they ought to deny that these things are, because they, with their blind minds, cannot discern them, they, too, who are blind from their birth, ought to deny that there is a sun. The light then shineth in darkness; but if the darkness comprehend it not,[131] let them first be illuminated by the gift of God, that they may be believers, and let them begin to be light in comparison with the unbelievers; and when this foundation is first laid, let them be built up to see what they believe, that at some time they may be able to see. For some things are so believed, that they cannot be seen at all. For Christ is not to be seen a second time on the cross; but unless this be believed which has been so done and seen, that it is not now to be hoped for as about to be and to be seen, there is no coming to Christ, such as without end He is to be seen. But as far as relates to the discerning in some way by the understanding that highest, ineffable, incorporeal, and unchangeable nature the sight of the human mind can nowhere better exercise itself, so only that the rule of faith govern it, than in that which man himself has in his own nature better than the other animals, better also than the other parts of his own soul, which is the mind itself, to which has been assigned a certain sight of things invisible, and to which, as though honorably presiding in a higher and inner place, the bodily senses also bring word of all things, that they may be judged, and than which there is no higher, to which it is to be subject, and by which it is to be governed, except God.

But among these many things which I have now said, and of which there is nothing that I dare to profess myself to have said worthy of the ineffableness of that highest Trinity, but rather to confess that the wonderful knowledge of Him is too great for me, and that I cannot attain[132] to it: O thou, my soul, where dost thou feel thyself to be? where dost thou lie? where dost thou stand? until all thy infirmities be healed by Him who has forgiven all thy iniquities.[133] Thou perceivest thyself assuredly to be in that inn whither that

[130] Serm. in *Joh. Evang. tract.* 99, n. 8, 9   [131] John i. 5   [132] Ps. cxxxix. 5   [133] Ps. ciii. 3

Samaritan brought him whom he found with many wounds inflicted by thieves, half-dead.[134] And yet thou hast seen many things that are true, not by those eyes by which colored objects are seen, but by those for which he prayed who said, "Let mine eyes behold the things that are equal." [135] Certainly, then, thou hast seen many things that are true, and hast distinguished them from that light by the light of which thou hast seen them. Lift up thine eyes to the light itself, and fix them upon it if thou canst. For so thou wilt see how the birth of the Word of God differs from the procession of the Gift of God, on account of which the only-begotten Son did not say that the Holy Spirit is begotten of the Father, otherwise He would be His brother, but that He proceeds from Him. Whence, since the Spirit of both is a kind of consubstantial communion of Father and Son, He is not called, far be it from us to say so, the Son of both. But thou canst not fix thy sight there, so as to discern this lucidly and clearly; I know thou canst not. I say the truth, I say to myself, I know what I cannot do; yet that light itself shows to thee these three things in thyself, wherein thou mayest recognize an image of the highest Trinity itself, which thou canst not yet contemplate with steady eye. Itself shows to thee that there is in thee a true word, when it is born of thy knowledge, *i.e.* when we say what we know: although we neither utter nor think of any articulate word that is significant in any tongue of any nation, but our thought is formed by that which we know; and there is in the mind's eye of the thinker an image resembling that thought which the memory contained, will or love as a third combining these two as parent and offspring. And he who can, sees and discerns that this will proceeds indeed from thought (for no one wills that of which he is absolutely ignorant what or of what sort it is) yet is not an image of the thought: and so that there is insinuated in this intelligible thing a sort of difference between birth and procession, since to behold by thought is not the same as to desire, or even to enjoy will. Thou, too, hast been able [to discern this], although thou hast not been, neither art, able to unfold with adequate speech what, amidst the clouds of bodily likenesses, which cease not to flit up and down before human thoughts, thou hast scarcely seen. But that light which is not thyself shows thee this too, that these incorporeal likenesses of bodies are different from the truth, which, by rejecting them, we contemplate with the understanding. These, and other things similarly certain, that light hath shown to thine inner eyes. What reason, then, is there why thou canst not see that light itself with steady eye, except certainly infirmity? And what has produced this in thee, except iniquity? Who, then, is it that healeth all thine infirmities, unless it be He that forgiveth all thine iniquities? And therefore I will now at length finish this book by a prayer better than by an argument.

[134] Luke x. 30, 34   [135] Ps. xvii. 2

CHAPTER XXVIII

THE CONCLUSION OF THE BOOK WITH A PRAYER, AND AN APOLOGY
FOR MULTITUDE OF WORDS

O Lord our God, we believe in Thee, the Father and the Son and the Holy Spirit. For the Truth would not say, Go, baptize all nations in the name of the Father and of the Son and of the Holy Spirit, unless Thou wast a Trinity. Nor wouldest thou, O Lord God, bid us to be baptized in the name of Him who is not the Lord God. Nor would the divine voice have said, Hear, O Israel, the Lord thy God is one God, unless Thou wert so a Trinity as to be one Lord God. And if Thou, O God, wert Thyself the Father, and wert Thyself the Son, Thy Word Jesus Christ, and the Holy Spirit your gift, we should not read in the book of truth, "God sent His Son;" [136] nor wouldest Thou, O Only-begotten, say of the Holy Spirit, "Whom the Father will send in my name;" [137] and, "Whom I will send to you from the Father." [138] Directing my purpose by this rule of faith, so far as I have been able, so far as Thou hast made me to be able, I have sought Thee, and have desired to see with my understanding what I believed; and I have argued and labored much. O Lord my God, my one hope, hearken to me, lest through weariness I be unwilling to seek Thee, "but that I may always ardently seek Thy face." [139] Do Thou give strength to seek, who hast made me find Thee, and hast given the hope of finding Thee more and more. My strength and my infirmity are in Thy sight: preserve the one, and heal the other. My knowledge and my ignorance are in Thy sight; where Thou hast opened to me, receive me as I enter; where Thou hast closed, open to me as I knock. May I remember Thee, understand Thee, love Thee. Increase these things in me, until Thou renewest me wholly. I know it is written, "In the multitude of speech, thou shalt not escape sin." [140] But O that I might speak only in preaching Thy word, and in praising Thee! Not only should I so flee from sin, but I should earn good desert, however much I so spake. For a man blessed of Thee would not enjoin a sin upon his own true son in the faith, to whom he wrote, "Preach the word: be instant in season, out of season." [141] Are we to say that he has not spoken much, who was not silent about Thy word, O Lord, not only in season, but out of season? But therefore it was not much, because it was only what was necessary. Set me free, O God, from that multitude of speech which I suffer inwardly in my soul, wretched as it is in Thy sight, and flying for refuge to Thy mercy; for I am not silent in thoughts, even when silent in words. And if, indeed, I thought of nothing save what pleased Thee, certainly I would not ask Thee to set me free from such multitude of speech. But many are my thoughts, such as Thou knowest, "thoughts of man, since they are vain." [142] Grant to me not to consent to them; and if ever they de-

[136] Gal. iv. 5 and John iii. 17   [137] John xiv. 26   [138] John xv. 26   [139] Ps. cv. 4
[140] Prov. x. 19   [141] 2 Tim. iv. 2   [142] Ps. xciv. 11

light me, nevertheless to condemn them, and not to dwell in them, as though I slumbered. Nor let them so prevail in me, as that anything in my acts should proceed from them; but at least let my opinions, let my conscience, be safe from them, under Thy protection. When the wise man spake of Thee in his book, which is now called by the special name of *Ecclesiasticus*, "We speak," he said, "much, and yet come short; and in sum of words, He is all." [143] When, therefore, we shall have come to Thee, these very many things that we speak, and yet come short, will cease; and Thou, as One, wilt remain "all in all." [144] And we shall say one thing without end, in praising Thee in One, ourselves also made one in Thee. O Lord the one God, God the Trinity, whatever I have said in these books that is of Thine, may they acknowledge who are Thine; if anything of my own, may it be pardoned both by Thee and by those who are Thine. Amen.

[143] Ecclus. xliii. 29   [144] 1 Cor. xv. 28

Venus, a peculiar candelabrum in a temple of, 571.

Venus, the planet, a strange prodigy that occurred to, 575.

Vestal virgin, a, to prove her innocence, carries water in a sieve from the Tiber, 631.

Vice, not nature, contrary to God, and hurtful, 180.

Vicissitudes of life, the, on what dependent, 47.

Victoria, the goddess, 52.

Virgil, quoted, 4, 5, 6, 7, 8, 25, 71, 121, 122, 242, 419, 550, 572, 583.

Virgin Mary, the, 395.

Virgins, the violation of, by force, does not contaminate, 22.

Virtue and Faith, honored by the Romans with temples, 53; the Romans ought to have been content with, and Felicity, 53; the war waged by, 395.

Virtues, as disgraceful to make them serve human glory as to serve bodily pleasure, 85; true, necessary to true religion, 504, 505.

Vision, the beatific, 656-660.

WARFARE, the Christian, 586.

Wars, against the Albans, 48; the Punic, 49; the civil, of the Gracchi, 49; the civil, between Marius and Sylla, 49; the Gothic and Gallic, 49; severe and frequent, before the advent of Christ, 49; the duration of various, 87; with Radagaisus, 88; the miseries of, 481.

Waters, the separation of the, 176.

Wicked, the, the ills which alone are feared by, 48; God makes a good use of, 460; going out to see the punishment of, 546; the end of, 506; and the good, one event befalls, 11, 510; the connection of, and the good together, 12.

Wickedness, not a flaw of nature, 596.

Will, the consent of, to an evil deed, makes the deed evil, 22; is it ruled

by necessity? 68; the enemies of God are so by, 180, 183; no efficient cause of an evil, 185; the misdirected love by which it fell away from the immutable to the mutable good, 186; whether the angels received their good, from God, 186; the character of, makes the affections of the soul right or wrong, 245, etc.; free in the state of perfect felicity, 660.

Will of God, the eternal and unchangeable, 610.

Wisdom, described in the Book of Proverbs, 401.

Wisdom, the Book of, a prophecy of Christ in, 400.

Woman, shall she retain her sex in the resurrection? 636; the formation of, from a rib of sleeping Adam, a type, 637.

World, the, not eternal, 145; the infinite ages before, not to be comprehended, 147; and time, had both one beginning, 148; falseness of the history which ascribes many thousand years to the past existence of, 188; of those who hold a plurality of worlds, 190; predictions respecting the end of, 549, etc.

Worlds without end, or ages of ages, 200, etc.

Wonders, lying, 618.

Worm, the, that dieth not, 546, 578.

Worship of God, 140, 141.

XENOCRATES, 114.

YEARS, in the time of the antediluvians, 288, etc., 293, etc.; in the words, "their days shall be an hundred and twenty years," 310, etc.; the thousand, of the Book of Revelation, 517; the three and a half, of the Book of Revelation, 548.

ZOROASTER, 584.

INDEX OF SUBJECTS
ON THE TRINITY